Japan and Korea

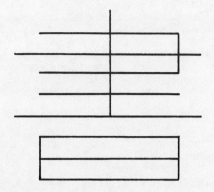

Japan and Korea

AN ANNOTATED BIBLIOGRAPHY
OF DOCTORAL DISSERTATIONS
IN WESTERN LANGUAGES
1877–1969

Compiled and edited by
Frank J. Shulman
for the Center for Japanese Studies,
The University of Michigan

AMERICAN LIBRARY ASSOCIATION
Chicago 1970

International Standard Book Number 0-8389-0085-2 (1970)

Library of Congress Catalog Card Number 71-127675

Printed in the United States of America

To John Bowden,

Roger F. Hackett,

and

Robert M. Spaulding, Jr.

Contents

Japan

Korea

Foreword

This annotated bibliography of doctoral dissertations on Japan and Korea grew out of a decision to expand and bring up to date an earlier list entitled Unpublished Doctoral Dissertations Relating to Japan, Accepted in the Universities of Australia, Canada, Great Britain, and the United States, 1946-1963, compiled by Peter Cornwall and issued by the Center for Japanese Studies in 1965. Like its predecessor, the present work is primarily intended to make more accessible, hence more useful, an impressive number of scholarly studies in the form of dissertations which by and large remain unpublished. An up-to-date inventory of doctoral dissertations, this book should be a valuable aid to students, teachers, librarians, and others who seek to trace through the scholarship of dissertations a bibliographic panorama of Japanese and Korean studies in Western languages.

Many institutions and individuals have generously contributed to its compilation, but Mr. Frank J. Shulman deserves full credit for the comprehensive search for dissertation titles, the planning and organization of the bibliography, and the writing of most and the editing of all the entries. As a specialist in library science as well as in East Asian history, Mr. Shulman has applied a distinctive combination of knowledge and skill to the exacting work of compilation. His desire to enhance its usefulness for teachers and students led him to expand the information conventionally furnished in an annotated bibliography to include related publications based on the author's dissertation. This unique feature greatly augments its value as an aid to research.

The work affords, both to Westerners and to Japanese and Korean scholars, a view of the main topics and research interests which have been pursued in Western universities over the past nine decades. By the same token, it will also serve to identify neglected themes and furnish guides for the direction of future research efforts. The inclusion of the original dissertations in addition to derivative publications adds immeasurably to the value of the bibliography as a research aid and provides an important measure of the extent and variety of Japanese and Korean studies in Western universities. The book is, in other words, both a general bibliographic reference tool and an instrument for the guidance of future research.

Prepared for the Center for Japanese Studies, this bibliography is the first in a projected series of bibliographies of Western-language works on special aspects of the study of Japan. It complements the Center's Bibliographical Series which list and evaluate major Japanese-language works pertaining to the humanities and social sciences. The Center wishes to express appreciation to the Social Science Research Council-American Council of Learned Societies' Joint Committee on Japanese Studies and the Joint Committee on Korean Studies for financial assistance in preparing this publication.

Roger F. Hackett
Director, Center for Japanese Studies
The University of Michigan

Acknowledgments

Without the extensive cooperation and assistance of the many individuals and institutions who generously contributed to the compilation of this bibliography, it would not have been possible to compile as comprehensive and complete a listing. Among the many overseas contributors who provided invaluable information are: Edwin S. Crawcour, Australian National University, Canberra, Australia; Josef Kreiner, Institut für Japanologie, Universität Wien, Vienna, Austria; Jaroslav Bărinka, Universita Karlova, Prague, Czechoslovakia; Eric Grinstead, Scandinavian Institute of Asian Studies, Copenhagen, Denmark; Wolfgang Bauer, Seminar für Ostasiatische Kultur- und Sprachwissenschaft, Universität, München, Munich, Germany; Bernhard Grossmann, Institut für Asienkunde, Hamburg, Germany; Bruno Lewin, Ostasien Institut, Bochum, Germany; Wolfgang Seuberlich, Stiftung Preussischer Kulturbesitz, Ostasiatische Abteilung, Marburg/Lahn, Germany; Barry C. Bloomfield, The Library, School of Oriental and African Studies, University of London, London, England, and his assistant, Miss B. A. Brown; Timothy Wixted, Oxford University, Oxford, England; Mrs. E. Hosszú, Center for Afro-Asian Research of the Hungarian Academy of Sciences, Budapest, Hungary; Girja Kumar, The Library, Indian School of International Studies, New Delhi, India; Sutinder Singh, The Library, Inter-University Board of India and Ceylon, New Delhi, India; Akira Tabohashi, Ministry of Education, Tokyo, Japan; Frits Vos, Japanologisch Instituut, Leiden, The Netherlands; Mikołaj Melanowicz, Oriental Institute, University of Warsaw, Warsaw, Poland; Cornelius Ouwehand, Ostasiatisches Seminar der Universität Zürich, Zürich, Switzerland; Alexander Bendik and Yvetta Perskaya, The Library, Institut Narodov Azii, Moscow, USSR.

Among those within the United States who deserve especial mention for providing necessary supplementary information regarding dissertations submitted to their respective institutions are: Kay Schmidt, The Library, American University; Raymond Tang and Mrs. Gloria Novak, East Asiatic Library, University of California at Berkeley; Mrs. Man-Hing Yue Mok and Che-Hwei Lin, The Library, University of California at Los Angeles; James Morita, Far Eastern Library, University of Chicago; Stanleigh H. Jones, Jr., Asian Studies Program, Claremont Graduate School; Frank Baldwin, Jr., East Asian Institute, Columbia University; Richard C. Howard, Wason Collection, Cornell University Library; Nancy W. Stadelman, Rose Memorial Library, Drew University; Stephen Uhalley, Department of History, Duke University; R. H. Reed, The Library, George Washington University; Ann C. Clark and Jeanne Conway, The Library, Georgetown University; staff of the Harvard University Archives; staff of the Reference Department at Indiana University Library; Ada M. Stoflet, The Library, University of Iowa; Theodore McNelly, Department of Government and Politics, University of Maryland; Iwao Ishino, Department of Anthropology, Michigan State University; Kazuko Abe, East Asian Library, University of Minnesota; Gary N. Denue, The Library of the University of Nebraska; Stephen M. O'Brien, New York University Library; William S. Wong, Chinese and Japanese Collection, and Thomas R. Buckman, Northwestern University Library; Eleanor R. Devlin, Ohio State University Library; Thomas T. Winant, Department of History, University of Pennsylvania; John Singleton, School of Education, University of Pittsburgh; Henry D. Smith, II, Department of History, Princeton University; Dorothea B. Shultes, Syracuse University Library; Curtis W. Stucki, The Library, University of Washington (Seattle); Chester Wang, The Library, University of Wisconsin; William J. Bogaty, Yale University.

Several specialists in Japanese and Korean studies within the United States kindly reviewed selected sections of the manuscript (as indicated in parentheses below) and provided valuable suggestions concerning its comprehensiveness and arrangement: Richard K. Beardsley (Anthropology, Archaeology, Psychology, Social Psychology, and Sociology), Calvin L. French (Art and Architecture), William Hauser (Premodern History), Susumu Nagara (Language and Linguistics), Kazuya Sato (Political Science), Robert M. Spaulding, Jr. (History and International Relations), and David J. Steinberg (International Relations), all of the University of Michigan; Akira Iriye (International Relations) and Joseph M. Kitagawa (Religion and Philosophy) of the University of Chicago; Victor Kobayashi (Education), University of Hawaii; Thomas Swann (Literature) and Edward Wagner (Korea) of Harvard University; David K. Wyatt (International Relations), Cornell University; Kozo Yamamura (Demography and Economics), Boston College; and Key P. Yang (Korea), Orientalia Division, The Library of Congress.

Particular thanks should go to the Joint Committee on Japanese Studies (John Hall, chairman) and the Joint Committee on Korean Studies (Gari Ledyard, chairman) of the Social Science Research Council and the American Council of Learned Societies both for the generous financial assistance and for the endorsement of the project that they have provided; to the Committee on East Asian Libraries (CEAL) for its early endorsement of the project; to Katharina Winokurow (Bochum, Germany), who painstakingly annotated nearly all the German dissertation entries, and to the

Stiftung Volkswagenwerk, which sponsored her contribution; to Peter Berton (School of Politics and International Relations, University of Southern California), Mrs. Raissa Berstein, George Ginsburgs (New School for Social Research), and Joseph A. Placek (Slavic Section, University of Michigan Library), to all of whom I am greatly indebted for their invaluable cooperation in romanizing, translating, supplementing, and editing the listing of Russian dissertations contributed by Alexander Bendik and Yvetta Perskaya of the Institut Narodov Azii; to Thomas Swann, Harvard University, for his constant encouragement and advice; to Hans-B. and Marianne Buergi, François Van Rosevelt, and Frithjof Schneider, all of the University of Michigan, for their help in translating both the titles of and the annotations for the German-language dissertations into English; to the staff of the Reference Desk, General Library, University of Michigan, for their many endeavors in facilitating the use of library reference materials; to Miss Choo-won Suh, Senior Japanese-Korean Librarian at the Asia Library of the University of Michigan for her considerable assistance with the Korean entries; to the graduate students and secretaries associated with the University of Michigan's Center for Japanese Studies, who assisted in proofreading the final typescript and in other matters; to University Microfilms, Inc., which provided a specially prepared DATRIX Key Word listing of relevant theses as well as permission to examine their file of recently completed American dissertations; to Yukihisa Suzuki (former head of the Asia Library of the University of Michigan) for his advice and initial support of the project; to Judy Hopkins, Susan Hochendoner, and Sue Dawkins, who managed to overcome the innumerable problems involved in typing the main body of the manuscript; and to Marion Dittman and Richard Gray of the American Library Association for the many hours that they spent in determining the format and arrangement of the entire bibliography and in providing invaluable editorial advice.

Finally, a very special expression of gratitude should be extended to: John Bowden, Ann Arbor, Michigan, whose constant assistance in many phases of the project was beyond what I had any right to expect; Roger F. Hackett, Director of the Center for Japanese Studies, The University of Michigan, without whose support the project could not have been completed; and Robert M. Spaulding, Jr., Research Associate of the Center, whose suggestion that led to the initiation of the project was but the first of many stimulating ideas. It is to these three friends that this work has been dedicated.

Frank J. Shulman

Ann Arbor, Michigan

Introduction

With the rapid, postwar development of Japanese and Korean studies at institutions throughout the West, the value, indeed the necessity, of maintaining bibliographic control over relevant doctoral dissertations has become increasingly recognized. Pioneering efforts have already been made by Curtis W. Stucki and Peter Cornwall in bringing together large numbers of dissertations on Asia and on Japan respectively.[1] Nonetheless, many scholars have continued to feel the need for a more comprehensive and detailed listing of such theses. The present bibliography has been compiled in response to this need, with the hope that it will serve as the definitive reference guide to this significant but widely scattered body of research materials on Japan and Korea. It is also hoped that the compilation will establish for others a useful bibliographic method for approaching the entire corpus of doctoral dissertations and will greatly increase the extent to which dissertations can and will be used for research and study.

SCOPE

Japan and Korea: An Annotated Bibliography of Doctoral Dissertations in Western Languages attempts to be a comprehensive, interdisciplinary guide to all Western-language dissertations, 1877-1969, dealing in whole or in part with Japan and Korea. Numerous bibliographies, checklists, dissertation typescripts, abstracts, unpublished records, and bulletins — many of which are listed on page 307 of this volume — have been carefully examined for pertinent information. As a result, the compiler has succeeded in identifying 2,586 relevant titles (2077 for Japan, 509 for Korea; see Appendixes A and B) in English, French, German, Russian, and ten additional European languages and in preparing descriptive annotations for the vast majority of them. Every effort has been made to be as retrospectively thorough and as up to date as possible: the earliest dissertation listed was submitted by Henry S. Munroe to Columbia University in 1877; the latest entries represent dissertations submitted for degrees in the Fall of 1969. Although the great majority of dissertations are for the degree of Doctor of Philosophy, no differentiation has been made between this degree and other doctoral degrees with the exception of the German- and Russian-language entries. Here distinction has been made between the terms Habilitationsschrift and Kandidat nauk for "Candidate's degree" and the terms Doktorat and Doktor nauk for "Doctor's degree".

In the compilation of this bibliography, many titles have been incorporated that would normally be overlooked because they do not directly relate to the Japanese home islands or to the Korean peninsula. Thus, among those included, are those which while focusing on other geographical areas of the world contain one or two chapters on such subjects as Japanese relations with China, Southeast Asia, or various Western countries, as well as those which treat overseas Japanese communities and the influence of Japanese culture abroad. Furthermore, while the compilation emphasizes the social sciences and the humanities, it also includes a number of relevant theses completed in the natural sciences. No attempt has been made to select or discard any title on the basis of its intrinsic merit or relative lack of value; it is assumed that doctoral candidates will want to know at the very least what topics have already been chosen by their predecessors.

ARRANGEMENT

All dissertations have been classified on the basis of their contents, regardless of the department to which they have been submitted, and specific cross references have been made from other sections to the main entries where appropriate. Within each subsection the arrangement is chronological by date of completion rather than alphabetical by author. This will provide the reader with rapid access to the most recent titles and will also indicate long-term trends in doctoral research on various subjects. Dissertations in the fields of economics, education, history, and political science concerned primarily with events prior to August 1945 are entered under History or under International Relations, depending on whether they focus on internal developments or on overseas activities and diplomatic relations. Readers approaching the listing by subject are advised also to look under related topics, to check the Addenda, and to note the general cross-reference statements at the head of each section and subsection. The three indexes to the compilation — (1) an alphabetical listing by author and main-entry code number, (2) an index by degree-awarding institution, and (3) a register of all dissertations that are primarily biographical in nature — furthermore should be consulted for effective use of the bibliography.

[1] Curtis W. Stucki, American Doctoral Dissertations on Asia—1933-June 1966 (3d ed.; Ithaca, N.Y.: Southeast Asia Program, Cornell University, 1968); Peter Cornwall, Unpublished Doctoral Dissertations Relating to Japan, Accepted in the Universities of Australia, Canada, Great Britain, and the United States, 1946-1963 (Ann Arbor: Center for Japanese Studies, University of Michigan, 1965).

ENTRIES

The information furnished for each main dissertation entry appears in the following sequence: (1) the consecutive entry number; (2) the author's name in full; (3) the complete title and subtitle of the dissertation (with an English translation where necessary); (4) the name of the university or institution in abbreviated form; (5) the year in which the degree was conferred; (6) the pagination; (7) the location of the abstract (if one exists); (8) information regarding the best means for obtaining a photographic reproduction of the dissertation typescript; (9) a descriptive annotation; and (10) a listing of related books and articles by the dissertation author. Keys to the abbreviations and symbols used in the various entries are given on page xix; a listing of universities with their complete names may be found in the Institutional Index (page 329).

When consulting the various entries, the reader should keep the following points particularly in mind:

Year of the dissertation. The year in which the degree was conferred, not the year in which the thesis was written, is normally provided; but there are a number of exceptions to this rule due to inadequate information.

Pagination. Dissertations for which abstracts have been published in Dissertation Abstracts indicate the pagination of the microfilm copy available from University Microfilms, Inc. In all other cases the pagination specified is that of the actual typescript.

Annotations. Annotations have been prepared primarily to assist the reader in rapidly obtaining an idea of the scope, character, or contents of the dissertation; to call his attention to certain of its noteworthy features; or, on occasion, to justify the inclusion of a title that appears to be unrelated to Japan or Korea. In most cases these annotations are based entirely on published abstracts and introductory statements to particular dissertations, or consist of a listing of the chapter headings found in the dissertation tables of contents (preceded in the entry by the word Contents). They are not meant to be evaluative or critical in nature, and their length, which varies from one entry to the next, depends solely upon the amount of information readily available to the compiler and, therefore, should not be regarded as indicative of the relative importance of respective titles. All quotations within the annotations, it should also be noted, are taken directly from the dissertation typescript or from its abstract.

Related publications. Full bibliographic information about books and articles by the dissertation author that either are based on his doctoral research or are outgrowths of it and of subsequent research on the same or on a closely related subject, is provided whenever known. Book-length monographs are listed first; their titles are abbreviated whenever they are identical with those of the dissertations themselves. Following are the titles of related articles listed in order of publication date. Every effort has been made to be as inclusive as possible in this respect, but periodical citations generally have not been verified and, in most cases, related articles have not been compared with the dissertation typescript for the purpose of determining just how closely they are related.

Translations of foreign-language titles. All translations have been made by the compiler or by contributors to the bibliography. Emphasis has been placed on providing a meaningful equivalent, rather than a literal translation, of all such titles.

AVAILABILITY OF DISSERTATIONS

While many doctoral dissertations are available in published form at major university libraries (e.g., Harvard University, The University of Michigan) or at the Center for Research Libraries (5721 South Cottage Grove Ave., Chicago, Ill. 60637), the majority of titles in this bibliography have never appeared in print except as journal articles. Most of these, nonetheless, are available for purchase on microfilm or in Xerox form. The following guide outlines the availability of such unpublished works country by country:

Australia. For copies of dissertations submitted to the Australian National University, write to: The Library, Australian National University, P.O. Box 4, Canberra, A.C.T. Photocopies of theses less than five years old may be obtained only after the author's written permission has been secured.

Austria. Refer to the dissertation desired by author, title, and inventory number (Nr.) as specified in the bibliography and write to either: (1) Die Universitätsbibliothek der Universität Wien, A-1010 Wien, Dr. Karl Lueger-Ring 1; or (2) Die Österreichische Nationalbibliothek, A-1010 Wien, Josefsplatz 1.

Belgium. Write directly to the library of the university where the dissertation has been accepted.

Brazil. Consult relevant entries in the bibliography.

Canada. For microfilm copies of dissertations available from the National Library of Canada, write to: Canadian Theses on Microfilm, Cataloguing Branch, Room 414, National Library of Canada, Ottawa 4, Ontario. Inter-library loan requests for these same theses should be addressed to the Reference Branch of the library. For all other dissertations, write directly to the university where the dissertation has been accepted.

Czechoslovakia. For Xerox or microfilm copies, write to: (1) Filosofická fakulta University Karlovy, děkanát; Praha 1; Náměstí Krasnoarmějců 2; or (2) Orientální ústav ČSAV; Praha 3; Lázeňská 4.

Denmark. Write to the library of the university where the dissertation has been accepted.

France. For copies of dissertations submitted to the Université de Paris, write to: Bibliothèque de la Sorbonne; 47, rue des Écoles; 75-Paris (5e). For a dissertation submitted to another institution, write directly to the library of the university where it has been accepted.

Germany. Copies of dissertations indicated as being available at Marburg/Lahn, Universitätsbibliothek, may be ordered directly from that institution. In all other cases, write directly to the university library of the institution at which the dissertation has been deposited. Refer to the dissertation by author, title, and inventory number (Nr.) as specified in the bibliography.

Great Britain. Regulations vary from institution to institution, but in most cases the written consent of the author or of his university must be obtained before photocopies can be provided. Write directly to the university library or consult the editorial note of the latest volume of the Association of Special Libraries and Information Bureaux (ASLIB), Index to Theses Accepted for Higher Degrees in the Universities of Great Britain and Ireland for further details.

Hungary. Consult relevant entries in the bibliography.

India. Consult relevant entries in the bibliography.

Italy. Write to the library of the university where the dissertation has been accepted.

Japan. Write to the library of the university where the dissertation has been accepted.

Korea. Write to the library of the university where the dissertation has been accepted.

Mexico. Consult relevant entries in the bibliography.

Netherlands. Write to the library of the university where the dissertation has been accepted.

New Zealand. Consult relevant entries in the bibliography.

Philippines. Write to the library of the university where the dissertation has been accepted.

Poland. Write to the library of the university where the dissertation has been accepted.

Sweden. Write to the library of the university where the dissertation has been accepted.

Switzerland. Write to the library of the university where the dissertation has been accepted.

United States. Copies of dissertations abstracted in Dissertation Abstracts and in Microfilm Abstracts may be purchased directly from University Microfilms, Inc., 300 North Zeeb Road, Ann Arbor, Mich. 48106. Order by the author's name and the dissertation's UM number, specifying whether a microfilm or xerographic copy is desired. Prices listed in Dissertation Abstracts are subject to change without notice. At the present time, the rate is 1 1/4¢ per microfilm frame and 4 1/2¢ per Xerox page. The minimum charge for any order is $3.00 plus shipping and handling. Customers are requested not to enclose payment with their orders; they will be billed at the time of shipment.

Dissertations submitted to the University of Chicago may be ordered directly from the Photoduplication Department, University of Chicago Library, Swift Hall, Chicago, Ill. 60637.

Dissertations submitted to Harvard University and to Radcliffe College are available at the Harvard University Archives, Widener Library, Cambridge, Mass. 02138. Xerox and microfilm copies of any dissertation over five years old can be ordered directly from the library. Dissertations less than five years old may be reproduced only with the author's written permission (his address may be obtained from the University Archives). Harvard University dissertations also are available on inter-library loan unless restricted. The reader should note that restrictions are automatically applied for a period of five years after the award of the Ph.D. degree for a dissertation written in History or in History and Far Eastern Languages. For further details, write directly to the University Archives.

For copies of all other American dissertations, write directly to the library of the university where the dissertation has been accepted. The reader should keep in mind, however, that recently completed dissertations lacking a UM number will likely become available from University Microfilms by December 1970.

USSR. Copies of all dissertations completed in the Soviet Union since 1945 are regularly deposited in the V. I. Lenin State Library of the USSR, Dr. Kalinina 3, Moscow; inquiries should be directed to the library. The reader should note, however, that photocopies are very difficult to obtain outside the Soviet Union and that the U.S. Library of Congress is among those institutions that have not yet been successful in acquiring such copies.

The compiler personally supervised the composition of the book.

Abbreviations and Symbols

AB	abstract of the dissertation (appearing in a source other than Dissertation Abstracts)
Contents:	a listing of the chapter headings in the dissertation's table of contents
DA	Dissertation Abstracts with volume and page numbers (example: DA 27 (July 1966), 167-68-A)
diss.ms.	dissertation manuscript or typescript
ed.	edited
no.; Nr.	library catalog or inventory number
Rel.Publ.:	related publications (articles and books)
UM	University Microfilms, Inc., with order number (example: UM 66-6370)
v.; t.; Bd.	volume

ABBREVIATIONS OF JOURNALS FREQUENTLY APPEARING IN LISTINGS OF RELATED PUBLICATIONS

FEQ	Far Eastern Quarterly
FES	Far Eastern Survey
HJAS	Harvard Journal of Asiatic Studies
JAOS	Journal of the American Oriental Society
JAS	Journal of Asian Studies
MN	Monumenta Nipponica
MOAG	Mitteilungen der Deutschen Gesellschaft für Natur- und Völkerkunde Ostasiens
PHR	Pacific Historical Review

Japanese and Korean names are listed in their "Oriental" order, i.e., surname followed by forename, but without diacritical marks in the case of Orientals whose dissertations are included within the bibliography

Wherever possible, the romanization systems generally regarded as standard in the English-speaking world have been used: Hepburn for Japanese; McCune-Reischauer for Korean; and Wade-Giles for Chinese.

Japan

Anthropology and Sociology

GENERAL

See also: Demography (pages 19-20), Economics--labor (pages 40-43), Psychology and Social Psychology (pages 219-20), and Overseas Japanese Communities (pages 198-208).

1
LAMPE, William Edmund. The Japanese Social Organization. Princeton, 1908. Diss. ms. not available.

Contents: The Social History (The Origin of the Japanese, The Japanese in Their Earliest History, The Great Reform, Development and Assimilation, The Shogunate and Feudalism); The Social Structure (The Family, The Emperor and the Kuge, Feudal Society, Buddhist Priests); The Changing Social Order (Changes Due to the Opening of the Country, The Levelling Process, Japan's Industrial Future, Estimate of the Stability of the Present Social Order).

Rel.Publ.: The Japanese...Organization. Princeton: Princeton University Press, 1910. 84p.

2
KAWAMURA, Tadao. The Class Conflict in Japan as Affected by the Expansion of Japanese Industry and Trade. Chicago, 1928. 329, xii p. AB: University of Chicago. Abstracts of Theses, Humanistic Series. v.6 (1927/28), p. 255-62.

Studies social changes in Japan from the Tokugawa period through the mid-1920's.

3
FILLA, Martin. Grundlagen und Wesen der altjapanischen Sportkünste [The Basis for and the Characteristics of Early Japanese Athletic Arts]. Leipzig, 1938. Text in German. The dissertation in its published form is available at Marburg/Lahn, Bücherei für Leibesübungen, Nr. T III 3.

Contents: Ethics and Morals as a Basis; Geographical, Racial, Aesthetic, and Cultural Prerequisites; The Nature and Objectives of Early Japanese Athletic Arts (Sumō, Kendō, Jūdō, Kyūdō, Hira suiei, Naginata, Kemari, Oibane).

Rel.Publ.: Grundlagen...Sportkünste. Würzburg-Aumühle: Triltsch, 1939. xii, 57p. (Kőrperliche Erziehung und Sport. Beiträge zur Sportswissenschaft. Schriften des Institutes für Leibesübungen der Universität Leipzig, 1)

4
PELZEL, John Campbell. Social Stratification in Japanese Urban Economic Life. Harvard, 1950. iii, 371p. AB: 4p. summary appended to diss. ms.

Contents: An Industrial Community (Location, Early History, The Hinterland and the Growth of the City, The Postwar City); Livelihood (A Community Living Pattern, Income and Living Standards); Work Life in and about the Factory (The Medium and Small Factory, Work Society in the Traditional Medium and Small Factory, Master and Enterpriser, The Union). Centers of life in Kawaguchi City, Saitama prefecture.

Rel.Publ.: "Some Social Factors Bearing upon Japanese Population," American Sociological Review, 15 (Feb. 1950), 20-25; "The Small Industrialist in Japan," Explorations in Entrepreneurial History, 7 (Dec. 1954).

5
JACOBS, Norman Gabriel. The Societal System: A Method for the Comparative Analysis of Social Institutions with Special Reference to China and Japan. Harvard, 1951. 646p. (2v.) AB: United States Department of State, External Research Office. Abstracts of Completed Doctoral Dissertations for the Academic Year 1950/51. p.347-49.

See especially Ch.5, "The Feudal-Industrial Societal System, Japan" (p.305-496) and Ch.6, pt.3, "Societal Change, Japan" (p. 574-99).

6
BELLAH, Robert Neelly. Religion and Society in Tokugawa Japan. Harvard, 1955. ii, 362p. AB: 5p. summary appended to diss. ms.

Contents: Religion and the Rise of Modern Industrial Societies; An Outline of Japanese Social Structure in the Tokugawa Period; Japanese Religion: A General View; Religion and the Polity; Religion and the Economy; Shingaku and Its Founder, Ishida Baigan.

Rel.Publ.: Tokugawa Religion: The Values of Pre-Industrial Japan. Glencoe, Ill.: Free Press, 1957. 249p.; "Research Chronicle: Tokugawa Religion," in Sociologists at Work: Essays on the Craft of Social Research, ed. by Phillip Hammond (New York: Basic Books, 1964), 142-60.

MUNAKATA, Peter F. The Application of Western Sociological Theory to the Analysis of Bureaucratic Structure in Japan: A Pilot Study and Its interpretation. 1956. See no.293.

RABINOWITZ, Richard W. The Japanese Lawyer: A Study in the Sociology of the Legal Profession. 1956. See no.1556.

KASAHARA, Yoshiko. The Influx and Exodus of Migrants among the 47 Prefectures in Japan, 1920-1935. 1958. See no.131.

7
REILING, John Thomas. The Origin of War. Indiana,

1958. 250p. DA 19 (June 1959), 3402-03; UM 58-2932.

India, Japan, and particularly China are studied in an effort to verify the hypothesis "that contemporary warfare is the product of a unique origin in the Near East...and that it has been diffused from that area to wherever it is presently found."

SKILLMAN, John H. A Study of the Relationship Between Participation in Various Types of Extra-Class Activities and Academic Performance in Three Private Japanese Secondary Schools. 1958. See no.449.

8
CHEE, Chang-boh. Development of Sociology in Japan: A Study of Adaptation of Western Sociological Orientations into the Japanese Social Structure. Duke, 1959. 289p. DA 20 (Mar. 1960), 3875-76; UM 60-402.

Essentially an historical study, from the early Meiji Period through the mid-1950's. Contents: Some Prerequisites to the Study of Japan's Adaptation of Western Society; A Sociological Analysis of the Meiji Restoration: Its Significance to Westernization; The Period of Encyclopedic and Organic Sociology (1870's-1918) and the Rise of Psychologicalism; High Tide of German Influence upon Japanese Sociology; Movement to Develop Japan's Own Sociology; The Postwar Trends of Japanese Sociology: Influence of American Sociology (1945-).

9
NIYEKAWA, Agnes Mitsue. Factors Associated with Authoritarianism in Japan. New York, 1960. 175p. DA 21 (July 1960), 255; UM 60-2300.

The sample for the study consisted of 543 subjects from two urban high schools and four rural high schools. The study demonstrated that authoritarianism in Japan is characterized by acquiescence, i.e., by the conviction of many Japanese that the words of the authority are right.

Rel.Publ.: "Authoritarianism in an Authoritarian Culture: The Case of Japan," International Journal of Social Psychiatry, 12 (Aug. 1966), 283-88.

KURODA, Yasumasa. Political Socialization: Personal Political Organization of Law Students in Japan. 1962. See no.1796.

10
PLATH, David William. The Strung and the Unstrung: Holidays in Japanese Life. Harvard, 1962. v, 225p.

"Ch. 1 examines the calendries of holidays in Japanese life...and points out that though these cultural charts of time serve to canalize behavior, they do not bind it rigidly: each group guides itself by these charts but must find its own way. Ch. 2 illustrates this by comparing the holiday rounds of three households in the Anchiku region of Nagano prefecture...Ch. 3 takes up the dynamics of compulsion and release within the framework of the holiday as social drama...Ch. 4-6 present three examples of Japanese holidays as social drama--Bon, Christmas, and the weekly holiday--and discuss the manner in which they are performed."

Rel.Publ.: The After Hours: Modern Japan and the Search for Enjoyment. Berkeley: University of California Press, 1964. xi, 222p.; "Overworked Japan and the Holiday Demiurge," Today's Japan, 8 (Aug. 1960), 61-64; "Land of the Rising Sunday," Japan Quarterly, 7 (July/Sept. 1960), 357-61; "Will Success Spoil the Japanese?" Asian Survey, 1 (Nov. 1961), 27-30. "The Enjoyment of Daily Living: Some Japanese Popular Views," JAS, 22 (May 1963), 305-16; "The Japanese Popular Christmas: Coping with Modernity," Journal of American Folklore, 76 (Oct./Dec. 1963), 309-17.

11
AJAMI, Ismail. Land Reform: A Sociological Interpretation. Cornell, 1964. 139p. DA 25 (Feb. 1965), 4847-48; UM 65-3708.

"The thesis proposes to develop a sociological interpretation of land reform. Land reform is conceptualized as a social movement and is studied in terms of its organizational development as well as its societal context. The land reform movements of Japan, Mexico, and Rumania were selected as the cases for study."

12
HESSELGRAVE, David John. A Propagation Profile of the Sōka Gakkai. Minnesota, 1965. 305p. DA 26 (Mar. 1966), 5596; UM 65-15,264.

Examines and evaluates from a rhetorical point of view Sōka Gakkai's method of coercive propagation called shakubuku. The dissertation includes "a consideration of the Society's organizational structure, indoctrination program, leadership, propaganda organs, small group technique, political activity, and related concerns."

Rel.Publ.: "The Background and Methodology of Sōka Gakkai Propagation: An Overview and Brief Rhetorical Analysis," Studies on Asia, 1966, ed. by Robert K. Sakai (Lincoln: University of Nebraska Press, 1966), 65-75.

13
SOARES, Gláucio Ary Dillon. Economic Development and Political Radicalism. Washington, St. Louis, 1965. 304p. DA 26 (Nov. 1965), 2916-17; UM 65-9778.

"Investigates the political consequences of economic development" using post-World War II data for Japan and three other countries.

AZUMI, Koya. The Recruitment of University Graduates by Big Firms in Japan. 1966. See no.225.

14
BRYCE, Herrington Julian. Social Origin as an Obstacle or as an Aid to Mobility: A Comparative Analysis of Long-Run Occupational Mobility. Syracuse, 1966. 240p. DA 28 (Aug. 1967), 333-34-A; UM 67-7060.

"This is a cross-national comparison of long-run occupational mobility in the United States, Japan, Puerto Rico, and seven countries in Western Europe. Its purpose is to estimate the degree to which the social origin of males (indicated by their father's occupational class) affects their opportunities for mobility into those occupational classes to which their fathers do not belong."

Rel.Publ.: "Social Mobility and Economic Growth and Structure," Kölner Zeitschrift für Soziologie und Sozialpsychologie, Sonderheft 5 (1961), 303-15.

15
CUCELOGLU, Dogan Mehmet. A Cross-Cultural Study of Communication via Facial Expressions. Illinois, 1967. 288p. DA 28 (June 1968), 5167-A; UM 68-8046.

The study includes an analysis of the Japanese language/culture community.

PRICE, John Andrew. The Japanese Market System: Retailing in a Dual Economy. 1967. See no.232.

16
SHIMAHARA, Nobuo. A Study of the Enculturative Roles of Japanese Education. Boston, 1967. 406p. DA 29 (June 1969), 4202-03-A; UM 69-7833.

An anthropological case study whose chief purposes were "(1) to determine roles that compulsory schools as agents of culture play at a time when Japanese culture is undergoing tremendous change; (2) to identify the nature of relationships between formal education and informal education as indicated by processes of enculturation in selected communities."

WIMBERLEY, Hickman H. Seicho-no-Ie: A Study of a Japanese Religio-Political Association. 1967. See no. 1974.

COLE, Robert E. Japanese Blue Collar Workers: A Participant Observation Study. 1968. See no.303.

JETTMAR, Dieter. Der Fischereiwortschatz der am Kuroshio gelegenen Pazifikküste Japans. 1968. See no. 1458.

KIEFER, Christie Weber. Personality and Social Change in a Japanese Danchi. 1968. See no.1878.

17
SKELTON, T. Lane. Social Movements and Social Change: The Sōka Gakkai of Japan. California, Berkeley, 1968. 307p. DA 30 (Sept. 1969), 1246-A; UM 69-15,001.

"In this study...several general questions were addressed: First, what conditions are conducive to social movements in general and to a particular social movement? Second, how do leaders attract, integrate, motivate, and retain members-at-large, intermediate-level leaders, and top leadership? How do they seek to avoid schism and succession? Third, how do leaders handle the movement in relation to the outside environmental society? Contents: Historical and Descriptive Review; Antecedent Factors; The Leadership; Ideology; Organization; Tactics of Operation.

BIOLOGICAL ANTHROPOLOGY

18
WEAR, Robert Edward. Physical Fitness and Performance of a Medically Healthy Group of Adult Males of Mongoloid and Melanesian Racial Ancestry. Michigan, 1955. 195p. DA 15 (Sept. 1955), 1548; UM 12,665.

"Investigates the physical condition and ability of Mongoloids [Chinese and Japanese] and Melanesians between the ages of seventeen and fifty-six years through the use of physical tests and measurements."

19
IKEDA, Namiko. A Comparison of Physical Fitness of Children in Iowa, U.S.A., and Tokyo, Japan. Iowa, 1961. 87p. DA 22 (Nov. 1961), 1501; UM 61-4031.

"A subproblem of the study was to find the relationships between anthropometric measurements and the motor performances" of children in the two groups.

20
HARTLE, Janet Arcuni. A Study of Certain Features of the Mongoloid Face. Columbia, 1962. 188p. DA 23 (Mar. 1963), 3069-70; UM 63-1495.

Compares a Central Asiatic Mongol population with other Mongoloid (including Japanese) and non-Mongoloid populations.

21
OMOTO, Keiichi. Vergleichende Untersuchungen zur Allelenhäufigkeit des Gc-Systems bei asiatischen und europaischen Populationen [A Comparative Study of Allele Frequencies in the Gc System among Asian and European Populations]. Münster, 1963. Text in German. The dissertation in its published form is available at Marburg/Lahn, Staatsbibliothek Preussischer Kulturbesitz, Nr. Hsn 39,632; also at the University of Michigan, General Library, no.28,577.

A study of population genetics within the Gc system among Europeans and Asians based on a modification of the immuno-electrophoresis investigation of 1114 serum tests from Greece, Korea, and Japan. The discussion focuses on a number of evolutionary factors which may have played a role in the occurrence of varying distributions of Gc alleles among different populations.

Rel.Publ.: Vergleichende...Populationen. München: Charlotte Schön, 1963. 30p.

COMMUNITY STUDIES

For Japanese communities in Brazil, the United States, etc., see Overseas Japanese Communities (pages 198-208).

22
JONES, Thomas Elsa. Mountain Folk of Japan: A Study in Method. Columbia, 1926. v, 132p.

An analysis of the economic desires and standards, family and social mores, and community fears and beliefs of the inhabitants of certain isolated mountain villages in Gifu, Kumamoto, Ibaraki, Niigata, and Shimane prefectures. Based on an investigation carried out between 1917 and 1924.

Rel. Publ.: Mountain...Method. New York, 1926. v, 132p.

23
EMBREE, John Fee. Suye Mura: A Changing Economic Order. Chicago, 1937. 210p.

A comprehensive social study of a rural peasant village in Kumamoto prefecture with focus on village organization, families and households, forms of cooperation, social classes and associations, the life cycle of individuals, religious rituals, and the economic basis of life.

Rel.Publ.: Suye Mura: A Japanese Village. Chicago: University of Chicago Press, 1939. xxvii, 354p. (The University of Chicago Publications in Anthropology, Ethnological Services); "Notes on the Indian God Gavagriva (Godzu Tenno) in Contemporary Japan," JAOS, 59 (1939), 67-70; "Some Social Functions of Religion in Rural Japan," American Journal of Sociology, 47 (Sept. 1941), 184-89; "Sanitation and Health in a Japanese Village," Journal of the Washington Academy of Sciences, 34 (1944), 97-108; "Japanese Administration at the Local Level," Applied Anthropology, 3 (Sept. 1944), 11-18; "Gokkanosho: A Remote Corner of Japan," The Scientific Monthly, 59 (Nov. 1944), 343-55.

24
NORBECK, Edward. Takashima: A Fishing Community of Japan. Michigan, 1952. 426p. DA 12 (1952), 124-25; UM 3541.

Seeks "to provide ethnographic data on rural Japan, to describe changes in rural Japanese culture which have occurred as the result of contact with Western cultures, and to analyze the processes which underlie the changes." Based on fieldwork carried out at Takashima, Okayama prefecture. Contents: Gaining a Livelihood; The Household and House Life; The Buraku and the Community; Religion; The Life Cycle; The Impact of Westernization.

Rel.Publ.: Takashima...Japan. Salt Lake City, University of Utah Press, 1954. 231p.; "Westernization as Evident on the Buraku Level," Minzokugaku kenkyū, 16 (1951), 38-45; "Pollution and Taboo in Contemporary Japan," Southwestern Journal of Anthropology, 8 (1952), 269-85; "Age-grading in Japan," American Anthropologist, 55 (1953), 373-84; "Child Training in a Japanese Fishing Community" [by] Edward and Margaret Norbeck, in Personal Character and Cultural Milieu, 3d rev. ed., ed. by Douglas G. Haring (Syracuse: Syracuse University Press, 1956), 651-73.

25
CORNELL, John Bilheimer. Matsunagi: The Life and Social Organization of a Japanese Mountain Community. Michigan, 1953. 387p. DA 13 (1953), 623-24; UM 5657.

Describes and analyzes the social and kinship aspects of buraku life in Matsunagi (Okayama prefecture) with the aim of defining "local social features that also have a general validity in Japan." Contents: Native Resources and Material Culture; Household Organization, Housing, and Domestic Life; Buraku Social Organization and Community Life; External Relations in the Cultural Milieu; Household Precedence in Relations of Kin, Community, and Individuals. The dissertation also includes detailed appendices on (1) the life history of the individual in the household, and (2) religion.

Rel.Publ.: "Matsunagi: A Japanese Mountain Community," in Two Japanese Villages [by] Robert J. Smith and John B. Cornell (Ann Arbor: University of Michigan Press, 1956), xvii-xxii, 113-232. (University of Michigan, Center for Japanese Studies, Occasional Papers, 5); "Local Group Stability in the Japanese Community," Human Organization, 22 (Summer 1963), 113-25.

26
SMITH, Robert John. Kurusu: A Changing Japanese Agricultural Community. Cornell, 1953. 360p.

A study of life in Kurusu, a buraku in Kagawa prefecture, with a discussion of neighborly cooperation, land reform, agricultural methods and practices, and various aspects of change.

Rel.Publ.: "Kurusu: A Changing Japanese Agricultural Community," in Two Japanese Villages [by] Robert J. Smith and John B. Cornell (Ann Arbor: University of Michigan Press, 1956), xi-xvi, 1-112. (University of Michigan, Center for Japanese Studies, Occasional Papers, 5); "Cooperative Forms in a Japanese Agricultural Community," in University of Michigan, Center for Japanese Studies, Occasional Papers, 3 (Ann Arbor: University of Michigan Press, 1952), 59-70; "Community Interrelations with the Outside World: The Case of a Japanese Agricultural Community" [by] Robert J. Smith and Eudaldo P. Reyes, American Anthropologist, 59 (June 1957), 463-72.

27
YOSHINO, Ikuno Roger. Selected Social Changes in a Japanese Village, 1935-1953. Southern California, 1954. 188p. AB: University of Southern California. Abstracts of Dissertations for...1955. p.218-19.

Analyzes selected social changes that occurred in Suye mura (Kyushu) between the years 1935 (when the community was studied by John Embree) and 1953, and pays considerable attention to "the impact of occupation policies and legislation." The author concluded that while the family structure had resisted many social changes, the village youth had become much more receptive to individualism.

Rel.Publ.: "A Re-Study of Suye-Mura: An Investigation of Social Change," in State College of Washington Research Studies, 24 (June 1956), 182p.

28
DONOGHUE, John David. An Eta Community in Northern Japan: A Study in Intra-group Relations. Chicago, 1956. v, 163p.

Focuses on the dynamics of interpersonal and intergroup relations that are responsible for the Eta remaining a distinct, socially segregated, and isolated group. Based on research in Shinkoji-machi, a political subdivision of Hirosaki City, Aomori prefecture.

Rel.Publ.: "Eta Community in Japan: The Social Persistence of Outcaste Groups," American Anthropologist, 59 (Dec. 1957), 1000-17 [Reprinted in Japan's Invisible Race, Caste in Culture and Personality, ed. by George DeVos and Hiroshi Wagatsuma (Berkeley: University of California Press, 1966), 138-52].

LIEBAN, Richard W. Land and Labor on Kudaka Island. 1956. See no.691.

29
JOHNSON, Erwin Henry. Nagura Mura: An Historical Analysis of Stability and Change in Community Structure. Columbia, 1961. 221p. DA 22 (Aug. 1961), 391; UM 61-1077.

Analyzes "family and community structure in a mountain agricultural village in Aichi prefecture." Attempts to integrate available historical documentation dating back to the middle ages "with later records and with contemporary observations to present a developmental picture of family patterns, inheritance patterns, hamlet patterns, etc....Throughout the study, an effort is made to tie in change in community and family patterns with the local conditions."

Rel.Publ.: "Children's Play Groups and Village Social Organization," in Joint Meeting of the Anthropological Society of Nippon and the Japanese Society of Ethnology, Twelfth Session (Tokyo, 1958), Proceedings; "The Emergence of a Self-Conscious Entrepreneurial Class in Rural Japan," in Japanese Culture, ed. by Robert J. Smith and Richard K. Beardsley (Chicago: Aldine, 1962), 91-99; "Perseverance through Orderly Change: The 'Traditional' Buraku in a Modern Community," Human Organization, 22 (1963/1964), 218-23; "The Stem Family and Its Extension in Present Day Japan," American Anthropologist, 66 (Aug. 1964), 839-51; "Status Changes in Hamlet Structure Accompanying Modernization," in Aspects of Social Change in Modern Japan, ed. by Ronald P. Dore (Princeton: Princeton University Press, 1967), 153-83.

30
BEFU, Harumi. Hamlet in a Nation: The Place of Three Japanese Rural Communities in Their Broader Social Context. Wisconsin, 1962. 392p. DA 22 (May 1962), 3809-10; UM 62-2227.

Examines the interrelations of three buraku in northern Japan (Miyagi prefecture) with the outside world. Includes information on the economic background and internal social structure of the hamlets, on their dependence on outside sources for economic activities, and on the kinship ties with surrounding communities. The author also studies the administrative structure of the hamlets and shows how the government has implemented various local activities.

Rel.Publ.: "Network and Corporate Structure: A Structural Approach to the Community Interrelations in Japan," Studies on Asia, 1963, ed. by Robert K. Sakai (Lincoln: University of Nebraska Press, 1963), 27-41; "Patrilineal Descent and Personal Kindred in Japan," American Anthropologist, 65 (Dec. 1963), 1328-41; "The Political Relation of the Village to the State," World Politics, 19 (July 1967), 601-20.

31
HIRABAYASHI, James Akira. The Relations between National and Local Normative Systems: A Study of a Japanese Mountain Community. Harvard, 1962. iv, 209p.

A case study of the means of livelihood, social organization, social relationships with the outside world, and aspects of land tenure in Kaida-mura, Nishi Chikuma-gun, Nagano prefecture.

MARKAR'IAN, S. B. Rol' sel'skokhoziaistvennoi kooperatsii v poslevoennoi iaponskoi derevne. 1963. See no. 185.

32
PLUMMER, John Frederick. Oya: A Village of Northeast Japan. Michigan, 1963. 318p. DA 24 (Dec. 1963), 2217; UM 64-872.

"Describes the more usual dōzoku in various stages of dissolution and analyzes the part they play in the buraku in the village of Oya in Yamagata prefecture." Contents: Geographical and Historical Setting; People; Social Structure; Utilization of Land and Water; Land Ownership and Water Rights; Making a Living; Economic Organization; Local Government and Politics; Education; Religion.

33
CHANG, Kenne Hyun-kyun. The Dynamics of Cultural Ecology of Suruki Hamlet, Kagoshima Prefecture, Japan, in the Postwar Years. Stanford, 1968. 261p. DA 29 (Jan. 1969), 2267-68-B; UM 69-205.

"This is a study of changes and continuities in the ecology and social structure of Suruki Hamlet," 1945-1965. The author notes that "postwar socio-cultural changes in this locality appear to consist mainly of a gradual shift of emphasis, rather than drastic change; the cultural core is resistant to change, whereas the fringe areas are even exceptionally ready to experiment with it, and this readiness to accept change in the fringe areas may well stem, paradoxically, from the stability and security of the inner core.

34
SESHAIAH, S. The Sociological Impact of Postwar Land Reform on the Rural Community of Japan. Indian School of International Studies, New Delhi, 1968. 476, xxii p. + bibliog., maps.

A study undertaken in 1962 of the village of Kannari in Miyagi prefecture. Examines family, house-federations, hamlet organization, and municipal administration as altered by the erasure of power held over tenants by great and small landlords.

Rel.Publ.: "Postwar Reforms and Changes in the Leadership Structure of Village Japan: A Case Study," Eastern Anthropologist (Lucknow), 19 (Jan./Apr. 1966), 1-28.

35
RAMSEYER, Robert Lewis. Takachiho, 1868-1968: Evolving Patterns of Community Decision-Making in a Developing Nation-State. Michigan, 1969. 290p. DA 30 (Nov. 1969), 1998-99-B; UM 69-18,088.

An analysis at both the municipal and hamlet levels of changes in community power relationships and decision-making in a rural municipality in central Kyushu (Miyazaki prefecture). Contents: Problem, Aims, Method, Findings; Takachiho; Penetration by the Official Bureaucracy at All Levels; The Local Community in the Face of Bureaucratic Penetration; Stages in Transition; Status, Patronage, Merit; Local Political Power; Political Power and Reputation.

ETHNOGRAPHY

(includes race, manners and customs, mythology, folk tales and songs, beliefs and rites)

See also Religion and Philosophy (pages 221-32).

OGATA, Masakiyo. Beitrag zur Geschichte der Geburtshülfe in Japan. 1891. See no.2027.

OKASAKI, Tōmitsu. Das Manyōshū: Eine kritisch-ästhetische Studie. 1898. See no.1593.

36
TAKAHASHI, Seigo. A Study of the Origin of the Japanese State. Columbia, 1917. 97p.

This study questions the traditional theory of the patriarchal origins of the Japanese state. It deals with racial factors and examines ancient literary records in the light of anthropological and other scientific findings.

Rel.Publ.: A Study...State. New York: W.O. Gray, 1917. 97p.

37
MATSUMOTO, Nobuhiro. Recherches sur quelques thèmes de la mythologie japonaise [A Study of Some Themes in Japanese Mythology]. Paris, 1928. (thèse complémentaire). Text in French.

Focuses on the local gods at Izumo, the solar character of the ancestors of the Japanese Imperial House, and on mythical elements originating among the early Japanese residents in Kyushu.

Rel.Publ.: Recherches...japonaise. Paris: P. Geuthner, 1928. 136p. (Austro-asiatica; documents et travaux pub. sous la direction de Jean Przyluski, t. 2.)

38
HIMES, Norman Edwin. The Practice of Contraception and Its Relation to Some Phases of Population Theory. Harvard, 1932. xxix, 521p. AB: Harvard University. Summaries of Theses...1932. p.375-78.

A survey of contraception in early Japan is presented on p.136-58.

Rel.Publ.: Medical History of Contraception. New York: Gamut Press, 1963. liii, 520p.

39
SUDAU, Günther. Die religiöse Gedankenwelt der Japaner im Spiegel ihres Sprichworts [The World of Religious Ideas of the Japanese as Reflected in Their Proverbs]. Leipzig, 1932. Text in German. The dissertation in its published form is available at Marburg/Lahn, Universitätsbibliothek, Nr. III C; also at the University of Michigan, General Library, no. 5984.

Japanese proverbs are classified into eight categories: life and death; fate; Hades and Hell; enlightenment and salvation; God, the gods, and demons; prayer, sacrifice, and faith; sins and virtues; the clergy and the people. Three principal features of religious thought and experience are recognized: religious indifference, the idea of one's reward, and religious faith.

Rel.Publ.: Die religiöse...Sprichworts. Leipzig: Werkgemeinschaft, 1932. 95p.

40
OKA, Masao. Kulturschichten in Alt-Japan [Cultural Stratification of Early Japan]. Wien, 1933. 980p. (3v.) Text in German. Diss. ms. available at the Universitätsbibliothek der Universität Wien, Nr. 3321.

Reviews the conclusions of previous investigations of the subject and studies the material culture, economy, and religion of the early Japanese. The study is based in part on archaeological findings.

GULIK, Robert Hans van. Hayagrīva: The Mantrayānic Aspect of Horse-Cult in China and Japan. 1935. See no.1897.

41
HASHIMOTO, Jujiro. Grundlage der japanischen Sitten [The Basis of Japanese Customs]. Kiel, 1936. Text in German. The dissertation in its published form is available at Marburg/Lahn, Universitätsbibliothek, Nr. VII C; also at the University of Michigan General Library, no. BL 2220.H35

A survey of the different movements and philosophies underlying the development of Japanese customs before the mid-1700's. These include Shinto, Confucian and Buddhist ideas; bushidō; the Hōtoku and the Mito Schools; and the Shingaku movement.

Rel.Publ.: Grundlage...Sitten. Kiel, 1936. 103p.

42
MATSUDAIRA, Narimitsu. Étude sociologique sur les fêtes saisonnières dans la province de Mikawa du Japon [A Sociological Study of the Seasonal Festivals in the Province of Mikawa, Japan]. Paris, 1936. Text in French.

Presents the religious, moral, and social ideas inspired by the festivals. Contents: Description of the Festivals; Beliefs Inspired by the Festivals; Village Organization and Its Relationship to the Festivals. The study is an exposition and interpretation of Hayakawa Kotaro's Hanamatsuri (Tokyo, 1930).

Rel.Publ.: Les fêtes saisonnières au Japon (province de Mikawa): Etude descriptive et sociologique. Paris: G.-P. Maisonneuve, 1936. 175p.

43
PETRAU, Alfred. Schrift und Schriften im Leben der Völker: Ein kulturgeschichtlicher Beitrag zur vergleichenden Rassen und Volkstumskunde [Writing and Writing Systems in the Life of Different Peoples: A Contribution in Cultural History to Comparative Ethnology and Ethnography]. Berlin, 1939. Text in German. The dissertation in its published form is available at Bochum, Universitätsbibliothek, Nr. GB 181.

Information on the following subjects is included in the dissertation: the pictorial writing of the Ainu and theories about the oldest forms of writing in Japan; Chinese influence upon the development of writing in Japan; comments about the pronunciation and order of the kana syllabaries; the Japanese manner of writing and the European influence upon it; efforts to simplify the Japanese writing system; the printing of religious texts.

Rel.Publ.: Schrift...Volkstumskunde. Berlin-Charlottenburg: K.u.R. Hoffman, 1939. xiv, 657p.

44
NUMAZAWA, Franz Kiichi. Die Weltanfänge in der japanischen Mythologie [The Beginning of the World in Japanese Mythology]. Freiburg i.B., 1942. Text in German.

A study of early Chinese influence upon Japanese cosmogony, of the literary and imaginary association with the Chinese sources, and of the myth of Izanagi and Izanami and their role as the world's first married couple and as the creators of heaven and earth. The dissertation concludes with an ethnological interpretation of the myth that the world was created as a result of the separation of heaven and earth.

LEROI-GOURHAN, André. Archéologie du Pacifique-Nord: Materiaux pour l'étude des relations entre les peuples riverains d'Asie et d'Amerique. 1944. See no.89.

45
WANG, Thusnelda. Das Pferd in Sage und Brauchtum Japans: Spuren eines Pferdekultes [The Horse in the Saga and Folklore of Japan: Traces of a Horse-Cult]. Wien, 1946. xiii, 114p. Text in German. Diss. ms. available at the Universitätsbibliothek der Universität Wien, Nr. D 7227; also at the Österreichische Nationalbibliothek, Nr. 743.982 C.

An investigation and theological analysis of the role of the horse in the Japanese oral tradition and in Japanese folklore.

Rel.Publ.: Article published in Folklore Studies (Tokyo), v. 18 (1959), 145-288.

46
BUCHANAN, Percy Wilson. The Orientation of the Japanese. Princeton, 1947. 277p. DA 15 (Mar. 1955), 407 [Abstract not available]; UM 10,860.

Contents: Linguistic Evidence of Orientation; The Archaeological Evidences of Orientation; Orientation in Religion and Court; Ethnological Evidences of Orientation; The Lucky Side. The appendix contains wind and rainfall statistics.

47
HAGUENAUER, Moïse-Charles. Introduction a l'étude des origines de la civilisation japonaise: La préhistoire insulaire jusque vers 250 b.c. [Introduction to the Study of the Origins of Japanese Civilization: The Prehistory of the Islands up to ca. 250 b.c.]. Paris, 1947. Text in French.

Studies the origins of Japanese culture from the anthropological. ethnographical, linguistic, and archaeological points of view.

Rel.Publ.: Origines de la civilisation japonaise: Introduction a l'étude de la préhistoire du Japon. Paris: Impr. Nationale, 1956. x, 640p. [t.1]

48
KRAUS, Bertram Shirley. Constitutional Typology and Race: A Comparative Analysis of Somatotypes within the Japanese Population of Northern Honshu. Chicago, 1949. 83p.

Seeks to delineate the types of body builds and their relative frequencies in a segment of the Japanese population of northern Honshu and to compare the Japanese sample with data derived from an American Caucasoid population. The subjects in the study were adult residents of Sendai and Morioka.

Rel.Publ.: "Male Somatotypes among the Japanese of Northern Honshu," American Journal of Physical Anthropology, 9 (Sept. 1951), 347-66.

49
SAROT, Eden Emanuel. Folklore of the Dragonfly: A Linguistic Approach. Princeton, 1949. 79p. DA 12 (1952), 789-90; UM 2208.
Includes an examination of the dragonfly's role in Japanese literature, painting, and folklore.
Rel.Publ.: Folklore...Approach. Roma: Edizioni di Storia e Letteratura, 1958. 79p. (Letture di pensiero e d'arte, 29)

DREWS, Robin. The Cultivation of Food Fish in China and Japan: A Study Disclosing Contrasting National Patterns for Rearing Fish Consistent with the Differing Cultural Histories of China and Japan. 1951. See no.240.

50
HOLTZ, Günther. Rassengeschichte der Ostgebiete von Inner und Nord-Asien [The Racial History of the Eastern Regions of Inner and Northern Asia]. Tübingen, 1951. 554p. Text in German. Diss. ms. available at Universität Tübingen.
Contains considerable information on the origins of the Ainu and on their role in Japan's early history. Compares pottery, language, and various remains in eastern Europe and northern Asia.

51
LAEMMERHIRT, P. Anton. Gebet und Verwünschung in der altjapanischen Kultsprache [Prayer and Curses in the Early Japanese Cultic Language]. Bonn, 1953. 80p. Text in German. Diss. ms. available at Bonn, Universitätsbibliothek, Nr. U 4° 55/221.
A systematic examination of the religious writings of the Nara period with an analysis of the verbs kotomukeru and ushihaku, a study of the classical Japanese verbs for the verb "to pray," and a study of the curses tokou, norou, kajiri, and majinai.
Rel.Publ.: "Gebet in der altjapanischen Kultsprache," MN, 11 (Jan. 1956), 356-96; "Verwünschung in der altjapanischen Kultsprache," MN, 12 (Apr./July 1956), 51-63.

52
ROBERTS, Warren Everett. Aarne-Thompson Type 480 in World Tradition: A Comparative Folktale Study. Indiana, 1953. 396p. DA 13 (1953), 754-55; UM 5875.
The dissertation includes a discussion of the folktale Aa-Th type 480, "The Spinning Woman by the Spring," as it existed in Japan.
Rel.Publ.: The Tale of the Kind and the Unkind Girls: Aa-Th 480 and Related Tales. Berlin: W. de Gruyter, 1958. 164p. (Supplement-Serie zu Fabula; Zeitschrift für Erzählforschung. Reihe B: Untersuchungen, H.1)

SHIMOYAMA, Tokuji. Der Einfluss der schamanistisch-Shintoistischen Urreligion Japans auf den japanischen Buddhismus: Eine religionspsychologische Studie. 1954. See no.1904.

53
IKEDA, Hiroko. A Type and Motif Index of Japanese Folk-Literature. Indiana, 1956. 403p. DA 16 (Nov. 1956), 2129; UM 17,957.
"Correlates Japanese folktales with European tale-types indexed in the Aarne-Thompson Index." For each of the 205 types that are established for Japan, the author presents "the distribution of the versions in Japan, a comparative analysis of the material, and some references to the tales of neighboring countries."

54
LEVIN, M. G. Etnicheskaia antropologiia i problemy etnogeneza narodov Dal'nego Vostoka [Ethnic Anthropology and the Problems of Ethno-genesis of the Peoples of the Far East]. Moscow, Institut istorii material'noi kul'tury Akademii nauk SSR, 1957(?). (Doctor of Historical Sciences) Text in Russian. AB: 16p. summary published in 1957. [See also addenda entry no.25A.]

LEBRA, William P. Okinawan Religion. 1958. See no. 693.

SKILLMAN, John H. A Study of the Relationship between Participation in Various Types of Extra-Class Activities and Academic Performance in Three Private Japanese Secondary Schools. 1958. See no.449.

MELICHAR, Herbert. Zur Chronologie neolithischer Steinkreise in Japan. 1959. See no.92.

55
UEHARA, Toyoaki. The Dynamics of the Archetypes in Japanese Shinto Mythology. Southern California, 1960. 512p. DA 21 (Dec. 1960), 1650-51; UM 60-4490.
"This study is an analysis of Japanese mythology in the light of the hypotheses made available by some of the scholars of the Jungian tradition....It (1) treats the development of Japanese mythology and the emergence of...the 'Yamato mind'..., (2) notes the presence and development of so-called archetypal images as projected in the stories concerning the leading deities of the ancient Shinto pantheon, (3) analyzes each myth drama as a projection of certain conflicts in the human psyche..., (4) correlates, hypothetically, a sequence of the entire myth drama with the movement of ego-consciousness toward higher synthesis..., and (5) arrives at some understanding of Japanese mythology as a representation of what presumably took place when the Yamato mind was in process of formation."

56
ARUTIUNOV, S. A. Drevnii vostochno-aziatskii i ainskii komponenty v etnogeneze Iapontsev [Early East Asian and Ainu Components in the Ethno-genesis of the Japanese People]. Moscow, Institut etnografii im. N. N. Miklukho-Maklaia Akademii nauk SSSR, 1962. (Candidate of Historical Sciences degree) viii, 257p. Text in Russian.

57
SUGANO, Kazutoshi. Die Entwicklung des Gott-Mensch-Verhältnisses und des ethischen Bewusstseins in der Philosophie des antiken Japan [The Development of the God-Man Relationship and of Ethical Consciousness in the Philosophy of Early Japan]. Innsbruck, 1963. 179p. Text in German. Diss. ms. available at the Österreichische Nationalbibliothek, Nr. 947.664-C.
A study of the religious conceptions and the ethical values of the early Japanese, based on an examination of the earliest Japanese literature.

HAAS, Michael. Some Societal Correlates of International Political Behavior. 1964. See no.1798.

KREINER, Josef. Beiträge zur Erforschung von Religion und Gesellschaft auf den nördlichen Ryūkyū: Der Noro-Kult von Amami-Ōshima. 1964. See no.699.

58
REINMAN, Fred Marvin. Maritime Adaptation: An Aspect of Oceanic Economy. California, Los Angeles, 1965. 208p. DA 25 (June 1965), 6884-85; UM 65-4700.

"An examination of the utilization of the sea as a source of food by Pacific peoples [including Japanese] with an appraisal of its possible significance for culture history....Ethnographic data are surveyed for specific statements as to the part fishing played in the lives of the native peoples....Archaeological data are reviewed for the analysis of food remains in the site middens....In addition, artifacts related to fishing, especially the fishhook", are considered.

59
SAMPLE, Lillie Laetitia. Culture History and Chronology in South Korea's Neolithic. Wisconsin, 1967. 414p. DA 28 (Feb. 1968), 3142-B; UM 67-12,156.

"Relationships with Japan across the Straits of Tsushima are considered in the light of trade materials ceramic stylistic similarities, and absolute chronology."

Rel.Publ.: "Chōsen shinsekkijidai shoki no doki kennen ni kansuru shin shiryō" [by] Albert Mohr, C.S. Chard, and L.L. Sample, Chōsen gakuhō, 41 (Oct. 1966), 73-82; "Chōsen kogendo no kushimemon doki," Sekki jidai, Mar. 1967.

HUNTSBERRY, William R. Religion and Value-Formation in Japan. 1968. See no.1893.

60
MILLER, Alan Lee. Chinese Influences on the Indigenous Folk Religion of Japan. Chicago, 1968. 309p.

The study is divided into two parts: (1) a general discussion of the folk religious phenomenon, and (2) an examination of the folk phenomena of ancient Japan up until the Heian period. The Chinese-Japanese cultural encounter is discussed, and individual chapters are devoted to a study of the ritsuryō ideal and to the concept of the state as a liturgical community. A useful list of Japanese terms is appended.

TIERNEY, Emiko O. A Northwest Coast Sakhalin Ainu World View. 1968. See no.71.

FAMILY AND KINSHIP STUDIES

See also Demography (pages 19-20) and Overseas Japanese Communities (pages 198-208).

61
BÖX, Arno. Das japanische Familiensystem [The Japanese Family System]. Marburg, 1941. Text in German. The dissertation in its published form is available at Marburg/Lahn, Universitätsbibliothek, Nr. XVIII C.

A study of the Japanese family system in both premodern and modern times, of the law of family confederations (uji and later forms) during the period of the Taika Reforms and during the Feudal period, and of the Japanese Civil Code as well as of attempts at reforming family and inheritance laws.

Rel.Publ.: Das japanische Familiensystem. Gräfenhainichen: Schulze, 1940. viii, 140p. [also, Leipzig: Harrassowitz, 1940. (Sammlung orientalistischer Arbeiten, Heft 6)].

62
ROLL, Hans-Jürgen. Die Entwicklung des japanischen Familiensystems seit 1945 [The Evolution of the Japanese Family System since 1945]. Marburg, 1953. xi, 118p. Text in German. Diss. ms. available at Marburg/Lahn, Universitätsbibliothek, Nr. XVIII B.

A study of the traditional Japanese family system, of the postwar reforms affecting the legal position of the family, and of the history behind these reforms.

63
ISHINO, Iwao. The Oyabun-Kobun Institution: An Introductory Analysis of a Ritual Kinship System in Japan. Harvard, 1954. vii, 203p. AB: 7p. summary appended to diss. ms.

Includes analyses of ritual kinship relations within a construction company, among streetstall merchants, and in the farm tenancy system.

Rel.Publ.: Paternalism in the Japanese Economy: Anthropological Studies of Oyabun-Kobun Patterns [by] John W. Bennett and Iwao Ishino. Minneapolis: University of Minnesota Press, 1963. x, 307p.; The Japanese Labor Boss System: A Description and a Preliminary Sociological Analysis [by] Iwao Ishino and John W. Bennet. Columbus, Ohio, 1953. 67p. (Ohio State University Research Foundation and Department of Sociology, report no. 3); "The Oyabun-Kobun: A Japanese Ritual Kinship Institution," American Anthropologist, 55 (Dec. 1953), 695-707; "Patterns of Social Relationship," Engineering Experiment Station News, 26 (1954), 74-77.

MARETZKI, Thomas Walter. Child Rearing in an Okinawan Community. 1957. See no.692.

64
SANO, Chiye. Changing Values of the Japanese Family. Catholic, 1958. viii, 142p.

Examines the effect of industrialization and Westernization upon parental values and attitudes in both urban and rural communities in postwar Japan. Contents: The Japanese Family; Civil Code Revision: Its Background and Ramifications; Parental Responsibility for Children under Age; Changing Values of the Institutional Family.

Rel.Publ.: Changing...Family. Washington, D.C.: Catholic University of America Press, 1958. viii, 142p. (Catholic University of America, Anthropological Series, 18)

65
ROH, Chang Shub. A Comparative Study of Korean and Japanese Family Life. Louisiana State, 1959. 310p. DA 19 (June 1959), 3408; UM 59-1546.

"Special reference is made to historical developments, characteristics of family life, familial cultures, family functions, and changing family life."

66
LANHAM, Betty Bailey. Aspects of Child Rearing in Kainan, Japan. Syracuse, 1962. 432p. DA 23 (Oct. 1962), 1162-63; UM 62-4024.

Based on data gathered in 1951/52 and 1959/60. Contents: Summary of Statistical Materials; Formalized Learning Situations; Mother-Child Conversations; Interpretive Analysis of Data.

Rel.Publ.: "Aspects of Child Care in Japan: Preliminary Report," in Personal Character and Cultural Milieu, 3d rev. ed., ed. by Douglas G. Haring (Syracuse: Syracuse University Press, 1956), 565-83; "The Psychological Orientation of the Mother-Child Relationship in Japan," MN, 21 (1966), 322-33.

67
MOOS, Felix. Inertia and Change: Elements of the Japanese Family and Kinship Organization since 1945. Washington, Seattle, 1963. 297p. DA 24 (Jan. 1964), 2650; UM 64-422.

Focuses particularly on the impact of the American Occupation. Contents: Elements of the Japanese Family System; The Japanese Ie in Ideal and Practice; Aspects of Japanese Parent-Child Relations; The Family and Elements of the Kinship Structure; The Civil Code and the Family; The Family System and Women; Marriage.

Rel.Publ.: "Japan: Culture Change and Acculturation: Some Considerations," in International Conference of Orientalists in Japan, Transactions, 5 (1960), 104-09.

68
BROWN, Leonard Keith. Dōzoku: A Study of Descent Groups in Rural Japan. Chicago, 1964. 350p.

A very detailed structural and functional analysis of dōzoku groups in Nakayashiki, a rural hamlet in Iwate prefecture. Asserts that the Japanese descent groups are constituted by a cognatic rather than by a patrilineal rule of descent.

Rel.Publ.: "Bunke no bunshutsu ni tsuite" [by] K. Brown and M. Suenari, Minzokugaku kenkyū, 31 (Jan. 1966), 38-48; "Dōzoku and the Ideology of Descent in Rural Japan," American Anthropologist, 68 (Oct. 1966), 1129-51; "The Content of Dōzoku Relationships in Japan," Ethnology, 7 (Apr. 1968), 113-38.

MINORITY GROUPS
(Includes the Ainu, eta, and Koreans in Japan)

69
ROGERS, Spencer Lee. A Comparison between Aboriginal Archery in Western North America and Eastern Asia. Southern California, 1937. 234p. AB: University of Southern California. Abstracts of Dissertations for ...1937. p.68-72.

The author provides information on Japan and refers in particular to the Ainu within this comparative study of bow and arrow types and of forms of arrow release.

Rel.Publ.: "Aboriginal Bow and Arrow of North America and Eastern Asia," American Anthropologist, 42 (Apr. 1940), 255-69.

LEROI-GOURHAN, André. Archéologie du Pacifique-Nord: Materiaux pour l'étude des relations entre les peuples riverains d'Asie et d'Amerique. 1944. See no.89.

HOLTZ, Günther. Rassengeschichte der Ostgebiete von Inner- und Nord-Asien. 1951. See no.50.

LEE, Chung Myun. Recent Population Patterns and Trends in the Republic of Korea. 1961. See no.738.

ARUTIUNOV, S. A. Drevnii vostochno-aziatskii i ainskii komponenty v etnogeneze Iapontsev. 1962. See no.56.

LEWIN, Bruno. Aya und Hata: Bevölkerungsgruppen Altjapans kontinentaler Herkunft. 1962. See no.486.

70
MITCHELL, Richard Hanks. The Korean Minority in Japan, 1910-1963. Wisconsin, 1963. 265p. DA 24 (Oct. 1963), 1597-98; UM 63-7655.

"Traces the historical development of this minority and analyzes the various problems that arose between the Korean immigrants and the Japanese." Contents: Relations between Korea and Japan until 1910; The Growth of Korean Nationalism, 1910-1919; The Origin of the Korean Minority Problem, 1920-1930; Communism and Nationalism among Koreans in Japan; The Effect of Japan's War Efforts on the Korean Migrants; The Nonassimilable Koreans; The Korean Minority in Occupied Japan, 1945-1952; The Korean Minority in 'New Japan,' 1952-1960; Recent Developments, 1960-1963.

Rel.Publ.: The Korean...1963. Berkeley: University of California Press, 1967. 187p.

HAH, Chong-Do. The Dynamics of Japanese-Korean Relations, 1945-1963: An Interpretation of International Conflict. 1967. See no.1168.

SIMEON, George. The Phonemics and Morphology of Hokkaido Ainu. 1968. See no.1459.

71
TIERNEY, Emiko Ohnuki. A Northwest Coast Sakhalin Ainu World View. Wisconsin, 1968. 425p. DA 29 (June 1969), 4494-B; UM 68-16,027.

Contents: Pt.1:The Culture History of the Sakhalin Ainu: Location and Natural Habitat of the Sakhalin Ainu; The Ainu Identity; The Sakhalin Ainu in History. Pt.2:A Northwest Coast Sakhalin Ainu World View: Spatio-Temporal Orientations of the Ainu Universe [i.e., southern Sakhalin and the surrounding sea and sky]; The Important Inhabitants of the Ainu Universe [i.e., the Ainu themselves, and the deities and demons]; Communication among the Important Inhabitants of the Ainu Universe.

Rel.Publ.: "Concepts of Time among the Ainu of the Northwest Coast of Sakhalin," American Anthropology, 71 (June 1969), 488-92.

STEPHAN, John. Ezo under the Tokugawa Bakufu, 1799-1821: An Aspect of Japan's Frontier History. 1969. See no.544.

SOCIAL POLICY AND SOCIAL WELFARE
See also Demography (pages 19-20) and Overseas Japanese Communities (pages 198-208).

72
NOGUCHI, Shozo. Die Entwicklung des Versicherungsgedankens in Japan [The Development of the Idea of Insurance in Japan]. Göttingen, 1926. Text in German. The dissertation in its published form is available at Marburg/Lahn, Universitätsbibliothek, Nr. XVII C.

The materialization of the idea of insurance before and after the Meiji Restoration; private insurance in Japan illustrated through the founding and the development of insurance companies and insurance houses; national and social insurance in Japan undertaken by the State.

Rel.Publ.: Die Entwicklung...Japan. Göttingen: Dieterich, 1926. vi, 118p.

73
BANG, Kap Soo. A Proposed Social Security System for Korea Based on an Analysis of Programs in Great Britain, Japan, Malaya, and the United States. Pennsyl-

vania, 1961. 464p. DA 23 (July 1962), 108-09; UM 62-2818.

See Ch. 4, a history and description of Japanese social security programs (p.183-241).

74
YAMAZAKI, Koji. The Japanese National Pension Scheme and Economic Growth. Edinburgh, 1962. 314p.

Contents: Place of Finance of Social Services in the National Economy of Japan; Welfare Pension Insurance Scheme and National Pension Scheme; The National Pension Scheme and National Expenditure; Statistical Illustration; The National Pension Scheme and Economic Growth; Other Studies of the Future of Pensions in Japan.

75
SAGRISTA FREIXAS, Antonio. Social Security in Japan: Its Evolution, Present Status, and Economic Implications. Cornell, 1963. 290p. DA 24 (May 1964), 4850-51; UM 64-3711.

"The main conclusions: (1) Non-economic forces, in particular social and political forces, had a larger influence on the origin, development, and present status of Japanese Social Security than economic factors. (2) Japanese social security, as it now exists, has not yet reached the same degree of 'welfare-statism' as some European countries, though it is moving in that direction. (3) Though the growth of Japanese Social Security during the last decade has been impressive, its full macroeconomic implications are yet to be felt.... (4) A change in the dual structure both of the Japanese economy and of Japanese social security legislation is imperative if social security measures are to have more beneficial impact on the lower-income Japanese populations...."

VALUES AND ATTITUDES

See also: Anthropology and Sociology--family and kinship studies (pages 10-11), Economics--labor (pages 40-43), Psychology and Social Psychology (pages 219-20), and Overseas Japanese Communities --United States (pages 200-208).

76
MARUYAMA, Kazuteru. A Study of the Ideals of Japanese Children as Determined by Social Environment. New York, 1920. 130p.

Contents: Ideals as Social Heredity (Physical Environment, Ethnology, Civilization); Ideals as a Content of the Child's Mind (Ethical Ideals: Greatness, Goodness, and Patriotism; Practical Ideals: Ideal Person, Vocational Choice, and Sense of Money); Conclusion.

NAYLOR, Harry. A Psychocultural Study of Twenty-eight Ryukyuan Students. 1952. See no.690.

77
BAKER, Wendell Dean. A Study of Selected Aspects of Japanese Social Stratification: Class Differences in Values and Levels of Aspiration. Columbia, 1956. 120p. DA 16 (Nov. 1956), 2232; UM 19,232.

"Japanese public opinion data collected...in 1952/53 are analyzed with three basic problems in mind: (1) Do Japanese low status persons tend to devalue the high prestige goals of their culture, as do American low status persons? (2) Do lower class Japanese tend to reject certain critical goals instrumental to upward mobility such as formal education, as do lower class Americans? (3) Is there a general awareness among lower class Japanese that their ascent into high status positions in their society is not likely, as in the United States?"

78
MATSUMOTO, Yoshiharu Scott. Collectivity Orientations in Contemporary Japan. American, 1957. 278p. DA 17 (Nov. 1957), 2700; UM 21,967.

The study seeks to compare "the orientations and values of the 'traditional' Japanese society of the Edo period with those of postwar Japan." It concludes that "collectivity orientations remain a dominant part of the social environment of contemporary Japan. Where attitudinal changes are occurring, they are shifting from the traditional collectivity orientations based on unilateral ancestry, paternal authoritarianism, and hierarchical doctrines toward a new set of collectivity orientations based on collateral ties, peer groups, and egalitarian principles."

Rel.Publ.: Contemporary Japan: The Individual and the Group. Philadelphia: American Philosophical Society, 1960. 75p. (Transactions of the American Philosophical Society, new ser., v. 50, pt. 1)

79
SONG, Un Sun. A Sociological Analysis of the Value System of Pre-war Japan as Revealed in the Japanese Government Elementary School Textbooks, 1933-1941. Maryland, 1958. 300p. DA 20 (July 1959), 409-10; UM 59-1924.

An analysis of the shūshin and kokugo textbooks. Contents: The Problem and Its Significance; Textbooks Studied; The Meaning of Values; The Textbook in Society; The Religious Institution; The Political Institution: The State; Values in the Family; Values within the Economic System; Values within the Educational System; The Interrelations of Values; The Present and Future Values of Japan.

80
BECKER, Ernest. Zen Buddhism, "Thought Reform" (Brainwashing), and Various Psychotherapies: A Theoretical Study in Induced Regression and Cultural Values. Syracuse, 1960. 396p. DA 21 (Mar. 1961), 2431; UM 61-498.

Contents: Introduction: Stress and Regressive Adaptation; Three Methods of Induced Regression: Brain Washing, Psychotherapy, Zen Buddhism; Values.

Rel.Publ.: Zen: A Rational Critique. New York: Norton, 1961. 192p.

81
PINKERTON, Florence Stebe. The Concept of National Character: Its Historical Development, Its Study, and Its Relevance to International Relations. New York, 1960. 498p. DA 27 (Dec. 1966), 1891-92-A; UM 66-9741.

The dissertation includes "a critical review of representative research on German and Japanese national character by all the psycho-cultural disciplines during and since World War II", and it discusses the consequences of some of this research for the formulation of Allied Occupation policy in Japan.

82
LEWIS, David Michael. The Acceptance of Work-Related Values by Young Rural Japanese. Michigan State, 1963. 201p. DA 25 (Aug. 1964), 1390; UM 64-4985.

"Examines the relationship between position in the

rural Japanese family according to sex and order of birth, and the acceptance of selected work-related values." Based on a case study of ninth-grade students from Emi town, Chiba prefecture.

Rel.Publ.: "Rural-Urban Differences in Preindustrial and Industrial Evaluations of Occupations by Japanese Adolescent Boys" [by] David M. Lewis and Archibald O. Haller, Rural Sociology, 29 (Sept. 1964), 324-29; "The Hypothesis of Intersocietal Similarity in Occupational Prestige Hierarchies," American Journal of Sociology, 72 (Sept. 1966), 210-16; "The Perception of Entrepreneurial Prestige by Rural Japanese Boys," Rural Sociology, 33 (Mar. 1968), 71-79.

SUGANO, Kazutoshi. Die Entwicklung des Gott-Mensch-Verhältnisses und des ethischen Bewusstseins in der Philosophie des antiken Japan. 1963. See no.57.

83
WALLACE, William McDonald. Cultural Values and Economic Development: A Case Study of Japan. Washington, Seattle, 1963. 233p. DA 25 (Aug. 1964), 922; UM 64-6443.

The study relates Japanese cultural values to Japan's industrial development after the Meiji Restoration. Utilizing a conceptual framework based on Weber's analysis of the Protestant Ethic and its role in the Western world, the author shows the interrelationships among cultural values, agents of economic change, and industrial development in Japan. Loyalty, patriotism, the military virtues, ethnocentrism, hard work, austerity, filial piety, and pragmatism were found to be the values most important in Japan's economic development.

84
DUCHAC, René. La Jeunesse de Tokyo: Problèmes d'intégration sociale [The Youth of Tokyo: Problems of Social Integration]. Paris, 1965. Text in French. AB: Université de Paris. Faculté des Lettres et Sciences Humaines. Positions des thèses de troisième cycle soutenues devant la Faculté en 1965. p.167-68. (Série "Recherches," t. 32)

A psychosociological study of the attitudes and the opinions of Tokyo youth between the ages of 17 and 28. Considers their urban mobility, aspects of their daily life and leisure time, problems of marriage and of professional life, their relationships with society, attitudes towards the future, etc. Also seeks to determine the degree to which Tokyo's material and cultural environment may be considered a determining factor in their personalities.

Rel.Publ.:La Jeunesse...sociale. Paris: Presses Universitaires de France, 1968. 365p. (Bulletin de la Maison Franco-Japonaise, t. 8, no. 3/4)

85
CORWIN, Charles Mathias. Selected Concepts of Human Experiences as Seen in the Japanese Tradition and in the Biblical Tradition: A Comparative Study. Claremont, 1966. 901p. DA 29 (July 1968), 245-A; UM 67-9502.

"Makes a linguistic analysis of the Japanese verbal symbol system for discovering basic Japanese cultural patterns of thought" in the belief that "the concepts of the normal Japanese man can be pieced together by examining the verbal symbol system he employs to express reality." Contents: Concepts of Intellectual Experiences, Time, Beginning, End, Eternity, Reality, Cause and Effect, Change, Education, Knowledge, Wisdom, Insight, Truth, Thought, Illusion, and Error; Concepts of Emotional Experience, Love, Compassion, Beauty, Hope, Joy, Happiness, Pleasure, Hardship, Sorrow, Endurance, Anger; Concepts of Religious Experience, Faith, Prayer, Purity, Righteousness, Evil, Sin, Sacrifice; Conclusions.

Rel.Publ.: Biblical Encounter with Japanese Culture. Tokyo: Christian Literature Crusade, 1967. 172p; "Biblical Encounter with Japanese Culture," Japan Missionary Bulletin, 21 (Nov. 1967), 626-30.

86
TSURUMI, Kazuko. Adult Socialization and Social Change: Japan before and after Defeat in World War II. Princeton, 1967. 567p. DA 28 (Nov. 1967), 1913-14-A; UM 67-13,512.

"This is a study of the plausibility, both in theory and in substantive analysis, of the hypothesis that socialization takes place throughout an individual's life cycle, and that the individual as a result changes his personality through socialization in adulthood and in old age also. Adult-personality change is likely to occur in a society whose basic value-orientation undergoes a drastic change within a single generation. Members of such a society are likely to be subjected to the contrasting types of socialization before and after the change. Japan before and after defeat in World War II exemplifies such a society."

Rel.Publ.: Social Change and the Individual: Japan before and after World War II. Princeton: Princeton University Press, 1970. ca.492p.

HUNTSBERRY, William R. Religion and Value-Formation in Japan. 1968. See no.1893.

87
STEINHOFF, Patricia Golden. Tenkō: Ideology and Societal Integration in Prewar Japan. Harvard, 1969. iii, 269p.

"This report is limited to the historical tenkō [change of heart; defection] of persons imprisoned under the provisions of the Peace Preservation Law of 1925 for participation in the Communist movement, and the direct consequences of these tenkō." Contents: The Communist Movement as an Integrative Movement; A Legal Solution to the Integrative Problem; Japanese Communism: Organization and Membership; The Process of Tenkō; Three Types of Tenkō (common-man, political, spiritual); Resistance to Tenkō; The Institutionalization of Tenkō.

Archaeology

88
CHÊNG, Tê-k'un. Prehistoric Archaeology of Szechuan. Harvard, 1941. x, 294p. AB: Harvard University. Summaries of Theses...1941. p.156-58.

"The study also aims to see what bearing the early culture of this region has on the prehistory of Eastern Asia as a whole." Ch. 4 (p.81-176) includes a lengthy comparison of local stone artifacts with those from Japan and other parts of East Asia.

Rel.Publ.: Archaeological Studies in Szechwan. Cambridge: Cambridge University Press, 1957. xx, 320p.

89
LEROI-GOURHAN, André. Archéologie du Pacifique-Nord: Materiaux pour l'étude des relations entre les peuples riverains d'Asie et d'Amerique [Archaeology of the North Pacific: Materials for the Study of the Relations among the Riparian Peoples of Asia and America]. Paris, 1944. Text in French.

Based on a comparative study of the ax, adze, hoe, club, knife, dagger, harpoon, urn, pot, lamp, spoon, pestle, comb, and pipe found among the remains of the early Japanese, Ainu, and other North Pacific peoples.

Rel.Publ.: Archéologie...Amerique. Paris: Institut d'ethnologie, 1946. xviii, 542p. (Université de Paris, Travaux et mémoires de l'Institut d'ethnologie, 47)

HAGUENAUER, Moïse-Charles. Introduction a l'étude des origines de la civilisation japonaise: La préhistoire insulaire jusque vers 250 b.c. 1947. See no.47.

90
GROOT, Gerard Joseph, S.V.D. Proto-Zyōmon: The Bearing of Recent Discoveries on the Problem of the Origin of Zyōmon Culture. Cambridge, 1954. 516p. AB: University of Cambridge. Abstracts of Dissertations... 1954/1955. p.8-9.

Describes Japanese Neolithic Zyōmon (Jōmon) culture, the various Proto Zyōmon sites of one part of Japan, and the Proto Zyōmon remains (pottery, adzes, blades, bone and shell artifacts, etc.). Concludes that the Proto Zyōmon culture developed in Japan as the result of four cultural waves that reached the islands from the south as well as from the north.

Rel.Publ.: The Prehistory of Japan. New York: Columbia University Press, 1951. xvii, 128p.

91
KIDDER, Jonathan Edward, Jr. The Jōmon Pottery of Japan. New York, 1955. 279p. DA 15 (Aug. 1955), 1376; UM 12,858.

A comprehensive survey of the major prehistoric and proto-historic pottery finds in Japan.

Rel.Publ.: The Jōmon...Japan. Ascona, Switzerland: Artibus Asiae, 1957. xvi, 200p. ("Artibus Asiae," Supplement, 17); "A Jōmon Pottery Vessel in the Buffalo Museum of Science," Artibus Asiae, 15 (1952), 11-16; "The Kamegaoka Vessels in the City Art Museum, St. Louis," Artibus Asiae, 16 (1953), 198-208; "Reconstruction of the 'Pre-Pottery' Culture of Japan," Artibus Asiae, 17 (1954), 135-43; Japan before Buddhism, rev. ed. New York: Praeger, 1966. 284p. (Ancient Peoples and Places, 10); Prehistoric Japanese Arts: Jōmon Pottery. Tokyo: Kodansha International, 1968. 308p.

92
MELICHAR, Herbert. Zur Chronologie neolithischer Steinkreise in Japan [On the Chronology of Neolithic Stone-circles in Japan]. Wien, 1959. v, 304p. Diss. ms. available at the Universitätsbibliothek der Universität Wien, Nr. D 11,813.

A study of early stone-circles in Hokkaido and in northern Honshu. Attempts to determine their meaning and their chronology.

PEARSON, Richard Joseph. Temporal and Spatial Variation in the Culture History of the Ryūkyū Islands. 1966. See no.702.

93
MOHR, Albert Donald. Archaeological Research in Southwestern Japan. Wisconsin, 1968. 451p. DA 29 (June 1969), 4493-B; UM 68-17,922.

"In 1966, the Hakodate City Museum and the University of Wisconsin carried out stratigraphic excavations at two sites in western Kyushu which delineated the chronology and nature of late initial Jōmon and Early Jōmon. At the Hime Site (Nagasaki Prefecture) three stratigraphic units, named (earliest to latest) Hime, Todoroki, and Sobata, were defined on the basis of the ceramic complexes....Excavations at the Kuwazuru site revealed two well defined cultural horizons, the lower a late initial Jōmon occupation and above that evidence of the Sobata period."

Art and Architecture

GENERAL

See also Influence of Japanese Culture Abroad (pages 101-03) and Theatrical Arts (pages 239-40).

94
MATSUI, Nawakichi. On the Nature of the Materials Used in the Manufacture of the Arita Porcelain of Japan. Columbia, 1880. Diss. ms. not available.

95
REVON, Michel. De arte florali apud Japonenses [Floral Art among the Japanese]. Paris, 1896. Text in Latin.

A study of floral art in Japan, with particular emphasis on its historical development and on esthetic and poetic considerations.

Rel.Publ.: De arte...Japonenses. Paris:Libr. Lacène et Oudlin, 1896. 148p. AB: Maurier, Ath. et F. Deltour. Catalogue et analyse des thèses latines et françaises admises par les Facultés des Lettres. Année scolaire 1895/1896. p.41.

96
BACHHOFER, Ludwig. Die Kunst der japanischen Holzschnittmeister [The Art of the Japanese Woodcut Masters]. München, 1921. Text in German. The dissertation in its published form is available at München, Universitätsbibliothek; also at the University of Michigan, General Library, no. NE1310.B12.

I. The social and stylistic prerequisites for the development of Japanese wood-block printing. An attempt to classify the development of block printing into three periods: "primitive," "classic," and "late." II. A study of the lines, colors, perspective, structure, unity, and clarity of the engravings. The development of the drawing of trees, figures, and clothing in Japanese woodcuts and an attempt to show how the artistic representation of selected subjects evolved over time.

Rel.Publ.: Die Kunst...Holzschnittmeister. München: Wolff, 1922. 121p.

97
LOEWENSTEIN, Fritz E. Die Handzeichnungen der japanischen Holzschnittmeister [The Drawings of the Japanese Woodcut Masters]. Würzburg, 1922. Text in German. The dissertation in its published form is available at Marburg/Lahn, Universitätsbibliothek, Nr. XVI a B 81gy; also at the University of Michigan, General Library, no. NC1240.L83.

The drawings of more than sixty Japanese woodcut masters are arranged by school and in historical order. A study is then made of the design, composition, and execution of these drawings and of the means by which they were transferred onto wood blocks.

Rel.Publ.: Die Handzeichnungen...Holzschnittmeister. Plauen: Schulz, 1922. 71p. (Ostasiatische Graphik, 2)

PERZYNSKI, Friedrich. Die Masken der japanischen Schaubühne. 1925. See no.2042.

98
WANGENHEIM, Gisella. Der Einfluss der japanischen Malerei auf die japanische Lackkunst [The Influence of Japanese Painting on Japanese Lacquer Art]. Freiburg i.B., 1928. Text in German. The dissertation in its published form is available at Marburg/Lahn, Universitätsbibliothek, Nr. XVI a C.

A brief historical survey of Japanese painting and Japanese lacquer art, an investigation of their themes and of their mutual influence, and a study of the composition and coloring of Japanese lacquer art and of the relationship between the decor and the tools that are used.

Rel.Publ.: Der Einfluss...Lackkunst. Gotha: Schmidt und Thelow, 1928. 59p.

99
RUMPF, Fritz. Das Ise-monogatari von 1608 und sein Einfluss auf die Buchillustration des XVII. Jahrhunderts in Japan [The 1608 Edition of the Ise monogatari and Its Influence upon Japanese Book Illustrations during the Seventeenth Century]. Berlin, 1931. Text in German. The dissertation in its published form is available at Berlin West, Staatsbibliothek Preussischer Kulturbesitz, Nr. An 7908/25.

A study of printing during the Keichō period (1596-1615), of the Saga-bon [the Saga wood block book] and the Pseudo-Saga-bon, and of the Goshiki bon. Presents a detailed description of the origins, kinds of printing, illustrations, styles, editions, and differences in the Waka sanjūrokkasen, Nō kadensho, Honchō kokon meijin, Ōgi no sōshi, and Ise monogatari.

Rel.Publ.: Das Ise...Japans. Berlin-Lankwitz: Würfel, 1931. 59p.

NELSON, Andrew. The Origin, History, and Present Status of the Temples of Japan. 1939. See no.1978.

100
HEMPEL, Rose-Marie. 36 Shikishi aus dem Besitz der Staatlichen Museen Berlin: Ein Beitrag zum Kōetsu-Sōtatsu-Problem [36 Large Square Japanese Poetry Cards in the Collection of the State Museum in Berlin: A Contribution to the Kōetsu-Sōtatsu Problem]. Berlin, 1944. 87, xvii, 3p. Text in German. Diss. ms. available at Berlin, Humboldt Universität, Universitätsbibliothek, Nr. P41.

Describes Japanese shikishi (poetry cards), tanzaku

(long strips of paper for writing poetry on), and kaishi (paper used for writing tanka) with regard to the kinds of paper used, the coloring of the paper, and the lettering; translates the poems that appear on the 36 shikishi which are under study; compares the styles of Honami Kōetsu (1558-1637) and of Tawaraya Sōtatsu (1576-1643); and compares the shikishi in the Berlin Museum with other works by Kōetsu.

101
BOYER, Martha Hagensen. Japanese Export Lacquers from the Seventeenth Century in the National Museum of Denmark. Copenhagen, 1959. 149p., 60 plates.

Contents: Political and Commercial Relations between Europe and Japan from the Middle of the Sixteenth to the End of the Seventeenth Century; Possibilities of How and When Japanese Lacquers of the Seventeenth Century were Acquired and Incorporated in the National Museum of Denmark; Historical and Technical Development of the Japanese Lacquer Industry; Description of the Seventeenth Century Japanese Lacquers in the National Museum of Denmark.

Rel.Publ.: Japanese...Denmark. Copenhagen: National Museum, 1959. (Nationalmuseets Skrifter: Større beretninger, 5)

102
HELLER, Fritz. Kontur und Faltengebung im Japanholzschnitt: Studien über den Wandel vom vorklassischen zum klassischen Stil [Outline and Style of Drapery in Japanese Woodcuts: Studies of the Shift from the Pre-Classical to the Classical Style]. Köln, 1962. Text in German. The dissertation in its published form is available at Marburg/Lahn, Staatsbibliothek Preussischer Kulturbesitz, Nr. Hsn 33,888; also at the University of Michigan, General Library, no. 26,647.

Studies the characteristics of and stylistic differences between early and classical Japanese wood engraving, presents a structural analysis of the figure drawings of Hishikawa Moronobu (an ukiyoe artist of the early Tokugawa Period), and concludes with a discussion of the Seirō bijin awase sugata kagami and of its importance for the origins of the classical style.

Rel.Publ.: Kontur...Stil. Köln: A Kleinschmidt, 1961. 80, xl p.

103
TAKEDA, Tomiko. La Symbolique royale de Louis XIV dans les châteaux royaux, avec quelques notes en appendice sur la symbolique impériale chinoise et japonaise de l'âge classique, architecture, et urbanisme [The Royal Symbolism of Louis XIV in the Royal Chateaux, with Some Notes within the Appendix on the Imperial Chinese and Japanese Systems of Symbols during the Classical Age, on Architecture, and on Urban Planning]. Paris, 1962. 340p. (2v.) Text in French.

KLEINSCHMIDT, Peter. Die Masken der Gigaku, der ältesten Theaterform Japans. 1964(?) See no.2052.

104
GENS, I. IU. Iaponskoe nezavisimoe kino [The Independent Cinema in Japan]. Moscow, Institut istorii iskusstv, 1967. (Candidate of Art Sciences degree). 325p. Text in Russian.

105
NIKOLAEVA, N. S. Dekorativnoe iskusstvo Iaponii: Problemy evoliutsii stilia i sinteza iskusstv [The Decorative Art of Japan: Problems in the Evolution of Style and the Synthesis of the Arts]. Akademiia khudozhestv SSSR, Nauchno-issledovatel'skii institut teorii i istorii izobrazitel'nykh iskusstv, 1968. (Candidate of Art Sciences degree) Text in Russian. AB: 28p. summary published in 1968.

ARCHITECTURE

106
KUMÉ, Gonkuro. Verbesserung des japanischen Wohnhauses [The Improvement of Japanese Homes]. Stuttgart, Technische Hochschule, 1929. Text in German. The dissertation in its published form is available at Marburg/Lahn, Universitätsbibliothek, Nr. XVI a B.

The author focuses upon (1) the special characteristics of the Japanese home, (2) its construction and the materials used in building it, and (3) the effect of earthquakes and of fire upon Japanese buildings (with a comparison between houses built of brick and those of wood).

Rel.Publ.: Verbesserung...Wohnhauses. Stuttgart: Jung und Brecht, 1929. 45p.

107
SOPER, Alexander Coburn, III. The Evolution of Buddhist Architecture in Japan. Princeton, 1944. Diss. ms. not available.

Focuses on the Asuka, Nara, Heian, and Kamakura periods, but also surveys architectural developments during the Muromachi, Momoyama, and Edo periods.

Rel.Publ.: The Evolution...Japan. Princeton: Princeton University Press, 1942. xv, 330p. (Princeton Monographs in Art and Archaeology, 22)

108
ENGEL, Heinrich. Japans Wohnhaus für die Gegenwart [The Japanese Home and Modern Living]. Darmstadt, Technische Hochschule, 1959. 124p. Text in German. Diss. ms. available at Marburg/Lahn, Staatsbibliothek Preussischer Kulturbesitz, Nr. 4° Hsn 23,446.

The primary objective of the work is the adaptation of traditional Japanese architecture to present needs. The dissertation considers among other things the building materials used in Japanese homes, the actual construction, the kyō-ma and inaka-ma methods, and existing building ordinances.

109
QUERA, Leon Neal. Persistent Principles in Japanese Architecture. Ohio State, 1962. 246p. DA 23 (Nov. 1962), 1655; UM 63-78.

Examines eleven monuments of Japanese architecture built between the third and the twentieth centuries in order to "establish a set of principles that will assist architectural students in evaluating the aesthetic quality of Japanese buildings." The monuments studied are the Great Shoin at Nishihonganji, Ni-nomaru and Hon-maru at Nijō-jō, Katsura Rikyū, Ise-jingū, Hōryūji, Byōdōin, Kinkakuji, Ginkakuji, Tōshōgū, Meiji-jingū, and the monument of Hiunkaku.

PAINTING

See also Influence of Japanese Culture Abroad (pages 101-30).

110
REVON, Michel. Étude sur Hokusaï [A Study of Hokusai]. Paris, 1896. (thèse complémentaire). Text in French.

A study of Hokusai's life; the use of nature, mankind, and the gods as subjects in his work; and the conception and execution of his art.

Rel.Publ.: Étude...Hokusai. Paris: Librairie Lecène et Oudin, 1896. 362p. AB: Mourier, Ath. et Deltour. Catalogue et analyse des thèses latines et françaises admises par les Facultés des Lettres. Année Scholaire 1895/1896. p.41-42.

111
NAGASSÉ, Takeshiro. Le paysage dans l'art de Hokouçaï [Landscape in the Art of Hokusai]. Paris, 1937. Text in French.

Rel.Publ.: Le paysage...Hokouçaï. Paris: Éditions d'art et d'histoire, 1937. 281p.

112
COVELL, Jon Etta Hastings (Carter). Under the Seal of Sesshū. Columbia, 1942. 163p.

A study of Sesshū's life, his artistic styles, and his landscape, figure, bird, flower, and animal paintings.

Rel.Publ.: Under...Sesshū. New York: De Pamphilis Press, 1941. xii, 163p.

113
FONG, Wen. Five Hundred Lohans at the Daitokuji. Princeton, 1958. 274p. DA 20 (Apr. 1960), 4069-70; UM 59-1552.

A study of "the hundred pictures [of Chinese origin] depicting the 500 Lohans (Buddhist saints) once kept at the Daitokuji monastery in Kyoto."

114
ARMBRUSTER, Gisela. Das Shigisan Engi Emaki: Ein japanisches Rollbild aus dem 12. Jahrhunderts [The Shigisan Engi Picture Scroll: A Japanese Scroll of the Twelfth Century]. Heidelberg, 1960. Text in German. The dissertation in its published form is available at Marburg/Lahn, Universitätsbibliothek, Nr. VI b C 593 rq, 40; also at the University of Michigan, General Library, no. QH5.G38 v.40.

The Shigisan Engi picture scroll, a late twelfth century work now owned by the Chogosonshi Temple in Nara. The dissertation describes and interprets the pictures of the scroll and their contents, translates the accompanying text, examines the painting from a technical point of view, studies the work as a narrative picture scroll and as a religious work, and classifies the scroll within the context of Japanese art history.

Rel.Publ.: Das Shigisan...Jahrhunderts. Hamburg, Wiesbaden: Harrassowitz in Komm., 1959. v, 290, xxxiv p. (MOAG, 40)

115
STERN, Harold Phillip. Ukiyoe Painting: Selected Problems. Michigan, 1960. 516p. (2v.). DA 21 (Aug. 1960), 330; UM 60-2573.

Focuses on the development of ukiyoe painting and concludes that ukiyoe was a revival of the yamatoe tradition rather than a new artistic form. Contents: Origin and Founding of Ukiyoe; Hishikawa Moronobu; The Development of Ukiyoe after Moronobu-Itchō to Utamaro; The Dozo Sagami Painting of Kitagawa Utamaro; Katsushika Hokusai; Two Last Artists: The End of Ukiyoe.

Rel.Publ.: "Ukiyoe Paintings of Tokugawa Japan," in Japan Society of London, Bulletin, 36 (Feb. 1962), 5-11.

116
MURASE, Miyeko. The Tenjin Engi Scrolls: A Study of Their Genealogical Relationship. Columbia, 1962. 394p. DA 23 (Mar. 1963), 3309-10; UM 63-1507.

"As one of the earliest engi emaki of Japan, the Tenjin Engi scrolls have particular significance for demonstrating the effects of a long period of copying, for providing clues to the production processes peculiar to the painted narrative scrolls of Japan, and for revealing the attitude of copyists towards their models."

117
FONTEIN, Jan. The Pilgrimage of Sudhana: A Study of Gaṇḍavyūha Illustrations in China, Japan, and Java. Leiden, 1966.

The Gaṇḍavyūha, a Buddhist work narrating the travels of Sudhana, whose search for Supreme Enlightenment/Ultimate Truth took him all over India. The work became popular in Southeast Asia, China, and Japan, and many painters and sculptors subsequently were inspired to illustrate the story. The dissertation describes and catalogues the great variety of such works of art and examines related iconographical problems. Ch. 3, "The Gaṇḍavyūha in Japanese Art" (p. 78-115 of the publication), focuses on Sudhana as depicted in the art of the Kamakura period and on various scrolls and paintings illustrating Sudhana's pilgrimage.

Rel.Publ.: The Pilgrimage...Java. Den Haag: Mouton, 1967. viii, 229p.

118
FRENCH, Calvin Leonard. Shiba Kōkan: Pioneer of Western Art and Science in Japan. Columbia, 1966. 442p. DA 27 (Dec. 1966), 1729-30-A; UM 66-8513.

A biography of Shiba Kōkan (1747-1818), "the leading exponent in [Tokugawa] Japan of painting in the Western style" and a scholar of Western learning, and a discussion of his work and influence. Contents: Kōkan and Tokugawa Influences (Western Art and Science in the Japanese 'Christian Era', Western Art and Science Learned from the Dutch, Tokugawa Intellectual Currents); Shiba Kōkan's Early Life: 1747-1781; Kōkan's Early Western Art Studies: 1781-1788 (Western Painting, Copperplate Engraving, Paintings in Kōkan's Engraved Style); Nagasaki Journey and Kōkan's Art: 1788-1790; Art of Kōkan's Mature Years: 1789-1806 (Paintings, Writings on Art); Science: 1792-1816; Retirement Years: 1809-1818.

Rel.Publ.: "Shiba Kōkan and the Beginnings of Western Art in Japan," in Columbia University, East Asian Institute, Researches in the Social Sciences on Japan, 2 (1959), 9-11.

119
BRODSKII, V. E. Iaponskaia klassicheskaia zhivopis' i grafika: Problema evoliutsii iaponskogo srednevekovogo iskusstva [Japanese Classical Painting and Drawing: The Problem of the Evolution of Medieval Japanese Art]. Moskovskii gosudarstvennyi universitet imeni M. V. Lomonosova, Istoricheskii fakul'tet. Kafedra istorii zarubezhnogo iskusstva. 1967. (Candidate of Art Sciences degree) 250p. Text in Russian. AB: 27p. summary published in 1967.

DOMBRADY, Géza Siegfried. Watanabe Kazan: Ein japanischer Gelehrter des 19. Jahrhunderts. 1968. See no.539.

120
MARTINSON, Fred Helmer. Early Muromachi Screen Paintings. Chicago, 1968. 232p.
A study of the manner in which Muromachi painters adopted the monochrome landscapes on Japanese screen formats from Chinese and Korean models. The problem of attributions to Tenshō Shūbun is also tackled.

SCULPTURE

121
WITH, Carl. Frühbuddhistische Plastik in Japan bis in den Beginn des 8. Jahrhunderts [Early Buddhist Sculptures in Japan up to the Beginning of the 8th Century]. Wien, 1918. Diss. ms. not available. Text in German.
Discusses the historical background of Buddhist art in Japan and the system of Mahāyāna Buddhism, then focuses on problems of form and on artistic developments between the early 7th and the early 8th centuries. [Annotation based on the book].
Rel.Publ.: Frühbuddhistische...Jahrhunderts. Wien: A. Schroll, 1922. 64p. (Arbeiten des Kunsthistorischen Institutes der Wiener Universität, 11)

122
MÜNSTERBERG, Hugo. Buddhist Bronzes of the Six Dynasties Period. Harvard, 1941. ii, 181p. AB: Harvard University. Summaries of Theses...1941. p.160-64.
See Ch. 8, "Early Buddhist Bronzes of Korea and Japan" (p.155-81).
Rel.Publ.: "Buddhist Bronzes of the Six Dynasties Period," Artibus Asiae, 9 (1946), 275-315, and 10 (1947), 21-33.

123
SAUNDERS, Ernest Dale. Les Gestes symboliques dans la sculpture japonaise: Sceaux iconographiques (mudrâ) du bouddhisme [Symbolic Gestures in Japanese Sculpture: Iconographic Signs (Mudrâ) of Buddhism]. Paris, 1953. iv, 302p. Text in French.
"Japanese sculpture has been chosen as the basis of this study because Japan is the end point in the development of the Buddhist tradition, and Japanese art is illustrative of iconographic mutations at the extreme limit of Buddhist expansion."
Rel.Publ.: Mudrā: A Study of Symbolic Gestures in Japanese Buddhist Sculpture. New York: Pantheon, 1960. xxiii, 296p. (Bollingen Series, 58); "Symbolic Gestures in Buddhism," Artibus Asiae, 21 (1958), 47-63.

124
LA PLANTE, John-David Paul. An Investigation of a Common Source for the International Bodhisattva Style in Asia during the Seventh Century. Stanford, 1965. 172p. DA 26 (Jan. 1966), 3853-54; UM 65-12,805.
After establishing the prototypical image, La Plante investigates its significance for Bodhisattva production throughout most of east and south Asia including Japan and examines "the reasons for the development of the new style and its wide adoption" within various Asian cultures.
Rel.Publ.: "A Pre-Pāla Sculpture and Its Significance for the International Bodhisattva Style in Asia," Artibus Asiae, 26 (1963), 247-84.

Demography

HIMES, Norman. The Practice of Contraception and Its Relation to Some Phases of Population Theory. 1932. See no.38.

125
PENROSE, Ernest Francis. Is Japan Overpopulated? A Study in Population Theories and Their Application. Stanford, 1934. 250p. AB: Stanford University. Abstracts of Dissertations 1933/34. p.112-15.

Asserts that Malthusian theories are not applicable to Japan and that certain population factors in the Japanese case require Japan to expand her industrialization, commercialization, and foreign trade for the sake of the country's "economic future."

Rel.Publ.: Population Theories and Their Application: With Special Reference to Japan. Stanford: Stanford University, Food Research Institute, 1934. xiv, 374p.

126
ISHII, Ryoichi. A Study of the Growth of [the] Japanese Population with Special Reference to Its Economic Significance. Clark, 1935. xiii, 406p. AB: Clark University. Thesis Abstracts-1935. p.17-21.

Shows that the trend of population growth (since 1868) has followed the trend of economic development, and "considers the possibilities and limitations of proposed remedies for Japan's population increase."

Rel.Publ.: Population Pressure and Economic Life in Japan. London: P.S. King, 1937. xix, 259p.

127
SECRÉTAIN, François. Les Problèmes de la population et leurs solutions en Allemagne, en Italie, et au Japan [Population Problems and Their Solutions in Germany, Italy, and Japan]. Lyon, 1941. Text in French.

A study of demographic pressure and of some of the possible demographic and economic remedies for it. Contains considerable information on Japan.

Rel.Publ.: Le Problème de la population: Étude des solutions données aux problèmes démographiques en Allemagne, en Italie, et au Japon. Paris: Presses Universitaires de France, 1942. xiv, 279p. (Nouvelle bibliothèque économique)

128
KAGAN, Salomon Sioma Jacques. The Demographic Factor: An Obstacle to Economic Development with Special Reference to Japan. Columbia, 1954. 401p. DA 14 (Sept. 1954), 1313-14; UM 8694.

Asserts that the failure of the Japanese standard of living to progress between the 1920's and 1950 "can be accounted for in terms of the demographic factor alone." Contents: Population; Income; Agriculture; Fishing; Raw Materials; Energy; Industry; Summary and Conclusions.

129
AMUNDSON, Robert Harold. Population Problems and Policies in Puerto Rico, India, and Japan. Notre Dame, 1956. 435p. DA 16 (Nov. 1956), 2231-32; UM 18,072.

The objectives of the study are (1) "to describe and compare the problem of rapid growth in Puerto Rico, India, and Japan; (2) to describe and evaluate the methods of population control fostered by recent programs or policies; and (3) to consider the practical and ethical aspects of these programs or policies."

Rel.Publ.: "Japan's Population Problem: A Positive Approach," Review of Social Economics, 15 (Sept. 1957), 104-17; "Population Pressure and India's Five Year Plans," Review of Social Economics, 18 (Sept. 1960), 161-77.

130
WILKINSON, Thomas Oberson. Tokyo: A Demographic Study. Columbia, 1957. 189p. DA 17 (Sept. 1957), 2081; UM 22,068.

"This study is a demographic analysis of the city of Tokyo which seeks to determine in what respect Tokyo is demographically similar to urban populations of modern Western nations, and whether or not there are similarities in social responses to an urban context."

131
ZIMMERMAN, Reverend Anthony Francis, S.V.D. Overpopulation: A Study of Papal Teachings on the Problem, with Special Reference to Japan. Catholic, 1957. xi, 328p.

"Seeks out the broad and general principles on solving overpopulation problems as enunciated by the Pope" and sees how they may be applied to resolving the population problem of Japan.

Rel.Publ.: Overpopulation...Japan. Washington: Catholic University of America Press, 1957. xv, 328p. (Catholic University of America. Studies in Sacred Theology, 2d ser., no. 99); "Survey of Papal Teaching on Population, with Special Reference to Japan," Migration News, May/June 1957, 13-15.

132
KASAHARA, Yoshiko. The Influx and Exodus of Migrants among the 47 Prefectures in Japan, 1920-1935. Michigan, 1958. 185p. DA 19 (Sept. 1958), 591-92; UM 58-3684.

"This study aims at reconstructing the historic trends in migration in industrializing Japan between 1920 and 1935. On the basis of estimates of net migration by age and sex for the 47 prefectures, variations in the volume and rate of population growth and decline due to migration among the prefectures are examined. Analysis of the age-sex differentials in migration is of importance as the first step toward gaining insights into the significant implications--demographic, social, and economic--of the population redistribution that accompanied Japan's modernization."

133
KONO, Shigemi. The Japanese Work Force: A Demographic Analysis. Brown, 1958. 246p. DA 19 (Jan. 1959), 1856; UM 58-7652.

A study of "the way in which population factors affect the patterns of work force participation" in Japan. Contents: Economic Growth, Population, and Work Force in Japan, 1850-1950; Population Factors Affecting Work Force Participation Rate in Japan: Components Analysis; Population and Economic Factors Affecting Work Force Participation Rates: Multiple Regression Analysis; Length of Working Life.

Rel.Publ.: "Demographic Aspects of the Japanese Economically Active Population" [by] S. Kono and H. Smythe, Sociologus, 7 (1957), 75-77.

INABA, Masaharu G. Japan: Some Geographic Aspects of Industrialization and Population Correlates. 1959. See no.464.

MURAMATSU, Minoru. Studies of Induced Abortion in Japan: 1--Effect on the Reduction of Births; 2.--Effect on Weight at Birth. 1959. See no.2035.

134
RIALLIN, Jean-Louis. Économie et population au Japon [Economy and Population in Japan]. Paris, 1960. Text in French. 311p.

A demographic study of modern Japan that focuses on Japanese methods to limit population growth and on the relationship between economic growth and demographic factors in postwar Japan.

Rel.Publ.: Économie...Japon. Paris: Génin, 1962. 174p.; "La Prévention des naissances au Japon: Politique, intentions, moyens, et résultats," Population, Apr./May 1960, 333-51.

135
TAKESHITA, Yuzuru. Socioeconomic Correlates of Urban Fertility in Japan. Michigan, 1962. 575p. DA 23 (Mar. 1963), 3537-38; UM 63-453.

Describes differences in fertility characteristics among people living in the Osaka area through an examination of socioeconomic factors such as occupation, education, income, wife's labor force status, and community background. Contents: Data and Methods; Fecundity of the Osaka Area Couples; Ideals about Family Size; Attitudes toward Birth Control; The Practice of Contraception: Fertility Planning Status; Socioeconomic Correlates of Contraceptive Use and Effectiveness of Fertility Planning; Induced Abortion as a Means of Birth Control; Family Size in Different Social and Economic Groups.

Rel.Publ.: "Population Control in Japan: A Miracle or Secular Trend?" Marriage and Family Living, 25 (Feb. 1963), 44-52.

VIRA, Soma. Impact of Urban Population Pressure upon Municipal Government. A Comparative Study: Calcutta, Djakarta, Tokyo. 1967. See no.1848.

Economics

GENERAL

See also: Demography (pages 19-20), Economics --economic history (pages 33-35), History-- Japanese empire--Chōsen (pages 90-95), History --Japanese empire--Manchoukuo (pages 96-97), and International Relations (pages 104-63).

136
MORIMOTO, Kokichi. A Study on the Standard of Living in Japan. Johns Hopkins, 1916. iii, 54p. and tables.

The study focuses on the general cost of living and on the cost of food, clothing, and housing during the years 1913-1915.

Rel.Publ.: A Study...Japan. Baltimore: Johns Hopkins University Press, 1918. 150p. (Johns Hopkins University Studies in Historical and Political Science, v.36, no.1)

137
OGATA, Kiyoshi. The Co-operative Movement in Japan. London, 1923. xiii, 352p.

Contents: The Forerunners of Co-operative Societies in Japan; The Mujin [system of mutual finance]; The Hōtokusha, a Japanese Co-operative Credit Society; The Modern Co-operative Movement of Japan; Credit Societies; Marketing Societies; Purchasing Societies; Machinery Societies; Associations of Consumers; Review of Co-operative Progress in Japan with Special Reference to the Forms of Cooperation Absent from Japan.

Rel.Publ.: The Co-operative...Japan. London: P.S. King, 1923. xv, 362p.

138
WÄCHTER, Franz. Japans wirtschaftlicher Aufstieg [Japan's Economic Advance]. Erlangen, 1925. v, 399p. Text in German. Diss. ms. not available.

KAWAMURA, Tadao. The Class Conflict in Japan as Affected by the Expansion of Japanese Industry and Trade. 1928. See no.2.

139
ROSINSKI, Herbert. Studien zum Problem der Autarkie in Japan [A Study of the Problem of Economic Independence in Japan]. Berlin, 1930. Text in German. The dissertation in its published form is available at Marburg/Lahn, Universitätsbibliothek, Nr. XVII C.

A description of the Japanese economy focusing on Japan's efforts to achieve economic independence before, during, and after World War One. The wood, coal, petroleum, electricity, and iron and steel industries are used as case illustrations. References to Korea, Formosa, Micronesia, Sakhalin, and Shantung are also included.

Rel.Publ.: Studien...Japan. Berlin: Ebering, 1930. 58p.; "Unsere Kenntnis von der japanischen Volkswirtschaft," Yamato, 4 (1932), 11-24; "Japans Erdolversorgung und Erdolpolitik," Weltwirtschaftliches Archiv, 39 (1934), 382-414.

EMBREE, John. Suye mura: A Changing Economic Order. 1937. See no.23.

140
SPURR, William Alfred. Seasonal Variations in the Economic Activities of Japan. Columbia, 1940. ix, 129p.

A study of the seasonal fluctuations in Japanese prices, production, employment, stocks of goods, transportation, foreign trade, banking activity, and speculation from the 1890's to 1937.

Rel.Publ.: Seasonal...Japan. Lincoln, Neb., 1940. ix, 129p. (University of Nebraska, University Studies, v.40, no.1)

141
TAGAWA, Hiroso. Grundzüge der Entwicklung der japanischen Wirtschaft [Basic Characteristics of Japanese Economic Development]. München, 1940. Text in German. The dissertation in its published form is available at Marburg/Lahn, Universitätsbibliothek, Nr. XVII C.

The author contends that Japan succeeded in acquiring a share of the world market by making use of her feudal heritage and by building up her military power. He explains the semi-feudal, semi-military character of Japanese capitalism, describes the historical development of the state from its beginnings to 1868, and considers the growth of commerce in Japan after the Meiji Restoration.

Rel.Publ.: Grundzüge...Wirtschaft. Berlin und München: Puchelt, 1940. 79p.

TSURU, Shigeto. Development of Capitalism and Business Cycles in Japan, 1868-1897. 1940. See no.315.

142
LIF, Sh. B. Voina i ekonomika Iaponii [War and the Economy of Japan]. Moscow, Voenno-politicheskaia akademiia Krasnoi Armii imeni V. I. Lenina, 1941. (Doctor of Economic Sciences degree) 248p. Text in Russian.

Rel.Publ.: Voina...Iaponii, ed. by E. S. Varga. Moscow: Politizdat, 1940. 248p. (Institut mirovogo khoziaistva i mirovoi politiki Akademii nauk SSSR)

143
ADLER, Walter. Die Träger der japanischen Wirtschaftspolitik [The Pillars of Japan's Economic Policy]. Leipzig, 1944. vii, 143p. Text in German. Diss. ms. available at Leipzig, Universitätsbibliothek; refer to author, title, year, and no. U44.6123.

Studies (1) Japanese capitalism and its policy, (2) the zaibatsu and their importance, (3) the Japanese labor movement, the economic policies of social reformers, and the position and goals of Japanese trade unions, (4) the economic policies of the parties and the national integration movement, and (5) the growth of the government bureaucracy and of the military after 1868 (examined with regard to economic policy, their capacity for leadership, and their influence upon various sectors of the economy).

144
VAGANOV, N. A. Zemlevladenie i arenda v Iaponii [Land Ownership and Rent in Japan]. Moscow, Institut mirovogo khoziaistva i mirovoi politiki Akademii nauk SSSR, 1947. (Candidate of Economic Sciences degree) 270p. Text in Russian.

145
LOCKWOOD, William Wirt. The Economic Development of Japan: Growth and Structural Change, 1868-1938. Harvard, 1950. viii, 588p. (2v.) AB: 6p. summary appended to diss. ms.

Contents: Foundations of Industrialism: The Meiji Period; Japan's Economy in Transition; The Scale of Economic Growth; Population, Markets, Technology; Capital, Savings, Enterprise; Structural Change: The Redirection of Demand; Structural Change: Production and Employment.

Rel.Publ.: The Economic...1938. Princeton: Princeton University Press, 1954. xv, 603p.; "The State and Economic Growth in Japan," FES, 20 (May 16, 1951), 93-99; "The Scale of Economic Growth in Japan, 1868-1938," in Economic Growth: Brazil, India, Japan, ed. by Simon Kuznets, Wilbert Moore, and Joseph Spengler (Durham: Duke University Press, 1955), 129-78; "The State and Economic Enterprise in Modern Japan, 1868-1938," in Economic Growth: Brazil, India, Japan (Durham: 1955), 537-602.

146
CHANG, She-wo. Problems of Industrialization in Densely Populated Underdeveloped Countries. Iowa, 1953. 297p. DA 13 (1953), 679-80; UM 5460.

Includes references to Japan that point out how Japan is illustrative of labor force shifts resulting from industrial development, of the expansion of agricultural output 1880-1920 through land saving, of industrialization patterns, of educational and technical training expansion, of capital growth through government encouragement, of the role of foreign capital, and of the effect of industrialization on international trade. Japan is usually contrasted with such densely populated but underdeveloped countries as India, China, and Egypt.

COLLIER, David S. The Politico-Economic Position of Japan. 1953. See no.1821.

147
PHAN-tan-Chuc. L'Économie japonaise à la recherche de sa solution [The Japanese Economy in Search of Her Solution]. Toulouse, 1955. 268p. Text in French.

148
OSHIMA, Harry Tatsumi. A Critique of the National Income Statistics of Selected Asian Countries. Columbia, 1956. 380p. DA 16 (Aug. 1956), 1361; UM 16,292.

Japan is included in a critical evaluation of the accuracy of official national income statistics published in the postwar period.

Rel.Publ.: "Survey of Various Long Term Estimates of Japanese National Income," Keizai kenkyū, 4 (July, 1953), 248-56; "National Income Statistics of Underdeveloped Countries," in American Statistical Association. Journal, 52 (June 1957), 162-74; "The International Comparison of Size Distribution of Family Incomes with Special Reference to Asia," Review of Economics and Statistics, 44 (Nov. 1962), 439-45; "National Accounts for the Analysis of Asian Growth," in Asian Conference on Income and Wealth--1st, Hong Kong, 1960. Asian Studies in Income and Wealth (New York: Asia Publishing House, 1965), 1-47.

149
RANIS, Gustav. Japan: A Case Study in Development. Yale, 1956. 176p.

A study of Japan's economic development, 1878-1937. Attention is paid to the emergence of the entrepreneur and his exploitation of tradition, to the problem of capital formation, and to the use of techniques which had already become obsolete in other industrial nations. The author also asserts that "changes in the factor-price ratio as a result of the successful break-out in the nineteenth century, the influx of foreign capital, and the gradual advent of social welfare considerations" were responsible for further development.

Rel.Publ.: "The Community-Centered Entrepreneur in Japanese Economic Development," Explorations in Entrepreneurial History, 8 (Dec. 1955), 80-98; "Factor Proportions in Japanese Economic Development," American Economic Review, 47 (Sept. 1957), 594-607; "The Capital Output Ratio in Japanese Economic Development," Review of Economic Studies, 26 (Oct. 1958), 23-32; "The Financing of Japanese Economic Development," Economic History Review, 11 (Apr. 1959), 440-54; "Economic Development: A Suggested Approach," Kyklos, 12 (1959), 428-47.

HOLLERMAN, Leon. Japanese National Income and International Trade: A Structural Analysis. 1957. See no.260.

150
SHARRON, Arthur O. An Analysis of Japan's External Disequilibrium Ten Years after the End of World War II. American, 1958. 253p. DA 19 (July 1958), 63-64; UM 58-2412.

Analyzes the relative lag in Japan's postwar trade recovery; "the internal effects of the external disequilibrium in terms of the inter-relationships of low industrial wages, low agricultural productivity, and low levels of trade;" and Japan's postwar dependence on trade with the USA.

Rel.Publ. "Japanese Consumption, External Disequilibrium, and the Statistical Measurement," Review of Social Economy, 17 (Sept. 1959), 136-50.

151
ROSOVSKY, Henry. Japanese Capital Formation, 1868-1940. Harvard, 1959. ix, 551p. AB: 10p. summary appended to diss. ms.

"A major portion of the thesis is directed towards making the first long-term capital formation estimates for Japan, broken down into narrow economic components from 1868 to 1940." Contents: Pt.1: Introduction. Pt.2: Measurement of Capital Formation in the Public Sector: Government Construction, 1868-1940; Government Investment in Durable Equipment, 1868-1940. Pt.3: Measurement of Capital Formation in the Private Sector: Residential Construction in Japan, 1881-1940; Private Non-Residential Construction; Investment in Producers' Durable Equipment: The Private Sector; Investment in Inventories. Pt.4: Analysis: Capital Formation and the Public Sector; Capital Formation and the Private Sector; Japanese Capital Formation and the European Model.

Rel.Publ.: Capital Formation in Japan, 1868-1940. Glencoe, Ill.: Free Press, 1961. xiii, 358p.; "The Statistical Measurement of Japanese Economic Growth," Economic Development and Cultural Change, 7 (Oct. 1958), 75-84; "Japanese Capital Formation: The Role of the Public Sector," Journal of Economic History, 19 (Sept. 1959), 350-78; "Capital Formation in Prewar Japan: Current Findings and Future Problems," in The Economic Development of China and Japan, ed. by C. D. Cowan (New York, 1964), 205-19.

152
BARSS, Lawrence Whitcomb. Political Change and Economic Growth: A Methodology Applied to Japan, Turkey, and India. Massachusetts Institute of Technology, 1961. 642p. AB: Massachusetts Institute of Technology. Abstracts of Theses 1960/1961. p.122-24.

"This paper comprises a study of the interaction of certain political and economic variables during early phases of the development cycle. With respect to the three cases examined, it is shown that the actual rates of growth attained during the 'stages' of 'tradition' and 'preconditions' were to a large degree determined by policies established by political elite groups. ...Ultimately, the creation of policies specifically designed to bring about expansion of the capital stock came to be recognized as a desideratum by political elite groups anxious to buttress their positions of authority. From this point, attempts to move forward through 'take-off' were assured."

Rel.Publ.: Political...India. Cambridge: M.I.T. Center for International Studies, 1961. 2v.

153
MARTIN, Hans-Peter. Japans Bedeutung im ozeanischen Wirtschaftsraum: Struktur und raumliche Verflechtung seiner Wirtschaft [Japan's Economic Importance for the Countries Bordering on the Pacific Ocean: The Structure and the Geographical Involvement of Her Economy]. Münster, 1961. Text in German. The dissertation in its published form is available at Marburg/Lahn, Universitätsbibliothek, Nr. Z64/1974.

Japan's involvement in the world economy is considered from the viewpoints of economic geography and of economic history. Her present situation is illustrated by means of a study of her economic structure, the structure of her iron and steel industry, and changes in the market structure and commodity composition of her foreign trade in the years 1934-1936 and 1959. The dissertation concludes with information on Japanese economic trends.

Rel.Publ.: Japans...Wirtschaft. Göttingen: Vandenhoek und Ruprecht, 1962. 123p. (Institut für Verkhrswissenschaft an der Universität Münster, Weltschaftliche Studien, 1)

154
MINHAS, Bagicha Singh. An International Comparison of Factor Costs and Factor Use. Stanford, 1961. 180p. DA 22 (Aug. 1961), 461-62; UM 61-1031.

Includes a discussion of the estimated rate of return on industrial capital in Japan.

Rel.Publ.: An International...Use. Amsterdam: North-Holland Pub. Co., 1963. 124p. (Contributions to Economic Analysis, 31); "Capital-Labor Substitution and Economic Efficiency" [by] K.J. Arrow, H.B. Chenery, B.S. Minhas, and R.M. Solow, Review of Economics and Statistics, 43 (Aug. 1961), 225-50; "The Homohypallagic Production Function, Factor-Intensity Reversals, and the Heckscher-Ohlin Theorem," Journal of Political Economy, 70 (Apr. 1962), 138-56.

155
SHOSAKU, Tokunaga. Razvoj kapitalizma u Japanu: o formiranju manufakture i njenom karakteru [The Development of Capitalism in Japan: On the Formation of Manufacturing and Its Character]. Beograd, 1961. iii, 129p. Text in Serbo-Croatian.

Studies the formation of the city and the town economies as well as the growth of financial and commodity relations involving the villages. Particular attention is paid to the significance of mercantile capital in the origin and development of the "verlag" (putting out) system for the production of cotton and silk. Also analyzes the role of the state in the transition to mechanized modes of production.

156
JOACHIMI, Herbert. Der japanische Imperialismus: Seine ökonomische Entwicklung, seine Besonderheiten, und sein Verstoss auf dem kapitalistischen Weltmarkt nach dem 2. Weltkrieg [Japanese Imperialism: Its Economic Development, Its Special Characteristics, and Its Rejection by the Capitalistic World Market after World War II]. Berlin, Humboldt Universität, 1962. iii, 365p. (2v.) Text in German.

157
JUNIOR, Gerald. Grundfragen des internationalen Sozialproduktvergleichs zwischen Japan und der Bundesrepublik Deutschland [Basic Problems in the Comparison of the Gross National Product of Japan with that of West Germany]. Frankfurt a.M., 1963. 332p. Text in German. Diss. ms. available at Marburg/Lahn, Staatsbibliothek Preussischer Kulturbesitz, Nr. Hsn 55,099.

The dissertation begins with a theoretical discussion of personal income, national income, and gross national product as well as with a statistical comparison of supply and production. The author then studies the objectives, methods, and prerequisites for comparing the gross national product of Germany with that of Japan.

WALLACE, William M. Cultural Values and Economic Development: A Case Study of Japan. 1963. See no.83.

MÜLLER, Christa. Erziehung und industrielle Entwicklung: Die Bedeutung des Erziehungswesens für die industrielle Entwicklung, erlangt am Beispiel Japans, 1964. See no.401.

158
BIRÓ, Klára. A modern Japán fejlődésének főbb sajátosságai, eredményei, és problémái [The Principal Characteristics, Results, and Problems of the Development of Modern Japan]. Budapest, Hungarian Academy of Sciences, 1965. 235, viiip. Text in Hungarian. Xerographic and microfilm copies are available from

the Library of the Hungarian Academy of Sciences, Budapest, v., Akademia utca 2. (Permission of the author must be secured in advance.)

Contents: Introductory Notes on Japan's Geography and Demography; Japan's Economic Development up to 1945; Principal Results and Problems in Japanese Economic Development since 1945, Including Chapters on the Industrial and Agricultural Development and on the Social Conditions; Japan's Foreign Policy after World War II; Western and Marxist Interpretation of Japan's Economic Growth; Japan as Model for the Third World.

159
KUZNETSOV, Iu. D. Problemy imperialisticheskoi integratsii v Iaponii [Problems of Imperialistic Integration in Japan]. Moscow, Institut mirovoi ekonomiki i mezhdunarodnykh otnoshenii Akademii nauk SSSR, 1965, (Candidate of Economic Sciences degree) 205p. Text in Russian.

160
LEE, Feng-yao. An Econometric Analysis of the Demand for Basic Living Materials in Japan. Michigan State, 1965. 189p. DA 26 (Feb. 1966), 4287; UM 66-408.

"Information from both cross-section and time-series data was utilized to derive the statistical consumer demand functions for basic living materials (food, housing, fuel and light, and clothing) in Japan during the period 1951-1962."

SOARES, Gláucio Ary Dillon. Economic Development and Political Radicalism. 1965. See no.13.

BRYCE, Herrington J. Social Origin as an Obstacle or as an Aid to Mobility: A Comparative Analysis of Long-Run Occupational Mobility. 1966. See no.14.

IATSENKO, B.P. Severnye raiony Iaponii: Ekonomichesko-geograficheskaia kharakteristika khoziaistva, usloviia i osobennosti razvitiia Khokkaiko i Tokhoku. 1967. See no.467.

IGNATUSHCHENKO, S. K. Ekonomicheskaia ekspansiia Iaponii posle vtoroi mirovoi voiny. 1967. See no.851.

161
MORRISON, Thomas Andrews. A Comparative Evaluation of Accounting and Reporting Practices in Selected Countries. Pennsylvania State, 1967. 280p. DA 28 (Dec. 1967), 1962-A; UM 67-15,404.

"For the major part of the study, the author selected for analysis annual reports of companies in the automobile and steel industries in Germany, France, Japan, and Italy....The material is presented in separate chapters on each of the countries and in the appendices which detail the important accounting findings for each of the twenty companies" studied.

162
FUJITA, Yukio. An Analysis of the Development and Nature of Accounting Principles in Japan. Illinois, 1968. 263p. DA 29 (Jan. 1969), 1986-87-A; UM 69-1346.

Utilizes Talcott Parsons' framework in order to analyze the social function of each set of accounting principles in Japan since 1890. "For analytical purposes, the development of accounting principles in Japan was divided into three stages: (1) groping for uniformity in financial reporting (1890-1947), (2) establishment and improvement of A Statement of Business Accounting Principles (1947-1962), and (3) reconciliation of the Japanese Commercial Code and A Statement of Business Accounting Principles (1962-)."

AGRICULTURE AND SERICULTURE

(includes land reform) See also: Economics--economic history (pages 33-35), History--Japanese empire--Manchoukuo (pages 96-97), and History--Japanese empire--Taiwan (pages 98-99).

163
NAGAI, Shinkizi. Die Landwirthschaft Japans: Ihre Gegenwart und ihre Zukunft [Japanese Agriculture: Its Present Situation and Its Future]. Halle-Wittenberg, 1886. Text in German. The dissertation in its published form is available at Marburg/Lahn, Universitätsbibliothek, Nr. XII C.

The peculiar characteristics of Japanese agriculture as determined by Japan's geographical conditions and by national legislation. The author studies Japan's climate and its influence on the cultivation of the soil and the preparation of natural fertilizer, he describes in detail farming and cattle-breeding, and he critically evaluates the tax system, transportation conditions, and the level of farm technology. He also presents a number of proposals aimed at improving the level of Japanese agriculture.

Rel.Publ.: <u>Die Landwirthschaft</u>...Zukunft. Halle a.S., 1886. ii, 98p.

SHIMOYAMA, Yunichiro. Beiträge zur Kenntnis des japanischen Klebreises, <u>Mozigome</u>. 1886. See no.2010.

164
HIRAI, Masao. Über die landwirtschaftlichen Verhältnisse Japans mit Berücksichtigung der Grundsteuer und des landwirtschaftlichen Kredites [A Study of Japan's Agricultural Conditions with Regard to the Land Tax and to Agricultural Credit]. Jena, 1890. Text in German. The dissertation in its published form is available at Marburg/Lahn, Universitätsbibliothek, Nr. XII C.

A description of rural landholding, taxation methods, and agricultural profitability in Japan. The land-tax is regarded as the major obstacle to agricultural development, and proposals are presented for eliminating various unprofitable practices.

Rel.Publ.: <u>Über...Kredites</u>. Jena: Frommann, 1890. x, 77p.

165
NITOBE, Inazo Ota. Über den japanischen Grundbesitz: Dessen Verteilung und landwirtschaftliche Verwertung [Japanese Landed Property: Its Distribution and Its Agricultural Utilization]. Halle, 1890. Text in German. The dissertation in its published form is available at Marburg/Lahn, Universitätsbibliothek, Nr. XVII C.

An investigation of land ownership in its various forms based on a survey of Japanese economic history with emphasis on the principal features of Japanese feudalism. The division and distribution of state and private lands during the first part of the Meiji period is presented in statistical tables. The position of the peasantry and Japan's agricultural situation are of central concern.

Rel.Publ.: <u>Über...Verwertung</u>. Halle a.S., 1890. viii, 91p.

166
ICHIHARA, Morihiro. The Silk Trade of Japan. Yale,

1892. 200p.

Contents: Position of Silk in Japanese Foreign Trade; The History of Japanese Silk Industries and Trade; The Actual State of Silk Production in Japan; The Present Status of the Japanese Silk Trade; Substitutes for Silk and Foreign Competitors; The Future Prospects of the Japanese Silk Trade.

167
YOSHIDA, Tetsutaro. Entwicklung des Seiden und der Seidenindustrie vom Alterthum dis zum Ausgang des Mittelalters [The Development of the Silk Trade and of the Silk Industry from Ancient Times to the End of the Middle Ages]. Heidelberg, 1894. Text in German. The dissertation in its published form is available at Marburg/Lahn, Universitätsbibliothek, NR. XVII C.

Contents: Silk in Ancient Greece and Rome and the Silk Trade between the Orient and the Occident; The Chinese Silk Trade with Rome, Byzantium, and Persia and the Beginnings of Sericulture in Japan; The Growth of the Silk Trade and of the Silk Industry (800's-1300's) in Europe, Asia Minor, China, and Japan; The Silk Industry in North Italy (1400's-1600's).

Rel.Publ.: Entwicklung...Mittelalters. Heidelberg: J. Hörning, 1894. viii, 111p.

MAHOE, Künwoll. Vergleichende Untersuchung über die physikalischen und chemischen Eigenschaften der chinesischen und japanischen Seiden. 1915. See no.1995.

168
STAMM, Henri. L'Approvisionnement en soie: La soie grège du Japon [The Supply of Silk: Japanese Raw Silk]. Bern, 1922. Text in French.

The author reviews the marketing potentiality for Japanese silk, 1859-1922; studies the production, sales organization, and sales difficulties of the Japanese silk industry, 1859-1922; and forecasts the future of the industry.

Rel.Publ.: L'Approvisionnement...Japon. Weinfelden: Neuenschwander, 1922. 124p. (Schweizer Industrie- und Handelsstudien, 12)

169
RUELLAN, Francis. La Production du riz au Japon: Étude des conditions naturelles et historiques de la culture et des problèmes qui s'y rapportent [The Production of Rice in Japan: A Study of the Natural and Historical Conditions of the Culture and of the Problems Relating to It]. Paris, 1940. (thèse complémentaire) Text in French.

Contents: Cultivation (Distribution of Rice-Fields, Mode of Cultivation, Enlargement of Rice-Fields and Distribution of Population); Problems of Production (Progress and Variations in the Size of the Harvest, Factors Involved in Increasing Production, Cost Price of Rice); Conclusion (Population Growth and the Relationship between Production and Consumption, the Agricultural Crisis, Its Remedies).

Rel.Publ.: La Production...rapportent. Paris: Larose, 1940, 104p.

PERTSEVA, K. T. Sel'skokhoziaistvennaia kolonizatsiia Iaponiei Iuzhnogo Sakhalina, 1905-1945 gg. 1950. See no.761.

170
POPOV, V. A. Agrarnaia reforma v Iaponii, 1945-1949 [Land Reform in Japan, 1945-1949]. Moscow, Institut vostokovedeniia Akademii nauk SSSR, 1951. (Candidate of Historical Sciences degree) 348p. Text in Russian.

Rel.Publ.: Zemel'naia reforma i agrarnye otnosheniia v Iaponii posle vtoroi mirovoi voiny. Moscow: Sotsekgiz, 1959. 211p.; Krest'ianskoe dvizhenie v Iaponii posle vtoroi mirovoi voiny. Moscow: Izdatel' stvo vostochnoi literatury, 1961. 186p. (Institut narodov Azii Akademii nauk SSSR)

171
GUZEVATYI, Ia. N. "Prodovol'stvennyi vopros" v Iaponni i upadok iaponskogo sel'skogo khoziaistva v usloviiakh amerikanskoi okkupatsii ["The Food Question" and the Decline of Japanese Agriculture under the American Occupation]. Moscow, Moskovskii institut vostokovedeniia, 1953. (Candidate of Economic Sciences degree) 289p. Text in Russian. AB: 17p. summary published in 1953.

172
JOHNSTON, Bruce Foster. Food and Agriculture in Japan, 1880-1950. Stanford, 1953. 495p. DA 13 (1953), 691; UM 5799.

Describes the outstanding characteristics of Japan's agricultural economy (domestic production, imports, and population). Focuses particularly on the relationship between improvements in agricultural productivity and economic development, and on Japan's critical food shortage during the 1940's.

Rel.Publ.: "Japan: The Race between Food and Population," Journal of Farm Economics, May 1949; "Agricultural Productivity and Economic Development in Japan," Journal of Political Economy, 59 (Dec. 1951), 498-513; Japanese Food Management in World War II. Stanford: Stanford University Press, 1953. xii, 283p. (Food, Agriculture, and World War II); "The Nature of Agriculture's Contributions to Economic Development" [by] B. F. Johnston and J. W. Mellor, Food Research Institute Studies, 1 (Nov. 1960), 335-56; "The Role of Agriculture in Economic Development" [by] B. F. Johnston and J. W. Mellor, American Economic Review, 51 (Sept. 1961), 566-93; "Agricultural Development and Economic Transformation: A Comparative Study of the Japanese Experience," Food Research Institute Studies, 3 (Nov. 1962), 223-76; "Agriculture and Economic Development: The Relevance of the Japanese Experience," Food Research Institute Studies, 6 (1966), 251-312.

173
KAIHARA, Motosuke. Economic Development of Japanese Agriculture: An Appraisal of the Significance of Land Tenure in Agricultural Development. Wisconsin, 1955. 228p. DA 16 (Aug. 1956), 1358-59; UM 16,177.

Contents: The Concept of the Economic Development of Agriculture; Capital Formation of the Function of the Landlord in Japan; Shifts in Agricultural Production; Ownership of Cultivated Land as an Investment Opportunity; The Pattern of the Land Tenure System and Land Rent; Farmer's Movement; Tenure Ladder of Farm People and Social Relations between Landlord and Tenant; Economic Function of the Landlord as a Rice Seller; Some Changes in Function in the Land Tenure Systems. The period of coverage is 1868-1939.

174
PADGETT, Rose. An Analysis of the Silk Industry. Purdue, 1955. 391p. DA 16 (June 1956), 1133; UM 13,963.

The dissertation is entirely technical in nature, but reference is constantly made to the silk industry in Japan and China. Contents: World Sericulture and Silk through the Ages; Types of Fabric Design [including Japanese fabric]; Technology of Silk Production; Wild Silks; Properties of Silk and Its By-Products; Silk Processing; The Mulberry; Production of Silk; Cocoon Production; Silk Reeling and Raw Silk; World Raw Silk Production; Marketing of Silk; Silk Prices; World Trade in Silk; Consumption of Raw Silk; Fiber Inter-relationships [of Silk, Cotton, Wool, and Man-Made Fibers].

175
PITTS, Forrest Ralph. Comparative Land Fertility and Potential in the Inland Sea and Peripheral Areas of Japan. Michigan, 1955. 258p. DA 15 (Sept. 1955), 1594-95; UM 12,634.

The study analyzes the physical, historical, agricultural, cultural, and economic factors which account for the paradox of high rural prosperity in Kagawa prefecture, an area of Japan which is extremely productive despite the fact that it experiences high rainfall variability and frequent drought.

Rel.Publ.: "Rural Prosperity in Japan," in Studies on Economic Life in Japan, ed. by Richard K. Beardsley (Ann Arbor: University of Michigan, 1964), 95-124. (University of Michigan, Center for Japanese Studies, Occasional Papers, 8)

176
ANSTEY, Robert Lealand. A Comparative Study of the Agricultural Land Use of the Aso Highland and the Kumamoto Lowland of Central Kyushu. Maryland, 1957. 275p. DA 17 (Nov. 1957), 2560-61; UM 23,254.

Contents: Introduction (Agricultural Land Utilization in Central Kyushu, Method of Study, A Note on the Historical Development of Japanese Land Use Mapping); Physical Setting of Central Kyushu (Landforms and Drainage, Climate, Soils, Application of Regional Planning); Comparison of Major Types of Agriculture Land Use between the Aso Highland and the Kumamoto Lowland (Pastureland, Timberland) Cultivated Land, Wasteland, Comparison between the Two Areas); Agricultural Land Use Systems of the Aso Highland and Kumamoto Lowland (Highland Utilization System, at Kojo Mura and Nagamizu Mura, Diluvial Lowland Utilization System at Haramizu Mura and Hiroyasu Mura, Alluvial Lowland Utilization System at Tamukai Mura and Ugiguchi Mura); Conclusion.

177
KLEIN, Sidney. The Pattern of Land Tenure Reform in East Asia after World War II. Columbia, 1957. 412p. DA 17 (May 1957), 1006; UM 20,584.

The first section describes and analyzes the Japanese case.

Rel.Publ.: The Pattern...War II New York: Bookman Associates, 1958. 260p. (Bookman Monograph Series)

SUN, Mung-chio Chao. Japanese Raw Silk and American Raw Cotton. 1957. See no.1370.

178
KAKIUCHI, Hiroaki George. The Rise and Development of the Fruit Industry on the Okayama Plain. Michigan, 1958. 188p. DA 19 (May 1959), 2909; UM 58-3682.

Studies the geographical setting, the historical development, competing crops and side lines (minor grains, sugar cane, cotton, indigo, rice, straw-plaiting, hand-made vermicelli, sericulture, fruit), farm management, and the various types of marketing.

Rel.Publ.: "Stone Wall Strawberry Industry on Kuno Mountain, Japan," Economic Geography, 36 (Apr. 1960), 171-84.

179
NARASIMHA MURTHY, P. A. Crop Insurance System in Japan and Its Lessons for India. Delhi University (through the Indian School of International Studies), 1959. xxvii, 297p. Order microfilm copy directly from the Nehru Memorial Museum and Library, New Delhi, India.

180
LIU, John Jung-chao. An Econometric Model of the Rice Market in the Japanese Empire, 1910-1937. Michigan, 1960. 143p. DA 20 (June 1960), 4549; UM 60-1778.

An econometric case study of the role of Korean and Formosan rice in the Japanese rice market. Contents: The Role of Rice in the Economy; Fluctuations in Rice Production and Growth of Exports; Production of Rice; Interregional Price Relationships; The Demand for Rice; Integrated Rice Market.

181
OKABAYASHI, Toyoki. Measuring the Contributions of Natural Resources to the National Outputs of the United States and Japan. Oregon, 1960. 206p. DA 21 (Feb. 1961), 2141-42; UM 60-5400.

"Separate studies were made of the non-agricultural sectors and of the agricultural sectors of the economy." The year 1951 was chosen for particular study.

182
TSUZUKI, Toshio. Die Bodennutzungssysteme der japanischen Landwirtschaft [Japanese Agriculture: Its Methods for Working the Soil]. Kiel, 1961. ii, 155p. Text in German. Diss. ms. available at Kiel, Universitätsbibliothek, Nr. TU. 61.5653.

Studies the various factors (economic, social, climatic, etc.) that influence the Japanese exploitation of the soil, investigates the different methods of representative agricultural undertakings for working the soil, and provides a statistical evaluation of soil utilization in all of the prefectures of Japan. Concludes with a comparison of the twenty most important Japanese methods for working the soil.

Rel.Publ.: Die Betriebssysteme der japanischen Landwirtschaft. Hamburg: Cram, De Gruyter, 1964. 127p. (Deutsche-Japanische Studien)

183
TUMA, Elias Hanna. Economics, Politics, and Land Tenure Reform: A Comparative Study. California, Berkeley, 1962. 542p. DA 24 (Sept. 1963), 1007-08; UM 63-6048.

"Compares 12 reform movements including the Japanese one on 23 variables representing the backgrounds, processes, and effects of reform."

Rel.Publ.: Twenty-Six Centuries of Agrarian Reform: A Comparative Analysis. Berkeley: University of California Press, 1965. xi, 309p.

184
HOUGH, Richard Fairchild. The Impact of the Drastic Decline in Raw Silk upon Land Use and Industry in Selected Areas of Sericultural Specialization in Japan. Wisconsin, 1963. 313p. DA 24 (Dec. 1963), 2417; UM 64-647.

An investigation of four selected areas for the period 1930-1960: Gumma prefecture, "the leading prefecture for mulberry acreage and cocoon production during the post-war years;" the Sagami diluvial terrace region of central Kanagawa prefecture; and the

Suwa and Nagano Basins of Nagano prefecture, two intermontane basins in which silk reeling factories were concentrated.

Rel.Publ.: "Impact of the Decline in Raw Silk on the Suwa Basin of Japan," Economic Geography, 44 (Apr. 1968), 95-116; "Impact of the Decline in Raw Silk on Two Major Cocoon-Producing Regions in Japan," in Association of American Geographers, Annals, 58 (June 1968), 221-49.

185
MARKAR'IAN, S. B. Rol' sel'skokhoziaistvennoi kooperatsii v poslevoennoi iaponskoi derevne [The Role of Agricultural Cooperation in the Postwar Japanese Village]. Moscow, Institut narodov Azii Akademii nauk SSSR 1963. (Candidate of Economic Sciences degree) 354 + 23p. Text in Russian. [See also addenda entry no. 30A.]

186
PATEL, Jagannath Prasad. Studies on the Japanese Method of Rice Cultivation: To Assess the Values of Various Factors of the Japanese Method of Rice Cultivation in Increasing the Crop Yield per Acre and To Determine the Optimum Dose of Fertilizers and a Suitable Spacing for it in the Jabalpur District [India]. Jabalpur, 1963. 237p. No facilities for the acquisition of a microfilm copy of the dissertation are available at Jabalpur University.

The research work includes three experiments. In the first experiment, all the factors of the Japanese method of rice cultivation are tested with a view to assessing their relative values in contributing to the increase in the yield of the crop. In the second experiment, the author aims at determining the optimum dose of fertilizer and a suitable spacing for the method. In the last experiment, the effect of different nursery methods on seedling growth is studied.

Rel.Publ.: "Evaluating the Various Factors of the 'Japanese Method' of Rice Cultivation in India," Agronomy Journal (U.S.A.), 57 (1965), 567-72; "Effect of Different Nursery Methods on the Growth of Rice Seedlings," Proceedings of the Crop Science Society of Japan, 35 (1966), 115-19; "Interrelations of Different Proportions and Rates of N-P Fertilizer Application, and Planting Patterns of Rice in the Jabalpur District," Indian Journal of Agronomy, 7 (1967), 222-30; "Relationships of the Plant Characters Attributing to the Yield of Rice," Indian Journal of Agronomy, 7 (1967), 407-10.

187
KANEDA, Hiromitsu. Technical Change and Returns to Scale: An Econometric Study of Japanese Agricultural Development in the Postwar Years. Stanford, 1964. 209p. DA 25 (Aug. 1964), 887; UM 64-7654.

"An econometric analysis of the developments in the supply side of Japanese agriculture" with particular focus on the production relationships underlying Japanese agriculture during the postwar period.

Rel.Publ.: "Substitution of Labor-Non-Labor Inputs and Technical Change in Japanese Agriculture," Review of Economics and Statistics, 47 (May 1965), 163-71; "The Source of Rates of Productivity Gains in Japanese Agriculture, as Compared with the U.S. Experience," Journal of Farm Economics, 49 (Dec. 1967), 1443-51; "Long-Term Changes in Food Consumption Patterns in Japan, 1878-1964," Food Research Institute Studies, 8 (Spring 1968), 3-32.

NAKAMURA, James I. The Place of Agricultural Production in the Economic Development of Japan. 1964. See no. 576.

188
SCHUTJER, Wayne Alan. The Relationship between P[ublic] L[aw] 480 Title I Imports and Domestic Agricultural Production in Six Receiving Nations. Michigan State, 1964. 220p. DA 25 (Mar. 1965), 4985; UM 65-725.

An analysis of the experiences of six receiving nations: Columbia, India, Israel, Japan, Pakistan, and Turkey. The dissertation includes a study of the impact of Japanese imports of Title I wheat, feed grain, and tobacco upon Japan's domestic agricultural production and upon her commercial imports of those particular products after 1954.

189
UEMURA, Kenji. Entwicklung, gegenwärtiger Stand, und Tendenz der Agrarstatistik in Japan [The Development, Current Position, and Trend of Agrarian Statistics in Japan]. Bonn, 1964. Text in German. The dissertation in its published form is available at Bochum, Universitätsbibliothek, Nr. UA 25,504.

Contents: Historical Introduction and the Beginnings of Statistics (up to 1870); The First Stage in the Development of Agrarian Statistics (1871-1925); The Structure of Agricultural Societies and Their Function in Agrarian Statistics (1899-1945); The Reforms and Present Nature of Agrarian Statistics; Critical Examination of Some Statistical Results; Trends in the Development of Agrarian Statistics in Japan.

Rel.Publ.: Entwicklung...Japan. Bonn: Institut für Agrarpolitik und Marktforschung der Rheinischen Friedrich-Wilhelms-Universität Bonn, 1964. iii, 120p.

190
SEO, Joseph Wonsock. Der gegenwärtige Stand der Agrarwirtschaft in Ostasien (Japan, Korea, Taiwan): Unter besonderer Berücksichtigung der handelspolitischen Verflechtung mit der EWG [The Present Position of Agriculture in East Asia (Japan, Korea, Taiwan): With Special Consideration of the Area's Commercial and Related Political Involvement with the European Common Market]. Wien, 1965. 189p. Text in German. Diss.ms. available at the Universitätsbibliothek der Universität Wien, Nr. D 16,229.

191
MALLAMPALLY, Taraka R. Sarma. An Analysis of Factors Influencing Increases in Rice Yields in Japan. Chicago, 1966. 80p.

An analysis of the factors that brought about the rapid increase in rice yields within Japan in the postwar period: fertilizers, machinery, labor, educational levels of rural population, irrigation, crop intensity, total crop land, land reform, and actual precipitation during the production period. The years 1950 and 1960 are singled out for comparison.

192
OH, Ki Song. Land Reform in Communist China and Postwar Japan. Pennsylvania, 1966. 448p. DA 28 (Aug. 1967), 743-44-A; UM 67-7868.

The author compares the two land reform programs in order "to answer such key questions as: Why did Communist China adopt such a radical reform program? How was the Japanese land reform program accomplished without violent opposition? To what extent were the aims and consequences of the two land reform programs different? What differences may be observed in the structure and political impact of the respective reform programs? Was land distribution able to solve the age old problem of 'too many people and too little land' in the two countries? If not, what was the significance of these land reform efforts and why were they pursued with such vigor?

193
MACNAB, John William. Agricultural Use of Sloping Land in Whitireia Peninsula (Wellington, New Zealand), Kitaki Island (Japan), and North Carolina (USA). London, 1967. 348p. [See also addenda entry no.28A.]

Rel.Publ.: "The Misused Land of Japan," in New Zealand Geographical Society, Record of Proceedings, 37 (Jan./June 1964), 1-5.

VIRACH ARROMDEE. Economics of the Rice Trade among Countries of South East Asia. 1968. See no.1240.

194
DALL, John Joseph, Jr. Sources of Productivity Change in Paddy Rice Production in Japan: 1900-1965. Pennsylvania, 1968. 229p. DA 30 (Sept. 1969), 914-A, UM 69-15,048.

"Changes in the total productivity measure were viewed as the result of two movements: (1) exploitation of a backlog or catching up effect as backward regions adopt the methods of the more advanced areas; and, (2) the residual or new technology."

195
FILIPPELLO, Anthony Nicholas. A Dynamic Econometric Investigation of the Japanese Livestock Economy. Missouri, 1968. 86p. DA 29 (Mar. 1969), 2860-A; UM 69-3382.

Seeks to "relate the dynamic economic adjustments in the Japanese livestock economy" and to project certain future developments.

WHITNEY, Daniel D. The Flow of Agricultural Information in Okinawa. 1968. See no.705.

196
BRAGINA, N. M. Sel'skoe khoziaistvo Iaponii posle zemel'noi reformy 1946-1949 [Japanese Agriculture after the Land Reform of 1946-1949]. Moscow, Institut mirovoi ekonomiki i mezhdunarodnykh otnoshenii Akademii nauk SSSR, 1969. (Candidate of Economic Sciences degree) 236p. Text in Russian.

BUSINESS, INDUSTRY, AND DOMESTIC COMMERCE

See also: Economics--economic history (pages 33-35), Economics--foreign trade (pages 36-40), Economics--money, banking, and investment (pages 43-47), and History--Japanese empire--Chōsen (pages 90-95) and Manchoukuo (pages 96-97).

197
ONO, Yeijiro. The Industrial Transition in Japan. Michigan, 1889. Diss. ms. not available.

"Traces the industrial transition now in progress in Japan, suggests some measures by which the process of transition may be facilitated, and speculates upon the consequences which are likely to follow in a society so long accustomed to primitive methods of industry." Contents: The Present Industrial Status of Japan (Population, Agriculture, Manufacture, and Transportation); Steps Necessary to Complete the Industrial Transition (Laws of Industrial Development, Criticism of the Japanese Agriculture, How May Modern Manufacture be Established?); The Probable Social Consequences of the Industrial Transition.

Rel.Publ.: The Industrial...Japan. Baltimore: American Economic Association, 1890. 121p. (Publications of the American Economic Association, v.5, no.1.)

198
UTSUNOMIYA, Kanae. Die Warenpreisbewegung in Japan seit dem Jahre 1875: Ihre Ursachen und Einwirkung auf die Volkswirtschaft [Changes in the Price of Goods in Japan since 1875: Their Causes and Their Impact on the Economy]. Berlin, 1897. Text in German. The dissertation in its published form is available at Marburg/Lahn, Universitätsbibliothek, Nr. XVII C.

After reviewing Japanese economic developments between 1868 and the 1890's, the author tries to determine the reasons for the increase of commodity prices after 1875 and points out how this increase affected Japanese agriculture and the working class throughout the country.

Rel.Publ.: Die Warenpreisbewegung...Volkswirtschaft. Leipzig: Duncker & Humblot, 1897. 96p.

199
SHIRASU, Chohei. The Development of Commerce in Japan and Its Effect on Civilization. Columbian University [now George Washington], 1901.

A study of external and domestic commerce during the 1890's. Pages 2319-58 consist of detailed commercial statistics based on official Japanese government reports. [Annotation based on the book.].

Rel.Publ.: Commercial Japan in 1900: Area, Population, Production, Railways, Telegraphs, Transportation Routes, Foreign Commerce, and Commerce of the United States with Japan. Washington, D.C.: Government Printing Office, 1901. 139p. ("From the Summary of Commerce and Finance for December 1901," U.S. Bureau of Statistics, U.S. Treasury Department, p.2217-358.)

200
KINOSITA, Yetaro. Past and Present of Japanese Commerce. Columbia, 1902. 166p.

Contents: The Finance and Economy of the Primitive Japanese; The Intercourse with Korea and China and Commerce in the Middle Ages; The Beginning of European Trade; The Restoration of 1868; Governmental Activity.

Rel.Publ.: Past...Commerce. New York: Columbia University Press, 1902. 165p. (Studies in History, Economics, and Public Law, ed. by the Faculty of Political Science of Columbia University, v.16; no.1.)

201
NISHI, Hikotaro. Die Baumwollspinnerei in Japan [Cotton Spinning in Japan]. Leipzig, 1911. Text in German. The dissertation in its published form is available at Marburg/Lahn, Universitätsbibliothek, Nr. XVII C; also at the University of Michigan, General Library, no. H5.Z52 no.40.

The author first focuses his attention on the introduction, promotion, and spread of cotton growing in Japan, on the nature of the cotton trade during the Meiji era, and on the mechanization of cotton spinning within the country. He then studies the cotton spinning factories and examines their capital conditions and their sales as well as the working conditions of their employees.

Rel.Publ.: Die Baumwollspinnerei...Japan. Tübingen: Laupp, 1911. viii, 265p. (Zeitschrift für die gesammte Staatswissenschaft, Ergänzungsheft, 40)

202
PSCHYREMBEL, Wilibald. Entwicklung und Stand der Elektrotechnik in Japan [Development and State of Electrical Engineering in Japan]. Berlin, 1924. 138p. Text in German. AB: Jahrbuch der Dissertationen der Philosophischen Fakultät Berlin. 1923/1924. II, p.145-49. Diss. ms. available at Marburg/Lahn, Staatsbibliothek Preussischer Kulturbesitz, Nr. MS 24.890.

The author investigates the basic factors underlying Japan's rapid industrial development; surveys the Japanese supply of raw materials, Japan's industrialization, and the demographic situation in general; and examines the development of transportation, power plants, and the electrical industry. He notes various trends towards industrial concentration in Japan and points out how the United States, England, and Germany have been competing with one another in their sales to Japan.

JIZUKA, Hanye. Japanisches Industrierecht: Vergleichende Darstellung mit dem deutschen Industrierecht. 1927. See no.1541.

NAGATA, Kikushiro. Das Grundbuch und die Rollen des gewerblichen Rechtsschutzes im deutschen und japanischen Recht. 1929. See no.1543.

203
HAHN, Karl. Die Industrialisierung Japans [The Industrialization of Japan]. Giessen, 1933. Text in German. The dissertation in its published form is available at Marburg/Lahn, Universitätsbibliothek, Nr. XVII C; also at the University of Michigan, General Library, no. HC462.H15.

Studies the historical development of Japanese business and industry after the Meiji Restoration, the financing and promotion of this industry, and its consequences for Japanese commerce and for the formation of new capital resources. Particular attention is paid to the social and economic impact of industrialization on economic controls, on the distribution of wealth, on forms of social and economic organization, and on the standard of living. Attention is also focused on the influence that Japan's economic conditions had on working and living conditions in other countries.

Rel.Publ.: Die Industrialisierung Japans. Bochum-Langendreer: Pöppinghaus, 1932. v, 169p.

204
O'NEILL, Reverend Charles A., S.J. Japan's Industrial Development and Foreign Trade Expansion in Cotton Textiles. Fordham, 1936. 189p. AB: Fordham University. Dissertations Accepted for Higher Degrees in the Graduate School. v.13 (Mar. 1937), p.35-38.

Analyzes "present conditions" (1935-1936) with regard to the forms of organization, the operation, and the control of the cotton textile industries in Japan. For the sake of Japan's "future economic welfare," the author advocates a reorganization and reform of the cotton textile industry which would be "in harmony with the specific principles laid down in Pope Leo XIII's Encyclicals, The Condition of Labor and Reconstruction of the Social Order." These reforms include labor legislation, more effective collective bargaining, and the development of co-partnership between capital and labor.

205
WHITE, Bennett Sexton, Jr. American Cotton in Foreign Markets. Harvard, 1937. ix, 466p. AB: Harvard University. Summaries of Theses...1937. p.231-36.

For information on the Japanese cotton textiles industry, see Ch.3, "The Shift in the Centers of Cotton Manufacturing with Special Reference to Great Britain and the Orient," and Ch.4, "The Effect of the Shift in the Centers of Cotton Manufacturing upon the Foreign Demand for American Cloth."

206
WALKER, Melville Herman. Manufacturers' Guilds (Kōgyō Kumiai) in Japanese Small Scale Industries. California, Berkeley, 1940. 243p.

Contents: The Importance of Medium and Small Scale Enterprise in Japanese Industry; Reasons for the Concentration of Industrial Enterprise in Japan; The Organization of Small Scale Industries; Reasons for the Continuance of Small Scale Industry in Japan; Manufacturers Guilds and Related Types of Association in Japan; Provisions of the Manufacturers Guild Law and Related Legislation; The Growth of the Manufacturers Guild System, 1925-1935; Influences Affecting the Development of the Manufacturers Guild System; The Government's Financial Assistance to Manufacturers Guilds; The Cooperative Enterprises of Manufacturers Enterprises; Price and Production Control Enterprises of Manufacturers Guilds.

207
RÜHL, Ingeborg. Die Papierwirtschaft in China, Japan, und Mandschukuo [The Paper Industry in China, Japan, and Manchoukuo]. Erlangen, 1942. vi, 185p. Text in German. Diss. ms. available at München, Bayrische Staatsbibliothek, Nr. U42/2112.

A study of the major differences among the paper and wood pulp industries of China, Japan, and Manchoukuo. Particular attention is paid to their development, their production, and their sales.

SHELDON, Charles S.,II. The Japanese Shipping Industry: An Analysis of Some Phases of the Industry in Relation to International Economic Rivalries. 1942. See no.384.

208
POPOV, K. M. Tekhno-ekonomicheskaia baza Iaponii: I. Problemy energetiki i khimizatsii Iaponii. II. Problemy metallurgii, mashinostroitel'noi bazy i transportnaia sistema Iaponii [The Technical and Economic Base of Japan: I. Problems with Regard to Power Engineering and the Introduction of Chemical Processes into the National Economy of Japan. II. Problems with Regard to Metallurgy, the Industrial Base in Machine Building, and the Transportation System of Japan]. Leningrad, Leningradskii gosudarstvennyi universitet imeni A. A. Zhdanova, 1943. (Doctor of Economic Sciences degree) 506 + 464p. (2v.) Text in Russian.

Rel.Publ.: Tekhno-ekonomicheskaia baza Iaponii. Moscow and Leningrad: Sotsekgiz, 1934. 230p. (Institut mirovogo khoziaistva i mirovoi politiki kommunisticheskoi akademii); Ekonomika Iaponii. Moscow: Sotsekgiz, 1936. 551p. (Institut mirovogo khoziaistva i mirovoi politiki Akademii nauk SSSR)

209
HADLEY, Eleanor Martha. Concentrated Business Power in Japan. Radcliffe, 1949. iii, 432p. AB: 4p. summary appended to diss. ms.

Using the case method approach, the author analyzes three representative "older" zaibatsu--Mitsui, Mitsubishi, and Sumitomo--and one representative "newer" one: Nitchitsu. "As the foremost combine of Japan's enterprise system, Mitsui is singled out for...extensive treatment."

Rel.Publ.: Antitrust in Japan. Princeton: Princeton University Press, 1970. 528p.; "Trust Busting in Japan," Harvard Business Review, 26 (July 1948), 424-40.

210
CRAWCOUR, Edwin Sydney. Medium and Small-Scale Industry in the Japanese Economy. Australian National, 1954. 230p.

A study of the nature, development, and implications of small scale industry in the Japanese economy. Small scale industry is regarded as the modern development of native pre-modern industry.

211
CHAO, Lien Lincoln. Distinctive Patterns of Industrial Relations in Korea. Minnesota, 1956. 233p. DA 16 (Oct. 1956), 1813-14; UM 17,844.

Japanese industrial practices are compared with those in Korea in part of the dissertation.

LA TROBE, Frederick de. Das Element der Werbung in der Publizistik der japanischen Presse der Gegenwart. 1957. See no.1676.

212
NUNN, Godfrey Raymond. Modern Japanese Book Publishing. Michigan, 1957. 215p. DA 18 (June 1958), 2014; UM 58-1443

The author seeks "to determine in what ways Japanese publishing, in the publication and distribution of books, acts in a selective manner and influences the availability of these books to readers." Contents: Author-Publisher Relationship; The Japanese Publisher; Distribution through Wholesalers; The Market for Books and Promotion; Bookshops and Libraries.

Rel.Publ.: "Studies on Economic Life in Japan: Modern Japanese Book Publishing," in Studies on Economic Life in Japan, ed. by Richard K. Beardsley (Ann Arbor: University of Michigan Press, 1964), 57-94. (University of Michigan, Center for Japanese Studies, Occasional Papers, 8)

VITH, Fritz. Zaibatsu: Die Auflösung der Familienkombinate in Japan. 1957. See no.1827.

BURKE, William M. The Role of the Entrepreneur in Japanese Economic Development. 1958. See no.473.

213
SHIMANO, Takuji. Handel und Handwerk in Deutschland und Japan unter besonderer Berücksichtigung der Kapitalverhältnisse [Commerce and Handicrafts in Germany and Japan, with Special Consideration of the Availability of Capital]. Kiel, 1958. 140p. Text in German. Diss. ms. available at Kiel, Universitätsbibliothek, Nr. TU. 58.4428.

A comparison of bourgeois commercial enterprises and craft enterprises in Germany and in Japan which seeks to determine whether similar changes occurred and whether parallels existed in their structure, supply of capital, and size of operations during their respective periods of industrialization.

VLASOV, V. A. Zakabalenie melkikh predpriiatii Iaponii monopolisticheskim kapitalom, 1929-1937. 1958. See no.664.

CUKIERMAN, Roger. Le Capital dans l'économie japonaise. 1960. See no.330.

214
SCHWARTZER, Uwe. Die Struktur der industriellen Konzentrationsformen in der japanischen Wirtschaft und deren Einfluss auf die internationalen Absatzmärkte [The Structure of Industrial Complexes in the Japanese Economy and Its Influence upon the World Trading Markets]. Graz, 1960. 122,iii p. Diss. ms. available at the Österreichische Nationalbibliothek, Nr. 898.407-C.

Studies the historical development and structure of the zaibatsu as well as the steps that were taken to break up these industrial complexes after 1946. Also examines the position of Japan in the world export trade from a political point of view and considers the participation of the zaibatsu in the trade.

215
TERRAHE, Eduard. Die Wettbewerbsfähigkeit der deutschen Baumwollrohweberei (insbesondere Nesselweberei) gegenüber Ländern mit asiatischem Lohnniveau sowie Ländern mit amerikanischer Produktions- und Automatisierungsintensität: Möglichkeiten und Grenzen der Rationalisierung durch Automatisierung [The Competitive Ability of the German Cotton Industry (Especially Unbleached Cotton Industry) Compared with Its Counterparts in Asian Countries, Where Wage Levels are Relatively Low, and in Countries with American Production Methods and with Automation: The Possibilities and the Limitations of Rationalization through Automation]. Münster, 1960. Text in German. The dissertation in its published form is available at Marburg/Lahn, Universitätsbibliothek, Nr. Z65/1403.

Analyzes production costs in the German cotton weaving industry as well as the differences between Germany and those countries (e.g., the United States) with sophisticated production techniques and those countries (e.g., India, Japan) with low wages. In discussing Japan, the author investigates (1) the importance of textiles as a branch of Japanese industry, (2) the structure of the Japanese cotton weaving industry, (3) labor as a factor of production within the industry, (4) the actual process of production, and (5) the characteristics of the Japanese cotton weaving industry as compared with those of its counterparts in West Germany and the United States.

Rel.Publ.: Die Wettbewerbsfähigkelt...Automatisierung. Münster (Westf.): M. Kramer, 1960. 298, iv p.

216
VOACK, Norbert. Die japanischen Zaibatsu und die Konzentration wirtschaftlicher Macht in ihren Händen [The Japanese Zaibatsu and the Concentration of Economic Power in Their Hands]. Erlangen-Nürnberg, 1962. Text in German. The dissertation in its published form is available at Marburg/Lahn, Staatsbibliothek Preussicher Kulturbesitz, Nr. Hsn 37,927.

The author examines the growth of the zaibatsu from Tokugawa times to the end of World War II, their organization, and their importance in the prewar Japanese economy. He then uses Mitsubishi, Sumitomo, and Mitsui as case studies to illustrate both the dissolution (during the Occupation) and the rebuilding of these companies, and he tries to determine how they fit into Japan's basic economic structure.

Rel.Publ.: Die japanischen...Handen. Erlangen-Nürnberg, 1962. 330p.

217
GERHAN, Richard Carl. An Analysis of the First and Second Modernization Programs of the Japanese Iron and Steel Industry. Michigan, 1963. 215p. DA 25 (Aug. 1964), 898; UM 64-8165.

"Examines the character and achievement of the industry, concentrating on its raw material supply, labor and employee compensation, expansion and technology, financing, and costs and prices during" the period of the two modernization programs: 1951-1955 and 1956-1960.

218
SERGIENKO, I. S. Sdvigi v voenno-promyshlennoi baze Iaponii posle 2-oi mirovoi voiny [Changes in Japan's Military and Industrial Base after World War II]. Moscow, Moskovskii gosudarstvennyi institut mezhdunarodnykh otnoshenii, 1963. (Candidate of Economic Sciences degree) Text in Russian.

Rel.Publ.: Vozrozhdenie militarizma v Iaponii. Moscow: Voenizdat, 1968. 216p.

219
KURIYAMA, Morihiko. Die betriebswirtschaftliche Untersuchung der obersten Unternehmensorganisation in den deutschen und japanischen Aktiengesellschaften: Das deutsche Aufsichtsrat--Vorstand und das japanische Board--Vertretungsdirektorium--System in vergleichender Betrachtung [Text in German: An Analysis from the Viewpoint of Business Administration of the Highest Level of the Corporate Organization in German and Japanese Joint-Stock Companies: The German Supervisory Board--The Board of Executive Officers and the Japanese Board --The Representative Board of Directors--Seen in Comparative Perspective]. Köln, 1964. The dissertation in its published form is available at Marburg/Lahn, Staatsbibliothek Preussischer Kulturbesitz, Inv.Nr. Hsn 42,803; also at the University of Michigan, General Library, no. 29,113.

The combination of the functions of the highest corporate level with those of the entrepreneur who serves as the "bearer of functions." Analysis of the "bearers of functions" with regard to their positions within the corporate hierarchy. A comparison between the organizational relationship of the "bearer of the functions" and the leadership organs of German and Japanese joint-stock companies.

Rel.Publ.: Die Betriebswirtschaftliche...Betrachtung. Köln, 1964. eii, 191p.

220
PASHKIN, E. B. Avtomobil'naia promyshlennost' Iaponii: Tekhnichesko-ekonomicheskoe issledovanie [The Japanese Automobile Industry: A Technical and Economic Study]. Moscow, Institut mirovoi ekonomiki i mezhdunarodnykh otnoshenii Akademii nauk SSSR, 1964. (Candidate of Economic Sciences degree) 453p. Text in Russian. AB: 25p. summary published in 1965.

Rel.Publ.: Avtomobil'naia promyshlennost' Iaponii. Moscow, 1965. 61p. (Gos. kom. avtotrakt. i s.-kh. mashinostroeniia pri Gosplane SSSR. Nauch.-issled. in-t informatsii po aftotrakt. i s.-kh mashinostroeniiu. "MIINA Avtosel'khozmash," seriia "Avtomobilestroenie.")

221
YAMAMURA, Kōzō. Competition and Monopoly in Japan, 1945-1961. Northwestern, 1964. 316p. DA 25 (Jan. 1965), 3878-79; UM 64-12,356.

Examines the anti-monopoly policies of SCAP and of the postwar Japanese government with respect particularly to their "impact on economic recovery and growth and on behavior and structure of manufacturing firms and markets."

Rel.Publ.: Economic Policy in Postwar Japan: Growth Versus Economic Democracy. Berkeley: University of California Press, 1967. xvii,226p.; "An Observation on the Post-war Japanese Anti-Monopoly Policy," Indian Journal of Economics, 45 (July 1964), 31-68; "Zaibatsu, Prewar and Zaibatsu, Postwar," JAS, 23 (Aug. 1964), 539-54; "Concentration in the Postwar Japanese Economy: Comment," Journal of Political Economy, 73 (Oct. 1965), 523-25; "Wage Structure and Economic Growth in Postwar Japan," Industrial and Labor Relations Review, 19 (Oct. 1965), 58-69; "Market Concentration in Postwar Japan," Southern Economic Journal, 32 (Apr. 1966), 451-64; "Growth Versus Economic Democracy in Japan: 1945-1965," JAS, 25 (Aug. 1966), 713-28; "Development of Anti-Monopoly Policy in Japan: The Erosion of Japanese Anti-Monopolistic Policy, 1947-1967," in George Washington University, Law School, Studies in Law and Economic Development, 2 (May 1967), 1-22.

222
BERNSTEIN, Herbert Martin. The Significance of the Postwar Growth of the Japanese Photographic Industry. Western Reserve, 1965. 195p. DA 26 (May 1966), 6416-17; UM 66-3022.

Analyzes the factors underlying the industry's marked postwar growth.

223
RAMZES, V. B. Melkie i srednie predpriiatiia v poslevoennoi Iaponii [Small and Medium-sized Enterprises in Postwar Japan]. Moscow, Institut mirovoi ekonomiki i mezhdunarodnykh otnoshenii Akademii nauk SSSR, 1965. (Candidate of Economic Sciences degree) 272p. Text in Russian.

Rel.Publ.: Melkie...Iaponii. Moscow: "Nauka," 1965. 173p.

224
AMANO, Matsukichi. A Study of Employment Patterns and a Measurement of Employee Attitudes in Japanese Firms at Los Angeles. California, Los Angeles, 1966. 517p. DA 27 (Feb. 1967), 2221-A; UM 67-439.

"There are some 130 wholly or partially owned Japanese subsidiary firms in Los Angeles whose home offices are located in Japan. Among them, about 20 firms are conducting full-fledged business operations, employing a considerable number of people locally. This dissertation deals with a study of employment patterns of these Japanese firms and a measurement of the [attitudes of the] employees locally recruited toward the Japanese management."

225
AZUMI, Koya. The Recruitment of University Graduates by Big Firms in Japan. Columbia, 1966. 189p. DA 30 (Sept. 1969), 1239-A; UM 69-15,526. [See also addenda.]

"The institutional context of the recruitment of university graduates by big firms in Japan is provided with respect to basic structural tendencies in the social organization of Japan: familism, gerontocracy, and hierarchy, the educational system and its relation to the status system, and the patterns of Japanese employment."

226
HONG, Wontack. A Study of the Changes in the Structure of Manufacturing Industry and in the Trade Pattern of Manufactured Products in Korea, Taiwan, and Japan.

Columbia, 1966. 277p. DA 27 (Jan. 1967), 1968-69-A; UM 66-12,569.

"This study of Korea (1911-1964), Taiwan (1896-1964), and Japan (1868-1964) supports the hypothesis that the structure of manufacturing industry (composition of manufactured output) and the trade pattern in manufactured products tend to change systematically as the economic development of a country progresses."

Rel.Publ.: "Industrialization and Trade in Manufactures: The East Asian Experience," in The Open Economy: Essays on International Trade and Finance, ed. by P. B. Kenen and R. Lawrence (New York: Columbia University Press, 1968), 213-39.

227
MATSUSAKI, Hirofumi. The Adaptation and Marketing Strategies of the Japanese Manufacturing Firms Operating in the United States: An Ecological Analysis and an Introductory Survey. Michigan State, 1966. 346p. DA 27 (June 1967), 4008-09-A; UM 67-7575.

"Two hypotheses were tested and found to be tenable: (1) There are identifiable characteristics and patterns of adaptation in the behavior of the Japanese firms that operate in the United States. (2) The successful adaptation on the part of the Japanese manufacturing firms is dependent on the selective use of marketing strategies."

228
CHEN, Ching-chih. Crude Oil Prices and the Postwar Japanese Refining Industry. Massachusetts Institute of Technology, 1967. x, 265p. AB: 2p. summary appended to diss. ms.

The dissertation explores factors influencing the determination of crude oil prices by examining data on prices since 1954 for certain European and Latin American markets as well as for Japan. The Japanese market is examined intensively as a case study. See especially Ch.6, "The Japanese Oil Industry and Prices of Crude in Japan" (p.164-246), which discusses the matter of foreign capital and the growth of the industry and which presents a cross-section study of crude prices in Japan for April-September 1964 and a time series study of crude oil prices in Japan for 1958-1966.

229
ITO, Masami. Kooperation der mittleren und kleinen Unternehmen in Japan am Beispiel der Ibaragi-Schalttafel-Fabrikssiedlungsgenossenschaft [Cooperation among the Medium and Small Entrepreneurs in Japan as Exemplified by the Housing Cooperative of the Ibaragi Factory for the Production of Instrument Panels]. Innsbruck, 1967. vii, 201p. Text in German. Diss. ms. available at the Österreichische Nationalbibliothek, Nr. 1040.781-C.

Concludes that for medium and small companies, cooperative housing is not the solution to the housing problem. It appears that greater assistance must be obtained from government authorities on both the prefectural and the national levels.

230
KATAOKA, Takashi. A Statistical Analysis of the Size Structure of the Japanese Manufacturing Industries. Wayne State, 1967. 132p.

Analyzes the transition probabilities, equilibrium distribution, and firm mobility with regard to the size distribution of the Japanese machine manufacturing industry and of the food processing industry within the Japanese economy.

231
MISAWA, Mitsuru. The Historical and Comparative Study of the Postwar Japanese Securities Markets in the Light of Law and Business Practices. Michigan, 1967. 212p. DA 28 (June 1968), 4764-65-A; UM 68-7675.

"Examines the efficacy and functioning of government control and business practices of American origin [inherited from the Occupation] in the securities markets of Japan where customs and practices are mostly of pre-war German origin." Japanese and American business customs and legal practices are compared extensively. Contents: History of Postwar Japanese Securities Markets; A Comparative Study of Securities Regulation and Marketing Practices in Japan and Other Countries; Evaluation of the Effects of Different Regulatory Procedures and Different Practices; Conclusions and Recommendations.

232
PRICE, John Andrew. The Japanese Market System: Retailing in a Dual Economy. Michigan, 1967. 206p. DA 28 (Jan. 1968), 2704-05-B; UM 67-17,831.

"An ethnographical survey of retailing and the development of marketing facilities in Japan" based on case studies conducted in the Osaka area. Contents: Japan in World Perspective; Japanese Business Practices; The Shopping Areas of Osaka and Its Suburbs; Department Stores; The Supermarket and Other Self-service Stores; The Ichiba; The Shotengai; The Neighborhood Store; Unoke, A Rural Case Study.

233
PROKHOZHEV, A. A. Nekotorye voprosy razvitiia metodov planirovaniia i upravleniia proizvodstvom v Iaponii: v poslevoennyi period [Certain Problems in the Development of Industrial Planning and Management in Japan since World War II]. Moscow, Tsentral'nyi ekonomichesko-matematicheskii institut Akademii nauk SSSR, 1967. (Candidate of Economic Sciences degree) 199p. Text in Russian. AB: 32p. summary published in 1967.

234
DEBABOV, S. A. Osobennosti sovremennogo razmeshcheniia obrabatyvaiushchei promyshlennosti Iaponii [Characteristics of the Present Location of Japan's Manufacturing Industry]. Moscow, Moskovskii gosudarstvennyi universitet imeni M. V. Lomonosova, 1968. (Candidate of Economic Sciences degree) 307p. Text in Russian. AB: 23p. summary published in 1968.

235
DHAWAN, Kailash Chandra. Post World War II Marketing Policies and Practices of Japanese Consumer Goods Manufacturers: A Study of Consumer Oriented Characteristics and Their Cultural Explanation. New York, 1968. 297p. DA 29 (Oct. 1968), 1021-22-A; UM 68-13,482.

The dissertation research was guided by the following propositions: (1) "Japanese manufacturers' marketing philosophy, organization, and practices have become dynamic in order to meet the changing demands of the consumers." (2) "Action of the large manufacturers indicates increased interest in consumer-oriented and coordinated marketing policies and practices. The character of these adopted marketing policies and practices is conditioned by cultural and socio-economic factors." (3)"During the postwar period, the cultural and socio-economic factors have influenced Japanese consumers to accept new values and have been favorable to the adoption of consumer-oriented marketing policies and practices by the manufacturers."

236
KRESSLER, Peter Rockwell. An Evaluation of United States-Japanese Negotiations of Major Commerical Disputes during the 1930's. Pennsylvania, 1968. 193p. DA 30 (Sept. 1969), 902-03-A; UM 69-15,075.

The dissertation examines "the course of the negotiations and the circumstances surrounding each of four disputes involving American businesses...to determine whether the policy pursued by the United States Government at the negotiations was successful and whether more effective alternative courses of action were open to the United States." The four disputes respectively involved (a) the Japanese encroachment on the United States' share of the Filipino cotton cloth market, (b) the Japanese decision "to establish an automotive industry under the financial and managerial control of Japanese nationals to the detriment of United States automotive companies" already in Japan, (c) the Japanese decision to eliminate United States petroleum companies operating in Manchoukuo, and (d) the Japanese enactment of a petroleum law designed to eliminate foreign control of Japanese petroleum refining and distribution facilities.

TSURUMI, Yoshihiro. Technology Transfer and Foreign Trade: The Case of Japan, 1950-1966. 1968. See no.284.

RATCLIFFE, Charles T. Tax Policy and Investment Behavior in Postwar Japan. 1969. See no.366.

ECONOMIC HISTORY

(Only dissertations on domestic Japanese history and on the Japanese empire are cross-referred.) See also the listings of dissertations in each subsection of Economics, in particular those dissertations submitted to their respective academic institutions before 1935.

Japan Proper

For the period ca. 400 A.D. to 1945

ICHIHARA, Morihiro. The Silk Trade of Japan. 1892. See no.166.

FUKUDA, Tokuzo. Die gesellschaftliche und wirtschaftliche Entwicklung in Japan. 1900. See no.468.

YOKOYAMA, Masajiro. The Development of the Land Tax in Japan. 1904. See no.469.

BURKS, Ardath W. Economics in Japanese Thought, 1185-1905. 1948. See no.471.

BURKE, William M. The Role of the Entrepreneur in Japanese Economic Development. 1958. See no. 473.

For the period ca. 400 A.D. to 1868

YOSHIDA, Tetsutaro. Entwicklung des Seiden und der Seidenindustrie vom Alterthum bis zum Ausgang des Mittelalters. 1894. See no.167.

MANCHESTER, Curtis A. The Development and Distribution of Sekisho in Japan. 1947. See no. 479.

ISKENDEROV, A. A. Feodal'nyi gorod Iaponii XVI stoletiia. 1958. See no.499.

IWAMOTO, Kiyotoshi. Land and Society in Traditional Japan. 1964. See no.480.

For the period ca. 400-784

DETTMER, Hans A. Die Steuergesetzgebung der Nara-Zeit. 1959. See no.485.

For the period 1333-1500

BROWN, Delmer M. An Historical Study of the Use of Coins in Japan from 1432 to 1601. 1946. See no.494.

For the Tokugawa Period (1600-1868)

TAKIZAWA, Matsuyo. The Penetration of Money Economy in Japan and Its Effects upon Social and Political Institutions. 1927. See no.504.

ZAHL, Karl. Über die Ursachen der japanischen Revolution (Meiji-ishin). (Nach japanischen Quellen.) 1947. See no.511.

SMITH, Thomas C. Government Enterprise and the Initial Phase of Japanese Industrialization, 1850-1880. 1948. See no.512.

TSUKAHIRA, Toshio G. The Sankin Kōtai System of Tokugawa Japan, 1600-1868. 1955. See no.516.

SHELDON, Charles D. The Rise of the Merchant Class in Tokugawa, Japan, 1600-1868. 1955. See no.518.

NEVILLE, Edwin L., Jr. The Development of Transportation in Japan: A Case Study of Okayama Han, 1600-1868. 1959. See no.525.

CHIN, Tung-yuan. Sotsial'no-ekonomicheskoe polozhenie v iaponskoi derevne nakanune revoliutsii 1867-1868 gg. 1961. See no.528.

OBELSKY, Alvan J. Pre-Conditions of Economic Development: An Analysis of the Japanese Case. 1961. See no.529.

CHAMBLISS, William J. Chiaraijima Village: Land Tenure, Taxation, and Local Trade, 1818-1884. 1963. See no.530.

PHAM-van-Thuan. Les Fondements socio-économiques de la revolution industrielle du Japon. 1965. See no. 534.

FROST, Peter K. Tokugawa Monetary Policy. 1966. See no.535.

NISHIO, Harry K. Political Authority Structure and the Development of Entrepreneurship in Japan, 1603-1890. 1966. See no.536.

HAUSER, William B. Economic Institutional Change in Tokugawa Japan: The Osaka Cotton Trade. 1969. See no.543.

For the Modern Period, 1868-1945

HAHN, Karl. Die Industrialisierung Japans. 1933. See no.203.

GOL'DBERG, D. I. Rabochee dvizhenie v Iaponii do 1917g. 1938. See no.289.

TAGAWA, Hiroso. Grundzüge der Entwicklung der japanischen Wirtschaft. 1940. See no.141.

BOLDYREV, G. I. Istoriia iaponskikh gosudarstvennykh finansov. 1946. See no.316.

LOCKWOOD, William W. The Economic Development of Japan: Growth and Structural Change, 1868-1938. 1950. See no.145.

JOHNSTON, Bruce F. Food and Agriculture in Japan, 1880-1950. 1953. See no.172.

KOKORIS, James A. The Economic and Financial Development of Okayama Prefecture, Japan. 1956. See no.326.

RANIS, Gustav. Japan: A Case Study in Development. 1956. See no.149.

AUERBACH, Arnold. Capital étranger et développement économique au Japon (1868-1938). 1958. See no.329.

ROSOVSKY, Henry. Japanese Capital Formation, 1868-1940. 1959. See no.151.

CUKIERMAN, Roger. Le Capital dans l'économie japonaise. 1960. See no.330.

KANG, Moon Hyung. The Monetary Aspect of Economic Development in Japan with Special Reference to Monetary Policies: 1868-1935. 1960. See no.332.

OTT, David J. The Financial Development of Japan, 1878-1958. 1961. See no.335.

SAKURAI, Kinichiro. Financial Aspects of [the] Economic Development of Japan from 1868 to [the] Present. 1961. See no.336.

WALLACE, William M. Cultural Values and Economic Development: A Case Study of Japan. 1963. See no.83.

MARSHALL, Byron K. Ideology and Industrialization in Japan, 1868-1941: The Creed of the Prewar Business Elite. 1966. See no.554.

For the Meiji Period, 1868-1912

TAKAKI, Masayoshi. The History of Japanese Paper Currency. 1895. See no.305.

HOSHINO, Benzo. Die Finanzen und die Finanzpolitik Japans während und nach dem russisch-japanischen Kriege (1904-1908). 1908. See no.351.

IKÉMOTO, Kisao. La Restauration de l'ère de Meiji et sa répercussion sur les milieux agricoles japonais (1867-1930). 1930. See no.557.

TSURU, Shigeto. Development of Capitalism and Business Cycles in Japan, 1868-1897. 1940. See no.315.

SMITH, Thomas C. Government Enterprise and the Initial Phase of Japanese Industrialization, 1850-1880. 1948. See no.512.

EGGERS, Melvin A. Economic Development of Japan, 1850-1900. 1950. See no.562.

REUBENS, Edwin P. Foreign Capital in Economic Development: The Japanese Experience, 1868-1913. 1952. See no.319.

CHOI, Kee Il. Shibusawa Eiichi and His Contemporaries: A Study of Japanese Entrepreneurial History. 1958. See no.567.

HIRSCHMEIER, Johannes. The Genesis of Modern Entrepreneurs in Meiji Japan. 1960. See no.571.

BARSS, Lawrence W. Political Change and Economic Growth: A Methodology Applied to Japan, Turkey, and India. 1961. See no.152.

NESS, Gayl D. Central Government and Local Initiative in the Industrialization of India and Japan. 1961. See no.572.

CHAMBLISS, William J. Chiaraijima Village: Land Tenure, Taxation, and Local Trade, 1818-1884. 1963. See no.530.

NAKAMURA, James I. The Place of Agricultural Production in the Economic Development of Japan. 1964. See no.576.

CHUNG, Young-iob. The Role of Government in the Generation of Saving: The Japanese Experience, 1868-1893. 1965. See no.606.

PHAM-van-Thuan. Les Fondements socio-économiques de la revolution industrielle du Japon. 1965. See no.534.

TUSSING, Arlon R. Employment and Wages in Japanese Industrialization: A Quantitative Study of Yamanashi Prefecture in the Meiji Era. 1966. See no.301.

For the Twentieth Century

KRIANEVA, O. A. Polozhenie i bor'ba rabochego klassa Iaponii v gody pervoi imperialisticheskoi voiny, 1914-1918. 1954. See no.658.

KHANIN, Z. Ia. Agrarnye otnosheniia i krest'ianskoe dvizhenie v Iaponii, 1922-1929 gg. 1961. See no.667.

VASILJEVOVÁ, Zdeňka. Japonský fašismus: Hnutí služby vlasti v průmyslu jako prostředek fašistické diktatury. 1967/68. See no.646.

DALL, John J., Jr. Sources of Productivity Changes in Paddy Rice Production in Japan: 1900-1965. 1968. See no.194.

For the War Period, 1937-1945

COHEN, Jerome B. The Japanese War Economy, 1937-1945. 1949. See no.674.

LÊ-thanh-Khôi. L'Économie de guerre japonaise. 1949. See no.675.

ERSELCUK, Muzaffer M. Some Aspects of Japanese Economy, 1937-1945. 1950. See no.676.

DINKEVICH, A. I. Voennye finansy imperialisticheskoi Iaponii v period voiny 1937-1945 gg.: Kharakteristike finansovoi politiki iaponskogo pravitel'stva. 1951 See no.677.

MORGAN, Alfred D. The Fiscal Anatomy of Wartime Japan, 1937-1945: With Special Reference to the National Government during 1941-1945. 1951. See no.678.

LUK'IANOVA, M. I. Ekonomika Iaponii v gody vtoroi mirovoi voiny. 1952. See no.680.

BESSON-GUYARD, Maurice. Les Consequences de la guerre 1939-1945 sur l'économie japonaise. 1953. See no.681.

TAOKA, George M. The Role of the Bank of Japan in the Administration of the Government during National Emergencies: With Special Emphasis on the Sino-Japanese War and the World War II Periods. 1955. See no.323.

The Japanese Empire (1895-1945)
For Korea, 1910-1945

GRAJDANZEV, Andrew J. Modern Korea: Her Economic and Social Development under the Japanese. 1945. See no.715.

CHEN, Ilen. Kharakternye osobennosti razvitiia promyshlennosti i polozhenie rabochego klassa v Koree nakanune i vo vremia vtoroi mirovoi voiny. 1956. See no.728.

KAZAKEVICH, I. S. Agrarnye otnosheniia v Koree nakanune 2-oi mirovoi voiny 1930-1939 gg. 1956. See no.729.

LIU, John J.-c. An Econometric Model of the Rice Market in the Japanese Empire, 1910-1937. 1960. See no.180.

SONG, Ki-tschul. Die Industrialisierung Koreas (1876-1956) unter besonderer Berücksichtigung der Wirtschaftspolitischen Probleme. 1960. See no.735.

JUHN, Daniel S. Entrepreneurship in an Underdeveloped Economy: The Case of Korea, 1890-1940. 1965. See no.748.

SUH, Sang Chul. Growth and Structural Changes in the Korean Economy since 1910. 1967. See no.755.

For Manchoukuo, 1931-1945

DORFMAN, Ben D. The Currencies of the Northeastern Provinces of China (Manchuria). 1933. See no.762.

KIRBY, Edward S. The Economic Organization of Manchoukuo: With Particular Reference to Specific Features Exemplifying the Special Characteristics of the Modern Economic System in the Far East. 1938. See no.765.

TCHENG, Kui-i. La Compagnie du chemin de fer Sud-Manchourien et l'enterprise japonaise en Mandchourie. 1939. See no.767.

PEUVERGNE, Raymond. Le Développement agricole et industriel du Mandchukuo. 1942. See no.768.

CHANG, Tian-bin. Industrieplanung in Mandschukuo. 1944. See no.769.

DOCKSON, Robert R. A Study of Japan's Economic Influence in Manchuria, 1931-1941. 1946. See no. 770.

MYERS, Ramon H. The Japanese Economic Development of Manchuria, 1932 to 1945. 1959. See no.773.

KINNEY, Ann R. Investment in Manchurian Manufacturing, Mining, Transportation, and Communications, 1931-1945. 1962. See no.774.

For Taiwan, 1895-1945

BARCLAY, George W. Colonial Development and Population in Taiwan. 1952. See no.789.

HSIEH, James C.-m. Successive Occupance Patterns in Taiwan. 1953. See no.790.

LIU, John J.-c. An Econometric Model of the Rice Market in the Japanese Empire, 1910-1937. 1960. See no.180.

HO, Yhi-min. The Agricultural Development of Taiwan, 1903-1960: Its Patterns and Sources of Productivity Increases. 1965. See no.797.

LEE, Teng-hui. Intersectoral Capital Flows in the Economic Development of Taiwan, 1895-1960. 1968. See no.801.

FISHERIES, FORESTRY, AND MINING

RICHTER, Otto. Japans Versorgung mit Kohle, Eisen, und Oel [Japan's Supply of Coal, Iron, and Oil]. Berlin, 1922. iii, 101p. Text in German. AB: Jahrbuch der Dissertationen der Philosophischen Fakultät Berlin. 1921/1922. II, p.158-62. Diss. ms. available at Marburg/Lahn, Staatsbibliothek Preussischer Kulturbesitz, Nr. MS 27/352.

The problem of securing an adequate supply of raw materials for her overall development and its influence on her economic policy are studied through an examination of the various phases of Japan's economic development after 1868. The dissertation covers not only the Japanese home islands but also Korea, Manchuria, Formosa, Sakhalin, Kiaochow, and China; and in the concluding section, the author compares Japan's economic development with that of Great Britain.

238
BÜCHE, Karl. Zur Kennzeichnung der japanischen Kohlen und ihrer Verwertungsmöglichkeiten [Characteristics of Japanese Coal and the Possibilities for Utilizing It]. Halle, 1931. Text in German.

Rel.Publ.: Zur Kennzeichnung...Verwertungsmöglichkeiten. Kattowitz: Oberschles. Berg- und Hüttenmänn. Verein, 1930. 23p.; "Zur Kennzeichnung...Verwertungsmöglichkeiten" [by] M. Dolch and Karl Büche, Zeitschrift d. Oberschles. Berg- und Hüttenmänn. Vereins, 70 (1931), 271-81.

239
SCHEPERS, Hansjulius. Japans Seefischerei: Eine wirtschaftsgeographische Zusammenfassung [Japan's Maritime Fishing: A Concise View of the Economic and Geographic Conditions]. München, 1932. Text in German. The dissertation in its published form is available at Berlin West, Staatsbibliothek Preussischer Kulturbesitz, Nr. Un 9515/160; also at the University of Michigan, General Library, No. SH301.S25.

In describing the factors responsible for the success of Japan's maritime fishing industry, the author focuses upon Japan's geographical location, the climatic conditions of the country, her means of transportation, Japanese fishing vessels and fishing methods, and state assistance to the fishing industry. Reference is made to the major fishing areas and ports of the Japanese fishing industry as well as to the economic importance of maritime fishing for Japan.

Rel.Publ. Japans...Zusammenfassung. Breslau: Hirt, 1934. 224, ivp.

LEONARD, L. Larry. International Regulation of Fisheries. 1943. See no.843.

KUZ'MIN, P. A. Gospodstvo iaponskoi tselliulozno-bumazhnoi monopolii Odzi Seisi na Iuzhnom Sakhaline, 1905-1945 gg. 1950. See no.760.

240
DREWS, Robin Arthur. The Cultivation of Food Fish in China and Japan: A Study Disclosing Contrasting National Patterns for Rearing Fish Consistent with the Differing Cultural Histories of China and Japan. Michigan, 1951. 277p. DA 12 (1952), 240-41; UM 3582.

Describes and compares both the historical development and the modern patterns of the pond cultivation of food fish in Japan and China.

241
EYRE, John Douglas. Salt from the Sea: A Geographical Analysis of the National and International Patterns of Japanese Salt Production and Trade. Michigan, 1951. 137p. AB: Microfilm Abstracts, 11 (1951): 640-41. UM 2591.

"This study is a geographer's appraisal of the role of the salt industry in the economy of the Inland Sea region and in the economy and strategic considerations of Japan." Contents: Historical Development (The Tokugawa Pattern, Rise of Regional Monopolies, Meiji Period Problems); Inland Sea Production (The Inshore Method, Field Site, Climatic Limitations, Salt Distribution, Salt Towns); The Monopoly System; Importation of Salt.

Rel.Publ.: "Patterns of Japanese Salt Production and Trade," in University of Michigan, Center for Japanese Studies, Occasional Papers, 3 (Ann Arbor: University of Michigan Press, 1952), 15-46.

KOH, Kwang-lim. International Regulation of Fisheries with Special Reference to Those in the North Pacific Ocean. 1953. See no.845.

MEAD, Giles, Jr. The Food Habits of the North Pacific Fur Seal in Japanese Waters: With a Study of the Fishes Found on the Feeding Grounds. 1953. See no.2020.

242
COMITINI, Salvatore. A Sectoral Study of the Economic Development of Japanese Fisheries Exploitation. Washington, Seattle, 1960. 149p. DA 21 (Feb. 1961), 2135-36; UM 60-5960.

A descriptive and analytical view of the "development of the Japanese fisheries sector in the light of the development of the economy as a whole." Seeks to account for the various factors underlying the sector's spectacular rate of growth between the early 1900's and the 1950's.

Rel.Publ.: "Marine Resources Exploitation and Management in the Economic Development of Japan," Economic Development and Cultural Change, 14 (July 1966), 414-27.

OKABAYASHI, Toyoki. Measuring the Contributions of Natural Resources to the National Outputs of the United States and Japan. 1960. See no.181.

243
KHANDKER, Nurul Alam. A Program for Fisheries Development with Special Reference to the Underdeveloped Countries. Miami (Florida), 1963. 327p. DA 26 (Apr. 1966), 6059-60; UM 64-4035.

"Three countries, Japan, the United States, and the United Kingdom, which have developed fishing industries, were chosen for study here to find out what factors promoted their growth."

CHEE, Choung Il. National Regulation of Fisheries in International Law. 1964. See no.1165.

ESTERLY, Henry H. Japanese High Seas Fisheries and the International Politics of the Occupation, 1945-1951. 1965. See no.1831.

244
KEEN, Elmer A. Some Aspects of the Economic Geography of the Japanese Skipjack Tuna Fishery. Washington, Seattle, 1965. 205p. DA 26 (Feb. 1966), 4564-65; UM 65-15,389.

Focuses on "the regional pattern of activity in the home island ports of Japan connected with the fishery" (1952-1964).

JETTMAR, Dieter. Der Fischereiwortschatz der am Kuroshio gelegenen Pazifikküste Japans. 1968. See no.1458.

245
OSORGIN, A. N. Tendentsiia razvitiia lesnoi promyshlennosti i lesnogo rynka Iaponii v poslevoennyi period, 1946-1966 gg. [Trends in the Development of the Japanese Lumber Industry and Lumber Market, 1946-1966]. Vladivostok, Sibirskoe otdelenie Akademii nauk SSSR, Dal'nevostochnyi filial imeni V. L. Komarova, 1968. (Candidate of Economic Sciences degree) 312p. Text in Russian.

FOREIGN TRADE

Dissertations on trade regulations, organization, etc., and on foreign trade matters in general. For dissertations on Japanese trade with specific countries, see International Relations (pages 104-63). See also Economics--business, industry, and domestic commerce (pages 28-33) and Economics--transportation and communications (pages 50-51).

ICHIHARA, Morihiro. The Silk Trade of Japan. 1892. See no.166.

246
TATEISH, Sajiro. Japans internationale Handelsbeziehungen, mit besonderer Berücksichtigung der Gegenwart [Japan's International Trade Relations, with Special Consideration of Present Conditions]. Halle-Wittenberg, 1902. Text in German. The dissertation in its published form is available at Marburg/Lahn, Universitätsbibliothek, Nr. XVII C.

A study of the evolution of Japan's commodity trade, finance, and tariff and transportation systems since the opening of the country in 1854. The growth of imports and exports is examined with the country's industrial and economic development being kept constantly in mind.

Rel.Publ.: Japans...Gegenwart. Halle a.S.: C.A. Kaemmerer, 1902. 98p.

247
HATTORI, Yukimasa. The Foreign Commerce of Japan since the Restoration, 1869-1900. Johns Hopkins, 1903. 79p.
Contents: The Volume of Trade; The Character of Japan's Commerce; The Geographical Distribution of Trade.
Rel.Publ.: The Foreign...1900. Baltimore: Johns Hopkins Press, 1904. 79p. (Johns Hopkins University Studies in Historical and Political Science, v.22, no.9-10)

248
SAMSI SASTRAWIDAGA. De ontwikkeling der handelspolitiek van Japan [The Development of Japanese Trade Policy]. Rotterdam Handelshoogeschool, 1925. Text in Dutch. [See also addenda no.39A.]
Rel.Publ.: De ontwikkeling...Japan. Eduard Ijdo, 1925. ii, 90p.

249
FURUYA, Seikow Yoshisada. Japan's Foreign Exchange and Her Balance of International Payments: With Special Reference to Recent Theories of Foreign Exchange. Columbia, 1928. i,209p.
Focuses on the Yen exchange and on the Japanese balance of payments during the period 1914-1927.
Rel.Publ.: Japan's...Exchange. New York: Columbia University Press, 1928. i,209p. (Studies in History, Economics and Public Law, ed. by the Faculty of Political Science of Columbia University, 299)

250
REICHELT, Amélie. Japans Aussenhandel und Aussenhandelspolitik unter dem Einfluss des Weltkrieges [Japan's Foreign Trade and Foreign Trade Policy as Influenced by World War I]. Berlin, 1931. Text in German. The dissertation in its published form is available at Marburg/Lahn, Universitätsbibliothek, Nr. XVII C.
A study of the historical development of Japan's foreign trade and of her foreign trade policy presented within the framework of economic and geographic factors. Included are a discussion of the growth of Japan's internal trade and of her foreign trade markets, and a study of the steps taken to promote her foreign trade in order to prepare for postwar competition in the world trade markets.
Rel.Publ.: Japans...Weltkrieges. Cöthen-Anh.: Both, 1931. v, 56p.

251
FURUUCHI, Hiroo. Der japanische Aussenhandel im 20. Jahrhundert [Japanese Foreign Trade in the Twentieth Century]. Köln, 1934. 122p. Text in German. Diss. ms. available at Köln, Universitätsbibliothek.
Contents: Structure of the Japanese Economy; Economic Basis of Japanese Foreign Trade; Japanese Foreign Trade Policy; The Actual Organization of Japanese Foreign Trade and the Direction of Its Development.

252
NIEUWENHUIS, Jan Eltjo. De groei van den buitenlandschen handel en scheepvaart van Japan sedert het jaar 1900 en enkele beschouwingen naar aanleidung daarvan [The Growth of Japanese Foreign Trade and Shipping after the Year 1900 and Several Views of This Development]. Utrecht, 1935. Text in Dutch.
Rel.Publ.: De groei...daarvan. Wageningen: H. Veenman, 1935. 110p. [See also addenda entry no.32A.]

253
PRUNETTI, Yves-Joseph-Antoine. Le Succès de l'économie japonaise dans la lutte pour les marchés mondiaux [The Success of the Japanese Economy in the Struggle for World Markets]. Alger, 1935. Text in French.
Contents: Pt.1: Japanese Preparations for the Struggle for World Markets: Origins of Her Industrialization; Evolution of Her Industrialization; Results. Pt.2: Aspects of the Japanese Success in the Struggle for World Markets: General Aspects; The Development of Export Industries; The Export Markets of Japan. Pt.3: The Reasons for Japan's Success. Pt.4: The Future of the Japanese Economy in the Struggle for World Markets: The Situation of Japan in Regard to Elements Essential for Her Economic Future; Obstacles Capable of Hindering Japan's Economic Expansion.
Rel.Publ.: Le Succès...mondiaux. Alger: S. Crescenzo, 1935. 408p.

254
COLLADO, Emilio Gabriel. Japanese Competition in International Trade. Harvard, 1936. vii,348p. AB: Harvard University. Summaries of Theses...1936. p.243-46.
Particular focus is "placed on the great expansion in Japan's export trade after 1928." Contents: The Problem; The Method of Attack; The Balance of International Payments, The Foreign Exchanges, Monetary Policy, and the Price Level: (a) 1868-1913, (b) 1914-1918, (c) 1919-1928, (d) 1929-1935); Factors Affecting Prices (Raw Materials, Organization and Technical Efficiency, Labor, Supply of Capital); Some Further Considerations.

255
GLÜCK, Kurt. Japans Verdringen auf dem Weltmarkt [Japan's Advance within the World Market]. Frankfurt a.M., 1937. Text in German. The dissertation in its published form is available at Marburg/Lahn, Universitätsbibliothek, Nr. XVII C.
Studies the economic development of Japan; its industry, agriculture, and shipping; Japanese foreign trade, 1860-1935, with particular focus on the Japanese colonies and on Japanese penetration of the Chinese market; and the impact of certain Japanese attitudes on Japan's political and economic life.
Rel.Publ.: Japans...Weltmarkt. Würzburg: Mayr, 1937. 107p.

256
KIM, Young Tak. Evaluation of Factors in the International Trade of Japan, 1920-1935. Northwestern, 1938. 245p. AB: Northwestern University. Summaries of Doctoral Dissertations. v.5 (1937), p.69-74.
Contents: Japan's Balance of International Payments in Relation to the Rest of the World Prior to 1920; The Post-War Reactions in Japan and Their Effect on the Balance of Payments; The Earthquake and Its Effect; Retrenchment Policy of the Government and Its Influence on the Balance of Payments, 1925-1927; Tanaka Cabinet and Its Influence, 1928-1929; Restoration of the Gold Standard in January 1930 and the Subsequent Renewal of the Gold Embargo and Their Effect on Japan's Balance of Payments, 1930-1935.

257
CRONJÉ, Frans Johannes Cornelius. World Consumption of Clothing Wools. Cambridge, 1938/39. 186p. AB:

University of Cambridge. Abstracts of Dissertations ...1938/1939. p.18-19.
A discussion of wool imports and wool consumption in Japan, ca. 1900-1938, is included. See Ch.11, "Consumption in Japan," and Ch.14 in particular.

258
PATEL, Indraprasad Gordhanbhai. Studies in Economic Development and International Trade. Cambridge, 1949. 289p. AB: University of Cambridge. Abstracts of Dissertations...1949/1950. p.78-79.
Part one "studies the impact on international trade of rapid economic development" in Japan between 1868 and 1938.

WIGGLESWORTH, Edwin. An Appraisal of Allied Foreign Trade Policy for Japan. 1949. See no.1808.

259
WALDSTEIN, George. Japanese Viability in the Post-Treaty Period. Harvard, 1954. ii, 272p.
An investigation of the prospects for Japanese economic viability. Contents: Natural Resources; The Development of Japanese Industry; The Development of the Pattern of Japanese International Trade prior to 1937; Changes since 1937; A Theoretical Model; Characteristics of Japanese Imports; Japanese Ability to Compete in World Commerce; Long Run Prospects; The Short Run.

260
HOLLERMAN, Leon. Japanese National Income and International Trade: A Structural Analysis. California, Berkeley, 1957. 306p.
"Identifies patterns of structural stability in both the domestic and the international sectors of the economy and presents new statistical results which reveal the hitherto neglected qualitative dimension of Japan's postwar trade dependence."
Rel.Publ.: Japan's Dependence on the World Economy: The Approach toward Economic Liberalization. Princeton: Princeton University Press, 1967. xv, 291p.; "Japan's Foreign Trade Dependence and the Five Year Economic Plan," Review of Economics and Statistics, 40 (Nov. 1958), 416-19; "What Does 'Dependence' Mean in International Trade?", Kyklos, 13 (1960), 102-09; "The Logistic View Versus the National Income View of Foreign Trade Dependence, with Special Reference to Japan," Hitotsubashi Journal of Economics, 1 (Oct. 1960), 52-58; "Japan's Dependence on Trade with the United States," Proceedings of the Western Economic Association 1957, p.53-57.

261
KATAYAMA, Hiroya. Japan's Balance of International Payments between 1924 and 1936. Wisconsin, 1957. 302p. DA 17 (Mar. 1957), 523; UM 20,245.
"Deals with the disequilibrium in Japan's balance in international payments during the period 1924-1931 and with the restoration of equilibrium in the years 1932-1936." Also investigates "the relationship between the balance of payments and the level of domestic economic activity."

262
QUERIN, Emile Eugene. Terms of Trade and Economic Development. Princeton, 1959. 297p. DA 20 (Mar. 1960), 3544; UM 59-5213.
In part of the thesis, Japan is one of several recently developed countries studied to determine "the great variety of economic and sociological factors which play an active role in determining the course of the terms of their trade."

263
OZAKI, Robert Shigeo. Japan's Postwar Resurgence in International Trade. Harvard, 1960 ix, 313p. AB: 11p. summary appended to diss. ms.
"Appraises the highlights of Japan's recovery of foreign trade since World War II." Contents: Japan in a Changed World: The Initial Pessimism; The Structure of Japanese Foreign Trade; The Road to Recovery; Japanese Exports and World Import Demand, 1950-1957; Japanese Imports and Domestic Economy, 1950-1957; The Japanese Balance of Payments, 1946-1957.
Rel.Publ.: "Duality in the Structure of Japanese Exports," Shōgyō Eigo Monthly, May 1961; "Postwar Expansion of Japanese Exports," Western Economic Journal, 1 (Spring 1963), 140-43; "A Note on Duality in the Structure of Japanese Exports," Social and Economic Studies (Jamaica), 12 (Dec. 1963), 140-43; "Trade Growth and the Balance of Payments of Post-War Japan," Social and Economic Studies (Jamaica), 16 (June 1967), 169-90.

264
KAWAMURA, Itsuo. Foreign Trade and Economic Development of Japan. Johns Hopkins, 1961. 280p.

265
SCHERUHN, Alexander. Die Exportoffensive Japans seit 1945: Ziele, Mittel, Träger, Grenzen [The Japanese Export Offensive since 1945: Aims, Means, Support, Limits]. Innsbruck, 1961. 161,xvi p. Text in German. Diss. ms. available at the Österreichische Nationalbibliothek, Nr. 944.886-C.
The author first analyzes Japan's postwar export offensive. He then recommends (in economic and political terms) different ways of reacting to this offensive.

266
ADAMS, Nassau Alexander. Economic Growth and the Structure of Foreign Trade. Harvard, 1962. vii,362p. AB: 10p. summary appended to diss. ms.
Investigates some aspects of the relationship between foreign trade and economic growth. Japan is one of six countries subjected to analysis.

267
TAKEUCHI, Kenji. The "Classical" Theories of International Trade and the Expansion of Foreign Trade in Japan from 1859 to 1892. Duke, 1962. 240p. DA 24 (July 1963), 105-06; UM 63-4374.
Examines the relative validity of three theories of international trade--(1) the "vent-for-surplus" theory, (2) the "productivity" theory, and (3) the comparative-costs theory--in the case of Japan, 1859-1892. One of the author's conclusions is "that, except in the filature and copper-mining sectors, the productivity improvement in the 1859-1880 period was fairly limited, and that even in the 'quasi-underdeveloped' period (1880-1892) they were only moderate in the 'export-dependent' sectors as a whole."
Rel.Publ.: "Koten-gakuha ni okeru mittsu no bōeki riron to kaikoku-go no Nihon bōeki no shinten," Shogaku ronkyū, 12 (Nov. 1964), 135-45; "A Statistical Analysis of Foreign Trade in Japan, 1859-1867" in Kwansei Gakuin University, Annual Studies, 14 (1965), 135-55; "Technical Progress and Productivity Change

in the 'Export-Dependent' Sectors in Japan, 1859-1892," in Kwansei Gakuin University, Annual Studies, 15 (1966), 127-57.

268
KIM, Hyong Chun. Factors Contributing to the Rapid Growth of Japan's Exports of Manufactures, 1953-1961. Oregon, 1964. 275p. DA 25 (May 1965), 6285; UM 65-5745.

Contents: The Background of the Postwar Growth of the Japanese Economy; Domestic Demand and Exports: A Theoretical Analysis; Changes in World Demand and the Growth of Japan's Exports; Domestic Demand and Exports: An Empirical Analysis; Industrial Production and Exports: The Supply Effect of Investment; The Efficiency Effect of Investment: Cost-Price of Products and Exports.

269
KOIZUMI, Kihei. Japan's Economic Growth and Balance of International Payments in the 1950's. Ohio State, 1964. 277p. DA 25 (May 1965), 6267; UM 65-3876.

Contents: Japan's Record of Economic Growth; Analysis of Factors Related to Japan's Rapid Economic Growth in the 1950's; Japan's Balance of International Payments; An Analysis of the Major Items in the Japanese Balance of Payments in the 1950's; (1) Merchandise Trade, (2) Non-Merchandise Items of the Current Account, (3) Capital Movements; Policies Affecting Japan's Balance of International Payments; Prospect of Japan's Economic Growth and Balance of International Payments: Analysis of Ten-Year Income Doubling Plan; The Japanese Economy in the Early 1960's.

270
GOMEZ, Henry. Foreign Competition for Steel Markets: An Analysis of World Market Shares for Steel Products, 1913-1962. New York, 1965. 416p. DA 28 (Mar. 1968), 3344-45-A; UM 65-5853.

"Measures the extent to which America's competitive position in steel markets declined at periodic intervals from 1913 to 1962 in relation to producers in the United Kingdom, the European Economic Community, Japan, and elsewhere.

271
HAITANI, Kanji. Japan's Export Trade: Its Structure and Problems. Ohio State, 1965. 248p. DA 27 (July 1966), 19-20-A; UM 66-6262.

"A comprehensive analysis of the problems arising from the structural changes in Japan's export trade," 1953-1963, "with a particular emphasis on the second half of the decade."

272
LANDES, James Edward. Japan and the Contracting Parties to the General Agreement on Tariffs and Trade: A Case Study in Postwar Commercial Policy. Colorado, 1965. 281p. DA 28 (Feb. 1968), 2844-45-A; UM 66-2809.

The study seeks "to determine the extent and nature of discrimination against Japanese exports by the contracting parties to GATT from 1952 to 1963 and to consider the implications of such discrimination." Japan was chosen for study because a challenge to the fundamental GATT principle of non-discrimination ("defined as similar and equal treatment of trading partners in the administration tariffs and/or import restrictions") has arisen from the threat of "low price" exports from Japan.

Rel.Publ.: "A Note on Japan's Liberalization of International Investments," Aoyama keizai ronshū, 19 (June 1967), 63-69.

273
MALLAMPALLY, Padma. The Influence of Relative Prices on the Exports of Germany and Japan, 1950-1962. Chicago, 1965. 99p.

It is found that in the case of Japan, changes in market prices of exports during the period 1950-1962 were the result of domestic productivity and cost changes rather than of a policy of influencing prices.

274
NAYA, Seiji. The Leontief Paradox and the Factor Structure of Japanese Foreign Trade. Wisconsin, 1965. 158p. DA 26 (Jan. 1966), 3661-62; UM 65-11,165.

Contents: The Leontief Paradox; The Factor Intensity Reversal Issue; The Input-Output Procedure in the Traditional Theory; The Factor Structure of Japanese Foreign Trade; The Regional Capital-Labor Structure of Japanese Foreign Trade. Data for 1955 and for 1959 are used.

Rel.Publ.: "Natural Resources Factor Mix, and Factor Reversal in International Trade," American Economic Review, 57 (May 1967), 561-70.

275
REIERSON, Curtis Calvin. An Investigation of Attitudes towards the Products of Selected Nations among College Students and the Testing of Certain Methods for Changing Existing Attitudes. Texas, 1965. 119p. DA 26 (Oct. 1965), 1970; UM 65-10,763.

"The purpose of this study was to demonstrate the presence of American consumer stereotyping of foreign nations' products, and to indicate the effectiveness of various communication media in obtaining more favorable consumer attitudes....Italy and Japan were selected as the 'test' countries."

Rel.Publ.: "Current Importance of United States Trade with Italy and Japan," Baylor Business Studies, 66 (Jan. 1966), 28-36; "Are Foreign Products Seen as Traditional Stereotypes?" Journal of Retailing, 42 (Fall 1966), 33-40; "Attitude Changes toward Foreign Products," Journal of Marketing Research, 4 (Nov. 1967), 385-87.

276
ABDEL-BARR, Hussein Abdallah. The Market Structure of International Oil with Special Reference to the Organization of Petroleum Exporting Countries. Wisconsin, 1966. 363p. DA 28 (Sept. 1967), 838-A; UM 66-13,756.

Part 2 includes a study of the pattern and outlook for oil imports in four major submarkets, one of which is Japan.

277
BANDURA, Iu. N. Karteli vo vneshnei torgovle Iaponii [Cartels in Japanese Foreign Trade]. Moscow, Institut narodov Azii Akademii nauk SSSR, 1966. (Candidate of Economic Sciences) 251p. Text in Russian. AB: 20p. summary published in 1967. [See also addenda entry 5A.]

HONG, Wontack. A Study of the Changes in the Structure of Manufacturing Industry and in the Trade Pattern of Manufactured Products in Korea, Taiwan, and Japan. 1966. See no.226.

278
OZAWA, Terutomo. Imitation, Innovation, and Trade: A Study of Foreign Licensing Operations in Japan.

Columbia, 1966. 162p. DA 27 (Mar. 1967), 2668-69-A; UM 67-804.

"Focusing upon the structural change of product-composition in both production and export, the study explores the hypothesis that the fundamental impulse to Japan's postwar export growth has come from technological borrowing through licensing, which was instrumental in the development of new productive capacities. Discussed are the connection of licensing operations with (1) trade, (2) economic growth, (3) direct foreign investment, and (4) research and development in Japan."

Rel.Publ.: "Imitation, Innovation, and Japanese Exports," in The Open Economy: Essays on International Trade and Finance, ed. by Peter B. Kenen and Roger Lawrence (New York: Columbia University Press, 1968), 190-212.

279
BAUGE, Kenneth LeRoy. Voluntary Export Restriction as a Foreign Commercial Policy with Special Reference to Japanese Cotton Textiles. Michigan State, 1967. 290p. DA 28 (Mar. 1968), 3311-A; UM 68-4102.

Analyzes the case of voluntary "Japanese export limitations on cotton textiles to the United States when it became evident in the late 1930's and again after World War II that tariff rates almost certainly would be sharply increased."

280
LEE, Kie Bok. Measures of and Factors Affecting the Level of 'Trade Dependence' with Special Applications to Great Britain, Japan, and Taiwan. Virginia, 1967. 345p. DA 28 (Mar. 1968), 3319-20-A; UM 68-3113.

"In Part 2 an attempt was made to find the existence or absence of relationship between the various levels of 'trade dependence' and the standard of living for Great Britain, Japan, and Taiwan in the early and maturing phases of their economic development."

281
LYNCH, Reverend John. The Voluntary Export Quota as a Modern Type of Quantitative Research: A Case Study of Japanese Voluntary Controls on Cotton Textile Exports. Georgetown, 1967. 328p. DA 28 (Feb. 1968), 2845-46-A; UM 68-1910.

A study of cotton textiles in Japan's postwar trade with the United States. Contents: Free Trade and United States Foreign Economic Policy; The Japanese Cotton Textile Industry; Under Pressure from the United States; The Fate of the Japanese Anti-Monopoly Law; The Administration of the Controls; Various Effects of the Quotas.

Rel.Publ.: Toward an Orderly Market: An Intensive Study of Japan's Voluntary Quota in Cotton Textile Exports. Tokyo: Sophia University, 1968. 215p.

282
RAPP, William Venable. A Theory of Changing Trade Patterns under Economic Growth: Tested for Japan. Yale, 1967. 273p. DA 28 (July 1967), 16-17-A; UM 67-8412.

Using Japanese data for the years 1890-1962, the author "proposes and tests a theory explaining change in the industrial composition and country direction of foreign trade during the course of economic development. He argues that as countries grow, they develop new industries. The country first imports manufactured goods from more advanced countries. It then develops an import substitution industry which may later export, first to the underdeveloped countries and finally to more advanced countries. Growth is characterized, therefore, by changing relative comparative advantages among industries which are reflected both in the bill of goods and in the country direction of exports and imports."

Rel.Publ.: "A Theory...Japan," Yale Economic Essays, 7 (Fall 1967), 69-135.

283
RAPPORT, David Joseph. An Economic Analysis of Barriers to World Trade in Cotton Textiles, 1953-1964. Michigan, 1967. 197p. DA 28 (June 1968), 4778-79-A; UM 68-7702.

"Examines the economic consequences that the high-income country cotton-textile quota and tariff barriers have for the so-called low-cost producing countries." Japan is one of the Low-Cost Producing Countries included in the analysis. Contents: The World Cotton Textile Industry, 1953-1964; Cotton Textile Policies of the High-Income Countries, 1953-1964; Impact of High-Income Country Quotas upon the Low-Cost Producing Countries, 1953-1964; The Impact of Tariffs and Welfare-Cost Estimates of High-Income Country Cotton-Textile Policies.

284
TSURUMI, Yoshihiro. Technology Transfer and Foreign Trade: The Case of Japan, 1950-1966. Harvard, 1968. iv, 350p.

"The thesis reviews how Japan, one-time developing nation, absorbed foreign manufacturing technologies and developed her own manufacturing industries. The impact of technology transfer and cumulative technological experience of Japan upon her own export profiles of manufactured goods also is appraised....Among other things, the thesis determines that the export profiles of Japan's manufactured goods as well as the direction and the magnitude of change in such profiles over a period of time are largely determined not by capital intensity of the industries involved but by cumulative technological experience of Japanese manufacturing industries."

285
KOBAYASHI, Kazumi. World Competition in Coarse Grain Trade. Cornell, 1969. 218p. DA 30 (Sept. 1969), 898-A; UM 69-10,433.

Estimates the future international demand for American maize, oats, barley, sorghum, and millet, and includes a detailed analysis of the projected needs of Japan, Great Britain, and the European Common Market for these grains.

LABOR

(Includes wages, labor organization, and the working class.) See also Demography (pages 19-20) and Political Science--political interest groups (pages 216-17).

286
HARADA, Shuichi. Labor Conditions in Japan. Columbia, 1928. i, 295p.

Studies the effects of economic and social conditions particularly during the 1920's upon the welfare of the working class, and discusses trends in the Japanese labor movement at that time.

Rel.Publ.: Labor...Japan. New York: Columbia University Press, 1928. i, 295p. (Studies in History,

Economics and Public Law, ed. by the Faculty of Political Science of Columbia University, 301)

287
MATSUOKA, Asa. Protective Labor Legislation for Women and Children in Japan. Columbia, 1932. 177p.

"Presents...an account of the working conditions existing among women and children in the textile factories of Japan, with special reference to the international influences at work since the beginning of factory employment largely determining those conditions and the efforts to improve them through protective labor legislation."

Rel.Publ.: Protective...Japan. New York: Columbia University Press, 1931. xii, 102p. [Originally issued under the title Labor Conditions of Women and Children in Japan (as U.S. Bureau of Labor Statistics, Bulletin no.558).]

288
SINHA, Sasadha. Post-War Labour Legislation in India: Comparison with Japan. London, 1932. 421p.

Concludes that the superiority of Japan's industrial development can be attributed to exhaustive exploitation of all available resources, longer working hours, labor legislation to insure healthy working conditions progressive business and technological methods, excellent health insurance for mine and factory workers, and a growing acceptance of the trade union.

289
GOL'DBERG, D. I. Rabochee dvizhenie v Iaponii do 1917g. [The Labor Movement in Japan up to 1917]. Leningrad, Institut vostokovedeniia Akademii nauk SSSR, 1938. (Candidate of Historical Sciences degree) Text in Russian.

PELZEL, John C. Social Stratification in Japanese Urban Economic Life. 1950. See no.4.

290
THEYSSET, Édouard-Antoine-Marie-Joseph. L'Essor du mouvement ouvrier au Japon (1945-1948) [The Great Strides Made by the Labor Movement in Japan, 1945-1948]. Paris, 1950. 242p. Text in French.

CAMACHO, Martin T. The Administration of the SCAP Labor Policy in Occupied Japan. 1954. See no.1823.

291
GALKIN, L. G. Usilenie obnishchaniia rabochego klassa Iaponii posle vtoroi mirovoi voiny, 1945-1953 gg. [The Increasing Pauperization of the Japanese Working Class, 1945-1953]. Moscow, Moskovskii gosudarstvennyi universitet imeni M. V. Lomonosova, 1954. (Candidate of Economic Sciences degree) 229 + 13p. Text in Russian. AB: 16p. summary published in 1954.

292
KHLYNOV, V. N. Polozhenie rabochego klassa Iaponii posle 2-oi mirovoi voiny, 1945-1955 [The Position of the Working Class in Japan, 1945-1955]. Moscow, Institut vostokovedeniia Akademii nauk SSSR, 1956. (Candidate of Economic Sciences degree) 17 + 222 + 17p. Text in Russian. AB: 16p. summary published in 1956.

Rel.Publ.: Polozhenie rabochego klassa Iaponii: Posle 2-oi mirovoi voiny. Moscow: Sotsekgiz, 1958. 158p.

293
MUNAKATA, Peter Francis. The Application of Western Sociological Theory to the Analysis of Bureaucratic Structure in Japan: A Pilot Study and Its Interpretation. Fordham, 1956. 308p. AB: 6p. summary appended to diss. ms.

Western sociological theory is applied to trade unions in postwar Japan in order to test the validity of this Western theory of bureaucratic functioning when applied to Japan. With certain revisions, Western sociological theory was found to be a useful device in studying Japanese conditions.

KONO, Shigemi. The Japanese Work Force: A Demographic Analysis. 1958. See no.133.

294
BÖTTCHER, Siegfried. Das Einkommen der arbeitenden Schichten Japans, in seinen Grundlagen und Entwicklungstendenzen [The Income of Peasants and Industrial Workers in Japan: Its Basis and Trends in Its Development]. Kiel, 1961. Text in German. The dissertation in its published form is available at Marburg/Lahn, Staatsbibliothek Preussischer Kulturbesitz, Nr. Ser. 2547-9; also at the University of Michigan, General Library, no. DS2.H22 v.9.

The dissertation begins with a study of the religious and philosophical foundations of Japanese economic views and of the Japanese social structure. The author then describes Japanese industrial growth after the Meiji Restoration and points out how agriculture and industry became progressively differentiated and how wage levels between small and large enterprises became increasingly greater (particularly after World War I). He also investigates the persistence of these trends.

Rel.Publ.: Lebensverhältnisse in der japanischen Kleinindustrie: Zwischen Bauernhof und Grossindustrie. Frankfurt a.M.: Metzner, 1961. 122p. (Schriften des Instituts für Asienkunde in Hamburg, 9)

295
SIEGEL, Abraham J. Strike and Industrial Relations Experience in the Steel Industries of Selected Countries. California, Berkeley, 1961. 430p.

Presents the record of steel strike experiences in each of nine countries--including Japan--and describes the main features of the prevailing industrial relations system in their iron and steel industries. Particular attention is focused on the structure of bargaining, negotiations,machinery, privately established procedures for dispute settlement, and the role of government in the industry's industrial relations."

296
TAIRA, Kōji. The Dynamics of Japanese Wage Differentials, 1881-1959. Stanford, 1961. 271p. DA 22 (Nov. 1961), 1457-58; UM 61-4163.

The study is "devoted to the verification and analysis on the basis of Japanese data, of the hypothesis that wage differentials tend to narrow secularly with economic progress and that they vary in the short run in close association with variations in general economic conditions." Part 1 describes Japanese wages and wage differentials during the period 1881-1959, and part 2 focuses on the economic forces that were responsible for the cyclical behavior of wage differentials during those years.

Rel.Publ.: "The Dynamics of Wage Differentials

in Japanese Economic Development," Proceedings of the 35th Annual Conference of the Western Economic Association (1960), 19-24; "Japanese 'Enterprise Unionism' and Interfirm Wage Structure," Industrial and Labor Relations Review, 15 (Oct. 1961), 33-51; "The Characteristics of Japanese Labor Markets," Economic Development and Cultural Change, 10 (Jan. 1962), 150-68; "The Intersectoral Wage Differential in Japan, 1881-1959," Journal of Farm Economics, 44 (May 1962), 322-34; "Market Forces and Public Power in Wage Determination: Early Japanese Experiences," Social Research, 30 (Winter 1963), 434-57; "The Labor Market in Japanese Development," British Journal of Industrial Relations, 2 (July 1964), 207-27.

297
KOMAROV, A. V. Polozhenie rabochego klassa v sovremennoi Iaponii [The Position of the Working Class in Contemporary Japan]. Moscow, Institut narodov Azii Akademii nauk SSSR, 1965. (Candidate of Economic Sciences degree) 240 + 11p. Text in Russian.
Rel.Publ.: Polozhenie rabochego klassa Iaponii. Moscow: "Nauka," 1967. 168p. (Akademiia nauk SSSR, Institut Vostokovedeniia)

298
BLUMENTHAL, Tuvia. The Determination of Wage Differentials in the Japanese Economy. Ōsaka, 1966. 66p. For copies, write directly to the author: Department of Economics, Eliezer Kaplan School of Economic and Social Sciences, Hebrew University, Jerusalem, Israel.
The dissertation consists of six chapters which focus on (1) The Japanese Labor Market, in which such peculiar market features as the life-time commitment and seniority system, the dual structure, and the role of trade unions are discussed; (2) The Analysis of Variance Approach; (3) The Effect of Socio-Economic Factors, where the effect of age, sex, size of firm, education, industry, and type of employment on wages are considered; (4) Changes in the Labor Market (an analysis of the shift from a labor surplus to a labor shortage); (5) The Explanation of the Economic Factors, in which economic factors such as productivity and unemployment are added to the socio-economic ones; and (6) Conclusions.
Rel.Publ.: The Determination...Economy. Osaka, 1966. 66p. (Institute of Social and Economic Research, Osaka University, Discussion Paper, 41); "The Effect of Socio-Economic Factors on Wage Differentials in Japanese Manufacturing Industries," Kikan riron keizaigaku, 17 (Sept. 1966), 53-67; "Scarcity of Labor and Wage Differentials in the Japanese Economy, 1958-1964," Economic Development and Cultural Change, 17 (Oct. 1968), 15-32.

299
ITO, Satoshi. Probleme der Lohnstruktur in Japan [Wage Structure Problems in Japan]. Basel, 1966. viii, 111p. Text in German.
A discussion of the formation and the problems of the current Japanese wage structure. Contents: Characterization of the Wage Structure in Japan; A Cross-Section Analysis of Wage Differences According to the Size of Various Businesses; Origin of Wage Differences.
Rel.Publ.: Probleme...Japan. Stuttgart, 1966.

300
PIROGOVA, I. M. Izmeneniia v strukture rabochego klassa Iaponii [Changes in the Structure of the Japanese Working Class]. Moscow, Institut ekonomiki i mezhdunarodnykh otnoshenii Akademii nauk SSSR, 1966. (Candidate of Economic Sciences degree) 178 + 14p. Text in Russian.

301
TUSSING, Arlon Rex. Employment and Wages in Japanese Industrialization: A Quantitative Study of Yamanashi Prefecture in the Meiji Era. Washington, Seattle, 1966. 241p. DA 27 (Aug. 1966), 315-A; UM 66-7904.
"This study examines the growth of the labor force and the behavior of wage rates in one Japanese prefecture, using occupational data from population censuses in 1879 and 1920, and factory statistics from the prefectural yearbooks....The investigator concludes that one of the central features of economic growth in Meiji Japan was the more intensive utilization of available labor time; in other words, that the Japanese increased their per capita income largely by working longer and working harder."
Rel.Publ.: "The Labor Force in Meiji Economic Growth: A Quantitative Study of Yamanashi Prefecture," Journal of Economic History, 26 (Mar. 1966), 59-92.

302
ODAKA, Konosuke. A Study of Employment and Wage-Differential Structure in Japan. California, Berkeley, 1967. 240p. DA 28 (Jan. 1968), 2404-A; UM 68-128.
An empirical and theoretical investigation of such peculiar characteristics of the Japanese labor market as extremely low unemployment rates, the lifetime commitment of employees with the firm, wide wage differentials according to the size of the firm, and enterprise unionism.
Rel.Publ.: "On Employment and Wage Differential Structure in Japan: A Survey," Hitotsubashi Journal of Economics, 8 (June 1967), 41-64; "A History of Money Wages in the Northern Kyushu Industrial Area, 1898-1939," Hitotsubashi Journal of Economics, 8 (Feb. 1968), 71-100; "Indices of the Excess Demand for Labor in Prewar Japan, 1929-1939: A Preliminary Study," Hitotsubashi Journal of Economics, 10 (June 1969), 33-55.

303
COLE, Robert Evan. Japanese Blue Collar Workers: A Participant Observation Study. Illinois, 1968. 583p. DA 29 (Aug. 1968), 690-91-A; UM 68-12,096.
Based on research conducted at a diecast firm and at an auto parts firm, the study "describes and analyses the attitudes and behavior of present day blue collar workers with primary focus on their relationship to and involvement in the factory. This covers such areas as the rules of work and the nature of the reward system in the factory and worker response to this set of rules. Particular attention is paid to the economic and sociological meaning of the permanent employment system and the payment by age and length of service system."
Rel.Publ.: "Industrialization and the Convergence Hypothesis: Some Aspects of Contemporary Japan" [by] Bernard Karsh and Robert E. Cole, Journal of Social Issues, 24 (Oct. 1968), 45-64; Japanese Blue-Collar: The Changing Tradition. Berkeley: University of California Press, forthcoming; "Japanese Workers, Unions, and the Marxist Appeal," The Japan Interpreter, 6 (Summer 1970).

304
MUTHUCHIDAMBARAM, Subba Pillai. Determinants of Income in Madras Labor Market. Wisconsin, 1968. 208p.

DA 29 (June 1969), 4570-71-A; UM 68-17,923.
A case study of blue collar workers in Madras City, India. Japanese data and the same regression model and definition of variables are used to provide a cross-cultural comparison. Stresses the importance of experience and age as the major factors accounting for variations in income in Japan.

MONEY, BANKING, AND INVESTMENT

For financial matters related primarily to foreign trade, e.g. international balance of payments, see Economics--foreign trade (pages 36-40). See also: Economics--business, industry, and domestic commerce (pages 28-33), Economics--history (pages 33-35), and History--Japanese empire--Taiwan (pages 98-99).

305
TAKAKI, Masayoshi. The History of Japanese Paper Currency, 1868-1890. Johns Hopkins, 1895. 59p.
Studies the genesis, circulation, kinds, and redemption of paper currency.
Rel.Publ.: The History...1890. Baltimore: Johns Hopkins Press, 1903. 59p. (Johns Hopkins University Studies in Historical and Political Science, v.21, no.5)

306
LAHAYE, Paul-Louis. Recherches sur les chambres de compensation (Clearing-Houses): Création, organisation, et développement en France, Angleterre, Allemagne, Autriche, Italie, Australie, au Japon, et en Amérique [Study of the Clearing Houses: Their Creation, Organization, and Development in France, England, Germany, Austria, Italy, Australia, Japan, and the United States of America]. Caen, 1901. Text in French.
See especially Ch.10, "Clearing Houses in Japan" (p.184-92), which focuses on clearing houses in Tokyo, Osaka, Kobe, and Kyoto.
Rel.Publ.: Recherches...Amérique. Caen: C. Valin, 1901. iv, 274p.

307
HAMAOKA, Itsuo. A Study on the Central Bank of Japan. Michigan, 1902. Diss. ms. not available.
Contents: General Considerations; The Organization and Work of the Bank [studies the Bank's capitalistic, administrative, and supervisory organization]; The Essential Functions of the Bank [examines the Bank's role as the issuing body of Government paper money and its role as a major fiscal and economic organ]; Development of the Bank [its history]; The Public Policy Observed towards the Bank [with regard to the Bank's pecuniary duty and its administration].
Rel.Publ.: A Study...Japan. Tokyo: Tōkyō Senmon Gakkō Publishing Department, 1902. vii, 118p.

308
AKAMATSU, Kakujiro. The Financial Development of Japan since the Restoration. Michigan, 1903. 131p.
Contents: Pt.1: From the [Meiji] Restoration to the Outbreak of the Sino-Japanese War: Experiences in Monetary and Banking Systems; National Debts; Expenditures and Revenues; Systems of Financial Administration and Control. Pt.2: From the War to the Present: War Financiering [i.e. Financing]; Subsequent Expansion of Expenditures; Receipt and Disbursement of the War Indemnity; Recent Modifications of the Revenue System.

309
KIGA, Kanju. Das Bankwesens Japans [The Japanese Banking System]. Leipzig, 1903. Text in German. The dissertation in its published form is available at Berlin West, Staatsbibliothek Preussischer Kulturbesitz, Nr. Un 9513.
An historical survey of the development of the Japanese banking system through the Meiji period is followed by a careful examination of the beginnings of modern banking, the establishment of the national banks, and the enactment of related legislation. The organization of the Bank of Japan (Nihon Ginkō) and of large commercial, small business, and savings banks as well as the founding and organization of the Industrial Banks and the Hypothec Bank also are studied.
Rel.Publ.: Das Bankwesens Japans. Leipzig: A. Deichert, 1904. viii, 197p.

310
ODATE, Gyoju. Japan's Financial Relations with the United States. Columbia, 1922. 137p.
Examines the financial, banking, and capital investment relations that existed between the United States and Japan, 1914-1920. The study is expressly written from the Japanese point of view.
Rel.Publ.: Japan's...United States. New York: Columbia University, 1922. 137p. (Studies in History, Economics, and Public Law, ed. by the Faculty of Political Science of Columbia University. v.98, no.2; whole no.224)

311
KUSHIMOTO, Tomosaburo. Der Industriekredit der japanischen Banken [The Industrial Credit of Japanese Banks]. Breslau, 1924. 136p. Text in German. Diss. ms. available at Marburg/Lahn, Staatsbibliothek Preussischer Kulturbesitz, Nr. MS 25/735.
Japan as an industrial state and the importance of the credit system in general. An investigation of the various kinds of Japanese industrial credit and of the role of the banks as sources of credit. Concludes with a critique of the Japanese system of industrial credits.
Rel.Publ.: Das Industriekredit...Banken. Breslau: Bresl. Genossensch.-Buchdr., 1924. [excerpt].

312
KROLL, Karl. Die Bankenkrisen in Japan [Banking Crises in Japan]. Marburg, 1930. Text in German. The dissertation in its published form is available at Marburg/Lahn, Universitätsbibliothek, Nr. XVII C.
The author surveys Japan's development during the Meiji era and then focuses on the origin and the organization of modern Japanese banking and on the impact of the banking crises of 1920, 1923, and 1927 upon Japan's economy and banking regulations.
Rel.Publ.: Die Bankenkrisen...Japan. Marburg a.d. Lahn: Friedrich, 1930. v, 130p.

313
HUNSBERGER, Warren Seabury. The International Financial Position of Japan. Yale, 1937. 392p.
Contents: Historical Introduction; International Accounts; Foreign Trade; Shipping; Industry; Agriculture and Fishing; Finance; Capital Movements. Considerable statistical data may be found both in the text and in the statistical appendix.

314
GINETE, Pedro A. Post-War Banking and Monetary Reforms

in the United States, Japan, and India. New York, 1939. viii, 478p.
See especially Ch.8, "Japan's Post-War Banking Developments and Reforms" (p.263-97), Ch.9, "The Japanese Banking System" (p.298-326), and Ch.10, "Post-War Changes in Japan's Monetary System" (p.327-55).

315
TSURU, Shigeto. Development of Capitalism and Business Cycles in Japan, 1868-1897. Harvard, 1940. xi, 284p. AB: Harvard University. Summaries of Theses... 1940. p.294-96.
Primarily a case study of "the evolution of the phenomenon of business cycles in its relation to the development of capitalism" in Meiji Japan. Contents: Theoretical: Capitalism and Business Cycles; Historical: Development of Capitalism in Japan, 1868-1897 (Public Finance, Industrialization, Development of Money and Banking, Formation of Wage Labor); Interpretive: Economic Fluctuations in Japan, 1868-1897.
Rel.Publ.: "Economic Fluctuations in Japan, 1868-1893," Review of Economic Statistics, 23 (Nov. 1941), 176-89.

316
BOLDYREV, G. I. Istoriia iaponskikh gosudarstvennykh finansov [History of Japanese Government Finance]. Moscow, Moskovskii finansovo-ekonomicheskii institut, 1946 (Doctor of Economic Sciences degree) 719p. Text in Russian.
Rel.Publ.: Finansy Iaponii: Opyt istoricheskogo analiza. Moscow: Gosfinizdat, 1946. 289p.

317
VAINTSVAIG, N. K. Finansovaia oligarkhiia Iaponii: Osnovnye etapy razvitiia [The Financial Oligarchy of Japan: Basic Stages of Development]. Moscow, Moskovskii institut vostokovedeniia, 1946. (Doctor of Economic Sciences degree) 374 + 36p. Text in Russian.
Rel.Publ.: Iaponskie kontserny. Moscow and Leningrad: Sotsekgiz, 1935. 120p. (Institut mirovogo khoziaistva i mirovoi politiki)

318
MOHAN, Krishna. Capital Imports and Japanese Economic Development, 1870 to 1931. Wisconsin, 1952. 275p. AB: University of Wisconsin. Summaries of Doctoral Dissertations. v.13. p.135-37.
The dissertation analyzes some of the means by which Japan was able to finance most of her internal development without relying on heavy capital imports. The author also draws certain conclusions from Japan's experience for economic development in underdeveloped areas today.

319
REUBENS, Edwin Pierce. Foreign Capital in Economic Development: The Japanese Experience, 1868-1913. Columbia, 1952. 253p. DA 12 (1952), 685-86; UM 4235.
"The analysis centers on two principal relationships: the 'degree of dependence on foreign capital' and the 'capacity to absorb foreign capital inflow.'"
Rel.Publ.: "Foreign Capital in Economic Development: A Case Study of Japan," Milbank Memorial Fund Quarterly, 28 (Apr. 1950), 173-90; "Foreign Capital and Domestic Development in Japan, 1868-1930," in Economic Growth: Brazil, India, Japan, ed. by Simon Kuznets, Wilbert Moore, and Joseph Spengler (Durham: Duke University Press, 1955), 179-228.

320
SHURKIN, A. O. Gosudarstvennye finansy poslevoennoi Iaponii na sluzhbe amerikanskoi agressii [Postwar Japanese Government Finance in the Service of American Aggression]. Moscow, Moskovskii gosudarstvennyi institut mezhdunarodnykh otnoshenii Ministerstva Inostrannykh Del SSSR, 1953. (Candidate of Economic Sciences degree) 307p. Text in Russian. AB: 20p. summary published in 1953.

321
DOWD, Laurence Phillips. Japanese Foreign Exchange Policy, 1930-1940: An Account of the Development of Japanese Foreign Exchange Policy during the Nineteen-Thirty Decade and an Analysis of Its Influence on the Japanese Economy in Its International and Domestic Aspects. Michigan, 1954. 503p. DA 14 (Apr. 1954), 606; UM 7643.
Considers "what were the successive steps in the development of the exchange policy in Japan and to what extent each step was necessitated by previous action; and what was the impact of these successive steps and of the policy as a whole on Japan's international and domestic economy."
Rel.Publ.: "The Impact of Exchange Policy on the International Economy of Japan during the Period 1930-1940," Kobe Economic Business Review, 4 (1957), 1-58.

322
PICHUGIN, B. M. Vozrozhdenie konkurentsii iaponskikh monopolii na mirovom kapitalisticheskom rynke [The Revival of Japanese Monopolistic Competition in the World Capitalistic Market]. Moscow, Moskovskii gosudarstvennyi universitet imeni M. V. Lomonosova, 1955. (Candidate of Economic Science's degree) 261p. Text in Russian. AB: 18p. summary published in 1955.
Rel.Publ.: Iaponiia: Ekonomika i vneshniaia torgovlia. Moscow: Vneshtorgizdat, 1957. 215p.

323
TAOKA, George Mazumi. The Role of the Bank of Japan in the Administration of the Economic and Financial Controls of the Government during National Emergencies: With Special Emphasis on the Sino-Japanese War and the World War II Periods. Columbia, 1955. 251p. DA 15 (June 1955), 1008; UM 12,072.
Contents: The Development of Modern Financial Institutions; Organization and Powers of the Bank of Japan; Operations of the Bank of Japan during National Emergencies prior to 1937; The Period of Transition: February 26, 1936-July 7, 1937; Operations of the Bank of Japan: 1937-1941; Operations of the Bank of Japan: 1942-1945.

324
YAMANE, Taro. Postwar Inflation in Japan. Wisconsin, 1955. 319p. AB: University of Wisconsin. Summaries of Doctoral Dissertations. v.16. p.255-56.
A theoretical discussion, description, and analysis of postwar Japanese inflation for the period August 1945-December 1952.

325
ISLAM, Nurul. Studies in Foreign Capital and Economic Development: Some Aspects of Absorption of Foreign Capital in Canada, India, and Japan. Harvard, 1956. v, 323p. AB: 5p. summary appended to diss. ms.
Information on Japan is found throughout. Contents: Pt.1: Some Theoretical Considerations: Theories of International Investment in Retrospect; The Problems of

Absorption of Foreign Capital. Pt.2: The Pattern of Foreign Investment: The Magnitude, Significance, and Economic Environment of Capital Inflow; Forms of Investment: Fields of Investment. Pt.3: The Problems of Debt Service: Introduction; The Case Studies: Canada, Japan, and India. Pt.4: Relation between Foreign Capital and Domestic Capital and Enterprise: Introduction; Case Studies.

Rel.Publ.: Foreign Capital and Economic Development: Japan, India, and Canada: Studies in Some Aspects of Absorption of Foreign Capital. Tokyo: Tuttle, 1960. 251p.

326
KOKORIS, James A. The Economic and Financial Development of Okayama Prefecture, Japan. Michigan, 1956. 409p. DA 17 (June 1957), 1250; UM 21,191.

Contents: The Place of Okayama in the Economy of Japan; Okayama in the Period of Tokugawa Feudalism; Transition of Okayama from a Feudal to a Modern Economy; Origins of Modern Banking in Okayama; The National Banks; The Ōhara Local Zaibatsu of Okayama; The Development of Banking Institutions in Okayama Prefecture; Summary of Observations on Local Economic Development in Japan.

Rel.Publ.: "The Ōhara Zaibatsu of Okayama," in Studies on Economic Life in Japan, ed. by Richard K. Beardsley (Ann Arbor: University of Michigan Press, 1964), 37-55. (University of Michigan, Center for Japanese Studies, Occasional Papers, 8)

327
AUERBACH, Arnold. Capital étranger et développement économique au Japon (1868-1938) [Foreign Capital and Japan's Economic Development, 1868-1938]. Paris, 1958. 294p. Text in French.

328
SCHIFFER, Reverend Hubert F., S.J. The Modern Japanese Banking System. Fordham, 1958. 465p. AB: 8p. summary appended to diss. ms.

A descriptive study of the development of the modern Japanese banking and credit structure. Includes a discussion of the Bank of Japan and its role in economic stabilization, of the structure of liabilities and capital accounts, and of the nature of deposits, loans and discounts, and investments in postwar Japan.

Rel.Publ.: The Modern...System. New York: University Publishers, 1962. xxii, 240p.

329
PIROGOV, G. G. Bankovskie monopolii sovremennoi Iaponii [Banking Monopolies in Contemporary Japan]. Moscow, Institut mirovoi ekonomiki i mezhdunarodnykh otnoshenii Akademii nauk SSSR, 1959. (Candidate of Economic Sciences degree) 445p. Text in Russian. AB: 18p. summary published in 1959.

330
CUKIERMAN, Roger. Le Capital dans l'économie japonaise [Capital in the Japanese Economy]. Paris, 1960. 254p. Text in French.

Pt.1: The formation of capital in Japan, 1868-the mid 1950's. Pt.2: The utilization of capital, with particular reference to the dual structure of the Japanese economy.

Rel.Publ.: Le Capital...japonaise. Paris: Presses universitaires de France, 1962. 183p. (Études économiques internationales)

331
EHRLICH, Edna E. The Role of Banking in Japan's Economic Development. New School for Social Research, 1960. xii, 554p.

Contents: The Japanese Banks as Sources of Finance for Industry (The Banking System as the Supplier of Investment Capital, The Underdeveloped Securities Market); The Collecting of Savings and Credit Creation for Investment; Inflation and Economic Growth in Japan (The Monetary Authorities, Historical Development of the Easy Money Policy, The Money Supply and the Development of Prices, Economic Growth as the Cause of the Gap between Prices and Money Supply); The Concentration of Bank Credit on Industry; Credit Policies in the Japanese "Combines" (Form, Position, and Role of the Zaibatsu Banks); Credit Extended for the Advancement of Foreign Trade; Statistical Indicators of Bank Credit (Industry in General, Specific Industries); Widespread Discrimination in Credit Extension to Small Manufacturers; A Paradox: Underdeveloped Agriculture Financing the Development of Industry.

Rel.Publ.: "Japan" [by] Edna E. Ehrlich and Frank M. Tamagna, in Banking Systems, ed. by Benjamin H. Beckhart (New York: Columbia University Press, 1954), 517-72; "Note on Postwar Credit Policies in Japan," Review of Economics and Statistics, 39 (Nov. 1957), 469-71.

332
KANG, Moon Hyung. The Monetary Aspect of Economic Development in Japan with Special Reference to Monetary Policies: 1868-1935. Nebraska, 1960. 306p. DA 21 (Dec. 1960), 1398; UM 60-4504.

"Deals with the historical monetary adjustment processes in the course of Japan's economic development" and seeks to determine the ways in which Japanese monetary policies affected the rate of that country's rapid economic growth.

Rel.Publ.: "Some Aspects of Japanese Imports with Reference to Economic Growth and Balance of Payments, 1901-1933," Journal of Developing Areas, 2 (Jan. 1968), 241-51.

333
PATRICK, Hugh Talbot. The Bank of Japan: A Case Study in the Effectiveness of Central Bank Techniques of Monetary Control. Michigan, 1960. 333p. DA 21 (Feb. 1961), 2151-52; UM 60-6920.

Contents: The Setting; The Financial System; Flows through the Financial System; Open Market Operations; Reserve Requirements; Discount Policy: Interest Rate Adjustments; Discount Policy: Credit Rationing; Other Bank of Japan Techniques of Monetary Control; The Application of Bank of Japan Techniques of Monetary Control (1953-1954, 1957-1958).

Rel.Publ.: Monetary Policy and Central Banking in Contemporary Japan. Bombay, 1962. xii, 291p. (University of Bombay, Series in Monetary and International Economics, 5); "Monetary Policy in Japan's Economic Growth, 1945-1959," FES, 28 (May 1959), 65-71; "Cyclical Instability and Fiscal-Monetary Policy in Postwar Japan," in The State and Economic Enterprise in Japan, ed. by William W. Lockwood (Princeton: Princeton University Press, 1965), 555-618.

334
HOEKENDORF, William Carl. The Secular Trend of Income Velocity in Japan, 1879-1940. Washington, Seattle, 1961. 263p. DA 22 (May 1962), 3889; UM 62-2079.

Contents: Development of Japanese Currency and

Banking Systems; Description, Evaluation, and Comparison of Secular Income Velocity in Japan; Factors Influencing the Secular Trend of Income Velocity in Japan.

Rel.Publ.: "The Secular Trend of Income Velocity in Japan, 1879-1940," Journal of Finance, 18 (Sept. 1963), 566-67.

335
OTT, David Jackson. The Financial Development of Japan, 1878-1958. Maryland, 1961. 322p. DA 22 (Mar. 1962), 3031; UM 62-211.

Part 1 is a study of "the growth of primary securities issued by nonfinancial spending units in Japan and the net purchases by Japanese intermediaries of these primary issues," 1878-1958. Part 2 compares "the broad contours of Japanese economic development with those in the United States."

Rel.Publ.: "The Financial Development of Japan, 1878-1958," Journal of Political Economy, 69 (Apr. 1961), 122-41.

336
SAKURAI, Kinichiro. Financial Aspects of [the] Economic Development of Japan from 1868 to [the] Present. Syracuse, 1961. 235p. DA 23 (Aug. 1962), 486; UM 62-1145.

Focuses on the role of such financial intermediaries as postal savings accounts, zaibatsu banks, and the Bank of Japan.

Rel.Publ.: Financial Aspects of Economic Development of Japan, 1868-1958. Tokyo, 1964. ix, 155p. (Science Council of Japan. Division of Economics, Commerce and Business Administration. Economic Series, 34)

337
KAWAKATSU, Shigeyoshi. Bilanzvergleichende Untersuchung der eisen-und metallverbeitenden Industrie der Bundesrepublik Deutschland und Japans für die Jahre 1949-1956 [A Study Comparing the Balance Sheets of the Iron and Metal Processing Industry of West Germany with That of Japan for the Years 1949-1956]. Kiel, 1962. 173, ix p. Text in German. Diss. ms. available at Kiel, Universitätsbibliothek, Nr. TU 62.5574.

A study of the investment activities and the related financial problems of various German and Japanese enterprises within that sector of the economy which produces goods for the subsequent manufacture of various products. The dissertation examines the impact of capital investment upon the mechanization and the rationalization of these enterprises, analyzes the balance sheets of certain important companies and points out differences in the development of individual branches within the industry.

338
PHILLIPS, Philip Robert. Japanese Financial Development. New York, 1962.

339
KYMN, Kern O. The Demand for Currency in Japan. Chicago, 1964. 73p.

This work explains the shift in the demand for currency as a function of real income alone; studies the effect of the determinants of the demand for currency, with emphasis on the effect of the expected rate of price level changes on the demand for currency; and determines the degree to which the demand for money as a whole was affected by the same determinants affecting the demand for currency. Covers the period 1899-1960.

340
DINKEVICH, A. I. Finansy poslevoennoi Iaponii [Postwar Japanese Finance]. Moscow, Institut narodov Azii Akademii nauk SSSR, 1965. (Doctor of Economic Sciences degree) 1,221p. Text in Russian. AB: 51p. summary published in 1965.

Rel.Publ.: Gosudarstvennye finansy poslevoennoi Iaponii. Moscow: "Nauka," 1967. 406p.; Voennye finansy Iaponii, 1937-1945. Moscow; Izdatel'stov vostochnoi literatury, 1958. 116p. [See also addenda no. 10A.]

341
HIRAMATSU, Kenji. Kreditschöpfung beim Wirtschaftswachstum: Betrachtungen über die Kreditschöpfungseinrichtungen, unter besonderer Berücksichtigung der Bundesrepublik Deutschland und Japans [Obtaining Credit during Periods of Economic Growth: A Study of Institutions that Grant Credit, with Special Consideration of West Germany and of Japan]. Gottingen, 1965. Text in German. The dissertation in its published form is available at Marburg/Lahn, Staatsbibliothek Preussischer Kulturbesitz, Nr. 64,021.

A theoretical study of several economic concepts such as "rate of growth," "stock," and "flow" is followed by a study of credit markets and of the granting of credit in general. The author then examines West Germany's export surplus and provides a comparison with Japan. He also discusses the term "over loan" with special regard to Japan.

Rel.Publ.: Kreditschöpfung...Japans. Göttingen, 1965. 170p.

342
ENG, Maximo Va Fong. A New Requisite in Training Overseas Bank Management in the Far East. New York, 1966. 286p. DA 27 (Aug. 1966), 299-300-A; UM 66-7862.

Includes a study of the general background of American overseas banks in East Asia and an analysis of their overseas management training problems in that area.

343
KERAN, Michael William. Monetary Policy and the Business Cycle in Postwar Japan. Minnesota, 1966. 160p. DA 27 (Jan. 1967), 1994-A; UM 66-9025.

Asserts that the monetary policy pursued by Japan in the postwar period contributed to the sharp year-to-year variations in her growth rate, and that "the more expansionist monetary policy contributed to greater fluctuation."

344
KHONSARY, Reza. The Role of Commercial Banks in Financing [the] Economic Growth of Japan, 1951-1963. New York, 1966. 192p. DA 28 (Jan. 1968), 2419-20-A; UM 66-10,577.

"A detailed study of the postwar structure, development, and method of operation of Japanese commercial banks, with emphasis on the banks' strategic contribution to economic growth."

345
PIGULEVSKAIA, E. A. Monopolii i finansovaia oligarkhiia v sovremennoi Iaponii [The Monopolies and the Financial Oligarchy in Contemporary Japan]. Moscow, Institut mirovoi ekonomiki i mezhdunarodnykh otnoshe-

nii Akademii nauk SSSR, 1966. (Doctor of Economic Sciences degree) 356p. Text in Russian.
Rel.Publ.: Monopolii...Iaponii. Moscow: "Nauka," 1966. 356p. [See also addenda entry no.35A.]

346
BARINOV, E. A. Kreditnaia sistema sovremennoi Iaponii [The Credit System in Contemporary Japan]. Moscow, Moskovskii finansovyi institut, 1967. (Candidate of Economic Sciences degree) 258p. Text in Russian.
AB: 16p. summary published in 1967.

PUBLIC FINANCE

See also Economics--economic history (pages 33-35).

347
KUSSAKA, Johannes Tsiōsiro. Das japanische Geldwesen [The World of Japanese Money]. Jena, 1890. Text in German. The dissertation in its published form is available at Marburg/Lahn, Universitätsbibliothek, Nr. VII m C; also at the University of Michigan, General Library, no. HG1274K97/1890.
A study of the four periods into which the history of Japanese currency is divided (from early times to the Meiji era), a technical description of coins and paper money, an examination of the exchange relationship between gold and silver and of the depreciation of paper money, and a critical evaluation of Japanese monetary questions. The appendix contains translations of the most important ordinances pertaining to Japanese monetary matters that were issued by the Imperial Court and by the shogunate between 712 and 1871.
Rel.Publ.: Das japanische Geldwesen. Jena: Frommann, 1890. vi, 100p.

348
SUGI, Umesaburo. Die Reform des japanischen Geldwesens im Jahre 1897 [The Reform of the Japanese Monetary System in 1897]. Göttingen, 1901. Text in German. The dissertation in its published form is available at Marburg/Lahn, Universitätsbibliothek, Nr. XVII C.
I. The period from the first monetary law (1871) to currency reform in 1886. II. The period of the de facto silver standard. III. The new monetary law of March 26, 1897, and the abandonment of silver in favor of a gold standard. (Reasons for the introduction of the gold standard and for various currency reforms are presented.)
Rel.Publ.: Die Reform...1897. Göttingen: Dieterich, 1901. 56p.

349
KIKUCHI, Gunzo. Das Staatsschuldenwesen seit der Restauration Japans [The Japanese National Debt since the Meiji Restoration]. Halle-Wittenberg, 1904. Text in German. The dissertation in its published form is available at Marburg/Lahn, Universitätsbibliothek, Nr. XVII C.
A study of the introduction of paper money and of the adverse effect that it had upon fiscal legislation, commodity prices, and foreign trade. Measures taken by the Ministry of Finance with regard to outstanding debts are studied, and the handling of domestic and foreign loans as well as the handling of the conversion, consolidation, and amortization of State debts are discussed.
Rel.Publ.: Das Staatsschuldenwesen...Japans. Halle a.S.: C.A. Kaemmerer, 1904. 80p.

YOKOYAMA, Masajiro. The Development of the Land Tax in Japan. 1904. See no.469.

350
HATTORI, Bunshiro. Local Finance in Japan in Relation to Imperial Finance. Princeton, 1906. v, 90p.
Contents: Administrative Organization (The Central and Local Governments); Local Finance (The Revenue and Expenditure of Local Government, Budgetary Legislation and Administration of Local Government); The Problems of Local Finance in Japan and Their Discussion (The Causes of the Increase in Expenditure, How the Increased Expenditure is Met, Reform of Local Finance).
Rel.Publ.: Local...Finance. Princeton: Princeton University Press, 1906. v, 90p.

351
HOSHINO, Benzo. Die Finanzen und die Finanzpolitik Japans während und nach dem russisch-japanischen Kriege (1904-1908) [Japanese Finances and Financial Policy during and after the Russo-Japanese War, 1904-1908]. Halle, 1908. Text in German. The dissertation in its published form is available at Bochum, Universitätsbibliothek, Nr. UA 18,660; also at the University of Michigan, General Library, no. HJ1424.H82.
A study of the administration of government revenue in Japan, 1896-1908, and of the measures taken to cover the expenses of the Russo-Japanese War: the taxes and duties (luxury taxes, taxes on profits, and taxes on trade) that were levied and the extraordinary sources of government revenue as well as government loans during the period.
Rel.Publ.: Die Finanzen...1908. Halle a.S.: Kämmerer, 1908, 79p.

352
ISHIZAWA, Kyugoro. Japan's War Finances, 1904-1905. Clark, 1909 138, xiv p. [Diss. ms. not available]

353
BÜCHEL, Hermann. Das japanische Budget [The Japanese Budget]. Strassburg, 1910. Text in German.
The organization and handling of the budget and its supervision by the Government Audit Office are discussed. The apportionment of the budget is presented in a table showing income and outflow, following which a comparison is made with government budgets in Germany and Russia. The author also discusses the introduction of monopolies, provides a detailed treatment of taxation, criticizes various aspects of the Japanese economy, and makes a number of recommendations for its improvement.
Rel.Publ.: Das japanische Budget. Bochum: Stumpf, 1910. 38p.; Die Finanzen Japans. Essen: G.D. Bädeker, 1908. vi, 222p.

354
ASHIDA, Teruo. Das Geldwesen Japans: Entwicklung und Vergleichung mit demjenigen in europäischen Ländern. [The Finance of Japan: Development and Comparison with Finance in European Countries]. Erlangen, 1912. Text in German. The dissertation in its published form is available at Marburg/Lahn, Universitätsbibliothek, Nr. XVII C; also at the University of Michigan, General Library.
The historical development of specie and of paper money in Japan is followed by an examination of the influence that certain European countries and China had upon the Japanese monetary system, and by a study of the production and use of coins, government-backed

paper money, and banknotes. The dissertation concludes with some general considerations about currency values, types of credit, the circulation of money, precious metals, and exchange rates.

Rel.Publ.: Das Geldwesen...Landern. Nürnberg: Hilz, 1912. 147p.

355
KITASAWA, Shinjiro. A Study of the National Debt of Japan. Johns Hopkins, 1914. iv, 115p.

356
MATSUMOTO, Masao Suma. Administration of the Budget of the Japanese Government. Stanford, 1933. 308p. AB: Stanford University. Abstracts of Dissertations, 1932/33. p.159-62.

A descriptive study of the essential elements of the Japanese budgetary system.

357
NISHIKAWA, Isokichi. Oekonomische Folgewirkungen der japanischen Valutakurssenkungen in den Jahren 1931/1933 [Economic Results of the Reduction of the Value of the Yen during the Years 1931/1933]. Jena, 1935. Text in German. The dissertation in its published form is available at Marburg/Lahn, Universitätsbibliothek, Nr. XVII B; also at the University of Michigan, General Library, no. HC462.N72.

Shows Japan's general commercial situation up to the beginning of the gold embargo through an examination of the stages of Japanese economic development, 1870-1930. The reasons for the gold embargo and for other Japanese government measures designed to protect the economy are presented. The impact upon Japanese agriculture, industry, retail business, banking, and finance is also shown.

Rel.Publ.: Oekonomische...1931/1933. Kyoto: Naigai-Shuppan, 1934. iv, 82p.

358
HUTCHINSON, Edmond Carlton. Inflation and Stabilization in Post-War Japan. Virginia, 1954. 412p. DA 14 (Dec. 1954), 2217-18; UM 9649.

"An historical account of the efforts of the Japanese government and the occupation authorities to control the inflationary situation, and an analysis of the results of two different approaches adopted."

359
SINGER, Morris. Studies in the Policies of Economic Development: The Experiences of New Zealand and Japan. California, Berkeley, 1955. 340p.

"Concerns the kinds of public policies open to a community predominantly private enterprise in its economic organization and desirous of promoting its economic development." Focuses on the factors grouped under the headings "the dispersion of socioeconomic power; the promotion of socially desirable enterprises; the mitigation of cyclical severities; the encouragement of foreign trade; and the stimulation of foreign cultural intercourse."

360
BUI-tuong-Huan. La politique de déflation au Japon et ses effets (1953-1954) [The Policy of Deflation in Japan and Its Effects, 1953-1954]. Paris, 1958. 315p.

361
PEVZNER, Ia. Kh. Gosudarstvenno-monopolisticheskii kapitalizm v Iaponii [State Monopolistic Capitalism in Japan]. Moscow, Institut mirovoi ekonomiki i mezhdunarodnykh otnoshenii Akademii nauk SSSR, 1959. (Doctor of Economic Sciences degree) 447p. Text in Russian. AB: 29p. summary published in 1960.

Rel.Publ.: Gosudarstvenno-monopolisticheskii kapitalizm v Iaponii posle vtoroi morovoi voiny. Moscow: Izdatel'stvo Akademii Nauk SSSR, 1961. 424p. (Institut mirovoi ekonomiki i mezhdunarodnykh otnoshenii Akademii nauk SSSR)

RAGATZ, Janet E. American, Japanese, and Australian Economic Assistance to Southern Asia: A Comparison of Objectives. 1962. See no.905.

YAMAZAKI, Koji. The Japanese National Pension Scheme and Economic Growth. 1962. See no.74.

SAGRISTA FREIXAS, Antonio. Social Security in Japan: Its Evolution, Present Status, and Economic Implications. 1963. See no.75.

362
CHO, Sei Yong. Japanese Economic Planning, 1952-1962. Columbia, 1965. 249p. DA 27 (July 1966), 39-40-A; UM 66-4766.

Contents: Planning Attempts prior to the Self-Sufficiency Plan; The Self-Sufficiency Plan (1954-1960); The Self-Sufficiency Plan vs. the Actual Performance of the Economy; A Critical Review of the Self-Sufficiency Plan; The New Long-Range Plan (1958-1962); The New Plan vs. the Actual Performance of the Economy; A Critical Review of the New Plan; Doubling National Income Plan (1961-1970); Its Prospects.

CHUNG, Young-iob. The Role of government in the Generation of Saving: The Japanese Experience, 1868-1893. 1965. See no.606.

FROST, Peter K. Tokugawa Monetary Policy. 1966. See no.535.

363
RAMINENI, Ayyanna. A Comparative Analysis of the Kaldor Indian Tax Reforms and the Shoup Mission Japanese Tax Reforms. Minnesota, 1966. 87p. DA 27 (Sept. 1966), 587-A; UM 66-9038.

"The Japanese tax reform plan entitled Report on Japanese Taxation by the Shoup Mission was prepared in 1949 by a committee, composed of American specialists under the chairmanship of Professor Carl S. Shoup, in response to an invitation from SCAP." Contents: Outline of Kaldor's Proposal; Outline of the Shoup Mission's Tax Reform Proposals; Comparison; Evaluation.

364
TANZI, Vito. The Structure of the Individual Income Tax in Major Industrialized Countries: An International Comparison. Harvard, 1967. xi, 314p. AB: summary appended to diss. ms.

An analysis of the structure of the personal income tax in six countries including Japan. Focuses on (1) "the question of 'sacrifice' or 'burden' connected with these taxes; (2) the relationship between the individual income tax and the propensity to save of the household sector; and (3) the relationship of the individual income tax of each country to the growth of the economy."

Rel.Publ.: The Individual Income Tax and Economic Growth: An International Comparison--France, Germany,

Italy, Japan, United Kingdom, and United States. Baltimore: Johns Hopkins University Press, 1969. 136p.; "Comparing International Tax 'Burdens': A Suggested Method," Journal of Political Economy, 76 (Sept./Oct. 1968), 1078-84.

365
KIM, Wan-Soon. Budgetary Policy for Economic Growth in Postwar Japan: 1952-1965. Harvard, 1969. 193p. AB: 5p. summary appended to diss. ms.

Seeks to show that the Japanese budgetary policy was expansionary. "Analyzes ways in which the structure of the budget supported the process of economic growth and attempts to appraise the effects of budget policy in making possible a large flow of funds for financing growth-generating projects."

366
RATCLIFFE, Charles Tait. Tax Policy and Investment Behavior in Postwar Japan. California, Berkeley, 1969. iv, 248p.

Analyzes the determinants of investment behavior in postwar Japan and evaluates in particular the role of tax policy in determining the levels of investment by industry and by type of assets. Contents: The Postwar Tax System; Empirical Results: The Investment Function; Empirical Results: Tax Policy Simulation.

Rel.Publ.: "A Guide to Data Sources for the Study of Investment Behavior in Postwar Japan," Keio Review of Economic Studies, 6(April 1969), 22-40.

THEORY

(Includes theoretical case studies that use Japan as a model or utilize Japanese data.)

367
NGUYEN-xuan-Oanh. Some Aspects of the Theory of Economic Development. Harvard, 1954. vi, 237p. AB: 7p. summary appended to diss. ms.

Japan's economic development, 1890-1937, is used as a case study to verify the author's hypothesis about consumer demand in the underdeveloped economy. See especially "The Japanese Economy and the Japanese Data" (p.158-70).

368
SASAKI, Kyohei. A Western Influence on Japanese Economic Thought: The Marxian Non-Marxian Controversies in the 1920's and Their Significance for Today. Columbia, 1957. 166p. DA 19 (July 1958), 68-69; UM 58-2245.

Examines and evaluates a series of related theoretical controversies centering on the labor theory of value and its relation to price that took place during the 1920's between the Marxian and Non-Marxian Schools of economic thought. An "examination of the characteristics of Japanese economic thought in the past as well as its future prospects" is also included within the study.

TAKEUCHI, Kenji. The "Classical" Theories of International Trade and the Expansion of Foreign Trade in Japan from 1859 to 1892. 1962. See no.267.

369
NARASIMHAM, Gorti Venkata Lakshmi. Economic Models of Growth and Planning. Pittsburgh, 1964. 150p. DA 26 (Sept. 1965), 1380; UM 65-5214.

In one part of the thesis, the author attempted to study empirically the economic growth and fluctuations of Japan and of five other countries.

Rel.Publ.: "Measurement and Mechanism of Economic Growth with Particular Reference to India," Economia Internazionale, 18 (May 1965), 265-79; "Theory of Trend Movements in Aggregate Economic Growth Models" [by] G. Tintner and G.V.L. Narasimham, Metroeconomia, 18 (Apr. 1966), 31-39.

NAYA, Seiji. The Leontief Paradox and the Factor Structure of Japanese Foreign Trade. 1965. See no.274.

370
LEE, Pong Seok. The Doctrine of Balanced Growth: With Special Reference to Japan, 1878-1918. Yale, 1966. 155p. DA 27 (July 1966), 4-A; UM 66-4905.

Three closely interrelated hypotheses of balanced growth--"(1) a simultaneous diversification of economy, (2) a diversification for the domestic consumers' market rather than international specialization, and (3) growth rate of production in each industry is largely determined by the income elasticity of demand"--are tested with respect to the Japanese experience.

371
YOSHIHARA, Kunio. An Econometric Study of Japanese Economic Development. California, Berkeley, 1966. 436p. DA 27 (May 1967), 3602-03-A; UM 67-5197.

Uses four existing long-term models of Japan in order to explain Japanese economic development, and improves two of the functions that are unsatisfactory in all of them: the aggregate consumption and the demand functions. Contents: Long-Term Models of the Japanese Economy; Aggregate Consumption Function; Demand Functions: An Application to the Japanese Expenditure Pattern.

Rel.Publ.: "Juyō kansū no ichi kenkyū," Keizai kenkyū, 18 (Oct. 1967), 367-72; "Demand Functions: An Application to the Japanese Expenditure Pattern," Econometrica, 37 (Apr. 1969); "Long-Term Models of the Japanese Economy," Economic Studies Quarterly (Tokyo), 20 (Dec. 1969), 40-63.

372
BICKEL, Gary William. Factor Proportions and Relative Price under C.E.S. Production Functions: An Empirical Study of Japanese-U.S. Comparative Advantage. Stanford, 1967. 237p. DA 28 (Aug. 1967), 376-77-A; UM 67-7896.

"Utilizes detailed and complete factor-use data from the Japanese and United States input-output materials and detailed data on 1951 Japanese-United States relative commodity prices." Note: "C.E.S." refers to 'constant-elasticity-of-substitution.'

373
BARSBY, Steven Loren. An Empirical Examination of the Gerschenkron Hypothesis: Economic Backwardness and the Characteristics of Development. Oregon, 1968. 175p. DA 29 (Jan. 1969), 2023-A; UM 69-4.

Japan is one of eleven countries whose data was used to test the hypothesis.

Rel.Publ.: "Economic Backwardness and the Characteristics of Development," Journal of Economic History, 29 (Sept. 1969), 449-72.

374
SAKAKIBARA, Eisuke. Optimal Growth and Stabilization Policies. Michigan, 1969. 183p. DA 30 (Mar. 1970);

UM 70-4180.

"The purpose of this study is the construction and analysis of a theoretical model designed for the simultaneous determination of the optimal levels (over time) of actual and full employment GNP, given a specific social welfare function and a specific economy represented by a system of equations." Ch.10, "Evaluations of Economic Policies in Japan" (p.116-39), applies the theoretical concepts developed in the study to an evaluation of the effects of postwar economic policies in Japan.

TRANSPORTATION AND COMMUNICATIONS

See also History--Japanese empire--Manchoukuo (pages 96-97) and International Relations (pages 104-63).

375
KODAMA, Riotaro. Railway Transportation in Japan. Michigan, 1898. Diss. ms. not available.

Contents: General Remarks; History of Railway Development (State Railways, The Private Railways, The Railways of Hokkaido, Statistical Review of Railways); The Administration and Regulation of Railways (The Railroad Bureau, The Railway Council, The Legislature and Railways, State Railway Regulations, Private Railway Regulation); On Railway Improvement (The Principal Defects of the Existing Railway System, Suggestions as to Improvement); Our Future Railway Policy, with Reference to Remedies.

Rel.Publ.: Railway...Japan. Ann Arbor: Register Job Rooms, 1898. 72p.

376
GOTO, Rokuya. Die japanische Seeschiffahrt [Japanese Ocean Shipping]. Berlin, 1901. Text in German. The dissertation in its published form is available at Berlin West, Staatsbibliothek Preussischer Kulturbesitz, Nr. Ah 7856.

The historical development of steamship lines and shipping companies in Japan: The impact of the Tokugawa seclusion policy and the rapid growth of maritime shipping following the opening of the country and Japan's entrance into world trade.

Rel.Publ.: Dic japanische Seeschiffahrt. Berlin: E. Ebering, 1901. 30p.

377
WATARAI, Toshiharu. Nationalization of Railways in Japan. Columbia, 1915. 156p.

In addition to a detailed discussion of the state operation of railways in Japan, the dissertation includes chapters on the historical development of Japan's railways and on freight rate and passenger fare policies.

Rel.Publ.: Nationalization...Japan. New York: Columbia University, 1915. 156p. (Studies in History, Economics, and Public Law, ed. by the Faculty of Political Science of Columbia University. v.63. no.2; whole no.152)

378
CROCKATT, Peter Campbell. Trans-Pacific Shipping since 1914. California, Berkeley, 1922. 314p.

Includes a description of the development of Japanese shipping services in the Pacific, 1914-1920.

379
GOLDAMMER, Heinz. Seefahrt und Schiffbau Japans als Exponenten seiner gesamten Entwicklung [Japanese Overseas Shipping and Shipbuilding as an Indicator of Japan's Entire Development]. Heidelberg, 1922. xi, 129p. Text in German. Diss. ms. available at Heidelberg, Universitätsbibliothek, Nr. W 710.

Pt.1 studies the general economic foundations for Japanese shipping. Pt.2 presents an historical survey of Japanese overseas shipping before the Sino-Japanese War as well as a study of how the policies of the major powers, 1894-1914, served as the basic factor in the development of Japanese sea power. Pt.3 focuses on Japanese ship construction, fishing, government subsidies, and port development.

380
ZINDLER, Herbert Georg. Die Entwicklung der japanischen Handelsschiffahrt [The Development of the Japanese Merchant Marine]. Würzburg, 1925. viii, 314p. Text in German. Diss. ms. available at Marburg/Lahn, Staatsbibliothek Preussischer Kulturbesitz, Nr. MS 25/8381.

The author first presents an historical survey of Japanese shipping, then examines in detail the modernization of Japanese shipping and its development through 1923. He also studies the production of marine products, the training of crews to man the ships, the construction of modern harbors, and the development of a navy. Statistical tables for ship construction, the number of ships, and marine insurance are included.

381
HERRMANN, Gerhard. Die japanische seeschiffahrt vor und nach dem Weltkriege [Japanese Maritime Shipping before and after World War I]. Leipzig, 1926. ii, 144p. Text in German. Diss. ms. available at Leipzig, Universitätsbibliothek.

Pt.1 examines the significance of Japan's geographical position for her maritime shipping and presents the basic characteristics of Japan's foreign trade, 1913-1922. Pt.2 focuses on the organization of Japanese maritime shipping: the supply of ships and ship construction; the Japanese system of shipping subsidies; the position of Japanese shipping in the world; the Japanese shipping companies and the formation of Japanese maritime shipping associations.

382
TRIBOLET, Leslie Bennett. The International Aspects of Electrical Communications in the Pacific Area. Johns Hopkins, 1928. ii, 229p.

See especially Ch.4 of the book, "Japan."

Rel.Publ.: The International...Area. Baltimore: Johns Hopkins Press, 1929. vii, 282p. (Johns Hopkins University Series in Historical and Political Science. Extra v. New ser.,4)

383
SUGIMOTO, Yuzo. Die japanische seeschiffahrt [Japanese Ocean Shipping]. Hamburg, 1936. Text in German. The dissertation in its published form is available at Marburg/Lahn, Universitätsbibliothek, Nr. XVII C; also at the University of Michigan, General Library, no. HE891.S95.

The author discusses the importance of ocean shipping by examining the economic and geographical situation of Japan and by studying the role that Japanese shipping has played in the country's entire cultural development. He then points out how significant shipping has been for Japan's balance of payments. Finally he reviews the development of the Japanese shipbuilding industry (1636-1930's) and the growth of Japan's overseas shipping since the Tokugawa period, focusing on its organization and on the assistance that it received from the government.

Rel.Publ.: Die japanische Seeschiffahrt. Hamburg: Niemann und Moschinski, 1935. 155p.

384
SHELDON, Charles Stuart, II. The Japanese Shipping Industry: An Analysis of Some Phases of the Industry in Relation to International Economic Rivalries. Harvard, 1942. ix, 400p. AB: Harvard University. Summaries of Theses...1942. p.216-17.

Contents: Location Theory and Japanese Industrial Development; The Development of Japanese Shipping; Japanese Shipping as an Export Industry; Monopolistic Competition and Japanese Shipping; International Rivalries Related to the Economic Sphere.

POPOV, K. M. Tekhno-ekonomicheskaia baza Iaponii: I. Problemy energetiki i khimizatsii Iaponii. II. Problemy metallurgii, mashinostroitel'noi bazy i transportnaia sistema Iaponii. 1943. See no.208.

GINSBURG, Norton S. Japanese Prewar Trade and Shipping in the Oriental Triangle. 1949. See no.904.

385
GEYMÜLLER, Urs. Staatlicher Protektionismus zur See zwischen den beiden Weltkriegen unter besonderer Berücksichtigung der 6 Gross-Schiffahrtsländer Deutschland, Frankreich, Grossbritannien, Italien, Japan, und der Vereinigten Staaten [State Protectionism on the Sea between the Two World Wars, with Special Consideration of the Six Major Naval Powers: Germany, France, Great Britain, Italy, Japan, and the United States of America]. Basel, 1953. Text in German.

Discusses the economic and political goals of state protection and the various kinds of state subsidies to the shipping industry.

Rel.Publ.: Staatlicher...Staaten. Lorrach-Stetten: Karl Schahl, 1953. 142p.

NEVILLE, Edwin L., Jr. The Development of Transportation in Japan: A Case Study of Okayama Han, 1600-1868. 1959. See no.525.

386
RUSETSKII, S. B. Transport Iaponii posle 2-oi mirovoi voiny [Japanese Transportation after World War II]. Moscow, Institut mirovoi ekonomiki i mezhdunarodnykh otnoshenii Akademii nauk SSSR, 1963. (Candidate of Economic Sciences degree) 193p. Text in Russian.

387
LEVIKOV, G. A. Voprosy razvitiia morskogo sudokhodstva poslevoennoi Iaponii [Problems in the Development of Postwar Japanese Shipping]. Moscow, Moskovskii gosudarstvennyi universitet imeni M. V. Lomonosova, 1968. (Candidate of Economic Sciences degree) 246p. Text in Russian.

Rel.Publ.: Morskoi transport poslevoennoi Iaponii. Moscow: "Nauka," 1969. 263p.

Education

GENERAL

See also History--Japanese empire (pages 90-99) and Overseas Japanese communities (pages 198-208).

388
NISHIYAMA, Sekiji. The Educational History of Japan. New York, 1910. Diss. ms. not available.

389
HOFFSOMER, Walter Edward. The Japanese Middle School. Columbia (Teachers College), 1918. 158p.

Focuses on the development of the Japanese middle school and on its curriculum.

390
TAKEMAYE, Riotaro. Die Modernisierung des japanischen Erziehungswesens in den letzten 50 Jahren [The Modernization of the Japanese Educational System during the Past Fifty Years]. Jena, 1929. Text in German. The dissertation in its published form is available at Marburg/Lahn, Universitätsbibliothek, Nr. XV C; also at the University of Michigan, General Library, no. LA1311.7.T14.

The modernization of the educational system is shown by a study of (1) educational reforms undertaken during the Meiji era, (2) the influence of Buddhism, Confucianism, and Western educational methods upon the system, and (3) national elements present in the Japanese educational system during the 1920's.

Rel.Publ.: Die Modernisierung...Jahren. Jena: Peuvag-Filiale, 1929. 87p.

HATSUKADE, Itsuaki. Die Bildungsideale in der japanischen Kultur und ihr Einfluss auf das Erziehungswesen in der Yedo-Zeit. 1932. See no.507.

391
MURAKAMI, Komao. Das japanische Erziehungswesen [The Japanese Educational System]. Giessen, 1934. The dissertation in its published form is available at Marburg/Lahn, Universitätsbibliothek, Nr. XV C; also at the University of Michigan, General Library, no. LA1312.M97.

Contents: Development of Education in Japan; Characteristics of Japanese Education; The Imperial Rescript on Education; Family and School; The School System; Kindergarten and Elementary School; Higher Schools; Trade Schools, High Schools, and Universities; Business Schools; Teacher Training; System of Adult Education; Education in the Colonies; Schools and Middle-Class Society; The Future of Japanese Education.

Rel.Publ.: Das japanische Erziehungswesen. Tokyo: Fuzambō, 1934. viii, 286p.

392
ZIMMERMANN, Herbert. Politische Erziehung der Militärklasse (Samurai) in Japan zur Feudalzeit [The Political Education of the Samurai Class during the Feudal Period]. Leipzig, 1935. Text in German. The dissertation in its published form is available at Marburg/Lahn, Universitätsbibliothek, Nr. XVIII C.

Focuses on the social rank, political position, and political education of the samurai class during the Tokugawa period. The educational system and the various educational ideals of the samurai are studied and character education as a political goal of education is given special consideration.

Rel.Publ.: Politische...Feudalzeit. Würzburg: Triltsch, 1935. 81p.

393
FURUKAWA, Jiryo. Samurai und Bodhisattva: Die Bestimmung des japanischen Erziehungs-Ideal durch die buddhistische Ethik [Samurai and Bodhisattva: The Japanese Educational Ideal Determined by Means of Buddhist Ethics]. Heidelberg, 1939. Text in German. The dissertation in its published form is available at Marburg/Lahn, Universitätsbibliothek, Nr. XIV B.

A study of (1) the political and religious crisis that occurred as a result of Japan's cultural contacts with China, (2) the teachings and activities of Dengyō (767-822), and (3) the ensuing development of Japanese Buddhism, its position within the state, and the ideals of samurai education. The author pays special attention to the Japanese ideal of education and to the influence that Buddhist ethics have had in shaping it, and he seeks to determine how the nature of the Japanese people is reflected in it.

Rel.Publ.: Samurai...Ethik. Tokyo: Kyorinsha, 1938. 72p.

394
MIYAZAWA, Jiro. Das Erziehungswesen in der Tokugawa-Zeit in kultur- und sozialgeschichtlicher Beleuchtung [The Educational System during the Tokugawa Period: Its Cultural and Social Historical Aspects]. Berlin, 1942. iv, 184p. Diss. ms. available at Berlin, Humboldt Universität, Universitätsbibliothek, Nr. P8.

A study of Japanese society before and during the Tokugawa period, of the rise and decline of the samurai class and the growth of the middle class, of contemporary religious currents, and of the hangakkō (han schools), terakoya (temple schools), kajuku (private schools), and shijuku (private schools).

395
POUSSON, Leon Bernard. The Totalitarian Philosophy of Education. Catholic, 1944. 164p.
A study of "four distinct, but related, systems of education as evolved and put into practice in Germany, Italy, Japan, and Russia." See especially Ch.4, "Japan" (p.88-118), which deals with the earliest backgrounds of education in Japan, the effect of the Meiji Restoration on education, and administration, and elementary, secondary, higher, social, and adult education in Japan of the 1930's.
Rel.Publ.: The Totalitarian...Education. Washington: Catholic University of America Press, 1944. ix, 164p. (Catholic University of America Philosophical Studies, 80)

THONAK, Otto. Über den Ideengehalt der japanischen Herzenslehre und die Organisation der auf sie gegründeten Volkserziehungsbewegung. 1944. See no.1958.

SPAE, Joseph J. Itō Jinsai: A Philosopher, Educator, and Sinologist of the Tokugawa Period. 1947. See no.1959.

396
IBANEZ, Dalmyra Montgomery. A Study of the Cultural Background of Japanese Education. Southern California, 1948. 285p. AB: University of Southern California. Abstracts of Dissertations...1948. p.243-44.
"Presents the historical development of the Japanese educational system up to 1941 in relation to the cultural...movements throughout the nation's growth in order to determine how education was developed from and by these influences."

SCHWANTES, Robert S. American Influence in the Education of Meiji Japan, 1868-1912. 1950. See no.563.

397
CROSS, Edmond. Japanese Education, 1868-1953, with Emphasis on Various Phases of Education in Aomori Prefecture. Columbia (Teachers College), 1954. 302p.
A study of education in Japan both before and after the Occupation with emphasis on the prefectural and the local levels and on the Japanese teacher and the school curriculum.

398
MAMMARELLA, Raymond Joseph. Contemporary Education and the Spirit of Zen. Columbia (Teachers College), 1959. 144p.
The study includes a historical survey of Zen and outlines a plan for a humanistic education based on Zen principles that would be directed to the discovery of the "higher and wider significance of life."

399
LODUCHOWSKI, Heinrich. Progressive, demokratische koedukation: Ihre Entwicklung und Auswirkung in den USA und Japan [Progressive, Democratic Coeducation: Its Development and Consequences in the United States and in Japan]. Trier, Theologische Fakultät, 1960. Diss. ms. not available. Text in German.
Rel.Publ.: "Amerikanische Demokratie als Lebensform im japanischen Schul- und Familiensystem: Ein pädagogisches Experiment in einem moralischen Vakuum," MN, 17 (1962), 67-125.

IKEDA, Namiko. A Comparison of Physical Fitness of Children in Iowa, U.S.A., and Tokyo, Japan. 1961. See no.19.

KITAMURA, Fusako. A Study of the Japan Teachers Union and Recommendations for Improvement. 1962. See no. 1853.

AVEN, James S. The Organization of American Community Schools in the Far East. 1963. See no.1419.

400
KOBAYASHI, Victor Nobuo. John Dewey in Japanese Educational Thought. Michigan, 1964. 203p. DA 25 (June 1965), 7060; UM 65-5332.
A study of the growing Japanese interest in Dewey since 1945 and a consideration of "the way in which educationists came to study this major American thinker and how they viewed his ideas, particularly those on democratic education." The prewar progressive education movement also is examined.
Rel.Publ.: John...Thought. Ann Arbor, 1964. v, 198p. (University of Michigan, Comparative Education Dissertation Series, 2); "Nationalism and Educational Progressivism in Japan: 1900-1941," Educational and Psychological Review (Bombay), 6 (Apr. 1966), 82-92; "Japan Progressive Movement and the Rise of National Schools," Teachers College Record, 68 (Apr. 1967), 551-57.

401
MÜLLER, Christa. Erziehung und industrielle Entwicklung: Die Bedeutung des Erziehungswesens für die industrielle Entwicklung, erlangt am Beispiel Japans [Education and Industrial Development: The Importance of the Educational System for Industrial Development as Seen in the Case of Japan]. Frankfurt, 1964. Text in German. The dissertation in its published form is available at Marburg/Lahn, Staatsbibliothek Preussischer Kulturbesitz, Nr. Hsn 60,144; also at the University of Michigan, General Library, no. 32,338.
Studies the influence of the Japanese educational system upon Japan's industrial development: (1) the educational system in Japan before 1868, (2) the educational system between 1868 and World War II, with focus on the Japanese cultural tradition and its confrontation with the Western mind, and on the organization of the educational system and its objectives, and (3) the reform of the educational system after World War II.
Rel.Publ.: Erziehung...Japans. Frankfurt a.M., 1964. 226p.

CESSNA, William C., Jr. The Psychosocial Nature and Determinants of Attitudes toward Education and toward Physically Disabled Persons in Japan. 1967. See no.1876.

SHIMAHARA, Nobuo. A Study of the Enculturative Roles of Japanese Education. 1967. See no.16.

402
MEDALLADA, Jacinto Arevalo. Socio-Economic Development Practices through the Public Elementary and Secondary Schools in Taiwan, Japan, and Mexico and Their Applicability for the Bicol Region, Philippines. Nebraska, 1968. 290p. DA 29 (June 1969), 4238-39-A; UM 69-9632.
Includes data on fifteen socio-economic development practices in Japan.

HALL, Ivan P. Mori Arinori: A Reconsideration. 1969. See no.611.

403
YOSHIKAWA, Hildegard Fusae. A Comparative Study of the Philosophical Orientation of Catholic and Public High Schools in Japan. Catholic, 1969. 211p. DA 30 (Nov. 1969), 1930-31-A; UM 69-19, 776.

"It was determined that the Catholic high schools were distinguished from the public high schools in their educational purposes and their concrete educational content, both of which were governed by the philosophical foundation peculiar to the type of school in each instance. In attempting to approach educational problems, the public high schools were inclined to start with an explanation of 'existence,' that is, of prevailing personal and social needs. This tended to lead them to an exclusive reliance on the results of scientific inquiry of a psychological and sociological nature. As a result, they offered an anthrocentric type of education. In contrast to this, the Catholic high schools started from a reference to the 'reason for existence.' They first sought to determine the why of education and what education ought to do. Their education therefore was theocentric."

ADMINISTRATION AND POLICY

See also: Education--higher, adult, and teacher education (pages 56-57), Education--religious education (pages 57-58), and Overseas Japanese communities (pages 198-208).

404
STEIG, Milan B. The Administration of Schools in Tokyo, Japan, 1945-1950. Nihon University, Tokyo, 1950/51. AB: Bungaku, Tetsugaku, Shigaku Gakkai Rengo. Kenkyū rombun-shū. v.4, p.214-16.

A study of "the actual condition of school education in Tokyo during the post-war years, with particular reference to the recommendations of two United States education missions and to the way that the new educational program has been adopted and developed."

DOI, James I. Educational Reform in Occupied Japan, 1945-1950: A Study of Acceptance of and Resistance to Institutional Change. 1952. See no.1815.

405
KERLINGER, Frederick Nichols. The Development of Democratic Control in Japanese Education: A Study of Attitude Change in Shikoku, 1948-1949. Michigan, 1953. 254p. DA 13 (1953), 722-23; UM 5686.

"The main objective is to demonstrate that a change from authoritarianism to democracy has taken place in Japanese education and attitudes during the Allied Occupation of Japan....Japanese educational administration and ideology, together with the attitudes of educators and the people toward education before and during the occupation, are examined for evidence of change. The underlying hypotheses of the study are tested by examining the educational changes that occurred in one area of Japan, Shikoku, during one period, October 1948 to November 1949, to determine the extent and depth of Occupation influence."

Rel.Publ.: Techniques of Democracy: A Guide to Procedure for Japanese Organizations. Takamatsu, Japan, 1948. 66p.; "The Modern Origin of Morals Instruction in Japanese Education," History of Education Journal, 2 (Summer 1951), 119-26; "Decision-making in Japan," Social Forces, 30 (Oct. 1951), 36-41; "Local Associations of Shikoku," in University of Michigan, Center for Japanese Studies, Occasional Papers, 2 (Ann Arbor: University of Michigan Press, 1952), 59-72.

406
ANDERSON, Paul Seward. The Reorientation Activities of the Civil Education Section of the Osaka Civil Affairs Team: A Case Study in Educational Change. Wisconsin, 1954. 437p. AB: University of Wisconsin. Summaries of Doctoral Dissertations. v.15, p.510-12.

A description and analysis of SCAP's efforts to guide the reorientation activities of the Japanese educational program in Osaka prefecture from October 1945 until November 1949. Among the changes introduced were ones affecting school organizations and school boards, adult education, women's groups, information services, and cultural, religious, and youth activities.

CHAPMAN, John G. The Re-Education of the Japanese People. 1954. See no.1824.

407
ORR, Mark Taylor. Education Reform Policy in Occupied Japan. North Carolina, 1954. 278p. AB: University of North Carolina Record, 548 (Oct. 1955), 231-32.

Concerned with the reshaping of the Japanese educational system, 1945-1952. Examines Japanese educational policy and the governmental machinery for making reform policy, the reform policies themselves, and the ways in which policy was formulated and applied. Contents: Japanese Education Policy; Control of Education by the Japanese Government; The Organs of Educational Reform; Objectives of Allied Education Policy; Decentralization of Controls over Education; Procedures in the Formulation and Application of Education.

Rel.Publ.: "Military Occupation of Japan, 1945-1952," in Yearbook of Education, ed. by Robert K. Hall, N. Hans, and J. A. Lauwerys (London: Evans Bros., 1954), 413-24.

408
NAOI, John Yutaka. The Educational Reformation in Japan after World War II. Catholic, 1955. 305p. AB: Catholic Educational Review, 53 (Dec. 1955), 621-22.

Contents: Totalitarian Philosophy of Education in Prewar Japan (Development and Metaphysics of Totalitarianism, Man and Society, Principles of Life in Totalitarianism); Democratic Philosophy of Education; Philosophy of Education of New Democratic Japan (Meaning of Democracy, Man and Society, Democratic Principles, Educational Aims and Values); Educational Organization of Prewar Japan (Government and Education, Legal Status of Public School Teachers and Pupils); Educational Organization of Postwar Japan (Principles of Reorganization, Process of Legislation, Legal Basis of School Education, Administrative Organization for Education, Criticism of Administrative Reorganization).

MURRAY, Robert A. Education as an Instrument of Japanese Governmental Policy, 1918-1945. 1956. See no.633.

409
SCHMIDT, Erwin Alfred. Die ersten Hoch- und Privatschulen Japans im Lichte zeitgenossischer Gesetze und Verfügungen [Japan's First Higher Schools and First Private Schools in the Light of Contemporary Laws and Decrees]. München, 1956. 127p. Text in German. Diss. ms. available at München, Universitätsbibliothek, Nr. U1956.7028.

A study of the Japanese school ststem from its beginnings through the end of the Heian Period. Includes information on the higher schools and on the organization and educational activities of the provincial and private schools.

410
BLUMHAGEN, Herman Herbert. Nationalistic Policies and Japanese Public Education from 1928 to March 31, 1947. Rutgers, 1957. 314p. DA 18 (May 1958), 1708-09; UM 22,566.
Analyzes "the effects which nationalistic policies and the educational program had in making it possible for the Japanese to accept the government's propaganda leading to war."

BENOIT, Edward G. A Study of Japanese Education as Influenced by the Occupation. 1958. See no.1828.

COHEN, Abraham. The Impact of the American Occupation upon the Culture and Education of Okinawa. 1961. See no.695.

BALTZ, William M. The Role of American Educators in the Decentralization and Reorganization of Education in Postwar Japan (1945-1952). 1965. See no.1830.

411
HARSAGHY, Fred Joseph. The Administration of American Cultural Projects Abroad: A Developmental Study with Case Histories of Community Relations in Administering Educational and Informational Projects in Japan and Saudi Arabia. New York, 1965. 820p. DA 27 (Dec. 1966), 1899-A; UM 66-5730.
"Part two presents a major case history of an American education project in postwar Japan, with special reference to the Hakodate Information Center....Included are analyses and background materials covering: historical, geographical, and cultural aspects of Japanese life and customs; illustrations of political and personnel problems; personnel selection, staffing, and training of Japanese staffs; budgetary and financial control of information programs; and program planning of community functions and the public relations effort."

412
SINGLETON, John Calhoun. Education as an Instrument of National Policy: A Case Study of a Modern Japanese Middle School and Its Communities. Stanford, 1965. 345p. DA 26 (Jan. 1966), 3708-09; UM 65-12,865.
"Specific attention was given to identifying the Japanese government's national policy in education, the manner in which it is transmitted to local schools, and its effect upon the local school where it interacts with other sources of influence."

CURRICULUM, TEXTBOOKS, AND EDUCATIONAL MEDIA

(Includes course content and educational television.)
See also Education--higher, adult, and teacher education (pages 56-57) and Education--religious education (pages 57-58).

413
TAKAYAMA, Kiyoshi. Fundamental Considerations Underlying the Reconstruction of the School Curriculum in Japan: A Sociological Search for Criteria of the Reconstruction of the Public Elementary School Curriculum in View of the Modern Transition in the National Life of Japan, Especially since 1918. New York, 1928. 240p.
Contents: A Brief Historical Survey of the Origin of Contemporary Japan; A Political Diagnosis and Prognosis (The Japanese Constitution and Modern Political Development, The Working of Ruling Forces in Japanese Politics, The Growth of the Liberal Movement); A Social Diagnosis and Prognosis; The Industrial and Commercial Development of Japan; An Educational Diagnosis and Prognosis (Uniformity in Education, Moral Education, Religious Resources and Problems, A Critical Study of the Government Courses of the Elementary School); Proposed Criteria for Curriculum Reconstruction Based on the Nature of Modern Social Change in Japan.

414
KASUYA, Yoshi. A Comparative Study of the Secondary Education of Girls in England, Germany, and the United States, with a Consideration of the Secondary Education of Girls in Japan. Columbia (Teachers College), 1933. x, 211p.
See Ch.8, "The Secondary Education of Girls in Japan and a Tentative Application of the Findings of the Comparative Study to the Consideration of Its Reforms" (p.179-202).
Rel.Publ.: A Comparative...Japan. New York: Teachers College, Columbia University, 1933. x, 211p. (Teachers College, Columbia University. Contributions to Education, 566)

WUNDERLICH, Herbert J. The Japanese Textbook Problem and Solution, 1945-1946. 1952. See no.1819.

415
LEE, Sookney. Primary Arithmetic Textbooks in Korea, Japan, China, and the United States. Iowa, 1954. 401p. DA 14 (Oct. 1954), 1584; UM 9586.
Uses the Sansū no Gakushū series and the Atarashii Sansū series for Japan.

SAITO, Mitsuko. Speech Education in Japan in the Latter Half of the Nineteenth Century. 1957. See no.598.

SONG, Un Sun. A Sociological Analysis of the Value System of Pre-war Japan as Revealed in the Japanese Government Elementary School Textbooks, 1933-1941. 1958. See no.79.

416
WATANABE, Akira. Mass Communication and Education. Hiroshima, 1961. Diss. ms. available at the National Diet Library, Tokyo.

417
NISHIMOTO, Yoichi. Improving Moral Education in the Upper Elementary Grades in Japan. Columbia (Teachers College), 1962. 422p. DA 23 (Nov. 1962), 1628; UM 62-4909.
Contents: The Problem of Moral Education in Japan; Development of Japanese Moral Thought: An Historical Background; The Ideals of Democracy; Prospects for Democracy in Japan; Some Important Considerations that Make Moral Education in a Democracy Unique; Provisions for Moral Education in the School Program.

418
WATANABE, Sister St. John the Baptist, S.N.D. The Tradition of Filial Piety and Japanese Moral Education. Boston College, 1962. ii, 213p.
Contents: The Problem of Moral Education in Con-

temporary Japan; The Tradition of Filial Piety up to the Meiji Restoration; An Analysis of Morals Textbooks between 1868 and 1902; An Analysis of Morals Textbooks between 1903 and 1945; The Tradition of Filial Piety after 1945.

419
KAO, Ming-huey. An Analysis of Moral Education in Japanese Public Schools, 1945-1960. Southern Illinois, 1964. 398p. DA 26 (Apr. 1966), 5917; UM 66-1077.

"Traces and analyzes the development of three movements--the pragmatic, the conservative, and the socialistic--in postwar Japan's moral education from the viewpoints of historical background, social background, and the three corresponding centers of social forces: SCAP, the conservatives, and the 'progressives.'"

420
CAIGER, John Godwin. Education, Values, and Japan's National Identity: A Study of the Aims and Contents of Courses in Japanese History, 1872-1963. Australian National, 1967. 313p.

Rel.Publ.: "A 'Reverse Course' in the Teaching of History in Postwar Japan?" Journal of the Oriental Society of Australia, 5 (Dec. 1967), 4-16; "Aims and Content of School Courses in Japanese History, 1872-1945," in Japan's Modern Century, ed. by Edmund Skrzypczak (Tokyo: Sophia University Press, 1968), 51-81; "Ienaga Saburō and the First Postwar Japanese History Textbook," Modern Asian Studies, 3 (Jan. 1969), 1-16.

421
VERA, José María de. Educational Television in Japan. Michigan, 1967. 238p. DA 28 (Dec. 1967), 1980-A; UM 67-15,612.

"The first four chapters...cover the concept and philosophy of educational TV in Japan, the content of the programs, the audience, and the effects and effectiveness of TV on the learning process. A final chapter was devoted to an appraisal of Japanese educational TV." Considerable attention is paid to Nihon Hōsō Kyōkai [NHK], the Japan Broadcasting Corporation.

Rel. Publ.: Educational...Japan. Tokyo: Sophia University; Rutland, Vt.: Tuttle, 1968. x, 140p.

HIGHER, ADULT, AND TEACHER EDUCATION

See also Education--religious education (pages 57-58).

422
KAWACHI, Risaku. An Analytical Study of the Reorganization Movements and Their Underlying Philosophies of the Teacher Training System of Nippon, Compared with Those of Other Countries. Southern California, 1935. 415p.

"Attempts to discover characteristics and weaknesses of the present normal-school system in Japan, in respect to administration and underlying philosophies, for the purpose of aiding in the attainment of educational goals by means of reorganization."

423
GRIFFITH, Harry Elmer. Japanese Normal School Education. Stanford, 1950. 392p. AB: Stanford University. Abstracts of Dissertations, 1949/50. p.364-69.

Pt.1: History of Japanese education prior to 1867. Pt.2: The normal schools between 1867 and 1945. Pt.3: "The changes, both actual and proposed, that have taken place in normal school education since 1945." Pt.4: "Proposals for a program of normal school education that would incorporate democratic principles."

SUH, Doo Soo. The Struggle for Academic Freedom in Japanese Universities before 1945. 1953. See no.550.

NELSON, John M. The Adult-Education Program in Occupied Japan, 1946-1950. 1954. See no.1825.

424
MESHIZUKA, Tetsuo. A Program of Professional Training in Physical Education for Colleges and Universities in Japan. Iowa, 1956. 175p. DA 16 (Nov. 1956), 2087; UM 18,548.

The main objective of the author was to propose and to develop a specific program.

425
AOKI, Hideo. The Effect of American Ideas upon Japanese Higher Education. Stanford, 1957. 363p. DA 17 (July 1957), 1506; UM 21,563.

"Traces the evolution of Japanese higher education from 701 A.D. to 1945," appraises two early periods of American influence--the 1870's and 1920's--"in terms of their relationship and significance to the historical development of Japanese higher education," and pays particular attention to SCAP-initiated educational reforms.

426
MITA, Setsuko. A Comparative Study of the Preparation of School Music Teachers in Japan and the United States. Michigan State, 1957. 281p. DA 18 (Jan. 1957), 250; UM 23,468.

Contents: Brief History of Music Education in Japan up to World War II; After World War II; Development of Music Teacher Education in Japan (up to 1945); Present Music Teacher Education in Japan; The Evaluation of Music Teacher Education by Secondary School Music Teachers in Japan; Brief History of Music Education in the United States; Development of Music Teacher Education in the United States; Present Music Teacher Education in the United States; Evaluation of College Training by American Secondary School Music Teachers.

427
TSURU, Haruo. Japanese Universities in a Changing Society: A Study of Some Historical, Sociological, and Psychological Bases of Student Personnel Work in Japanese Universities. Columbia (Teachers College), 1958. 449p.

Investigates student personnel work in Japanese universities and traces the development of the officially stated aims of higher education in Japan from the pre-gakusei period (early ages to 1872) to the mid-1950's.

KING, Horace C. An Analysis of Educational-Administrative-Cultural Aspects of the Relationship between the University of the Ryukyus and Michigan State University. 1962. See no.696.

KURODA, Yasumasa. Political Socialization: Personal Political Organization of Law Students in Japan. 1962. See no.1796.

MELLOH, Sister M. Tolentine. Planning for the Development of a Home Economics Curriculum for a Japanese

College. 1963. See no.802.

428
KOBAYASHI, Tetsuya. General Education for Scientists and Engineers in the United States of America and Japan. Michigan, 1965. 401p. DA 26 (Nov. 1965), 2576; UM 65-10,984.

A comparative analysis of the trends in national policies and public opinion on the objectives of general education for scientists and engineers between 1945 and 1962.

Rel.Publ.: General...Japan. Ann Arbor, 1965. iv, 404p. (University of Michigan, Comparative Education Dissertation Series, 6); "Die Reform des japanischen Bildungswesen seit 1945 und ihr Einfluss auf die Gesellschaft," Internationales Jahrbuch für Geschichtsunterricht, 9 (1963/64), 65-70.

429
O'CONNELL, Alfred Christopher. Junior College Education in Japan. Columbia (Teachers College), 1965. 238p. DA 26 (Aug. 1965), 851; UM 65-8853.

Examines and assesses "in historical perspective the nature and development of junior college-level education in Japan," "determines the extent of American influence upon Japanese junior colleges, particularly since 1945," and "compares and contrasts the junior college scene in the United States and Japan."

430
OWADA, Yasuyuki. The Dynamics of College Administration: A Study of Interpersonal Relations in the X University Administration, Tokyo, Japan. Columbia (Teachers College), 1966. 454p. DA 27 (Oct. 1966), 911-12-A; UM 66-10,308.

A case study of the "interactions of Japanese and Americans who were engaged in the fourteen-year process of determining a site for the plant development for the university's physical education program."

431
RODIONOV, M. L. Obshcheobrazovatel'naia shkola Iaponii posle 2-oi mirovoi voiny [General Education Schools of Japan after the Second World War]. Moscow, Nauchno-issledovatel'skii institut teorii i istorii pedagogiki Akademii pedagogicheskikh nauk SSSR, 1967. (Candidate of Pedagogical Sciences degree) 274p. Text in Russian. AB: 21p summary published in 1967.

432
KAMITSUKA, Arthur Jun. A Conceptual Scheme for an Adaptation of Participation Training in Adult Education for Use in the Three Love Movement of Japan. Indiana, 1968. 308p. DA 29 (Mar. 1969), 2948-49-A; UM 69-4762.

The "Three Love Movement" is an adult education program of education extension sponsored by Rakunō Gakuen Daigaku (College of Dairy Agriculture) and the Hokkai Kyoku (Hokkaido District) of the Nihon Kirisuto Kyōden (United Church of Christ in Japan). Instruction is provided by specialists in agriculture, social studies, and religion. Emphasis is placed on the "three loves" idea: "Love for God, Man, and Soil." Contents: Review of Related Literature; Three Love Movement in Japan; Participation Training in Adult Education; Japanese Ideas and Practices Inimical to Democracy; A Conceptual Scheme for Adapting Participation Training in Group Discussion for the Three Love Movement.

433
MALIKAIL, Puthenpenpura Joseph Scaria. A Comparative Study of Teacher Education in India with Certain Selected Countries. Oregon, 1968. 205p. DA 29 (Apr. 1969), 3501-A; UM 69-6645.

Compares India with Japan, the Soviet Union, the United States, and the United Kingdom with respect to (1) philosophy of education, (2) organization of teacher education, (3) the program of teacher education, and (4) the examination and certification of teacher education students.

434
MIWA, Keiko. Analysis of the Effect of Major American Ideas upon the Organization of Japanese Higher Education from 1946 to 1967. Washington State, 1969. 106p. DA 30 (Sept. 1969), 933-34-A; UM 69-14,460.

Analyzes the impact of ideas introduced under the Occupation upon Japan's system of higher education. These ideas included "(1) structuring of the simplified four-year university, (2) introduction of the junior college, (3) multiplication of junior colleges and universities, (4) official recognition of women's higher education, and (5) higher institutions independent of government control."

SMITH, Henry D. Student Radicals in Prewar Japan. 1969. See no.673.

RELIGIOUS EDUCATION

435
WELLONS, Ralph Dillingham. The Organizations Set up for the Control of Mission Union Higher Educational Institutions. Columbia, 1927.

A comprehensive discussion of the organizational characteristics and functioning of various missionary colleges and universities in a number of countries including Japan and Korea. The following Japanese and Korean missionary colleges and universities are classified according to type of organizational control: (1) Control by a Board of Governors in the home-land and a Board of Managers in the field (examples: Kwansei Gakuin, Kobe); (2) Control by a Board of Governors located in the field and a co-operating committee in the home-land (examples: Chōsen Christian College, Seoul; Meiji Gakuin, Kobe; The Women's Christian College, Tokyo); and (3) Control by a Board of Governors located in the field (examples: Union Christian College, Pyongyang).

SCHILLING, Konrad. Das Schulwesen der Jesuiten in Japan (1551-1614). 1931. See no.498.

436
GILLETT, Clarence Sherman. To Formulate an Appropriate Philosophy of Mission Work and to Determine, for Work with Students of High School Age, in What Strategic Areas and in What Ways the American Board Missionary of Sendai, Japan, Can Make His Best Contribution. Columbia (Teachers College), 1936. 80p.

Covers the Japanese family system, political and economic conditions, religion, and education.

437
SCHROER, Gilbert William. A Religious Education Program for the Nihon Kirisuto Kyōkwai for Iwate Prefecture. Hartford School of Religious Education, 1938. 258p.

BOLLER, Paul F., Jr. The American Board and the Dōshisha, 1875-1900. 1947. See no.561.

438
FEELY, Gertrude Marie. A Program for Youth in Oita, Japan. Columbia (Teachers College), 1949. 142p. AB: Teachers College Record, 52 (Dec. 1950), 189; also in W. C. Eells. The Literature of Japanese Education, 1945-1954. p.42-43.

Surveys Japan's cultural heritage and developments in the country since 1941, and formulates plans for the organization of a city-wide youth program in the Church of Christ in Ōita, Japan.

439
MATSUMOTO, Toru. A Proposed Program of Voluntary Religious Education at Meiji Gakuin, Tokyo, Japan. Columbia (Teachers College), 1949. 224p. AB: Teachers College Record, 52 (Nov. 1950), 125-26.

Contents: The Problem; The General Post-War Situation in Japan; Orientation of Meiji Gakuin as a Christian School; Evaluating the Whole Situation; Some Fundamental Issues Involved; Basic Assumptions of the Project; Exploring Alternative Possibilities; Developing the Project; Voluntary Religious Education.

440
HIROSE, Hamako. A Guide for Curriculum Development for Religious Education Department of Seiwa Woman's College in Nishinomiya, Japan. Columbia (Teachers College), 1950.

Surveys the postwar period in Japan and the need for Christian workers.

441
OTAKE, Masuko. Education for Leadership in the Christian Colleges of Japan. Yale, 1951. 410p. AB: Religious Education, 47 (May/June 1952), 222-23.

Contents: Pt.1: The Current Situation: The Need for a New 'Spirit' in Postwar Japan. Pt.2: The Performance of Japan's Christian Colleges, the Results of a Survey, and Some Limiting Factors for a Success. Pt.3: Christian Leadership for a New Day; A Ten Point Program for Reorganization.

Rel.Publ.: "Education for Leadership in the Christian Colleges of Japan," Japan Christian Quarterly, 19 (Winter 1953), 9-21.

442
MERRITT, Richard Allen. Group Life and Christian Education in the Nippon Seikōkai. Columbia (Teachers College), 1960. 361p.

The study is concerned with the problems of employing a discipline of "group dynamics" in the guidance of young people's groups in the Anglican-Episcopal Church of Japan. It includes a chapter on the social behavior of Japanese youth.

443
TURRI, Arrigo Claudiano, O.F.M. De Catechesi in Ordine and Vitam Eucharisticam in Primitiva Ecclesia Japonensi Praesertim, Secundum Fratres Minores [Religious Instruction about the Eucharist in the Early Church of Japan as Taught in Particular by the Franciscans]. Santo Tomas, 1960. Text in Latin.

BURNSTEIN, Ira J. The American Movement to Develop Church Colleges for Men in Japan, 1868-1912. 1964. See no.574.

444
HOLLAWAY, Ernest Lee, Jr. Major Developments in Religious Education in the Japan Baptist Convention to 1961. Southwestern Baptist, 1965. 277p.

One chapter is devoted to general Christian religious education prior to 1945, but the main focus is on religious education in Japanese Baptist churches, 1946-1960. Includes information on the organization (ca. 1946) and reorganization (in 1959) of the Japan Baptist Convention, on church schools, the Baptist Training Union, the Women's Missionary Union, youth work, and church music education.

445
SHIODA, Sister Mary John Bosco, S.S.N.D. Cultural Basis for Teaching Religion in Catholic Women's Colleges in Japan. St. Louis, 1967. 248p. DA 28 (Feb. 1968), 2964-A; UM 68-1296.

Contents: Introduction; Historical Survey of Japanese Culture (Brief Review of the History of Japanese Culture, Continuity in the History of Japanese Culture, Characteristics of Japanese Personality); Changing Attitude of Japanese Youth; Nature and Practices of Catholic Schools in Japan (Modern Catechetical Movement and Missionary Apostolate, Bangkok Study Week, Nature of Catholic Schools in Japan, Administrator's Report, Reason and Nature of Religion Courses, General Policy, Content of Religion Courses); Conclusion and Recommendations.

YOSHIKAWA, Hildegard F. A Comparative Study of the Philosophical Orientation of Catholic and Public High Schools in Japan. 1969. See no.403.

TEACHING AND LEARNING

(Includes methods of instruction and studies of learning/teaching psychology.) See also Psychology and Social Psychology (pages 219-20).

446
OTOMO, Shigeru. An Experimental Study of the Eye Movements Made by Various Persons in Reading Japanese Texts of Different Forms. Chicago, 1924. ix, 148p. AB: University of Chicago. Abstracts of Theses, Humanistic Series. v.3 (1924/1925). p.75-80.

"Reports on several experiments dealing with the eye-movements of Japanese students in reading kanji, katakana, hiragana, and romaji."

447
PAIUSOV, N. G. Metodika ob"iasneniia i zakrepleniia ieroglifov na nachal'nom etape obucheniia iaponskomu iazyku [The Methodology of Explaining and Retaining Characters during the Beginning Stage of Teaching Japanese]. Moscow, Voennyi institut inostrannykh iazykov, 1954. (Candidate of Pedagogical Sciences degree) 275p. Text in Russian.

Rel.Publ.: Vvodnyi ieroglificheskii kurs. Moscow: 1953. 200p. (Voennyi institut inostrannykh iazykov); Ieroglificheskii minimum: Dlia studentov IVIa pri MGU, izuchaiuschchikh iaponskii iazyk. Moscow: Izdatel'stov Moskovskogo universiteta, 1968. 178p. (Institut vostochnykh iazykov, kafedra iazykov i literatur Dal'nego Vostoka)

448
KLEINJANS, Everett. A Descriptive-Comparative Study Predicting Interference for Japanese in Learning Eng-

lish Noun-Head Modification Patterns. Michigan, 1958. 205p. DA 19 (Dec. 1958), 1306; UM 58-7743.

"The study grew out of the belief that the best materials for the teaching of a foreign language [in this case, English to a Japanese student] are those which are based on a linguistic comparison of the language to be learned with the native language of the learner." "Tests were sent to Japan for administration to junior and senior high school students."

Rel.Publ.: Nichiei ryōgo no hikaku to eigo kyōiku. Tr. by Itō Tadashi. Tokyo: Taishūkan, 1961. 330p. [Translation of the thesis]; "A Comparison of Japanese-English Object Structures," Language Learning, 8, no.1-2 (1957-1958), 47-52.

449
SKILLMAN, John Harold. A Study of the Relationship between Participation in Various Types of Extra-Class Activities and Academic Performance in Three Private Japanese Secondary Schools. Syracuse, 1958. 116p. DA 19 (Feb. 1959), 1958; UM 58-7242.

The subjects were third year students at Aoyama Gakuin Senior High, Joshi-sei Gakuin Senior High, and Meiji Gakuin Senior High School (all in Tokyo).

KOHMOTO, Sutesaburo. Phonemics and Sub-Phonemic Replacement of English Sounds by Speakers of Japanese. 1960. See no.1452.

450
KIMIZUKA, Sumako. Problems in Teaching English Based upon a Contrastive Analysis of Japanese and English. California, Los Angeles, 1962. 249p.

Contents: Pt.1: English as a Subject in the School Curriculum: A Brief History of Language Teaching with Special Reference to the United States; A Brief History of Foreign Language Teaching in Japan; The Present Situation of English Teaching in Japanese Schools; Problems of Teaching and Learning English in Japanese Schools. Pt. 2: A Study of Errors Based upon a Constructive Analysis of the Sound and Structural Systems between English and Japanese: A Study of Phonological Errors; A Study of Structural Errors Revealed in English Compositions Written by Japanese Students; Cultural Difference as Reflected in Language. Pt.3: Principles of Teaching English Based upon an Analytical Study of English and Japanese: Assumptions and Principles of Teaching to Japanese Students; Teaching the Sound System; Teaching the Structural System; Teaching Vocabulary.

Rel.Publ.: "A Contrastive Study of Japanese suru and English do," in The Association of Teachers of Japanese, Journal-Newsletter, 3 (Apr. 1966), 22-29; "A Contrastive Study of the Japanese Structural Device 'Onomatopoeia + Verb' and Certain English Verbs," in The Association of Teachers of Japanese, Journal-Newsletter, 4 (Sept. 1967), 12-16.

NEY, James W. A Morphological and Syntactic Analysis of English Compositions Written by Native Speakers of Japanese. 1963. See no.1453.

NISHIYAMA, Reverend Toshiko P. Primary Relationships and Academic Achievement: A Comparative Study of American and Japanese Youth. 1965. See no.1875.

451
HASHIMOTO, Mitsuo George. From Japanese to English; A Contrastive Analysis Based on a Transformational Model. Georgetown, 1967. 148p. DA 28 (Sept. 1967), 1064-A; UM 67-9465.

"Predicts some of the possible interferences which the speakers of Japanese might encounter in learning English."

452
MISHIMA, Toshiko. An Experiment Comparing Five Modalities of Conveying Meaning for the Teaching of Foreign Language Vocabulary. Georgetown, 1967. 111p. DA 27 (Mar. 1967), 3030-31-A; UM 67-2922.

"The target language is Japanese and the subjects' native language is English."

453
FRENCH, Henry Pierson, Jr. A Study of Difference in Students' Learning of Chinese and Japanese Culture Concepts Using Lecture and Intrinsically Programmed Methods. Rochester, 1968. 203p. DA 29 (Dec. 1968), 1765-A; UM 68-15,876.

"The purpose of the study was two-fold: (a) to prepare instructional materials using a branching, programmed self-instruction paradigm; and (b) to evaluate students' learning using this method of instruction." The study included the designing of an evaluation instrument "to measure pre- and post-achievement knowledge of Chinese and Japanese culture concepts, and to measure attitude change regarding Chinese and Japanese culture concepts viewed both in Eastern and Western contexts."

454
RODGERS, Theodore Stephan. Measuring Vocabulary Difficulty: An Analysis of Item Variables in Learning Russian-English and Japanese-English Vocabulary Pairs. Stanford, 1968. 99p. DA 29 (Nov. 1968), 1528-29-A; UM 68-15,091.

"Examines some data on paired-associate learning with foreign language-English vocabulary lists."

455
SANCHES, Mary Mildred Snipes. Features in the Acquisition of Japanese Grammar. Stanford, 1968. 91p. DA 30 (Sept. 1969), 1161-A; UM 69-14,013.

"A corpus consisting of the early speech of three children (ages 24 plus to 29 plus months) learning Japanese as a native language is analysed for both syntactic and morphological patterns. Early syntactic classes and relations are discovered through the examination of: (1) distributional patterns, (2) intonation patterns, and (3) adult expansions of the child's utterances. The analysis reveals major 'pivot' and 'open' clauses and early elaborations of phrase-structure similar to those reported elsewhere in the speech of children learning other languages."

456
BRODKEY, Dean Guy. A Self-Instructional Program in English Article Usage for Chinese, Japanese, Korean, and Thai College Students. California, Los Angeles, 1969. 81p.

Contents: Article and Oriental; Principles of Second-Language Instruction; Patterns of Article Usage; Program Development; Experimental Procedures; Analysis of Data; Conclusions.

HANZEL, Louis F. A Contrastive Analysis of the Principal Predication Types of English and Japanese. 1969. See no.1460.

Geography

See also Economics--agriculture and sericulture (pages 24-28) and Economics--fisheries, forestry, and mining (pages 35-36).

457
HEIDER, Josef. Die Bedeutung der Jesuiten für die Geographie und Topographie Ostasiens [The Importance of the Jesuits for the Geography and Topography of East Asia]. Karlova Universita (German Branch), 1909/10. Pagination not known. Text in German.

458
GEZELIUS, Erik Birger. Japan i västerländsk framställning till omkring år 1700: Ett geografiskt--kartografiskt försök [The Western Conception of Japan up to ca. 1700 A.D.: A Geographical and Cartographical Study. Uppsala, 1910. 185p. Text in Swedish.

Rel.Publ.: Japan...forsok. Linköping, 1910. (Bilaga till Linköpings h. allm. läroverks årsredogörelse)

459
HAUSHOFER, Karl. Der deutsche Anteil an der geographischen Erschliessung Japans und des Subjapanischen Erdraums, und deren Förderung durch den Einfluss von Krieg und Wehrpolitik [The German Participation in the Geographical Opening of Japan and of Its Peripheral Areas, and Its Advancement through the Impact of War and of Military Policy]. Erlangen, 1914. Text in German. The dissertation in its published form is available at Bochum, Universitätsbibliothek, Nr. UA 18,656.

P. F. von Siebold's history of the geographical discoveries of Japan from early times until the period when Japanese geographical knowledge was influenced by the introduction of European geographical techniques. The life and the work of Siebold (a German scientist who was resident in Japan during the 1820's) as the beginning of a new study of Japanese geography and cartography. The relationship of the actual opening of Japan after Siebold's time to subsequent Japanese developments in the military sphere and in defense. Initial economic and political alienation of the Japanese. Trends in the present relationship of German geography to Japan and to neighboring areas. Limitations of an exclusively native geography. The role of German geographers in recognizing the importance of East Asia in terms of trade and politics.

Rel.Publ.: Der deutsch...Wehrpolitik, Erlangen: Junge und Sohn, 1914. 110p. (Mitteilungen der geographischen Gesellschaft in München, 9)

460
HAUSHOFER, Karl. Grundrichtungen in der geographischen Entwicklung des japanischen Reiches (1854 bis 1919) [Basic Tendencies Characterizing the Geographical Development of the Japanese Empire, 1854-1919]. München, 1919 (Habilitationsschrift). Text in German. Diss. ms. available at München, Universitätsbibliothek, Nr. U 1919/154, P2327.

Rel.Publ.: Das japanische Reich in seiner geographischen Entwicklung. Wien: Seidel, 1921. vii, 171p. (Angewandte Geographie, 50); "Die geographischen Grundrichtungen in der Entwicklung des japanischen Reiches von 1854-1919," Geographische Zeitschrift, 26 (1920), 8-25.

SCHEINPFLUG, Alfons. Die japanische Kolonisation in Hokkaido. 1935. See no.559.

461
SCHUBERT, Kurt. Die Grossstädte Japans [The Large Towns of Japan]. Hamburg, 1942. 180p. Text in German. Diss. ms. available at Hamburg, Staats- und Universitätsbibliothek. Nr. Diss. math.-nat. Mscr. 177.

The dissertation is designed to better our understanding of the close relationship between the formation of large towns in Japan and the country's natural environment. It therefore studies the growth and geographical location of these urban communities and discusses the most important activities going on within them (e.g. trade, industry, science, culture).

462
CRACY, Douglas Dunham. The Physical Geography of Iga-no-kuni, Japan. Michigan, 1947. xvii, 247p.

A study of the changing relationships between the physical features of the landscape of a portion of Mie prefecture. The study seeks to show that change in the physical aspect of the landscape according to geological processes is as significant as change in the cultural aspect of a landscape brought about by historical processes in the formation of the total landscape.

Rel. Publ.: "A Geographer Looks at the Landscape," Landscape, 9 (Autumn 1959), 22-25.

MANCHESTER, Curtis A. The Development and Distribution of Sekisho in Japan. 1947. See no.479.

WILSON, James N. A Handbook on the Political Geography of the Orient. 1949. See no.1434.

EYRE, John D. Salt from the Sea: A Geographical

Analysis of the National and International Patterns of Japanese Salt Production and Trade. 1951. See no.241.

PITTS, Forrest R. Comparative Land Fertility and Potential in the Inland Sea and Peripheral Areas of Japan. 1955. See no.175.

463
KORNHAUSER, David Henry. The Influence of Geography and Related Factors on the Rise of Japanese Cities. Michigan, 1956. 189p. DA 17 (June 1957), 1308-09; UM 21,139.

Focuses on "those factors which have led to differences in the characteristics of growth of" large, medium, and small cities. Two cities--Okayama (Okayama prefecture) and Matsuyama (Ehime prefecture)--are investigated as case studies. Contents: The Physical Base; The Historical Base; The Sites and Functions of Pre-Modern Cities; The Transition to the Modern Period; Urban Population Growth, 1888-1950: A Summary of Trends; The "Medium" City.

Rel.Publ.: "Urbanization and Population Pressure in Japan," Pacific Affairs, 31 (Sept. 1958), 275-85.

ANSTEY, Robert L. A Comparative Study of the Agricultural Land Use of the Aso Highland and the Kumamoto Lowland of Central Kyushu. 1957. See no.176.

KAKIUCHI, Hiroaki G. The Rise and Development of the Fruit Industry on the Okayama Plain. 1958. See no. 178.

464
INABA, Masaharu George. Japan: Some Geographic Aspects of Industrialization and Population Correlates. Columbia, 1959. 232p. DA 20 (Sept. 1959), 986; UM 59-3110.

A description and analysis of the industrialization and urbanization process in Japan and of "the chronological and geographical population correlates" that have accompanied it.

465
MASAI, Yasuo. Lansing, Michigan and Shizuoka, Japan: A Comparison of Areal Functional Organization in Two Different Environments. Michigan State, 1960. 224p. DA 21 (May 1961), 3413-14; UM 61-1184.

A systematic comparison of various features of the two areas including their cultural development, functional organization, land use, and division of labor.

Rel.Publ.: "Rural and Urban Land Uses of the Shimizu Area in Central Japan" [by] S. Yamamoto and Y. Masai, in Tōkyō Kyōiku Daigaku, Scientific Reports, Section C, 1965, nos. 83-84, p.17-66.

HOUGH, Richard F. The Impact of the Drastic Decline in Raw Silk upon Land Use and Industry in Selected Areas of Sericultural Specialization in Japan. 1963. See no.184.

KEEN, Elmer A. Some Aspects of the Economic Geography of the Japanese Skipjack Tuna Fishery. 1965. See no.244.

466
PEZEU-MASSABUAU, Jacques. La Maison japonaise et la neige: Études géographiques sur l'habitation du Hokuriku (côte occidentale du Japon central) [The Japanese House and the Snow: Geographical Studies of Dwellings in the Hokuriku Area (the Western Part of Central Japan)]. Paris, 1966. Text in French.

A study of the adaptation of the Japanese home to the snowy winters of the Hokuriku. Considerable attention is paid to the traditional forms of adaptation, life within the home during the winter, and the long-term effects of the snow on the house itself.

Rel.Publ.: La Maison...central. Paris: Presses universitaires de France, 1966. vi, 233p. (Bulletin de la Maison franco-japonaise, nouvelle série, t.8, n.1)

GORRIE, Averilda M. New Zealand's Future Export Trade with Japan: A Geographical Assessment in the Light of Recent Trends in Japanese Agriculture and Forestry. 1967. See no.1246.

467
IATSENKO, B. P. Severnye raiony Iaponii: Ekonomichesko-geograficheskaia kharakteristika khoziaistva, usloviia i osobennosti razvitiia Khokkaiko i Tokhoku [The Northern Regions of Japan: An Economic and Geographical Survey of the Economy and of the Conditions for and Characteristics of the Development of Hokkaido and Tōhoku]. Leningrad, Leningradskii gosudarstvennyi fakul'tet, 1967. (Candidate of Geographical Sciences degree) 301, xiii p. Text in Russian. AB: 19p. summary published in 1967.

MACNAB, John W. Agricultural Use of Sloping Land in Whitireia Peninsula (Wellington, New Zealand), Kitaki Island (Japan), and North Carolina (U.S.A.). 1967. See no.193.

History

Limited to internal developments only. For dissertations on Japanese relations with other countries, see International Relations (pages 104-63). See also: Economics (pages 21-51), Education (pages 52-59), Japan--The View from Abroad (pages 164-66), Law and the Judicial System (pages 176-81), and Religion and Philosophy (pages 221-32).

GENERAL: ca. 400 A.D.-1945

468
FUKUDA, Tokuzo. Die gesellschaftliche und wirtschaftliche Entwicklung in Japan [Social and Economic Development in Japan]. München, 1900. Text in German. The dissertation in its published form is available at Marburg/Lahn, Staatsbibliothek Preussischer Kulturbesitz, Nr. Fe 677-42.

The following are examined within the dissertation: the uji system, the Taika Reform, the Taihō Code, the five-man mutual responsibility groups and the handen system; manorial lords, feudal tenure, the cities, and guilds during the feudal period; the establishment and subsequent decline of the "Japanese police state;" the composition of the rural class, and property and inheritance regulations. The study concludes with a number of remarks about the social and economic situation in Japan in the year 1900.

Rel.Publ.: Die gesellschaftliche...Japan. Stuttgart: Cotta, 1900. x, 190p. (Münchener volkswirtschaftliche Studien, 42)

469
YOKOYAMA, Masajiro. The Development of the Land Tax in Japan. Yale, 1904. 329p.

An historical review of the land tax, the primary source of revenue for Japanese governments in pre-industrial society. The dissertation discusses various concepts of land ownership and tries to determine whether this revenue was in reality a "tax" or a form of "rent." Emphasis is placed upon the continued importance of the land tax after the Meiji Restoration and upon the promulgation of the Meiji Constitution.

470
RIESE, Friedrich. Japans staatsrechtliche und politische Modernisierung [The Constitutional and Political Modernization of Japan]. Würzburg, 1926. vii, 143p. Text in German. Diss. ms. available at Würzburg, Universitätsbibliothek, Nr. 6729.

A general, historical survey from the fifth century A.D. through the Tokugawa era; the development and organization of the Japanese feudal state along with a comparison with medieval European feudal states; and the transition from a feudal to a constitutional state with the promulgation of the Meiji constitution.

471
BURKS, Ardath Walter. Economics in Japanese Thought, 1185-1905. Johns Hopkins, 1949. 318p.

An identification and analysis of basic issues in Chinese and derived Japanese socio-economic thought.

GRIFFITH, Harry E. Japanese Normal School Education. 1950. See no.423.

472
YOUNG, John. Japanese Historians and the Location of Yamatai. Johns Hopkins, 1955. viii, 323p.

An historiographical study of the controversy over the location of Yamatai, Japan's proto-historic capital, which has confronted Japanese historians for centuries. The author traces the historical treatment of this controversy by scholars in Japan and points out how closely tied it is to the wider controversy over the early history of the Japanese Imperial Court.

Rel.Publ.: The Location of Yamatai: A Case Study in Japanese Historiography, 720-1945. Baltimore: Johns Hopkins Press, 1958. 199p. (Johns Hopkins University. Studies in History and Political Science, ser. 75, no.2)

473
BURKE, William Moran. The Role of the Entrepreneur in Japanese Economic Development. Georgetown, 1958. 215p.

Contents: Entrepreneur in Society; Entrepreneur in Japanese Society; Stationary State: Pre-Tokugawa; Stationary State: Tokugawa; Breakthrough; Entrepreneur in Contemporary Japan.

Rel.Publ.: "Creative Response and Adaptive Response in Japanese Society," American Journal of Economics and Sociology, 21 (Jan. 1962), 103-12.

MÜLLER, Christa. Erziehung und industrielle Entwicklung: Die Bedeutung des Erziehungswesens für die industrielle Entwicklung, erlangt am Beispiel Japans. 1964. See no.401.

PRE-MODERN: ca. 400 A.D.-1868

See also: Art and Architecture (pages 15-18), Literature (pages 183-84), & Religion and Philosophy (pages 221-32).

474
YOSHIDA, Sakuya. Geschichtliche Entwicklung der Staatsverfassung und des Lehnswesens von Japan [Historical Development of the Political Constitution and the Feudal System of Japan]. Bonn, 1890. Text in German. The dissertation in its published form is available at Marburg/Lahn, Universitätsbibliothek, Nr. VII m C 1232 ra.

The author examines the development of the Japanese feudal system--in particular, feudal law and the organization of the feudal policy--on the basis of an historical survey from ancient times to the decline of the Tokugawa Bakufu.

Rel.Publ.: Geschichtliche...Japan. Den Haag: M. M. Couvée, 1890. 124p.

475
OKUBO, Toshitake. Die Entwickelungsgeschichte der Territorialverfassung und der Selbstverwaltung Japans in politischer und insbesondere wirtschaftlicher Beziehung [The Historical Development of Local Systems of Government and of Autonomy in Japan with Reference to Politics and Especially to Administration]. Halle-Wittenberg, 1894. Text in German. The dissertation in its published form is available at Marburg/Lahn, Universitätsbibliothek, Nr. XVIII C.

I. Territorial origins and the transition to a centralized state. II. 654-1186: The development of territorial, manorial, and communal systems of government under Imperial rule. III. 1186-1600: The rise of the feudal state, the policies of the feudal lords, and administrative development in various regions. IV. 1600-1868: The Tokugawa system of government and the daimyo. Self-government in the Tokugawa regime (city rule and village rule).

Rel.Publ.: Die Entwickelungsgeschichte...Beziehung. Halle a.S.: E. Karras, 1894. viii, 190p.

476
LIU, Chiang. Isolation and Contact as Factors in the Cultural Evolution of China, Korea, and Japan prior to 1842. Iowa, 1923. 383p.

Contents: The Problem, Material, and Method; A General Survey; Art; Religion; Science; Language; Government; Conclusions.

Rel.Publ.: "Isolation...1842," Chinese Social and Political Science Review, 9 (1925), p.189-229, 502-29, 787-817; 10 (1926), p.212-29, 447-75, 728-45, 914-32; 11 (1927), p.142-54, 287-302, 491-509.

477
DONAT, Walter. Der Heldenbegriff im Schrifttum der älteren japanischen Geschichte [The Concept of the Hero in Early Japanese Historical Writings]. Hamburg, 1938. (Habilitationsschrift). Text in German.

A literary and historical study of the Japanese concept of the hero. Pt.1 examines early Japanese myths, sagas, and poetry. Pt.2 focuses on the absorption of Chinese culture, and on early Japanese lyric poetry, epic prose, and changes in the form of the warrior. Pt.3 studies the period of the great war chronicles: the origins of the gunkimono, the choice of subjects, historical and poetic representations. The dissertation concludes with some observations on the character and the ethos of the warrior class and of military types as well as on the development of heroic ideals.

Rel.Publ.: Der Heldenbegriff in der japanischen Literatur von den Anfängen bis zur epischen Gattung der Gunkimono. Tokyo: Deutsche Gesellschaft für Natur- und Völkerkunde Ostasiens, Leipzig: Harrassowitz, 1938. 130p. (MOAG, Bd 31, Teil A)

FURUKAWA, Jiryo. Samurai und Bodhisattva: Bestimmung des japanischen Erziehungs-Ideals durch die buddhistische Ethik. 1939. See no.393.

478
HEYER, Siegfried. Staatswirklichkeit und Staatsdenken in Japan zur Zeit des Shogunats [The Reality of the State and Political Thought in Japan at the Time of the Shogunate]. Marburg, 1942. xi, 190p. Text in German. Diss. ms. available at Marburg/Lahn, Universitätsbibliothek, Nr. XVIII B.

A history of the development of the Japanese state up to the Tokugawa period. The author focuses upon the development of the Tennō ideology and searches for its roots in the middle ages.

479
MANCHESTER, Curtis Alexander. The Development and Distribution of Sekisho in Japan. Michigan, 1947. xiii, 223p.

"Attempts to establish the distribution and function of the sekisho [road barriers, check points] at different periods of their development" from the Taika Reform to 1871. Shows the "relation of the early sekisho to the development of the frontiers...and shows how they retarded and handicapped the development of trade and communications in various periods" of Japanese history.

480
IWAMOTO, Kiyotoshi. Land and Society in Traditional Japan. Utah, 1964. 216p. DA 25 (Dec. 1964), 3315-16; UM 64-13,727.

"Analyzes the nature of social change in traditional Japanese society [from ancient times to the mid-1800's] with particular reference to the transformation of the ruling elite." Argues that in the Japanese case, "the process of social change has been significantly related to changes in the productive relationships associated with land."

EUCKEN-ADDENHAUSEN, Margarethe von. Die Wandlung der sozialen Struktur des Ritterstandes in der Muromachi-Zeit. 1968. See no.497.

The Beginning of Japanese History (ca. 400 A.D.-784)

See also Anthropology and Sociology--ethnography (pages 7-10) and Archaeology (page 14).

481
ASAKAWA, Kan'ichi. The Reform of 645: An Introduction to the Study of the Origin of Feudalism in Japan. Yale, 1902. 367p.

Deals with the institutions before the reform, events leading up to the reform, the political doctrine of Sui and T'ang China, and the reform itself.

Rel.Publ.: The Early Institutional Life of Japan: A Study in the Reform of 645 A.D. Tokyo: Shueisha, 1903; New York: Paragon, 1963. vi, 355p.

482
WEDEMEYER, André. Japanische Frühgeschichte: Untersuchungen zur Chronologie und Territorialverfassung von Altjapan bis zum 5. Jahrhundert n.Chr. [Early Japanese History: Studies of the Chronology of Early Japan and of the Country's System of Government up to

the Fifth Century A.D.]. Leipzig, 1924. (Habilitationsschrift). Text in German. The dissertation in its published form is available at Bochum, Bibliothek des Ostasien-Instituts, Abt. Japan; also at the University of Michigan, General Library, no. QH5.D486 suppl. v.11.

Seeks to determine the basic chronology of early Japanese history and attempts to study Japan's early system of government through an examination of Chinese and Korean sources: the kingdom of Queen Himiko and the states of Kunu and Iyo; the system of government as presented in the Kokuzō-hongi; a comparison of the Kojiki with the Kokuzō-hongi; and a study of the kuni-no-miyatsuko (landholders), the miyake (imperial granaries), and the royal socage-farms. Also includes a translation of the chapter entitled "Wa" (the early Chinese name for Japan) from the Chinese historical chronicle Hou-Han-shu and of the chapter "People of Wa" from the Weichi as well as an annotated translation of the Kokuzō-hongi.

Rel.Publ.: Japanische...n.Chr. Tokyo, 1930. xvi, 346p. (Deutsche Gesellschaft für Natur- und Völkerkunde Ostasiens. Supplementband 11)

SCHÜFFNER, Rudolf. Die Fünferschaft als Grundlage der Staats- und Gemeindeverwaltung und des sozialen Friedens in Japan zur Zeit der Taikwa-Reform und in der Tokugawa-Periode. 1938. See no.509.

483
ZACHERT, Herbert. Semmyō: Die kaiserlichen Erlasse des Shoku-Nihongi [Semmyō: The Imperial Proclamations of the Shoku-Nihongi]. Berlin, 1949. (Habilitationsschrift). Text in German. The dissertation in its published form is available at the University of Michigan, General Library, no. AS182.B517A3 no.4.

Presents a synopsis of the imperial genealogy, a discussion of the nature and significance of the Shoku-Nihongi, and an index, the text, and an annotated translation of the semmyō proclaimed between 697 and 789.

Rel.Publ.: Semmyō...Shoku-Nihongi. Berlin: Akademie Verl., 1950. 198p. (Deutsche Akademie der Wissenschaften zu Berlin, Institut für Orientforschung. Veröffentlichung, 4)

LINN, John K., Jr. The Imperial Edicts of the Shoku-Nihongi: An Annotated Translation of Edicts #30-62. 1950. See no.1553.

484
MILLER, Richard James. A Study of the Development of a Centralized Japanese State prior to the Taika Reform, A.D. 645. California, Berkeley, 1953. iv, 216p.

Focuses on the disintegration of the uji system as a social and political force in early Japan and on the assumption of paramount power by the Imperial clan and by the Soga family. Emphasis is on military and economic developments.

YOUNG, John. Japanese Historians and the Location of Yamatai. 1955. See no.472.

SCHMIDT, Erwin A. Die ersten Hoch- und Privatschulen Japans im Lichte zeitgenössischer Gesetze und Verfügungen. 1956. See no.409.

485
DETTMER, Hans Adalbert. Die Steuergesetzgebung der Nara-Zeit [The Tax Legislation of the Nara Period]. München, 1959. Text in German. The dissertation in its published form is available at Marburg/Lahn, Staatsbibliothek Preussischer Kulturbesitz, Nr. Ser. 4173-1; also at the University of Michigan, General Library, no. HJ2982.D48.

A study of the legislation for different kinds of tax payments, in particular (1) payments in kind such as the head tax, the tax paid to discharge one's labor duties, the field tax, tributary payments, and the tax on individual households, and (2) tax payments in the form of labor services to the state. The problem of tax evasion also is discussed. The author concludes the dissertation with a translation of those portions of the Yōrō Code that deal with taxation (koryō, denryō, buyakuryō).

Rel.Publ.: Die Steuergesetzgebung...Zeit. Wiesbaden: Harrassowitz, 1959. vii, 156p. (Studien zur Japanologie, 1)

486
LEWIN, Bruno. Aya und Hata: Bevölkerungsgruppen Altjapans kontinentaler Herkunft [Aya and Hata: Population Groups of Continental Origin in Early Japan]. München, 1962. (Habilitationsschrift). Text in German. The dissertation in its published form is available at Marburg/Lahn, Staatsbibliothek Preussischer Kulturbesitz, Nr. Ser. 4173-3; also at the University of Michigan, General Library.

An historical study of the origins and of the settlement in Japan of immigrants who came to the country from the continent between the fourth and the eighth centuries, of their social and professional organization, of their political position, and of their influence on early Japanese religion and early Japanese literature. The dissertation concludes with information on how events in early Korean history influenced this flow of immigration.

Rel.Publ.: Aya...Herkunft. Wiesbaden: Harrassowitz, 1962. 238p. (Studien zur Japanologie, 3)

487
HERAIL, Francine M. Yodo no tsukai: le système des quatre envoyés: Un des rouages de l'administration provinciale du Japon antique [Yodo no Tsukai: The System of the Four Envoys: An Organ of Provincial Administration in Early Japan]. Paris, 1966. 186p. Text in French. AB: Université de Paris. Faculté des Lettres et Sciences Humaines. Positions des thèses de troisième cycle soutenues devant la Faculté en 1966. (Série "Recherches," t.42), p.133-34.

A study of the evolution of the system from its inception at the time of the Taika Reform to its abandonment during the Heian period. Under the system, each province dispatched four envoys annually to the central government to report on economic and military developments in their provinces, to submit the provincial census and tribute registers, and to inform the central authorities about local officials' activities.

Rel.Publ.: Yodo no tsukai ou le système des quatres envoyés. Paris: Presses Universitaires de France, 1966. 214p. (Bulletin de la Maison Franco—Japonaise, n.s.8, no.2); "A propos du séjour à la capital des envoyés des provinces," in International Conference of Orientalists in Japan, Transactions, 8 (1963), 42-47.

488
TANAKA, Kashiki. A Comparison of the Tz'u-ling and the Jingi ryō. Claremont, 1966. 151p. DA 28 (Apr. 1967), 4077-A; UM 68-4627.

"The purpose...is to try to see what basic differences there are between the ancient Chinese attitude toward their indigenous religion and the early Japanese attitude toward their indigenous religion, as seen in the oldest extant law codes dealing with religious rituals in each of the traditions": the "law of rituals" of T'ang China and the "law of Shinto" of Nara Japan.

Heian Period (784-1185)

489
KLUGE, Inge-Lore. Miyoshi Kiyoyuki: Sein Leben und seine Zeit [Miyoshi Kiyoyuki: His Life and His Times]. Berlin/Humboldt, 1950. 143p. Text in German. The dissertation in its published form is available at Marburg/Lahn, Staatsbibliothek Preussischer Kulturbesitz, Nr. 4° Ser. 2200-35.

Pt.1: Miyoshi Kiyoyuki (847-918) and his times: Cultural developments, the beginning of political and economic decline, and attempts at reform during the Kampyō and Engi eras. Pt.2: The life of Miyoshi Kiyokuki, his activities as a court official, and his memorials. Pt.3: A translation of the memorials of the Councillor of State: Kiyoyuki Ason.

Rel.Publ.: Miyoshi...Zeit. Berlin: Akademie-Verlag, 1958. 80p. (Deutsche Akademie der Wissenschaften zu Berlin, Institut für Ostasienforschung, Veröffentlichung, 35)

SHIMIZU, Osamu. Nihon Montoku Tennō jitsuroku: An Annotated Translation with a Survey of the Early Ninth Century in Japan. 1951. See no.1615.

SCHMIDT, Erwin A. Die ersten Hoch- und Privatschulen Japans im Lichte zeitgenossischer Gesetze und Verfügungen. 1956. See no.409.

490
BOCK, Felicia Gressitt. Engi-shiki: Ceremonial Procedures of the Engi Era, 901-922. California, Berkeley, 1966. 317p. DA 27 (Sept. 1966), 741-42-A; UM 66-8277.

The "procedures for both civil and religious (Shintō) administration and ceremonial" are presented. Books four and five of the first section of the procedures for official matters under the Jingikan are translated.

Rel.Publ.: Monograph forthcoming from Sophia University Press (Tokyo); "Some Notes on the Itsuki-nomiya," Phi Theta Papers (Berkeley, Calif.), 7 (May 1962), 23-32.

Kamakura Period (1185-1333)

See also Literature--classical (pages 183-90) and Religion and Philosophy (pages 221-32).

McCULLOUGH, Helen Craig. A Study of the Taiheiki: A Medieval Japanese Chronicle. 1955. See no.1624.

491
SHINODA, Minoru. The Founding of the Kamakura Shogunate, 1180-1185: Based on the Azuma kagami. Columbia, 1957. 446p. DA 17 (Aug. 1957), 1733-34; UM 21,128.

Essentially an historical study to which the author has appended selected translations of the first five chapters of the Azuma kagami.

Rel.Publ.: The Founding...kagami. New York: Columbia University Press, 1960. xii, 385p. (Records of Civilization: Sources and Studies, 57)

492
McCULLOUGH, William Hoyt. Shōkyūki and Azuma kagami: Sources for the Shōkyū War of 1221. California, Berkeley, 1962. ii, 619p.

Translates the two accounts of the Shōkyū War and supplements them with material drawn from the Rokudai shōjiki, Shōkyū sannen yonen hinami no ki, Masu kagami, and other early sources.

Rel.Publ.: "Shōkyūki: An Account of the Shōkyū War of 1221," MN, 19, nos. 1-2 (1964), 163-215, and nos. 3-4 (1964), 186-221; "Azuma kagami: Account of the Shōkyū War," MN, 23 (1968), 102-55.

MÜLLER, Klaus. Das Nakatsukasa no Naishi nikki: Ein Spiegel höfischen Leben in der Kamakura-Zeit. 1965. See no.1628.

493
HORI, Kyotsu. The Mongol Invasions and the Kamakura Bakufu. Columbia, 1967. 273p. DA 28 (Nov. 1967), 1787-A; UM 67-14,051.

A description and analysis of the expansion of Bakufu authority into the western provinces of Japan at the time of the Mongol crisis and of the economic and political problems that resulted from this extension of shogunal power. The author concludes that "the Kamakura Bakufu would most likely have come to an end not long after it actually did even without the Mongol crisis. However, the crisis undoubtedly hastened its final demise in 1333, despite the fact that the power of the military regime was greatly expanded during this unprecedented emergency."

1333-1500

494
BROWN, Delmer Myers. An Historical Study of the Use of Coins in Japan from 1432 to 1601. Stanford, 1946. 184p. AB: Stanford University. Abstracts of Dissertations, 1946/1947. p.88-91.

Focuses on the importation of copper coins from China, their extended use within the Japanese economy, and the development of local coinage of copper, gold, and silver.

Rel.Publ.: Money Economy in Medieval Japan: A Study in the Use of Coins. New Haven: Yale University Press, 1951. 128p. (Far Eastern Association Monographs, 1); "The Importation of Gold into Japan by the Portuguese during the Sixteenth Century," PHR, 16 (May 1947), 125-33.

495
PRETZELL, Klaus-Albrecht. Das Bunmei-itto-ki und das Shōdan-chiyō: Zwei Lehrschriften des Ichijō Kanera [Bunmei itto ki and Shōdan chiyō: Two Didactic Writings of Ichijō Kanera]. Hamburg, 1964. Text in German. Diss. ms. available at Hamburg, Staats- und Universitätsbibliothek.

A study of the cultural history of the Muromachi period, of the life and work of the scholar and statesman Ichijō Kanera (1402-1481), and of Ichijō's intellectual and cultural influence. Concludes with an annotated translation and an interpretation of Bunmei ittoki and Shōdan chiyō.

Rel.Publ.: "Das Bunmei-itto-ki...Kanera," Oriens Extremus, 12 (Dec. 1965), 161-219, and 13 (Aug. 1966), 1-80.

496
VARLEY, Herbert Paul, Jr. The Origins and Institutional Significance of the Ōnin War. Columbia, 1964. 351p.

DA 28 (Dec. 1967), 2165-A; UM 67-16,051.

"An examination both of the institutional development of military government from its inception until the mid-fifteenth century and of the Ōnin War, which marked the end of this initial attempt at central control." Appended "is an annotated translation of selected portions of the Ōnin-ki, a record based on the Ōnin War."

Rel.Publ.: The Ōnin War: History of Its Origins and Background with a Selective Translation of the Chronicle of Ōnin. New York: Columbia University Press, 1967. x, 238p. (Studies in Oriental Culture, 1)

497
EUCKEN-ADDENHAUSEN, Margarethe von. Die Wandlung der sozialen Struktur des Ritterstandes in der Muromachi-Zeit [Changes in the Social Structure of the Warrior Class during the Muromachi Period]. Hamburg, 1968. Text in German. Diss. ms. available at Hamburg, Staats- und Universitätsbibliothek.

Pt. 1 is a study of the shōen from a legal and economic point of view, of the growth of the warrior class and the establishment of feudalism during the Kamakura period, and of the hegemony that the military aristocracy established over the court nobility. Pt.2 focuses upon the social order among the buke (military families) and upon the evolution of the warrior class during the Sengoku and Tokugawa periods.

Rel.Publ.: "Die Wandlung...Muromachi-Zeit," Oriens Extremus, 14 (Aug. 1967), 69-128; (Dec. 1967), 199-234.

1500-1600

See also Religion--Christianity (pages 224-28).

498
SCHILLING, Konrad. Das Schulwesen der Jesuiten in Japan (1551-1614) [The Educational System of the Jesuits in Japan, 1551-1614]. Münster i.W., 1931. Text in German. The dissertation in its published form is available at Marburg/Lahn, Universitätsbibliothek, Nr. VII C.

An investigation of the organization, administration, and financing of the Jesuit schools in Japan during the sixteenth century. Considerable attention is devoted to the founding of elementary schools and to their activities as well as to the development of the medical institute and of the schools in Ōita which specialized in religious instruction and in translating work.

Rel.Publ.: Das Schulwesen...1614. Münster i.W.: Regensberg, 1931. xxviii, 86p.

BROWN, Delmer Myers. An Historical Study of the Use of Coins in Japan from 1432 to 1601. 1946. See no.494.

BOURDON, Marie-Antoine-Léon. Alexandre Valignano: Visiteur de la Compagnie de Jésus (1573-1583). 1949. See no.1929.

BOURDON, Marie-Antoine-Léon. La Compagnie de Jésus et le Japon. 1949. See no.1930.

499
ISKENDEROV, A. A. Feodal'nyi gorod Iaponii XVI stoletiia [The Feudal Town in Sixteenth Century Japan]. Moscow, Institut vostokovedeniia Akademii nauk SSSR, 1958. (Candidate of Historical Sciences degree) 222p. Text in Russian. AB: 23p. summary published in 1958.

Rel.Publ.: Feodal'nyi...stoletiia. Moscow: Izdatel'stvo vostochnoi literatury, 1961. 116p. (Institut narodov Azii Akademii nauk SSSR)

500
SCHWADE, Auctore Arcadio. Ōtomo Sōrins Kampf um die Rettung seines Landes Bungo und des Christentums in Südjapan (1578-1587) [Ōtomo Sōrin's Struggle for the Preservation of His Realm, Bungo, and of Christianity in Southern Japan, 1578-1587]. Dissertation completed at an unspecified institution in Rome (Italy) in 1961. xxii, 92, 341p. Text in German.

The dissertation discusses the position of the Ōtomo and the Shimazu families within the framework of Japan's overall political situation. The relationship of these families with Christianity during the 1580's is examined, their role in the growth of Japan's early ties with the Western powers is pointed out, and Ōtomo Sōrin's personal gains as a result of the propagation of Christianity within his realm are noted. The dissertation also includes a detailed study of European missionary activities in Kyushu during this period.

501
POZDNIAKOV, I. G. Zakreposhchenie iaponskogo krest'ianstva vo vtoroi polovine XVI v. [The Enslavement of the Japanese Peasantry during the Second Half of the Sixteenth Century]. Moscow, Institut narodov Azii Akademii nauk SSSR, 1963. (Candidate of Historical Sciences degree) 404p. Text in Russian. [See also addenda]

502
COOPER, Michael, S.J. João Rodrigues and His Description of Japan: Translation and Editing of an Early 17th Century Manuscript Describing Social Life in Contemporary Japan, with an Assessment of Its Accuracy and Value. Oxford, 1969.

João Rodrigues, S.J. (1561-1634), a native of Sernancelhe, Portugal, who sailed to Japan in 1576 where he became a Jesuit. Prior to his expulsion from the country in 1612, he served as interpreter for both Hideyoshi and Ieyasu. He was the author of História da Igreja do Japão and of Arte da Lingoa de Japam.

Rel.Publ.: They Came to Japan: An Anthology of European Reports on Japan, 1543-1640. Berkeley: University of California Press, 1965. xviii, 439p. (Publication of the Center for Japanese and Korean Studies)

503
ELISON, George Saul. Deus Destroyed: The Image of Christianity in Early Modern Japan. Harvard, 1969. 381p.; 503, lxvi p. (2v.).

A study of Japanese reaction to and ultimate rejection of Christianity during the 16th and 17th centuries. Contents: Attitudes of Entry; Misunderstanding and Appeal; Method in Accommodation; The Donation of Bartolomeu; Hideyoshi and the Sectarians; Fabian Fucan: The Apostate's Progress; The Final Solution. Volume 2 consists of translations of (1) Deus Destroyed by Fabian Fucan, (2) Deceit Disclosed by Christavão Ferreira sive Sawano Chūan, (3) Kirishitan monogatari, an anonymous Chapbook, and (4) Christians Destroyed by Suzuki Shōsan.

Tokugawa Period (1600-1868)

See also Religion and Philosophy--Confucianism, Bushidō, Kokugaku, Yōgaku (pages 228-30).

504
TAKIZAWA, Matsuyo. The Penetration of Money Economy

in Japan and Its Effects upon Social and Political Institutions. Columbia, 1927. 304p.

A study of the transition from a natural economy to a money economy and of the concurrent institutional changes (latter part of the Tokugawa era).

Rel.Publ.: The Penetration...Institutions. New York: Columbia University Press, 1927. 159p. (Studies in History, Economics and Public Law, ed. by the Faculty of Political Science of Columbia University, 285)

505
RAMMING, Martin. Russland-Berichte schiffbrüchiger Japaner aus den Jahren 1793 und 1805 und ihre Bedeutung für die Abschliessungs politik der Tokugawa [Reports of Russia from the Years 1793 and 1805 Held by Shipwrecked Japanese and Their Significance for the Tokugawa Policy of Seclusion]. Berlin, 1930. Text in German. The dissertation in its published form is available at Marburg/Lahn, Universitätsbibliothek, Nr. II B.

The study focuses on (1) the development of shipping during the Tokugawa period; (2) the literary genre entitled hyōmindan (reports of shipwrecked people); (3) the history of shipwrecked people from the provinces of Ise and Mutsu; and (4) the impact that the reports brought back from Russia by Kōdayū and other Japanese had on the closed door policy of the Tokugawa government and on the growth of Dutch studies in Japan.

Rel.Publ.: Reisen schiffbrüchiger Japaner im XVIII. Jahrhundert. Berlin: Würfel, 1930. 86p.; Über den Anteil der Russen an der Eröffnung Japans für den Verkehr mit den westlichen Mächten. Tokyo, 1926. i, 36p. (MOAG, Bd 21, Teil B)

506
MATSUMOTO, Kaoru. Die Beziehung zwischen Mikado und Schogun vor 1868 im Spiegel der europäischen Schriftsteller: Eine kritische Untersuchung [The Relations between the Emperor and the Shogun before 1868 as Seen in the Works of European Authors: A Critical Study]. Heidelberg, 1931. Text in German. The dissertation in its published form is available at Marburg/Lahn, Universitätsbibliothek, Nr. VII C.

A critical comparison of European reports of the Meiji Restoration and of the actual events as presented by Japanese historians. Contents: A Survey of the History of the Empire, 1853-1858; Critical Comments about Individual Writers and Their Works; Three Ways of Interpreting the Relationship Existing between the Emperor and the Shogun; Debates over the Title "Shogun;" The Role and the Authority of the Emperor before the Restoration.

Rel.Publ.: Die Beziehung...Untersuchung. Wertheim a.M.-Heidelberg: E. Bechstein, 1931. 99p.

507
HATSUKADE, Itsuaki. Die Bildungsideale in der japanischen Kultur und ihr Einfluss auf das Erziehungswesen in der Yedo-Zeit [Educational Ideals in Japanese Culture and Their Influence on the Educational System of the Tokugawa Period]. Leipzig, 1932. Text in German. The dissertation in its published form is available at Marburg/Lahn, Universitätsbibliothek, Nr. XV C; also available at the University of Michigan, General Library, no. 10,900.

The following subjects are examined within the dissertation: (1) the educational ideals of the followers of Chu Hsi, Wang Yang-ming, and Yamaga Sokō; (2) the influence of the Tokugawa seclusion policy upon education; (3) educational ideals in early Confucian philosophy; (4) Ishida Baigan and the cultivation of the early Japanese spirit; (5) influence of Western culture; (6) the educational system under Matsudaira Norihira and the Mito daimyo families; (7) the influence of renewed contacts with the outside world on the educational system.

Rel.Publ.: Die Bildungsideale...Yedo-Zeit. Würzburg: Triltsch, 1932. ii, 86p.

ZIMMERMANN, Herbert. Politische Erziehung der Militärklasse (Samurai) in Japan zur Feudalzeit. 1935. See no.392.

508
BORTON, Hugh. Peasant Uprisings in Japan of the Tokugawa Period. Leiden, 1936.

A study of peasant uprisings as they appeared in the Tokugawa period, with particular focus on their origin and development, on the breakdown of centralized feudal control, and on the various regional types of uprisings. Contents: Characteristics of the Tokugawa Regime; Peasant Uprisings and Feudalism; Growth and Development of Peasant Uprisings; Further Uprisings Reveal the Real Weakness of the Central Government: Early Bakumatsu; Breakdown of Centralized Feudal Control: Late Bakumatsu; Regional Studies.

Rel.Publ.: Peasant...Period. Tokyo, 1938. xv, 219p. (Transactions of the Asiatic Society of Japan, 2d. ser., v.16). New York: Paragon, 1968 [2d. ed.].

HAENISCH, Wolfgang. Die auswartige Politik Ryūkyūs seit dem Anfang des 17. Jahrhunderts und der Einfluss der Fürsten von Satsuma. 1937. See no.688.

509
SCHÜFFNER, Rudolf. Die Fünferschaft als Grundlage der Staats- und Gemeindeverwaltung und des sozialen Friedens in Japan zur Zeit der Taikwa-Reform und in der Tokugawa-Periode [The Five-Man Mutual Responsibility Groups as a Basis for Administering the State and Community and for Maintaining Social Peace in Japan at the Time of the Taika Reform and during the Tokugawa Era]. Hamburg, 1938. Text in German. The dissertation in its published form is available at Marburg/Lahn, Staatsbibliothek Preussischer Kulturbesitz, Nr. Ser. 1171/30,E.

Part 1 is a study of the mutual responsibility groups--their organization, duties, and decline--during the period of the Taika reform. Part 2 examines the social structure, regional and central administration, local (i.e. village and city) organization, and finally the goningumi-system of the Tokugawa era. The appendix contains a translation of 40 articles found in the ordinances governing the five-man mutual responsibility system in 1853.

Rel.Publ.: Die Fünferschaft...Tokugawa-Periode. Tokyo: Deutsche Gesellschaft für Natur- und Völkerkunde Ostasiens; Leipzig: Harrassowitz, 1938. iii, 127p. (MOAG, Bd 30, Teil E)

510
PODPALOVA, G. I. Krest'ianskoe dvizhenie v Iaponii XVII-go i nachalo XVIII-go vekov: Petitsionnye vystupleniia [The Peasant Movement in Japan during the Seventeenth and the First Part of the Eighteenth Centuries: Appeals (Made to the Tokugawa Authorities)]. Moscow, Moskovskii institut vostokovedeniia, 1946. (Candidate of Historical Sciences degree) 404 + 10p. Text in Russian.

Rel.Publ.: Krest'ianskoe petitsionnoe dvizhenie v Iaponii vo vtoroi polovine XVII v. -- nachale XVIII v.

Moscow: Izdatel'stvo vostochnoi literatury, 1960. 278p. (Institut vostokovedeniia Akademii nauk SSSR)

511
ZAHL, Karl. Über die Ursachen der japanischen Revolution (Meiji-ishin). (Nach japanischen Quellen) [On the Causes of the Japanese Revolution: The Meiji Restoration. (According to Japanese Sources]. Hamburg, 1947. 179p. Text in German. Diss. ms. available at Hamburg, Staats- und Universitätsbibliothek, Nr. Diss. phil. Mscr. 43.

Contents: The Breakdown of Shogunal Finances and the Attempt to Bring About an Economic Adjustment; The Collapse of the Feudal Hierarchy, and the Gentry Transformed into a Bourgeoisie; The Intellectual Representation of the Tokugawa State; The Advance of the Western Powers into East Asia and Their Role in the Opening of Japan.

512
SMITH, Thomas Carlyle. Government Enterprise and the Initial Phase of Japanese Industrialization, 1850-1880. Harvard, 1948. v, 247p. AB: 5p. summary appended to the diss. ms.

"By studying the first three decades of modern industry in Japan, it is hoped to discover the decisive force (or forces) in initiating the process of industrialization." The author seeks to determine what considerations underlay the particular form of the government's industrial program, what enterprises were established by the Government in each field of industry and why, and what importance these enterprises had in terms of the early development of Japanese industry.

Rel.Publ.: Political Change and Industrial Development in Japan: Government Enterprise, 1868-1880. Palo Alto: Stanford University Press, 1955. x, 126p.; "The Introduction of Western Industry to Japan during the Last Years of the Tokugawa Period," Harvard Journal of Asiatic Studies, 11 (1948), 130-52.

513
STRAELEN, Henricus van, J.J.M. Yoshida Shōin: Forerunner of the Meiji Restoration. Cambridge, 1949. 252p. AB: University of Cambridge. Abstracts of Dissertations...1948/1949. p.120.

Studies the life of Yoshida Shōin (1830-1859) in its historical context, assesses Shōin's merits as a thinker by "tracing the sources of his ideas and by explaining his basic conceptions" as found in his writings, expounds his educational principles, and attempts to explain the reasons for his great influence. Included within the dissertation are translations of some of Yoshida Shōin's major writings.

Rel.Publ.: Yoshida...Restoration. Leiden: E. J. Brill, 1952. viii, 149p. (T'oung Pao Monographs, 2); "Yoshida Shōin as a Poet," in International Conference of Orientalists in Japan, Transactions, 5 (1960), 33-47; "Yoshida Shōin: Forerunner of the Meiji Restoration," in International Congress of Orientalists, 25th, Moscow, 1960, Trudy XXV Mezhdunarodnogo Kongressa Vostokovedov (Moscow: Izd.-vo vostochnoi lit-ry, 1963), v.5, p.382-86.

514
HALL, John Whitney. Modern Trends in Tokugawa Japan: The Life and Policies of Tanuma Okitsugu. Harvard, 1950. iii, 290p. AB: 6p. summary appended to diss. ms.

Contents: Characteristics of the Tokugawa Administrative System; Tanuma Okitsugu [1719-1788], Favorite of the Tenth Shogun; Filling the Bakufu Coffers; The Dutch and the Russians; Political Decline and Social Unrest; The Triumph of Reaction; In Retrospect.

Rel.Publ.: Tanuma Okitsugu (1719-1788): Forerunner of Modern Japan. Cambridge: Harvard University Press, 1955. xii, 208p. (Harvard-Yenching Monograph Series, 14); "The Tokugawa Bakufu and the Merchant Class," in University of Michigan, Center for Japanese Studies, Occasional Papers, 1 (Ann Arbor: University of Michigan Press, 1951), 26-33.

515
ACKROYD, Joyce Irene. Arai Hakuseki: Being a Study of His Political Career and Some of His Writings, with Special Reference to the Hankampu. Cambridge, 1951. 519p. AB: University of Cambridge. Abstracts of Dissertations...1951/1952. p.154-55.

It is noted that Arai "produced a quantity of Chinese classic poetry, wrote on philology in the Tōga, on economics in the Hakuseki kengi, on Western affairs in the Seiyō kibun and Sairan igen, on philosophy and religion in the Seiyō kibun and Kishin ron, on antiquities in the Honchō gunkikō, on botany in the Boke kō and most important of all on the history of Japan in the Hankampu and the Tokushi yoron, to mention a few titles."

516
TSUKAHIRA, Toshio George. The Sankin Kōtai System of Tokugawa Japan, 1600-1868. Harvard, 1951. iii, 241p. AB: United States Department of State, External Research Office. Abstracts of Completed Doctoral Dissertations for the Academic Year 1950/1951. p.357-59.

"A survey of the sankin kōtai system as it developed and functioned within the political and economic setting of Tokugawa Japan." Focuses on the economic impact of the system on daimyo finances. Contents: The Tokugawa Regime; The Origins and Development of the Sankin Kōtai; Structure and Operation of the System; The Economic Effects of the Sankin Kōtai; Contemporary Critiques of the System; The End of the System. The appendix contains a detailed table of the 265 daimyo han as of 1853.

Rel.Publ.: Feudal Control in Tokugawa Japan: The Sankin Kōtai System. Cambridge: Harvard University Press, 1966. xii, 228p. (Harvard East Asian Monographs, 20)

517
BUGAEVA, D. P. Krest'ianskoe dvizhenie v Iaponii vo vtoroi polovine XVIII v. -- v pervoi polovine XIX v. [The Peasant Movement in Japan in the Second Half of the Eighteenth Century and in the First Half of the Nineteenth Century]. Leningrad, Leningradskii gosudarstvennyi universitet imeni A. A. Zhdanova, 1953. (Candidate of Historical Sciences degree) 238p. Text in Russian. AB: 20p. summary published in 1953.

GOODMAN, Grant Kohn. The Dutch Impact on Japan (1640-1853). 1955. See no.1302.

HENDERSON, Dan. The Pattern and Persistence of Traditional Procedures in Japanese Law. 1955. See no.1554.

518
SHELDON, Charles David. The Rise of the Merchant Class in Tokugawa Japan, 1600-1868. California, Berkeley, 1955. 291p.

A survey description of the merchant class and of its major institutions.

Rel.Publ.: The Rise...1868. Locust Valley, N.Y.: J. J. Augustin, 1958. ix, 206p. (Association for Asian Studies: Monographs and Papers, 5)

519
EARL, David Magarey. Loyalty to Emperor and Nation in the Thinking of the Tokugawa Period. Columbia, 1957. 427p. DA 17 (Oct. 1957), 2302-03; UM 23,073.

A study of developments in political thinking during the Tokugawa period. "The closing section of the study is a detailed analysis of the political thinking of Yoshida Shōin."

Rel.Publ.: Emperor and Nation in Japan: Political Thinkers of the Tokugawa Period. Seattle: University of Washington Press, 1964. x, 270p.

520
MIYAUCHI, Dixon Yoshihide. Yokoi Shōnan: A Pre-Meiji Reformist. Harvard, 1957. v, 269p.

"The primary aim is to find out how Yokoi Shōnan [1809-1869], a Confucian samurai scholar from Higo han, managed to rise to a position of national prominence and helped carry out sweeping reforms during the chaotic final years of the Tokugawa shogunate." Contents: The Higo Background; Yokoi Shōnan's Life (Early Life and Education, Shōnan as a Teacher, Shōnan as a Political Advisor); Yoko; Shōnan's Ideas (Early Phase, Post-Perry Phase, Phase of Application in National Affairs, Influence and Significance of Shōnan's Ideas). The appendices include an annotated translation of the Kokuze sanron.

Rel.Publ.: "Kokuze sanron: Three Major Problems of State Policy...an Annotated Translation," MN 23 (1968), 156-86; "Yokoi Shōnan (1809-1869): A National Political Adviser from Kumamoto Han in Late Tokugawa Japan," Journal of Asian History, 3 (1969), 23-33.

521
SIGUR, Gaston Joseph, Jr. A History of Administration in Bizen Han. Michigan, 1957. 189p. DA 18 (Apr. 1958), 1409-10; UM 58-991.

Examines the central, rural, and municipal administration of Bizen during the Tokugawa period "in order to ascertain the degree of centralization achieved by its officials."

CHOI, Kee Il. Shibusawa Eiichi and His Contemporaries: A Study of Japanese Entrepreneurial History. 1958. See no.567.

522
KIM, Young-Chin. Disintegration of Political Power: An Analytical Study of the Genesis of the Meiji Restoration. Pennsylvania, 1958. 286p. DA 19 (Oct. 1958), 860; UM 58-3345.

"The objective of the study was to formulate and verify generalizations relevant to the political process in Japan, more specifically, to the occurrence and resolution of revolutionary crisis. Factors were identified and analyzed which seemed to have a significant impact on the disintegration and mortality of power in the Tokugawa society leading up to the Meiji Restoration."

Rel.Publ.: "On Political Thought in Tokugawa Japan," Journal of Politics, 23 (Feb. 1961), 127-45.

523
WEBB, Herschel Ferdinand. The Thought and Work of the Early Mito School. Columbia, 1958. 306p. DA 19 (Aug. 1958), 316; UM 58-2719.

A description of the principles of ethics and politics which the compilers of the Dai Nihon shi incorporated into the work and a study of the means by which the principles were expressed within it. The dissertation also includes translations of certain sections of the Dai Nihon shi and of related works by Mito scholars.

Rel.Publ.: "The Mito Theory of the State," in Columbia University, East Asian Institute, Researches in the Social Sciences on Japan, 4 (Feb. 1957), 33-52; "What is the Dai Nihon shi?," JAS, 19 (Feb. 1960), 135-49; The Japanese Imperial Institution in the Tokugawa Period. New York: Columbia University Press, 1968. xiii, 296p. (Studies of the East Asian Institute, Columbia University)

524
CRAIG, Albert Morton. Chōshū and the Meiji Restoration, 1840-1868. Harvard, 1959. ii, 459p.

Examines and analyzes the structure of Chōshū han and its role in the Restoration movement. Contents: Background: The Position of Chōshū in Tokugawa Japan; Background: Chōshū's Finances and the Tokugawa Economy; Chōshū and the Tempō Reform; The Early Stage of Bakumatsu Politics, 1853-1861; The Intellectual Background in Chōshū; The Rise of Chōshū in National Politics, 1861-1863; The Decline of the Chōshū Sonnō Jōi Movement, 1863-1864; The Chōshū Civil War; The March to Power.

Rel.Publ.: Chōshū in the Meiji Restoration. Cambridge: Harvard University Press, 1961. 385, xxxix p. (Harvard Historical Monographs, 47); "The Restoration Movement in Chōshū," JAS, 18 (Feb. 1959), 187-97.

525
NEVILLE, Edwin Lowe, Jr. The Development of Transportation in Japan: A Case Study of Okayama Han, 1600-1868. Michigan, 1959. 187p. DA 20 (Oct. 1959), 1334; UM 59-3947.

Chapters 1-3 present a general description of transportation and communication in Tokugawa Japan. Chapters 4-5 focus on the land and sea transportation systems specifically in Okayama han.

526
IWATA, Masakazu. Ōkubo Toshimichi: The Leading Protagonist on the Stage of the Restoration Drama. California, Los Angeles, 1960. 588p.

A biographical study focusing on Ōkubo's role in the Meiji Restoration. Contents: The Spirit and Structure of Tokugawa Japan; Ōkubo's Formative Years; Ōkubo, The Champion of Court-Camp Unity; Ōkubo, The Champion of the Restoration; Ōkubo, The Architect of Modern Japan; Ōkubo, The Statesman and Soldier; Ōkubo, The Statesman Diplomat.

Rel.Publ.: Ōkubo Toshimichi: The Bismarck of Japan. Berkeley: University of California Press, 1964. viii, 376p. (Publications of the Center for Japanese and Korean Studies)

527
LEE, Edwin Borden, Jr. The Political Career of Ii Naosuke. Columbia, 1960. 200p. DA 21 (Nov. 1960), 1175-76; UM 60-3104.

A descriptive biography. Contents: The Ii Family; The Impact of the Perry Expedition; From Perry to Harris: Domestic Problems; Hotta Masayoshi's Journey to Kyoto; Ii Takes Control; Kyoto Challenges Ii; The Ansei Daigoku; Ii at the Height of His Power; The Assassination of Ii Naosuke.

528
CHIN, Tung-yuan. Sotsial'no-ekonomicheskoe polozhenie v iaponskoi derevne nakanune revoliutsii 1867-1868 gg. [Socio-Economic Conditions in the Japanese Village on the Eve of the Meiji Revolution]. Moscow, Moskovskii gosudarstvennyi universitet imeni M. V. Lomonosova, Institut vostochnykh iazykov, 1961. (Candidate of Historical Sciences degree) 127p. Text in Russian.

529
OBELSKY, Alvan Jerome. Pre-Conditions of Economic Development: An Analysis of the Japanese Case. Michigan, 1961. 222p. DA 22 (Feb. 1962), 2625-26; UM 61-6403.

Certain factors crucial to Japan's successful development during the Meiji period--"the presence of highly favorable economic propensities and of a vigorous entrepreneurial group"--are explained in terms of the prevailing social value system and of the characteristics of economic and political institutions existing in the late Tokugawa period.

Rel.Publ.: "Japan's Transition: A Socio-Economic Interpretation," Kobe University Economic Review, 9 (1963), 1-12.

530
CHAMBLISS, William Jones. Chiaraijima Village: Land Tenure, Taxation, and Local Trade, 1818-1884. Michigan, 1963. 241p. DA 24 (June 1964), 5353-54; UM 64-6663.

Seeks to "determine the effect of commerce and taxation on peasant land tenure and the relation between landed status and the holding of village office." Contents: Pt.1: Chiaraijima Village during the Late Tokugawa Period: Village and Domain; Village Commerce and Peasant Traders; The Village Land and Its Division among the Peasants; Taxation during the Late Tokugawa Period. Pt.2: Chiaraijima Village after the Meiji Land Tax Reform: Land Tenure and Village Office Following the Meiji Land Tax Reform; Taxation during the Early Meiji Period. Appendix 2 (p.169-86) discusses the peasant background of Shibusawa Eiichi (1940-1931).

Rel.Publ.: Chiaraijima...1884. Tucson: University of Arizona Press, 1965. xiv, 159p. (Association for Asian Studies: Monographs and Papers, 19)

531
CHANG, Richard Taiwon. Fujita Tōko and Sakuma Shōzan: Bakumatsu Intellectuals and the West. Michigan, 1964. 336p. DA 25 (Dec. 1964), 3530-31; UM 64-12,574.

"An examination of the changing image of the West held by two leading early nineteenth-century intellectuals: Fujita Tōko (1806-1855) of Mito and Sakuma Shōzan (1811-1864) of Matsushira."

Rel.Publ.: "Yokoi Shōnan's View of Christianity," MN, 21 (1966), 266-72; "Fujita Tōko's Image of the West," Journal of Asian History, 2 (1968), 130-40.

532
TOTMAN, Conrad Davis. Politics in the Tokugawa Bakufu. Harvard, 1964. xiii, 328p. AB: 3p. summary appended to diss. ms.

"The thesis is a study of the internal political development of the Tokugawa shogunate. It discusses the overall situation of the Tokugawa house: Its origins and early development, its lands, its fiscal arrangements, its military system, the structure of the Tokugawa castle, site of its political activities, its formal administrative organization, and the character of the major groups which had a role in Tokugawa affairs. Then it describes the informal organization of the house government, the Bakufu, outlining its internal power structure and the operating techniques of Bakufu leaders. Finally it traces the gradual evolution of this power structure and of its leadership from the establishment of the Bakufu until the mid-nineteenth century."

Rel.Publ.: Politics in the Tokugawa Bakufu, 1600-1843. Cambridge: Harvard University Press, 1967. 346p. (Harvard East Asian Series, 30); "Political Succession in the Tokugawa Bakufu: Abe Masahiro's Rise to Power, 1843-1845," Harvard Journal of Asiatic Studies, 26 (1966), 102-24.

WERNECKE, Wolfgang. Maejima Hisoka (1835-1919) und seine Vorschläge zur japanischen Sprache und Schrift: Die Anfänge des Reformgedankens in der japanischen Sprache um die Zeit der unvollendeten bürgerlichen Revolution in Japan. Mit Einschluss von 3 Arbeiten des Maejima zum Gegenstand, darunter der originären Denkschrift an den Shōgun Tokugawa Yoshinobu vom Jahre 1866 dargestellt. 1964. See no. 1508.

ALTMAN, Albert Avraham. The Emergence of the Press in Meiji Japan. 1965. See no. 605.

533
OPITZ, Fritz. Die Lehensreformen des Tokugawa Nariaki nach dem Hitachi-obi des Fujita Tōko: Ein Beitrag zur Lehensgeschichte der Tokugawa-Zeit [The Feudal Reforms of Tokugawa Nariaki According to the Hitachi obi of Fujita Tōko: A Contribution to the Feudal History of the Tokugawa Period]. München, 1965. Text in German. The dissertation in its published form is available at München, Universitätsbibliothek; also at the University of Michigan, General Library, no.33,210.

I. An historical survey of the great reforms of the Tokugawa period that were carried out by Arai Hakuseki and Tokugawa Yoshimune, Matsudaira Sadanobu, and Mizuno Tadakuni. II. The growth of Mito han, together with the family tree of the daimyo of the han. III. The reforms of Tokugawa Nariaki: (1800-1860): methods of feudal administration, economy measures and economic reforms in Mito han, reorganization of the system of defense, and reform of the educational system. IV. The personality of Fujita Tōko (a leading adviser to Tokugawa Nariaki), the origins of his work Hitachi obi, and an annotated translation of it.

Rel.Publ.: Die Lehensreformen...Tokugawa-Zeit. München, 1965. 69p.

534
PHAM-van-Thuan. Les Fondements socio-économiques de la revolution industrielle du Japon [The Socio-Economic Foundations of the Japanese Industrial Revolution]. Lausanne, 1965. Text in French.

Part 1 is a study of Tokugawa society and Tokugawa economic organization. Part 2 examines the manner in which the Meiji leaders launched Japan on the path towards economic modernization.

Rel.Publ.: La Construction du Japon moderne. Lausanne: Centre de Recherches Européennes, 1966. 195p.

535
FROST, Peter Kip. Tokugawa Monetary Policy. Harvard, 1966. v, 251p.

Seeks to "judge the nature of the bakufu by analyzing the development of its monetary policy between 1600 and 1867." Contents: (1) Establishment: The Demand for Money; The Supply of Precious Metals; The Copper, Silver, and Gold Coinage Systems; Gold and

Silver Circulation; Paper Money; Exchange Rates and Prices. (2) Debasement: The Decision to Debase the Coinage System; Growth of Monetary Controls; Copper Coinage, Silver and Paper Money, and Gold Coinage Changes; Profit and Loss. (3) Collapse: Admiral Perry's Exchange Rate; Townsend Harris' Exchange Rate; The Ansei Recoinage 1858-1859; The Treasure Trade; The Man'en Currency Reform (1860); The Mexican Silver Dollar; Inflation.

536
NISHIO, Harry Kaneharu. Political Authority Structure and the Development of Entrepreneurship in Japan (1603-1890). California, Berkeley, 1966. 289p. DA 27 (Sept. 1966), 577-78-A; UM 66-8350.

The study "pays particular attention to relationships between samurai elites, and wealthy merchants in order to assess the influence of political leadership and ideas upon developing entrepreneurial institutions and ideas" during the Tokugawa and early Meiji periods.

537
KEMPER, Ulrich. Arai Hakuseki und sein Geschichtsauffassung: Ein Beitrag zur Historiographie Japans in der Tokugawa-Zeit [Arai Hakuseki and His View of History: A Contribution to the Historiography of Japan during the Tokugawa Period]. München, 1967. Text in German. The dissertation in its published form is available at Bochum, Universitätsbibliothek, Inv. Nr. GB 37,877; also at the University of Michigan, General Library, no. D5834.9.A66K32.

A descriptive and critical essay over Oritaku shibanoki, the memoirs of Arai Hakuseki (1657-1725), and over Hakuseki's historical writings in general is followed by an examination of his views of history, a study of his Dokushi-yoron, and information on various changes that he advocated regarding Tokugawa authority and the Buke Sho-Hatto ("the Laws Governing the Military Households"). The dissertation concludes with an examination of the views that later generations have had of Arai Hakuseki and of the positions that have been taken by a number of authors who have written about him.

Rel.Publ.: Arai...Tokugawa-Zeit. Wiesbaden: Harrassowitz, 1967. 105p. (Studien zur Japanologie, 9)

538
MAËS, Hubert. Hiraga Gennai et son temps [Hiraga Gennai and His Times]. Paris, 1967. 170p. Text in French. AB: Université de Paris. Faculté des Lettres et Sciences Humaines. Positions des thèses de troisième cycle soutenues devant la Faculté en 1967. (Série "Recherches," t.52), p.215-16.

A descriptive study of the life and activities of Hiraga Gennai (1729-1779) and of Japanese society during the eighteenth century.

MATSUDA, Mitsugu. The Government of the Kingdom of Ryukyu, 1609-1872. 1967. See no.704.

ORDRONIC, Walter John. Kodō taii (An Outline of the Ancient Way): An Annotated Translation with an Introduction to the Shintō Revival Movement and a Sketch of the Life of Hirata Atsutane. 1967. See no.1965.

539
DOMBRADY, Géza Siegfried. Watanabe Kazan: Ein japanischer Gelehrter des 19. Jahrhunderts [Watanabe Kazan: A Nineteenth Century Japanese Scholar]. Hamburg, 1968. (Habilitationsschrift) Text in German. The dissertation in its published form is available at Bochum, Bibliothek des Ostasien—Instituts; also at the University of Michigan, General Library, no. QH5.G38 v.47.

A biographical study of Watanabe Kazan (1793-1841) which focuses on Watanabe's intellectual development, his views as a moralist and as a teacher, his study of yōgaku and his political concepts, and his artistic and poetic endeavors. A translation of Watanabe's Shinkiron is found in the appendix.

Rel.Publ.: Watanabe...Jahrhunderts. Hamburg, 1968. 226p. (MOAG, 47)

540
LAMBERTI, Matthew V. A Political Study of Tokugawa Nariaki of Mito: 1800-1860. Columbia, 1968. 381p. DA 29 (Feb. 1969), 2623-A; UM 69-415.

"Examines the political ideas of a daiymo as one of several currents of thought during the nineteenth century." Also studies Nariaki's personal rise to a position of influence and his role as patron of the Mito school.

541
MOORE, Ray Arvil. Samurai Social Mobility in Tokugawa Japan. Michigan, 1968. 413p. DA 30 (Aug. 1969), 664-A; UM 64-12,189.

"Concerned with the extent and means of change in social status as the Tokugawa system matured and as long-term changes began to make their influence felt." Following a presentation of the nature of the Tokugawa stratification system, the author explains why he has selected the size and kind of samurai stipend as "the most sensitive and available indicator of status" within the society. He then analyzes data collected from extant records for four han (Hikone, Kaga, Owari, Sendai) for three time periods (1680-1700; 1750-1780; 1830-1860) to determine the patterns and channels of mobility within the elite samurai class.

Rel.Publ.: "Samurai Discontent and Social Mobility in the Late Tokugawa Period," MN, 24 (1969), 79-91.

542
BOLITHO, Harold. The Fudai Daimyo and the Tokugawa Settlement. Yale, 1969. 299p. DA 30 (Feb. 1970); UM 70-2699.

Studies the role and power of the fudai daimyo in the Bakufu, concluding that it was their collective power and competing baronial interests which prevented the accumulation of great power in the central government. The author asserts that "historians, believing too readily that the fudai were more bureaucrats than barons, have...assumed that they were the model servants of centralized feudalism. An examination of their roles, however, supports no such belief."

543
HAUSER, William Barry. Economic Institutional Change in Tokugawa Japan: The Osaka Cotton Trade. Yale, 1969. ix, 303p.

The dissertation attempts to show the relationship between innovation in the commercial sector and changing commercial policies of the Tokugawa bakufu. Contents: Tokugawa Commerce: Phase of Dynamic Growth; Tokugawa Commerce: Maturity and the Critical Confrontation; The Osaka Cotton Trade: Establishment and Consolidation; The Osaka Cotton Trade: Institutional Decline [from the Kansei Reforms through the Tempō Reforms]; The Edo Cotton Trade: Four Case Studies [Kashiwaya, Hasegawa, Shirokiya, Daimaruya]; Conclusions: A

New Perspective for Institutional Change.

544
STEPHAN, John Jason. Ezo under the Tokugawa Bakufu, 1799-1821: An Aspect of Japan's Frontier History. London, 1969. 344p.
Examines Japan's northern frontier in Ezo (Hokkaido), Karafuto, and Chishima (Kurile Islands) when these areas were administered for the first time by the Tokugawa Bakufu. The author concludes that the Japanese administration of these areas witnessed the implementation of dynamic social and economic policies that not only changed the areas' relationship to Japan and led to the promotion of Japanese markets and of Ainu culture but also were responsible for subsequent Russian hostilities and Russo-Japanese boundary disputes.

MODERN

Modern, 1868-1945: General

545
IWASAKI, Uichi. The Working Forces in Japanese Politics: A Brief Account of Political Conflicts, 1867-1920. Columbia, 1921. 143p.
Examines the working forces in Japanese politics as dynamic forces rather than as static conditions. Contents: The Emperor; The Genrō, or the Elder Statesmen; The Peers; The Bureaucrats; The Militarists; The Political Parties; The Capitalists; The Workers.
Rel.Publ.: The Working...1920. New York: Columbia University, 1921. 143p. (Studies in History, Economics, and Public Law, ed. by the Faculty of Columbia University, v.97, no.1; whole no.220)

546
SATO, Hiroshi. Democracy and the Japanese Government. Columbia, 1921. Diss. ms. not available.
A study of the interrelationship of the democratic processes and of (1) the Executive Department, (2) the Legislative Department, (3) the Japanese Election Law before 1919, (4) the Movement for the Extension of the Suffrage, (5) local government, and (6) municipal government.
Rel.Publ.: Democracy...Government. New York: Arbor Press, 1920. iv, 97p.

FAHS, Charles Burton. The Japanese House of Peers. 1933. See no.1571.

HAHN, Karl. Die Industrialisierung Japans. 1933. See no.203.

547
YANAGA, Chitoshi. Theory of the Japanese State. California, Berkeley, 1934. 345p.
Discusses the nature of the Japanese state with emphasis on its totalitarian, Imperial, and theocratic aspects. Contents: The Nature of the Japanese State; The Emperor; Bushidō; Religion and the State; The Constitution.

GOL'DBERG, D. I. Rabochee dvizhenie v Iaponii do 1917g. 1938. See no.289.

548
WENCK, Günther. Die japanischen Minister als politische Führung [The Japanese Ministerial Office as a Form of Political Leadership]. Leipzig, 1940. Text in German. The dissertation in its published form is available at Marburg/Lahn, Universitätsbibliothek, Nr. XVIII C.
The following problems are treated within the dissertation: (1) The Japanese constitution, the position of the Emperor, the Emperor's sovereign rights, and his relationship with his ministers. (2) The internal structure of the Cabinet and its political basis; and the responsibility of the Cabinet to and its position within the Privy Council and the two branches of the Diet. (3) The balance of power between the Lower House and the government. (4) The problem of Japanese political leadership and Japan's constitutional and parliamentary system.
Rel.Publ.: Die japanischen...Führung. Leipzig: Meiner, 1940. viii, 139p. (Abhandlungen des Instituts für Politik, ausländisches öffentliches Recht, und Völkerrecht an der Universität Leipzig. N.F., Heft 6)

549
BAKER, Alonzo Lafayette. The Influence of the Divine Emperor Doctrine upon Japan. Southern California, 1948. 421p. AB: University of Southern California. Abstracts of Dissertations for...1948. p.147-50.
Attempts to ascertain the role of the doctrine of a divine Emperor in the development of Japan, 1868-1945. Concludes that "without the divine Emperor doctrine, the forces always generated by industrialism, and by the impact of modern science and the scientific method would have in due time liberalized and perhaps even democratized Japan. But the greatest of all repressive agents--the divine Emperor doctrine--blocked the way to democratization.

JOHNSTON, Bruce F. Food and Agriculture in Japan, 1880-1950. 1953. See no.172.

550
SUH, Doo Soo. The Struggle for Academic Freedom in Japanese Universities before 1945. Columbia, 1953. 493p. DA 13 (1953), 201; UM 4901.
Focuses on the history of government restrictions on academic freedom and on the struggle for some degree of academic freedom in Japanese universities.

551
SUTTON, Joseph Lee. A Political Biography of Inukai Tsuyoshi. Michigan, 1954. 291p. DA 14 (Aug. 1954), 1246; UM 8421.
The political development, the methods, and the problems of democratic parties in Japan before 1932 as well as the background and activities of their members are all examined within the framework of Inukai's life. Contents: Setting the Scene; The Beginnings of Inukai the Politician; The First Election; Clan Violence and Party Victory; Inukai's Local Machine; Inukai's Role in the Party Movement; The Spokesman for Japan's Alternative to Militarism; The Anti-Climax; Inukai and Japanese Politics.

ANDERSON, Ronald S. Nishi Honganji and Japanese Buddhist Nationalism, 1862-1945. 1956. See no.1905.

KOKORIS, James A. The Economic and Financial Development of Okayama Prefecture, Japan. 1956. See no.326.

RANIS, Gustav. Japan: A Case Study in Development. 1956. See no.149.

AOKI, Hideo. The Effect of American Ideas upon Japanese Higher Education. 1957. See no.425.

AUERBACH, Arnold. Capital étranger et développement économique au Japon: 1868-1938. 1958. See no.327.

552
JOSHIDA, Miriam Misao. Politische Parteien und Gruppen in Japans Innenpolitik von 1886-1931 [Political Parties and Groups in Japanese Domestic Politics, 1886-1931]. Würzburg, 1958. iv, 205p. Text in German. Diss. ms. available at Würzburg, Universitätsbibliothek, Nr. U 58.7885.

Contents: Japan's Internal Development up to the Beginning of the Meiji Era; Assumptions and Effects of Japan's Domestic Policy; The Formation of the Parties and the First Imperial Diet (1874-1894); The Sino-Japanese War and Japan's First Move towards Expansion [and] the Growth of the Parties (1894-1904); The Russo-Japanese War and the Political Struggle among the Parties (1904-1916); The Consequences of World War I and the First Party Cabinets (1916-1928); The Manchurian Incident and the Military Seizure of Power (1928-1940).

ROSOVSKY, Henry. Japanese Capital Formation, 1868-1940. 1959. See no.151.

KANG, Moon Hyung. The Monetary Aspect of Economic Development in Japan with Special Reference to Monetary Policies: 1868-1935. 1960. See no.332.

COGSWELL, James A. A History of the Work of the Japan Mission of the Presbyterian Church in the United States, 1885-1960. 1961. See no.1937.

OTT, David J. The Financial Development of Japan, 1878-1958. 1961. See no.335.

SAKURAI, Kinichiro. Financial Aspects of [the] Economic Development of Japan from 1868 to [the] Present. 1961. See no.336.

LEE, Kun Sam. The Christian Confrontation with Shinto Nationalism: A Historical and Critical Study of the Conflict of Christianity and Shinto in Japan in the Period between the Meiji Restoration and the End of World War II (1868-1945). 1962. See no.1939.

WALLACE, William M. Cultural Values and Economic Development: A Case Study of Japan. 1962. See no.83.

553
BAGGS, Albert Edward. Social Evangel as Nationalism: A Study of the Salvation Army in Japan, 1895-1940. State University of New York at Buffalo, 1966. 407p. DA 27 (Dec. 1966), 1905-A; UM 66-12,103.

"This study probes the causes and effects of the Japanese Salvation Army's deep commitment to the spirit of nationalism." It explores the Salvation Army's English origins and its basically conservative nature, presents a biographical study of the Army's first native Japanese officer, Yamamura Gumpei, and "explains how and why the Army in the space of twelve years rose from obscurity to national reknown and gained official recognition from the state." The Army's social service work "is explored in depth by describing its relief program at the time of the Kanto Earthquake of 1923 and by dissecting the various aspects and purposes of its work" during the height of Japan's economic depression (1931/32). The final chapter analyzes the struggle of the Japanese branch of the Salvation Army for a greater degree of autonomy within the Army's worldwide power structure.

554
MARSHALL, Byron Kipling. Ideology and Industrialization in Japan, 1868-1941: The Creed of the Prewar Business Elite. Stanford, 1966. 254p. DA 27 (July 1966), 167-68-A; UM 66-6370.

"The chief purpose of this dissertation is to analyze the factors that account for the reluctance of Japanese businessmen to break with the values of the past to seek a more adequate ideological justification for the private enterprise system. The character of the Meiji Restoration, the climate of nationalism, the economic role of government, the social background of the business elite itself, the problem of recruiting an industrial workforce, and the significance of the example of labor relations in the West are discussed in relation to the development of business ideology up to 1941."

Rel.Publ.: Capitalism and Nationalism in Prewar Japan: The Ideology of the Business Elite, 1868-1941. Stanford: Stanford University Press, 1967. xi, 163p.

555
BENJAMIN, Roger Wayne. Military Influence in Foreign Policy-Making. Washington, St. Louis, 1967. 252p. DA 28 (Jan. 1968), 2754-A; UM 67-17,176.

Formulates a series of generalizations concerning the role of military leaders in foreign policy-making by "analyzing the level of military influence in 57 foreign policy issues from the USA (1918-1954), Japan (1894-1945), France (1904-1954), and Germany (1871-1938)."

CAIGER, John G. Education, Values, and Japan's National Identity: A Study of the Aims and Contents of Courses in Japanese History, 1872-1963. 1967. See no.420.

556
MIWA, Kimitada. Crossroads of Patriotism in Imperial Japan: Shiga Shigetaka (1863-1927), Uchimura Kanzō (1861-1930), and Nitobe Inazō (1862-1933). Princeton, 1967. 467p. DA 28 (June 1968), 4996-97-A; UM 68-8952.

The dissertation is "a study of patriotism conceived of as a condition of mind, not as a system of thought." It is based on a study of the lives of three prominent men who "shared a similar social background and education" but whose ideas and activities were strikingly different.

Meiji Period, 1868-1912: General

See also History--Modern, 1868-1945 (pages 72-73).

YOKOYAMA, Masajiro. The Development of the Land Tax in Japan. 1904. See no.469.

KAWABÉ, Kisaburō. The Press and Politics in Japan: A Study of the Relations between the Newspaper and the Political Development of Modern Japan. 1919. See no.1673.

557
IKÉMOTO, Kisao. La Restauration de l'ère de Meiji et sa répercussion sur les milieux agricoles japonais, 1867-1930 [The Meiji Restoration and Its Impact on the Agricultural Classes of Society]. Nancy, 1930. Text in French.

Contents: The Feudal Regime; Disintegration of the Feudal Regime and the Meiji Restoration (Collapse of the Tokugawa Shogunate, Internal Situation at the Time of the Restoration, External Influences); The Restoration's Impact on the Peasantry (Meiji Political Reforms, Impact of the Reforms on the Peasantry, Revision of Agricultural Regulations, Agricultural Riots, The Warrior Class and Its Participation in Rural Affairs).

Rel.Publ.: La Restauration...1930. Paris: Les presses universitaires de France, 1931. 370p.

558
REISCHAUER, Robert Karl. Alien Land Tenure in Japan. Harvard, 1935. viii, 257p. AB: Harvard University. Summaries of Theses...1935. p.172-77.

Contents: Before the Coming of Perry; The Period of the "Old Treaties" and the Treaty Ports, 1854-1899 (Treaties Opening Japan, Establishment and History of the Foreign Settlements, Land Rights and Taxation, Promulgation of the New Treaties and the End of Extraterritoriality); The Controversy over Perpetual Leases, 1899-1934 (Controversy over (a) the Status of Lands and Buildings on Them, (b) National and Municipal Taxation); Land Tenure of Aliens since 1899.

Rel.Publ.: Alien...Japan. Tokyo: Asiatic Society of Japan, 1936. iii, 137p. (TASJ. 2d ser., v.13, 1936)

559
SCHEINPFLUG, Alfons. Die japanische Kolonisation in Hokkaido [The Japanese Colonization of Hokkaido]. Leipzig, 1935. Text in German. The dissertation in its published form is available at Marburg/Lahn, Universitätsbibliothek, Nr. VI C; also at the University of Michigan, General Library, no. DS895.H72S3.

Studies the geography of Hokkaido, the island's colonization during the Meiji era, and its development. Includes a description of the rural and urban settlements established along the island's coasts and in the interior, of Hokkaido's economy, and of the distribution of population throughout the area.

Rel.Publ.: Die japanische...Hokkaido. Leipzig: Hirt, 1935. 132p. (Mitteilungen der Gesellschaft für Erdkunde zu Leipzig, 53)

560
JENSEN, Gustav. Japans Wille und Weg zur Seemacht: Ein Beitrag zu Japans Kampf um selbstbehauptung und Gleichberechtigung in den Jahren 1853-1895 [Japan's "Will and Way" to the Attainment of Naval Power: A Contribution to the History of Japan's Struggle for Self-Determination and Equality during the Years 1853-1895]. Hamburg, 1937. Text in German. The dissertation in its published form is available at Berlin West, Staatsbibliothek Preussischer Kulturbesitz, Nr. Un 19323; also at the University of Michigan, General Library, no. VA653.J54.

The study focuses on the development of Japanese shipping, the growth of Japan's merchant marine, the organization of her army and navy, the construction of the country's first capital ships, and the arms race with China.

Rel.Publ.: Japans...1895. Berlin: Siegismund, 1938. 379p. [Also published under the title Japans Seemacht: Der schnelle Aufstieg in Kampf um Selbstbehauptung und Gleichberechtigung in den Jahren 1853-1895. Berlin: Siegismund, 1938. 379p.]

TSURU, Shigeto. Developments of Capitalism and Business Cycles in Japan, 1868-1897. 1940. See no.315.

561
BOLLER, Paul Franklin, Jr. The American Board and the Dōshisha, 1875-1900. Yale, 1947. 307p. DA 28 (May 1968), 4456-A; UM 65-7519.

"A study of a quarter of a century of co-operation between American missionaries and the Japanese at Dōshisha University, one of the largest private universities in Japan, with an emphasis on the impact of nineteenth-century American Protestantism upon Japanese thought, and the gradual evolution in attitudes which took place among the Japanese and Americans working at the school."

562
EGGERS, Melvin Arnold. Economic Development of Japan, 1850-1900. Yale, 1950. 230p.

Japan's economic development is examined in order to test the theory that economic development in general is a process of social learning. As a result of his study, the author is able to point to the following factors as being critical in the growth of economic activity in Japan: (1) the motivation of a minority of men to seek new ways of achieving status, (2) the success of the strongly motivated minority in gaining control of the central government, and (3) the ability of these men, who desired change, to agree as to what the nature of the change should be.

563
SCHWANTES, Robert Sidney. American Influence in the Education of Meiji Japan, 1868-1912. Harvard, 1950. iv, 370p. AB: 4p. summary appended to diss. ms.

Contents: Japan's Educational Problem; The American Teacher in Japan; Higher Education in Tokyo: American Influence on the Japanese Public School System; Japanese Students in America, 1865-1885; Wider Ranges of Thought; Vocational and Professional Education; Art and Music; Education of Women; Christianity vs. Materialism; American Influence in a Period of Reaction; The Importance of Cultural Relations. Appendices: (1) American Teachers in Japan, 1860-1912; (2) Japanese Students in America, 1865-1885.

Rel.Publ.: "Results of Study Abroad: Japanese Students in America, 1865-1885," School and Society, 72 (Dec. 9, 1950), 375-76; "Christianity versus Science: A Conflict of Ideas in Meiji Japan," FEQ, 12 (Feb. 1953), 123-32; Japanese and Americans: A Century of Cultural Relations. New York: Harper, 1955. xi, 380p.; "The Teacher as Carrier of Culture: Japan in the Meiji Era," in Japanese National Commission for UNESCO, International Symposium on History of Eastern and Western Cultural Contacts, Tokyo and Kyoto, 1957, Collection of Papers Presented (Tokyo, 1954), 121-25; "Educational Influence of the United States of America," Contemporary Japan, 26 (May 1960), 442-58.

REUBENS, Edwin P. Foreign Capital in Economic Development: The Japanese Experience, 1868-1913. 1952. See no.319.

564
CODY, Cecil Earl. A Study of the Career of Itagaki Taisuke (1837-1919), a Leader of the Democratic Movement in Meiji Japan. Washington, Seattle, 1955. 361p. DA 15 (Dec. 1955), 2388; UM 14,245

Contents: Itagaki's Career through the Restoration Reforms, 1837-1873; The Parliamentary Period, 1874-1889; Leader of a Parliamentary Party, 1890-1900; Retirement, 1900-1919.

Rel.Publ.: "A Japanese Liberal's Response to Europe," Historian, 21 (Feb. 1959), 176-86.

565
HACKETT, Roger Fleming. Yamagata Aritomo: A Political Biography. Harvard, 1955. iii, 417p. AB: 6p. summary appended to diss. ms.

A descriptive study of Yamagata's career which focuses on his role in the building of Japanese institutions and on his influence as a leading Meiji political figure. Contents: The Making of an Oligarch; Consolidating the Imperial Rule; Establishing the Political Framework; Leading the Nation; The Elder Statesman.

Rel.Publ.: "Yamagata and the Taishō Crisis, 1912-1913," in Studies on Asia, 1962, ed. by Sidney D. Brown (Lincoln: University of Nebraska Press, 1962), 21-38; "The Meiji Leaders and Modernization: The Case of Yamagata Aritomo," in Changing Japanese Attitudes toward Modernization, ed. by Marius B. Jansen (Princeton: Princeton University Press, 1965), 243-73; "Political Modernization and the Meiji Genrō," in Political Development in Modern Japan, ed. by Robert E. Ward (Princeton: Princeton University Press, 1968), 65-97; Yamagata Aritomo. Cambridge: Harvard University Press, forthcoming.

566
TETERS, Barbara Joan. The Conservative Opposition in Japanese Politics, 1877-1894. Washington, Seattle, 1955. 253p. DA 15 (Nov. 1955), 2278; UM 14,264.

A study of "the conservative opposition that emerged in protest against the solutions offered by both the government and the political parties to the political, constitutional, and foreign policy problems" of Japan, 1877-1894.

Rel.Publ.: "The Genrō In and the National Essence Movement," PHR, 31 (Nov. 1962), 359-78.

BEST, Ernest E. The Influence of Political and Economic Factors upon the Development of Protestant Christianity in Japanese Society, 1859-1911. 1958. See no.1935.

567
CHOI, Kee Il. Shibusawa Eiichi and His Contemporaries: A Study of Japanese Entrepreneurial History. Harvard, 1958. x, 333p. AB: 4p. summary appended to diss. ms.

Shibusawa Eiichi (1840-1931), peasant-born entrepreneur and leader in Japan's early industrialization. Contents: Factors in the Emergence of New Leadership in the Nineteenth Century; Shibusawa's Life in His Native Village; The Crucial Years of Shibusawa's Life; The Milieu of the Early Meiji Era; Shibusawa as Treasury Official; Shibusawa's First Three Years as a Banker.

Rel.Publ.: "Tokugawa Feudalism and the Emergence of the New Leaders of Early Modern Japan," Explorations in Entrepreneurial History, 9 (Dec. 1956), 72-90.

568
LEBRA, Joyce Chapman. Japan's First Modern Popular Statesman: A Study of the Political Career of Ōkuma Shigenobu (1838-1922). Radcliffe, 1958. ii, 302p. AB: 7p. summary appended to diss. ms.

"A political biography concentrating chiefly on Ōkuma's role in domestic political developments...and particularly on those events which form a part in Japan's development in parliamentary government." Contents: Ōkuma in the Restoration Government; The 1881 Political Crisis; The Kaishintō; The Kuroda Cabinet; Party Development and the Second Matsukata Cabinet; The Kenseitō Cabinet; Ōkuma's Taishō Cabinet; Epilogue.

Rel.Publ.: "Ōkuma Shigenobu and the 1881 Political Crisis," JAS, 18 (Aug. 1959), 475-87; "Ōkuma Shigenobu: Meiji Statesman without a Regional Base of Power," in International Conference of Orientalists in Japan, Transactions, 5 (1960), 58-68; "Kaishintō no sōritsusha oyobi rironka Ōno Azusa," Nihon rekishi, 149 (Oct. 1960), 61-67; "Yano Fumio: Meiji Intellectual, Party Leader, and Bureaucrat," MN, 20 (1965), 1-14; "The Kaishintō as a Political Elite," in Modern Japanese Leadership: Transition and Change, ed. by Bernard S. Silberman and Harry D. Harootunian (Tucson: University of Arizona Press, 1966), 371-83; "Ōkuma Shigenobu, Modernization, and the West," in Japan's Modern Century, ed. by Edmund Skrzypczak (Tokyo: Sophia University Press, 1968), 27-40.

569
BAILEY, Jackson Holbrook. Prince Saionji: A Study in Modern Japanese Political Leadership. Harvard, 1959. ii, 223p.

"An attempt to assess Saionji's political background, philosophy, and actions and to relate these factors to the development of the modern Japanese state." Contents: Saionji as a Kuge; Saionji and the Restoration; Saionji's Ten Years as a Student Abroad; Relationship with the Liberal Movement; Experience in Government Service: Bureaucrat and Diplomat; Saionji's Relationship with Itō and the Establishment of the Seiyūkai; Saionji as Party President and Prime Minister [Saionji Kimmochi, 1849-1940].

Rel.Publ.: "Prince Saionji and the Popular Rights Movement," JAS, 21 (Nov. 1961), 49-63; "Prince Saionji and the Taishō Political Crisis, 1912-1913," Studies in Asia, 1962, ed. by Sidney D. Brown (Lincoln: University of Nebraska Press, 1962), 39-57.

570
AKITA, George. Development of Parliamentary Government in Meiji Japan. Harvard, 1960. viii, 348p.

Contents: The Question of Assemblies and a Constitution during the Early Meiji Period; Itagaki and the Movement for Parliamentary Government; Itō and Ōkuma: The Crisis of 1881; Itō and the Drafting of the Meiji Constitution; The Philosophy behind the Constitution; The Constitution in Practice: The First Diet; Itō and Yamagata: The Nature and Role of Parties; The Second Itō Ministry: Itō as a Constitutional Statesman.

Rel.Publ.: Foundations of Constitutional Government in Modern Japan, 1868-1900. Cambridge: Harvard University Press, 1967. viii, 292p. (Harvard East Asian Series, 23); "The Meiji Constitution in Practice: The First Diet," JAS, 22 (Nov. 1962), 31-46.

571
HIRSCHMEIER, Johannes, S.V.D. The Genesis of Modern Entrepreneurs in Meiji Japan. Harvard, 1960. vii, 389p. AB: 6p. summary appended to diss. ms.

By "entrepreneur" is meant the "businessmen (bankers, traders, and industrialists) who somehow excelled and contributed by their economic activity toward the introduction of modern industry or business organization of some kind." Contents: The Background (The Merchant Class, The Samurai Class); The Problems (The Formative Process, Profits and the Profit Motive); The Men (The Zaibatsu Builders, Analysis of Fifty Leading Entrepreneurs, The Entrepreneurs in Cotton Spinning).

Rel.Publ.: The Origins of Entrepreneurship in Meiji Japan. Cambridge: Harvard University Press, 1964. x, 354p. (Harvard East Asian Series, 17); "Shibusawa Eiichi: Industrial Pioneer," in The State and Economic Enterprise in Japan, ed. by William W. Lockwood (Princeton: Princeton University Press, 1965), 209-47.

572
NESS, Gayl Deforrest. Central Government and Local Initiative in the Industrialization of India and Japan. California, Berkeley, 1961. 405p.

Analyzes the early industrialization of Japan and the effect of central control and local initiative on industrialization. Also compares the industrialization of India and Japan with one another.

573
LIE, Tek-tjeng. Mutsu Munemitsu: 1844-1897: A Machiavellian Portrait. Harvard, 1962. iv, 162p. AB: 2p. summary appended to diss. ms.

"The present biography maintains that Mutsu could best be described as a ressentiment-laden person who... became a Machiavelli...Chapter 2 discusses Mutsu's early years and shows how the interaction between his basic character, a certain event while he was still a child, and the life he led during the years of his personality formation, led to his development into a Machiavelli. Chapters 3 and 4...describe how Mutsu's orientation towards reality, rationality, and expediency enabled him to climb from a minor official in the Foreign Affairs Bureau of the Meiji Government to Foreign Minister. The final chapter demonstrates how Mutsu's policy of raison d'état enabled him to accomplish the task of treaty revision in 1894."

574
BURNSTEIN, Ira Jerry. The American Movement to Develop Church Colleges for Men in Japan, 1868-1912. Michigan, 1964. 222p. DA 25 (June 1965), 7059-60; UM 65-5278.

Contents: Christian Higher Education: A Perspective; The Foundations for Christian Higher Education and the Rage for Western Learning; Government Resistance to Christian Schools; A Decade of Hardship for the Christian Educational System, 1890-1900; Order Number 12; Christian Higher Education: A Peripheral Role; The Christian University Movement: As a Solution.

Rel.Publ.: The American Movement to Develop Protestant Colleges for Men in Japan, 1868-1912. Ann Arbor: University of Michigan, School of Education, 1967. v, 158p. (University of Michigan. Comparative Education Dissertation Series, 11)

575
EPP, Robert Charles. Threat to Tradition: The Reaction to Japan's 1890 Civil Code. Harvard, 1964. ii, 307p.

This study of the compilation of the civil code and of Japanese reactions to it "attempts to focus attention on the changes in social values which Japanese of the late nineteenth century thought were challenging their traditional values." Contents: Early Work on the Civil Code (1866-1878); Compilation of the First Civil Code (1879-1890); Debate in the Senate and the First Diet (1889-1890); The Barristers' Attack on the Civil Code (1889-1893); Postponement of the Code (1892-1893).

Rel.Publ.: "The Challenge from Tradition: Attempts to Compile a Civil Code in Japan, 1866-78," MN, 22, (1967), 15-48.

576
NAKAMURA, James I. The Place of Agricultural Production in the Economic Development of Japan. Columbia, 1964. 239p. DA 28 (Aug. 1967), 375-A; UM 67-10,382.

Attempts to correct the understatement of production, which is a major defect of Japanese official agricultural statistics of the Meiji period, and "analyzes the significance of the findings in understanding the economic development of Japan."

Rel.Publ.: Agricultural Production and the Economic Development of Japan, 1873-1922. Princeton: Princeton University Press, 1966. xxiii, 257p.; "Growth of Japanese Agriculture, 1875-1920," in The State and Economic Enterprise in Japan, ed. by William W. Lockwood (Princeton: Princeton University Press, 1965), 249-324; "Meiji Land Reform, Redistribution of Income, and Savings from Agriculture," Economic Development and Cultural Change, 14 (July 1966), 428-39.

577
HAVENS, Thomas Robert Hamilton. Nishi Amane (1829-1897) in Japanese Intellectual History. California, Berkeley, 1965. 303p. DA 26 (June 1966), 7280-81; UM 66-3610.

Contents: The Early Development of Nishi's Thought; Gaining Knowledge Abroad and Applying It at Home; A Leader in Enlightening Japan; Attack on Shushi Confucianism; Ethics for the New Society; Nishi and the Meiji Six Society; Civil and Military Society.

Rel.Publ.: "Comte, Mill, and the Thought of Nishi Amane in Meiji Japan," JAS, 27 (Feb. 1968), 217-28; "Scholars and Politics in Nineteenth-Century Japan: The Case of Nishi Amane," Modern Asian Studies, 2 (Oct. 1968), 315-24; Nishi Amane and Modern Japanese Thought. Princeton: Princeton University Press, 1970. 260p.

HOWES, John F. Japan's Enigma: The Young Uchimura Kanzō. 1965. See no.1944.

578
PYLE, Kenneth Birger. The New Generation: Young Japanese in Search of National Identity, 1887-1895. Johns Hopkins, 1965. 265p. DA 26 (May 1966), 6679-80; UM 66-4961.

A study of the Minyūsha and the Seikyōsha, "two rival groups of young intellectuals who, in the period from 1887 to 1895, debated the issues raised by abrupt cultural change." These included the overall problem of Japan's cultural identity as well as basic questions concerning the directions Japan should take in reforming and in modernizing her cultural, educational, political, and social institutions.

Rel.Publ.: The New Generation in Meiji Japan: Problems of Cultural Identity, 1885-1895. Stanford: Stanford University Press, 1969. ix, 240p.

579
SPAULDING, Robert Miller, Jr. Imperial Japan's "Higher Examinations." Michigan, 1965. 378p. DA 26 (Dec. 1965), 3288-89; UM 65-11,041.

Focuses on the "recruitment of higher civil servants through competitive examinations "during the Meiji Era and on its implications for Japan's political modernization. Also includes information on recruitment by non-examination methods. Contents: The Decision to Examine; Changes in the Twentieth Century; The Examinations and the Examiners.

Rel.Publ.: Imperial Japan's Higher Civil Service Examinations. Princeton: Princeton University Press, 1967. xiv, 416p.

TUSSING, Arlon R. Employment and Wages in Japanese Industrialization: A Quantitative Study of Yamanashi Prefecture in the Meiji Era. 1966. See no.301.

580
JONES, Hazel J. The Meiji Government and Foreign Employees, 1868-1900. Michigan, 1967. 472p. DA 28 (Feb. 1968), 3113-14-A; UM 67-17,789.

Contents: Foreign Employees in Pre-Meiji Japan, 1854-1868; The New Policy of Meiji Leaders; The Administrative Policy; Expenditures for Foreign Employees; Contracts for Foreign Employees; Treatment of Foreign Employees; Jurisdiction over Foreign Employees; Their Quality and Functions; Termination of Their Services.

Rel.Publ.: "The Formulation of Meiji Policy toward the Employment of Foreigners," MN, 23 (1968), 9-30.

581
YAMAMOTO, Masaya. Image-Makers of Japan: A Case Study in the Impact of the American Protestant Foreign Missionary Movement, 1859-1905. Ohio State, 1967. 406p. DA 28 (Dec. 1967), 2194-A; UM 67-16,349.

Contents: A Survey of the Home Ground: The U.S.A.; The Field: Japan in Perspective; The Preparatory Period, 1858-1873 (The First Japanese Mission to the U.S., Beginning of Missionary Activity in Japan, Griffis in Fukui, The De Facto Recognition of Christianity); The Flowering Years, 1873-1889 (The Promising Start, Joseph Hardy Neesima, Griffis in Tokyo and the U.S., Japan's Modernization, Satsuma Rebellion, Cries for Equality, Mission Apogee); The Era of Reaction, 1889-1895 ("Japan for the Japanese", Lafcadio Hearn in Japan, "Evangelization of the World in This Generation," Rise of Nationalism, Sino-Japanese War); The Age of Readjustment, 1895-1905.

582
LEE, Hongkoo. Social Conservation and Political Development: A Normative Approach to Political Change with Special Reference to Meiji Japan. Yale, 1968. 217p. DA 29 (June 1969), 4532-A; UM 69-8378.

The author concludes that (1) "the political and social leaders in Meiji Japan possessed historical consciousness and recognized the threats of identity crisis and legitimacy crisis, (2) Meiji nationalism was created as a set of political prescriptions derived from the ultimate social values of Japan, and it determined the nature and course of popular consensus in Meiji Japan, (3) Meiji Japan chose an oligarchy of elites who possessed historical consciousness as the best constitution, and (4) the Meiji oligarchy played an important role in creating political parties and the Diet which gave the Meiji polity both stability and dynamics." These factors led to political development, i.e. to change derived from and intended to conserve the ultimate values of society.

583
MINEAR, Richard Hoffman. Hozumi Yatsuka and the Conservative Interpretation of the Meiji Constitution. Harvard, 1968. ii, 332p.

Not a biography of Hozumi Yatsuka (1860-1912) but "an analysis of the ideas which were available to him and of the ideas which he used." Contents: Hozumi Yatsuka: The Early Years; The German Background; Hozumi's General Theory: The State; Law, Constitutions, and Constitutionalism; The Meiji Constitution; Hozumi Yatsuka's Theory: A Critique.

Rel.Publ.: Japanese Tradition and Western Law: Emperor, State, and Law in the Thought of Hozumi Yatsuka. Cambridge: Harvard University Press, forthcoming; "Hozumi Yatsuka: The Early Years," Hōgaku ronsō (Kyoto), 79 (June 1966), 1-14.

584
POWLES, Cyril Hamilton. Victorian Missionaries in Meiji Japan: The Shiba Sect 1873-1900. British Columbia, 1968. ix, 370p. DA 30 (Aug. 1969), 666-A. Order microfilm copy directly from the National Library of Canada at Ottawa.

An investigation of the careers and writings of three early, upper or upper-middle class, Anglican missionaries who lived in Japan between 1873 and 1900. The dissertation seeks to show that Anglicanism tended to affirm traditional institutions while American Protestantism constantly sought to change important aspects of the Japanese way of life.

Meiji Period: First Half (1868-1890)

See also Law--constitutions of Japan (pages 180-81) and History--Meiji Period: General (pages 73-77).

585
IYENAGA, Toyokichi. The Constitutional Development of Japan from 1853 to 1881. Johns Hopkins, 1890. 56p.

Contents: Beginnings of the Constitutional Movement (1853-1868); The Restoration (1868-1869); The Abolition of Feudalism (1869-1871); Influences That Shaped the Growth of the Representative Idea of Government; Progress of the Constitutional Movement from the Abolition of Feudalism to the Proclamation of October 12, 1881.

Rel.Publ.: The Constitutional...1881. Baltimore: Johns Hopkins Press, 1891. 56p. (Johns Hopkins University. Studies in History and Political Science, ser. 9, no.9)

586
JACOB, Erich. Der Zwischenfall von Sakai (L'incident du Dupleix): Nach Aufzeichnungen von Teilnehmern und Zeitgenossen zusammengestellte japanische Darstellung: Ein Kulturbild aus dem Beginn der Meiji-Zeit. Text und Übersetzung [The Incident at Sakai (Dupleix): A Japanese Representation Based on the Accounts of the Participants and Their Contemporaries: A Cultural Protrait of the Beginning of the Meiji Period. Text and Translation]. Leipzig, 1939. Text in German. The dissertation in its published form is available at Marburg/Lahn, Universitätsbibliothek, Nr. VII C.

A translation and commentary on the "Sakai jiken" (the incident at Sakai, February 1868) and the "Myōkoku jiken" as well as on their consequences. The author studies these two military clashes involving soldiers from Tosa han and French sailors in order to present a picture of Japanese life at that time.

Rel.Publ.: Der Zwischenfall...Übersetzung. Berlin-Schöneberg: Bolach, 1939. 91p.

587
NORMAN, Egerton Herbert. Japan's Emergence as a Modern State. Harvard, 1940. Diss. ms. not available. AB: Harvard University. Summaries of Theses...1940. p.196-200.

A study of the Meiji Restoration and its background, Japan's early industrialization, the agrarian settlement and its social consequences, and early Meiji parties and politics.

Rel.Publ.: Japan's Emergence as a Modern State: Political and Economic Problems of the Meiji Period. New York: Institute of Pacific Relations, 1940. xvi, 254p.

SMITH, Thomas C. Government Enterprise and the Initial Phase of Japanese Industrialization, 1850-1880. 1948. See no.512.

588
HARRISON, John Armstrong. Yezo, the Japanese Northern Frontier, 1854-1882: A Preliminary Study in Japanese Expansion and Colonization with Particular Reference to the Role of the Kaitakushi in Modern Japanese History. California, Berkeley, 1949. 260p.

Includes materials on Russian interest in Hokkaido during the Tokugawa period. Concludes that Japanese activities in Hokkaido were closely related to "the rise of military feudalism, the growth of Russophobia in Japan, the futility of the forced overseas migration of the Japanese, and the establishment of constitutional government in Japan."

Rel.Publ.: Japan's Northern Frontier: A Preliminary Study in Colonization and Expansion with Special Reference to the Relations of Japan and Russia. Gainesville: University of Florida Press, 1953. xii, 202p.; "Notes on the Discovery of Yezo," Annals of the Association of American Geographers, 40 (Sept. 1950), 254-66; "The Capron Mission and the Colonization of Hokkaido, 1868-1875," Agricultural History, 25 (July 1951), 135-42.

589
IKE, Nobutaka. The Democratic Movement in Meiji Japan. Johns Hopkins, 1949. ix, 259p.

Traces and explains the origins, growth, and decline of the Jiyu minken undō.

Rel.Publ.: The Beginnings of Political Democracy in Japan. Baltimore: Johns Hopkins Press, 1950. xvi, 246p.

590
WILSON, Robert Arden. A Study of the Political Institutions and Ranking Personnel of the New Meiji Government, 1868-1871. Washington, Seattle, 1949. 325p.

Contents: The Establishment of the Restored Government; The Impact of Western Ideas on Japanese Government; A More Authoritarian Government Structure; An Analysis of Developments. Tables of offices and personnel are included in the appendix.

Rel.Publ.: Genesis of the Meiji Government in Japan, 1868-1871. Berkeley: University of California Press, 1957, iv, 149p. (University of California Publications in History, 56); "The Seitaishō: A Constitutional Experiment," FEQ, 11 (May 1952), 297-304.

591
ANTHONY, David Forsyth. The Administration of Hokkaido under Kuroda Kiyotaka--1870-1882: An Early Example of Japanese-American Cooperation. Yale, 1951. 161p. AB: United States Department of State, External Research Staff. Abstracts of Completed Doctoral Dissertations for the Academic Year 1950/1951. p.360-62. Also listed in DA 29 (July 1968), 198-A, but without an abstract; UM 65-7527.

A study of the career of Kuroda Kiyotaka [1840-1900]; the historical origins and activities of the Kaitakushi; land settlement problems; the development of agriculture, communications, education and industry in Hokkaido; and the assistance of American advisors.

592
BECKMANN, George Michael. The Constitutional Development of Japan in the Early Meiji Period, 1868-1890. Stanford, 1952. 246p. AB: Stanford University. Abstracts of Dissertations, 1951/1952. p.265-66.

A survey of the origins and development of the Meiji Constitution.

Rel.Publ.: The Making of the Meiji Constitution: The Oligarchs and the Constitutional Development of Japan, 1868-1891. Lawrence: University of Kansas Press. 158p.; "The Meiji Restoration and Constitutional Development of Japan 1868-1871," Hōgaku kenkyū, 26 (June 1953), 458-68; "The Oligarchs and the Origins of Constitutional Thought in Japan," Hōgaku kenkyū, 27 (Sept. 1954); "Political Crises and the Crystallization of Japanese Constitutional Thought," PHR, 23 (1954), 259-70; "The Democratic Movement and the Constitutional Policy of the Satsuma-Chōshū Oligarchs, 1876-1881," Hōgaku kenkyū, 28 (Apr. 1955); "The Constitutional Debate in Japan, 1881-1885," Hōgaku kenkyū (Fall 1955); "Political Thought and the Meiji Oligarchs," in International Christian University, Asian Cultural Studies, 3 (Oct. 1962), 87-102.

593
BROWN, Sidney DeVere. Kido Takayoshi and the Meiji Restoration: A Political Biography, 1833-1877. Wisconsin, 1953. 440p. AB: University of Wisconsin. Summaries of Doctoral Dissertations. v.14, p.205-07.

Focuses on Kido's role in the early Meiji government. Contents: Young Revolutionary, 1833-1868; Expel the Barbarians, 1853-1868; The Destruction of Feudalism, 1868-1871; The Occident through Japanese Eyes, 1871-1873; Expansion or Reform, 1868-1873; Proponent of Peaceful Progress, 1874-1876; Champion of Constitutional Government, 1873-1875; Defender of the Disinherited, 1875-1877; The End of an Era: Passing of the Three Heroes of the Restoration.

Rel.Publ.: "Kido Takayoshi (1833-1877): Meiji Japan's Cautious Revolutionary," PHR, 25 (May 1956), 151-62.

594
IOFAN, N. A. Krest'ianskoe dvizhenie v Iaponii v 1868-1873 godakh [The Peasant Movement in Japan, 1868-1873]. Moscow, Institut vostokovedeniia Akademii nauk SSSR, 1954. (Candidate of Historical Sciences degree) 200p. Text in Russian. [See also addenda entry 18A.]

595
BLACKER, Carmen Elizabeth. Fukuzawa Yukichi: A Study in the Introduction of Western Ideas into Japan in the Meiji Period. London, 1957. iii, 201p.

Focuses on Fukuzawa's role in advocating the introduction of a new body of knowledge into Japan. His views on Western ethics, family relationships, history, politics, and Western techniques are studied in some detail.

Rel.Publ.: The Japanese Enlightenment: A Study of the Writings of Fukuzawa Yukichi. Cambridge: Cambridge University Press, 1964. xiii, 185p. (University of Cambridge. Oriental Publications, 10); "Kyūhanjō, by Fukuzawa Yukichi," MN, 9 (Apr. 1953), 304-29; "The First Japanese Mission to England," History Today, 7 (Dec. 1957), 840-47; "Fukuzawa Yukichi on Family Relationships," MN, 14 (Apr./July 1958), 40-60.

596
HANE, Mikiso. English Liberalism and the Japanese Enlightenment, 1868-1890. Yale, 1957. 327p. DA 26 (June 1966), 7279-80; UM 66-6567.

Contents: Popularity of England; The Champions of English Liberalism; The Roots of Liberalism; The Sources of English Ideas; Liberal Principles: Individualism [Independence and Self-Regret, Laissez Faire, Freedom and Liberty, Equality]; Liberal Principles: Utilitarianism-Materialism; Liberal Principles: Reason, Science, and Progress; Attitude toward Government; Activities in the Political Field.

Rel.Publ.: "Nationalism and the Decline of Liberalism in Meiji Japan," in Studies on Asia, 1963, ed. by Robert K. Sakai (Lincoln: University of Nebraska Press, 1963), 69-80; "The Sources of English Liberal Concepts in Early Meiji Japan," MN 24 (1969), 259-72.

597
HAROOTUNIAN, Harry D. The Samurai Class during the Early Years of the Meiji Period in Japan, 1868-1882. Michigan, 1957. 226p. DA 18 (Apr. 1958), 1407; UM 58-925.

Studies the problem of samurai absorption into the emerging industrial society of Japan on both the national and local levels. Includes an analysis of the samurai opposition to government policies. Contents: Pt.1: Shizoku at the National Level: The Dissolution of Tokugawa Polity and the Establishment of the Meiji State; Shizoku and Government Policy; Shizoku Opposition to Government Policy. Pt.2: Shizoku at the Local Level: The Shizoku as a Class; The Problems of Status and Livelihood; Shizoku and Administrative Changes; Shizoku in Education and Military Service; Shizoku in Land and Business.

Rel.Publ.: "The Progress of Japan and the Samurai Class, 1868-1882," PHR, 28 (Aug. 1959), 255-66; "The Economic Rehabilitation of the Samurai in the Early Meiji Period," JAS, 19 (Aug. 1960), 433-44.

598
SAITO, Mitsuko. Speech Education in Japan in the Latter Half of the Nineteenth Century. Northwestern, 1957. 338p. DA 18 (Feb. 1958), 698-99; UM 24,921.

"An historical study of the development and nature of speech education and public speaking activities in Japan," 1872-1890. The dissertation includes one chapter on the life of Fukuzawa Yukichi and on his contributions to the creation of a favorable environment for the introduction of speech.

599
BUCK, James Harold. The Satsuma Rebellion of 1877: An Inquiry into Some of Its Military and Political Aspects. American, 1959. 285p. DA 20 (Aug. 1959), 649-50; UM 59-2833.

"Early chapters treat the decline of Tokugawa feudalism, the "formal" abolition of feudalism by the oligarchy, and the series of recurring crises which split irrevocably the Restoration Government. A middle chapter is devoted to the events [e.g. the lesser revolts of the 1870's] which precipitated the Rebellion. Later chapters consider in detail the military operations, and a final chapter summarizes the causes of the Rebellion and offers an assessment of its results."

Rel.Publ.: "Japan's Last Civil War: The Satsuma Rebellion of 1877," Military Review, 40 (Sept. 1960), 22-29.

IWATA, Masakazu. Ōkubo Toshimichi: The Leading Protagonist on the Stage of the Restoration Drama. 1960. See no.526.

600
FRASER, Andrew. The Evolution of the Council in the Japanese Government, 1868-1890. Australian National, 1962. 263p.

A study of the supreme decision-making body, its membership, the issues it determined, and its relationship to other arms of the government.

Rel.Publ.: "The Osaka Conference of 1875," JAS, 26 (Aug. 1967), 589-610.

601
SOVIAK, Eugene. Baba Tatsui: A Study of Intellectual Accumulation in the Early Meiji Period. Michigan, 1962. 342p. DA 23 (Mar. 1963), 3342-43; UM 63-446.

Baba's "entire life, career, and writings are studied in an effort to determine how such a Meiji Japanese intellectual was produced, how he employed Western ideas in his own thinking and writing, and how he sought to transform Japanese society on the basis of these ideas. Contents: Pt.1: The Double Context (1850-1878); The Japanese Background; England--The First Phase; Japan Revisited (January 1875-April 1875); England--The Second Phase (1875-1878). Pt.2: The Cultural Hybrid in Action (1878-1888): The Intellectual as Emissary of Western Enlightenment (1878-1881); The Intellectual as Political Party Member (1881-1886); The Intellectual as Exile (1886-1888); Conclusion: Baba in Retrospect.

Rel.Publ.: "The Case of Baba Tatsui: Western Enlightenment, Social Change, and the Early Meiji Intellectual," MN, 18 (1963), 191-235; "An Early Meiji Intellectual in Politics: Baba Tatsui and the Jiyūtō," in Modern Japanese Leadership: Transition and Change, ed. by Bernard S. Silberman and Harry D. Harootunian (Tucson: University of Arizona Press, 1966), 121-70.

CHAMBLISS, William Jones. Chiaraijima Village: Land Tenure, Taxation, and Local Trade, 1818-1884. 1963. See no.530.

602
CH'EN, Hsien-t'ing. The Japanese Government and the Creation of the Imperial Army, 1870-1873. Harvard, 1963. xxii, 241p. AB: 7p. summary appended to diss. ms.

Contents: Pt.1: The Background of the Creation of the Imperial Army, September 1870-January 1872: The Appointment of Yamagata Aritomo, September 1870, and the State of Military Affairs; The Formation of the Emperor's Personal Force (Goshimpei); Effects of the Formation of the Emperor's Personal Force: The Abolition of the Han and the Assumption of Control of all Military Forces. Pt.2: The Creation of the Imperial Army, January 1872-April 1873: A New Military Policy Defined and the Major Military Reforms in 1872; Designing the Conscript System; The Enactment of the Conscript Act; The Establishment of the Conscript System.

603
PITTAU, Joseph, S.J. Ideology of a New Nation: Authoritarianism and Constitutionalism, Japan 1868-1890. Harvard, 1963. viii, 411p. AB: 6p. summary appended to diss. ms.

"Examines the political concepts of the articulate elite of early Meiji life and sees what kind of state the Meiji leaders envisaged as they built the new nation and discussed the pros and cons of a representative constitutional government." Contents: The Meiji Political System: Different Interpretations; Political Thought in Pre-Meiji Japan; Antifeudal National Unification; Gradualism versus Radicalism; Towards a Constitutional Government; The Debate on Sovereignty and National Rights; The German Influence: Roesler and the Making of the Constitution; The New Theory of the State: Inoue Kowashi, Itō Hirobumi, and the Constitution.

Rel.Publ.: Political Thought in Early Meiji Japan, 1868-1889. Cambridge: Harvard University Press, 1967. vi, 259p. (Harvard East Asian Series, 24); "The Meiji Political System: Different Interpretations," in Studies in Japanese Culture, ed. by Joseph Roggendorf (Tokyo: Sophia University Press, 1963), 99-122; "Inoue Kowashi, 1843-1895, and the Formation of Modern Japan," MN, 20 (1965), 253-82.

604
ABOSCH, David. Katō Hiroyuki and the Introduction of German Political Thought in Modern Japan: 1868-1883. California, Berkeley, 1964. 500p. DA 25 (May 1965), 6558; UM 65-2938.

Concludes that Katō "made it possible for the Japanese to modernize their government while stoutly maintaining the unchanging essence of their state."

605
ALTMAN, Albert Avraham. The Emergence of the Press in Meiji Japan. Princeton, 1965. 192p. DA 26 (Jan. 1966), 3893-94; UM 65-13,123.

A study of the development of the newspaper in Meiji Japan. Ch.1 "examines some of the features of Tokugawa society that prepared the ground for the emergence of the press in Meiji Japan....Ch.2 begins with a detailed examination of the news publications issued by the Bakufu in the early 1860's and speculates upon the considerations inducing it to make foreign news publicly available." Ch.3 describes "how metal type printing was re-introduced into Japan during the final years of the Tokugawa period," while the concluding chapter studies Japanese newspaper developments following the abolition of the feudal polity (1871).

Rel.Publ.: "Modernization of Printing in Mid-Nineteenth Century Japan," Asian and African Studies (Jerusalem, Israel), 4 (1968), 85-105.

606
CHUNG, Young-iob. The Role of Government in the Generation of Saving: The Japanese Experience, 1868-1893. Columbia, 1965. 397p. DA 26 (Mar. 1966), 5074-75; UM 65-13,928.

Explains how Japanese government efforts led to a relatively high rate of private saving and, therefore, to an unusually high rate of capital formation. Contents: Economic Development of Japan, 1868-1893; Tax Policy; Government Borrowing Policy; Monetary Policy; Banking Policy; Other Government Policies.

PHAM-van-Thuan. Les Fondements socio-économiques de la revolution industrielle du Japon. 1965. See no.534.

607
MOORE, George Eagleton. Kozaki Hiromichi and the Kumamoto Band: A Study in Samurai Reaction to the West. California, Berkeley, 1966. 192p. DA 27 (Feb. 1967), 2483-A; UM 66-15,451.

Considerable attention is devoted to Captain Leroy L. Janes' conversion of many samurai to Christianity.

Rel.Publ.: "Samurai Conversion: The Case of Kumamoto," Asian Studies, Apr. 1966.

NISHIO, Harry K. Political Authority Structure and the Development of Entrepreneurship in Japan (1603-1890). 1966. See no.536.

608
SCHEINER, Irwin. The Beginning of Modern Social Criticism in Japan: A Study of the Samurai and Christian Values, 1867-1891. Michigan, 1966. 193p. DA 28 (Dec. 1967), 2187-88-A; UM 67-15,734.

"An analysis of the intellectual process by which samurai came to understand and adapt Christianity for their own social needs and then, because of their new doctrine, to reject many of the political assumptions of Meiji society." Contents: Protestant Evangelists and Christian Samurai; Alienation and Conversion; Westernization and Conversion; Toward Social Criticism; Niijima Jo: The Conscience of a Christian; The Founding of a School and the Cultivation of a Nation.

Rel.Publ.: "Christian Samurai and Samurai Values," in Modern Japanese Leadership: Transition and Change, ed. by Bernard S. Silberman and Harry D. Harootunian (Tucson: University of Arizona Press, 1966), 171-94.

609
TSURUTANI, Taketsugu. Tension, Consensus, and Political Leadership: A New Look into the Nature and Process of Modernization. Wisconsin, 1967. 297p. DA 28 (Aug. 1967), 748-49-A; UM 67-528.

Explores the interrelationship of tension, consensus, and political leadership and examines "their respective relevances to the process of modernization." Then analyzes (as a case study) the nature and pattern of Japan's modernization, 1868-1890.

610
DAVIS, Sandra Toby Weisman. Ono Azusa: A Meiji Intellectual. Pennsylvania, 1968. 444p. DA 30 (Sept. 1969), 1104-A; UM 69-15,049.

Considerable attention is devoted in particular to (1) Ono's organization of the Kyōzon Dōshū, an early Meiji intellectual society, (2) his career in the government's legislative and auditing bureaus and his developing friendship with Ōkuma Shigenobu, (3) his responsibility for bringing about the political change of 1881, (4) his role as "the founder, organizer, and leading political theorist of the Kaishintō and as the author of its major policy statements," and (5) his ideas on constitutional theory as expressed in Kokken hanron.

611
HALL, Ivan Parker. Mori Arinori: A Reconsideration. Harvard, 1969. ii, 928p. (3v.).

Contents: Satsuma Origins: 1847-1865; Awakening to the West: 1865-1866 (Britain and Russia: The West Observed, Letters to Yokohama: Observations on the West); The Student Turned Pilgrim: 1866-1868 (Harris, Oliphant, and the Japanese, The Rigors of Brockton, The Appeal of the New Life); In and Out of the New Government: 1868-1870; Representing Japan at Washington: 1871-1873; The Extracurricular Harvest of America: 1871-1873; Apostle of Enlightenment: 1873-1876; The Diplomat as Kibitzer on Politics: 1877-1884; The Making of an Education Minister: 1879-1884; Mori at the Monbushō: 1884-1889; Conclusion: The Image [of Mori] Revised.

Rel. Publ.: "Mori Arinori: The Formative Years (1847-1875)," in Harvard University, East Asian Research Center, Papers on Japan, 3 (1965), 52-124.

Meiji Period: Second Half (1890-1912)

See also History--Meiji Period: General (pages 73-77).

612
FURUYA, Hisatsuna. Système représentatif au Japon [The Representative System in Japan]. Bruxelles, 1899. xi, 262p. Text in French.

Contents: The Origin of the Representative System in Japan; The Composition of the Japanese Diet; The Functioning of the Japanese Diet; Criticisms of the Representative System in Japan.

Rel.Publ.: Système...Japon. Bruxelles: Henri Lamertin, 1899. xi, 262p.

WILDES, Harry E. The Press and Social Currents in Japan. 1927. See no.1674.

613
COPELAND, Edwin Luther. The Crisis of Protestant Missions in Japan, 1889-1900. Yale, 1949. 398p. DA 26 (July 1965), 512; UM 65-6546.
Contents: Human and Historical Factors in the Background; The Beginning: Its Character and Causes; The Japanese Government and Protestant Christianity; The Clamor for Independence: Theological; The Clamor for Independence: Ecclesiastical and Administrative; The Crisis: Its End and Effects.
Rel.Publ.: "The Japanese Government and Protestant Christianity," Contemporary Japan, 22 (1953), 650-71, and 23 (1954), 101-26.

614
IVANOVA, G. D. Kōtoku kak publitsist: K istorii progressivnoi iaponskoi publitsistiki nachala XX v. [Kōtoku (Shūsui, 1871-1911) as a Journalist: From the History of Progressive Japanese Journalism of the Early Twentieth Century]. Moscow, Institut vostokovedeniia Akademii nauk SSSR, 1953. (Candidate of Philological Sciences degree) 286p. Text in Russian. AB: 15p. summary published in 1953.
Rel.Publ.: Kōtoku: Revoliutsioner i literator. Moscow: Izdatel'stvo vostochnoi literatury, 1959. 129p. (Institut vostokovedeniia Akademii nauk SSSR)

615
MARTIN, Harris Inwood. The Early Life and Thought of Kita Ikki. Stanford, 1959. 236p. DA 20 (Oct. 1959), 1343-44; UM 59-3713.
"A description of Kita Ikki in his 'formative years,' and an attempt to place him and his thought as expressed in his first book, Kokutairon oyobi junsei shakaishugi, in the perspective of rapidly changing Japan at the turn of the twentieth century."

616
MASON, Richard Henry Pitt. Japan's First General Election, 1890. Australian National, 1962. 448p.
A descriptive and analytical account of Japan's first parliamentary election--the issues, principles, parties, election campaign, and results--based primarily on contemporary newspaper accounts.
Rel.Publ.: Japan's...1890. Cambridge: Cambridge University Press, 1969. xv, 284p. (University of Cambridge Oriental Publications, 14)

617
NAJITA, Tetsuo. The Seiyūkai in the Politics of Compromise, 1905-1915. Harvard, 1965. iii, 385p. AB: 4p. summary appended to diss. ms.
Studies "the politics underlying the steady growth of party power between 1905 and 1915 in order to see how the parties penetrated the political structure and with what kinds of consequences," and focuses on the Seiyūkai, the dominant party at this time, and on its leader Hara Kei. Contents: Hara Kei and the Politics of of Compromise; Home Minister Hara: The Uses of Power (1906-1908); Cultivation of a Local Power Base (1909-1911); Prelude to Conflict (1911-1912); Movement for Constitutional Government: December 1912; Akatsura and the Formation of the Dōshikai: January 1913; The Taishō Political Crisis at Its Height: February 1913; Compromise and Reform in the Political Settlement; Stemming the Anti-Seiyū Tide (1913-1915).
Rel.Publ.: Hara Kei in the Politics of Compromise, 1905-1915. Cambridge: Harvard University Press, 1967. xvii, 314p. (Harvard East Asian Series, 31); "Inukai Tsuyoshi: Some Dilemmas in Party Development in Pre-World War II Japan," American Historical Review, 74 (Dec. 1968), 492-510.

618
BERNAL, Martin Gardiner. Chinese Socialism to 1913. Cambridge, 1966. 501p.
Includes information on Japanese Socialism at the turn of the century and on its influence upon Chinese Socialism. Contents: Socialism in Japan up to 1901; Traces of Socialism in China before 1902; Liang Ch'i-ch'ao and the Introduction of Socialism from 1902 to 1905; Japanese Socialism between 1901 and 1905; Sun Yat-sen and the Origin of Min-sheng Chu-i; The Socialism of the Min-pao Group 1905-1906; Liang Ch'i-ch'ao's Attack on the Social Policies of Min-pao; Chiang K'ang-hu and the Chung-kuo She-hui Tang; Chiang K'ang-hu's Political Thought.
Rel.Publ.: "The Tzu-yu tang and Tai Chi t'ao, 1912-1913," Modern Asian Studies, 1 (Apr. 1967), 133-54.

619
FRIDELL, Wilbur Medbury. The Policy of the Japanese Government toward Shinto Shrines at the Town and Village Level, 1894-1914. California, Berkeley, 1966. 432p. DA 27 (May 1967), 3808-09-A; UM 67-5053.
Focuses on "the manner in which Japanese government leaders pressed national religious traditions into service on behalf of modernization in the Meiji period, and the consequences of those actions for the religious traditions, the modernization process, and the people themselves."

620
BERNSTEIN, Gail Lee. Kawakami Hajime: Portrait of a Reluctant Revolutionary. Harvard, 1968. xiii, 277p. AB: 3p. summary appended to diss. ms.
Biography of Kawakami Hajime (1879-1946), "who was influential in the translation, interpretation, and popularization of Marxism in Japan in the 1920's." Contents: A Young Man of Meiji; The "Way" in the Modern World; The Road to Marxism; The End of the Road; Prison Years.

621
NOTEHELFER, Frederick George. Kōtoku Shūsui: Portrait of a Japanese Radical. Princeton, 1968. 322p. DA 29 (Feb. 1969), 2652-53-A; UM 69-2772.
An examination of the life and thought of the man who was executed in 1911 for plotting against the life of the Meiji Emperor. In the dissertation, the author challenges the contention that Kōtoku Shūsei was "a political visionary far ahead of his time both in values and ideas." He asserts that Kōtoku was not a modern revolutionary but rather a "revolutionary in the tradition of the shishi loyalist" and that his action and thoughts "had their roots within traditional, not modern, values."

622
OKAMOTO, Shumpei. The Oligarchic Control of Foreign Policy: Japan's Experience in the Russo-Japanese War. Columbia, 1969. 415p. DA 30 (Apr. 1970); UM 70-7041.
This study examines the formulation and execution of Japan's foreign policy during the Russo-Japanese War in terms of those factors that contributed to the

successful prosecution of the war. It attempts to answer two questions: (1) What are the strengths and weaknesses of oligarchic control of foreign policy? (2) What bearing did such strengths and weaknesses have on the conduct of Japan's prewar foreign policy?

623
SIEVERS, Sharon Lee. Kōtoku Shūsui, The Essence of Socialism: A Translation and Biographical Essay. Stanford, 1969. 213p.

Twentieth Century: General

See also History--Modern, 1868-1945 (pages 72-73).

624
REED, John Paul. Kokutai: A Study of Certain Sacred and Secular Aspects of Japanese Nationalism. Chicago, 1937. ii, 274p.
Contents: The Study of "The Spirit of Nippon"; Shinto; Dangerous Thoughts; Thought Problems; Gimbura and Moral Censorship; Traditional and Foreign Literature; The "Two-Twenty-Six Affair"; Patriotic Societies; The Good Japanese; The Role of the Sacred in the Secular.
Rel.Publ.: Kokutai...Nationalism. Chicago, 1940. ii, 274p. ("Private edition, distributed by the University of Chicago libraries.")

625
ZHUKOV, E. M. Istoriia iaponskoi voenshchiny [History of the Japanese Militarists]. Leningrad, Nauchno-issledovatel'skii institut vostokovedeniia Akademii nauk SSSR, Leningradskoe otdelenie, 1940. (Doctor of Historical Sciences degree) Text in Russian.

626
MAKI, John McGilvrey. Japanese Militarism: Its Cause and Cure. Harvard, 1948. Diss. ms. unavailable.
Contents: The War against Japan; The Political Oligarchy; The Economic Oligarchy; The Emperor Idea; Foreign Influences and Anti-Foreignism; The Authoritarian State; Background of War; The Future of Japan.
Rel.Publ.: Japanese...Cure. New York: Knopf, 1945. x, 258p.

627
SCALAPINO, Robert Anthony. An Analysis of Political Party Failure in Japan. Harvard, 1948. iv, 508p. AB: 5p. summary appended to diss. ms.
"Analyzes the nature, causes, and results of political party failure in pre-World War II Japan." Contents: The Impact of Feudalism on Political Party Emergence; Party Emergence and the Philosophic Struggle within the Government; The Popular Basis of Early Japanese Parties; Early Party Organization and the Problem of Factionalism; The Evolution of Political Parties in Japanese Institutional Structure and Theory: (a) 1890-1913, (b) 1913-1932; Japanese Capitalism and the Political Party Movement; Political Parties and the Japanese People; The Era of Militarism and Party Collapse.
Rel.Publ.: Democracy and the Party Movement in Prewar Japan: The Failure of the First Attempt. Berkeley: University of California Press, 1953. xi, 471p.

628
TURNER, John Elliott. The Kenseikai (Constitutional Party) of Japan, 1913-1927: A Study of Its History, Organization, and Domestic and Foreign Policies. Minnesota, 1950. 702p.
Contents: Pt.1: Introduction: Feudal Influences on the Politics of the Era; The Restoration, and Its Aftermath; Restoration Reforms and the Role of the Political Party. Pt.2: The Kenseikai in Historical Context: The Birth of the Dōshikai; The Dōshikai and the Ōkuma Cabinet, 1914-1916; The Kenseikai: The Lean Years, 1916-1924; The Kenseikai under Katō and Wakatsuki, 1924-1927. Pt.3: The Kenseikai in Operation: Party Structure, Personnel, and Political Techniques. Pt.4: The Policies of the Kenseikai: The Kenseikai and the Problem of the Continent; The Kenseikai and the Problem of the Military; The Kenseikai and Japan's Colonies; The Kenseikai and Individual Rights: (1) Manhood Suffrage, (2) Civil Liberties; Socio-Economic Policy of the Kenseikai.
Rel.Publ.: "The Kenseikai: Leader vs. Party Liberal," FEQ, 11 (May 1952), 317-34.

629
MAXON, Yale Candee. Control of Japanese Foreign Policy, 1930-1945. California, Berkeley, 1952. 621p.
A descriptive history of the military-civilian rivalry for control. Contents: Pt.1: The Problem: General Factors; Specific Limitations of the Meiji Constitution; In Search of a Coordinating Instrument. Pt.2: Toward a Coordinated Policy: Emergence of Dual Government 1930-1936; Failure of Attempted Coordination 1936-1940; Coordination and the Eclipse of Civil Authority 1940-1944; The Reemergence of Civil Authority. Pt.3: Evaluation.
Rel.Publ.: Control of Japanese Foreign Policy: A Study of Civil-Military Rivalry, 1930-1945. Berkeley: University of California Press, 1957. vi, 286p. (University of California Publications in Political Science, 5)

630
MIWA, Ralph Makoto. The Ideology of Imperialism and Its Implications for Constitutional Reforms in Japan. Johns Hopkins, 1953. iv, 273p.
An attempt to understand the development of the Japanese rationale for expansionism with a view to finding out the degree to which it reflected prevailing socio-economic-political conditions. Based on the assumption that the history of ideas provides clues to the value structure of a nation as well as to significant conditioning factors.
Rel.Publ.: "The Anatomy of an Ideology: Japanese Imperialism," Studies on Asia, 1961, ed. by Robert K. Sakai (Lincoln: University of Nebraska Press, 1961), 38-52.

631
SWEARINGEN, Arthur Rodger. The Japanese Communist Party and the Comintern, 1919-1943: A Study of the Relationship between the Japanese Party and Moscow and of the Success of the Japanese Special Higher Police (Thought Police) in Combating Communism in Japan. Harvard, 1953. iii, 164p. AB: 3p. summary appended to diss. ms.
Contents: The Japanese setting; The Comintern Blueprint for Asia and the Establishment of a Communist Party in Japan; Comintern Influence during the Early Period, 1922-1927; Systematic Suppression by the Special Higher Police (Thought Police), 1927-1929; Armed Interlude, 1930; Intensified Comintern Activity: Reorganization from Moscow, 1931-1934; Comintern Assistance through the American Communist Party, 1935-1937; The Comintern and the Communist Party in Wartime Japan,

1937-1945; Japanese Communist Operations in Communist China, 1940-1945.

Rel.Publ.: Red Flag in Japan: Communism in Action, 1919-1951 [by] Rodger Swearingen and Paul F. Langer. Cambridge: Harvard University Press, 1952. xii, 276p.; Japanese Communism: An Annotated Bibliography of Works in the Japanese Language with a Chronology, 1921-1952 [by] Paul F. Langer and Rodger Swearingen. New York: International Secretariat, Institute of Pacific Relations, 1953. xii, 95p.; "Nosaka and the Cominform," FES, 19 (May 17, 1950), 98-101.

632
OLSON, Lawrence Alexander, Jr. Hara Kei: A Political Biography. Harvard, 1955. vii, 350p. AB: 6p. summary appended to diss. ms.

"This thesis describes Hara's career and writings as as a leading representative of the generation of bureaucrat-politicians which followed the early Meiji leaders and inherited their position. Set against a shifting background of military and industrial growth, it stresses how Hara differed from his elders and represented a new stage in Japanese political evolution."

633
MURRAY, Robert Allen. Education as an Instrument of Japanese Governmental Policy, 1918-1945. Kansas State, 1956. 87p.

634
PERRY, Walter Scott. Yoshino Sakuzō, 1878-1933: Exponent of Democratic Ideals in Japan. Stanford, 1956. 497p. DA 16 (Nov. 1956), 2144-45; UM 17,734.

A biographical study of Yoshino Sakuzō, "the foremost champion of democracy during his generation," who not only served on the faculty of Tokyo Imperial University but also sponsored the post-World War I student organization, the Shinjinkai, helped found the Shakai minshutō, and wrote numerous articles on political affairs and related questions. Part of the dissertation focuses on Yoshino's concept of democracy, its origins, and its variance with Western democratic concepts.

BLUMHAGEN, Herman H. Nationalistic Policies and Japanese Public Education from 1928 to March 31, 1947. 1957. See no.410.

635
HAY, Stephen Northrup. India's Prophet in East Asia: Tagore's Message of Pan-Asian Spiritual Revival and Its Reception in Japan and China, 1916-1929. Harvard, 1957. ix, 281p. AB: 5p. summary appended to diss. ms.

Contents of Pt.2: "Tagore and Japan" (p.54-158): The Japanese Background; Tagore's 1916 Itinerary; Japanese Responses to His Message in 1916; Tagore's 1924 Itinerary and Responses to His Message; Tagore's 1929 Itinerary and Responses to His Message.

Rel.Publ.: Asian Ideas of East and West: Tagore and His Critics in Japan, China, and India. Cambridge: Harvard University Press, 1969. 600p. (Harvard East Asian Series, 40)

636
POOS, Frederick William. Kawakami Hajime (1879-1946): An Intellectual Biography. Stanford, 1957. 169p. DA 17 (Nov. 1957), 2586; UM 23,212.

This is essentially a study of Kawakami's ideas with particular emphasis on his views of the classical economists, his Marxist ideology, and the ideas that he expressed in Bimbō monogatari, his most outstanding book (published in 1917).

637
HOLLAND, Harrison Melsher. The Rikken Minseitō (Constitutional Democratic Party) of Japan (1927-1940): Its Antecedents, Structure, and Operations. George Washington, 1958. viii, 216p. AB: George Washington University. Summaries of Doctoral Dissertations - 1958. p.26-32.

Contents: Pt.1: Political Party Development prior to 1927: The Political Setting - The Early Days of Meiji (1868-1873); The Antecedents of the Minseitō; The Intervening Years (1886-1927). Pt.2: The Minseitō - Its Formation and Development, 1927-1940: Events Leading to the Formation of the Minseitō; The Minseitō in Power; The Decline and Dissolution of the Minseitō, 1932-1940. Pt.3: The Minseitō - Formal Organization: Constitutional Framework; System of Organization; Selection of Party Officials; Party Finance. Pt.4: The Minseitō; Informal Structure and Operation: The Power Structure; The Process of Decision-Making; Assignment and Selection of Party Officials and Candidates for Public Office; Party Discipline; Intra-Party Tensions: Factionalism; Party Leadership.

KASAHARA, Yoshiko. The Influx and Exodus of Migrants among the 47 Prefectures in Japan, 1920-1935. 1958. See no.132.

638
OHASHI, Marshall Masashi. Japan's Southward Movement as Seen through Japanese Eyes. New York, 1959. xiii, 398p.

Contents: Japan's Ideological Response to the Western Intrusion into Asia; Ideological Response through World War I; The Twenties and Ideological Reappraisal; The Thirties and the Ideology of Direct Action; The China Incident and the Concept of Tōa ("East Asia"); Ideological Foundations; Ideological Principles; Greater East Asianism: Destructive [Characteristics]; Greater East Asianism: Constructive; Putting Japan's Ideology to Work; Toward the Evaluation of an Idea; The Meaning Today.

639
LIN, Jung-shun. Popular Movements in Japan during the Taishō Era. Pennsylvania, 1960. 527p. DA 21 (Nov. 1960), 1238-39; UM 60-3598.

Pt.1: The political and economic legacies inherited by Japan from the Meiji Era. Pt.2: Evolution of parliamentarianism. Pt.3: The impact of Western ideologies upon the Japanese and the development of mass organizations. Pt.4: The proletarian movement.

640
ARIMA, Tatsuo. The Failure of Freedom: An Intellectual Portrait of Taishō Japan. Harvard, 1962. iv, 467p. AB: 3p. summary appended to diss. ms.

"Shows how various intellectual groups in Taishō Japan failed to see the virtues of their constitutional form of government however clumsily inaugurated." Contents: Uchimura Kanzō: The Politics of Spiritual Despair; The Anarchists: The Negation of Politics; Japanese Naturalism: The Limitation of Experience; The Shirakaba-ha: The Tyranny of Art in Politics; Arishima Takeo: Bourgeois Criticism; Akutagawa Ryūnosuke: The Literature of Defeatism; Proletarian Literature: The Tyranny of Politics in Art.

Rel.Publ.: The Failure of Freedom: A Portrait of Modern Japanese Intellectuals. Cambridge: Harvard University Press, 1969. xiii, 296p. (Harvard East Asian Series, 39); "Uchimura Kanzō: A Study of the Post-Meiji Intelligentsia," in Harvard University, East Asian Research Center, Papers on Japan, 1 (1961), 130-88.

641
KÜMMEL, Hans Peter. Ōyama Ikuo: Sein Beitrag zum japanischen Sozialismus [Ōyama Ikuo: His Contribution to Japanese Socialism]. Hamburg, 1962. The dissertation in its published form is available at Marburg/Lahn, Universitätsbibliothek, Nr. Z63/1391; also at the University of Michigan, General Library, no.28,470.

Studies (1) the formation and the growth of Japanese socialism up to World War II; (2) the life of Ōyama Ikuo (1880-1955), (3) Ōyama's publications and the influence of his political ideas upon Japanese socialism and upon Japanese internal politics, and (4) his relationship with the Japan Social Democratic Party (Shakai Minshutō) and with the Labor-Farmer Party (Rōdō Nōminto). Concludes with some observations on Ōyama's position within the Japanese pacifist movement.

Rel.Publ.: Ōyama...Sozialismus. Hamburg, 1962. 139p.

MITCHELL, Richard Hanks. The Korean Minority in Japan, 1910-1963. 1963. See no.70.

642
QUO, Fang-quei. Japanese Liberalism: A Case Study in the Transplantation of Political Theory. Southern Illinois, 1964. 207p. DA 25 (Mar. 1965), 5366; UM 65-1334.

The study seeks "to derive a hypothetical theory for transplanting an alien political idea into a society of different cultural and historical backgrounds," and examines the transplantation of liberalism into Japan both before and after World War II as a case study. The appendices (p.168-203) contain chronologies of the life and works of Kawai Hijiro (1891-1944), Yoshino Sakuzō (1898-1933), and Minobe Tatsukichi (1893-1948), and a chronological bibliography of major Japanese writings in political science, 1865-1945.

Rel.Publ.: "Jiyūshugi: Japanese Liberalism," Review of Politics, 28 (Oct. 1966), 477-92.

643
DUUS, Peter. The Kenseikai and the Politics of Taishō Japan. Harvard, 1965. ii, 403p. AB: 5p. summary appended to diss. ms.

Focuses on "the process by which party government became possible in Japan and the uses to which the parties put power once they had acquired it." Contents: Trends in Party Development, 1900-1927; The Formation of the Dōshikai; The Rise of Katō Kōmei; From Dōshikai to Kenseikai, 1914-1916; The Seiyūkai in Power, 1918-1922; The Universal Manhood Suffrage Question, 1919-1920; Party Instability and the "Movement for Constitutional Government" 1921-1924; The Kenseikai in Power: (1) Attempt at Reform, 1924-1925, (2) Triumph of Politics over Reform, 1925-1927.

Rel.Publ.: Party Rivalry and Political Change in Taishō Japan. Cambridge: Harvard University Press, 1968. x, 317p. (Harvard East Asian Series, 35); "The Universal Manhood Suffrage Issue (1919-1925): From Popular Protest to Party Policy," in Harvard University, East Asian Research Center, Papers on Japan, 1 (1961), 227-60.

644
GRIFFIN, Edward Geary. The Adoption of Universal Manhood Suffrage in Japan. Columbia, 1965. 269p. DA 27 (July 1966), 164-A; UM 66-6934.

Contents: An Emerging Issue and a False Start; The Reappearance of the Issue in the Parties; Liberalization of the Kenseikai Suffrage Policy (1919-1922); Non-Party Governments and Universal Suffrage (1922-1924); Seiyūkai Resistance and Conversion (1919-1924); Passage of the Universal Suffrage Law (1924-1925).

645
WILSON, George Macklin. Kita Ikki and the Roots of Japanese Fascism. Harvard, 1965. vii, 287p.

"Charts the process by which Kita arrived at his ideas and relates them to the overall development of ideology in modern Japan." Contents: Kita Ikki in Ideological History; Life of a Political Romantic; Kita Ikki and Socialism; Kita Ikki and Fascism; Kita Ikki in Japanese Historiography.

Rel.Publ.: Radical Nationalist in Japan: Kita Ikki, 1883-1937. Cambridge: Harvard University Press, 1969. xii, 230p. (Harvard East Asian Series, 37); "Kita Ikki, Ōkawa Shūmei, and the Yūzonsha: A Study in the Genesis of Shōwa Nationalism," in Harvard University, East Asian Research Center, Papers on Japan, 2 (1963), 139-81; "Kita Ikki's Theory of Revolution," JAS, 26 (Nov. 1966), 89-99; "Reflections on Japanese Imperialist Ideology," in Imperial Japan and Asia: A Reassessment, compiled by Grant K. Goodman (New York: Columbia University, East Asian Institute, 1967), 46-51; "A New Look at the Problem of 'Japanese Fascism'," Comparative Studies in Society and History, 10 (July 1968), 401-12.

646
VASILJEVOVÁ, Zdeňka. Japonský fašismus: Hnutí služby vlasti v průmyslu jako prostředek fašistické diktatury [Japanese Fascism: The "Movement for Service to the State through Industry" (Sangyō Hōkoku) as an Instrument of the Fascist Dictatorship]. Universita Karlova, 1967/68. 176p. Text in Czech.

An interpretation of the documents related to Japanese fascism focusing on the problem of total integration and control of the society and on the position of the social organizations within the society.

Rel.Publ.: "Sensō ninshiki to Nihon fashizumu no tokushitsu," Rekishi hyōron, 180 (Aug. 1965), 1-19; Le nationalisme japonais et la seconde guerre mondiale," La pensée, 128 (Aug. 1966), 102-18.

647
BRITSCH, Ralph Lanier. Early Latter-Day Saint Missions to South and East Asia. Claremont, 1968. 392p. DA 29 (Aug. 1968), 537-38-A; UM 68-10,498.

Includes material on the history of the Japan Mission (1901-1924) of the Church of Jesus Christ of Latter-Day Saints (Mormon). See especially Chapters 11-16: The Instigation of the Japan Mission; The Early Months of the Japan Mission; Late 1901 to Early 1903: A Period of Many Firsts; From 1903 through 1905: The Ensign Period; From 1905 through 1909: The Taylor Period; From 1910 through 1924: The Unsuccessful Struggle.

DALL, John Joseph, Jr. Sources of Productivity Change in Paddy Rice Production in Japan: 1900-1965. 1968. See no.194.

648
WASWO, Barbara Ann Lardner. Landlords and Social Change in Prewar Japan. Stanford, 1969. 217p. DA 30 (Nov. 1969), 1971-A; UM 69-17,459. [See also addenda entry no.44A.]

1912-1937

See also History--modern, 1868-1945 (pages 72-73) and History--twentieth century: general (pages 82-84).

649
KLINGHAMMER, Helmut. Die Hirota-Doktrin [The Hirota Doctrine]. Greifswald, 1935. Text in German. The dissertation in its published form is available at Marburg/Lahn, Universitätsbibliothek, Nr. XVIII C.

The origin of the Hirota Doctrine and the interpretation that it is a terminal point of Japan's political development since 1853; the form, political motives, and aims of the Doctrine; and an investigation of its legal and political meaning.

Rel.Publ.: Die Hirota-Doktrin. Greifswald: Adler, 1935. 150p.

650
KAEMPF, Christopher. Der Tennō: Ein Organ des Staates? Betrachtung über den Wandel im japanischen Staatsdenken [The Emperor: An Organ of the State? Reflections on Changes in the Theories Concerning the Japanese State]. Leipzig, 1937. Text in German. Available at Marburg/Lahn, Institut für öffentliches Recht der Universität Marburg/Lahn, Nr. E IIIx 245.

The basis of the Japanese state is studied by means of an examination of Japanese theology, the Japanese family system, and early Chinese cultural influence upon Japan. In analyzing the confrontation that developed between Western political science and the Japanese concept of the state, the author considers the relationship existing among the Emperor, his ministers, and the Diet, as well as the relationship of the people to the State. He concludes with a study of the changes in Japanese political thought during the 1930's.

Rel.Publ.: Der Wandel im japanischen Staatsdenken der Gegenwart unter besonderer Berücksichtigung der Stellung des Tennō. Leipzig: Meiner, 1938. xv, 76p. (Abhandlungen des Instituts für Politik, ausländisches öffentliches Recht, und Völkerrecht an der Universität Leipzig. N.F. H.1)

651
EIDUS, Kh. T. (U. Khaiama). Iaponiia v period obshchego krizisa kapitalizma [Japan during the Period when Capitalism Underwent a General Crisis]. Moscow, Institut mirovogo khoziaistva i mirovoi politiki Akademii nauk SSSR, 1940. (Doctor of Historical Sciences) 237p. Text in Russian.

652
WARD, Robert Edward. Party Government in Japan: A Preliminary Survey of Its Development and Electoral Record, 1928-1937. California, Berkeley, 1948. 636p.

Studies the laws and ordinances regulating the election system, the development and the organization of parties before 1928, and the general elections of 1928, 1930, 1932, 1936, and 1937. For each of the elections, the following information is presented: (1) the political background, (2) a general survey of election results, (3) an analysis of the party vote, and (4) the characteristics of successful candidates.

653
WALD, Royal Jules. The Young Officers Movement in Japan, ca. 1925-1937: Ideology and Actions. California, Berkeley, 1950. 268p.

Focuses on Kita Ikki's ideology and on the series of conspiracies and attempted coups d'état that occurred during the 1930's.

654
ROSE, Saul Rose. The Functioning of Parliamentary Government in Japan, 1918-1932, with Special Reference to the Control of Foreign Policy. Oxford, 1951. xii, 877p.

Contents: Prologue [From the Restoration to 1918]; Seiyūkai Government (The Hara Ministry, Takahashi Ministry); Bureaucratic Interlude (Admiral Katō's Ministry, Yamamoto Ministry, Kiyoura Ministry); Party Government (The Coalition Ministry), Viscount Katō's Second Ministry, Wakatsuki's First Ministry, Tanaka Ministry, Hamaguchi Ministry, Wakatsuki's Second Ministry, Inukai Ministry).

655
ZHUKOVA, I. I. Burzhuazno-pomeshchich'ia partiia seiiukai: Posobnik agressii i fashizma v Iaponii, 1931-1941 [The Bourgeois-Landowners' Party, the Seiyūkai: An Accomplice in Aggression and Fascism in Japan, 1931-1941]. Moscow, Moskovskii institut vostokovedeniia, 1952(?). (Candidate of Historical Sciences degree) Text in Russian. AB: 12p. summary published in 1952.

656
DURKEE, Travers Edgar. The Communist International and Japan, 1919-1932. Stanford, 1954. 208p. DA 14 (Oct. 1954), 1691-92; UM 9488.

"This study examines the record of international communism in Japan from 1919 (the formation of the Communist International) to 1932 (the destruction of the pre-war Japanese Communist Party and the last Comintern analysis of Japan). Three main problems are investigated: (1) The Bolshevik historical analysis of Japanese society and the strategy and tactics based on it; (2) Whether the Bolsheviks, as they claim, adhere to their theory in practice; and (3) Whether the pre-World War II Marxist-Leninist analysis of Japan accords with the facts of Japanese society."

657
GEORGIEV, Iu. V. Bor'ba kommunisticheskoi partii Iaponii za revoliutsionnyi put' razvitiia iaponskogo professional'nogo dvizheniia, 1922-1928 gg. [The Struggle of the Japan Communist Party for Revolutionary Means of Developing the Japanese Trade Union Movement, 1922-1928]. Moscow, Moskovskii institut vostokovedeniia, 1954. (Candidate of Historical Sciences degree) 314 + 21p. Text in Russian. AB: 15p. summary published in 1954.

658
KRIANEVA, O. A. Polozhenie i bor'ba rabochego klassa Iaponii v gody pervoi imperialisticheskoi voiny, 1914-1918 [The Position and the Struggle of the Japanese Working Class during the First Imperialist War, 1914-1918]. Leningrad, Leningradskii gosudarstvennyi universitet imeni A. A. Zhdanova, 1954. (Candidate of Historical Sciences degree) 214p. Text in Russian. AB: 14p. summary published in 1954.

659
SYRITSYN, I. M. Antivoennoe i antifashistskoe dvizhenie v Iaponii v 1935-1937 gg. [The Anti-Fascist and Antiwar Movement in Japan, 1935-1937]. Moscow, Moskovskii gosudarstvennyi universitet imeni M. V. Lomonosova, 1954. (Candidate of Historical Sciences) 10 + 402p. Text in Russian. AB: 12p. summary published in 1954.

Rel.Publ.: Bor'ba iaponskikh trudiashchikhsia protiv voiny i fashizma, 1935-1937 gg. Moscow, Izdatel'stvo vostochnoi literatury, 1960. 107p. (Moskovskii gosudarstvennyi universitet imeni M. V. Lomonosova, Institut vostochnykh iazykov, Institut narodov Azii Akademii nauk SSSR)

660
TOTTEN, George Oakley, III. Japanese Social Democracy: An Analysis of the Background, Leadership, and Organized Support of the Social Democratic Movement in Prewar Japan. Yale, 1954. iv, 397p. DA 15 (Mar. 1955), 447. Order microfilm copy directly from Yale University library.

Contents: Background (Historical Development, Environmental Conditions); Leadership (Shaminkei, Nichirokei, Rōnōha, and Other Leftist Groupings); Party Support (The Electorate, Organized Labor, Organized Farmers, Women and Minority Groups).

Rel.Publ.: The Social Democratic Movement in Prewar Japan. New Haven: Yale University Press, 1966. xv, 455p.; "Problems of Japanese Socialist Leadership," Pacific Affairs, 28 (June 1955), 160-69.

661
LIEBERMAN, Mary Estes. Ōkawa Shumei and Japan's "Divine Mission." California, Berkeley, 1956. 119p.

Ōkawa Shumei (1886-1957), the jurist and politician who founded the nationalistic Yūzonsha and Jimmukai and who participated in the March Affair (1931) and in the May 15th Incident (1932). Contents: Ōkawa's Early Life; Meeting with Kita Ikki; The Climax of Ōkawa's Career: The Incidents of 1931 and 1932; Later Career; Arraignment as a War Crimes Suspect; Ōkawa's Ideological Heritage; Pan-Asianism; Internal Reform.

662
SILBERMAN, Bernard Samuel. The Democracy Movement in Japan, 1916-1921: A History of a Social Movement. Michigan, 1956. 264p. DA 17 (Aug. 1957), 1743; UM 21,947.

Contents: Introduction: The Meiji Social Background; The Social and Political Origins of the Democracy Movement; The Theoretical Bases, the Beginnings, and the Active Phase of the Democracy Movement; The Movement to the Left; The Aftermath of the Democracy Movement.

Rel.Publ.: "The Political Theory and Program of Yoshino Sakuzō," Journal of Modern History, 31 (Dec. 1959), 310-24.

663
McGOVERN, James Richard. American Christian Missions to Japan, 1918-1941. Pennsylvania, 1957. 306p. DA 17 (Dec. 1957), 2994-95; UM 23,614.

Examines "the operation and results of American Protestant and Catholic missions in Japan," 1918-1941, and the status of Christianity in Japan during that period. Concludes that "the Japanese were too oriental and the Christian enterprises too western for Christianity to make any sizable gains during that period."

SASAKI, Kyohei. A Western Influence on Japanese Economic Thought: The Marxian Non-Marxian Controversies in the 1920's and Their Significance for Today. 1957. See no.368.

664
VLASOV, V. A. Zakabalenie melkikh predpriiatii Iaponii monopolisticheskim kapitalom, 1929-1937 [The Enslavement of Small Japanese Enterprises by Monopolistic Capital, 1929-1937]. Moscow, Institut vostokovedeniia Akademii nauk SSSR, 1958. (Candidate of Economic Sciences degree) 201p. Text in Russian.

Rel.Publ.: Zakabalenie...1937. Moscow: Izdatel'stvo vostochnoi literatury, 1958. 116p. (Institut vostokovedeniia Akademii nauk SSSR)

665
TIEDEMANN, Arthur Everett. The Hamaguchi Cabinet: First Phase July 1929-February 1930: A Study in Japanese Parliamentary Government. Columbia, 1959. 410p. DA 20 (Mar. 1960), 3719; UM 60-50.

An examination of the first eight months of the Hamaguchi Cabinet. "While giving a full account of the events of the period, the dissertation also uses them as a point of departure for the description of certain Japanese political processes and for the statistical analysis of a number of important Japanese political groups."

666
CROWLEY, James Buckley. Japan's China Policy, 1931-1938: A Study of the Role of the Military in the Determination of Foreign Policy. Michigan, 1960. 344p. DA 20 (June 1960), 4640; UM 60-1751.

"Aims to discover who the decision-makers were and to ascertain the precise content of the official China policy." The investigation focuses on the bureaucratic and military elites and seeks to determine whether the leaders of the Imperial Army, especially the so-called Tōsei faction, were the one's most responsible for the direction of Japan's China policy.

Rel.Publ.: Japan's Quest for Autonomy: National Security and Foreign Policy, 1930-1938. Princeton: Princeton University Press, 1966. xviii, 428p.; "Japanese Army Factionalism in the Early 1930's," JAS, 21 (May 1962), 309-26; "A Reconsideration of the Marco Polo Bridge Incident," JAS, 22 (May 1963), 277-91.

667
KHANIN, Z. Ia. Agrarnye otnosheniia i krest'ianskoe dvizhenie v Iaponii, 1922-1929 gg. [Agrarian Relationships and the Peasant Movement in Japan, 1922-1929]. Leningrad, Leningradskii gosudarstvennyi universitet imeni A. A. Zhdanova, 1961. (Candidate of Historical Sciences degree) 266p. Text in Russian.

668
MILLER, Frank Owen. Minobe Tatsukichi: The Interpreter of Constitutionalism in Japan. California, Berkeley, 1961. 551p. (2v.).

"An explication of Minobe's constitutional theory and of his part as an exponent of an important and controversial school of constitutional interpretation in Japan."

Rel.Publ.: Minobe...Japan. Berkeley: University of California Press, 1965. xi, 392p. (Publications of the Center for Japanese and Korean Studies)

669
LI, San Cho. Ideologiia "Kodo" na sluzhbe iaponskogo militarizma [The Ideology of Kōdō ("The Imperial Way") in the Service of Japanese Militarism]. Minsk, Institut filosofii Akademii nauk Belorusskoi SSR, 1962. (Candidate of Philosophical Sciences degree) 251p. Text in Russian.

670
GAMAZKOV, K. A. Rol' "Obshchestva Iuibutsuron kenkiukai" v rasprostranenii marksizma-leninizma v Iaponii, 1932-1938 gg. [The Role of the Yuibutsuron Kenkyūkai

(The Society for the Study of Historical Materialism) in the Dissemination of Marxism-Leninism in Japan, 1932-1938]. Moscow, Institut narodov Azii Akademii nauk SSSR, Ekonomicheskaia sektsiia, 1965(?). (Candidate of Historical Sciences degree) Text in Russian. AB: 18p. summary published in 1965. [See also addenda.]

NAJITA, Tetsuo. The Seiyūkai in the Politics of Compromise, 1905-1915. 1965. See no.617.

671
SMETHURST, Richard Jacob. The Social Basis for Japanese Militarism: The Case of the Imperial Military Reserve Association. Michigan, 1968. 366p. DA 30 (July 1969), 260-A; UM 69-12,239.
A study of "part of the central leadership of the [Shōwa] government--the Imperial Military Reserve Association (Teikoku zaigō gunjinkai)--an organization which was used to maintain and to spread the leaders' ideology, to create a social basis for Japanese militarism, and, thereby, to strengthen the role of the military in determining the future of the nation."

672
DINGMAN, Roger Vincent. Power in the Pacific: The Evolution of American and Japanese Naval Policies. Harvard, 1969. 504, cxxxiip. AB: 10p. summary appended to diss. ms.
"Analyzes the choices and decisions before Japanese and American policy-makers during the critical postwar years...and focuses on the motives which guided naval policy-makers toward new definitions of naval adequacy." Contents: Backgrounds to Controversy; Context for Choice: Politics, Diplomacy, and American Naval Policy, 1919-1920; Towards Postwar Naval Excellence: The Imperial Navy and the National Defense Compromises of 1918; The Eight Eight Fleet Attained: The Politics of Japanese Naval Expansion, 1919-1920; Republicans and the Choices of Postwar Naval Policy, November 1920-July 1921; The Standards of American Naval Strength, July-November 1921; Japan's Turn toward Disarmament, August 1920-July 1921; Hara, Kato, and Japan's Naval Security, July-October 1921; Conclusion: The Nature of Naval Change, 1918-1921.

673
SMITH, Henry DeWitt, II. Student Radicals in Prewar Japan. Harvard, 1969. 525p.
Contents: The Prewar Japanese University System; The Prehistory of the Modern Student Movement; The Early Shinjinkai ["The New Man Society"]; The Evolution of a National Student Movement, 1922-1925; Shinjinkai Activity on the University Campus; The Nature of Student Communism; Suppression and the Student Movement Underground; The Shinjinkai Membership Origins and Careers; The Legacy to the Postwar Student Movement.
Rel.Publ.: "The Shinjinkai (1918-1921): The Making of an Intelligentsia," in Harvard University, East Asian Research Center, Papers on Japan, 3 (1965), 162-229.

STEINHOFF, Patricia G. Tenkō: Ideology and Societal Integration in Prewar Japan. 1969. See no.87.

1937-1945

674
COHEN, Jerome Bernard. The Japanese War Economy, 1937-1945. Columbia, 1949. 262p.
Describes the planned industrial expansion of the Japanese economy prior to 1941 and surveys the war years, showing how the Japanese sought (1) to develop their war industries, (2) to meet various emergencies, and (3) to cope with problems of labor and supply of material. Based largely on reports of the United States Strategic Bombing Survey.
Rel.Publ.: Japan's Economy in War and Reconstruction. Minneapolis: University of Minnesota Press, 1949. xix, 545p.; "The Japanese War Economy: 1940-1945," FES, 15 (Dec. 4, 1946), 361-70.

675
LÊ-thành-Khôi. L'Économie de guerre japonaise [The Japanese War Economy]. Paris, 1949. 402p. Text in French.

676
ERSELCUK, Muzaffer Mehmet. Some Aspects of Japanese Economy, 1937-1945. Indiana, 1950. 248p.
Contents: Pt.1: Introduction: Method and Scope--Historical Background. Pt.2: Labor. Pt.3: Japanese Food Situation: Agriculture; Rice. Pt.4: Energy Resources: Coal; Liquid Fuels; Electric Power Industry. Pt.5: Japanese War Finance: State Finance; Banking. Pt.6: Conclusion.
Rel.Publ.: "Japan's Oil Reserves," Economic Geography, 22 (Jan. 1946), 14-23; "Electricity in Japan," FEQ, 6 (May 1947), 283-95.

677
DINKEVICH, A. I. Voennye finansy imperialisticheskoi Iaponii v period voiny 1937-1945 gg.: Kharakteristike finansovoi politiki iaponskogo pravitel'stva [Imperial Japan's War Finances, 1937-1945: Characteristics of the Japanese Government's Financial Policy]. Moscow, Moskovskii institut vostokovedeniia, 1951. (Candidate of Economic Sciences degree) 389p. Text in Russian.

678
MORGAN, Alfred Davidson. The Fiscal Anatomy of Wartime Japan, 1937-1945: With Special Reference to the National Government during 1941-1945. Harvard, 1951. x, 712p. AB: United States Department of State, External Research Staff. Abstracts of Completed Doctoral Dissertations for the Academic Year 1950/1951. p.353-56.
Contents: Conceptual Framework; The Budget Structure; Structure of Expenditures; Structure of Taxation; The Burden of Taxation; The Structure of Deficit-Finance.

679
LATYSHEV, I. Z. Ustanovlenie voenno-fashistskogo rezhima v Iaponii nakanune voiny na Tikhom okeane, 1940-1941 [The Establishment of a Military and Fascist Regime in Japan on the Eve of the Pacific War, 1940-1941]. Moscow, Moskovskii institut vostokovedeniia, 1952(?). (Candidate of Historical Sciences degree) Text in Russian. AB: 52p. summary published in 1952.
Rel.Publ.: Vnutrenniaia politika iaponskogo imperializma nakanune voiny na Tikhom okeane. Moscow, 1955. 232p.

680
LUK'IANOVA, M. I. Ekonomika Iaponii v gody vtoroi mirovoi voiny [The Japanese Economy during World War II]. Moscow, Institut vostokovedeniia Akademii nauk SSSR, 1952. (Doctor of Economic Sciences degree) 827p. Text in Russian. AB: 31p. summary published

in 1952.
Rel.Publ.: Iaponskie monopoli v gody vtoroi mirovoi voiny. Moscow: Izdatel'stvo Akademii Nauk SSSR, 1953. 396p.

681
BESSON-GUYARD, Maurice. Les Conséquences de la guerre 1939-1945 sur l'économie japonaise [The Consequences of the Second World War for the Japanese Economy]. Paris, 1953. 258p. Text in French.

682
BUTOW, Robert Joseph Charles. Japan's Decision to Surrender: A Study in Policy Evolution. Stanford, 1953. 565p. DA 13 (1953), 221; UM 4656.
History of "the behind-the-scenes activities of those Japanese whose thoughts and actions spawned Japan's decision to surrender."
Rel.Publ.: Japan's...Evolution. Stanford: Stanford University Press, 1954. xi, 259p. (The Hoover Library on War, Revolution, and Peace. Publication no.24)

TAOKA, George M. The Role of the Bank of Japan in the Administration of the Economic and Financial Controls of the Government during National Emergencies: With Special Emphasis on the Sino-Japanese War and the World War II Periods. 1955. See no.323.

683
KIM, Chonghan. Konoye Fumimaro and Japanese Foreign Policy: 1937-1941. Indiana, 1956. 337p. DA 16 (Oct. 1956), 1937; UM 17,964.
"Examines the development of Japan's military-controlled politics as it affected the conduct of Japan's foreign policy in the period prior to the Pacific War and appraises the role of Konoye Fumimaro therein during his tenure of the premiership."

684
LU, David Kun-hsi. From the Marco Polo Bridge to Pearl Harbor: Japan's Entry into the Second World War. Columbia, 1960. 503p. DA 21 (Oct. 1960), 949-50; UM 60-3111.
"Describes the interplay of domestic and foreign policy considerations that ultimately led Japan to war."
Rel.Publ.: From...War. Washington: Public Affairs Press, 1961. 274p.

TSUNEISHI, Warren M. The Japanese Emperor: A Study in Constitutional and Political Change. 1960. See no.1829.

685
CHAPMAN, J. W. M. Japanese Military Cooperation, 1936-1945. Oxford, 1967.

OGASAWARA (BONIN ISLANDS)

686
KUBLIN, Hyman. The Bonin Islands, 1543-1875. Harvard, 1947. ii, 163p. AB: 4p. summary appended to diss. ms.
See especially "Early Japanese Relations with the Bonin Islands" (Ch.2); "The Japanese Colony" (Ch.7); and "Annexation by Japan" (Ch.8).
Rel.Publ.: "The Ogasawara Venture, (1861-1863)," HJAS, 14 (1951), 261-84; "Commodore Perry and the Bonin Islands," United States Naval Institute Proceedings, 78 (Mar. 1952), 283-91; "The Discovery of the Bonin Islands: A Reexamination," Annals of the Association of American Geographers, 43 (Mar. 1953), 27-46; "The Bonin Islands: An Essay on the Western Language Literature," Kokusai-hō gaikō zasshi, 54 (Dec. 1955), 1-16.

THE RYUKYUS

(Includes dissertations in anthropology, political science, and religion, etc. that focus on the Ryukyu Islands as a geographical and historical entity.)

687
SIMON, Edmund M. H. Liu-ch'iu-kuo: Beiträge zur Kenntnis der Riu-kiu Inseln [Liu-ch'iu-kuo: Contributions to Our Knowledge of the Ryukyu Islands]. Leipzig, 1913. Text in German.
Contents: Pt.1: Geography: The Various Characteristics of the Region; The Geography of the Region; Its Rivers; The Geology of the Region; Meteorological Conditions; Topography (Okinawa, Naha, Shuri, Shimajiri, Nakagami, Kunchan, Sakishima); Transportation. Pt.2: Ethnography: Residential Buildings; The Origin of Related Customs and Practices; Marriage; Death and Burial; Clothing, Tatooing, and Related Things; Social Organization; Religious Ideas (Primitive Ideas, Buddhism, The Influence of Chinese Religious and Moral Ideas).
Rel.Publ.: Liu-ch'iu-kuo...Inseln. Leipzig: R. Voigtländer, 1913. xiv, 182p.; "Die wirtschaftlichen Verhältnisse der Riukiu-Inseln, (Japan)," Berichte über Handel und Industrie, 14 (1910), 522-31; "Ein alter Plan der beiden Hauptstädte des ehemaligen Kōnig reiches Chusan," T'oung Pao, 2d ser., 12 (1911), 728-35; "Eine ethnographische-interessante Kakemono," T'oung Pao, 2d ser., 13 (1912), 113-16; "Riukiu: Ein Spiegel für Altjapan," MOAG, v.15, pt.B (1914), 1-31; "Über Knotenschriften und ähnliche Knotenschnüre der Riukiu Inseln," Asia Major (Leipzig), 1 (1924), 659-67; "Der Feuergott der Riu-kiu Inseln," in Deutsche Gesellschaft für Natur- und Völkerkunde Ostasiens, Nachrichten, 8 (1927), 4-5.

MATSUMOTO, Nobuhiro. Le Japonais et les langues austroasiatiques: Étude de vocabulaire comparé. 1928. See no.1495.

LUDWIG, Albert Philip. Li Hung-chang and Chinese Foreign Policy, 1870-1885. 1936. See no.916.

688
HAENISCH, Wolfgang. Die auswärtige Politik Ryūkyūs seit dem Anfang des 17. Jahrhunderts und der Einfluss der Fürsten von Satsuma [The Foreign Policy of the Ryukyus since the Beginning of the Seventeenth Century and the Influence of the Daimyo of Satsuma]. Berlin, 1937. Text in German. The dissertation in its published form is available at Marburg/Lahn, Universitätsbibliothek, Nr. VII C.
Focuses on the politically undefined situation of the Ryukyus during the Tokugawa period, a situation in which the inhabitants of the islands found themselves caught in the middle between two great powers, China and Japan.
Rel.Publ.: Die auswärtige...Satsuma. Erlangen-Bruck: Krahl, 1937. 41p.

EDER, Matthias. Das Lautwesen des Yaeyama-Dialektes: Ein Beitrag zur Dialektkunde Japans. Mit Parallelen aus anderen Dialekten der Ryūkyū-Inseln. 1939. See no.1449.

689
LA RUE, Adrian Jan Pieters. The Okinawan Classical Songs: An Analytical and Comparative Study. Harvard, 1952. vii, 260p. AB: 12p. summary appended to diss. ms.

Contents: The History and Culture of Okinawa; Musical Instruments and Vocal Style; The Okinawan Notation System; Form; Texts; Melody; Rhythm; The Varied Unison Style; Connections with Other Oriental Styles. A microfilm of transcriptions of the entire Okinawan repertory is on deposit with the dissertation.

Rel.Publ.: "Native Music on Okinawa," Musical Quarterly, 33 (Apr. 1946), 157-70; "The Okinawan Notation System," Journal of the American Musicological Association, 4 (Spring 1951), 25-35.

690
NAYLOR, Harry Lee. A Psychocultural Study of Twenty-eight Ryukyuan Students. New Mexico, 1952. viii, 180p. + appendix.

Contents: History of the Psychocultural Approach; The Cultural History of the Ryukyus; Ethnology of the Ryukyu Islands; The Personality Structure of Twenty-eight Ryukyuan Students.

691
LIEBAN, Richard Warren. Land and Labor on Kudaka Island. Columbia, 1956. 125p. DA 16 (July 1956), 1198; UM 16,903.

Studies communal land tenure as a functioning system of Kudaka, a small island off the coast of Okinawa, which since 1899 has resisted the changeover to a system of private land ownership. Also concerned with the theoretical implications involved in the perpetuation of communal tenure there.

Rel.Publ.: "The Land System of Kudaka Island," Sociologus, 5 (1955), 150-56.

TIGNER, James L. The Okinawans in Latin America. 1956. See no.1698.

692
MARETZKI, Thomas Walter. Child Rearing in an Okinawan Community. Yale, 1957. 535p.

Contents: The Setting; Property; Basic Economy; Food and Eating; Social Organization; Political Organization and Social Control; Religion; Health; Status of Men and Women; Recreation; Daily Routine; Life Crises; Child Rearing Agents; Infancy Training; Childhood Training; Formal Education; Dependence and Independence; Social Structure and Socialization.

Rel.Publ.: Taira: An Okinawan Village [by] Thomas and Hatsumi Maretzki. New York: Wiley, 1966. xxxv, 176p. (Six Culture Series, 7) [Also in Six Cultures: Studies of Child Rearing, ed. by Beatrice B. Whiting (New York: John Wiley, 1963), 363-539.]

693
LEBRA, William Philip. Okinawan Religion. Harvard, 1958. iii, 362p.

"A systematic, descriptive account of the indigenous religion of contemporary Okinawa taking into account its historical development." Focuses on concepts of the supernatural, religious practices, religious organization and specialists, state religion, community religion, kin group religion, and household religion.

Rel.Publ.: Okinawan Religion: Belief, Ritual, and Social Structure. Honolulu: University of Hawaii Press, 1966. xiv, 241p.; "Client and Shaman in Okinawa," in Mental Health Research in Asia and the Pacific, ed. by W. Caudill and Tsung-yi Lin (Honolulu: East-West Center Press, 1969).

694
STIRES, Frederick Hand. The Ryukyus, an American Dependency: An Analysis of the Military and Civil Administration of the Ryukyu Islands, 1945-1958. Georgetown, 1960. 226p.

Contents: Background from Earliest Times to 1945; Period of Military Government, 1945-1950; San Francisco Peace Treaty; Civil Administration and Ryukyan Self-Government; Economic Development; Military Land Problem; Political Parties and Reversion Movement.

ARNAUD, Paul H., Jr. The Heleid Genus Culicoides in Japan, Korea, and Ryukyu Islands (Insecta: Diptera) 1961. See no.2022.

695
COHEN, Abraham. The Impact of the American Occupation upon the Culture and Education of Okinawa. Columbia (Teachers College), 1961. 223p.

696
KING, Horace Clifford. An Analysis of Educational-Administrative-Cultural Aspects of the Relationship between the University of the Ryukyus and Michigan State University. Michigan State, 1962. 199p. DA 23 (Apr. 1963), 3725-26; UM 63-1735.

The study covers the period 1951-1961. Contents: Description of the Problem and Method of Research; The Identity of Forces Having Influence on the Ryukyuan Culture; Education in Okinawa and the Evolution of the University of the Ryukyus; Major Factors in the Establishment and Development of the University of the Ryukyus (Purposes of the University of the Ryukyus, Financial and Related Resources, Michigan State University Advisory Group, Leadership, Internal Structure, and Program Performance at the University, Interaction between the University, the Ryukyuan Community, and the International Community, Concern for the University's Future); Conclusions and Recommendations.

697
CH'EN, Ta-tuan. Sino--Liu-ch'iuan Relations in the Nineteenth Century. Indiana, 1963. 238p. DA 24 (Jan. 1964), 2875-76; UM 64-452.

"A study of the tribute system pattern of relations between the Chinese Empire and the kingdom of Liu-ch'iu (Ryukyu) as they developed prior to the Japanese annexation of the latter in 1879."

698
LOVELESS, Owen Robert. The Okinawan Language: A Synchronic Description. Michigan, 1963. 246p. DA 26 (Apr. 1966), 6032; UM 64-6715.

A description of the phonology, inflectional system, word-classes, and syntax of the language spoken by monolingual persons of Shuri, the former capital city of the Ryukyus.

699
KREINER, Josef. Beiträge zur Erforschung von Religion und Gesellschaft auf den nördlichen Ryūkyū: Der Noro-Kult von Amami-Ōshima [Contributions to the Investigation of Religion and Society in the Northern Ryukyus: The Noro Cult of Amami-Ōshima]. Wien, 1964. vii, 344p. Text in German. Diss. ms. available at the Universitätsbibliothek der Universität Wien, Nr. D 15,595; also at the Österreichische Nationalbibliothek,

Nr. 990.645-C.

A survey of the problems of cultural history that relate to the Ryukyus and particularly to Amami-Ōshima with a monographic study of religious life on the island of Kakeroma. Analyses the Noro cult in regard to the structure of the cult group and its conception of god.

Rel.Publ.: Beiträge...Ōshima. Wien: 1965. v, 200p. (Beiträge zur Japanologie, 2); "Noro saishi shūdan ni okeru kamiyaku no keishō ni tsuite: Amami Kakeroma-shima no ba'ai," Minzokugaku kenkyū, 27 (1962), 382-87; "Amami Ōshima no sonraku kōzō to saishi soshiki: Kakeroma-shima Sukumo bunraku no Noro Seido," Shakai to denshō, 7 (1963), 43-63; "Maskenbrauchtum der Tokara-Inseln, Japan," Archiv für Völkerkunde, 19 (1964/65), 90-91.

700
HEWETT, Robert Foster, Jr. United States Civil Administration of the Ryukyu Islands, 1950-1960: An Historical Analysis and Appraisal of a Decade of Civil Administration of an Asian Area. American, 1966. 299p. DA 26 (May 1966), 6824; UM 66-3395.

Contents: Background Information; United States Civil Administration of the Ryukyus; Government of the Ryukyu Islands; The Ryukyuan Economy; Development of Public Activities.

701
HSU, Tsu-wei. Le Statut international de l'archipel de Ryukyu [The International Status of the Ryukyu Islands]. Paris, 1966. 147,iv p. Text in French. AB: Université de Paris. Annales de l'Université de Paris. v.37, no.4 (Oct./Dec. 1967), p.625.

The author argues that China, which was the suzerain over the Ryukyus from 1372 until their seizure by Japan in 1879, still has ultimate sovereignty over the islands. Japan, it is maintained, has no right to reclaim them and the United States has no right to return them to her inasmuch as she renounced them in Article 3 of the 1951 Peace Treaty in San Francisco.

702
PEARSON, Richard Joseph. Temporal and Spatial Variation in the Culture History of the Ryūkyū Islands. Yale, 1966. 355p. DA 28 (July 1967), 34-B; UM 67-8405.

"Presents an archaeological chronology, extending in time from about 2000 B.C. to 1700 A.D., of the Ryūkyū Islands....Sites and types of artifacts excavated by the author, as well as those of many other archaeologists, are outlined, and phases of cultural development are formulated." Excavations in southern Kyushu are also discussed.

Rel.Publ.: Archaeology of the Ryūkyū Islands: A Regional Chronology from 3000 B.C. to the Historic Period. Honolulu: University of Hawaii, 1969. 228p.

703
WATANABE, Akio. Japanese Attitudes towards the Okinawa Project, 1945-1965. Australian National, 1966. 200p.; 135p. (2v.).

A general discussion of the merits of the Okinawan issue and of the groups involved.

Rel.Publ.: "Okinawa in United States Strategy," Australia's Neighbours, 4th ser., no.8/9 (Sept./Oct. 1963), 6-8; "The Okinawa Conflict and the U.S.-Japan Alliance," Australian Outlook, 20 (Apr. 1966), 36-42; "Government Departments and the Making of Foreign Policy towards Okinawa," in Australian National University, Department of International Relations, Papers on Modern Japan, 1968 (Canberra, 1968), 46-61.

704
MATSUDA, Mitsugu. The Government of the Kingdom of Ryukyu, 1609-1872. Hawaii, 1967. 346p. DA 28 (Nov. 1967), 1767-A; UM 67-13,704.

Focuses on the organization and expansion of the Ryukyuan system of government following the occupation of the kingdom by Shimazu forces in 1609 and discusses the relationship that existed between the Ryukyus and Satsuma han during the Tokugawa period.

705
WHITNEY, Daniel De Wayne. The Flow of Agricultural Information in Okinawa. Michigan State, 1968. 295p. DA 30 (Aug. 1969), 478-B; UM 69-11,183.

Analyzes the dissemination of agricultural information from national agencies in Okinawa to individual farmers. Contents: The Island of Okinawa; The Sources of Agricultural Information; Channel: Agricultural Extension (Agriculture and Home Demonstration System, Farm Management Advisors); Channel: Township and Village Administration; Channel: Formal Associations (Women's Association, Youth Association, Cooperatives); Channel: Mass Media and Education (Newspapers, Magazines, Government Publications, Television and Radio, Closed Circuit Broadcasting System, Education); Receivers of Agricultural Information.

THE JAPANESE EMPIRE

(Dissertations that focus on the Japanese acquisition of Karafuto, Korea, Manchoukuo, Micronesia, and Taiwan are not included)

General

706
ASAMI, Noboru. Japanese Colonial Government. Columbia, 1925. v, 82p.

Contents: Colonial Institutions in the Motherland; The Legal Sources of Colonial Government; The Organization of the Colonial Governments in Chōsen, Formosa, Sakhalin, Kwantung, and the South Sea Islands.

Rel.Publ.: Japanese...Government. New York, 1925. v, 82p.

Chōsen [Korea] (1910-1945)

See International Relations--Korea (pages 133-36) for dissertations on the Japanese rivalry over and annexation of Korea.

707
CHUNG, Henry. Case of Korea: [A] Collection of Evidence on the Japanese Domination of Korea [and] on the Development of [the] Korean Independence Movement. American, 1921. 289p.

Contents: Diplomatic Relations between Korea and Japan; Political and Judicial Oppression; The Official "Paddle"; Prison and Prison Tortures; Economic Exploitation; Intellectual Strangulation; Imposition of Social Evils; Persecution of the Church; Indignities to Missionaries; The Movement to Restore Independence; Japan Amuck; Massacres; "Speaking Officially" ; Japan's Alleged Reforms; Korean and Japanese Characters Contrasted.

Rel.Publ.: Case...Movement. New York: F. H. Revell, 1921.

708
UNDERWOOD, Horace Morton. Outline History of Modern Education in Korea. New York, 1926. viii, 393p.
For information on Korean education under Japanese rule, see Ch.5, "Government Education since 1910" (p. 207-308). Within this chapter the author focuses on Japanese educational policy (the Educational Ordinance of 1911, the 1915 revision of private school regulations, the Educational Ordinance of 1922, the Governor-General's ruling on private schools in 1923, etc.) and on the Government-General's educational work.
Rel.Publ.: Modern Education in Korea. New York: International Press, 1926. xv, 336p.

709
FISHER, James Earnest. Democracy and Mission Education in Korea. Columbia (Teachers College), 1928. xiii, 187p.
See Ch.4, "The Relation of Mission Education to the Japanese Government, and Government Control of Education" (p.65-93).
Rel.Publ.: Democracy...Korea. New York: Teachers College, Columbia University. Contributions to Education, 306)

710
AUH, Paul (Chunsuk). Education as an Instrument of National Assimilation: A Study of the Educational Policy of Japan in Korea. Columbia, 1931. 246p.
The dissertation examines Japan's policy of denationalizing the Korean people by means of an assimilationist educational policy. Among the subjects discussed are (1) Korean nationality, (2) political relations between Japan and Korea, (3) education under the Yi dynasty, (4) Japan's educational policy in Korea, (5) Japan's colonial policy in Korea and education as an instrument of that policy, (6) resistance to the assimilation policy, and (7) the Independence Movement and the student uprising.

711
WASSON, Alfred Washington. Factors in the Growth of the Church in Korea. Chicago, 1931. 229p.
"The history of the Southern Methodist mission in Korea." Contains considerable information on the impact that Japanese rule had upon church development.
Rel.Publ.: Church Growth in Korea. Concord, N.H.: Rumford Press, 1934. xii, 175p. (Studies in the World Mission of Christianity)

712
LINKE, Johannes Christian. Veränderung der wirtschaftsgeographischen Beziehungen in Korea unter dem Einfluss der Erschliessung: Die Grundlagen und ursprüngliche Ausgestaltung [Changes in Economic and Geographical Relations within Korea as Influenced by the Opening of That Country: Their Basis and the Initial Arrangement That They Took]. Leipzig, 1932. 134p. Text in German. The dissertation in its published form is available at Leipzig, Universitätsbibliothek, Nr. U 33,1413.
In part of the dissertation the author studies Japan's economic impact upon Korea, exploring how geographical circumstances influenced the nature and course of Japanese economic penetration.
Rel.Publ.: Veränderung...Ausgestaltung. Stuttgart: Metzler, 1932. 134p.

713
KIM, Che-won. Die Volksschule in Korea: Die japanische Assimilationserziehung [Primary Schools in Korea: The Assimilation to Japanese Educational Ideas]. The dissertation in its published form is available at Marburg/Lahn, Universitätsbibliothek, Nr. XV C; also at the University of Michigan, General Library, no. LA1331.KS.
Studies the accommodation of the Korean primary schools to the Japanese educational system, the goals of elementary education in Korea, and the attitude of the pupils to the authority of their teachers. Also includes Japanese ideas on assimilation.
Rel.Publ.: Die Volksschule...Assimilationserziehung. Antwerpen [Belgium]: "De Sikkel", 1934. 69p.

714
CHO, Seung-hak. A Study of the Korean Elementary School Curriculum. Wisconsin, 1937. iii, 200p. AB: University of Wisconsin. Summaries of Doctoral Dissertations. v.2, p.243-44.
Chapters 2-4 include critical discussions of the impact of Japanese educational policy upon Korean education.

715
GRAJDANZEV, Andrew Jonah. Modern Korea: Her Economic and Social Development under the Japanese. Columbia, 1945. x, 330p.
A comprehensive review covering the following subjects: population; agriculture, forestry, and fishery; power and mineral resources; industrial development; transport and communications; money and banking; public finance; external trade; the government; courts, prisons, police; health, education, and religion; Problems of Korean independence.
Rel.Publ.: Modern...Japanese. New York: Institute of Pacific Relations, 1944. x, 330p.

716
SHVER, M. K. Iaponskoe kolonial'noe gospodstvo v Koree i ego krakh [Japanese Colonial Rule in Korea and Its Collapse]. Leningrad, Leningradskii gosudarstvennyi universitet imeni A. A. Zhdanova, 1947. (Candidate of Economic Sciences degree) iv, 574p. Text in Russian. AB: 3p. summary published in 1948.

717
MEADE, Edward Grant. A Military Government Experiment in Korea. Pennsylvania, 1948. xi, 410p.
A study of the United States military occupation of South Korea in 1945-1946. Includes considerable information on the liquidation of Japanese colonial rule there.
Rel.Publ.: American Military Government in Korea. New York: King's Crown Press, 1951. xii, 281p.

718
MITCHELL, Charles Clyde, Jr. The New Korea Company, Limited: Land Management and Tenancy Reform in Korea against a Background of United States Army Occupation, 1945-1948. Harvard, 1949. xv, 365p. AB: 5p. summary appended to diss. ms.
See Ch.2, "Predecessors of the New Korea Company" (p.15-31), for information on prewar Japanese land management activities in Korea, and Ch.3, "Early Land Management and Tenancy Reform Operations of the Military Government" (p.32-59), for information on the American seizure and operation of the agricultural properties formerly owned by the Japanese in Korea.
Rel.Publ.: Final Report and History of the New Korea Company. Seoul: Headquarters, United States Army Military Government in Korea, National Land Administra-

tion, 1948. 65p.; "South Korean Tenants Become Landowners," Foreign Agriculture, 12 (Oct. 1948), 217-20; "Land Reform in South Korea," Pacific Affairs, 22 (June 1949), 144-54.

GANE, William Joseph. Foreign Affairs of South Korea, August, 1945 to August, 1950. 1951. See no.1811.

719
HU, Hung-lick. Le Problème coréen [The Korean Problem]. Paris, 1951. Text in French.

Pt.2, "The Loss and Recovery of Independence, 1895-1945" (p.53-78), deals with the Russo-Japanese rivalry for Korea, the Japanese annexation of the country, and the Korean independence movement.

Rel.Publ.: Le Problème coréen. Paris: A. Pedone, 1953. 191p.

720
CHUNG, Han Pom. The Republic of Korea in Power Politics. American, 1952. 395p.

The contents of pt.2, "Tragedy of Korea under Japan, 1910-1945": Japan's Policy in Korea after Annexation; Heroes of Korean Independence Movements; Korea's International Relations between the Imposition of the Protectorate and Liberation.

721
RIM, Han Young. The Development of Higher Education in Korea during the Japanese Occupation (1910-1945). Columbia (Teachers College), 1952. 246p.

The study includes chapters on the Japanese annexation of Korea, the establishment of Japanese control over education, and Japanese special schools. There is much information on the impact of the Japanese annexation, contemporary Korean society, Korean educational reforms, the role of students in the Independence Movement, and institutions of higher learning in Korea.

Rel.Publ.: "Japanese Totalitarian Education in Korea, 1910-1945," Koreana Quarterly, 2 (Spring 1960), 85-92.

722
SEMENOVA, N. P. Kolonial'naia politika iaponskogo imperializma v Koree i natsional'no-osvoboditel'naia bor'ba koreiskogo naroda (1910-1918 gg.) [Japanese Colonial Policy in Korea and the Korean Struggle for National Liberation, 1910-1918]. Moscow, Ministerstvo kul'tury SSSR, Moskovskii institut vostokovedeniia, 1953. (Candidate of Historical Sciences degree) viii, 454p. Text in Russian. AB: 16p. summary published in 1953.

723
ARNOLD, Dean Alexander. American Economic Enterprises in Korea, 1895-1939. Chicago, 1954. 515p.

Ch.3 [p.79-123] examines the international rivalries in Korea, 1897-1898; Ch.6 [p.235-90] focuses on the Russo-Japanese War; and Ch.7-9 [p.291-479] studies three different American enterprises and concessions in Korea during the period of Japanese colonial rule.

724
SHIPAEV, Viktor Ivanovich. Natsional'no-osvoboditel'naia bor'ba koreiskogo naroda protiv iaponskogo imperializma (1918-1931) [The National-Liberation Struggle of the Korean People against Japanese Imperialism, 1918-1931]. Moscow, Akademiia nauk SSSR, Institut vostokovedeniia, 1954. xviii, 282p. (Candidate of Historical Sciences degree) Text in Russian. AB: 15p. summary published in 1954.

Rel.Publ.: Koreiskaia burzhuaziia v natsional'no-osvoboditel'nom dvizhenii. Moscow: "Nauka," 1966. 299p.

725
KARPOVICH, N. I. Kolonial'naia politika iaponskogo imperializma v Koree (1931-1941 gg.) [The Colonial Policy of Japanese Imperialism in Korea, 1931-1941]. Moscow, Institut vostokovedeniia Akademii nauk SSSR, 1955. (Candidate of Historical Sciences degree) 204p. Text in Russian. AB: 16p. summary published in 1955.

726
KIM, In Dia. Shkola i prosveshchenie v Koree (1910-1945 gg.) [Schools and Enlightenment in Korea, 1910-1945]. Moscow, Moskovskii ordena Lenina gosudarstvennyi universitet imeni M. V. Lomonosova, Filosofskii fakultet 1955. (Candidate of Pedagogical Sciences degree) ii, 243p. Text in Russian. AB: 15p. summary published in 1955.

727
LIEROP, Peter van. The Development of Schools under the Korea Mission of the Presbyterian Church in the U.S.A., 1919-1950. Pittsburgh, 1955. 276p. DA 16 (Jan. 1956), 170; UM 15,109.

Much of the dissertation focuses on developments in Korea during the period of Japanese rule.

Rel.Publ.: "The Place of Christian Schools in Korea Past and Present," in Korean Research Center, Seoul, Seminar Series, 1 (1962), 48-63.

728
CHEN, Ilen. Kharakternye osobennosti razvitiia promyshlennosti i polozhenie rabochego klassa v Koree nakanune i vo vremia vtoroi mirovoi voiny [The Characteristic Pecularities of the Development of Industry and the Position of the Working Class in Korea on the Eve of and during the Second World War]. Moscow, Moskovskii ordena Lenina i ordena Trudovogo Krasnogo Znameni gosudarstvennyi universitet imeni M. V. Lomonosova, Ekonomicheskii fakultet, 1956. (Candidate of Economic Sciences degree) 300p. Text in Russian. AB: 16p. summary published in 1956.

729
KAZAKEVICH, I. S. Agrarnye otnosheniia v Koree nakanune 2-oi mirovoi voiny 1930-1939 gg. [Agrarian Relations in Korea on the Eve of World War II]. Moscow, Institut vostokovedeniia Akademii nauk SSSR, 1956. (Candidate of Economic Sciences degree) xviii, 233p. Text in Russian.

Rel.Publ.: Agrarnye...1930 gg. Moscow: Izd. vostochnoi literatury, 1958. 127p. (Akademiia nauk SSSR, Institut vostokovedeniia)

729a
YUN, Sung Bum. Der Protestantimus in Korea, 1930-1955 [Protestantism in Korea, 1930-1955]. Basel, 1956. Text in German.

Concerned with the difficulties of the Korean Christian Church in regard to the Shinto religion during the 1930's, with the Japanese attempt in 1938 to compel Korean Christians to revere Shinto, and with the Church's amazing prosperity during and after the Korean War.

730
PAIK, Young Hoon. Industrialisierungsprozess Korea [The Process of Industrialization in Korea]. Nürnberg, 1957. 123, vi p. Text in German. Diss. ms. available

at Marburg/Lahn, Staatsbibliothek Preussischer Kulturbesitz, Nr. 15,883.

A study of the economic and social structure of Korea before the beginning of industrialization, of Korea's industrialization under Japanese rule, and of the development of Korean industry following the division of the country in 1945.

Rel.Publ.: "Das Autarkieproblem in der koreanische Wirtschaft," Koreana Quarterly, 1 (1959), 91-112.

731
LEE, Sung-hwa. The Social and Political Factors Affecting Korean Education, 1885-1950. Pittsburgh, 1958. 235p. DA 19 (Dec. 1958), 1284-85; UM 58-5619.

Ch.3, "Japanese National Education, 1910-1945" (p.71-143), "covers the duration of Japanese domination in Korea, during which time the Japanese national system of education was used as a means of control of the life and thought of the Korean people." Contents: Sociopolitical Development; Basic Philosophy of Japanese National Education; Major Policies of Japanese National Education in Korea; Western Influence in Educational Philosophy.

732
MAZUROV, Viktor Mikhailovich. Antiiaponskaia vooruzhennaia bor'ba koreiskogo naroda (1931-1940 gg.) [The Anti-Japanese Armed Struggle of the Korean People, 1931-1940]. Moscow, Institut vostokovedeniia Akademii nauk SSSR, 1958. (Candidate of Historical Sciences degree) 104p. Text in Russian.

Rel.Publ.: Antiiaponskaia...1940 gg. Moscow Izd. vostochnoi literatury, 1958. 104p. (Akademiia nauk SSSR. Institut Vostokovedeniia)

733
KIM, Chong-Ik Eugene. Japan in Korea (1905-1910): The Techniques of Political Power. Stanford, 1959. 333p. DA 20 (Aug. 1959), 722-23; UM 59-2831.

"Evaluates...how successfully Japan solved various problems involved in annexing Korea."

Rel.Publ.: "A Problem in Japan's Control of the Press in Korea, 1906-1909," PHR, 31 (Nov. 1962), 393-402; Korea and the Politics of Imperialism, 1876-1910 [by] C. I. Eugene Kim and Han-kyo Kim. Berkeley: University of California Press, 1967. x, 260p. (Publications of the Center for Japanese and Korean Studies)

734
LI, Den Iur. Sostoianie zdoroviia naseleniia i deiatel'nost' organov zdravo-okhraneniia KNDR do i posle osvobozhdeniia [The State of Public Health and the Activity of Public Health Organs in the Korean People's Democratic Republic before and after Liberation]. Moscow, 1-i. Moskovskii ordena Lenina meditsinskii institut imeni I. M. Sechenova, 1960. (Candidate of Medical Sciences) Text in Russian. AB: 24p. summary published in 1960.

LIU, John Jung-chao. An Econometric Model of the Rice Market in the Japanese Empire, 1910-1937. 1960. See no.180.

735
SONG, Ki-tschul. Die Industrialisierung Koreas (1876-1956) unter besonderer Berücksichtigung der Wirtschaftspolitischen Probleme [The Industrialization of Korea, 1876-1956, with Special Consideration of Political and Economic Problems]. Köln, 1960. Text in German. The dissertation in its published form is available at the University of Michigan, General Library, no. 22,930.

The dissertation focuses on the period 1945-1956, but it does include some information on Korean industrial development during the period of Japanese rule.

Rel.Publ.: Die Industrialisierung...Probleme. Köln, 1960. 151p.

736
KIM, Sung-Il. A Study of Certain Aspects of Educational Administration and Their Historical Roots in the Republic of Korea. Syracuse, 1961. 656p. DA 22 (June 1962), 4240; UM 62-1106.

The degree to which the Japanese government influenced certain aspects of post-1945 Korean educational administration by means of its colonial policies is indicated in the dissertation.

Rel.Publ.: "A Study of Historical Roots of Educational Administration in the Republic of Korea," in Hanguk Yŏngu Tosŏgwan, Seoul, Bulletin of the Korean Research Center: Journal of Social Science and Humanities, 22 (June 1965), 1-25.

737
LEE, Chong-sik. The Korean Nationalist Movement, 1905-1945. California, Berkeley, 1961. 836p.

A study of Korean attempts to regain national independence. The author contends that during these years "Japan awakened and sustained Korean nationalism."

Rel.Publ.: The Politics of Korean Nationalism. Berkeley: University of California Press, 1963. xiv, 342p. (Publications of the Center for Japanese and Korean Studies); "The Origins of the Korean Communist Movement" [by] Robert A. Scalapino and Chong-sik Lee, JAS, 20 (Nov. 1960), 9-31, and 20 (Feb. 1961), 149-67; "Korean Communists and Yenan," China Quarterly, 9 (Jan./Mar. 1962), 182-92; "Witch Hunt among the Guerrillas: The Min-Sheng-T'uan Incident," China Quarterly, 26 (Apr./June 1966), 107-17.

738
LEE, Chung Myun. Recent Population Patterns and Trends in the Republic of Korea. Michigan, 1961. 228p. DA 21 (June 1961), 3745; UM 61-1760.

Much of the dissertation studies developments during the period of Japanese rule. See also the sections dealing with Korean migration to Japan and to Manchuria (p.106-24).

Rel.Publ.: "Population Movement of Korea: International Movement," Korean Affairs (1963), 20-37; "Population Increases and Food Problem in Korea," Korean Affairs, 3 (July 1964), 168-85; "The Impact of Emigration upon the Korean People," in Kyung Hee University, Seoul, Theses Collection, 3 (1964), 44-65.

739
BARK, Dong Suh. Public Personnel Administration in Korea: A Mixed Heritage in Contemporary Practice. Minnesota, 1962. 469p. DA 23 (Apr. 1963), 3959-60; UM 63-2306.

The dissertation includes a study of the influence of the Japanese colonial personnel system on the structure of the postwar personnel system.

Rel.Publ.: For related publications, see entry no.2498.

740
CHANG, Dae Hong. The Historical Development of the Korean Socio-Family System since 1392: A Legalistic Interpretation. Michigan State, 1962. 312p. DA 23 (Apr. 1963), 4011; UM 63-1716.

Devotes considerable attention to the impact of

Japanese rule on "the structure and function of the family and social system."

Rel.Publ.: "The Historical...Interpretation," Journal of East Asiatic Studies (Manila), 11 (Sept. 1967), pt.2, 1-124.

741
KIM, Han-Kyo. The Demise of the Kingdom of Korea: 1882-1910. Chicago, 1962. 440p.

The final two chapters (p.263-414), treating the years 1895-1910, describe the Russo-Japanese rivalry and the final domination of Korea by the Japanese.

Rel.Publ.: Korea and the Politics of Imperialism, 1876-1910 [by] C. I. Eugene Kim and Han-Kyo Kim. Berkeley: University of California Press, 1967. x, 260p. (Publications of the Center for Japanese and Korean Studies)

742
REW, Joung Yole. A Study of the Government-General of Korea, with an Emphasis on the Period between 1919 and 1931. American, 1962. 312p. DA 23 (Mar. 1963), 3460-61; UM 62-4526.

The study focuses on (1) "the impact of the Government-General of Korea upon the Japanese expansion in Asia in order to determine whether and to what extent the Government-General participated in expanding the Japanese empire; (2) the reaction of the Koreans towards the Government-General in order to find out to what extent the Japanization of Korea was possible; and (3) the impact of internal politics of Japan, as well as that of international affairs, upon the development of the Government-General."

743
KIM, Changyup Daniel. Seventy-Eight Years of the Protestant Church in Korea. Dallas Theological Seminary, 1963. xvii, 330p.

Includes information on relations between the Church and Japanese authorities in Korea, 1910-1945. See Ch.5, "Period of Development (1913-1934)," and Ch.6, "The Period of Persecution (1935-1945)."

MITCHELL, Richard Hanks. The Korean Minority in Japan, 1910-1963. 1963. See no.70.

744
WOO, Philip Myungsup. The Historical Development of Korean Tariff and Customs Administration, 1875-1958. New York, 1963. 292p. DA 27 (June 1967), 4321-A; UM 64-1792.

See especially Ch.3, "The Japanese Era, I: The Korean Customs in the Period of a Vanished Kingdom, 1905-1919" (p.89-104), Ch.4, "The Japanese Era, II: The Korean Customs, 1910-1945" (p.105-29), and Ch.5, "The Japanese Tariff System" (p.130-59).

745
GÖTHEL, Ingeborg. Der Kampf des koreanischen Volkes für die Schaffung einer nationalen Einheitsfront gegen den japanischen Imperialismus in den Jahren 1930-1940 [The Struggle of the Korean People for the Creation of a National Front against Japanese Imperialism, 1930-1940]. Leipzig, 1964. iv, 139p. Text in German. Diss. ms. available at Leipzig, Universitätsbibliothek; refer to author, title, year, and Nr. U 64.7556.

Studies Korean resistance to Japanese colonial rule during the 1910's and 1920's, the characteristics of Japanese imperialism, the impact of the world economic crisis of the 1930's upon Korea and upon the Korean socio-economic structure, Korea's participation in the international, united front against fascism, and the Soviet liberation of Korea in 1945.

746
SUH, Dae-Sook. Korean Communism and the Rise of Kim. Columbia, 1964. 544p. DA 28 (Dec. 1967), 2317-18-A; UM 67-16,049.

A study of the origins and development of the Korean Communist movement during the period of Japanese rule.

Rel.Publ.: The Korean Communist Movement, 1918-1948. Princeton: Princeton University Press, 1967. xix, 406p. (Studies of the East Asian Institute, Columbia University)

747
DONG, Wonmo. Japanese Colonial Policy and Practice in Korea, 1905-1945: A Study in Assimilation. Georgetown, 1965. 542p. DA 26 (Dec. 1965), 3466-67; UM 65-12,510.

An analytical study aimed at "determining the characteristics, scope, instruments, and some results of assimilation which served as the governing principle of Japanese colonial rule in Korea." The author concludes that "the overemphasis of one common language, in absence of other factors of political socialization, in the pluralistic, colonial society of Korea proved to be most costly in terms of the administration of the colony and that it inhibited the process of assimilation in a larger sense."

748
JUHN, Daniel Sungil. Entrepreneurship in an Underdeveloped Economy: The Case of Korea, 1890-1940. George Washington, 1965. 225p. DA 27 (Oct. 1966), 863-64-A; UM 65-14,632.

Includes consideration of the effects of Japanese rule on Korean entrepreneurial expansion.

749
PAK, Boris Dmitrievich. Osvoboditel'naia bor'ba koreiskogo naroda nakanune pervoi mirovoi voiny [The Struggle of the Korean People to Liberate Themselves on the Eve of the First World War]. Moscow, Moskovskii gosudarstvennyi pedagogicheskii institut imeni V. I. Lenina, 1965 (Candidate of Historical Sciences degree) 297p. Text in Russian. AB: 16p. summary published in 1965.

Rel.Publ.: Osvoboditel'naia...voiny. Moscow, "Nauka," 1967. 167p.; "Iz istorii koreiskoi emigrantskoi pechati (1909-1914)," Narody Azii i Afriki, 3 (1965), 172-78.

750
PAK, Hyung Kao. Social Changes in the Educational and Religious Institutions of Korean Society under Japanese and American Occupations. Utah State, 1965. 258p. DA 26 (Dec. 1965), 3522-23; UM 65-12,601.

See especially Ch.3, "Social Changes in the Educational Institutions of Korean Society: Under Japanese Occupation" (p.60-113), and Ch.5, "Social Changes in the Religious Institutions of Korean Society: Under Japanese Occupation" (p.143-202).

751
CHUNG, In Teak. The Korean Minority in Manchuria (1900-1937). American, 1966. 213p. DA 28 (Aug. 1967), 584-A; UM 66-13,586.

"Treats the general problems of the Korean minority in Manchuria with a particular emphasis on the Korean Communist movements up to 1937." Includes considerable information on Japanese attempts to control these Koreans both before and after 1931.

HONG, Wontack. A Study of the Changes in the Structure of Manufacturing Industry and in the Trade Pattern of Manufactured Products in Korea, Taiwan, and Japan. 1966. See no.226.

752
KIM, Eui Whan. The Korean Church under Japanese Occupation with Special Reference to the Resistance Movement within Presbyterianism. Temple, 1966. 253p. DA 27 (Oct. 1966), 1103-04-A; UM 66-9214.

See especially Ch.3, pt.3, "The Growth and Trial of the Church: The Christian Encounter with the Early Japanese Persecution" (p.100-23), Ch.4, "The Challenge of Shintoism to the Korean Church" (p.124-63), and Ch.5, "The Korean Church in Conflict with Shinto Nationalism" (p.164-223).

753
CHANG, Yunshik. Population in Early Modernization: Korea. Princeton, 1967. 433p. DA 28 (Nov. 1967), 1909-A; UM 67-9594.

Focuses on Korea while it was under Japanese rule and includes an analysis of the impact of Japanese colonial administration.

754
KANG, Wi Jo. The Japanese Government and Religions in Korea, 1910-1945. Chicago, 1967. 258p.

Describes and analyzes Japanese government policies toward Korean religions. The sources are official publications of the Japanese Governor-General of Chōsen and reports of church organizations (mainly Presbyterian).

755
SUH, Sang Chul. Growth and Structural Changes in the Korean Economy since 1910. Harvard, 1967. xvi, 313p. AB: 10p. summary appended to diss. ms.

"Measures quantitatively the growth and structural changes in the Korean economy during the colonial period (1910-1941), evaluates critically the pattern of the colonial development, and endeavors to show the relation of the colonial development to postwar economic growth."

756
CHEN, I-te. Japanese Colonialism in Korea and Formosa: A Comparison of Its Effects upon the Development of Nationalism. Pennsylvania, 1968. 376p. DA 29 (Jan. 1969), 2317-A; UM 69-76.

"In Pt.1 a brief survey of the history of Japanese-Korean and Japanese-Formosan relations is presented in order to ascertain whether nationalism had already developed among Koreans and Formosans before annexation. Pt.2 deals with the impact of Japanese rule on various facets of native life [local government, educational systems and policies, economic effects]....In Pt.3 are presented the different ways in which Koreans and Formosans responded to the Japanese rule: the nature of their resistance movements, the techniques they employed, and the repression they invited from the Japanese."

757
BALDWIN, Frank. The March First Movement: Korean Challenge and Japanese Response. Columbia, 1969. 343p.

Contents: Agent Provocateur: Woodrow Wilson; Doubts and Decisions: November 1918 to January 1919; Planning the Movement: January 28 to February 28, 1919; Korean Demands for Independence, March 1 to December 1919; Self-Determination and the Paris Peace Conference; The Japanese Response; The Saitō Administration.

Karafuto [Sakhalin] (1905-1945)

See International Relations--Russia/1860-1917 (pages 150-52) for dissertations on the Russo-Japanese War.

758
ISBERT, Heinrich. Geschichte, Natur, und Bedeutung der Insel Sachalin [The History, Nature, and Importance of Sakhalin]. Bonn, 1907. Text in German. The dissertation in its published form is available at Bonn, Universitätsbibliothek.

The dissertation discusses (1) the 1905 treaty of peace between Russia and Japan that led to the cession of southern Sakhalin to Japan, (2) Japanese and European exploratory expeditions to the island, 1613-1875, and the earliest Japanese colonization of Sakhalin, (3) the size, climate, surface features, flora, and fauna of Sakhalin, (4) the early inhabitants of the island (Ainu, Gilyaks, Tungus), and (5) the economic and social importance of Sakhalin (its agriculture, fisheries, and coal deposits as well as its use as a penal settlement).

Rel.Publ.: <u>Geschichte...Sachalin</u>. Bonn: A Broch, 1907. 63p.

759
SCHWIND, Martin. Die Gestaltung Karafutos zum japanischen Raum [Developing Karafuto into a Japanese Area]. Leipzig, 1941. (Habilitationsschrift) Text in German. The dissertation in its published form is available at Marburg/Lahn, Universitätsbibliothek, Nr. VI a B gf, Erg.H 239.

A detailed study of the nature, history, colonial development, and inhabitants of Karafuto (Sakhalin). Contents: Pt.1: The Nature of the Land: The Surface Area; Climate; Flora; Soil; Indigenous Population. Pt.2: Pre-Colonial History. Pt.3: The Economy of the Colony: Fisheries; Mining; Forests and Industry; Agriculture. Pt.4: The Inhabitants of the Colony: The Colonial Population; Colonial Settlements in General; Individual Settlements (Otomari, Maoka, Honto, Noda and Tomarioru, Esutoru, Shikuka, Shiritori and Motodomari, Ochiai, Toyohara); Trade. Pt.5: Concluding Remarks: Karafuto's Significance as Part of Greater Japan; Karafuto as a Japanese Area.

Rel.Publ.: <u>Die Gestaltung...Raum</u>. Gotha: J. Perthes, 1942. 230p. (Petermanns geographische Mitteilungen. Erg. H. Nr. 239)

760
KUZ'MIN, P. A. Gospodstvo iaponskoi tselliuloznobumazhnoi monopolii Odzi Seisi na Iuzhnom Sakhaline, 1905-1945 gg. [The Dominance of Oji Seishi, the Japanese Paper and Pulp Monopoly, in Southern Sakhalin, 1905-1945]. Moscow, Moskovskii gosudarstvennyi universitet imeni M. V. Lomonosova, 1950. (Candidate of Economic Sciences degree) 255p. Text in Russian.

761
PERTSEVA, K. T. Sel'skokhoziaistvennaia kolonizatsiia Iaponiei Iuzhnogo Sakhalina, 1905-1945 gg. [Japanese Agricultural Colonization in Southern Sakhalin, 1905-1945]. Moscow, Tikhookeanskii institut Akademii nauk

SSSR, 1950. (Candidate of Economic Sciences degree) 253p. Text in Russian.

Manchoukuo [Manchuria] (1931-1945)

See International Relations--China: 1894-1931 (pages 113-17) and succeeding sections for dissertations on the steps leading up to the Japanese seizure of Manchuria.

762
DORFMAN, Ben David. The Currencies of the Northeastern Provinces of China (Manchuria). California, Berkeley, 1933. 179p.
The chief purposes of the study were "to explain how the currency chaos prevailing in Manchuria prior to the establishment of Manchoukuo came about, and how it contributed to the Sino-Japanese difficulties; and to state and evaluate the respective Chinese and Japanese contentions vis-à-vis the responsibility for this chaos."

763
BEHR, Hugo. Die völkerrechtliche Anerkennung von Mandschukuo [International Recognition of Manchoukuo]. Hamburg, 1936. Text in German. The dissertation in its published form is available at Berlin West, Staatsbibliothek, Preussischer Kulturbesitz, Nr. Un 15,817/12.
General theories regarding international recognition of states, drawn from the Belgian and Iraqi cases, are applied to the Manchurian question. The author then examines China's ties to Manchuria; the development of Japan's "special position" in Manchuria (1894-1917); the sharp difference in the views of China, Japan, and the commission of the League of Nations regarding the Mukden incident; the nature of Japan's relationship with the state of Manchoukuo; and the views of the League, China, Russia, and others about the entire matter.
Rel.Publ.: Die völkerrechtliche...Mandschukuo. Würzburg: Trilts h, 1936. viii, 77p.

764
CHEN, Chao-shung. La Vie du paysan en Mandchourie (les trois provinces de l'est de la Chine) [Peasant Life in Manchuria]. Paris, 1937. Text in French.
A study of agricultural conditions and peasant life and organization before and after the Japanese seizure of Manchuria. Also includes one chapter (Ch.7) on the village life and organization of Japanese immigrants in Manchuria.
Rel.Publ.: La Vie...Chine. Paris: P. Bossuet, 1937. 160p.

765
KIRBY, Edward Stuart. The Economic Organisation of Manchoukuo: With Particular Reference to Specific Features Exemplifying the Special Characteristics of the Modern Economic System in the Far East. London, 1938. xi, 360p.
Explores the nature of the Japanese economic organization of Manchoukuo in terms of the general Japanese political character, the prewar divergence between rigid government control and the powerful monopolistic Houses, and the effect of Japanese immigration into Manchoukuo. The author emphasizes the "organisational point of view."

766
MEYN, Erich. Die japanische Wirtschaftspolitik in der Mandschurei [Japanese Economic Policies in Manchuria]. Handelshochschule Leipzig, 1938. Text in German.
Rel.Publ.: Die japanische...Mandschurei. Leipzig: Moltzen, 1938. 110p.

767
TCHENG, Kui-i. La Compagnie du chemin de fer Sud-Manchourien et l'enterprise japonaise en Mandchourie [The South Manchurian Railway Company and Japanese Enterprise in Manchuria]. Paris, 1939. Text in French.
Contents: A General Survey of Manchuria; The South Manchurian Railway (S.M.R.) Company; The Activities of the S.M.R. (Financial, Economic, Its Relationship to Other Japanese Economic Activities in Manchuria, Its Contribution to Economic Development in Manchuria, Its Political Activities); International Activities in Manchuria; Chinese Efforts.
Rel.Publ.: La Compagnie...Mandchourie. Paris: P. Bossuet, 1939. 316p.

768
PEUVERGNE, Raymond. Le Développement agricole et industriel du Mandchukuo [The Agricultural and Industrial Development of Manchukuo]. Grenoble, 1942. Text in French.
Contents: Agriculture (Soil, Agricultural Population, Agricultural Exploitation, Agricultural Production and Revenue, Cereal Crops, Industrial Crops); Communications (Railways, Road and River Networks, Ports, Airlines); Mining and Metallurgical Industries (Coal, Iron and the Metallurgical Industry, Petroleum, Aluminum, Magnesium, Gold); Manufacturing Industries (Electrical, Wood, Chemicals, Food, Textiles, Machinery); Capital Investments in Manchuria (Nature and Size of Investments, Movements and Origin of Capital, Investment Organs).
Rel.Publ.: Le Développement...Mandchukuo. Grenoble: Boissy et Colomb, 1942. 159p.

RÜHL, Ingeborg. Die Papierwirtschaft in China, Japan, und Mandschukuo. 1942. See no.207.

769
CHANG, Tian-bin. Industrieplanung in Mandschukuo [Industrial Planning in Manchukuo]. Berlin, 1944. ii, 92p. Text in German.

770
DOCKSON, Robert Ray. A Study of Japan's Economic Influence in Manchuria, 1931-1941. Southern California, 1946. 349p. AB: University of Southern California. Abstracts of Dissertations for...1947, p.53-54.
Focuses on the nature and extent of Japanese influence in the fields of agriculture, currency, reform, the light and heavy industries, and trade and transportation. Concludes that by 1941, the entire Manchurian economy was government controlled and was subservient to the Japanese economy.

771
PETROV, Victor P. Manchuria as an Objective of Russian Foreign Policy. American, 1954. 373p.
Ch.10, "Ten Years of Japanese Domination" (p.282-303), focuses on the Japanese position in Manchuria during the 1930's and 1940's and on the provisions within the Yalta Agreement that concerned Manchuria.

772
STAUFFER, Robert Burton, Jr. Manchuria as a Political Entity: Government and Politics of a Major Region of

China, Including Its Relations to China Proper. Minnesota, 1954. 627p. DA 15 (Oct. 1955), 1890; UM 13,370.

A study of regionalism in Manchuria during the twentieth century which shows in part how "Manchurian nationalism was used--and changed and strengthened--by Japan" when she set up Manchoukuo as an industrial colony.

773
MYERS, Ramon Hawley. The Japanese Economic Development of Manchuria, 1932 to 1945. Washington, Seattle, 1959. 340p. DA 20 (Apr. 1960), 3976; UM 60-867.

Contents: Economic Development of Manchuria prior to 1931; Economic Planning and Organization; Agriculture; Industry; Labor; Foreign Trade; Finances.

774
KINNEY, Ann Rasmussen. Investment in Manchurian Manufacturing, Mining, Transportation, and Communications, 1931-1945. Columbia, 1962. 191p. DA 23 (Nov. 1962), 1550-51; UM 62-5186.

Contents: The Setting: Manchuria, 1930-1945; Estimated Investment in Current Prices in Manchoukuo Industry, 1931-1942; Institution Supplying the Capital for Manchurian Economic Development; An Evaluation of Manchurian Industrial Investment, the Amount, and Its Sources; Summary and Conclusion: The Lessons of the Manchurian Experience.

775
KUO, Heng-yü. Die japanische Pressekontrolle in der Mandschurei von 1931 bis 1941 [Japanese Press Control in Manchuria, 1931-1941]. Berlin, Freie Universität, 1963. Text in German. The dissertation in its published form is available at Marburg/Lahn, Staatsbibliothek Preussischer Kulturbesitz, Nr. 39,910; also at the University of Michigan, General Library, no. 28,775.

Focuses on the origins and the development of the Japanese control of the Manchurian press. Included within the dissertation is a study of the "three press laws" and of the organization of the press control system as well as a comparison of Japanese press laws with Nazi Germany's editorial law and with Soviet Russia's TASS regulations.

Rel.Publ.: Die japanische...1941. Berlin: Ernst-Reuter, 1963. 113p.

CHUNG, In Teak. The Korean Minority in Manchuria (1900-1937). 1966. See no.751.

Micronesia (1920-1945)

776
ANDREWS, Fannie Fern. The Mandatory System after the World War. Harvard, 1923. xxiii, 904p. (2v.) AB: 6p. summary appended to diss. ms.

Includes information on the Japanese mandated islands and on Japanese efforts to secure them.

777
EVANS, Luther Harris. The Mandates System and the Administration of Territories under C Mandate. Stanford, 1927. 373p. DA 25 (Jan. 1965), 4240; UM 64-12,767.

Includes a discussion of the Japanese mandate over Micronesia.

Rel.Publ.: "The General Principles Governing the Termination of a Mandate," American Journal of International Law, 26 (1932), 735-58; "Would Japanese Withdrawal from the League Affect the Status of the Japanese Mandate?" American Journal of International Law, 27 (1933), 140-42.

778
PAUWELS, Peter Carel. The Japanese Mandate Islands. Batavia Rechtshoogeschool (Dutch East Indies), 1936.

An historical survey of Micronesia under Spanish, German, and Japanese rule which focuses on the Japanese acquisition and administration of the islands.

Rel.Publ.: The Japanese...Islands. Bandoeng, Dutch East Indies: G. C. T. van Dorp, 1936. 157p.

779
REIMERS, Jacobus. Das japanische Kolonialmandat und der Austritt Japans aus dem Völkerbund [The Japanese Colonial Mandate and Japan's Withdrawal from the League of Nations]. Göttingen, 1937. Text in German. The dissertation in its published form is available at Marburg/Lahn, Universitätsbibliothek, Nr. XVIII C; also at the University of Michigan, General Library, no. DU500.R36.

The weakness of the mandate system is shown through an examination of the Japanese mandate over Micronesia. The mandated area is examined with regard to its location, commercial value, and political and strategic importance. The actual administration of Micronesia, the question of sovereignty over the islands, and the legal situation also are studied.

Rel.Publ.: Das japanische...Völkerbund. Quackenbrück: Trute, 1936. viii, 60p.

780
DECKER, John Alvin. Labor Problems in the Pacific Mandates. Columbia, 1941. xiii, 246p.

See Ch.2, "Japanese Immigrant Labor in the Pacific Mandates," and Ch.5, "Native Contract Labor in the Phosphate Mines of the Japanese Mandated Territory."

Rel.Publ.: Labor...Mandates. New York: Institute of Pacific Relations, 1940. xiii, 246p.

781
EFIMENCO, Nicholas Marbury. Imperialism and the League Experiment with the Mandates System. Minnesota, 1949. 786p.

Includes information on Japan's position and powers relative to the Mandate question at the Paris Peace Conference.

782
STEVENS, William Delos. A Study of Depopulation on Yap Island. Harvard, 1949. vii, 215p. AB: 6p. summary appended to diss. ms.

Information on the Japanese administration of Yap may be found throughout the dissertation.

783
BOWERS, Neal Monroe. Problems of Resettlement on Saipan, Tinian, and Rota, Mariana Islands. Michigan, 1951. 492p. AB: Microfilm Abstracts, 11 (1951), 314-15; UM 2382.

Includes a discussion of the islands' prewar standard of living, of the struggle for the islands during World War II, and of the immediate postwar repatriation of the Japanese residents, who comprised seven-eighths of the population.

Rel.Publ.: Problems...Islands. Ann Arbor, Michigan, 1950. viii, 258p. (National Research Council. Pacific Science Board. Coordinated Investigation of Micronesian Anthropology. Final Report, 31)

784
FORCE, Roland Wynfield. Leadership and Cultural Change in Palau. Stanford, 1958. 312p. DA 19 (Mar. 1959), 2211-12; UM 59-265.
An anthropological study which includes information on Palau for the years when it was administered by Japan as a mandated island.
Rel.Publ.: Leadership...Palau. Chicago: Chicago Natural History Museum, 1960. 211p.

785
ANTILLA, Elizabeth Kelley. A History of the Peoples of the Trust Territory of the Pacific Islands and Their Education. Texas, 1965. 547p. DA 26 (Nov. 1965), 2574-75; UM 65-10,706.
Includes considerable information on education under the Japanese.

786
PURCELL, David Campbell, Jr. Japanese Expansion in the South Pacific, 1890-1935. Pennsylvania, 1967. 375p. DA 28 (Apr. 1968), 4102-A; UM 68-4607.
The dissertations "begins with a discussion of the efforts of the Japanese government to purchase the island of Santos, New Hebrides, of Japanese immigrant labor in New Caledonia, Fiji, Ocean Island, and Makatea, and of attempts by Japanese entrepreneurs to develop commercial and industrial interests in the Marianas, Marshalls, and Carolines." It then discusses Germany's prewar administration of Micronesia, Japan's efforts to gain control of the islands during and after World War I, and the dispute between Japan and the United States over the control of Yap Island. "The remainder of the dissertation describes in detail Japan's administration of the mandated islands to 1935."

787
SMITH, Donald Francis. Education of the Micronesian with Emphasis on the Historical Development. American, 1968. 328p. DA 29 (Nov. 1968), 1435-36-A; UM 68-14,968.
"Traces the development of the Micronesian educational system under the Spanish, German, Japanese, and American administrations."

Taiwan (1895-1945)

See International Relations--China/1860-1894 (pages 112-13) for dissertations on early Japanese interest in Taiwan and on the Japanese acquisition of the island.

788
FENG, Yueh-tseng. Formose: Sa Situation historique et les problèmes de son statut actuel [Formosa: Its Historical Position and the Problems Surrounding Its Present Status]. Paris, 1951. Text in French.

789
BARCLAY, George Watson. Colonial Development and Population in Taiwan. Princeton, 1952. 186p.
Focuses on "the aims and policies of Japan's colonial development and their consequences for the population." Includes information on economic activities and social change, the disposition of manpower, migration and the growth of cities, public health and the risks of death, the setting for family life, patterns of marriage and divorce, and the fertility of the Taiwanese.
Rel.Publ.: Colonial...Taiwan. Princeton: Princeton University Press, 1954. xvii, 274p.

790
HSIEH, James Chiao-min. Successive Occupance Patterns in Taiwan. Syracuse, 1953. 417p.
See Ch.10, "The Japanese Industrial Period" (p.192-252), for information on the Japanese population and occupation in Taiwan; the "intensification of agriculture" with regard to the growing of rice, sugar cane, and fruit; and the development of the electric power industry and of transportation.
Rel.Publ.: "Sequent Occupance of Formosa," in International Geographical Congress, 17th, Washington, D.C., 1952, Proceedings, 481-85.

LIU, John Jung-chao. An Econometric Model of the Rice Market in the Japanese Empire, 1910-1937. 1960. See no.180.

791
GORDON, Leonard H. D. Formosa as an International Prize in the Nineteenth Century. Michigan, 1961. 336p. DA 22 (Jan. 1962), 2372; UM 61-6355.
"An examination of the interest shown in Formosa by the United States, England, France, and Japan" primarily between 1840 and 1895. See especially Ch.4, "The Beginnings of Modern Japanese Colonialism: The Formosa Expedition, 1874" (p.134-222), and Ch. 6, "The Cession of Formosa to Japan" (p.267-99).
Rel.Publ.: "Early American Relations with Formosa, 1849-1870," Historian, 19 (May 1957), 262-89; "Diplomacy of the Japanese Expedition to Formosa, 1874," in International Conference of Orientalists in Japan, Transactions, 5 (1960), 48-57; "Japan's Interest in Taiwan, 1872-1895," Orient/West, 9 (Jan./Feb. 1964), 49-59; "Japan's Abortive Colonial Venture in Taiwan, 1874," Journal of Modern History, 37 (June 1965), 171-85; "Charles W. LeGendre: A Heroic Civil War Colonel Turned Adventurer in Taiwan," Smithsonian Journal of History, 3 (Winter 1968/69); "Taiwan and the Powers, 1840-1895," in Taiwan: Studies in Chinese Local History, ed. by Leonard Gordon (New York: Columbia University Press, 1970), 93-116. (Columbia University, East Asian Institute, Occasional Papers)

792
XUTO, Manaspas. United States Relations with Formosa, 1850-1955. Fletcher, 1961. 401p.
See Pt.2, "The Japanese Interlude, 1895-1945" (p.127-208): Fifty Years of Japanese Rule; Formosa in World War II; War-Time Arrangements for Post-War Formosa.

793
TSAI, Pao-tien. Development of a System of Teacher Education in Taiwan with Emphasis upon the Period of 1945-1962. Indiana, 1963. 128p. DA 25 (Sept. 1964), 1702-03; UM 64-5144.
Includes information on Taiwan under Japanese rule. Contents: Historical and Cultural Background of the Educational System in Taiwan (see the section subtitled "General Culture and Education in Taiwan under Japanese Rule"); Development of a Teacher Education System on the Chinese Mainland and in Taiwan, 1895-1945; Teachers in Taiwan, 1945-1962.

794
LAMLEY, Harry Jerome. The Taiwan Literati and Early Japanese Rule, 1895-1915: A Study of Their Reactions to the Japanese Occupation and Subsequent Responses to

Colonial Rule and Modernization. Washington, Seattle, 1964. 530p. DA 25 (Mar. 1965), 5240; UM 65-1883.

Parts 2 and 3 of the study discuss the activities of the literati in 1895--their resistance, flight, and submission--and their subsequent responses to Japanese rule. Contents: Taiwan during the Ch'ing Period; The Taiwan Literati prior to 1895; Gentry Resistance to the Japanese Take-Over; Other Reactions of the Literati to the Occupation; General Background of the Early Japanese Period; The Taiwan Literati and Colonial Rule; Adjustment to Change: Modernization, Reform, and Assimilation.

Rel.Publ.: "The 1895 Taiwan Republic," JAS, 27 (Aug. 1968), 739-62.

795
TZENG, Jenn. Taiwanian Vocational Education in Agriculture, 1945-1963. Colorado State, 1964. 193p. DA 25 (July 1964), 268-69; UM 64-8530.

The study includes information on the "transformation from a Japanese to a Chinese educational system" during the immediate postwar years as well as a discussion of the repatriation of Japanese teachers.

796
WU, Ping-lin. The Development of Taiwan Education from 1946 to 1962. New York, 1964. 188p. DA 26 (Feb. 1966), 4413; UM 65-6612.

One section of the dissertation is concerned with "the status and background of Taiwan education throughout Japanese rule (1895-1945)."

797
HO, Yhi-min. The Agricultural Development of Taiwan, 1903-1960: Its Patterns and Sources of Productivity Increases. Vanderbilt, 1965. 215p. DA 26 (Oct. 1965), 1953-54; UM 65-10,474.

"Analyzes the sources and patterns of Taiwan's successful agricultural growth...and illustrates the role of land-saving and labor-intensive devices in agricultural improvement under the condition of a small farm-holding system."

Rel.Publ.: The Agricultural...Increases. Nashville: Vanderbilt University Press, 1966. xii, 172p.

HONG, Wontack. A Study of the Changes in the Structure of Manufacturing Industry and in the Trade Pattern of Manufactured Products in Korea, Taiwan, and Japan. 1966. See no.226.

798
LI, Weng-lang. Inter-Prefectural Migration of the Native Population in Taiwan, 1905-1940. Pennsylvania, 1967. 213p. DA 29 (July 1968), 334-A; UM 68-9217.

Contents: Historical Setting; Pattern of Internal Migration, 1905-1940; Streams of Migration; Differentails of Migration; Socio-Economic Correlates of Interprefectural Migration; Summary and Conclusions.

799
BUXBAUM, David Charles. Some Aspects of Substantive Family Law and Social Change in Rural China (1896-1967): With a Case Study of a North Taiwan Village. Washington, Seattle, 1968. 391p. DA 29 (Jan. 1969), 2289-A; UM 69-1148.

"Certain marriage, adoption, divorce, and inheritance practices in Taiwan from late Ch'ing times until the present, 1896-to 1967, are examined in detail. The creative legislation and court decisions in China from the early twentieth century to the present, including those occurring during the Japanese occupation of Taiwan, are similarly examined."

CHEN, I-te. Japanese Colonialism in Korea and Formosa: A Comparison of Its Effects upon the Development of Nationalism. 1968. See no.756.

800
JANG, John Lun. A History of Newspapers in Taiwan. Claremont, 1968. 174p. DA 30 (July 1969), 247-48-A; UM 68-18,274.

With regard to the period of colonial rule, the author notes that "when Japan gained control of Taiwan, a daily newspaper, the first on the island, was immediately established to propagate its colonial policy. By the first years of the twentieth century, a number of modern periodicals had been founded in Taiwan. However, this rapid growth of the press was limited only to the Japanese community on the island. The native people were forbidden to publish their own newspaper until 1927."

801
LEE, Teng-hui. Intersectoral Capital Flows in the Economic Development of Taiwan, 1895-1960. Cornell, 1968. 408p. DA 29 (Dec. 1968), 1641-A; UM 68-16,755.

The dissertation studies Taiwanese agricultural development and the relationship of economic growth within this sector with development in the remainder of the island's economy. Considerable attention is paid to the period of Japanese colonial rule.

Home Economics

802
MELLOH, Sister M. Tolentine, S.S.N.D. Planning for the Development of a Home Economics Curriculum for a Japanese College. Southern Illinois, 1963. 269p. DA 24 (June 1964), 5375; UM 64-4475.

A descriptive background study written for the purpose of developing a Home Economics Department at Notre Dame Women's College in Kyoto.

803
MATSUSHIMA, Chiyono. Connotative Meaning Structure of Home Economics and Related Concepts Assessed in Two Cultures. Cornell, 1966. 274p. DA 27 (Sept. 1966), 868-69-B; UM 66-7853.

"This cross-cultural study is concerned with the connotations that home economics has for professional people in the field of home economics in the United States and Japan."

Influence of Japanese Culture Abroad

(Japanese influence on Western literary and artistic developments)

804
TUTTLE, Allen Edmond. Lafcadio Hearn and Herbert Spencer. Northwestern, 1950. 213p. AB: Northwestern University. Summaries of Doctoral Dissertations. v.18 (1950), p.30-34.

Includes a discussion of Hearn's admiration of Japan's traditional values and the agony he experienced as Japanese ethics changed. Contents: The American Hearn among Bohemian Idols; Preparation for Synthesis; The Meeting of Minds; The Spencerian in Unfamiliar Japan.

Rel.Publ.: "Lafcadio Hearn and the Soul of the Far East," Contemporary Japan, 23 (July/Sept. 1955), 529-52.

805
WULF, Ingeborg. Das Japanbild Lafcadio Hearns [Lafcadio Hearn's Image of Japan]. Berlin, Freie Universität, 1951. 194p. Text in German. Diss. ms. available at Berlin, Freie Universität, Universitätsbibliothek, Nr. U51.521.

A study of Hearn's ties to Japan and of the way in which he depicts the land, the people, and the culture of Japan in his works. The author also seeks to determine how accurate a picture Hearn had of Japan.

806
YOUNG, Myrl Marvin. The Impact of the Far East on the United States, 1840-1860. Chicago, 1951. 185p.

Commercial, missionary, immigrant, and other types of contacts with the Orient (including Japan) are described. Their impact on American agriculture (e.g. Chinese and Japanese plants, tea, cotton) and subsequently upon scholarship (linguistic and religious studies), literature, and the arts is then analyzed.

807
CARMINEOVÁ, Eva. Lafcadio Hearn, 1850-1904. Universita Karlova, 1952. 142p. Text in Czech. Diss. ms. available at the University archives, no. AUK 3160a.

Presents a survey of Hearn's activity before his arrival in Japan and a study of the three periods of his literary work in Japan. Included within the dissertation is an evaluation of Hearn's understanding of Japanese folklore and religion.

808
NAUSS, George Murray. Poems of Paper Fish and Lanterns. Iowa, 1953. 55p. DA 13 (1953), 812; UM 5487.

The dissertation consists of original poems describing the author's observations of life in East Asia in general and in Japan in particular.

809
MINER, Earl Roy. The Japanese Influence on English and American Literature, 1850-1950. Minnesota, 1955. 504p. DA 15 (June 1955), 1075; UM 11,988.

Contents: The First Era of Western European Consciousness of the Orient: 1550-1850; America Awakens to Japan; Japan and the Victorian Muse: The Romantic Afterglow and the Fruits of Imperialism; Japonisme and Impressionism: The Change from Nineteenth to Twentieth Century Artistic and Poetic Modes; Japan and the Forms of Western Fiction; Lafcadio Hearn; Transition to the 'New Poetry'; Ezra Pound and T. S. Eliot; Amy Lowell; Imagists, Amygists, and Others; Wallace Stevens; A Japanese Miscellany; The Japanese Subject on the Stage; Kabuki and Nō as Dramatic Criteria; W. B. Yeats.

Rel.Publ.: The Japanese Tradition in British and American Literature. Princeton: Princeton University Press, 1958. 312p.; "Pound, Haiku, and the Image," Hudson Review, 9 (Winter 1956/57), 570-84.

810
KITZINGER, Angela Mae. Lafcadio Hearn and French Literature. Southern California, 1958. 398p. AB: University of Southern California. Abstracts of Dissertations for...1958. p.43-45.

Includes a discussion of Hearn's teaching activities at Tokyo University and of his continued interest in French literature even while in Japan.

811
SHINODA, Yujiro. Degas: Der Einzug der Japanischen in die französische Malerei [Degas: The Japanese Influence on French Painting]. Koln, 1958. Text in German. The dissertation in its published form is available at Marburg/Lahn, Staatsbibliothek Preussischer Kulturbesitz, Nr. Hsn 16,093.

An investigation of the influence of the Japanese woodcut masters upon French art as seen in the case of the French painter Degas (1834-1917). Topics covered include the introduction of Japanese pictures into Europe (particularly France); Degas and Ukiyo-e; and a comparison of the works of Degas and of various Japanese artists with regard to their use of themes, scenery, construction, and in particular principles of composition.

Rel.Publ.: Degas...Malerei. Tokyo: Toppan-Dr., 1957. 118, 48p.

812
YU, Beongcheon. An Ape of Gods: A Study of Lafcadio Hearn. Brown, 1958. 371p. DA 19 (Jan. 1959), 1765;

UM 58-7673.

The thesis is not a biography of Lafcadio Hearn (1850-1904) but an examination of his art, thought, criticism, and philosophy. Part of the study focuses on Hearn's "Japanese period."

Rel.Publ.: An Ape of Gods: The Art and Thought of Lafcadio Hearn. Detroit: Wayne State University, 1964. xiv, 346p.; "Lafcadio Hearn's Aesthetics of Organic Memory," in English Literary Society of Japan, Studies in English Literature, 38 (Nov. 1961), 1-28; "Lafcadio Hearn's Twice-Told Legends Reconsidered," American Literature, 34 (Mar. 1962), 56-71.

813
BECKER, Eugene Matthew. Whistler and the Aesthetic Movement. Princeton, 1959. 341p. DA 20 (Jan. 1960), 2744; UM 59-5133.

"How James McNeill Whistler--carrying with him from France the art for art's sake ideas of Baudelaire and a revived interest in Japanese decorative art--followed the English aesthetes...is the central focus of this dissertation."

814
REBAY, Luciano. Le origini della poesia di Giuseppe Ungaretti, 1914-1935 [The Origins of the Poetry of Giuseppe Ungaretti, 1914-1935]. Columbia, 1960. 271p. Text in Italian. DA 24 (Aug. 1963), 748; UM 63-6126.

Ch.2 describes the vogue for Japanese haiku poetry launched in Italy as a result of the publication of Ungaretti's Porto Sepolto, which was influenced by haiku aesthetics. A literary analysis of the resemblance of Ungaretti's work to haiku also is presented.

Rel.Publ.: Le Origini...1935. Roma: Edizioni di storia e letteratura, 1962. 202p. (Uomini e dottrine, 10)

815
NISHIMOTO, Kōji. Le Japon chez Pierre Loti [Japan in the Works of Pierre Loti]. Laval, 1961. 198p. Text in French.

Contents: Japan at the Time of Loti's Two Visits (Japan's Modern Development, Japan in 1885, Japan in 1900-1901); Japan as Seen by Pierre Loti (Impressions of Japan, The Basis for These Impressions); Loti and Japan (French Knowledge of Japan during the 1800's, Loti's Antipathy towards Japan—An Explanatory Essay, Loti's Search for Childhood in Japan, Loti as an Impressionist, Loti as a Pseudo-initiate in an Exotic World, Loti as an Impressionist in Japan).

Rel.Publ.: Loti en face du Japon. Québec: Presses de l'Université Laval, 1962. 50p. ("Extrait de la Revue de l'Université Laval, t. xvi, no.4-5-6, déc. 1961, jan. et fév. 1962.")

816
STEPHENS, Edna Buell. The Oriental Influence in John Gould Fletcher's Poetry. Arkansas, 1961. 330p. DA 22 (July 1961), 264-65; UM 61-1351.

Includes his attempt to fuse the spirit of haiku and the doctrine of Zen into his poetry.

Rel.Publ.: John Gould Fletcher. New York: Twayne, 1967. 160p. (Twayne's United States Authors Series, 118)

817
TILLEUX, Geneva Frances Morgan. The Paintings of James McNeil Whistler, 1857-1873. Wisconsin, 1962. 384p. DA 23 (Oct. 1962), 1318; UM 62-4749.

An examination of the early years of Whistler's painting which contends that ukiyo-e prints had a greater influence on the development of Whistler's mature style than had hitherto been supposed.

818
PAGE, John G. José Juan Tablado: Introductor del haikai en Hispanoamérica [José Juan Tablado: The Man Who Introduced Haikai into the Spanish-Speaking Countries of Latin America]. Universidad Nacional Autónoma de México, 1963. 94p. Text in Spanish. A copy of the dissertation has been deposited at the University of Texas Library, Latin American Collection.

Contents: Lyrical Poetry in the Spanish Language; Some Forms of Japanese Poetry; The Journey to Japan, Chronicles; José Juan Tablado [1871-1945] and Modernism; The Introduction of Haikai.

819
BOWDITCH, James Rogers. The Impact of Japanese Culture on the United States, 1853-1904. Harvard, 1964. ii, 533p. (2v.) AB: 6p. summary appended to diss. ms.

"Attempts to answer five broad questions about the nature and extent of the impact of Japan: What, at any given period, was the American attitude toward Japan? What aspects of its culture seemed most worthy of notice and how accurate was American knowledge? What were the sources of this attitude and knowledge? What were the conditions, both in Japan and in the United States, which facilitated or hindered understanding and appreciation? What effect did Japanese culture, or any aspect of that culture, have upon the thoughts and actions of nineteenth century Americans?"

820
HARPER, Howard Morrall, Jr. Concepts of Human Destiny in Five American Novelists: Bellow, Salinger, Mailer, Baldwin, Updike. Pennsylvania State, 1964. 340p. DA 25 (May 1965), 6625-26; UM 65-4380.

Includes a discussion of the influence of Zen Buddhism on J. D. Salinger (1919-).

Rel.Publ.: Desperate Faith: A Study of Bellow, Salinger, Mailer, Baldwin, and Updike. Chapel Hill: University of North Carolina Press, 1967. 200p.

821
PERSICK, William Thomas. Three Concepts of Pottery. Ohio State, 1964. 129p. DA 25 (Aug. 1964), 1136; UM 64-9584.

Ch.3--the biography and thought of Bernard H. Leach --discusses the influence of Japanese aesthetic concepts upon his work.

822
CEIDE-ECHEVARRÍA, Gloria. El haikai en la lírica Mexicana [The Haikai in Mexican Lyric Poetry]. Illinois, 1965. 236p. Text in Spanish. DA 26 (Mar. 1966), 5410-11; UM 66-4155.

Presents "a general view of Japanese haikai, its adaptation to Mexican lyric poetry, and the establishment of the nexus and differences between them."

Rel.Publ.: El haikai...Mexicana. Mexico City: Ediciones de Andrea, 1967. 165p. (Colección studium, 58)

823
BROWER, Gary Layne. The Haiku in Spanish American Poetry. Missouri, 1966. 232p. DA 27 (Mar. 1967), 3036-37-A; UM 67-2849.

"The trajectory of this work is predicated on an analysis of the haiku as a verse form of Japanese origin, as it has been employed by Spanish American poets.

As Spanish American haiku stands, it can be divided by function into three groupings: those poems which function only as Western poetry, those which function as Westernized haiku, and those which do not even seem to function as 'good' poetry." Contents: The Basis for the Misunderstanding of Haiku in the West; A Comparison of the Technical Devices of Spanish American and Japanese Haiku; Spanish American Interpretations of Haiku; A Comparison of Themes and Images; Spanish American Haiku.

Rel.Publ.: "The Japanese Haiku in Hispanic Poetry," MN, 23 (1968), 187-89.

824
LIN, Choate. Chinoiserie and Japonisme in French Literature. Michigan, 1966. 348p. DA 27 (Jan. 1967), 2155-A; UM 66-14,550.

"Studies the role which China and Japan have played in French literature." Contents: The First Contact: Around "la question des rites;" Chinoiserie and French Men of Letters; Japonisme and French Men of Letters (Japonisme and the Artists, Japonisme and the Goncourt "Grenier," "Le Haïkaï Français," Eyewitnesses: Pierre Loti and Paul Claudel).

825
VINCENT, Mary Louise. Lafcadio Hearn and Late Romanticism. Minnesota, 1967. 436p. DA 28 (June 1968), 5075-A; UM 68-7400.

"Considers Hearn's position in the artistic milieu of the period from 1870 to 1904" and includes a discussion of the influence of his stay in Japan upon his work.

826
WEISBERG, Gabriel Paul. The Early Years of Philippe Burty: Art Critic, Amateur, and Japoniste 1855-1875. Johns Hopkins, 1967. 358p. DA 28 (Feb. 1968), 3091-A; UM 67-13,840.

A biographical study of Philippe Burty (1830-1890), one of the first Frenchmen to become very interested in Japanese art. In different parts of the dissertation, the author discusses Burty's early interest in Japan, his participation in the Société du Jing-lar (a French society interested in Japan), his study of Buddhism, and his large collection of Japanese art objects, prints, and European publications on Japan.

827
KLONER, Jay Martin. The Influence of Japanese Prints on Edouard Manet and Paul Gauguin. Columbia, 1968. 318p.

Artistic Japanism during the second half of the nineteenth century in France is reassessed in the light of new evidence. A comprehensive survey of prior research, primary sources, and possibilities of iconographic and stylistic impact is made in regard to Manet and Gauguin, with added reference to Bracquemond, Whistler, and Degas. The dissertation amplifies to a greater degree the significance of iconographic influences, especially by determining the specific Japanese prints and books owned by, or known to, the artists concerned. Contents: Pt.1: Introduction to the Problem: Manet and Gauguin; Cultural Parallels in Japan and France; The Dispersion of Ukiyo-e; Bracquemond; Whistler; Degas. Pt.2: Manet: Primary Evidence; Iconography; Style; Conclusions. Pt.3: Gauguin: Primary Evidence; Iconography; Style; Conclusions.

International Relations

[Political, historical, and economic]

GENERAL AND MULTILATERAL

Before 1905

See also: Economics--foreign trade (pages 36-40), International Relations--Europe (pages 144-55), and International Relations--United States (pages 155-63).

MATSUDAIRA, Yorikadzu von. Die völkerrechtlichen Verträge des Kaiserthums Japan in wirtschaftlicher, rechtlicher, und politischer Bedeutung. 1890. See no.1530.

828
MÜNSTERBERG, Oskar. Japans Edelmetall-Handel von 1542-1854 [Japan's Trade in Valuable Metals, 1542-1854]. Freiburg i.B., 1895. 38p. Text in German. The dissertation in its published form is available at Marburg/Lahn, Staatsbibliothek Preussicher Kulturbesitz, Nr. Fe 677.

A study of European trade with Japan before and during the Tokugawa era with information on the various forms of the trade, commercial negotiations, trade commodities, and prices.

Rel.Publ.: Japans auswärtiger Handel von 1542-1854. Stuttgart: J. G. Cotta'sche, 1896. xxxviii, 312p. (Münchener volkswirtschaftliche Studien, 10)

SENGA, Tsurutaro. Gestaltung und Kritik der heutigen Konsulargerichtsbarkeit in Japan. 1897. See no.1535.

829
HISHIDA, Seiji George. The International Position of Japan as a Great Power. Columbia, 1906.

A history of Japanese foreign relations from ancient times to the Treaty of Portsmouth (1905).

Rel.Publ.: The International...Power. New York: Columbia University Press, 1905. 291p. (Studies in History, Economics, and Public Law, ed. by the Faculty of Political Science of Columbia University, v.24, no.3); "Formosa: Japan's First Colony," Political Science Quarterly, 2 (1907), 267-82.

830
YAMASAKI, Naozo. L'Action de la civilisation européene sur la vie japonaise avant l'arrivée du commodore Perry [The Impact of European Civilization on Japanese Life before the Arrival of Commodore Perry]. Paris, 1910. Text in French.

Rel.Publ.: L'Action...Perry. Paris, 1910. 130p.

LIU, Chiang. Isolation and Contact as Factors in the Cultural Evolution of China, Korea, and Japan prior to 1842. 1923. See no.476.

831
TCHEN, Yaotong. De la disparition de la jurisdiction consulaire dans certains pays d'Orient. Tome 1: Japon, Turquie, Siam, Perse [On the Disappearance of Consular Jurisdiction in Certain Countries of the Orient. Volume 1: Japan, Turkey, Siam, Persia]. Paris, 1931. Text in French.

The chapter devoted to Japan (p.67-94) surveys the system of consular jurisdiction in Japan, Japanese moves to abolish it, and the new treaties and statutes that replaced it in the late 1890's.

Rel.Publ.: De la disparition...Perse. Paris: Presses modernes, 1931. 186p.

832
SIEMERS, Bruno. Japan und die Mächte 1853-1869 [Japan and the Powers, 1853-1869]. Kiel, 1937. Text in German. The dissertation in its published form is available at Marburg/Lahn, Universitätsbibliothek, Nr. VIIa C 29º; also at the University of Michigan, General Library, no. DS882.S62.

A review of Japanese history from the opening of Japan by the West through the Meiji Restoration. Particular attention is paid to Spanish and Portuguese ties with Japan before 1853, the American efforts to reopen Japan, Japan's commercial treaties with various Western countries, and Chōshū's resistance and opposition to Tokugawa policies.

Rel.Publ.: Japan...1869. Berlin: Ebering, 1937. 139p.; also as Japans Eingliederung in den Weltverkehr, 1853-1869. Berlin: Ebering, 1937. 139p. (Beiträge zur Weltpolitik, Heft 1)

833
HECKHOFF, Heinz. Die Seeschiffahrt in der Aussenwirtschaftspolitik [Ocean Shipping in Foreign Economic Policy]. Köln, 1938. Text in German. The dissertation in its published form is available at Marburg/Lahn, Staatsbibliothek Preussischer Kulturbesitz, Nr. Fb 9509/12-6.

Includes a brief study of the role of Japanese shipping in the country's foreign economic policy, an historical survey of Japanese foreign trade, 1542-1854, and a description and evaluation of the most important commercial and shipping treaties concluded between Japan and the West, 1854-1927.

Rel.Publ.: Die Seeschiffahrt...Aussenwirtschaftspolitik. Köln: Orthen, 1938. 222p.

834
ECKEL, Paul Edward. The Revival of European Economic Interest in Japan from 1800 to 1955. Southern California, 1941. 118p. AB: University of Southern California. Abstracts of Dissertations for...1941. p.100-03.

"Traces the sharp commercial competition that took place among the chief Western nations [Great Britain, Russia, and the United States] interested in again opening Japan to the trade and manufactures of their respective countries." Also includes consideration of the Dutch position during this period.

Rel.Publ.: "Challenges to Dutch Monopoly of Japanese Trade during the Wars of Napoleon," FEQ, 1 (Feb. 1942), 173-79; "A Russian Expedition to Japan in 1852," Pacific Northwest Quarterly, 34 (Apr. 1943), 159-67; "The Crimean War and Japan," FEQ, 3 (Feb. 1944), 109-18.

835
VEENHOVEN, Willem Adriaan. Strijd om Deshima: Een onderzoek naar de aanslagen van Amerikaanse, Engelse, en Russische zijde op het Nederlandse handelsmonopolie in Japan gedurende de periode 1800-1817 [The Struggle over Deshima: An Investigation of the American, English, and Russian Assaults on the Dutch Trade Monopoly during the Period 1800-1817]. Leiden, 1950. Text in Dutch, with a summary in English.

Focuses on the attempts of the English to establish commercial relations with Japan during the Napoleonic period and on the actions taken by Dutch representatives at Deshima to thwart their efforts.

Rel.Publ.: Strijd...1817. Bloemendaal: J. B. Hemelsoet, 1950. 104, xcvi p.

836
KERST, Georg. Die Anfänge der Erschliessung Japans im Spiegel der zeitgenossischen Publizistik: Untersucht auf Grund der Veröffentlichungen der Kölnischen Zeitung [The Opening of Japan as Reflected in Contemporary Publications of the Kölnische Zeitung]. Kiel, 1953. 191p. Text in German. The dissertation in its published form is available at Berlin West, Staatsbibliothek Preussischer Kulturbesitz, Nr. 23,767. [See also addenda 20A.]

The author seeks to determine how much one can rely on mid-nineteenth century German political publications for new information about the changing political situation in Japan and about the importance of this change. He considers Japan's policy of seclusion and Western efforts to end it, using the Kölnische Zeitung as an historical source with regard to Commodore Perry's negotiations, Admiral James Stirling's treaty with Japan (on behalf of England), and the danger of war in the Far East between England and Russia during the late 1850's.

837
ARAKI, Tadao Johannes. Geschichte der Entstehung und Revision der ungleichen Verträge mit Japan (1853-1894) [History of the Origin and Revision of the Unequal Treaties with Japan, 1853-1894]. Marburg, 1959. Text in German. The dissertation in its published form is available at Marburg/Lahn, Staatsbibliothek, Preussischer Kulturbesitz, Nr. Hsn 27,883; also at the University of Michigan, General Library, no.24,841.

A study of the Treaty of Kanagawa (1854) and the first unequal treaties concluded with Great Britain, Russia, and Holland, of the origins and significance of the Ansei Treaty with the United States, of the consequences of the jōi movement and the collapse of the bakufu, and of the eventual revision of the unequal treaties.

Rel.Publ.: Geschichte...1894. Marburg: Nolte, 1959. v, 152p.

838
MAYO, Marlene June. The Iwakura Embassy and the Unequal Treaties, 1871-1873. Columbia, 1961. 358p. UM 61-2661.

"A study of how the Japanese came to consider the pre-Meiji treaties unequal, of the motives which led to the dispatch of an embassy of almost fifty members in December 1871, and of what the embassy did to help solve the problem of diplomatic immunity."

Rel.Publ.: "The Iwakura Mission to the United States and Europe, 1871-1873," in Columbia University, East Asian Institute, Researches in the Social Sciences on Japan, 2 (1959), 28-47; "Rationality in the Meiji Restoration: The Iwakura Embassy," in Modern Japanese Leadership: Transition and Change, ed. by Bernard S. Silberman and Harry D. Harootunian (Tucson: University of Arizona Press, 1966), 323-69; "A Catechism of Western Diplomacy: The Japanese and Hamilton Fish, 1872," JAS, 26 (May 1967), 389-410; Book-length manuscript for publication being prepared for submission to the East Asian Institute, Columbia University (Tentative title: "In Search of Enlightenment and Equality: The Iwakura Mission.").

JONES, Hazel J. The Meiji Government and Foreign Employees, 1868-1900. 1967. See no.580.

After 1905

See also: Economics--foreign trade (pages 36-40), History--Japanese empire: Micronesia (pages 97-98), International Relations--Europe (pages 144-55), and International Relations--United States (pages 155-63).

839
ULLRICH, Richard. Die politische Entwicklung Japans seit dessen Erschliessung im Jahre 1854: Eine völkerrechtliche Studie [The Political Development of Japan since the Opening of the Country in 1854: A Study in International Law]. Würzburg, 1923. iv, 263p. Text in German. Diss. ms. available at Marburg/Lahn, Staatsbibliothek Preussischer Kulturbesitz, Nr. MS 23/10,761.

A study of Japan's internal political development through 1889, of the development of her foreign policy since 1854 (her expansion within East Asia, her position during World War I, and her relations with the United States), and of the influence of her diplomacy upon various European states. Germany's East Asian policy also is critically reviewed and its deficiencies are noted.

840
MATSUSHITA, Masatoshi. Japan in the League of Nations. Columbia, 1929. ii, 177p.

"The official utterances of the Japanese delegates in the League of Nations Commission for the drafting of the Covenant and in the various organs of the League are examined in order to determine the significance of Japan's membership in the League.

Rel.Publ.: Japan...Nations. New York: Columbia University Press, 1929. ii, 177p. (Studies in History, Economics, and Public Law, ed. by the Faculty of Political Science of Columbia University, 314)

841
ROOS, Herman, Jr. Japan in den Grooten Oceaan [Japan

in the Pacific Ocean]. Amsterdam Gemeente, 1929. xii, 204p. Text in Dutch.

Contents: Relations between "White and Black" (up to the Peace of Portsmouth); Expectation and Disappointment (after the Victory over Russia); The Population Problem; The Emigration Question; Japan's Maritime Position.

Rel.Publ.: Japan...Oceaan. Amsterdam: H. J. Paris, 1929. xii, 204p.

842
TAKEUCHI, Sterling Tatsuji. The Control of Foreign Relations in Japan. Chicago, 1931. 559p.

Discusses Japan's constitutional structure and examines the processes of formulating, executing, and controlling Japanese foreign policy, 1890-1930.

Rel.Publ.: War and Diplomacy in the Japanese Empire. Chicago: University of Chicago Press, 1935. xix, 505p.

843
LEONARD, Leonard Larry. International Regulation of Fisheries. Columbia, 1943. 203p.

Includes information on the Russo-Japanese controversy over fishing rights off Kamchatka, on the American-Japanese dispute over salmon fishing off Alaska, on Japanese participation in the 1911 convention for the protection of fur-seals, and on Japanese whaling activities.

Rel.Publ.: International...Fisheries. Washington, D.C.: Carnegie Endowment for International Peace, Division of International Law, 1944, x, 201p. (Monograph Series, 7)

844
WU, Teh-yao. The Balance of Power in the Far East, 1921-1931. Harvard, 1946. iv, 285p. AB: 7p. summary appended to diss. ms.

Contents: The Balance of Power; The Factors Affecting the Balance of Power in the Far East; Nationalism vs. Imperialism; Foreign Policy and the Balance of Power; The Balance of Power in Action (The Washington Conference, China's Civil Strife, The Sino-Soviet Dispute, The Manchurian Incident).

845
KOH, Kwang-lim. International Regulation of Fisheries with Special Reference to Those in the North Pacific Ocean. Rutgers, 1953. 331p.

Ch.1 deals with the historical background of American-Japanese fisheries relations prior to World War II. Ch.2 and 3 include post World War II treaties and regulations and United Nations regulatory activities. Ch.4 and 5 examine fisheries relations among East Asian countries and Russo-Japanese relations.

846
GOL'DBERG, David Isaakovich. Vneshniaia politika Iaponii v period vtoroi mirovoi voiny [Japanese Foreign Policy during World War II]. Leningrad, Leningradskii gosudarstvennyi universitet imeni A. A. Zhdanova, 1956. (Doctor of Historical Sciences degree) 1,894 + 267 + 92p. Text in Russian. AB: 46p. summary published in 1955.

Rel.Publ.: Vneshniaia politika Iaponii (Sent. 1939 --dek. 1941 g.). Moscow: Izdatel'stvo vostochnoi literatury, 1959. 303p. (Leningradskii gosudarstvennyi universitet imeni A. A. Zhdanova)

847
OKAJIMA, Eiichi. The Japanese Peace Treaty and Its Implications for Japan's Post-War Foreign Policy. New York, 1956. 651p. DA 20 (July 1959), 360-61; UM 59-945.

Focuses on the issues of Japanese rearmament, Japanese irredentist sentiments, criminal jurisdiction over the foreign forces in Japan, and Japanese reparations to Southeast Asian countries.

848
TAKEUCHI, Tatsuji. War and Diplomacy in the Japanese Empire. Ritsumeikan, 1958. Diss. ms. available at the National Diet Library, Tokyo.

849
PETROV, Dmitrii Vasil'evich. Vneshniaia politika Iaponii posle 2-oi mirovoi voiny, 1945-1963 gg. [Japanese Foreign Policy after World War II, 1945-1963]. Moscow, Institut mirovoi ekonomiki i mezhdunarodnykh otnoshenii Akademii nauk SSSR, 1964. (Doctor of Historical Sciences degree) 1,076p. Text in Russian. AB: 30p. summary published in 1964.

Rel.Publ.: Vneshniaia politika Iaponii posle 2-oi mirovoi voiny. Moscow: "Mezhdunarodnye otnosheniia," 1965. 400p.

850
WEISE, Ronald Eric. Japan and Postwar International Organization. Indiana, 1966. 183p. DA 28 (Jan. 1968), 2756-57-A; UM 67-15,174.

Focuses on Japan's participation in the United Nations. Contents: Japan's Failure to Adjust to Post-World War I Responsibilities Leads to War, Defeat, and a Restructuring of the State; Russia Opposes United Nations Membership for Japan in the Absence of a Russo-Japanese Treaty of Peace; Japan Formally Rejoins the Community of Nations; A Dilemma--The Search for Security: Non-Alignment, Military Alliance, and the United Nations; Membership, the China Problem, and the Struggle for Hegemony in the Far East; The Economic and Social Council Provides a Forum for Cooperation.

851
IGNATUSHCHENKO, Stepan Kirillovich. Ekonomicheskaia ekspansiia Iaponii posle vtoroi mirovoi voiny [Japanese Economic Expansion after World War II]. Moscow, Institut narodov Azii Akademii nauk SSSR, 1967. (Candidate of Economic Sciences degree) Text in Russian.

Rel.Publ.: Ekonomicheskaia ekspansiia iaponskikh monopolii posle vtoroi mirovoi voiny. Moscow: "Nauka," 1966. 296p. (Ministerstvo vneshnei torgovli SSSR, Nauchno-issledovatel'skii kon'iunkturnyi institut)

852
TAKIZAWA, Makoto. Japanese Rearmament: A Dilemma in the Search for Peace and Security. Florida State, 1967. 229p. DA 28 (July 1967), 279-80-A; UM 67-8474.

The major topics of concern are: (1) the origins of Japanese rearmament during the American occupation period, (2) the reversal of Japanese demilitarization in the face of the Korean crisis, (3) the impact of Japanese rearmament upon public opinion and party politics and upon administrative and judicial attitudes (1950-1966), (4) the influence of Japan's security commitment upon its relations with the United States, the U.S.S.R., and Communist China, and (5) the status of Japan's security issue in 1965-1966.

853
EDINGTON, Robert van. Japan in the United Nations on the Issues of Nuclear Weapons. Washington, Seattle,

1968. 280p. DA 30 (Aug. 1969), 787-A; UM 69-13,554.

"The Japanese speeches, memoranda, resolutions, and communiqués in the General Assembly all point to the conclusion that Japan's policy has been independent of both major Cold-War protagonists in the struggle over the questions concerning nuclear weapons control." Contents: Japan: Defeated, Demilitarized, and Democratized; Control of Nuclear Weapons; Registration of Nuclear Explosions; Playing the International Game; End Nuclear Explosions Immediately: Japan Protests to Allies and Antagonists; The Test Ban Treaty and Beyond; Voting on Nuclear Weapons Issues.

854
WADHVA, Charan Dass. Regional Payments Arrangements: An Application to Asia and the Far East. Yale, 1968. 207p. DA 30 (Aug. 1969), 473-A; UM 69-13,514.

Concludes that regional payments arrangements have an importance of their own even if unaccompanied by other elements of regional economic integration. Gains from this arrangement would be greatest if the entire region of Asia and the Far East, including developed countries, were included. Japan is treated as a developed country, along with Australia and New Zealand.

DISARMAMENT DURING THE 1920's AND 1930's

See also International Relations--China: World War I, Shantung Controversy, & Washington Conf. (pp. 121-25).

855
HOSONO, Gunji. International Disarmament. Columbia, 1926. Diss. ms. not available.

A study of disarmament in Europe and in East Asia during the late nineteenth and early twentieth centuries with particular focus on the problem of naval disarmament. See especially chapters 14: "The Naval Policy of the Three Powers," 15: "The Washington Conference," 16: "The Question of Capital Ships," 17: "The Question of Submarines," 18: "Land Armament and New Agencies of War," 19: "The Washington Conference and After," 24: "The Treaty of Mutual Assistance," 25: "The Limitation of Naval Armament," and 26: "The Geneva Protocal" for information on Japan. [Annotation based on the published dissertation.]

Rel.Publ.: International Disarmament. New York: Columbia University Press, 1926. 314p.; Histoire du désarmement. Paris: A. Pedone, 1933. 253p.

856
WANG, Tsao-shih. Disarmament in the Foreign Policy Programs of the Great Powers since 1919. Wisconsin, 1929. 421, xvii p.

857
CHANG, Liang-sau. Les Dernières tentatives de désarmement naval et l'équilibre des Puissances en Extrême-Orient [The Last Attempts at Naval Disarmament and the Balance of Power among the Powers in the Far East]. Dijon, 1935. Text in French.

Contents: The Evolution of Naval Disarmament in the Early 1900's; The Naval Disarmament Negotiations at London in 1934; Japan's Denunciation of the Washington Conference and World Opinion; Taking up Once Again the Question of the Pacific and the Far East; The General Nature of Naval Armament Limitations and Their Drawbacks; Preliminary Agreements Concerning the Eventual Limitation of Naval Forces prior to the Next Naval Conference.

Rel.Publ.: Les Dernières...Extrême-Orient. Dijon: M. Pornon, 1935. 132p.

858
CHAPUT, Rolland Aimé. Disarmament in British Foreign Policy. Genève, 1935.

Traces the policy and attitude of the British Government throughout the various negotiations for naval, military, and air disarmament during the 1920's and the early 1930's. Constant reference is made to Japan.

Rel.Publ.: Disarmament...Policy. London: Allen and Unwin, 1935. 432p.

859
BARR, Eric Lloyd. The International Regulation of Naval Armaments. Washington, Seattle, 1938. 244p. AB: University of Washington. Abstracts of Theses and Faculty Bibliography. v.3. p.357-62.

A history of the regulation of naval armaments from the early 1800's through 1937. Includes considerable information on Japan, particularly in regard to the Washington Treaty of 1922, the London Naval Treaty of 1930, and the London Naval Conference of 1935.

860
HEICHER, Winchester Hallock. Great Britain and Naval Disarmament. New York, 1939. iv, 216p.

Considerable information on Japan is found throughout the dissertation. Contents: The Two-Power Stand; The Washington Conference; Great Britain at the League; The Three-Power Conference; The Anglo-French Naval Compromise; Anglo-American Conversations in 1929-1930; The London Naval Conference of 1930; The End of Naval Disarmament.

Rel.Publ.: Great...Disarmament. New York: New York University, 1944. iv, 216p.

861
MITCHELL, Donald William. The History of the United States Navy (1883-1939). Southern California, 1939. 733p. AB: University of Southern California. Abstracts of Dissertations for...1939. p.85-89.

Includes a discussion of American naval activities in East Asia and information on negotiations with the Japanese following World War I to limit the size of naval forces in the Pacific.

Rel.Publ.: History of the Modern American Navy: From 1883 through Pearl Harbor. New York: Knopf, 1946. xiv, 477, xxv p.

862
SHAW, Roger. The London Naval Conference of 1930: A Study in Naval and Political Relations among the Western Powers. Fordham, 1946. 155p. AB: Fordham University. Dissertations Accepted for Higher Degrees in the Graduate School. v.13 (1946), p.69-72.

Focuses on the activities and attitudes of France, Great Britain, Italy, and the United States, but also includes considerable information on Japan.

863
ATKINSON, James David. The London Naval Conference of 1930. Georgetown, 1949. 329p.

Examines in part the problem "of bringing the third large naval power, Japan, into the agreement with America and Britain."

864
GROELING, Dorothy Trautwein. Submarines, Disarmament, and Modern Warfare. Columbia, 1950. 211p. AB: Microfilm Abstracts, 10 (1950), 200-01; UM 1854.

Two chapters discuss the naval conferences of 1929-1930 and the Disarmament Conference of 1931-1932. They include information on proposed regulations for restricting submarine warfare and information on some of the Japanese reactions.

865
FAGAN, George Vincent. Anglo-American Naval Relations: 1927-1937. Pennsylvania, 1954. 378p. DA 14 (May 1954), 819; UM 7784.

A study of Anglo-American cooperation in the area of naval disarmament. Such cooperation was brought about by a common fear of Japan's growing power in the Pacific.

866
MICKEY, David Hopwood. Senatorial Participation in Shaping Certain United States Foreign Policies, 1921-1941: Being Largely a Study of The Congressional Record. Nebraska, 1954. 737p. DA 14 (Aug. 1954), 1203; UM 8526.

Ch.4 contains the Congressional reaction to the armament reduction treaties of the 1920's and 1930's and includes considerable information on Japan.

867
OLIVER, John B. Japan's Role in the Origins of the London Naval Treaty of 1930: A Study on Diplomatic History. Duke, 1954. 514p.

Contents: Japan as a Naval Power, 1922-1928; The Naval Question in Japan's Internal Affairs, January-March, 1929; The Naval Question in Japan's Foreign Affairs, April-June, 1929; Japan's Position in the Beginning of British-American Negotiations, June, 1929; Japan as an Obstacle to British-American Agreement, July-August, 1929; Tentative British-American Agreement, September, 1929; Japan's Case Examined and Decided, October-November, 1929; Preliminary 'Negotiations' with Japan, December 1929-January 1930; Japan at the Conference: (1) January-February 1930, (2) February-March, 1930; Acceptance, March-April 1930; Aftermath and Summary.

WHEELER, Gerald E. Japan's Influence on American Naval Policies, 1922-1931. 1954. See no.1388.

868
MAYER-OAKES, Thomas Francis. Prince Saionji and the London Naval Conference: Being Part of Volume One of the Memoirs of Harada Kumao, Entitled: Prince Saionji and the Political Situation, Translated into English, with Annotations.

A translation of that portion of Baron Harada's memoirs (published in Japanese as Saionji-kō to seikyoku, Tōkyō: Iwanami Shoten, 1950), which describes the controversy that arose between the civilian government and military authorities over acceptance of the 1930 London Naval Treaty. Focuses on Prime Minister Hamaguchi's efforts--with the aid of Prince Saionji--to obtain ratification of the treaty in the face of powerful opposition.

Rel.Publ.: Fragile Victory: Prince Saionji and the 1930 London Treaty Issue. From the Memoirs of Baron Harada Kumao. Detroit: Wayne State University Press, 1968. 328p.

869
BOWEN, Adelphia Dane, Jr. The Disarmament Movement, 1918-1935. Columbia, 1956. 402p. DA 16 (Aug. 1956), 1433-34; UM 17,041.

"Attempts to describe the movement for international disarmament [in Europe and the United States]...and to survey press opinion and other developments related to the movement." Attention is focused on several conferences in which Japan participated.

870
MILLION, Paul Eugene, Jr. The Influence of the Washington Naval Conference upon American Sea Power. Georgetown, 1956. 264p.

Includes information on the rise of Japanese and American sea power and its threat to British naval supremacy, the Japanese acquisition of Micronesia and its impact on the balance of power in the Pacific, the American view of Japan as a Pacific power, and the Japanese reaction to the Washington treaties.

871
O'CONNOR, Raymond Gish. The United States and the London Naval Conference of 1930. Stanford, 1957. 308p. DA 17 (July 1957), 1543; UM 21,576.

A discussion and analysis of the Conference "within the framework of American foreign policy and naval policy," with considerable information on Japan and on her reactions to the efforts aimed at achieving naval limitation in the Pacific.

Rel.Publ.: Perilous Equilibrium: The United States and the London Naval Conference of 1930. Lawrence: University of Kansas Press, 1962. iii, 188p.; "The 'Yardstick' and Naval Disarmament in the 1920's," Mississippi Valley Historical Review, 45 (Dec. 1958), 441-63.

872
COOPER, Harold. United States Default of World Leadership: Its Major Treaty Negotiations of the Nineteen-Twenties. Nebraska, 1959. 480p. DA 20 (July 1959), 277-78; UM 59-1781.

Includes the issues of naval limitation and disarmament that involved Japan. See especially Ch.3, "Disarmament Pressures Force Harding to Call a Conference," which discusses in part the Anglo-Japanese Alliance, Ch.5, "Japanese Demands and United States Concessions" (the Washington Conference), Ch.7, "The Collapse of the Coolidge Conference," which includes information on the Japanese involvement in the Geneva Conference, and Ch.9, "The London Rearmament Conference."

873
ANDRADE, Ernest, Jr. United States Naval Policy in the Disarmament Era, 1921-1937. Michigan State, 1966. 448p. DA 27 (Mar. 1967), 2973-A; UM 67-1594.

Examines "the effect of the naval disarmament treaties upon American naval policy in the interwar period." Information on contemporary Japanese naval development and its impact on American policy is included.

Rel.Publ.: "The United States Navy and the Washington Conference," The Historian, 31 (May 1969), 345-63.

874
BERG, Meredith William. The United States and the Breakdown of Naval Limitation, 1934-1939. Tulane, 1966. 295p. DA 27 (Apr. 1967), 3390-91-A; UM 67-3829.

"A study of United States policy toward the extension of naval limitations past 1936, the year that the Washington and the first London treaties expired. The major emphasis is on the second London Naval Conference of 1936-1936." Constant reference is made to Japan.

CAINE, Philip D. The American Periodical Press and Military Preparedness during the Hoover Administration.

1966. See no.1411.

ALLIED PARTICIPATION IN WORLD WAR II
For dissertations focusing on the Japanese military occupation of Southeast Asia, see International Relations--Southeast Asia during World War II (pages 138-43). See also International Relations--China: Sino-Japanese War (pages 131-32).

875
FIELD, James Alfred, Jr. The Sho Operation. Harvard, 1947. iii, 213p. AB: 5p. summary appended to diss. ms.
The Battle for Leyte Gulf (autumn 1944): A reconstruction in detail of "the Japanese planning and execution of the last and greatest naval battle of World War II."
Rel.Publ.: The Japanese at Leyte Gulf: The Sho Operation. Princeton: Princeton University Press, 1947. xiv, 162p.

876
CLINE, Ray Steiner. United States Army in World War II; High Command: The Operations Division of the War Department General Staff. Harvard, 1949. vii, 1453p. AB: 4p. summary appended to diss. ms.
See especially Ch.9, "The Role of WPD [War Plans Division] in the Pearl Harbor Attack" (p.251-71), and Ch.26, "Case History: Planning for the End of the War against Japan" (p.1259-320).
Rel.Publ.: Washington Command Post: The Operations Division. Washington: Office of the Chief of Military History, Department of the Army, 1951. xvi, 413p. (United States Army in World War II: The War Department)

877
HARKNESS, Albert, Jr. Retreat in the Southwest Pacific, December 8, 1941-March 4, 1942. Brown, 1949. Diss. ms. not available. AB: ii, 25p. summary available at Brown University Library.
"The original manuscript, which was never presented to Brown University for record, was written in two parts: one was used by Samuel Eliot Morison as the basis of sections [Chapters 6-10, 14-19] of his book History of United States Naval Operations. v.3: The Rising Sun in the Pacific (Boston: Little, Brown, 1948). The other was turned over to the United States Office of Naval History as the official history of the Seventh Fleet. The latter has not yet been published (9/28/51)." [From a letter to the compiler sent by Mr. I-min Chiang, Curator, East Asian Collection, Brown University, August 1969].

878
RICHARD, Dorothy Elizabeth. The United States Navy in World War II: A Chronology. Georgetown, 1949. 525p.
Primarily a day by day chronology of American naval events. The first division under each date lists operations in the Pacific Ocean and Pacific Ocean areas. The fourth division under each date lists ship losses and ship damages including those sustained by the Japanese.

879
TURNER, Gordon Brinkerhoff. The Amphibious Complex: A Study of Operations at Saipan. Princeton, 1950. 416p.
Contents: The Marianas: Heart of Central Pacific Strategy; Plans in Concert; Forces Joined in Combat; Unity in the Amphibious Assault; Fire Power in Support of Manpower; Logistics Complex; Post-Amphibious Tactics; Battle Lessons.

880
VATCHER, William Henry, Jr. Combat Propaganda against the Japanese in the Central Pacific. Stanford, 1950. 405p. AB: Stanford University. Abstracts of Dissertations, 1949/1950. p.171-72.
Studies the use of propaganda to entice Japanese soldiers to surrender.

881
HIGGINS, Trumbull. The Problem of a Second Front: An Interpretation of Coalition Strategy before and during the Turning Point of the Second World War. Princeton, 1951. vi, 394p. AB: United States Department of State, External Research Staff. Abstracts of Completed Doctoral Dissertations for the Academic Year 1950/1951. p.139-140.
Ch.2 studies the causes for the Japanese decision to continue moving south instead of carrying through their policy of 1938-1939 of waging war against the USSR.
Rel.Publ.: Winston Churchill and the Second Front, 1940-1943. New York: Oxford University Press, 1957. 281p.

882
ANDERS, Ray Leslie, Jr. A History of the Construction of the Ledo Road by the United States Army Corps of Engineers. Missouri, 1954. 371p. DA 15 (Feb. 1955), 256-57; UM 10,097.
The history of the reopening of an Allied land route to China through upper Burma during World War II.
Rel.Publ.: The Ledo Road: General Joseph W. Stilwell's Highway to China. Norman: University of Oklahoma Press, 1965. xv, 255p.; "The Engineers at Myitkyina," Military Engineer, 44 (Nov./Dec. 1952), 446-50; "Engineer Reconnaissance in Forbidden North Burma," Military Affairs, 20 (Fall, 1956), 129-38.

McINTYRE, Stuart H. Legal Effect of World War II on Treaties of the United States. 1956. See no.1555.

883
MATLOFF, Maurice. Strategic Planning for Coalition Warfare, 1943-1944. Harvard, 1956. ix, 1232p. (2v.).
"Sets forth the principal steps in the development of the American strategic case and attempts to view, through the eyes of the Washington high command, the war as a whole and in its main components." (January 1943-summer 1944). Contains considerable information the war against Japan. See especially Ch.1, "Casablanca: Beginning of an Era, January 1943," Ch.3, "Mounting Pressures in the Pacific-Far East, January-May 1943," Ch.5, "The Trident Conference: New Patterns, May 1943," Ch.7, "Current Plans and Future Operations in the War against Japan, June-August 1943," Ch.8, "Quadrant: Shaping the Patterns, August 1943," Ch.12, "Final Rehearsals en Route to Cairo," and Ch.13, "Cairo-Tehran: A Goal is Reached."
Rel.Publ.: Strategic Planning for Coalition Warfare, 1943-1944 [by] Maurice Matloff and Edwin M. Snell. Washington: Office of the Chief of Military History, Dept. of the Army, 1953-1959. xvi, 454p.; xvii, 640p. [2v., v.1: 1941-42; v.2: 1943-44].

KREPS, Leslie R. The Image of Japan in the Speaking of United States Congressmen, 1941-1953. 1957. See no.1437.

884
VORONTSOV, Vladilen Borisovich. Koreia v planakh SShA v gody vtoroi mirovoi voiny [Korea in American Planning during the Second World War]. Moscow, Institut narodov Azii Akademii nauk SSSR, 1961. (Candidate of Historical Sciences degree) 222p. Text in Russian.
Rel.Publ.: Koreia...voiny. Moscow: Izd-vo vostochnoi literatury, 1962. 138p. (Institut narodov Azii, Akademiia nauk SSSR); "SShA i problema nezavisimosti Korei v period vtoroi mirovoi voiny," in Institut naradov Azii, Akademiia nauk SSSR, Protiv fal'sifikatstii istorii Vostoka (Moscow, 1961), 113-23.

885
CRABBE, William Mervin, Jr. Consensus through Slogan: The Policy of Unconditional Surrender in the Second World War. George Washington, 1963. v, 354p. AB: George Washington University. Summaries of Doctoral Dissertations-1963. p.31-38.
Some information on the Japanese reactions to the Allied policy of unconditional surrender is included.

886
ALPEROVITZ, Gar. The Influence of the Atomic Bomb upon Certain Military and Political Questions, April-September, 1945. Cambridge, 1964. 557p.
Focuses on the role that the atomic bomb played in the formulation of American policy towards Japan and the U.S.S.R. in particular. For information on Japan, see especially Ch.4 (of the book), "The Far East and Two Faces of the Strategy of Delay." [Annotation based on the book.].
Rel.Publ.: Atomic Diplomacy: Hiroshima and Potsdam: The Use of the Atomic Bomb and the American Confrontation with Soviet Power. New York: Simon and Schuster, 1965. 317p.

887
BOYLE, James Michael. The XXI Bomber Command: Primary Factor in the Defeat of Japan. St. Louis, 1964. 254p. DA 25 (Feb. 1965), 4668; UM 64-13,442.
The study "traces the organization and training in the United States [of the XXI Bomber Command of the United States Twentieth Air Force], its movement overseas, the initial period of failure in its operations against Japan, and finally, the months from March to August, 1945, when the [aerial] onslaught [against Japan], reached its peak. It is a statistical analysis of achievements, with an aim toward proving that by the last month of the war the B-29's had destroyed a very substantial percentage of Japanese industry, wrought havoc on her economy, and greatly undermined the morale of her people, thus bringing about the conditions for surrender, and making a costly land invasion unnecessary."

888
BRESLER, Robert Joel. American Policy toward International Control of Atomic Energy 1945-1946. Princeton, 1964. 178p. DA 26 (Sept. 1965), 1750-51; UM 65-2115.
Ch.2 is an account of the decision to use the atomic bomb against Japan and of the Potsdam Conference.

889
REYNOLDS, Clark Gilbert. History and Development of the Fast Carrier Task Forces, 1943-1945. Duke, 1964. 603p. DA 28 (Apr. 1968), 4102-03-A; UM 68-5237.
Includes their role in the war against Japan.
Rel.Publ.: The Fast Carriers: The Forging of an Air Navy. New York: McGraw-Hill, 1968. xvi, 498p.; "Submarine Attacks on the Pacific Coast," PHR, 33 (1964), 183-93.

890
HAGERTY, James Joseph, Jr. The Soviet Share in the War with Japan. Georgetown, 1966. 245p. DA 27 (May 1967), 3811-A; UM 67-5223.
Focuses on the development of Soviet policy toward Japan and on the Soviet Far Eastern campaign. Concludes that (1) "World War II would have taken another course if the Soviet Union and Japan had not maintained their mutual neutrality;" (2) "from a military-technical standpoint, Soviet forces performed adequately in situations more like maneuvers than combat;" (3) although the campaign lasted only eleven days, Soviet industrial and political gains were astounding;" and (4) "Soviet participation in the war against Japan was not essential."

891
HOSKA, Lukas Ernest, Jr. Summit Diplomacy during World War II: The Conferences at Tehran, Yalta, and Potsdam. Maryland, 1966. 281p. DA 27 (Mar. 1967), 3100-A; UM 67-2334.
Examines several items relating to Japan which were considered at all three conferences, including (1) bases and strong points in the vicinity of Japan, (2) disposition of Japanese conquests in China and Korea, and (3) Soviet desires in East Asia.

892
WILSON, Theodore Allen. Meeting at Argentia. Indiana, 1966. 371p. DA 27 (June 1967), 4209-A; UM 67-3727.
Includes discussions held between Churchill and Roosevelt in August 1941 on the problem of their respective policies toward Japan.
Rel.Publ.: The First Summit: Roosevelt and Churchill at Placentia Bay 1941. Boston: Houghton Mifflin, 1969. xvi, 344p.

893
BEITZELL, Robert Egner. Major Strategic Conferences of the Allies, 1941-1943: Quadrant, Moscow, Sextant, and Eureka. North Carolina, 1967. 518p. DA 28 (Mar. 1968), 3594-95-A; UM 68-2153.
References to Allied policy towards Japan are included.

894
MOON, John Ellis van Courtland. Confines of Concept: American Strategy in World War II. Harvard, 1968. xix, 1120p. (2v.).
Studies the evolution of American strategic thought during the years immediately preceding Pearl Harbor. Contains considerable information concerning American views of Japan. See especially Ch.13, "The Temporal Imperative: The Race Against Time in the Pacific (p.443-501), for information on American preparations to meet the potential Japanese threat.

895
PARRISH, Noel Francis. Behind the Sheltering Bomb: Military Indecision from Alamogordo to Korea. Rice, 1968. 406p. DA 29 (Nov. 1968), 1500-A; UM 68-15,650.
Includes a discussion of the American policy decision to use atomic bombs on Hiroshima and Nagasaki and of the reactions to their use.

896
REED, John Jay. American Diplomatic Relations with

Australia during the Second World War. Southern California, 1969. 360p. DA 30 (May 1970); UM 70-8540.

TOKYO WAR CRIMES TRIALS

897
GORBUNOV, D. I. Vopros ob agressivnoi voine na tokiiskom protesesse glavnykh voennykh prestupnikov [The Problem of Aggressive War at the Tokyo War Crimes Trials]. Moscow, Moskovskii gosudarstvennyi institut mezhdunarodnykh otnoshenii Ministerstva Inostrannykh Del SSSR, 1950. (Candidate of Juridical Sciences degree) 266p. Text in Russian.

898
WADSWORTH, Lawrence W., Jr. A Short History of the Tokyo War Crimes Trials with Special Reference to Some Aspects of Procedures. American, 1955. 238p.
Contents: The Origins of the Tokyo Trials; The Establishment of the Tribunal: Its Powers and Functions; The Indictment; The Case for the Prosecution; The Case for the Defense; Court Procedure and Conduct of Trial; Judgments and Sentences.

899
RILEY, Walter Lee. The International Military Tribunal for the Far East and the Law of the Tribunal as Revealed by the Judgment and the Concurring and Dissenting Opinions. Washington, Seattle, 1957. 218p. DA 18 (Apr. 1958), 1481; UM 58-1092.
Focuses on the Tribunal's assertedly unprecedented ex post facto decision to declare "that international law provided for the punishment of persons found guilty of war crimes." "What is questioned," the author writes, "is the propriety of throwing the onus of punishment into legalistic form and interpreting for history the appearance of an international judicial process for judging political and military leaders."

900
TSAI, Paul Chung-tseng. Judicial Administration of the Law of War: Procedures in War Crimes Trials. Yale, 1957. 462p.; 327p. (2v.).
A comprehensive analysis of war crimes trials procedures which concludes with a formulation of standards for such trials. Information on the Tokyo war crimes trials may be found throughout.

901
HELLER, Maxine Jacobson. The Treatment of Defeated War Leaders. Columbia, 1965. 500p. DA 26 (Feb. 1966), 4786; UM 65-13,954.
Studies the treatment of leaders of defeated nations after the Napoleonic Wars and after World Wars I and II. Includes the debate among the Allies that led to the Tokyo war crimes trial.

AFRICA

902
LEHMANN, Hans-Wilhelm. Der japanische Afrika-Handel während der japanischen Export-Offensive 1931-1937 [Japanese Trade with Africa during the Period of Japan's Export Offensive, 1931-1937]. Hamburg, 1951. x, 105, xv p. Text in German. Diss. ms. available at Hamburg, Staats- und Universitätsbibliothek, Nr. Diss.jur. Mscr. 690.
Studies the structure of Japanese foreign trade in general and the significance of the devaluation of the yen for Japanese exports, the growth and organization of Japanese-African trade, and Japan's trade and trade measures with regard to individual African countries.

ASIA

General

903
FIFIELD, Russell Hunt. Regionalism as a Principle in International Relations. Clark, 1942. 489p. AB: Clark University. Thesis Abstracts-1942. p.43-47.
A study of the attempts of Nazi Germany, Japan, and the United States of America "to organize large areas of the world...into political, economic, and cultural units under" their respective leaderships. Within this context the author discusses Japan's "New Order in Greater East Asia" in some detail.
Rel.Publ.: Geopolitics in Principle and Practice [by] Russell H. Fifield and G. Etzel Pearcy. Boston: Ginn, 1944. iv, 203p.

904
GINSBURG, Norton Sydney. Japanese Prewar Trade and Shipping in the Oriental Triangle. Chicago, 1949. xi, 308p.
The "Oriental triangle" is the area between India, Kamchatka, and New Zealand. An examination of the nature of Japan's prewar trade as a whole and of the characteristics of its shipping industry is made. The key year is 1936. Each country within the triangle is accorded separate treatment within the thesis.
Rel.Publ.: Japanese...Triangle. Chicago, 1949. xi, 308p. (University of Chicago. Department of Geography. Research Paper, 6)

905
RAGATZ, Janet Evans. American, Japanese, and Australian Economic Assistance to Southern Asia: A Comparison of Objectives. Ohio State, 1962. 370p. DA 24 (July 1963), 375; UM 63-4695.
The author characterizes Japanese aid-giving as being motivated primarily by economic considerations.

906
ALEKSEEV, V. V. Ekonomicheskaia ekspansiia Iaponii v slaborazvitye strany posle 2-oi mirovoi voiny [Japan's Postwar Economic Expansion in the Underdeveloped Part of the World]. Moscow, Moskovskii gosudarstvennyi institut mezhdunarodnykh otnoshenii, 1963. (Candidate of Economic Sciences degree) 16 + 200p. Text in Russian.

907
CHIN, Ming-shan. Ekonomicheskaia ekspansiia iaponskogo imperializma v ekonomicheski slaborazvitye strany posle vtoroi mirovoi voiny [The Postwar Economic Expansion of Japanese Imperialism into Economically Underdeveloped Countries]. Moscow, Institut mirovoi ekonomiki i mezhdunarodnykh otnoshenii Akademii nauk SSSR, 1963. (Candidate of Economic Sciences) 226p. Text in Russian.

908
JO, Yung-Hwan. Japanese Geopolitics and the Greater East Asia Co-Prosperity Sphere. American, 1964. 301p. DA 25 (Jan. 1965), 4241-42; UM 64-12,804.
"The purposes of the study are (1) to examine a hypothesis that the GEACPS was a formulation by Japanese policy-makers out of geographical concepts bor-

rowed from Germany, reinforced by the Japan-centric ideology of expansion, and used in interpreting the pressing conditions in and around the Japanese empire; (2) to engage extensively in an objective analysis of various theories advanced for the organization of the GEACPS; and (3) to compare the policies that were actually implemented in the building of the GEACPS with the theories advanced by Japanese students of geopolitics."

Rel.Publ.: "An Interpretation of Professor Kamikawa's View of Japanese Diplomacy," in Studies on Asia, 1964, ed. by Robert K. Sakai (Lincoln: University of Nebraska Press, 1964), 51-61.

909
SEELIG, Rosemarie. Die diplomatischen Beziehungen zwischen Japan und den weissen Mächten in Ost- und Südöstasien zwischen 1919 and 1925 [Diplomatic Relations between Japan and the Caucasian Powers in East and Southeast Asia, 1919-1925]. Würzburg, 1964. iii, 162p. Text in German. The dissertation in its published form is available at Marburg/Lahn, Staatsbibliothek Preussischer Kulturbesitz, Nr. Hsn 55,385; also at the University of Michigan, General Library, no. 30,708.

Studies the renewal of the Anglo-Japanese Alliance before the convening of the Washington Conference, its termination, and the origins of the Four-Power Treaty; Japan's policy in Siberia; and Japanese relations with the Dutch East Indies, the Philippines, Great Britain, the United States, Germany, and the U.S.S.R. The study is based primarily upon German documentary materials.

Rel.Publ.: Die diplomatischen...1925. Würzburg, 1964. iii, 162p.

910
HUH, Kyung-Mo. The Development and Prospects of Japan's Trade in Asia. Michigan, 1965. 382p. DA 28 (Jan. 1968), 2402-03-A; UM 66-6620.

"Investigates the development of Japan's trade relations with the ten major ECAFE countries since the middle 1920's and explores the prospects for the expansion of her trade with these countries by 1970."

Rel.Publ.: Japan's Trade in Asia: Developments since 1926, Prospects for 1970. New York: Praeger, 1966. xx, 283p. (Praeger Special Studies in International Economics and Development)

911
YEH, Yeong-Her. Economies of Scale, Market Size, and Degree of Concentration in a Hypothetical Common Market for the ECAFE Region. Minnesota, 1965. 242p. DA 27 (Sept. 1966), 561-A; UM 66-8964.

"The primary purpose of the thesis is to evaluate a possible common market for the ECAFE [United Nations, Economic Commission for Asia and the Far East] Region from one particular viewpoint: namely would a common market permit a greater exploitation of economies of scale in manufacturing." Japan is one of the countries within the region, and the study is in part based on data gathered for Japan.

China

(Dissertations on Japanese relations with Germany, Great Britain, Russia, and the United States that deal with Japanese activities in China are entered in this section. See also History --the Japanese Empire (pages 90-99).

Early to 1860

REISCHAUER, Edwin Oldfather. Nittō guhō junrei gyōki: Ennin's Diary of His Travels in T'ang China, 838-847. 1939. See no.1610.

912
WANG, Yi-t'ung. Official Relations between China and Japan, 1368-1549. Harvard, 1949. ii, 215p. AB: 5p. summary appended to diss. ms.

Contents: 1368-1403: Early Attempts to Establish Relations; 1404-1419: Profit and Patriotism: Amicable Relations under Yoshimitsu Interrupted by Yoshimochi; 1432-1549: Trade and Profit: Chinese Opposition to an Adverse Trade Balance; Economic Aspects of Official Ming-Japanese Relations, 1368-1549.

Rel.Publ.: Official...1549. Cambridge: Harvard University Press, 1953. ix, 128p. (Harvard-Yenching Institute series, 9)

913
MESKILL, John Thomas. A Record of Drifting across the Sea: P'yohae-rok. Columbia, 1958. 380p. DA 19 (Jan. 1959), 1724-25; UM 58-3237.

This journal by a Korean confucian official records many observations of fifteenth century China including the problem of the Japanese wakō.

Rel.Publ.: Ch'oe Pu's Diary: A Record of Drifting across the Sea. Tucson: University of Arizona Press, 1964. 177p. (Association for Asian Studies Monographs and Papers, 17)

914
WIETHOFF, Bodo. Die chinesische Seeverbotspolitik und der private Überseehandel von 1368 bis 1567 [The Chinese Prohibition of Maritime Trade and Private Overseas Trade, 1368-1567]. Hamburg, 1963. Text in German. The dissertation in its published form is available at Marburg/Lahn, Universitätsbibliothek, Nr. VIb C 593 rq, 45- ; also at the University of Michigan, General Library, no. QH5.G38v.45.

Reference is frequently made to trade with Japan.

Rel.Publ.: Die chinesische...1567. Wiesbaden: Harrassowitz, 1963. ix, 235p. (MOAG, 45)

HORI, Kyotsu. The Mongol Invasions and the Kamakura Bakufu. 1967. See no.493.

MILLER, Alan L. Chinese Influences on the Indigenous Folk Religion of Japan. 1968. See no.60.

1860-1894

915
TCHEN, Hoshien. Les Relations diplomatiques entre la Chine et le Japon de 1871 à nos jours [Diplomatic Relations between China and Japan from 1871 to the Present (1919)]. Paris, 1920. Text in French.

"Investigates the causes underlying the difficulties involved in the relations between China and Japan."

Rel.Publ.: Les Relations...jours. Paris: Editions de "La Vie universitaire," 1921. 328p.

916
LUDWIG, Albert Philip. Li Hung-chang and Chinese Foreign Policy, 1870-1885. California, Berkeley, 1936. 443p.

Focuses on the negotiations for the Tientsin Treaty of 1871 with Japan and on the Sino-Japanese controversies over Taiwan, the Ryukyus, and Korea.

917
QUIMBY, Paul Elmore. A Study of the Foreign Policies of Li Hung-chang. Southern California, 1940. 310p. AB: University of Southern California. Abstracts of Dissertations for...1940. p.78-81.

Includes information on Sino-Japanese relations between 1874 (the Japanese expedition to Taiwan) and 1895.

MASLENNIKOV, V. A. Iapono-kitaiskie ekonomicheskie otnosheniia, 1860-1940 gg. 1947. See no.951.

918
TODER, F. A. Istoriia zakhvata Formozy Iaponiei [The History of the Japanese Seizure of Taiwan]. Moscow, Moskovskii gosudarstvennyi universitet imeni M. V. Lomonosova, 1948. (Candidate of Historical Sciences degree) 13 + 35 + 300p. Text in Russian.

919
ZENINA, L. V. Nachalo iaponskoi agressii v Kitae: 70-90-e gody XIX stoletiia [The Beginning of Japanese Aggression in China: From the 1870's to the 1890's]. Leningrad, Leningradskii gosudarstvennyi universitet imeni A. A. Zhdanova, 1951. (Candidate of Historical Sciences degree) 268p. Text in Russian. AB: 20p. summary published in 1951.

920
ATKINS, Emily Howard. General Charles LeGendre and the Japanese Expedition to Formosa, 1874. Florida, 1953. 261p.

"To summarize, the Formosan expedition settled for the future the jurisdiction of China over Formosa and her responsibility for the future protection of the mariners; it provided groups for dissatisfaction in China with Japan over the sovereignty of the Liu-chiu Islands; it revealed the weakness of China and the rising strength of Japan; it served as an example to show how the foreign representatives interfered with the Japanese plans; it disclosed the struggle which was going on between the English Minister and the United States Minister for the controlling influence in the Japanese Government; and it proved that General LeGendre's motives were peaceful ones."

DONG, Chon. Japanese Annexation of Korea: A Study of Korean-Japanese Relations to 1910. 1955. See no.1148.

921
YEN, Sophia Su-fei. Taiwan in China's Foreign Relations, 1836-1874. Yale, 1962. 417p.

Pt.3--"The Problem of China's Sovereignty over Taiwan"--presents a lengthy description and analysis of the 1874 Japanese expedition to Taiwan, its background, and its outcome.

Rel.Publ.: Taiwan...1874. Hamden, Conn.: Shoe String Press, 1965. xii, 404p.

922
CARUTHERS, Sandra Carol Taylor. Charles LeGendre, American Diplomacy, and Expansion in Meiji Japan, 1868-1893. Colorado, 1966. 377p. DA 28 (Oct. 1967), 1367-A; UM 67-10,031.

Focuses on the Japanese expedition to Taiwan. Contents: American Diplomacy and Meiji Japan; LeGendre and Formosa; A Hiring and a Firing; Soejima's Mission to Peking; The Formosa Expedition; Crisis Averted; Advice from the General; Aftermath and Conclusion.

Rel.Publ.: "Anodyne for Expansion: Meiji Japan, the Mormons, and Charles LeGendre," PHR, 38 (May 1969), 129-40.

1894-1931

See also International Relations--China: 1894-1911 (pages 117-19) and International Relations--China: 1911-1931 (pages 119-21).

923
TYAU, Min-ch'ien Tuk-zung. The Legal Obligations Arising Out of Treaty Relations between China and Other States. London, 1916. 861p.

Contains information on Chinese disputes and treaties with Japan and on cessions and leases made to Japan.

Rel.Publ.: The Legal...States. Shanghai: Commercial Press, 1917. xxii, 304p.

924
NEDERBRAGT, Johan Alexander. "Penetration Pacifique" in China [The "Peaceful Penetration" of China]. Rotterdam Handelshoogeschool, 1918. Text in Dutch.

A study of Western economic and political penetration into China. Includes considerable information about Japanese activities in China during the early 1900's.

Rel.Publ.: "Penetration...China. 'sGravenhage: Voortvaren, 1918. v, 231p.

925
TAI, En-sai. Treaty Ports in China: A Study in Diplomacy. Columbia, 1918.

Constant reference is made to Japanese activities in China.

Rel.Publ.: Treaty...Diplomacy. New York: Columbia University, 1918. x, 202p.

926
OVERLACH, Theodore William. Foreign Financial Control in China. California, Berkeley, 1920. 317p.

See especially Ch.6, "Sino-Japanese Relations, 1894-1917."

Rel.Publ.: Foreign...China. New York: Macmillan, 1919. xiii, 295p.

TCHEN, Hoshien. Les Relations diplomatiques entre la Chine et le Japon de 1871 à nos jours. 1920. See no.915.

927
BAU, Ming-chien Joshua. The Foreign Relations of China: Part III: The Policy of Japan in China. Johns Hopkins, 1921. 594p.

Discusses and analyzes the development of Japanese policies in China, 1894-1918, under such headings as "Economic Exploitation," "Territorial Expansion," "Paramount Influence," "Political Control," and "The Asiatic Monroe Doctrine."

Rel.Publ.: The Foreign Relations of China: A History and a Survey. New York: Fleming H. Revell, 1921. xii, 508p.

928
OHLY, Waldemar Hazama. Das wirtschaftliche Vordringen Japans in China seit dem Frieden von Portsmouth (New Hampshire, U.S.A.), 5. September 1905 [Japan's Economic Advance in China since the Treaty of Portsmouth,

September 5, 1905]. Kiel, 1922. xviii, 356p. Text in German. Diss. ms. available at Marburg/Lahn, Staatsbibliothek Preussischer Kulturbesitz, Nr. MS 22/5511.

A study of the Japanese economic expansion and its significance for both the Japanese and the Chinese economies is made on the basis of an exhaustive examination of Japanese and Chinese trade statistics.

Rel.Publ.: "Das wirtschaftliche...1905," Weltwirtschaftliches Archiv, 20 (1924), 377-79.

929
REMER, Charles Frederick. The Foreign Trade of China. Harvard, 1923. v, 356p.

Sino-Japanese trade is discussed in Chapters 3-6 entitled "Foreign Trade of China, 1871-1921."

Rel.Publ.: The Foreign...China. Shanghai: Commercial Press, 1926. xii, 269p.

930
CLYDE, Paul Hibbert. International Rivalries in Manchuria, 1689-1922. Stanford, 1925.

Focuses on the Russo-Japanese competition for Manchuria, the Portsmouth Treaty and the Treaty of Peking, subsequent Japanese and American activities in Manchuria, and Sino-Japanese relations, 1906-1922.

Rel.Publ.: International...1922. Columbus: Ohio State University Press, 1926. x, 217p.; "The Manchurian Freight-Rate Controversy, 1914-1916," Far Eastern Review, 26 (1930), 410-12; "The Open Door Policy of John Hay," Historical Outlook, 22 (1931), 210-14.

931
HSU, Shu-hsi. China and Her Political Entity: A Study of China's Foreign Relations with Reference to Korea, Manchuria, and Mongolia. Columbia, 1925. xxiv, 438p.

Focuses on the role of Manchuria in China's relations with Japan and with Russia during the latter half of the nineteenth and the early part of the twentieth centuries.

Rel.Publ.: China...Mongolia. New York: Oxford University Press, 1926. xxiv, 438p.; "Japan and Manchuria," Pacific Affairs, 3 (Sept. 1930), 854-64.

932
SZE, Tsung-yu. China and the Most-Favored-Nation Clause. Columbia, 1925. 268p.

Constant reference is made to Japan and to Japanese activities in China under the most-favored-nation clause.

Rel.Publ.: China...Clause. New York: Fleming H. Revell, 1925. 268p.

933
LI, Banghan. Die chinesische Volkswirtschaft und der Einfluss der fremden Mächte [The Chinese Political Economy and the Influence of the Foreign Powers]. Frankfurt, 1926. Text in German. The dissertation in its published form is available at Marburg/Lahn, Universitätsbibliothek, Nr. XVII C.

Information on the following subjects concerning Japan is scattered throughout the dissertation: (1) Japan and Korea as countries to which Chinese emigrants went in search of work; (2) the influence of Japanese diplomacy upon China; (3) relations between Japan and the United States and the protection of their respective Asian interests; (4) Sino-Japanese commercial ties before, during, and after World War I; (5) the competition among Japan, England, and the United States for the Chinese market.

Rel.Publ.: Die Chinesische...Mächte. Borna-Leipzig: Noske, 1926. 126p.

934
WOU, Kienpang. La Chine et les grandes Puissances: Étude d'histoire diplomatique contemporaine [China and the Great Powers: A Study of Contemporary Diplomatic History]. Louvain, 1926.

Chapters on the Sino-Japanese war and on Sino-Japanese relations, 1900-1925, are included.

Rel.Publ.: La Chine...contemporaine. Gand: S. Hussein 1926. ix, 414p. (Université catholique de Louvain. Collection de l'Institut des sciences politiques et sociales)

935
TCHAI, Henri Tsoun-tchun. Essai historique et analytique sur la situation internationale de la Chine: Conséquences des traités sino-étrangers [An Historical and Analytical Essay on China's International Situation: The Consequences of China's Foreign Treaties]. Lyon, 1927. Text in French.

Rel.Publ.: Essai...étrangers. Paris: P. Geuthner, 1929. 235p. (Bibliotheca Franco-Sinica Lugdunensis. Études et documents publiés par l'Institut franco-chinois de Lyon, 3)

936
WEIGH, Ken Shen. The Diplomatic Relations between China and Russia. Johns Hopkins, 1927. vi, 394p.

Includes considerable information on the Russo-Japanese rivalry over Manchuria.

Rel.Publ.: Russo-Chinese Diplomacy. Shanghai: Commercial Press, 1928. xxi, 382p.

937
THUNG, Soey-hay. De internationaalrechtelijke betrekkingen tusschen China en Japan [Sino-Japanese Relations from the Viewpoint of International Law]. Rotterdam Handelshoogeschool, 1928. Text in Dutch.

Rel.Publ.: De internationaalrechtelijke...Japan. Rotterdam: F. Bosman, 1928. vi, 215p. [See also addenda.]

938
CHANG, Chung-tao. Les Traités inegaux de la Chine et l'attitude des puissances [The Unequal Treaties with China and the Attitude of the Powers]. Paris, 1929. Text in French.

Includes some information on Sino-Japanese relations 1894-1922.

Rel.Publ.: Les Traités...puissances. Paris: M. Rivière, 1929. 216p.

939
YOUNG, Carl Walter. Japan's Jurisdiction and International Legal Position in Manchuria. Johns Hopkins, 1931. vii, 647p.

Presents a detailed background of the development of Japanese interests in Manchuria.

Rel.Publ.: The International Legal Status of the Kwantung Leased Territory. Baltimore: Johns Hopkins University Press, 1931. xxx, 254p.; Japan's Special Position in Manchuria: Its Assertion, Legal Interpretation, and Present Meaning. Baltimore: Johns Hopkins University Press, 1931. xxxiv, 412p.; Japanese Jurisdiction in the South Manchurian Railway Areas. Baltimore: Johns Hopkins University Press, 1931. xxxv, 323p.; "Sino-Japanese Interests and Issues in Manchuria," Pacific Affairs, 1 (Dec. 1928), 1-20; "Manchurian Questions at Kyoto. (IPR Conference)," Pacific Affairs, 3 (Mar. 1930), 249-65.

940
HOH, Yam-tong. The Boxer Indemnity Remissions and Education in China: Being an Historical and Analytical Study of the China Indemnity of 1901 as Remitted to China by the United States, Great Britain, France, Belgium, Italy, Soviet Russia, and the Netherlands, and the Application of These Remissions to Educational and Cultural Purposes, together with a Chapter on Japan's Use of Her Share "for Cultural Work in China." Columbia, 1933. 485p.

Chapter Y, "Japanese Share of the Boxer Indemnity" (p.426-40), deals with the uses made by the Japanese government of the Boxer indemnities. The author notes that the ostensibly honorific intentions of the Japanese "law of special accounts for cultural work in China" were merely a sham for Japanese penetration and exploitation of Chinese educational institutions.

941
LONG, Johnson. La Mandchourie et la doctrine de la porte ouverte [Manchuria and the Open Door Policy]. Paris, 1933. Text in French.

Pt.3, "The Application of the Open Door Policy to Manchuria" (p.113-94), contains considerable information on its application with respect to Japan as well as on Japan's military and political expansion into Manchuria.

Rel.Publ.: La Mandchourie...ouverte. Paris: A. Pedone, 1933. 208p.

942
MENG, Chu-ju. La Position juridique du Japon en Mandchourie. [The Legal Position of Japan in Manchuria]. Grenoble, 1933. Text in French.

Seeks to prove that with the exception of certain special and concrete cases, Japan does not possess any legal rights in Manchuria. Contents: Pt.1: Japanese Rights in Manchuria: Japanese Rights with Regard to the South Manchurian Railway; Japanese Claims to a Railway Monopoly in Manchuria. Pt.2: Japan's Special Position in Manchuria: Japanese Claims to a Sphere of Influence (1905-1914); Japan's Attempts to Acquire a Special Position in Manchuria during World War One; The Breakdown of Japanese Claims during the Negotiations of the International Banking Consortium and at the Washington Conference; The Japanese Monroe Doctrine.

Rel.Publ.: La Position...Mandchourie. Paris: A. Pedone, 1933. 265p.

943
MICHAEL, Franz. Die chinesisch-japanischen Rechtsbeziehungen in den "drei östlichen Provinzen" Chinas (Mandschurei) vor Ausbruch des Konfliktes im September 1931 [Sino-Japanese Jurisdictional Relations in the "Three Eastern Provinces" of China (Manchuria) before the Outbreak of the Conflict in September 1931]. Freiburg i.B., 1933. Text in German. The dissertation in its published form is available at Freiburg i.B, Universitätsbibliothek, Nr. P 1801 i; also at the University of Michigan, Law Library.

The study focuses on (1) the development of Japan's special interests in China as a consequence of Sino-Japanese treaties concerning Manchuria, (2) the problems ensuing from Japan's special position in Manchuria, and (3) the legal validity of Japanese claims. The dissertation also clarifies the meaning of the concepts "open door," "spheres of influence," "spheres of interest," and "special interests: with regard to Manchuria in particular.

Rel.Publ.: Die chinesisch...1931. Borna-Leipzig: Noske, 1933. viii, 100p. (Abhandlungen des Instituts für Politik, ausländisches öffentliches Recht, und Völkerrecht an der Universität Leipzig, Heft 29); "Japan's 'Special Interests' in China," Pacific Affairs, 10 (Dec. 1937), 407-11.

PRICE, Ernest B. The Russo-Japanese Treaties of 1907-1916 Concerning Manchuria and Mongolia. 1933. See no.1312.

944
CHANG, Tao-shing. International Controversies over the Chinese Eastern Railway. Iowa, 1934. 350p.

"A descriptive, analytical, and critical study of the major international disputes over the railway, 1895-1935. In the published version, see especially Ch.3, "The Construction and Extension of the Railway and the Russo-Japanese War;" Ch.6, "Japanese Encroachment upon the Railway during the World War;" Ch.9, "Russia's Proposal to Sell Her Interest in the Railway (1933);" and Ch.10, "The Cession of the Railway to Manchoukuo (1933-1935)." [Annotation based on the book.]

Rel.Publ.: International...Railway. Shanghai: Commercial Press, 1936. ix, 289p.

945
KLÉVANSKI, Georges. Le "Monroïsme" japonais [The Japanese Monroeism]. Paris, 1935. 174p. Text in French.

Contents: Pt.1: The Origin and Meaning of Japanese Monroeism. Pt.2: Japanese Monroeism in Practice: Japanese Expansion in Korea and in Southern Manchuria; The Twenty-One Demands and the Occupation of Eastern Siberia; The Washington Conference and the Nine Power Treaty; The Creation of the State of Manchukuo.

Rel.Publ.: Le "Monroïsme" japonais. Paris: A. Rousseau, 1935. 174p.

946
CHANG, Yu-shin. Die Entwicklungstendenzen des chinesischen Aussenhandels nach dem Weltkriege: Eine Untersuchung über die internationale Wirtschaftsverflechtung Chinas [Developing Trends in China's Foreign Trade after World War I: An Examination of the International Multilateral Economic Relations of China]. Frankfurt a.M., 1936. Text in German. The dissertation in its published form is available at Marburg/Lahn, Universitätsbibliothek, Nr. XVII C.

A study of China's foreign trade policies from early times through the postwar era. The dissertation includes information on the following matters pertaining to Japan: the Treaty of Shimonoseki; Chinese territorial concessions to Japan; the question of war indemnity payments following the Sino-Japanese War; Japanese demands on China; the growth of Japanese-American commercial relations and its impact on China; Japan's predominance in Manchuria; the decline of China's trade with Japan; and Japan's capital investments in China.

Rel.Publ.: Die Entwicklungstendenzen...Chinas. Gelnhausen: Kalbfleisch, 1936. 93p.

947
HSU, Oscar T. Handel und Handelspolitik Chinas [China's Trade and Trade Policy]. Hamburg, 1936. Text in German. The dissertation in its published form is available at Marburg/Lahn, Universitätsbibliothek, Nr. XVII B; also at the University of Michigan, General Library, no. HF1588.H87.

Includes considerable information on Sino-Japanese trade relations, Chinese boycotts of Japanese goods, special treaties between China and Japan, Japanese economic expansion into China, and Japan's "Twenty-One

Demands" and its consequences.
Rel.Publ.: Handel...Chinas. Lyon, 1934. 54p.

CHEN, Tai-chu. China's Frontier Problems. 1937. See no.1313.

948
CHIN, Rockwood Quock-ping. Japanese Owned Cotton Mills in China: A Study in International Competition. Yale, 1937. 371p.
Contents: Cotton Textile Competition in the China Market; Extension of the Japanese Cotton Industry to China; Competition of the Japanese-Owned Cotton Mills with Chinese Mills and with Japanese Mills; Economic Factors in the Success of the Competition of Japanese-Owned Cotton Mills; Political Aspects of Japanese Ownership of Cotton Mills in China.
Rel.Publ.: "Cotton Mills: Japan's Economic Spearhead in China," Far Eastern Survey, 6 (Nov. 17, 1937), 251-67.

949
KUO, Chao-lin. Die Macht Bewerbung von Japan und U.S.A. in Ost-Asie [The Power Struggle between Japan and the United States in East Asia]. Berlin, 1938. Text in German.

950
JENZOWSKI, Siegfried. Die chinesisch-japanischen Boykottfälle als völkerrechtliches Problem [The Sino-Japanese Boycotts as an International Legal Problem]. Koln, 1939. Text in German. The dissertation in its published form is available at Marburg/Lahn, Universitätsbibliothek, Nr. XVIII C.
Presents an historical survey of boycotts in China's internal affairs and in her foreign relations, studies the various Sino-Japanese boycotts that occurred after 1908 as well as the political motivations that were behind them, and examines the boycott as a violation of international law.
Rel.Publ.: Die chinesisch...Problem. Köln: Orthen, 1939. 61p.

951
MASLENNIKOV, V. A. Iapono-kitaiskie ekonomicheskie otnosheniia, 1860-1940 gg. [Sino-Japanese Economic Relations, 1860-1940]. Moscow, Institut mirovogo khoziaistva i mirovoi politiki, 1947. (Doctor of Economic Sciences degree) Text in Russian.

952
GRAA, Frederick Albert. The Open Door Policy of the United States: A Fundamental Cause of War between the United States and Japan. St. John's, 1948. vi, 152p.
Contents: A New Policy is Born; England Plays a Part; The Role of Japan in the Far East, 1900-1922; Japanese Expansion Challenges the Open Door; America's Reaction, 1900-1922; A Fundamental Cause of War.

953
KRUSE, Arthur Paul. The Territorial Integrity and Administrative Entity of China as a Phase of the Far Eastern Policy of the United States, 1900-1921. Chicago, 1948. 537p.
Includes information on the Russo-Japanese competition for Manchuria, 1901-1912, the Japanese administration of Shantung province, railway concessions to Japan, and Japanese diplomacy with respect to China's demands at the Paris Peace Conference.

954
JANSEN, Marius Berthus. The Japanese and the Chinese Revolutionary Movement, 1895-1915. Harvard, 1950. 329p. AB: 5p. summary appended to diss. ms.
"The motives which lay behind the cooperation of the Japanese with the Chinese revolutionary movement constitute the primary focus of this study; they are traced from the anti-foreign and expansionist theories of the late Tokugawa Period and the political currents of the early part of the Meiji Period." Contents: The Tokugawa Background: Loyalism and Chauvanism; The Meiji Context of Expansionist Thought; The Problem of Asia; Sun Yat-sen; The Year 1900; The T'ung-meng-hui; The 1911 Revolution; 1913: Afterglow; 1915: Guidance by Force; Sun Yat-sen and Japanese Aid.
Rel.Publ.: The Japanese and Sun Yat-sen. Cambridge: Harvard University Press, 1954. viii, 274p. (Harvard Historical Monographs, 27); "The Japanese and Sun Yat-sen," in Harvard University, East Asian Research Center, Papers on China, 1 (1947), 37-73; "Opportunists in South China during the Boxer Rebellion," PHR, 20 (Aug. 1951), 241-50.

955
CHU, Charles Chia-hwei. The China Policy of the Taft-Knox Administration, 1909-1913. Chicago, 1956. 565p.
Analyzes in great detail the central China railway projects, the Manchurian policy of Knox, the Chinese revolution, and American policy and the reorganization loans. Touches repeatedly upon Japanese foreign policy.

956
GÜTTER, Charlotte. Das imperiale Kraftfeld Ostasiens 1904-1914 [Imperialism in East Asia, 1904-1914]. Erlangen, 1960. Text in German. The dissertation in its published form is available at Marburg/Lahn, Staatsbibliothek Preussischer Kulturbesitz, Nr. Hsn 29,869; also at the University of Michigan, General Library, no. 25,272.
I. The imperialistic goals of the great powers in East Asia and the consequences of imperialism; England as the leading imperialistic nation. II. England's efforts to bring Japan into her system of alliances and the precautions that were taken simultaneously. III. Japan's diplomatic policy: her efforts to free herself from dependence upon the Western powers. IV. The growth of Sino-Japanese relations.
Rel.Publ.: Das imperiale...1914. Spiegelberg/Württ: Richter, 1960. 156p.

957
BOCAGE, Leo Joseph. The Public Career of Charles R. Crane. Fordham, 1962. 347p. DA 23 (Oct. 1962), 1169-70; UM 62-3756.
Includes a discussion of his anti-Japanese attitudes while serving as American minister to China (in 1909 and in 1920-1921).

958
WOLFF, Ernst. Chou Tso-jên: Modern China's Pioneer of the Essay. Washington, Seattle, 1966. 239p. DA 27 (June 1967), 4271-A; UM 67-7690.
A biographical study of Chou Tso-jên (born in 1885). Includes information on Chou's studies in Japan, the influence of Japanese methods and ideas upon his work, and his participation in the Wang Ching-wei regime during World War Two.

959
CHONG, Ken Ray. The Sources and Development of Sun

Yat-sen's Nationalistic Ideology as Expressed in His San Min Chu I. Claremont, 1967. 297p. DA 29 (Aug. 1968), 647-A; UM 68-10,501.

Includes a discussion of the influence of Japanese thinkers and of their writings on Sun's philosophy and ideology.

960
ISRAEL, Jerome Michael. Progressivism and the Open Door: America and China, 1901-1921. Rutgers, 1967. 407p. DA 28 (Nov. 1967), 1764-65-A; UM 67-14,721.

Includes information on American-Japanese diplomatic relations during this era and relates various aspects of these relations to concurrent developments in the United States.

Rel.Publ.: "Manchu and Muckrake: The Image of China in the American Press, 1900-1912," in Rutgers University Library, Journal, 31 (June 1968), 58-64.

1894-1911

See also International Relations--China: 1894-1931 (pages 117-19).

961
TCHOU, Louis Ngaosiang. Le Régime des capitulations et la reforme constitutionnelle en Chine [Government by Capitulation and Constitutional Reform in China]. Louvain, 1915. Text in French.

A study of the extraterritorial rights held by various Western nations and by Japan in China. Includes a section entitled "Japanese Politics and the Question of Kiaochow" (p.116-24).

Rel.Publ.: Le Régime...Chine. Cambridge: Cambridge University Press, 1915. viii, 230p. (Université catholique de Louvain. Collection de l'Institut des sciences politiques et sociales)

962
JOSEPH, Philip. China's Political fin-de-siècle, 1894-1900: A Study in the Diplomatic Relations of the Powers with China. London, 1926. xxv, 201p.; 223, xi p. (2v.).

Sino-Japanese relations included.

Rel.Publ.: Foreign Diplomacy in China, 1894-1900: A Study in Political and Economic Relations with China. London: G. Allen & Unwin, 1928. iii, 458p.

963
SWARTZ, Willis George. Anglo-Russian Rivalry in the Far East, 1895-1905. Iowa, 1929. 478p. AB: University of Iowa. Studies in the Social Sciences. v.10, no.2 (1932), 158-70.

Includes considerable information on Anglo-Japanese, Russo-Japanese, and Sino-Japanese relations. See especially Ch.1, "The Japan-China War (1894-1895)," Ch.2, "Russia Supreme in China and Korea (1895-1897)," and Ch.10, "The Russo-Japanese War (1904-1905)."

McCORDOCK, Robert S. British Far Eastern Policy, 1894-1900. 1931. See no.1275.

964
WANG, Feng-gang. Japanese Influence on Educational Reform in China from 1895 to 1911. Stanford, 1931. 185p. AB: Stanford University. Abstracts of Dissertations, 1930/1931. p.66-68.

A study of the "proposition that the real impetus towards the introduction of Western civilization into China came chiefly from Japan, and that from 1895 to 1911 the predominant influence on educational reform in China was Japanese."

Rel.Publ.: Japanese...1911. Peiping: Author's Bookstore, 1933. viii, 204p.

965
REID, John Gilbert. The Manchu Abdication and the Powers, 1908-1912. California, Berkeley, 1934. 590p.

Discusses the lack of support of the foreign powers for the Manchu dynasty. Concerning Japan the author asserts that "Japanese policy was directed, by means of ententes, to insure Tokyo's paramount role in the Far East and its greatest influence with the Chinese government."

Rel.Publ.: The Manchu Abdication and the Powers, 1908-1912: An Episode in Pre-War Diplomacy: A Study of the Role of Foreign Diplomacy during the Reign of Hsüan-T'ung. Berkeley: University of California Press, 1935. xiii, 497p.

966
BEE, Benjamin Ming-chu. The Leasing of Kiaochow: A Study in Diplomacy and Imperialism. Harvard, 1935. vii, 450p. AB: Harvard University. Summary of Theses ...1935. p.136-39.

"A detailed examination of the diplomatic history of the leasing of Kiaochow from the preparations during the Sino-Japanese War to the conclusion of the convention of March 1898." Information on Sino-Japanese and on German-Japanese relations is included.

Rel.Publ.: "Origins of German Far Eastern Policy," Chinese Social and Political Science Review, 21 (Apr. 1937), 65-97.

967
SWEN, Wen-ming. Étude sur les traités politiques sino-étrangers [A Study of China's Political Treaties with Foreign Countries]. Paris, 1936. Text in French.

Studies the conclusion of these treaties from an historical standpoint, examines the politics involved in treaty revision, and investigates the theoretical and legal foundations for revising the unequal treaties. Contains considerable information on Japan.

Rel.Publ.: Étude...étrangers. Paris: P. Bossuet, 1936. 255p.

968
MILLER, Jessie Ashworth. China in American Policy and Opinion, 1906-1909. Clark, 1940. 340, xvi p. AB: Clark University. Thesis Abstracts-1940. p.24-29.

Analyzes Japanese-American as well as Sino-American relations and often highlights the issue of Japanese interests in China.

969
CHEN, Changbin. La Presse française et les questions chinoises (1894-1901): Étude sur la rivalité des puissances étrangères en Chine [The French Press and the Chinese Questions, 1894-1901: A Study of Foreign Power Rivalry in China]. Paris, 1941. Text in French.

See especially Ch.1, "The French Press and the Sino-Japanese War" (p.9-31), dealing with the Korean question and the ensuing conflict and with the attitudes of the Western powers at the outbreak of the war; and Ch.3, "The French Press and the Triple Intervention" (p.55-78), focusing on the Treaty of Shimonoseki and on French reactions to it.

Rel.Publ.: La Presse...Chine. Paris: Impr. R. Foulon, 1941. 208p.

CRIST, David S. Russia's Manchurian Policy, 1895-1905. 1941. See no.1316.

970
ZABRISKIE, Edward Henry. American-Russian Rivalry in the Far East from 1895 to 1914. Chicago, 1942. 262p.
Includes considerable information on Japanese activities in China and Manchuria as well as on Japan's relations respectively with Russia and the United States. Contents: Tradition of Friendship; The United States and Russia Look Eastward; Friendship Gives Way to Rivalry; Crisis in American-Russian Relations; Roosevelt's Policy of Balanced Antagonisms; Formation of the Anti-American Front in Manchuria; Failure of Dollar Diplomacy in Manchuria.
Rel.Publ.: American...1914. Philadelphia: University of Pennsylvania Press, 1946. vii, 226p.

971
CHEN, Tieh-ming. The Sino-Japanese War, 1894-1895: Its Origin, Development, and Diplomatic Background. California, Berkeley, 1944. 291p.
Contents: Moves and Counter Moves; Japan in Korean Politics; Chinese Ascendency in Korea, 1885-1894; Revival of Japan's Intense Intervention in Korea; Japan's War Preparations and Offensive Diplomacy; Failure of Western Mediation; The Question of War and Peace; The Treaty of Shimonoseki.

972
SUHL, Marga. Die Grossmächte und die chinesische Revolution bis zum Ausbruch des ersten Weltkrieges [The Great Powers and the Chinese Revolution up to the Outbreak of World War One]. Kiel, 1945. 115p. Text in German. Diss. ms. available at Kiel, Universitätsbibliothek, Nr. Tu 45/48.7732.
Includes information on Japan's industrialization, Russo-Japanese relations, the Russo-Japanese War and its influence upon great power politics, and the interests of the great powers (including Japan) in Manchuria.

973
CHANG, Tennyson Po-hsun. China's Revolution, 1911-1912, and Its Foreign Relations: A Study of the Fall of the Manchu Empire and the Founding of the Chinese Republic. Georgetown, 1948. 376p.
The author regards Japan as a copartner of the Western powers in their aggression against China. He describes this development and includes information on the Sino-Japanese War, its origins, and its aftermath.

974
DOTSON, Lillian Ota. The Sino-Japanese War of 1894-1895: A Study in Asian Power Politics. Yale, 1951. 260p. DA 27 (June 1967), 4190-A; UM 67-6898.
Focuses on "the contrasting attitudes and practices of foreign relations of China and Japan during this period."

975
KUO, Sung-ping. Chinese Reaction to Foreign Encroachment: With Special Reference to the First Sino-Japanese War and Its Immediate Aftermath. Columbia, 1953. 331p. DA 14 (Jan. 1954), 99-100; UM 6652.
Contents: The Setting: (a) China's Internal Weaknesses, (b) Onslaught of Western Capitalist-Imperialism, (c) China's First Attempt at Tzu-ch'iang, (d) Sino-Japanese Rivalry Prior to the War; First Encounter with Japan; A Debacle; Peace at all Costs; Veering toward Russia; On the Verge of Partition; Self-Appraisal; Rebuttal against Reform.

976
VEVIER, Charles. The United States and China: Diplomacy and Finance, 1906-1913. Wisconsin, 1953. 146p. AB: University of Wisconsin. Summaries of Doctoral Dissertations. v.14. p.219-20.
Includes a discussion of Japanese resistance to efforts made by Edward Harriman, Willard Straight, and others to expand American financial holdings in China and particularly in Manchuria.
Rel.Publ.: The United...1913. New Brunswick, N.J.: Rutgers University Press, 1955. ix, 229p.; "The Open Door: An Idea in Action, 1906-1913," PHR, 24 (Feb. 1955), 49-62.

977
MALIN, Morton Victor. American Economic Interests in China, 1900-1908. Maryland, 1954. 183p. AB: University of Maryland. Abstracts of Dissertations...for 1952/53 and 1953/54. p.68.
Discusses American economic interests in China and shows how they competed there with the activities of other countries including Japan.

978
BOWER, Leon McKinley. Willard D. Straight and the American Policy in China, 1906-1913. Colorado, 1955. 247p.
Reference is constantly made to Japanese interests and activities in China during these years.

ROSEN, Oscar. German-Japanese Relations, 1894-1902: A Study of European Imperialism in the Far East. 1956. See no.1259.

979
GILLIN, Donald George. Tradition and Revolution in Modern China: Yen Hsi-shan in Shansi Province 1911-1930. Stanford, 1959. 249p. DA 20 (Aug. 1959), 651-52; UM 59-2817.
A study of the career and regime of one of the most prominent of the Chinese warlords, Yen Hsi-shan (1883-1960). Included within the dissertation is information on Yen's studies at the Imperial Military Academy in Tokyo and on the impact of Japan's modernization and development upon his own ideas and actions.
Rel.Publ.: Warlord: Yen Hsi-shan in Shansi Province, 1911-1949. Princeton: Princeton University Press, 1967. xiv, 334p.; "Portrait of a Warlord: Yen Hsi-hsan in Shansi Province, 1911-1930," JAS, 19 (Mar. 1960), 289-306; "Education and Militarism in Modern China: Yen Hsi-shan in Shansi Province, 1911-1930," Journal of Modern History, 34 (June 1962), 161-67; "China's First Five-Year Plan: Industrialization under the Warlords as Reflected in the Policies of Yen Hsi-shan in Shansi Province, 1930-1937," JAS, 24 (Feb. 1965), 245-59.

980
RAWLINSON, John Lang. The Chinese Navy, 1839-1895. Harvard, 1959. xii, 891p. (2v.). AB: 5p. summary appended to diss. ms.
See Ch.15, "Selective Commentary on the Sino-Japanese War, 1894-1895" (p.721-814): "The Feng-tao Fight and the Problem of Strategy; the Yalu Battle, September 17, 1894; the End of Li Hung-chang's Fleet; Rewards and Punishments."
Rel.Publ.: China's Struggle for Naval Development,

1839-1895. Cambridge: Harvard University Press, 1967. xii, 318p. (Harvard East Asian Series, 25)

981
CHENG, Shelley Hsien. The T'ung-meng-hui: Its Organization, Leadership, and Finances, 1905-1912. Washington, Seattle, 1962. 391p. DA 23 (Dec. 1962), 2105-06; UM 62-6625.

Inasmuch as the T'ung-meng-hui was founded in Tokyo in 1905 and its nucleus was the Tokyo student group, the author devotes considerable attention to the party's activities in Japan.

Rel.Publ.: "The T'ung-meng-hui and Its Financial Supporters, 1905-1912," in University of Malaya, Chinese Language Society, Journal, 2 (1963/1964), 43-126.

982
KELLY, John S. A Forgotten Conference: The Negotiations at Peking, 1900-1901. Genève, 1962. 193p.

A study of the diplomatic conference that was held subsequent to the Boxer revolt. Constant reference is made to Japan.

Rel.Publ.: A Forgotten...1901. Genève: Droz, 1963. 192p. (Travaux de droit, d'économie, et de sociologie, 5)

983
LUNG, Chang. La Chine à l'aube du 20e siècle: Les relations depuis la guerre sino-japonaise jusqu'à la guerre russo-japonaise [China at the Dawn of the Twentieth Century: China's Diplomatic Relations with the Powers between the Sino-Japanese and Russo-Japanese Wars]. Fribourg, 1962. Text in French.

Includes very lengthy discussions of the Korean question and the Sino-Japanese War and of the Manchurian question and the Russo-Japanese War.

Rel.Publ.: La Chine...japonaise. Paris: Nouvelles éditions latines, 1962. 503p.

BERNAL, Martin G. Chinese Socialism to 1913. 1966. See no.618.

984
HUANG, Philip Chung-chih. A Confucian Liberal: Liang Ch'i-ch'ao in Action and Thought. Washington, Seattle, 1966. 251p. DA 27 (Mar. 1967), 2988-89-A; UM 67-2166.

"This study traces and accounts for the changes in Liang Ch'i-ch'ao's (1873-1929) thinking from 1890 to 1929. It examines the sources of inspiration for Liang's ideas and analyzes the interactions between Liang's Confucian and liberal ideas." Included within the dissertation is an examination of Liang's writings about Meiji Japan and Japanese thinkers. The mass of contemporary Japanese police reports on Liang, moreover, are used extensively by the author.

985
RANKIN, Mary Backus. Student Revolutionaries in Shanghai and Chekiang 1902-1907. Harvard, 1966. v, 458p. (2v.) AB: 4p. summary appended to diss. ms.

Ch.2, "The Tokyo Influence" (p.13-34), and Ch.3, "Ideology of the Student Revolutionaries" (p.35-72), in particular contain information on the Japanese influence on Chinese students in the early 1900's.

Rel.Publ.: Early Chinese Revolutionaries: Radical Intellectuals in Shanghai and Chekiang, 1902-1911. Cambridge: Harvard University Press, forthcoming.

986
CHANG, Hao. Liang Ch'i-ch'ao's Early Intellectual Life: 1873-1903. Harvard, 1967. ii, 472p.

For information on Liang's sojourn in 1898 and thereafter, see p.167-93.

987
KAHN, Helen Dodson. The Great Game of Empire: Willard D. Straight and American Far Eastern Policy. Cornell, 1968. 599p. DA 29 (Dec. 1968), 1848-A; UM 68-15,750.

An examination of American East Asian policy between 1904 and 1913 through a biography of Willard D. Straight (1880-1928), "an important figure in the formulation and execution of American Far Eastern policy" who worked during those years as Consul General in Manchuria, acting chief of the United States State Department's Far Eastern Affairs Division, and representative of American business interests in China. Japan's efforts to build up her position in Manchuria during the years immediately following the Russo-Japanese War and American attempts to prevent her from completely dominating the region form one of the major themes of the entire dissertation.

1911-1931

See also International Relations--China/1894-1931 (pages 113-17) and International Relations--China/World War I, the Shantung Controversy, and the Washington Conference (pages 121-25)

988
TUPPER, Eleanor. American Sentiment toward Japan, 1904-1924. Clark, 1929. 532p. AB: Clark University. Thesis Abstracts-1929. p.39-43.

Focuses on the attitudes of the American public towards Japanese expansion in East Asia and Japanese immigration to the United States.

Rel.Publ.: Japan in American Public Opinion [by] Eleanor Tupper and George E. McReynolds. New York: Macmillan, 1937. xix, 465p.

989
PARK, No-yong. China in the League of Nations: A Chapter on China's Foreign Relations. Harvard, 1932. v, 299p. AB: Harvard University. Summaries of Theses... 1932. p.142-46.

Includes information on Sino-Japanese relations. See especially Ch.1, "China's Entry into the League" (p.10-47), which focuses on the Shantung Question, and Ch.2, "China in the Commission on the Covenant" (p.48-58), which focuses on the discussion of the Monroe Doctrine and the Japanese Race Equality Clause.

DORFMAN, Ben D. The Currencies of the Northeastern Provinces of China (Manchuria). 1933. See no.762.

990
CHEN, Tsung-ching. Les Relations commerciales entre la Chine et le Japon depuis l'avènement de la République chinoise à nos jours [The Commercial Relations between China and Japan since the Establishment of the Chinese Republic]. Paris, 1936. Text in French.

A study of the trade, the manner in which it was carried on, the efforts of Japan to penetrate the Chinese market, and the influence of politics (treaties, boycotts) on Sino-Japanese relations.

Rel.Publ.: Les Relations...jours. Paris: P. Bossuet, 1936. ix, 333p.

991
VERHAGE, William. The Negotiation of International Public Loans to China, 1895-1920: With Reference to the Theory and Practice of International Cooperation. Minnesota, 1940. 627p. AB: University of Minnesota. Summaries of Ph.D. Theses. v.4 (1949), p.251-55.

Includes considerable information on Japanese loans and investments in China after 1909 and on Western efforts to check Japanese ambitions there during this period.

992
WATKINS, James Thomas, IV. China and the League of Nations, 1919-1935. Stanford, 1941. AB: Stanford University. Abstracts of Dissertations, 1940/1941. p.203-06.

Sino-Japanese issues brought before the League of Nations during the period covered are examined within the dissertation.

WU, Teh-yao. The Balance of Power in the Far East, 1921-1931. 1946. See no.844.

993
CHAN, Yu-lai. A History of the Alien Conquests of China through the Liao Area. Georgetown, 1951. 419p. AB: United States Department of State, External Research Staff. Abstracts of Completed Doctoral Dissertations for the Academic Year 1950/1951. p.342-45.

Includes a study of Japanese expansionist activities in Manchuria during the first half of the twentieth century.

994
PU, Shu. The Consortium Reorganization Loan to China 1911-1914: An Episode in Pre-War Diplomacy and International Finance. Michigan, 1951. 693p. AB: Microfilm Abstracts, 11 (1951), 326; UM 2446.

A detailed discussion of the six power consortium loan to the Yuan Shih-kai government which includes information on Japan's participation in the consortium. Contents: Origins of the Consortium, 1895-October 9, 1911; The Chinese Revolution of 1911 and the Powers, October 10, 1911-February 12, 1912; Negotiations in Peking: The Reorganization Loan, February 13-July 15, 1912; Negotiations in Europe: The Six Power Consortium, February 13-July 15, 1912; The Ups and Downs of the Six Power Consortium, July 16, 1912-January 9, 1913; The "Battle for Advisers," January 10-March 3, 1913; The Conclusion of the Five Power Consortium's Reorganization Loan, March 4-May 10, 1913; The Chinese "Second Revolution" of 1913 and the Powers, May 11-September 12, 1913; The Futile Negotiations for the Second Series of the Reorganization Loan, September 13, 1913-December 1915.

995
OKONISHNIKOV, A. P. Iaponskii imperializm v gody podgotovki vtorzheniia v Severo-Vostochnyi Kitai (Man'chzhuriiu) 1929-1931 gg. [Japanese Imperialism during the Years of Japan's Preparation for the Invasion of Northeast China (Manchuria), 1929-1931]. Moscow, Moskovskii institut vostokovedeniia, 1952. (Candidate of Historical Sciences degree) 322p. Text in Russian. AB: 17p. summary published in 1952.

996
UVAROVA, T. V. Agressivnaia politika iaponskogo imperializma v otnoshenii Kitaia v period 1924-1927 gg. [Japan's Agressive Policy towards China, 1924-1927]. Moscow, Institut vostokovedeniia Akademii nauk SSSR, 1952. (Candidate of Historical Sciences degree) 343p. Text in Russian. AB: 16p. summary published in 1953.

997
LANGDON, Frank Corriston. The Japanese Policy of Expansion in China, 1917-1928. California, Berkeley, 1953. 282p.

Contents: The Period of Sino-Japanese Collaboration (Japan's War Aims, Her Policies with Relation to the Allies, Political Background of China Policy: Tuan Aid Policy, The Financial Policy of Economic and Military Assistance to the Chinese Government to Attain a Sino-Japanese Economic Union, the Strategic Policy of Military Alliance and Cooperation with China, Appraisal of the Policy of 1917 and 1918); Failure of International Cooperation to Unify and Strengthen China; Loss of Japan's Special Position in China Proper (Military Agreement to Siberian Evacuation, Surrender of Japan's Special Position in China, End of Seiyūkai Positive Financial Policy in China); The Positive Approach to China (Rights Recovery Movement, Conciliatory Policy, Tanaka Policy, A Certain Grave Incident: Assassination of Chang Tso-lin, Comparison of Terauchi, Hara, and Tanaka Policies).

Rel.Publ.: "Japan's Failure to Establish Friendly Relations with China in 1917-1918," PHR, 26 (Aug. 1957), 245-58.

998
SOTER, Richard Paul. Wu P'ei-fu: Case Study of a Chinese Warlord. Harvard, 1959. iv, 266p.

Examines Wu's ideological commitments, his role in military affairs, and his relations with "such influential nations as Japan, Soviet Russia, England, and the United States." See especially Ch.6, "Relations with the Japanese" (p.211-51), for information on Sino-Japanese relations during the 1920's and 1930's.

999
SNITWONGSE, Kusuma. United States Policy toward China, 1921-1927. Fletcher, 1960. v, 399p.

See especially Ch.2, "China at the Washington Conference" (p.43-112), for information on Japanese activities in China and on the Shantung controversy.

1000
IRIYE, Akira. American Diplomacy and Sino-Japanese Relations, 1926-1931. Harvard, 1961. iii, 531p. (2v.) AB: 6p. summary appended to diss. ms.

Contents: Pt.1: The Washington System and Chinese Nationalism. Pt.2: American and Japanese Responses: Patience and Watchfulness; Co-existence and Co-prosperity. Pt.3: The Role of the Kuomintang "Moderates": The Nanking Incident; Kuomintang "Moderates" and the Powers. Pt.4: Japan's "Problem of Life and Death": The Eastern Conference; Backdoor Negotiations; The Open Door in Manchuria. Pt.5: The Completion of the Nationalist Revolution: The Worsening of Sino-Japanese Relations; The Last Days of Chang Tso-lin; The Nationalist Unification of China; America between China and Japan. Pt.6: Steps toward Free China: The United States and Chinese Reconstruction; Sino-Japanese Rapprochement.

Rel.Publ.: After Imperialism: The Search for a New Order in the Far East, 1921-1931. Cambridge: Harvard University Press, 1965. viii, 375p. (Harvard East Asian Series, 22); "Shōwa shoki ni okeru Amerika no kyokutō seisaku," in Nihon Kokusai Seiji Gakkai, Kokusai seiji, 1960, no.1, p.104-19; "Chang Hsueh-liang and the Japanese," JAS, 20 (Nov. 1960), 33-43; "Kindai Nihon gaikō no isan," Chūō kōron, 80 (Jan. 1965), 171-205;

"Shidehara Kijūrō to Washinton taisei," Chūō kōron, 80 (May 1965), 370-76.

1001
RAMSDELL, Daniel Bailey. Japan's China Policy, 1929-1931: A Fateful Failure. Wisconsin, 1961. 336p. DA 22 (Dec. 1961), 1968-69; UM 61-5976.

The dissertation "aims to show how the basic drive of Japan to expand in Asia together with the Japanese constitutional system, in whose framework a fierce struggle for power went on, served to frustrate the conciliatory power of Baron Shidehara and made rapprochement impossible."

Rel.Publ.: "The Nakamura Incident and the Japanese Foreign Office," JAS, 25 (Nov. 1965), 51-67.

1002
CHENG, Emily Hwa. United States Policy during the Chinese Revolution. South Carolina, 1963. 212p. DA 25 (July 1964), 426; UM 64-7306.

Discusses American efforts to prevent Japan as well as other nations from taking advantage of the revolution to advance their own interests in China.

ELMAR, Peter. Die bedeutung Chinas in der deutschen Ostasienpolitik (1911-1917). 1965. See no.1266.

1003
ROY, David Tod. Kuo Mo-jo: The Early Years. Harvard, 1965. v, 249p.

Kuo lived and studied in Japan during the 1910's and 1920's, where he was exposed to various aspects of Japanese and Western civilization. See especially p.52-114.

Rel.Publ.: "Kuo Mo-jo: The Pre-Marxist Phase (1892-1924)," in Harvard University, East Asian Research Center, Papers on China, 12 (1958), 69-146.

1004
FALCONERI, Gennaro Sylvester. Reactions to Revolution: Japanese Attitudes and Foreign Policy toward China, 1924-1927. Michigan, 1967. 456p. DA 28 (June 1968), 4986-87-A; UM 68-7591.

Studies the impact of contemporary events in China upon Japan, the reactions of Japanese military, political and economic groups to these events, Japanese disillusionment with the Wakatsuki government's China policy, and the debate in the Privy Council that brought down the government. Contents: The Post Washington Conference Sino-Japanese Setting and Japan's Foreign Policymaking Bureaucracy; Prelude to Revolution: Strikes in Japanese Industries in China; Prelude to Reaction: The May 30th Period; Reaction to Warlord Unrest in Manchuria: The Kuo Sung-ling Rebellion; Militant Revolution: The Anti-British Kuomintang Northern March; Militant Revolution: The Antiforeign Kuomintang Northern March; Reactions to Revolution: Disenchantment with Non-Intervention; Domestic Reaction: Collapse of the Kenseikai Government.

1005
HUANG, Chinliang Lawrence. Japan's China Policy under Premier Tanaka, 1927-1929. New York, 1968. 306p. DA 30 (May 1970); UM 70-7405.

1006
MUNSON, Vivian Lorraine. American Merchants of Capital in China: The Second Chinese Banking Consortium. Wisconsin, 1968. 197p. DA 30 (July 1969), 252-A; UM 69-966.

A study of the consortium of American, British, French, and Japanese bankers that was formed ca. 1918 for the purpose of cooperative investment in China and an examination of American moves to utilize the consortium as a means to further American policy in East Asia during the ensuing years--primarily at Japanese expense.

1007
MORTON, William Fitch. Traditional Foreign Policy and National Revolution: The Tanaka Cabinet and China, 1927-1929. Columbia, 1969. ix, 510p.

Contents: A Half-Century of Sino-Japanese Relations: A Summary; The New Trend of the Times; Opposition to the Kenseikai Cabinet, Winter and Spring 1927; China Policy and the Tanaka Cabinet: (1) Early Phase, (2) Second Phase.

Rel.Publ.: "The Tsinan Incident, 1928-1929: Failure of Tanaka's 'Positive Policy' in China," in Columbia University, East Asian Institute, Researches in the Social Sciences on Japan, 2 (1959), 82-90.

1008
WANG, Chi. Young Marshall Chang Hsueh-liang and Manchuria: 1928-1931. Georgetown, 1969. 235p. DA 30 (Apr. 1970); UM 70-5926.

World War I, the Shantung Controversy, and the Washington Conference

See also International Relations--Disarmament during the 1920's and 1930's (pages 107-09).

1009
FOTH, Werner. Der politische Kampf im Fernen Osten und Chinas finanzielle Schwäche [The Political Struggle in the Far East and China's Financial Weakness]. Berlin, 1919. Text in German. The dissertation in its published form is available at Berlin West, Staatsbibliothek Preussischer Kulturbesitz, Nr. Ah 7856. (In: Berlin, Philosophische Diss. 1919, Bd 2, Eh-G).

A study of the struggle that was waged among Japan, Great Britain, the United States, Russia, and China. The author describes Japanese policy towards China during World War One in great detail, focusing on Japanese goals, the Twenty-One Demands, Japanese relations with the countries surrounding China, the development of the Japanese merchant marine, and the entire situation as of 1918.

Rel.Publ.: Der politische...Schwäche. Gotha: F.A. Perthes, 1919. xi, 118p.

1010
WEI, Sidney Kok. International Relationship in China and Its Ethical, Social, and Political Interpretation. Chicago, 1920. 103, xviii p. AB: University of Chicago. Abstracts of Theses, Humanistic Series. v.1 (1922/23), p.67-75.

Includes arguments for the restoration of Chinese sovereignty over Japanese-occupied Shantung.

1011
HICKMANN, Ernst. Der Einfluss des Weltkrieges auf den chinesischen Aussenhandel [The Influence of World War I on China's Foreign Trade]. Berlin, 1921. 193p. Text in German. AB: Jahrbuch der Dissertationen der Philosophischen Fakultät Berlin. 1921/1922. II, p.74-83. Diss. ms. available at Marburg/Lahn, Staatsbibliothek Preussischer Kulturbesitz, Nr. MS 27/248.

The dissertation includes considerable information on the growth of Sino-Japanese trade during the war (the enlargement of Japan's merchant marine, the expansion of her overseas markets, and the ways in which Japan acquired raw materials from China), on the elimination of European commercial competition in Asia, and on Japan's aggressive policies vis-à-vis China.

1012
DONOHUE, James Lane. The Shantung Question. American, 1922. 120p.
Contents: Beginnings of the Shantung Question; The Development of Japanese Influence in China; Japan and the World War; The Shantung Question.

1013
YEN, En-tsung. Diplomatic History Pertaining to Shantung since Germany's Advent into the Far Eastern Politics to the Close of the Washington Conference. George Washington, 1922. iii, 301p. (2v).
Includes considerable information on Japanese activities in China during the early 1900's.
Rel.Publ.: The Open Door Policy. Boston: Straford, 1923. vi, 191p.

1014
BUELL, Raymond Leslie. The Washington Conference. Princeton, 1923. xiii, 461p.
A chronological account of the Washington Conference. Contents: Forces in the Background (Nibbling at Asia, A Japanese Monroe Doctrine, Militarism in Japan, The Anglo-Japanese Alliance); The Conference (The Passing of the Battleship, The Four-Power Treaty, Future Weapons of War, The Defeat of China, Propositions in Principle, The Crux of the Situation).
Rel.Publ.: The Washington Conference. New York: D. Appleton, 1922. xiii, 461p.

1015
GODSHALL, Wilson Leon. The International Aspects of the Shantung Question. Pennsylvania, 1923. ii, 172p.
Contents: Foreign Encroachments in China; The Province of Shantung; Shantung, 1914-1919; Shantung in the Peace Negotiations; Shantung in the Disarmament Conference.
Rel.Publ.: The International...Question. Philadelphia, 1923. ii, 172p.

1016
WOU, Saofong. La Chine et la conférence de Washington [China and the Washington Conference]. Paris, 1927. 232p. Text in French.
A study of the various issues raised by the Chinese delegation to the Washington Conference. See especially Ch.11, "The Question of Shantung and Japan's Twenty-One Demands" (p.154-84).

1017
HICKS, Charles Roger. Foreign Control in Shantung Province, China. Clark, 1931. iii, 249p. AB: Clark University. Thesis Abstracts-1931. p.20-24.
Focuses on the Japanese efforts to secure control of Shantung, 1914-1922.
Rel.Publ.: Japan's Entry into the War, 1914. Reno: University of Nevada Press, 1944. 8p.

1018
DAI, Poeliu. The Diplomacy of Cooperative Action in China: With Special Reference to the Washington Conference and Its Aftermath. Johns Hopkins, 1934. 172p.

1019
YONG, Thaddée Ann-yuen. Chine et Japon à la conférence de la paix [China and Japan at the Peace Conference]. Louvain, 1934. Text in French.
Actually a study of Sino-Japanese relations, 1914-1919, with considerable focus on Japan's seizure of Kiaochow, the "21 Demands," Japan's role in the attempt to restore the monarchy (1915), and the secret Sino-Japanese treaties of 1918-1919; as well as information on the questions of Shantung and the "21 Demands" that were taken up at the peace conference.
Rel.Publ.: Chine...paix. Lophem-lez-Bruges: Abbaye de Saint-André, 1934. viii, 304p. (Université catholique de Louvain. Collection de l'Institut des sciences politiques et sociales)

1020
LAFARGUE, Thomas Edward. China and the World War. Stanford, 1935. 357p. AB: Stanford University. Abstracts of Dissertations. 1934/35. p.119-24.
Studies the Japanese seizure of Kiaochow, the 21 demands, Western pressures upon China to enter the war, the Peace Conference, and the Shantung Question.
Rel.Publ.: China...War. Stanford: Stanford University Press, 1937. x, 278p. (Hoover War Library Publications, 12); "The Entrance of China into the World War," PHR, 5 (1936), 222-33.

1021
KANE, Albert Eli. China, the Powers, and the Washington Conference. Columbia, 1938. vi, 233p.
Contents: Some Cooperative Elements in China's International Relations; Attitudes toward Foreign Supervision; The Four Power Treaty; Some Problems Affecting China's Territorial Integrity and Administrative Independence; The Nine Power Treaty; Estimates of the Conference.
Rel.Publ.: China...Conference. Shanghai: Commercial Press, 1937. vi, 233p.

1022
GAGE, Daniel James. Paul S. Reinsch and Sino-American Relations. Stanford, 1939. 593p. AB: Stanford University. Abstracts of Dissertations, 1938/1939. p.156-59.
The dissertation focuses on Reinsch's activities as a diplomat to China and includes considerable information on his efforts to check Japanese expansion in that country during World War I.

1023
DULL, Paul Shirley. An Analysis of the Open Door Policy of the United States as Incorporated in the Washington Treaties, 1922-1928. Washington, Seattle, 1940. 354p. AB: University of Washington. Abstracts of Theses and Faculty Bibliography. v.5, p.325-27.
Includes information on Japanese participation in the Nine Power Treaty.
Rel.Publ.: "America's Foreign Policy and the China Trade," Oregon Business Review, 6 (Mar. 1947), 1-3.

1024
YUI, Ming. The Principles and Policies of the Nine Power Treaty of 1922 in the Light of Subsequent Developments. Oxford, 1941. 497p.
Contents: The Setting of the Washington Conference; The Making of the Nine Power Treaty; Analysis (Article by Article, Political and Strategic Significance); Application of Principles and Policies to the Problems at Washington (Procedure Used, Foreign Post Offices, Armed Troops, and Radio Stations, Customs Tariff, Extra-

territoriality, Leased Territories); Application during the Period of Unification; Revision of Treaties [1927-1930]; The Sino-Japanese Conflict of 1931-1932; The Brussels Conference.

1025
JENKINS, Warren Gard. The Foreign Policy of the Chicago Tribune, 1914-1917: A Program of National Self-Interest. Wisconsin, 1943. ii, 391p. AB: University of Wisconsin. Summaries of Doctoral Dissertations. v.8, p.111-13.
A discussion of the Tribune's fears of Japanese expansion in the Pacific and in Asia and of suggested American countermoves is included.

1026
TEKUT'EVA, E. T. Agressivnaia politika Iaponii v Kitae v period pervoi mirovoi voiny [Japan's Aggressive Policy in China during the First World War]. Tomsk, Tomskii gosudarstvennyi universitet imeni V. V. Kuibysheva, 1943. (Candidate of Historical Sciences degree) 111p. Text in Russian.

1027
BRODSKII, Roman Mikhailovich. 21 trebovanie Iaponii k Kitaiu v 1915 godu [Japan's Twenty-One Demands, 1915]. Leningrad, Leningradskii gosudarstvennyi universitet imeni A. A. Zhdanova, 1947. (Candidate of Historical Sciences degree) 380p. Text in Russian.

1028
TOMPKINS, Pauline. American-Russian Relations in the Far East, 1914-1933: A Study of American Far Eastern Policy and Its Effect on Russian Interest. Fletcher, 1948. iv, 466p.
Considerable information on American-Japanese and Russo-Japanese relations is found throughout the thesis. Contents: Traditions and Realities, 1775-1914; War, Revolution, and Intervention, 1914-1918; America, Russia, and Japan, 1918-1925; America, Russia, and China, 1919-1929; America and Russia in Asia, 1931-1933.
Rel.Publ.: American...Interest. New York: Macmillan, 1949. xiv, 426p.

1029
PRESCOTT, Francis Calvin. The Lansing-Ishii Agreement. Yale, 1949. 255p. DA 27 (Sept. 1966), 734-35-A; UM 66-8542.
Traces the course of American-Japanese relations from the signing of the Lansing-Ishii Agreement in November 1917 to its termination at the Washington Conference. Discusses the needs of the Allies during the war and the problems that arose out of America's traditional open door policy in China.

1030
VINSON, John Chalmers. The Senate and the Washington Conference, 1921-1922. Duke, 1949. 414p.
Studies the role of the senate in shaping American foreign policy during the early 1920's. Constant reference is made to Japan and to Japanese-American relations.
Rel.Publ.: The Parchment Peace: The United States Senate and the Washington Conference, 1921-1922. Athens: University of Georgia Press, 1955. xi, 259p.; "The Drafting of the Four-Power Treaty of the Washington Conference," Journal of Modern History, 25 (Mar. 1953), 40-47; "The Annulment of the Lansing-Ishii Agreement," PHR, 27 (Feb. 1958), 57-69; "The Imperial Conference of 1921 and the Anglo-Japanese Alliance," PHR, 31 (Aug. 1962), 257-66.

1031
LI, Tien-yi. Woodrow Wilson's China Policy, 1913-1917. Yale, 1950. 313p.
Includes an analysis of the new imperialistic role of Japan in China that developed as the result of the shift in the balance of power at the beginning of World War I. See especially Ch.5, "The Threatened Japanese Protectorate" (p.105-63).
Rel.Publ.: Woodrow...1917. Kansas City, Mo.: University of Kansas City Press, 1952. 268p.

CURRY, Roy W. Woodrow Wilson and the Far East. 1952. See no.1386.

1032
NIKOLAEVA, O. S. Razvitie iaponskogo imperializma v gody 1-oi mirovoi voiny [The Development of Japanese Imperialiam during the First World War]. Leningrad, Leningradskii gosudarstvennyi universitet imeni A. A. Zhdanova, 1953. (Candidate of Historical Sciences degree) 502p. Text in Russian. AB: 15p. summary published in 1954.

1033
NAVLITSKAIA, Galina Bronislavovna. Iaponiia na Vashingtonskoi konferentsii, 1921-1922 gg. [Japan at the Washington Conference, 1921-1922]. Moscow, Moskovskii gosudarstvennyi universitet imeni M. V. Lomonosova, 1954. (Candidate of Historical Sciences degree) xxi, 255p. Text in Russian. AB: 15p. summary published in 1954.

1034
KHODOSH, I. A. Amerikano-iaponskie imperialisticheskie protivorechiia i shan'dunskii vopros na Parizhskoi mirnoi konferentsii 1919 g. [American-Japanese Imperialistic Contradictions and the Shantung Question at the Paris Peace Conference of 1919]. Moscow, Moskovskii gosudarstvennyi universitet imeni M. V. Lomonosova, 1955. (Candidate of Historical Sciences degree) 268p. Text in Russian.

1035
BEERS, Burton Floyd. Robert Lansing and the Far East, 1914-1917. Duke, 1956. 283p.
Studies the East Asian policy of Woodrow Wilson's administration by focusing on the ideas for dealing with East Asian problems which Lansing developed and sought to incorporate into official United States policy.
Rel.Publ.: Vain Endeavor: Robert Lansing's Attempts to End the American-Japanese Rivalry. Durham, N.C.: Duke University Press, 1962. 207p. (Duke Historical Publications); "Robert Lansing's Proposed Bargain with Japan," PHR, 26 (Nov. 1957), 391-400.

1036
TILLMAN, Seth Phillip. Cooperation and Conflict between the United States and the British Empire at the Paris Peace Conference of 1919. Fletcher, 1959. ix, 597p.
See Ch.16, "Anglo-American Approaches to the Claims of Japan: Racial Equality in the Covenant and the Shantung Controversy" (p.447-69). Examines the Background of the Japanese claims, the North Pacific Islands, and the controversies over the proposed racial equality clause in the covenant and over Shantung.
Rel.Publ.: Anglo-American Relations at the Paris

Peace Conference of 1919. Princeton: Princeton University Press, 1961. xiv, 442p.

1037
ERICH, Wolfgang. Die amerikanische Chinapolitik von 1911 bis 1918 [America's China Policy, 1911-1918]. Kiel, 1961. v, 385p. Text in German. Diss. ms. available at Kiel, Universitätsbibliothek, Nr. TU.62.5618.

Focuses on the American position vis-à-vis Japanese wartime policy in China and the 21 Demands; the American-Japanese rivalry in China and the Lansing-Ishii Agreement; and Japan's successful "Yen diplomacy" as well as America's return to Consortium policy.

BURNS, Roy G., Jr. American-Japanese Relations, 1920-1925. 1962. See no.1390.

ASADA, Sadao. Japan and the United States, 1915-1925. 1963. See no.1391.

FRY, Michael G. Anglo-American-Canadian Relations: With Special Reference to Far Eastern and Naval Issues, 1918-1922. 1963. See no.1288.

1038
YIM, Kwanha. Japanese Policy toward China during World War I. Fletcher, 1963. vii, 226p. AB: 3p. summary appended to diss. ms.

Asserts that "Japanese policy during this period was, by and large, guided by moderate aims reflecting the limits of Japanese power....The thesis is divided into seven chapters: Ch.1, 'Japan Enters the War;' Ch.2, 'The Coming of the Twenty-One Demands;' Ch.3, 'The Sino-Japanese Negotiations of 1915;' Ch.4, 'Yuan Shih-k'ai and the Japanese;' Ch.5, 'The Search for a New Direction;' Ch.6, 'When the Chips Were Down;' and Ch.7, 'A Balance Sheet.' The climactic episode here is the fall of Yuan Shih-k'ai, which...can be regarded as the turning point. Before the fall of Yuan, conditions approximated normalcy. Immediately after his fall, chaos prevailed. Partly for this reason, the focus of the narratives in the first three chapters is primarily on the diplomatic manouvers, while in the later chapters it is broadened to take into account the intricacies of political development."

Rel.Publ.: "Yuan Shih-k'ai and the Japanese," JAS, 24 (Nov. 1964), 63-73.

1039
BIRN, Donald S. Britain and France at the Washington Conference, 1922. Columbia, 1964. 324p. DA 26 (Oct. 1965), 2156; UM 65-7340.

Contents: Naval Rivalries and Post-War Politics; The Calling of the Washington Conference; The Opening Stages of the Conference; Capital Ships and Naval Supremacy; The Submarine Controversy and Settlement in Asia; Public Opinion and the Press at the Conference; The Conference and the Quest for European Security; Aftermath of the Conference.

1040
PETER, Elmar. Die Bedeutung Chinas in der deutschen Ostasienpolitik (1911-1917) [The Importance of China in German East Asian Policy, 1911-1917]. Hamburg, 1965. Text in German. The dissertation in its published form is available at Marburg/Lahn, Staatsbibliothek Preussischer Kulturbesitz, Nr. Hsn 64,332; also available at the University of Michigan, General Library, no. 33,760.

Germany and the great powers in China, 1894-1911; Germany and China from the Chinese revolution to the outbreak of World War I; German ties with China during World War I; Japan's declaration of war against China and her entrance into the war; German East Asian policy during the first years of the war; efforts to reach a German-Japanese accord; the Twenty-one Demands and the reactions of the great powers; the rupture in Germany's relations with China; Germany's East Asian policy, 1911-1917: Its goals, methods, and results.

Rel.Publ.: Die Bedeutung...1917. Hamburg, 1965. vi, 296p.

1041
PUGACH, Noel Harvey. Progress, Prosperity, and the Open Door: The Ideas and Career of Paul S. Reinsch. Wisconsin, 1967. 630p. DA 28 (Feb. 1968), 3120-A; UM 67-12,148.

"Explores Reinsch's assumptions, his ideas and programs, and examines his method of operation" during the period he served as United States Minister to China and as adviser to the Chinese government (1913-1922). Includes considerable information on Japanese activities in China and on Japanese-American relations during the period.

Rel.Publ.: "Making the Open Door Work: Paul S. Reinsch in China, 1913-1919," PHR, 38 (May 1969), 157-76.

1042
RATTAN, Sumitra. The Four-Power Treaty of 1921 and the American National Interest. American, 1967. 282p. DA 28 (Oct. 1967), 1377-78-A; UM 67-12,040.

"An examination of the forces which prompted the Treaty and a narration of the negotiations as well as the results of the Four-Power Treaty" that were concluded at the time of the Washington Conference. The author argues that "the question of disarmament was intimately connected with the Anglo-Japanese alliance" and with the controversy over the awarding of a Pacific Mandate to Japan.

1043
CHI, Madeleine Sung-chun, R.S.C.J. The Chinese Question during the First World War. Fordham, 1968. 409p. DA 29 (Aug. 1968), 538-A; UM 68-11,008.

Focuses on the Japanese exploitation of China and on Japanese attempts to gain a paramount position on the mainland during World War I. Contents: The Outbreak of the War in the Far East; The Japanese Challenge: The Twenty-One Demands; Yuan Shih-kai's Monarchical Scheme; The European Diplomatic Retreat (French Desire for Japanese Military Assistance, Russia and Japan, 1914-1916, British-Japanese Negotiations Affecting China); The American Compromise; China's Entry into the War, 1917.

Rel.Publ.: The Chinese...War. Cambridge: Harvard University Press, 1970. (Harvard East Asian Monographs, 31)

1044
STREMSKI, Richard. Britain's China Policy 1920-1928. Wisconsin, 1968. 314p. DA 29 (Sept. 1968), 859-A; UM 68-9133.

Includes information on Britain's Japan policy. See especially Ch.2, "The Anglo-Japanese Alliance and the Washington Conference."

1045
GRANAT, Stanley Jerome. Chinese Participation at the Washington Conference, 1921-1922. Indiana, 1969.

384p. DA 30 (May 1970); UM 70-7525.

SARGENT, Thomas A. America, Britain, and the Nine Power Treaty: A Study of Inter-War Diplomacy and Great Power Relationships. 1969. See no.1065.

1931-1945: General

See also International Relations--China/The Manchurian Incident and the Shanghai Crisis (pages 127-31) and International Relations--Sino-Japanese War (pages 131-32).

CHANG, Tao-shing. International Controversies over the Chinese Eastern Railway. 1934. See no.944.

KUO, Chao-lin. Die Macht Bewerbung von Japan und U.S.A. in Ost-Asie. 1938. See no.949.

1046
TCHENG, Kia-kan. Le Conflit sino-japonais et l'équilibre des puissances en Extrême-Orient [The Sino-Japanese Conflict and the Balance of Power in East Asia]. Dijon, 1938. Text in French.

Contents: China's Foreign Relations; Japanese Expansion before 1931; The Respective Positions of the Powers with Regard to Sino-Japanese Relations; The Power Balance in East Asia: The Washington Conference; Upsetting the Balance of Power: Japanese Infiltration into China (1931-1937); Japanese Violations of International Law; The Reestablishment of the Balance of Power in East Asia Following Japanese Aggression There: The Brussels Conference of 1937.

Rel.Publ.: Le Conflit...Extrême-Orient. Dijon: Bernigaud et Privat, 1938. 190p.

1047
HOGAN, Willard Newton. International Violence and Third States since the World War. Chicago, 1939. 147p.

The League of Nations' application of sanctions against Japan is touched upon, and the American neutrality legislation of 1937 and the principle of differential treatment with regard to the Sino-Japanese conflict are studied.

Rel.Publ.: Chicago, 1941. (Abstract) "Private edition, distributed by the University of Chicago libraries;" International Conflict and Collective Security: The Principle of Concern in International Organization. Lexington: University of Kentucky Press, 1955. 202p.

JENZOWSKI, Siegfried. Die chinesisch-japanischen Boykottfälle als völkerrechtliches Problem. 1939. See no.950.

1048
PECHOTA, Henry Lee. Neutrality Legislation and the Foreign Policy of the United States with Special Reference to Neutrality Statutes of 1935, 1936, and 1937. Southern California, 1939. 644p. AB: University of Southern California. Abstracts of Dissertations for...1939. p.107-10.

Part of the dissertation analyzes the application of neutrality legislation to the Sino-Japanese conflict.

CH'EN, Yao-sheng. The International Settlement at Shanghai. 1940. See no.1695.

1049
FRIEDMAN, Irving Sigmund. British Relations with China, 1931-1939. Columbia, 1940. xv, 255p.

Focuses on "Great Britain's attempt to maintain her position in China during this period, in which Japanese aggression threatened China's independence and British interests in China." Includes considerable information on Anglo-Japanese relations.

Rel.Publ.: British...1939. New York: Institute of Pacific Relations, 1940. xv, 255p. (Inquiry Series)

1050
WEI, Henry. The Sino-Japanese Hostilities and International Law. Chicago, 1942. 253p.

The study sketches the development of these hostilities and examines Japan's plea for self-defense, the attitudes of third states, the status of the puppet governments, and the problem of responsibility for damages in the hostilities.

CAUSEY, Beverley D., Jr. German Policy towards China, 1918-1941. 1943. See no.1255.

1051
WEISS, Karl Günther. Ostasien und der Wandel des Völkerrechts [East Asia and the Change in International Law]. München, 1944. xvi, 313p. Text in German. Diss. ms. available at München, Universitätsbibliothek, Nr. U 1944.6537.

Studies political events in East Asia during the first four decades of the twentieth century, examines the position of China, the problem of neutrality, and --from the standpoint of international law (the League, the Brussels Conference)--the Sino-Japanese Conflict; and describes the political development of the "Greater East Asia Co-Prosperity Sphere" concept.

MASLENNIKOV, V. A. Iapono-kitaiskie ekonomicheskie otnosheniia, 1860-1940 gg. 1947. See no.951.

1052
SHEN, Yun-kung. American Official Attitudes toward Governments in China, 1898-1947. Wisconsin, 1948. iv, 217p. AB: University of Wisconsin. Summaries of Doctoral Dissertations. v.10. p.349-51.

Includes a discussion of American "non-recognition of Manchukuo in 1932, of the Japanese-made autonomy in north China in 1935, and of the puppet regimes in occupied China" in 1937 and thereafter.

1053
WANG, Samuel Hsuan. The Sino-Japanese War and American Far Eastern Policy, 1931-1941. Cornell, 1948. 373p.

Contents: The Background of the Manchurian Crisis; The Outbreak of the Manchurian Crisis; The Aggravation of the Situation; The Establishment of Manchukuo; The Sino-Japanese Rapprochement; The North China Independence Movement; The Sino-Japanese Negotiations, 1936; The Outbreak of the Sino-Japanese War; Japan's New Order in East Asia; Japan's Southward Move.

1054
CHOU, I-kua. The American Policy in China, 1929-1939. Fletcher, 1949. vi, 352p. AB: Fletcher School of Law and Diplomacy. Thesis Abstract, 1949, no.2.

"Traces the various phases through which the integration of American policy toward China into a foreign policy toward the world as a whole was achieved." "Particular attention is given to the relationship of the United States to the League of Nations during the Manchurian crisis of 1931, and to the so-called 'Middle of the Road' policy of the late nineteen thirties. A comparison has been made between the policies of the Hoover

Administration with those of the Roosevelt period, and ...the study includes the reactions" of Japan and China to American Far Eastern policy. "The scope of the work may be divided into four phases: The Russo-Chinese controversy in 1929, the Manchurian crisis of 1931-1933, the interim between wars, and the undeclared war between China and Japan since 1937."

1055
KAWAHARA, Hattie Masuko. Diplomatic Relations between the United States and Japan from 1931 to 1941. Minnesota, 1949. 424p.
Contents: Introduction: Bases of American and Japanese Policies in the Far East. Pt.1: The Manchurian Crisis: "Cooperative" Efforts at Settlement; American Leadership: The Non-Recognition Doctrine; The Shanghai Controversy; American Rights and Interests under Manchukuo. Pt.2: Pattern for Conflict: Beginnings of the Roosevelt-Hull Policy toward the Far East; The Diplomatic Revolution in Japanese Foreign Policy; Rivalry in China. Pt.3: Prelude to Pearl Harbor: The Sino-Japanese Conflict and American Diplomatic Efforts; Implications of the European War on American-Japanese Relations; Matsuoka Diplomacy and Its Repercussions on American Foreign Policy; The Last Phase.

1056
GRIGG, Richard James. Japanese-American Relations, 1931-1937. Georgetown, 1950. 243p.
Contents: Early Reactions to the Manchurian Incident; American Cooperation with the League of Nations: The October Session at Geneva; General Dawes and the Paris Session of the Council of the League, November 16-December 10; The United States Stands Alone: The Stimson Doctrine of January 7, 1932; The Shanghai Crisis Leads to a New Statement of American Policy; Boycott of Japan?; Secretary Stimson Plays a Leading Role in Compelling Japan to Leave the League of Nations; Secretary Hull Continues the Stimson Policy towards Japan; Japan Moves Forward in North China to Establish a Bulwark of Defense against the Menace of Soviet Influence in East Asia; The American Press Disapproves of the Quarantine against Japan.

1057
LIU, Tzu-chien. Sino-Japanese Diplomacy during the Appeasement Period, 1933-1937. Pittsburgh, 1950. 242p.
Contents: Prelude to Appeasement (May 1933); The Progress of Appeasement (May 1933-May 1935); Crises in Appeasement (May 1935-February 1936); The End of Appeasement (February 1936-July 1937).

CHAN, Yu-lai. A History of the Alien Conquests of China through the Liao Area. 1951. See no.993.

THOMSON, John S. The Government of the International Settlement at Shanghai: A Study in the Politics of an International Area. 1953. See no.1696.

SOTER, Richard P. Wu P'ei-fu: Case Study of a Chinese Warlord. 1959. See no.998.

CROWLEY, James B. Japan's China Policy, 1931-1938: A Study of the Role of the Military in the Determination of Foreign Policy. 1960. See no.666.

1058
GARDNER, Lloyd Calvin, Jr. American Foreign Policy in a Closed World: 1933-1945. Wisconsin, 1960. 385p. DA 21 (Sept. 1960), 604-05; UM 60-3196.
Includes information on American-Japanese relations. See especially Ch.5, "Relations with the World of Colonialism," and Ch.7, "An Unfulfilled Promise: China."
Rel.Publ.: Economic Aspects of New Deal Diplomacy. Madison: University of Wisconsin Press, 1964. ix, 409p.

1059
AKASHI, Yoji. The Boycott and Anti-Japanese National Salvation Movement of the Nanyang Chinese, 1908-1941. Georgetown, 1963. 381p.
Contents: Boycott Movement 1905-1921; National Salvation Movement: Tsinan Incident, 1928; China's Policies towards Nanyang Chinese; Manchurian Incident 1931-1932; Sino-Japanese War (1937-1941) and the Nanyang Chinese National Salvation Movement, First Phase; The Nanyang Chinese Anti-Japanese and National Salvation Movement, Second Phase; Contributions of the Nanyang Chinese National Movement and Its Economic Effectiveness. Note: The term "Nanyang" refers to the Chinese communities of Southeast Asia.
Rel.Publ.: "The Nanyang Chinese Anti-Japanese Boycott Movement, 1908-1928: A Study of Overseas Chinese Nationalism," in International Conference of Asian History, Proceedings (Kuala Lumpur: 1968).

1060
CHEN, Chin-shan. American Recognition and Non-Recognition Policies in China: A Legal, Historical, and Political Analysis. Southern Illinois, 1963. 353p. DA 24 (June 1964), 5520-21; UM 64-4464.
Includes American non-recognition of Manchoukuo and of the Wang Ching-wei regime.

1061
ISRAEL, John Warren. The Chinese Student Movement, 1927-1937. Harvard, 1963. xv, 434p. AB: 7p. summary appended to diss. ms.
Includes information on the Chinese reaction to Japanese aggression in China.
Rel.Publ.: Student Nationalism in China, 1927-1937. Stanford: Stanford University Press, 1966. ix, 253p. (Hoover Institution Publications); The Chinese Student Movement, 1927-1937: A Bibliographical Essay Based on the Resources of the Hoover Institution. Stanford: Hoover Institution on War, Revolution, and Peace, Stanford University, 1959. v, 29p.

1062
BUHITE, Russell Devere. Nelson T. Johnson and American Policy toward China, 1925-1941. Michigan State, 1965. 278p. DA 26 (Feb. 1966), 4600; UM 65-14,197.
Includes considerable information on American reactions to Japanese expansion in China. Contents: The Education of a Diplomat; Nelson Johnson and Chinese Nationalism; Discussing Extraterritoriality; The Chinese Eastern Railway Dispute and the Kellogg Pact; Japanese Aggression in Manchuria, 1931-1932; Johnson and a Stronger Policy toward Japan; Nelson Johnson and United States Silver Policy; From the Outbreak of the Undeclared War to May 1941; In Retrospect.
Rel.Publ.: Nelson...1941. East Lansing: Michigan State University Press, 1969. 163p.; "Nelson Johnson and American Policy toward China, 1925-1928," PHR, 35 (Nov. 1966), 451-66.

1063
GILBERT, Carl L. The Hirota Ministries: An Appraisal. Japan's Relations with China and the U.S.S.R., 1933-1938. Georgetown, 1967. 337p. DA 28 (Feb. 1968),

3108-A; UM 68-1917.

The dissertation examines "the role of Russo-Japanese relations as they bore on the formulation of Japan's policies to 1935," analyzes Hirota Kōki's attempts "to ease tensions with Soviet Russia and to effect a rapprochement with China," traces developments during "the crucial year of 1936," and studies "the deterioration and collapse of Sino-Japanese negotiations" after July 1937.

1064
CHIANG, Wen-hsien. Dohihara Kenji and the Japanese Expansion into China (1931-1937): A Case Study of the Role of a Young Officer in Decision-Making. Pennsylvania, 1969. 336p. [See also addenda entry no. 9A.]

1065
SARGENT, Thomas Andrew. America, Britain, and the Nine Power Treaty: A Study of Inter-War Diplomacy and Great Power Relationships. Fletcher, 1969. ix, 581p. AB: 5p. summary appended to diss. ms.

"The history of the Treaty is traced through the diplomacy of the United States and Great Britain as they carried out their policies in the Far East between World Wars One and Two." Contents: From the Open Door to the Washington Conference; The Washington Conference and the Nine Power Treaty; Treaty Implementation and Post-Conference Diplomacy, 1922-1931; Manchuria and the Nine-Power Treaty; The Sino-Japanese Conflict and the Brussels Conference of 1937; The End of the Nine-Power Treaty: From the Brussels Conference to Pearl Harbor.

Manchurian Incident and the Shanghai Crisis (1931-1933)

See also International Relations--China/1931-1945 (pages 125-27). For events leading up to the Manchurian Incident, see International Relations--China/1894-1931 (pages 113-17) and International Relations--China/1911-1931 (pages 119-21).

1066
ALBRECHT, Dietger. Der chinesisch-japanische Konflikt und das Völkerrecht [The Sino-Japanese Conflict and International Law]. Königsberg, 1933. Text in German. The dissertation in its published form is available at Marburg/Lahn, Staatsbibliothek Preussischer Kulturbesitz, Nr. Fm 3081-41; also at the University of Michigan Law Library.

The dissertation begins with a short description of Japanese treaty rights in Manchuria. It then studies in detail the Sino-Japanese conflict (the Manchurian crisis and the Incident at Shanghai) between September 1931 and May 1933. A legal evaluation of the entire conflict and an examination of the attitudes of the League of Nations towards the conflict conclude the work.

Rel.Publ.: Der chinesisch...Völkerrecht. Leipzig: Noske, 1933. vi, 163p. (Frankfurter Abhandlungen zum modernen Völkerrecht, 41)

1067
CHAN, Mark Fung. Le Conflit sino-japonais en Mandchourie et le droit international [The Sino-Japanese Conflict over Manchuria and International Law]. Nancy, 1933. Text in French.

Contents: Japan's Legal Position in Manchuria; The Invasion of China; The Causes of the Conflict; The Conflect Brought before the League of Nations; The Attitudes of the United States and the Soviet Union; The Consequences of the Conflict.

Rel.Publ.: Le Conflit...international. Nancy: Société d'impressions typographiques, 1933. 131p.

1068
LING, Chong-yun. La Position et les droits du Japon en Mandchourie [The Position and the Rights of Japan in Manchuria]. Paris, 1933. Text in French.

Pt.1: An historical, legal, ethnographic, and economic survey of Manchuria. Pt.2: A lengthy and detailed exposition of the evolution of the Japanese position in Manchuria, 1895-1931. Pt.3: A study of Japanese administrative, legal, military, and economic rights in Manchuria (as of 1931).

Rel.Publ.: La Position...Mandchourie. Paris: A. Pedone, 1933. ii, 464p. (Publications de la Revue générale du droit international public, 7)

1069
COOPER, Russell Morgan. American Consultation in World Affairs for the Preservation of Peace. Columbia, 1934.

See Ch.5, "The Contest between China and Japan" (p.192-284 of the book): The League Acts under Article XI; The United States Cooperates Readily; Prentiss Gilbert at the Council; The Draft Resolution of October 24; Dawes and the Council in Paris; The United States Acts Independently; Consultation on the Shanghai Affair; Moral Suasion Wins at Shanghai; The Enquiry Commission Reports; Japan Bars Non-Members from Conciliation; The Assembly Adopts Its Report; The United States Backs up the League; Consultation on the Advisory Committee; The Record of Consultation.

Rel.Publ.: American...Peace. New York: Macmillan, 1934. xiv, 406p.

1070
HOLDCAMPER, Forrest Robert. A History of American Diplomatic Relations Regarding Manchuria. Clark, 1934. vii, 367p. AB: Clark University. Thesis Abstracts-1934. p.38-41.

Much of the dissertation discusses the American reaction to Japanese activities in Manchuria during the Russo-Japanese War and again in 1931-1932.

1071
MUELLER, Hans Joachim. Die Rechtslage im chinesisch-japanischen Konflikt 1931-1933 [The Legal Situation in the Sino-Japanese Conflict, 1931-1933]. Marburg, 1934. Text in German. The dissertation in its published form is available at Marburg/Lahn, Universitätsbibliothek, Nr. XVIII C.

An examination of the political situation between China and Japan before the outbreak of the conflict, of the arguments of both sides from the standpoint of international law, of the League of Nations' consideration of the entire conflict, and of the legal situation after February 24, 1933.

Rel.Publ.: Die Rechtslage...1933. Jena: Neuenhahn, 1933. vii, 74p.

1072
SHARP, Roland Hall. Nonrecognition as a Legal Obligation, 1795-1934. Genève, 1934.

Ch.7 (p.134-80) discusses the nonrecognition of Manchoukuo.

Rel.Publ.: Nonrecognition...1934. Liège, Belgium: G. Thone, 1934. x, 234p.

1073
KAO, Kouei-fen. Politique intérieure et extérieure de la Chine depuis 1926 jusqu'à nos jours [The Internal and External Policies of China from 1926 to the Present Time]. Nancy, 1935. Text in French.
See Ch.7, "The Sino-Japanese Conflict" (p.100-17).
Rel.Publ.: Politique...jours. Nancy: Grandville, 1935. 160p.

1074
TULLIÉ, A. R. La Mandchourie et le conflit sino-japonais devant la Société des Nations [Manchuria and the Sino-Japanese Conflict before the League of Nations]. Toulouse, 1935. Text in French.
Examines the political, economic, and social factors underlying Japan's seizure of Manchuria, the immediate and long-term causes for Sino-Japanese animosities, and the case of Japan's intervention in Manchuria as brought before the League of Nations.
Rel.Publ.: La Mandchourie...Nations. Paris: Librairie du Recueil Sirey, 1935. 381p.

1075
WU, Cheng-hwa. The Sino-Japanese Crisis and the World Peace Machinery. Washington, Seattle, 1935. 377p. (2v.) AB: University of Washington. Abstracts of Theses and Faculty Bibliography. v.2. p.695-701.
Contents: Japan's China Policy: A Record of Aggression; The Conflict of Sovereign Rights, Exceptional Rights, and Open Door in Manchuria; The Mukden Clash and the Sino-Japanese Manchurian Issue before the League of Nations; Shanghai Crisis and International Intervention; Japan's Recognition of Manchukuo; World Action on the Lytton Commission Report; General Consideration of Japan's Pleas for Justification; Significance of the Crisis; Question of Solution.

1076
CHENG, Kang-chi. The Presentation of the Manchurian Question in the English Press, 1931-1933. London, 1936. vii, 423p.
Background information concerning the origin of the crisis is provided in the first chapter, and the author suggests that the Japanese success in Manchuria set a precedent for the testing of the League's system of war limitation. The thesis, however, deals mainly with the League activities and the press responses to them.

1077
WANG, Kiding. La Société des Nations et la paix du monde [The League of Nations and the Peace of the World]. Bruxelles, 1936. Text in French.

1078
CHU, Hung-t'i. China and the League of Nations. Illinois, 1937.
Contains considerable information on the League of Nations' involvement in the Manchurian controversy.
Rel.Publ.: China...Nations. Urbana, Ill., 1937. 13p. [Abstract].

1079
PATIJN, Constantijn Leopold. De geschiedenis der Japansche penetratie in Mantsjoerije als volkenrechtelijk probleem [The History of Japanese Penetration into Manchuria as a Problem of International Law]. Utrecht, 1937. vii, 221p. Text in Dutch.
Contents: Pt.1: Manchuria with Respect to China. Pt.2: Japanese Penetration into Manchuria: Japanese Rights; Japan's Concerns and Ambitions. Pt.3: The Points of Dispute between Japan and China: The 21 Demands; The South Manchurian Railway; Other Railway Issues; The Position of the Korean Minority in Manchuria; The Rights of Residence in Manchuria; Law and Reality in the Far East. Pt.4: The Problem of Legal Change.
Rel.Publ.: De geschiedenis...probleem. Amsterdam: H. J. Paris, 1937. ix, 221p.

1080
QUAN, Lau-king. China's Relations with the League of Nations, 1919-1936. New York, 1937. iii, 364p.
Chapter 3 (p.58-117 of the book) studies the entire Manchurian controversy.
Rel.Publ.: China's...1936. Hong Kong: Asiatic Litho. Printing Press, 1939. xviii, 414p.

1081
CARTER, Gwendolen Margaret. The British Dominions and Collective Security through the League of Nations: With Particular Reference to the Sino-Japanese Dispute and the Italo-Ethiopian Conflict. Radcliffe, 1938. ii, 529p. AB: Radcliffe College. Summaries of Theses... 1935-1938. p.153-56.
Includes a discussion of the positions taken by Great Britain, Australia, Canada, Ireland, New Zealand, and South Africa at the time when the League of Nations was considering the Sino-Japanese dispute.
Rel.Publ.: The British Commonwealth and International Security: The Role of the Dominions, 1919-1939. Toronto: Ryerson Press, 1947. xx, 326p.

1082
MOULIN, Pierre. Expériences récentes de non-reconnaissance en droit international: Mandchoukouo, Espagne nationaliste [Recent Experiences of Non-Recognition in International Law: Manchoukuo, Nationalist Spain]. Lyon, 1938. Text in French.
Rel.Publ.: Expériences...nationaliste. Lyon: Bosc frères, M. et L. Riou, 1938. 211p.

1083
PAN, Stephen Chao-ying. American Diplomacy Concerning Manchuria. Catholic, 1938. vii, 385p.
See especially Ch.5, "The Open-Door Doctrine: Application in Manchuria before 1922," Ch.6. "The Open-Door Doctrine at the Washington Conference," Ch.8, "American Diplomacy Concerning the Manchurian Controversy," Ch.9, "The Open Door in Manchukuo," Ch.10, "The Hoover-Stimson Non-Recognition Policy toward Manchukuo," and Ch.11, "The Roosevelt-Hull Policy toward Manchukuo."
Rel.Publ.: American...Manchuria. Washington: Catholic University of America, 1938. xvi, 385p.

1084
MORINO, Masayoshi. The Stimson Policy of Non-Recognition as Applied to Manchoukuo. California, Berkeley, 1939. 180p.
An analysis of the strengths and weaknesses of the Stimson policy. Contents: The Enunciation of the Policy (The Stimson Note of January 7, 1932, The Stimson Letter to Borah of February 23, 1932); The Meaning of the Policy (Non-Recognition, Fruits of Force, Means Contrary to); The Application of the Policy to Manchoukuo (Recommendations of the League Advisory Committee, Effects of the Policy, Utility of the Policy); Conclusion.

1085
BURTON, Margaret Ernestine. The Assembly of the League

of Nations. Columbia, 1941. xi, 441p.
Includes a discussion and analysis of the Sino-Japanese dispute as dealt with by the League of Nations (p.293-332).
Rel.Publ.: The Assembly...Nations. Chicago: University of Chicago Press, 1941. xi, 441p.

WATKINS, James T., IV. China and the League of Nations 1919-1935. 1941. See no.992.

1086
CHU, Esther Briney. The Policy of Secretary of State Henry L. Stimson toward China, 1929-1933. Northwestern, 1943. 243p. AB: Northwestern University. Summaries of Doctoral Dissertations. v.11 (1943), p.126-30.
Contents: Secretary Stimson and the Sino-Soviet Railway Controversy; Stimson's Policy in Regard to the Manchurian Crisis: First Phase; Stimson's Policy in Regard to the Manchurian Crisis: Non-Recognition; The Policy of the State Department toward Nationalistic Aspirations.

1087
LANGER, Robert. Seizure of Territory, the Stimson Doctrine, and Related Principles in Legal Theory and Diplomatic Practice. Columbia, 1946.
Includes chapters on the American refusal to recognize and sanction the Japanese seizure of Manchuria.
Rel.Publ.: Seizure...Practice. Princeton: Princeton University Press, 1947. viii, 313p.

1088
LEE, Meng-ping. The Geneva Treatment of the Manchurian and Abyssinian Crises. London, 1946. iv, 352p.
Part I contains separate accounts of the Manchurian and Ethiopian crises, related in terms of League articles. Part II is a comparative study, centered around the actions of the League in both instances.

1089
CHRISTOPHER, James William. American Diplomatic Policy in China, 1928-1933. Oxford, 1948. xi, 405p.
Contents: The Chinese Background; The Tradition of American Policy towards China; The Problem of Manchuria; The Kuomintang in Power; The Chinese Eastern Railway Crisis; The Opening Phase; The Development of the Crisis; The Russian Invasion; Stimson Invokes the Kellogg Pact; The C.E.R. Crisis: The Settlement; The Problem of Relinquishing Extraterritoriality; Protection of American Lives in China; The Case of Captain Nakamura; The Mukden Incident; Japan Plays for Time; Japan Defies the World; The Attack on Shanghai; The Triumph of Japan.
Rel.Publ.: Conflict in the Far East: American Diplomacy in China from 1928-1933. Leiden: E. J. Brill, 1950. xiv, 335p.

1090
OPPENHEIMER, Ernest Julius. A Comparative Study of Selected World Opinion about the Sino-Japanese Conflict, 1931-1932. Chicago, 1948. 223p.
An analysis of American, British, French, German, Russian, and Communist journals on the subject.

TOMPKINS, Pauline. American-Russian Relations in the Far East, 1914-1933: A Study of American Far Eastern Policy and Its Effect on Russian Interest. 1948. See no.1028.

1091
KISELEVA, M. A. Iaponskaia agressiia i geroicheskaia oborona Shankhaia v 1932g. [Japanese Aggression and the Heroic Defense of Shanghai in 1932]. Moscow, Akademiia obshchestvennykh nauk pri Tsentral'nom Komitete Vsesoiuznoi Kommunisticheskoi Partii (bol'shevikov), 1949. (Candidate of Historical Sciences degree) 330p. Text in Russian.

1092
PETERSEN, Keith Stuart. The United States, Great Britain, and the Far Eastern Crisis of 1931-1933. Chicago, 1949. 326p.
A detailed analysis of the diplomatic side of the Manchurian incident with special stress upon the role of the American Secretary of State, Henry L. Stimson, in the entire crisis.

1093
RAMSEY, Julia Havlicek. The Foreign Policy of the British Dominions, 1931-1936. Georgetown, 1949. xiii, 324p.
See especially Ch.1, "Dominion Foreign Policy before 1931," Ch.3, "The Invasion of Manchuria before the Council of the League of Nations," Ch.4, "The Sino-Japanese Dispute before the Assembly of the League of Nations," and Ch.5, "The Press," which contains a section on the press and public opinion on the conflict in East Asia.
Rel.Publ.: The Foreign...1936. Rochester, N.Y.: University of Rochester Press, 1954. (University of Rochester Canadian Studies Series, 8) [Microprint copy of typescript, 8 cards]

1094
SMITH, Sara Rector. The Manchurian Crisis, 1931-1932: A Tragedy in International Relations. Columbia, 1949. ix, 281p.
Focuses on the handling of the Manchurian crisis by the Council of the League of Nations and points out the quandry that the Council was in. Contents: The Stage is Set; The 65th Session of the Council, September, 1931; First Interlude: October 1 to 12; Prentiss Gilbert Sits with the Council; Second Interlude: October 24 to November 16; The Paris Meeting; Anticlimax.
Rel.Publ.: The Manchurian...Relations. New York: Columbia University Press, 1948. ix, 281p.

1095
HAMILTON, Thomas T. The Impact of the Shanghai Incident of 1932 upon the United States and the League of Nations. Duke, 1953. 389p.
Contents: The Background; The Crisis; The Japanese Attack; The Chinese Defense; The Japanese Victory; The Truce.

1096
YOSHIHASHI, Takehiko. The Background of the Manchurian Crisis and the Rise of the Japanese Military. Yale, 1957. 272p.
Contents: Introduction: The Mukden Incident; Portents of Crisis; Tensions within Japan: Contributing Causes to the Manchurian Crisis; Mounting Crisis in Japanese-Chinese Relations; The Mukden Incident; Chain of Actions following the Mukden Incident; The Collapse of the Wakatsuki Cabinet; Conclusions.
Rel.Publ.: Conspiracy at Mukden: The Rise of the Japanese Military. New Haven: Yale University Press, 1963. xvi, 274p. (Yale Studies in Political Science, 9)

1097
SÉNAT, Philippe. La Politique de reconnaissance des États-Unis en Chine, 1911-1953 [The American Policy of Diplomatic Recognition in China, 1911-1953]. Toulouse, 1958. ix, 200p. Text in French.

1098
CHOWDHURY, Chinmoy. The United States, the League, and the Manchurian Crisis. London, 1960. viii, 513p.

Concludes that a firm opposition to the Japanese in Manchuria after the Mukden affair would have eliminated the subsequent need for force. The author condemns the policy of the American Republican Party, with its "tendency to judge the Manchurian issue in moral terms, and, at the same time, regard it as of no concern to the United States."

1099
SHÊN, Mo. Japan in Manchuria: A Documentary Study. Santo Tomas, 1960.

"Deals with Japan in relation to the Open Door policy and foreign interests in Manchuria,...presents a detailed treaty study of Japan's 'special rights and interests' in Manchuria [up to 1931],...and studies the Manchurian crisis and the international intervention in the light of international laws."

Rel.Publ.: Japan in Manchuria: An Analytical Study of Treaties and Documents. Manila, 1960. 463p.

1100
WÜNSCHE, Renate. Die Haltung des deutschen Imperialismus zum japanisch-chinesischen Konflikt von 1931-1933 und der Kampf der Kommunistischen Partei Deutschlands gegen die fernöstliche Kriegsgefahr [The Attitude of German Imperialism towards the Sino-Japanese Conflict of 1931-1933 and the Struggle of the German Communist Party against the Dangers of War in East Asia]. Potsdam, Deutsche Akademie für Staats- und Rechtswissenschaft "Walter Ulbricht," 1961. 257p. Text in German.

1101
OGATA, Sadako Nakamura. Japanese Foreign Policy Making in the Manchurian Affair. California, Berkeley, 1963. 386p. DA 24 (June 1964), 5516; UM 64-5274.

The author reconstructs the step-by-step decision making of the Manchurian Affair in order to determine the immediate impact of the Affair upon the Japanese political power structure as well as the Affair's effects upon the formulation of Japan's foreign policy objectives. The policy statements and programs of the Kwantung Army in particular are studied in depth.

Rel.Publ.: Defiance in Manchuria: The Making of Japanese Foreign Policy, 1931-1932. Berkeley: University of California Press, 1964. xvi, 259p. (Publications of the Center for Japanese and Korean Studies)

1102
HUBERT, Sister Mary Gabriel, O.P. The Role of Nelson Trusler Johnson in Sino-American Diplomatic Relations, 1930-1935. Catholic, 1964. 305p. DA 25 (Oct. 1964), 2474; UM 64-11,063.

Nelson T. Johnson, United States Minister and Ambassador to China during the 1930's. Discusses both Johnson's views of the Sino-Japanese conflict and the role that he played "in the formulation and execution of America's China policy during the early 1930's."

1103
AMBROS, Heino. Nonrecognition: Its Development in International Law and Application by the United States with Particular Reference to the Baltic States. New York, 1965. 362p. DA 28 (Mar. 1968), 3740-41-A; UM 66-5714.

The step by step analysis of the origin and development of the Hoover-Stimson Doctrine of Nonrecognition and of its success and failure as a new principle of American foreign policy constitutes the nucleus of the thesis. Information on the Doctrine as applied to Japan in the early 1930's is included.

1104
DOENECKE, Justus Drew. American Public Opinion and the Manchurian Crisis, 1931-1933. Princeton, 1966. 291p. DA 27 (Jan. 1967), 2108-09-A; UM 66-13,304.

The author seeks to "measure the range of American pacifism and isolationism at the time when the post-Versailles order faced its first onslaught." As his means of doing so, he examines the response of the leaders of American public opinion to various proposals for coercion against Japan in the early 1930's.

1105
NORTON, Nile Brown. Frank R. McCoy and American Diplomacy, 1928-1932. Denver, 1966. 372p. DA 27 (Mar. 1967), 2995-96-A; UM 67-1543.

Includes an examination of McCoy's participation in the Lytton Commission, which investigated the situation in and the Sino-Japanese dispute over Manchuria in 1931-1932.

1106
STARR, Daniel Phillips. Nelson Trusler Johnson: The United States and the Rise of Nationalist China, 1925-1937. Rutgers, 1967. 367p. DA 28 (Nov. 1967), 1775-A; UM 67-14,765.

Considerable attention is devoted to the views of Nelson T. Johnson towards the Sino-Japanese conflict. See especially Ch.6, "The Manchurian Crisis," and Ch.7, "The Resurgence of Nationalist China, 1933-1937."

1107
STEVENS, Donald George. The United States and the League of Nations during the Manchurian Crisis, September-December 1931. St. John's, 1967. 286p. DA 28 (Mar. 1968), 3619-20-A; UM 68-4370.

The author argues that Secretary of State Stimson did not cooperate with the League as much as people have assumed he did.

1108
PEARSON, Alden Bryan, Jr. The American Christian Press and the Sino-Japanese Crisis of 1931-1933: An Aspect of Public Response to the Breakdown of World Peace. Duke, 1968. 319p. DA 29 (June 1969), 4437-38-A; UM 69-9071.

"This study analyzes the challenge to peace and the reactions of the editors of various Christian journals as part of the public response of Americans to an international crisis which seemed to herald the collapse of international morality and peace. The editors were conscious of themselves as Christians struggling to think and react in a Christian way; many Americans shared their attitudes and responses." The journals surveyed included the Christian Century, the World Tomorrow, and America.

1109
DONNELLY, James Baker. Prentiss Bailey Gilbert, The League Council, and the Manchurian Crisis of 1931. Virginia, 1969. 432p. DA 30 (Apr. 1970), UM 70-4781.

1110
MALPASS, Elizabeth Deanne. Sir John Simon and British Diplomacy during the Sino-Japanese Crisis, 1931-1933. Texas Christian, 1969. 171p. DA 30 (Feb. 1970), UM 70-1990.

1111
HECHT, Robert A. Britain and America Face Japan, 1931-1933: A Study of Anglo-American Far Eastern Diplomacy during the Manchurian and Shanghai Crises. City University of New York, 1970. 253p. DA 30 (June 1970), UM 70-10,412.

Sino-Japanese War (1937-1945)

See also International Relations--China/1931-1945 (pages 125-27).

1112
HUANG, Robert Feng-chang. A Survey of the Development of the Present Undeclared War between China and Japan. Santo Tomas, 1940. 213p.

1113
MA, Chih-cheng. Controverses et conventions internationales au regard de la guerre sino-japonaise [International Controversies and Agreements Concerning the Sino-Japanese War]. Paris, 1941. Text in French.
Contents: Sino-Japanese Relations, 1931-1937; The Incident at Lukouchiao and Its Consequences; Agreements and Treaties Related to the Incident at Lukouchiao; The Incident at Shanghai (1937); The Sino-Japanese War and the League of Nations (Articles X, XI, XVI, and XVII of the Covenant Examined from a Theoretical Standpoint, History of Chinese Appeals to the League, Commentary); The Sino-Japanese War and the Nine-Power Treaty.
Rel.Publ.: Controverses...japonaise. Paris: Recueil Sirey, 1941. 218p.

1114
NIKIFOROV, V. N. Izmennicheskaia politika Gomin'dana v voine s Iaponiei 1937-1945 gg. [The Traitorous Policy of the Kuomintang in the War with Japan, 1937-1945]. Moscow, Moskovskii gosudarstvennyi universitet imeni M. V. Lomonosova, 1950. (Candidate of Historical Sciences) 395p. Text in Russian.
Rel.Publ.: Gomin'danovskie reaktsionery-predateli Kitaia, 1937-1945. Moscow: Izdatel'stvo Moskovskogo universiteta, 1953. 246p.

1115
TSIEN, Tche-hao. Les Violations du droit international commises par le Japon au cours des hostilités contre la Chine: 1937-1945 [The Violations in International Law Committed by Japan in the Course of Her War with China, 1937-1945]. Paris, 1951. Text in French.

1116
BEDNIAK, Inessa Iakovlevna. Miunkhenskaia politika SShA i Anglii, kak faktor usileniia iaponskoi imperialisticheskoi agressii (iul' 1937-sentiabr' 1939) [The Munich Policy of the United States and Great Britain as a Factor in the Growth of Japanese Imperialistic Aggression, July 1937-September 1939]. Moscow, Institut vostokovedeniia Akademii nauk SSSR, 1952. (Candidate of Historical Sciences degree) xv, 452p. Text in Russian. AB: 12p. summary published in 1952.
Rel.Publ.: Iaponskaia agressiia v Kitae i pozitsiia SShA, 1937-1939. Moscow: Izdatel'stvo Akademii nauk SSSR, 1957. 175p. (Institut vostokovedeniia Akademii nauk SSSR); "K voprosu o neitralitete SShA v iapono-kitaiskoi voine: Zaiavlenie gos. departamenta SShA ot 14 sent. 1937 g.," in Instituta Vostokovedeniia, Akademiia nauk SSSR, Kratkie soobshcheniia, 16 (1955), 18-29.

1117
TAI, Erh-ching. British Opinion of the Sino-Japanese War, 1937-1941. London, 1952. v, 240p.
Portrays Great Britain's position in 1937-1941 as being balanced between the fear of war with Japan and the fear of losing important economic and political ties with China. The role of the League of Nations, the situation in Europe, the strong anti-Japanese popular opinion, and relations with the United States are cited as complicating factors.

1118
PHILLIPS, Claude S. Questions of International Law in the Consideration of Selected Issues by the United States Congress, 1937-1941. Duke, 1954. 296p.
Ch.4 deals with the Sino-Japanese conflict and with the "domestic" neutrality of the United States.

KIM, Chonghan. Konoye Fumimaro and Japanese Foreign Policy: 1937-1941. 1956. See no.683.

1119
QUALE, Gladys Robina. The Mission Compound in Modern China: The Role of the United States Protestant Mission as an Asylum in the Civil and International Strife of China, 1900-1941. Michigan, 1957. 321p. DA 18 (Apr. 1958), 1409; UM 58-1453.
"Part 3 depicts the revival of the inviolability of United States Protestant missions in the struggle between Japan and China," 1937-1941.

1120
SHAO, Otis Hung-i. American Far Eastern Policy in 1937. Brown, 1957. 347p. DA 18 (Feb. 1958), 642; UM 23,454.
Studies the events in East Asia during the 1930's that led up to the Sino-Japanese conflict in 1937, the 1937 crisis itself, and American foreign policy during this period in order to determine (1) how the Roosevelt Administration understood and applied traditional United States East Asian policy at this time, (2) what the response of the Administration to the crisis was, and (3) what the "principal contending interpretations and recommendations among men influential in policy-making" were.
Rel.Publ.: "The Conference of Brussels, 1937," International Review of History and Political Science, 2 (June 1965), 138-52.

1121
SEVOST'IANOV, Grigorii Nikolaevich. Politika imperialisticheskikh derzhav na Dal'nem Vostoke, iul' 1937 - dekabr' 1941 [The Policies of the Imperialist Powers in East Asia, July 1937-December 1941]. Moscow, Institut istorii Akademii nauk SSSR, 1958(?) (Doctor of Historical Sciences degree) Text in Russian. AB: 48p. summary published in 1958.
Rel.Publ.: "Russo-Japanese War of 1938-1939," History Today, 8 (Mar. 1958), 196-97 [Abstract]; Podgotovka voiny na Tikhom okeane, sentiabr' 1939 g. - dekabr' 1941 g. Moscow: Idz-vo Akademii nauk SSSR, 1962. 590p. (Akademiia nauk SSSR. Institut istorii)

LU, David K.-h. From the Marco Polo Bridge to Pearl

Harbor: Japan's Entry into the Second World War. 1960. See no.684.

1122
CLIFFORD, Nicholas Rowland. British Policy in the Far East, 1937-1941. Harvard, 1961. viii, 541p. AB: 5p. summary appended to diss. ms.

Contents: The British Position in East Asia in 1937; The Outbreak of War, July-October 1937; Attempts to End the War through Collective Action: The League of Nations and the Nine Power Conference; The West Involved: The Japanese Attack on Foreign Interests; British Interests in China, 1938; The Larger Diplomatic Issues, January-October 1938; The Growing Challenge to the West: Japan's New Order and the British Reaction, November 1938; January 1939; 1939: The Diplomatic Background; The Campaign against the Foreign Settlements: Shanghai, Amoy, Tientsin; The Coming of the European War and Its Effects in the Far East; The Increase of Japanese Pressure, January to July 1940; Conclusion: July 1940 to December 1941.

Rel.Publ.: Retreat from China: British Policy in the Far East, 1937-1941. Seattle: University of Washington Press, 1967. ix, 222p.; "Britain, America, and the Far East, 1937-1940: A Failure in Co-operation." Journal of British Studies, 3 (Nov. 1963), 137-54.

DRECHSLER, Karl. Die Beziehungen Hitlerdeutschlands zu China und Japan 1936-1939: Ein Beitrag zur Vorgeschichte des zweiten Weltkrieges. 1962. See no.1265.

1123
KENNEDY, Jesse Carl. American Foreign Policy in China, 1937-1950: An Analysis of Why It Failed. Chicago, 1962. 514p.

See Ch.4, "The War with Japan, 1937-1941," and Ch.5, "Chinese Communist Resistance to Japan, 1937-1941."

1124
WHITEHURST, George William. Quarantine the Aggressor: Roosevelt's Attempt at Collective Security in 1937. West Virginia, 1962. 278p.

"An analysis of the Far Eastern policy of the Roosevelt Administration in 1937. It covers a five month period, from the outbreak of the undeclared Sino-Japanese War in July to the failure of the Brussels Conference to end the conflict in November." Contents: The China Incident; Public Opinion and the Problem of Neutrality; Groping for a Far Eastern Policy; Quarantine the Aggressor; National and International Reaction; Parallel Action with the League of Nations; Setting the Stage for Brussels; The Welles Plan; The Brussels Conference.

1125
CASELLA, Alessandro. Le Conflit sino-japonaise de 1937 et la société des nations [The Sino-Japanese Conflict of 1937 and the League of Nations]. Genève, 1966. Text in French.

Demonstrates that the League of Nations failed not so much for lack of material means as for lack of efforts in trying to find an equitable solution.

Rel.Publ.: Le Conflit...nations. Genève: Librairie générale de droit et de jurisprudence, 1967. 136p.

WOLFF, Ernst. Chou Tso-jên: Modern China's Pioneer of the Essay. 1966. See no.958.

1126
ALDRED, Francis Kazimer. The Brussels Conference: A Study of Efforts during 1937 to Formulate a Joint Anglo-American Far Eastern Policy. Virginia, 1967. 309p. DA 28 (Mar. 1968), 3592-A; UM 68-3102.

"The history of Anglo-American relations during the last half of 1937 is largely the story of the failure of efforts to reach agreement on common measures...for stopping the onrushing Japanese" in China. The failure "was due...to shortcomings of Statesmanship on both sides of the Atlantic, to preoccupation of government and peoples with domestic issues, to mutual distrust and suspicion, and to a lack of understanding of the kaleidoscopic shifts of power taking place in Asia."

1127
LIN, Han-sheng. Wang Ching-wei and the Japanese Peace Efforts. Pennsylvania, 1967. 607p. DA 28 (Oct. 1967), 1359-A; UM 67-12,773.

"Attempts to ascertain both the causes of the Sino-Japanese conflict and the reasons for its prolongation to 1945. Wang Ching-wei is the central figure of the thesis."

1128
RHEE, Tong-chin. Sino-American Relations from 1942 through 1949: A Study of Efforts to Settle the China Problem. Clark, 1967. 570p. DA 28 (Nov. 1967), 1773-74-A; UM 67-13,546.

"Emphasizes the entanglement of Washington's initial military commitment against Japan in China in the complex domestic struggle between the Kuomintang and the Chinese Communists." Chapters 3-5 deal with the war years and are concerned with Japan as a military opponent.

Rel.Publ.: "American Military Mission to Yenan and the Chinese Communists, 1944-1945," University of Dayton Review, 1968.

1129
BOYLE, John Hunter. Japan's Puppet Regimes in China, 1937-1940. Stanford, 1968. 468p. DA 29 (Jan. 1969), 2170-71-A; UM 69-197.

A study of several local and regional public regimes that were sponsored by the nearly autonomous Japanese army commands in China during the late 1930's and of the government that was established under Wang Ching-wei in March 1940. The dissertation "views the puppet regimes from Japanese eyes as expressions of Japanese policy and ideology," and it studies them in order to "illustrate the nature of Japanese imperialism and Pan-Asianism."

1130
NGOK, Lee. The Chinese Communist Bases (Ken-Chü-Ti) in North China, 1938-1943: A Study of Their Growth and Anti-Japanese Activities, with Special Reference to Administration and Mass Mobilization Programmes at the Village Level. London, 1968.

1131
BUNKER, Edward Gerald. A Political Tragedy: The Story of Wang Ching-wei's Peace Movement. Harvard, 1970.

Since World War II
(Includes both Communist China and Taiwan)

1132
SUGIYAMA, Yasushi. Japan's Policies towards Communist China, 1949-1963. Maryland, 1965. 352p. DA 26 (Mar. 1966), 5535-36; UM 65-4475.

"Examines the responses made by successive governments, political parties, and interest groups in Japan to meet the challenge presented by Communist China."

1133
WANG, Yu-san. Sino-Japanese Peace Making and Settlement. Pennsylvania, 1968. 331p. DA 29 (Jan. 1969), 2335-A; UM 69-182.
"Investigates the plans for peace between China and Japan from 1937 to 1950, analyzes why China was excluded from the Japanese Peace Treaty at San Francisco, describes the positions of Japan and Nationalist and Communist China toward the Sino-Japanese peace settlement, and discloses the details of the making of the Peace Treaty between Nationalist China and Japan."

Korea

Early to 1860

YOON, Hong Sub. Korea in International Far Eastern Relations. 1935. See no.1138.

NELSON, Melvin F. The International Status of Korea, 1876-1910. 1940. See no.1139.

1134
McCUNE, George McAfee. Korean Relations with China and Japan, 1800-1864. California, Berkeley, 1941. xiii, 292p.
Pt.2--an analysis of the ceremonial diplomatic relations and the trade relations between Korea and Japan --includes information on the contacts of the Korean court with the Tokugawa shogun and with the daimyo of Tsushima.
Rel.Publ.: "The Exchange of Envoys between Korea and Japan during the Tokugawa Period," FEQ, 5 (May 1946), 308-25; "The Japanese Trading Post at Pusan," Korean Review, 1 (June 1948), 11-15.

DONG, Chon. Japanese Annexation of Korea: A Study of Korean-Japanese Relations to 1910. 1955. See no.1148.

1135
HAZARD, Benjamin Harrison, Jr. Japanese Marauding in Medieval Korea: The Wakō Impact on Late Koryŏ. California, Berkeley, 1967. 379p. DA 28 (Jan. 1968), 2617-18-A; UM 68-76.
Contents: Relations between Japan and Koryŏ before the First Wakō Raids; A Century of Sporadic Raiding; Conditions in Korea and Japan Immediately before 1350; Wakō Raids in the Reigns of Ch'ungjŏng Wang, Kongmin Wang, Sin U, Sin Ch'ang, and Kang'yang Wang; The Wakō and Their Impact on Korea.
Rel.Publ.: "The Formative Years of the Wakō, 1223-63," MN, 22 (1967), 260-77.

1860-1910

For dissertations on the Russo-Japanese dispute over Korea, see International Relations--Russia: 1860-1917 (pages 150-52). See also History--Japanese empire --Chōsen (pages 90-95).

1136
TYLER, Alice Felt. The Foreign Policy of James G. Blaine. Minnesota, 1927. Diss. ms. not available.
Includes information on the Japanese-Korean Treaty of 1876 and on Li Hung-chang's diplomacy, which sought to counteract Japanese influence in Korea.
Rel.Publ.: The Foreign...Blaine. Minneapolis: University of Minnesota Press, 1928. 411p.

1137
JONES, Francis Clifford. Foreign Diplomacy in Korea, 1866-1894. Harvard, 1935. ii, 567p. AB: Harvard University. Summaries of Theses...1935. p.163-66.
Includes a discussion of Japan's Korean policy, of her diplomatic activities in Korea, and of the origins of the Sino-Japanese War.

1138
YOON, Hong Sub. Korea in International Far Eastern Relations. American, 1935. 450p.
Includes information on Japanese relations with Koryŏ, Japanese attempts to conquer Korea under Hideyoshi, the conclusion of the Kanghwa Treaty, the Tonghak movement and the Sino-Japanese War, and the Russo-Japanese War and its consequences.

LUDWIG, Albert P. Li Hung-chang and Chinese Foreign Policy, 1870-1885. 1936. See no.916.

1139
NELSON, Melvin Frederick. The International Status of Korea, 1876-1910. Duke, 1940. 434p.
Also includes considerable information on Japanese-Korean relations between the fourth century A.D. and the mid-1800's.
Rel.Publ.: Korea and the Old Orders in Eastern Asia. Baton Rouge: Louisiana State University Press, 1945. xvi, 326p.

1140
STAROSELTSEV, N. D. Kolonial'naia politika Iaponii v Koree ot "otkrytiia" ee do iapono-kitaiskoi voiny (1876-1894 gg.) [Japan's Colonial Policy in Korea from the "Opening" of the country to the Sino-Japanese War, 1876-1894]. Moscow, Moskovskii gosudarstvennyi universitet imeni M. V. Lomonosova, 1941. (Candidate of Historical Sciences degree) xiii, 235p. Text in Russian.

1141
SUNOO, Hag-won. A Study of the Korean Treaties: 1876 and 1882. The Opening of Korea. Universita Karlova, 1949/50. 181, xxii p. Diss. ms. available at the University archives, no. AUK 2583.
One section deals with the conclusion of the Kanghwa treaty between Korea and Japan in 1876.

1142
TIAGAI, Galina Davidovna. Koreia v 1893-1896 gg.: Krest'ianskoe vosstanie i bor'ba koreiskogo naroda protiv iaponskikh militaristov i ikh amerikanskikh posobnikov [Korea in 1893-1896: Peasant Uprisings and the Struggle of the Korean People against the Japanese Militarists and Their American Accomplices]. Moscow, Institut vostokovedeniia Akademii nauk SSSR, 1951. (Candidate of Historical Sciences degree) vii, 334p. Text in Russian.
Rel.Publ.: Krest'iankie vosstaniia v Koree 1893-1895 gg. Moscow: Izd. Akademii nauk SSSR, 1953. 208p.

1143
BRIDGHAM, Philip Low. American Policy toward Korean Independence, 1866-1910. Fletcher, 1952. iv, 179p. AB: Fletcher School of Law and Diplomacy. Thesis Abstract, 1951. no.2.

"Analyzes the origin, development, and denouement of American governmental policy toward Korean independence." For information on Japan's relations with Korea and with the United States, see especially Ch.3, "The United States, Korea, and the Sino-Japanese War" (p.39-68), Ch.4, "Retreat to Neutrality: American Policy toward Korea, 1896-1904" (p.69-106), Ch.5, "From Neutrality to Complicity: America's Role in Promoting a Japanese Protectorate over Korea, 1904-1905" (p.107-61), and Ch.6, "A Postscript: America's Indifference toward Japanese Annexation of Korea, 1906-1910" (p.162-71).

1144
BARTZ, Carl Frederick, Jr. The Korean Seclusion Policy, 1860-1876. California, Berkeley, 1953. 246p.

A descriptive history of the seclusion policy that the Koreans carried out against the United States, Europe, and Japan.

1145
VASILEVSKAIA, I. I. Politika iaponskogo imperializma v Koree nakanune anneksii (1905-1910 gg.) [The Policy of Japanese Imperialism in Korea on the Eve of the Annexation, 1905-1910]. Moscow, Moskovskii ordena Lenina gosudarstvennyi universitet imeni M. V. Lomonosova, Istoricheskii fakultet, 1953. (Candidate of Historical Sciences degree) xviii, 247p. Text in Russian. AB: 16p. summary published in 1953.

Rel.Publ.: "Nekotorye voprosy iaponskogo okkupatsionnogo rezhima v Koree v 1904-1905 gg.," in Akademiia nauk SSSR, Institut Vostokovedeniia, Kratkie soobshcheniia, 16 (1955), 57-67; "K voprosu ob ekonomicheskom zakabalenii i ograblenii Korei Iaponskim imperial'izmom v gody protektorata (1905-1910 gg.)," in Akademiia nauk SSSR, Institut vostokovedeniia, Kratkie soobshcheniia, 34 (1958), 28-34.

1146
MERRILL, John Espy. American Official Reactions to the Domestic Policies of Japan in Korea, 1905-1910. Stanford, 1954. 388p. DA 14 (Oct. 1954), 1698; UM 9510.

Pt.1 examines "the foreign attitudes toward the various steps preparatory to the establishment of the protectorate." Pt.2 "deals with the first two years of the protectorate and details the American and European reactions to that government's establishment, to Prince Itō's efforts to reform the Korean government by advisory means, and to the failure of such efforts. ...The third part delineates a period in which the old Emperor of Korea was forced to abdicate and Korean riots and attempted Japanese reforms played an alternating tattoo on the senses of the foreigners in Korea.... It concludes with the foreign reactions, generally acquiescence, to the outstanding events of the last year of the protectorate." Pt.4 focuses on the annexation and on related developments.

1147
WEEMS, Clarence Norwood, Jr. The Korean Reform and Independence Movement (1881-1898). Columbia, 1954. 557p. DA 14 (Oct. 1954), 1704-05; UM 8859.

Includes chapters discussing the reform efforts of Japanese-supported Korean modernizers, the Japanese opposition to Korean independence, and the Western-style reformers in Korea who were overshadowed by Japanese influence (1881-1884, 1894-1895).

1148
DONG, Chon. Japanese Annexation of Korea: A Study of Korean-Japanese Relations to 1910. Colorado, 1955. 391p. DA 17 (Sept. 1957), 1992; UM 16,932.

Pt.1: From the earliest contacts through the era of Hideyoshi's invasion. Pt.2: The Sino-Russo-Japanese contest over Korea (1876-1905). Pt.3: The final stages of annexation, based almost entirely on the Nikkan Gappō hi-shi.

Rel.Publ.: "Korea and the Russo-Japanese War," Koreana Quarterly, 1 (Winter 1959), 22-72; "The United States Attitude towards the Sino-Russian-Japanese Policies in Korea, 1891-1898," in Hanguk Yŏngu Tosŏgwan, Seoul, Bulletin of the Korean Research Center: Journal of the Social Sciences and Humanities, 23 (Dec. 1965), 1-28.

1149
KIM, Chang Hoon. Relations internationales de la Corée de la seconde moitié du XIXe siècle à la perte de son indépendance (1910) [The International Relations of Korea from the Second Half of the Nineteenth Century to the Loss of Her Independence (1910)]. Paris, 1959. 224, xlvi p. Text in French.

1150
CHOE, Ching-young. A Decade of the Taewŏngun: Reform, Seclusion, and Disaster. Harvard, 1960. vii, 592p. (2v.).

Ch.7, "The Taewŏngun's Foreign Policy: Korean-Japanese Relations, 1864-1873" (p.391-484), deals with the Bakufu's proposed mediation and the Yabe incident of 1867, the Taewŏngun's opposition to Japan's efforts to change the nature of the four-century old Korea-Japan relationship, the An-Urase compromise plan, and the Sada, Yoshioka, Sagara, and Hanabusa Missions.

1151
NAHM, Andrew Changwoo. Kim Ok-kyun and the Korean Progressive Movement, 1882-1884. Stanford, 1961. 406p. DA 22 (Nov. 1961), 1603-04; UM 61-4149.

Includes Japan's support of the Korean Progressives and her involvement in the coup d'état of 1884.

Rel.Publ.: "Korea's Response to International Rivalries: Korean Domestic Policies, 1876-1884," in Michigan Academy of Science, Arts, and Letters, Papers, 50 (1964), 445-65; "Reaction and Response to the Opening of Korea, 1876-1884," in Studies on Asia, 1965, ed. by Robert K. Sakai (Lincoln: University of Nebraska Press, 1965), 61-80.

1152
CHIEN, Frederick Foo. The Opening of Korea: A Study of Chinese Diplomacy, 1876-1885. Yale, 1962. 415p.

Japanese-Korean relations are also examined within the dissertation. Contents: The Treaty of Kanghwa; The Initial Modifications of China's Korea Policy; The Opening of Korea: The United States-Korean Treaty of May 1882; The Émeute of 1884; The Opening of Korea: Treaties with Other Powers; The Active Policy of China in Korea; The Émeute of 1884; The Inception of International Competition in Korea: To the End of 1884.

Rel.Publ.: The Opening...1885. Hamden, Conn.: Shoe String Press, 1967. xiii, 364p.

1153
KHAN, Marks. Osvoboditel'naia bor'ba koreiskogo naroda v gody iaponskogo protektorata (1905-1910 gg.) [The Struggle of the Korean People to Liberate Themselves during the Period of the Japanese Protectorate, 1905-1910]. Moscow, Institut narodov Azii Akademii nauk SSSR, 1963. (Candidate of Historical Sciences degree)

177p. Text in Russian.
Rel.Publ.: Osvoboditel'naia...1910 gg. Moscow: Izd. vostochnoi literatury, 1961. 71p.

1154
KIM, Yoon Young. National Images of Korea, 1850-1910: A A Study on the National Survival of a Small Power. Chicago, 1963. 493p.
Includes information about several matters involving Japan: the Tientsin Treaty between China and Japan, the Tonghak Rebellion and Japanese intervention, the Russo-Japanese understandings and clashes, the Russo-Japanese War, and the period of Japan's protectorate preceding annexation.

1155
CHAY, Jongsuk. The United States and the Closing Door in Korea: American-Korean Relations, 1894-1905. Michigan, 1965. 192p. DA 27 (Aug. 1966), 435-A; UM 66-6581.
Japan is constantly referred to in this dissertation which examines America's Korean policy and which evaluates it in the light of American interests in Korea, 1894-1905, and of the situation in East Asia at that time.
Rel.Publ.: "The Taft-Katsura Memorandum Reconsidered," PHR, 37 (Aug. 1968), 321-26.

1156
CHOI, Dong Hoon. The United States Policy toward the Japanese Protectorate and Annexation in Korea, 1904-1910. Fletcher, 1965. iv, 228p. AB: 3p. summary appended to diss. ms.
Contents: Korea and the Outside World: From the Treaty of Kanghwa (1876) to the Japanese Annexation of Korea (1910); Korean-American Relations: From the Treaty of Shimonoseki to the Russo-Japanese War; United States Policy toward the Japanese Protectorate of Korea; United States Policy toward the Japanese Absorption from the Protectorate Agreement to the Hague Affair; United States Policy toward the Japanese Annexation of Korea.

1157
KIM, Yung Chung. Great Britain and Korea, 1883-1887. Indiana, 1965. 247p. DA 26 (Nov. 1965), 2712; UM 65-10,856.
Examines British policy toward Korea during the initial period of British-Korean relations. Includes information on the Sino-Japanese intervention of 1884 and on Japanese protests regarding the British naval occupation of Port Hamilton, an island in the Korea Strait.

1158
MacDONALD, Donald Ross Hazelton. Russian Interest in Korea, to 1895: The Pattern of Russia's Emerging Interest in the Peninsula from the Late Seventeenth Century to the Sino-Japanese War. Harvard, 1966. [Dissertation actually completed in 1957]. xi, 535p.
Includes information on Japanese activities in Korea in the 1880's and on the development of Russian scholarship on Japan in general.

1159
RO, Kwang Hai. Power Politics in Korea and Its Impact on Korean Foreign and Domestic Affairs, 1882-1907. Oklahoma, 1966. 202p. DA 27 (Dec. 1966), 1893-A; UM 66-10,191.
The thesis "examines the policies and methods used by Korea to retain her independence during the struggle between China and Japan" and [later] Russia and Japan for the possession of the country.

1160
DEUCHLER, Martina. The Opening of Korea, 1875-1884. Harvard, 1967. v, 322p.
Includes considerable information on Japanese relations with and activities in Korea.

1161
SUH, Byung Han. Die internationalen Beziehungen Koreas von der Mitte des 19. Jahrhunderts bis zum Ende der Unabhängigkeit [The International Relations of Korea from the Mid-1800's to 1910]. Wien, 1967. v, 340p. Text in German. Diss. ms. available at the Österreichische Nationalbibliothek, Nr. 1040.461-C.
Overall presentation of the Korean conduct of foreign affairs from the mid-1800's to 1910, with particular attention being paid to the views then current about the principles of modern international law.

1162
PALAIS, James Bernard. Korea on the Eve of the Kanghwa Treaty, 1873-1876. Harvard, 1968. v, 955p. (2v.)
A study of the years immediately preceding the conclusion of the Kanghwa Treaty between Japan and Korea. Pt.2, which focuses on Korea's foreign policy, examines (among other things) the Taewŏngun's policy with regard to Japan, "the nature of the change in Korea's Japan policy that emerged after 1874 and the reasoning that lay behind it," and "the conduct of negotiations with Japan that culminated in the Kanghwa Treaty.

1163
COOK, Harold Francis. Kim Ok-kyun and the Background of the 1884 Émeute. Harvard, 1969. vi, 708p. (2v.).
A study of Kim Ok-kyun (1851-1894) and of the events leading up to the attempted coup d'état of 1884 in which he and other Korean reformers sought to overthrow the conservative, pro-Chinese government in Seoul. Information on Kim's visits to Japan, his relationship with Fukuzawa Yukichi, and his failure to obtain Meiji government support for his activities is included.

Since World War II

1164
LEE, Jin Won. Political Issues between Japan and Korea, Post-War Period, 1952-1962. Oxford, 1963/64.
Rel.Publ.: "Brief Survey of Korean-Japanese Relations (Post-War Period)," Koreana Quarterly, 1 (Winter, 1959), 64-85.

1165
CHEE, Choung Il. National Regulation of Fisheries in International Law. New York, 1964. 329p. DA 27 (Sept. 1966), 812-A; UM 65-6624.
The Korea-Japan fishing dispute is one of "four post-war fishing disputes singled out for the purpose of analyzing the legal, economic, and technical aspect of the fishing dispute."

1166
LEE, Chong Ha. A Study of Bonded Processing Trade in Korea: Analysis of the Feasibility of the Korean Garment Industry's Moving toward a Full Processing Trade System. Washington, St. Louis, 1964. 311p. DA 26 (Aug. 1965), 767; UM 65-6844.
Includes a study of the role in this trade of Japanese consignors, who "provide raw materials and tech-

nical assistance and who assume responsibility for inspecting and guaranteeing processed products."

1167
CHAI, Nam-Yearl. Asian Attitudes toward International Law: A Case Study of Korea. Pennsylvania, 1967. 303p. DA 28 (June 1968), 5125-26-A; UM 68-9189.
Includes an analysis of the Korean-Japanese disputes concerning Korea's claim to sovereignty over the adjacent seas and the Japanese claim to property in Korea.

1168
HAH, Chong-Do. The Dynamics of Japanese-Korean Relations, 1945-1963: An Interpretation of International Conflict. Indiana, 1967. 372p. DA 28 (May 1968), 4677-A; UM 68-7234.
Analyzes the various sources of discord, with particular emphasis on the period 1951-1960. Also includes a study on the life of the Korean minority living in Japan.
Rel.Publ.: "Bitter Diplomacy: Postwar Japan-Korea Relations," in Studies on Asia, 1964, ed. by Robert K. Sakai (Lincoln: University of Nebraska Press, 1964), 63-93; "National Image and the Japanese-Korean Conflict, 1951-1965," in Studies on Asia, 1967, ed. by Sidney D. Brown (Lincoln: University of Nebraska Press, 1967), 33-69.

1169
KIM, Ok Yul. The American Role in Korean-Japanese Relations. Bryn Mawr, 1967. 235p. DA 28 (Apr. 1968), 4239-A; UM 68-4695.
A study of the United States role in the achievement of the Normalization Treaty between Japan and Korea.
Rel.Publ.: "American Views of Korean-Japanese Rapprochement," in Hanguk Yŏngu Tosŏgwan, Seoul, Bulletin of the Korean Research Center: Journal of Social Science and Humanities, 28 (June 1968), 18-30.

1170
LEE, Soon-won Stewart. Korean-Japanese Discord, 1945-1965: A Case Study of International Conflict. Rutgers, 1967. 304p. DA 28 (Aug. 1967), 752-53-A; UM 67-9253.
Contents: Pt.1: Introduction. Pt.2: Historical Background: Japanese-Korean Relations to 1945. Pt.3: Issues in Conflict: The Issue of Property Claims; The Fishery Line; The Territorial Dispute; Koreans in Japan; Japanese Repartriation of Koreans to North Korea; Political Questions. Pt.4: Negotiations for Normalization: Postwar Developments and Japan-ROK Relations under SCAP; Negotiation Efforts under Syngman Rhee's Regime; Negotiations under Post-Rhee Governments; The Terms of Settlement. Pt.5: Analysis: United States Involvement in the Japan-ROK Controversy; Japanese Policy toward the Republic of Korea; ROK's Policy toward Korea.

Mongolia and Tibet

1171
FRITERS, Gerard Martin. The International Position of Outer Mongolia: A Contribution to Russia's and Japan's Policies in the Far East. Geneve, 1939. 165p.
Rel.Publ.: The International...East. Dijon: Darantière, 1939; Outer Mongolia and Its International Position. Ed. by Eleanor Lattimore. Baltimore: Johns Hopkins Press, 1949. xlvii, 358p.

1172
HYER, Paul V. Japan and the Lamaist World: Part I, Japanese Relations with Tibet. California, Berkeley, 1961. 274p.
Contents: Kawaguchi Ekai: Japan's Pioneer to Tibet at the Turn of the Century (Origins of Japanese-Tibetan Contact, Kawaguchi's Adventure in Lhasa, Kawaguchi as a Japanese and Tibet's First Impression of Japan); Teramoto Enga's Tibetan Enterprises, 1900-1910; Tibet's Independence Movement and the Japanese (Establishing Relations between Honganji and the Dalai Lama, Aoki Bunkyō Enters Tibet, The Beginning of New Developments in Tibet, Yajima Yasujirō, Military Adviser of the Dalai Lama, The Decline of Japanese-Tibetan Relations Following World War I); Tibet, Japan, and the Coming of the War (The Nature of Japanese-Tibetan Relations during the Late 1930's, Plan to Establish a Base in Tibet for Operations in Mongolia); Tibet and Japan's Greater East Asia (Developments Following Pearl Harbor, Visit to Japan of Tibetan Government Representatives, Kimura Hisao, Japanese Agent in Tibet).
Rel.Publ.: "Japaner und Lama," Zeitschrift für Geopolitik, Aug. 1954.

South Asia

1173
BOCK, Robert Leroy. Subhas Chandra Bose: Bengali Revolutionary Nationalist, 1897-1945. American, 1960. 286p. DA 21 (Nov. 1960), 1236-37; UM 60-3022.
Includes a discussion of Bose's Japanese association during World War II and of his connections with Asian Communism.
Rel.Publ.: "The Political Philosophy of Subhas Chandra Bose: Bengali Revolutionary Nationalist, 1897-1945," in Arkansas Academy of Science, Proceedings, 16 (1962), 30-36.

1174
LAL, Gopal. India's Trade Relations with South-East Asia and the Far East since Independence. Bhagalpur, 1963. ii, 304, xxiii p.
Pinpoints some of the weaknesses in India's trade relations with Southeast Asia and East Asia and suggests measures for the removal of obstacles hindering the development of such trade relations. Ch.1 deals with the scope and plan of the work, Ch.2 with the economy of East and Southeast Asia, Ch.3 with Indian government policy, and Ch.4 with trade development measures. Ch.5 and 6 examine Indian exports to and imports from the two regions. Ch.7 discusses India's balance of payments with East and Southeast Asia, and Ch.8 examines the problem of regional cooperation. In Ch.9 an analysis of India's trade agreements is presented, and Ch.10 sets forth the main conclusions of the study.

1175
GHOSH, Kalyan Kumar. Dissertation on the history of the Indian National Army during World War II [Exact title unknown]. Indian School of International Studies, New Delhi, 1965.
A study of the I.N.A., that portion of the Indian army which transferred its loyalty to Japan upon the fall of Singapore in 1942 and which participated in subsequent military campaigns along the Indo-Burmese border.
Rel.Publ.: "The Indian National Army: Motives, Problems, and Significance," Asian Studies (Manila),

7 (Apr. 1960), 4-30.

Southeast Asia before World War II

See also International Relations--
Asia: general (pages 111-12).

Early to 1860

1176
RÖHL, Wilhelm. Die ersten diplomatischen Beziehungen zwischen Japan und Siam zu Beginn des 17. Jahrhunderts [The First Diplomatic Relations between Japan and Siam, at the Beginning of the Seventeenth Century]. Hamburg, 1955. iv, 148p. Text in German. Diss. ms. available at Hamburg, Staats- und Universitätsbibliothek, Nr. Diss. phil. Mscr. 356.

Studies Japanese-Siamese relations during the late 1500's and early 1600's, focusing in part on the letters that Tokugawa Ieyasu and Honda Masazumi sent to Siam at that time and on the first Siamese ships and embassies sent to Japan. The appendix contains (in translation) the correspondence exchanged between Siam and Japan during the years 1606-1623 as well as Japanese reports about the visit of a Japanese delegation to the court of the shogun.

Rel.Publ.: "Japanische Siam-Kaufleute um 1600," in Gesellschaft für Natur- und Völkerkunde Ostasiens, Nachrichten, 78 (1955), 12-17.

1177
IRIKURA, James Kensuke. Trade and Diplomacy between the Philippines and Japan, 1585-1623. Yale, 1958. 270p.

An investigation of early Spanish and Japanese activities in the Philippines and of their effect upon the area.

1178
MEILINK-ROELOFSZ, Marie Antoinette Petronella. Asian Trade and European Influence in the Indonesian Archipelago between 1500 and about 1630. Amsterdam Gemeentelijke, 1962.

Information on Japanese trade with China and with Southeast Asia during the sixteenth and seventeenth centuries is incorporated in various sections of the thesis.

Rel.Publ.: Asian...1630. The Hague: M. Nijhoff, 1962. viii, 471p.

1860-1941: The Philippines

1179
CRUZ, Cornelio Castor. Commercial Relations of the Philippine Islands with Other Regions. Chicago, 1928. xxvii, 391p. AB: University of Chicago. Abstracts of Theses, Science Series, 7 (1928/29), p.251-57.

Information on Filipino-Japanese trade during the 1920's and on the activities of Japanese commercial organizations in the Philippines is included.

1180
PROVIDO, Generoso Pacificar. Japanese Interests in the Philippines. Stanford, 1936. 164p. AB: Stanford University. Abstracts of Dissertations, 1936/37. p.131-33.

Primarily a discussion of Japanese economic activities in the Philippines during the first four decades of the twentieth century. Includes information on trade and competition between Japan and the Philippines as well as on Japanese investments in the archipelago, particularly in Davao.

1181
BALDORIA, Pedro Laeda. A Study of the Problems Involved in the Neutralization of the Philippines. Southern California, 1940. 295p.

Deals in part with Philippine-Japanese-American relations. It indicates the factors underlying Japanese policy in the Philippines and Japan's attitude toward the neutralization of the islands following the anticipated termination of American colonial rule.

1182
EYRE, James Kline, Jr. The Philippines, the Powers, and the Spanish-American War: A Study of Foreign Policies. Michigan, 1940. iii, 315p. AB: Microfilm Abstracts. v.2, no.2 (1940), p.111-12; UM 154.

See Chapters 14-17 (p.233-296): Japan, Spain, and the Philippines; Japan Favorable to the United States; The Philippines: A Japanese-American Clash of Interests; The Ponce Mission to Japan.

Rel.Publ.: "Japan and the American Annexation of the Philippines," PHR, 11 (Mar. 1942), 55-71; "Japanese Imperialism and the Aguinaldo Insurrection," in United States Naval Institute, Proceedings, 75 (Aug. 1949), 901-07; "Early Japanese Imperialism and the Philippines," in United States Naval Institute, Proceedings, 75 (Nov. 1949), 1267-75.

1183
CASES, Manuel Tandas. The Philippines in Foreign Relations since 1895. California, Berkeley, 1941. 607p. (2v.).

Focuses on the role that the Philippines played in American-Japanese relations, 1895-1940.

1184
LONG, Robert Eli. A Study of the Naval Base with Particular Reference to the Philippine Islands. Yale, 1942. 311p.

Ch.6, "The Element of Strength" (p.237-86), describes the strategic, tactical, and logistical factors influencing Japanese strength and weakness in the home islands, Taiwan, Mainland China, the South Pacific, and the East Indies. The author concludes that postwar strategic control of the Philippines by the United States would assure it of control over the western Pacific.

1185
FRIEND, Theodore Wood, III. The Politics and Strategy of Philippine Independence, 1929-1936. Yale, 1958. 243p.

See especially Ch.12, "The Deepening Strategic Quandry: 1898-1936," which deals almost entirely with Japanese-American relations and with Japan's impact on the formation of American Philippine policy.

Rel.Publ.: Between Two Empires: The Ordeal of the Philippines 1929-1946. New Haven: Yale University Press, 1965. xviii, 312p. (Yale Historical Publications, 22); "The Philippine Sugar Industry and the Politics of Independence, 1929-1935," JAS, 22 (Feb. 1963), 179-92; "American Interests and Philippine Independence, 1929-1933," Philippine Studies, 11 (Oct. 1963), 505-23; "Philippine Interests and the Mission for Independence, 1929-1932," Philippine Studies, 12 (Jan. 1964), 63-82; "Philippine Independence and the Last Lame-Duck Congress," Philippine Studies, 12 (Apr. 1964), 260-76;

"Veto and Repassage of the Hare-Howes-Cutting Act: A Catalogue of Motives," Philippine Studies, 12 (Oct. 1964), 666-80; "Manuel Quezon: Charismatic Conservative," Philippine Historical Review, 1 (1965), 153-69.

1186
SANIEL, Josefa M. Lucero. Japan and the Philippines, 1868-1898. Michigan, 1962. 470p. DA 23 (July 1962), 216; UM 62-2782.

Contents: Antecedent Relations between Japan and the Philippines, 1565-1868; A Period of Probing: 1868-1888; The Ideological Basis of Japanese Expansion towards the Philippines: (1) Nationalism and Expansion, (2) Elaboration on Expansionist Programs; Japan and the Philippines: Trade Relations (1889-1898); Spanish Apprehensions over Japanese Intentions; The Philippine Revolution and the Japanese Involvement, 1896-1898: (1) Official Relations: Japan and the Philippines, (2) Unofficial Relations: The Japanese and the Philippines.

Rel.Publ.: Japan...1898. Quezon City: University of the Philippines, 1962. xvi, 409p.; "Four Japanese: Their Plans for the Expansion of Japan to the Philippines," Journal of Southeast Asian History, 4 (Sept. 1963), 1-12. [Also in Asian Studies (Quezon City), 1, special issue (1963), 52-63]; "Okuma Shigenobu and the 1898 Philippine Problem," Philippine Historical Review, 1 (1965), 298-319.

1860-1941: Burma, Indochina, Indonesia, Malaya, and Thailand

1187
MORICE, Jean. Les Accords commerciaux entre l'Indochine et le Japon [The Commerical Agreements between Indochina and Japan]. Paris, 1933. Text in French.

A study of Japan's relations with France and with French Indochina (1500's-1932). Special emphasis is placed on the Franco-Japanese commercial agreement of May 13, 1932, relating to Japanese trade with Indochina.

Rel.Publ.: Les Accords...Japon. Paris: F. Louiton, 1933. viii, 187p.

1188
JAQUET, Louis George Martin. De industrialisatie van Japan in verband met de Japansche handelsexpansie naar Nederlandsch-Indië [The Industrialization of Japan and Its Relation to Japanese Trade Expansion towards the Dutch East Indies]. Leiden, 1935. Text in Dutch.

1189
LIJNKAMP, Henricus Anthonius Franciscus. De "Japannerwet:" Onderzoek naar de wording [The "Japannerwet:" An Investigation of Its Origins]. Utrecht, 1938. x, 115p. Text in Dutch.

The "Japannerwet" refers to the ordinance which placed all Japanese nationals in the Dutch East Indies on an equal footing with Europeans insofar as civil law was involved. It went into effect in 1899. Contents: A Short Historical Survey of the Legal Distinctions among the Inhabitants of the Dutch East Indies According to Their National Origins; An Historical Survey of the International Legal Relations between Holland and Japan, 1605-1896; The Reasons for the Creation of the "Japannerwet."

Rel.Publ.: De "Japannerwet"...wording. Utrecht: A. Oosthoek, 1938. 115p. (Utrechtsche bijdragen tot de geschiedenis, het staatsrecht, en de economie van Nederlandsch-Indië, 12)

AKASHI, Yoji. The Boycott and Anti-Japanese National Salvation Movement of the Nanyang Chinese, 1908-1941. 1963. See no.1059.

1190
FLOOD, Edward Thadeus. Japan's Relations with Thailand: 1928-1941. Washington, Seattle, 1967. 835p. DA 29 (July 1968), 210-A; UM 68-9283.

Seeks to explain the remarkable rapprochement that the Thai-Japanese Treaty of Alliance of December 21, 1941, signified through an analysis of earlier relations between the two countries.

Rel.Publ.: "The 1940 Franco-Thai Border Dispute and Phibuun Sankhraam's Commitment to Japan," Journal of Southeast Asian History, 10 (Sept. 1969), 304-25.

WOLTHUIS, Robert K. United States Foreign Policy towards the Netherlands Indies: 1937-1945. 1968. See no.1224.

Southeast Asia during World War II

Burma, Indochina, Malaya, and Thailand

1191
KUYPERS, Cornelis Anthonie. Klinische waarnemingen bij beri-beri in een Japans Krijgsgevangenkamp te Singapore (1944-1945) [Clinical Observations of Beri-beri in a Japanese Prisoner-of-war Camp in Singapore, 1944-1945]. Leiden, 1948. 158p. Text in Dutch, with a summary in English.

A detailed report of an epidemic of cardio-vascular oedematous, or "wet" beri-beri, which ravaged a Japanese p.o.w. camp on Pulu Damar, a small island off Singapore, in late 1944 and early 1945.

Rel.Publ.: Klinische...1945. n.p., 1948.

1192
AMES, Carleton Cecil. Impact of British Rule in Burma, 1900-1948. Wisconsin, 1950. iii, 287p. AB: University of Wisconsin. Summaries of Doctoral Dissertations. v.11, p.181-82.

For information on the wartime Japanese occupation see Ch.5, "Self-government and Occupation," and Ch.6, "Liberation and Reconstruction."

1193
HINNERS, David Gardner. British Policy and the Development of Self-Government in Burma, 1935-1948. Chicago, 1951. vii, 373p. AB: United States Department of State, External Research Staff. Abstracts of Completed Doctoral Dissertations for the Academic Year 1950/1951. p.400-05.

Ch.3, "Burma under the Japanese Occupation" (p.140-212), studies the Japanese administration in Burma, the anti-Japanese underground movement, and the liberation of Burma.

1194
HAMMER, Ellen Joy. The Emergence of Vietnam. Columbia, 1952. 342p.

Includes information on the Japanese in Indochina during World War II.

Rel.Publ.: The Struggle for Indochina. Stanford: Stanford University Press, 1954. 342p.

1195
DMITRIEV, A. A. Ekspansiia iaponskogo imperializma v strany Iugo-Vostochnoi Azii v gody 2-oi mirovoi

voiny [The Expansion of Japanese Imperialism into the Countries of Southeast Asia suring the Second World War]. Moscow, Moskovskii gosudarstvennyi institut mezhdunarodnykh otnoshenii Ministerstva Inostrannykh Del SSSR, 1955. (Candidate of Economic Sciences degree) 274p. Text in Russian.

1196
MAHAJANI, Usha Ganesh. The Roles of the Indian Minorities in Burmese and Malayan Nationalisms. Johns Hopkins, 1957. ix, 464p.
See Ch.5, "The Japanese Occupation of Burma and Malaya" (p.139-70 of the published version).
Rel.Publ.: The Role of Indian Minorities in Burma and Malaya. Bombay: Vora, 1960. xxx, 344p.

1197
KOZICKI, Richard Joseph. India and Burma, 1937-1957: A Study in International Relations. Pennsylvania, 1959. 513p. DA 20 (Nov. 1959), 1850; UM 59-4640.
See Ch.4 (p.150-89) for a descriptive study of Burma during the Japanese Occupation.

BOCK, Robert L. Subhas Chandra Bose: Bengali Revolutionary Nationalist, 1897-1945. 1960. See no.1173.

1198
SACKS, Isaac Milton. Communism and Nationalism in Viet Nam: 1918-1946. Yale, 1960. 296p. DA 28 (Dec. 1967), 2309-A; UM 67-15,561.
Information on the Japanese occupation is included. See especially Ch.7, "The Japanese Occupation and Vietnamese Nationalism" (p.150-76), and Ch.9, "'Independent' Viet Nam under Japanese Auspices" (p.198-218).

1199
CHAWAN CHAWANIDCHAYA. Thai Irredentism and French Indochina: A Study of a Controversial Aspect of Thai Nationalism. Yale, 1962. 372p.
Pages 232-55 discuss Japan's role in settling Franco-Thai disputes and in diverting and containing Thai irredentism under the "Pax Nipponica," 1941-1945. The Thai disillusionment with Japanese tutelage and the Thai attempt to return to status quo ante late in World War II also are examined in some detail.

1200
KAHLER, John Knapp. The Genesis of the American Involvement in Indochina, 1940-1954. Chicago, 1964. 163p.
See Ch.1, "The Establishment of Japanese Domination over Indo-China, 1940-1941."

1201
SEIN MAUNG, Maung. Socio-Cultural Values and Economic Backwardness: A Case Study of Burma. New York, 1964. 279p. DA 26 (July 1965), 474; UM 65-1648.
Includes a discussion of the Japanese impact on religio-cultural values and economic developments in Burma during World War II.

GHOSH, Kalyan K. Dissertation on the history of the Indian National Army during World War II. 1965. See no.1175.

1202
GUYOT, Dorothy Hess. The Political Impact of the Japanese Occupation of Burma. Yale, 1966. 498p. DA 27 (Feb. 1967), 2570-A; UM 67-71.
"For the ethnic Burmese majority of the population events of the war had four major political consequences:" (1) independence became a realistic expectation, (2) government ceased to be basically an administrative matter, (3) a new political elite arose, and (4) the gap separating the political elite from the mass was bridged by cohesive secular organizations.
Rel.Publ.: "The Burma Independence Army: A Political Movement in Military Garb," in Southeast Asia in World War II: Four Essays, ed. by Josef Silverstein (New Haven: Yale University, Southeast Asia Studies, 1966), 51-65; "The Uses of Buddhism in Wartime Burma," Asian Studies (Manila), 7 (Apr. 1969), 50-80.

1203
McALISTER, John Thomas, Jr. The Origins of the Vietnamese Revolution. Yale, 1966. 450p. DA 28 (Aug. 1967), 754-55-A; UM 66-14,984.
Includes an analysis of the impact of the Japanese occupation.
Rel.Publ.: Viet Nam: The Origins of Revolution. New York: Knopf, 1969. 377p.

Indonesia

1204
WIJN, Jan Frederik de. Deficiëntie-verschijnselen bij krijgsgevangenen, waargenomen bij langdurige ondervoeding in krijgsgevangen-kampen te Batavia en Fukuoka (Japan) gedurende de Japanse bezetting van Nederlandsch Oost-Indië (1942-1945): In het bijzonder over haematologische bevindingen bij pellagra sine pellagra [Evidence of General Physical Deficiency in Prisoners-of-war Found after Longstanding Malnutrition in p.o.w. Camps in Batavia and in Fukuoka (Japan) during the Japanese Occupation of the Dutch East Indies, 1942-1945, with Particular Emphasis on Haemotological Findings of Pellagra Sine Pellagra]. Utrecht, 1947. Text in Dutch with summaries in English, French, and German.
An analysis of the food-rations supplied to the camp inmates and of the resulting deficiencies in certain vitamins, protein, and fat.
Rel.Publ.: Deficientie...pellagra. n.p., 1947. 132p.

1205
POPPE, Janus. Political Development in the Netherlands East Indies during and Immediately after the Japanese Occupation. Georgetown, 1948. 339p.
Contents: Japanese Plans for the Netherlands East Indies; Initial Political Development during the Japanese Occupation; Progressive Administration during the Japanese Occupation; The Independence Movement in the Netherlands East Indies during the Japanese Occupation; Final Development towards Independence; Birth of the Republic of Indonesia.

1206
WOLF, Charles, Jr. The Indonesian Story: The Birth, Growth, and Structure of the Indonesian Republic. Harvard, 1949. Diss. ms. not available.
Ch.1, "Birth of the Republic," deals with the Japanese occupation.
Rel.Publ.: The Indonesian...Republic. New York: John Day, 1948. x, 201p.; "The Men Who Made Merdeka," FES, 16 (Sept. 3, 1947), 181-84.

1207
KAHIN, George McTurnan. Nationalism and Revolution in Indonesia. Johns Hopkins, 1951. 986, xvii p.

See Chapter 5, "The Japanese Occupation."
Rel.Publ.: Nationalism...Indonesia. Ithaca: Cornell University Press, 1952. xii, 490p.

1208
ELSBREE, Willard Hubbard. Japan and the National Movements in Southeast Asia, 1940-1945: With Special Attention to Developments in Indonesia. Harvard, 1952. 260p. AB: 5p. summary appended to diss. ms.
Seeks to define the official Japanese attitude toward various national movements in Southeast Asia and to evaluate the ways in which the wartime occupation affected local nationalist developments. Contents: The Japanese Blueprint; Some Revisions in the Blueprint; The Development of Political Participation in Indonesia; National Unity; National Minorities.
Rel.Publ.: Japan's Role in Southeast Asian Nationalist Movements, 1940 to 1945. Cambridge: Harvard University Press, 1953. 182p.

1209
ZORAB, Arratoon Albert. De Japanse Bezetting van Indonesië en haar volkenrechtelijke zijde [The Japanese Occupation of Indonesia in Regard to International Law]. Leiden, 1954. Text in Dutch, with a summary in English.
An account of the occupation with particular emphasis on Japanese rule in Java.
Rel.Publ.: De Japanse...zijde. Leiden: Universitaire Pers Leiden, 1954. viii, 173p.

1210
AZIZ, Muhammad Abdul. Japan's Colonialism and Indonesia. Leiden, 1955. 264p.
Contents: Pt.1: Japan Starts Conquering Dependencies; Policy in Formosa and Korea; Plans for Further Conquest, 1911-1930; Policy in Manchuria; Internal Preparations for Further Expansion, 1931-1936; Japanese Blueprint, 1937-1941. Pt.2: Plans for Indonesia; Preparations for Conquest: Negotiations; Conquest and Occupation Policy (Military Government, Elimination of Western Influence, Economic Reorganization, Policy towards Islam, Policy towards Nationalism).
Rel.Publ.: Japan's...Indonesia. The Hague: M. Nijhoff, 1955. x, 271p. (Publications under the Direction of the Netherlands Institute of International Affairs, 1)

1211
BENDA, Harry Jindrich. The Crescent and the Rising Sun: Indonesian Islam under the Japanese Occupation of Java, 1942-1945. Cornell, 1955. 352p. DA 15 (Nov. 1955), 2274-75; UM 12,364.
Contents: Pt.1: The Colonial Heritage: The Foundation of Dutch Moslem Policy; The Development of Indonesian Islam, 1918-1931; Dutch Islamic Policy in Transition, 1926-1931; Indonesian Islam during the Closing Years of Dutch Rule. Pt.2: The Japanese Occupation: The Rebirth of M.I.A.I.: April to December 1942; Indonesian Islam and the Spirit of Dai Nippon; The Consolidation of Japanese Moslem Policy during 1943; The Rise of Masjumi: November 1943-September 1944; Towards Independence: September 1944-August 1945.
Rel.Publ.: The Crescent...1945. The Hague: W. van Hoeve, 1958. xiv, 320p.; "Indonesian Islam under the Japanese Occupation, 1942-1945," Pacific Affairs, 28 (Dec. 1955), 350-62; "The Beginnings of the Japanese Occupation of Java," FEQ 15, (Aug. 1956), 541-60.

1212
DEMIN, Lev Mikhailovich. Iaponskaia agressiia v Indonezii v gody vtoroi mirovoi voiny [Japanese Aggression in Indonesia during the Second World War]. Moscow, Institut vostokovedeniia Akademii nauk SSSR, 1955(?) (Candidate of Historical Sciences degree) Text in Russian. AB: 16p. summary published in 1955.
Rel.Publ.: Iaponskaia okkupatsiia Indonezii, 1942-1945 gg. Moscow: Izd-vo Vostochnoi literatury, 1963. 234p. (Akademiia nauk SSSR. Institut narodov Azii)

DMITRIEV, A. A. Ekspansiia iaponskogo imperializma v strany Iugo-Vostochnoi Azii v gody 2-oi mirovoi voiny. 1955. See no.1195.

1213
STELTZER, Hans-Jürgen. Die Indonesienpolitik der Vereinigten Staaten 1940 bis 1949 [The Indonesian Policy of the United States, 1940-1949]. Hamburg, 1956. iii, 200, xvii p. Text in German. Diss. ms. available at Hamburg, Staats- und Universitätsbibliothek, Nr. Mscr. 429.
Studies the influence of American and Japanese foreign policy upon one another particularly with regard to the interests that the two countries had in Indonesia. The Japanese dependence on the United States for raw materials and the political consequences of this factor as well as the American embargo of Japan and its influence upon American-Indonesian relations are among the subjects handled within the dissertation.

1214
HARPER, Robert William. An Analysis of the Development of the International Relations of Indonesia. American, 1957. 254p. DA 17 (July 1957), 1583; UM 21,404.
See Ch.5, "The Japanese Occupation" (p.87-105), and Ch.8, "Contemporary International Relations."

1215
AMSTUTZ, James Bruce. The Indonesian Youth Movement, 1908-1955. Fletcher, 1958. v, 424p.
Includes information on the movement during the period of Japanese occupation. See especially Ch.3, "The Youth Movement during the Japanese Occupation" (p.76-111), and Ch.4, "The Proclamation of Independence" (p.112-23).

1216
SELO SOEMARDJAN. Social Changes in Jogjakarta. Cornell, 1959. 552p. DA 20 (June 1960), 4746-47; UM 60-1886.
Pt.1 includes a discussion of changes in the political status of the Jogjakarta administration during the Japanese occupation of Indonesia.
Rel.Publ.: Social...Jogjakarta. Ithaca: Cornell University Press, 1962. xxvii, 440p.

1217
SUTTER, John Orval. Indonesianisasi: A Historical Survey of the Role of Politics in the Institutions of a Changing Economy from the Second World War to the Eve of the General Elections (1940-1955). Cornell, 1959. 1335p. DA 21 (Nov. 1960), 1240; UM 60-2494.
See Pt.2, "The Reorganization of the Indonesian Economy under the Japanese.
Rel.Publ.: Indonesianisasi: Politics in a Changing Economy, 1940-1955. Ithaca, 1959. xxi, 1312p. (4v.) (Cornell University. Department of Far Eastern Studies. Southeast Asia Program. Data Paper no.36, I-IV)

1218
MESTENHAUSER, Josef Arthur. Ideologies in Conflict in Indonesia, 1945-1955. Minnesota, 1960. 410p. DA 21 (July 1960), 230-31; UM 60-2049.

"In Ch.3 ideological developments under the Japanese occupation are surveyed with a view toward ascertaining the importance of personalities, communications, institutionalization, and development of means to pursue ideological objectives."

1219
VELDEN, Doetje van. De Japanse interneringskampen voor burgers gedurende de tweede wereldoorlog [The Japanese Civil Internment Camps during the Second World War]. Utrecht, 1963. Text in Dutch, with summary in English.

A detailed description of Japanese internment camps for enemy civilians in China, Hong Kong, Japan, and Southeast Asia, with particular emphasis on Java. Describes Japanese policies, camp conditions, and relations between inmates and camp personnel.

Rel.Publ.: De Japanse...wereldoorlog. Groningen: J. B. Wolters, 1963. viii, 628p.

1220
DAHM, Bernhard. Sukarnos Kampf um Indonesiens Unabhängigkeit: Werdegang und politische Ideen bis zu seiner Wahl zum 1. Präsidenten der Republik Indonesien im August 1945 [Sukarno's Struggle for Indonesien Independence: His Career and Political Ideals until His Election as the First President of the Republic of Indonesia in August 1945]. Kiel, 1964. xi, 406p. Text in German. Diss. ms. available at Kiel, Universitätsbibliothek, Nr. P 717.

Pages 159-239 focus on Sukarno's struggle for Indonesian independence during the Japanese occupation period: his activities against both Western and Japanese imperialism; the guiding principles of the Japanese occupation; Sukarno's efforts to form a partnership with the Japanese in Indonesia; the various stages in Japanese policy through the conclusion of the war.

Rel.Publ.: Sukarnos...1945. Frankfurt a.M. und Berlin: Metzner, 1966. xvi, 295p. (Institut für Asienkunde in Hamburg. Schriften, 18); Soekarno en de strijd om Indonesie's onafhankelijkheid. Meppel: J. A. Boom, 1964. 399p.; Sukarno and the Struggle for Indonesian Independence. Ithaca: Cornell University Press, 1969.

1221
SMAIL, John Richard Wharton. Bandung in the Early Revolution, 1945-1946. Cornell, 1964. 310p. DA 25 (Sept. 1964), 1882; UM 64-8758.

"The thesis deals with events in and around the city of Bandung in West Java during the first seven months of the Indonesian Revolution...August 17, 1945-March 24, 1946." Throughout the thesis there is information on the wartime Japanese occupation, the Japanese surrender and disarmament upon the conclusion of World War Two, and the Japanese influence on Indonesian nationalism.

Rel.Publ.: Bandung in the Early Revolution, 1945-1946: A Study in the Social History of the Indonesian Revolution. Ithaca: Cornell University, Southeast Asia Program, Department of Asian Studies, 1964. xi, 169p. (Modern Indonesia Project. Monograph Series)

1222
ANDERSON, Benedict Richard O'Gorman. The Pemuda Revolution: Indonesian Politics 1945-1946. Cornell, 1967. 668p. DA 28 (Oct. 1967), 1476-A; UM 67-12,325.

The thesis explores in part "the sociological, political, and psychological background to the outbreak of the Indonesian national revolution in the fall of 1945." See especially Ch.1, which "covers the experience of various pemuda elements in the late Japanese colonial period...and the formation of a specifically pemuda political consciousness and style," and Ch.2, which includes information on the rise to power of politicians who had collaborated with the Japanese.

Rel.Publ.: Some Aspects of Indonesian Politics under the Japanese Occupation: 1944-1945. Ithaca, 1961. ix, 126p. (Cornell University. Department of Far Eastern Studies. Modern Indonesian Project. Interim Reports Series); "Japan: 'The Light of Asia,'" in Southeast Asia in World War II: Four Essays, ed. by Josef Silverstein (New Haven: Yale University, Southeast Asia Studies, 1966), 13-50.

1223
KANAHELE, George Sanford. The Japanese Occupation of Indonesia: Prelude to Independence. Cornell, 1967. 343p. DA 28 (Oct. 1967), 1486-A; UM 67-12,617.

"Traces the growth of Indonesian nationalism during the Japanese occupation...not only in Java but also in the outer Islands....The bulk of the study is a complex narrative of the interaction between Indonesian nationalists and Japanese authorities."

1224
WOLTHUIS, Robert K. United States Foreign Policy towards the Netherlands Indies, 1937-1945. Johns Hopkins, 1968. 476p. DA 30 (July 1969), 375-76-A; UM 68-10,579.

Includes information on Japanese interest in the Indies before World War II and on American policy towards the Indies while they were under Japanese occupation.

Philippines

1225
PRIEST, Bill Jason. Philippine Education in Transition, 1941-1946. California, Berkeley, 1947. 287p.

The study seeks "to trace the development of Philippine public education during this period of Japanese Occupation, to discern the views of Filipino educators toward the educational offering of this period, and to analyze postwar educational problems of the Philippines."

1226
VAUGHAN, Elizabeth Head. A Japanese Internment Camp: A Sociological Study of Bacolod Camp, Negros Island, Philippines. North Carolina, 1947. 182p.

Contents: Social and Economic Structure of the Philippines; Opening of the Bacolod Camp; Bacolod Camp Organization: The Pooling of Food Supplies; Bacolod Camp Organization: Work and Health; Bacolod Camp Organization: Recreation, Religion, and Communication; The Japanese; Development of Artifacts in the Bacolod Camp; Adjustment of Individuals to the New Culture; A Community under Stress.

1227
SORIANO, Rafaelita Vasquez Hilario. Japanese Occupation of the Philippines, with Special Reference to Japanese Propaganda 1941-1945. Michigan, 1948. 451p. AB: Microfilm Abstracts, v.8, no.2 (1948), p.147-48; UM 1078.

Contents: The Filipino Nation; Philippine-Japanese Relations prior to the American Regime; Japanese Commercial Penetration and Propaganda: Background for Invasion and Occupation; The Establishment of the Puppet Philippine Government; Japanese Propaganda Media and

Techniques; Japan's Propaganda Lines; The Philippine Guerilla Resistance Movement.

1228
LEAR, Elmer Norton. Collaboration, Resistance, and Liberation: A Study of Society and Education in Leyte, the Philippines, under Japanese Occupation. Columbia, 1951. [Ph.D. degree] 745p. DA 12 (1952), 340-41; UM 3358.

"This study aims to present a documented analysis of the life of a community under enemy rule....Chapter 2 concerns itself with the governing policy and activities of the Japanese Military Administration in Leyte, and the adaptation of the Filipino 'puppet' administration and the people to enemy occupation....Chapter 3, the analysis of the resistance movement in Leyte, constitutes the heart of the study....The study carries over into the Liberation period, tracing the aftermath of resistance and collaboration, and pointing out the difficulties of reconstruction."

Rel.Publ.: The Japanese Occupation of the Philippines, Leyte, 1941-1945. Ithaca: Cornell University, Department of Far Eastern Studies, Southeast Asia Program, 1961. xvi, 246p. (Cornell University. Southeast Asia Program. Data Paper, 42); "Collaboration in Leyte: The Philippines under Japanese Occupation," FEQ, 11 (Feb. 1952), 183-206; "Education in Guerrilla Territory under a Regime of Enemy Occupation," History of Education Quarterly, 7 (Fall 1967), 312-28.

1229
WURFEL, Violet Elizabeth. American Implementation of Philippine Independence. Virginia, 1951. vii, 774p. (2v.) AB: University of Virginia. Abstracts of Dissertations, 1951. p.77-82.

For information on the wartime Japanese occupation of the Philippines, see Ch.3, "Final Preparations for Independence" (p.149-262), which contains material on Japan and the Philippine wartime government, Philippine collaboration with Japan, and American attitudes towards collaboration. The emphasis, however, is strongly on Philippine internal problems rather than on the Japanese Occupation itself.

DMITRIEV, A. A. Ekspansiia iaponskogo imperializma v strany Iugo-Vostochnoi Azii v gody 2-oi mirovoi voiny. 1955. See no.1195.

1230
RUTLAND, Lolita Garcia. The History of Teacher Education in the Philippines to 1955. Florida, 1955. 120p. DA 15 (Dec. 1955), 2463; UM 14,328.

The dissertation includes information on Japanese wartime efforts "to indoctrinate Filipino teachers with the tenets and principles of the 'co-prosperity sphere.'"

1231
HOEKSEMA, Renze Lyle. Communism in the Philippines: A Historical and Analytical Study of Communism and the Communist Party in the Philippines and Its Relations to Communist Movements Abroad. Harvard, 1956. iv, 507p. AB: 4p. summary appended to diss. ms.

Ch.5, "The Wartime History of the CPP and Hukbalahap" (p.231-74), discusses Japanese actions against the Communist Party as well as the Party's anti-Japanese stand.

1232
JENSEN, Khin Khin Myint. The Chinese in the Philippines during the American Regime, 1898-1946. Wisconsin, 1956. 415p. DA 16 (Nov. 1956), 2143; UM 19,099.

See Ch.7, "The Chinese Community during the Japanese War" (p.333-68), which focuses on Chinese collaboration in the underground resistance movement.

1233
GARCIA, Alfonso Gonzales. An Historical Study of the Legal and Constitutional Bases of Public Elementary Education in the Philippines. Michigan, 1959. 440p. DA 19 (June 1959), 3171; UM 59-2116.

See Ch.7 (p.241-82) for a study of the Japanese impact on Philippine education.

1234
LEAR, Elmer Norton. The Legitimation of Resistance: A Case Study. New School for Social Research, 1964. [D.S.Sc. degree]. 266p. DA 26 (Aug. 1965), 1204-05; UM 65-1109.

"This is a study in the political sociology of guerrilla resistance. It centers upon the efforts of a Philippines-based guerrilla organization to gain recognition as the legitimate resistance movement combatting an enemy occupation power. Specifically, this is a study in failure--the failure of the Western Leyte Guerrilla Warfare Forces, the best organized and strongest anti-Japanese force on Leyte, to win American endorsement as the official resistance organization on the island of Leyte."

Rel.Publ.: See main entry no.1228.

1225
STEINBERG, David Joel. The Philippines during World War Two: A Study in Political Collaboration. Harvard, 1964. xii, 463p. AB: 4p. summary appended to diss. ms.

"The thesis is a study of what happened during the war in the Philippines. It attempts to relate the Japanese aspirations and achievements. It also recounts how the Filipinos, especially the Filipino oligarchy, responded to the Japanese occupation. Most of the prewar elite chose to remain in office under the Japanese, and their reaction to the Japanese demand for cooperation is of central concern. Thus, this monograph attempts to analyse whether the perjorative 'collaborator' has any valid meaning within the Philippine context." Contents: "The Philippine Executive Commission; The Laurel Republic; The Motivation for Collaboration; The Post-War Era.

Rel.Publ.: Philippine Collaboration in World War II. Ann Arbor: University of Michigan Press, 1967. viii, 235p.; "Jose P. Laurel: A 'Collaborator' Misunderstood," JAS, 24 (Aug. 1965), 651-65; "The Philippine 'Collaborators:' Survival of an Oligarchy," in Southeast Asia in World War II: Four Essays. ed. by Josef Silverstein (New Haven: Yale University, Southeast Asia Studies, 1966), 67-86.

1236
FERNANDEZ, Alejandro M. International Law in Philippine Relations, 1898-1946. Duke, 1966. 355p. DA 27 (Dec. 1966), 1886-A; UM 66-11,092.

Includes "a detailed description of the Japanese administration of the Philippines as a belligerent occupant" and "an analysis of the legal consequences of that occupation in terms of the rights and duties of the belligerent occupant and the validity of its acts and judgments."

Southeast Asia since World War II

1237
ANGELES, Conrado P. Dissertation on the Resumption of Trade between the Philippines and Japan. Santo Tomas, 1952.

1238
IDLE, Dunning, IV. Indonesia's Independent and Active Foreign Policy. Yale, 1956. 489p. DA 25 (Dec. 1964), 3669-70; UM 64-11,376.

Two chapters (p.52-70 and p.375-89) discuss Japanese-Indonesian relations. The former reviews postwar relations through the mid-1950's; the latter views the negotiations over the Treaty of Peace with Japan as an aspect of Indonesian domestic politics.

1239
SANVICTORES, Lourdes Lauchengco. Philippine-Japan World Trade: Its Impact on Philippine Economy. Santo Tomas, 1966.

1240
VIRACH ARROMDEE. Economics of the Rice Trade among Countries of South East Asia. Minnesota, 1968. 362p. DA 30 (Aug. 1969), 462-A; UM 69-11,365.

A study of the trade with particular emphasis on Thailand. For information on Japan as an export market for Thai rice, see p.228-57. This section includes an historical analysis of rice production and consumption for Japan, analyses of supply and demand for Japan, and projections of Japanese rice imports in 1975.

AUSTRALIA AND NEW ZEALAND

See also International Relations--Allied participation in World War II (pages 109-11) and International Relations --China: Mancurian Incident (pages 127-31).

WYNNE, Edward C. Racial Discrimination in the Attitude of Australia towards the Japanese. 1927. See no.1688.

TUELLER, Dallas A. Australian-American Relations, 1901-1940. 1946. See no.1396.

1241
MONTGOMERY, Clifford Corey. The External Policy of the Australian Commonwealth. Wisconsin, 1949. 250p. AB: University of Wisconsin. Summaries of Doctoral Dissertations. v.11. p.194-95.

Includes information on Australia's ban on Oriental immigration and on Australian trade with Japan during the 1920's and the 1930's.

1242
ROACH, James Robert. The Background of Australian Foreign Policy. Harvard, 1950. iv, 495p. AB: 6p. summary appended to diss. ms.

For information on Australian-Japanese relations and on immediate postwar Australian attitudes toward Japan, see especially the two chapters entitled "Australia as an Asiatic Power" (p.298-315) and "Japan" (p.315-30).

Rel.Publ.: "Australia and the Japanese Treaty," FES, 20 (Nov. 21, 1951), 206-08.

1243
WALTER, Austin Frederick. Australia's Relations with the United States: 1941-1949. Michigan, 1954. 411p. DA 14 (Aug. 1954), 1247; UM 8432.

Includes a consideration of "the Australian and American positions on the status of Pacific island bases and island territories occupied by Japan, the machinery and policies devised for the Allied occupation of Japan, and the character of the eventual peace settlement with Japan." See especially Ch.3, "The Search for a Peace Settlement in the Pacific: Australia's Place in the Pacific" (p.63-96), Ch.4, "Status of Pacific Islands" (p. 97-147), Ch.5, "Occupied Japan" (p.148-89), and Ch.6, "Making Peace with Japan" (p.190-215).

1244
ROSECRANCE, Richard Newton. Australian Foreign Policy and the Problem of Japan: 1945-1951. Harvard, 1957. ix, 429p. AB: 5p. summary appended to diss. ms.

Analyses the gradual change in Australian policy toward Japan: from one advocating military and economic suppression to one supporting the conclusion of a peace treaty and a security pact. Contents: The Japanese Surrender: Its Prologue and Aftermath; Jurisdictional Disagreements; Dispute over Manus Island; Divergence and Rapprochement; Three Negatives; Growing Disaffection; Second Overture for a Pacific Pact; Second Initiative for a Japanese Treaty; Australian Policy and Japanese Peace Proposals; United States Initiative Resumed; Autumn Negotiations; Second Dulles Mission to the Far East; Prelude to the Peace Conference; Treaty Conference and Australian Ratification.

Rel.Publ.: Australian Diplomacy and Japan, 1945-1951. New York: Cambridge University Press, 1962. xii, 288p.

BENNETT, Neville R. The Anglo-Japanese Alliance and the Dominions, 1902-1911. 1966. See no.1291.

1245
DRYSDALE, Peter David. Japanese-Australian Trade: An Approach to the Study of Bilateral Trade Flows. Australian National, 1967. 318p.

An analysis of the pattern of Japanese-Australian trade based on the application of the index of mutual trade dependence.

Rel.Publ.: "Japanese-Australian Trade," in Australian National University, Department of International Relations, Papers on Modern Japan, 1965 (Canberra, 1965), 83-98.

1246
GORRIE, Averilda Margaret. New Zealand's Future Export Trade with Japan: A Geographic Assessment in the Light of Recent Trends in Japanese Agriculture and Forestry. Auckland, 1967. xiii, 315p. For microfilm and xerox copies, write to the Reference Librarian, the University of Auckland, P.O.B. 2175, Auckland, New Zealand.

A study of recent trends in Japan's agricultural economy with estimates of future Japanese requirements and with information on New Zealand's future prospects as an exporter of wool, mutton and lamb, beef, and logs and forest products to Japan. Contents: Introduction; General Description and Evaluation of Selected Trends in Agriculture in Japan with Special Reference to Arable Farming; Grassland; Animal Husbandry; Sheep Farming; Mutton and Lamb; Dairying in Japan; Beef Cattle Raising in Japan; Forestry in Japan; New Zealand's Trade Rivals in Japan.

EUROPE

General

See also International Relations--general and multilateral (pages 104-07).

1247
NAGAOKA, Haruichi. Histoire des relations du Japon avec l'Europe aux XVIe et XVIIe siècles [History of Japan's Relations with Europe during the Sixteenth and Seventeenth Centuries]. Paris, 1905. 326p. Text in French.

Contents: Introduction; Prosperity and Decadence of Christianity in Japan; Commercial Ties between Japan and Europe. Appendix: The Embassy of the Daimyo of Kyushu to the Pope; The Embassy of Date Masamune to Europe.

Rel.Publ.: Histoire...siècles. H. Jouve, 1905. 326p.; "Les premières relations de l'Europe avec le Japon," in Société franco-japonaise, Bulletin, 4 (1906), 35-48.

SEO, Joseph W. Der gegenwärtige Stand der Agrarwirtschaft in Ostasien (Japan, Korea, Taiwan): Unter besonderer Berücksichtigung der handelspolitischen Verflechtung mit der EWG. 1965. See no.190.

1248
BOSCARO, Adriana. Il Giappone del XVI secolo: Il momento socio-politico e il momento culturale nei primi contatti con l'occidente Europeo [Japan during the Sixteenth Century: The Socio-Political Moment and the Cultural Moment in Japan's First Contacts with Western Europe]. Venezia, 1969. xix, 278p. Text in Italian with a summary in Japanese.

A study of Japanese contacts with Europeans during the 1500's with consideration (among other things) of the attitudes of the daimyo towards Westerners, the growth of Nagasaki and Sakai, and contemporary social and economic reforms. Contents: Japan at the End of the Ashikaga Period; Europe from the Opening of Japan to the Religious and Mercantile Penetration of That Country; Europeans in Kyushu: Initial Reactions and Political and Economic Consequences; European Involvement in Japanese Reunification; Western Presence in Sixteenth Century Japanese Culture. The appendix includes the reactions and comments to the visit made by a Japanese embassy in 1585 to Pope Gregory XIII.

Austria and Austria-Hungary

1249
PANTZER, Peter. Japan und Österreich-Ungarn: Die diplomatischen, wirtschaftlichen, und kulturellen Beziehungen, von ihrer Aufnahme (1869) bis zum Ausbruch des ersten Weltkrieges [Japan and Austria-Hungary: Their Diplomatic, Economic, and Cultural Ties, 1869-1914]. Wien, 1968. 218p. (2v.) Text in German. Diss. ms. available at the Österreichische Nationalbibliothek, Nr. 1,040.585 C.

A comprehensive study focusing on the Austro-Hungarian expedition of 1868/69, the visit made to Japan by Franz-Ferdinand (the successor to the Imperial throne), and the entrance of Japan into World War One.

France

See also International Relations--disarmament during the 1920's and 1930's (pages 107-09) and International Relations--China (pages 112-33).

1250
MEDZINI, Meron. French Policy in Japan during the Closing Years of the Tokugawa Regime. Harvard, 1964. vii, 404p. AB: 4p. summary appended to diss. ms.

Contents: Pt.1: France and the Powers in Japan 1859-1864: France and Japan before 1844; Missionary Activities and Naval Interests 1830-1858; The Mission of Baron Gros; The Foundation of French Policy in Japan; The Japanese Mission to Europe 1862; Years of Crisis: 1862-1863; Franco-Japanese Commercial Relations 1859-1863. Pt.2: Roches Seeks French Hegemony in Japan 1864-1867: The Ikeda Mission; Léon Roches and the New French Policy; First Anglo-French Differences; Commerical Relations 1864-1867; The Yokosuka Arsenal; Military Assistance; Roches and Tokugawa Keiki; The Meiji Restoration and the Failure of Roches' Policy; Aftermath.

Rel.Publ.: "Léon Roches in Japan (1864-1868)," in Harvard University, East Asian Research Center, Papers on Japan, 2 (1963), 182-228.

1251
SIMS, Richard Leslie. French Policy towards Japan, 1854-1894. London, 1968. 411p.

Examines Franco-Japanese relations prior to the Sino-Japanese War, focusing on the differences of opinion between the Quai d'Orsay (the French Foreign Office) and the diplomats actually living in Japan. Suggests that through the efforts of diplomats such as Léon Roches, France became increasingly involved in Japanese affairs.

Germany

See also International Relations--China (pages 112-33) for dissertations on German interests and activities in China and their consequences for German-Japanese relations.

1252
BAKER, Dwight Condo. Germany and the Far East, 1895-1908. California, Berkeley, 1927. 434p.

Contents: Germany and the Liaotung Intervention in 1895; Germany and the South Pacific Base; Germany Occupies Kiaochow; Germany and the Overcommand in the Boxer War; Germany as the "Honest Broker" in Shantung and the Yangtze Valley; The Conclusion of the Anglo-German Agreement concerning China; The Anglo-Japanese Alliance and Germany's Position in 1902; Germany and the United States Mediate in the Russo-Japanese War; The Quadruple Entente in Asia; Germany's Encirclement; The Way Out: A German-Chinese-American Entente Project in 1907 and 1908.

1253
KOEPSEL, Kurt. Die Entwicklung des japanischen Aussenhandels, insbesondere der deutsch-japanischen Handelsbeziehungen vor dem weltkriege [The Development of Japanese Foreign Trade, Especially German-Japanese Commercial Relations, before World War I]. Köln, 1928. Text in German. The dissertation in its published form is available at Marburg/Lahn, Universitätsbibliothek, Nr. XVII C.

The Japanese feudal economy and the impact of the Meiji Restoration; economic conditions before World War

I with reference in particular to agriculture, business, and industry; Japanese foreign trade before and after the opening of the country; German-Japanese trade relations before World War I; treaty conditions and their impact on Japanese foreign trade.

Rel.Publ.: Die Entwicklung...Weltkriege. Kassel: Kasseler Post, 1929. 96p.

1254
KIEL, Erich. Die handelspolitischen Beziehungen zwischen Deutschland und Japan in der Nachkriegszeit [Commercial Ties between Germany and Japan in World War I]. Münster, 1934. Text in German. The dissertation in its published form is available at Marburg/Lahn, Universitätsbibliothek, Nr. XVII C; also at the University of Michigan, General Library, no. HF 1545.K47

Contents: Pt.1: A Summary of Commercial Ties between Germany and Japan before World War I Based on an Examination of the Commercial Treaties of 1861, 1869, 1896, and 1911. Pt.2: The Economic Development of Both Countries after World War I. Pt.3: Foreign Trade Relations of the Two Countries after the War.

Rel.Publ.: Die handelspolitischen...Nachkriegszeit. Münster: Gutenberg-Dr., 1934. 107p.

1255
CAUSEY, Beverley Douglas, Jr. German Policy towards China, 1918-1941. Harvard, 1943. xii, 460p. AB: Harvard University. Summaries of Theses...1943-1945. p.218-21.

An analysis of Germany's East Asian policy and of German-Japanese relations during the inter-war years. See especially Ch.5, "The Manchurian Crisis, 1931-1933," Ch.7, "The German-Japanese Rapprochement, 1933-1936," Ch.8, "The China Incident, 1937-1939, and Ch.9, "War Diplomacy in China."

Rel.Publ.: "Why Germany Never Signed the Nine-Power Treaty," FEQ, 1 (Aug. 1942), 364-77.

1256
KIEHL, Rudolf. Die Entwicklung der handelspolitischen Beziehungen zwischen Deutschland und Japan bis zum Jahre 1938 [The Development of German-Japanese Commercial Relations up to the Year 1938]. Dresden, Technische Hochschule, 1943. 168, xix p. Text in German. Diss. ms. available at Dresden, Bibliothek der Technischen Hochschule, Nr. 2792 U 4°.

Contents: The Development of Commercial Ties between Germany and Japan up to World War I; World War I, Its Impact on German-Japanese Trade, and Its Consequences for the Japanese Economy; German-Japanese Commercial Ties from the End of World War I to the Conclusion of the German-Japanese Economic Agreement of 1939.

1257
IKLE, Frank William. German-Japanese Relations, 1936-1940: A Study of Totalitarian Diplomacy. California, Berkeley, 1953. 352p.

A study primarily of the Japanese side of these relations. Includes information on the pressures that the Japanese army brought to bear upon Japanese policy towards Germany.

Rel.Publ.: German...Diplomacy. New York: Bookman Associates, 1956. 243p.

1258
PRESSEISEN, Ernst Leopold. Germany and Japan: A Study in Totalitarian Diplomacy, 1933-1941. Harvard, 1955. v, 542p. AB: 6p. summary appended to diss. ms.

Contents: Background to an Alliance: (1) Nazi Views, (2) Geopolitical Plans; The League of Nations Loses Two Members; The Shaping of German Far Eastern Policy; The Anti-Comintern Pact; The First Crisis, 1937-1938: (1) Attempts at Mediation, (2) The German Commerical Retreat; The Axis Becomes a Triangle; Negotiations for an Alliance; The Second Crisis, 1939; From Triangle to Tripartite Pact; Alliance without Allies.

Rel.Publ.: Germany...1941. The Hague: Martinus Nijhoff, 1958. xii, 368p.; "Le racisme et les Japonais: Un dilemma nazi," Revue d'Histoire de la Deuxième Guerre Mondiale, 13 (July 1963), 1-14.

1259
ROSEN, Oscar. German-Japanese Relations, 1894-1902: A Study of European Imperialism in the Far East. Wisconsin, 1956. 339p. DA 16 (Dec. 1956), 2441-42; UM 19,132.

The author attributes the gradual deterioration of German-Japanese relations largely to the conflicting policies of the two countries with regard to the situation in China and to Germany's increasingly pro-Russian policy.

1260
HARUKI, Takeshi. The Tripartite Pact and Japanese Foreign Policy. Southern California, 1957. 496p. AB: University of Southern California. Abstracts of Dissertations for...1957. p.241.

Focuses particularly on Japan's relations with Germany, 1936-1941.

1261
MACK, Karlheinz. Die Antikominternverträge: Ein Beitrag zur Geschichte der Aussenpolitik Deutschlands, Italiens, Japans, und ihrer Satelliten [The Anti-Comintern Pacts: A Contribution to the History of the Foreign Policy of Germany, Italy, Japan, and Their Satellite States]. Wien, 1957. viii, 243p. Text in German. Diss. ms. available at the Universitätsbibliothek der Universität Wien, Nr. D 12,418.

Elucidates one aspect of German, Italian, and Japanese foreign policy during the period 1935-1941. Relevant documents are translated into German.

1262
MENZEL, Johanna Margarete. German-Japanese Relations during the Second World War. Chicago, 1957. 539p.

The major portion of the thesis deals with diplomatic relations 1939-1941. In addition, one chapter is devoted to the remainder of the war and two chapters study the Soviet Union as a subject of concern to both Germany and Japan, economic relations between the two countries, and military assistance.

Rel.Publ.: "Der geheime deutsch-japanische Notenaustausch zum Dreimächtpakt," Vierteljahrsheft für Zeitgeschichte, 5 (1957), 182-93; Hitler and Japan: The Hollow Alliance [by] Johanna M. Meskill. New York: Atherton, 1966. x, 245p.

1263
PRINZ, Lore Emma. Deutsche Ostasienpolitik: Ihre Ergebnisse und Versäumnisse unter besonderer Berücksichtigung des deutsch-japanischen Verhältnisses vor dem 1. Weltkrieg [Germany's East Asian Policy: Its Results and Its Shortcomings with Special Consideration of German-Japanese Relations before World War I]. München, 1957. 259p. Text in German. Diss. ms. available at München, Bayrische Staatsbibliothek, Nr. 1957. 7181.

A study of German-Japanese relations from their origins to the end of the nineteenth century and an examination of the German errors and shortcomings during the prewar and wartime periods that precluded early collaboration between the two countries.

1264
SOMMER, Theodor. Deutschland und Japan zwischen den Mächten 1935-1940: Vom Antikominternpakt zum Drei-Mächtepakt: Eine Studie zur diplomatischen Vorgeschichte des Zweiten Weltkriegs [Germany and Japan between the Powers, 1935-1940: From the Anti-Comintern Pact to the Tripartite Pact: A Study of the Diplomatic Antecedents of World War II]. Tübingen, 1960. 700p. Text in German. The dissertation in its published form is available at Marburg/Lahn, Staatsbibliothek Preussischer Kulturbesitz, Nr. Ser. 1974-15.

A detailed description of the alliance negotiations conducted between Germany and Japan prior to World War II: (1) the alliance "without a backbone;" (2) the Anti-Comintern Pact, 1935-1938; (3) alliance negotiations, 1938-1939; (4) the alliance consummated--1940; (5) the ineffectual alliance. The appendix contains thirteen documents regarding the Anti-Comintern Pact and the Tripartite Pact.

Rel.Publ.: Deutschland...Weltkriegs. Tübingen: J. C. B. Mohr (Paul Seibeck), 1962. xii, 540p. (Tübingen Studien zur Geschichte und Politik, 15)

1265
DRECHSLER, Karl. Die Beziehungen Hitlerdeutschlands zu China und Japan 1936-1939: Ein Beitrag zur Vorgeschichte des zweiten Weltkrieges [Nazi Germany's Relations with China and Japan, 1936-1939: A Contribution to the Antecedents of World War II]. Halle, 1962. v, 297p. Text in German. The dissertation in its published form is available at Marburg/Lahn, Staatsbibliothek Preussischer Kulturbesitz, Nr. Ser. 2900-1,25.

I: The dilemma of Germany's East Asian policy, 1933-1937: Germany's interest in China (a country of many business opportunities) versus her interest in Japan (a partner in the repartition of the world). II: The Sino-Japanese conflict, July 1937-January 1938, arguments within Germany over the direction of the country's East Asian policy, and German efforts to mediate the conflict. Japanese demands of Germany and the German reorientation in favor of Japan.

Rel.Publ.: Deutschland-China-Japan 1933-1939: Das Dilemma der deutschen Fernostpolitik. Berlin: Akademie-Verlag, 1964. 180p. (Akademie der Wissenschaften, Berlin. Institut für Geschichte. Schriften, Reihe 1: Allgemeine und deutsche Geschichte, 25)

1266
ELMAR, Peter. Die Bedeutung Chinas in der deutschen Ostasienpolitik (1911-1917) [China's Importance in German East Asian Policy, 1911-1917]. Hamburg, 1965. Text in German. The dissertation in its published form is available at the University of Michigan, General Library, no. 33,760.

Includes information on Japanese activities in China and on the influence that Japan exerted on German foreign policy.

Rel.Publ.: Die Bedeutung...1917. Hamburg, 1965. vi, 296p.

1267
DOLMAN, Arthur. The Third Reich and Japan: A Study in Nazi Cultural Relations. New York, 1966. 244p. DA 27 (May 1967), 3807-A; UM 67-6013.

Focuses on the attitudes of Nazi Germany toward Japan, 1933-1940.

1268
GLADE, Dieter. Bremen und der Ferne Osten [Bremen and the Far East]. Kiel, 1966. Text in German. The dissertation in its published form is available at the University of Michigan, General Library, no. DD 901. B71A45 v.34.

A study of the commercial, consular, cultural, and political ties of the German port city of Bremen with East Asia particularly during the latter half of the nineteenth century. Some information on Bremen's relations with Japan is included.

Rel.Publ.: Bremen...Osten. Bremen: Schünemann, 1966. 170p. (Veröffentlichungen aus dem Staatsarchiv der Freien Hansestadt Bremen, 34)

Great Britain

Early to 1894

See also International Relations--China: 1860-1894 (pages 112-13) for dissertations on British interests and activities and the consequences for Great Britain's relations with Japan.

1269
BEASLEY, William Gerald. Great Britain and the Opening of Japan, 1834-1858. London, 1950. iii, 313p.

Focuses on British policy towards Japan up to the conclusion of the Elgin Mission, 1857-1858.

Rel.Publ.: Great...1858. London: Luzac, 1951. xix, 227p.; "The Language Problem in the Anglo-Japanese Negotiations of 1854," in University of London, School of Oriental and African Studies, Bulletin, 13 (1950), 746-58.

1270
KLIMENKO, N. P. Kolonial'naia ekspansiia Anglii na Dal'nem Vostoke v 1856-1858 gg. i otnoshenie k nei klassov i partii angliiskogo obshchestva [The Relationship of English Social Classes and Parties to Great Britain's Colonial Expansion in East Asia, 1856-1858]. Moscow, Moskovskii gorodskoi pedagogicheskii institut imeni Potemkina, 1962. (Candidate of Historical Sciences degree) 390p. Text in Russian.

1271
McMASTER, John. British Trade and Traders in Japan, 1859-1869. London, 1962. 316p.

Concludes that the establishment of normal trade relations with Japan was to her benefit and that the apparent ill effects (i.e. inflation) were due to the intensification of longstanding deficiencies. Improved transportation, the disposal of surplus goods, the introduction of technology--all occurred as the result of trade. The author argues that the impression that such trade was harmful has been created by writers of the classes whose interests were threatened by its change: the Japanese samurai and the British leisure class.

Rel.Publ.: "The Japanese Gold Rush of 1859," JAS, 19 (May 1960), 273-87; "The Takashima Mine: British Capital and Japanese Industrialization," Business History Review, 37 (Autumn 1963), 217-39; Jardines in Japan, 1859-1867. Groningen: Druk, V.R.B., 1966. 162p.; "Alcock and Harris: Foreign Diplomacy in Bakumatsu Japan," MN, 22 (1967), 305-67.

1272
PERRY, John Curtis. Great Britain and the Imperial Japanese Navy, 1858-1905. Harvard, 1962. iii, 273p. AB: 4p. summary appended to diss. ms.

"A study of the relationship between the Royal Navy and the Imperial Japanese Navy and of the assistance given by Great Britain in the creation of a modern Japanese navy." Concludes that although British naval thinking (e.g. attitudes toward politics and towards civil-military relations) had little impact on the Japanese, "British material aid to the Japanese navy was substantial and significant. British-built ships formed the backbone of the Meiji navy. British naval officers gave sound professional training to many Japanese men. ...And during the years immediately after the signing of the Anglo-Japanese Alliance, a close bond of friendship united the two navies."

Rel.Publ.: "Great Britain and the Emergence of Japan as a Naval Power," MN, 21 (1966), 305-21.

MORE, Lois Alma. American Diplomacy in Japan, 1853-1869: From Advantage Gained to Advantage Lost. 1963. See no.1366.

KIM, Yung Chung. Great Britain and Korea, 1883-1887. 1965. See no.1157.

1273
DANIELS, Gordon. Sir Harry Parkes: British Representative in Japan, 1865-1882. Oxford, 1967. xxii, 392p.

Contents: The Formative Years (1828-1865); Anglo-Japanese Relations: The Background (1853-1865); Bakumatsu (1865-1867); The Country at War (1868-1869); The Beginning of Reconstruction (1869-1871); Home Away from Home (1871-1873); The New Japan: Restive and Adventurous (1873-1874); Korea and Kagoshima (1875-1877); Diplomacy by Other Means (1878-1879); Honoured and Reviled (1880-1881); Japan Rebuffed, Parkes Promoted (1882-1883).

Rel.Publ.: "The Japanese Civil War (1868): A British View," Modern Asian Studies, 1 (July 1967), 241-63; "The British Role in the Meiji Restoration: A Re-interpretive Note," Modern Asian Studies, 2 (Oct. 1968), 291-313.

1894-1922

1274
CHANG, Chung-fu. The Anglo-Japanese Alliance. Johns Hopkins, 1929. iii, 340p.

Studies the origins of the Alliance, the Alliance itself (1902-1921), and the manner in which the Alliance affected the interests of China, Korea, the United States, and other Western states.

Rel.Publ.: The Anglo-Japanese Alliance. Baltimore: Johns Hopkins Press, 1931. ix, 317p. (Johns Hopkins University Series in Historical and Political Science; Extra v., New ser., no.12)

SWARTZ, Willis G. Anglo-Russian Rivalry in the Far East, 1895-1905. 1929. See no.963.

1275
McCORDOCK, Robert Stanley. British Far Eastern Policy, 1894-1900. Columbia, 1931. 377p.

Includes some information on Anglo-Japanese and Sino-Japanese relations, particularly with regard to the Sino-Japanese War and its aftermath and the first origins of the Anglo-Japanese Alliance.

Rel.Publ.: British...1900. New York: Columbia University Press, 1931. 377p. (Studies in History, Economics, and Public Law, ed. by the Faculty of Political Science of Columbia University, 346)

1276
MINRATH, Paul. Das englisch-japanische Bündnis von 1902: Die Grundlegung der Ententepolitik im Fernosten [The Anglo-Japanese Alliance of 1902: Laying the Foundation of "Entente" Politics in East Asia]. Bonn, 1932. Text in German. The dissertation in its published form is available at Marburg/Lahn, Universitätsbibliothek, Nr. VII C; also at the University of Michigan, General Library, no. DA 47.9.J3M7/1933.

Part 1 studies the decline of continental (European) policy following the intervention at Shimonoseki, 1895-1900. Part 2, a study of the 1902 Alliance and of the rise of the oceanic powers (1900-1905), investigates the European alliance negotiations and the impact of events in East Asia upon European politics.

Rel.Publ.: Das englisch...Fernosten. Stuttgart: W. Kohlhammer, 1933. ix, 112p. (Beiträge zur Geschichte der nachbismarckischen Zeit und des Weltkriegs, Heft 20); "Frankreich-Russland und das englische-japanische Bündnis von 1902," Berliner Monatshefte, 15 (Feb. 1937), 1939-53.

1277
CRAMER, Anneliese. Die Beziehungen zwischen England und Japan von 1894-1902 [Anglo-Japanese Relations, 1894-1902]. Hamburg, 1935. Text in German. The dissertation in its published form is available at Marburg/Lahn Universitätsbibliothek, Nr. VII C; also at the University of Michigan, General Library, no. DA 47.9.J3C89.

A study of Anglo-Japanese relations following the end of the first Sino-Japanese War. Particular attention is paid to the effect that the Russian-French-German intervention of 1895 had on England and on Japan, to the politics of the foreign powers in China which were menacing British and Japanese interests there, to the Boxer Rebellion, and to the conclusion of the negotiations that resulted in the formation of the Anglo-Japanese Alliance.

Rel.Publ.: Die Beziehungen...1902. Zeulenroda: Sporn, 1935. 79p.

1278
WILLISTON, Frank Goodman. The End of British Isolation: The Origins of the Anglo-Japanese Alliance. Chicago, 1935. 273p.

The British imperial position at the turn of the century is examined with particular attention to Great Britain's position in East Asia in 1898-1901. The negotiations and the reception of the treaty of alliance are studied in the last two chapters.

Rel.Publ.: The End...Alliance. Chicago, 1937. 18p. abstract. ("Private edition, distributed by the University of Chicago libraries.")

1279
SPINKS, Charles Nelson. A History of the Anglo-Japanese Alliance, 1902-1922. Stanford, 1936. 816p. AB: Stanford University. Abstracts of Dissertations. 1935/36. p.145-50.

The alliance is presented "in its broader setting, as a part of the world diplomatic system."

Rel.Publ.: "Japan's Entrance into the World War," PHR, 5 (Dec. 1936), 297-311; "The Termination of the Anglo-Japanese Alliance," PHR, 6 (Dec. 1937), 321-40; "The Background of the Anglo-Japanese Alliance," PHR, 8 (Sept. 1939), 317-39.

1280
WENIGER, Irene Margarete. Die historischen Hintergründe des englisch-japanischen Bündnisses von 1902: Zur Kennzeichnung der Diplomatie der Empire-Politik [The Historical Background of the Anglo-Japanese Alliance of 1902: A Characterization of the Diplomacy of Imperial Politics]. Halle, 1943. xvi, 450p. Text in German.

1281
TARKOW-NAAMANI, Israel. The Abandonment of "Splendid Isolation:" A Study of British Public Opinion and Diplomacy, 1895-1902. Indiana, 1946. vii, 311p.
See especially Ch.6, "The Anglo-Japanese Alliance: The End of Isolation."
Rel.Publ.: "Abandonment of Splendid Isolation by Great Britain in 1902: Influence of Public Opinion in the 1890's," Canadian Historical Review, 27 (June 1946), 163-88.

1282
GAL'PERIN, Aleksandr L'vovich. Iz istorii anglo-iaponskikh otnoshenii: Tri soiuznykh dogovora, 1901-1911 gg. [Aspects of the History of Anglo-Japanese Relations: Three Treaties of Alliance, 1901-1911]. Moscow, Moskovskii gosudarstvennyi universitet imeni M. V. Lomonosova, 1947. (Doctor of Historical Sciences degree) 819p. Text in Russian.
Rel.Publ.: Anglo-iaponskii soiuz 1902-1921 gg. Moscow: Gospolitizdat, 1947. 448p. (Tikhookeanskii institut Akademii nauk SSSR)

WHITNEY, Henry N. British Foreign Policy and the Russo-Japanese War. 1949. See no.1320.

1283
GOUDSWAARD, Johan Marius. Some Aspects of the End of Britain's "Splendid Isolation," 1898-1904. Rotterdam Nederlandse Economische Hogeschool, 1952.
See Ch.4, "The Anglo-Japanese Alliance."
Rel.Publ.: Some...1904. Rotterdam: W. L. & J. Brusse, 1952. 123p.

1284
GRENVILLE, John Ashley Soames. British Foreign Policy, 1899-1902. London, 1954. x, 474p.
Includes a discussion of Anglo-Japanese and Anglo-Korean relations in 1899 and a detailed account of the Anglo-Japanese Alliance.
Rel.Publ.: Lord Salisbury and Foreign Policy: The Close of the Nineteenth Century. London: Athlone Press, 1964. 451p. (University of London Historical Studies, 14)

1285
STEINER, Zara Shakow. The Formulation of British Foreign Policy, 1898-1914: With Special Reference to the Conservative Administrations. Radcliffe, 1957. v, 512p. AB: 3p. summary appended to diss. ms.
See Ch.8, "Case History: Anglo-Japanese Negotiations" (p.242-74).
Rel.Publ.: "Great Britain and the Creation of the Anglo-Japanese Alliance," Journal of Modern History, 31 (Mar. 1959), 27-36; "Last Years of the Old Foreign Office, 1898-1905," Historical Journal, 6 (1963), 59-60.

GÜTTER, Charlotte. Das imperiale Kraftfeld Ostasiens 1904-1914. 1960. See no.956.

1286
MONGER, George W. The End of Isolation: British Foreign Policy, 1900-1905. Cambridge, 1962. 377p.
Contents: Splendid Isolation; The Approach to Germany, 1900-1901; The Japanese Alliance, 1901-1902; British Diplomacy in 1902; C.I.D. and Foreign Office: Currents of Thought; 1903 and the Turn to France and Russia; The Russo-Japanese War, 1903-1905.
Rel.Publ.: The End of Isolation: British Foreign Policy, 1900-1907. London: T. Nelson, 1963. vi, 343p. (Nelson's Studies in Modern History); "The End of Isolation: Britain, Germany, and Japan, 1900-1902," in Royal Historical Society, Transactions, 5th ser., v.13 (1963), 103-21.

1287
NISH, Ian Hill. The Diplomacy of the Anglo-Japanese Alliance, 1902-1907. London, 1962. 210, xxii p.
A study of the limited alliance that was negotiated in 1902 between Great Britain and Japan, of its revision and extension in 1905, and of its anti-Russian character and its origins in general.
Rel.Publ.: The Anglo-Japanese Alliance: The Diplomacy of Two Island Empires, 1894-1907. London: Athlone, 1966. xi, 420p. (London University. Historical Studies, 18); "Japan's Indecision during the Boxer Disturbances," JAS, 20 (Aug. 1961), 449-61; "Australian and the Anglo-Japanese Alliance, 1901-1911, Australian Journal of Politics and History, 9 (Nov. 1963), 201-12; "Japan Reverses the Unequal Treaties: The Anglo-Japanese Commercial Treaty of 1894," Papers of the Hong Kong International Conference on Asian History, 20; "Korea: Focus of Russo-Japanese Diplomacy, 1898-1903," Asian Studies, v.2, no.7.

PERRY, John C. Great Britain and the Imperial Japanese Navy, 1858-1905. 1962. See no.1272.

1288
FRY, Michael Graham. Anglo-American-Canadian Relations: With Special Reference to Far Eastern and Naval Issues, 1918-1922. London, 1963. v, 561p. AB: University of London. Institute of Historical Research. Bulletin, v.39, no.99 (May 1966), 110-13.
A study of the policies of Great Britain, the United States, and Canada with regard to the controversies surrounding the Anglo-Japanese Alliance.
Rel.Publ.: "The Imperial War Cabinet, the United States, and the Freedom of the Seas," in Royal United Service Institution (London), Journal, 110 (Nov. 1965), 353-63; "The North Atlantic Triangle and the Abrogation of the Anglo-Japanese Alliance," Journal of Modern History, 39 (March 1967), 46-64; "Great Britain, the Allies, and the Problem of Russia, 1918-1919," Canadian Journal of History, 2 (Sept. 1967), 62-84.

1289
HONG, Choon Sik. The Termination of the Anglo-Japanese Alliance, 1920-1921. Iowa, 1965. 217p. DA 26 (Apr. 1966), 5997; UM 66-3441.
Contents: The Anglo-Japanese Rapprochment in Asia, 1902-1911; The Alliance of 1911 and the Bryan Peace Commission, 1914; The Alliance during the First World War; Technicalities Involved in the Renewal of the Alliance, 1920-1921; Negotiations to End the Alliance, 1921-1922.

1290
REMMEY, Paul Baker Jr. British Diplomacy and the Far East, 1892-1898. Harvard, 1965. ix, 335p. AB: 3p.

summary appended to diss. ms.

See especially Ch.2, "The Sino-Japanese War: Britain's Shock of Recognition," and Ch.3, "The Move toward Japan, April 1895."

1291
BENNETT, Neville Richard. The Anglo-Japanese Alliance and the Dominions, 1902-1911. London, 1966. xiii, 376p.

A study of the effect of Dominion opinion on Britain's policy of exclusion towards Japanese immigration. Suggests that direct dealings between Japan and the Dominions led to the latter's increasing independence from British authority; also that Britain's Japanese policy encouraged Japan's extreme nationalism.

1292
LOWE, Peter C. British Policy in the Far East, 1911-1915: With Special Reference to Relations with Japan. Wales, 1967.

Studies the beginnings of Great Britain's decline as a world power and the effects of her decline upon her East Asian policy, and examines the evolution of the Anglo-Japanese Alliance as relations between the two countries deteriorated.

Rel.Publ.: Great Britain and Japan, 1911-1915: A Study of British Far Eastern Policy. London: Macmillan, New York: St. Martin's, 1969. 343p.; "The British Empire and the Anglo-Japanese Alliance, 1911-1915," History, 54 (June 1969), 212-25.

1293
SIMKIN, Arnold P. Anglo-Russian-American Relations in the Far East, 1897-1904. London, 1967. 715p. (2v.)

The major consideration of Japanese interests is given in Appendix 6, p.630-57, where the Anglo-Japanese Alliance is discussed in some detail. Reference also is made to Japanese interests in the sections dealing with Manchuria.

1294
WELLS, Samuel Fogle, Jr. Anglo-American Friendship, 1904-1914: The Strategic Aspect. Harvard, 1967. ii, 478p. AB: 4p. summary appended to diss. ms.

In Ch.7, "The United States, the Anglo-Japanese Alliance, and Arbitration" (p.376-439), the author shows how "Great Britain attempted to eliminate the possibility of Japanese-American conflict by including the United States in most of her plans for the area and by twice modifying the Anglo-Japanese Alliance in order to exclude the United States from its terms of operation."

1295
MOORE, John Edward. Admiralty Politics and the Redistribution of the British Fleet (1904-1912). Columbia, 1968. 343p. DA 30 (Oct. 1969), 1340-41-A; UM 69-15,697.

A chapter on the Admiralty's role in the renewal of the Anglo-Japanese Alliance in 1905 is included. The author indicates in this connection that "the Admiralty urged the renewal and modification of the Alliance in order to avoid having to match the Japanese battle fleet in the Far East."

STREMSKI, Richard. Britain's China Policy 1920-1928. 1968. See no.1044.

1922-1945

See also: International Relations--Disarmament during the 1920's and 1930's (pages 107-09), International Relations--Allied participation in World War II (pages 109-11), and International Relations--China (pages 112-33).

1296
MILLER, Eugene Herbert. The Singapore Naval Base. Clark, 1940. 293, xxiii p. AB: Clark University. Thesis Abstracts-1940. p.20-24.

Includes the Japanese reaction to the establishment of the base [built between 1923 and 1938].

Rel.Publ.: Strategy at Singapore. New York: Macmillan, 1942. viii, 145p.

1297
CALDERWOOD, James Dixon. The International Implications of British Economic Foreign Policy, 1931-1939. Ohio State, 1943. 486p. AB: Ohio State University. Abstracts of Doctoral Dissertations. no.44. p.13-18.

Shows how England's abandonment of free trade, her adoption of a system of imperial preference, the closing of the "Open Door" in her colonies, and her conclusion of a series of bilateral trade agreements with foreign countries affected world trade. A discussion of the impact of British policy on Japan is included.

1298
SOULE, Vivian Joan. The Embassy of Sir Robert Craigie to Tokio, 1937-1941. London, 1966. iv, 460p.

A consideration of Great Britain's East Asian policy prior to Pearl Harbor, comparing her policy favorably with that of the United States. Particular reference is made to the Craigie-Clark-Kerr correspondence and to the relations among Great Britain, Germany, and Japan at the time.

Netherlands

See also International Relations--Southeast Asia (pages 137-43).

1299
NACHOD, Oskar. Die Beziehungen der Niederländischen Ostindischen Kompagnie zu Japan im siebzehnten Jahrhundert [The Relations of the Dutch East India Company with Japan during the Seventeenth Century]. Leipzig, 1897. Text in German. The dissertation in its published form is available at Berlin West, Staatsbibliothek, Preussischer Kulturbesitz, Nr. Un 9510.

The dissertation opens with a survey of Japanese history prior to 1600 and with a study of the origins and the organization of the Dutch East India Company. It then focuses on the initiation of trade relations between the Netherlands and Japan, discusses contemporary developments in Japan, and examines the company's relationship with the Japanese while its factories at Hirado and Deshima were in operation.

Rel.Publ.: Die Beziehungen...Jahrhundert. Leipzig: R. Friese, 1897. xxxiv, 444, ccx p.

1300
KRIEGER, Carel Coenraad. The Infiltration of European Civilization in Japan during the 18th Century. Leiden, 1940.

The dissertation is "part of the translation of a study by Ōtsuki Nyoden, entitled Shinsen yōgaku nempyō

(Revised chronological tables of Western learning), which was published in 1927. It is a revised and considerably enlarged edition of Nihon yōgaku nempyō, composed by the same author, signed Ōtsuki Shūji, and printed in 1878." The tables cover the period 1700-1799 and present a chronological review of the introduction and Japanese adoption of Western science, ideas, languages, and technology.

Rel.Publ.: The Infiltration...Century. Leiden: E. J. Brill, 1940. x, 125p.

1301
CARES, Paul Benjamin. The Dutch Conquest of the Malay Archipelago, Ceylon, Formosa, and the European Trade with Japan. Michigan, 1941. 373p.

See Ch.5, "The Establishment of Commercial Contacts with Japan, 1600-1613" (p.204-61), and Ch.6 "The Conquest of the European Trade with Japan" (p.262-322).

1302
GOODMAN, Grant Kohn. The Dutch Impact on Japan: 1640-1853. Michigan, 1955. 325p. DA 15 (Aug. 1955), 1375-76; UM 12,575.

Contents: The Dutch at Hirado; The Island of Deshima; Visits to Edo; The Nagasaki Interpreters and Early Medical and Astronomical Studies; Arai Hakuseki and Intellectual Developments in Genroku and Shōtoku; Tokugawa Yoshimune and Western Learning; Aoki Bunzō and Noro Genjō and Their Mentors; The Kohōka, Maeno Ryotaku, and Sugita Gempaku; The Advent of Heliocentricity and Its Social Implications; Ōtsuki Gentaku and the Spread of Rangaku; Tanuma Okitsugu and Matsudaira Sadanobu and Western Learning; Western Learning in Various Domains; Western Learning in Certain Private Schools; Some Further Influences of European Civilization on Feudal Japan; Western Learning and the "Open Country" Policy.

Rel.Publ.: The Dutch...1853. Leiden: E. J. Brill, 1967. 167p. (T'oung Pao, Monographs, 5); "A Translation of Ōtsuki Gentaku's Ransetsu benwaku," in University of Michigan, Center for Japanese Studies, Occasional Papers, 3 (Ann Arbor: University of Michigan Press, 1952), 71-99.

1303
GLAMANN, Kristof. Dutch-Asiatic Trade, 1620-1740. Copenhagen, 1958. Text in English, with a summary in Danish.

A commercial history of the Dutch East India Company with one chapter devoted to the Company's trade in Japanese copper and with frequent references to other aspects of the Dutch trade with Japan. [Annotation based on the book.]

Rel.Publ.: Dutch...1740. Copenhagen: Danish Scientific Press, 1958. xi, 334p.

Russia

Early to 1860

1304
GOLDER, Frank Alfred. Russian Voyages in the North Pacific Ocean to Determine the Relation between Asia and America. Harvard, 1908. 249p.

Ch.2, "Terra de Jeso," is a discussion of the various cartographical accounts of Japan during the sixteenth, seventeenth, and eighteenth centuries. See also Ch.7, "The Second Kamchatka Expedition: Spanberg's Voyages to Japan--1738-1739."

Rel.Publ.: Russian Expansion on the Pacific, 1641-1850. Cleveland: Clark, 1914. 368p.

RAMMING, Martin. Russland-Berichte schiffbrüchiger Japaner aus den Jahren 1793 und 1805 und ihre Bedeutung für die Abschliessungspolitik der Tokugawa. 1930. See no.505.

HARRISON, John A. Yezo, the Japanese Northern Frontier, 1854-1882: A Preliminary Study in Japanese Expansion and Colonization with Particular Reference to the Role of the Kaitakushi in Modern Japanese History. 1949. See no.588.

1305
LENSEN, George Alexander. Russia's Japan Expedition of 1852 to 1855. Columbia, 1951. 259p. AB: Microfilm Abstracts, v.11 (1951): 1004-05.

A description of the activities of the expedition of Vice-Admiral Evfimii Vasil'evich Putiatin in Japanese waters. Includes information on the Russian motives for sending the expedition, on its reception by the Japanese, and on its influence upon Tokugawa foreign policy.

Rel.Publ.: Russia's...1855. Gainesville: University of Florida Press, 1955. xxvii, 208p.; "Early Russo-Japanese Relations," FEQ, 10 (1950), 3-38; "Russians in Japan, 1858-1859," Journal of Modern History, 26 (June 1954), 162-72; The Russian Push toward Japan: Russo-Japanese Relations, 1697-1875. Princeton: Princeton University Press, 1959. xv, 553p.

1306
FAINBERG, Esfir' Iakovlevna. Russko-iaponskie otnosheniia, 1792-1875 [Russo-Japanese Relations, 1792-1875]. Moscow, Institut vostokovedeniia Akademii nauk SSSR, 1955. (Doctor of Historical Sciences degree) 744p. Text in Russian.

Rel.Publ.: Russko...1875 gg. Moscow: Izdatel'stvo vostochnoi literatury, 1960. 314p. (Moskovskii gosudarstvennyi institut mezhdunarodnykh otnoshenii); "Iz istorii ustanovleniia ofitsial'nykh otnoshenii mezhdu Rossiei i Iaponiei," Sovetskaia Vostokovedenie, 1955, no.3, 56-70.

1307
KONSTANTINOV, V. M. Orosiiakoku suimudan kak pamiatnik rannikh russko-iaponskikh otnoshenii [Oroshiakoku suimudan as a Source for the Study of Early Russo-Japanese Relations]. Moscow, Institut vostokovedeniia Akademii nauk SSSR, 1959. (Candidate(?) of Historical Sciences degree) 360p. Text in Russian. AB: 16p. summary published in 1959.

Rel.Publ.: Orosiiakoku suimudan: Sny o Rossii. Tr. and ed. with an introductory article and notes by V. J. Konstantinov, ed. by N. I. Konrad. Moscow: Izdatel'stvo vostochnoi literatury, 1961. 133p.; "Pervyi v Iaponii krupnyi nauchnyi trud o Rossii," Narody Azii i Afriki, 4 (1963), 99-108.

STEPHAN, John J. Ezo under the Tokugawa Bakufu, 1799-1821: An Aspect of Japan's Frontier History. 1969. See no.544.

1860-1917

1308
DAS, Taraknath. Russo-Japanese Relations. Georgetown, 1924. Diss. ms. not available.

1309
DENNETT, Tyler. Roosevelt and the Russo-Japanese War: A Critical Study of American Policy in Eastern Asia in 1902-1905, Based Primarily upon the Private Papers of Theodore Roosevelt. Johns Hopkins, 1924. 445p.

An investigation of American policies towards Japan, Korea, and China during these years.

Rel.Publ.: Roosevelt...Roosevelt. Garden City, N.Y.: Doubleday, Page, 1925. xi, 357p.; "President Roosevelt's Secret Pact with Japan," Current History, 21 (Oct. 1924), 15-21.

1310
MEHNERT, Klaus. Der Einfluss des Russisch-Japanischen Krieges auf die grosse Politik [The Influence of the Russo-Japanese War on the World Powers]. Berlin, 1930. Text in German. The dissertation in its published form is available at Marburg/Lahn, Universitätsbibliothek, Nr. VII C.

A study of the political events of the period 1901-1914, of the events leading up to the Russo-Japanese War, of the war itself, and of its consequences and impact upon world politics.

Rel.Publ.: Der Einfluss...Politik. Berlin, 1930. 68p.

1311
STEINMANN, Friedrich von. Russlands Politik im Fernen Osten und der Staatssekretär Bezobrazov: Ein Beitrag zur Vorgeschichte des russisch-japanischen Krieges [Russia's Policy in the Far East and Secretary of State Bezobrazov: A Contribution to the Antecedents of the Russo-Japanese War]. Berlin, 1931. Text in German. The dissertation in its published form is available at Marburg/Lahn, Universitätsbibliothek, Nr. VII C.

Ch.1 examines the origins of the Russo-Japanese conflict, 1898-1904. Ch.2 focuses on the concessions in Korea and on the personality, political goals, and activities of Bezobrazov in East Asia in general and in Korea in particular.

Rel.Publ.: Russlands...Krieges. Leipzig: Werkgemeinschaft, 1931. 61, iii p.

1312
PRICE, Ernest Batson. The Russo-Japanese Treaties of 1907-1916 Concerning Manchuria and Mongolia. Johns Hopkins, 1933. xii, 158p.

Contents: The Background of International Relations in Northeastern Asia; Early Efforts at Russo-Japanese Understanding; The Treaties of July 30, 1907; The Treaties of July 4, 1910; The Secret Treaty of July 8, 1912; The Treaties of July 3, 1916; The Present Status.

Rel.Publ.: The Russo...Mongolia. Baltimore: Johns Hopkins Press, 1933. xiv, 158p.

1313
CHEN, Tai-chu. China's Frontier Problems. London, 1937. vii, 445p.

Parts of the dissertation deal with the Russo-Japanese agreements of 1907, 1910, 1912, and 1916 concerning Mongolia and discuss the Russo-Japanese conflict in Mongolia.

1314
STEWART, Edgar Irving, Jr. American Foreign Policy Incident to the Russo-Japanese War, 1904-1905. California, Berkeley, 1938. 329p.

Describes and analyzes the international political factors that led President Roosevelt to mediate the Russo-Japanese peace negotiations.

TSAI, Wei-ping. The Russo-Japanese Conflict in the Far East. 1938. See no.1328.

1315
KRUPINSKI, Kurt. Die russisch-japanischen Beziehungen von ihren Anfängen bis zum Frieden von Portsmouth [Russo-Japanese Relations from Their Beginnings to the Peace of Portsmouth]. Berlin, 1939. Text in German. The dissertation in its published form is available at Berlin West, Staatsbibliothek Preussischer Kulturbesitz, Nr. Ue 516-N.F. 27.

The following subjects are treated: (1) Japanese relations with Europe through 1639; (2) Russo-Japanese relations until 1850 and the role of Count Murav'iev Amurskij; (3) the Sino-Japanese War and Russia's East Asian policy from 1896 until Russia leased Port Arthur; (4) Japan's policy towards Russia, 1898-1901; (5) the Anglo-Japanese Alliance; (6) diplomatic and military preparations for the impending conflict, and the Treaty of Portsmouth.

Rel.Publ.: Der russisch...Portsmouth. Tilsit: V. Mauderode, 1939. vi, 126p.; also published under the title Russland und Japan: Ihre Beziehungen bis zum Frieden von Portsmouth. Königsberg und Berlin: Ost-Europa-Verlag, 1940. viii, 126p. (Osteuropäische Forschungen. N.F., Bd 27)

1316
CRIST, David Scott. Russia's Manchurian Policy, 1895-1905. Michigan, 1941. vii, 261p.

A narrative account of Russian expansion in Manchuria with considerable information on Russo-Japanese relations between 1894 and 1905.

1317
ROMANOV, Boris Aleksandrovich. Russko-iaponskaia voina 1904-1905 gg.: Politiko-istoricheskii ocherk [The Russo-Japanese War of 1904-1905: A Political and Historical Survey]. Moscow, Institut istorii Akademii nauk SSSR, 1941. (Doctor of Historical Sciences degree) 504p. Text in Russian.

Rel.Publ.: Ocherki diplomaticheskoi istorii russko-iaponskoi voiny. 2d ed. Moscow and Leningrad: Izdatel'stvo Akademii nauk SSSR, 1955. 695p. (Institut istorii Akademii nauk SSSR)

1318
VYGOTSKII, S. Iu. Portsmutskii dogovor i ego sud'by [The Peace Treaty of Portsmouth and Its Fate]. Tashkent, Sredneaziatskii gosudarstvennyi universitet, 1942. (Candidate of Historical Sciences degree) 307p. Text in Russian.

KALISCH, Gertrude. Der russisch-japanische Krieg im Spiegel der österreichischen Presse. 1944. See no.1429.

SÜHL, Marga. Die Grossmächte und die chinesische Revolution bis zum Ausbruch des ersten Weltkrieges. 1945. See no.972.

1319
DOBRYNIN, Anatolii Fedorovich. Dal'nevostochnaia politika SShA v period russko-iaponskoi voiny, 1904-1905 gg. [American Far Eastern Policy during the Russo-Japanese War, 1904-1905]. Moscow, Vysshaia diplomaticheskaia shkola Ministerstva inostrannykh del SSSR, 1947. (Candidate of Historical Sciences degree) xviii, 388p. Text in Russian.

1320
WHITNEY, Henry Norman. British Foreign Policy and the Russo-Japanese War. Pennsylvania, 1949. iv, 327p.
Contents: The Far Eastern Problem, 1894-1902; The Prelude to War; The Pursuit of a Middle Course; The Predominance of Western Affairs.

BRAISTED, William R. The Development of the Far East as an American Naval Problem, 1897-1909. 1950. See no.1376.

1321
FORD, Harold Perry. Russian Far Eastern Diptomacy, Count Witte, and the Penetration of China, 1895-1904. Chicago, 1950. 428p. AB: United States Department of State, External Research Staff. Abstracts of Completed Doctoral Dissertations for the Academic Year 1950/1951. p.275-80.
A case study of Russia's role in the Triple Intervention against Japan, the penetration of Manchuria, the scramble for concessions, the seizures of Kiaochow and Port Arthur, the Boxer Rebellion, the conclusion of the Anglo-Japanese Alliance, and the advent of the Russo-Japanese War.

1322
MALOZEMOFF, Andrew Alexander. Russian Far Eastern Policy, 1881-1904: With Special Emphasis on the Causes of the Russo-Japanese War. California, Berkeley, 1952. 659p. (2v.).
Chapters 8-9 study the Russo-Japanese dispute that led to war.
Rel.Publ.: Russian...War. Berkeley: University of California Press, 1958. 358p.

1323
HUCUL, Walter Charles. The Evolution of Russian and Soviet Sea Power, 1853-1953. California, Berkeley, 1953. 521p.
The author devotes one chapter to the Russo-Japanese War, in which he includes a discussion of the Tsushima Operation. His comments on the post-World War II buildup in the Pacific do not specifically mention Japan but could be applied to her.

1324
BERTON, Peter Alexander Menquez. The Secret Russo-Japanese Alliance of 1916. Columbia, 1956. 460p. DA 16 (Aug. 1956), 1432-33; UM 16,272.
A study of the background, formation, and consequences of the Alliance. Contents: Russo-Japanese Relations, 1905-1914; Efforts to Conclude an Alliance at the Outbreak of World War I; Russo-Japanese Relations during the Early Part of World War I; Negotiations in Tokyo; Negotiations in Petrograd; The 1916 Treaties, China, and the Powers. The lengthy appendices include "16 drafts or texts of treaties and diplomatic notes."
Rel.Publ.: "Russo-Japanese Relations during the First World War," in International Conference of Orientalists, Transactions, 5 (1960), 95-101.

1325
VERCHAU, Ekkhard. Europa und der Ferne Orient 1894 bis 1898: Studien über Erscheinung und Wesen des Imperialismus in dieser Zeit [Europe and East Asia, 1894-1898: Studies of the Appearance and the Reality of Imperialism during This Period]. Tübingen, 1957. v, 268p. Text in German. Diss. ms. available at Tübingen, Universitätsbibliothek, Nr. Um 7729.
Discusses Russian, French, and German penetration into China and Korea, Britain's loss of her dominant position in China, and the struggle between Russia and Japan over conflicting interests in Korea.

BURGMAN, Torsten. Svensk opinion och diplomati under rysk-japanska Kriget 1904-1905. 1965. See no.1430.

1326
TRANI, Eugene Paul. The Treaty of Portsmouth: An Adventure in Rooseveltian Diplomacy. Indiana, 1966. 220p. DA 27 (Apr. 1967), 3414-A; UM 67-3719.
Focuses on the role that Theodore Roosevelt played in bringing about an end to the Russo-Japanese War.
Rel.Publ.: The Treaty...Diplomacy. Lexington: University of Kentucky Press, 1969. 208p.

1327
SYNN, Seung Kwon. The Russo-Japanese Struggle for Control of Korea, 1894-1904. Harvard, 1967. iv, 479p.
"The purpose...is to present a comprehensive analysis of the policies of Russia and Japan toward Korea from 1894 to 1904." Contents: Sino-Japanese Rivalry over Korea, 1873-1893; The Outbreak of the Sino-Japanese War; Japan's Attempt to Seize Korea, 1894-1895; Russian Policy toward Korea, 1894-1895; The Murder of Queen Min; Russo-Japanese Rivalry over Korea, 1896-1898; The Rise of Japanese Influence, 1898-1900; On the Eve of the Russo-Japanese War.

EMERY, Michael C. The American Mass Media and the Coverage of Five Major Foreign Events, 1900-1950: The Russo-Japanese War, Outbreak of World War I, Rise of Stalin, Munich Crisis, Invasion of South Korea. 1968. See no.1445.

OKAMOTO, Shumpei. The Oligarchic Control of Foreign Policy: Japan's Experience in the Russo-Japanese War. 1969. See no.622.

1917-1945

See also: International Relations--Allied participation in World War II (pages 109-11), International Relations--China (pages 112-33), and International Relations--Russia: Siberian Intervention (pages 153-54).

1328
TSAI, Wei-ping. The Russo-Japanese Conflict in the Far East. Illinois, 1938. 264p.
Contents: Pt.1: Historical Background of Russo-Japanese Relations: Early Relations between Russia and Japan; The World War and the Far Eastern Situation; Soviet Russia and Japan in the Post War Period. Pt.2: The Russo-Japanese Railroad Rivalry on the Asiatic Mainland: The Rivalry in Manchuria, 1906-1922; The Rivalry in Manchuria, 1922-1931; Rivalry on the Asiatic Mainland, 1932-1937. Pt.3:The Russo-Japanese Conflict over Sakhalin: The Political History of Sakhalin; The Dispute over North Sakhalin. Pt.4: The Russo-Japanese Conflict over the Northern Seas Fisheries: The Negotiations over the Fishing Rights and the Rate of Exchange; The Disputes over the Use of the Fishing Waters. Pt.5: The Outer Mongolian Question.
Rel.Publ.: The Russo...East. Urbana, Ill., 1938. 12p. [Abstract].

1329
FOSTER, Hazel Elizabeth. The Development of Public In-

ternational Law Relating to Fisheries Interests of Selected Major States, 1910-1938. Duke, 1941. 425p.

Ch.5, "Conventional Law," discusses Russo-Japanese treaties relevant to the author's subject.

SWEARINGEN, Arthur R. The Japanese Communist Party and the Comintern, 1919-1943: A Study of the Relationship between the Japanese Party and Moscow and of the Success of the Japanese Special Higher Police (Thought Police) in Combating Communism in Japan. 1953. See no.631.

DURKEE, Travers E. The Communist International and Japan, 1919-1932. 1954. See no.656.

1330
OSKOLKOV, Iu. N. Agressivnaia politika iaponskogo imperializma protiv SSSR v 1939-1941 gg.: Ot nachala voiny v Evrope do voiny na Tikhom okeane [The Aggressive Policy of Japanese Imperialism against the U.S.S.R., 1939-1941: From the Outbreak of the War in Europe until the (Outbreak of the) Pacific War]. Leningrad, Leningradskii gosudarstvennyi universitet imeni A. A. Zhdanova, 1954. (Candidate of Historical Sciences degree) xxx, 458p. Text in Russian. AB: 15p. summary published in 1954.

1331
LUPKE, Hubertus. Japans Russlandpolitik von 1939-1941 [Japan's Policy towards Russia, 1939-1941]. Hamburg, 1961. viii, 233p.

An examination of the moves that the Japanese government made to resolve such outstanding problems with the U.S.S.R. as the dispute over Japanese fishing rights in Russian waters and the delineation of the Manchoukuo-Mongolian border, and of the efforts made to eliminate the possibility of a major conflict with Soviet Russia.

Rel.Publ.: Japans...1941. Frankfurt a.M.: Metzner, 1962. viii, 189p. (Schriften des Instituts für Asienkunde in Hamburg, 10)

1332
CLAYBERG, Anna Marie Anderson. Soviet Policy toward Japan, 1923-1941. California, Berkeley, 1962. iv, 373p.

Focuses on (1) Soviet moves to keep the Japanese from interfering in the Russian and the Chinese revolutions, (2) Soviet reaction to the Japanese occupation of Manchuria and Soviet efforts "to keep Japanese armies moving southward away from Siberia," and (3) Soviet efforts during the late 1930's to keep Japan preoccupied with areas other than northeast Asia.

1333
BUZINKAI, Donald Imrich. Soviet-League Relations, 1919-1939: A Survey and Analysis. New York, 1964. 263p. DA 25 (Apr. 1965), 6042-43; UM 65-1609.

Includes a discussion of Soviet Russia's reaction to the threat posed by Japanese expansionism during the 1930's and a study of Soviet attempts to utilize the League of Nations in order to gain greater security.

1334
THORNTON, Sandra Winterberger. The Soviet Union and Japan, 1939-1941. Georgetown, 1964. 368p.

Contents: Japanese Foreign Relations in 1939; Nazi-Soviet Pact; Japan Considers Rapprochement with the Soviet Union, September 1939-July 1940; Determination of Japanese Foreign Policy, July 1940-April 1941; Role of Richard Sorge; Soviet-Japanese Neutrality Pact; Soviet-German War; Decision: South.

GILBERT, Carl L. The Hirota Ministries: An Appraisal: Japan's Relations with China and the U.S.S.R., 1933-1938. 1967. See no.1063.

1335
YOUNG, Katsu Hirai. The Japanese Army and the Soviet Union: 1936-1941. Washington, Seattle, 1968. 434p. DA 29 (Sept. 1968), 860-A; UM 68-12,725.

A study of the army-dominated foreign policy of Imperial Japan toward the U.S.S.R., 1936-1941. Contents: The Crisis of 1935-1936; The Anti-Comintern Pact of 1936; The Phantom Sino-Japanese Anti-Comintern Pact; The Hayashi Cabinet and the Army's Preparation for War; The China Incident to the Fall of Nanking; The China Incident and the Soviet Union: "The Wolf at the Back Door"; The Nomonham Incident; The Effect of the German-Soviet Non-Aggression Pact; The Tripartite Pact: The German Victories in Europe and the Army's Foreign Policy; The Japanese-Soviet Neutrality Pact; The Japanese Army and the German Invasion of the Soviet Union.

Rel.Publ.: "The Nomonhan Incident: Imperial Japan and the Soviet Union," MN, 22 (1967), 82-102.

Siberian Intervention

1336
SCHUMAN, Frederick Lewis. American Policy toward Russia, 1917-1927. Chicago, 1927. 662, vii p. AB: University of Chicago. Abstracts of Theses, Humanistic Series. v.5 (1926/27), p.221-25.

Includes information on American-Japanese relations with regard to the Allied intervention in Siberia, 1918-ca.1922.

Rel.Publ.: American Policy toward Russia since 1917: A Study of Diplomatic History, International Law, and Public Opinion. New York: International Publishers, 1928. ix, 399p.

1337
REIKHBERG, G. E. Podgotovka i nachalo interventsii na Dal'nem Vostoke v 1917-1918 gg. [The Preparation for and the Beginning of Intervention in the Far East, 1917-1918]. Moscow, Institut istorii, filosofii, i literatury, 1937. (Candidate of Historical Sciences degree) Text in Russian.

Rel.Publ.: Razgrom iaponskoi interventsii na Dal'nem Vostoke, 1918-1922, ed. by B. Rubtsova. Moscow: Sotsekgiz, 1940. 212p.

1338
BOCK, Benjamin. The Origins of the Inter-Allied Intervention in Eastern Asia, 1918-1920. Stanford, 1940. 347p. AB: Stanford University. Abstracts of Dissertations, 1940/41. p.184-87.

Focuses particularly on Japanese and American participation in the intervention.

1339
PELZEL, Sophia Rogoski. American Intervention in Siberia, 1918-1920. Pennsylvania, 1943. iv, 98p.

Contents: Principles of American Foreign Policy in the Far East; The Sequence of Russian-European Events toward Intervention; Administration and Development of American Intervention. Information on Japan is found throughout.

Rel.Publ.: American...1920. Philadelphia, 1946. iv, 98p.

1340
BRANDENBURG, William Aaron, Jr. The Origins of American Military Intervention in Russia, 1918-1920. Colorado, 1947. 295p.
Includes information on the Japanese intervention in Siberia. Concludes that "Japanese-American tension in Siberia" revealed, "among other things, that the Asiatic Ally was seeking to establish herself permanently in Manchuria and Siberia, as Wilson suspected, and that American influence was exerted to defeat this ambition."

1341
WHITE, John Albert. Siberian Intervention: The Allied Phase. Stanford, 1947. 491p. AB: Stanford University. Abstracts of Dissertations, 1947/1948. p.156-60.
Includes considerable information on the Japanese participation in the Allied intervention and on the Russo-Japanese "duel for possession of the Far Eastern areas of the former Russian empire" (1920-1922).
Rel.Publ.: The Siberian Intervention. Princeton: Princeton University Press, 1950. xi, 471p.

1342
FIKE, Claude Edwin, Jr. A Study of Russian-American Relations during the Ominous Years, 1917-1921. Illinois, 1950. 302p. AB: Microfilm Abstracts, v.10, no. 4 (1951). p.195-96.
Includes information on the Japanese and the American intervention in Siberia. See especially Ch.6, "Siberian Quicksand" (p.109-35).
Rel.Publ.: "The United States and Russian Territorial Problems, 1917-1920," Historian, 24 (May 1962), 331-46.

1343
UNTERBERGER, Betty Miller. America's Siberian Expedition 1918-1920: A Study of National Policy. Duke, 1950. 456p.
Includes information on the Japanese intervention in Siberia.
Rel.Publ.: America's...Policy. Durham, N.C.: Duke University Press, 1956. 271p.; "President Wilson and the Decision to Send American Troops to Siberia," PHR, 24 (Feb. 1955), 63-74.

1344
BACON, Eugene Haywood. Russian-American Relations, 1917-1921. Georgetown, 1951. 354p.
Ch.5, "Siberia: The Adventure Perilous," and Ch.6, "Motives for Intervention," deal with the Japanese intervention in Siberia.

1345
GRIGORTSEVICH, Stanislav Seliverstovich. Razgrom iaponskoi interventsii i krakh proiskov amerikanskikh imperialistov na sovetskom Dal'nem Vostoke, 1920-1922 [The Failure of Japanese Intervention and the Collapse of American Imperialist Intrigues in the Soviet Far East, 1920-1922]. Moscow, Institut vostokovedeniia Akademii nauk SSSR, 1951(?) (Candidate of Historical Sciences degree) Text in Russian. AB: 27p. summary published in 1951.
Rel.Publ.: Amerikanskaia i iaponskaia interventsiia na sovetskom Dal'nem Vostoke i ee razgrom. Moscow, 1957. 199p.

1346
MALYSHEV, V. P. Bor'ba rabochikh i krest'ian za ustanovlenie sovetskoi vlasti na Amure v 1917-1922 (Amurskaia oblast') [The Struggle of the Workers and the Peasants for the Establishment of the Soviet Government in the Amur Oblast (Province), 1917-1922]. Moscow, Moskovskii gosudarstvennyi pedagogicheskii institut imeni V. P. Potemkina, 1954(?) (Doctor of Historical Sciences degree) Text in Russian. AB: 31p. summary published in 1954.

1347
MORLEY, James William. Samurai in Siberia: The Origins of Japan's Siberian Expedition, 1918-1922: A Case Study in the Formation of Japan's Foreign Policy. Columbia, 1954. 679p. DA 14 (Dec. 1954), 2328; UM 10,180.
Contents: Samurai in Siberia; Clansmen and Politicians; Enemies and Allies; Reconnaisance in Siberia; The Manchurian Sanctuary; International Complications; A Crisis Weathered; The Army's Problems; Unruly Proteges; Unaccommodating Allies; The Impasse Broken; A Decision Forced; Hidden Meanings.
Rel.Publ.: The Japanese Thrust into Siberia, 1918. New York: Columbia University Press, 1957. xiii, 395p. (Studies of the Russian Institute, Columbia University)

1348
STAMATOPULOS, Stephen. Woodrow Wilson's Russian Policy: A Case Study of American-Russian Relations, 1913-1921. Harvard, 1957. v, 398p. AB: 7p. summary appended to diss. ms.
Considerable information on Japanese relations with Russia and the United States and on the Siberian intervention can be found in Ch.5, "The Road to Brest-Litovsk" (p.150-92), Ch.6, "The United States, Russia, and the Far East" (p.193-221), and Ch.7, "Wilson and Siberian Intervention" (p.222-61).

1349
ULLMAN, Richard Henry. British Intervention in Russia, November 1917 to February 1920: A Study in the Making of Foreign Policy. Oxford, 1960. xii, 823p.
Contains considerable information on the Japanese intervention in Siberia and on Allied-Japanese relations. See especially Ch.7, "London-Tokyo-Washington: The Crucial Negotiations" (p.277-332).
Rel.Publ.: Intervention and the War: Anglo-Soviet Relations, 1917-1921. Princeton: Princeton University Press, 1961 and 1968. xvi, 360p.; xix, 395p. (2v).

LEVIN, Norman G., Jr. The Response of Wilsonian Liberalism to War and Revolution, 1914-1919. 1967. See no.1393.

1350
LEONG, Sow-theng. The Soviets and China: Diplomacy and Revolution, 1917-1923. Harvard, 1969. iv, 395p.
Ch.1, "Soviet Problems in the East 1917-1920" (p.1-61), focuses on "the Bolshevik heritage of a position of weakness vis-à-vis other powers" in Manchuria and eastern Siberia and on the Japanese bid to gain control of these areas.

Since World War II

SCOTT, John R. The Effect of the Cold War upon the Occupation of Japan. 1952. See no.1818.

HELLMANN, Donald C. Japanese Foreign Policy and Domestic Politics: The Peace Agreement with the Soviet Union. 1964. See no.1799.

1351
CHEREVKO, Iu. M. Iapono-sovetskaia torgovlia posle 2-oi mirovoi voiny, 1945-1964 [Soviet-Japanese Trade after the Second World War, 1945-1964]. Moscow, Institut narodov Azii Akademii nauk SSSR, 1965. (Candidate of Economic Sciences degree) 319p. Text in Russian. AB: 18p. summary published in 1965.
Rel.Publ.: "Nekotorye problemy vneshnei torgovli Iaponii v poslednie gody," in Institut narodov Azii, Akademiia nauk SSSR, Kratkie soobshcheniia, 81 (1964), 59-71.

Switzerland

1352
DESLARZES, Jean-Pierre. Les Relations commerciales entre la Suisse et le Japon [Commercial Relations between Switzerland and Japan]. Fribourg, 1958. 103p. Text in French.
Contents: The Characteristics of the Two Economies; Commerical Relations between Switzerland and Japan from the Period of the Earliest Contacts to the Establishment of Normal Relations between the Two Countries; The Treaty of 1911 and Its Application; Swiss-Japanese Commerce; Other Aspects of the Balance of Payments between Switzerland and Japan.
Rel.Publ.: Les Relations...Japon. Zürich: Jean Herbst, 1957. 103p.

1353
NAKAI, Paul Akio. Das Verhältnis zwischen der Schweiz und Japan: Vom Beginn der diplomatischen Beziehungen 1859 bis 1868 [Relations between Switzerland and Japan from the Inception of Diplomatic Relations in 1859 until 1868]. Bern, 1967. x, 150p. Text in German.
Contents: Swiss Knowledge of Japan before the 1859 Expedition; The 1859 Trade Mission to Japan of the "Union Horlogère" of La Chaux-de-Fonds and Le Locle and of the Commercial Board of Directors of St. Gallen; The Conclusion of a Treaty of Friendship and Commerce between Japan and Switzerland; Commerce and Trade between Switzerland and Japan following the Conclusion of the Treaty (1864/1868).
Rel.Publ.: Das Verhältnis...1868. Bern und Stuttgart: Paul Haupt, 1967. x, 150p.

LATIN AMERICA

For Japanese immigration to and settlement in Latin America, see Overseas Japanese Communities--Latin America (pages 199-200).

1354
MURAKAMI, Naojiro. Japan's Attempts to Establish Commercial Relations with Mexico in the Seventeenth Century. Tokyo, 1921. Diss. ms. available at the National Diet Library, Tokyo.

NORTH AMERICA

Canada

For Japanese immigration to and settlement in Canada, see Overseas Japanese Communities--Canada (pages 198-99).

WOODSWORTH, Charles J. Canada and the Far East. 1940. See no.1691.

BENNETT, Neville R. The Anglo-Japanese Alliance and the Dominions, 1902-1911. 1966. See no.1291.

1355
GOWEN, Robert Joseph. Canada's Relations with Japan, 1895-1922: Problems of Immigration and Trade. Chicago, 1966. 332p.
Essentially a study of the decision-making process in Canadian foreign policy.

United States

For Japanese immigration to and settlement in the United States as well as American-Japanese diplomacy concerning the immigration problem, see Overseas Japanese Communities--United States (pages 200-08). For dissertations on Japan and the United States during World War II, see International Relations--Allied participation in World War II (pages 109-11) and International Relations--Southeast Asia during World War II (pages 138-43).
Also see International Relations--China (pages 112-33), which includes dissertations on American-Japanese relations revolving around Japanese activity and aggression in China.

1800-1900

See also International Relations--general and multilateral (pages 104-07).

1356
HINCKLEY, Frank Erastus. American Consular Jurisdiction in the Orient. Columbia, 1905. xx, 283p.
Contains considerable (but scattered) information on American consular extraterritorial jurisdiction in Japan.
Rel.Publ.: American...Orient. Washington: Lowdermilk, 1906. xx, 283p.

1357
WADA, Totaro. The Foreign Policy of the United States toward Japan from 1832 to 1901. Iowa, 1915. 416p.
Contents: The Interest of the United States in the Orient with Especial Reference to Japan before 1832; The Policy of the United States toward Japan from 1832 to 1847; The Policy of the United States toward Japan from 1847 to 1851; The Policy of the United States toward Japan from 1852 to 1855; The Political Foreign Policy of the United States toward Japan from 1855 to 1901; The Commercial Policy of the United States toward Japan from 1855 to 1901; The Quasi-Politico-Social Policy of the United States toward Japan from 1855 to 1901; The Policy of the United States toward Japan with Reference to Their International and National Events.
Rel.Publ.: American Foreign Policy towards Japan during the Nineteenth Century [by] Wada Teijun. Tokyo: Tōyō Bunko, 1928. xi, 575p. (Tōyō Bunko. Publications, Ser. D., v.1)

1358
BASS, Harold James. The Policy of the American State Department toward Missionaries in the Far East. Washington State, 1937. 462p.
See especially Ch.11, "The American State Department

and Missionary Work in Japan prior to the Toleration Decrees of 1873" (p.306-47), and Ch.12, "Religious Liberty in Modern Japan, 1873-1937" (p.348-65).

1359
GRIFFIN, Eldon. The United States and Eastern Asia, 1845-1860, with Special Reference to Consuls and Commerce. Yale, 1937. 456p.

A general study of American consular processes and procedures, their strengths and their weaknesses, and the modifications that were made necessary by American contact with a variety of cultures in East Asia. American diplomatic offices and officials in Japan are included in the study, but the work is not organized on a country by country basis.

Rel.Publ.: Clippers and Consuls: American Consular and Commercial Relations with Eastern Asia, 1845-1860. Ann Arbor, Mich.: Edwards Brothers, 1938. xxii, 533p.

1360
DAVIS, George Theron. The Naval Policy of the United States, 1880-1917. Yale, 1938. 543p.

Pages 302-25 examine in some detail Japanese-American relations, 1898-1914, in the context of American naval policies. Japan's victory in the Russo-Japanese War stimulated anxieties about the safety of the West Coast and led to suggestions that naval power be reallocated to the Pacific. Debates over naval appropriations increasingly concerned Japan.

Rel.Publ.: A Navy Second to None: The Development of Modern American Naval Policy. New York: Harcourt, Brace, 1940. xiii, 508p. (Institute of International Studies, Yale University)

1361
COLE, Allan Burnett. The Dynamics of American Expansion toward Japan, 1791-1860. Chicago, 1940. 674p.

Includes an outline of the political events of the period and a description of the expansionist ideologies of mid-nineteenth century America.

Rel.Publ.: The Dynamics...1860. Chicago, 1943. 14p. ("Private edition, distributed by the University of Chicago libraries"); "Japan's First Embassy to the United States, 1860," Pacific Northwest Quarterly, 32 (Apr. 1941), 131-66; "Plans of Edmund Roberts for Negotiations in Nippon," MN, 4 (1941), 497-513; A translation of 13 interviews of Townsend Harris with Inouye Shinano no Kami and Iwase Higo no Kami appearing in "Japan: 1858 and 1859," in Treaties and Other International Acts of the United States of America, ed. by Hunter Miller (Washington: United States Government Printing Office, 1942), v.7, Document no.200 (p.1094-1170); "The Mount Vernon's Voyage from Batavia to Nagasaki in 1807," American Neptune, 5 (Oct. 1945), 255-65; "The Ringgold-Rodgers-Brooke Expedition to Japan and the North Pacific, 1853-1859," PHR, 16 (May 1947), 152-62.

EYRE, James K., Jr. The Philippines, the Powers and the Spanish-American War: A Study of Foreign Policies. 1940. See no.1182.

1362
SAKAMAKI, Shunzo. Japan and the United States: A Study of Japanese Contacts with and Conceptions of Its People prior to the American Expedition of 1853-1854. Columbia, 1940. ix, 204p.

Presents accounts "of American ships and seamen that came to Japan between 1790 and 1853 and cases of Japanese shipwrecks in which Americans were concerned in one way or another." Also "seeks to indicate the type and extent of Japanese knowledge, or lack of knowledge, of things American before 1854."

Rel.Publ.: Japan and the United States, 1790-1853. Tokyo, 1939. ix, 204p. (Transactions of the Asiatic Society of Japan. 2d ser., v.18, 1939); "Western Concepts of Japan and the Japanese," PHR, 6 (1937), 1-14.

BOLLER, Paul F., Jr. The American Board and the Dōshisha, 1875-1900. 1947. See no.561.

CONROY, Francis H. The Japanese Expansion into Hawaii, 1868-1898. 1949. See no.1741.

1363
SCRIBNER, Robert Leslie. The Diplomacy of William L. Marcy, Secretary of State, 1853-1857. Virginia, 1949. iii, 590p. AB: University of Virginia. Abstracts of Dissertations, 1949. p.57-61.

Ch.14, "Taiping and Tokugawa" (p.480-528), deals with Marcy and Japan.

SCHWANTES, Robert S. American Influence in the Education of Meiji Japan, 1868-1912. 1950. See no.563.

ANTHONY, David F. The Administration of Hokkaido under Kuroda Kiyotaka, 1870-1882: An Early Example of Japanese-American Cooperation. 1951. See no.591.

1364
GRAFF, Henry Franklin. Bluejackets with Perry in Japan: A Day-by-Day Account Kept by Master's Mate John R. C. Lewis and Cabin Boy William B. Allen. Columbia, 1952. 181p.

The edited manuscripts are preceded by an introduction focusing on early American interest in Japan.

Rel.Publ.: Bluejackets...Allen. New York: New York Public Library, 1952. 181p. [Reprinted from the Bulletin of the New York Public Library, 1950-1951.]

1365
PETROV, Dmitrii Vasil'evich. Amerikanskaia ekspansiia v Iaponii v seredine XIX veka, 1853-1868 [American Expansion in Japan, 1853-1868]. Moscow, Moskovskii institut vostokovedeniia, 1952. (Candidate of Historical Sciences degree) 495, xxv p. Text in Russian. AB: 20p. summary published in 1952.

Rel.Publ.: Kolonial'naia ekspansiia Soedinennykh Shtatov Ameriki v Iaponii v seredine XIX veka. Moscow: Gospolitizdat, 1955. 280p.

1366
MORE, Lois Alma. American Diplomacy in Japan, 1853-1869: From Advantage Gained to Advantage Lost. Columbia, 1963. 265p. DA 24 (June 1964), 5522-23; UM 64-4329.

"Concludes that while the Americans maintained their diplomatic advantage in Japan until 1865, in the following four years that advantage was lost to the British...because of the policies pursued by the American and British representatives in connection with the Japanese civil war of 1868/69. The British representative, Sir Harry Parkes, supported the successful Imperialists while the Americans adhered to the losing Shogun...." While the Japanese-American relations remained strong and friendly during the ensuing decades, "for the period after 1869...it was the British who particularly influenced Japanese policy."

CARUTHERS, Sandra C. T. Charles LeGendre, American Diplomacy, and Expansion in Meiji Japan, 1868-1893. 1966.

See no.922.

1367
HARBERT, Mary Elizabeth Mack. The Open Door Policy: The Means of Attaining Nineteenth Century American Objectives in Japan. Oregon, 1967. 485p. DA 28 (Sept. 1967), 1031-A; UM 67-10,783.

Argues that although historians have failed to apply the term "Open Door" to American relations with Japan before 1900, American foreign policy towards Japan--the maintenance of equal opportunity--was founded on the same policy as that developed in China.

1900-1941: General

See also International Relations--United States: [1] 1900-1914, [2] 1914-1930, and [3] 1930-1941 (pages 157-62).

BASS, Harold J. The Policy of the American State Department toward Missionaries in the Far East. 1937. See no.1358.

CASES, Manuel T. The Philippines in Foreign Relations since 1895. 1941. See no.1183.

GRAA, Frederick A. The Open Door Policy of the United States: A Fundamental Cause of War between the United States and Japan. 1948. See no.952.

1368
IN'KOV, Iu. I. Ekonomicheskie vzaimootnosheniia mezhdu SShA i Iaponiei posle 1931 g. [Economic Relations between the United States and Japan after 1931]. Moscow, Vsesoiuznaia akademiia vneshnei torgovli, 1948. (Candidate of Economic Sciences degree) 269p. Text in Russian.

1369
SNOWBARGER, Willis Edward. The Development of Pearl Harbor. California, Berkeley, 1950. 306p.

From 1907, Pearl Harbor was planned as an operating base from which the United States Navy could oppose and attempt to contain the Japanese.

ARNOLD, Dean A. American Economic Enterprises in Korea, 1895-1939. 1954. See no.723.

1370
SUN, Mung-chio Chao. Japanese Raw Silk and American Raw Cotton. Michigan, 1957. 205p. DA 18 (May 1958), 1671; UM 58-1468.

Studies the relationship between raw silk and raw cotton--two commodities of outstanding importance--in the trade between Japan and the United States (1893-1955).

1371
JOHNSSON, Stephen Henning. The Influence of Special Interests upon American Far Eastern Relations from Versailles to Teheran. Georgetown, 1959. 699p. (2v.).

"Deals with important groups and individuals and the influence which they exerted upon policy-making during this period....Emphasis was placed upon the diplomatic relations between the United States and Japan and China."

STEMEN, John R. The Diplomacy of the Immigration Issue: A Study in Japanese-American Relations, 1894-1941. 1960. See no.1728.

1372
BURKE, Robert Louis. Franklin D. Roosevelt and the Far East: 1913-1941. Michigan State, 1969. 238p. DA 30 (May 1970); UM 70-9505.

1900-1914

For dissertations on the American diplomatic involvement in the Russo-Japanese War, see International Relations--Russia: 1860-1917 (pages 150-52).

1373
SHIMAN, Russell Gardner. The United States and Old World Diplomacy, 1898-1914: With Special Reference to China. London, 1929. v, 399p.

Includes a discussion of the American role in the Sino-Japanese conflict, of the Anglo-Japanese Alliance, and of the American attitude of "benevolent neutrality" towards Japan during the Russo-Japanese War. The author attempts to reevaluate the question of America's isolationist policy (especially in East Asia) in order to show how crucial United States involvement actually was.

1374
CLINARD, Outten Jones. The National Strategy of the United States in the Pacific, 1897-1917: A Study in American Naval Policy. California, Berkeley, 1942. 570p.

A study in Japanese-American relations that discusses the growing conflict of interest between Japan and the United States and the effect that this had on American naval developments.

Rel.Publ.: Japan's Influence on American Naval Power, 1897-1917. Berkeley: University of California Press, 1947. iv, 235p. (University of California Publications in History, 36)

1375
LIVERMORE, Seward Wright. American Naval Development, 1898-1914: With Special Reference to Foreign Affairs. Harvard, 1943. xviii, 572p. AB: Harvard University. Summaries of Theses...1943-1945. p.243-48.

For information on naval and diplomatic relations with Japan, see Ch.4, "Naval Base Policy: The Pacific, 1898-1914" (p.149-94), and Ch.9, "The Navy in the Far East" (p.363-422).

Rel.Publ.: "American Strategy Diplomacy in the South Pacific, 1890-1914," PHR, 12 (Mar. 1943), 33-51; "American Naval-Base Policy in the Far East, 1850-1914," PHR, 13 (June 1944), 113-35; "The American Navy as a Factor in World Politics, 1903-1913," American Historical Review, 63 (July 1958), 863-79.

1376
BRAISTED, William Reynolds. The Development of the Far East as an American Naval Problem, 1897-1909. Chicago, 1950. 564p.

A study of "the relation of the naval and diplomatic policies of the United States in the Pacific" with some attention devoted to the Russo-Japanese War and its aftermath and to the matter of Japan as America's Pacific naval problem, 1906-1907.

Rel.Publ.: The United States Navy in the Pacific, 1897-1909. Austin: University of Texas Press, 1958. xii, 282p.; "The United States Navy's Dilemma in the Pacific, 1906-1909," PHR, 26 (Aug. 1957), 235-44.

BRIDGHAM, Philip L. American Policy toward Korean Independence, 1866-1910. 1952. See no.1143.

MERRILL, John E. American Official Reactions to the Domestic Policies of Japan in Korea, 1905-1910. 1954. See no.1146.

1377
ESTHUS, Raymond Arthur. Diplomatic Relations between the United States and Japan. Duke, 1956. 474p.

Contents: Roosevelt and the Russo-Japanese War; Japan, Korea, and the United States; The Open Door in Manchuria, 1905-1906; The Open Door in Manchuria, 1906-1907; The School Segregation Crisis; Settlement of the School Segregation Crisis; Riots and Discrimination in San Francisco; The War Scare of 1907; The Quest for an Immigration Treaty; The Immigration Démarché of November, 1907; Achieving Anglo-American Solidarity vis-à-vis Japanese Immigration; Straight's Crusade in Manchuria; The Beginning of the Japanese-American Rapprochement; The Root-Takahira Exchange of Notes; The Renewal of Anti-Japanese Agitation in California.

Rel.Publ.: Theodore Roosevelt and Japan. Seattle: University of Washington Press, 1966. viii, 329p.; "The Taft-Katsura Agreement: Reality or Myth?" Journal of Modern History, 31 (Mar. 1959), 46-51; "The Changing Concept of the Open Door, 1899-1910," Mississippi Valley Historical Review, 46 (Dec. 1959), 435-54.

1378
GRAF, Helga. Die Aussenpolitik der Vereinigten Staaten von Amerika in Ostasien von 1905-1914 [American Foreign Policy towards East Asia, 1905-1914]. München, 1957. iii, 370p. Text in German. Diss. ms. available at München, Universitätsbibliothek, Nr. U 1957.7138.

The author focuses on the following aspects of American foreign policy when discussing American-Japanese relations: (1) the initiation of diplomatic relations between the two countries; (2) Japan's political position before 1905, the attitude of the United States before and during the Russo-Japanese War, and the Taft-Katsura Agreement; (3) the problem of United States-Japanese trade and of Japanese immigration to the United States; and (4) the Japanese state of affairs, 1904-1914.

1379
KACHI, Teruko Okada. The Treaty of 1911 and the Immigration and Alien Land Law Issue between the United States and Japan, 1911-1913. Chicago, 1957. 266p.

Contents: Pt.1: The Treaty of Commerce and Navigation between the United States and Japan, 1911: Preparation for the Treaty, 1908-1910; Negotiations for the Treaty, 1910-1911; Conclusion of the Treaty, 1911. Pt.2: The Japanese Immigration and Alien Land Law Issue, 1911-1913: The Japanese Immigration Issue; Anti-Japanese Bills in the California Legislature, 1911; The California Anti-Alien Land Law, 1913; Conclusions.

Rel.Publ.: "Nihon tsūshō kōkai jōyaku to Kariforunia-shū tochi hō," in Nihon Kokusai Seiji Gakkai, Kokusai seiji, 1961, no.1, p.21-45.

KNUTH, Helen E. The Climax of American Anglo-Saxonism 1898-1905. 1958. See no.1724.

1380
MINGER, Ralph Eldin. William Howard Taft: The Development of His Conceptions of American Foreign Policy, 1900-1908. Southern California, 1958. 310p. AB: University of Southern California. Abstracts of Dissertations for...1958. p.184-87.

Chapter 6 studies Taft's missions to Japan (1905 and 1907) as a special representative of President Roosevelt.

Rel.Publ.: "Taft's Missions to Japan: A Study in Personal Diplomacy," PHR, 30 (Aug. 1961), 279-94.

1381
HART, Robert Allen. The Voyage of the Great White Fleet, 1907-1909. Indiana, 1964. 314p. DA 26 (Aug. 1965), 1003; UM 65-3484.

A descriptive and analytical study of the actual voyage and of its impact on American relations with Japan as well as with several other Asian and European countries.

Rel.Publ.: The Great White Fleet: Its Voyage around the World, 1907-1909. Boston: Little, Brown, 1965. xvi, 362p.

1382
NEU, Charles Eric. The Far Eastern Policy of Theodore Roosevelt, 1906-1909. Harvard, 1964. iv, 338p. (2v.). AB: 4p. summary appended to diss. ms.

Primarily a study of United States-Japanese relations, 1906-1909, with particular emphasis on the problem of Japanese immigration. Contents: California and Japan; The Widening Crisis; "The Need of Preparedness"; A Summer of Uncertainties; Taft and Aoki; Pressure on Japan; Strategy in the Pacific; A Heritage of Strength; Reconciliation with Japan; The Final Crisis; Roosevelt's Legacy.

Rel.Publ.: An Uncertain Friendship: Theodore Roosevelt and Japan, 1906-1909. Cambridge: Harvard University Press, 1967. x, 347p.; "Theodore Roosevelt and American Involvement in the Far East, 1901-1909," PHR, 35 (Nov. 1966), 433-49.

CHAY, Jongsuk. The United States and the Closing Door in Korea: American-Korean Relations, 1894-1905. 1965. See no.1155.

CHOI, Dong Hoon. The United States Policy toward the Japanese Protectorate and Annexation in Korea, 1904-1910. 1965. See no.1156.

ISRAEL, Jerome M. Progressivism and the Open Door: America and China, 1901-1921. 1967. See no.960.

1383
COSTELLO, Daniel Joseph. Planning for War: A History of the General Board of the Navy, 1900-1914. Fletcher, 1969. xi, 348p. AB: 6p. summary appended to diss. ms.

"Analyzes the [American] Board's origin and describes its organization, operation, and relationship with other Navy Department components. Also examined are the Board's estimates as to the 'threats' to United States security, and its proposals relative to naval bases, ship strength, and the strategical disposition of the fleet." Includes considerable information on Japanese naval activities in the Pacific and Japan's potential threat to the Philippines in particular and the United States in general.

1914-1930

See also: International Relations--Disarmament during the 1920's and 1930's (pages 107-09), International Relations--Russia: Siberian intervention (pages 153-54), and International Relations--United States: 1900-1941 (pages 157).

ODATE, Gyoju. Japan's Financial Relations with the United States. 1922. See no.310.

TUPPER, Eleanor. American Sentiment toward Japan, 1904-1924. 1929. See no.988.

1384
LAHEE, Arnold Warburton. Our Competitors and Markets. Harvard, 1933. Diss. ms. not available. AB: Harvard University. Summaries of Theses...1933. p.245-48.
Japan is studied as one of several countries trading with the United States. See Ch.11, "Japan and the Eastern Question."
Rel.Publ.: Our Competitors and Markets: An Introduction to Foreign Trade. New York: H. Holt, 1934. xix, 477p.

1385
ISHII, John David. Japanese-American Diplomatic Relations, 1919-1929. Georgetown, 1950. 447p.
Contents: Background to Conflict; Organization of a New Financial Consortium; Japan versus Wilson at the Peace Conference; Settlement of the Shantung Question; Yap Island Controversy; Japanese Withdrawal from Siberia; Japan at Washington; The Japanese Immigration Problem; 1926-1929.

1386
CURRY, Roy Watson. Woodrow Wilson and the Far East. Duke, 1952. 679p.
A study of East Asian developments during the administration of Woodrow Wilson (1913-1921) with particular focus on Japanese expansion in East Asia and on Japanese-American relations. Contents: Enter the Crusader; Money, Recognition, and Representation in China; The California Crisis; Men and Policy for the Philippines; War and Consequences; Minor Conflicts of Japanese-American Relations; War and Its Adjustments; A Consortium of Troubles; The Siberian Fracas; Paris, Peace, and the Far East; The Course is Run.
Rel.Publ.: Woodrow Wilson and Far Eastern Policy, 1913-1921. New York: Bookman Associates, 1957. 411p. (Bookman Monograph Series); "Woodrow Wilson and Philippine Policy," Mississippi Valley Historical Review, 41 (Dec. 1954), 435-52.

1387
SCHILLING, Warner Roller. Admirals and Foreign Policy, 1913-1919. Yale, 1954. 375p. DA 26 (Oct. 1965), 2306; UM 64-11,383.
Studies the foreign policy views of high-ranking American naval officers with particular regard to the other major naval powers: England, Germany, and Japan.
Rel.Publ.: "Civil-Naval Politics in World War I," World Politics, 7 (July 1955), 572-91.

1388
WHEELER, Gerald Everett. Japan's Influence on American Naval Policies, 1922-1931. California, Berkeley, 1954. 300p.
Focuses on American naval preparations to meet the growing Japanese threat in the Pacific and on some of the policy disagreements regarding these preparations that developed between the United States Navy Department on the one hand and Congress and the President on the other.
Rel.Publ.: Prelude to Pearl Harbor: The United States Navy and the Far East, 1921-1931. Columbia, Mo.: University of Missouri Press, 1963. 212p.; "The United States Navy and the Japanese 'Enemy': 1919-1931," Military Affairs, 21 (1957), 61-74; "Republican Philippine Policy, 1921-1933," PHR, 28 (Nov. 1959), 377-90; "Isolated Japan: Anglo-American Diplomatic Co-operation, 1927-1936," PHR, 30 (May 1961), 165-78.

1389
WINTERS, Richard John. The United States Foreign Policy and Japan: From the Washington Conference to the Manchurian Incident. Fordham, 1959. 206p. AB: 9p. summary appended to diss. ms.
Contents: Introduction (Scope of the Problem, Conflict and Issues); The Washington Conference; Liberal and Reactionary Governments of Japan; The Liberal Government Returns; From Liberalism to Militarism.

1390
BURNS, Roy Gene, Jr. American-Japanese Relations, 1920-1925. Missouri, 1962. 246p. DA 23 (Jan. 1963), 2501; UM 63-1573.
Focuses particularly on the events leading up to the Washington Conference and on immediate subsequent developments. Contents: The Origin of the Conference; Battle-Fleets and the Pacific; The Problem of China; End of an Era.

1391
ASADA, Sadao. Japan and the United States, 1915-1925. Yale, 1963. 466p. DA 27 (July 1966), 158-59-A; UM 66-7562.
"Alternating between Tokyo and Washington, the narrative follows the process of decision making and closely analyzes the conflict of aims and policies, the confusion of views and images during the years 1915-1925."
Rel.Publ.: "Japan's 'Special Interests' and the Washington Conference, 1921-1922," American Historical Review, 67 (Oct. 1961), 62-70.

1392
MADDOX, Robert James. William E. Borah and American Foreign Policy: 1907-1929. Rutgers, 1964. 393p. DA 25 (Oct. 1964), 2476; UM 64-10,933.
The views of the Japanese held by Senator Borah, who "thought that Russian and American interests coincided in the Far East and that collaboration between them might curb Japanese expansion," are included and discussed.
Rel.Publ.: "William E. Borah and the Crusade to Outlaw War," Historian, 29 (Feb. 1967), 200-21; "Keeping Cool with Coolidge," Journal of American History, 53 (Mar. 1967), 772-80; "Woodrow Wilson, the Russian Embassy, and Siberian Intervention," PHR, 36 (Nov. 1967). [See also addenda entry no.29A.]

1393
LEVIN, Norman Gordon, Jr. The Response of Wilsonian Liberalism to War and Revolution, 1914-1919. Harvard, 1967. ii, 378p. AB: 4p. summary appended to diss. ms.
Contains information on American-Japanese relations, the Japanese intervention in Siberia, and Japanese claims to Shantung. See especially Ch.7, (p.308-52): "Peace and Revolution, IV: The Wilsonian Search for

Postwar Liberal Order in Siberia and the Underdeveloped World."

Rel.Publ.: Woodrow Wilson and World Politics: America's Response to War and Revolution. New York: Oxford University Press, 1968. xii, 340p.

1930-1941

See also International Relations--Disarmament during the 1920's and 1930's (pages 107-09) and International Relations--United States: 1900-1941: General (page 157)

1394
McREYNOLDS, George Edgar. American Sentiment Regarding Japan 1924-1934. Clark, 1937. xi, 270p. AB: Clark University. Thesis Abstracts-1937. p.43-47.

"Ascertains the attitude of Americans towards the immigration and naval questions and Japan's China policy during the decade 1924-1934." Contents: The Immigration Question; The London Conference and After; War in the Far East, 1931-1933; Guardians of the "Peace" of Asia.

Rel.Publ.: Japan in American Public Opinion [by] Eleanor Tupper and George E. McReynolds. New York: Macmillan, 1937. xix, 465p.

1395
MASLAND, John Wesley, Jr. Group Interests in American Relations with Japan. Princeton, 1938. 403p. DA 12 (1952), 327 [Abstract not available]; UM 3005.

Contents: The Executive Formulates Policy; The Navy Supports Administration Policy; An Isolationist Congress; Peace Societies, Churches, and Missions; American Patriots; Labor and Agriculture; American Business Groups; In Conclusion.

Rel.Publ.: "Missionary Influence upon American Far Eastern Policy," PHR, 10 (Sept. 1941), 279-96; "Commercial Influence upon American Far Eastern Policy, 1937-1941," PHR, 11 (Sept. 1942), 281-99.

BALDORIA, Pedro L. A Study of the Problems Involved in the Neutralization of the Philippines. 1940. See no.1181.

LONG, Robert E. A Study of the Naval Base with Particular Reference to the Philippine Islands. 1942. See no.1184.

1396
TUELLER, Dallas Alma. Australian-American Relations, 1901-1940. Stanford, 1946. 464p. AB: Stanford University. Abstracts of Dissertations, 1946/47. p.115-19.

Devotes considerable attention to American and Australian attitudes towards Japanese aggression during the 1930's and discusses the various points on which they diverged.

1397
RODOV, B. V. Iapono-Amerikanskie peregovory 1941 goda: K voprosu o proiskhozhdenii Tikhookeanskoi voiny [Japanese-American Negotiations in 1941: Concerning the Origin of the Second World War in the Pacific Area]. Moscow, Moskovskii institut vostokovedeniia, 1947. (Candidate of Historical Sciences degree) 265p. Text in Russian.

Rel.Publ.: Rol' SShA i Iaponii v podgotovke i razviazyvanii voiny na Tikhom okeane 1938-1941 gg. Moscow: Gospolitizdat, 1951. 200p. [TRANSLATIONS: (1) Die USA in Japan bei der Vorbereitung und Entfesselung des Krieges im Stillen Ozean 1938-1941. Ins. deutsche Übertr. von B. Sommer. Berlin: Rütten und Loening, 1953; (2) Rola USA i Japonii w przygotowsniu i rozpataniu wojnu na pacyfiku 1938-1941. z ros. tłum J. Nowacki. Warszawa: M-wo obrony narodowej, 1952. 209p.; (3) Podíl USA a Japonska na přípravě a rozpoutání války v Tichomoří, 1938-1941. Přel. z rus. kpt. K. A. Krejei. Praha: Naše vojsko, 1952. 162p.]

1398
PERMIAKOV, P. A. Amerikano-iaponskie otnosheniia v nachale 2-oi mirovoi voiny: Amerikanskaia politika "umirotvoreniia" Iaponii v 1939-1941 gg. [American-Japanese Relations at the Beginning of World War Two: The American Policy of "Appeasement" vis-à-vis Japan, 1939-1941]. Moscow, Akademiia obshchestvennykh nauk pri Tsentral'nom Komitete Vsesoiuznoi Kommunisticheskoi Partii (bol'shevikov), 1948. (Candidate of Historical Sciences degree) 312p. Text in Russian.

1399
DRUMMOND, Donald Francis. From Peace to War: A Study of the Neutrality and Nonbelligerency of the United States, 1937-1941. Michigan, 1949. xii, 651p. AB: Microfilm Abstracts, v.9 (1949), p.114-15; UM 1296.

"Charts the whole pattern of American foreign policy as it evolved through the years 1937-1941, shows its connection with the policies and actions of other states, and aligns it with such imponderables as the growth of public opinion and the force of executive resolve." Contains considerable information on Japanese-American relations.

Rel.Publ.: The Passing of American Neutrality, 1937-1941. Ann Arbor: University of Michigan, 1955. vi, 409p. (University of Michigan Publications. History and Political Science, 20)

KAWAHARA, Hattie M. Diplomatic Relations between the United States and Japan from 1931 to 1941. 1949. See no.1055.

1400
KUUSISTO, Allan Andrew. The Influence of the National Council for Prevention of War on United States Foreign Policy, 1935-1939. Harvard, 1950. iii, 308p. AB: 7p. summary appended to diss. ms.

See especially, "The Far East Crisis-1937" (p.170-88) and "Fortification of Guam" (p.237-46).

1401
LENG, Shao-chuan. United States-Japanese Negotiations in 1941. Pennsylvania, 1950. 301p. DA 13 (1953), 1242-43; UM 6319.

"Covers the nature of the negotiations, the reasons for their failure, and the responsibility for the coming of war." Contents: The Early Stage of Negotiations; Stalemate of Negotiations; The Proposed Meeting of President Roosevelt and Premier Konoye; Kurusu's Mission; The Reactions of China and the Powers to the Negotiations; The Final Phase; The Myth of "Maneuvering the Japanese Into Firing the First Shot."

1402
BUDKEVICH, S. L. Razvitie iapono-amerikanskikh protivorechii na Dal'nem Vostoke v 1931-1941 gg. [The Growing Conflict between Japan and the United States in East Asia, 1931-1941]. Moscow, Institut vostokovedeniia Akademii nauk SSSR, 1953. (Candidate of Historical Sciences degree) 435p. Text in Russian. 27p. summary

published in 1953.

Rel.Publ.: Iapono-amerikanskaia bor'ba za Iugo-Vostochnuiu Asiiu v nachale vtoroi mirovoi voiny, in Akademiia nauk SSSR, Institut Vostokovedeniia, Kratkie soobshcheniia, 35 (1959), 49-61; "Ob odnoi neudavsheisia popytke imperialisticheskogo sgovora: Po povodu iapono-amerikanskikh peregovorov 1941 g.," in Institut narodov Azii, Akademiia nauk SSSR, Kratkie soobshcheniia, 50 (1962), 3-18; "Po povodu provala odnoi diplomaticheskoi intrigi Iaponii: Iun'--dekabr' 1941 g.," in Institut narodov Azii, Akademiia nauk SSSR, Kratkie soobshcheniia, 64 (1963), 60-74.

1403
KUBEK, Anthony N. Japanese-American Relations, 1937-1945. Georgetown, 1956. 518p.

Contents: Historical Introduction; Secretary Hull Adopts a Policy of Watchful Waiting; Soviet Russia Makes Certain that War in the Far East will Serve Her Purposes; The Problems of the Far East: Clamour for Settlement; The Negotiations for a Triple Alliance; The United States Exerts Pressure upon Japan; Secretary Hull Makes a Faint Effort to Find a Path to Peace with Japan; Japanese-American Relations Concerning the Tripartite Pact; Roosevelt Refuses to Meet Konoye; Japan Seeks A Truce with the United States; The Problem of Pearl Harbour; Yalta, Prologue to Tragedy: (1) First Phase, (2) Second Phase.

STELTZER, Hans-Jürgen. Die Indonesienpolitik der Vereinigten Staaten 1940 bis 1949. 1956. See no. 1213.

1404
BADER, Ernest Birny. Some Aspects of American Public Reaction to Franklin D. Roosevelt's Japanese Policy, 1933-1941. Nebraska, 1957. 460p. DA 18 (Jan. 1958), 209-10; UM 23,656.

Seeks to "discover how much of President Roosevelt's Japanese policy was revealed to the American people before Pearl Harbor, and how the public reacted to the information it possessed." Concludes that "the Roosevelt Administration...was less than candid in dealing with public information. Nevertheless, the American people were adequately informed about basic Japanese foreign policy. Although Americans were more hostile toward the Japanese than they were toward the Germans, there was little support of any truly vigorous Japanese policy. The charge that the Roosevelt Administration maneuvered the nation into war is not sustained by the evidence."

FRIEND, Theodore W., III. The Politics and Strategy of Philippine Independence, 1929-1936. 1958. See no.1185.

1405
OYOS, Lynwood Earl. The Navy and the United States Far Eastern Policy, 1930-1939. Nebraska, 1958. 333p. DA 19 (Dec. 1958), 1356-57; UM 58-3773.

"Analyzes and discusses the efforts of the Executive department from 1930 to 1939 to ready the American navy for the Pacific contingency which erupted in 1941."

1406
BURNS, Richard Dean. Cordell Hull: A Study in Diplomacy: 1933-1941. Illinois, 1960. 355p. DA 21 (Mar. 1961), 2685; UM 61-94.

Studies Secretary of State Hull's philosophy and influence in the formulation of American foreign policy, particularly in regard to developments in Europe and East Asia. Contents: The Curtain Rises; Prosperity and Peace; The Challenge of the Dictators; From Madrid to Munich; Closing the Open Door; The Collapse of Neutrality; A Prelude to War.

1207
TOWNE, Ralph Louis, Jr. Roosevelt and the Coming of World War II: An Analysis of the War Issues Treated by Franklin D. Roosevelt in Selected Speeches, October 5, 1937 to December 7, 1941. Michigan State, 1961. 205p. DA 22 (Dec. 1961), 2108-09; UM 61-4992.

Includes his views on the international situation in East Asia.

1408
TULEJA, Thaddeus Vincent. United States Naval Policy in the Pacific, 1930-1941. Fordham, 1961. 315p. DA 23 (July 1962), 217; UM 62-1045.

Focuses on developments directly or indirectly affecting American-Japanese relations and American defence policies in the Pacific.

Rel.Publ.: Statesmen and Admirals: Quest for a Far Eastern Naval Policy. New York: W. W. Norton, 1963. 256p.

1409
HERZOG, James Henry. The Role of the United States Navy in the Evolution and Execution of American Foreign Policy Relative to Japan, 1936-1941. Brown, 1963. 224p. DA 24 (Mar. 1964), 3822-23; UM 64-1977.

Contents: Historical Background; The Chief of Naval Operations and Extra-Service Cooperation; The Evolution of American War Plans against Japan; The Evolution of British-American Cooperation in the Pacific; The Quest for a Cooperative Defense against Japan by the American, British, and Dutch Military Commands in the Far East; The Asiatic Fleet in Japanese-American Relations; Relations Resulting from Visits by American and Japanese Naval Ships; The Role of the Navy in the Embargo of Oil to Japan; The Role of the Navy in the Deterrent Strategy in the Pacific.

Rel.Publ.: "Influence of the United States Navy in the Embargo of Oil to Japan, 1940-1941," PHR, 35 (Aug. 1966), 317-28.

1410
MURAKAMI, Yoshio. Japanese-American Negotiations, 1940-1941. Fletcher, 1965. vii, 269p. AB: 4p. summary appended to diss. ms.

"Analyzes the negotiations between Tokyo and Washington which took place during the period between June 1940 and October 1941...and demonstrates how far apart the positions of the two countries were and how small the chances were for improving their relations in the Pacific." Contents: An Introduction: Arita-Grew Conversations of June 1940; Matsuoka and the Axis Alliance; Winter of 1940-1941; Negotiations in Washington and the Russo-German War; Dismissal of Matsuoka and the Fall of the Konoe Cabinet.

BERG, Meredith W. The United States and the Breakdown of Naval Limitation, 1934-1939. 1966. See no.874.

1411
CAINE, Philip David. The American Periodical Press and Military Preparedness during the Hoover Administration. Stanford, 1966. 285p. DA 27 (June 1967), 4189-A; UM 67-4330.

"Seeks to determine the amount of public concern about preparedness, to survey the viewpoints that were presented to the public by the magazines, and to discover the degree to which Hoover's military policies were in harmony with" popular sentiment. The study centers around the London Naval Conference, the Manchurian Incident, and the Geneva Disarmament Conference.

1412
KOGINOS, Emmanuel Theodore. The Panay Incident: Prelude to War. American, 1966. 278p. DA 26 (May 1966), 6675-76; UM 66-3392.
"Examines the Panay crisis [1937] and reviews the episode's impact on American foreign and domestic policies." Contents: Diplomatic Background; The Crisis; The Settlement; The Ludlow Referendum; Naval Expansion.
Rel.Publ.: The Panay...War. Lafayette, Ind.: Purdue University Studies, 1967. ix, 154p.

SOULE, Vivian J. The Embassy of Sir Robert Craigie to Tokio, 1937-1941. 1966. See no.1298.

BAUGE, Kenneth L. Voluntary Export Restriction as a Foreign Commercial Policy with Special Reference to Japanese Cotton Textiles. 1967. See no.279.

KRESSLER, Peter R. An Evaluation of United States-Japanese Negotiations of Major Commercial Disputes during the 1930's. 1968. See no.236.

MOON, John E. Confines of Concept: American Strategy in World War II. 1968. See no.894.

1413
PAPACHRISTOV, Judith Reisner. American-Soviet Relations and United States Policy in the Pacific, 1933-1941. Colorado, 1968. 568p. DA 29 (Sept. 1968), 856-57-A; UM 68-12,421.
"Evaluates the influence of American-Soviet relations on the formation of American policy in the Pacific." Also discusses American policy towards Japan at considerable length.

1414
HOLBROOK, Francis Xavier. United States National Defense and Trans-Pacific Commercial Air Routes 1933-1941. Fordham, 1969. 430p. DA 31 (July 1970); UM 70-11,435.

Since World War II

For dissertations on the Allied occupation of Japan, see Political Science--Allied occupation (pages 210-14).

1415
SAPIN, Burton Malcolm. The Role of the Military Establishment in the Japanese Peace Treaty: A Case Study in American Foreign Policy Decision-Making. Princeton, 1953. Diss. ms. not available.
Rel.Publ.: The Role of the Military in American Foreign Policy [by] Burton M. Sapin and Richard C. Snyder. Garden City, N.Y.: Doubleday, 1954. viii, 84p. (Doubleday Short Studies in Political Science, 7); An Appropriate Role for the Military in American Foreign Policy-Making: A Research Note [by] Burton Sapin, Richard C. Snyder, and H. W. Bruck. Princeton: Organizational Behavior Section, Princeton University, 1954. 64p. (Foreign Policy and Analysis Series, 4).

1416
CHANG, Yu-nan. American Security Problems in the Far East, 1950-1952. Washington, Seattle, 1954. 356p. DA 14 (Nov. 1954), 2114-15; UM 10,002.
Includes a discussion of the United States-Japan Security Treaty as well as information on non-military aspects of American-Japanese relations.

1417
SHATOV, L. G. San-frantsisskii "mirnyi dogovor" s Iaponiei i iapono-amerikanskii "dogovor bezopasnosti" ot 8 sentiabria 1951 g. [The San Francisco "Peace Treaty" with Japan and the Japanese-American "Security Treaty" of September 8, 1951]. Moscow, Moskovskii gosudarstvennyi institut mezhdunarodnykh otnoshenii Ministerstva Inostrannykh Del SSSR, 1954. (Candidate of Juridical Sciences degree) 475p. Text in Russian.

OKAJIMA, Eiichi. The Japanese Peace Treaty and Its Implications for Japan's Post-War Foreign Policy. 1956. See no.847.

1418
SULLIVAN, Sister Maria Regina, S.J. United States-Japanese Relations and Public Opinion 1945-1955. St. John's, 1959. vi, 241p.
Contents: Japan in World War II; Fundamental Principles of the Occupation; Demilitarization and Democratization; Period of Recovery and Stabilization; Japan: A Possible Bastion of the Western World in the Far East.

1419
AVEN, James Stephen. The Organization of American Community Schools in the Far East. California, Los Angeles, 1963. 209p. DA 24 (Nov. 1963), 1893; UM 63-7700.
"Concerned with the policy of the indigenous governments, non-government agencies, and the United States government toward American community schools in the Far East." Includes a discussion of the development and present status of American schools in Japan.

CHO, Sung Yoon. Jurisdiction over Foreign Forces in Japan, 1945-1960. 1963. See no.1557.

PACKARD, George R., III. Japan's Reaction to the American Alliance 1960: A Study of Japan's Political Processes. 1963. See no.1797.

1420
CHENG, Peter Ping-chii. A Study of John Foster Dulles' Diplomatic Strategy in the Far East. Southern Illinois, 1964. 674p. DA 25 (Apr. 1965), 6043; UM 65-1320.
A study of "Dulles' general principles, his policies in the Far East,...and the views of his critics and supporters," 1950-1959. The author notes that in the case of Japan, "Dulles was able to bring Japan as a nation to a firm commitment in association with free nations."

1421
KOBAYASHI, A. Hiroaki. Der amerikanisch-japanische Sicherheitspakt [The United States-Japan Security Treaty]. Würzburg, 1964. ix, 412p. Text in German. Diss. ms. available at Würzburg, Universitätsbibliothek, Nr. U 64.11,153.
A very detailed study of the historical background, origins, and development of the two security treaties that have been concluded between Japan and the United States since World War II. The dissertation concludes with an examination of the relationship between Japan's postwar constitution and the security pact.

HARSAGHY, Fred J. The Administration of American Cultural Projects Abroad: A Developmental Study with Case Histories of Community Relations in Administering Educational and Informational Projects in Japan and Saudi Arabia. 1965. See no.411.

AMANO, Matsukichi. A Study of Employment Patterns and a Measurement of Employee Attitudes in Japanese Firms at Los Angeles. 1966. See no.224.

KAWAMURA, Yoshitaka. Les Traités de sécurité de 1951 et de 1960 entre le Japon et les États-Unis et le problème de leur compatabilité avec la constitution du Japon de 1946. 1966. See no.1575.

TOMIKAWA, Soji. Impact of Public Opinion on the Postwar Administration of Japan: Problems Connected with the Supplying of Facilities and Areas for Use by United States Forces. 1966. See no.1801.

WATANABE, Akio. Japanese Attitudes toward the Okinawa Project, 1945-1965. 1966. See no.703.

1422
WINIATA, Whatarangi. United States Managerial Investment in Japan, 1950-1964: An Interview Study. Michigan, 1966. 170p. DA 28 (July 1967), 9-A; UM 67-8368.

A "fact-finding effort" focusing on the decision-making process that led to sizable direct investments by United States corporations in Japanese enterprises. Contents: Preview of This Study; Background of United States Postwar Ownership Interests in Japan; Preinvestment Relationship and Major Obstacles Associated with United States Managerial Investment in Japan; The Decisions to Commit Resources to United States-Japanese Business Enterprises in Japan; Major Findings.

1423
DAOUST, George Arlington, Jr. The Role of Air Power in U.S. Foreign Policy in the Far East, 1945-1958. Georgetown, 1967. 235p. DA 28 (Feb. 1968), 3243-44-A; UM 68-1901.

From the use of the atomic bomb against Japan to the Taiwan crisis of 1958.

KIM, Ok Yul. The American Role in Korean-Japanese Relations. 1967. See no.1169.

1424
MORIYA, Etsuro. A Study of the Export Marketing Policy of Selected United States Firms in the Changing Japanese Market. George Washington, 1967. 164p. DA 27 (June 1967), 4009-10-A; UM 67-8439.

Analyzes the export marketing policies of 66 United States manufacturing firms doing business with Japan according to standards relating to "formulation of the marketing mix, overseas operation philosophy, organizational framework, effectiveness of channels of communication, and market survey practices."

1425
AMRAVATI, Mallappa. Relations between Japan and the United States since 1945 with Special Reference to the Peace Treaty and the Security Pact. Indian School of International Studies, 1969. iv, 391p.

"The first three chapters are concerned with the surrender, organization of SCAP, reforms, and an evaluation of the impact of allied reforms on Japanese society. Ch.4 deals with the shift in American policy vis-à-vis Japan and its implications for the occupied country. Ch.5 is devoted to American views on the Japanese peace settlement and the security problem in the Far East. Ch.6 is concerned with the stands taken by the members of the Far Eastern Commission on the peace settlement. The seventh chapter deals with the peace conference held in San Francisco in September 1951. It also contains a critical review of the peace treaty and the security pact. Ch.8 is concerned with the divisions in Japanese society on the peace settlement. The concluding chapter deals with some tentative conclusions reached by the author regarding foreign occupations, reforms, peace conferences and content of peace treaties."

WEINSTEIN, Martin E. Japan's Postwar Defense Policy. 1969. See no.1805.

Japan: The View from Abroad

Limited primarily to non-political attitudes held by people outside of Japan and to foreign knowledge and images of Japan and of Japanese civilization. For Western reactions to Japanese aggression in East Asia, see especially International Relations--China/Manchurian Incident (pages 127 - 131). For Chinese attitudes towards Japanese activities and aggression in China, see International Relations--China (pages 112 - 133) and History--Japanese Empire/Taiwan (pages 98 - 99). For Korean attitudes towards Japan, see History--Japanese Empire/Chōsen (pages 90 - 95) and International Relations--Korea (pages 133 - 136). For Southeast Asian attitudes, see in particular International Relations--Southeast Asia during World War II (pages 138 - 143). Canadian and American attitudes towards Japanese immigration are entered under Overseas Japanese Communities--Canada (pages 198 - 199) and Overseas Japanese Communities--United States (pages 200 - 208).

EUROPE

GEZELIUS, Erik B. Japan i västerländsk framställning till omkring år 1700: Ett geografiskt-kartografiskt försök. 1910. See no.458.

1426
SCHWARTZ, William Leonard. The Imaginative Interpretation of the Far East in Post-Classical French Literature. Stanford, 1926.

Contents: The Gautiers and the Interpretation of the Far East [Japan and China] through Book Sources, 1800-1870; The Goncourt Brothers and French Appreciation of Japanese Art, 1860-1895; The First Literary Observers in the Far East, Loti and His Successors, 1885-1905; Recent Progress and Recent Tendencies in the Imaginative Interpretation of the Far East, 1905-1925.

Rel.Publ.: The Imaginative Interpretation of the Far East in Modern French Literature, 1800-1925. Paris: E. Champion, 1927. xiii, 246p. (Bibliothèque de la Revue de littérature comparée. T.40)

1427
EHLER, Karl. Japan im Urteil europäischer Grossmächte 1894-1906 [The View of Japan Held by the European Powers]. Universita Karlova (German Branch), 1940. Text in German. Pagination not available.

1428
FREITAG, Adolf. Die Japaner im Urteil der Meiji-Deutschen [The Japanese in the Opinion of the Germans Living in Japan during the Meiji Era]. Leipzig, 1940. Text in German. The dissertation in its published form is available at Marburg/Lahn, Staatsbibliothek Preussischer Kulturbesitz, Nr. Ser. 1171-31, C.

A study of their views of (1) the Japanese state, race, personality, intellect, and abilities, (2) of the relationship of the Japanese people with nature and with art, (3) of the Japanese way of life, and (4) of the Western impact on Japanese culture.

Rel.Publ.: Die Japaner...Deutschen. Leipzig: Harrassowitz in Komm., 1939. iv, 144p. (MOAG, Bd 31, Teil c)

1429
KALISCH, Gertrude. Der russisch-japanische Krieg im Spiegel der österreichischen Presse [The Russo-Japanese War as Reflected in the Austrian Press]. Wien, 1944. ii, 179p. Text in German. Diss. ms. available at the Universitätsbibliothek der Universität Wien, Nr. D 7937.

An examination of the attitudes of the Austrian press and the Austrian public towards the Russo-Japanese war. Underlines its importance for Austria-Hungary's East European policy.

ASHMEAD, John, Jr. The Idea of Japan, 1853-1895: Japan as Described by Americans and Other Travellers from the West. 1951. See no.1435.

1430
BURGMAN, Torsten. Svensk opinion och diplomati under rysk-japanska kriget 1904-1905 [Swedish Public Opinion and Foreign Policy during the Russo-Japanese War, 1904-1905]. Uppsala, 1965. Text in Swedish, with a summary in English.

Portions of the dissertation study the reactions of the Swedish press to wartime developments and the attitudes of the Swedish public towards Japan and Russia at that time. The author points out that Swedish admiration of the Japanese was in part due to Swedish resentment of Russia's treatment of Finland, and he notes that Russian attempts to appeal to Swedish public opinion by raising the specter of a "yellow tide" [i.e. "yellow peril"] sweeping over the west failed completely.

[Annotation based on the book].
Rel.Publ.: Svensk...1905. Stockholm: Svenska bokförlaget/Norstedts, 1965. viii, 282p. (Studia Historica Upsaliensia, 18).

1431
SCHWARTZ, Ronald. José María Gironella as Shown in His Works. Connecticut, 1967. 236p. DA 28 (Mar. 1968), 3684-A; UM 68-1405.
Includes a detailed analysis of Gironella's El Japón y su duende (Japan and its Ghosts) and of his attempts to promote within Spain a wider awareness of the modern world including Japan.

UNITED STATES

1432
CHURCH, Alfred Madison. The Study of China and Japan in American Secondary Schools: What Is Worth Teaching and What Is Being Taught? Harvard, 1939. vii, 305p.
"The problem of the thesis is threefold: (1) What should Americans know about China, Japan, and the interests of the United States in the western Pacific area? (2) What are American secondary schools now teaching about this region? (3) In the light of what is considered important, of what is now being taught, and of the factors conditioning the secondary School program, what should the curriculum aim to do?"

1433
CECIL, Levi Moffitt, Jr. Our Japanese Romance: The Myth of Japan in America, 1853-1905. Vanderbilt, 1947. 268p. DA 12 (1952), 791; UM 4390.
"Ch.1, 'The Isle of Mystery,'...gives a summary account, drawn from books of the period, of 1850 America's fanciful impressions of the impregnable island kingdom. Ch.2, 'Pioneering Diplomats,' describes the visit of Commodore Perry to Japan and characterizes the reports of that country that were published as a result of his mission....Ch.3, 'Western Spokesmen for Japan,' tells of the influx of foreign teachers, missionaries, and 'experts' into Japan after 1868. It...indicates the profound influence that their writings and opinions had in coloring America's attitude toward the country. Ch 4, 'Jinrikisha Run,' follows the trail of the tourist through Japan and estimates the results of scores of colorful travel books upon the myth of Japan in America. And Ch.5, 'Lacquered Literature,' interprets numerous novels and stories with Japanese settings produced during the period...."

1434
WILSON, James Newton. A Handbook on the Political Geography of the Orient. Columbia (Teachers College), 1949. 61p.
An elementary school children's workbook with questions on Japan's location and place relations, her physical characteristics and population, and her industry and commerce.

1435
ASHMEAD, John, Jr. The Idea of Japan, 1853-1895: Japan as Described by Americans and Other Travellers from the West. Harvard, 1951. ii, 631p. (2v.). AB: United States Department of State, External Research Staff. Abstracts of Completed Doctoral Dissertations for the Academic Year 1950/1951. p.350-52.
Analyzes the writings of approximately two hundred travellers to Japan (primarily Americans and Englishmen) and studies their influence on Western art and literature and on the growth of Western knowledge of Japan.
Rel.Publ.: "Lafcadio Hearn in Japan: The Matsue Period," Occasional Papers of the Kansai Asiatic Society, 10 (1961), 1-14.

1436
TAKAKI, Tori. The Treatment of Japan and Peoples of Japanese Descent in Senior High School American History Textbooks. Michigan, 1954. 297p. DA 14 (Apr. 1954), 626; UM 7744.
Analyzes eighty-seven textbooks published between 1895 and 1950 in order to determine and to evaluate the change in treatment that occurred during this period.

1437
KREPS, Leslie Roy. The Image of Japan in the Speaking of United States Congressmen, 1941-1953. Northwestern, 1957. 370p. DA 18 (Feb. 1958), 696; UM 24,908.
"By 'image' is meant the assumptions as to national character upon which speaking about Japan is based." Contents: The Pre-War Image; The Wartime Image: Debate on the Treatment of Japanese-Americans; The Wartime Image: The speaking of Senator Elbert B. Thomas (The Thomas Broadcasts to Japan, Classification and Analysis of the Thomas Broadcasts, Speaking in Explanation and Defense of the Broadcasts); Speaking on the Conduct of the War and Surrender Terms; Speaking on Immigration Policy; Speaking on Occupation Policy and Peace Treaty Terms.

1438
URDANG, Miriam E. Images of Asia Held by Sixth Grade Pupils in New York State: Implications for Instruction. Columbia (Teachers College), 1961. 134p.
Includes a lengthy chapter on the notions held by American school children about social life and customs in Japan.

1439
ZENNER, Sister Mary Emilene, O.S.F. A Study of the Ideology of an Eastern Culture in the College Curriculum. St. Louis, 1962. 253p. DA 24 (Apr. 1964), 3928; UM 64-3775.
In order to investigate "the patterns of existing college and university programs dealing with Eastern cultures with particular reference to the Far East," the author studies the knowledge and views that 373 college history majors from twenty-seven small liberal arts colleges had of Japan and of its culture.

REIERSON, Curtis C. An Investigation of Attitudes towards the Products of Selected Nations among College Students and the Testing of Certain Methods for Changing Existing Attitudes. 1965. See no.275.

1440
BÖGER, Gerd. A Content Analysis of Selected Children's Books on the Negro and on Japan. Michigan State, 1966. 121p. DA 28 (July 1967), 46-A; UM 67-7522.
"Submitted to analysis were books listed in the Children's Catalog, 1941-1965, under 'Negroes' and under 'Japan,' classified as 'Fiction' or as 'Easy Books,' and designated for grades kindergarten through [grade] 4.... It was concluded that the books on Japan were slightly more adequate than the books on the Negro in terms of the definition of a realistic story as 'a tale that is convincingly true to life.'"

1441
JACKSON, Charles Wayne. Construction and Use of a Test to Measure Knowledge High School Seniors Have of the Far East. Arkansas, 1966. 92p. DA 27 (Sept. 1966), 603-04-A; UM 66-7039.

"Constructed from materials found in high school textbooks, courses of study..., magazine articles, and news reports," the test "was designed to measure the student's knowledge of the economic history, political history, religions, and geography of the Far East."

1442
BERNARDI, Ralph Eugene. Social Distance, Stereotypes, and Knowledge as Affected by Modern Foreign Language Education: An Assessment of Changes in the Dimensions of Ethnic Attitudes after a Course in Secondary School French. New York, 1967. 172p. DA 28 (Oct. 1967), 1522-23-A; UM 67-11,096.

Analyses the "changes in factual knowledge and negative stereotypes about the French and Japanese" brought about among students taking a secondary school course in French or in Latin.

1443
SCHMIDT, Carl Peter. Familial Relations in Modern Japanese Fiction. New York, 1967. 309p. DA 28 (Nov. 1967), 1828-A; UM 67-11,125.

Analyzes one hundred fifty-five Japanese novels and short stories that were written between 1902 and 1963 and that were translated into English in order "to determine the image of familial relations presented to American readers."

1444
SHAW, Larry James. A Comparative Image Study of the Japanese Culture as Presented in Secondary Social Studies Textbooks and Expressed by Nebraska Secondary Teachers and Japanese Citizens. Nebraska (Teachers College), 1967. 269p. DA 28 (Dec. 1967), 1998-99-A; UM 67-15,993.

Determined that "significant differences in image portrayal existed among the three sources of information."

1445
EMERY, Michael Charles. The American Mass Media and the Coverage of Five Major Foreign Events, 1900-1950: The Russo-Japanese War, Outbreak of World War I, Rise of Stalin, Munich Crisis, Invasion of South Korea. Minnesota, 1968. 447p. DA 30 (Aug. 1969), 675-A; UM 69-11,386.

See CH.1, "The Sun-Flag Rises" (p.1-81): First on the Scene; Melville Stone and the Czar; The S.S. Haimun; Novelist on Horseback; The Professional Palmer; Low Mark in a Great Career; Siege of Port Arthur; Understanding the Japanese; American Press Coverage; Togo Sinks the Russian Fleet.

FRENCH, Henry P. Jr. A Study of Difference in Students' Learning of Chinese and Japanese Culture Concepts Using Lecture and Intrinsically Programmed Methods. 1968. See no. 453.

1446
SAIKI, Patsy Sumie. A Unit in Japanese Literature: Developed as an Example of the Utilization of Non-Western Literature in High School Language Arts Programs to Deepen Understandings of Other Cultures. Columbia, 1968. 413p. DA 29 (June 1969), 4200-01-A; UM 69-9915.

"The purpose of this study was to explore how selected translated literature of representative non-Western countries might be studied in high schools....To achieve the purpose, an illustrative unit on Japanese literature was developed. Because many schools may be unable to purchase an unlimited number of books on foreign literature from a single country, selections from Japanese literature, combined with facts and concepts from history, religion, art, and other disciplines, were gathered into a book for the students. A teacher's guide was also developed."

OTHER COUNTRIES

1447
HELLING, George Clifford. A Study of Turkish Values by Means of Nationality Stereotypes. Minnesota, 1959. 534p. DA 20 (Apr. 1960), 4205-06; UM 60-926.

Includes the verbal stereotype of the Japanese that the Turkish respondents presented.

Language and Linguistics

GENERAL

1448
HAGUENAUER, Moïse-Charles. Introduction a l'étude de la langue japonaise [Introduction to the Study of the Japanese Language]. Paris, 1947. (thèse complémentaire) Text in French.

Rel.Publ.: "Études de linguistic japonaise: I. Les enclitiques -wa et -ga en japonais 'ancien', 'classique', et 'moyen,'" Mélanges 2 (1960), 170-405.

APPLIED LINGUISTICS
(Includes contrastive analysis, dialectology, language contact, psycho-linguistics, and socio-linguistics) See also Education--teaching and learning (pages 58-59) and Psychology and Social Psychology (pages 219-20).

1449
EDER, Matthias. Das Lautwesen des Yaeyama-Dialektes: Ein Beitrag zur Dialektkunde Japans: Mit Parallelen aus anderen Dialekten der Ryūkyū-Inseln, vergleichen mit dem Japanischen und einer Wortwurzelstudie auf phonetischer Grundlage [The Sound Structure of the Yaeyama Dialect: A Contribution to the Dialectology of Japan with Parallels from Other Dialects of the Ryukyu Islands and Comparisons with Japanese, and a Study of Word Stems on a Phonetic Basis]. Berlin, 1939. Text in German. The dissertation in its published form is available at Marburg/Lahn, Universitätsbibliothek, Nr. V C.

After discussing previously completed research on Ryukyuan dialects that had been undertaken by other scholars, the author works out the special characteristics of the Yaeyama dialect by means of a detailed comparison of its sound structure with parallels in Japanese. He points out analogous tendencies in the sound changes and uses the course of sound change in the Yaeyama dialect and in Japanese to derive a heuristic principle for the investigation of Japanese word stems.

Rel.Publ.: Das Lautwesen...Grundlage. Berlin: Triltsch und Huther, 1938. 93p.

1450
MULDER, Robert Leonard. A Comparative Study of the Competence of Groups of International and Native Students in Aspects of Language that Hold Special Relevance to Speech. Ohio State, 1953. 221p. DA 19 (Jan. 1959), 1863-66; UM 58-7160.

The subjects were twenty native speakers each of English, Japanese, and Spanish.

KUMATA, Hideya. A Factor Analytic Study of Semantic Structures across Three Selected Cultures. 1958. See no.1870.

1451
KNOWLTON, Edgar Colby, Jr. Words of Chinese, Japanese, and Korean Origin in the Romance Languages. Stanford, 1959. 904p. DA 20 (Aug. 1959), 665; UM 59-2822.

"This dissertation contains a set of indexed lists of 298 Chinese, 325 Japanese, and 138 Korean words in the Romance languages. The arrangement is alphabetical by etymon. Indices record all spellings given in quotations or citations from other sources, so that the reader may find (by reference to the etymon) a treatment of any specific Far Eastern word included, together with its Romance language reflexes, or discover to what Far Eastern source a given exoticism may be referred."

1452
KOHMOTO, Sutesaburo. Phonemics and Sub-Phonemic Replacement of English Sounds by Speakers of Japanese. Michigan, 1960. 186p. DA 21 (Aug. 1960), 340; UM 60-2545.

Attempts "to find replacement of English consonants and vowels commonly made by native speakers of Japanese in learning English pronunciation," and "determines the relative degree of difficulty that each pronunciation problem presents to the Japanese learner."

Rel.Publ.: Applied English Phonology: Teaching of English Pronunciation to the Native Japanese Speaker. Tokyo: Tanaka Press, 1965. xvii, 205p.

LOVELESS, Owen R. The Okinawan Language: A Synchronic Description. 1963. See no.698.

1453
NEY, James Walter. A Morphological and Syntactic Analysis of English Composition Written by Native Speakers of Japanese. Michigan, 1963. 355p. DA 24 (Aug. 1963), 735; UM 63-5000.

"A study designed as a preliminary to providing material which can be used to facilitate the teaching of English to native speakers of Japanese."

NAKANO, Terumi. The Effect of a Subject's Native Language upon His Choice of Alternative "Syntactical Arrangements" of a Set of Pictures. 1964. See no.1873.

1454
BENDIX, Edward Herman. Componential Analysis of General Vocabulary: The Semantic Structure of a Set of Verbs in English, Hindi, and Japanese. Columbia, 1965. 242p. DA 28 (Apr. 1968), 4153-A; UM 68-5637.

Contents: Semantic Interpretation and Semantic Tests; On Defining Have; Minimal Definitions for a Selected Set of English Verbs; Semantic Analysis of a Set of Verbal Constructions in Hindi; A Set of Verbs and Constructions in Japanese.

Rel.Publ.: Componential...Japanese. Bloomington: Indiana University, 1966. ix, 190p. (International Journal of American Linguistics, v.32, no.2, pt.2)

1455
BRANNEN, Noah Samuel. The Dialect of Oomišima in Three Generations: A Tagmemic Approach. Michigan, 1966. 436p. DA 27 (Apr. 1967), 3439-A; UM 66-14,495.

"The dissertation describes a dialect of the Japanese language spoken by the people of Oomišima, Ehime prefecture, and measures significant differences within the dialect in three generations." Ch.1 presents the orientation of the study within the field of dialect studies in Japan. "Ch.2 describes the locale in which the data were recorded and identifies the principal informants....Ch.3, the main body of the thesis, is a description of syntagmemic classes (or grammatical constructions) beginning with the sentence and proceeding through the clause, phrase, and word level structures of the language....Ch.4...demonstrates the usefulness of several techniques in measuring differences within the dialect from one generation to another."

CORWIN, Charles M. Selected Concepts of Human Experience as Seen in the Japanese Tradition and in the Biblical Tradition: A Comparative Study. 1966. See no.85.

1456
LAVRENT'EV, B. P. Kitaiskie ieroglify i kitaiskie zaimstvovaniia v obshchestvenno-iazykovoi praktike sovremennoi Iaponii [Chinese Characters and Chinese Borrowings in the Socio-Linguistic Usage of Contemporary Japan]. Moscow, Moskovskii gosudarstvennyi institut mezhdunarodnykh otnoshenii, 1966. (Candidate of Philological Sciences degree) 422p. Text in Russian. AB: 15p. summary published in 1966.

1457
NEVEROV, S. V. Inoiazychnye slova v obshchestvenno-iazykovoi praktike sovremennoi Iaponni (Foreign Loan Words in the Socio-Linguistic Usage of Contemporary Japan]. Moscow, Moskovskii gosudarstvennyi institut mezhdunarodnykh otnoshenii, 1966. (Candidate of Philological Sciences degree) 328, xxvii p. Text in Russian. AB: 16p. summary published in 1966.

Rel.Publ.: "Zametki o inoiazychnykh slovakh v sovremennom iaponskom iazyke," Narody Azii i Afriki, 4 (1965), 154-57.

CUCELOGLU, Dogan M. A Cross-Cultural Study of Communication via Facial Expressions. 1967. See no.15.

HASHIMOTO, Mitsuo G. From Japanese to English: A Contrastive Analysis Based on a Transformational Model. 1967. See no.451.

PAE, Yang Seo. English Loanwords in Korean. 1967. See no.1515.

1458
JETTMAR, Dieter. Der Fischereiwortschatz der am Kuroshio gelegenen Pazifikküste Japans [The Vocabulary of the Fishing Industry Operating off That Part of Japan's Pacific Coast Which Lies along the Kuroshio] Wien, 1968. 151, xxiv p. [and 59 maps]. Text in German. Diss. ms. available at the Österreichische Nationalbibliothek, Nr. 894.829-C Per. S.

Studies the diffusion of dialect words in connection with fishing along the Kuroshio (the Black Current) and inquires into the non-linguistic causes of this diffusion.

1459
SIMEON, George John. The Phonemics and Morphology of Hokkaido Ainu. Southern California, 1968. 81p. DA 29 (Dec. 1968), 1888-A; UM 68-17,042.

A synchronic description of three southern Hokkaido Ainu dialects: the Horobetsu, the Hiratori, and the Higashi Shizunai.

Rel.Publ.: "Hokkaido Ainu Morphophonemics," Studies in Linguistics, 20 (1968), 53-57.

1460
HANZEL, Louis Francis, S.V.D. A Contrastive Analysis of the Principal Predication Types of English and Japanese. Georgetown, 1969. 220p. DA 30 (Mar. 1970), UM 70-4637.

"Chapters 3 and 4 establish the principal predication types of English and Japanese....In Ch.5 we perform the actual contrastive analysis of the surface features and attempt to predict the level of difficulty the native speaker will encounter in these predication types. Ch.6 describes the constitution and administration of the test and states the results. Ch.7 concludes that there are four levels of difficulty, that we can theoretically predict just how difficult the native speaker of Japanese will find the predication types of English, and that consequently contrastive analysis is highly reliable."

NAGARA, Susumu. A Bilingual Description of Some Linguistic Features of Pidgin English Used by Japanese Immigrants on the Plantations of Hawaii: A Case Study in Bilingualism. 1969. See no.1757.

1461
REE, Joe Jungno. Some Aspects of Korean Syntax. Indiana, 1969. 301p. DA 30 (Sept. 1969), 1160-A; UM 69-14,715.

Japanese sentences are compared with Korean sentences throughout much of the dissertation with regard to "various aspects of relativization, i.e., postposition deletion, relative clause reduction, the formal distinction between restrictive and non-restrictive relative clauses, etc."

GRAMMAR

(Includes morphemics, problems of translation, and syntax) See also Language and Linguistics--historical and comparative studies (pages 171-73).

1462
CARR, Denzel Raybourne. Certain Verb Formations in Modern Japanese. Yale, 1937. 63p.

Ch.1 presents an analysis of the structure of the Japanese verb, Ch.2 deals with aspects of verbs in Japanese, and Ch.3 is a study of "derivational aspects or praxitypes."

1463
YAMAGIWA, Joseph Koshimi. The Older Inflected Forms Surviving in the Modern Japanese Written Language. Michigan, 1942. 467p. AB: Microfilm Abstracts, v.7,

no.2 (1947), 100-02; UM 889.

The study focuses on the verb, adjective, adjectival verb, and verb auxiliary. Contents: The Inflected Word-Classes in Japanese as Treated by Professors Hashimoto, Yamada, and Matsushita; Towards Another System of Paradigms for the Inflected Word-Classes in Japanese; The Older Inflected Literary Forms in the Modern Written Language; Summary of Findings.

1464
FEL'DMAN, Nataliia Isaevna. Poslelogi v sovremennom iaponskom iazyke [Postpositions in Modern Japanese]. Moscow, Moskovskii institut vostokovendeniia, 1944. (Candidate of Philological Sciences degree) 281p. Text in Russian.

1465
KOLPAKCHI, Evgeniia Maksimova. Formant "ga" kak pokazatel' sub"ekta v drevneiaponskom iazyke [The Formant "ga" as an indicator of Subject in Classical Japanese]. Leningrad, Leningradskii gosudarstvennyi universitet imeni A. A. Zhdanova, 1946(?) (Doctor of Philological Sciences) Text in Russian. AB: Nauchnyi biulleten' Leningradskogo gosudarstvennogo universiteta. 97(1946), 28-30.

1466
NAVRON-VOITINSKAIA, E. L. Lichnaia forma iaponskogo glagola [Personal Form of the Japanese Verb]. Moscow Institut vostokovedeniia Akademii nauk SSSR, 1946. (Candidate of Philological Sciences degree) 150p. Text in Russian.

1467
GARDNER, Elizabeth Frances. The Inflections of Modern Literary Japanese. Yale, 1948. 71p.

The inflected forms are analyzed into morphs, the smallest recurrent meaningful partials. These morphs are then classified according to their phonemic shape and environment; and on the basis of meaning and distribution, they are grouped into morphemes.

Rel.Publ.: The Inflections...Japanese. Baltimore: Linguistic Society of America, 1950. 46p. (Supplement to Language, 26, Oct./Dec. 1950)

1468
KHOLODOVICH, A. A. Ocherki po stroiu iaponskogo iazyka [Essays on the Structure of the Japanese Language]. Leningrad, Leningradskii gosudarstvennyi universitet imeni A. A. Zhdanova, 1949. (Doctor of Philological Sciences degree) xxxix, 804p. Text in Russian. AB: 23p. summary published in 1949.

1469
HARTMANN, Peter. Einige Grundzüge des japanischen Sprachbaus gezeigt an den Ausdrücken für das Sehen [Several Characteristics of the Japanese Language as Shown in the Different Expressions for the verb "to see"]. Münster, 1950. iv, 102p. Text in German. The dissertation in its published form is available at Berlin West, Staatsbibliothek Preussischer Kulturbesitz, Nr. 19,496.

Pt.1: Characteristics of Japanese verbal expression the root of a word as the means for conveying its meaning; the forms of the verb expanded by means of suffixes; the position of the verb within the sentence as the subject, predicate, or object as well as its use as a grammatical particle. Pt.2: The verbs "to see," "to appear," "to be visible," and "to be invisible" in the Manyōshū and Kokinshū.

Rel.Publ.: Einige...Sehen. Heidelberg: Carl Winter, 1952. 123p. (Bibliothek der allgemeinen Sprachwissenschaft, Dritte Reihe, Darstellungen und Untersuchungen aus einzelnen Sprachen)

1470
JORDEN, Eleanor Harz. The Syntax of Modern Colloquial Japanese. Yale, 1950. 198p.

"Japanese utterances as spoken by educated natives of Tokyo are divided into successively shorter maximally independent sequences by a specifically described technique, and the sequences isolated at each stage of analysis are classified according to a limited number of syntactic types."

Rel.Publ.: The Syntax...Japanese. Baltimore: Linguistic Society of America, 1955. v, 135p. (Supplement to Language, v.31, no.1, pt.3, Jan./Mar. 1955)

1471
KOTAŃSKI, Wiesław. Jezykoznawcza problematyka przekładu ze współczesnego jezyka japońskiego [Linguistic Problems Involved in Translating from Modern Japanese]. Warsaw, 1951. 122p. Text in Polish.

A Japanese text is characterized as a structure where all relevant explicit and implicit, morphological, and syntactical properties must be formally and semantically evaluated, in order to enable a translator to formulate in another language the full expressive value of the original.

1472
GOLOVIN, I. V. Glagol'nye vremena v sovremennom iaponskom literaturnom iazyke [Verb Tenses in Modern Literary Japanese]. Moscow, Voennyi institut inostrannykh iazykov, 1952(?) (Candidate of Philological Sciences degree) Text in Russian. AB: 19p. summary published in 1952.

1473
PASHKOVSKII, A. A. Slovoobrazovanie v sovremennom iaponskom iazyke: Tipy slozhnykh i affiksirovannykh slov [Word Formation in Modern Japanese: The Typology of Compound and Affixed Words]. Moscow, Voennyi institut inostrannykh iazykov, 1952. (Candidate of Philological Sciences degree) 434p. Text in Russian. AB: 29p. summary published in 1952.

1474
POPOV, K. L. Glagol'noe upravlenie v sovremennom iaponskom iazyke [Verbal Government in Modern Japanese]. Moscow, Institut vostokovedeniia Akademii nauk SSSR, 1953. (Candidate of Philological Sciences degree) 168 + 62p. Text in Russian.

1475
CHASOVITINA, L. A. Leksicheskie sredstva vyrazheniia modal'nosti v sovremennom iaponskom iazyke [Lexical Means of Expression of Modality in Japanese]. Moscow, Moskovskii institut vostokovedeniia, 1954. (Candidate of Philological Sciences degree) 225p. Text in Russian. AB: 15p. summary published in 1954.

1476
RIAVKIN, A. G. Ogranichitel'nye chastitsy v sovremennom iaponskom iazyke [Restrictive Particles in Modern Japanese]. Moscow, Voennyi institut inostrannykh iazykov, 1954(?) (Candidate of Philological Sciences degree) Text in Russian. AB: 17p. summary published in 1954.

Rel.Publ.: "Ogranichitel'nye...iazyke," in Akademiia

nauk SSSR, Institut Vostokovedeniia, Kratkie soobshcheniia, 24 (1958), 75-93; "Chastitsa mo v sovremennom iaponskom iazyke," in Institut narodov Azii, Akademiia nauk SSSR, Iaponskii iazyk: Sbornik statei (Moscow, 1963), 106-20.

1477
LEPESHKO, M. F. Uchenie o predlozhennii iaponskogo iazyka prof. Iamada Esio v svete istorii iaponskoi grammatiki [Professor Yamada Yoshio's Theory of the Japanese Sentence in the Light of the History of Japanese Grammar]. Moscow, Moskovskii gosudarstvennyi institut mezhdunarodnykh otnoshenii, 1955. (Candidate of Philological Sciences degree). 498p. Text in Russian.
Rel.Publ.: Ocherki po istorii iaponskoi grammatiki. Moscow, 1955. 135p.

1478
SYROMIATNIKOV, Nikolai Aleksandrovich. Vremena glagolov i prilagatel'nykh novoiaponskogo iazyka kak sistema dvukh otnositel'nykh vremen [The Tense Systems of Verbs and Adjectives in Modern Japanese as a System of Two Relative Tenses]. Moscow, Institut vostodovedeniia Akademii nauk SSSR, 1956. (Candidate of Philological Sciences degree) 952p. (2v.) Text in Russian.
Rel.Publ.: Stanovlenie novoiaponskogo iazyka. Moscow: "Nauka," 1965. 306p. (Institut narodov Azii Akademii nauk SSSR); "O sisteme vremen novoiaponskogo iazyka," in Akademiia nauk SSSR, Institut Vostokovedeniia, Kratkie soobshcheniia, 24 (1958), 75-93; "Problemy izucheniia grammaticheskikh vremen," in Institut narodov Azii, Akademiia nauk SSSR, Kratkie soobshcheniia, 72 (1963), 206-22.

1479
CHEW, John James, Jr. A Transformational Analysis of Modern Colloquial Japanese. Yale, 1961. 177p. DA 25 (Aug. 1964), 1204; UM 64-8236.
Contents: Background; Outline of a Generative Grammar (The Kernel, Constructionally Included Cores, Conjunctions, Element-Sharing, Nominalizing and Tightening, The Interrogative, The Idenfinite, the Negative, Restricting and Emphasizing Units, Transforms of Relational Phrases, the Honorific, Emphasis Transforms, Connecting Sentences, Transforms of Style, Pauses, Unit Classes and Elements); The Generating of an Actual Text.

1480
JINUSHI, Toshiko Suzuki. The Structure of Japanese: A Study Based on a Restatement of Phonology and an Analysis of Inflected Words. State University of New York at Buffalo, 1963. 197p. DA 24 (Dec. 1963), 2469; UM 63-5874.
"Presents the phonological and morphological structures of colloquial Japanese in terms of a methodology of linguistic analysis developed by George L. Trager and Henry Lee Smith, Jr., and employed in their book, An Outline of English Structure, and in their teaching." Contents: Introduction; Phonology; Morphemics; Syntax; Summary.
Rel.Pub.: A Grammar of Japanese. Norman, Okla., 1967. 140p. (Studies in Linguistics, Occasional Papers, 11)

1481
BEIKO, B. V. Kategoriia prilagatel'nykh v sovremennom iaponskom iazyke [The Category of Adjectives in Modern Japanese]. Moscow, Institut vostochnykh iazykov PRi Moskovskom gosudarstvennom universitete imeni M. V. Lomonosova, 1964. (Candidate of Philological Sciences degree) 554p. Text in Russian.

1482
CHEREVKO, K. E. Narechie v sovremennom iaponskom iazyke [The Adverb in Modern Japanese]. Moscow, Institut narodov Azii Akademii nauk SSSR, 1964. (Candidate of Philological Sciences degree) 185p. Text in Russian.

1483
INOUE, Kazuko. A Study of Japanese Syntax. Michigan, 1964. 221p. DA 25 (Apr. 1965), 5918-19; UM 65-5322.
"An attempt at a generative grammar of Japanese with emphasis on the relationships between certain particles and the predicate." Contents: Problems and Preliminaries; Phrase Structure; Embedding Transformations; Preliminary Simple Transformations; Conjoining Transformations; Final Simple Transformations; Conclusion.
Rel.Publ.: A Study...Syntax. The Hague: Mouton, 1969. 160p. (Janua Linguarum, Series Practica, 41)

1484
TRET'IAK, N. N. O strukture slova v sovremennom iaponskom iazyke: Iaponskii sloi leksiki [On Word Structure in Modern Japanese: The Japanese Lexical Stratum]. Leningrad, Institut narodov Azii Akademii nauk SSSR, 1964. (Candidate of Philological Sciences degree) 220p. Text in Russian.

1485
KURODA, Sige-yuki. Generative Grammatical Studies in the Japanese Language. Massachusetts Institute of Technology, 1965. 234p.
"An attempt to apply the theory of transformational grammar to the Japanese language." Pt.1--devoted to syntax--deals with attachment transformations and with the problem of pronominalization, and "reveals the formal character of the particles ga and o." Pt.2 deals with the problem of consonant morae.
Rel.Publ.: "Causative Forms in Japanese," Foundations of Language, 1 (Jan. 1965), 30-50.

BRANNEN, Noah S. The Dialect of Oomišima in Three Generations: A Tagmemic Approach. 1966. See no.1455.

1486
PRIDEAUX, Gary Dean. The Syntax of Japanese Honorifics. Texas, 1966. 156p. DA 27 (Feb. 1967), 2516-A; UM 66-14,430.
"Provides a transformational grammar of Japanese which utilizes the syntactic distinctive feature theory, and accounts for the syntax of the various levels of politeness and formality in terms of such features."
Rel.Publ.: The Syntax...Honorifics. The Hague: Mouton, forthcoming. (Janua Linguarum, Series Practica, 102)

1487
SAINT-JACQUES, Bernard. Analyse structurale de la syntaxe du japonais moderne [A Structural Analysis of the Syntax of Modern Japanese]. Paris, 1966. 210p. Text in French. AB: Université de Paris. Faculté des Lettres et Sciences Humaines. Positions des thèses de troisième cycle soutenues devant la Faculté en 1966. (Série "Recherches", t.42) p.69-70.
In pt.1, three forms of "minimal statements" are established, and these are examined from the standpoint of the Japanese language. In pt.2, a study is made of linguistic autonomy in Japanese. The author also analyzes the structure of Japanese sentences and compares

the basic characteristics of Japanese with those of the Indo-European languages.

Rel.Publ.: Analyse...moderne. Tokyo: Salesian Press, Paris: C. Klincksieck, 1966. 122p.

1488
SOGA, Matsuo. Some Syntactic Rules of Modern Colloquial Japanese. Indiana, 1966. 338p. DA 27 (Feb. 1967), 2519-A; UM 66-14,892.

"Based upon the generative transformational view of language, this study attempts to characterize some of the more important syntactic rules operating in modern colloquial Japanese."

1489
UEDA, Akiko Watanabe. The Adnominal Modification in Japanese. Texas, 1966. 161p. DA 28 (Aug. 1967), 659-A; UM 66-7381.

"The adnominal modification is defined as an embedded sequence placed in front of the noun which it modifies." Contents: The Transformational Rule of Modification; Similar Constructions; Subsequent Changes; N + no Construction as the Modifying Sequence; A Required Modifying Sequence; A Further Restriction on T 20 ob; The NP + wa + NP + ga Construction; Multiplicity of Modifying Sequences; Permutations and Deletions. The appendices include phrase-structure, transformational, and phonological rules; and a sample text.

1490
JACKSON, Kenneth Leroy. Word Order Patterns Involving the Middle Adverbs of English and Their Lexically Similar Counterparts in Japanese: A Contrastive Study. Columbia (Teachers College), 1967. 159p. DA 28 (Apr. 1968), 4159-A; UM 67-16,760.

Includes a description of "the points of correlation and difference in form, meaning, and distribution of these patterns on the syntactical level;" and a study of the "problems of recognition and production a Japanese student would encounter in learning these patterns in English."

1491
BEDELL, George Dudley, IV. Kokugaku Grammatical Theory. Massachusetts Institute of Technology, 1968. viii, 280p.

"The primary objectives are to describe the linguistic theory which is inherent in kokugaku grammar and to assess the impact of this theory on the subsequent development of grammar in Japan. The dissertation discusses (1) the content of the theory comparable in most respects to that of European traditional grammatical theory; (2) the contact and cross-fertilization of kokugaku grammar and European traditional grammar; and (3) the conflict between kokugaku grammar and the tenets of some forms of modern linguistics." The appendices include a translation of Suzuki Akira's Gengyo shishu ron.

1492
MAKINO, Seiichi. Some Aspects of Japanese Nominalizations. Illinois, 1968. 326p. DA 30 (July 1969), 306-A; UM 69-10,780.

"The aspects discussed are relativizing and non-relativizing nominalizations and the nominal compounds that result from the application of the first two nominalizations."

1493
MATHIAS, Gerald Barton. The Selectional Features of Japanese Verbs. California, Berkeley, 1968. 194p. DA 30 (Sept. 1969), 1159-60-A; UM 69-14,949.

The author asserts that "the selection of verbal complements must be based on distinct characteristics of the referents of the verbal complements." Contents: General Theoretical Considerations; Strict Subcategorization of Japanese Verbs; Verb Complements; Verbal Suffixes; The Semantic Features of NP and the Semantic Features of Verbs as "Conceptual Ions"; The Selectional Features of Some Japanese Verbs.

Rel.Publ.: "Toward the Semantics of -te-i- Attachment," in The Association of Teachers of Japanese, Journal-Newsletter, 6 (Apr. 1969), 51-57.

HISTORICAL AND COMPARATIVE STUDIES
(Includes problems of linguistic affiliations of Japanese.)

1494
KITASATO, Takeshi. Zur Erklärung der altjapanischen Schrift [An Explanation of the Early Japanese Writing System]. Leipzig, 1901. Text in German. The dissertation in its published form is available at Marburg/Lahn, Universitätsbibliothek, Nr. II C.

Studies the allegedly "early Japanese" writing systems (Ana'ichi, Moritsune, Iyo, Taneko, Chikugo, Koretari, Ahiru, and Ainu) and their derivation from the Indian alphabet, surveys the analogous origins of the Korean writing system, and considers their impact on the subsequent evolution of the kana syllabary.

Rel.Publ.: Zur Erklärung...Schrift. Leiden: E. J. Brill, 1901. 38p.

1495
MATSUMOTO, Nobuhiro. Le Japonais et les langues austroasiatiques: Étude de vocabulaire comparé [Japanese and the Austro-Asiatic Languages: A Study of Comparative Vocabulary]. Paris, 1928. Text in French.

Compares classical Japanese with the Ryukyuan, Indo-Chinese, Mon-Khmer, and Munda languages and shows that classical Japanese vocabulary contains "an important element introduced from the South."

Rel.Publ.: Le japonais...comparé. Paris. P. Geuthner, 1928. x, 114p. (Austro-asiatica; documents et travaux pub. sous la direction de Jean Przyluski, t.1)

1496
PETERSDORFF, Fritz-Julius von. Beiträge zur altjapanischen Phonetik: Bericht über Takeshi Kitasato: "Forschungen über das altjapanische Sprachlautsystem" mit einer Übersetzung im Auszuge [Contributions to Early Japanese Phonetics: An Account of Takeshi Kitasato's "Investigations of the Early Japanese Phonetic System," with a Partial Translation]. Leipzig, 1931. Text in German. The dissertation in its published form is available at Berlin West, Staatsbibliothek Preussischer Kulturbesitz, Nr. Ah 8884, in: Phil. Diss. Leipzig, Bd 13, Ne-P, 1931; also available at the University of Michigan, General Library, no. 6684.

Attempts to establish the phonetics of the characters used in Japanese texts between the seventh and the tenth centuries with the help of Chinese-language dictionaries. Investigates the use of these characters to represent Sanskrit syllables in the Sino-Japanese Buddhist literature. Comparisons are also made between the Sanskrit alphabet and the Japanese kana syllabary.

Rel.Publ. Beiträge...Auszuge. Shanghai: A.B.C. Press, 1931. vi, 67p.

1497
KOLPAKCHI, Evgeniia Maksimova. Drevneiaponskii literaturnyi iazyk po pamiatnikam epokhi Nara [Early Literary Japanese as Found in Outstanding Literary Works of the Nara Period]. Leningrad, Institut vostokovedeniia Akademii nauk, 1945. (Doctor of Philological Sciences degree) 461p. Text in Russian. AB: Nauchnyi biulleten' Leningradskogo gosudarstvennogo universiteta, 1946, no. 10, p.37-39.
Rel.Publ.: Ocherki po istorii iaponskogo iazyka. v.1. Moscow-Leningrad: Izdatel'stvo Akademii nauk SSSR, 1956. 234p. (Akademiia nauk SSSR, Institut vostokovedeniia)

PETROVA, Ol'ga P. Iaponskaia voenno-morskaia terminologiia: Istoriko-leksikologicheskie ocherki. 1946. See no.1512.

1498
SCHEPPACH, Walter. Die Schrift als Grundlage einer vergleichenden Grammatik zu den Schwierigkeiten der japanischen Sprache [The Writing System as a Basis for a Comparative Grammar about the Difficulties of the Japanese Language]. Wien, 1946. 97p. Text in German. Diss. ms. available at the Universitätsbibliothek der Universität Wien, Nr. D 7246; also at the Österreichische Nationalbibliothek, Nr. 598.842 C.
The writing system as a basis for the study of Japan. Reviews the history and development of Chinese writing and the problems imvolved in its adoption by the Japanese.

1499
LÖER, Wilhelm Ferdinand. Das Problem der japanischen Schrift: Grundlagen zu einer neuen Darstellung der japanischen Sprache und Schrift für praktische Zwecke [The Problem of the Japanese Writing System: The Basis for a New and More Practical Representation of the Japanese Language and Writing System]. Bonn, 1947. 65p. Text in German. Diss. ms. available at Bonn, Universitätsbibliothek, Nr. U 4° 47/178.
The objective of the work is to present a theoretical clarification of the entire problem of writing Chinese characters. The author first studies Chinese grammar, language, and writing, and compares Chinese with Sanskrit. He then covers the origins of the Japanese language, the Japanese adoption of Chinese and the use of the Chinese script to represent Japanese words, the development of the kana script, the divergence between the written and the spoken language, and the Western influence upon the Japanese language.

1500
KAROW, Otto. Wamyōruijushō: Ein Betrag zur Geschichte der Lexikographie und Sprache der Nara- und Heianperiode mit Berücksichtigung der medizinischen Literatur [The Wamyōruijushō: A Contribution to the Lexicographical and Linguistic History of the Nara and Heian Periods, with Consideration of the Medical Literature]. Bonn, 1949. 93, xvi p. Text in German. Diss. ms. available at Bonn, Universitätsbibliothek, Nr. U 4° 48/110.
Studies the historical evolution of speech, writing, and vocabulary during the Nara and Heian periods through an examination of the Wamyōruijushō; covers the history of early Japanese lexicography, examines problems of the standard (educated) language and of the dialects, and notes the divergence of the literary and colloquial languages during the later part of the Heian period; and attempts to classify early Japanese dialects.
Rel.Publ.: "Die Wörterbücher der Heianzeit und ihre Bedeutung für die japanische Sprachgeschichte: Teil I: Das Wamyōruijushō des Minamoto no Shitagau," MN, 7 (1951), 156-97.

1501
YOKOYAMA, Masako. The Inflections of 8th-Century Japanese. Yale, 1949. 129p.
A purely descriptive structural analysis of the inflected forms of eighth-century Japanese.
Rel.Publ.: The Inflections...Japanese. Baltimore: Linguistic Society of America, 1950. vi, 96p. (Supplement to Language, v.26, no.3, July/Sept. 1950)

1502
BINKENSTEIN, Rolf. Die historische Entwicklung der Studien und der Ideen über Sprache in Japan [The Historical Development of Linguistic Studies and Ideas in Japan]. München, 1951. 71, xviii p. Text in German. Diss. ms. available at München, Universitätsbibliothek, Nr. U 1951.7533.
A study of the linguistic theories and writings of various Japanese scholars: the beginning of scientific investigations of language and literature; the beginning of Kokugaku and of such scientific studies as those focusing on the Manyōshū; scholarly work during the Tokugawa period; the influence of European philology after the Meiji Restoration.

1503
SHEMANAEV, P. I. K istorii obrazovaniia sovremennogo iaponskogo literaturnogo iazyka [Toward the History of the Formation of Modern Literary Japanese]. Moscow, Voennyi institut inostrannykh iazykov, 1951(?) (Candidate of Philological Sciences degree) Text in Russian. AB: 12p. summary published in 1951.

1504
SOKOLOV, A. N. Sistema pis'ma v Iaponii, ee istoriia i sovremennoe sostoianie [The Japanese System of Writing: Its History and Its Present State]. Moscow, Moskovskii institut vostokovedeniia, 1952. (Candidate of Philological Sciences degree) 207p. Text in Russian. AB: 22p. summary published in 1952.

LAEMMERHIRT, P. Anton. Gebet und Verwünschung in der altjapanischen Kultsprache. 1953. See no.51.

1505
SKILLEND, William Edward. The Vocabulary of the Manyoosyuu as a Basis for the Comparison of Japanese with Other Languages. Cambridge, 1956. 265p. AB: University of Cambridge. Abstracts of Dissertations...1955/1956. p.186-87.
Studies in particular the morphological features found in the text.

1506
BAILEY, Don Clifford. The Rakuyōshū and Its Place in the History of Dictionaries in Japan. Michigan, 1960. 344p. DA 21 (Feb. 1961), 2290-91; UM 60-6835.
"Presents a summary of dictionaries used in Japan before the seventeenth century, describes the format and contents of the Rakuyōshū as compared with earlier Japanese dictionaries, and, through collation, establishes some of the sources used in its compilation."
Rel.Publ.: "Early Japanese Lexicography," MN, 16 (Apr./July 1960), 1-52; "The Rakuyōshū," MN, 16 (Oct. 1960/Jan. 1961), 69-156, and 17 (1962), 214-64.

1507
KWON, Hyogmyon. Das Koreanische Verbum verglichen mit dem altaischen und japanischen Verbum: Zur Typologie des Koreanischen [The Korean Verb Compared with the Altaic Verb and with the Japanese Verb: A Study of the Typology of the Korean Language]. München, 1963. Text in German. The dissertation in tis published form is available at Marburg/Lahn, Staatsbibliothek Preussischer Kulturbestz, Nr. Hsn 45,233; also at the University of Michigan, General Library, no.30,702.

Surveys various theories centering on the interrelationship of the Korean, Altaic, and Japanese languages; compares polite forms, the imperative and the optative moods, and the structure of the verb in the three languages; and studies various indicative verb forms and various nouns that are derived from verbs. One portion of the dissertation also seeks to determine the origin of the Korean language.

Rel.Publ.: Das koreanische...Koreanischen. München, 1963. xii, 144p.

1508
WERNECKE, Wolfgang. Maejima Hisoka (1835-1919) und seine Vorschläge zur japanischen Sprache und Schrift: Die Anfänge des Reformgedankens in der japanischen Sprache um die Zeit der unvollendeten bürgerlichen Revolution in Japan. Mit Einschluss von 3 Arbeiten des Maejima zum Gegenstand, darunter der originären Denkschrift an den Shōgun Tokugawa Yoshinobu vom Jahre 1866 dargestellt. [Maejima Hisoka (1835-1919) and His Proposals for the Reform of the Japanese Language and of Japanese Writing: The Beginning of Ideas for Reforming the Japanese Language at the Time of the Uncompleted Bourgeois Revolution in Japan, with Three of Maejima's Works on the Subject Including the Original Memorial Submitted to Shogun Tokugawa Yoshinobu in 1866]. Berlin, Humboldt Universität, 1964. 124p. Text in German. Diss. ms. available at Humboldt Universität, Universitätsbibliothek, Nr. Phil. Diss. 1964, P 10/66.

Maejima Hisoka, a late Tokugawa and Meiji bureaucrat who advocated the reform of the Japanese writing system, served as chief of the Postal Service Bureau, participated in the Kaishintō Party, and became a director of Tōkyō Sermon Gakkō (later Waseda University).

1509
SPEAR, Richard Lansmon. A Grammatical Study of Esopono Fabulas: A 16th Century Text in Colloquial Japanese. Michigan, 1966. 256p. DA 27 (Apr. 1967), 3445-A; UM 66-14,598.

Describes the grammatical structure of medieval Japanese as reflected in the 1593 translation of Esop's Fables by the Jesuit Fathers at Amakusa. Contents: Introduction; Phonology; Morphology I (Non-Inflected Forms); Morphology II (Inflected Forms); Syntax.

Rel.Publ.: "Research on the 1593 Jesuit Mission Press Edition of Esop's Fables," MN, 19 (1964), 222-31.

1510
LANGE, Roland Albin. The Phonology of Eighth-Century Japanese. Michigan, 1968. 390p. DA 30 (Aug. 1969), 708-A; UM 69-12,162.

Reconstructs, analyzes, and describes "the phonemic system of the dialect of Japanese spoken by members of the Japanese aristocracy living in and around Nara in the middle of the eighth century A.D." Concludes that the eighth century Japanese sound system can be adequately described in terms of five vowel phonemes (rather than eight) and that consonant plus semivowel clusters were a feature of the early Japanese language and therefore not something borrowed from China.

LEXICON
(Includes lexical studies and semantics)

1511
TRAUTZ, Friedrich Max. Der Stûpa in Japan: Eine Übersicht literarischer japanischer Quellen, nebst Texten und Übersetzung [The Stupa in Japan: A Survey of Japanese Literary Sources, with Texts and Translations]. Berlin, 1921. 305p. Text in German. AB: Jahrbuch des Dissertationen der Philosophischen Fakultät Berlin. 1920/21. I. p.239-46. Diss. ms. available at Berlin, Universitätsbibliothek, Nr. Phil. Diss. 1921.

A lexical study of the religious term "stupa" with translations from the Buddhist Tripitaka, the Nihon shakai jii, and the Kokushi daijiten.

Rel.Publ.: "Japanische wissenschaftliche Hilfsmittel zur Kultur- und Religionsgeschichte Zentral- und Ostasiens," Asia Major, 1 (1924), 147-75, 197-242.

1512
PETROVA, Ol'ga Petrovna. Iaponskaia voenno-morskaia terminologiia: Istoriko-leksikologicheskie ocherki [Japanese Military and Naval Terminology: Historical and Lexicological Essays]. Moscow, Institut vostokovedeniia Akademii nauk SSSR, 1946. (Candidate of Philological Sciences degree) 262p. Text in Russian.

1513
KAPUL, N. P. Ocherki iaponskoi onomastiki [Essays on Japanese Onomastics]. Moscow, Institut narodov Azii Akademii nauk SSSR, 1965. (Candidate of Philological Sciences degree) 267p. Text in Russian. AB: 24p. summary published in 1965.

Rel.Publ.: "Iaponskie psevdonimy," in Institut narodov Azii, Akademiia nauk SSSR, Kratkie soobshcheniia, 72 (1963), 168-77; "K voprosu ob etimologii i strukture iaponskikh imen sobstvennykh: Na materiale imen i familii," in Institut narodov Azii, Akademiia nauk SSSR, Iaponskii iazyk: Sbornik statei. (Moscow, 1963), 42-59.

LAVRENT'EV, B. P. Kitaiskie ieroglify i kitaiskie zaimstvovaniia v obshchestvenno-iazykovoi praktike sovremennoi Iaponii. 1966. See no.1456.

1514
MIYAJI, Hiroshi. A Frequency Dictionary of Japanese Words. Stanford, 1966. 908p. DA 27 (Apr. 1967), 3442-43-A; UM 67-4406.

"Mechanical and electronic devices were extensively used in order to handle a sample" of 250,000 words from the genres of fiction, drama, didactic prose, periodicals and scientific writings "and to perform quantitative analysis."

Rel.Publ.: Frequency Dictionary of Japanese Words. The Hague: Mouton, 1970.

1515
PAE, Yang Seo. English Loanwords in Korean. Texas, 1967. 199p. DA 28 (June 1968), 5038-39-A; UM 68-4326.

Ninety-two percent of the loanwords treated in the study were borrowed before 1945 and hence "channeled through Japanese." Some are direct loans, others Japanese corruptions.

1516
BURKART, Edward Ingersoll. A Procedure for Decomposing Chinese-Japanese Ideographs. Pennsylvania, 1968. 65p.

DA 29 (Jan. 1969), 2241-A; UM 69-69.
Attempts "to gain insight into the internal structuring of Chinese-Japanese ideographs by developing a mechanical procedure for decomposing individual ideographs and converting them into strings in a linear notation."

PHONOLOGY
(Includes morphophonemics, phonemics, and phonetics) See also Language and Linguistics--historical and comparative studies (pages 171-73).

1517
EDWARDS, Ernest Richard. Étude phonétique de la langue japonaise [A Phonetic Study of the Japanese Language]. Paris, 1903. Text in French.
An analysis of the sounds of Japanese (Tokyo dialect). Also uses phonetic texts and grammatical notes to present a general idea of the spoken language.
Rel.Publ.: Étude...japonaise. Leipzig: B. G. Teubner, 1903. 208p.

1518
GERHARD, Robert Hassler. Japanese Pronunciation. Ohio State, 1945. iii, 284p.; three 78 RPM Records (6 sides) boxed separately. AB: Ohio State University. Abstracts of Doctoral Dissertations. no.51. p.55-64.
"Presents a detailed analysis and description of the pronunciation of Japanese, particularly in comparison with the sounds of English and American speech." Emphasizes "the characteristically syllabic make-up of the language."

1519
WENCK, Günther. Japanische Phonetik [Japanese Phonetics]. Hamburg, 1949. (Habilitationsschrift) Text in German. The dissertation in its published form is available at Marburg/Lahn, Universitätsbibliothek, Nr. II C 203q1; also at the University of Michigan, General Library, no. PL541.W47.
Rel.Publ.: Japanische Phonetik. Wiesbaden: Harrassowitz, 1954-1959. 4v. (I. Die Lautlehre des modernen Japanischen: Die Geschichte des Lautbewusstseins und der Lautforschung in Japan: Die Quellen der japanischen Lautgeschichte. (vi, 373p.) II. Die Phonetik der Man-yōgana (x, 328p.) III. Die Phonetik des Sinojapanischen. (411p.) IV. Erscheinungen und Probleme des japanischen Lautwandels. (496p.).

1520
MARTIN, Samuel Elmo. Morphophonemics of Standard Colloquial Japanese. Yale, 1950. 228p.
A systematic study of Japanese morphophonemics on a synchronic level.
Rel.Publ.: Morphophonemics...Japanese. Baltimore: Linguistic Society of America, 1952. 115p. (Supplement to Language, v.28, no.3, pt.2, July/Sept. 1952)

1521
TSOI, Den-Khun. Foneticheskaia struktura zaimstvovannykh kitaiskikh leksicheskikh elementov v koreiskom i iaponskom iazykakh [The Phonetic Structure of Borrowed Chinese Lexical Elements in the Korean and Japanese Languages]. Moscow, Moskovskii ordena Lenina gosudarstvennyi universitet imeni M. V. Lomonosova, 1954. (Candidate of Philological Sciences degree) iii, 214p. Text in Russian. AB: 15p. summary published in 1954.

1522
HAN, Mieko Shimizu. Japanese Phonology: An Analysis Based upon Sound Spectrograms. Texas, 1961. 139p. DA 22 (Dec. 1961), 1987-88; UM 61-4694.
"Presents the phonology of standard colloquial Japanese based on phonetic data recorded on a...sound spectrograph."
Rel.Publ.: Japanese...Spectograms. Tokyo: Kenkyūsha, 1962. 154p.; "Internal Juncture in Japanese," Studies in Linguistics, 16 (Spring 1962), 49-61.

1523
FILLMORE, Charles John. A System for Characterizing Phonological Theories. Michigan, 1962. 215p. DA 23 (July 1962), 230; UM 62-3411.
Ch.4 (p.167-198) presents several interpretations of Japanese phonology: Bloch 1946, Bloch 1950, Kokutei Rōmazi, Jones, and Trubetzkoy.

1524
KOMAI, Akira Alan. A Generative Phonology of Standard Colloquial Japanese. Michigan, 1963. 155p. DA 25 (July 1964), 463-64; UM 64-6703.
"The type of Japanese language to be generated by this phonological model is Colloquial Standard Japanese, spoken by educated Japanese, native to the Yamanote district of metropolitan Toyko....The model presented generates a formal, precise style of speech by obligatory rules; informal rapid speech can be derived from the formal one by applying some of the optional rules." The dissertation also includes a detailed discussion of Japanese grammar.
Rel.Publ.: "Re-examination of Descriptive Phonemics: Japanese Phonemics," in The Association of Teachers of Japanese, Journal-Newsletter, 1 (Oct. 1963), 8-12.

1525
NEUSTUPNÝ, Jiři V. K fonologii japonského přízvuku: Pokus o analysu vágnosti [The Phonology of the Japanese Accent: An Attempt at an Analysis of Vagueness]. The Oriental Institute of the Czechoslovak Academy of Sciences, Prague, 1963. 214, viii p. Text in Czech.
Focuses on the vagueness of the opposition of phonemic and prosodic systems in Japanese as exemplified by the free accent and its variants.
Rel.Publ.: "The Assymetry of Phonological Oppositions," Bulletin of the Phonetic Society of Japan, 106 (Apr. 1961), 1-6; "Gengo to inbun no kankei ni tsuite: Nihongo inbun no kyakuin to inyu," in International Conference of Orientalists in Japan, Transactions, 6 (1961), 19-26; "Nihongo no mitsu no akusento tan'i no kanōsei ni tsuite," Onsei kenkyū, 11 (1965), 233-39; "Gengo ruikeigaku to Nihongo on'in taikei no bunseki," Onsei no kenkyū, 12 (1966), 337-46; "'Hana' to 'hana' no hatsuon wa hatashite chigau ka?" Gengo seikatsu, 172 (Jan. 1966), 80-87; "Nihongo no akusento wa kōtei akusento ka?" Onsei gakkai kaihō, 121 (1966), 1-7; "On the Analysis of Linguistic Vagueness," Travaux linguistiques de Prague, 2 (1966), 39-51.

1526
HEINEMANN, Robert Klaus. Le Système prosodique de la langue japonaise [The Prosodic System of the Japanese Language]. Paris, 1965. 133p. Text in French.

1527
McCAWLEY, James David. The Accentual System of Standard Japanese. Massachusetts Institute of Technology, 1965. i, 222p.
Contents: (1) a sketch of generative phonological

theory; (2) a description of the rules relating to segmental phonology in a transformational grammar of Japanese; (3) a treatment of the accentual system of standard Japanese; (4) a list of "pre-accenting" and "de-accenting" morphemes in Japanese.

Rel.Publ.: The Phonological Component of a Grammar of Japanese. The Hague: Mouton, 1968. 206p. (Monographs on Linguistic Analysis, 2); "The Accentuation of Japanese Noun Compounds," in The Association of Teachers of Japanese, Journal-Newsletter, 5 (Apr. 1968), 1-9.

1528
SWINDELL, Kimie Mushiaki. A Dictionary of Japanese Syllables. Stanford, 1968. 727p. DA 29 (Aug. 1968), 588-A; UM 68-11,357.

Defines the Japanese syllable, distinguishing it from the mora, and establishes a dictionary based on the Nihongo akusento jiten "which will serve as a basis for a later study of the syllable structure of Japanese."

1529
WEITZMAN, Raymond Stanley. Japanese Accent: An Analysis Based on Acoustic-Phonetic Data. Southern California, 1969. xi, 169p. DA 30 (May 1970); UM 70-8548.

The dissertation presents an acoustic-phonetic and phonological analysis of Japanese accent. Previous studies by both Western and Japanese scholars are reviewed. Two experiments are carried out by instrumental means to determine the nature and extent of fundamental frequency and intensity as acoustic correlates of accent. The results of these experiments are presented in detail. Previous theories of Japanese accent are examined in light of the experimental findings, and a new phonological interpretation is proposed.

Rel.Publ.: To be published in 1970 as a research monograph by the Acoustic Phonetics Research Laboratory, the University of Southern California.

Law and the Judicial System

See also International Relations, especially International Relations--China: The Manchurian Incident (pages 127-31) for matters of international law involving or affecting Japan.

GENERAL

1530
MATSUDAIRA, Yorikadzu von. Die völkerrechtlichen Verträge des Kaiserthums Japan in wirtschaftlicher, rechtlicher, und politischer Bedeutung [The International Treaties of the Empire of Japan: Their Economic, Legal, and Political Importance]. Tübingen, 1890. Text in German. The dissertation in its published form is available at Marburg/Lahn, Staatsbibliothek Preussicher Kulturbesitz, Nr. Fl 9561; also at the University of Michigan, Law Library.

Includes a history of Japan's commercial relations with the West that focuses upon trade geography and upon cultural and political relations, and systematically lists all Japanese political treaties with other countries and all subsequent revisions up to ca. 1890. The author also provides a systematic description of all treaties concluded between 1854 and 1884 as well as several supplements covering the treaties of subsequent years.

Rel.Publ.: Die völkerrechtlichen...Bedeutung. Stuttgart, Leipzig, Berlin, Wien: Deutsche Verl.-Anst., 1890. xv, 527, ii p.

1531
TAKAKI, Simpe. Die stille Gesellschaft, die Participations- und die Gelegenheits-Gesellschaft nach den Entwurfen eines Handelsgesetzbuches für Japan [The Silent Partnership, the Stockholding Company, and the "Risk-Taking Company" According to the Drafts of a Commercial Code for Japan]. Halle-Wittenberg, 1890. Text in German. The dissertation in its published form is available at Marburg/Lahn, Universitätsbibliothek, Nr. XVIII f C.

Compares the proposals made in 1884 for Japan's commercial code with the existing commercial laws of various European states. Also tries to determine whether Japan should create her own legal forms or adopt those exchange, maritime, and commercial regulations that are in effect elsewhere. As part of the study, the author surveys the feudal period and investigates the origins of various laws in individual Japanese provinces.

Rel.Publ.: Die stille...Japan. Halle a.S.: Waisenhaus, 1890. iv, 55p.

1532
KISHI, Kosaburo. Das Erbrecht Japans, insbesondere Kritik des Intestaterbrechtes der Codification vom Jahre 1890 [The Inheritance Laws in Japan: With a Critique of the Inheritance Law Appearing in the Code of 1890 That Deals with People Who Die Without Leaving a Will]. Göttingen, 1891. Text in German. The dissertation in its published form is available at Marburg/Lahn, Universitätsbibliothek, Nr. XVIII f C.

A study of the principles underlying Japanese family and inheritance laws, an examination of the basic features of the inheritance law that was promulgated in 1890, and a critique of the law with related suggestions for legal reforms.

Rel.Publ.: Das Erbrecht...1890. Göttingen: W. F. Kästner, 1891. 65p.

1533
TORII, Seiya. Das Contumacialverfahren im japanischen Strafprocess [Non-Appearance in Court According to Japanese Criminal Law]. Göttingen, 1891. Text in German. The dissertation in its published form is available at Marburg/Lahn, Universitätsbibliothek, Nr. XVIII h C.

The dissertation opens with a comparison of the Japanese and German laws of criminal procedure in regard to actions against people in absentia, and with a discussion of the Japanese law of procedure before the Meiji Restoration as well as of the European influences upon it after 1868. It then goes on to describe the differences between Japanese and German law in the adjudication of court costs, the procedure in cases of non-appearance, the resumption or revision of court proceedings, and the execution of judgment.

Rel.Publ.: Das Contumacialverfahren...Strafprocess. Göttingen: W. F. Kästner, 1891. 37p.

1534
ARAKI, Torataro. Japanisches Eheschliessungsrecht: Eine historisch-kritische Studie [Marital Law in Japan: An Historical and Critical Study]. Göttingen, 1893. Text in German. The dissertation in its published form is available at Marburg/Lahn, Universitätsbibliothek, Nr. XVIII C.

The author first studies the evolution of monogamous marriage and of other forms of marriage in Japan. He then critically comments about the Civil Code's provisions on marital law regarding the requisites for contracting a marriage, marriage by Japanese abroad, and marriage by foreigners in Japan. The dissertation concludes with a translation of paragraphs 30-60 of the Civil Code of 1890, which pertain to marriage.

Rel.Publ.: Japanisches...Studie. Göttingen: W. F.

Kästner, 1893. 53p.

1535
SENGA, Tsurutaro. Gestaltung und Kritik der heutigen Konsulargerichtsbarkeit in Japan [The Character of Present-Day Consular Jurisdiction in Japan and Some Criticism of It]. Berlin, 1897. Text in German. The dissertation in its published form is available at Marburg/Lahn, Universitätsbibliothek, Nr. XVIII C.

The dissertation opens with a study of the legal foundations and character of consular jurisdiction in Japan during the Meiji era. The author then investigates the competence of the consular courts, their organization, and their special status with regard to civil and criminal proceedings. He concludes with an examination of the consul's police powers and of his position in both civil and criminal law.

Rel.Publ.: Gestaltung...Japan. Berlin: L. Simion, 1897. iv, 106p.

1536
SAKAMOTO, Saburo. Das Ehescheidungsrecht Japans [The Law of Divorce in Japan]. Heidelberg, 1903. Text in German. The dissertation in its published form is available at Marburg/Lahn, Staatsbibliothek Preussischer Kulturbesitz, Nr. Fi 1275 (In: Heidelberg, Juristische Diss. 1903).

The evolution of Japanese divorce law (Nara period to Meiji period) is followed by a study of divorce according to Meiji law, which focuses on (1) divorce on grounds of mutual consent, (2) judicial divorce, and (3) the impact of divorce on the husband and the wife as well as on the children.

Rel.Publ.: Das Ehescheidungsrecht Japans. Berlin: G. Pintus, 1903. viii, 107p.

1537
MINAKUCHI, Kichizo. Das internationale Privatrecht der Wechselordnung und des Scheckgesetzes, verglichen mit Bürgelichem Gesetzbuch und japanischem Recht [The Law on Bills of Exchange and on Checks in Private International Law, Compared with Their Treatment in the Civil Code and in Japanese Law]. Heidelberg, 1911. Text in German.

Rel.Publ.: Das internationale...Recht. Heidelberg: K. Rössler, 1911. 125p.

1538
OTTO, Günther von. Geschichte des japanischen Strafrechts [History of Japanese Criminal Law]. Leipzig, 1913. Text in German. The dissertation in its published form is available at Marburg/Lahn, Universitätsbibliothek, Nr. XVIII C.

A study of penal law in ancient times, the reception of Chinese law (with particular focus on the yōrōritsu), criminal law during the Tokugawa period, and the adoption of European law. The Shinritsukōryō, Kaiteiritsurei, the Criminal Code of 1880, and the revised criminal code of 1907 are also examined in some depth.

Rel.Publ.: Geschichte...Strafrechts. Borna-Leipzig: Noske, 1913. vii, 152p.

1539
YOKOYAMA, Tomikichi. The Japanese Judiciary: Its Historical Development and Present Organization. Johns Hopkins, 1915.

1540
BECKMAN, Paul. Japanisches Neutralitätsrecht [The Japanese Neutrality Law]. Marburg, 1918. 120, xvi p. Text in German. Diss. ms. available at Marburg/Lahn, Universitätsbibliothek, Nr. XVIII B.

A study of the principles underlying Japan's attitude towards the question of wartime neutrality. Part 1 examines Japan's attitudes towards neutrality in coastal waters as found in her laws, as put into practice, and as expressed at the Hague Conference. Part 2 considers Japan's attitude towards contraband and naval blockade as found in her laws, as seen in past incidents (in 1884/85 and in 1904/05), and as expressed by her representatives at the London Conference.

1541
JIZUKA, Hanye. Japanisches Industrierecht: Vergleichende Darstellung mit dem deutschen Industrierecht [Japanese Industrial Law: A Study Comparing It with German Industrial Law]. Hamburg, 1927. Text in German. The dissertation in its published form is available at Marburg/Lahn, Staatsbibliothek Preussischer Kulturbesitz, Nr. Fi 1220 (In: Hamburg, Rechtes- u. Staatswiss. Dissertationen, 1929, Bd 7, Heq-In.); also at the University of Michigan, General Library, no. T201.I8 no.2.

Studies patent laws and the laws regarding industrial designs and trademarks. Concludes with information on Japanese regulations against unfair competition.

Rel.Publ.: Japanisches...Industrierecht. Berlin-Grunewald: Rothschild, 1926. xi, 99p. (Industrierechtliche Forschungen, veröffentlicht vom Seminar für Industrierecht der Universität Hamburg, 2)

1542
PLAGE, Wilhelm. Der Hausverband im modernen japanischen Zivilrecht [The Household Group in Modern Japanese Civil Law]. Hamburg, 1927. Text in German. The dissertation in its published form is available at Marburg/Lahn, Universitätsbibliothek, Nr. (XVIIIaC-9547: 43).

After defining the concept of household group (Hausverband), the author makes some general comments about the head of the household/family, the members of the family, and the family name; indicates how one can become head of the household and can subsequently lose this position; and discusses the rights and duties of the head of the household. He also touches upon the acquisition and the loss of family membership, and he concludes the dissertation with a translation of sections #732 and 764 of the Japanese civil code regarding the household group.

Rel.Publ.: Der Hausverband...Zivilrecht. Stuttgart: Enke, 1927. 150p. (Zeitschrift für vergleichende Rechtswissenschaft, 43)

1543
NAGATA, Kikushiro. Das Grundbuch und die Rollen des gewerblichen Rechtsschutzes im deutschen und japanischen Recht [The Land Register and Registers of Industrial Property Rights in German and in Japanese Law]. Hamburg, 1929. Text in German. Diss. ms. available at München, Universitätsbibliothek, Nr. U 1930.3321.

A comparative study of German and Japanese legislation and of the land registers and the registers of patents, trademarks, and design patents.

Rel.Publ.: Das Grundbuch...Recht. München: Berlin und Leipzig: Schweitzer, 1929. x, 127p.

1544
SCHALKHAUSSER, Friedrich. Die deutsche Auswanderungsgesetzgebung im Vergleich zur italienischen und japani-

schen [German Emigration Legislation Compared with That of Italy and Japan]. Würzburg, 1929. Text in German. The dissertation in its published form is available at Marburg/Lahn, Universitätsbibliothek, Nr. XVIII C.

A comparison of German emigration legislation with that of Italy and of Japan respectively in regard to their historical development, their formal arrangement, and their contents.

Rel.Publ.: Die deutsche...japanischen. Schwabach: Schwabacher Tagblatt, 1930. vi, 48p.; "Die japanische Auswanderungsgesetzgebung," Archiv für Wanderungswesen, 3 (1930), 89-94.

1545
MATSUDAÏRA, K. Le Droit conventionnel international du Japon [The International Treaty Law of Japan]. Paris, 1931. Text in French.

A study of the legal regulations found in the bilateral treaties that are in force within Japan.

Rel.Publ.: Le Droit...Japon. Paris: Libr. du "Recueil Sirey," 1931. 223p.

MATSUOKA, Asa. Protective Labor Legislation for Women and Children in Japan. 1932. See no.287.

1546
SANO, Shigeo. Japanisches und deutsches Seeversicherungsrecht: Ein Vergleich [Japanese and German Maritime Insurance Law: A Comparison]. Erlangen, 1936. Text in German. The dissertation in its published form is available at Marburg/Lahn, Universitätsbibliothek, Nr. XVIII C.

Using a number of case studies, the author discusses the nature of maritime insurance contracts and the objectives, risks, and certain financial aspects of maritime insurance.

Rel.Publ.: Japanisches...Vergleich. Würzburg: Mayr, 1936. 84p.

1547
BREUER, Richard. Die Stellung der Staatsanwaltschaft in Japan: Ihre Entwicklung, die gegenwärtige Lage, und die Hauptverschiedenheiten gegenüber dem deutschen Recht [The Position of the Prosecuting Attorney in Japan: Its Development, Present Situation, and Major Differences When Compared with the German Law]. München, 1940. Text in German. The dissertation in its published form is available at Berlin West, Staatsbibliothek Preussischer Kulturbesitz, Nr. Ag 7288/1099/23.

Studies the historical development of a Japanese civil service empowered with the functions of a state prosecuting attorney as well as the Japanese reception of the European system of prosecution by attorney. Also compares Japanese law with German law. Concludes with a translation of the 1922 Japanese law of criminal procedure.

Rel.Publ.: Die Stellung...Recht. Berlin: Triltsch, 1940. 125p. (Neue deutsche Forschungen, Abt. Strafrecht, 5)

1548
RUETE, Hans Hellmuth. Der Einfluss des abendländischen Rechtes auf die Rechtsgestaltung in Japan und China [The Influence of Western Law on the Formation of Law in Japan and in China]. Marburg, 1940. Text in German. The dissertation in its published form is available at Marburg/Lahn, Universitätsbibliothek, Nr. XVIII C.

Part 2 is a study of the influence of early Chinese culture and of Western law (1869-1930) on the growth of Japanese law.

Rel.Publ.: Der Einfluss...China. Bonn: Röhrscheid, 1940. xxii, 122p. (Rechts vergleichende Untersuchungen zur gesamten Strafrechtswissenschaft, 12)

1549
AN, Yü-kun. Reform von Vermögensverbrechen im deutschen, chinesischen, und japanischen Strafrecht [Reform of the German, Chinese, and Japanese Penal Law with Regard to Damage Done to Property]. Berlin, 1941. Text in German. The dissertation in its published form is available at Bochum, Universitätsbibliothek, Nr. RB 396; also at the University of Michigan, Law Library.

The historical development of Chinese and Japanese penal law. Chinese and Japanese definitions of the following unlawful acts are compared with regard to German penal law: theft, fraud, embezzlement, and receipt of stolen goods.

Rel.Publ.: Reform...Strafrecht. Berlin: E. Ebering, 1940. 80p. (Rechtswissenschaftliche Studien, 90)

1550
FISCHER, Erich. Die Konkursmasse im japanischen Konkursrecht nebst Übersetzung des ersten Buches der japanischen Konkursordnung [The Estate of an Insolvent Person in Japanese Bankruptcy Law together with the Translation of the First Book of the Japanese Bankruptcy Law]. Halle-Wittenberg, 1941. Text in German. The dissertation in its published form is available at Marburg/Lahn, Universitätsbibliothek, Nr. XVIII C.

Part 1: A translation of Book One, Regulations Concerning Substantial Law. Part 2: The estate of an insolvent person according to Japanese bankruptcy law; bankruptcy proceedings in ordinary cases and in cases of inheritance, settlement of the estate by means of separation and compensation; settlement of disputes among the individual creditors; the influence of German banking laws upon the contents of the Japanese laws in question including those cases where they overlap with the domains of family law and of inheritance law.

Rel.Publ.: Die Konkursmasse...Konkursordnung. Burg b.M.: Hopfer, 1941. 37p.

1551
HUCH, Richard. Japanisches internationales und interlokales Privatrecht: Allgemeine Lehren [Japanese Private Law between Nations and between Local Units of Government: General Patterns]. Hamburg, 1941. iv, 266p. Text in German. Diss. ms. available at Hamburg, Staats- und Universitätsbibliothek, Nr. Diss. jur. Mscr. 1192.

A translation of the following legal texts: the statutes (hōrei) of 1890 and 1898; the law concerning the simultaneous application of statutes; conflicting rules, appropriate substantial laws, the provisions of Japanese laws concerning foreign law, and questions of civil procedure; the law of nationality. Also a discussion of Japanese private international law, a history of the codification of international private law, and the pattern of private law between local units in Japan.

Rel.Publ.: Japanisches...Lehren. Würzburg: K. Triltsch, 1941. ix, 154p. (Hansische Universität, Abhandlungen und Mitteilungen aus den Seminaren für öffentliches Recht und für ausländisches und internationales Privatrecht, 40)

1552
FRIESE, Curt. Die neuzeitliche Strafrechtsentwicklung in Japan [The Development of Modern Penal Law in Japan].

Berlin, 1943. 118, xx, 79p. Text in German. Diss. ms. available at Berlin, Humboldt Universität, Universitätsbibliothek, Nr. Jur. Diss. 1943, J 19.

The dissertation presents the development of Japanese penal law since the introduction of European law and compares it with its counterpart in German law. The work focuses on (1) the development of penal law in Japan up to the outbreak of the war with China; (2) wartime penal law since 1937; (3) efforts at reforming the law; (4) general characteristics of the Japanese penal law; (5) the concepts of "crime" and "punishment" in Japanese law; and (6) the actual penal system and the application of penal laws. The appendix contains a translation of the "draft for an improved penal code."

ZACHERT, Herbert. Semmyō: Die kaiserlichen Erlasse des Shoku-Nihongi. 1941. See no.483.

1553
LINN, John Kenneth, Jr. The Imperial Edicts of the Shoku-Nihongi: An Annotated Translation of Edicts #30-62. Yale, 1950. 112p. DA 26 (June 1966), 7298; UM 66-5388.

In the dissertation, thirty-three of the sixty-two Imperial edicts issued between 697 A.D. and 789 A.D. are translated from the original Chinese. A "Linguistic Note" (p.98-106) on the rendering of Japanese particles in Chinese characters concludes the work.

1554
HENDERSON, Dan Fenno. The Pattern and Persistence of Traditional Procedures in Japanese Law. California, Berkeley, 1955. 524p.

"This study is an analysis of the traditional role of conciliation in the settlement of civil disputes in Japan, beginning with the dominance of conciliation in civil trials of the Tokugawa period and tracing its persistence in the modern practice up to the Civil Conciliation Law of 1951." [Emphasizes the Tokugawa period in analysis.]

Rel.Publ.: Conciliation and Japanese Law: Tokugawa and Modern. Seattle: University of Washington Press, 1964. 420p. (2v.) (Association for Asian Studies Monographs and Papers, 13); "Some Aspects of Tokugawa Law," Washington Law Review, 27 (1952), 85-109; "Japanese Legal History of the Tokugawa Period: Scholars and Sources," in Five Studies in Japanese Politics, ed. by Robert E. Ward (Ann Arbor: University of Michigan, 1957), 100-21. (University of Michigan, Center for Japanese Studies, Occasional Papers, 7); "The Evolution of Tokugawa Law," in Studies in the Institutional History of Early Modern Japan, ed. by John W. Hall and Marius B. Jansen (Princeton: Princeton University Press, 1968), 203-29.

1555
McINTYRE, Stuart Hall. Legal Effect of World War II on Treaties of the United States. Columbia, 1956. 585p. DA 17 (Mar. 1957), 669-70; UM 20,059.

Includes a study of the war's effect upon the legal status of those treaties with Japan that were in force at the outbreak of World War II.

Rel.Publ.: Legal...States. The Hague: M. Nijhoff, 1958. ix, 392p.

1556
RABINOWITZ, Richard William. The Japanese Lawyer: A Study in the Sociology of the Legal Profession. Harvard, 1956. x, 438p. AB: 4p. summary appended to diss. ms.

A study of the occupational role of the lawyer in Japanese society. "Compares the role as it is performed in different geographical areas of the society [Tokyo, Osaka, Iwate and Gifu prefectures] in order to see whether or not it is possible to discern systematic differences which can be related to differences in the socio-economic structure of the areas under investigation." Contents: The Sociology of Law; History of the Japanese Bar; Statistical Aspects of the Growth and Distribution of the Japanese Bar; Field Work (includes age, composition, education, family background, career motivation, motive for community selection, career pattern, content of the lawyer role, income hierarchy, intra-professional status hierarchy, and the weltanschauung of the lawyer); Law and the Lawyer in Japanese Society.

Rel.Publ.: "Bibliography on Japanese Law in Western Languages," American Journal of Comparative Law, 4 (Winter 1955), 97-104; "The Historical Development of the Japanese Bar," Harvard Law Review, 70 (Nov. 1956), 61-81.

1557
CHO, Sung Yoon. Jurisdiction over Foreign Forces in Japan, 1945-1960. Tulane, 1963. 356p. DA 24 (Feb. 1964), 3404-05; UM 64-1804.

"Examines the Japanese experience with problems of jurisdiction, both criminal and civil, arising from the presence of American troops, 1945-1960."

EPP, Robert C. Threat to Tradition: The Reaction to Japan's 1890 Civil Code. 1964. See no.575.

1558
TSAI, Tun-ming. Die Bande als Verbrechensform im deutschen, chinesischen, und japanischen Strafrecht [Gang Activities as a Form of Crime in German, Chinese, and Japanese Criminal Law]. Freiburg i.B., 1964. Text in German. The dissertation in its published form is available at Marburg/Lahn, Staatsbibliothek Preussischer Kulturbesitz, Nr. Hsn 55,915.

The dissertation first studies the concept of a "gang," the phenomenon of criminal acts committed by a gang, and their treatment in Roman and German law. It then contrasts this with the treatment of criminal gang activities in Chinese and Japanese law and views this treatment in historical perspective as well as from the standpoint of jurisprudence.

Rel.Publ.: Die Bande...Strafrecht. Freiburg i.B., 1964. xiii, 159p.

1559
GROBE, Hans Martin. Die Entstehung und Funktion des Familiengerichts: Eine rechstvergleichende Darstellung der amerikanischen und japanischen Familiengerichte im Hinblick auf eine entwaige Einführung von Familiengerichten in Deutschland [The Origin and Function of the Domestic Relations Court: A Comparative Legal Presentation of the American and Japanese Domestic Relations Courts with a View to the Eventual Introduction of Such Courts into Germany]. Hamburg, 1965. Text in German. The dissertation in its published form is available at the University of Michigan, General Library, no. 31820.

Following a study of the domestic relations court in the United States, the author examines the historical development, organization, competence, and procedures of the its Japanese counterpart. He then compares the two, and seeks to determine whether the introduction of such courts into Germany would be significant

Rel.Publ.: Die Entstehung...Deutschland. Hamburg, 1965. 95p.

1560
TANIGUCHI, Yasuhei. Shareholders' Judicial Remedies: A Comparative Study, Japanese-American. Cornell, 1965. 305p.
Contents: Pt.1: Exposition of Japanese System: Historical Development of Corporation Law (Pre-1950 Situation, 1950 Amendment); Present Situation of Judicial Remedial System (General Doctrine Concerning Judicial Remedies, Judicial Remedies Concerning Corporate Disputes). Pt.2: American Law and Comparison: Remedies Concerning Shareholders' Meetings; Dichotomy of Shareholders' Remedies.

1561
LIN, Chü-chih. Elterliche Gewalt im deutschen, japanischen und chinesischen Recht [Parental Authority According to German, Japanese, and Chinese Law]. München, 1966. 82p. Text in German.

1562
KIM, Sung Bae. Die Behandlung asozialer und straffälliger Jugendlicher im japanischen Jugendrecht [Japanese Juvenile Law and the Manner of Dealing with Antisocial Teenagers Who Are Liable to Punishment]. Köln, 1967. Text in German. The dissertation in its published form is available at Bochum, Universitätsbibliothek, Nr. UA 5917; also available at the University of Michigan, General Library, no. 34,940.
Contents: The Scope of the Juvenile Law of July 15, 1948, with Regard to People and to Things; Punishments and Measures; Procedures.
Rel.Publ.: Die Behandlung...Jugendrecht. Köln: Universitätsdruck, 1967. vii, 102p.

MISAWA, Mitsuru. The Historical and Comparative Study of the Postwar Japanese Securities Markets in the Light of Law and Business Practices. 1967. See no.231.

HARARI, Ehud. The Politics of Labor Legislation in Japan. 1968. See no.1856.

1563
ITOH, Hiroshi. Japanese Supreme Court: Judicial Decision-Making Analysis. Washington, Seattle, 1968. 256p. DA 29 (Apr. 1969), 3652-53-A; UM 69-7059.
Traces the development of Japanese studies of the judicial decision-making process, shows the complexity and multiplicity of the factors involved in the judicial decision-making process of the Japanese Supreme Court, examines the consistency and predictability of judicial outcomes, and analyzes "judicial behavior with respect to the political question doctrine, within the context of a judicial activism-judicial restraint dichotomy."

PARK, Yung Ho. The Electoral Reform Laws of 1962: A Case Study of the Japanese Policy-Making Process. 1968. See no.1866.

CONSTITUTIONS OF JAPAN
(The Meiji Constitution and the postwar constitution of 1946.)

1564
ARIMORI, Sinkiti. Das Staatsrecht von Japan [Japanese Constitutional Law]. Strassburg, 1892. Text in German. The dissertation in its published form is available at Marburg/Lahn, Universitätsbibliothek, Nr. XVIII b. c.
In order to explain the principles that determine the relationship between the Japanese state and its subjects, the author presents an introduction to the development of Japan's system of government. He then compares the Japanese system with European counterparts from a constitutional point of view.
Rel.Publ.: Das Staatsrecht...Japan. Strassburg: K. J. Trübner, 1892. ii, 111p.

1565
NOSAWA, Takematsu. Étude sur la constitution du Japon [A Study of the Japanese Constitution]. Genève, 1895. Text in French.
Rel.Publ.: Étude...Japon. Genève: R. Burkhardt, 1896. 188p.

1566
TANAKA, Yudourou. La Constitution de l'empire du Japon [The Constitution of the Japanese Empire]. Paris, 1899. Text in French.
Discusses the Japanese constitution as a whole and studies the settlement of certain controversies surrounding particular portions of its text. Contents: The Emperor; The Rights and Duties of the Subjects; The Imperial Assembly; State Ministers and Private Councillors; Justice; Finance; Additional Matters.
Rel.Publ.: La Constitution...Japon. Paris: L. Larose, 1899. 176p.

1567
KOBAYASHI, Takejiro. Die japanische Verfassung, verglichen mit ihren europäischen Vorbildern [The Japanese Constitution: A Comparison with Its European Prototypes]. Rostock, 1902. Text in German. The dissertation in its published form is available at Rostock, Bibliotheca Academiae.
Pt.1 examines the characteristics of the Belgian and Prussian constitutions, that served as models for the Meiji constitution. Pt.2 surveys the historical development of the Japanese constitution and discusses the Japanese executive power and its organization including the political powers and personal position of the Meiji Emperor, the Diet, and the administrative authorities.
Rel.Publ.: Die japanische...Vorbildern. Rostock: H. Winterberg, 1902. 121p.

1568
UEBERSCHAAR, Johannes. Die Stellung des Kaisers in Japan: Eine staatsrechtlich-historische Skizze [The Position of the Emperor in Japan: A Constitutional and Historical Survey]. Leipzig, 1913. Text in German. The dissertation in its published form is available at Marburg/Lahn, Universitätsbibliothek, Nr. XVIII C.
Within the section on constitutional law, the author focuses on the Japanese Imperial system, the Imperial prerogatives, the law of succession to the throne, and the constitution. In the historical section, he examines the significance of ancestor worship, Confucianism, and Feudalism for Japan and briefly surveys the historical evolution of Japanese society.
Rel.Publ.: Die Stellung...Skizze. Borna-Leipzig: Noske, 1912. iv, 87p.

1569
NAKANO, Tomio. The Ordinance Power of the Japanese Emperor. Johns Hopkins, 1922. iii, 229p.
Examines the Japanese constitution from the standpoints of political science and of general constitution-

al jurisprudence. Contents: Fundamental Characteristics of the Constitution of Japan; Conception of an Ordinance; Constitutional Limitations upon the Ordinance Power of the Emperor; The Power to Issue the Ordinances Necessary for the Execution of the Laws; The Emperor's Power to Fix the Administrative Organization; Police Ordinance and Ordinance for the Welfare of the People; Ordinances Issued by Virtue of Statutory Delegation of Power; Legislative Delegations of Power to Colonial Governments; The Power to Confer Titles of Nobility, Rank, and Decorations; The Pardoning Power; Military Power of the Emperor; Temporary Suspension of Constitutional Guarantees; Emergency Ordinances; Guarantees of the Constitutionality and Legality of Ordinances; European Sources of the Japanese Constitution.

Rel.Publ.: The Ordinance...Emperor. Baltimore, 1923. xviii, 269p. (Johns Hopkins University Studies in Historical and Political Science. Extra Volumes, New Ser., no.2); Tōsui ken no dokuritsu. Tokyo: Yūhi Kaku, 1934. 729p.

1570
TICHY, Alois. Die staatsrechtliche Stellung des Kaisers von Japan unter besonderer Berücksichtigung des Kaiserlichen Hausgesetzes [The Constitutional Position of the Japanese Emperor: With Special Consideration of the Imperial Household Law]. Breslau, 1928. Text in German. The dissertation in its published form is available at Marburg/Lahn, Universitätsbibliothek, Nr. XVIII C.

Resolves the contradictions between the traditional and the modern elements in Japanese national law, and examines the reasons for the adoption of the constitutional form of government. Also studies the personal rights of the Emperor as well as his rights as head of state, the position of the Emperor within the Imperial family, the matter of the succession to the throne, the Emperor's monetary rights and his personal representatives, and the relationship between the Emperor and the Privy Council.

Rel.Publ.: Die staatsrechtliche...Hausgesetzes. Ohlau in Schles.: Eschenhagen, 1928. x, 52p.

1571
FAHS, Charles Burton. The Japanese House of Peers. Northwestern, 1933. 221p. AB: Northwestern University. Summaries of Doctoral Dissertations. v.1 (1933), p.102-09.

A study of the House of Peers under the Meiji Constitution. Contents: Origin and Purpose; The Fundamental Laws; Membership; Sessions, Organization, and Procedure; Powers of the House of Peers; The House of Peers in the Governmental System; Parties; Reform of the House of Peers.

Rel.Publ.: "Political Groups in the Japanese House of Peers," American Political Science Review, 34 (Oct. 1940), 896-919.

1572
LIM, Manuel. The Constitution of Japan. Santo Tomas, 1937.

1573
REID, Ralph Waldo Emerson. Post War Constitutional Reform in Japan, 1945-1947. Harvard, 1949. 861p. AB: 7p. summary appended to diss. ms.

Describes the postwar constitution and its implementing legislation in considerable detail. Contents: Drafting the Constitution; The Diet; The Cabinet and the Ministries; The Judiciary; The Emperor; Local Government; Civil and Economic Liberties; Renunciation of War; The Future: Constitutional Problems; The Future: Other Problems. In the concluding 282 pages of the thesis are translations of major postwar laws.

BROWN, Richard G. Ministerial Responsibility in Japan. 1952. See no.1813.

INAGAKI, Bernard R. The Constitution of Japan and the Natural Law. 1955. See no.1886.

1574
BEER, Lawrence Ward. The Doctrine of the Public Welfare and the Freedom of Assembly under the Constitution of Japan. Washington, Seattle, 1966. 273p. DA 27 (Mar. 1967), 3098-A; UM 67-2140.

Focuses particularly on the judicial use of the public welfare and freedom-of-assembly standards. Contents: Constitutions, Freedom, and the Public Welfare in Japan; The Settling of Japanese Constitutional Law; Constitutional Interpretation in Japan; The Public Welfare Standard and Freedom of Assembly: The Supreme Court's Position; The Public Welfare in Japanese Constitutional Debate; Freedom and Public Welfare under the "Living Constitution" of Japan.

1575
KAWAMURA, Yoshitaka. Les Traités de sécurité de 1951 et de 1960 entre le Japon et les États-Unis et le problème de leur compatibilité avec la constitution du Japon de 1946 [The United States-Japan Security Treaties of 1951 and of 1960 and the Problem of Their Compatibility with the Japanese Constitution of 1946]. Paris, 1966. 230p. + appendices. Text in French.

Library Science

NUNN, Godfrey R. Modern Japanese Book Publishing. 1957. See no.212.

1576
INADA, Hide Ikehara. Translations from the Japanese into Western Languages from the 16th Century to 1912. Michigan, 1967. 298p. DA 28 (Dec. 1967), 2274-A; UM 67-15,638.

"Studies the achievements of early European and American Japanologists in the field of translation of Japanese works, and discerns how early the Westerners began to study the Japanese language and make translations." Pt. 1 is a general survey. In pt.2--the bibliography--"the translations are listed chronologically under the name of the translator if known and under the title of the translation if the translator is unknown. In the annotation the name of the original author and the title of the original work are given whenever they are identified."

Rel.Publ.: "Translators and Translations of the Meiji Era," in Japan's Modern Century, ed. by Edmond Skrzypczak (Tokyo: Sophia University Press, 1968), 133-59; Book forthcoming from Sophia University Press (Tokyo).

Literature

For dissertations on foreign literary works in which Japan appears as a major theme, see Japan: The View from Abroad (pages 16[illegible] See also Influence of Japanese Culture Abroad (pages 101-0[illegible]

GENERAL

1577
FRANZ, Eckart. Die Beziehungen der japanischen Mythologie zur griechischen [The Connections between Japanese and Greek Mythology]. Bonn, 1932. Text in German. The dissertation in its published form is available at Marburg/Lahn, Universitätsbibliothek, Nr. VII C.

A comparison of Japanese and Greek cosmogony and myths about the underworld. The author seeks to determine whether the correspondence of motifs in Greek and Japanese mythology is based on actual historical contacts between Greece and Japan.

Rel.Publ.: Die Beziehungen...griechischen. Bonn: Duckwitz, 1932. 129p.

1578
ASHIYA, Mizuyo. Japanische und deutsche Tiermärchen, besonders Fuchsmärchen, in ihrem Wesen und nach ihrer volkstümskundlichen Grundlage [Japanese and German Animal Tales, Especially Fox Tales: Their Nature and Their National Basis]. Köln, 1939. Text in German. The dissertation in its published form is available at Marburg/Lahn, Universitatsbibliothek, Nr. XVI C.

A study of the nature of Japanese folk tales and a comparative study of the animals appearing in Japanese and in German stories. The author also investigates the characteristics that the Japanese and the Germans have attributed to the fox and compares those fox tales which contain motifs of witchcraft, of rewards for good deeds, and of marriages between human beings and foxes.

Rel.Publ.: Japanische...Grundlage. Köln: Orthen, 1939. 82p.

1579
HIBBARD, Esther Lowell. The Yuriwaka Tradition in Japanese Literature. Michigan, 1944. viii, 180p.; 222p.; 327p. (3v.).

Presents a synopsis of the Yuriwaka tradition in Japan; reconstructs a theoretical prototype of the tradition and compares it with the Greek tale of Ulysses; considers the problem of the tradition's age and origin; and discusses the influence of religion, history, Tokugawa social institutions, and Japanese literary taste upon the tradition. Volumes 2 and 3 contain annotated translations of Yuriwaka texts. The Yuriwaka tradition in Japanese literature has its roots in a mid-seventeenth century tale based on the adventures of a hero called Minister Yuriwaka. This tale was prevalent in several versions during the Tokugawa period and was embodied in Chikamatsu's play Yuriwaka nomori kagami as well as in a number of other works.

Rel.Publ.: "The Ulysses Motif in Japanese Literature," Journal of American Folklore, 59 (July/Sept. 1946): 221-46.

SAROT, Eden E. Folklore of the Dragonfly: A Linguistic Approach. 1949. See no.49.

IKEDA, Hiroko. A Type and Motif Index of Japanese Folk-Literature. 1956. See no.53.

1580
OSBORN, Marijane Louis. Foreign Studies of Beowulf: A Critical Study of Beowulf Scholarship outside English-Speaking Countries and Germany, with Bibliographies. Stanford, 1969. 257p. DA 30 (Sept. 1969), 1146-A; UM 69-13,998.

A study of Beowulf scholarship in twenty different nations including Japan. Japan is stated to be the only Asian country where any work of great interest has appeared. Indeed, forty-three relevant Japanese works are listed and the author notes in particular the "translation of Beowulf by the philologist Kuriagawa into Middle Japanese in the style of a biwa romance."

CLASSICAL

Drama

1581
TAKEHARA, Tsuneta. Chikamatsu: The Marionette Playwright. New York, 1915.

1582
GUNDERT, Wilhelm. Der Schintoismus im japanischen Nō-Drama [Shinto in Japanese Noh Drama]. Hamburg, 1925. Text in German. The dissertation in its published form is available at Berlin West, Staatsbibliothek Preussischer Kulturbesitz, Nr. Uk 452-19.

The Nō plays that are predominantly Shinto in character are arranged in order by scenes, and the religious ideas that are found within them and in related myths are carefully studied. Excerpts from various Nō plays also are translated.

Rel.Publ.: Der Schintoismus...Drama. Hamburg und Berlin: Behrend; Tokyo, 1925. ix, 275p. (MOAG, 19); "Gedanken über das japanische Nō-drama," Transactions of the Meiji Seitoku Kinen Gakkai, 27 (1927), 1-8, and 28 (1928), 1-10.

1583
McKINNON, Richard Nichols. Zeami on the Nō: A Study of Fifteenth Century Japanese Dramatic Criticism. Harvard, 1951. 181p. AB: 4p. summary appended to diss. ms.

Contains (1) a discussion of some of the outstanding characteristics of the Nō as a stage art, (2) a biographical sketch of Zeami, (3) a brief comparative study of Zeami and his father Kan'ami, (4) a consideration of the nature and contents of Zeami's theoretical essays and some general observations on the development of his ideas, and (5) a full translation of the Yūgaku shūdō fūken.

Rel.Publ.: "The Nō and Zeami," FEQ, 11, (May 1952), 355-61; "Zeami on the Art of Training," Harvard Journal of Asiatic Studies, 16 (June 1953), 200-25.

1584
SHIVELY, Donald Howard. A Japanese Domestic Tragedy of the Eighteenth Century: An Annotated Translation of Shinjū Ten no Amijima. Harvard, 1951. 308p. AB: 6p. summary appended to diss. ms.

The introduction describes the social environment and the cultural tradition in which the work was produced, the influence of poetic style on the jōruri of Chikamatsu, the subject matter of Chikamatsu's sewamono (domestic plays), and the content, style, and textual history of Ten no Amijima.

Rel.Publ.: The Love Suicide at Amijima (Shinjū Ten no Amijima: A Study of a Japanese Domestic Tragedy by Chikamatsu Monzaemon. Cambridge: Harvard University Press, 1953. 173p. (Harvard-Yenching Institute. Monograph Series, 15)

1585
KEENE, Donald Lawrence. The Battles of Coxinga: Chikamatsu's Puppet Play: Its Background and Importance. Columbia, 1952. 205p.

The dissertation provides a short history of jōruri, a discussion of Chikamatsu's career and its place in The Battles of Coxinga (Kokusenya kassen), information on the sources and influences of the play, a literary analysis of the play, and a translation of it. The introduction focuses on the blending of Chinese and Japanese cultures as seen in The Battles of Coxinga.

Rel.Publ.: The Battles...Importance. London: Taylor's Foreign Press, 1951. 205p. (Cambridge Oriental Series, 4)

1586
WEBER-SCHÄFER, Peter. Ono no Komachi: Gestalt und Legende im Nō-Spiel [Ono no Komachi: Her Appearance and Legends about Her in the Noh Play]. München, 1960. Text in German. The dissertation in its published form is available at Marburg/Lahn, Staatsbibliothek Preussischer Kulturbesitz, Nr. Ser. 4173-2; also at the University of Michigan, General Library, no. PL 898. O58Z5W38.

The author first studies the life and work of the ninth century poetess Ono no Komachi and the legends that subsequently grew up around her. He then translates five Noh plays by Kan'ami and Zeami in which they utilize these legends: Sōshi arai [Komachi], Sekidera Komachi, Ōmu Komachi, Sotoba Komachi, and Kayoi Komachi. Appendix A is a translation of Tamatsukuri Komachi-ko sōsui sho. Appendix B contains numerous poems written by Komachi that appear in various anthologies of Heian poetry.

Rel.Publ.: Ono...Spiel. Wiesbaden: Harrassowitz, 1960. vii, 176p. (Studien zur Japanologie, 2)

UEDA, Makoto. Zeami, Bashō, Yeats, Pound: A Study in Japanese and English Poetics. 1961. See no. 1603.

1587
MOTOFUJI, Francis Toshiyuki. A Study of Narukami: An Eighteenth-Century Kabuki Play. Stanford, 1964. 238p. DA 26 (Aug. 1965), 1024-25; UM 65-2890.

An annotated translation of a representative early kabuki play, with a discussion of its author, sources, and characteristics.

1588
TSUKUI, Nobuko. Ezra Pound and the Japanese Noh Plays. Nebraska, 1967. 199p. DA 28 (Dec. 1967), 2267-68-A; UM 67-15,842.

Studies the nature and the quality of Pound's translations of the fifteen Noh plays which Ernest Fenollosa had not time to finish before his death. The author focuses on five plays--Sotoba Komachi, Kayoi Komachi, Kinuta, Aoi no ue, and Nishikigi--and points out "the most essential characteristics, both merits and demerits, of Pound's translations of these plays in comparison with their Japanese originals." She then examines the translations of the remaining plays, determines some of their most common characteristics, and suggests a number of reasons for the inadequacies of Pound's work.

1589
KIM, Myung Whan. Mythopoetic Elements in the Later Plays of W.B. Yeats and the Noh. Indiana, 1969. 237p. DA 30 (May 1970), UM 70-7467. [See also addenda 22A.]

1590
TAKAYA, Ted Terujiro. An Inquiry into the Role of the Traditional Kabuki Playwright. Columbia, 1969. v, 202p.

With the exception of Chikamatsu Monzaemon (1653-1724), the role of the playwright was subordinate to both the actor and the manager throughout the entire history of kabuki. Even an outstanding playwright like Kawatake Mokuami (1816-1893), who bridged the Tokugawa and Meiji periods, remained essentially within this mold. Thoroughly committed to the preservation of its Tokugawa heritage, kabuki could not develop into a modern theater.

1591
TERASAKI, Etsuko Takemoto. A Study of Genzai Plays in Nō Drama. Columbia, 1969. 216p.

Contents: The Classification of Nō Drama; What are Genzai Plays?; Muromachi Dramatists; The World as Revealed in Genzai Plays.

Poetry

1592
GRAMATZKY, August Julius Wilhelm Paul. Kokinwakashū maki no dai roku Tōkagami Fuyu no Uta...Altjapanische

Winterlieder aus dem Kokinwakashū (Grundschrift, Umschrift, und Übersetzung) nebst Motooris Prosaumschreibung (Grundschrift und Umschrift), Wörter- und Formenverzeichnis und Zusammenstellung der chinesischen und japanischen Schriftzeichen (Sōsho und Hiragana) [Kokinwakashū maki no dai roku Tōkagami fuyu no uta... Early Japanese Poems about the Winter from the Kokinwakashū (Original, Transcription, and Translation) Compared with Motoori's Prose Transcription (Original and Transcription) with a Word and Character Index and with a Synopsis of the Chinese and Japanese Writing Systems (Sōsho and Hiragana)]. Halle-Wittenberg, 1892. Text in German.

A translation of the poems about winter accompanied with a translation of Motoori Norinaga's commentary Tōkagami.

Rel.Publ.: Kokinwakashū...Hiragana. Leiden: E.J. Brill, 1892. x, 32p.

1593
OKASAKI, Tōmitsu. Das Manyōshū: Eine kritisch-ästhetische Studie [The Manyōshū: A Critical and Esthetic Study]. Leipzig, 1898. Text in German. The dissertation in its published form is available at Marburg/Lahn, Universitätsbibliothek, Nr. II C.

Includes a general survey of the Manyōshū, an essay on its authorship, textual criticism and evaluation of the work, and information on fashions, customs, and early Japanese society as reflected in the Manyōshū. The dissertation concludes with a study of the "Azuma people" (the people in eastern Japan) and their poetry.

Rel.Publ.: Das Manyōshū...Studie. Leipzig: Duncker & Humblot, 1898. 67p.

1594
CHANOCH, Alexander. Die Herbstlieder des Kokinshū und die altjapanische Jahreszeitenpoesie [The Autumn Songs of the Kokinshū and Early Japanese Poetry about the Seasons]. Hamburg, 1924. iii, 165p. Text in German. Diss. ms. available at Marburg/Lahn, Staatsbibliothek Preussischer Kulturbesitz, Nr. MS 25/4331.

Based on a study of the first six books of the Kokinshū, the dissertation is an examination of the literary genre known as early Japanese seasonal poetry. A brief survey of the most important official collections of early Japanese poetry and of the use of seasonal poetry within them is followed by a study of certain aspects of the structure of the poems written about autumn: the makura-kotoba, kenyōgen (twice-used word), and jo (poetic preface). In addition, the author examines the change of mood in Japanese poetry from the beginning of spring to the end of winter and provides an annotated translation of poems 1-80 of book 4 of the Kokinshū and poems 1-65 of book 5. The appendix contains biographical notes about individual poets.

Rel.Publ.: "Die altjapanische Jahreszeitenpoesie aus dem Kokinshū," Asia Major, 4 (1927), 240-376 [Also published as a monograph under the title Die altjapanische Jahreszeitenpoesie aus dem Kokinshū: In Text und Übersetzung mit Erläuterungen. Leipzig: Asia Major, 1928. 148p. (Veröffentlichungen des Seminars für Sprache und Kultur Japans an der Hamburger Universität, 2).]

1595
LORENZENY, Alfred. Die Gedichte Hitomaro's aus dem Manyōshū in Text und Übersetzung mit Erläuterungen [Hitomaro's Poetry in the Manyōshū: Text and Annotated Translation]. Hamburg, 1927. Text in German. The dissertation in its published form is available at Bochum, Bibliothek des Ostasien-Instituts, Abt. Japan, Nr. C gc 20.

Pt.1: Translation of Hitomaro's poetry. Pt.2: Consideration of the contents, themes, and structure of his longer poems; consideration of his stylistic characteristics; the shorter poems and comparisons with Chinese poetry; the makura-kotoba and the jo (poetic preface); an index of the makura-kotoba employed in Hitomaro's poetry.

Rel.Publ.: Die Gedichte...Erläuterung. Hamburg: L. Friederichsen, 1927. 95p. (Veröffentlichungen des Seminars für Sprache und Kultur Japans an der Hamburgischen Universität,1)

1596
PIERSON, Jan Lodewijk, Jr. The Manyōshū: Translated and Annotated. [Book 1.] Leiden, 1929.

Book one consists of an introductory essay discussing the composition of the Manyōshū and an annotated translation (emphasizing various grammatical points) of 82 poems.

Rel.Publ.: The Manyōshū...Annotated. Leiden: E.J. Brill, 1929. x, 240p. [The entire text of the Manyōshū was published in 20 volumes by E.J. Brill between 1929 and 1964.]; The Makura-Kotoba of the Manyōshū. Leiden: E.J. Brill, 1964. 223p.; Selection of Japanese Poems Taken from the Manyōshū. Leiden: E.J. Brill, 1966. xvii, 46p.; Character Dictionary of the Manyōshū. Leiden: E.J. Brill, 1967. 839p.; plus several periodical articles on the Manyōshū and its grammar, etc.

NAKARAI, Toyozo W. A Study of the Impact of Buddhism upon Japanese Life as Revealed in the Odes of the Kokin-shū. 1930. See no.1896.

1597
HLA-DORGE, Gilberte. Une Poétesse japonaise au XVIIIe siècle: Kaga no Tchiyo-jo [A Japanese Poetess of the Eighteenth Century: Kaga no Chiyo-jo]. Paris, 1936. Text in French.

Contents: Introduction (Japanese Poetry in General, Historical Development and Technique of the Haikai); Japanese Authoresses and Writers of Haikai; The Life of Kaga no Chiyo-jo (Her early years, Her Youth, Her Pilgrimages, Her Final Years); Kaga no Chiyo-jo, Poetess of Nature. The Appendix contains 454 of her haikai transliterated and translated into French.

Rel.Publ.: Une Poétesse...Tchiyo-jo. Paris: G.-P. Maisonneuve, 1936. 256p.; "La poétesse Kaga no Chiyo-jo," France-Japon. 20 (May/June 1937), 97-100.

1598
SCHREIBER, Helga. Tennō-Idee und Vaterlandsliebe der Japaner im Spiegel der Liedersammlung Manyōshū [The Tennō-Idea and Japanese Patriotism as Reflected in the Manyōshū]. Leipzig, 1945. v, 91p. Text in German. Diss. ms available at Leipzig, Universitätsbibliothek; refer to author, year, title, and no. U44.6186.

Following an historical survey of the period 665-770, the author studies the Tennō (Emperor) ideas that are in the Manyōshū through an examination of the poetry within the work and of the designations that were used to refer to the ruler of the country. The author also studies the expression of Japanese patriotism in the Manyōshū through a consideration of those poems which deal with the countryside, the capital, the imperial court, and the Emperor. The concluding section compares the concept of patriotism in early Japan with that in twentieth century Europe.

1599
BENL, Oscar. Die Entwicklung der japanischen Poetik bis zum 16. Jahrhundert [The Development of Japanese Poetics up to the Sixteenth Century]. Hamburg, 1951. (Habilitationsschrift) Text in German. The dissertation in its published form is available at Marburg/Lahn, Universitätsbibliothek, Nr. XVII B 57grb, 56.

Studies the various stylistic periods of Japanese poetry by means of a systematic and chronological description and evaluation of the most important Japanese poetry written between the ninth and the sixteenth centuries: early Japanese poetry; the beginnings of pure Japanese poetry during the Heian period; Fujiwara Shunzei (1114-1204) and his times; Fujiwara Teika (1162-1241) and the golden age of Japanese peotry; Fujiwara Teika's poetic tradition in the hands of the Nijō school; poetry and Buddhism during the Muromachi period; the decline of Japanese poetry.

Rel.Publ.: Die Entwicklung...Jahrhundert. Hamburg: Cram, de Gruyter, 1951. xiii, 133p. (Abhandlungen aus dem Gebiet der Auslandskunde Bl 56, Reihe B. Völkerkunde, Kulturgeschichte, und Sprachen, 31)

1600
NOVAK, Miroslav. Haiku: japonská přírodní lyrika [Haiku: The Japanese Lyric Poetry of Nature]. Universita Karlova, 1952. 116p. Text in Czech. Diss. ms. available at the University archives, no. AUK 2958.

Focuses on the euphonic and thematic aspects of the haiku as they have been developed by Bashō and his followers.

Rel.Publ.: "Euphonie im Haiku," Archiv orientální, 30 (1962), 192-210.

1601
DOMBRADY, Géza Siegfried. Das Ora ga haru des Kobayashi Issa. [The Ora ga haru of Kobayashi Issa]. München, 1956. 216p. Text in German. Diss. ms. available at München, Universitätsbibliothek, Nr. U 1956.6948.

A biography of Kobayshi Issa (1763-1827), the construction and thematic arrangement of his prose-poem Ora ga haru, and a study of some motifs, the contents and style of his haibun and haikai, and his personality as reflected in Ora ga haru. The concluding portion of the dissertation is an annotated translation of Ora ga haru.

Rel.Publ.: Kobayashi Issa's Ora ga haru. Tokyo: Deutsche Gesellschaft für Natur- und Völkerkunde Ostasiens, 1959. (MOAG, supplement 23); "Issa und seine Gedanken zur Dichtung," in Gesellschaft für Natur- und Völkerkunde Ostasiens, Nachrichten, 85/86 (1959), 50-59; "Ein Haikai des Kobayashi Issa," in Deutsche Gesellschaft für Natur- und Völkerkunde Ostasiens, Nachrichten, 82 (1957), 15-25.

1602
YASUDA, Kenneth Kenichiro. On the Essential Nature and Poetic Intent of Haiku. Tokyo, 1956.

Rel.Publ.: The Japanese Haiku: Its Essential Nature, History, and Possibilities in English, with Selected Examples. Rutland, Vt.: Tuttle, 1957. xx, 232p.; A Pepper-pod: Classic Japanese Poems Together with Original Haiku. New York: Knopf, 1947. xl, 104p.

1603
UEDA, Makoto. Zeami, Bashō, Yeats, Pound: A Study in Japanese and English Poetics. Washington, Seattle, 1961. 179p. DA 22 (May 1962), 4007-08; UM 62-2097.

Seeks to "illuminate some essential features of poetry which transcend the difference of language and literary convention by bringing together the ideas of poetry held by four writers of different age and nationality."

Rel.Publ.: Zeami...Poetics. The Hague: Mouton, 1965. 165p. (Studies in General and Comparative Literature, 1); "The Nature of Poetry: Japanese and Western Views," Yearbook of Comparative and General Literature (Bloomington, Indiana), 11 (1962), 142-48; "Bashō and the Poetics of Haiku," Journal of Aesthetics and Art Criticism, 21 (Summer 1963), 423-31; "The Modes of Progression in English and Japanese Poetry," Yearbook of Comparative and General Literature (Bloomington, Indiana), 15 (1966), 166-73.

1604
NAUMANN, Wolfram. Hitorigoto: Eine Haikai-Schrift des Onitsura [Hitorigoto: A Haikai Composition of (Kamijima) Onitsura]. München, 1963. Text in German. The dissertation in its published form is available at Marburg/Lahn, Staatsbibliothek Preussischer Kulturbesitz, Nr. Ser. 4173-4; also at the University of Michigan, General Library, no. PL 795.K15H5N3.

After studying the life of Kamijima Onitsura (1661-1738), the author examines Onitsura's theories about poetry, paying special attention to his concepts of makoto and shugyō. He concludes the work with a partial translation of Hitorigoto.

Rel.Publ.: Hitorigoto...Onitsura. Wiesbaden: Harrassowitz, 1963. vii, 103p. (Studien zur Japanologie, 4)

1605
BORONINA, I. A. Kakekotoba kak odin iz spetsificheskikh priemov iaponskoi klassicheskoi poezii: Po pamiatnikam Kheianskogo perioda [Kakekotoba as One Specific Device Used in Classical Japanese Poetry: As Seen in Heian Period Literature]. Moscow, Institut narodov Azii Akademii nauk SSSR, 1965. (Candidate of Philological Sciences degree) 215p. Text in Russian. AB: 23p. summary published in 1965.

Rel.Publ.: "O roli omonima v iaponskoi klassicheskoi poezii, Narody Azii i Afriki, 2 (1964), 147-55; "Poetika iaponskoi tanka," Narody Azii i Afriki, 3 (1965), 100-12; "Poetika Kokinshu: Priemy kakekotoba i engo i ikh vliianie na poetiku tanka," in Akademiia nauk SSSR, Institut narodov Azii, Literatura i fol'klor narodov Vostoka (Moscow, 1967), 18-38.

1606
NAUMANN, Wolfram. Die japanische Kettendichtung des Mittelalters mit besonderer Berücksichtigung Shinkeis und der buddhistischen Lebenshaltung [Medieval Japanese "Chain Poems" (Renga) with Particular Consideration of Shinkei and of the Buddhist Attitude towards Life]. München, 1967. (Habilitationsschrift) Text in German. Diss. ms. available at München, Universitätsbibliothek.

A study of the development of renga--its form and its contents--and of the literaty contribution of Shinkei (1406-1475). The author discusses the theory of poetry underlying Shinkei's renga, its connections with shorter Japanese poems (e.g. tanka), and the influence of Chinese theories on the writing of poetry. He also studies the construction and contents of renga and analyzes the basic themes found in the renga that Shinkei composed.

Rel.Publ.: Shinkei in seiner Bedeutung fur die japanische Kettendichtung. Wiesbaden: Harrassowitz, 1967. viii, 166p. (Studien zur Japanologie, 8); "Oi no kurigoto von Shinkei (1406-1475): Eine Quelle zur Poetik des Renga, Oriens Extremus, 7 (Dec. 1960),

185-211.

1607
WEHLERT, Heide. Imagawa Ryōshun und sein Nigenshō: Ein Beitrag zur Waka-Poetik der Muromachi-Zeit [Imagawa Ryōshun and His Nigenshō: A Contribution to Waka Poetry of the Muromachi Period]. Bochum, 1968. Text in German.

The following topics are among those examined within the dissertation: the life and personality of Imagawa Ryōshun (1325-1420); his development as a poet and his studies of waka and renga; his systemization and continuation of the Reizei school of poetry; Imagawa's traditional consciousness; the purity and spontaneity of poetry as well as the original moment of creation. The dissertation concludes with a study of the style of the Nigenshō and a translation of the text.

Rel.Publ.: Imagawa...Muromachi-Zeit. Wiesbaden: Harrassowitz, 1969. 106p. (Studien zur Japanologie, 11)

Prose

Heian Period

ISHIKAWA, Takeshi. Étude sur la littérature impressioniste au Japon. 1909. See no.1623.

1608
BEAUJARD, André. Les Notes de Chevet de Séi Shōnagon', dame d'honneur au Palais de Kyōto: Essai de traduction [The Pillow Book of Sei Shōnagon, Lady of Honor at the Palace in Kyoto: Translation]. Paris, 1935. (thèse complémentaire) Text in French.

A translation without any introductory essay.

Rel.Publ.: Les Notes...Traduction. Paris: G.-P. Maisonneuve, 1934. xxii, 331p.

1609
BEAUJARD, André. Séi Shōnagon', son temps, et son oeuvre: Une femme de lettres de l'Ancien Japon [Sei Shōnagon, Her Times, and Her Work: A Lady of Letters of Ancient Japan]. Paris, 1935. Text in French.

A study of tenth century Japan (political organization, religion, social life and customs, important families), the work of Sei Shōnagon (its form, style, and background), and Sei Shōnagon's knowledge and ideas.

Rel.Publ.: Sei..Japon. Paris: G.-P. Maisonneuve, 1934. 380p.

1610
REISCHAUER, Edwin Oldfather. Nittō guhō junrei gyōki: Ennin's Diary of His Travels in T'ang China, 838-847. Harvard, 1939. 260p. AB: Harvard University. Summaries of Theses...1939. p.66-68.

An introduction and annotated translation of the first four chapters of the "Record of Pilgrimage to China in Search of the Holy Law." Ennin (794-864), an important Heian Buddhist monk, sailed to China as a member of Tsunetsugu's embassy. In his diary he recorded details of his travels and information about contemporary conditions in China.

Rel.Publ.: Ennin's Travels in T'ang China. New York: Ronald Press, 1955. 454p.

1611
FOKKEN, Julia. Beitrag zur Stilgeschichte der Monogatari an Hand des Taketorimonogatari und des Makura no sōshi [A Contribution to the Stylistic History of the Monogatari by Means of an Examination of the Taketori monogatari and of the Makura no sōshi]. Bonn, 1941. Text in German. The dissertation in its published form is available at Bonn, Universitätsbibliothek, Nr. Phil. 1941, U 48/4632; also at the University of Michigan, General Library, no. PL 787.T32F66.

The dissertation contains (1) general information on the Taketori monogatari and the Makura no sōshi with annotated translations of portions of these two works; (2) a study of the principles of sentence structure; the structure and function of verbs, nouns and their equivalents, adjectives, and adverbs; comments on poetry as prose and on the style of Sei Shōnagon; and (3) a comparison of the two works with regard to their contents, style, and grammar.

Rel.Publ.: Beitrag...sōshi. Botrop i.W.: W. Postberg, 1941. 63p.

1612
HRDLIČKOVÁ-STUNOVÁ, Věnceslava. Ki no Curajuki, průkopník japonské prosy [Ki no Tsurayuki: The Pioneer of Japanese Prose]. Karlova Universita, 1950. 136p. Text in Czech. Diss. ms. available at the University archives, no AUK 2550.

Presents an annotated translation of the introductory sections of the Kokinwakashū and of the Tosa nikki, evaluates Ki no Tsurayuki's contribution to the development of prose in Japan, and examines the concept of time in the Tosa nikki.

LINN, John K. Jr. The Imperial Edicts of the Shoku-Nihongi: An Annotated Translation of Edicts #30-62. 1950. See no.1553.

1613
ZIEGLER, Edwin Bořivoj. Deník Sarašina (Sarašina nikki): Studie, překlad, a komentář [The Sarashina nikki: A Study, Translation, and Commentary]. Universita Karlova, 1950. Text in Czech. Diss ms. available at the University archives, no. AUK 2508.

Includes a brief introduction to the Sarashina nikki and a discussion of its place in Japanese literature.

1614
MORRIS, Ivan Ira. The Style of Murasaki Shikibu with Particular Reference to Literary Influences. London, 1951. xxiv, 424p.; 137, lxxxviii p. (2v.)

1615
SHIMIZU, Osamu. Nihon Monotoku Tennō jitsuroku: An Annotated Translation with a Survey of the Early Ninth Century in Japan. Columbia, 1951. 619p. DA 12 (1952), 71. UM 3383.

Part 1 contains background material for the period 781-967, a biographical account of Emperor Montoku (who reigned from 850 to 858), and a bibliographical analysis of the work. Part 2 is a translation of the Montoku jitsuroku, the fifth of the "Six National Histories" (Rikkokushi).

1616
BROWER, Robert Hopkins. The Koñzyaku monogatarisyū: An Historical and Critical Introduction, with Annotated Translations of Seventy-Eight Tales. Michigan, 1952. 1067p. (3v.) DA 12 (1952), 420; UM 3724.

Contents of v.1 (Introduction): Some Early Buddhist Tale Collections in India, China, and Japan; Non-Buddhist Narrative Writing in Japan from the Beginnings to the Late Heian Period; The Social and Literary Scene in the Late Heian Period (ca.1025-1160); The Contents of the Konzyaku monogatarisyū [Konjaku monogatari], Their Topical Arrangement, and the Basis for the Selection of the Tales Translated; The Sources of the Konzyaku monogatarisyū, the Structure and Style of the Tales, and the Purpose for Which the Collection Was Compiled; The Problems of the Authorship and Date of the Konzyaku monogatarisyū; The Position of the Konzyaku monogatarisyū in the Stream of Japanese Literature. NOTE: "The 78 tales translated and annotated are selected in such a way as to provide at least one example from each of the major topical groups under which the Japanese stories are arranged in the original work."

1617
BÜCHELE, Hanna Yuki. Saga und Monogatari als Werke früher Kunstprosa: Versuch eines Vergleiches [Saga and Monogatari as Works of Early Literary Prose: An Attempt at a Comparison of the Two]. Tübingen, 1954. ii, 108p. Text in German. Diss. ms. available at Tübingen, Universitätsbibliothek, Nr. UM 6154.

A comparison of the saga and the monogatari as literary genres with regard to their thematic material, form, transmission from generation to generation, origin and development, contents, and composition. Included is a study of their historical credibility, of the magic that is characteristic of supernatural forces, and of the sense of reality as a stylistic medium.

1618
MÜLLER, Wolfram Harald. Das Mumyōzōshi und seine Kritik am Genji-monogatari [The Mumyōzōshi and Its Criticism of the Genji monogatari]. Hamburg, 1956. 95p. Text in German. Diss. ms. available at Hamburg, Staats- und Universitätsbibliothek, Nr. Diss. phil. Mscr. 466.

Begins with a survey of the criticism levied against the Genji monogatari from the eleventh century to the Mumyōzōshi (the diary of Murasaki Shikibu, the Sarashina nikki, and the beginnings of Buddhist criticism). It continues with a study of the origins, authorship, and arrangement of the Mumyōzōshi and its criticism of the characters and events in the Genji monogatari.

Rel.Publ.: "Das Mumyōzōshi...monogatari," Oriens Extremus, 3 (Dec. 1956), 205-14, and 4 (1957), 70-103.

1619
VOS, Frits. A Study of the Ise-monogatari: With the Text According to the Den-Teika-hippon, and an Annotated Translation. Leiden, 1957. [See also addenda 43A]

Rel.Publ.: A Study...Translation. The Hague: Mouton, 1957. xii, 271p.; 208p. (2v.)

1620
MILLS, Douglas Edgar. The Uji-shūi-monogatari. London, 1963. 416p.

A study of the "tale collection" Uji-shūi-monogatari (ca. 11th century) against the background of its genre. Part 1 deals with the style and quality of the book; part 2 consists of a comparative analysis of the tales in terms of other works of the same period; and part 3 deals with the question of dating the work and establishing its authorship.

BOCK, Felicia G. Engi-shiki: Ceremonial Procedures of the Engi Era, 901-922. 1966. See no.490.

1621
CRANSTON, Edwin Augustus. The Izumi Shikibu nikki: A Study and Translation. Stanford, 1966. 458p. DA 27 (July 1966), 176-77-A; UM 66-6332.

An introductory study (the life of Izumi Shikibu, textual history of Izumi Shikibu nikki, problems of date and authorship, the nikki as a genre) and an annotated translation.

Rel.Publ.: The Izumi Shikibu Diary: A Romance of the Heian Court. Cambridge: Harvard University Press, 1969. xii, 332p. (Harvard-Yenching Institute Monograph Series, 19)

1622
BREWSTER, Jennifer E. Sanuki no suke nikki: Tribute to Emperor Horikawa: An Introduction and Translation. Australian National, 1969. 314p.

The introductory essay presents a biography of Fujiwara Nagako (1029-1103), the author of the work, a stylistic analysis and the historical background of the Sanuki no suke nikki, and a study of the nikki as a literary genre.

Kamakura and Muromachi Periods

1623
ISHIKAWA, Takeshi. Étude sur la littérature impressioniste au Japon [A Study of Impressionist Literature in Japan]. Paris, 1909. Text in French.

Contents: Pt.1: Kenkō and the Tsurezuregusa: Life of Kenkō; The Tsurezuregusa; Analysis of the Tsurezuregusa; Character of Kenkō; Public Reception of the Tsurezuregusa. Pt.2: Chōmei and the Hōjōki: Life of Chōmei; The Hōjōki; Character of Chōmei. Pt.3: Sei Shōnagon and the Makura no sōshi: Life of Sei Shōnagon; The Makura no sōshi; Character of Sei Shōnagon.

Rel.Publ.: Étude...Japon. Paris: A. Pedone, 1909. 190p.; "Une Poétesse japonaise et son oeuvre: Sei Shōnagon et le Makura no sōshi," Bulletin de la Société Franco-japonaise de Paris, 18 (Mar. 1910), 36-52.

DONAT, Walter. Der Heldenbegriff im Schrifttum der älteren japanischen Geschichte. 1937. See no.477.

1624
McCULLOUGH, Helen Craig. A Study of the Taiheiki: A Medieval Japanese Chronicle. California, Berkeley, 1955. 427p.

The dissertation consists of an introduction to and translation of four of the first five scrolls of the Taiheiki, the fourteenth-century chronicle of the Hojo family.

Rel.Publ.: The Taiheiki: A Chronicle of Medieval Japan. New York: Columbia University Press, 1959. xlix, 401p. (Records of Civilization: Sources and Studies, 59); "Some Notes on the Translation of Japanese Offices and Titles," Phi Theta Annual (Berkeley, Calif.), 5 (1954/1955), 45-60.

1625
NIWA, Tamako. Nakatsukasa Naishi nikki. Radcliffe, 1956. iv, 201p. AB: 1p. summary appended to diss. ms.

Pt.1 surveys the travel journals and court diaries written before 1280. Pt.2 contains a translation of this thirteenth century diary and also includes "a brief study of the Nakatsukasa Naishi nikki itself, its historical background and value as an historic source, its author, and the various existing texts."

GLAUBITZ, Joachim. Das Hokke-shuhō-ippyakuza-kikigakishō: Übersetzung, textkritische und grammatische Bearbeitung eines buddhistischen Erzählungstextes. 1959. See no.1907.

ARAKI, James T. The Kōwakamai: A Survey of Its Development as a Medieval Performed Art and a Study of Its Texts. 1961. See no.1681.

McCULLOUGH, William H. Shōkyūki and Azuma kagami: Sources for the Shōkyū War of 1221. 1962. See no.492.

1626
BUTLER, Kenneth Dean, Jr. The Birth of an Epic: A Textual Study of the Heike monogatari. Harvard, 1964. iii, 458p.

Contents: The Early Variant Texts of the Heike monogatari; The Authorship and Date of the Shibu Text; The Shibu Text as the Original Heike monogatari; The Rokudai Gozen monogatari; The Heike monogatari and the Rokudai Gozen monogatari; The Basis of the Heike monogatari in Oral Composition. Appendices contain translations, romanized transliterations, and the Japanese texts of the Rokudai Gozen monogatari and of the Rokudai Gozen story in the Shibu, Yashiro, and Kakuichi variants of the Heike monogatari.

Rel.Publ.: "The Textual Evolution of the Heike monogatari," Harvard Journal of Asiatic Studies, 26 (1966) 5-51; "The Heiki monogatari and Theories of Oral Epic Literature," in Seikei University (Tokyo), Bulletin of the Faculty of Letters, 2 (1966), 37-54; "Seikai no jojishi kenkyū to Heike monogatari no ichi," in Nihon koten hyōshaku zen chūshaku sōsho geppō 5 (Tōkyō: Kadokawa, 1967); "The Heike monogatari and the Japanese Warrior Ethic," Harvard Journal of Asiatic Studies, 29 (1969), 93-108; "Heike monogatari to Yōroppa jojishi bungaku," in Heike monogatari no oitachi, ed. by Tomikura Tokujiro (Tōkyō: Komine, 1968).

1627
GOREGLIAD, Vladimir Nikanorovich. Tsuredzuregusa: Vydaiushchiisia pamiatnik iaponskoi esseisticheskoi literatury [Tsurezuregusa: An Outstanding Example of the Essay as a Genre in Japanese Literature]. Leningrad, Leningradskii gosudarstvennyi universitet imeni A. A. Zhdanova, 1964. (Candidate of Philological Sciences degree) 228p. Text in Russian.

Rel.Publ.: "O nekotorykh khudozhestvennykh osobennostiakh 'Zapisok ot skuki' Kenko-khosi," in Institut narodov Azii, Akademiia nauk SSSR, Kratkie soobshcheniia, 63 (1963), 23-38.

1628
MÜLLER, Klaus. Das Nakatsukasa no Naishi nikki: Ein Spiegel höfischen Leben in der Kamakura-Zeit [The Nakatsukasa no Naishi nikki: A Mirror of Court Life during the Kamakura Period]. München, 1965. Text in German. The dissertation in its published form is available at Bochum, Universitätsbibliothek.

An historical survey of the thirteenth century in Japan, a biographical study of the author, an examination of the work with particular regard to the time when it was written as well as to the period covered in the diary, a consideration of the diary's position within the mainstream of medieval Japanese literature, a discussion of the contents of the work, and an annotated translation of the Nakatsukasa no Naishi nikki. The appendix contains poems of Nakatsukasa that appear in the court anthology Gyokuyōshū (compiled about 1313) and an index of the names appearing in the text.

Rel.Publ.: Das Nakatsukasa...Zeit. Bamberg: K. Urlaub, 1969. 156p.

1629
RUCH, Barbara Ann. Otogi bunko and Short Stories of the Muromachi Period. Columbia, 1965. 304p. DA 26 (Feb. 1966), 4645; UM 65-13,987.

"An examination is made of the Tokugawa period publication by Shibukawa Seiemon of the twenty-three story set of books called Otogi bunko, the first anthology of Muromachi stories, and an attempt is made to clarify the differences between the Edo view of these stories and their actual origins and uses during the Muromachi period." The appendix contains a list of titles and alternate titles of extant Muromachi short stories.

SCHNEIDER, Roland. Kōwaka-mai: Sprache und Stil einer mittelalterlichen japanischen Rezitationskunst. 1967. See no.1684.

1630
WILSON, William Ritchie. Hōgen monogatari: Tale of the Disorder in Hōgen. Washington, Seattle, 1967. 297p. DA 28 (Nov. 1967), 1800-01-A; UM 67-14,237.

An annotated translation of the Rufubon Hōgen monogatari, one of Japan's five major gunkimono. An essay follows the translation which "first identifies the Hōgen in its relation to other gunkimono and historical writing of the time; next, identifies the Rufubon Hōgen in its relationship to other variant versions of the work; and finally, deduces how an earlier refinement of the tale purely in the verbal tradition would compare with the final Rufubon, intended for a large, but not highly educated, readership."

1631
BRAZELL, Karen Woodard. A Study and Partial Translation of Towazugatari. Columbia, 1969. 405p.

Towazugatari is the autobiography of a court lady of the Kamakura period who first became a concubine of the retired emperor Gofukakusa (reigned 1246-1259) and who later became a wandering nun. Part one of the thesis examines the author's life, the history of the text, and the literary position and value of the work. Part two is an annotated translation of the first three books of Towazugatari.

1632
MORRELL, Robert Ellis. Representative Translations and Summaries from the Shasekishū with Commentary and Critical Introduction. Stanford, 1969. 581p. DA 30 (Sept. 1969), 1144-A; UM 69-13,987.

"The bulk of the dissertation consists of translations of representative portions of the Shasekishū [a late Kamakura period example of the didactic and anecdotal literary genre known as Buddhist setsuwa] with detailed summaries of the remainder." The introductory portion is an examination of the life and background of Mujū Ichien (1226-1312), the author, and a study of the work's extant texts, structure, style, content, and place in the Japanese literary tradition.

Tokugawa Period

1633
HIBBETT, Howard Scott, Jr. Ejima Kiseki and the Hachimonjiya: A Study in Eighteenth-Century Japanese Fiction. Harvard, 1950. ii, 184p. AB: 2p. summary appended to diss ms.

Surveys popular prose in Japan during the seventeenth and early eighteenth centuries, studies the history of the Hachimonjiya publishing house, with which

Ejima Kiseki (1667-1736) was closely associated, and discusses Kiseki's principal works. Also includes an annotated translation of the first two of the five sections of Seken musuko katagi (Characters of Modern Sons).

Rel.Publ.: "Ejima Kiseki (1667-1736) and His Katagi-mono,: Harvard Journal of Asiatic Studies, 14 (Dec. 1951), 404-32; The Floating World in Japanese Fiction. New York: Oxford University Press, 1959. xiii, 232p.

1634
SARGENT, Geoffrey Willis. The Nippon Eitai-gura and Chōnin Ideology in the Seventeenth Century. Cambridge, 1954. 272p. AB: University of Cambridge. Abstracts of Dissertations...1953/1954. p.191-92.

"The dissertation is an investigation into the ideological background to the Nippon Eitai-gura (1688) of Ihara Saikaku" and an annotated translation of the entire text of this work. Included within the introduction are an analysis of three works in the 'Chōja-kyō' tradition, a study of "the relationship of Eitai-gura ideology with that expressed in The Seventeen Injunctions (1610) of the Hakata merchant Shimai Sōshitsu," and an investigation of indications within the Eitai-gura which foresaw coming changes in chōnin thought.

Rel.Publ.: The Japanese Family Storehouse, or the Millionaires' Gospel Modernized. Cambridge: Cambridge University Press, 1959. xlix, 281p. (University of Cambridge, Oriental Publications, 3)

1635
LANE, Richard Douglas. Saikaku: Novelist of the Japanese Renaissance. Columbia, 1957. 417p. DA 18 (Apr. 1958), 1432-33; UM 58-1344.

A biographical account and discussion of Saikaku's literary activities. The appendix includes "an account of Saikaku's literary contemporaries and followers, and a comprehensive bibliographical study of Saikaku's prose works."

Rel.Publ.: "Ibara Saikaku: Realistic Novelist of the Tokugawa Period," Journal of Oriental Literature, 11 (June 1948), 15-29; "Postwar Japanese Studies of the Novelist Saikaku," Harvard Journal of Asiatic Studies, 18 (June 1955), 181-99; "Saikaku and Burlesque Fiction," Harvard Journal of Asiatic Studies, 20 (June 1957), 53-73; "Saikaku bungaku no muzukashisa," Jimbutsu ōrai, 11 (Aug. 1957), 23-25; "The Beginnings of the Modern Japanese Novel: Kana-zōshi, 1600-1682," Harvard Journal of Asiatic Studies, 20 (Dec. 1957), 644-701; "Saikaku and the Japanese Novel of Realism," Japan Quarterly, 4 (Apr. 1957), 178-88; "Saikaku to Bokkachio," Bungaku, 26 (May 1958), 27-41; "Saikaku's Prose Works: A Bibliographical Study," MN, 14 (Apr./July 1958), 1-26; "Saikaku's Contemporaries and Followers: The Ukiyo-zōshi 1680-1780," MN, 14 (Oct. 1958/Jan. 1959), 125-37; "Saikaku and Boccaccio: The Novella in Japan and Italy," MN, 15 (Apr./July 1959), 87-118.

1636
BACKUS, Robert Lee. Matsudaira Sadanobu as a Moralist and Litterateur. California, Berkeley, 1963. 615p. DA 24 (Sept. 1963), 1158; UM 63-5475.

Focuses on the non-political aspects of the life and writings of Matsudaira Sadanobu (1758-1829), the daimyo who led the Kansei Reform. Included are translations of the Kagetsutei hikki and of excerpts from the Daigaku keibun kōgi and Sekizen shū, all of which present his ethical ideas; and translations of his tanka, the Seki no akikaze, and the Iizaka Travelogue.

1637
DONATH-WIEGAND, Margarete. Zur literarhistorischen Stellung des Ukiyoburo von Shikitei Samba [The Position of Shikitei Samba's Ukiyoburo in Japanese Literary History]. München, 1963. Text in German. The dissertation in its published form is available at Marburg/Lahn, Staatsbibliothek Preussischer Kulturbesitz, Nr. Ser. 4173-5; also at the University of Michigan, General Library, no. PL 798.2.U5D68.

An introduction to the sōshi (picture book) literature and to various kinds of Tokugawa period kokkeibon (comic books) as well as to the works and the life of Shikitei Samba (1776-1822) is followed by a study of the origins, arrangement, and language of the Ukiyoburo. The thesis concludes with a translation of parts 1 and 2 of Ukiyoburo and with a summary of the entire work.

Rel.Publ.: Zur...Samba. Wiesbaden: Harrassowitz, 1963. vi, 280p. (Studien zur Japanologie, 5)

1638
ZOLBROD, Leon Max. Takizawa Bakin: Major Edo Author (1767-1848). Columbia, 1963. 318p. DA 27 (Dec. 1966), 1845-46-A; UM 65-7482.

Contents: The Growth of Edo Literature; A Rōnin Becomes a Writer; Journey to Kyoto; The Leading Author (1803-1813); Respectability in Scholarship; Life in Kanda: A Restoration that Failed (1818-1835); Satomi and the Eight "Dogs": The Culmination of a Lifetime of Toil; The Blind Author (1835-1848).

Rel.Publ.: Takizawa Bakin. New York: Twayne, 1967. 162p. (Twayne's World Authors Series, 20); "Takizawa Bakin 1767-1848: A Restoration that Failed," MN, 21 (1966), 1-46; "Yomihon: The Appearance of the Historical Novel in Late Eighteenth Century and Early Nineteenth Century Japan," JAS, 25 (May 1966), 485-98.

1639
BEFU, Ben. Worldly Mental Calculations: An Annotated Translation of Ihara Saikaku's Seken munezan'yō. Stanford, 1966. 381p. DA 27 (Jan. 1967), 2144-A; UM 66-14,634.

Includes a "survey of Saikaku's times and of his prose writings, a brief discussion of his townsman pieces (chōninmono), and comments on his style."

1640
BOHÁČKOVÁ, Libuše. Ueda Akinari Ugecu monogatari: Rozbor sbírky a jednotlivých povídek a jejich motivických prvků [The Ugetsu monogatari of Ueda Akinari: An Analysis of the Collection, of the Individual Stories, and of Their Motifs]. Universita Karlova, 1966/67. 209p.

Compares the motifs found in the Ugetsu monogatari with their counterparts in those works of Chinese literature from which they were adapted, and examines Ueda Akinari's method of adapting those motifs in order to understand his attitude toward literary creation.

1641
JONES, Stanleigh Hopkins, Jr. Scholar, Scientist, Popular Author: Hiraga Gennai (1728-1780). Columbia, 1968. vii, 302p.

A biography covering selected aspects of Hiraga Gennai's career including his scientific endeavors, his novels, puppet plays, and social criticism.

MODERN

1642
PINUS, E. M. Peizazhnaia lirika Tokutomi [The Landscape

Lyric of Tokutomi (Roka)]. Moscow, Institut vostokovedeniia Akademii nauk SSSR, 1946. (Candidate of Philological Sciences degree), xiv, 214p. Text in Russian.
Tokutomi Roka, the pen name of the novelist Tokutomi Kenjirō (1868-1927).

1643
MORRISON, John Wilson. A Study in Modern Japanese Literature with a Translation of Arishima Takeo's Descendants of Cain. Washington, Seattle, 1948. 345p.
Contents: Post-Meiji Literature, 1868-1931; Background; The Career of Fukuzawa Yukichi; Translators and Early Naturalists; Naturalism at Its Height, 1900-1912; The Leisure School of Esthetics; Humanism; Intellectuals and Independents; The Proletarian School; Descendants of Cain [Kain no matsuei].
Rel.Publ.: Modern Japanese Fiction. Salt Lake City: University of Utah Press, 1955. xiii, 230p.; "Japan and the West: Backgrounds," Western Humanities Review, 7 (Spring 1953), 111-24; "Japan and the West: The Career of Fukuzawa Yukichi," Western Humanities Review, 7 (Summer 1953), 233-44.

1644
IOFFE, I. L. Tvorchestvo Khiguti Itie [The Work of Higuchi Ichiyō]. Moscow, Moskovskii institut vostokovedeniia, 1949. (Candidate of Philological Sciences degree) 291 + 99 + 34p. Text in Russian.
Higuchi Ichiyō (1872-1896), novelist.

1645
KARLINA, R. G. Roman Ftabateia Plyvushchee oblako i romany Goncharova i Turgeneva: Vliianie russkoi khudozhestvennoi literatury i kriticheskoi mysli XIX v. na protsess vozniknoveniia i stanovleniia realisticheskogo napravleniia v novoi iaponskoi literature [Futabatei (Shimei)'s Novel The Drifting Cloud (Ukigumo) and the Novels of Goncharov and Turgenev: The Influence of Nineteenth Century Russian Belles-Lettres and Critical Thought upon the Emergence and Development of the Realist School in Modern Japanese Literature]. Leningrad, Leningradskii gosudarstvennyi universitet imeni A. A. Zhdanova, 1950. (Candidate of Philological Sciences degree) 368p. Text in Russian. AB: 7p. summary published in 1950.

1646
SCHNITZER, Annelotte. Die Entwicklung der japanischen Shintaishi-Dichtung von der Meijizeit bis zur Gegenwart [The Development of Japanese Shintaishi Poetry from the Meiji Period up to the Present]. Hamburg, 1950. 124p. Text in German. Diss. ms. available at Hamburg, Staats- und Universitätsbibliothek, Nr. Diss. phil. Mscr. 147.
Following a survey of Meiji period literature, the author examines the beginnings of Shintaishi poetry (Shintaishishō and Shintaishika) and its early development (from the realism of Tsubouchi Shōyō to the Waseda School). She then discusses the heyday of this literature, focusing on (1) romanticism, symbolism, and humanism, (2) reaction and renewal in naturalism, and (3) development in aestheticism and the period of decline. The poetry of Takamura Kōtarō and of Murō Saisei as well as the writings of the neo-romantics and of the symbolists are considered.
Rel.Publ.: "Das Shi als Ausdruck des japanischen Lebensgefühls in der Taishōzeit: Hagiwara Sakutarō und Takamura Kōtarō" [by] Annelotte Piper, in Gesellschaft für Natur- und Völkerkunde Ostasiens, Nachrichten, 77 (1955), 8-21, and 79/80 (1956), 110-30; "Moderne Strömungen in der japanischen Dichtung," Akzente, 4 (1957), 425-36; "Fuyuhiko Kitagawa: Ein japanischer Dichter der Gegenwart: Das Shi als Ausdruck des japanischen Lebensgefühls der Shōwa-Zeit" [by] Annelotte Piper, Oriens Extremus, 6 (Mar. 1959), 75-103.

1647
FELDMAN, Horace Ziegler. The Growth of the Meiji Novel. Columbia, 1952. 326p. DA 12 (1952), 422-23; UM 3882.
A survey of literary trends as reflected in the prose literature of the Meiji period.
Rel.Publ.: "The Meiji Political Novel: A Brief Survey," FEQ, 9 (May 1950), 245-55.

1648
POSPELOV, B. V. Iaponskii realisticheskii roman 1906-1910 gg.: Proizvedeniia Simadzaki Tosona Narushennyi zavet, Vesna, Sem'ia [The Japanese Realistic Novel, 1906-1910: The Works of Shimazaki Tōson: The Broken Commandment (Hakai), Spring (Haru), Family (Ie)]. Moscow, Moskovskii institut vostokovedeniia, 1953. (Candidate of Philological Sciences degree) 294, xviii p. Text in Russian. 16p. summary published in 1953.

1649
LEWIN, Bruno. Futabatei Shimei in seinen Beziehungen zur russischen Literatur [Futabatei Shimei and His Connections with Russian Literature]. München, 1954. 197p. Text in German. The dissertation in its published form is available at Marburg/Lahn, Universitätsbibliothek, Nr. V1 b C 593rq, 38; also at the University of Michigan, General Library, no QH5.G38 v.38.
Studies the life of the nineteenth century author Futabatei Shimei and his work with Japanese and Russian works on literary theory. Examines his prose works Ukigumo, Sono omokage, Heibon) and his translation of Russian and Polish literary works by Turgenev, Gogol, Goncharov, Tolstoy, Garshin, Andreev, and Gorkii as well as his translations into Russian. The dissertation concludes with an evaluation of the influence that Futabatei's translations of Russian novels had upon Japanese literature during the latter part of the Meiji period.
Rel.Publ.: Futabatei...Literatur. Wiesbaden: Harrassowitz, 1955. 100p. (MOAG, 38).

1650
HUBRICHT, Manfred. Die Haiku-Poetik des Masaoka Shiki [Masaoka Shiki's Theory of Haiku Poetry]. Hamburg, 1955. 65p. Text in German. Diss. ms. available at Hamburg, Staats- und Universitätsbibliothek, Nr. Diss. phil. Mscr. 355.
The dissertation includes a biographical sketch of Masaoka Shiki (1867-1902), a study of his haiku poetry, information about his Bashō zōdan and Haijin buson, and a discussion of his views and theories about the writing of haiku poetry.
Rel.Publ.: "Die ästhetischen Abschnitte aus Masaoka Shiki's Haijin buson," Oriens Extremus, 3 (July 1956), 116-27.

1651
VIGLIELMO, Valda Humbert. The Later Natsume Sōseki: His Art and Thought. Harvard, 1956. ii, 224p. AB 4p. summary appended to diss. ms.
Ch.1-3 analyze Higan sugi made, Kōjin, and Kokoro. Appendices contain translations of significant passages from Wagahai wa neko de aru, Sore kara, Michikusa, and Meian.
Rel.Publ.: "Watakushi no mita Sōseki," Bungei: Natsume Sōseki tokuhon (June 1954), 28-35; "Ōgai to Sōseki," Kōza: Gendai rinri, 11 (1959), 305-08; "An

Introduction to the Later Novels of Natsume Sōseki," MN, 19, (1964), 1-36; "The Hero in Natsume Sōseki's Novels," in The Association of Teachers of Japanese, Journal-Newsletter, 4 (Aug. 1966), 1-18.

1652
SHEA, George Tyson. The Japanese Proletarian Literary Movement, Theory and Fiction: 1921-1934. Michigan, 1956. 526p. DA 17 (Aug. 1957), 1770; UM 21,673.

"The evolution of proletarian literary theory and the proletarian short story and novel are traced through a succession of alignments and realignments of proletarian literary leagues and federations." Pt.1--a "prehistory of the proletarian literary movement"--discusses the rise of socialist literature, Ishikawa Takuboku's critical realism, the rise of the popular arts and the labor literature theory, and Socialist writers and worker writers during the years 1907-1922. Pt.2, the main body of the thesis, examines the organizational and theoretical developments of the magazines Tane-maku hito and Bungei sensen and of NAPF and KOPF, and studies the fiction of the period 1921-1934. Pt.3 "traces the survival of the proletarian tradition in Japanese literature between 1934 and 1950."

Rel.Publ.: Leftwing Literature in Japan: A Brief History of the Proletarian Literary Movement. Tokyo: Hōsei University Press, 1964. v, 478p.

1653
McCLELLAN, Edwin. An Introduction to Sōseki, a Japanese Novelist. Chicago, 1957. 89p.

A study of the life of Natsume Sōseki (1867-1916) and of some of his writings. Contents: The Novelist's Background; The Major Novels.

Rel.Publ.: "The Implications of Sōseki's Kokoro," MN, 14 (Oct. 1958/Jan. 1959), 110-24; "An Introduction to Sōseki," HJAS, 22 (Dec. 1959), 150-208; Kokoro. Tr. by Edwin McClellan. Chicago: Regnery, 1957. 248p.; Two Japanese Novelists: Sōseki and Tōson. Chicago: University of Chicago Press, 1969.

1654
TOMITA, Takemasa. Goethe in Japan. München, 1957. ii, 169p.; 49p. (2v.) Text in German. Diss. ms. available at München, Universitätsbibliothek, Nr. U 1957. 7211.

Contents: An Historical Survey of the Intellectual Ties between European and Japanese Literature; Goethe's Work in Japan [Goethe's initial reputation in Japan, Japanese translations of his major works, and his influence upon Japanese literature]; The Development of Studies about Goethe in Japan [a discussion of the research of Chino Shōshō, Kimura Kinji, and Okutsu Hikoshige; and a tabular survey of translations and editions of Goethe's works as published in Japan and of Japanese works about Goethe].

1655
GRIGOR'EVA, Tat'iana Petrovna. Zhizn' i tvorchestvo Kunikida Doppo [The Life and Work of Kunikida Doppo]. Moscow, Institut vostochnykh iazykov pri Moskovskom gosudarstvennom universitete imeni M. V. Lomonosova, 1959. (Candidate of Philological Sciences degree) 334p. Text in Russian.

Kunikida Doppo, 1871-1908.

Rel.Publ.: Odinokii strannik: O iaponskom pisatele Kunikida Doppo. Moscow: "Nauka," 1967. 255p. (Institut narodov Azii Akademii nauk SSSR); "Tvorcheskii put' Kunikida Doppo," in Akademiia nauk SSSR, Institut Vostokovedeniia, Kratkie soobshcheniia, 34 (1958), 52-63.

1656
CHEGODAR', Nina Ivanovna. Znachenie povesti "Snegozashchitnaia roshcha" v tvorchestve Kobaiasi Takidzi [The Importance of the Story "Bōsetsurin" among the Works of Kobayashi Takiji]. Moscow: Institut vostokovedeniia Akademmi nauk SSSR, 1960. (Candidate of Philological Sciences degree) 307p. Text in Russian.

"Bosetsurin," literally translated as "a small forest which was planted as a protection against the snow," was one of the early works of Kobayashi Takiji (1903-1933).

Rel.Publ.: Kobaiasi Takidzi: Zhiszn' i tvorchestvo. Moscow: "Nauka," 1966. 95p. (Akademiia nauk SSSR. Institut narodov Azii)

ARIMA, Tatsuo. The Failure of Freedom: An Intellectual Portrait of Taishō Japan. 1962. See no.640.

1657
KIM, Le Chun. M. Gor'kii i iaponskaia literatura [Maxim Gorky and Japanese Literature]. Moscow, Moskovskii gosudarstvennyi universitet imeni M. V. Lomonosova, 1962. (Candidate of Philological Sciences degree) 249p. Text in Russian.

1658
BERNDT, Jürgen. Miyamoto Yuriko: Ihre Entwicklung von einer bürgerlich-demokratischen zur sozialistischen Schriftstellerin: Dargestellt im Zusammenhang mit einigen Grundproblemen der modernen japanischen Literatur [Miyamoto Yuriko: Her Development from a Bourgeois-Democratic to a Socialistic Writer, Shown in Connection with Some Fundamental Problems in Modern Japanese Literature]. Berlin, Humboldt, 1963. 338p. (2v.) Text in German. Diss. ms. available at Berlin, Humboldt-Universität, Universitätsbibliothek, Nr. P34/64.

A study of the evolution and of the characteristics of modern Japanese literature is followed by an examination of Miyamoto Yuriko's (1898-1951) early work (her first work: Mazushiki hitobito no mure), her critical and realistic writings (the novel Nobuko), her proletarian and revolutionary works (the narrative Chibusa), and her postwar writings (the narratives Banshū-ebene and Fūchisō).

1659
MATHY, Reverend Hamlin Francis, S.J. Kitamura Tōkoku: Between East and West. Michigan, 1963. 348p. DA 24 (Nov. 1963), 2017; UM 63-8144.

Seeks to determine the manner in which Tōkoku sought to fuse Japanese and Western literature and thought "into a coherent, harmonious view of life and literature transcending both East and West." Contents: The Age; The Man; Tōkoku's Criticism of Pre-Meiji Japan; Tōkoku's Criticism of Meiji Japan; Tōkoku and the Japanese Fūryū Tradition; Tōkoku and Byron; Tōkoku and Carlyle; Tōkoku and Emerson; Two Narrative Poems; Early Essays; Kakujin shinkyū-nai no hikyū and Other Essays; The Inner Life; Final Essays; The Last Days; The Meaning of Tōkoku.

Rel.Publ.: "Kitamura Tōkoku: The Early Years," MN, 18 (1963), 1-44; "Kitamura Tōkoku: Essays on the Inner Life," MN, 19 (1964), 66-110; "Kitamura Tōkoku: Final Essays," MN, 20 (1965), 41-63.

1660
IWAMOTO, Yoshio. The Relationship between Literature and Politics in Japan, 1931-1945. Michigan, 1964.

452p. DA 25 (June 1965), 7270-71; UM 65-5323.
Contents: The Literature of the Left (Proletarian Literature to 1934, Conversion Literature, Proletarian Literature after 1934); The Literature of the Center (Liberal Writers, Literary Resistance); The Literature of the Right (War Literature, Literature of National Policy, Nationalist Litterateurs).
Rel.Publ.: "Sensō to tenkō," Hihyō (Winter 1966), 55-65; "The Changing Hero Image in Japanese Fiction of the Thirties," in Association of Teachers of Japanese, Journal-Newsletter, 4 (Aug. 1966), 28-36; "Aspects of the Proletarian Literary Movement in Japan," forthcoming in a book ed. by Bernard Silberman and Harry Harootunian.

1661
NAFF, William Edward. Shimazaki Tōson: A Critical Biography. Washington, Seattle, 1965. 316p. DA 26(Aug. 1965), 1047-48; UM 65-8523.
Contents: The Meiji Literary Scene; Home and Family; Education and Apprenticeship; Fame and Success; The Shinsei Affair; Tōson's Career in His Last Two Decades.
Rel.Publ.: Book on Shimazaki Tōson is forthcoming from the University of Washington Press.

1662
RYAN, Marleigh Myrna. Futabatei Shimei and the Creation of Ukigumo: Japan's First Modern Novel. Columbia, 1965. 447p. DA 26 (Oct. 1965), 2222; UM 65-10,221.
"The first modern Japanese novel in colloquial language specifically designed to reveal the psychological nature of its characters."
Rel.Publ.: Japan's First Modern Novel: Ukigumo of Futabatei Shimei. New York: Columbia University Press, 1967. xvi, 381p. (Studies of the East Asian Institute); "A Study of Futabatei Shimei, 1864-1909," in Columbia University, East Asian Institute, Researches in the Social Sciences on Japan, 2 (1959), 55-76; "Futabatei Shimei and the Superfluous Hero," in the Association of Teachers of Japanese, Journal-Newsletter, 4 (Aug. 1966), 19-27.

1663
SATO, Toshihiko. Henrik Ibsen in Japan. Washington, Seattle, 1966. 267p. DA 27 (Dec. 1966), 1836-37-A; UM 66-12,043.
Discusses the reception of the Norwegian playwright's works in Japan, the growth of Japanese interest in his work, his impact on Japanese literature in general and on drama in particular, his role in the formation of the Seitōsha under the leadership of Hirazuka Raichō, and his contribution to the development of the emancipation of women movement in Japan.
Rel.Publ.: "Henrik Ibsen and the Modern Japanese Theater," Orient/West, 7 (Jan. 1962), 45-49; "Ibsen Parallels in Modern Japanese Drama," Yearbook of Comparative and General Literature (Bloomington, Indiana), 11 (1962), 183-90; "Ibsen and Emancipation of Women in Japan," Orient/West, 9 (Sept./Oct. 1964), 73-77; "Nakamura Kichizo's A Vicarage and Ibsen," Modern Drama, 9 (Feb. 1967), 440-50.

1664
FISCHER, Claus M. Lev N. Tolstoi in Japan: Meiji- und Taishō-Zeit [Leo Tolstoy in Japan during the Meiji and Taishō periods]. Bochum, 1967. Diss. ms. available at Bochum, Universitätsbibliothek.
I. Tolstoy in Japanese translations of the Meiji and Taishō periods. II. The attitudes of Japanese writers and critics towards Tolstoy as a novelist and philosopher and towards his literary works. III. Tolstoy's influence upon Japanese writers (Tokutomi Roka, Kinoshita Naoi, Mushakōji Saneatsu, and Arishima Takeo) and the significance of Tolstoy's influence in Japan. The appendix contains translations of four critical essays about Tolstoy (by Kōtoku Shūsui, Hirotsu Kazuo, Masamune Hakuchō, and Mushakōji Saneatsu) as well as two very detailed listings of the Japanese-language translations of Tolstoy's works and of critical Japanese writings about him.
Rel.Publ.: Lev...Zeit. Wiesbaden: Harrassowitz, 1969. x, 219p.

1665
TSUKIMURA, Reiko. The Language of Symbolism in Yeats and Hagiwara. Indiana, 1967. 214p. DA 28 (Mar. 1968), 3689-A; UM 68-2370.
A comparative study dealing in part with Hagiwara Sakutarō (1886-1942), "the first poet in whom Japanese poetry in colloquial style attained perfection and who succeeded in assimilating French symbolism into Japanese poetic sensibility." Contents: Introduction: The Literary Situation; Symbolist Phase: The Wind among the Reeds and Baying at the Moon [Tsuki ni hoeru]; Metaphysical Phase: The Tower and A Blue Cat [Aoneko]; Vacillation: "The Winding Stair" and "After a Blue Cat"; Passion is Reality: Last Poems and The Iceland [Hyōtō]; Conclusion: Poetics.

1666
TSURUTA, Kinya. Akutagawa Ryūnosuke: His Concepts of Life and Art. Washington, Seattle, 1967. 246p. DA 28 (Mar. 1968), 3689-90-A; UM 68-3886.
"This dissertation is neither a full scale biographical study of Akutagawa Ryūnosuke [1892-1927], nor is it a pure aesthetic evaluation of his literary work; it is a study of a nebulous area which lies between his concepts of life and art. It examines his relationship with nature, society, family, and women in search of an underlying principle and then tries to relate the findings to his concepts of art."
Rel.Publ.: "Akutagawa Ryūnosuke ni okeru ahō to tensai," Kokubungaku, 13 (Dec. 1968), 23-26.

1667
MAMONOV, A. I. Svobodnyi stikh v iaponskoi poezii [Free Verse in Japanese Poetry]. Moscow, Institut narodov Azii Akademii nauk SSSR, 1968. (Candidate of Philological Sciences degree) 402p. Text in Russian. AB: 31p. summary published in 1968.

1668
MORITA, James R. Yamada Bimyō as Novelist. Chicago, 1968. 199p.
A study of the life, works, and achievement of Yamada Bimyō (1868-1910), a novelist and poet of the Meiji era.

1669
RECK, Michael. Masaoka Shiki und seine Haiku-Dichtung [Masaoka Shiki and His Haiku Poetry]. München, 1968. Text in German. The dissertation in its published form is available at München, Universitätsbibliothek; also at the University of Michigan, General Library, no. 38,459.
Surveys Japanese literature during the Meiji period, discusses Masaoka Shiki's (1867-1902) life and works, and studies his haiku, his ideals of haiku composition, and his influence upon the subsequent development of haiku. The appendix contains the texts and annotated

translations of 550 of Masaoka Shiki's haiku.
Rel.Publ.: Masaoka...Dichtung. München: Salzer, 1968. 128p.

1670
MELANOWICZ, Mikołaj. Twórczość Hagiwara Sakutarō [The Works of Hagiwara Sakutarō]. Warsaw, 1968/69. 382p. Text in Polish. For microfilm copies, write to the Central Library of the University of Warsaw (Biblioteka Główna Uniwersytetu Warszawskiego), Warsaw, Poland.
Pt.1: Genesis of free verse poetry in Japan and the early free verse poetry of Hagiwara (1886-1942). Pt.2: "The World of Solitude:" An analysis and categorical arrangement of Hagiwara's poetry. Pt.3: A model of the "lyric hero" of Hagiwara Sakutarō: the problems of the structure of the protagonist, his manner of existence, and his relation to other poetic elements.

1671
IRIYE, Mitsuko Maeda. Quest for Literary Resonance: Young Nagai Kafū and French Literature. Harvard, 1969. 224p.
A study of Kafū's relationship with Western and, in particular, with French literature during the Meiji period." Contents: The Early Years; American and France' The Return I; The Return II.

1672
O'BRIEN, James Aloysius. A Biographical and Literary Study of Dazai Osamu. Indiana, 1969. 200p. DA 30 (May 1970); UM 70-7486.
The author maintains that "studying the particular period of Dazai Osamu's life in which a given work was composed provides the best possible context for understanding that work, and that studying the successive stages of Dazai's entire life provides the best possible context for interpreting the whole corpus of Dazai literature." Accordingly, the dissertation divides Dazai's life up into five periods--the pre-Bannen, the Bannen, the pre-war, the war, and the post-war--and determines the manner in which Dazai's life at that time found expression in his works of fiction.

TAKAYA, Ted T. An Inquiry into the Role of the Traditional Kabuki Playwright. 1969. See no.1590.

Mass Media: Radio, Television, and the Press

1673
KAWABÉ, Kisaburō. The Press and Politics in Japan: A Study of the Relations between the Newspaper and the Political Development of Modern Japan. Chicago, 1919. xiii, 190p.

A study of the influence of the press upon Japanese political life, primarily during the Meiji period.

Rel.Publ.: The Press...Japan. Chicago: University of Chicago Press, 1921. xiii, 190p.

1674
WILDES, Harry Emerson. The Press and Social Currents in Japan. Pennsylvania, 1927. ix, 390p.

Primarily an analysis of the Japanese press in the early 1900's. Contents: The Culture Clash of East and West; The Press Seeks Freedom; Press Tendencies; The Anti-Alien Tide; Censorship and Extra-Legal Supervision; Safeguards against Radicalism; International News Agencies; Correcting Misconceptions; Creating a Pleasant Impression; Interpreting Japan to Foreigners; The Friendly Foreign Press; The Japan Advertiser: America's Newspaper; Libeling the Japanese.

Rel.Publ.: Social Currents in Japan. Chicago: University of Chicago Press, 1927. ix, 390p.

1675
KIM, Heun-chun. Die Aufmachung der modernen Zeitung in Ostasien: Japan, China, und Korea [The Make-Up of the Modern Newspaper in East Asia: Japan, China, and Korea]. Leipzig, 1928. Text in German. The dissertation in its published form is available at Marburg/Lahn, Universitätsbibliothek, Nr. VII C.

Focuses on the historical development of the daily press in East Asia and on the make-up and various parts of the daily newspaper (especially the parts featuring politics, trade, advertisements, local news, and feuilletons). The author also critically compares the press in East Asia with that in Europe, and his appendix contains statistical information on the development and the present-day [i.e. 1920's] position of the press in Japan, Korea, and China.

Rel.Publ.: Die Aufmachung...Korea. Leipzig: Twietmeyer, 1928. 61p.

IVANOVA, G. D. Kōtoku kak publitsist: K istorii progressivnoi iaponskoi publitsistiki nachala XX v. 1953. See no.614.

1676
LA TROBE, Frederick de. Das Element der Werbung in der publizistik der japanischen Presse der Gegenwart [Advertising as an Element in the Present-Day Japanese Press]. Berlin, Freie Universität, 1957. i, 158p. Text in German. Diss. ms. available at Berlin West, Freie Universität.

A study of the history of the press and of advertising methods in Japan, of advertising in Japanese newspapers, of the market-value of Japanese newspapers, and of the interrelationship between the press and advertising in Japan.

KUO, Heng-yü. Die japanische Pressekontrolle in der Mandschurei von 1931 bis 1941. 1963. See no.775.

ALTMAN, Albert A. The Emergence of the Press in Meiji Japan. 1965. See no.605.

VERA, José María de. Educational Television in Japan. 1967. See no.421.

JANG, John L. A History of Newspapers in Taiwan. 1968. See no.800.

Music

1677
ARIMA, Daigoro. Japanische Musikgeschichte auf Grund der Quellenkunde [Japanese Musical History Based on Knowledge of the Sources]. Wien, 1933. xxii, 246p. Text in German. Diss. ms. available at the Universitätsbibliothek der Universität Wien, Nr. D 3817.

LA RUE, Adrian J.P. The Okinawan Classical Songs: An Analytical and Comparative Study. 1952. See no.689.

1678
ECKARDT, Hans. Das Kokonchomonshū des Tachibana Narisue als musikgeschichtliche Quelle [The Kokonchomonshū of Tachibana Narisue as a Source for the History of Music]. Berlin, Freie Universität, 1954. (Habilitationsschrift). Text in German. The dissertation in its published form is available at Marburg/Lahn, Universitätsbibliothek, Nr. III C 5fks, 6.

Part 1 provides an historical survey of the flowering of Japanese music during the Heian period, a reconstruction of the life of Tachibana Narisue and a description of his intellectual surroundings, a discussion of the most important sources for the history of music from the twelfth through the seventeenth centuries, and a list of musical terms. Part 2 contains an annotated translation of "Kangen kabu" (music, song, and dance) taken from the Kokonchomonshū, completed in 1254.

Rel.Publ.: Das Kokonchomonshū...Quelle. Wiesbaden: Harrassowitz, 1956. 432p. (Göttinger asiatische Forschungen, 6); "Die geistige Umwelt des Tachibana Narisue," in Gesellschaft für Natur- und Völkerkunde Ostasiens, Nachrichten, 74 (1953), 16-32.

MITA, Setsuko. A Comparative Study of the Preparation of School Music Teachers in Japan and the United States. 1957. See no.426.

1679
MAY, Elizabeth. Japanese Children's Music before and after Contact with the West. California, Los Angeles, 1958. 205p.

Studies the shōgaku shōka (primary school songs) of the Meiji period and the introduction of music into the Japanese public school system during the late 1800's. Also discusses the nature of children's folk songs and the teaching of music in pre-Meiji Japan, before they were affected by the West.

Rel.Publ.: The Influence of the Meiji Period on Japanese Children's Music. Berkeley and Los Angeles: University of California Press, 1963. xi, 95p. (University of California Publications in Music, 6); "Japanese Children's Folk Songs before and after Contact with the West," in International Folk Music Council, Journal, 11 (1959), 59-65; "The Influence of the Meiji Period on Japanese Children's Music," Journal of Research in Music Education, 13 (Summer 1965), 110-20.

1680
MALM, William Paul. Japanese Nagauta Music. California, Los Angeles, 1959. 475p. (2v.)

Contents: Pt.1: History and Theory: A Short History of Nagauta Music; Classifications of the Nagauta Repertoire; Form in Nagauta. Pt.2: Music and Instruments: The Nagauta Voice; The Shamisen and Its Music; Drums of the Hayashi Ensemble; Flutes of the Hayashi Ensemble; The Off-Stage Ensemble and Its Music. Pt.3: Analysis: Analysis of Tsuru-kame; Analysis of Gorō Tokimune. Volume 2 contains various transcriptions of nagauta.

Rel.Publ.: Nagauta: The Heart of Kabuki Music. Rutland, Vt., and Tokyo, Japan: Charles E. Tuttle, 1963. xvi, 239p.; "The Essentials of Naga Uta Form," in International Conference of Orientalists in Japan, Transactions, 2 (1957), 46-47; "A Short History of Nagauta Music," Journal of the American Oriental Society, 80, (Apr./June 1960), 124-31; "Japanese Nagauta Music," in Festival of Oriental Music and the Related Arts (Los Angeles: University of California Press, 1960), 33-36.

1681
ARAKI, James Tomomosa. The Kōwakamai: A Survey of Its Development as a Medieval Performed Art and a Study of Its Texts. California, Berkeley, 1961. 346p.

Pt.1 describes the history and tradition of the kōwaka as a performing art, tracing and delineating all artistic elements that may have contributed to its formation. Pt.2 analyzes and describes the kōwaka libretto.

Rel.Publ.: The Ballad-Drama of Medieval Japan. Berkeley: University of California Press, 1964. xvi, 289p. (Publications of the Center for Japanese and Korean Studies); "Kōwakamai kenkyū no ichi hōhō," Chūsei bungaku no janru, 1 (1960), 7-8; "Kōwaka: Ballad-Dramas of Japan's Heroic Age," Journal of the American Oriental Society, 82 (Oct./Dec. 1962), 545-52; "Medieval Artistic Elements in Japanese Folk Theater," Modern Drama, 9 (Feb. 1967), 373-88.

1682
ADRIAANSZ, Willem Rudolf Cornelis. The Kumiuta and Danmono Traditions of Japanese Koto Music. California, Los Angeles, 1965. 589p. (2v.) DA 26 (Feb. 1966), 4708; UM 66-210.

Contents: Pt.1: Introduction: Introduction to the History of Koto Music; The Instrument; Scales and Tunings; Notation; Playing Techniques. Pt.2: Danmono: The First Dan; The Later Dan; Other Considerations. Pt. 3: Kumiuta: Fuki, the First Kumiuta; Kumiuta in Hirajōshi; Kumiuta in other Chōshi; The Vocal Part. Volume two contains transcriptions of selected kumiuta and danmono following the tradition of the Ikuta-ryū in Kyoto.

Rel.Publ.: "Research into the Chronology of Danmono," Ethnomusicology, 11 (Jan. 1967) 25-53; "On the Evolution of the classic Repertoire of the Koto," in Proceedings of the Centennial Workshop in Ethnomusicology Held at the University of British Columbia, Vancouver, June 19 to 23, 1967, ed. by Peter Crossley-Holland (Victoria, 1968), 68-78.

1683
GARFIAS, Robert A. The Tōgaku Style of Japanese Court Music: An Analysis of Theory in Practice. California, Los Angeles, 1965. 500p. (2v.) DA 26 (Jan. 1966), 3993-94; UM 66-215.

Contents: Historical Backgrounds; The Instruments of the Tōgaku Ensemble; Theory and Notation; Performance Practice and Musical Forms in the Repertoire; Rhythmic and Melodic Structure in Tōgaku; Tōgaku Ornamentation Technique and Its Earlier Variants; Modal Practice and Ornamentation; Analysis of Two Tōgaku Compositions; Conclusion: The Continuous Evolution of the Tōgaku Tradition. Volume 2 contains musical transcriptions.

Rel.Publ.: "Gagaku: Subdivisions of the Repertoire," in Festival of Oriental Music and the Related Arts (Los Angeles: University of California Press, 1960), 24-32.

1684
SCHNEIDER, Roland. Kōwaka-mai: Sprache und Stil einer mittelalterlichen japanischen Rezitationskunst [Kōwakamai: The Language and Style of a Medieval Japanese Performing Art]. Hamburg, 1967. Text in German. The dissertation in its published form is available at Bochum, Bibliothek des Ostasien-Instituts, Abt. Japan; also available at the University of Michigan, General Library, no. QH5. G38 v.49.

Pt.1: Questions and essence of the art of kōwakamai. Pt.2: The texts of the kōwakamai as literary works. Pt.3: The Texts as linguistic documents. Pt.4: Annotated translations of the kōwakamai entitled Kosodegoi and Takadachi.

Rel.Publ.: Kōwaka-mai...Rezitationskunst. Hamburg, 1968. viii, 305p. (MOAG, 51)

1685
FREEBERN, Charles L. The Music of India, China, Japan, and Oceania: A Source Book for Teachers. Arizona, 1969. 176p. DA 30 (Apr. 1970); UM 70-6670.

In the belief that there is an urgent need to make much more use of ethnic music at all levels of education in music, the author has sought to compile a source book on Asian music which can serve as a resource guide for those teachers wishing to teach ethnic music but unable to learn about the subject except through their own self-initiated, continuing educational endeavors. The main body of the dissertation includes source materials concerning four cultures--Oceania, China, Japan, and India--in the following categories: history; geography; notational systems; instruments; performance practices; and suggested music literature for use in classroom presentations. An annotated list of books, periodicals, recordings, and films, as well as a glossary of terms which can be used in teaching non-Western music also are included.

Overseas Japanese Communities

(Historical as well as contemporary developments. Includes studies on Japanese emigration; immigrant problems and legislation affecting immigration; and Japanese settlement, activities, and assimilation abroad.)

GENERAL

SCHALKHAUSSER, Friedrich. Die deutsche Auswanderungsgesetzgebung im Vergleich zur italienischen und japanischen. 1929. See no.1544.

1686
NOPITSCH, Toni. Die japanische Auswanderung: Eine Studie ihrer Entwicklung und ihrer Ursachen [Japanese Emigration: A Study of Its Development and of Its Origins]. München, 1930. vi, 135p. Text in German. Diss. ms. available at München, Universitätsbibliothek, Nr. U1930/5366.

A study of the Japanese emigration quotas and of the objectives of emigration. The author tries to determine whether the causes of emigration are economic, social, or political in nature, and he describes emigration policies and emigration organization.

1687
DJU, Peter. L'Émigration japonaise depuis 1918 [Japanese Emigration since 1918]. Paris, 1937. Text in French.

Contents: Historical Survey of Japanese Emigration before 1918; The Population of Japan; The Economic Foundations of the Japanese People; Emigration and Its Relationship to Japanese Politics; Japanese Emigration and Japanese Economic Activities in China; Japanese Emigration to Other Countries.

Rel.Publ.: L'Émigration...1918. Paris: P. Bossuet, 1937. 158p.

AUSTRALIA

1688
WYNNE, Edward Cyril. Racial Discrimination in the Attitude of Australia towards the Japanese. Harvard, 1927. 265p; 371p. (2v.) AB: Harvard University. Summaries of Theses...1927. p.102-06.

Focuses on the legal measures employed by Australia *ca*. 1894-*ca*. 1905 to restrict Japanese immigration.

Rel.Publ.: Immigration Laws: Australia, Canada, New Zealand, and Japan [by] George G. Wilson and Edward C. Wynne. Cambridge: Harvard University Press, 1926(?). 122p.

CANADA

1689
KING, William Lyon Mackenzie. Oriental Immigration to Canada. Harvard, 1909. Diss. ms. unavailable.

The contents of pt. 1, "Immigration from Japan" (p.17-68): The Regulation of emigration in Japan; The Immigration of Previous years [1901-1906]; The Immigration of 1907; The Tokio Emigration Company and the Canadian Nippon Supply Company; The Alleged Connection of the Grand Trunk Pacific; The Immigration from Hawaii; The Immigration from Other Sources.

Rel.Publ.: Report of the Royal Commission Appointed to Inquire into the Methods by which Oriental Labourers Have Been Induced to Come to Canada. Ottawa: Government Printing Bureau, 1908. 81p.

1690
CHÊNG, Tien-fang. Oriental Immigration to Canada. Toronto, 1926. x, 306p.

An historical and political survey of Oriental immigration to Canada and a study of the economic and social conditions of the Oriental immigrants there. See especially chapters 5-6 for information on Japanese immigration before and after 1908.

Rel.Publ.: Oriental Immigration in Canada. Shanghai: Commercial Press, 1931. x, 306p.

1691
WOODSWORTH, Charles James. Canada and the Far East. London, 1940. vii, 359p.

A study of Canadian ties with East Asia between the mid-1800's and the late 1930's. Much of the dissertation deals with Chinese and Japanese immigration to Canada and with Canada's "Oriental problem" in the province of British Columbia. Also includes information on Canada's political and commercial relations with Japan and China and a section on Canadian missionary influence in those countries.

Rel.Publ.: Canada and the Orient: A Study in International Relations. Toronto: Macmillan, 1941. xii, 321p.; "Canada and the Far East," FES, 10 (July 28, 1941), 159-64.

1692
HOCKIN, Margaret Lillian. A Study of the Process of Acculturation as Revealed in Canadian Japanese Family Life. Cornell, 1949. 536p.

Studies the behavior of the issei and nisei generations of the Suzuki-Namba family, focusing on the manner and degree of their deviation from Japanese cultural expectations and on trends in their behavior during periods of acculturation.

1693
STEWART, John Benjamin. Parliament and Executive in Wartime Canada, 1939-1945. Columbia, 1953. 281p. DA 14 (Jan. 1954), 173-74; UM 6717.

In one portion of the thesis, "the importance of the [wartime] power devolved upon Ministers and their assistants is illustrated by noting the modifications in the customary rights of the subject concerning freedom of speech and publication association, movement, and freedom of the person made in three instances," one of which was the discriminatory treatment of Japanese Canadians. See especially p.161-75.

1694
ANDRACKI, Stanislaw. The Immigration of Orientals into Canada with Special Reference to Chinese. McGill, 1958. 244p.

Outlines the development of Canada's Chinese immigration policy. The matter of Japanese immigration is dealt with as part of the broader Oriental question. See especially p.78-85 (pre-1903 situation), p.119-22. (Vancouver riots, 1907), p.132-37 (1907-1922 period), p.186-91 (1923-1941 period), and p.215-18 (post World War II Period).

GOWEN, Robert J. Canada's Relations with Japan, 1895-1922: Problems of Immigration and Trade. 1966. See no.1355.

CHINA

For Japanese communities in Manchuria and Taiwan see History--Japanese Empire: Manchoukuo (pages 96-97) and History--Japanese Empire: Taiwan (pages 98-99).

1695
CH'EN, Yao-Sheng. The International Settlement in Shanghai. London, 1940. iv, 531p.

Chapter 12--a discussion of Shanghai's international character--deals with the question of the Japanese community in Shanghai. The author suggests that Japan's domination led to the curtailment of foreign interests, interference with individual rights, general demoralization, and grave international diplomatic conquences.

1696
THOMSON, John Seabury. The Government of the International Settlement at Shanghai: A Study in the Politics of an International Area. Columbia, 1953. 414p. DA 14 (Jan. 1954), 178-79; UM 6722.

A study of "the competition among the national communities for representation on the municipal government and the impact of international power relations on the Shanghai scene." Part of the work focuses on the efforts of the Japanese community during the 1930's to overcome Anglo-American opposition and to win control of the government machinery.

LATIN AMERICA

1697
LOFTIN, Marion Theo. The Japanese in Brazil: A Study in Immigration and Acculturation. Vanderbilt, 1952. 372p. DA 12 (1952), 759; UM 3974.

"The objectives of this study include (1) an analysis of Japanese immigration to Brazil [1903-1941], (2) a description of the location and distribution of the immigrants within the country and of the demographic characteristics of the Japanese element in the Brazilian population, and (3) an analysis of certain aspects of acculturation among the immigrants and their descendants."

1698
TIGNER, James Lawrence. The Okinawans in Latin America. Stanford, 1956. 683p. DA 16(Oct. 1956), 1894-95; UM 17,742.

A study of Okinawan emigration, 1900-1940, with focus on the historical development of Okinawan communities in Argentina, Bolivia, Brazil, Mexico, and Peru, and with a study of contemporary conditions (economic status, demographic situation, social and political behavior, degree of assimilation and acculturation, etc.) and of settlement possibilities there. While the dissertation deals primarily with the former residents of pre-war Okinawa, it also includes important information about non-Ryukyuan Japanese in Latin America. Fully two-thirds of the entire dissertation is devoted to the Okinawan population in Brazil.

Rel.Publ: The Okinawans in Latin America: Investigation of Okinawan Communities in Latin America, with Exploration of Settlement Possibilities. Washington: Pacific Science Board, National Research Council, 1954. xx, 656p. (Its Scientific Investigations in the Ryukyu Islands Report, 7); "The Ryukyuans in Bolivia," Hispanic American Historical Review, 43 (May 1963), 206-29; "The Ryukyuans in Argentina," Hispanic American Historical Review, 47 (May 1967), 203-24.

1699
STEWART, Norman Reginald. Japanese Colonization in Eastern Paraguay: A Study in the Cultural Geography of Pioneer Agricultural Settlement. California, Los Angeles, 1963. 485p. DA 25 (Mar. 1965), 5208-09; UM 64-5557.

A case study of the pioneer agricultural colony of La Colmena with descriptions of its land use and land occupance patterns and with an analysis of the cultural changes that have occurred within the immigrant community as it has adapted to the physical and cultural environment of Paraguay.

Rel.Publ.: Japanese Colonization in Eastern Paraguay. Washington, D.C.: National Academy of Sciences, National Research Council, 1967. 202p. (Foreign Field Research Program, Report no.30); "Recent Trends in Paraguayan Immigration and Pioneer Settlement," Geographical Review, 51 (July 1961), 431-33; "Foreign Agricultural Colonization as a Study in Cultural Geography," Professional Geographer 15 (Sept. 1963), 1-5.

1700
STANIFORD, Philip. Political Organization in a North Brazilian Community: With Special Reference to Japanese Immigrants. London, 1967. iv, 247p.

A study of the Japanese community of Tomé-Açú in Pará State. Discusses the varying sorts of social grouping within the isolated Japanese community: the family as primary and politically limiting; the "aggregates" of immigrants formed by situation rather than by shared interest; the purposive association; and the community networks. Within this context the labor exchange and the political organization are given specific attention.

1701
VIEIRA, Francisca Isabel Schurig. A Absorçao de Japones em Marilia [The Absorption of Japanese in Marilia]. São Paulo (Brazil), 1967. v, 276p. Text in Portuguese. For microfilm copies, contact: Dr. Nettie Lee Benson, Librarian; Latin American Collections; University of Texas; Austin, Texas 78712.

An anthropological study of the Japanese in Marilia, a city in the state of São Paulo, Brazil. Part one of the work focuses on the immigration of Japanese settlers to the state of São Paulo. It includes a discussion of the activities of early emigration companies and information on Japanese settlement during the period 1925-1941, when there was considerable Japanese capital investment in the area. Part 2 focuses on the Japanese ethnic group in Marilia during the years 1964-1966: the various factors influencing the system of marriage, the family, and various ethnic associations; the organization of the family, the maintenance of the family work force, and patterns of family entrepreneurial organization; and the system of marriage as a mechanism of reinforcement of ethnic solidarity through intra-ethnic marriage alliances.

UNITED STATES

General

1702
KUKI, Basil Ichizo. Anthropological Study of the Japanese in the United States. New York, 1914. 165p.

The author's investigation included a study of (1) the ethnic characteristics of the Japanese male adult, (2) physical characteristics of infants and adults, (3) physical growth in relation to education, place of growth, father's occupation, and one's own occupation, (4) physical growth in relation to the mother's age when one was born, the difference in age of the two parents, and whether one was the oldest child or not, and (5) child birth and death rates in relation to the mother's age at marriage.

1703
STEINER, Jesse Frederick. The Japanese Invasion: A Study in the Psychology of Inter-racial Contacts. Chicago, 1915. 231p.

A psychological study of the racial aspects of Japanese immigration to the United States, with emphasis on "the changing mental attitudes of the Japanese immigrants and on their reaction to the race prejudice they are compelled to face."

Rel.Publ.: The Japanese...Contacts. Chicago: A.C. McClung, 1917. 231p.

1704
DARSIE, Marvin Lloyd. The Mental Capacity of American-Born Japanese Children. Stanford, 1924. 210p.

Contents: Introduction, Methodology, and General Results; Performance of Japanese Children in the Separate Tests of the Stanford-Binet Scale; Analysis of Binet and Beta Results; Mental Capacity as Associated with Environment; Teachers' Estimates of Japanese; Comparative Mental Capacity of Orientals.

Rel.Publ.: The Mental...Children. Baltimore: Williams & Wilkins, 1926. 89p. Comparative Psychology Monographs. v.3, ser.no.15)

1705
SAVOY, Prew. La Question japonaise aux États-Unis [The Japanese Question in the United States]. Paris, 1924. Text in French.

Contents: Pt.1: Historical Survey: From Early Times to the Twentieth Century; Immigration and Japanese-American Relations. Pt.2: Judicial Questions: The Japanese and the Naturalization of Foreigners in the United States; The Alien Land Laws (Do the Alien Land Laws Violate the 1911 Treaty or the 14th Amendment of the Constitution?); The Power to Make Treaties and the Alien Land Law. Pt.3: Critical Examination of the Social and Economic Bases: Population and the Gentlemen's Agreement; Japanese Possessions and Economic Power; Assimilation.

Rel.Publ.: La Question...États-Unis. Paris: E. de Boccard, 1924. 256p.

1706
PAN, Nai-wei. L'Immigration asiatique aux États-Unis d'Amérique [Asian Immigration to the United States]. Lyon, 1926. Text in French.

A Study of immigration to the United States from China, Japan, and other Asian countries. Contents: The History of Asian Immigration to the United States; The Immigrant Exclusion Law of May 24, 1924; The Exclusion of Asians Seen from an Economic Viewpoint; The Exclusion of Asians Seen from the Viewpoint of International Politics.

Rel.Publ.: L'Immigration...d'Amérique. Lyon: Bosc, frères M. & L. Riou, 1926. 163p.

1707
YOSHITOMI, Masaomi. Les Conflits nippo-américains sur l'immigration japonaise [The Japanese-American Conflict over Japanese Immigration]. Bordeaux, 1926. Text in French.

A descriptive and critical study of anti-Japanese sentiment in the United States (1853-1925) with consideration of sociological, economic, political, and legal factors.

Rel.Publ.: Les Conflits nippo-américains et le problème du Pacifique. Paris: A. Pedone, 1926.

1708
GARIS, Roy Lawrence. Immigration Restriction: A Study of the Opposition to and Regulation of Immigration into the United States. Columbia, 1927. xv, 376p.

Ch.10 studies the problem of Japanese immigration (p.308-55).

Rel.Publ.: Immigration...States. New York: Macmillan, 1927. xv, 376p.

1709
WU, Charles Ling. Attitudes towards Negroes, Jews, and Orientals in the United States. Ohio State, 1927. 442p.

See Ch.5, "Attitudes towards Orientals" (p.216-74), which deals with attitudes towards the West Coast Japanese and Chinese communities.

Rel.Publ.: Attitudes...States. Columbus, Ohio: H.L. Hendrick, 1930. 13p. (Abstract).

1710
ROSS, Verne Ralph. The Relation between Intelligence, Scholastic Achievement, and Musical Talent of Three Racial Groups. Southern California, 1931. 285p.

Compares 365 Japanese-American children with 427 American Indian and 1541 White American children. Concludes that "the musical talent of the Japanese children as measured by the Seashore test compares favorably at all grade levels with that of the whites."

Rel.Publ.: Relationship between Intelligence, Achievement, and Musical Talent. Claremont, Calif.: California Bureau of Juvenile Research, 1937. ix, 37p.; "Musical Tests of Indian and Japanese Children," Journal of Juvenile Research, 20 (July 1936), 47-64.

1711
BELL, Reginald. A Study of the Educational Effects of Segregation upon Japanese Children in American Schools. Stanford, 1932. 203p. AB: Stanford University. Abstracts of Dissertations. 1932/1933. p.15-18.

"The population studied was made up of the school children of Japanese parentage, prevailingly American born, in the third to the eight grades in eight school districts."

Rel.Publ.: Public School Education of Second-Generation Japanese in California. Stanford: Stanford University Press, 1935. 116p. (Stanford University Publications. University Series. Education-Psychology, v.1, no.3); Educational Status of Japanese Americans in California. Stanford: Stanford University Press, 1933. 94p.

1712
PAJUS, Jean. The Real Japanese California. Dijon, 1937.

Contents: Immigration; Restrictive Legislation; Japanese Land Holdings; Legislation Affecting Use and Tenure: Urban Activities; Educational and Economic Status.

Rel.Publ.: The Real...California. Berkeley, Calif.: J.J. Gillick, 1937. xii, 275p.

1713
HALE, Robert Moffett. The United States and Japanese Immigration. Chicago, 1945. ii, 188p.

Contents: From Perry to the Portsmouth Conference; The Gentlemen's Agreement; The 1913 California Alien Land Law; The War Years and After; The Johnson Immigration Act of 1924; Wanted: A Quota for Japan.

1714
NETTLER, Gwynne. The Relationship between Attitude and Information Concerning the Japanese in America. Stanford, 1945. 290p. AB: Stanford University. Abstracts of Dissertations, 1945/46. p.141-44.

Attempts to determine the extent to which attitudes towards Japanese-Americans held by Caucasian Americans are a function of knowledge. Attitudes are measured according to the Thurstone method of equal-appearing intervals.

Rel.Publ.: "The Relationship between Attitude and Information Concerning the Japanese in America," American Sociological Review, 11 (Apr. 1946), 177-91; "The Measurement of Attitudes toward the Japanese in America" [by] Gwynne Netler and Elizabeth H. Golding, American Journal of Sociology, 52 (July 1946), 31-39.

1715
LA VIOLETTE, Forrest Emmanuel. Americans of Japanese Ancestry: A Study of Assimilation in the American Community. Chicago, 1946. xi, 185p.

Based upon research which the author conducted in West Coast communities between 1934 and 1942, the dissertation studies "the social context of the term 'nisei' as it had developed between the cessation of immigration in 1924 and Pearl Harbor in 1941, with the chief emphasis placed upon Japanese family and community life." Contents: The Japanese Family; The Japanese Community; The Vocational Problem; Meeting the Vocational Problem; Problems of Marriage; Community Problems; Discrimination and Feelings of Inferiority; Assimilation.

Rel.Publ.: Americans...Community. Toronto: Canadian Institute of International Affairs, 1946. xi, 185p.

1716
HENRY, Burton. The Intercultural Knowledge and Attitudes of Prospective Teachers in the United States. Southern California, 1948. 423p. AB: University of Southern California. Abstracts of Dissertations for... 1948. p.109-14.

A study of attitudes towards minority groups in the United States, among them Japanese-Americans.

1717
CAUDILL, William Abel. Japanese-American Acculturation and Personality. Chicago, 1950. 364p.

Studies the social structure, behavior patterns, and personality configurations of Japanese immigrants to the United States and of second-generation Japanese-Americans.

Rel.Publ.: Japanese-American Personality and Acculturation. Provincetown, Mass.: Journal Press, 1952. 102p. (Genetic Psychology Monographs, 45); "Achievement, Culture, and Personality: The Case of the Japanese Americans" [by] William Caudill and George DeVos, American Anthropologist, 58 (Dec. 1956), 1102-26; "Personal and Cultural Factors in the Treatment of a Nisei Man" [by] Charlotte G. Babcock and William Caudill, in Clinical Studies in Culture Conflict. ed. by Georgene Seward (New York: Ronald Press, 1958), 409-48.

1718
DE VOS, George Alphonse. Acculturation and Personality Structure: A Rorschach Study of Japanese Americans. Chicago, 1951. 309p.

The study starts with a sketch of the nature of traditional Japanese society and of Japanese-American acculturation. Pt.2 discusses the use of the Rorschach technique in cross-cultural research. Pt.3 examines the prevalent personality attributes of Japanese Americans: patterns of rigidity, intellectual organization, ego controls, control mechanisms, and affective loadings.

Rel.Publ.: "A Comparison of the Personality Differences in Two Generations of Japanese Americans by Means of the Rorschach Test," Nagoya Journal of Medical Science, 17 (1954), 153-265; "A Quantitative Rorschach Assessment of Maladjustment and Rigidity in Acculturating Japanese Americans," Genetic Psychology Monographs (Provincetown, Mass.), 52 (1955), 51-87; "Achievement, Culture, and Personality: The Case of the Japanese Americans" [by] William Caudill and George DeVos, American Anthropologist, 58 (Dec. 1956), 1102-26.

1719
KIMURA, Yukiko. A Comparative Study of the Collective Adjustment of the Issei, the First Generation Japanese, in Hawaii and in the Mainland United States since Pearl Harbor. Chicago, 1952. 510p.

"Emphasis is placed on the development of a corporate self-image as an ethnic group in 3 different social environments." The comparison is not only spatial, between Hawaii and the West Coast, but also temporal, comparing the adjustment before, during, and after the war.

TAKAKI, Tori. The Treatment of Japan and Peoples of Japanese Descent in Senior High School American History Textbooks. 1954. See no.1436.

1720
ISHIDA, Gladys. The Japanese-American Renunciants of Okayama Prefecture: Their Accomodation and Assimilation to Japanese Culture. Michigan, 1956. 339p. DA 17 (June 1957), 1406-07; UM 21,138.

"Describes and interprets the behavior and adjustment...of those persons of Japanese ancestry...who renounced their citizenship while still in the United States and then went to live in post-war Japan." Contents: The Background of the Japanese on the West Coast from the Frontier Period to the Relocation Period; The Relocation and Segregation Sectors; The Assimilation of the Kibei Renunciants in Okayama Prefecture; The Accomodation of the Nisei in Japan.

KACHI, Teruko O. The Treaty of 1911 and the Immigration and Alien Land Law Issue between the United States and Japan, 1911-1913. 1957. See no.1379.

1721
THOMPSON, Richard Austin. The "Yellow Peril," 1890-1924. Wisconsin, 1957. 510p. DA 17 (Nov. 1957), 2589; UM 24,331.

An examination of the fears caused by increasing Japanese and Chinese immigration to Hawaii and to the West Coast as "expressed in the United States between 1890 and 1924 under the general heading of the 'yellow peril'."

1722
ABE, Stephen Kiyoshi. Nisei Personality Characteristics as Measured by the Edwards Personal Preference Schedule and Minnesota Multiphasic Personality Inventory. Utah, 1958. 100p. DA 19 (Apr. 1959), 2648; UM 58-7942.

This study is based on the results of tests taken by 207 adult Nisei men and women from several Western states. The author tentatively concludes that "cultural variables have been a dominant factor in the personality development of Nisei" and that "as a result, they tend to have a closer identification with each other than with their respective sexual counterparts in the Normative Samples."

1723
GRAHAM, Lloyd Barner. The Adoption of Children from Japan by American Families, 1952-1955. Toronto, 1958. 285p.

Contents: The Method of the Study; Orphan Immigration Legislation and Children Admitted from Japan; The Circumstances of the Children prior to Adoptive Placement; The Adoptive Parents in General and "Non-Proxy" Parents in Particular; Adoption by Couples Living in the United States; The Situation of the Children since Their Arrival in the United States.

1724
KNUTH, Helen Elizabeth. The Climax of American Anglo-Saxonism 1898-1905. Northwestern, 1958. 348p. DA 19 (Dec. 1958), 1355-56; UM 58-5763.

Includes a discussion of "the opposition to oriental immigration and the fear of the yellow peril in America and in Asia."

1725
BARGELT, Hal James. An Experimental Investigation of the Intelligibility of Japanese-Born American-Speaking Male College Students. Southern California, 1959. 172p. DA 20 (Nov. 1959), 1895; UM 59-3505.

The author sought to determine whether characteristically Japanese vowel, consonant, and nonarticulatory speech errors equally affect the intelligibility of acquired American speech of Japanese-born male students.

1726
HONG, Sung-chick. Majority Perception of Minority Behavior and Its Relationship to Hostility toward Ethnic Minorities: A Test of George A. Lundberg's Hypotheses. Washington, Seattle, 1959. 217p. DA 20 (June 1960), 4748-49; UM 60-858.

Explores the attitudes held by University of Washington students toward eighteen different groups including the Japanese-American minority.

1727
HUMISTON, Thomas Frederick. Participation of Ethnic Groups in Student Activities at a Junior College. Stanford, 1959. 149p. DA 20 (Feb. 1960), 3424-25; UM 59-3665.

The representative sample group included 31 Japanese-Americans.

1728
STEMEN, John Roger. The Diplomacy of the Immigration Issue: A Study in Japanese-American Relations, 1894-1941. Indiana, 1960. 355p. DA 21 (Mar. 1961), 2697; UM 60-6330.

"Largely an account of actions taken by the Japanese Government on behalf of Japanese subjects who were deprived of or denied real or potential rights and privileges by various governments and governmental agencies in the United States."

1729
LYMAN, Stanford Morris. The Structure of Chinese Society in Nineteenth-Century America. California, Berkeley, 1961. 439p.

Compares the isolation and communal life of the Chinese in the United States with the rapid acculturation and integration of the Japanese.

Rel.Publ.: The Oriental in North America. Vancouver, B.C.: University of British Columbia, 1962.(11 v. in 1) (University Extension Series. Lectures no.1-11)

1730
GOLDEN, Loretta. The Treatment of Minority Groups in Primary Social Studies Textbooks. Stanford, 1964. 352p. DA 25 (Jan. 1965), 3912; UM 64-13,549.

Orientals in the United States were among the five minority groups studied.

1731
GAST, David Karl. Characteristics and Concepts of Minority Americans in Contemporary Children's Fictional Literature. Arizona State, 1965. 206p. DA 27 (Aug. 1966), 390-91-A. UM 66-6902.

Japanese-Americans are included.

1732
KUROKAWA, Minako. Acculturation and Childhood Accidents among Chinese- and Japanese-Americans. California, Berkeley, 1967. 422p. DA 28 (May 1968), 4726-A; UM 68-5754.

Studies the sociocultural factors rather than the personality factors "that are related to the incidence and types of childhood accidents in different cultural and social groups." Particular focus is on Oriental children resident in California.

Rel.Publ.: Acculturation and Childhood Accidents among Chinese and Japanese Americans. Provincetown, Mass.: Provincetown Journal Press, 1969. (Genetic Psychology Monographs, 79).

1733
OGAWA, Dennis Masaaki. Small Group Communication Stereotypes and Actual Communicative Behavior of Japanese Americans in Discussion. California, Los Angeles, 1969. 194p. DA 30 (May 1970), UM 70-8183.

Contents: Stereotype: Definition and Research; Research Objectives; Research: Phase 1 Methodology and Results; Research: Phase II Methodology; Results: Phase II Research; Explanation of Results; General Interpretation of Phase II Results; Projected Research and Implications of the Study.

Hawaii

1734
LIND, Andrew William. Economic Succession and Racial Invasion in Hawaii. Chicago, 1931. 434p.

Includes information on Japanese immigration to Hawaii.

Rel.Publ.: Economic...Hawaii. Chicago: University of Chicago Press, 1936. ("Private edition, distributed by the University of Chicago libraries."); "Occupational Attitudes of Orientals in Hawaii, "Sociology and Social Research, 12 (Jan./Feb. 1929), 244-45.

1735
LIVESAY, Thayne Miller. A Study of Public Education in Hawaii with Special Reference to the Pupil Population. Washington, Seattle, 1931. AB: University of Washington. Digests of Theses, 1914-1931. p.103-09.

Presents considerable information throughout the dissertation on the Japanese-American school population.

Rel.Publ.: A Study...Population. Honolulu: University of Hawaii, 1932. vii, 120p. (University of Hawaii. Research Publications, 7).

1736
MIDKIFF. Frank Elbert. Economic Determinants of Education in Hawaii. Yale, 1935. 429p.

A study of the economic and social factors influencing the various racial groups in Hawaii that seek to appraise the effectiveness of education as a factor of social change. References to the Japanese occur throughout, and chapter 2, "The Social Status of the Peoples of Hawaii," and chapter 3, "The Effects of Economics upon Social Conditions," both contain analyses by race.

1737
LADENSON, Alex. The Japanese in Hawaii. Chicago, 1938. 205p.

Describes Japanese immigration to and settlement in Hawaii and studies the economic evolution and assimilation of the immigrants. Covers the period 1884-1924.

Rel.Publ.: "The Background of the Hawaiian-Japanese Labor Convention of 1886," PHR, 9 (Dec. 1940), 389-400.

1738
LEITER, Russell Graydon. A Comparative Study of the General Intelligence of Caucasian, Chinese, and Japanese Children as Measured by the Leiter International Performance Scale. Southern California, 1938. 618p. AB: University of Southern California. Abstracts of Dissertations for...1938. p.25-29.

Compares two Oriental groups living in Hawaii with a Caucasian group in Los Angeles.

1739
MASUOKA, Jitsuichi. The Westernization of the Japanese Family in Hawaii. Iowa, 1940. 326p. AB: University of Iowa. Doctoral Dissertations, Abstracts, and References. v.4, p.355-61.

Describes the manner in which the traditional Japanese family organization in Hawaii has been breaking down in response to Western cultural, economic, and moral forces and how it has been evolving into a husband-wife centered unit.

Rel.Publ.: "The Changing Moral Basis of the Japanese Family in Hawaii, "Sociology and Social Research, (Nov./Dec. 1936), 158-69; "The Japanese Patriarch in Hawaii," Social Forces, 17 (Dec. 1938), 240-48; "The Structure of the Japanese Family in Hawaii," American Journal of Sociology, 46 (Sept. 1940), 168-78; "The Life Cycle of an Immigrant Institution in Hawaii: The Family," Social Forces, 23 (Oct. 1944), 60-64; "Changing Food Habits of the Japanese in Hawaii," American Sociological Review, 10 (Dec. 1945), 759-65.

1740
LARRY, Etta Cynthia. A Study of the Sounds of the English Language as Spoken by Five Racial Groups in the Hawaiian Islands. Columbia, 1942. iv, 79p.

"Determines the characteristic production of the sounds of the English language as spoken by the descendants of five...racial groups living on Oahu...including the Japanese."

Rel.Publ.: A Study...Islands. New York: 1942. iv, 79p.

1741
CONROY, Francis Hilary. The Japanese Expansion into Hawaii, 1868-1898. California, Berkeley, 1949. 310p.

A study of the interaction of the Japanese and the Americans in Hawaii before its annexation by the United States.

Rel.Publ.: The Japanese Frontier in Hawaii, 1868-1898. Berkeley: University of California Press, 1953. vi, 175p. (University of California Publications in History, 46).

1742
BITNER, Harold Miller. Ethnic Inter-Group Differences in Personality, General Culture, Academic Ability, and Interests in a Geographically Restricted Area. Ohio State, 1954. 135p. DA 20 (Aug. 1959), 772-74; UM 59-2543.

The subject group--freshmen at the University of Hawaii (1948)--included 409 Japanese-Americans.

1743
KAWAHARA, Hatsuko Furuhashi. An Interpretation of Cultural Factors Affecting Child-Parent Relationships and Its Use in Improving Relations. Columbia (Teachers College), 1954. 110p.

A study of child-parent relationships among Japanese-Americans in Hawaii, with emphasis on generational change and acculturation.

1744
ALLER, Curtis Cosmos, Jr. Evolution of Hawaiian Labor Relations: From Benevolent Paternalism to Mature Collective Bargaining. Harvard, 1958. xii, 676p. AB: 5p.

summary appended to diss. ms.

Frequent reference is made to the Japanese as sugar plantation workers during the nineteenth and twentieth centuries.

Rel.Publ.: Labor Relations in the Hawaiian Sugar Industry. Berkeley: Institute of Industrial Relations, University of California, 1957. viii, 108p.

1745
DEDMON, Donald Newton. An Analysis of the Arguments in the Debate in Congress on the Admission of Hawaii to the Union. Iowa, 1961. 487p. DA 22 (Nov. 1961), 1744-45; UM 61-4024.

The congressional debate, 1935-1959, centered around the issue whether statehood should be given to a territory whose population was predominantly oriental.

1746
VOSS, Harwin LeRoy. Insulation and Vulnerability to Delinquency: A Comparison of the Hawaiians and Japanese. Wisconsin, 1961. 486p. DA 22 (Dec. 1961), 2100; UM 61-6013.

Attempts to determine whether the differential involvement of Japanese residents in Hawaii and of Hawaiians in juvenile delinquency is due to differences in self conception and in association.

1747
STUEBER, Ralph Kant. Hawaii: A Case Study in Development Education 1778-1960. Wisconsin, 1964. 422p. DA 25 (Jan. 1965), 3959-60; UM 64-13,927.

The impact of Japanese-Americans residing in Hawaii on local educational developments is included.

1748
WITTERMANS-PINO, Elizabeth. Inter-Ethnic Relations in a Plural Society. Leiden, 1964. viii, 180p.

A study of race relations--past and present--in Hawaii. References to the Japanese living in Hawaii are found throughout much of the dissertation. Contents: The Social Structure of Hawaii in Historical Perspective; Hawaiian Society at Present; A Plural Society and Its Ideology; Ideology and Practice; The Dynamics of Inter-Ethnic Relations.

Rel.Publ.: Inter-Ethnic...Society. Groningen: J. B. Wolters, 1964. viii, 180p.

1749
SAKUMOTO, Raymond Eiji. Social Areas of Honolulu: A Study of the Ethnic Dimensions in an Urban Social Structure. Northwestern, 1965. 166p. DA 26 (Dec. 1965), 3523-24; UM 65-12,159.

Contents: The Problem; Social Scale and Ethnic Differentiation in Hawaii; Ethnic Differentiation and Residential Segregation; Empirical Identification of the Ethnic Dimension by Means of Factor Analysis; Urban Differentiation and Political Behavior; Summary and Conclusions. The Shevsky-Bell Method of social area analysis is applied in the study.

1750
FULTZ, Jane Nakano. A Study of Status Systems and Related Value Orientations among Adolescents of an Ethnically Plural High School Community in Hawaii. New York, 1966. 176p. DA 27 (May 1967), 3772-A; UM 67-4920.

"Subjects of the study consisted predominantly of 17 year olds of second generation Japanese (55%), cosmopolitan (20%), and Chinese (11%) background in Hawaii."

1751
GARSIDE, Jayne Gillette. A Cross-Cultural Comparison of Personality. Brigham Young, 1966. 66p. DA 26 (Apr. 1966), 5864; UM 65-14,604.

The study was designed "to determine personality differences among Polynesian, Oriental, and Caucasian college students [at the Church College of Hawaii] as measured by scales of the MMPI." Many of the Oriental subjects were Japanese-Americans.

1752
RICHSTAD, Jim Andrew. The Press and the Courts under Martial Rule in Hawaii during World War II: From Pearl Harbor to Duncan v. Kahanamoku. Minesota, 1967. 425p. DA 28 (Dec. 1967), 2197-A; UM 67-14,643.

Contents: Introduction and Prewar Hawaii; Hawaii after Pearl Harbor; The Press under Military Control; The impact of Military Control; Military Courts and Early Habeas Corpus Cases; Ex Parte Duncan; Duncan v. Kahanamoku.

1753
HARTLE, Helen Weisner. An Analysis of Certain Achievement Patterns of Four Language Speaking Groups of Sixth Grade Students in Hawaii. State University of New York at Albany, 1968. 266p. DA 29 (May 1969), 3913-A; UM 69-6690.

The study sample--722 Sixth grade students from the Waianae-Campbell complex of the Leeward Oahu School District--included students who spoke Japanese first and who used English as a second language. The author notes that it is a common practice among Japanese and Chinese students to attend language classes after school to maintain proficiency in their first languages.

1754
IGE, Philip Keimin. Paradise and Melting Pot in the Fiction and Nonfiction of Hawaii: A Study of Cross-cultural Record. Columbia (Teachers College), 1968. vi, 677p.

See especially Ch.8, "The Melting Pot Image: Duality of Vision in Contemporary Hawaiian Fiction, 1900-1959" (p.360-532), and Ch.9 "The Melting Pot Image: Duality of Vision in the Factual Record of Hawaii, 1900-1959" (p.533-654).

1755
NAGASAWA, Arthur. The Governance of Hawaii from Annexation to 1908: Major Problems and Developments. Denver, 1968. 339p. DA 29 (Apr. 1969), 3563-A; UM 69-7013.

Information on the Japanese in Hawaii is included.

1756
MEREDITH, Gerald Marvin. Acculturation and Personality among Japanese-American College Students in Hawaii. Hawaii, 1969. 104p. DA 30 (June 1970); UM 70-9975.

1757
NAGARA, Susumu. A Bilingual Description of Some Linguistic Features of Pidgin English Used by Japanese Immigrants on the Plantations of Hawaii: A Case Study in Bilingualism. Wisconsin, 1969. 605p. DA 30 (June 1970), UM 69-22,449.

Includes an investigation of the psychological capacity that an immigrant must have to be bilingual in English and Japanese. Appendices: (1) "Brief History of Language Contacts in Hawaii, 1778-Present;" (2) "Number of Speakers of Japanese Dialects in Hawaii in 1924 and 1960."

Mainland

See also Overseas Japanese Communities--United States: wartime evacuation and internment (pages 206-07).

1758
ICHIHASHI, Yamato. Emigration from Japan and Japanese Immigration into the State of California. Harvard, 1914. vi, 427p.

Contents: History of Early Japanese Emigration; History of Modern Japanese Colonization; History of Modern Japanese Emigration; Japanese Immigration to the United States; Japanese in the City Trades of California; Japanese Farmers and Farm Hands in California; Channels for Assimilation; Anti-Japanese Agitation; Causes of Japanese Emigration; Population and Emigration; Effects of Japanese Emigration.

Rel.Publ: Japanese Immigration: Its Status in California. San Francisco: Japanese Association of America, 1913. iii, 48p.; Japanese in the United States: A Critical Study of the Problems of the Japanese Immigrants and Their Children. Palo Alto: Stanford University Press, 1932. x, 426p.

1759
REYNOLDS, Charles Nathan. Oriental-White Race Relations in Santa Clara County, California. Stanford, 1927. 396p. AB: Stanford University. Abstracts of Dissertations, 1926/1927. p.182-88

A study of the relations existing between the Japanese and Chinese residents of Santa Clara County and their Caucasian neighbors, 1912-1927. Particular emphasis has been placed on news material found in the San Jose Mercury Herald.

1760
THOMSON, Ruth Haines. Events Leading to the Order to Segregate Japanese Pupils in the San Francisco Public Schools. Stanford, 1931. 176p. AB: Stanford University. Abstracts of Dissertations, 1931/1932. p.43-45.

A study of events leading to the local Board of Education's segregation order of October 11, 1906, which resulted in international controversy and was rescinded in March 1907. The author concludes that the order "was inspired by racial antagonism and economic fear; was promulgated by labor through all of its organizations; was sponsored by Mayor Schmitz as a means of insuring labor support and distracting public attention from administrative graft; was passed by the Board of Education, a tool of the mayor; and was repealed by that body when expediency demanded."

1761
LUKE, Orral Stanford. Differences in Musical Aptitude in School Children of Different National and Racial Origin. California, Berkeley, 1939. 157p.

Attempts to determine the comparative aptitude among five junior high school groups in the San Francisco area (one being Japanese) in pitch discrimination, musical memory, and tonal memory. In this manner, the author seeks to measure quantitatively the intellectual, perceptual, and sensory aspects of music appreciation for each of the groups.

1762
RADEMAKER, John Adrian. The Ecological Position of the Japanese Farmers in the State of Washington. Washington, Seattle, 1939. 377p. AB: University of Washington. Abstracts of Theses and Faculty Bibliography. v.5. p.331-36.

A study of the relationships of local Japanese farmers with the inhabitants and with the natural resources of the state of Washington. Contents: The Cultural Conditions of Land Holding by Japanese Farmers; Significance of the Land Acts to Dynamics of Position; The Division of Labor as a Definition of the Position of Japanese Farmers in the State of Washington; Spacial Distribution of Japanese Farmers; Temporal Factors in the Sustenance Relations of Japanese Farmers.

1763
McENTIRE, Davis. An Economic and Social Study of Population Movements in California, 1850-1944. Havard, 1947. ix, 635p. AB: 5p. Summary appended to diss. ms.

Includes information on Japanese immigration to and life in California. See especially Ch.8, "The Composition of the Population," Ch.14, "Occupational Opportunities of Minority Racial Groups," and the supplement entitled "Ways of Living in California: Racially Distinct Groups: The Japanese in California."

1764
UYEKI, Eugene Shigemi. Process and Patterns of Nisei Adjustment to Chicago. Chicago, 1953. 295p.

A sample study of the changes in self-conception of Chicago nisei.

1765
BLEYHL. Norris Arthur. A History of the Production and Marketing of Rice in California. Minnesota, 1955. 547p. DA 17 (Mar. 1957), 525; UM 17,893.

Information on Japanese farming in California during the early 1900's and on Japanese pioneering efforts in the production of rice is included. See especially Ch.3, "How Rice Came to be a Significant California Crop."

1766
IGA, Mamoru. Acculturation of Japanese Population in Davis County, Utah. Utah, 1955. ix, 271p.

Contents: Review of Literature (Traditional Japanese Culture, Acculturation Processes and Results); Methodology and Procedure; Presentation of Data; Traditional Japanese Culture (Customs, Values); Analysis and Discussion (Comparison of Japanese Americans according to Generation, Cross-Cultural Groups, Sex Differences; Family Membership: Comparison of the Issei Male Family Members and the Issei Male Nonfamily Members; Language Facility; Religion: Comparison of Christians and Non-Christians of the Same Age Level; Economic Status: Comparison of the Issei who, or whose Family Members, Own Land and the Nonlandowning Issei); Summary.

Rel.Publ.: "The Japanese Social Structure and the Source of Mental Strains of Japanese Immigrants in the United States," Social Forces, 35 (Mar. 1957), 371-78.

1767
WALDRON, Gladys Hennig. Antiforeign Movements in California, 1919-1929. California, Berkeley, 1956. 322p.

Discusses the most prevalent anti-Japanese activities of the decade. These included not only daily social and economic discrimination but also the anti-Japanese actions of California governor William D. Stephens and of publisher V. S. McClatchy as well as the Alien Land Acts and the 1924 National Origins Act.

1768
KESSLER, James Bewley. The Political Factors in California's Anti-Alien Land Legislation, 1912-1913. Stanford, 1958. 221p. DA 19 (Mar. 1959), 2380; UM 59-608.

Studies the role of various groups, personalities, and other factors in the enactment of legislation that prohibited Japanese Americans from owning land and that limited their tenure of the land to which they held leases.

1769
DANIELS, Roger. The Politics of Prejudice: The Anti-Japanese Movement in California and the Struggle for Japanese Exclusion. California, Los Angeles, 1962. Diss. ms. not available.

Contents: The Issei Generation; Labor Takes the Lead; Segregation and Diplomacy; The Progressives Draw the Color Line; The Yellow Peril; The Pressure Groups Take Over; Exclusion in 1924. [Annotation based on the book.]

Rel.Publ.: The Politics...Exclusion. Berkeley: University of California Press, 1962. ix, 165p. (University of California Publications in History, 71)

1770
NISHI, Setsuko Matsunaga. Japanese American Achievement in Chicago: A Cultural Response to Degredation. Chicago, 1963. 454p.

This study examines Japanese American mobility, the role of values in shaping collective adaptation rationale, their institutionalization, and their socialization.

1771
UNO, Raymond S. Japanese Old Age Recipients of the Salt Lake City Welfare Department. Utah, 1963. v, 89p.

Contents: Review of Literature (Aging, The Japanese Culture, The Japanese in Utah); Methodology; Presentation and Analysis of Data (Background, Internment, Income Maintenance, Health and Medical Care, Education and Language, Free Time Activities, Public Assistance, Comparison of Not Lonesome and Lonesome Recipients); Summary, Conclusions, and Recommendations.

1772
BUNCH, Ralph Elliot. The Political Orientations of Japanese Americans. Oregon, 1968. 216p. DA 29 (Sept. 1968), 938-39-A. UM 68-11,946.

"This work is a replication of the survey of Almond and Verba's Civic Culture study applied to a sample of 300 Japanese Americans in the Portland, Oregon, metropolitan area in 1967." It "describes the political attitudes and behavior of the Japanese Americans according to 'orientational categories.'"

1773
KAGIWADA, George. Ethnic Identification and Socio-Economic Status: The Case of the Japanese-Americans in Los Angeles. California, Los Angeles, 1969. 335p. DA 30 (Oct. 1969), 1651-A; UM 69-16,917.

"This study attempted to explore selected aspects of the interrelationship of ethnicity and social stratification using a purposive sample of 178 native-born Japanese-American heads of household in the Los Angeles area." It was concerned in particular with the effects that assimilation have had upon the attitudes and behavior of various individuals.

1774
MODELL, John. The Japanese of Los Angeles: A Study in Growth and Accomodation, 1900-1946. Columbia, 1969. 463p. DA 30 (Apr. 1970); UM 70-7033. [See also addenda entry no.31A.]

Wartime Evacuation and Internment

1775
GRODZINS, Morton Melvin. Political Aspects of the Japanese Evacuation. California, Berkeley, 1945.

Through an examination of public opinion, administrative implementation, and legislative sanctions in 1941-1942, the dissertation determines the process by which the West Coast evacuation became an established federal policy.

Rel.Publ.: Americans Betrayed: Politics and the Japanese Evacuation. Chicago: University of Chicago Press, 1949. xvii, 444p; The Loyal and the Disloyal: Social Boundaries of Patriotism and Treason. Chicago: University of Chicago Press, 1956. x, 320p.

1776
O'BRIEN, Robert William. The Changing Role of the College Nisei during the Crisis Period, 1931-1943. Washington, Seattle, 1945. 215p. AB: University of Washington. Abstracts of Theses and Faculty Bibliography 1945/1946, p.71-73.

Contents: Assimilation of the College Nisei; Reaction of the College Nisei to Japan and Japanese Foreign Policy from 1931 to Pearl Harbor; Changing Role of the College Nisei after Pearl Harbor; The Effects of Relocation Center Life; The Dominance of Loyalty as a Symbol for the College Nisei; The Role of the College Student Relocation in the Dispersion of the Nisei.

Rel.Publ.: The College Nisei. Palo Alto, Calif: Pacific Books, 1949. viii, 165p.

1777
FOX, Rollin Clay. The Secondary School Program at the Manzanar War Relocation Center. California, Los Angeles, 1946. 263p.

Contents: The Background for the Study; The High School Students; The Secondary School Program; Survey of Educational Needs of Japanese Americans; Implications for the Educational Adjustment of Japanese Americans; Summary, Conclusions, and Implication for Education.

1778
LIGHT, Jerome Thomas. The Development of a Junior-Senior High School Program in a Relocation Center for People of Japanese Ancestry during the War with Japan. Stanford, 1947. 549p. + v.2 (appendix). AB: Stanford University. Abstracts of Dissertations, 1946/47. p. 184-87.

Documents the attempts of the high school at the Minidoka Relocation Center, Hunt, Idaho, to "bring about appropriate readjustments among the evacuees to the end that they would make a successful resettlement into normal American communities" after the war.

1779
VICKERY, William Edwin. Prejudice in a Government Policy: The West Coast Evacuation and Its Implications for Intercultural Education. Harvard, 1948. xiii, 478p. 9p. summary appended to diss. ms.

Focuses on the attitudes and behavior of Japanese-Americans on the West Coast, the prejudices of government authorities, and the evacuation itself. Contents: The Term "Prejudice" as a Concept in Social Science; The Development of Government Policy toward the American Japanese, 1941-1942; The Reasons Advanced for Evacuation; Historical Antecedents of the Charges against the American Japanese; The Factual Basis of the "Japanese Menace"; The Necessity for Mass Evacuation; An Analysis of Prejudice: (1) The Role of Rumor in the

Case for Mass Evacuation, (2) Elements of Irrationality in the Evacuation Decision; Prejudice in a Government Policy; Implications of the Evacuation for Intercultural Education.

1780
SAKODA, James Minoru. Minidoka: An Analysis of Changing Patterns of Social Interaction. California, Berkeley, 1949. 429p.
Analyses the changing patterns of social and political interaction in one of the Japanese relocation centers, Minidoka, during World War II.

1781
SMITH, Mildred Joan. Backgrounds, Problems, and Significant Reactions of Relocated Japanese American Students. Syracuse, 1949. 230p.
Contents: Detailed Description of Procedures; Backgrounds of the Japanese American Students; Conditions Affecting the Relocated Students' College Experiences; College Problems of Nisei Students; Some Significant Attitudes of Nisei Students.

1782
MIYAMOTO, Shotaro Frank. The Career of Intergroup Tensions: A Study of the Collective Adjustments of Evacuees to Crises at the Tule Lake Relocation Center. Chicago, 1950. 410p.
A Study of Japanese Americans facing acute stress in the early phases of the establishment of a relocation center. Tension is studied as a process, rather than as a static condition; hence the word "career" in the title.

1783
WAX, Rosalie Hankey. The Development of Authoritatianism: A Comparison of the Japanese-American Relocation Centers and Germany. Chicago, 1950. 277p.
A study of the influences of the deterioration of the life situation in relocation centers upon group action, developing from conservative libertarian to radical authoritarian.

1784
YATSUSHIRO, Toshio. Political and Socio-Cultural Issues at Poston and Manzanar Relocation Centers: A Themal Analysis. Cornell, 1953. 618p.
Contents: Theory and Method; The Pre-War Japanese Community on the West Coast; The Setting; Themes in the Center Culture of the West Coast Japanese.
Rel.Publ.: "The Japanese American Looks at Resettlement," Public Opinion Quarterly, 8 (Summer 1944), 188-201.

1785
JACKMAN, Norman Richard. Collective Protest in Relocation Centers. California, Berkeley, 1955. 251p.
Discusses the nature of collective protest in relocation centers established for the detention of people of Japanese ancestry resident in the United States at the time of the outbreak of the war with Japan. Includes a brief history and description of the ten relocation centers during their existence from 1942 to 1945.
Rel.Publ.: "Collective Protest in Relocation Centers," American Journals of Sociology, 63 (Nov. 1957), 264-72.

1786
NISHI, Midori. Changing Occupance of the Japanese in Los Angeles County, 1940-1950. Washington, Seattle, 1955. 229p. DA 15 (Oct. 1955), 1831, UM 13,000.
Contents: Japanese Migration to the United States; The Japanese in Los Angeles County, 1940; Influence of World War II; Postwar Rural Resettlement and Economy; Postwar Urban Occupance.

1787
PURSINGER, Marvin Gavin. Oregon's Japanese in World War II: A History of Compulsory Relocation. Southern California, 1960. 496p. DA 22 (Mar. 1962), 3179, UM 61-6304.
Concludes that "the uprisings in early 1942 to effect an evacuation and again in early 1945 to prevent the Japanese from returning to their former residences" were the result of "deep-seated prejudices on the part of a very limited number of Oregonians."
Rel.Publ.: "The Japanese Settle in Oregon," Journal of the West, 5 (Apr. 1966), 251-62.

1788
ZELLER, William Dean. The Educational Program Provided the Japanese Americans during the Relocation Period 1942-1945. Michigan State, 1963. 345p. DA 25 (July 1964), 269-70; UM 64-5014.
Describes "the philosophical framework and curriculum development of the schools which were established to educate the nearly 30,000 youngsters of Japanese descent." The thesis is based primarily on a study of the educational and related activities of the War Relocation Authority.

1789
TURNER, Albert Blythe. The Origins and Development of the War Relocation Authority. Duke, 1967. 276p. DA 28 (Apr. 1968), 4108-09-A; UM 68-5248.
A study of the war time relocation of West Coast Japanese-Americans. Focuses on the "economic, social, and political pressures that affected the establishment of the WRA and its subsequent policies and administration."

Japanese Students at American Universities

See also Psychology and Social Psychology (pages 219-20).

1790
GRAHAM, Grace. Foreign Students in an American University. Stanford, 1952. 269p. AB: Stanford University. Abstracts of Dissertations, 1951/1952. p.563-65.
A description and analysis of the social relationships of foreign students --including Japanese--at an American university, *ca*. 1950-1951.

1791
HO, Genevieve Po-ai. Factors Affecting Adaptation to American Dietary Pattern by Students from the Oriental Countries. Pennsylvania State, 1961. 114p. DA 22 (May 1962), 3977-78, UM 62-1719.
Twenty-five (out of 120) subjects were Japanese.

1792
BURROUGHS, Franklin Troy. Foreign Students at U.C.L.A.: A Case-Study in Cross-cultural Education. California, Los Angeles, 1964. 252p. DA 25 (Sept. 1964), 1711, UM 64-8321.
The dissertation studies (1) the types of problems the foreign students (including 624 Japanese foreign

students for the period 1951-1963) have faced, (2) the way in which the university and the community have served the foreign students, and (3) the efforts of the foreign students to effect their own organizations.

1793
BRISTOW, Ronald Milton. English and Native Language Test Score Relationships to College Grade Point Average for Japanese Students. Southern California, 1966. 218p. DA 27 (Jan. 1967), 2062-63-A; UM 67-395.

"The purpose of this research was to investigate the predictive validity in relationship to college grade point averages of the American College Testing Program examination for Japanese students in its original English version as well as a version in which the English subtest was in English and the Mathematics, Social Science, and Science subtests had been translated into Japanese. The test group consisted of sixty-four students of Japanese citizenship attending the California state colleges in the Spring Semester of 1965 and represented a sample of a hypothetical population of Japanese students in these colleges."

1794
SUGIMOTO, Roy Atsuro. The Relationship of Selected Predictive Variables to Foreign Student Achievement at the University of California, Los Angeles. Southern California, 1967. 154p. DA 28 (July 1967), 65-A; UM 67-8032.

"This analytical-descriptive study was designed to discover the relationship between certain items found on forms in admission offices dealing with foreign students and the eventual academic success or lack of success of these students." The study dealt in part with students from Japan.

Political Science

Limited primarily to domestic politics during the postwar era. For dissertations on Japanese foreign relations, see the various subsections under International Relations. For dissertations on domestic political developments before 1945, see History (pages 62-99). Dissertations focusing on the Meiji and the Postwar Constitutions may be found under Law and the Judicial System--constitutions of Japan (pages 180-81), while dissertations on the historical development of these two constitutions are entered respectively under History--Meiji Period: First Half, 1868-1890 (pages 77-80) and Political Science--Allied Occupation (pages 210-14).

GENERAL

1795
POBELENSKII, Ia. A. Bor'ba iaponskogo naroda za mir i nezavisimost', 1949-1955 gg. [The Struggle of the Japanese People for Peace and Independence, 1949-1955]. Kharkov, Khar'kovskii gosudarstvennyi universitet imeni A. M. Gor'kogo, 1959. (Candidate of Historical Sciences degree) 15 + 326 + 24p. Text in Russian. AB: 18p. summary published in 1959.

1796
KURODA, Yasumasa. Political Socialization: Personal Political Organization of Law Students in Japan. Oregon, 1962. 232p. DA 22 (June 1962), 4397; UM 62-2065.

"This is a research report on one aspect of a study of the political socialization of Japanese law students, which is itself a part of a cross-cultural survey that was carried out at the Institute for Community Studies, University of Oregon, on the political socialization of future political leaders. "It seeks to explain the [type and] degree of personal political involvement of Japanese law students" through an analysis of their "ideological orientation, social class, primary groups, career orientation, and personality."

Rel.Publ.: "Agencies of Political Socialization and Political Change: Political Orientation of Japanese Law Students," Human Organization, 24 (Winter 1965), 328-31; "Sociability and Political Involvement," Midwest Journal of Political Science, 9 (May 1965), 133-47. "The Political Cynicism of Law Students in Japan," MN, 22 (1967), 147-61.

1797
PACKARD, George Randolph, III. Japan's Reaction to the American Alliance 1960: A Study of Japan's Political Processes. Fletcher, 1963. xi, 479p.

"The thesis begins with a discussion of the original United States-Japan security treaty and reactions in Japan during 1951-1952 (Ch.1), and then takes up the origins of the treaty revision controversy during 1957-1959 (Ch.2-4). Ch.5 tells of the leftist campaign to prevent the signing of the treaty, Ch.6 of the great debate over ratification, and Ch. 7-8 of the protest after approval in the Lower House, May 19-20, 1960. Ch.9 discusses the political situation in the wake of the crisis, and Ch.10 contains some concluding observations. I have tried throughout to show that the crisis resulted from the convergence of international and domestic forces, and that no simplistic explanation of the causes is acceptable."

1798
HAAS, Michael. Some Societal Correlates of International Political Behavior. Stanford, 1964. 176p. DA 25 (Jan. 1965), 4240-41; UM 64-13,591.

Japan is one of ten countries from which data for the period 1900-1960 has been collected in order "to test the theory that international stresses and strains in social systems lead to warlike behavior." "Five indicators of internal stress and strain--unemployment, industrialization rate (annual per capita kilowatt-hour electricity production increments), suicides, homicides, and deaths due to alcoholism--are correlated with the outbreak of war and with military expenditures."

Rel.Publ.: "Societal Approaches to the Study of War," Journal of Peace Research, 2 (1965), 307-23.

1799
HELLMANN, Donald Charles. Japanese Foreign Policy and Domestic Politics: The Peace Agreement with the Soviet Union. California, Berkeley, 1964. 247p. DA 25 (May 1965), 6738-39; UM 65-3005.

"In analyzing the role of domestic Japanese politics in the negotiation of this agreement, the focus is on the effective influence of the major components in this process: public opinion, the political parties, and the formal governmental institutions concerned with international affairs."

Rel.Publ.: Japanese...Union. Berkeley: University of California Press, 1969. viii, 202p.

1800
NEUBAUER, Deane Edward. On the Theory of Polyarchy: An Empirical Study of Democracy in Ten Countries. Yale, 1965. 252p. DA 27 (July 1966), 232-A; UM 66-4920.

Japan is one of the ten countries studied. See especially Ch.3, "Polyarchal Performance," and the tables scattered throughout the thesis.

Rel.Publ.: "Some Conditions of Democracy," American Political Science Review, 61 (Dec. 1967), 1002-09.

SOARES, Gláucio A. Economic Development and Political Radicalism. 1965. See no.13.

1801
TOMIKAWA, Soji. Impact of Public Opinion on the Postwar Administration of Japan: Problems Connected with the Supplying of Facilities and Areas for Use by United States Forces. Syracuse, 1966. 375p. DA 27 (Nov. 1966), 1418-A; UM 66-9868.

The major case studies presented illustrate the role of important institutions and influences in shaping postwar Japanese public opinion and, in turn, the impact of this public opinion upon the Japanese government. "The case studies include the Uchinada Proving Ground case in 1953, the Sunakawa incident in 1957, the problems involving the revised [United States-Japan] Security Treaty in 1960, the Fuji Maneuver Area problem, LORAN [Long-Range Aid to Navigation] base questions, and the Laotian crisis."

1802
GOUIFFES-LESOUT, Suzanne. L'Information d'État au Japon [State Information in Japan]. Paris, 1967. 453p. Text in French.

1803
SAVEL'EV, V. I. Vysshie organy vlasti Iaponii [The Highest Organs of Government in Japan]. Moscow, Institut gosudarstva i prava Akademii nauk SSSR, 1967. (Candidate of Juridical Sciences degree) 391p. Text in Russian. AB: 20p. summary published in 1967.

LEE, Hongkoo. Social Conservation and Political Development: A Normative Approach to Political Change with Special Reference to Meiji Japan. 1968. See no.582.

1804
MARKOV, A. P. Politika perevooruzheniia Iaponii posle vtoroi mirovoi voiny, 1945-1967 gg. [Japan's Rearmament Policy after the Second World War, 1945-1967]. Moscow, Institut narodov Azii Akademii nauk SSSR, 1968. (Candidate of Historical Sciences degree) 334, x p. Text in Russian.

1805
WEINSTEIN, Martin Emmanuel. Japan's Postwar Defense Policy. Columbia, 1969. 209p. DA 30 (Dec. 1969), 2472-A; UM 69-20,197.

Covering the 1950's and 1960's, the dissertation examines Japan's geographical and historical background, the origins and basic conceptions of her postwar defense policy, the 1951 Security Treaty, Security Treaty diplomacy from 1952 to 1957, defense policy and the 1960 Treaty, and defense policy and the self-defense forces.

Rel.Publ.: "Defending Postwar Japan," New Leader, 50 (July 3, 1967), 12-14; "Japanese Air Self-Defense Force: Restrained, but Powerful," Air Force and Space Digest, 50 (Dec. 1967), 56-60, 63; "The Origins and Basic Conception of Japan's Postwar Defense Policy," in International Conference of Orientalists in Japan, Transactions, 13 (1968), 21-30; "Defense Policy and the Self-Defense Forces," The Japan Interpreter, 6 (Summer 1970).

ALLIED OCCUPATION, 1945-1952

See also Law--constitutions of Japan (pages 180-81) for the postwar constitution as well as International Relations--United States: Since World War II (pages 162-63).

1806
GINSBURGH, Robert Neville. Between War and Peace: An Administrative and Organizational Analysis of Selected Military Government Experiences of the United States Army during the Transition Phase. Harvard, 1948. 507p. AB: 2p. summary appended to diss. ms.

Contents of Ch.6, "Rulers of Japan: An Administrative Study of the Japanese Occupation" (p.376-449): Plans and Policies; United States Agencies: Organization and Functioning; The United States and the Far Eastern Commission; McArthur and the Allied Council for Japan.

1807
BRAIBANTI, Ralph J. D. The Occupation of Japan: A Study in Organization and Administration. Syracuse, 1949. xxii, 970p.

Contents: Training of Military Government Personnel; Top Level Policy and Advisory Organizations (Initial Post-Surrender Policy Formulation, SWNCC, Far Eastern Commission, Allied Council for Japan, Impact of Top Level Policy on Local Military Government Administration); Transition from Planning to Effective Operation of Military Government (Organization, Accomplishments, and Dissolution of Military Government Section); Military Government versus Civil Affairs; Balancing Military and Military Government Interests within One Unified Command; Procedural Controls over Japanese Government and People; Relations with Subordinate Military Agencies; Coordination of Military Government at the Intermediate Levels (Role of Eighth Army, Role of the Counter-Intelligence Corps, Military Government Regional Headquarters); Military Government at the Prefectural Level (General Attitude of the Japanese toward Military Government, Initial Establishment of Combat Type Military Government in the Prefectures, Reorganization on Territorial Basis, Relations with other Occupation Forces and with the Japanese Government and People).

Rel.Publ.: "State and Religion in Japan," FES, 6 (Sept. 3, 1947), 185-87; "Neighborhood Associations in Japan and Their Democratic Potentialities," FEQ, 7 (Feb. 1948), 136-65; "Occupation Controls in Japan," FES, 7 (Sept. 22, 1948), 215-19; The Administration of Occupied Areas: A Study Guide [by] Ralph J. Braibanti and P. H. Taylor. Syracuse: Syracuse University Press, 1948. iv, 111p.; "Japan's New Police Law," FES, 18 (Jan. 24, 1949), 17-22; "Administration of Military Government in Japan at the Prefectural Level," American Political Science Review, 43 (Apr. 1949), 250-74; "The Role of Administration in the Occupation of Japan," Annals of the American Academy of Political and Social Science, 267 (Jan. 1950), 154-63; "Executive Power in the Japanese Prefectural Government," FEQ, 9 (May 1950), 231-44.

REID, Ralph W. Post War Constitutional Reform in Japan, 1945-1947. 1949. See no.1573.

1808
WIGGLESWORTH, Edwin French. An Appraisal of Allied Foreign Trade Policy for Japan. New York, 1949. 408p.

Contents: Pt.1: Basic Factors in the Reestablishment of Japan's Trade: The Pre-War Pattern of the Foreign Trade of Japan; Basic Changes in the Asiatic Markets; Social Philosophy and Economic Development; Postwar Economic Conditions. Pt.2: Allied War Aims and Trade Policy: War and Postwar Aims; Making Foreign Trade Policy; The Foreign Trade Policy: Definition and Implementation. Pt.3: Factual Results of Allied Foreign Trade Policies. Pt.4: Appraisal of Results of Allied War Aims and Foreign Trade Policies: Allied Policies and the Basic Factors; Allied Policies and the Reestablishment of Trade; Appraisal of the Policy-Making Organization; Appraisal of Detailed Allied Foreign Trade Policy; Conclusions and Recommendations.

1809
GADDIS, John Wilson. Public Information in Japan under American Occupation: A Study of Democratization Efforts through Agencies of Public Expression. Genève, 1950.

Concerned with the philosophy, methods, and international implications of the American effort to purge the Japanese of their autocratic ideology and to indoctrinate them in peace and democracy.

Rel.Publ.: Public...Expression. Genève: Impr. Populaires, 1950. 199p.

GRIFFITH, Harry E. Japanese Normal School Education. 1950. See no.423.

1810
PARONG, Simplicio. A Critical Study of the Present Government of Japan under the Supreme Commander of the Allied Powers. Manila, 1950. 145p.

STUART, Gordon H. Public Health in Occupied Japan. 1950. See no.2033.

THEYSSET, É. L'Essor du mouvement ouvrier au Japon: 1945-1948. Text in French. 1950. See no.290.

STEIG, Milan B. The Administration of Schools in Tokyo Japan, 1945-1950. 1950/51. See no.404.

1811
GANE, William Joseph. Foreign Affairs of South Korea, August, 1945, to August, 1950. Northwestern, 1951. 444p. AB: Northwestern University. Summaries of Doctoral Dissertations. v.19 (1951). p.352-57.

Devotes considerable attention to the repatriation of Japanese civilian residents and military personnel and to the supervision of relations between South Korea and Japan between 1945 and 1948 by SCAP General Headquarters.

POPOV, V. A. Agrarnaia reforma v Iaponii, 1945-1949. 1951. See no.170.

1812
TOPEKHA, Petr Pavlovich. Iaponskie pravye sotsialisty na sluzhbe u amerikanskogo imperializma [Japanese Right-Wing Socialists in the Service of American Imperialism]. Moscow, Institut vostokovedeniia Akademii nauk SSSR, 1951. (Candidate of Historical Sciences degree) 478p. Text in Russian. AB: 28p. summary published in 1951.

Rel.Publ.: Antinarodnaia politika pravykh liderov iaponskoi sotsialisticheskoi partii, 1945-1951 gg. Moscow: Izdatel'stvo Akademii nauk SSSR, 1954. 244p. (Institut vostokovedeniia Akademii nauk SSSR)

1813
BROWN, Richard Gerard. Ministerial Responsibility in Japan. Northwestern, 1952. 503p. AB: Northwestern University. Summaries of Doctoral Dissertations. v.19 (1951), p.347-51.

Examines the nature and status of the responsibility of Cabinet members to the Prime Minister and to the Diet during the Occupation period "within the larger context of parliamentary government in the light of...contemporary developments." Contents: Philosophical Concepts in Japanese Politics; The Two Constitutions; Drafting a New Constitution; The New Constitution; The Prime Minister and the Cabinet; The Diet and the Cabinet; Selection of the Prime Minister under the New Constitution; Comparative Aspects of Japanese Parliamentary Government.

1814
DENISOV, V. V. Vozstanovlenie amerikanskim imperializmom voenno-promyshlennogo potentsiala Iaponii posle vtoroi mirovoi voiny [American Imperialism and the Restoration of Japan's Military-Industrial Potential after World War II]. Moscow, Moskovskii institut vostokovedeniia, 1952. (Candidate of Economic Sciences degree) 445 + 17p. Text in Russian. AB: 68p. summary published in 1953.

1815
DOI, James Isao. Educational Reform in Occupied Japan, 1945-1950: A Study of Acceptance of and Resistance to Institutional Change. Chicago, 1952. vii, 390p.

Studies the general social setting, the methods of educational reform, some of the more important changes attempted, and the reactions of the Japanese to the educational changes in an attempt "to determine whether or not the perspectives and attitudes of the Japanese people concerning the schools and the education of their children underwent change" between 1945 and 1950.

1816
KASTELEINER, Rolf H. Die staatsrechtliche Entwicklung Japans seit 1945 [The Constitutional Development of Japan since 1945]. Marburg, 1952. 98p. Text in German. Diss. ms. available at Marburg/Lahn, Universitätsbibliothek, Nr. XVIII B.

Part 1 studies Japan's constitutional development from the end of World War II to May 1947, when the new constitution came into force, and includes information on the Allied occupation, the organization of SCAP, military occupation policy, and events of those two years. Part 2 focuses on the Japanese constitution of 1947 and on its effect on Japan's constitutional development, 1947-1951.

1817
McNELLY, Theodore Hart. Domestic and International Influence on Constitutional Revision in Japan, 1945-1946. Columbia, 1952. 451p. DA 12 (1952), 747-48; UM 4216.

Contents: The Need for Constitutional Revision in Japan; Prince Konoye's Attempt to Revise the Japanese Constitution; The Shidehara Cabinet and the Matsumoto Proposals; The Political Parties and Their Proposals; Some Proposals of Private Individuals and Groups; SCAP Headquarters and the New Japanese Constitution; The Far Eastern Commission and the Japanese Constitution; Japanese Public Opinion and the Yoshida Government; The House of Representatives and the House of Peers and the New Constitution; Conclusions.

Rel.Publ.: "American Influence and Japan's No-War Constitution," Political Science Quarterly, 67 (Dec. 1952) 589-98; "The Japanese Constitution: Child of the Cold War," Political Science Quarterly, 74 (June 1959), 176-95.

1818
SCOTT, John Richard. The Effect of the Cold War upon the Occupation of Japan. Illinois, 1952. 368p. DA 12 (1952), 750; UM 4012.
Contents: The Aggressors Prepare; Wartime Collaboration in Planning the Peace Settlement; Japanese Surrender and Allied Control; SCAP and Allied Control; Original Goals and Policies; Change in Goal for Japan; The Right Favored over the Left; Allied Reaction to American Policies; The Background of the Peace Treaty; The Peace Conference; Problems of Ratification.

1819
WUNDERLICH, Herbert John. The Japanese Textbook Problem and Solution, 1945-1946. Stanford, 1952. 382p. AB: Stanford University. Abstracts of Dissertations, 1951/1952. p.726-27.
A study of the efforts of SCAP's educational division "to replace the spirit of Japanese kokutai with democratic tendencies" by eliminating wartime texts permeated by militaristic and ultranationalistic ideology and by introducing new classroom materials.

1820
CARROLL, Holbert Nicholson. The House of Representatives and Foreign Affairs. Harvard, 1953. vi, 494p. AB: 4p. summary appended to diss. ms.
A study of the United States House of Representatives and its involvement in foreign affairs. For information on Japan see appendix I (p.405-29), "The Control of Occupation Policy [especially in Germany and Japan] by the Committee on Appropriations."
Rel.Publ.: The House...Affairs. Pittsburgh: University of Pittsburgh, 1958. 365p.

1821
COLLIER, David Swanson. The Politico-Economic Position of Japan. Northwestern, 1953. 360p. AB: Northwestern University. Summaries of Doctoral Dissertations. v.20 (1952), p.364-68.
Contents: The Politico-Economic Position of Japan; The Economic Development of Japan; The Development of Labor; Labor under the Occupation; The Politico-Economics of Labor; Politico-Economic Policy and the Program of Economy under the Occupation; The Problems of the Japan Trade, 1946-1951; International Politico-Economic Interests and the Communist Asia Trade; Japan, the United States, and the Politico-Economic Development of Asia.

1822
GRISHELEVA, L. D. Bor'ba iaponskogo naroda za demokraticheskuiu natsional'nuiu kul'turu v usloviiakh amerikanskoi okkupatsii [The Struggle of the Japanese People for a Democratic National Culture during the American Occupation]. Moscow, Institut vostokovedeniia Akademii nauk SSSR, 1953. (Candidate of Historical Sciences degree) 228 + 82p. Text in Russian. AB: 16p summary published in 1953.

GUZEVATYI, Ia. N. "Prodovol'stvennyi vopros" v Iaponii i upadok iaponskogo sel'skogo khoziaistva v usloviiakh amerikanskoi okkupatsii. 1953. See no.171.

KERLINGER, Frederick N. The Development of Democratic Control in Japanese Education: A Study of Attitude Change in Shikoku, 1948-1949. 1953. See no.405.

SHURKIN, A. O. Gosudarstvennye finansy poslevoennoi Iaponii na sluzhbe amerikanskoi agressii. 1953. See no.320.

ANDERSON, Paul S. The Reorientation Activities of the Civil Education Section of the Osaka Civil Affairs Team: A Case Study in Educational Change. 1954. See no.406.

1823
CAMACHO, Martin Thomas. The Administration of the SCAP Labor Policy in Occupied Japan. Harvard, 1954. v, 783p. (2v.) AB: 7p. summary appended to diss. ms.
Contents: Structure and Composition of Occupation Agencies; Genesis: Theory of Occupational Control; Operating Policies and Directives; The Labor Division, Economics and Scientific Section; Administration of the SCAP Labor Policy at the Local Level; Japanese Government Labor Agencies; The Labor Movement in Japan before 1945; The Postwar Labor Movement and Communist Infiltration; Occupation Policies and Personnel and the Communist Infiltration of the Labor Movement; The Democratization Movement: Labor's Counter-Communist Offensive; Occupation Counter-Communist Policies and Programs; The Occupation Inspired Red-Purge Program of 1950; Simplification and Unification of the Japanese Labor Movement.

1824
CHAPMAN, John Griffin. The Re-Education of the Japanese People. Houston, 1954. 288p. DA 14 (Nov. 1954), 1988-89; UM 9847.
Discusses the efforts of the American Occupation authorities to "achieve cultural and social changes through re-education of the Japanese people" and the consequences of their actions. The author concludes that "the American Occupation Forces not only succeeded in re-educating the Japanese youth but also re-directed the thought and energy of all the people toward the building of a more democratic way of life than the Japanese had ever known in the past."

CROSS, Edmond. Japanese Education, 1868-1953: With Emphasis on Various Phases of Education in Aomori Prefecture. 1954. See no.397.

HUTCHINSON, Edmond C. Inflation and Stabilization in Post-War Japan. 1954. See no.358.

1825
NELSON, John Monniger. The Adult-Education Program in Occupied Japan, 1946-1950. Kansas, 1954. 448p. (2v.)

ORR, Mark T. Education Reform Policy in Occupied Japan. 1954. See no.407.

WALTER, Austin F. Australia's Relations with the United States: 1941-1949. 1954. See no.1243.

YAMANE, Taro. Postwar Inflation in Japan. 1955. See no.324.

1826
BAERWALD, Hans Herman. The Purge of Japanese Leaders under the Occupation. California, Berkeley, 1956. 202p.
"The purge...was the principal tool for the effectuation of changes in the personnel who constituted the leadership of Japan during its period of occupation. This study is an endeavor to appraise the strengths and weaknesses of this policy and its implementation." Focuses on the problems encountered in administratively implementing the purge, on the limitations of the purge, and on its impact upon the dominant power groups in Japanese society.

Rel.Publ.: The Purge...Occupation. Berkeley: University of California Press, 1959. 111p. (University of California Publications in Political Science, 8)

BRETT, Cecil C. The Government of Okayama Prefecture: A Case Study of Local Autonomy in Japan. 1956. See no.1847.

EDWARDS, Marie A. Political Activities of Japanese Postwar Labor Unions. 1956. See no.1851.

AOKI, Hideo. The Effect of American Ideas upon Japanese Higher Education. 1957. See no.425.

KLEIN, Sidney. The Pattern of Land Tenure Reform in East Asia after World War II. 1957. See no.177.

1827
VITH, Fritz. Zaibatsu: Die Auflösung der Familienkombinate in Japan [Zaibatsu: The Dissolution of the Family Financial Combines in Japan]. Marburg, 1957. ii, 136p. Text in German. Diss ms. available at Marburg/Lahn, Universitätsbibliothek, Nr. 4° Z 58/12.

A study of the zaibatsu problem from a constitutional and administrative standpoint: the zaibatsu system, its development, and its structure; the American policy and program for breaking up the zaibatsu; and the outcome of American policies in Japan. The appendices contain a collection of documents, materials on the history of the Mitsui, Mitsubishi, and Sumitomo families, and a tabular summary of their spheres of interest.

1828
BENOIT, Edward George. A Study of Japanese Education as Influenced by the Occupation. Michigan State, 1958. 303p. DA 19 (June 1959), 3168; UM 59-1319.

Examines some of the changes in Japanese education that occurred between 1945 and 1955. Contents: Introduction to the Problem and Its Scope; The Geographical Background; The Historical Background; The Occupation and Japanese Education; Legislative "Milestones"; Aims and Organization of Japanese Education; The Problems of Japanese Education; A Survey of Japanese Educational Thought; A Survey of Teacher and Student Attitudes in Gumma Prefecture.

SULLIVAN, Sister Maria R. United States-Japanese Relations and Public Opinion 1945-1955. 1959. See no. 1418.

1829
TSUNEISHI, Warren Michio. The Japanese Emperor: A Study in Constitutional and Political Change. Yale, 1960. 307p. DA 27 (Dec. 1966), 1884-A; UM 66-12,883.

Focuses on the changes that occurred during the 1930's and 1940's. Contents: Introduction: The Final Imperial Conference of August 14, 1945; Historical and Constitutional Background; The Political Background: The Supreme Council for the Direction of the War and Its Predecessors; Imperial Decisions of the Shōwa Period; The Final Imperial Conferences; Political and Constitutional Reform; The Emperor and Symbol: His Constitutional Reform; Changing Attitudes towards the Emperor.

PETTY, Edward A. Directed Change and Culture Adhesion: A Study of Functional Integration in the Police Administration of Japan. 1961. See no.1835.

YAMAMURA, Kōzō. Competition and Monopoly in Japan, 1945-1961. 1964. See no.221.

1830
BALTZ, William Matthew. The Role of American Educators in the Decentralization and Reorganization of Education in Postwar Japan (1945-1952). State University of New York at Buffalo, 1965. 212p. DA 26 (May 1966), 6495; UM 65-8894.

"An historical account of the part played by the Education Division of the Civil Information and Education Section of the Headquarters of SCAP in the administrative reorganization of Japan." The role of the individuals who made up the staff of the Education Division is emphasized.

1831
ESTERLY, Henry Hermon. Japanese High Seas Fisheries and the International Politics of the Occupation, 1945-1951. Columbia, 1965. 408p. DA 29 (July 1968), 305-06-A; UM 68-5646.

Focuses on the power struggle among the Allies over the control of Japan's fishing policy and over the "question of whether or not Japan should be permitted to regain her preeminent role in the exploitation of oceanic resources."

Rel.Publ.: "Japan's Reentry into Pelagic Fisheries: From Surrender to the North Pacific Fisheries Convention, 1945-1952," in The Law of the Sea: The Future of the Sea's Resources, ed. by Lewis M. Alexander (Kingston: University of Rhode Island, 1968), 151-53.

OH, Ki Song. Land Reform in Communist China and Postwar Japan. 1966. See no.192.

RAMINENI, Ayyanna. A Comparative Analysis of the Kaldor Indian Tax Reforms and the Shoup Mission Japanese Tax Reforms. 1966. See no.363.

1832
SVENSSON, Eric H. F. The Military Occupation of Japan: The First Years. Planning, Policy Formulation, and Reforms. Denver, 1966. 427p. DA 27 (June 1967), 4205-06-A; UM 67-4793.

"Investigates planning and policy formulation for the occupation of Japan and the implementation of some of the more important reforms initiated during the early years of the occupation." Contents: Early Planning; Policy Formulation; Pacific Planning; Occupation Beginings; Organization for Occupation; Constitutional Reform; Economic Reform; Labor Reform; Agricultural Reform; Reorientation; Assessment.

DENUDOM, Maitrée. Système politique et vie politique au Japon depuis l'entrée en vigueur de la constitution de 1946. 1967. See no.1862.

1833
MONNIER, Claude. Les Américains et Sa Majesté l'Empereur: Étude du conflit culturel d'où naquit la Constitution japonaise de 1946 [The Americans and His Majesty the Emperor: A Study of the Cultural Conflict Which Produced the Japanese Constitution of 1946]. Neuchâtel, 1967. Text in French.

Discusses and compares the conflicting American and Japanese attitudes towards the imperial institution and explains how the Japanese constitution was born out of this conflict of opinions.

Rel.Publ.: Les Américains...1946. Neuchâtel: Ed. de la Baconnière, 1967. 223p. (Histoire et Société d'aujourd'hui); "Attitudes américaines et japonaises à l'égard du principe impérial nippon," Revue de psychologie des peuples, 22 (1967), 366-97.

AMRAVATI, Mallappa. Relations between Japan and the United States since 1945 with Special Reference to the Peace Treaty and the Security Pact. 1969. See no. 1425.

1834
MURATA, Suzuko. A Study of the Impact of the American Educational System on Higher Education in Japan. Indiana, 1969. 247p. DA 30 (Nov. 1969), 1838-A; UM 69-17,755.

An assessment of "the impact of changes in Japanese higher education imposed by SCAP and recommended by the United States Education Mission." After describing the impact of western ideas on prewar Japan, the dissertation reviews the postwar educational system "with special reference to implementing democratic principles in higher education as exemplified by increased enrollments, equality of opportunity for both sexes, and the introduction of general education. The failure of SCAP and the Mission to fully understand and appreciate Japanese history and culture is noted. Four major problems--entrance examinations, education for women, financing private universities, and relations between the state and higher education--also are considered."

BUREAUCRACY AND PUBLIC ADMINISTRATION

For the postwar period only. For the prewar period, see Economics--public finance (pages 47-49) and History--modern period (pages 72-88).

1835
PETTY, Edward Avin. Directed Change and Culture Adhesion: A Study of Functional Integration in the Police Administration of Japan. Southern California, 1961. 386p. DA 22 (Nov. 1961), 1707; UM 61-3823.

"The purpose of this study is to analyze directed social change in Japan under the special conditions of a military occupation and the process of cultural adhesion which made it possible for the Japanese to markedly modify aspects of the new postwar system after the occupation had ended. The specific subject of the study is police service and administration. It focuses on the efforts of the American occupying forces in Japan to adapt the police system of one culture to another culture."

1836
KIM, Paul Sunik. The Higher Public Service in Japan: An Introductory Analysis of Japanese Administrative Behavior. New York, 1964. 265p. DA 26 (Sept. 1965); 1757-58; UM 65-1641.

"Emphasis is placed on determinants of administrative system, recruitment policy, and education which have helped to determine the attitude of the higher civil servants toward their subordinates in particular and the people in general." Covers both pre- and post-war Japan. Contents: Environmental Conditions of Administrative Behavior; Administrative Heritage; Administrative Structure under the New Constitution of 1947; Public Personnel Management in Japan; Social Background of Higher Public Servants; Administrative Process: Social Aspects.

1837
KANG, Pyung Kun. The Role of Local Government in Community Development in Korea. Minnesota, 1966. 428p. DA 28 (Feb. 1968), 3236-37-A; UM 68-1177.

"Korean administrative processes and organizational behavior were compared with those of the Japanese."

Rel.Publ.: "Administrative Structure and Management in Regional Development: Case of Korea," Koreana Quarterly, 10 (Summer 1968), 121-32.

1838
KUBOTA, Akira. Higher Civil Servants in Post-War Japan: A Study of Their Social Origins, Educational Backgrounds, and Career Patterns. Michigan, 1966. 219p. DA 27 (Apr. 1967), 3505-A; UM 67-1764.

"Examines the composition of higher civil service personnel in the 1949-1959 period and identifies major characteristics of the postwar Japanese higher civil service." Contents: Social Origins; Educational Backgrounds; Career Patterns; Retirement; The Postwar Japanese Bureaucracy.

Rel.Publ.: Higher...Patterns. Princeton: Princeton University Press, 1969. 197p.

LONG, Theodore D. Science Policy in Postwar Japan. 1968. See no.1991.

1839
HIGA, Mikio. The Role of Bureaucracy in Contemporary Japanese Politics. California, Berkeley, 1968. 398p. DA 29 (Mar. 1969), 3194-A; UM 69-3612.

The objective is "to explore the policy-making role of the bureaucracy in modern Japanese politics and to identify those factors which seem most helpful in expanding this role." Contents: The Emergence of Modern Bureaucrats; The Nature and Dynamics of Early Meiji Bureaucracy; The Prewar Governmental Structure; Institutionalization of Privileged Status; Stability of the Established Status; Characteristics of the Prewar Bureaucracy; The Purge Program; Constitutional Revision; Initial Civil Service Reform; Bureaucratic Manipulation; Revision of the National Public Service Law; Readjustment and Resistance; Characteristics of the Postwar Bureaucracy.

ELECTION PROCESS

For the postwar period only. For the prewar period see History--modern period (pages 72-88). See also Political Science--political leadership and political parties (pages 217-18).

1840
CLUBOK, Alfred Bernard. Electoral Politics in Rural Japan: A Case Study of Okayama Prefecture. Michigan, 1962. 219p. DA 23 (Mar. 1963), 3453; UM 63-324.

"Analyzes the legal framework of the Japanese election system; analyzes statistically the electoral support of the conservatives and left-wing in rural Okayama at both the national and prefectural levels; differentiates conservative and left-wing party and electoral organization membership on the basis of socioeconomic, community leadership, and political orientation characteristics; examines the structure of political power in the villages of Okayama; and examines the campaign organization and activities of the two wings in Japanese politics and relates these to rural politics.

Rel.Publ.: "Political Party Membership and Sub-Leadership in Rural Japan: A Case Study of Okayama Prefecture," in Modern Japanese Leadership: Transition and Change, ed. by Bernard S. Silberman and Harry D.

Harootunian (Tucson: University of Arizona Press, 1966), 385-409.

1841
RICHARDSON, Bradley Moore. Political Attitudes and Voting Behavior in Contemporary Japan: Rural and Urban Differences. California, Berkeley, 1966. 269p. DA 27 (Nov. 1966), 1416-A; UM 66-8368.

Compares and discusses the attitudes and behavior of Japanese living in Yokohama, Atsugi (a farm village in Kanagawa prefecture), and Nita (a village in Shimane prefecture) at the time of the 1963 national and local elections.

Rel.Publ.: "Japanese Local Politics: Support Mobilization and Leadership Styles," Asian Studies, 7 (Dec. 1967), 860-75.

1842
IKEDA, George Kiyoshi. Ishikawa: Electoral Politics in a Japanese Prefecture. Harvard, 1968. v, 222p.

"Attempts to show the electoral process as a whole by examining the electoral structure which begins at the local grass-roots level and culminates in the Lower House election of a Diet member." Contents: Municipal Elections; Prefectural Elections; Diet Elections.

PARK, Yung Ho. The Electoral Reform Laws of 1962: A Case Study of the Japanese Policy-Making Process. 1968. See no.1866.

1843
CURTIS, Gerald Leon. Mobilizing Electoral Support: A Study of a Liberal Democratic Party Candidate's Campaign Strategies in the 1967 Lower House Election in Japan. Columbia, 1969. 414p. DA 30 (Apr. 1970); UM 70-6956.

This study examines the strategies of support mobilization utilized by a candidate for election to the lower house of the Japanese Diet. It deals with the following issues: the process of receiving LDP endorsement as an official party candidate; the differing structures of campaign organization in rural and urban sectors of the constituency; the function of kōenkai, a "supporter's organization"; the role played in the campaign by interest groups; and the conduct of both the unofficial and the official campaigns.

Rel.Publ.: "The Kōenkai and the Liberal Democratic Party," The Japanese Interpreter, 6 (Summer 1970).

ELITE STUDIES

HADLEY, Eleanor M. Concentrated Business Power in Japan. 1949. See no.209.

WILSON, Robert A. A Study of the Political Institutions and Ranking Personnel of the New Meiji Government, 1868-1871. 1949. See no.590.

BAERWALD, Hans H. The Purge of Japanese Leaders under the Occupation. 1956. See no.1826.

VITH, Fritz. Zaibatsu: Die Auflösung der Familienkombinate in Japan. 1957. See no.1827.

KIM, Paul Sunik. The Higher Public Service in Japan: An Introductory Analysis of Japanese Administrative Behavior. 1964. See no.1836.

KURIYAMA, Morihiko. Die betriebswirtschaftliche Untersuchung der obersten Unternehmensorganisation in den deutschen und japanischen Aktiengesellschaften: Das deutsche Aufsichtsrat--Vorstand und das japanische Board--Vertretungsdirektorium--System in vergleichender Betrachtung. 1964. See no.219.

1844
McGARRY, James Frederick, Jr. A Study of Decision-Making in Japan's Postwar Foreign Economic Policy: Some Aspects of Elite Influences in a Modern Non-Western Political System. Pennsylvania, 1964. 428p. DA 25 (Oct. 1964), 2601; UM 64-10,401.

"Examines changes and continuity in the decision-making elite and the concepts which motivate them and which they articulate." Contents: The Structure of Postwar Japan's Foreign Economic Policy; The Importance of Elite Groups in Postwar Japan's Foreign Economic Policy; Some Ideas Concerning Historic Patterns in the Formation of Japanese Government Policies; The Rise and Fall of the Co-Prosperity Spirit Concept; Survivors and Newcomers: The Postwar Elite; Some Elite Views on the Elements of Foreign Economic Policy (National Bureaucracy, Permanent Majority, Business Leadership, New Socialism and Old, Moderate Intellectuals); Consensus and Collectivities; Some Examples of Foreign Economic Policy Formulation.

SPAULDING, Robert M. Jr. Imperial Japan's "Higher Examinations." 1965. See no.579.

KUBOTA, Akira. Higher Civil Servants in Post-War Japan: A Study of Their Social Origins, Educational Backgrounds, and Career Patterns. 1966. See no.1838.

MARSHALL, Byron K. Ideology and Industrialization in Japan, 1868-1941: The Creed of the Prewar Business Elite. 1966. See no.554.

NISHIO, Harry K. Political Authority Structure and the Development of Entrepreneurship in Japan (1603-1890). 1966. See no.536.

BENJAMIN, Roger W. Military Influence in Foreign Policy-Making. 1967. See no.555.

TSURUTANI, Taketsugu. Tension, Consensus, and Political Leadership: A New look into the Nature and Process of Modernization. 1967. See no.609.

1845
TRIMBERGER, Ellen Kay. Revolution by Elites: A Comparative Study of Political Change in Japan and Turkey. Chicago, 1969. 328p.

LOCAL GOVERNMENT

For the postwar period only. For the prewar period, see History--modern period (pages 72-88).

1846
STEINER, Kurt. Local Government in Japan. Stanford, 1955. 384p. DA 15 (June 1955), 1103-04; UM 12,273.

The author seeks to "determine the degree of local self-government actually existing in Japan" during both the pre-war and the post-war periods. He therefore analyses "not only the institutions of local government but also their operation and the sociological and historical forces influencing them."

Rel.Publ.: Local...Japan. Stanford: Stanford University Press, 1965. ix, 564p.; "Local Government in Japan: Reform and Reaction," FES, 13 (July 1954), 97-102; "The Japanese Village and Its Government," FEQ, 15 (Feb. 1956), 185-99; "Bibliographical Article: Selected Materials for a Comparative Study of Local Government; Japanese Local Government," American Political Science Review, 50 (Dec. 1956), 1126-33; "Japan's Prefectural System," Toshi mondai, 43 (Apr. 1957), 107-16; "Popular Political Participation and Political Development in Japan: The Rural Level," in Political Development in Modern Japan, ed. by Robert E. Ward (Princeton: Princeton University Press, 1968), 213-47.

1847
BRETT, Cecil Carter. The Government of Okayama Prefecture: A Case Study of Local Autonomy in Japan. Michigan, 1956. 305p. DA 17 (June 1957), 1371; UM 21,152.
Studies "the extent to which the Occupation sponsored decentralization and democratization measures were carried into practice" in Okayama prefecture. Contents: Post-War Reforms in Local Government; Structure and Function of the Prefectural Government (Okayama Prefecture, Machinery of Prefectural Government, Local Agencies of the National Government, Judicial Affairs); The Executive (The Governor, Prefectural Officials, Liaison with Tokyo); The Legislature (Political Parties, Legislative Process, Bylaws Passed by the Prefectural Assembly); Legislation by Negotiation (The Education Supplementary Appropriations Measure: A Case Study); Agriculture and the National Subsidy; Education and Police: Decentralization in Theory and Practice (The Prefectural Board of Education, The Prefectural Police, The Public Safety Commission).
Rel.Publ.: "The Japanese Prefectural Legislature," Parliamentary Affairs, 11 (Winter 1957/1958), 23-38.

1848
VIRA, Soma. Inpact of Urban Population Pressure upon Municipal Government: A Comparative Study: Calcutta, Djakarta, Tokyo. New York, 1967. 549p. DA 29 (Aug. 1968), 661-62-A; UM 68-10,100.
"The central idea is to find whether or not population increases in rapidly industrializing urban areas generate conditions or problems which are largely similar in more than one metropolis."

RAMSEYER, Robert L. Takachiho, 1868-1968: Evolving Patterns of Community Decision-Making in a Developing Nation-State. 1969. See no.35.

POLITICAL IDEOLOGY AND PHILOSOPHY

For the postwar period only. For the prewar period, see History--modern period (pages 72-88) and Religion and Philosophy--Confucianism, Bushidō, Kokugaku, and Yōgaku (pages 228-30).

1849
HAM, Euiyoung. Ideology in the Foreign Policy of Japanese Socialism. Wisconsin, 1964. 504p. DA 26 (Feb. 1966), 4785-86; UM 64-13,883.
Analyzes the extent to which "Japanese socialism and its inherent ideological factionalism as well as socialist internationalism are reflected in the making of socialist foreign policy proposals and the attitudes of Japanese socialists toward international affairs."

QUO, Fang-quei. Japanese Liberalism: A Case Study in the Transplantation of Political Theory. 1964. See no.642.

1850
KRIEGER, David Malcolm. Personality and Political Ideology. Hawaii, 1968. 124p. DA 29 (Dec. 1968), 1933-A; UM 68-16,952.
"A multivariate statistical approach was used to assess the relationship between a broad range of personality traits and factorially derived dimensions of attitudinal space in a sample of Japanese university students."

POLITICAL INTEREST GROUPS

1851
EDWARDS, Marie Alice. Political Activities of Japanese Postwar Labor Unions. Northwestern, 1956. 470p. DA 17 (Feb. 1957), 393-94; UM 18,981.
Pt.1 is devoted to an exposition of the postwar development of the labor union movement in Japan with special attention to the basic labor legislation and the development and activities of the major national unions and federations. Pt.2 focuses on the identification of labor unions with political parties, the use of labor to further political programs, the attempt of the government to control leftist activities, and the position of the Japan Communist Party with regard to labor unions.

1852
SOUKUP, James Rudolph. Labor and Politics in Postwar Japan: A Study of the Political Attitudes and Activities of Selected Labor Organizations. Michigan, 1957. 336p. DA 18 (Apr. 1958), 1479-80; UM 58-1464.
Pt.1 is a general account of postwar trade union developments (September 1945-September 1954). Pt.2 examines the attitudes of major labor organizations and their leaders towards domestic economic policy, Japan's foreign policy, and labor's role in domestic politics. Pt.3 investigates the various political activities of the major labor organizations (e.g. election activities, lobbying, strikes).
Rel.Publ.: "Reflections on Japanese Labor," Today's Japan, 5 (Jan./Feb. 1960), 59-66; "Labor and Politics in Japan: A Study of Interest-Group Attitudes and Activities," Journal of Politics, 22 (May 1960), 314-37; "Japanese Labor: Goals and Political Tactics," Orient/West, 7 (Mar. 1962), 15-24.

1853
KITAMURA, Fusako. A Study of the Japan Teachers Union and Recommendations for Improvement. Columbia (Teachers College), 1962. 605p. DA 23 (May 1963), 4189; UM 63-2264.
"Analyzes the purposes, organization, and program of the Teachers Union."

1854
STESLICKE, William Eugene. The Politics of Medical Care: A Study of the Japan Medical Association. Michigan, 1965. 599p. DA 27 (Aug. 1966), 517-18-A; UM 66-6712.
Contents: Interest Groups and the Political Process in Modern Japan; Health and Welfare Administration and Policy; The Japanese Medical Profession; The Japan Medical Association: Organization, Objectives, and Activities; The "Four Demands "of the Japan Medical Association; The Second Ikeda Cabinet and the "Struggle to Break through the Medical Care Crisis"; "Medical Holi-

days," Negotiations, and Compromise: The Final Phase of the Japan Medical Association's 1960-61 Campaign; The Japan Medical Association and the Politics of Medical Care.

Rel.Publ.: "The Japan Medical Association and the Liberal Democratic Party: A Case Study of Interest Group Politics in Japan," in Studies on Asia, 1965, ed. by Robert K. Sakai (Lincoln: University of Nebraska Press, 1965), 143-61.

1855
KAPUSTIN, A. V. General'nyi sovet profsoiuzov Iaponii (Sokhë): Progressivnyi tsentr iaponskogo profsoiuznogo dvizheniia, 1950-1965 gg. [The General Council of Trade Unions of Japan (Sōhyō): The Progressive Center of the Japanese Trade Union Movement, 1950-1965]. Moscow, Akademiia obshchestvennykh nauk pri TsK KPSS, Kafedra istorii mezhdunarodnogo kommunisticheskogo i rabochego dvizheniia, 1966. (Candidate of Historical Sciences degree) 337 + 11p. Text in Russian. AB: 16p. summary published in 1966.

1856
HARARI, Ehud. The Politics of Labor Legislation in Japan. California, Berkeley, 1968. 444p. DA 30 (Sept. 1969), 1212-13-A; UM 69-14,902.

"This study traces the evolution of labor legislation as an issue area in Japanese politics. It identifies the types of demands made by domestic and international actors and explains their transformation into political issues....Included is a case study of the ratification of ILO Convention No.87 (Freedom of association and protection of the right to organize, 1948) and the concomitant revision of several Japanese labor laws." Contents: The Pre-1945 Legacy; The Allied Occupation; The Emergence of a Political Issue through the Internationalization of a Domestic Demand: 1952-1957; The Legislative Package: 1958-1966.

POLITICAL LEADERSHIP AND POLITICAL PARTIES

For the postwar period only. For the prewar period, see Economics--public finance (pages 47-49) and History--modern period (pages 72-88).

BROWN, Richard G. Ministerial Responsibility in Japan. 1952. See no.1813.

1857
MENDEL, Douglas Heusted, Jr. Political Behavior in Post-Treaty Japan: A Survey of Constituents and Leaders in Two Selected Areas. Michigan, 1955. 309p. DA 15 (Apr. 1955), 621-22; UM 11,326.

"Analyzes the relationship of political party identification and rural-urban residence to measures of political consciousness, political participation, and voting motivation in Osaka City and the Izumo plain area of Shimane prefecture during the spring of 1953.

1858
PAK, Kun. Political Parties in Postwar Japan. Pennsylvania, 1958. 441p. DA 19 (Oct. 1958), 861-62; UM 58-3366.

Investigates the degree to which the postwar Japanese parties are democratic and the extent to which they have become imbued in the Japanese political fabric. The various chapters deal primarily with the history, ideology, and organization of the Liberal Democratic Party and the Social Democratic Party.

1859
FARNSWORTH, Lee Winfield. Factionalism in Recent Japanese Politics: Theory and Practice. Claremont, 1963. 299p. DA 25 (Dec. 1964), 3654 [Abstract not available]; UM 63-7746.

A descriptive study of the types of factions, the patterns of recruiting faction members, the nature of the factional leadership, and the nature of intra-factional politics. Contents: The Political Bases of Factionalism; Socio-Cultural Aspects of Factionalism; in Japanese Politics: A Historical View; Factionalism in Recent Conservative Politics; Factionalism in Recent Radical Politics; The Politics of Factions.

Rel.Publ.: "Challenges to Factionalism in Japan's Liberal Democratic Party," Asian Survey, 6 (Sept. 1966), 501-09; "Social and Political Sources of Political Fragmentation in Japan," Journal of Politics, 29 (May 1967), 287-301.

1860
CHUNG, Sung Beh. Le Système des partis au Japon [The Party System in Japan]. Paris, 1965. 288, iv p. Text in French.

1861
STOCKWIN, James Arthur Ainscow. The Neutralist Policy of the Japan Socialist Party. Australian National, 1965. 300p.; 192p. (2v.)

Discusses the factors related to the JSP policy of neutralism including the history and structure of the party and the factional divisions within it. Focuses on the party's ideology and on its foreign policy decision-making process.

Rel.Publ.: The Japanese Socialist Party and Neutralism. Melbourne: Melbourne University Press, New York: Cambridge University Press, 1968. xv, 197p.; "'Positive Neutrality': The Foreign Policy of the Japanese Socialist Party," Asian Survey, 2 (Nov. 1962), 33-41; "Faction and Ideology in Postwar Japanese Socialism," in Australian National University, Department of International Relations, Papers on Modern Japan, 1965 (Canberra, 1965), 34-49; "The Japanese Socialist Party under New Leadership," Asian Survey, 6 (Apr. 1966), 187-200.

1862
DENUDOM, Maitrée. Système politique et vie politique au Japon depuis l'entrée en vigeur de la constitution de 1946 [The Political System and Political Life in Japan since the 1946 Constitution Came into Force]. Paris, 1967. 765, vi p. (2v.). Text in French.

1863
FUKUI, Haruhiro. The Japanese Liberal-Democratic Party and Policy-Making. Australian National, 1967. 352p.; 183p. (2v.)

Three case studies figure prominently in this dissertation: (1) the question of constitutional reform, (2) the question of Japanese relations with Communist China, and (3) the question of compensating landlords for dispossession during the era of the postwar land reform.

Rel.Publ.: "The Associational Basis of Decision-Making in the Liberal-Democratic Party," in Australian National University, Department of International Relations, Papers on Modern Japan, 1965 (Canberra, 1965), 18-33; "The Liberal-Democratic Party and Constitutional Revision," in Australian National University, Department of International Relations, Papers on Modern Japan, 1968 (Canberra, 1968), 26-45; Jiyū minshutō no seisaku kettei. Tōkyō: Fukumura, 1969; Party in Power: The Japanese Liberal-Democrats and Policy-Making. Berkeley: University of California Press, 1970. (Publications of the Center for Japanese and Korean Studies)

1864
LATYSHEV, Igor' Aleksandrovich. Praviashchaia Liberal'no-demokraticheskaia partiia Iaponii i ee politika [Japan's Ruling Liberal-Democratic Party and Its Policies]. Moscow, Institut narodov Azii Akademii nauk SSSR, 1967. (Doctor of Historical Sciences degree) 338p. Text in Russian.
Rel.Publ.: Praviashchaia...politika. Moscow, "Nauka,: 1967. 338p. (Institut narodov Azii Akademii nauk SSSR); "Fraktsionnye techeniia v liberal'no-demokraticheskoi partii Iaponii," Narody Azii i Afriki, 4 (1965), 48-59.

1865
THAYER, Nathaniel Bowman. How the Conservatives Rule Japan: A Study of Personality and Institutions in the Liberal Democratic Party. Columbia, 1967. 436p.
A study examining the factions and party organs of the Liberal Democratic Party. The dissertation includes information on the role of factions, the LDP's relations with the economic community, the organization and financing of elections, the selection of a party president, the formation of the cabinet, and policy- and decision-making within the party.
Rel.Publ.: How the Conservatives Rule Japan. Princeton: Princeton University Press, 1969. xiv, 349p. (Studies of the East Asian Institute, Columbia University) [TRANSLATION: Jimintō. Tr. by Kobayashi Katsumi. Tōkyō: Sekkasha, 1968. 283p. (Nihon o ugokasu soshiki shirizu)]; "The Election of a Japanese Prime Minister," Asian Survey, 9 (July 1969), 477-97.

1866
PARK, Yung Ho. The Electoral Reform Laws of 1962: A Case Study of the Japanese Policy-Making Process: Illinois, 1968. 304p. DA 29 (Aug. 1968), 652-A; UM 68-12,176.
"The major objective is to demonstrate the proposition that the Liberal-Democratic Dietmen, in spite of their access to and involvement in all the stages of policy-making, are far from being the omnipotent political force, and that they are subject to numerous limitations in their attempt to influence policy-making."

1867
WHITE, James Wilson. Mass Movement, Military Religion, and Democracy: Sōka Gakkai in Japanese Politics. Stanford, 1969. 856p. DA 30 (Nov. 1969), 2100-21-A; UM 69-17,461.
A political study and an extensive description of the membership and the ideology of the Sōka Gakkai. The thesis "problem is approached through William Kornhauser's model of a mass movement. Two independent variables, the Gakkai membership and the Gakkai as a formal organization, are tested against over 20 indicators of congruence with the three basic aspects of a mass movement: detachment from the social environment, alienation from this environment, and inclinations toward deviant, direct action. As an intervening variable, the mutual influences of membership and organization upon each other (the Gakkai's internal micro-macro interaction) are examined in order to evaluate the dependent variable, the implications of the Gakkai as an interactive social and organizational whole, for the Japanese polity as a democratic system."
Rel.Publ.: The Sokagakkai and Mass Society. Stanford: Stanford University Press, 1970. (Stanford Studies in Comparative Politics); "Mass Movement and Democracy: Sōka Gakkai in Japanese Politics," American Political Science Review, 61 (Sept- 1967), 744-50.

1868
PALMER, Arthur Arvin. Buddhist Politics: Japan's Clean Government Party. Claremont, 1970. 190p. DA 31 (July 1970); UM 70-11,910.
A study of the Kōmeitō.

Psychology and Social Psychology

See also Overseas Japanese Communities (pages 198-208).

1869
HOFSTÄTTER, Peter Robert. Testuntersuchungen an japanischen Kindern und das Reifungsproblem [Projective Testing of Japanese Children and the Problem of Maturation]. Wien, 1936. 111p. Text in German. Diss.ms. available at the Universitätsbibliothek der Universität Wien, Nr. D 5014.

A study of the process of maturation among Japanese children living in an industrial community in northern Korea. The Bühler Test was used in the study.

ISHIDA, Gladys. The Japanese-American Renunciants of Okayama Prefecture: Their Accomodation and Assimilation to Japanese Culture. 1956. See no.1720.

1870
KUMATA, Hideya. A Factor Analytic Study of Semantic Structures across Three Selected Cultures. Illinois, 1958. 316p. DA 18 (May 1958), 1881-82; UM 58-1716.

Explores "the feasibility of using Osgood's Semantic Differential as a cross-cultural measuring instrument and the tenability of the Sapir-Whorf linguistic relativity hypothesis in the area of connotative meaning." Based on a case study of monolingual college students in Japan and in the United States and of bilingual Japanese and Korean exchange students in the United States.

TSURU, Haruo. Japanese Universities in a Changing Society: A Study of Some Historical, Sociological, and Psychological Bases of Student Personnel Work in Japanese Universities. 1958. See no.427.

1871
KRAMER, Ernest Franklin. Judgment of Portrayed Emotion from Normal English, Filtered English, and Japanese Speech. Michigan, 1963. 49p. DA 24 (Oct. 1963), 1699-70; UM 63-6914.

"Japanese was selected as a foreign language with which to investigate the problem of judging emotions from speech in a language with which the listener is unfamiliar."

1872
TANAKA, Yasumasa. A Test of Congruity Hypothesis across Three Language/Culture Communities. Illinois, 1963. 117p. DA 24 (June 1964), 5589; UM 64-6164.

A cross-cultural and cross-linguistic experiment involving undergraduate students in Japan (at Kuwazawa College of Arts and Design in Tokyo), Finland, and the United States that was designed to examine the codability of eight perceptual signs: two high-codable and two low-codable line forms and two high codable and two low-codable colors. The author concluded from the experiment "that the laws governing the dynamics of cognitive interaction have a universal character."

Rel.Publ.: "Affective Dimension of Colors: A Cross-Cultural Study" [by] Tadasu Oyama and Yasumasa Tanaka, Japanese Psychological Research, 4 (July 1962), 78-91; "A Cross-Culture and Cross-Concept Study of the Generality of Semantic Spaces" [by] Y. Tanaka, T. Oyama, and C.E. Osgood, Journal of Verbal Learning and Verbal Behavior, 2 (Dec. 1963), 392-405; "The Use of the Entrophy Measure, H, as an Index of Perceptual Sign and Codability: A Cross-Cultural Study," Japanese Psychological Research, 6 (Apr. 1964), 38-45; "A Test of the Congruity Hypothesis across Three Language/Culture Communities," in Gakushuin University (Tokyo), Seikei Gakubu, Kenkyū nempō, 9 (1964); "Cross-Culture, Cross-Concept, and Cross-Subject Generality of Affective Meaning Systems" [by] C.E. Osgood and Y. Tanaka, Journal of Personality and Social Psychology, 2 (Aug. 1965), 143-53; "SD-ho o mochiita kokka-kan taibutsu ninchi sokutei no hikaku bunka kenkyū," Nempō shakai-shinri-gaku, 6 (1965), 100-24; "Cross-Cultural Compatability of the Affective Meaning Systems: Measured by Means of Multilingual Semantic Differentials," Journal of Social Issues, 23 (Jan. 1967), 27-46.

1873
NAKANO, Terumi. The Effect of a Subject's Native Language upon His Choice of Alternative "Syntactical Arrangements" of a Set of Pictures. Indiana, 1964. 214p. DA 25 (Feb. 1965), 4547. UM 65-404.

Sought to determine "whether or not there were different modal patterns in the way pictorial signs are arranged to state a message by people whose native languages are different." The subjects were thirty native speakers of English and eighteen of Japanese.

DUCHAC, René. La Jeunesse de Tokyo: Problèmes d'intégration sociale. 1965. See no.84.

1874
FLEISZ, Ida. Experimentelle Untersuchungen zur Existenz von inhärenten Laut-Sinn Beziehungen: Eine Durchführung des Czurda-Tests an japanischen Kindern [Experimental Investigations Dealing with the Existence of Inherent Relationships between Sounds and Their Meanings: A Practical Application of the Czurda Test Involving Japanese Children]. Wien, 1965. 132p. Text in German. Diss.

ms. available at the Universitätsbibliothek der Universität Wien, Nr. D 16,318; also at the Österreichische Nationalbibliothek, Nr. 1,013.343-C.

A contribution to the study of the relationship between things and their names, and words and their meanings, by means of the Czurda Test. Children in Kyoto served as subjects for the test.

1875
NISHIYAMA, Reverend Toshiko Peter. Primary Relationships and Academic Achievement: A Comparative Study of American and Japanese Youth. St. Louis, 1965. 327p. DA 28 (Sept. 1967), 1136-A; UM 65-14,654.

Examines and compares in the Japanese case "the influence of family and friend groups" on (1) Japanese students who go on to college, and (2) Japanese students who do not continue their formal education beyond high school.

OWADA, Yasuyuki. The Dynamics of College Administration: A Study of Interpersonal Relations in the X University Administration, Tokyo, Japan. 1966. See no. 430.

1876
CESSNA, William Conrad, Jr. The Psychosocial Nature and Determinants of Attitudes toward Education and toward Physically Disabled Persons in Japan. Michigan State, 1967. 355p. DA 28 (Nov. 1967), 1674-A; UM 67-14,486.

A study conducted in Tokyo in 1965 investigating "the relationship between (a) attitudes, (b) interpersonal attitudes, (c) personal contact with education and disabled persons, and (d) certain demographic variables."

1877
FRAGER, Robert David. Conformity in Japan. Harvard, 1967. vi, 101p.

An investigation of the Japanese concern for social opinion and its effect on their behavior. Contents: Conformity and Need for Social Approval; Patterns in Japanese Society Related to Conformity (Traditional Values, Modern Japan, Alienation); Experimental Procedures (The Need for Social Approval Scale, The Traditionalism Scale, The Conformity Experiment); Results; Conclusions.

1878
KIEFER, Christie Weber. Personality and Social Change in a Japanese Danchi. California, Berkeley, 1968. 285p. DA 29 (Oct. 1968), 1246-B; UM 68-13,926.

In this study the author sought "to gain a general familiarity with life in a single danchi [apartment complex], to assess the typicality of this danchi among others of its kind throughout the country, and to compare danchi life with life in 'ordinary' Japanese communities....Special reference is made to the interplay of personality factors and aspects of social change peculiar to the danchi setting."

1879
KRETSCH, Rina Anne. Communication of Emotional Meanings across National Groups. Columbia, 1968. 81p. DA 29 (Apr. 1969), 3914-B; UM 69-3083.

The author "investigated vocal communication of emotional meaning among speakers from Japan, Israel, and the United States."

KRIEGER, David M. Personality and Political Ideology. 1968. See no.1850.

1880
SCHEINER, Suzanne Beatrice. Differential Perception of Personality Characteristics in Cross-Cultural Interaction. California, Los Angeles, 1968. 215p. DA 30 (Aug. 1969), 477-78-B; UM 69-11,912.

The study "investigates the effect of culturally patterned personality characteristics on cross-cultural person-perception....The primary comparison groups were drawn from foreign students attending the two major universities in the Los Angeles area and consisted of 31 Buddhist Japanese and 16 Moslem Middle Eastern students who had been in the United States for less than one year. Respondents used the Interpersonal Check List (LaForge & Suczec, 1955) to describe themselves, their culture-ideal, and the average American of their experience."

1881
SIMPSON, Miles Edward. Status Inconsistency, Social Mobility, Self, and Society. Michigan State, 1968. 264p. DA 29 (Apr. 1969), 3683-84-A; UM 69-5949.

Based on data from Japan and three other countries, the study "proposes a self-esteem theory to account for the effects of status inconsistencies in (1) self-perceived autonomy, (2) authoritarianism, (3) expectations for future life conditions, and (4) alienation, as manifested in a sense of powerlessness, normlessness, and social isolation."

1882
KOBAYASHI, Reverend Michael Junichi, S.J. Relationship of Intelligence and Creativity to Anxiety and Extroversion-Introversion in Ninth Grade Japanese Boys. Boston College, 1969. 121p. DA 30 (Mar. 1970); UM 70-2013.

Contents: Design of the Study; Statistical Data on Analysis of Variance for Anxiety; Statistical Data on Analysis of Variance for Extroversion-Introversion; Summary and Implications of the Data.

Religion and Philosophy

GENERAL

See also Anthropology-Sociology--values and attitudes (pages 12-13)

1883
KISHINAMI, Tsunezō. The Development of Philosophy in Japan. Princeton, 1914.
Studies the development of Western philosophy during the Meiji Era and its relation to Japanese religion and to contemporary social and ethical problems.
Rel.Publ.: The Development...Japan. Princeton: Princeton University Press, 1915. 27p.

1884
OSHIMO, Raymond Kakuichi. The Development of Social Idealism in Modern Japan. Chicago, 1931. 221p.
The first part describes Tokugawa feudalism while in the second part an analysis is made of the forces that contributed to the development of liberal movements.
Rel.Publ.: The Development...Japan. Chicago, 1930. 22p. (Private edition, distributed by the University of Chicago Libraries)

1885
ROY, Andrew Tod. Modern Confucian Social Theory and Its Concept of Change. Princeton, 1948. 538p. DA 15 (Mar. 1955), 430-31; UM 11,014.
Includes consideration of "the Japanese appeal to Confucian beliefs."

STRAELEN, Henricus van, J.J.M. Yoshida Shōin: Forerunner of the Meiji Restoration. 1949. See no.513.

1886
INAGAKI, Bernard R. The Constitution of Japan and the Natural Law. Catholic, 1955. v, 194p.
The dissertation "analyzes the 1946 Constitution in the light of the basic principles of the Thomistic social philosophy. It begins with a discussion of the basic elements of the Thomistic concept of the natural law....It then delineates the natural law elements in the Constitution and investigates the problems of adjusting the relationship between the Constitution and the actual conditions of social life in Japan."
Rel.Publ.: The Constitution...Law. Washington, 1955. 27p. (Catholic University of America. Philosophical Series, 164; Abstract Series, 19)

1887
OTAKE, Masaru Victor. A Study of Japanese Taste with An Observation Concerning Fūryū and The Structure of Iki by Kuki Shūzō. Syracuse, 1956. 236p. DA 17 (June 1957), 1357-58; UM 19,386.
Investigates the history of mono no aware ("the spirit of seeing things through empathy and achieving harmony with Nature, love, and the world after death"), fūryū (the spirit which "strives to bring the work-a-day life towards art rather than art towards life"), and iki ("the sensibility of Edo, particularly of its common people"). Also presents a "philosophical exposition of fūryū and iki executed by Dr. Kuki Shūzō (1888-1941), one of the foremost modern philosophers in Japan."

BLACKER, Carmen E. Fukuzawa Yukichi: A Study in the Introduction of Western Ideas into Japan in the Meiji Period. 1957. See no.595.

LEBRA, William P. Okinawan Religion. 1958. See no. 693.

1888
ÖRNEK, Sedat Veyis. Die religiösen, kulturellen, und sozialen Reformen in der neuen Türkei (von 1920 bis 1938), verglichen mit der Modernisierung Japans [The Religious, Cultural, and Social Reforms of the New Turkey, 1920-1938, Compared with Japan's Modernization]. Tübingen, 1960. iii, 113p. Text in German. Diss. ms. available at Tübingen, Universitätsbibliothek, Nr. Um 8485.
The first three chapters focus on social, cultural, and religious reforms in Turkey. Chapter 4 presents a general survey of Turkey's cultural history and calls attention to parallels respectively in the Japanese and in the Turkish process of modernization. Finally, chapter 5 compares the religion and the culture of Turkey with their Japanese counterparts.

1889
SHINTO, William Mamoru. The Role of the Prophet in Japanese Religion. Southern Baptist, 1960. xxvi, 275p.
Contents: The Role of the Prophet in Non-Japanese Cultural Religions [Semitic, Aryan, and non-Japanese East Asian peoples]; Factors in Ancient Japan (Pre-History to 794 A.D.) Contributing to Conditions Favorable for the Growth of the Japanese Prophet; Rise of Japanese Buddhism and Buddhist Prophets (794-1568); The Japanese Prophet in the Tokugawa Period; The Prophet and Modern Japan (1868-1960).

1890
KOZLOVSKII, Iu. B. Filosofiia Nisida i ee idealisticheskaia sushchnost' [Nishida (Kitarō)'s Philosophy and Its Idealistic Nature]. Moscow, Institut filosofii Akademii nauk SSSR, 1963. (Candidate of Philosophical Sciences degree) 195p. Text in Russian.

1891
TAKENO, Keisaku. Pascal et la philosophie de Nishida [Pascal and the Philosophy of Nishida]. Paris, 1961. ix, 210p. Text in French.
Blaise Pascal (1623-1662), French mathematician and philosopher, and Nishida Kitarō (1870-1945).

1892
SAITO, Niyoshi. Étude sur la philosophie de Nishida (1870-1945) [A Study of the Philosophy of Nishida (Kitarō), 1870-1945]. Paris, 1965. 97p. Text in French.
Nishida Kitarō, Japan's most important pre-war philosopher, who sought to synthesize Western philosophical thought with Japanese tradition.

CORWIN, Charles M. Selected Concepts of Human Experience as seen in the Japanese Tradition and in the Biblical Tradition: A Comparative Study. 1966. See no.85.

1893
HUNTSBERRY, William Randall. Religion and Value-Formation in Japan. Harvard, 1968. ii, 232p. AB: 5p. summary appended to diss. ms.
Examines the images and myths propagated by the ancient Japanese in order to determine "the paradigmatic model which governed the way the contents of these stories were put together" and to clarify "the relationship of religion and value-formation in ancient Japan." Also seeks to determine whether "there is a continuity in Japanese values from ancient times to the present."

1894
KAMMER, Reinhard. Die Kunst der Bergdämonen: Zen-Lehre und Konfuzianismus in der japanischen Schwertkunst. Das Tengu-geijutsu-ron des Shissai Chozan [The Art of the Mountain Demons: Zen Teachings and Confucianism in the Japanese Art of the Sword. The Tengu geijutsuron of Shissai Chozan]. Bochum, 1968. Text in German. The dissertation in its published form is available at Bochum, Universitätsbibliothek.
Surveys the historical development of Japanese swordsmanship, provides an annotated translation of the Tengu geijutsuron, and examines the influence of Zen and Confucianism upon the Japanese art of the sword and Shissai Chozan's interpretation of swordsmanship.
Rel.Publ.: Die Kunst...Chozan. Weilheim/OBB.: Otto Wilhelm Barth Verl., 1969. 165p.

BUDDHISM

See also: Religion-- Confucianism, Bushidō, Kokugaku, and Yōgaku (pages 228-30), Religion--Zen Buddhism (pages 231-32), and Overseas Japanese Communities-- United States (pages 200-08).

TRAUTZ, Friedrich M. Der Stupa in Japan: Eine Ubersicht literarischer japanischen Quellen, nebst Texten und Übersetzungen. 1921. See no.1511.

1895
HILBURN, Samuel Milton. A Social History of the Rise of Amida Buddhism in Japan. Chicago, 1930. 148p. AB: University of Chicago. Abstracts of Theses, Humanistic Series, v.8 (1929/30), p.305-09.
Five stages are distinguished: The pre-Buddhist religious development in Japan, the entrance of Buddhism, the first century of Buddhism, the Nara period, and Heian Buddhism.

1896
NAKARAI, Toyozo Wada. A Study of the Impact of Buddhism upon Japanese Life as Revealed in the Odes of the Kokinshū. Michigan, 1930. vi, 171p.
Analyzes the religious ideas found in the Kokinshū.
Rel.Publ.: A Study...Kokin-shū. Greenfield, Indiana: Wm. Mitchell Printing Co., 1931. 130p.

1897
GULIK, Robert Hans van. Hayagrīva: The Mantrayānic Aspect of Horse-Cult in China and Japan. Utrecht, 1935.
See especially Ch.4, "Hayagrīva in Japan" (p.76-94), which studies the horse-cult in Japan before the introduction of Buddhism, the Buddhist Hayagrīva, and Hayagrīva in the Japanese canon.
Rel.Publ.: Hayagrīva...Japan. Leiden: E.J. Brill, 1935. iv, 103p. (Internationales Archiv für Ethnographie...Supplement zu Bd. 33)

1898
TAJIMA, Ryūjun. Étude sur le Mahavairocana-Sutra (Dainichikyō), avec la traduction commentée du premier chapitre [Study of the Mahavairocana Sutra (Dainichikyō), with an Annotated Translation of the First Chapter]. Paris, 1936. Text in French.
Includes background information on the Shingon sect. Contents: A General Study of the Dainichikyō; Translation of Its First Chapter; Doctrinal Analysis of the First Chapter; Resume of Chapters 2-31.
Rel.Publ.: Étude...chapitre. Paris: Nizet et Bastard, 1936. 228p.

1899
SHACKLOCK, Floyd. The Amida Sects of Japanese Buddhism. Hartford Seminary Foundation, 1937. v, 406p.
Contents: The Amida Teachings; Introduction and Growth of Amida Teachings; Hōnen and the Jōdo Sect; Development of Amida Sects; Shinran and the Shin Sect; Modern Awakening (Meiji Era); Temples, Priesthood, and Rituals; Sects and Sub-sects; Present Tendencies; Sacred Scriptures, Suffering and Karma, Man; Amida; Sin and Salvation, Paradise; Amidism in Daily Life.

FURUKAWA, Jiryo. Samurai und Bodhisattva: Die Bestimmung des japanischen Erziehungs-Ideals durch die buddhistische Ethik. 1939. See no.393.

NELSON, Andrew. The Origin, History, and Present status of the Temples of Japan. 1939. See no.1978.

1900
BUTSCHKUS, Horst. Luthers Religion und ihre Entsprechung im japanischen Amida-Buddhismus [Luther's Religion and Its Equivalent in Japanese Amida Buddhism]. Bonn, 1944. Text in German. The dissertation in its published form is available at Marburg/Lahn, Staatsbibliothek Preussischer Kulturbesitz, Nr. Hsn 11,076.
The author studies and compares the two with regard to (1) the concept of good deeds, (2) the phenomenon of faith, (3) precepts of law, (4) types of experience, (5) questions concerning the nature and the content of religion, (6) predestination, and (7) concepts concerning man and his individuality as well as his libertinism. There is also a comparison of the Afterworld, the Western Paradise in Amida Buddhism, and Paradise.
Rel.Publ.: Luthers...Buddhismus. Emsdetten (Westf.): Lechte, 1940. iii, 92p.

1901
HARRIS, Lindell Otis. The Doctrine of Salvation in

Japanese Buddhism. Southwestern Baptist, 1949. 214p.
Contents: The Doctrine of Salvation in Original Buddhism; The Rise and Spread of Mahayana Buddhism and the Comparison of Mahayana and Hinayana; A View of Buddhism in Japan; The Doctrine of Salvation in the Hinayana Sects (Kusha, Jō-Jitsu, and Ritsu Sects); In the Quasi-Mahayana Sects (Sanron and Hossō Sects); In the Kegon Mahayana, Tendai Mahayana, Shingon Mahayana, Zen Mahayana, Jōdo Mahayana, Shin Mahayana, and Nichiren Mahayana Sects; The Doctrine of Salvation in Japanese Buddhism; The Future of Buddhism in Japan.

1903
KITAGAWA, Joseph Mitsuo. Kōbō-Daishi and Shingon Buddhism. Chicago, 1951. 302p.
The first two chapters sketch the religious development of Japan before and during the Nara period. Then the background and life of Kōbō Daishi (774-835) are described, and finally the development of the Shingon sect is studied.

1904
SHIMOYAMA, Tokuji. Der Einfluss der schamanistisch-shintoistischen Urreligion Japans auf den japanischen Buddhismus: Eine religionspsychologische Studie [The Influence of the Shamanistic-Shintoistic Primitive Religion of Japan upon Japanese Buddhism: A Study in the Psychology of Religion]. Bonn, 1954. 94p. Text in German. Diss. ms. available at Bonn, Universitätsbibliothek, Nr. U 4° 54/414.
The author first studies Japanese mentality with regard to the reception of foreign religious ideas, and the essence of Japan's indigenous religion. He then compares Shamanistic psychology with the Shinto concepts of the gods. Finally, he studies the transformation of Buddhism as a foreign religion in Japan, examining Japanese sculpture from the period when Buddhism was introduced into the country.

1905
ANDERSON, Ronald Stone. Nishi Honganji and Japanese Buddhist Nationalism, 1862-1945. California, Berkeley, 1956. vii, 313p.
Contents : Pt.1: The Setting: Buddhism and Nationalism in Japan: The Beginnings of Nationalism and the Role of Religion in Its Rise; Buddhism and the Japanese State: An Historical Resumé; The Meiji Restoration and the Use of Religion; Renewed Pressures by the Totalitarian Government on Religion; Utilizing Buddhism to Win the Hearts of the People of Asia. Pt.2: Nishi Honganji and the Rise of Nationalism: The First Stage: Co-operation with the Early Meiji Government; The Second Stage: Sect Leadership in Nationalism during the Decade of Abbot Ōtani Kōzui; The Third Stage: Co-operation with the Ultranationalists. Pt.3: Kōzui, Case History of a Buddhist Nationalist: Kōzui as Abbot; Kōzui as an Independent, in Business, and Religion; Kōzui and the National Reconstruction Movement; Kōzui's Political Philosophy and Position; Kōzui's Impact on Japan.

1906
CALLAWAY, Tucker Noyes. A Comparison of the Christian Doctrine of Salvation with That of Some of the Major Sects of Japanese Buddhism. Southern Baptist, 1956. xx, 339p.
"The purpose of this thesis is to provide material which would assist a Christian in making an effective evangelistic approach to informed adherents of Japanese Buddhism." Contents: General Considerations Concerning Salvation in Japanese Buddhism; Salvation in the Zen Sect; Salvation in the Jōdo-Shin Sect; Salvation in the Nichiren Sect; Comparison between the Buddhist and Christian Doctrines of Salvation.
Rel.Publ.: Japanese Buddhism and Christianity: A Comparison of the Christian Doctrine of Salvation with that of some Major Sects of Japanese Buddhism. Tokyo: Shinkyō Shuppansha. 1957. 320p.; "The World-View of Japanese Buddhism," Japan Christian Quarterly, 24 (Apr. 1958), 98-102.

1907
GLAUBITZ, Joachim. Das Hokke-Shuhō-ippyakuza-kikigaki-shō: Übersetzung, textkritische und grammatische Bearbeitung eines buddhistischen Erzählungstextes [The Hokke-shuhō-ippyakuza-kikigaki-shō: Translation, Textual Criticism, and Grammatical Analysis of a Buddhist Narrative Text]. Hamburg, 1959. ii, 305p. Text in German. Diss. ms. available at Hamburg, Staats- und Universitätsbibliothek, Nr. Diss. phil. Mscr. 678.
The dissertation includes an annotated translation of the work, a study of the text and of its arrangement, and a grammatical analysis that focuses upon verbs, the imperative mood, the pronouns ware and waga, and the particles na, ga, o, ya, and ka.

1908
KAMSTRA, Jacques H. The Hīna- and Mahāyānism of the Japanese Nara Sects. Nijmegen, Katholieke Universiteit, 1962.
Rel.Publ.: Encounter or Syncretism: The Initial Growth of Japanese Buddhism. Leiden: E.J. Brill, 1967. viii, 505p.

1909
KOHLER, Werner. Die drei grossen Lotus-Bewegungen in Japan [The Three Great Lotus Movements in Japan]. Zürich, 1962. ii, 301p. Text in German.
Contents: What are Modern Religions in Japan?; Religions in Japan, Past and Present; Typical Modern Religions; The Lotus Sutra; The Prophet Nichiren; The Three Great Lotus Movements; Ancestor Worship and Shamanism; Modern Japanese Religion and Us.
Rel.Publ.: Die Lotus-Lehre und die modernen Religionen in Japan. Zürich: Atlantis, 1962. 299p.

1910
BLOOM, Alfred. Shinran: His Life and Thought. Harvard, 1963. iii, 299p. AB: 8p. summary appended to diss. ms.
Contents: Shinran's World: The Age of Transition from Heian to Kamakura; Shinran's Life: The Journey toward Self Acceptance; Shinran's Thought: A Religion of Pure Grace.
Rel.Publ.: "Shinran's Philosophy of Salvation by Absolute Other Power," Contemporary Religions in Japan, 5 (June 1964), 119-42; "Shinran's Gospel of Pure Grace," Journal of Bible and Religion, 32 (Oct. 1964), 305-16; Shinran's Gospel of Pure Grace. Tucson: University of Arizona Press, 1965. xiv, 97p. (Association for Asian Studies, Monographs and Papers, 20); "Shinran and Nichiren: A Comparison," Maha bodhi (Calcutta), 74 (May/June 1966), 115-18; "The Sense of Sin and Guilt and the Last Age (mappō) in Chinese and Japanese Buddhism," Numen, 14 (July 1967), 144-49; The Journey to Self-Acceptance. Leiden: E.J. Brill, 1968. 62p.[Also published as "The Life of Shinran Shonin: The Journey to Self-Acceptance," Numen, 15 (Feb. 1968), 1-62.]

1911
ORLOFF, Alicia Catherine. The Influence of Buddhist Negation on the Concept of Divinity 'Indian Background of Honji Suijaku'. Claremont, 1964. 305p.
Contents: The Concept of Negation in Indian Buddhism; Gods in Early Buddhism: Buddhist Transformation of Indian Gods; Influence of Mādhyamika and Vijñānavada Negation upon the Notion of Divinity; Tantrism; Influence of the Chinese Affirmation; The Concept of Buddhism in Japan and the Rise of Shunbutso Shugo; Development of the Theory of Honji Suijaku; Epilogue.
Rel.Publ.: The Buddhist Philosophy of Assimilation: The Historical Development of the Honji-Suijaku Theory. Tokyo: Tuttle, 1969. 310p; "The Land of Natural Affirmation: Pre-Buddhist Japan," MN 21 (1966) 203-09.

1912
EARHART, Harry Byron. A Religious Study of the Mount Haguro Sect of Shugendō: An Example of Japanese Mountain Religion. Chicago, 1965. 683p. (2v.)
A detailed treatment of the development and religious life of a very eclectic Japanese sect which developed from indigenous beliefs and religious practices in the mountains. This religious movement previously was studied only as a Shinto-Buddhist aspect of folk religion.
Rel.Publ.: "Four Ritual Periods of Haguro Shugendō in Northeastern Japan," History of Religions, 5 (Summer 1965), 93-113; "Shugendō, the Traditions of En no Gyōja, and Mikkyō Influence," in Studies of Esoteric Buddhism and Tantrism (Koyasan, Japan: Koyasan University, 1965), 297-317; "Ishikozume: Ritual Execution in Japanese Religion, Especially in Shugendō," Numen, 13 (Aug. 1966), 116-27; "Toward a Unified Interpretation of Japanese Religion," in The History of Religions: Essays on the Problem of Understanding, ed. by Joseph M. Kitagawa (Chicago: University of Chicago Press, 1967), 195-225; Japanese Religion: Unity and Diversity. Belmont, Calif.: Dickenson, 1969. 115p.

1913
REID, James David. Revelation and the Religions: A Theological Inquiry into the meaning of the Final Revelation through a Critical Analysis of the Problem as It Emerges in Selected Writings of Ernst Troeltsch, Karl Barth, and Hendrik Kraemer, with Limited Reference to the Diverse Claims to Ultimate Truth Made by the non-Christian Religions as Instanced by the Jōdo Shinshū, and with Specific Reference to the Problem of Religious Encounter. Harvard, 1965. iv, 417p. AB: 1p. summary appended to diss. ms.
See Pt.2, Ch.6, "The Jōdo Shinshū" (p.316-69).

1914
KIM, Hee-Jin. The Life and Thought of Dōgen. Claremont, 1966. 342p. DA 28 (Aug. 1967), 728-29-A; UM 67-9513.
"Dōgen's (1200-1253) thought, developed chiefly in the Shōbō-genzō, is examined in terms of (1) method, (2) cosmology, and (3) mystical realism." Contents: Dōgen's Life; Language, Action, and Understanding; The Cosmology of Impermanence: The Buddha-Nature; Mystical Realism: The Acting Buddha.

1915
WEINSTEIN, Stanley. The Kanjin kakumushō. Harvard, 1966. vi, 596p. (2v.)
"The only work of manageable size in Japanese Buddhist literature that contains a detailed, systematic discussion of all of the major doctrines of the Hosso School" (Kamakura Period). Contains an annotated translation of the Kanjin kakumushō with a philological study of the Chinese Buddhist terminology that is employed.

1916
ROTERMUND, Hartmut O. Die Yamabushi: Aspekte ihres Glaubens, Lebens, and ihrer sozialen Funktionen im japanischen Mittelalter [The Yamabushi: Aspects of Their Faith, Their Lives, and Their Social Functions in Japan during the Middle Ages]. Hamburg, 1967. Text in German. The dissertation in its published form is available at Hamburg, Staats- und Universitätsbibliothek; also at the University of Michigan, General Library, no.GN37. H2A4 no.5.
Studies the importance of the yamabushi (Buddhist hermits who lived in the mountains) in Japanese religious and cultural history, their religious and worldly behavior during the Kamakura and Muromachi periods, their religious beliefs, and the austerities that they practiced.
Rel.Publ.: Die Yamabushi...Mittelalter. Hamburg: Cram, de Gruyter in Komm., 1968. xiv, 257p. (Monographien zur Völkerkunde, herausgegeben vom Hamburgischen Museum für Vökerkunde, 5); Die Legende des Enno-Gyōja, Oriens Extremus, 12 (Dec. 1965), 221-42.

1917
INGRAM, Paul Owens. Pure Land Buddhism in Japan: A Study of the Doctrine of Faith in the Teachings of Hōnen and Shinran. Claremont, 1968. 113p. DA 29 (Aug. 1968), 667-68-A; UM 68-10,511.
"The main question of the study concerns the basis for Hōnen's and Shinran's rejection of all traditional Buddhist methods of personal efforts in the quest for nirvana, and their emphasis upon a doctrine of the salvation by faith through grace in Japanese Pure Land Buddhism. Contents: Introduction; Indian Pure Land Buddhism, Chinese Pure Land Buddhism; Japanese Pure Land Buddhism; Conclusion.

PALMER, Arthur A. Buddhist Politics: Japan's Clean Government Party. 1970. See no.1868.

CHRISTIANITY
See also Education--religious education (pages 57-58) and History--The Japanese Empire: Chōsen (pages 90-95).

1918
ISHIZAKA, Masanobu. Christianity in Japan, 1859-1883. Johns Hopkins, 1894. 35p.
Contents: Opening of the Door to the Gospel; Breaking up of the Barriers; Indirect Obstacles to the Spread of Christianity; Progress of the Work; Rise of Nationalistic Church.
Rel.Publ.: Christianity...1883. Baltimore, 1895. 35p.

1919
FAUST, Allen Klein. Christianity as a Social Factor in Modern Japan. Pennsylvania, 1909. 96p.
Contents: The Antecedents of Christianity in Japan; The second Coming of Christianity: Its Influence on Government and Education in Japan; Influence of Christianity on Literature, Morals, and Religions of Japan; Influence of Christianity on Philanthropic and Social Work in Japan; The Japanese Christian Church.
Rel.Publ.: Christianity...Japan. Lancaster, Pa.: Steinman & Foltz, 1909. 96p.

1920
KATO, Katsuji. The Psychology of Oriental Religious Experience: A Study of Some Typical Experiences of Japanese Converts to Christianity. Chicago, 1913.
"A psychological interpretation of the phenomenon of conversion and various phases of religious experience attendant upon it, as seen in a group of arbitrarily selected Japanese Christians."
Rel.Publ.: The Psychology...Christianity. Menasha, Wisc.: George Banta, 1915. 102p.

1921
GOETZE, Walter. Franz Xaviers Missionsarbeit in Japan und sein Ende [Francis Xavier's Missionary Work in Japan and His Death]. Berlin, 1930. Text in German. The dissertation in its published form is available at Marburg/Lahn, Universitätsbibliothek, Nr. XIX c.
A study of Xavier's missionary work in Japan with particular emphasis upon (1) his life, (2) reports of his journeys, (3) the miracles he performed, (4) the organization of missionary outposts, and (5) Xavier's image among Catholics and Protestants.
Rel.Publ.: Franz...Ende. Berlin: Emil Ebering, 1930. 47p.

1922
IGLEHART, Charles Wheeler. The Japanese Spirit as a Conditioning Factor in the Further Integration of the Christian Movement in Japan: A Study in Education. Drew, 1934. 211p. AB: Selected Graduate Theses in Religious Education, 1934. p.36-37.
Contents: Pt.1: Sources and Development of the Japanese Spirit: Aesthetic and Cultural Aspects; Religious and Philosophical Aspects; Ethical and Social Aspects (Early Communal Life, Family System, Bushidō, The Nation). Pt.2: The National Spirit in Present-Day Japan: The Current Political Philosophy of Japan (Theory of the Origin and Nature of the State, The Emperor and His Subjects, The Place of the Individual, Messianic Destiny of the State); Cultivation of the State Cult. Pt.3: The Integration of the Christian Movement in Japanese Society: The Present Factors; The Problem of Further Integration.

1923
RYDER, Stephen Willis. A Historical-Educational Study of the Japanese Mission of the Reformed Church in America. Columbia (Teachers College), 1935. 172p.
Examines from an educational viewpoint the history of the Japan Mission of the Reformed Church of America from the inauguration of its work in 1859 through 1930. Contents: History of the Japan Mission of the Reformed Church in America: Beginnings and Working Out of Methods; The Mission's Schools; The Mission and Its Relation to Other Groups; Some Major Issues in the History of the Japan Mission of the Reformed Church.
Rel.Publ.: A Historical...America. York, Pa.: York Printing Co., 1935. 172p.; A Historical Sourcebook of the Japan Mission of the Reformed Church in America (1859-1930). York, Pa.: York Printing Co., 1935. 156p.

BASS, Harold J. The Policy of the American State Department toward Missionaries in the Far East. 1937. See no.1358.

1924
FLOYD, Arva Colbert. The Founding of the Japan Methodist Church: From the Point of View of the Methodist Episcopal Church, South. Yale, 1939. 367p.
A description of the establishment of a unified Japanese Methodist Church controlled by Japanese from the missionary churches founded by the two Methodist bodies in the United States and by the Methodist Church of Canada. The study concludes with the unification and the founding of the indigenous church in 1907.

1925
THOMAS, Winburn Townsend. A History of Protestant Christianity in Japan 1883-1889. Yale, 1942. xii, 218p.
Contents: Factors Affecting the Introduction and spread of Protestantism; The Spread of Protestantism in Japan; Reasons for the Spread of Protestantism, 1883-1889; Reasons for Retardation in the Spread of Protestantism; Conclusion.
Rel.Publ.: Protestant Beginnings in Japan: The First Three Decades, 1859-1889. Tokyo, Rutland, Vt.: Tuttle, 1959. 258p.

1926
NOSS, George Sherer. An Inquiry into the Background of and an Interpretation of the Critical Issues Confronting the Japanese Church in Its Struggle with the Japanese Totalitarian State: Together with Some Suggestions for a Solution. Union, 1943. 348, xix p. (2v.)
Contents: The Christian Church in Japan until the Death of Hideyoshi (1598); Ieyasu and His Policy toward the Church; The Efforts of Ieyasu's Successors to Extirpate Christianity; Japan's Period of Isolation and Its Effects; The Imperial Restoration of 1868; Japanese Progress from the Restoration of 1868 until the Sino-Japanese War; To the American Exclusion Act of 1924; From the Exclusion Act of 1924 to the War on China in 1937; The Japanese Church and the Growing Crisis in Its Relations with the Totalitarian State; What of the Future?

1927
DYER, Robert A. The Development of Christian Unity in Japan between 1859 and 1941. Southern Baptist, 1946 171p.

1928
KNUDTEN, Arthur Christian. Toyohiko Kagawa and Some Social, Economic, and Religious Tendencies in Modern Japan. Southern California, 1946. 392p. AB: University of Southern California. Abstracts of Dissertations for...1946. p.45-49
"Examines the life, work, and Christian Philosophy of Kagawa with a view to an analysis of some of the elements in the socioethical structure of the Japanese nation and their manifestations" in contemporary life.

1929
BOURDON, Marie-Antoine-Léon. Alexandre Valignano: Visiteur de la Compagnie de Jésus (1573-1583) [Alexandre Valignano: Inspector for the Society of Jesus, 1573-1583]. Paris, 1949. (Thèse complémentaire) Text in French. Diss. ms. not available.

1930
BOURDON, Marie-Antoine-Léon. La Compagnie de Jésus et le Japon [The Society of Jesus and Japan]. Paris, 1949. Text in French. Diss. ms. not available.

COPELAND, Edwin Luther. The Crisis of Protestant Missions in Japan, 1889-1900. 1949. See no.613

1931
UDY, James Stuart. Attitudes within the Protestant Churches of the Occident toward Propagation of Christianity in the Orient: An Historical Survey Up to 1914. Boston, 1952.

1932
HAYS, George Howard. The Problem of the Development of the Christian Ethic in Japanese Culture. Southern Baptist, 1954. xvi, 461p.

An historical and critical study emphasizing the postwar problem. Contents: Historical Background; Analysis of Japanese Culture: The Religious Heritage; Analysis of Japanese Culture: Social and Political Heritage; Analysis of Japanese Culture: The Ethical and Linguistic Heritage; Christian Ethic; Influence of the Christian Ethic on Japanese Culture; Factors both Conducive and Detrimental to the Development of the Christian Ethic in Japanese Culture; Obstacles Intrinsic in the Nature of the Christian Ethic.

1933
TAKENAKA, Masao. The Relation of Protestantism to Social Problems in Japan, 1900-1941. Yale, 1955. 348p. DA 27 (Dec. 1966), 1921-A [Abstract not available]; UM 65-1970.

Contents: Background Study: The Rise of the Protestant Movement in Japan [during the 1800's]; The Rise of the Christian Socialist Movement; Uchimura and the Non-Church Group; Attitudes of the Orthodox Churches; The Impact of Kagawa and His Movement; The Movement of Social Christianity and the Churches.

1934
HUDDLE, Benjamin Paul. History of the Lutheran Church in Japan. Temple, 1956. 270p.

Contents: Pt.1: Background: Roman Catholic Missions; Protestant and Greek Orthodox Missions. Pt.2: Lutheran Work: Initiations, 1892-1905; Growth and Organization, 1906-1920; Mission-Church, 1920-1930 (Personnel and Reorganization, Educational and Social Work, Problems and Wider Relations); The Church in Emergency, 1930-1940 (The Picture of Emergency, Reaction in the Church, Some Specific Effects); Period of Crisis, 1940-1946; Reorganization and Expansion, 1946-1954.

McGOVERN, James R. American Christian Missions to Japan, 1918-1941. 1957. See no.663.

ZIMMERMAN, Reverend Anthony F. Overpopulation: A Study of Papal Teachings on the Problem, with Special Reference to Japan. 1957. See no.131.

1935
BEST, Ernest Edwin. The Influence of Political and Economic Factors upon the Development of Protestant Christianity in Japanese Society, 1859-1911. Drew, 1958. 377p.

Contents: Pt.1: Prelude to the Restoration: Political Considerations and Social Background (Internal Conditions, External Pressures); Christian Beginnings. Pt.2: The Period of Flux (1868-1889): The Effect of Political and Economic Developments on the Structure of Japanese Society; The Development of Christianity in Relation to the Changing Order. Pt.3: The New Nation (1890-1911): The Structure of the New Nation. Its Political and Social Consequences; The Developing Economy; The Impact of the New Order on the Development of Christianity in Japan.

Rel.Publ.: Christian Faith and Cultural Crisis: The Japanese Case. Leiden: E.J. Brill, 1966. xv, 199p.; "Christian Faith and Cultural Crisis," Journal of Religion (Chicago), 41 (Jan. 1961), 17-27.

1936
GERMANY, Charles Hugh. Dominant Theological Currents in Japanese Protestant Christianity from 1920 to 1958 with Particular Reference to the Nature of Their Understanding of the Responsibility of Christianity to Society. Columbia, 1959. 346p. DA 20 (Mar. 1960): 3867. UM 60-11.

"The central section of the dissertation deals with the confrontation of liberal and dialectical theology within the Christian scene in Japan."

Rel.Publ.: Protestant Theologies in Modern Japan: A History of Dominant Theological Currents from 1920-1960. Tokyo: IISR Press, 1965. xv, 239p.

1937
COGSWELL, James Arthur. A History of the Work of the Japan Mission of the Presbyterian Church in the United States, 1885-1960. Union Theological Seminary in Virginia, 1961. xv, 611p.

Contents: Background of our Mission's Work (1859-1885); Beginning of Our Mission's Work (1885-1905); Its Growth (1906-1930); Our Mission's Work under Stress (1931-1945); Post-War Development of Our Mission's Work (1946-1960).

Rel.Publ.: Until the Day Dawn. [Nashville?]: Board of World Missions, Presbyterian Church U.S., 1957. 226p.

1938
HAGIWARA, Itsue. No-Church Movement: Ein Vergleich des Kirchenbegriffs von Sebastian Franck und Kanzo Utschimura [The "No-Church" Movement: A comparison of the Ecclesiastical Concepts of Sebastian Franck and Uchimura Kanzō]. Marburg, 1962. Text in German. The dissertation in its published form is available at Marburg/Lahn, Staatsbibliothek Preussischer Kulturbesitz, Nr. Hsn 39,454; also at the University of Michigan, General Library, no.28,482.

A comparative Study of Franck and Uchimura and of the criticism they levelled against the institutionalized churches of their times: the established church of the Reformation in Europe, and the church established by foreign missionary societies in Japan. The outcome of their actions also is considered.

Rel.Publ.: No-Church...Utschimura. Marburg: Nolte, 1962. ix, 172p.

1939
LEE, Kun Sam. The Christian Confrontation with Shinto Nationalism: A Historical and Critical Study of the Conflict of Christianity and Shinto in Japan in the Period between the Meiji Restoration and the End of World War II (1868-1945). Amsterdam Vrije Universiteit, 1962.

The introductory chapters examine the development of Shinto nationalism and of Emperor worship as well as the early confrontations of Christianity with Japan. The main chapters study the conflict between Christianity and Shinto nationalism under the two headings "compromise" and "resistance" and deal with both Japan and Korea.

Rel.Publ.: The Christian...1945. Amsterdam: van Soest, 1962. 210p.

1940
SCHNELLBACH, Jörg. Amt und Gemeinde als Unionsproblem asiatischer und afrikanischer Kirchen [Ecclesiastical Duty and the Congregation as a Problem in the Unification of the Asian and African Churches]. Heidelberg, 1962. Text in German. The dissertation in its published form is available at Marburg/Lahn, Staatsbibliothek Preussischer Kulturbesitz, Nr. Hsn 42,515.

Includes information on the Mukyōkai, on state participation in the federation of churches known as the Kyōdan, and on the coexistence of the church and the "non-church" in Japan.

Rel.Publ.: Amt...Kirchen. Heidelberg, 1962. xiii, 245p.

1941
GURGANUS, George Pope. An Audience Analysis of Three Missionary-Supported and Three Indigenous Christian Congregations in Tokyo, Japan. Pennsylvania State, 1963. 171p. DA 25 (Aug. 1964), 1406; UM 64-7714.

"Sought to test whether there were significant differences between three indigenous (self-supporting, self-governing, and self-propagating) congregations and three missionary-supported congregations in their (1) attitude toward Christ and His teachings, (2) attitude toward organized Christianity, (3) attitude toward Euro-Americans, (4) growth in finances, and (5) growth in membership."

1942
NEBREDA, Alfonso M., S.J. Jalones para una preevangelizacion en Japón [Approaches to pre-Evangelization in Japan]. Pontifical Gregorian University, Rome, 1964. Text in Spanish.

"Pre-evangelization", a recently coined term, refers to the creation of an atmosphere that is conducive to the preaching of the Gospel and to the spread of Christian ideals and values.

1943
FALLS, Helen Emery. An Examination of Changes Made Necessary in the Work of the Baptist Foreign Missionary by Changes in Society. Columbia, 1965. 232p. DA 26 (July 1965), 513; UM 65-6162.

Includes information on Baptist Church leadership in Japan as well as on financial conditions of the church there.

1944
HOWES, John Forman. Japan's Enigma: The Young Uchimura Kanzō. Columbia, 1965. 355p. DA 26 (Feb. 1966), 4607-08; UM 65-13,956.

Focuses on the years 1861-1903. Contents: The Ceremony; "A Fretful Timid Child"; The Education of a Chosen Man; The Unhappy Bureaucrat; The Penitent Expatriate; Repatriation; The Resignation; The Birth of a Writer; Lamentation and Literature; Justification of Self and Nation; National Mission and Individual Responsibility; Prophecy with Honor; Out into the World; In enemy Territory; Conclusion: Uchimura Kanzō in History.

Rel.Publ.: "Kanzō Uchimura: Teacher and Writer," Japan Christian Quarterly, 23 (Apr. 1957), 150-56; "Kanzō Uchimura: Social Reformer," Japan Christian Quarterly, 23 (July 1957), 243-52; "Two Works by Uchimura Kanzō until Recently Unknown in Japan," in International Conference of Orientalists in Japan, Transactions, 3 (1958), 25-31; "Kanzō Uchimura on War," Japan Christian Quarterly, 24 (Oct. 1958), 290-92; "Uchimura Kanzō on Christopher Columbus," in International Conference of Orientalists in Japan, Transactions, 5(1960), 109-11 [Also in Japan Christian Quarterly, 26 (Oct. 1960), 239-45]; "The Chijinron of Uchimura Kanzō," in International Conference of Orientalists in Japan, Transactions, 5(1960), 116-26; "Japanese Christians and American Missionaries," in Changing Japanese Attitudes toward Modernization, ed. by Marius B. Jansen (Princeton: Princeton University Press, 1965), 337-68; "Western Words and Japanese Preoccupations: The English-Language Works of Uchimura Kanzō," Pacific Affairs, 38 (1965/66), 307-25; "The Man Kanzō Uchimura," Japan Studies, 13 (Spring 1968), 7-27.

BAGGS, Albert E. Social Evangel as Nationalism: A Study of the Salvation Army in Japan, 1895-1940. 1966. See no.553.

1945
HORI, Mitsuo. Die Kontinuität der einen apostolischen Kirche und die Bedeutung des Bekenntnisses für den Protestantismus ohne Reformation: Dargestellt am Beispiel d. Nihon-Kirisuto-Kyōdan (Verein. Kirche Christi in Japan) [The Continuity of an Apostolic Church and the Meaning of Confession for Protestantism without Reformation: The Case of the Nihon Kirisuto Kyōdan (Church of Christ in Japan)]. Tübingen, 1966. v, 256p. Text in German.

1946
LÓPEZ-GAY, Jesús, S.J. El Catecumenado en la Misión del Japón del siglo XVI [The State of Preparation as a Catechumen in the Mission of Japan of the Sixteenth Century]. Pontifical Gregorian University, Rome, 1966. Text in Spanish.

A "catechumen" is a person under instruction in the rudiments of Christianity.

Rel.Publ.: El Catecumenado...siglo XVI. Roma: Universitas Gregoriana, 1966. 252p. (Studia Missionalia, Documenta et Opera, 2); "Las organizaciones de laicos en el apostolado de la primitiva misión del Japón," Archivum historicum Societatis Iesu, 36, no.71 (Jan./June 1967), 1-31.

1947
NISHIMURA, Ken. Idea of Redemption in the Writings of Toyohiko Kagawa. Emory, 1966. 282p. DA 28 (July 1967), 288-89-A; UM 67-8830.

Presents Kagawa's ideas of God, Christ, man, evil, salvation, and the church; evaluates his theological significance; and seeks to show that the central theme of shokuzaiai (redemptive love) was the fundamental motif which characterized Kagawa's theology as a whole.

SCHEINER, Irwin. The Beginning of Modern Social Criticism in Japan: A Study of the Samurai and Christian Values, 1867-1891. 1966. See no.608.

1948
WEBER, Hans-Ruedi. Asia and the Ecumenical Movement (1895-1961). Genève, 1966.

A descriptive study of the manner in which Asian Christians and churches have been drawn into the ecumenical movement. Concentrates on Japan, China, and Korea.

Rel.Publ.: Asia...1961. London: S.C.M. Press, 1966. 319p.

1949
NOHARA, Thomas K. Institutum Saeculare Ancillae Domini in Japonia: Nagasaki [The Secular Institute of the

Ancillae Domini ("Handmaidens of the Lord") in Nagasaki, Japan]. Pontifical Urban University, 1966/67. Text in Latin.

YAMAMOTO, Masaya. Image-Makers of Japan: A Case Study in the Impact of the American Protestant Foreign Missionary Movement, 1859-1905. 1967. See no.581.

1950
ADAMS, Evyn Merrill. An Elucidation of Soren Kierkegaard's Categories of Communication and Their Application to the Communication of Christian Existence in Japan. Drew, 1968. 505p. DA 30 (Nov. 1969), 1885-86-A; UM 69-18,620.
Contents: The Map of Existence; Reduplication: Christian Experience; Applying the Military Science; The Japanese Aesthetic Attitude (The Shinto Myth and the Japanese Love of Nature, Japanese Aesthetic Vocabulary, Contemporary Aesthetic Expressions in Japan, The Transition from the Aesthetic); The Ethical in Japanese Life (Confucian Roots of Japanese Ethical Relationships, Vocabulary of Japanese Ethical Relationships, Expressions of Ethical Conflicts in Japanese Literature and Popular Media); The Religiosity of the Japanese (Hōnen, Tenrikyō, Zen Buddhism, Nishida Kitarō); Becoming; The Role and Task of the Christian Communicator in Japan; The Pathos of Becoming a Christian in Japan.

1951
BIKLE, George Brown, Jr. The New Jerusalem: Aspects of Utopianism in the Thought of Kagawa Toyohiko. California, Berkeley, 1968. 369p. DA 29 (June 1969), 4412-A; UM 69-10,251.
"We advance a dual theme: On the one hand, we trace the development of that strand of rationality of planning which infused Kagawa's perspective of the New Jerusalem and suggest the contribution such modes of thought may have made to the Japanese modernization process. On the other hand, we examine the social psychology of Kagawa's contemplative mystic beliefs and the secular rationalization of his spiritual relationship to the Divine. We conclude that the modes of Utopian planning Kagawa espoused were thoroughly consonant with the ends of modernization."

BRITSCH, Ralph L. Early Latter-Day Saint Missions to South and East Asia. 1968. See no.647.

1952
IZUMI, Akio. The Theology of Seiichi Hatano. Southwestern Baptist, 1968. 233p.
Contents: The Life and Thought of Seiichi Hatano, 1877-1950; Hatano's Philosophy of Religion (The Essence of Religion, The Basic Features of Philosophy of Religion and Its Method, Personalism as a Basic Feature of Philosophy of Religion, The Content of the Religious Life, Time and Eternity); Hatano's Understanding of Christianity (Judaism, Jesus, Paul); Theological Significance of Hatano's Thought.

ELISON, George S. Deus Destroyed: The Image of Christianity in Early Modern Japan. 1969. See no.503.

CONFUCIANISM, BUSHIDŌ, KOKUGAKU, AND YŌGAKU

See also History--pre-modern: Tokugawa period (pages 66-71).

1953
KAWABE, Jiroku. The Development of Confucianism in Japan under the Influence of the Philosophy of Shushi. Yale, 1904. 205p.
Presents an intellectual history of both Japan and China, analyzes the thought of Shushi (Chu Hsi), Rikushozan, and Ōyōmei, and then relates their thought to three schools of Japanese Confucianism: Yamaga Sokō, Ogyū Sorai, and Itō Jinsai. Finally, the dissertation offers a criticism of Confucian philosophy and analyzes the "moral crisis of Japan."

1954
ARMSTRONG, Robert Cornell. Light from the East: Studies in Japanese Confucianism. Toronto, 1914. xv, 326p.
Contents: Studies in the Early History of Confucianism in Japan; Studies in the Shushi School of Confucianism (Fujiwara Seika, Hayashi Razan, Amenomori Hōshū and Andō Seian, Muro Kyūsō, Nakamura Tekisai, Kaibara Ekken, Yamazaki Ansai and Asami Keisai, Mito School, Shushi Scholars after the Kansei Era); Studies in the Ō-Yōmei School (Nakae Tōju and His School, Kumazawa Banzan, Kitajima Setsuzan, Miwa Shitsusai, Nakane Tōri and Ōshio Chūsai, Several Yōmei Scholars, Fujita Tōko, Saigō Takamori, Yoshida Shōin and Others at the Time of the Restoration); Studies in the Classical School (Yamaga Sokō, Itō Jinsai, Ogyū Sorai, Itō Tōgai, Dazai Shundai and Others); The Eclectic School of Confucianism (Hosoi Heishū and Uesugi Yōzan, Katayama Kenzan and others).
Rel.Publ.: Light...Confucianism. Toronto: University of Toronto Press, 1914. xv, 326p. (University of Toronto Studies. Philosophy).

HATSUKADE, Itsuaki. Die Bildungsideale in der japanischen Kultur und ihr Einfluss auf das Erziehungswesen in der Yedo-Zeit. 1932. See no.507.

HASHIMOTO, Jujiro. Grundlage der japanischen Sitten. 1936. See no.41.

1955
GRAF, Olaf. Kaibara Ekiken's Daigiroku. Leiden, 1941. i, 116p. Text in German.
A detailed biography of Kaibara Ekken (1630-1714) and an annotated translation of the Daigiroku, one of his philosophical treatises.
Rel.Publ.: Kaibara Ekiken: Ein Beitrag zur japanischen Geistesgeschichte des 17. Jahrhunderts und zur chinesischen Sung-Philosophie. Leiden: E.J. Brill, 1942. ii, 545p.

1956
DUMOULIN, Heinrich. Kamo Mabuchi, 1697-1769: Ein Beitrag zur japanischen Religions- und Geistesgeschichte [Kamo Mabuchi, 1697-1796: A Contribution to the History of Japanese Religion and Ideas]. Tokyo, 1943 (?). Text in German. AB: Bungaku, Tetsugaku, Shigaku Gakkai Rengō. Kenkyū rombun-shu. v.1, p.241-42.
Includes a detailed account of the life and literary works of Kamo Mabuchi, a study of his thought and of his fight against religious and cultural syncretism, and translations of some of his writings.
Rel.Publ: Kamo...Geistesgeschichte. Tokyo: Sophia University Press, 1943. vii, 317p. (Monumenta Nipponica Monographs, 8); "Kamo Mabuchi: Kokuikō, Gedanken über den 'Sinn des Landes,'" MN, 2 (Jan. 1939),

165-92; "Zwei Texte zum Kadō des Kamo Mabuchi: (1) Uta no kokoro no uchi, (2) Niimanabi," MN, 4 (1941), 192-206, 566-84; "Die Erneuerung des Liederwegs durch Kamo Mabuchi," MN, 6 (1943), 110-45; "Kamo Mabuchi und das Manyōshū," MN, 9 (Apr. 1953), 34-61; "Zwei Texte Kamo Mabuchis zur Wortkunde," MN, 11 (Jan. 1955), 268-83, and 11 (Oct. 1955), 48-63; "Kamo Mabuchis Kommentar zum Norito des Toshigoi-no-matsuri," MN, 12 (Apr./July 1956), 121-56, and 12 (Oct. 1956/Jan. 1957), 101-30.

1957
MIBACH, Karl. "Der Leitfaden der Ritterlehre" von Yamaga Sokō (1622 bis 1685): Unter Berücksichtigung des Kommentars von Joshida Shōin ["The way of the Warrior" (Shidō) by Yamaga Sokō (1622-1685): With Consideration of Yoshida Shōin's Commentary to It]. Bonn, 1944. 160p. Text in German. Diss. ms. available at Bonn, Universitätsbibliothek, Nr. 4° (U 45/642).

Discusses Yamaga Sokō's life and evaluates his works, provides a detailed study of Bukyō shōgaku based on Bukyō kōroku (Yoshida Shōin's commentary to it), and concludes with an annotated translation of Shidō.

1958
THONAK, Otto. Über den Ideengehalt der japanischen Herzenslehre und die Organisation der auf sie gegründeten Volkserziehungsbewegung [The Intellectual Content of Shingaku ("Learning of the Mind") in Japan and the Organization of the National Education Movement that was Based Upon It]. Berlin, 1944. viii, 226p. (2v.) Text in German. Diss. ms. available at Berlin, Humboldt Universität, Universitätsbibliothek, Nr. P.13

Studies the historical background of Shingaku, its founding by Ishida Baigan, its growth as an ethical and national movement, and its subsequent development.

1959
SPAE, Joseph John. Itō Jinsai: A Philosopher, Educator, and Sinologist of the Tokugawa Period. Columbia, 1947. xv, 278p.

Contents: Historical Notes on Confucianism in Japan with Special Reference to the Classics; Biography of Itō Jinsai [1627-1705]; Jinsai as Philosopher and Moralist (Cosmology, Theism, Human Nature, Virtue and the Virtues); Jinsai as Educator; Jinsai as Sinologist; The Kogidō and Jinsai's Successors; Conclusion.

Rel.Publ.: Itō...Period. Peiping: Catholic University of Peking, 1948. xv, 278p. (Monumenta Serica, Monograph Series, 12)

1960
McEWAN, John Robertson. Ogyū Sorai. Cambridge, 1951. 314p. AB: University of Cambridge. Abstracts of Dissertations...1951/1952. p.156-57.

Pt.1: "His biography, his studies in the Chinese language, and the development of his Confucian doctrines." Pt.2: A description of two of his works, Taiheisaku and Seidan.

Rel.Publ.: The Political Writings of Ogyū Sorai. Cambridge: Cambridge University Press, 1962. viii, 153p. (University of Cambridge. Oriental Publications, 7); "Some Aspects of the Confucianism of Ogyū Sorai," Asia Major, 8 (1961), 199-214.

BELLAH, Robert N. Religion and Society in Tokugawa Japan. 1955. See no.6.

WEBB, Herschel F. The Thought and Work of the Early Mito School. 1958. See no.523.

1961
BRÜLL, Lydia. Ōkuni Takamasa und seine Weltanschauung: Ein Beitrag zum Gedankengut der Kokugaku [Ōkuni Takamasa and His Philosophy of Life: A Contribution to the Ideological Content of Kokugaku]. München, 1964. Text in German. The dissertation in its published form is available at Bochum, Universitätsbibliothek, Nr. GB 27,806; also at the University of Michigan, General Library, no. DS881.5.048B88.

A study of the ideological background of Ōkuni Takamasa's (1793-1871) teachings. The author investigates the structure of the world outlook and the system of values that developed out of his teachings and provides an annotated translation of his work Hongaku Kyōyō.

Rel.Publ.: Ōkuni...Kokugaku. Wiesbaden: Harrassowitz, 1964. 111p. (Studien zur Japanologie, 7)

1962
MIYOSHI, Mother Setsuko, R.S.C.J. The Role of Kokugaku and Yōgaku during the Tokugawa Period. Georgetown, 1965. 134p. DA 26 (Dec. 1965), 3269-70; UM 65-4122.

Considerable attention is devoted to the teachings of Hirata Atsutane (1776-1843), in whom the tendency to regard the Kokugaku movement "as the true expression of Japanese national feeling untainted by alien culture" reached its height.

1963
LIDIN, Olof Gustaf. Ogyū Sorai: Life and Philosophy, with Full Translation of His Work Bendō and Partial Translation of His Work Seidan. California, Berkeley, 1967. 551p. DA 28 (May 1968), 4603-04-A; UM 68-5766.

Contents: The Life of Ogyū Sorai; Essay on Sorai's Philosophy, Based Mainly on His Work, the Bendō; Some of Sorai's Political Ideas, as Contained in the First kan of the Seidan; Translations.

Rel.Publ.: "Annotated Translation of the Preface and First Chapter of Seidan (first kan) by Ogyū Sorai," Phi Theta Papers (Berkeley, Calif.), (Fall 1963), 17-33.

1964
MATSUMOTO, Shigeru. Motoori Norinaga. Harvard, 1967. iv, 483p. AB: 8p. summary appended to diss. ms.

Focuses on "the personal or motivational level, together with the social and cultural levels, of Norinaga's thought." "Chapter 1 is concerned with Norinaga's family background and with his early experiences and problems....Chapter 2 considers the way in which the developed the idea of mono no aware on the basis of his study of ancient Japanese (particularly Heian) literature and through his encounter with Confucian and Buddhist ideas....Chapter 3 deals with his thirties and forties, when he established his idea of the "Ancient Way" on the basis of his study of ancient Japanese texts, the Kojiki in particular." Chapter 4 discusses his personal maturity and social activity in his old age.

Rel.Publ.: Motoori Norinaga (1730-1801). Cambridge: Harvard University Press, forthcoming.

1965
ODRONIC, Walter John. Kodō taii (An Outline of the Ancient Way): An annotated Translation with an Introduction to the Shintō Revival Movement and a Sketch of the Life of Hirata Atsutane. Pennsylvania, 1967. 259p. DA 28 (Apr. 1968), 4258-59-A; UM 68-4599.

Contents of the Introductory Section: Summary of Shintō History; Kada no Azumamaro; Kamo no Mabuchi; Motoori Norinaga; Hirata Atsutane; Studies of the Kokugakusha; Kodō taii.

1966
SCHUSTER, Ingrid. Kamada Ryūkō und seine Stellung in der Shingaku [Kamada Ryūkō and His Position within Shingaku]. München, 1967. Text in German. Diss. ms. available at München, Universitätsbibliothek.

Studies the intellectual background of Shingaku and its objectives as determined by Ishida Baigan, the three main directions in its later development, the life and work of Kamada Ryūkō (1754-1821?), and Kamada's teachings as illustrated in his book Michi no kodama. The dissertation concludes with an assessment of Kamada Ryūkō's position within Shingaku and with a translation of Michi no kodama.

Rel.Publ: Kamada...Shingaku. Wiesbaden: Harrassowitz, 1967. 137p. (Studien zur Japanologie, 10)

1967
McMULLEN, Ian James. Kumazawa Banzan: The Life and Thought of a Seventeenth Century Japanese Confucian. Cambridge, 1969. 462p.

Kumazawa Banzan (1619-1691), the chief minister to Ikeda Mitsumasa (the daimyo of Bizen han), a student of the Yōmei school of Confucianism, and the author of such works as Daigaku wakumon, Shintō taigi, and Miwa-monogatari. Contents: Pt.1: Short Biography. Pt.2: Confucian Ritual. Pt.3: Anti-Buddhism. Pt.4: Forestry.

NEW RELIGIONS OF JAPAN (Konkokyō, Ōmotokyō, P.L. Kyōdan, Seichō no Ie, Soka Gakkai, etc.)

1968
CLARKE, Edward Maurice. Konko-kyō, or Modern Sect of Shintoism. Edinburgh, 1924. iv, 148p. A copy of the dissertation has been deposited at the University of Michigan, General Library.

Section 1 focuses on the following aspects of Konko-kyō: (a) Its historical development; (b) Its business organization and methods; (c) Its ceremonies and worship; (d) Its doctrinal content (scriptural basis, theological tenets, and anthropological, ethical, social, and philosophical speculations). Section 2 elaborates on the above points, translates the sect's "constitution," and compares certain tenets of Konko-kyō with those of other religions.

1969
HEPNER, Charles William. The Kurozumi Sect of Shinto. Yale, 1933. 298p.

"Shows the relationship of the Kurozumi sect to the historical antecedents of Shinto development," studies the life and work as well as the teaching of Kurozumi Munetada, (1780-1850), and explains the organization, constitution, and activities of the Kurozumi sect.

Rel.Publ.: The Kurozumi...Shinto. Tokyo: Meiji Japan Society, 1935. xviii, 263p.

1970
BAIRY, Mauritius A. Japans "Neue Religionen" in der Nachkriegszeit [Japan's "New Religions" since World War II]. Bonn, 1959. Text in German. The dissertation in its published form is available at Marburg/Lahn, Staatsbibliothek Preussischer Kulturbesitz, Nr. Ser. 3905-3.

Determines those factors that account for the newness and originality of Japan's "new religions" and studies the present state of religion in Japan from the social, psychological, religious, and political points of view. Includes an examination of the characteristics of the new religions and studies in particular P.L. Kyōdan within an historical and religious framework.

Rel.Publ.: Japans...Nachkriegszeit. Bonn: Rohrscheid, 1959. 135p. (Untersuchungen zur allgemeinen Religionsgeschichite, N.F. Bd 3)

1971
HAMMER, Raymond Jack. The Idea of God in Japan's New Religions: With Special Reference to Tenrikyō, Konkokyō, Sekai Kyuseikyō, Ōmotokyō, Reiyukai, Risshokoseikai, P.L. Kyōdan, Seichō no Ie, and Ananaikyō. London, 1961. vi, 334p.

Examines the religions of postwar Japan in terms of their development from the "Shinto-Buddhist substratum," and the influence of Christian vocabulary and concepts. Maintains that these religions remain primarily Oriental in such things as adapting charismatic traditions.

1972
OFFNER, Clark Benjamin. The Doctrine and Practice of Faith Healing in Modern Japanese Religions. Northern Baptist Theological Seminary, 1961. 318p.

Includes the Ōmoto-related religions and PL Kyōdan, and Nichiren-related Buddhistic religions. Contents: Background Elaboration; Relevant Metaphysical Concepts; Cause of Sickness; Cure of Sickness; Primary Methods Employed in Healing; Types of People and Sicknesses Healed; Secondary Factors Conducive to Healing; Conclusion; Recapitulation, Evaluation, and Application of Findings.

Rel.Publ: Modern Japanese Religions: With Special Emphasis upon Their Doctrines of Healing [by] Clark B. Offner and Henry van Straelen. New York: Twayne, 1963. 296p.

1973
SCHNEIDER, Delwin Byron. Dissertation on Konkokyō [Exact title unknown]. Rikkyō, 1961.

Studies the background of Konkokyō in Shintoism; the nature of kami, religious leadership, and the Japanese world view; the beginnings of Konkokyō, its scriptures, and its attitudes; and toritsugi (mediation) and Tenchi Kane no Kami.

Rel.Publ.: Konkokyō: A Japanese Religion: A Study in the Continuities of Native Faiths. Tokyo: International Institute for the Study of Religions (ISR) Press, 1962. xv, 166p.

HESSELGRAVE, David J. A Propagation Profile of the Sōka Gakkai. 1965 See no.12.

LEBRA, Takie. An Interpretation of Religious Conversion: A Millennial Movement among Japanese-Americans in Hawaii. 1967. See no.24A.

1974
WIMBERLEY, Hickman Howard. Seichō-no-Ie: A Study of a Japanese Religio-Political Association. Cornell, 1967. 261p. DA 28 (Dec. 1967), 2245-B; UM 67-17,258.

A study of Seichō-no-Ie, one of Japan's "new religions", which seeks to explain why it "is supported by its adherents and why it has assumed the form that it has, a form including a number of cultural components such as Japanese ultranationalism and ancestor worship which are significant features of Japanese society."

SKELTON, T. Lane. Social Movements and Social Change: The Sōka Gakkai of Japan. 1968. See no.17.

White, James W. Mass Movement, Military Religion, and Democracy: Sōka Gakkai in Japanese Politics. 1969. See no.1867.

SHINTO

See also Anthropology and Sociology--ethnography (pages 7-10).

1975
HOLTOM, Daniel Clarence. The Political Philosophy of Modern Shinto: A Study of the State Religion of Japan. Chicago, 1919.

Focuses on some of the problems that developed as a consequence of the close relationship between the modern Japanese state and the Shinto shrines.

Rel.Publ: The Political...Japan. Tokyo, 1922. iv, 325p. (Transactions of the Asiatic Society of Japan. v.49, pt.2); The National Faith of Japan. London: Kegan Paul, Trench, Trubner, 1938. xiii, 329p.; Modern Japan and Shinto Nationalism. Chicago: University of Chicago Press, 1943. ix, 178p.

CLARKE, Edward M. Konko-kyō, or Modern Sect of Shintoism. 1924. See no.1968.

GUNDERT, Wilhelm. Der Schintoismus im japanischen Nō-Drama. 1925. See no.1582.

HEPNER, Charles W. The Kurozumi Sect of Shinto. 1933. See no.1969.

1976
BUCHANAN, Daniel Crump. Inari: Its Origin, Development, and Nature. Hartford Seminary Foundation, 1934. v, 211p.

Contents: The Origin of Inari; Phallicism and Inari; The Fox and Inari; The Cult in Historical Development; The Inari Pantheon; Shrines and Festivals; Worship. (Inari is a Shinto agricultural deity.)

Rel.Publ.: Inari...Nature. Tokyo, 1935. vi, 191p. (Transactions of the Asiatic Society of Japan. 2d. ser., v.12)

1977
HAMMITZSCH, Horst. Yamato-hime no mikoto seiki: Bericht über den Erdenwandel Ihrer Hoheit der Prinzessin Yamato. Eine Quelle zur Frühgeschichte der Shinto-Religion übersetzt und erklärt [Yamato-hime no mikoto seiki: Report of the Life on Earth of Her Highness, Princess Yamato. An Annotated Translation of a Source for the Early History of Shinto]. Leipzig, 1937. Text in German.

A study of the Shintō-gobusho and particulary of one of its parts, the Yamato-hime no mikoto seiki, in which the history and the founding of the two Ise shrines is presented. The Seiki and the Nihongi are compared with regard to the establishment of Ise Shrine, the personality of the shrine's founder, and the dates of the period during which Yamato-hime no mikoto served as high priestess at the shrine. Also includes an annotated translation of Seiki.

Rel.Publ.: Yamato...erklärt. Leipzig: A. Richter, 1937. 92p.

1978
NELSON, Andrew Nathaniel. The Origin, History, and Present Status of the Temples of Japan. Washington, Seattle, 1939. 732p. (2v.) AB: University of Washington. Abstracts of Theses and Faculty Bibliography. v.4. p.355-69.

A detailed history of the origins and historical evolution of Shinto shrines and Buddhist temples in Japan with particular focus on their architecture, their artistic ornamentations, and the sculpture within them. Also investigates the legal and political status of the shrines and temples during the 1930's.

UEHARA, Toyoaki. The Dynamics of the Archetypes in Japanese Shinto Mythology. 1960. See no.55.

LEE, Kun Sam. The Christian Confrontation with Shinto Nationalism: A Historical and Critical Study of the Conflict of Christianity and Shinto in Japan in the Period between the Meiji Restoration and the End of World War II (1868-1945). 1962. See no.1939.

1979
CREEMERS, Wilhelmus Helena Martinus. Shrine Shinto after World War II, 1945-1965. Columbia, 1966. 337p. DA 27 (Oct. 1966), 1101-A; UM 66-9356.

Seeks "to analyze the reasons why and the manner in which State Shinto was disestablished after the war; to observe how Shrine Shinto has tried, and still tries, to re-establish itself in the postwar situation; and to investigate what are its main problems in defining its status in view of postwar developments which made necessary a thorough reexamination of the values of Shrine Shinto."

Rel.Publ.: Shrine...1965. Leiden: E.J. Brill, 1968. xviii, 261p.

FRIDELL, Wilbur M. The Policy of the Japanese Government toward Shinto Shrines at the Town and Village Level, 1894-1914. 1966. See no.619.

TANAKA, Kashiki. A Comparison of the Tzu-ling and the Jingi ryō. 1966. See no.488.

1980
ELLWOOD, Robert S., Jr. Shinto Worship of the Heian Court as Presented in the Engi-shiki. Chicago, 1967. 404p.

An analysis of four liturgies presented in the Engi-shiki: Spring rite, rebuilding of the Grand Shrine at Ise, the imperial priestess at Ise, and the imperial accession ceremony. Substantial portions of the Engi-shiki are translated. A glossary with characters is included.

ZEN BUDDHISM

See also Influence of Japanese Culture Abroad (pages 101-03).

1981
BROWNE, Robert Charles. Some Functional Theories of Religion and Their Philosophical Bases: An Essay in the Integration of Philosophy, Religion, and Social Science. Syracuse, 1959. 163p. DA 20 (May 1960), 4408-09; UM 59-6296.

"The case of zen is provided as an illustration of the regenerative functioning of religion."

MAMMARELLA, Raymond J. Contemporary Education and the Spirit of Zen. 1959. See no.398.

BECKER, Earnest. Zen Buddhism, "Thought Reform" (Brainwashing), and Various Psychotherapies: A Theoretical Study in Induced Regression and Cultural Values. 1960. See no.80.

1982
CHUCK, James. Zen Buddhism and Paul Tillich: A Comparison of Their Views on Man's Predicament and the Means of Its Resolution. Pacific School of Religion, 1962. 356p. DA 23 (Feb. 1963), 3004; UM 62-5726.
Explores the nature and the scope of Western interest in Zen Buddhism and seeks to determine "how the interpreters of Zen to the West relate themselves to the Christian faith."

1983
MAUPIN, Edward Wolfe. An Exploratory Study of Individual Differences in Response to a Zen Meditation Exercise. Michigan, 1962. 99p. DA 23 (Apr. 1963), 3978; UM 63-403.
"The study is designed to give basic information about how people respond during the early stages of meditation and what personality factors are involved in differences in response." The subjects were Americans.
Rel.Publ.: "Individual Differences in Response to a Zen Meditation Exercise," Journal of Consulting Psychology, 29 (Apr. 1965), 139-45.

COLBATH, James A. The Japanese Noh Drama and Its Relation to Zen Buddhism. 1963. See no.2051.

1984
UEDA, Shizuteru. Die Gottesgeburt in der Seele und der Durchbruch zur Gottheit: Die mystische Anthropologie Meister Eckhardts und ihre Konfrontation mit der Mystik des Zen-Buddhismus [The Birth of God in One's Soul and the Break-Through to Divinity: The Mystical Anthropology of Master Eckhardt and Its Confrontation with the Mysticism of Zen Buddhism]. Marburg, 1963. 174p. Text in German.
Rel.Publ.: Die Gottesgeburt...Buddhismus. Gütersloh: Gütersloher Verl.-Haus G. Mohn, 1965. 174p. (Studien zu Religion, Geschichte, und Geisteswissenschaft, 3)

1985
VERDÚ, Alfonso. Die noetische Bedeutung der nichtchristlichen religiösen Erfahrungen: Ein Beitrag zur Phänomenologie und Metaphysik der konistischen Mystik, unter besonderer Berücksichtigung des Zen-Buddhismus [The Noetic significance of non-Christian Religious Experiences: A Contribution to the Phenomenology and Metaphysics of Monistic Mysticism, with Special Regard to Zen Buddhism]. München, 1965. Text in German.
Rel.Publ.: Abstraktion und Intuition als Wege zur Wahrheit in Yoga und Zen: Ein Beitrag zur Phänomenologie und Metaphysik der nicht-christlichen Mystik. München: Pustet, 1965. 309p. (Epimeleia, 1)

1986
HASUMI, Toshimitsu. La Formation philosophique de la pensée du Zen [The Philosophical Formation of Zen Thought]. Paris, 1967. Text in French. AB: Université de Paris. Faculté des Lettres et Sciences Humaines. Positions des thèses de troisième cycle soutenues devant la Faculté en 1967. (Serie "Recherches," t. 52) p.163-64.
Studies Zen thought from a philosophical rather than from a religious viewpoint in order to determine whether one may validly regard Zen as a philosophy or not. Considerable attention is devoted to an exploration of the central Zen concept of Nothingness.

1987
ROSEMONT, Henry, Jr. Logic, Language, and Zen. Washington, Seattle, 1967. 164p. DA 28 (Mar. 1968), 3717-18-A; UM 68-3877.
A critique of the influence of the writings of Daisetz T. Suzuki on the subject of Zen Buddhism. The author argues that "the influence of Suzuki's writings has not been and cannot be altogether salutary from the standpoint of the philosopher, owing in large measure to his inattentiveness to logical and linguistic detail when working with and in the literature of Zen."

1988
BARRANDA, Natividad Gatbonton. The Concept of Personhood in the Thought of Martin Buber, Daisetz Suzuki, and Muhammad Iqbal. Claremont, 1968. 273p. DA 30 (Sept. 1969), 1200-A; UM 69-8931.
"An endeavor to point out and explore the concept of personhood from a philosophical, psychological, and religious point of view....The main objective of this essay is to investigate and to understand personality as these three men of different backgrounds and different religious traditions examine selfhood."

1989
De MARTINO, Richard Joseph. The Zen Understanding of Man. Temple, 1969. 302p. DA 30 (Dec. 1969), 2602-A; UM 69-19,952.
A study of the Zen understanding of (1) the fundamental nature of the ordinary man, (2) the nature of the fundamental problem of the ordinary man, (3) the nature of the resolution to the ordinary man's fundamental problem, (4) the nature of man's true self-awakening, (5) the nature of man's true self, and (6) the nature of authentic non-dualism. Also included are an examination of the basic methodology of Zen Buddhism and a study of Zen's "methodology" and "ontology."

1990
DORNISH, Margaret Hammond. Joshu's Bridge: D.T. Suzuki's Message and Mission, the Early Years, 1897-1927. Claremont, 1969. 193p. DA (June 1970). UM 70-9813.
Contents: Discipleship and Friendship: Suzuki and His Mentors; The Apologia for Buddhism: Interpreting the Mahayana; The Apologia for Zen: Interpreting Zen; The True Spirit of Buddhism: The Eastern Buddhist.

Science, Medicine, and Technology

GENERAL

KOBAYASHI, Tetsuya. General Education for Scientists and Engineers in the United States of America and Japan. 1965. See no.428.

1991
LONG, Theodore Dixon. Science Policy in Postwar Japan. Columbia, 1968. x, 479p.

Rel.Publ.: "Development of Modern Science Policy in Japan," in Columbia Essays in International Affairs; the Dean's Papers, 1965, ed. by Andrew W. Cordier (New York: Columbia University Press, 1966), 205-25. "Policy and Politics in Japanese Science: The Persistence of a Tradition," Minerva, 7 (Spring 1969), 426-53.

EARTH SCIENCES
(Chemistry, Geology, Meteorology, Mineralogy, and Seismology)

1992
MUNROE, Henry S. Yesso Coals. Columbia, 1877. Diss. ms. not available.

The published dissertation is a geological survey of the deposits of coal found on the island of Hokkaido (Yesso). The author focuses on the physical properties of the coal and studies the Kayanoma coal from the province of Shiribetsu and the Horumui and Sorachi coal of the province of Ishikari. For the sake of comparison, assays are also made of coal found elsewhere in Japan.

Rel.Publ.: Yesso Coals. Tokyo: The Kaitakushi, 1874. 39p. [Also published in Reports and Official Letters to the Kaitakushi [by] Horace Capron, Commissioner and Adviser, and His Foreign Assistants (Tokei [i.e. Tokyo]: The Kaitakushi, 1875), 163-99]; "The Gold Fields of Yesso," in Reports and Official Letters to the Kaitakushi [by] Horace Capron et al. (Tokei: The Kaitakushi, 1875), 665-774.

1993
BACHER, Carl. Über die Laven der kleineren Izu-Inseln: Ein Beitrag zur Petrographie Japans [On the Different Kinds of Lava Found on the Smaller Izu Islands: A Contribution to the Petrography of Japan]. München, Technische Hochschule, 1914. Text in German. The dissertation in its published form is available at Marburg/Lahn, Universitätsbibliothek, Nr. IX C.

Studies various rocks found on the Izu islands for the purpose of determining the physical origins of the archipelago.

Rel.Publ.: Über...Japans. München: Wolf, 1914. 38p.

1994
WIEDENHOFF, Siegfried. Der tägliche Gang der Bewölkung in Japan [The Daily Movements of Clouds in Japan]. Berlin, 1914. Text in German. The dissertation in its published form is available at Berlin West, Staatsbibliothek Preussischer Kulturbesitz, Nr. Ah 7856. (In: Berlin, Philosophische Diss. Wen-Z, 1914, Bd 22.)

Studies the different types of cloud formations in the skies over Japan and their distribution, the extent of their daily movement, and the varying degrees of cloudiness and their frequency. The author determines that the distribution of various types of clouds is dependent upon temperature changes, wind direction, and the degree of humidity.

Rel.Publ.: Der tägliche...Japan. Essen: Girardet, 1914. 111p.

1995
MAHOE, Künwoll. Vergleichende Untersuchung über die physikalischen und chemischen Eigenschaften der chinesischen und japanischen Seiden [A Comparative Study of the Physical and Chemical Characteristics of Chinese and Japanese Silk]. Berlin, Technische Hochschule, 1915. Text in German. The dissertation in its published form is available at Berlin West, Staatsbibliothek Preussischer Kulturbesitz.

A brief study of the cultural history of silk in China; an examination of the chemical make-up of Chinese and Japanese silk; an analysis of the fineness, durability, and elasticity of the two kinds of silk; and an investigation of the gloss, the suppleness, and the color properties of silk.

Rel.Publ.: Vergleichende...Seiden. Berlin: Ebering, 1915. 18p.

1996
CHU, Co-ching. A New Classification of the Typhoons of the Far East. Harvard, 1918. iii, 95p. AB: 2p. summary appended to diss. ms.

Contents: Historical Review of Typhoon Classifications; The New Classification; The Characteristics of Each Type of Typhoon; Seasonal Variation of Typhoon Tracks; The Origin and Recurvature of Typhoons; Rate of Progression of Typhoons-Temperature Conditions in the Center of the Storm; Wind and Pressure Conditions in the Center of the Storm.

Rel.Publ.: "Some New Facts about the Centers of Typhoons," United States Department of Agriculture, Weather Bureau, Monthly Weather Review, 46 (1918), 417-19.

1997
PAUL, H. Wilhelm. Der Bergbau Japans während des Krieges 1914-1918 [Mining in Japan during World War

One]. Aachen, Technische Hochschule, 1924. 152p. Text in German. Diss. ms. available at Marburg/Lahn, Staatsbibliothek Preussischer Kulturbesitz, Nr. MS 24/9362.

A survey of mining and metallurgical conditions and development in Japan, the Japanese colonies, and China both prior to and during World War I.

1998
KIENAPFEL, Georg. Die Vulkanlandschaften der ostasiatischen Randbögen: Ein Beitrag zur Landschaftskunde Monsunasiens mit Ausschluss Formosas [Volcanic Regions along the Rim of East Asia: A Contribution to the Topography of Monsoon Asia Excluding Taiwan]. Königsberg, 1931. Text in German. The dissertation in its published form is available at Marburg/Lahn, Universitätsbibliothek, Nr. VI a B 9 10.

Attempts to determine whether the type of volcanic landscape that is characterized by S. Passarge is found along the rim of East Asia. The author focuses on the Kurile Islands, Japan, and the Ryukyus and describes their morphology and their vegetation as well as the relation of the two to the present surface features of the aforementioned islands.

Rel.Publ.: Die Vulkanlandschaften...Formosas. Königsberg i. Pr.: Gräfe und Unzer, 1931. v, 126p. (Veröffentlichungen des Geographischen Instituts der Albertus Universität zu Königsberg i. Pr., N.F., Reihe Geographie Nr. 3)

1999
HODGSON, Ernest Atkinson. A Seismometric Study of the Tango Earthquake, Japan, March 7, 1927. St. Louis, 1932. 207p.

Two new probability methods for locating the epicenter of the earthquake from arrival times only are developed and tested in connection with the data recorded for the Tango earthquake.

Rel.Publ.: "Two Probability Methods for the Determination of Earthquake Epicentres," Gerlands Beiträge zur Geophysik, 37 (1932), 390-409; "The P-Curve and the S-Curve Resulting from a Study of the Tango Earthquake, Japan, March 7, 1927," in Seismological Society of America, Bulletin, 22 (Mar. 1932), 38-49; "Epicentral Time and Surface Structure Determined for the Tango Earthquake, Japan, March 7, 1927," in Seismological Society of America, Bulletin, 22 (Dec. 1932), 270-87.

2000
STECHSCHULTE, Victor Cyril, S.J. The Japanese Earthquake of March 29, 1928, and the Problem of Depth of Focus. California, Berkeley, 1932. 105p.

Seismograms and other reports received from 82 observatories throughout the world and information based on the seismographic recordings of 62 stations in Japan were used to measure the depth of focus of this Japanese earthquake. The depth was calculated to be 410 $\pm$ 30 km.

Rel.Publ.: "The Japanese Earthquake of March 29, 1928, and the Problem of Depth of Focus," in Seismological Society of America, Bulletin, 22 (June 1932), 81-137.

2001
BÖTTGE, Johannes. Die Erdbebentätigkeit Ostasiens sowie ihre Beziehungen zur Tektonik [Seismological Activity in East Asia and Its Relationship to Tectonics]. Jena, 1935. 98p. Text in German. Diss. ms. available at Jena, Universitätsbibliothek.

Studies the geology and tectonics of Japan, seismological activity in the northern, central, and southern parts of the country, and the characteristics and frequency of Japanese earthquakes.

Rel.Publ.: Die Erdbebentätigkeit...Tekonik. Potsdam: Hayn, 1933. 31p.

2002
HUANG, Hsia-chien. Frontogenetic Regions in the Far East. California Institute of Technology, 1938. vi, 86p.

Discusses the frontogenetic lines of East Asia during the four seasons of the year. Includes information about meteorological conditions over Japan.

2003
RUELLAN, Francis. Le Kwansai: Étude géomorphologique d'une région japonaise [The Kansai: A Geomophological Study of a Region of Japan]. Paris, 1940. Text in French.

The area's geological and morphological development.

Rel.Publ.: Le Kwansai...japonaise. Tours: Impr. de Arrault, 1940. ix, 823p.

2004
LEE, Donald Edward. A Mineralogical Study of Some Manganese Ores from Japan. Stanford, 1954. 107p. DA 14 (Dec. 1954), 2362; UM 10,378.

"Many small deposits of manganese ore are found in Paleozoic chert beds, exposed over wide areas throughout the four main islands of Japan. A detailed mineralogical study has been made of specimens from eleven scattered deposits of this type."

2005
HANAI, Tetsuro. Studies on the Ostracoda from Japan: I Subfamilies Leptocytherinae, n. Subfam., "Toulminiinae," n. Subfam., and Cytherurinae G. W. Muller. Louisiana State, 1956. 142p. DA 17 (Mar. 1957), 600; UM 17,443.

A descriptive study of certain subfamilies of small marine crustaceans having bodies enclosed in hinged, bi-valved shells. The dissertation is "part of a basic taxonomic study of Ostracoda found living in the sea surrounding Japan and as fossils in Pliocene and Miocene deposits in Japan."

2006
RUDICH, Evgenii Markovich. Osnovnye zakonomernosti tektonicheskogo razvitiia Primor'ia, Sakhalina i Iaponii kak zony perekhoda ot kontinenta k okeanu [Basic Laws Governing the Tectonic Development of the Maritime (Province), Sakhalin, and of Japan as Zones of Transformation from Continent to Ocean]. Moscow, Moskovskii geo.-razved. institut imeni S. Ordzhonikidze, 1962. (Candidate of Geological and Mineralogical Sciences degree) 474p. Text in Russian.

Rel.Publ.: Osnovnye...okeanu. Moscow, Izdatel'stovo Akademii nauk SSSR, 1962. 272p. (Institut fiziki zemli imeni O. Iu. Shmidta Akademii nauk SSSR)

2007
TARAKANOV, R. Z. Skorostnye razrezy i stroenie verkhnei mantii: Kurile-Iaponskogo regiona [High-Speed Cuts and the Formation of the Upper Mantle of the Kurile Islands and of Japan]. Novoaleksandrovsk, Sakhalinskii kompleksnyi nauchno-issledovatel'skii institut, 1969. (Candidate of Physical and Mathematical Sciences degree) 169, xii p. Text in Russian.

HISTORY OF SCIENCE

See also Science, Medicine, and Technology--Medicine and Public Health (pages 237-38).

2008
NAKAYAMA, Shigeru. An Outline History of Japanese Astronomy: Western Impact vs. Chinese Background. Harvard, 1960. viii, 343p.

Contents: Pt.1:The Early Impact of Chinese Astronomy: From the 6th century A.D. to the First Half of the 16th century: Historical Introduction; The Institutional Framework of Astronomical Learning and Related Subjects; Astrology and the Occult Science; Introduction of Chinese Calendrical Science. Pt.2:The Early Impact of the West: From the Latter Part of the 16th Century to the Early Part of the 18th Century: Jesuit Influence; The Impact of Aristotelian Cosmology: Conceptual Aspects, I; The First Native Calendar Reform: Technical Aspects, I; Institutional Features and Background Attitudes in the Tokugawa Period. Pt.3:The Period of Recognition of Western Supremacy: The Inception of "Dutch Learning"; Introduction of the Copernican and Newtonian Theories: Conceptual Aspects, II; Continued Efforts at Calendar Reform: Technical Aspects, II; The Responses of Buddhists and Others to Western Cosmological Theories; The Transition to Modern Astronomy.

Rel.Publ.: A History of Japanese Astronomy; Chinese Background and Western Impact: Cambridge: Harvard University Press, 1969. xiii, 329p. (Harvard-Yenching Institute Monograph Series, 18); "On the Introduction of the Heliocentric System into Japan," in Tokyo University, Papers of the College of General Education, 11 (1961), 163-76; "Japanese Studies in the History of Astronomy," Japanese Studies in the History of Science, 1 (1962), 14-22; "Characteristics of Chinese Astrology," ISIS, 57 (Winter 1966), 442-54.

FRENCH, Calvin L. Shiba Kōkan: Pioneer of Western Art and Science in Japan. 1966. See no.118.

JONES, Stanleigh H. Jr. Scholar, Scientist, Popular Author: Hiraga Gennai (1728-1780). 1968. See no.1641.

LIFE SCIENCES

(Biology, Botany, Marine Biology, and Zoology)
See also Anthropology-Sociology--Biological Anthropology (page 5).

2009
APPELLÖF, Jakob Johan Adolf. Japanska Cephalopoder [Japanese Cephalopodes]. Uppsala, 1886. Text in Swedish, with a summary in German.

Anatomical study of certain cuttlefish, octopuses, and squids within the families Loliginidae, Octopodidae, Ommastrephidae, Sepiidae, and Sepiolidae of the class Cephalopoda.

Rel.Publ.: "Japanska Cephalopoder," in Kungliga Svenska Vetenskapsakademien, Handlingar, v.21 (1884/1885), no.13. [40 pages].

2010
SHIMOYAMA, Yunichiro. Beiträge zur Kenntnis des japanischen Klebreises, Mozigome [Contributions to the Study of Japanese Glutinous Rice, Mochigome]. Strassburg, 1886. Text in German. The dissertation in its published form is available at Marburg/Lahn, Universitätsbibliothek, Nr. IX C.

A study of glutinous rice and its uses, a chemical analysis of the starch content of mochi rice and a comparison with the starch content of ordinary rice, an examination of maltose, and an investigation of the ability of reducing the derived dextrin.

Rel.Publ.: Beiträge...Mozigome. Strassburg: Heitz und Mündel, 1886. 40p.

2011
NAKAMURA, Yaroku. Über den anatomischen Bau des Holzes der wichtigsten japanischen Coniferen [The Anatomical Structure of the Wood of the Most Important Japanese Conifers]. München, 1892. Text in German. The dissertation in its published form is available at München, Bayr. Staatsbibliothek, Nr. Phyt. 475t.

Begins with a survey of Japanese woodland flora, of Japanese climatic conditions, and of the distribution of various species of wood within Japan. The dissertation then describes 22 different conifers within the families Taxaceae (evergreens and shrubs), Cupressaceae (cedars and junipers), and Abietineae (pines, spruces, hemlocks, and firs) and discusses their geographical distribution and growth, the quality of their wood, their hardiness, and their utilization.

Rel.Publ.: Über...Coniferen. München, 1892. 34, iv p.

FRITZE, Adolf. Die Fauna der Liu-Kiu-Insel Okinawa. 1894. See addenda entry no. 13A.

2012
HONGO, Takanori. Forstlich und gärtnerisch empfellenswerte Halbbäume und Sträucher der japanischen Flora [Japanese Dwarf Trees and Bushes Recommended for Use in Wooded Areas and in Gardens]. München, 1910. Text in German. The dissertation in its published form is available at Marburg/Lahn, Universitätsbibliothek, Nr. XII C.

A study of 121 species of Japanese dwarf trees and bushes that are hardly known in Europe, of their occurrence in Japan (they are grouped together according to the climatic zones in which they are found), and of the possibility of cultivating them in European gardens.

Rel.Publ.: Forstlich...Flora. München: Kastner und Callwey, 1911. 70p.

2013
LEBWOHL, Friedrich. Japanische Tetraxonida [Japanese Tetraxons]. Karlova Universita (German Branch), 1912/13. Text in German.

2014
ENGELHARDT, Robert. Monographie der Selachier der Münchener Zoologischen Staatssamlung (mit besonderer Berücksichtigung der Haifauna Japans): I. Teil: Tiergeographie der Selachier [A Study of the Selachii Found in the Munich State Zoological Collection (with Special Consideration of Japanese Sharks and Rays): Part 1: The Animal Geography of Selachii]. Freiburg i.B., 1913. Text in German. The dissertation in its published form is available at Marburg/Lahn, Universitätsbibliothek, Nr. IX B.

The distribution of Selachii from a bionomical and a geophysical point of view; the classification of the various species of Selachii according to the three different parts of the sea in which they live, and an explanation of the causal relationships among their ethology, morphology, and their geographical distribution; the occurrence and the kinds of sharks and rays, etc. that are found in Japanese waters (the area between Taiwan and the Bōsō Peninsula; the Oyashio, off the northern coast of Japan); a comparison with sharks and rays found in the waters surrounding the Malay peninsula and in the Arctic region.

Rel.Publ.: Monographie...Selachier. München: K. B. Akademie der Wissenschaften in Komm., 1913.

2015
FRICKHINGER, Hans Walter. Japanische Polychaeten: I. Amphinomidae. Aphroditidae. Polynoidae [Japanese Polychaeta: Part 1: Amphinomidae, Aphroditidae, and Polynoidae]. Freiburg i.B., 1923. 134p. Text in German. Diss. ms. available at Marburg/Lahn, Staatsbibliothek Preussischer Kulturbesitz, Nr. 23/3238.

Classification and study of the three families of marine annelid worms: Amphinomidae, Aphroditidae, and Polynoidae. In the part which deals with animal geography, there is a study of the distribution of Polychaeta. In the biological section there is an examination of those forms which are found in the Arctic region and in the deep sea. Part 3 considers all members of the three families that were known as of 1923.

Rel.Publ.: Japanische Polychäten aus der Sammlung Doflein. n.p., 1916.

2016
STEWARD, Albert Newton. The Polygoneae of Eastern Asia. Harvard, 1930. Diss. ms. not available. AB: Harvard University. Summaries of Theses...1930. p.24-25.

An identification as well as a descriptive and contrastive study of the genera Tovara, Koenigia, and Polygonum found in parts of eastern Asia including Japan.

Rel.Publ.: The Polygoneae...Asia. Cambridge: Gray Herbarium of Harvard University, 1930. lxxxviii, 129p. (Contributions from the Gray Herbarium of Harvard University)

2017
KURONUMA, Katsuzo. Studies on the Heterosomate Fishes of Japan. Michigan, 1938. 119, vi p.

A Study of the flounders and soles found in the seas surrounding Japan, Korea, the Ryukyus, and Taiwan. Particular attention is paid to "comparative studies of the structure of the olfactory laminae, gill-rakers and lower pharyngeals, and of the variations in meristic characters."

2018
WALKER, Egbert Hamilton. A Revision of the Eastern Asiatic Myrsinaceae. Johns Hopkins, 1940.

A study of those members of this family of tropical trees and shrubs (order Primulales) found in East Asia, including Japan.

2019
JAHN, Hermann. Zur Oekologie und Biologie der Vögel Japans [On the Ecology and Biology of Japanese Birds]. Kiel, 1942. 164p. Text in German. Diss ms. available at Kiel, Universitätsbibliothek, Nr. TU 42.4118.

Contents: Part 1: Characteristics of Japanese Birds; The Flight of Migratory Birds in Japan; The Japanese Islands South of Hokkaido; Hokkaido. Part 2: The Range, Ecology, and Biology of Individual Species.

2020
MEAD, Giles Willis, Jr. The Food Habits of the North Pacific Fur Seal in Japanese Waters: With a Study of the Fishes Found on the Feeding Grounds. Stanford, 1953. 141p. DA 13 (1953), 922; UM 5805.

"The study was an analysis of the relationships existing between the North Pacific fur seal (Callorhinus ursinus) while wintering off Japan, the marine organisms on which it feeds, and the Japanese commercial fisheries. It was part of the survey designed to collect information on which an international agreement for the protection of the seal could be reached among the countries bordering the North Pacific."

2021
GELHAUSEN, Ursula. Die amolytische Aktivität des Rhizopus Japonicus unter verschieden Kulturbedingungen [The Amymolytic Activity of the Rhizopus Japonicus under Different Growing Conditions]. Kiel, 1955. 62p. Text in German. Diss. ms. available at Kiel, Universitätsbibliothek, Nr. TU 55.5166.

The author searches for the appropriate conditions for cultivating Rhizopus Japonicus (a genus of fungi used in Japan to prepare sake) in order to obtain a usable preparation of amylase (an enzyme). She investigates the influence of light, temperature, and various substrates on the formation of amylase. She also describes the brewing of sake in Japan and provides information on the basic process of sake fermentation.

HANAI, Tetsuro. Studies on the Ostracoda from Japan: I Subfamilies Leptocytherinae, n. subfam., "Toulminiinae," n. subfam., and Cytherurinae G. W. Muller. 1956. See no.2005.

2022
ARNAUD, Paul Henri, Jr. The Heleid Genus Culicoides in Japan, Korea, and Ryukyu Islands (Insecta: Diptera). Stanford, 1961. 126p. DA 23 (July 1962), 358; UM 62-286.

A "study of the speciation and distribution of the biting midge genus Culicoides" in the area.

2023
KAWANO, Shoichi. A Biosystematic and Phytogeographical Study on the Alpine Flora of Hokkaido, Japan. Montréal, 1962. 1104p. (4v.)

Presents a complete taxonomic revision of the alpine flora of Hokkaido. Includes a discussion of the distribution patterns of the alpine plants, of the biological significance of their geographical distribution, and of their evolution. Contents: Brief Notes on the History of the Botanical Explorations in the Alpine Zone of Hokkaido; Geography and Geology; Climate; Notes on Plant Habitat and Ecology; Composition of the Flora; Evolution of the Flora; Systematic Categories and Arrangement; Cytological Materials and Methods; Systematic Comments on the Flora [the main body of the thesis].

2024
MURDOCH, Wallace Pierce. The Female Tabanidae of Japan, Korea, and Manchuria. Utah, 1962. 437p. DA 24 (July 1963), 448; UM 63-1385.

Includes a discussion of their "life history, economic and medical importance, control, morphology, classification, evolution and geologic history, and distribution."

2025
KUWAHARA, Yukinobu. The Family Metzgeriaceae of North and South East Asia, Pacific Oceania, Australia, and New Zealand. Columbia, 1964. 136p. DA 26 (July 1965), 48; UM 65-2083.

The author studies the morphology, phylogeny, phytogeography, and taxonomic features of this family. Coverage extends to all reported species.

2026
GREEN, Detroy Edward. Inheritance of Soybean Seed

Quality Characters. Missouri, 1965. 246p. DA 26 (Sept. 1965), 1266; UM 65-9112.

Experiments conducted with two commercial varieties and three Japanese strains (Wasedaizu No.1, Matsuura, and Kimusume) of soybeans.

MEDICINE AND PUBLIC HEALTH

See also Demography (pages 19-20) and Overseas Japanese Communities--United States--Mainland (pages 205-06).

2027
OGATA, Masakiyo. Beitrag zur Geschichte der Geburtshülfe in Japan [A Contribution to the History of Midwifery in Japan]. Freiburg i.B., 1891. Text in German. The dissertation in its published form is available at Marburg/Lahn Universitätsbibliothek, Nr. XI f C.

Provides a brief summary of the history of Japanese midwifery (from the Nara period to the Meiji period); information on (1) the treatment of pregnancies before during, and after childbirth, (2) the mode of life during the period of pregnancy, (3) care for the newborn, and (4) the husband's assistance during the actual delivery; and a description of new medical practices and of the influence of European medicine upon obstetrical practices in Japan.

Rel.Publ.: Beitrag...Japan. Freiburg i.B.: H. Epstein, 1891. 48, xiii p.

2028
GOTOH, Shimpei. Vergleichende Darstellung der Medizinalpolizei und Medizinalverwaltung in Japan und anderen Staaten [A Comparative Study of Health Inspection and Its Administration in Japan and Other Countries]. München, 1892. Text in German. The dissertation in its published form is available at Marburg/Lahn, Universitätsbibliothek, Nr. XI C.

Studies the organization of the Japanese public health system and the administration, duties, and structure of its central and provincial organs. The author is concerned with improving the system and compares it with its counterparts in the United States and in Europe.

Rel.Publ.: Vergleichende...Staaten. München: M. Ernst, 1891. 34p.

2029
SASAKI, Djundiro. Unterschiede der japanischen und deutschen Geburtshilfe: Ein Beitrag zur japanischen Tokologie [Differences between Japanese and German Midwifery: A Contribution to Japanese Tocology]. Würzburg: 1895. Text in German. The dissertation in its published form is available at Marburg/Lahn, Universitätsbibliothek, Nr. XI C.

A study of the anatomical differences between German and Japanese women; the time, duration, and frequency of births; and the European and the Japanese methods of delivery with the use of forceps.

Rel.Publ.: Unterschiede...Tokologie. Würzburg: F. Schreiner, 1895. 40p.

2030
MUNRO, Neil Gordon. Cancer in Japan. Edinburgh, 1909. 20p. + tables.

This account of cancer in Japan is based upon official statistics of cancer returns. The author also investigates the incidence of cancer among the European residents of Yokohama.

2031
SAITO, Hisashi. Über die Entwicklung der Orthodontie in Japan [The Development of Orthodontia in Japan]. Leipzig, 1932. Text in German. The dissertation in its published form is available at Marburg/Lahn, Universitätsbibliothek, Nr. XI C.

A study of the origins of orthodontia in Japan, of orthodontic instruction in that country, and of the use of orthodontic equipment there. Also includes information on the frequency of denture anomalies in Japan.

Rel.Publ.: Über...Japan. Leipzig: Edelmann, 1932. 28p.

2032
WAGNER, Walther. Die Ernährung Japans [The Nutritional System in Japan]. Frankfurt a.M., 1947. 72p. Text in German. Diss. ms. available at Frankfurt a.M., Senckenbergische Bibliothek, Bockenheimer Landstrasse 134-138. Nr. U45/48.2866.

Geographical and historical facts about nutrition in Japan; an investigation of nutrients with respect to their variety and occurrence, cultivation, preparation, nutritional value, and consumption; a critical discussion of malnutrition and vitamin deficiencies in Japan and of their causes; and recommendations for nutritional improvement.

2033
STUART, Gordon Hackworth. Public Health in Occupied Japan. London, 1950. iii, 93p.

A discussion of the postwar reconstruction of the Japanese health standard and the efforts to prevent the spread of disease and to maintain an adequate level of hygiene through the combined use of previously established (traditional) Japanese practices and of modern methods. A section on Japanese social habits is included. The author concludes that overpopulation is the major problem of the future.

2034
HSÜ, Shu-ying Li. On the Interstrain Variation of Schistosoma Japonicum. Iowa, 1957. 41p. DA 17 (Sept. 1957), 1986-87; UM 22,085.

"Cercariae of Schistosoma japonicum from the infected oncomelanian snails originating from four endemic areas--the Chinese mainland, Formosa, Japan, and the Philippines--were used to infect a number of laboratory animals for the study of the interstrain variations of this parasite."

2035
MURAMATSU, Minoru. Studies of Induced Abortion in Japan: 1.--Effect on the Reduction of Births; 2.--Effect on Weight at Birth. John Hopkins, 1959.

Rel.Publ.: "Effect of Induced Abortion on the Reduction of Births in Japan," Milbank Memorial Fund Quarterly, 38 (Apr. 1960), 153-66.

2036
NEHEMIAS, John Vincent. The Effects of Atomic Bomb Radiations upon the Growth of Children Present at Hiroshima on August 6, 1945. Michigan, 1960. 199p. DA 21 (Feb. 1961), 2252-53; UM 60-6913.

Seeks to determine whether or not exposure to radiation affected the children's growth and skeletal development.

2037
CHU, Kuang-yu. Drug Susceptibility of Geographic Strains of Schistosoma Japonicum. Iowa, 1961. 33p.

DA 22 (July 1961), 232-33; UM 61-1914.
A comparative study of the Japanese, Taiwan, and Philippine strains.

2038
MILLER Robert Warwick. A Study of Factors Associated with Loss of Distant Visual Acuity among Children Five to Eleven Years of Age in Hiroshima and Nagasaki. Michigan, 1961. 142p. DA 23 (Aug. 1962), 610; UM 62-3219.
"Evaluates the effect of inheritance and the environment on the loss of distant visual acuity."

STESLICKE, William E. The Politics of Medical Care: A Study of the Japan Medical Association. 1965. See no.1854.

2039
SASANUMA, Sumiko. A Description of the Disfluent Speech Behavior of Stuttering and Non-Stuttering Japanese Children. Iowa, 1968. 138p. DA 29 (Dec. 1968), 2231-B; UM 68-16,858.
Contents: Introduction; Procedure; Results; Discussion; Summary. "Implications of the findings in terms of the cultural, social, and linguistic variables are discussed."

TECHNOLOGY

See also Art and Architecture--architecture (page 16).

POPOV, Konstantin M. Tekhno-ekonomicheskaia baza Iaponii: I. Problemy energetiki i khimizatsii Iaponii. II. Problemy metallurgii, mashinostroitel'noi bazy i transportnaia sistema Iaponii. 1943. See no.208.

PASHKIN, E. B. Avtomobil'naia promyshlennost' Iaponii: Tekhnichesko-ekonomicheskoe issledovanie. 1964. See no.220.

TSURUMI, Yoshihiro. Technology Transfer and Foreign Trade: The Case of Japan, 1950-1966. 1968. See no. 284.

2040
JALAL, Kazi Abul Farhad Mohammad. Excreta Disposal in East Asia: A Systems Approach. Harvard, 1969. xiv, 263p.
"The work presented in this thesis is the result of an attempt to evaluate the technological feasibility of composting as a means of nightsoil disposal in East Asia and to make an economic analysis of such processes." Japan is one of the major countries investigated. Contents: Epidemiology of Fecal Borne Diseases; Technological Evaluation of the Composting Process; Benefit-Cost Analysis; Error Analysis and Refinement of Cost Estimate.

Theatrical Arts

2041
BÉNAZET, Alexandre. Le Théâtre au Japon: Esquisse d'une histoire littéraire [The Theater in Japan: Survey of a Literary History]. Paris, 1902. Text in French.

Contents: Traditional Festivals and Mystery Plays; Sacred Drama; Popular Drama; Techniques and Subjects; Music, Material Arrangements, Performance.

Rel.Publ.: Le Théâtre au Japon: Contribution à l'étude comparée des littératures. Paris: E. Leroux, 1901. viii, 302p. (Annales du Musée Guimet, 13)

2042
PERZYNSKI, Friedrich. Die Masken der japanischen Schaubühne [Masks in the Japanese Theater]. Hamburg, 1925. 243p.; 184p. (2v.). Text in German. Diss ms. available at Marburg/Lahn, Staatsbibliothek Preussischer Kulturbesitz, Nr. MS 25/4391 I + II.

Pt.1: The orgins of the Nō drama; the historical development of Japanese masks used in various dances between the fourteenth and the twentieth centuries; an historical consideration of Japanese sculpture. Pt.2: An alphabetically arranged survey of the most frequently occurring types of masks used in Nō and in Kyōgen.

Rel.Publ.: Japanische Masken: Nō und Kyōgen. Berlin: Walther de Gruyter, 1925. xii, 426p.; vi, 235p. (2v.); "Nō und Nō-Masken," Jahrbuch der Asiatischen Kunst, 1 (1924), 211-16; "The Collection of Nō Masks in the Section of Eastern Asiatic Art in the Berlin Museum," Year Book of Oriental Art and Culture, ed. by Arthur Waley (London: E. Benn, 1925), 4-8.

2043
BENL, Oscar. Das künstlerische Ideal Seami's [Zeami's Artistic Ideal]. Hamburg, 1947. 121p. Text in German. Diss. ms. Available at Hamburg, Staats- und Universitätsbibliothek, Nr. Diss phil. Mscr. 11.

Studies the historical development of Sarugaku-Nō; presents a biography of Zeami (1363-1443) and a survey of his critical writings; examines the development of the concepts mono-mane, hana, and yūgen, and Zeami's use of them; and provides an annotated translation of Zeami's Kyūi shidai and of books 1-7 of Kadensho, the major critical and theoretical work on Nō.

Rel.Publ.: Seami Motokiyo und der Geist des Nō-Schauspiels: Geheime kunstkritische Schriften aus dem 15. Jahrhundert. Wiesbaden: Steiner, 1953. 149p. (Akademie der Wissenschaften und der Literatur, Mainz, Abhandlungen der Klasse der Literatur, Jahrgang 1952, Nr. 5); "Zwei Spätschriften Seami Motokiyo's," in Gesellschaft für Natur- und Völkerkunde Ostasiens. Nachrichten, 73 (1952), 29-44.

2044
SCOTT, Joseph Wright. The Japanese Noh Play: The Essential Elements in its Theatre Art Form. Ohio State, 1949. 394p. AB: Ohio State University. Abstracts of Doctoral Dissertations. no.60. p.267-73.

"Investigates the form, the aesthetic function, and the art techniques of the following elements which comprise the theatrical production of the Noh play: the Noh texts, the Noh Stage, the acting, dance, music, masks, and the costumes."

2045
LOGUNOVA, Vera Vasil'evna. Personazhi iaponskikh kegenov v svete epokhi: Antifeodal'nyi i antibuddiiskii fars XIV-XV vv. [Dramatic Characters Appearing in the Japanese Kyōgen Seen in Historical Perspective: The Anti-Feudal and Anti-Buddhist Farce of the Fourteenth and Fifteenth Centuries]. Moscow, Institut vostokovedeniia Akademii nauk SSSR, 1951. (Candidate of Philological Sciences degree) 237p. Text in Russian. AB: 15p. summary published in 1951.

2046
YOUNG, Margaret Hershey. Japanese Kabuki Drama: The History and Meaning of the Essential Elements and of Its Theatre Art Form. Indiana, 1954. 397p. DA 14 (Apr. 1954), 737-38; UM 7551.

The elements analyzed are stage and stagecraft, actors and acting, dance and music, costume and make-up, and plays and playwrights.

2047
O'NEILL, Patrick Geoffrey. Sarugaku, Dengaku, and Kuse-mai in the Creation of Nō Drama, 1300-1450. London, 1957. iv, 451p.

A study of the origins and development of the Nō.

Rel.Publ.: Early Nō Drama: Its Background, Character, and Development, 1300-1450. London: Lund Humphries 1958. 223p.; "The Nō Plays Koi no Omoni and Yuya," MN, 10 (Apr. 1954), 203-26; "The Special Kasuga Wakamiya Festival of 1349," MN, 14 (Oct. 1958/Jan. 1959), 162-83.

2048
DUNN, Charles James. The Development of Zyooruri up to 1686. London, 1960. 219p.

A study of several different aspects of the early Japanese puppet theater including jōruri reciting, puppetry, and texts. Appendices of the publication contain translations of the early jōruri play Munewari and of the old jōruri play Kimpira tengu mondō.

Rel.Publ.: The Early Japanese Puppet Drama. London: Luzac, 1966. 153p.

2049
BLAU, Hagen. Sarugaku und Shushi: Beiträge zur Ausbildung dramatischer Elemente im weltlichen und religiösen Volkstheater der Heian-Zeit, unter besonderer Berücksichtigung seiner sozialen Grundlagen [Sarugaku and Shushi: Contributions to the Development of Dramatic Elements in the Secular and Religious Folk Theater of the Heian Period, with Special Regard to Its Social Foundations]. Berlin, 1961. Text in German. The dissertation in its published form is available at Bochum, Universitätsbibliothek, Nr. GB 31,987; also at the University of Michigan, General Library, no. PN2922. B64.

Contents: Distinctive Features of Early Japanese Dances and Ceremonies; Gigaku: The First Continental Stage Play in Japan; Sangaku and Sarugaku: Representative Folk Drama of the Heian Period; Shushi: Representative Temple Drama of the Late Heian Period. Also includes information on the origins, lives, and group organization of Heian period dancers and actors.

Rel.Publ.: Sarugaku...Grundlagen. Wiesbaden: Harrassowitz, 1966. xi, 481p. (Studien zur Japanologie, 6).

2050
ORTOLANI, Benito. Die Anfänge des Kabuki-Theaters [The Beginnings of the Kabuki Theater]. Wien, 1961. Text in German. Diss ms. available at the Österreichische Nationalbibliothek, Nr. 942.387 C Th.

A brief survey of the general history of the Japanese theater and of the cultural background of the kabuki is followed by an analysis of the origins of the kabuki (Okuni-kabuki, Onna-kabuki, Wakashū-kabuki, and Yarō-kabuki).

Rel.Publ.: Das Kabukitheater: Kulturgeschichte der Anfänge. Tokyo: Sophia University Press, 1964. 169p. (Nonumenta Nipponica Monographs, 19); "Okuni-kabuki und Onna-kabuki," MN, 17 (1962) 163-213; "Das Wakashū-kabuki und das Yarō-kabuki," MN, 18 (1963), 89-127.

2051
COLBATH, James Arnold. The Japanese Noh Drama and Its Relation to Zen Buddhism. Case Western Reserve, 1963.

Contents: Pt.1: History: The Origins and History of the Noh. Pt.2: Production and Performance Elements: The Stage; Properties; Apparel (Masks, Wigs, Costumes); The Music (The Flute, Drums, Score, Chanting and Singing); The Actors and the Acting (The Roles, Mimetic Action, The Dance). Pt.3: The Plays: The Texts and Sources of the Plays; The Form. Pt.4: Zen Buddhism in the Noh: Zen Buddhism; Zen and the Arts; Its Relation to Noh.

2052
KLEINSCHMIDT, Peter. Die Masken der Gigaku, der ältesten Theaterform Japans [The Masks of Gigaku, Japan's Oldest Theatrical Form]. 1964 (?). Text in German. The dissertation in its published form is available at Bochum Universitätsbibliothek, Nr. GB 33,303; also at the University of Michigan, General Library, no. DS503.A83v.21.

The following topics are explored in the dissertation with regard to the carved wooden and laquer dance masks that were used in gigaku performances at various temples in Japan: (1) the number and types of gigaku masks that have been preserved, (2) the manufacture of gigaku masks and of copies made during the nineteenth century, (3) the methods and criteria for classifying the types of masks, (4) the typology of the masks that have been preserved, (5) the problems of dating and the attempts at reconstructing some sets of masks, and (6) the dramatic techniques of gigaku. There also is a detailed listing of 250 masks which characterizes each mask according to its type, the material of which it is made, color, outer and inner dimensions, inscriptions, attributions, dating, owners, and origin.

Rel.Publ.: Die Masken...Japans. Wiesbaden: Harrassowitz, 1966. xi, 458p. (Asiatische Forschungen, 21).

2053
HOFF, Frank Paul. A Theater of Metaphor: A Study of the Japanese Nō Form. Harvard, 1966. iii, 123p.

A study of four plays of the Yamabushi Kagura theater: Kinuta ("the classical theater of metaphor"), Hataori ("the theater of gesture metaphor"), Warabiori ("a discontinued dramatic form"), and Nenju (an early form of Nō drama).

2054
TSUBAKI, Andrew Takahisa. An Analysis and Interpretation of Zeami's Concept of Yūgen. Illinois, 1967. 243p. DA 28 (June 1968), 5183-A; UM 68-8253.

"The study examines the conditions of the early Nō theater, the influence of Kannami on his son, Zeami, and the transition of the concept of yūgen as an aesthetic ideal in the middle ages. Zeami's life and his works in general are also dealt with....The major emphasis, however, is focused on defining his concept of yūgen, analyzing its relationship with other important elements of Nō, and interpreting the significance of the transformation of the concept in his later years."

2055
SATO, Kioko (Kyoko). Sovremennyi iaponskii dramaticheskii teatr Singeki [Shingeki: The Modern Japanese Dramatic Theater]. Moscow, Gosudarstvennyi institut teatral'nogo iskusstva imeni A. V. Lunacharskogo, 1968. (Candidate of Art Sciences degree) 281p. Text in Russian. AB: 17p. summary published in 1968.

2056
LESSLEY, Merrill Joe. A Comparative Study of Oriental and Occidental Acting Theories. Utah, 1969. 118p. DA 30 (Nov. 1969), 2817-88-A; UM 69-18,485.

"This study compares oriental and occidental acting theories, focusing upon the works of [the Russian actor, producer, and theoretician] Constantin Stanislavski, the most influential and systematic occidental theorist thus far, and the writings of Zeami Motokiyo and Bharata Muni [author of the second century A.D. work, Natyaśāstra], two of the most important genuises of oriental theater."

Korea

Anthropology, Sociology, Psychology, and Social Psychology

GENERAL

2057
KARL, Hong Kee. A Critical Evaluation of Modern Social Trends in Korea. Chicago, 1934. 243p.

The study traces "the causal factors responsible for the destruction of old securities and describes the new attitudes arising out of...the past." Special emphasis is placed upon relevant economic and political factors.

Rel.Publ.: A Critical...Korea. Chicago, 1938. 11p. ("Private edition, distributed by the University of Chicago libraries.")

2058
PAK-IR, P. A. Klassovaia sushchnost' narodnoi demokratii Korei [The Class Nature of the People's Democracy of Korea]. Alma-Ata, Kazakhskii gosudarstvennyi universitet imeni S. M. Kirova, 1954. (Candidate of Philosophical Sciences degree) 280p. Text in Russian. AB: 20p. summary published in 1954.

2059
CHAO, Lien Lincoln. Distinctive Patterns of Industrial Relations in Korea. Minnesota, 1956. 233p. DA 16 (Oct. 1956), 1813-14; UM 17,844.

"The primary objective...is to inquire into the existing industrial relations practices and working conditions in South Korea. More specifically, the study is intended to investigate the extent of labor force participation by men, women, and children, levels and structures of wages, hours of work, health and safety in employment, the legal status of unions, and experience in industrial disputes." Industrial relations practices in Korea, moreover, are compared with those in Japan and the United States.

2060
KUMATA, Hideya. A Factor Analytic Study of Semantic Structures across Three Selected Cultures. Illinois, 1958. 316p. DA 18 (May 1958), 1881-82; UM 58-1716.

Explores "the feasibility of using Osgood's Semantic Differential as a cross-cultural measuring instrument and the tenability of the Sapir-Wharf linguistic relativity hypothesis in the area of connotative meaning." Based on a case study of monolingual college students in Japan and in the United States and of bilingual Japanese and Korean exchange students in the United States.

2061
SMITH, Melton Vern. Self Representations of American and Korean Youth. Texas, 1958. 154p. DA (June 1958), 2065; UM 58-1670.

"The purpose of the investigation was to test the proposition that certain 'experience' variables provide significant components of variation in the relative emphases placed by youth upon three self mechanisms (ego, superego, and ego-ideal) and five behavioral contexts (somatoself, psychoself, age-mates, family, and school)."

LEE, Reverend Gabriel G.-S. Sociology of Conversion: Sociological Implications of Religious Conversion to Christianity in Korea. 1961. See no.2533.

2062
OMOTO, Keiichi. Vergleichende Untersuchungen zur Allelen-häufigkeit des Gc-Systems bei asiatischen und europäischen Populationen [A Comparative Study of Allele Frequencies in the Gc System among Asian and European Populations]. Münster, 1963. Text in German. The dissertation in its published form is available at Marburg/Lahn, Staatsbibliothek Preussischer Kulturbesitz, Nr. Hsn 39,632; also at the University of Michigan, General Library, no.28,577.

A Study of population genetics within the Gc system among Europeans and Asians based on a modification of the immuno-electrophoresis investigation of 1114 serum tests from Greece, Korea, and Japan. The discussion focuses on a number of evolutionary factors which may have played a role in the occurrence of varying distributions of Gc alleles among different populations.

Rel.Publ.: Vergleichende...Populationen. München: Charlotte Schön, 1963. 30p.

2063
YUH, Ki Sup. The Development of a Korean Group Intelligence Test. Boston, 1964. 240p. DA 26 (Apr. 1966), 5887; UM 65-5532.

A study designed "to develop a valid and reliable group test for evaluating the intelligence of Korean children between the ages of 9 to 12."

2064
HURH, Won Moo. Über die Grenzen der Imitation der abendländischen Kultur und ihre Problematik im Prozess der Kulturdiffusion in Korea [Concerning the Limits of Imitating Western Culture and the Difficulties Encountered in the Process of Cultural Diffusion in Korea]. Heidelberg, 1965. Text in German. The dissertation in its published form is available Marburg/Lahn, Staatsbibliothek Preussischer Kulturbesitz, Nr. Hsn 62,840; also at the University of Michigan, General Library, no.32,205.

In pt.1--a survey of Korea's heritage--the author

discusses Korea's geography, her population, the symbols that have been handed down during the course of Korean history (language, writing, myths, and religion), and Korea's socio-cultural setting. In pt.2 he theorizes about the role of "imitation" in the process of cultural diffusion and notes some of the limitations inherent in this process. Pt.3 focuses on Korea's postwar efforts to imitate other cultures, noting some of the actual attempts at and problems of cultural borrowing and pointing out the modification of foreign cultural elements that has accompanied the process of cultural diffusion in Korea.

Rel.Publ.: Über...Korea. Heidelberg, 1965. iii, 149p.

2065
PAK, Hyung Koo. Social Changes in the Educational and Religious Institutions of Korean Society under Japanese and American Occupations. Utah State, 1965. 258p. DA 26 (Dec. 1965), 3522-23; UM 65-12,601.

Contents: Theoretical Orientation; Historical Background; Social Changes in the Educational Institutions of Korean Society: (1) Under Japanese Occupation, (2) Under American Occupation; Social Changes in the Religious Institutions of Korean Society: (1) Under Japanese Occupation, (2) Under American Occupation; Analysis and Conclusion.

2066
HOWELL, Richard Wesley. Linguistic Choice as an Index to Social Change. California, Berkeley, 1967. 180p. DA 28 (Jan. 1968), 2701-02-B; UM 68-85.

Studies the basic patterns of linguistic choice through an examination of the linguistic behavior of Koreans resident in the Berkeley (California) area. Asserts that linguistic choice is an index to social change and that this can be seen in the case of Korean society, where modern patterns of verbal interaction reflect the changes that have occurred during the past century as a result of industrialization.

COMMUNITY STUDIES

2067
HAN, Chungnim Choi. Social Organization of Upper Han Hamlet in Korea. Michigan, 1949. 238p. AB: Microfilm Abstracts, v.9, no.2 (1949), 180-81; UM 1245.

A case study of an agricultural society near Pukch'ŏng (in South Hamgyŏng province). Focuses on economic and social controls, social structure (the family and the kinship system), reciprocal behavior patterns, farm economy, and religion.

2068
IONOVA, Iu. V. Koreiskaia derevnia v kontse XIX i nachale XX vv.: Istoriko-etnograficheskii ocherk [The Korean Village at the End of the Nineteenth and at the Beginning of the Twentieth Centuries: An Historical and Ethnographic Essay]. Leningrad, Institut etnografii imeni N. N. Miklukho-Maklaia Akademii nauk SSSR, 1953. (Candidate of Historical Sciences degree) 267p. Text in Russian. 16p. summary published in 1953.

2069
KNEZ, Eugene Irving. Sam Jong Dong: A South Korean Village. Syracuse, 1959. 283p. DA 20 (Feb. 1960), 3016-17; UM 59-6308.

"This is an ethnographic presentation of cultural behavior" in Sam Jong Dong, Kyongsang Namdo province, that is primarily based upon field work done in the winter of 1951-1952. "An attempt has been made here to treat only certain facets of village life associated mainly with its geographical setting, its historical antecedents, the interplay of some social factors, and its value orientation as expressed in ethical and religious behavior."

2070
WANG, In Keun. Relationship of Adoption of Recommended Farm Practices with Selected Variables in Three Korean Communities. Wisconsin, 1967. 128p. DA 28 (Sept. 1967), 1138-39-A; UM 67-6843.

The "study is directed toward understanding the time lag between scientific discovery and the actual use of new developments in agriculture."

2071
BRANDT, Vincent Selden Randolph. A Structural Study of Solidarity in Ŭihang Ni. Harvard, 1969. vii, 301p.

An ethnographic study of a Korean farming-fishing village situated on the Yellow Sea in Chungch'ŏng Namdo province. Contents: Methodology and Intent; Environment and Economy; Class, Status, and Mobility (Fifty Years Ago, Age Grading, Personal Status, Mobility, Hierarchy, Leadership, and Status); Lineage and Household (Structure of the System, Kinship Ideology and Ritual, Marriage Rules and Affinal Relations, Wives and the Status of Women, Behavior among Kin); Beyond Kinship: The Anatomy of Solidarity (Interpersonal Relations, Ideology, Topography and Interaction); Conflict and Mal-Integration (Mal-Integration, Social Control, Disputes and Their Settlement).

ETHNOGRAPHY

(Includes race, manners and customs, mythology, folk tales and songs, beliefs and rites)
See also Religion and Philosophy--Buddhism, Confucianism, and Other Non-Christian Movements (pages 295-96).

2072
SLAWIK, Alexander. Kulturschichten in Altkorea [Cultural Stratification of Ancient Korea]. Wien, 1935. xvii, 229p. Text in German. Diss. ms. available at the Universitätsbibliothek der Universität Wien, Nr. D 4162.

A comprehensive study of the material culture and the economy of ancient Korea up to the Silla period. Based on early Chinese and Korean literature, and on prehistoric and ethnological studies.

2073
SAMPLE, Lillie Laetitia. Culture History and Chronology in South Korea's Neolithic. Wisconsin, 1967. 414p. DA 28 (Feb. 1968), 3142-B; UM 67-12,156.

The chronology is based on a stratigraphic analysis of Tongsamdong Shellmound on Yongdo, an island in Pusan harbor. Includes a general interpretation of culture history at Tongsamdong and a consideration of early Korean relationships with Japan.

Rel.Publ.: "Chōsen shinsekkijikai shoki no doki kennen ni kansuru shin shiryō [by] Albert Mohr, C. S. Chard, and L. L. Sample, Chōsen gakuhō, 41 (Oct. 1966) 73-82; "Chōsen kogendo no kushimemon doki," Sekki jidai, Mar. 1967.

FAMILY AND KINSHIP STUDIES
See also Demography (page 247).

2074
ROH, Chang Shub. A Comparative Study of Korean and Japanese Family Life. Louisiana State, 1959. 310p. DA 19 (June 1959), 3408; UM 59-1546.
"Special reference is made to historical developments, characteristics of family life, familial cultures, family functions, and changing family life."

2075
YIM, Seong Hi. Die Grundlage und die Entwicklung der Familie in Korea [The Foundation and Development of the Family in Korea]. Köln, 1961. Text in German. The dissertation in its published form is available at Marburg/Lahn, Staatsbibliothek Preussischer Kulturbesitz, Nr. Hsn 29,900; also at the University of Michigan, General Library, no.25,100.
The structure of Korean society since the fifteenth century is studied through an examination of the concepts of "kinship," "marriage," and "ancestor worship," and considerable attention is paid to the matter of hierarchical status within the family and to patrimonial rights. A comparison of Korean and American social structure also is presented (see the chapter entitled "Foundation and Development of the Family in Modern Times, 1860-1960").
Rel.Publ.: Die Grundlage...Korea. Köln: W. Kleipkamp, 1961. iv, 181p.

2076
CHAI, Alice Yun. Kinship and Mate Selection in Korea. Ohio State, 1962. 164p. DA 23 (Aug. 1962), 392; UM 62-3577.
"Attempts to describe kinship organizations and mate selection patterns among the urban people of Korea, and examines the changes that have occurred in the mate selection patterns between two generations of upper-class Korean urban women."

2077
CHANG, Dae Hong. The Historical Development of the Korean Socio-Family System since 1392: A Legalistic Interpretation. Michigan State, 1962. 312p. DA 23 (Apr. 1963), 4011; UM 63-1716.
Contents: A Historical Background of the Traditional Family System prior to the Yi Dynasty; The Family System during the Yi Dynasty (Structure and Function of the Traditional Korean Family, Parental Authority and Socialization of the Young, Junior Members' Duties toward Their Parents, Relationships among the Junior Members of the Family, Family Registry, The Greater Family and Clan Village); Marriage Rules during the Yi Dynasty; Legal Interpretation of the Korean Family System from 1910-1945 and 1945 to the Present.
Rel.Publ.: "The Historical...Interpretation," Journal of East Asiatic Studies (Manila), 11 (Sept. 1967), pt.2, 1-124.

2078
BIERNATZKI, William Eugene, S.J. Varieties of Korean Lineage Structure. St. Louis, 1967. 635p. DA 28 (Feb. 1968), 3141-B; UM 68-1251.
"Field research was conducted in three separate areas of Korea, first, to obtain an empirical description of Korean lineage organizations and closely related institutions as they now exist, and, second, to determine whether accessibility to Seoul, the dominant city and source of Westernizing influences, is significantly related to the variances observed."

VALUES AND ATTITUDES

2079
KOH, Hesung Chun. Religion, Social Structure, and Economic Development in Yi Dynasty Korea. Boston, 1959. 267p. DA 20 (Nov. 1959), 1888-89; UM 59-3459.
In investigating the key variables related to the economy of pre-modern Korean society, the dissertation seeks to determine why pre-modern Korea failed to develop the social and cultural bases for a modern industrial society. "The major findings are that the pre-modern Korean value system put more stress upon the integrative value as compared with the political or economic values than did Ch'ing dynasty China or Tokugawa Japan. This integrative value appears in the emphasis on the harmony and the solidarity of the family rather than that of the state....Moreover, Korean religion reinforced the primacy of the integrative value through the yangban class...and failed to help the efforts of the chungin to emphasize political economic values."
Rel.Publ.: "Yungt'ongsŏng," Shin Tong-A, Dec. 1968, 156-58.

2080
BARRINGER, Herbert Reese. The Aesthetic-Theoretical Continuum: Primary and Secondary Social Values in Korea and in the United States. Northwestern, 1964. 286p. DA 25 (Jan. 1965), 4289; UM 64-12,250.
Examines the contention "that Orientals (as represented by Koreans) tend to be more aesthetic (hence primary) than Westerners."

2081
CHO, Tae Kyung. Das Bild der Geschlechter bei Koreanern: Eine experimentelle-statistische Untersuchung [The Image of the Two Sexes among Koreans: An Experimental and Statistical Inquiry]. Heidelberg, 1965. Text in German. The dissertation in its published form is available at Marburg/Lahn, Staatsbibliothek Preussischer Kulturbesitz, Nr. Hsn 62,850.
The study aims (1) to determine the image of the two sexes in Korea on the basis of specimens of writing, (2) to provide information about the validity (and degree of validity) of the sexual stereotypes that are found among Koreans, (3) to compare the stereotypes with the actual roles of the two sexes in Korean social and family life, and (4) to make a contribution to the study of the images that people in general have of the two sexes.
Rel.Publ.: Das Bild...Untersuchung. Heidelberg, 1965. 97p.

Archaeology, Art, and Architecture

2082
CHÊNG, Tê-k'un. Prehistoric Archaeology of Szechuan. Harvard, 1941. x, 294p. AB: Harvard University. Summaries of Theses...1941. p.156-58.

"The study also aims to see what bearing the early culture of this region has on the prehistory of Eastern Asia as a whole. Ch.4 (p.81-176) includes a lengthy comparison of local stone artifacts with those from Korea and neighboring countries.

Rel.Publ.: Archaeological Studies in Szechwan. Cambridge, Eng.: Cambridge University Press, 1957. xx, 320p.

2083
MÜNSTERBERG, Hugo. Buddhist Bronzes of the Six Dynasties Period. Harvard, 1941. ii, 181p. AB: Harvard University. Summaries of Theses...1941. p.160-64.

See Ch.8, "Early Buddhist Bronzes of Korea and Japan" (p.155-81).

Rel.Publ.: Buddhist Bronzes of the Six Dynasties Period," Artibus Asiae, 9 (1946), 275-315, and 10 (1947), 21-33.

2084
KIM, Dzhin Khi (Kim Chinhi). Osnovnye printsipy vosstanovleniia i rekonstruktsii gorodov Koreiskoi Narodno-Demokraticheskoi Respubliki [Basic Principles for Restoring and Reconstructing the Cities of the Korean People's Democratic Republic]. Moscow, Moskovskii arkhitekturnyi institut, 1953. (Candidate of Architectural Sciences degree) 373p. Text in Russian.

Rel.Publ.: "Arkhitektura koreiskogo naroda," Sovetskaia arkhitektura, 2 (1952), 88-100.

2085
KIM, Won-Yong. Studies on Silla Pottery. New York, 1959. 237p. DA 20 (July 1959), 260-61; UM 59-2447.

Ch.1 provides a brief survey of the political history of the Silla dynasty and background information on Silla pottery. Ch.2, "The Origins of Silla Pottery," discusses prehistoric Korean potteries and Kimhae pottery as well as the problems involved in determining the origins of Silla pottery. Ch.3 focuses on the stylistic development and the actual dating of various regional groups of Silla pottery. Note: "The term 'Silla Pottery' is applied to the hard grey stoneware of the Silla dynasty."

Rel.Publ.: Studies...Pottery. Seoul: Eul-yoo pub. co., 1960. 137, xviii p. (Publication of the National Museum of Korea. Series A, v.9)

2086
TIAN, Khi Un. Arkhitekturno-planirovochnye priemy i konstruktivnye resheniia 4-6 etazhnykh zhilykh domov dlia stroitel'stva v KNDR: Na osnove izucheniia opyta proektirovaniia v SSSR [Architectural-Planning Techniques and Decisions for the Construction of Four and Six Story Residential Houses in the Korean People's Democratic Republic]. Kiev, Kievskii inzhenerno-stroitel'nyi institut, 1959. (Candidate of Architectural Sciences degree) 218p. Text in Russian.

SAMPLE, Lillie L. Culture History and Chronology in South Korea's Neolithic. 1967. See no.2073.

Demography

2087
LEE, Chung Myun. Recent Population Patterns and Trends in the Republic of Korea. Michigan, 1961. 228p. DA 21 (June 1961), 3745; UM 61-1760.

Contents: Physical Setting of Korea's Population; Population History of Korea; Population Patterns, Composition, Growth, and Movement; Possible Solutions to the Population Movement. Focuses on the period 1910-1955.

Rel.Publ.: "The Impact of Emigration upon the Korean Population," in Kyung Hee University, Seoul, Theses Collection, 3 (1964), 44-65; "Population Movement of Korea: International Movement," Korean Affairs (1963), 20-37; "Population Increase and Food Problem in Korea," Korean Affairs, 3 (July 1964), 168-85.

IM, Ik-Soon. A Program for Effective Utilization of Surplus Rural Labor in the Republic of Korea: With Special Reference to Domestic Capital Formation. 1964. See no.2099.

2088
CHANG, Yunshik. Population in Early Modernization: Korea. Princeton, 1966. 433p. DA 28 (Nov. 1967), 1909-A; UM 67-9594.

Studies population developments throughout the Korean peninsula during the period of Japanese rule and in the Republic of Korea after World War Two.

2089
BANG, Sook. A Comparative Study of the Effectiveness of a Family Planning Program in Rural Korea. Michigan, 1968. 262p. DA 29 (Oct. 1968), 1419-20-B; UM 68-13,798.

Determines that "an organized family planning program to promote the use of contraception control is feasible in rural Korea." Contents: Data and Methods; Nature of the Family Planning Program: Koyang and Kimpo; Overall Program Effect: (1) Changes in Fertility, (2) Changes in Knowledge, Attitudes, and Practice of Family Planning; Program Participation and Changes in Fertility, Behavior, and Attitude; Family Planning Knowledge, Attitudes, and Practice and Fertility: An Examination of Interrelationships.

Rel.Publ.: "Fertility and Family Planning in Rural Korea" [by] Jae Mo Yang, Sook Bang, Myung Ho Kim, and Man Gap Lee, Population Studies, 18 (1965), 237-50; "The Koyang Study: Results of Two Action Programs," Studies in Family Planning, 11 (1966), 5-12.

YU, Yeun-chung. The Development of the Economically Active Population in East Asia, 1947-1966. 1969. See no.2106.

Economics

GENERAL

LINKE, Johannes C. Veränderung der wirtschaftsgeographischen Beziehungen in Korea unter dem einfluss der Erschliessung: Die Grundlagen und ursprüngliche Ausgestaltung. 1932. See no.2210.

NAM, In Kho. Voprosy planirovaniia narodnogo khoziaistva v Koreiskoi Narodno-Demokraticheskoi Respublike (do Otechestvennoi osvoboditel'noi voiny). 1951. See no.2495.

2090
HENNING, Charles Nathaniel. The Economic Basis of an Independent Korea. California, Los Angeles, 1953. 614p. (2v.)
Contents: The Geographic, Political, and Demographic Setting of Korea's Economy: The Structure and Problems of Korea's Agriculture; The Utilization of Forest and Marine Resources; The Basis of Industrialization: Electric Power; The Variety of Korea's Mineral Resources; Partial Industrialization of Korea; Economic Aspects of Transportation and Communications; External Trade and Balance of Payment Position; The Political and Demographic Setting, and Developments in Agriculture, Forestry, and Fishing, South Korea, 1945-1950; Economic Development in Power, Mining, Industry, Transportation, and Foreign Trade, South Korea, 1945-1950; The Economic Basis of an Independent Korea.

2091
CHUNG, Nam Kyu. The Economic Development of the Republic of Korea. Wisconsin, 1954. v, 394p. AB: University of Wisconsin. Summaries of Doctoral Dissertations. v.16. p.185-86.
"Not a presentation of programs or blueprints for Korean economic development" but rather a statement of "fundamental prerequisites for concrete programming under changing conditions."

2092
KHESSINA, E. I. Ekonomicheskie preobrazovaniia v Severnoi Koree (1945-1950 gg.) [Economic Transformations in North Korea, 1945-1950]. Moscow, Moskovskii ordena Lenina universitet imeni M. V. Lomonosova, 1954. (Candidate of Economic Sciences degree) iv, 375p. Text in Russian. AB: 16p. summary published in 1954.

IM, Khe. Planirovanie narodnogo khoziaistva v Koreiskoi Narodno-Demokraticheskoi Respublike. 1955. See no.2496.

2093
TSOI, Ben Chol. Razvitie mobilizatsii sredstv i gosudarstvennyi biudzhet v SSSR i Koreiskoi Narodno-Demokraticheskoi Respublike [Stages in the Mobilization of Resources and the State Budget in the USSR and in the Korean People's Democratic Republic]. Leningrad, Leningradskii finansovo-ekonomicheskii institut, 1956. (Candidate of Economic Sciences degree) x, 301p. Text in Russian.

2094
ALEXANDRIDES, Costas George. The United Nations Economic Assistance to the Republic of Korea: A Case Study of Economic Reconstruction and Development. New York, 1960. 359p. DA 27 (Nov. 1966), 1149-50-A; UM 66-9659.
Contents: Pt.1: The Organization of Economic Assistance in the Republic of Korea: The Korean Question in the United Nations; The UN Civil Assistance Command in Korea; The UN Commission for the Unification and Rehabilitation of Korea; The UN Korean Reconstruction Agency; The Economic Coordinator; An Evaluation of the Organization of Economic Aid. Pt.2: Economic Assistance to the Republic of Korea during the Financial Years 1950-1958: The Economic Situation; Agriculture; Forestry; Fisheries; Mining; Power; Transportation and Communications; Manufacturing Industries; Foreign Trade; Housing; Education; Health; Relief and Social Services. Pt.3: The Economy of the Republic of Korea in the Financial Year 1959.

2095
KIM, S. V. Voprosy teorii i praktiki stroitel'stva osnov sotsializma v KNDR: Perekhodnyi period ot kapitalizma k sotsializmu [Questions of Theory and Practice Regarding the Construction of the Basis for Socialism in the Korean People's Democratic Republic: The Transition from Capitalism to Socialism]. Moscow, Institut ekonomiki Akademii nauk SSSR, 1962. (Candidate of Economic Sciences degree) xx, 255p. Text in Russian.
Rel.Publ.: "Voprosy stroitel'stva osnov sotsializma v Koreiskoi Narodno-Demoktraticheskoi Respublike, Narody Azii i Afriki, 2 (1962), 18-29.

2096
LEE, Joe Won. The Nathan Economic Commission and Korean Development. Indiana, 1962. 728p.
Contents: The Historical Background of the Nathan Economic Mission to Korea; The Quantitative Data Situation; The Nathan Economic Mission's "Diagnosis" of the Korean Economic Situation and Problems; The Mission's General Planning Methodology: The "Overall" Total Requirements-Personal Approach; The Development Scheme: The Quantitative Program; The Development Scheme:

Qualitative Economic Policies; The Development Scheme: Qualitative, Administrative, and Political Strategies; Inter-Governmental Relations: The Aid-to-Korea Effort; Summary and Conclusion: A Net Hindsight Approach.

Rel.Publ.: "Planning Efforts for Economic Development," in Patterns of Economic Development: Korea, ed. by Joseph Sang-hoon Chung (Kalamazoo, Mich., 1966), 1-24.

2097
RO, Chung-Hyun. A Comparative Study of Manpower Administration in Developing Countries: With special Reference to South and North Korea. New York, 1962. 173p. DA 29 (July 1968), 313-14-A; UM 63-7197.

Includes a comparative examination of the patterns of supply and utilization of trained manpower in North and South Korea.

Rel.Publ.: "Economic Growth and Manpower Administration in North Korea," Korean Affairs, 2 (1963), 150-61.

2098
CHUNG, Joseph Sang-hoon. The North Korean Economy: Structure and Development. Wayne State, 1964. 294p. DA 26 (Feb. 1966), 4283; UM 65-7720.

"A case study of the actual performance and operational problems of a centrally planned, collectivized, and completely socialized economy attempting to recover from a war, to develop, and industrialize." Contents: Agricultural Development; Industrial Development; The Wartime Economy; External Financing: Trade and Aid.

Rel.Publ.: "The North Korean Industrial Enterprise: Control, Concentration, and Managerial Functions," Studies on Asia, 1966, ed. by Robert K. Sakai (Lincoln: University of Nebraska Press, 1966), 165-85; "Industrial Development of North Korea, 1945-1964: Some Strategic Quantitative Indicators," in Patterns of Economic Development: Korea, ed. by Joseph Sang-hoon Chung (Kalamazoo, Mich., 1966), 104-44; "A Pattern of Agricultural Development: Size, Organization, and Work Incentives of the North Korean Collection and State Farms," in Patterns of Economic Development: Korea, ed. by Joseph Sang-hoon Chung (Kalamazoo, Mich., 1966), 55-79; "Trends in the North Korean Industrial Enterprise: Control, Concentration, and Managerial Functions," in Patterns of Economic Development: Korea, ed. by Joseph Sang-hoon Chung (Kalamazoo, Mich., 1966), 80-103.

2099
IM, Ik-Soon. A Program for Effective Utilization of Surplus Rural Labor in the Republic of Korea: With Special Reference to Domestic Capital Formation. Washington, St. Louis, 1964. 241p. DA 26 (Oct. 1965), 1965; UM 65-6841.

"The purpose...is to estimate the magnitude of rural surplus labor in Korea and to seek methods for the productive employment of such surplus labor." The dissertation surveys the history of capital formation in Korea, discusses "the problems of rapid population growth," analyzes the composition of the Korean labor force compared with that of other countries, explores and estimates capital requirements and sources of capital to alleviate unemployment, and "presents suggested programs for the effective utilization of surplus labor and for the enhancement of capital formation and economic development."

Rel.Publ.: "Population Growth and Economic Development in Korea," Korean Affairs, 3 (Apr. 1964), 73-88; "Composition of Labor Force and Its Influence upon the Income Level of Korea," Korean Affairs, 3 (July 1964), 186-98; "Population Growth and Economic Development," in Patterns of Economic Development: Korea, ed. by Joseph Sang-hoon Chung (Kalamazoo, Mich., 1966), 29-45.

2100
LEE, Samuel Sang-ok. The Effects of Inflation and Legal Remedies on Accounting in Korea Since 1945. Columbia, 1964. 171p. DA 25 (June 1965), 7006; UM 65-5858.

"Studies two Korean laws (1958 and 1962) relating to price-level adjustment, and their background; evaluates them; and suggests better ways for Korean accounting to meet the problem of inflation."

2101
WINSTON, Ralph John. Studies of Korean Accounting Procedures with Suggestions for System Improvements. Washington, St. Louis, 1965. 314p. DA 26 (June 1966), 7099; UM 66-1630.

Contents: Introduction and Statement of the Problem; Research Methodology; General Description of Current Accounting Procedures; Description of Procedures at Selected Companies: (a) Cash Receipts and Disbursements, (b) Purchases, Material Control, and Accounts Payable, (c) Sales, Accounts Receivable, and Finished Goods Inventories, (d) Payroll Activities, (e) Cost Accounting Systems, (f) Budgeting and Control, (g) Bank Loans, Notes Payable, and Post-dated Checks, (h) Withholding and Payment of Taxes, (i) Plant Assets; Loan Procedures at the Korean Reconstruction Bank; Comparison of Korean and Japanese Accounting Methods; Conclusions and Recommendations.

2102
KUARK, John Yoon Tai. A Comparative Study of Economic Development in North and South Korea during the Post-Korean War Period. Minnesota, 1966. 327p. DA 27 (May 1967), 3558-59-A; UM 67-5211.

"Examines the significance of the contrasting economic development under Communism in North Korea and a mixed system of public and private enterprises in South Korea."

Rel.Publ.: "North Korea's Industrial Development during the Post-War Period," China Quarterly, 14 (Apr./June 1963), 51-64; "North Korea's Agricultural Development during the Post-War Period," China Quarterly, 14 (Apr./June 1963), 82-93; "Economic Development Contrast between South and North Korea," in Patterns of Economic Development: Korea, ed. by Joseph Sang-hoon Chung (Kalamazoo, Mich., 1966), 145-200.

2103
KIM, Yang Han. Empirical and Theoretical Analysis of Balanced and Unbalanced Growth Theories with Reference to South Korea, 1953-1960. Utah, 1967. 226p. DA 28 (Sept. 1967), 842-43-A; UM 67-11,464.

The dissertation first evaluates "the applicability of two different investment approaches developed by P. N. Rosenstein-Rodan, Ragnar Nurkse, and Albert O. Hirshman" to the South Korean Economy. It then "proposes an investment strategy for the South Korean economy which places strategic importance on the initial development of agricultural and capital goods industries rather than consumer goods industries within the general manufacturing sector....This proposal is made with special reference to the development policy adopted in South Korea during the years 1953-1960."

2104
SUH, Sang Chul. Growth and Structural Changes in the Korean Economy since 1910. Harvard, 1967. xvi, 313p.

AB: 10p. summary appended to diss. ms.

"Measures quantitatively the growth and structural changes in the Korean economy during the colonial period (1910-1941), evaluates critically the pattern of the colonial development, and endeavors to show the relation of the colonial development to postwar economic growth." Contents: Korea's Transition to the Colonial Period; The Colonial Policy and Scale of Development; Structural Changes: (1) Domestic Production, (2) Domestic Use of Commodity-Product; Comparative Economic Structure: South versus North; Conclusion: Postwar Growth of the South Korean Economy in Historical Perspective.

WHANG, In-Joung. Elites and Economic Programs: A Study of Changing Leadership for Economic Development in Korea, 1955-1967. 1968. See no.2501.

YOO, Jong Hae. National Planning for Development: The Case of Korea. 1968. See no.2502.

2105
SONG, Yoon Keun. A Quantitative Model for the Korean Economy. Illinois, 1969. 218p. DA 30 (Jan. 1970); UM 70-987.

The author develops a quantitative model for the Korean economy, which consists of an econometric macromodel and an input-output model, and then analyzes its predictability and its relative stability.

2106
YU, Yeun-chung. The Development of the Economically Active Population in East Asia, 1947-1966. Pennsylvania, 1969. 303p. DA 30 (May 1970); UM 70-7869.

AGRICULTURE

See also Geography (page 261).

2107
HAN, Sang-uk. Die Landwirtschaft von Korea [The Agriculture of Korea]. Zürich, 1927. Text in German.

A study of the natural basis, political and social organization, agricultural products, foreign trade, and actual performance of Korean agriculture.

Rel.Publ.: Die Landwirtschaft...Korea. Zürich: H. A. Gutzwiller, 1927. 96p.

2108
KIM, To Youn. Rural Economic Conditions in Korea. American, 1931. 245p.

Contents: Land and Climate; The Korean People; Agricultural Industry; Ownership and Tenancy; Agricultural Credit Organizations; Taxation of Land; Rural Market Conditions; Rural Communities and Organizations.

Rel.Publ.: Rural...Korea. Washington, D. C.(?), 1931. vii, 245p.

2109
MITCHELL, Charles Clyde, Jr. The New Korea Company, Limited: Land Mangement and Tenancy Reform in Korea against a Background of United States Army Occupation, 1945-1948. Harvard, 1949. xv, 365p. AB: 5p. summary appended to diss. ms.

"The thesis is a historical record of the author's own experience in Korea as director, for two years, of one of the largest of the country's economic activities, the New Korea Company." It studies (1) the land management activities of the United States in its operation of the agricultural properties formerly owned by the Japanese in Korea; (2) the development of the American-sponsored land-reform program and its results; (3) the outlook for additional rural reform measures in Korea; and (4) the administrative difficulties which threatened and continue to threaten to wreck the entire economic rehabilitation program of Korea."

Rel.Publ.: Final Report and History of the New Korea Company. Seoul: Headquarters, United States Army Military Government in Korea, National Land Administration, 1948. 65p.; "South Korean Tenants Become Landowners," Foreign Agriculture, 12 (Oct. 1948), 217-20; "Korean Farm Tenant Purchase Program," Land Economics, 24 (Nov. 1948), 402-05; "Land Reform in South Korea," Pacific Affairs, 22 (June 1949), 144-54.

2110
LI, Ne-Diu. Agrarnaia reforma /1946g./ i preobrazovanie sel'skogo khoziaistva Narodno-Demokraticheskoi Respubliki Korei [The Agrarian Reform (of 1946) and the Transformation of Agriculture in the People's Democratic Republic of Korea]. Moscow, Moskovskaia sel'skokhoziaistvennaia Akademiia imeni K. A. Timiriazeva, 1952. (Candidate of Economic Sciences degree) 239p. Text in Russian.

2111
BAICK, Dai Hyen. Pasture Establishment and Management for Students of Vocational Agriculture in Korea. Louisiana State, 1956. 146p. DA 18 (Mar. 1958), 723; UM 18,728.

"Develops a plan for the introduction of a new type of agricultural science in Korea known as grassland farming." The dissertation contains data on the establishment, management, and utilization practices of pasture land as well as an assessment of the benefits that would accrue to Korea through the introduction of grassland farming.

2112
KAZAKEVICH, Igor' Stepanovich. Agrarnye otnosheniia v Koree nakanune 2-oi mirovoi voiny 1930-1939 gg. [Agrarian Relations in Korea on the Eve of World War II]. Moscow, Institut vostokovedeniia Akademii nauk SSSR, 1956. (Candidate of Economic Sciences degree) xviii, 233p. Text in Russian.

Rel.Publ.: Agrarnye...1939 gg. Moscow: Izd. vostochnoi literatury, 1958. 127p. (Akademiia nauk SSSR, Institut Vostokovedeniia)

2113
PAK, Ki Hyuk. Economic Analysis of Land Reform in the Republic of Korea with Special Reference to an Agricultural Economic Survey, 1954-1955. Illinois, 1956. 214p. DA 16 (Nov. 1956), 1977; UM 18,183.

"This study is concerned especially with analyses of the effects of land reform upon (1) agricultural productivity, (2) marketing of farm products, (3) the status of the tenant-purchaser and his former landlord, (4) the agricultural policies of the government and its actions with respect to land reform, farm credit, farm taxation, and other farm problems, and (5) methods for promptly improving the changing agricultural community."

2114
KLEIN, Sidney. The Pattern of Land Tenure Reform in East Asia after World War II. Columbia, 1957. 412p. DA 17 (May 1957), 1006; UM 20,584.

Includes discussions of land reform in both North and South Korea.

Rel.Publ.: The Pattern...War II. New York: Bookman Associates, 1958. 260p. (Bookman Monograph Series)

2115
LIU, John Jung-chao. An Econometric Model of the Rice Market in the Japanese Empire, 1910-1937. Michigan, 1960. 143p. DA 20 (June 1960), 4549; UM 60-1778.
A case study focusing on the role played by Korea and Taiwan in the price stability of the Japanese rice market and on the competition with Japanese farmers created by the expansion of rice production in and exports from these two colonies to Japan.

McRAITH, James F. The Marketing of Rice in the Republic of Korea: Problems of an Underdeveloped Oriental Country. 1960. See no.2129.

2116
CHO, Yong Sam. Disguised Unemployment in South Korean Agriculture. California, Los Angeles, 1961. 205p.
Contents: The Literature of "Disguised Unemployment"; An Alternative Theoretical Model of Manpower Utilization: Voluntary and Involuntary Underemployment; Measurement of Underemployment: Voluntary and Involuntary Underemployment; The Nature of Korean Agriculture; "Surplus Labor" and Real Capital Formation; The Way Out: A Proposed Program.
Rel.Publ.: "Disguised Unemployment" in Underdeveloped Areas; With Special Reference to South Korean Agriculture. Berkeley: University of California Press, 1963. xiv, 163p. (Publications of the Bureau of Business and Economic Research, University of California, Los Angeles)

2117
PARK, Jin Hwan. Economics of Resource Use on Rice Farms in Korea. Minnesota, 1963. 241p. DA 25 (July 1964), 155-56; UM 64-7114.
Focuses on the problem of increasing food production through a reallocation of resources from rice to other crops and through greater use of supplementory crops.

2118
TRIGUBENKO, M. E. Sotsialisticheskie preobrazovaniia sel'skogo khoziaistva v Koreiskoi Narodno-Demokraticheskoi Respublike [The Socialist Transformation of Agriculture in the Korean People's Democratic Republic]. Moscow, Institut ekonomiki mirovoi sotsialisticheskoi sistemy Akademii nauk SSSR, 1963. (Candidate of Economic Sciences degree) 273p. Text in Russian.

2119
CHO, Jae Hong. Post-1945 Land Reforms and Their Consequences in South Korea. Indiana, 1964. 215p. DA 26 (Aug. 1965), 740-41; UM 64-12,012.
Investigates "(1) the nature of the impact of the reforms on agricultural productivity, (2) whether the reforms improved the farmers' living conditions on a permanent basis without having adverse effects on agricultural production, and (3) the impact of this land and income redistribution on agricultural production for sale."

2120
IUN, A. D. Deiatelnost' Trudovoi Partii Korei po sotsialisticheskomu preobrazovaniiu sel'skogo khoziaistva strany (1954-1956 gg.) [The Activity of the Korean Workers' Party in the Socialist Transformation of Korean Agriculture]. Tashkent, Tashkentskii gosudarstvennyi universitet imeni V. I. Lenina, 1964(?) (Candidate of Historical Sciences degree) 322p. Text in Russian.
Rel.Publ.: "Trudovaia partiia Korei v bor'be za organizatsiiu massovogo kooperativnogo dvizheniia sredi krest'ian: K 15-letiiu so dnia osvobozhdeniia Korei," Izvestiia Akademii nauk UzSSSR. Seriia obshchestvennykh nauk, 1960, no.5.

2121
SEO, Joseph Wonsock. Der gegenwärtige Stand der Agrarwirtschaft in Ostasien (Japan, Korea, Taiwan): Unter besonderer Berücksichtigung der handelspolitischen Verflechtung mit der EWG [The Present Position of Agriculture in East Asia (Japan, Korea, Taiwan): With Special Consideration of the Area's Commercial and Related Political Involvement with the European Common Market]. Wien, 1965. 189p. Text in German. Diss. ms. available at the Universitätsbibliothek der Universität Wien, Nr. D 16,229.

2122
KIM, Sun Kee. A Solution to the Problem of Food Shortages in Korea. Southern California, 1966. 253p. DA 26 (June 1966), 7080; UM 66-5485.
"One of the outstanding problems of the Korean economy is the persistent and large scale hunger which is spreading among a large proportion of the population. This study provides a strategy for the solution of this problem within the constraints of the Korean economy." Contents: The Extent of Food Shortages; Possibilities of Increasing the Supply of Food; The Cost of Increasing the Supply of Food; Output, Income, Expenditure, and the Price Level; Financing Capital Expenditure; Increase in the Food Supply and Economic Development.

2123
ELLO, Paul Stephen. The Commissar and the Peasant: A Comparative Analysis of Land Reform and Collectivization in North Korea and North Vietnam. Iowa, 1967. 564p. DA 28 (July 1967), 268-69-A; UM 67-9051.
Primarily a political analysis of land reform and collectivization in the two countries. Includes consideration of the Russian influence on North Korea's land reform and collectivization policies, 1945-1960's.

WANG, In Keun. Relationship of Adoption of Recommended Farm Practices with Selected Variables in Three Korean Communities. 1967. See no.2070.

2124
YOON, Tae Hee. Benefit-Cost Analysis of Two Alternatives for Increasing Food Output in the Republic of Korea. Connecticut, 1967. 149p. DA 28 (May 1968), 4347-A; UM 68-1426.
Seeks "to provide an economic guide for public investment in achieving self-sufficient food production in Korea." Concludes that programs for the greater intensive use of chemical fertilizer and for the expansion of agricultural land through conversion of idle uplands are both economically profitable but that the fertilizer program would bring greater benefits than the land program.

2125
LEE, Kie Wook. Efficiency of Resource Allocation in Traditional Agriculture: A Case Study of South Korea. Vanderbilt, 1968. 147p. DA 29 (Jan. 1969), 2011-A; UM 68-17,980.
"This study examines the efficiency of traditional agriculture in allocating scarce resources, with special reference to the case of South Korea. The concept of efficiency refers to that of using resources according to returns and opportunity costs, while the tradi-

tional agriculture is used to designate an agriculture which uses traditional inputs under the condition of static technology and thus contributes little to economic growth either directly or indirectly."

BUSINESS, INDUSTRY, AND DOMESTIC COMMERCE
See also Economics--money, banking, and investment (pages 254-55).

2126
BAGRIANSKAIA, L. S. Vosstanovlenie i razvitie promyshlennosti severnoi chasti Koreiskoi Narodno-Demokraticheskoi Respubliki (1945-1950 gg.) [The Reestablishment and Development of Industry in the Northern Part of the Korean People's Democratic Republic, 1945-1950]. Moscow, Ministerstvo vysshego obrazovaniia, Moskovskii institut vostokovedeniia, 1954. (Candidate of Economic Sciences degree) 296p. Text in Russian. AB: 16p. summary published in 1954.

CHAO, Lien L. Distinctive Patterns of Industrial Relations in Korea. 1956. See no.2059.

2127
PAIK, Young Hoon. Industrialisierungsprozess Korea [The Process of Industrialization in Korea]. Nürnberg, 1957. 123, vi p. Text in German. Diss. ms. available at Marburg/Lahn, Staatsbibliothek Preussischer Kulturbesitz, Nr. 15,883.

Studies the economic and social structure of Korea before the beginning of industrialization, Korea's industrialization under Japanese rule, and the development of Korean industry following the division of the country in 1945. Also attempts to isolate and analyze the factors that were significant in Korea's process of industrialization.

Rel.Publ.: "Das Autarkieproblem in der koreanische Wirtschaft," Koreana Quarterly, 1 (1959), 91-112.

2128
BELIAEV, Iu. N. Sotsialisticheskaia industrializatsiia Koreiskoi Narodno-Demokraticheskoi Respubliki [The Socialist Industrialization of the Korean People's Democratic Republic]. Moscow, Institut ekonomiki Akademii nauk SSSR, 1959. (Candidate of Economic Sciences degree) xv, 295p. Text in Russian. AB: 18p. summary published in 1959.

Rel.Publ.: "Building Socialist Industry in the Korean People's Democratic Republic," Problems of Economics (Moscow), 1 (Jan. 1959), 33-38.

2129
McRAITH, James Fredrick. The Marketing of Rice in the Republic of Korea: Problems of an Underdeveloped Oriental Country. Columbia, 1960. 186p. DA 21 (Apr. 1961), 2934; UM 60-5833.

"This study seeks first, to describe and to analyze domestic rice marketing institutions and techniques in the Republic of Korea and second, to make specific recommendations for improving the country's system of rice marketing." The latter include "public works projects to relieve unemployment and to construct transportation and communication facilities; a true agricultural cooperative system free of political control from the Executive Department of the government; construction of storage facilities to meet the collateral requirements of banks; judicious use of grain received in foreign aid to stabilize domestic rice prices; and a concerted effort to halt the inflation spiral."

2129a
SONG, Ki-tschul. Die Industrialisierung Koreans (1876-1956) unter besonderer Berücksichtigung der wirtschaftspolitischen Probleme [The Industrialization of Korea, 1876-1956, with Special Consideration of Political and Economic Problems]. Köln, 1960. Text in German. The dissertation in its published form is available at the University of Michigan, General Library, no.22,930.

Contents: Theoretical Basis for Industrialization in Underdeveloped Lands; An Historical Survey of Korean Economic Development with Particular Focus on Industrialization (Political History, Social Structure, The Intellectual Situation, Korea's Industrialization); Problems Regarding the Growth of South Korean Industry (Natural Factors including Climate, Population, and Raw Materials/Economic Difficulties); An Examination of Economic Policy in South and North Korea.

Rel.Publ.: Die Industrialisierung...Probleme. Köln, 1960. 151p.

2130
KIM, Hae-chun. Die industriellen Mittel- und Kleinunternehmen in Korea als Basis der wirtschaftlichen Entwicklung [Medium and Small-Sized Industrial Enterprises in Korea as a Base for Economic Development]. Köln, 1961. Text in German. The dissertation in its published form is available at Marburg/Lahn, Staatsbibliothek Preussischer Kulturbesitz, Nr. 28,414; also at the University of Michigan, General Library, no.24,583.

The foundations of the Korean economy and its present development are shown through a study of overall consumption, national income, and industrial production. The author also studies the structure and the productivity of Korean industry and the reasons for its unsatisfactory progress, and he concludes the dissertation with an examination of the aims and demands of American economic aid.

Rel.Publ.: Die industriellen...Entwicklung. Köln: Universität, 1961. 120p.

2131
LEE, Chong Ha. A Study of Bonded Processing Trade in Korea: Analysis of the Feasibility of the Korean Garment Industry's Moving toward a Full Processing Trade System. Washington, St. Louis, 1964. 311p. DA 26 (Aug. 1965), 767; UM 65-6844.

Analyzes the feasibility of the "industry's expanding exports by moving toward a full processing trade from its present bonded processing trade."

2132
YU, Se Hwan. The Adoption of Business Accounting Systems in Korean Municipal Water Utilities. Washington, 1964. 175p. DA 26 (Aug. 1965), 776-77; UM 65-6845.

Seeks "to demonstrate the vital necessity of adopting business accounting systems in Korean municipal water utilities to enable them to achieve rational management by making use of such analytical tools as budgetary control, cost analysis, and periodic financial reporting."

2133
JUHN, Daniel Sungil. Entrepreneurship in an Underdeveloped Economy: The Case of Korea, 1890-1940. George Washington, 1965. 225p. DA 27 (Oct. 1966), 863-64-A; UM 65-14,632.

"An historical study of indigenous Korean entrepreneurship." Contents: The Deterrents to Entrepreneurship in Pre-Japanese Korea; Some Aspects of Business and Economic Growth: (a) 1910-1930, (b) 1930-1940;

Entrepreneurship by Type of Activity; Analysis of Korean Entrepreneurship in Two Selected Cities; Analysis of Japanese Entrepreneurship in Korea; Other Factors in Entrepreneurial Change in Korea.

2134
CHO, Young Rin. The Structure of Demand and Economic Development. Massachusetts, 1966. 200p. DA 28 (Oct. 1967), 1195-96-A; UM 67-269.
"To find out whether 'reorganization of market within-the-industry' would in some real underdeveloped economies be sufficient to create a market to accomodate a modern efficient plant, the paper [includes] a case study involving the present and future prospects of a synthetic fiber industry in Korea."

2135
HONG, Wontack. A Study of the Changes in the Structure of Manufacturing Industry and in the Trade Pattern of Manufactured Products in Korea, Taiwan, and Japan. Columbia, 1966. 277p. DA 27 (Jan. 1967), 1968-69-A; UM 66-12,569.
"This study of Korea (1911-1964), Taiwan (1896-1964), and Japan (1868-1964) supports the hypothesis that the structure of manufacturing industry (composition of manufactured output) and the trade pattern in manufactured products tend to change systematically as the economic development of a country progresses."
Rel.Publ.: "Industrialization and Trade in Manufactures: The East Asian Experience," in <u>The Open Economy: Essays on International Trade and Finance</u>, ed. by P. B. Kenen and R. Lawrence (New York: Columbia University Press, 1968), 213-39.

2136
KIM, Jongbin. The Korean Cotton Manufacturing Industry. California, Berkeley, 1966. 288p. DA 27 (Apr. 1967), 3189-90-A; UM 67,5095.
"An economic analysis of the Korean cotton manufacturing industry." Contents: A Survey of the Korean Cotton Manufacturing Industry; Foreign Aid Programs to Korea; Market Structure in the Korean Cotton Manufacturing Industry; Market Conduct in the Industry; Market Performance in the Industry; Can the Korean Cotton Manufacturing Industry Survive without U.S. Aid Raw Cotton to Korea?

2137
LEE, Henry Farrow. Relative Prices and Cereal Consumption Functions: Korea, 1952 to 1962. Pennsylvania, 1966. 164p. DA 27 (Apr. 1967), 3181-A; UM 67-3085.
"Monthly family budget data from a panel of salary and wage earner families in Seoul, Korea from 1952 to 1962 provided...[the basis for] estimating how consumers' monthly cereal demand is influenced by food expenditure, by a proxy for income, and by the relative price of cereals."

2138
SHIN, Paul Yong Hak. The Significance of the Role of Insurance in Economic Development with Special Emphasis on Korea. Nebraska, 1968. 163p. DA 29 (Dec. 1968), 1637-38-A; UM 68-18,030.
Contents: The Conceptual Analysis of the Role of Insurance in Economic Theory; Historical Development of Insurance in Korea; Analytical Theories of Underdeveloped Economies; The Contribution of Insurance to Economic Development; Policy Implications of Insurance for Underdeveloped Countries.

ECONOMIC HISTORY

LEE, Hun-gu. A History of Land Systems and Politics in Korea. 1923(?) See no.2217.

ARNOLD, Dean A. American Economic Enterprises in Korea, 1895-1939. 1954. See no.2289.

CHEN, Ilen. Kharakternye osobennosti razvitiia promyshlennosti i polozhenie rabochego klassa v Koree nakanune i vo vremia vtoroi mirovoi voiny. 1956. See no.2308.

KOH, Hesung C. Religion, Social Structure, and Economic Development in Yi Dynasty Korea. 1959. See no.2079.

LIU, John J.-C. An Econometric Model of the Rice Market in the Japanese Empire, 1910-1937. 1960. See no.2115.

SONG, Ki-tschul. Die Industrialisierung Koreas (1876-1956) unter besonderer Berücksichtigung der wirtschaftspolitischen Probleme. 1960. See no.2129a.

WOO, Philip M. The Historical Development of Korean Tariff and Customs Administration, 1875-1958. 1963. See no.2499.

JUHN, Daniel S. Entrepreneurship in an Underdeveloped Economy: The Case of Korea, 1890-1940. 1965. See no. 2133.

SUH, Sang C. Growth and Structural Changes in the Korean Economy since 1910. 1967. See no.2104.

FISHERIES, FORESTRY, AND MINING

2139
MARTYNOV, V. V. Ekonomiko-statisticheskoe izuchenie toplivno-energeticheskoi bazy Koreiskoi Narodno-Demokraticheskoi Respubliki [An Economic and Statistical Examination of the Fuel and Power Resources of the Korean People's Democratic Republic]. Moscow, Moskovskii ekonomiko-statisticheskii institut, 1963. (Candidate of Economic Sciences degree) 193p. Text in Russian.

FOREIGN TRADE

(Includes dissertations on Korean trade with specific countries as well as on trade regulations, organization, and foreign trade matters in general)

2140
HUH, Kyung-Mo. The Development and Prospects of Japan's Trade in Asia. Michigan, 1965. 382p. DA 28 (Jan. 1968), 2402-03-A; UM 66-6620.
Includes a study of Japanese-Korean trade.
Rel.Publ.: <u>Japan's Trade in Asia: Developments Since 1926, Prospects for 1970</u>. New York: Praeger, 1966. xx, 283p. (Praeger Special Studies in International Economics and Development)

HONG, Wontack. A Study of the Changes in the Structure of Manufacturing Industry and in the Trade Pattern of Manufactured Products in Korea, Taiwan, and Japan. 1966. See no.2135.

2141
PARK, Seong Ho. Export Expansion and Import Substitution in the Economic Development of Korea, 1955-1965. American, 1969. 165p. DA 30 (Nov. 1969), 1700-A; UM 69-18,811.

A quantitative assessment of the impact of foreign trade as well as of domestic demand and technology factors on the expansion of Korea's economic output, 1955-1965. Contents: Export Expansion and Import Substitution in Economic Development; Korea's Changing Foreign Trade; Analytical Model and Its Application; Analysis of the Sources of Economic Expansion.

2142
LEE, Dae Sung. International Trade in the Economic Development of the Korean Economy. Massachusetts, 1970. 165p. DA 30 (June 1970); UM 70-9857. [See also addenda]

MONEY, BANKING, AND INVESTMENT

For financial matters related primarily to foreign trade, e.g. international balance of payments, see Economics--foreign trade (pages 253-54).

2143
LI, Von Gen. Voprosy kreditnogo planirovaniia v Koreiskoi Narodno-Demokraticheskoi Respublike [Questions of Credit Planning in the Korean People's Democratic Republic]. Leningrad, Leningradskii finansovo-ekonomicheskii institut, 1956. (Candidate of Economic Sciences degree) xi, 267p. Text in Russian.

2144
JOEL, Clark. Korea: A Case Study in Inflation. Wisconsin, 1961. 339p. DA 22 (Dec. 1961), 1863-64; UM 61-5943.

Studies the background and causes of the inflation that occurred in Korea during the 1950's and the successful stabilization program that was launched in 1957.

2145
NAM, Duck Woo. Monetary Expansion and Capital Formation in Korea, 1954-1958. Oklahoma State, 1961. x, 196p.

Contents: Foreign Economic Aid and Domestic Production; The Expansion of the Money Supply; The Velocity of Money and Prices; The Causes and Extent of Deficit Spending and Its Allocation; The Causes of Expansion of Bank Credit and Its Allocation; Actual Performance in Capital Formation and Its Relation to Deficit Spending and Credit.

Rel.Publ.: "Deficit Financing and Economic Development in Underdeveloped Economics," Koreana Quarterly, 93-102.

2146
CHUNG, Nae Hoon (Paul). The Role of the Central Bank and Inflation in Korea, 1945-1960. Michigan State, 1963. 274p. DA 24 (May 1964), 4460; UM 63-6144.

Systematically tries to determine "whether or not the Bank of Korea achieved the goals of monetary policy: maintaining price stability and inducing economic growth."

Rel.Publ.: "Monetary Policy in Korea 1945-1960," Economics (Seoul), 11 (Nov. 1963), 14-28.

2147
SONG, Chang-Jin. Die Neugestaltung des koreanischen Bankwesens nach dem zweiten Weltkrieg: Ihre Notwendigkeit und Auswirkungen [The Reform of the Korean Banking System after World War II: Its Necessity and Its Consequences]. München, 1963. Text in German. The dissertation in its published form is available at Marburg/Lahn, Staatsbibliothek Preussischer Kulturbesitz, Nr. Hsn 39,106; also at the University of Michigan, General Library, no. 28,193.

Focuses on the postwar establishment of the Bank of Korea, the formation of a central banking system, the Korean credit system, and the control and organization of credit within the country.

Rel.Publ.: Die Neugestaltung...Auswirkungen. München: Universitätsdruck, 1963. vii, 118p.

2148
LEE, Bumsun. Central Banking and Monetary Control in Korea, 1950-1963. New York, 1966. 157p. DA 28 (Jan. 1968), 2420-21-A; UM 66-10,580.

"Evaluates the effectiveness of the monetary control exercised by the Bank of Korea between 1950 and 1963 (and particularly 1957-1963) and examines the comparative usefulness of the various monetary control instruments."

2149
KIM, Hyung Kon. Korean Monetary and Credit Policy: A Study of Financial Policy in an Underdeveloped Country. Washington, Seattle, 1967. 238p. DA 28 (Aug. 1967), 367-68-A; UM 67-9913.

Studies the performance of the Bank of Korea between 1953 and 1960 in an attempt "to analyze the particular economic conditions and financial markets influencing the development of central banking operations and to illuminate the financial problems of reconstruction of a wartorn economy and achievement of relative price stability."

2150
LEE, Joong Koon. Behavior of Money and Prices in the Korean Inflation, 1953-1964. Columbia, 1967. 196p. DA 28 (Oct. 1967), 1188-A; UM 67-9350.

"The purpose of this study is to analyze the Korean inflation and to suggest a way to explain the historical rate of inflation in Korea....The results show that changes in agricultural output gave rise to changes in price expectations such that they significantly influence the demand for real money and for real liquid assets in Korea."

2151
AHN, Seung Chul. A Monetary Analysis of the Korean Economy, 1954-1966, on the Basis of Demand and Supply Functions of Money. California, Berkeley, 1968. 88p. DA 29 (Mar. 1969), 2847-A; UM 69-3555.

"Explores two policy issues: (1) a search for the 'safe' limit of monetary expansion in a developing economy like Korea, and (2) an examination of the extent of the inflation-financed economic growth in the case of Korea."

2152
RHA, Woong Bae. An Application of Mathematical Programming to the Choice of Investments: The Case of the Electric Power Industry in Korea. California, Berkeley, 1968. 144p. DA 29 (June 1969), 4142-A; UM 69-10,371.

"The thesis is an attempt to develop mathematical programming models for investment problems in the electric power industry and to apply those models to power development planning in Korea....The significance of impacts of some important factors (e.g. discount rate, investment funds, technical progress, and fuel prices, etc.) on power development planning is investigated by sensitivity analysis. The results are interesting and suggestive in finding the proper direction of a long-run power development program in Korea."

2153
SHIN, Bong Ju. Inflation and Economic Growth: An Empirical Study Based on the Korean Experience 1948-1967. Ohio State, 1969. 313p. DA 30 (Apr. 1970); UM 70-6881.

2154
WESTPHAL, Larry Edward. A Dynamic Multi-Sectoral Programming Model Featuring Economies of Scale: Planning Investment in Petrochemicals and Steel in Korea. Harvard, 1969. xxv, 341p. AB: 6p. summary appended to diss. ms.

The mixed integer-continuous variable programming model is applied to planning the timing of investment in a petro-chemicals plant and in an integrated iron and steel mill in the Republic of Korea. Contents: Economies of Scale in Capital Accumulation Models; A Dynamic, General Equilibrium Investment Planning Model; Programming the Growth of the Korean Economy: The Basic Solution; The Use of Balanced Growth Models to Determine Comparative Advantage; Programming the Growth of the Korean Economy: Effects of Changing the Welfare Function and the Timing of Foreign Capital Inflows; Capital Accumulation Paths in the Presence of Increasing Returns.

PUBLIC FINANCE

2155
KAY, Bong Hyok. Fiscal and Taxation Policy in a Developing Economy with Special Reference to the Republic of Korea. Wisconsin, 1958. 386p. DA 18 (June 1958), 2017-18; UM 58-1910.

Explores the conditions necessary to raise per capita income in Korea. Focuses on "(1) the obstacles to economic development, (2) the government's share in financing economic development, (3) foreign aid's contribution to internal development, and (4) the government's revenue system in promoting economic growth."

2156
BANG, Kap Soo. A Proposed Social Security System for Korea Based on an Analysis of Programs in Great Britain, Japan, Malaya, and the United States. Pennsylvania, 1961. 464p. DA 23 (July 1962), 108-09; UM 62-2818.

"The purpose of this study is to suggest social security programs for Korea which would alleviate economic insecurity and poverty, and stimulate efforts for progress of the Korean economy." Both short-range and long-range social security programs are proposed.

2157
HAN, Kee Chun. A Study of the Interregional Economics of Korea. Boston, 1963. 269p. DA 24 (Aug. 1963), 544-45; UM 63-5908.

Creates an interregional input-output model for the Korean economy and uses it to "measure the regional and interregional implications of the Investment Program projected for 1962 and 1963 in The First Five Year Plan (1962-1966)."

2158
YU, Hoon. The Budgetary Process in Korea. Minnesota, 1964. 297p. DA 25 (Feb. 1965), 4807; UM 65-1026.

Describes and analyzes the Korean budget system as it operated during the early 1960's. Contents: The Development of Budgeting in Korea; The Korean Government's Organization for Budget Administration; The Budget Accounts; Legal Basis of the Budget; Budget Classification; Preparation of the Budget; Authorization of the Budget; The Execution of the Budget; Audit; Performance Budgeting in Korea; Economic Development and the Budget.

2159
CHOUGH, Soon. Financing of Economic Development in South Korea, 1954-1964. California, Berkeley, 1967. 247p. DA 30 (July 1969), 40-A; UM 68-46.

"The first part of the study analyzes those aspects of fiscal and monetary frameworks of the economy which are relevant to development financing. The second part deals with analyses of operations of development banks [government lending institutions created by special legislation] and economic impacts emanating therefrom.... Two such banks are dealt with in the study: the National Agricultural Cooperatives and the Korean Reconstruction Bank."

2160
SONG, Young-dahl. The Tax System of the Republic of Korea. Pennsylvania, 1967. 303p. DA 28 (Apr. 1968), 3859-A; UM 68-4615.

"An attempt to describe and critically appraise the several taxes comprising the fiscal structure, to appraise the functioning of the entire tax system, and to suggest means whereby the tax system might be improved in the interest of equity, more effective administration, and desirable economic effects."

2161
KIM, Seung Hee. The Korean Balance of Payments and Economic Development. New York, 1969. 246p. DA 30 (Nov. 1969), 1720-A; UM 69-16,765.

Develops a theoretical framework in order to estimate the amount of foreign capital that Korea will need to help finance internal economic development over a ten year period. The author estimates that $3,900,000,000 in external capital will be required to achieve the 8% target growth of GNP during the 1967-1976 projection period.

TRANSPORTATION AND COMMUNICATIONS

2162
LEE, Hyun Jong. Die Tarifpolitik der Eisenbahn im Güterverkehr: Unter besonderer Bezugnahme auf die koreanische National-Eisenbahn [The Tariff Policy of the Railways with Regard to Freight Traffic: With Special Reference to the Korean National Railways]. Wien, 1967. 122p. Text in German. Diss. ms. available at the Österreichische Nationalbibliothek, Nr. 1,040.6460.

Pt.2 examines the policies of the Korean National Railways during the twenty years following World War II and recommends ways for improving its services.

Education

See also History and International Relations--The Period of Japanese Rule, 1910-1945: Education (page 272).

GENERAL

2163
UNDERWOOD, Horace Horton. Outline History of Modern Education in Korea. New York, 1926. viii, 393p.
Contents: Education under the Korean Government; Missionary Education (Early Beginnings and Indirect Education, Elementary and Secondary Education, Industrial Education, Higher Education, Other Educational Work); Korean Private Education; Government Education since 1910 (Educational Policy, Educational Work of the Government-General since 1910); Opportunities.
Rel.Publ.: Modern Education in Korea. New York: International Press, 1926. xv, 336p.

2164
ROE, Chungil Yhan. The True Function of Education in Social Adjustment, as Comparative Estimate and Criticism of the Educational Teachings of Confucius and the Philosophy of John Dewey with a View to Evolving a Project for a System of National Education which will Meet the Needs of Korea. Nebraska, 1927. 60p.
Ch.3 applies the theoretical aspects of the paper to a concrete situation in Korea. It also includes several designs for secondary and college curriculums in Korean Schools.
Rel.Publ.: The True...Korea. Lincoln, Neb., 1927. 60p.

2165
KIM, Helen Kiteuk. Rural Education for the Regeneration of Korea. Columbia (Teachers College), 1931. vii, 124p.
Contents: The Life Situations of Rural Korea and the Educational Problems (The Economic, Health, Social and Recreational, and Cultural Situations, Summary of the Educational Problems Rising Out of the Life Situations); How the Present Educational System Meets the Educational Problems of the Rural People (Elementary, Secondary, and Agricultural Schools, Facilities for Adult Rural Education, Is the Educational System Meeting the Problems Rising Out of the Rural Life Situations? The Underlying Principles as an Explanation for the Present Policies and Practices); Contribution of Other Agencies towards the Education of the Rural People; What Other Countries [Denmark and Russia] are Doing under Similar Circumstances; What May Be Some Reasonable Objectives and Means of Rural Education in Korea.
Rel.Publ.: Rural...Korea. New York: Teachers College, Columbia University, 1931. vii, 124p.

2166
KIM, Hyun-chul. History of Education in Korea. American, 1931. 291p.
Contents: Beginning of Educational Effort; Development of Education during (a) the Three Kingdom Period, (b) the Koryŏ Dynasty, (c) the Lee Dynasty; System of Education and the Method of Education; Transition to Modern Education.

2167
YUN, Sŏng-sun. The Influence of Confucianism and Christianity upon Korean Education. American, 1932. 240p.
Contents: Brief Survey of Korean Education; Influence of Confucian Education from Its Dominance over Buddhism until 1885 A.D.; Early Influence of Christianity upon Confucian Education, 1886-1895; Christian Influence upon Secondary and Higher Education, 1896-1931.

2168
KIM, Son Gi. Uchenie Lenina-Stalina o kulturnoi revoliustii i rol' narodnogo obrazovaniia v osushchestvlenii kulturnoi revoliutsii v Koreiskoi Narodno-Demokraticheskoi Respublike [The Teachings of Lenin and Stalin on the Cultural Revolution and the Role of National Education in the Implementation of the Cultural Revolution in the Korean People's Democratic Republic]. Moscow, Moskovskii gosudarstvennyi pedagogicheskii institut imeni V. I. Lenina, 1954. (Candidate of Pedagogical Sciences degree) Text in Russian. AB: 8p. summary published in 1954.

2169
ADAMS, Donald Kendrick. Education in Korea 1945-1955. Connecticut, 1955. 328p. DA 16 (Sept. 1956), 1630; UM 18,314.
"A descriptive analysis of the major developments of Korean education from 1945 through 1954 including an examination of the goals, organizational structure, and administrative and teaching practices as they evolved" during that time.
Rel.Publ.: "Teacher Education in Modern Korea," School and Society, 88 (Apr. 23, 1960), 207-09; Higher Educational Reforms in the Republic of Korea. Washington: United States Department of Health, Education, and Welfare, Office of Education, 1965. vi, 63p. (United States Office of Education, Bulletin,1964 [i.e. 1965] no.27)

2170
PAK, Khyn-Sen. Osushchestvlenie vseobshchego obiazatel'nogo nachal'nogo obucheniia v SSSR i KNDR [The Completion of Universal Compulsory Primary Education in the USSR and the KPDR]. Moscow, Moskovskii gosudarstvennyi pedagogicheskii institut imeni V. I. Lenina, 1956. (Candidate of Pedagogical Sciences degree) ix, 224p. Text in Russian. AB: 15p. summary published in 1956.

2171
LEE, Sung-hwa. The Social and Political Factors Affecting Korean Education, 1885-1950. Pittsburgh, 1958. 235p. DA 19 (Dec. 1958), 1284-85; UM 58-5619.

Contents: Introduction of Modern Education, 1885-1910; Japanese National Education, 1910-1945; Educational Reform since Liberation, 1945-1950.

2172
YOO, Hyung Jin. An Intellectual History of Korea from Ancient Times to the Impact of the West with Special Emphasis upon Education. Harvard, 1958. vii, 292p. AB: 5p. summary appended to diss. ms.

"The primary purpose of the thesis is to trace the general trend of social, political, and intellectual forces in Korean history that provided the foundation upon which her educational system was based, until the influence of Western civilization became active in the 19th century." The dissertation includes a clarification of "the relationship between the total dependency of the Korean culture on that of China and the deadening effects which resulted therefrom in the sphere of learning and education."

2173
WILSON, Elizabeth Cecil. The Problem of Value in Technical Assistance in Education: The Case of Korea, 1945-1955. Maryland, 1959. 349p. DA 20 (Apr. 1960), 4006; UM 60-1286.

"Attempts to compare and contrast the major values which dominated Korean education in 1945 with those imported by American teachers working in technical assistance programs in South Korea between 1945 and 1955."

2174
CHOI, Sung Pyo. The Problem of Reconstructing Korean Education in Historical Perspective. Illinois, 1960. 350p. DA 21 (Mar. 1961), 2575-76; UM 61-103.

"Studies the social and intellectual foundations of Korean education throughout its history" and compares them with the foundations of American education.

2175
AVEN, James Stephen. The Organization of American Community Schools in the Far East. California, Los Angeles, 1963. 209p. DA 24 (Nov. 1963), 1893; UM 63-7700.

"Concerned with the policy of the indigenous governments, non-government agencies, and the United States government toward American community schools in the Far East." Includes a discussion of the development and present status of American schools in Seoul.

2176
USHKOV, A. M. Progressivnaia prosvetitel'naia mysl' v Koree: v kontse XIX-nachale XX vv. [Progressive Educational Thought in Korea at the End of the Nineteenth and at the Beginning of the Twentieth Centuries]. Moscow, Institut filosofii Akademii nauk SSSR, 1963. (Candidate of Pholosophical Sciences degree) viii, 180p. Text in Russian.

2177
PARK, Bong Mak. An Analysis of the Ideas of John Dewey and Reinhold Niebuhr on Social Justice and the Implications of These Ideas for Korean Education. New York, 1968. 262p. DA 30 (Aug. 1969), 624-A; UM 69-11,767.

In Ch.5, the author indicates the relevance of some of Dewey's and Niebuhr's mutually-held ideas to Korean education, particularly "in such areas as: teaching of the scientific and pragmatic approach in the classroom and in social research; decentralization of the educational system; reform of the examination system; the role of teachers organizations; and the social and democratic values of individual freedom and equality."

2178
KIM, Hyung-chan. A Study of North Korean Education under Communism since 1945. George Peabody College for Teachers, 1969. 1162p. (2v.) DA 30 (May 1970); UM 70-7615.

Contents: Introduction to Korea, Her People, and Culture; History of Korean Education prior to 1945; An Overview of the Communist System of Education; Educational Reforms during the Period 1946-1967; Decision-Making Processes and the Financial Costs of Education; Pre-School Education; Primary Education; Secondary Education; Higher Education; International Education and Cultural Exchanges. Volume 2 (409p.) "presents a hitherto uncollected and largely untranslated compilation of key educational documents."

Rel.Publ.: "Ideology and Indoctrination in the Development of North Korean Education," <u>Asian Survey</u>, 9 (Nov. 1969), 831-41.

2179
SESSIONS, Eldred Steed. An Analysis of the Contribution of the Educational Establishment to the Emergence of Korean National Identity: A Case Study of the Role of Education in Formulating a National Ethic in a Developing Country. Catholic, 1969. 209p. DA 30 (Dec. 1969), 2269-70-A; UM 69-19,693.

An analysis of the origin and development of traditional patterns of Korean moral education, the historical relationships that have existed between students and governmental authority, and the prospects for inculcating national cognition and patriotic ideals in a developing country through democratic institutions fostered by a viable philosophy of education.

ADMINISTRATION AND POLICY

2180
CHOY, Young Ho. Reorganization of Private Education in Korea: With Special Emphasis on the Rural Secondary Phase. Indiana, 1930. 139p.

Contents: Historical Background of Korean Education; Private Education in Korea; Mission Education in Korea; Government Education in Korea; Educational Needs of Korea; Reorganization and Suggested Reconstruction.

2181
BARNES, Elaine Milam. The Schools of Taegu, Kyongsang Pukto Province, Korea, in 1954-1955: An Investigation into the Interaction between Culture and Education. Maryland, 1960. 310p. DA 22 (Dec. 1961), 1873; UM 61-5391.

Describes and analyzes the educational organization which the Taegu City Education Bureau developed in response to the laws of the Republic of Korea requiring the development of democratic concepts and practices in Korean primary schools. It shows how the educational system reflected the unique historical, cultural, and political facets of this region."

2182
YOO, Young Dae. Suggestions for the Improvement of Korean Educational Laws in Terms of the Democratic Principles. George Peabody College for Teachers, 1960. 257p. DA 21 (Sept. 1960), 533-34; UM 60-2910.
"Points out the provisions in Korean educational laws which contradict the democratic principles, and suggests ways for improving the laws."

2183
KIM, Sung-Il. A Study of Certain Aspects of Educational Administration and Their Historical Roots in the Republic of Korea. Syracuse, 1961. 656p. DA 22 (June 1962), 4240; UM 62-1106.
The dissertation "describes educational aims and policies, organization, staffing, facilities and equipment, financing, and problems" of educational administration under the present ROK government; and it "traces the historical roots of current concepts, practices, and problems" through a study of Korean education between 1392 and 1948.
Rel.Publ.: " A Study of Historical Roots of Educational Administration in the Republic of Korea," in Hanguk Yŏngu Tosŏgwan, Seoul, Bulletin of the Korean Research Center; Journal of Social Science and Humanities, 22 (June 1965), 1-25.

2184
NAM, Byung Hun. Educational Reorganization in South Korea under the United States Army Military Government, 1945-1948. Pittsburgh, 1962. 275p. DA 23 (Dec. 1962), 1996-97; UM 62-6677.
A descriptive analysis of (1) the administrative reorganization of the educational system, (2) the reorganization of Korean schools, and (3) the reorganization of higher education.

2185
CHUNG, Yong Hwan. A Study of Some Aspects of Educational Administration with Implications for the Korean Public School System. Oklahoma, 1965. 163p. DA 26 (Sept. 1965), 1445; UM 65-9743.
The objective of the study: "To make some proposals for improving and introducing into Korean public education certain principles and practices found to be effective in modern democratic forms of school administration."

2186
KHON, K. E. Prosvetitel'naia politika marionetochnykh vlastei i shkola v Iuzhnoi Koree (1945-1965) [The Educational Politics of the Puppet Authorities and the School in South Korea, 1945-1965]. Moscow, Moskovskii oblastnoi pedagogicheskii institut imeni N. K. Krupskoi, 1966. (Candidate of Pedagogical Sciences degree) xiv, 230p. Text in Russian.

2187
PARK, Young Youl. Education in South Korea: Schools in Transition. California, Los Angeles, 1967. 232p. DA 28 (Aug. 1967), 548-49-A; UM 67-7396.
A critical analysis of postwar educational reforms. Contents: Education prior to 1945; Postwar Trend in Korean Education; The Implications of Educational Reform; A Search for Democratic Pedagogical Methods.

CURRICULUM, TEXTBOOKS, AND EDUCATIONAL MEDIA

See also Education--higher, adult, and teacher education (pages 259-60) and Education--religious education (page 260).

2188
CHO, Seung-Hak. A Study of the Korean Elementary School Curriculum. Wisconsin, 1937. iii, 200p. AB: University of Wisconsin. Summaries of Doctoral Dissertations. v.2 (1936/1937), p.243-44.
Studies "(1) the development and present status of the educational system in Korea, and (2) the extent to which psychological principles have been applied to elementary education in general and to the curriculum in particular."

WILSON, James N. A Handbook on the Political Geography of the Orient. 1949. See no.2213.

PULTR, Alois. Učebnice Korejštiny. 1951/52. See no.2427.

2189
SUHR, Myong Won. Together we Live: A Proposed Civics Textbook for the Elementary Schools in the New Korea. George Peabody College for Teachers, 1953. 168p. AB: George Peabody College for Teachers. Abstracts of Dissertations for the Year 1953. p.205-13.
This is the result of the author's attempt to write a civics textbook based on modern educational theories and practices.

2190
LEE, Sookney. Primary Arithmetic Textbooks in Korea, Japan, China, and the United States. Iowa, 1954. 401p. DA 14 (Oct. 1954), 1584; UM 9586.
The dissertation analyzes the primary arithmetic textbooks of four countries in order to select from them certain instructional materials of value for Korean education. The Sembon series of Korean textbooks is among the series analyzed and evaluated.

2191
PAK, N. T. Metodika obucheniia russkomu predlozhnomu upravleniiu v koreiskoi semiletnei shkole [Methods of Teaching Russian Prepositional Cases in the Korean Seven-Year School]. Moscow, Akademiia pedagogicheskikh nauk RSFSR, Nauchno-issledovatel'nyi institut metodov obucheniia, 1955. (Candidate of Pedagogical Sciences degree) Text in Russian. AB: 15p. summary published in 1955.

2192
PAIK, Hyung Ki. Designing County Cooperative Services for the Improvement of the School and Community in the Rural Areas of Korea with Special Attention to Audio-Visual Service. Columbia (Teachers College), 1956. 246p.
The study presents the background of educational organizations in Korea, a description of the rural Korean school and community, and a plan for improving Korean schools through the use of audio-visual materials.

LAH, Kihough H. Geography of Korea. 1957. See no.2215.

2193
LEE, Yung Dug. The Contribution of the Ohio State University School to a Proposal for the Development of Core Programs in the Campus Secondary Schools of Korea. Ohio State, 1959. 396p. DA 20 (Dec. 1959), 2177-78; UM 59-5913.

Contents: The Background of the Educational Programs of the Campus Laboratory Secondary Schools of Korea; The Theoretical Foundations of General Education in American Secondary Schools; The Nature of Core Program, and Procedures for Developing a Core Program Based on Adolescent Problems; The Ohio State University School: Historical Background and General Setting; The Core Program of the University School in Action; A Proposed Plan for Developing Core Programs in the Campus Laboratory Schools of Korea.

2194
PARK, Thomas Choonbai. Proposal for Improvement of Korean Schools through Development of a Cocurricular Program. Florida, 1961. 195p. DA 24 (Nov. 1963), 1945; UM 63-7495.

Contents: The Cocurricular Program in the United States: Survey of Literature; A Brief Description of Korean Education with Emphasis on the Cocurricular Program; Bases of a Cocurricular Program; A Recommended Cocurricular Program for Korean Elementary and Secondary Schools.

2195
LIMBACHER, Karl Frederick. A First Book of English for Use in the Korean Public Schools. Columbia, 1968. 178p. DA 29 (Apr. 1969), 3598-99-A; UM 69-6380.

The dissertation is "the result of a textbook project that was begun under the joint auspices of the United Nations Korean Reconstruction Agency and the Korean Ministry of Education in 1953 and was continued during 1957-1960 under the auspices of the ministry and of UNESCO. It consists of two parts: a rationale and the textbook.

HIGHER, ADULT, AND TEACHER EDUCATION

See also Education--religious education (page 260).

2196
CHEY, Soon Ju. A Suggested Commercial Curriculum for the Chōsen Christian College of Korea. New York, 1930. viii, 271p.

Contents: A Brief Historical Background of General Education; A Detailed Study of the Development of Commercial Education in Korea; The General Trend of Economic Conditions; The Economic Defects in Terms of Existing Economic Conditions, and the Educational Aims Correcting These Defects; The Evaluation of the Present Curriculum of the Chōsen Christian College; Summary and Conclusions; A Proposed Commercial Curriculum of Chōsen Christian College.

Rel.Publ.: A Suggested...Korea. New York, 1930. 8p. (Abstract of thesis)

2197
DIETZ, Elisabeth Hoffman-Warner. Normal School Education in the Republic of Korea, 1952-1953. New York, 1955. 361p. DA 16 (Mar. 1956), 501-02; UM 15,541.

Contents: The Problem of the Study; Background of the Study; The Economic Basis for the Development of Korean Education; Education in Korea; The Findings of the Study: Part 1 (The Aims and Objectives of the ROK and the UN as They Bear upon Education, General Information about Korean Education, 1952-1953); The Findings: Part 2 (The Present Status of Elementary and Normal School Education, Problems Identified by the Koreans Represented in the Study); Recommendations.

2198
MASTON, Robert Edward. English Language Workshops for English Teachers of South Korea: In-Service Experiences Leading to a Mastery of English Structures through an Audio/Lingual Pattern Practice Approach. Michigan, 1963. 306p. DA 24 (Nov. 1963), 1931; UM 63-8147.

"Examines critically the needs of South Korea for a means by which international understanding and communication may be effected and describes the development of methods for improving instruction in English in Korean Schools." Contents: Korea's Need for English; Education and English; An English Program and Barriers to Progress; Pre-Workshop Planning; The Workshop Design and the Workshop Series; Residues and Recommendations.

2199
BURROUGHS, Franklin Troy. Foreign Students at U.C.L.A.: A Case-Study in Cross-Cultural Education. California, Los Angeles, 1964. 252p. DA 25 (Sept. 1964), 1711; UM 64-8321.

The dissertation studies (1) the types of problems the foreign students (including 247 Korean foreign students for the period 1951-1963) have faced, (2) the way in which the university and the community have served the foreign students, and (3) the efforts of the foreign students to effect their own organizations.

2200
CHANG, Yong. Development of Korean Journalism Education Based on American Practices. Missouri, 1967. 303p. DA 28 (Nov. 1967), 1778-79-A; UM 67-13,844.

The study was designed "with the objective of adapting suitable methods, techniques, policies, and curricula of American journalism education to Korean journalism education at the university level."

2201
SUGIMOTO, Roy Atsuro. The Relationship of Selected Predictive Variables to Foreign Student Achievement at the University of California, Los Angeles. Southern California, 1967. 154p. DA 28 (July 1967), 65-A; UM 67-8032.

"This analytical-descriptive study was designed to discover the relationship between certain items found on forms in admission offices dealing with foreign students and the eventual academic success or lack of success of these students." The study dealt in part with students from Korea.

2202
KIM, Young Shik. Education of Elementary School Teachers and Administrators in the Republic of Korea, 1958-1964. George Peabody College for Teachers, 1968. 333p. DA 29 (Nov. 1968), 1465-A; UM 68-16,344.

Contents: Historical Background of Teacher Education from the Late 1890's through the 1950's; Pre-Service Education of Elementary Teachers from the Late 1950's through 1964; The In-Service Education of Elementary School Teachers and Administrators from the Late 1950's through 1964.

2203
MONCUR, Earl. Structural Elements of Extension Systems in Selected Developing Countries. Cornell, 1968. 241p.

DA 29 (Dec. 1968), 1749-A; UM 68-16,758.
Korea is one of twenty countries investigated in this study.

2204
SITLER, Lydia Arlene. An Investigation of the Need for Increased Support and Improvement of Indigenous Graduate Education in Korea. Indiana, 1968. 350p. DA 29 (Apr. 1969), 3400-01-A; UM 69-6774.
"Explores the underlying causes and ensuing effects of the 'brain drain' or the migration of Korean students and faculties to United States graduate schools and employment opportunities on the current staffing needs of Korean higher education, and ascertains...that Korean development is at a stage where a national program for strengthening...indigenous graduate education is imperative."

RELIGIOUS EDUCATION

2205
WELLONS, Ralph Dillingham. The Organizations Set Up for the Control of Mission Union Higher Educational Institutions. Columbia, 1927.
A comprehensive discussion of the organizational characteristics and functioning of various missionary colleges and universities in a number of countries including Japan and Korea. The following Japanese and Korean missionary colleges and universities are classified according to type of organizational control: (1) control by a Board of Governors in the homeland and a Board of Managers in the field (Examples: Kwansei Gakuin, Kobe); (2) control by a Board of Governors located in the field and a co-operating committee in the homeland (Examples: Chōsen Christian College, Seoul; Meiji Gakuin, Kobe; The Women's Christian College, Tokyo); and (3) control by a Board of Governors located in the field (Examples: Union Christian College, Pyongyang).
Rel.Publ.: The Organizations...Institutions. New York, 1927. vi, 138p.

2206
FISHER, James Earnest. Democracy and Mission Education in Korea. Columbia (Teachers College), 1928. xiii, 187p.
Contents: A General Survey of the Situation, and an Outline of the Problem; Modern Conceptions of Democracy in Education: Some Basic Assumptions and Experimental Results; A Criticism of the Aims of Mission Education in Korea from the Viewpoint of Democracy; The Relation of Mission Education to the Japanese Government, and Government Control of Education; The Relation of Mission Education to Political and Economic Problems of the Korean People; The Relation of Mission Education to Indigenous Korean Culture; Problems in Individual and Social Adjustment between Missionary and Native Educational Workers; The Growing Conflict between Intellectual Liberalism and Religious Authoritarianism in Korea.
Rel.Publ.: Democracy...Korea. New York: Teachers College, Columbia University, 1928. xiii, 187p. (Teachers College, Columbia University, Contributions to Education, 306)

2207
KIM, Tuk Yul (Andrew). The Problem of Growing Disunity in the Presbyterian Church in Korea and a Suggested Approach for the Christian Education of Young Koreans. Hartford Seminary Foundation, 1961. 259p. DA 23 (July 1962), 332-33; UM 62-145.
Contents: The General Background of the Problem; Some Factors Operating in the Growing Disunity in the Presbyterian Church in Korea; A Critical Restatement of the Problem and Related Factors with Implications for Christian Education; An Approach to the Christian Education of Young People.

2208
MOON, Stephen Tongwhan. First Century Christ for Twentieth Century Korean Youth. Hartford Seminary Foundation, 1961. 365p. DA 22 (May 1962), 3932-33; UM 62-2028.
Aims at discovering a way whereby Korean youth can learn about Christ in a meaningful fashion.

2209
YOU, In Jong. The Impact of the American Protestant Missions on Korean Education from 1885 to 1932. North Carolina, 1967. 324p. DA 28 (Feb. 1968), 2999-A; UM 68-2254.
A study of four missions: "The Presbyterian Church in the U.S.A., the Presbyterian Church in the U.S., the Methodist Episcopal Church, and the Methodist Episcopal Church, South." Contents: Social and Educational Backgrounds before the coming of the American Protestant Missionary; The Establishment of American Protestant Missions and Their Early Educational Activities, 1885-1896; The Establishment of Mission Schools, 1897-1910; The Development of the Secondary Mission Schools, 1911-1932; The Development of Mission Colleges as Union Institutions, 1911-1932.

Geography

2210
LINKE, Johannes Christian. Veränderung der wirtschaftsgeographischen Beziehungen in Korea unter dem Einfluss der Erschliessung: Die Grundlagen und ursprüngliche Ausgestaltung [Changes in Economic and Geographical Relations within Korea as Influenced by the Opening of That Country: Their Basis and the Arrangement That They Initially Took]. Leipzig, 1932. 134p. Text in German. The dissertation in its published form is available at Leipzig, Universitätsbibliothek, Nr. U 33,1413.

A survey of Korea's climate, mineralogy, flora, and settlement patterns is followed by a discussion of the changes that occurred in the country's economic and geographic development after 1905, of the influence of geography upon these changes, and of the form that they took. Japan's economic impact also is studied, and the author tries to determine how geographic circumstances determined the nature and course of Japanese economic penetration.

Rel.Publ.: Veränderung...Ausgestaltung. Stuttgart: Metzler, 1932. 134p.

2211
McCUNE, Shannon Boyd-Bailey. Climatic Regions of Tyosen (Korea). Clark, 1939. xii, 431p. AB: Clark University. Thesis Abstracts-1939. p.26-31.

Using winter temperatures as a base inasmuch as they control the single-crop and the double-crop agricultural systems within the country, the author divides Korea into ten climatic regions and analyzes and describes the climate and the natural resources (especially the agriculture) of each one of them.

Rel.Publ.: "Climatic Regions of Korea and Their Economy," Geographical Review, 31 (Jan. 1941), 95-99; Climate of Korea. Hamilton, N.Y.: Korean Research Associates, 1941. (Research Monographs on Korea, Series B, nos. 1-4); Climatic Regions. Hamilton, N.Y.: Korean Research Associates, 1945. (Research Monographs on Korea, Series E, nos. 1-11); Korea's Heritage: A Regional and Social Geography. Rutland, Vt.: Tuttle, 1956. xiii, 250p.

2212
SCHUMACHER, Gerhard. Das Klima Südkoreas auf Grund der japanischen Wetterbeobachtungen der Jahre 1914 bis 1933 [The Climate of South Korea: Based on Japanese Meteorological Observations during the Years 1914-1933]. Greifswald, 1939. Text in German. The dissertation in its published form is available at Marburg/Lahn, Universitätsbibliothek, Nr. VI B.

Part 1: The calculation, cartographic interpretation, and textual interpretation of wind, temperature, and precipitation conditions. An overall picture of cyclical changes in weather conditions. Part 2: Genetic considerations of the yearly weather cycle. Particular attention is paid to typical weather and atmospheric conditions and to the extent of their influence. Part 3: South Korea is divided into climatic regions on the basis of conclusions drawn in parts 1 and 2.

Rel.Publ.: Das Klima...1933. Hamburg: Hansischer Gilden-Verlag, 1939. 86p.

2213
WILSON, James Newton. A Handbook on the Political Geography of the Orient. Columbia (Teachers College), 1949. 61p.

An elementary school children's workbook. It includes one chapter containing questions on Korea's location, her physical characteristics and population, and her industry and commerce.

2214
ZAICHIKOV, V. T. Koreia [Korea]. Moscow, Institut geografii Akademii nauk SSSR, 1951. (Doctor of Geographical Sciences degree) 477p. Text in Russian.

Rel.Publ.: Koreia. 2d ed. Moscow: Geografgiz, 1951. 477p.

2215
LAH, Kihough H. Geography of Korea. Columbia (Teachers College), 1957. 204p.

"This project is a text on Korean geography suitable for the South Korean secondary schools....They need a modern geography of Korea with emphasis on human elements and the world peace." The study contains information on Korea's physical features, population, agriculture, forestry, fisheries, power, mining, transportation and communication, and regional geography.

2216
KIM, Su-san. Ocherki fizicheskoi geografii Korei [Outlines of the Physical Geography of Korea]. Moscow, Moskovskii ordena Lenina i Trudovogo Krasnogo Znameni gosudarstvennyi universitet imeni M. V. Lomonosova, 1958. (Candidate of Geographical Sciences) i, 378p. Text in Russian. AB: 23p. summary published in 1958.

History and International Relations

GENERAL

2217
LEE, Hun-gu. A History of Land Systems and Politics in Korea. Wisconsin, 1923(?)

2218
LIU, Chiang. Isolation and Contact as Factors in the Cultural Evolution of China, Korea, and Japan prior to 1842. Iowa, 1923. 383p.

Contents: The Problem, Material, and Method; A General Survey; Art; Religion; Science; Language; Government; Conclusions.

Rel.Publ.: "Isolation...1842," Chinese Social and Political Science Review, 9 (1925), p.189-229, 502-29, 787-817; 10 (1926), p.212-29, 447-75, 728-45, 914-32; 11 (1927), p.142-54, 287-302, 491-509.

2219
CYONG, Ho Do. Probleme der koreanischen Geschichte in kulturellem Zusammenhang [Problems of Korean History in the Cultural Context]. Wien, 1935. Text in German. Diss. ms. not available.

2220
YOON, Hong Sub. Korea in International Far Eastern Relations. American, 1935. 450p.

Contents: Pt.1: Ancient Age (57 B.C.-918 A.D.), Period of the Three Kingdoms: Traditions Pertaining to Political Thought and Diplomatic Intercourse in Earliest Times; The Three Kingdoms and Their Transformation into Two Larger States; Militarism of Koguryuh; Industrialism of Paik-cheh; Unification of Sinla; Creation of the State of Palhai. Pt.2: Medieval Age (918-1392 A.D.): Increased Foreign Intercourse and Consequent Results; Political Organization and Foreign Affairs; Foreign Relations under Aristocratic Regime; Emancipation of Slaves and Its Influence. Pt.3: Modern Age (1392-1910 A.D.): Beginning of New Dynastic Government and Foreign Relations; Economic Intercourse; Foreign Relations under an Autocratic Regime; The Open Door and Evolution.

YOO, Hyung Jin. An Intellectual History of Korea from Ancient Times to the Impact of the West with Special Emphasis upon Education. 1958. See no.2172.

KIM, Sung-Il. A Study of Certain Aspects of Educational Administration and Their Historical Roots in the Republic of Korea. 1961. See no.2183.

EARLY TO 935 A.D.

PAK, Mikhail N. Kim Busik: Samkuk Sagi. 1960. See no.2228.

2221
GARDINER, Kenneth Herbert James. The Rise and Development of the Korean Kingdom of Koguryŏ from the Earliest Times to A.D. 313. London, 1964. x, 527p.

A presentation of Korean history from before the Han conquest in 108 B.C. with close reference to the available sources, indicating possible variations in interpretation and hypotheses concerning social, economic, and cultural activities, seen in terms of Chinese references and counterparts. Includes chronological tables based on dynastic succession in China.

Rel.Publ.: The Early History of Korea: The Historical Development of the Peninsula up to the Introduction of Buddhism in the Fourth Century A. D. Honolulu: University of Hawaii Press, 1969. 87p.; "The Beginnings of Korean History," in Oriental Society of Australia, Journal, 4 (June 1966), 77-92.

2222
KANG, Hi Woong. The Development of the Korean Ruling Class from Late Silla to Early Koryŏ. Washington, Seattle, 1964. 357p. DA 28 (July 1967), 166-A; UM 65-5432.

"Attempts to establish the thesis that there was a basic continuity in the social composition and power configuration of the Korean ruling class between the Kingdom of Silla and the Koryŏ Dynasty before 1170." Contents: The Silla Aristocracy; The Eclipse of the Silla Aristocracy; The Founding of the Koryŏ Dynasty; The Emergence of the Yangban System; The Current of Thought; The Recognition of Koryŏ Government; The Power of the Aristocratic Yangban; The Ruling Stratum of Early Koryŏ.

2223
KIM, Chong Sun. The Emergence of Multi-Centered Despotism in the Silla Kingdom: A Study of the Origin of Factional Struggles in Korea. Washington, Seattle, 1965. 585p. DA 27 (Aug. 1966), 427-28-A; UM 65-15,391.

Contents: Historical Background; On the Question of the Emergence of the Silla Kingdom; On the Question of the Formation of the Classical Economic Structure; On the Question of the 8th Century Census; On the Question of the Kolp'um System; Hwarang under State Ownership of Land; Factionalism in Action; Silla's Contribution to Koryŏ and the Yi Dynasty.

Rel.Publ.: "Sources of Cohesion and Fragmentation in the Silla Kingdom," Journal of Korean Studies (University of Washington), Aug. 1968.

2224
JAMIESON, John Charles. The Samguk sagi and the Unification Wars. California, Berkeley, 1969. 351p. DA 30 (Nov. 1969), 1984-A; UM 69-18,938.
The author's primary concern is to determine how Silla, during the reign of Kim Pŏmmin (660-681), rose "from a position as weakest of three peninsular kingdoms to one of a strength sufficient to absorb both neighbors...and to repulse T'ang China in order to maintain her newly unified territory's integrity." "The bulk of the dissertation consists of an integral translation, with annotations, of Samguk sagi materials which relate to the unification wars, including the Silla Annals for the years 660-681 and biographies of personalities active in those decades."

2225
RIU, Khakku. Iaponskaia istoriografiia po istorii Korei rannego perioda [Japanese Historiography on Early Korean History]. Moscow, Institut vostochnykh iazykov pri Moskovskom gosudarstvennom universitete imeni M. V. Lomonosova, 1969. (Candidate of Historical Sciences degree) 284p. Text in Russian.

SEO, Kyung Bo. A Study of Korean Zen Buddhism Approached through the Chodangjip. 1969. See no.2521.

918-1392 (KORYŎ DYNASTY)

2226
BREHER, P. Theodor. Das Toung tien des Tou über Ko Kou rye: Materialien zur Geschichte Koreas [The Toung tien of Tou on Ko Kou rye: Materials on Korean History]. Berlin, 1921. 72p. Text in German. AB: Jahrbuch der Dissertationen der Philosophischen Fakultät Berlin. 1920/1921. p.63-65. Diss. ms. available at Marburg/Lahn, Staatsbibliothek Preussischer Kulturbesitz, Nr. MS 23/405.
The text and an annotated translation of the Toung tien.

2227
MESKILL, John Thomas. A Record of Drifting across the Sea: P'yohae-rok. Columbia, 1958. 380p. DA 19 (Jan. 1959), 1724-25; UM 58-3237.
An annotated translation of P'yohae-rok, by Ch'oe Pu (1454-1504), a Korean Confucian official.
Rel.Publ.: Ch'oe Pu's Diary: A Record of Drifting across the Sea. Tucson: University of Arizona Press, 1964. 177p. (Association for Asian Studies: Monographs and Papers, 17)

2228
PAK, Mikhail Nikolaevich. Kim Busik: Samkuk Sagi [Samguk Sagi by Kim Pu-sik]. Moscow, Institut vostokovedeniia Akademiia nauk SSSR, 1960. (Doctor of Historical Sciences degree) vi, 384p. + vii, 202p. (2v.) Text in Russian.
Consists of an introduction, edited text, and annotated translation of this Koryŏ historical compilation.
Rel.Publ.: Kim...Sagi. Moscow: Izd. vostochnoi literatury, 1959. vii, 384p.; vii, 202p. (2v.); "O Kharaktere sotsial'no-ekonomicheskikh otnoshenii v gosudarstve Silla (III-VI vv.)," Voprosy istorii, 7 (1956), 49-85.

2229
VANIN, Iu V. Feodal'naia Koreia v XIII-XIV vv. [Feudal Korea during the Thirteenth and Fourteenth Centuries]. Moscow, Institut narodov Azii Akademii nauk SSSR, 1962. (Candidate of Historical Sciences degree) 199p. Text in Russian.
Rel.Publ.: Feodal'naia...XIX vv. Moscow: Izd. vostochnoi literatury, 1962. 198p. (Akademiia nauk SSSR, Institut narodov Azii); "Istochniki po istorii pozdnego feodalizma v Koree," in Institut narodov Azii, Akademiia nauk SSSR, Kratkie soobshcheniia, 85 (1964), 30-42.

2230
HENTHORN, William Ellsworth. Korea: The Mongol Invasions. Leiden Rijksuniversiteit, 1963.
Studies the thirteenth century Mongol invasions of Koryŏ as a development in Korean history. Contents: Pt.1: The Mongol Invasion: The Initial Phase; The Invasions of Sartaq; The Invasions of Tanqut-bātur and Prince Yekü; The Invasions of J̌alairtai-gorči; Submission and Alliance; The Rebellion of the Three Patrols, Sam pyŏlch'o. Pt.2: Mongol Demands upon Koryŏ: The Instructions for Surrendering States; Mongol Military-Administration in Koryŏ; Tribute, Levies, and Gifts; Mongol Military Colonies in Koryŏ; Ship Construction; Post-Stations; Military Support; Hostages.
Rel.Publ.: Korea...Invasions. Leiden, E.J. Brill, 1963. xii, 252p.; "Monggo Kojonsol e tae hae so," Pusan Hakpo, 1958; "Some Notes on Koryŏ Military Units," Transactions of the Korea Branch of the Royal Asiatic Society, 35 (1959), 67-75.

KANG, Hi Woong. The Development of the Korean Ruling Class from Late Silla to Early Koryŏ. 1964. See no.2222

2231
SEROV, V. M. Krest'ianskie vosstaniia v Koree v XII veke [Peasant Uprisings in Korea in the Twelfth Century]. Leningrad, Leningradskii ordena Lenina gosudarstvennyi universitet imeni A. A. Zhdanova, Vostochnyi fakultet, 1964. (Candidate of Historical Sciences degree) 180p. Text in Russian.

2232
HAZARD, Benjamin Harrison, Jr. Japanese Marauding in Medieval Korea: The Wakō Impact on Late Koryŏ. California, Berkeley, 1967. 379p. DA 28 (Jan. 1968), 2617-18-A; UM 68-76.
Contents: Relations between Japan and Koryŏ before the first Wakō Raids; A Century of Sporadic Raiding; Conditions in Korea and Japan Immediately before 1350; Wakō Raids in the Reigns of Ch'ungjŏng Wang, Kongmin Wang, Sin U, Sin Ch'ang, and Kong'yang Wang; The Wakō and Their Impact on Korea.
Rel.Publ.: "The Formative Years of the Wakō, 1223-63," MN, 22 (1967), 260-77.

2233
RECK, Karl-Heinz. Die Mongolen in Korea: Kommentierte Übersetzung des Korea-Kapitels 208 im Yuanshi [The Mongols in Korea: An Annotated Translation of the Chapters in the Yuanshi Dealing with Korea]. Berlin, Humboldt, 1968. 288p. (2v.) Text in German. Diss. ms. available at Berlin, Universitätsbibliothek, Nr. 68 HB 975 I./II.
A reinterpretation of the Mongol domination of Korea during the thirteenth century that is based on a careful examination and textual comparison of Chinese and Korean sources for this period. The author focuses primarily on the forms and content of Mongol policy towards Koryŏ and on the Korean reaction to Yuan foreign policy as it affected them.

1392-1860

2234
McCUNE, George McAfee. Korean Relations with China and Japan, 1800-1864. California, Berkeley, 1941. xiii, 292p.

Pt.1 is a systematic analysis of the ceremonial diplomatic relations between Korea and China and of the trade between the two countries. Pt.2 studies Korean-Japanese relations in a similar fashion and includes information on the contacts between the Korean court and the Tokugawa shogun on the one hand and the court and the daimyo of Tsushima on the other.

Rel.Publ.: "The Exchange of Envoys between Korea and Japan during the Tokugawa Period," FEQ, 5 (May 1946), 308-25; "The Japanese Trading Post at Pusan," Korean Review, 1 (June 1948), 11-15.

2235
KHVAN, Don-Min (I. I.). Li Sun-Sin [Yi Sun-sin (1545-1598)]. Moscow, Moskovskii institut vostokovedeniia, 1948. (Candidate of Historical Sciences degree) ii, 266p. Text in Russian.

2236
WAGNER, Edward Willett. The Literati Purges: Case Studies in the Factionalism of the Early Yi Dynasty. Harvard, 1959. xvi, 474p. (2v.).

Contents: The Setting; The Purge of 1498; The Purge of 1504; The Purge of 1519; The Summing Up.

Rel.Publ.: "The Recommendation Examination of 1519: Its Place in Early Yi Dynasty History," Chōsen gakuhō, 15 (1960), 1-80.

2237
CHOI, Andreas. L'Érection du premier vicariat apostolique et les origines du catholicisme en Corée 1592-1837 [The Establishment of the First Apostolic Vicariate and the Origins of Catholicism in Korea, 1592-1837]. Bonn, 1961. Text in French. The dissertation in its published form is available at Bochum, Universitätsbibliothek, Nr. GB 9801.

Studies the first reports of the infiltration of Catholics into Korea (1592-1783), secular Christianity in Korea (1784-1790), the Korean persecution of Christians (1791-1802), Catholic efforts to set up a new church organization within the country (1802-1831), and the beginnings of the apostolic vicariate in Korea (1831-1837).

Rel.Publ.: L'Érection...1837. Bonn, 1961. xii, 136p. (Neue Zeitschrift für Missionswissenschaft, suppl. 11); "L'Église catholique au service de la langue coréenne au cours du XIXe siècle," Neue Zeitschrift für Missionswissenschaft, 17 (1961), 175-90.

2238
SOHN, Pow-key. Social History of the Early Yi Dynasty 1392-1592: With Emphasis on the Functional Aspects of Governmental Structure. California, Berkeley, 1963. 523p. DA 24 (June 1964), 5368; UM 64-5307.

Concludes that (1) "the governmental structure of the early Yi dynasty was definitely a variant of the Chinese monarchical system" and that (2) "in Korea it was the yangban who dominated the monarchy and not the reverse as was true in China."

1860-1945: GENERAL

2239
HSU, Shu-hsi. China and Her Political Entity: A Study of China's Foreign Relations with Reference to Korea, Manchuria, and Mongolia. Columbia, 1925. xxiv, 438p.

See especially Ch.1, Pt.4, "China and the Kingdoms: Korea" (p.25-31), and Ch.3, "The Korean Problem" (p.102-49).

Rel.Publ.: China...Mongolia. New York: Oxford University Press, 1926. xxiv, 438p.

2240
BASS, Harold James. The Policy of the American State Department toward Missionaries in the Far East. Washington State, 1937. 462p.

See Ch.13, "The Attitude of the American State Department toward Missionary Work in Korea, 1882-1937" (p.366-407).

HU, Hung-lick. Le Problème coréen. 1951. See no.2335.

2241
CHUNG, Han Pom. The Republic of Korea in Power Politics. American, 1952. 395p.

Contents: Pt.1: Tragedy of Korea under Despotism and Power Politics: Korea...and the Signing of the First Treaties with the Great Powers; Internal Politics and International Intrigues in Korea, 1876-1905. Pt.2: Tragedy of Korea under Japan, 1910-1945: Japan's Policy in Korea after Annexation; Heroes of Korean Independence Movements; Korea's International Relations between the Imposition of the Protectorate and Liberation. Pt.3: Korea since Its Liberation August 15, 1945: Liberation and Disillusionment; The Vicissitudes of the Young Republic of Korea; The Start of Aggression by North Korea; Korea's Ever Perilous International Position; Korea's Immediate Relations with America, China, and Japan.

BROWN, George T. A History of the Korea Mission, Presbyterian Church, U.S., from 1892 to 1962. 1963. See no.2534.

2242
PALMER, Spencer John. Protestant Christianity in China and Korea: The Problem of Identification with Tradition. California, Berkeley, 1964. 199p. DA 25 (Jan. 1965), 4111-12; UM 64-13,073.

Argues that "in Korea, Christianity could be identified with national feelings involving a continuity with tradition" and that Christianity "was not a target of nationalism partly because Japan, a non-Christian country, was the target."

Rel.Publ.: Korea and Christianity: The Problem of Identification with Tradition. Seoul: Hollym, 1967.

2243
NAMGUNG, Yun. Image de la Corée en France au XIXe siècle [The Image of Korea in France during the Nineteenth Century]. Paris, 1967. 369p. Text in French.

2244
KWAK, Tae-Hwan. United States-Korean Relations: A Core Interest Analysis prior to U.S. Intervention in the Korean War. Claremont, 1969. 306p. DA 30 (June 1970); UM 70-9824.

Contents: A Conceptual Framework: The Concept of Core Interests as an Analytical Tool in the Study of United States-Korean Relations; The Nature of American-Korean Relations (1882-1945); United States-Soviet Military Occupation of Korea; United States Policy of Military Disengagement from Korea; United States Military

Intervention in Korea.

1860-1910

See also History and International Relations--
1860-1895 (pages 265-68),
1895-1910 (pages 268-69),
and 1905-1910 (pages 269-70).

PAIK, Lark-June George. The History of Protestant Missions in Korea, 1832-1910. 1927. See no.2522.

2245
NELSON, Melvin Frederick. The International Status of Korea, 1876-1910. Duke, 1940. 434p.

"Traces the growth of Korea from barbarism to brotherhood in the Confucian system and attempts a reconstruction of that system as it existed and confronted the eastward expansion of the Western powers...; studies the conflict of the two systems in Korea and Korea's attainment of full membership in the Western state system; and considers Korea's loss of statehood."

Rel.Publ.: Korea and the Old Orders in Eastern Asia. Baton Rouge: Louisiana State University Press, 1945. xvi, 326p.

2246
PAK, Mikhail Nikolaevich. Ocherki iz politicheskoi istorii Korei vo vtoroi polovine XIX v. [Essays on the Political History of Korea during the Second Half of the Nineteenth Century]. Moscow, Moskovskii gosudarstvennyi universitet imeni M. V. Lomonosova, 1946. (Candidate of Historical Sciences degree) xxxix, 289p. Text in Russian.

2247
BRIDGHAM, Philip Low. American Policy toward Korean Independence, 1866-1910. Fletcher, 1952. iv, 179p. AB: Fletcher School of Law and Diplomacy. Thesis Abstract, 1951. no.2.

"The thesis is...a synthesis based largely on the contributions of earlier scholars in the field." It analyzes the origin, development, and denouement of American governmental policy toward Korean independence. Contents: The United States Opens Korea to the West; Early American Policy in Korea; The United States, Korea, and the Sino-Japanese War; Retreat to Neutrality: American Policy toward Korea, 1896-1904; From Neutrality to Complicity: America's Role in Promoting a Japanese Protectorate over Korea, 1904-1905; A Postscript: America's Indifference toward Japanese Annexation of Korea, 1906-1910.

2248
WEEMS, Clarence Norwood, Jr. The Korean Reform and Independence Movement (1881-1898). Columbia, 1954. 557p. DA 14 (Oct. 1954), 1704-05; UM 8859.

Analyzes the failure of the nineteenth century Korean reform movement in terms of the failure of the reformist Tonghak Society and the independence movement to combine forces.

2249
DONG, Chon. Japanese Annexation of Korea: A Study of Korean-Japanese Relations to 1910. Colorado, 1955. 391p. DA 17 (Sept. 1957), 1992; UM 16,932.

Pt.1: From the earliest contacts through the era of Hideyoshi's invasion. Pt.2: The Sino-Russo-Japanese contest over Korea (1876-1905). Pt.3: The final stage of annexation, based almost entirely on the Nikkan kappo Hi-shi.

Rel.Publ.: "Korea and the Russo-Japanese War," Koreana Quarterly, 1 (Winter 1959), 22-72; "The United States Attitude towards the Sino-Russian-Japanese Policies in Korea, 1891-1898," in Hanguk Yŏngu Tosŏgwan, Seoul, Bulletin of the Korean Research Center: Journal of the Social Sciences and Humanities, 23 (Dec. 1965), 1-28.

2250
KIM, Chang Hoon. Relations internationales de la Corée de la seconde moitié du XIXe siècle à la perte de son indépendance (1910) [The International Relations of Korea from the Second Half of the Nineteenth Century to the Loss of Her Independence (1910)]. Paris, 1959. 224, xlvi p. Text in French.

2251
KIM, Han-Kyo. The Demise of the Kingdom of Korea: 1882-1910. Chicago, 1962. 440p.

Contents: The Climax in the "Opening" of Korea (The Chemulpo Treaty of 1882 between Korea and the United States, Treaties with Other Western Nations); Political Disturbances after the "Opening" (The Soldiers' Mutiny of 1882, The Progressives and the Coup of 1884, The 1885 Treaty Settlement); The Decade of Chinese Dominance, 1885-1894; Rebellion, War, and Reforms, 1894-1895; Russo-Japanese Rivalry in Korea, 1895-1904; Japanese Domination of Korea, 1904-1910.

Rel.Publ.: Korea and the Politics of Imperialism, 1876-1910 [by] C. I. Eugene Kim and Han-Kyo Kim. Berkeley: University of California Press, 1967. x, 260p. (Publications of the Center for Japanese and Korean Studies)

2252
KIM, Yoon Young. National Images of Korea, 1850-1910: A Study on the National Survival of a Small Power. Chicago, 1963. 493p.

2253
RO, Kwang Hai. Power Politics in Korea and Its Impact on Korean Foreign and Domestic Affairs, 1882-1907. Oklahoma, 1966. 202p. DA 27 (Dec. 1966), 1893-A; UM 66-10,191.

"Examines the policies and methods used by Korea to retain her independence during the struggle between China and Japan"--and later, Russia and Japan--for control and possession of the country.

2254
SUH, Byung Han. Die internationalen Beziehungen Koreas von der Mitte des 19. Jahrhunderts bis zum Ende der Unabhängigkeit [The International Relations of Korea from the Mid-1800's to 1910]. Wien, 1967. v, 340p. Text in German. Diss. ms. available at the Österreichische Nationalbibliothek, Nr. 1040.461-C.

An overall presentation of the Korean conduct of foreign affairs from the mid-1800's to 1910, with particular attention being paid to the views then current about the principles of modern international law.

1860-1895

See also History and International Relations--
1860-1910 (page 265).

2255
KIM, Ryea Sik. The Early Relations between Korea and the United States. American, 1924. 226p.

Contents: Beginning of Intercourse; An Armed Conflict; Commodore Shufeldt's Policy; Korean Troubles and American Policy; Coup d'Etat of 1884; The Russian-British Menace and the American Attitude; Foulk and the Chinese Intrigues; International Status of Korea.

2256
TYLER, Alice Felt. The Foreign Policy of James G. Blaine. Minnesota, 1927. Diss. ms. not available.
Includes information on the Kanghwa Treaty (1876) and the diplomacy of Li Hung-chang to counteract Japanese influence in Korea.
Rel.Publ.: The Foreign...Blaine. Minneapolis: University of Minnesota Press, 1928. 411p.

2257
NOBLE, Harold Joyce. Korea and Her Relations with the United States before 1895. California, Berkeley, 1932. 606p. (2v.).
Focuses on the negotiation of the Korean-American treaty of 1882, on the activities of American diplomatic representatives in Seoul, and on relations in general between the two countries before the outbreak of the Sino-Japanese War.
Rel.Publ.: "The Korean Mission to the United States in 1883; The First Embassy Sent by Korea to an Occidental Country," Transactions of the Korea Branch of the Royal Asiatic Society, 18 (1929), 1-21; "The Former Foreign Settlements in Korea," American Journal of International Law, 23 (Oct. 1929), 776-82; "The United States and Sino-Korean Relations, 1885-1887," PHR, 2 (Sept. 1933), 292-304; "Political Activities of American Missionaries in Korea before 1905," Nankai Social and Economic Quarterly, 9 (1936).

2258
DJANG, Chu. Chinese Suzerainty: A Study of Diplomatic Relations between China and Her Vassal States (1870-1895). Johns Hopkins, 1935. iv, 203p.

2259
JONES, Francis Clifford. Foreign Diplomacy in Korea, 1866-1894. Harvard, 1935. ii, 567p. AB: Harvard University. Summaries of Theses...1935. p.163-66.
Contents: William H. Seward and the French Expedition of 1866; George F. Seward and the American Expedition, 1868-1871; The Korean Policy of Japan, 1871-1876; The British Government and a Korean Treaty; The Shufeldt Mission and Japanese "Good Offices"; Great Britain and the Korean Question, 1880-1881; The Shufeldt Treaty; The Unratified British and German Treaties; The Assertion of Chinese Suzerainty over Korea; The Treaties of 1883; The Crisis of 1884-1885; The British Occupation of Port Hamilton; American Policy in Korea, 1885-1894; The Origins of the Sino-Japanese War.

2260
LUDWIG, Albert Philip. Li Hung-Chang and Chinese Foreign Policy, 1870-1885. California, Berkeley, 1936. 443p.
Includes a study of the Sino-Japanese controversy over Korea.

2261
KIM, M. P. "Otkrytie" Korei i vosstanie tonkhakov [The "Opening" of Korea and the Uprising of the Tonghaks]. Moscow, Moskovskii gosudarstvennyi universitet imeni M. V. Lomonosova, 1939. (Candidate of Historical Sciences degree) 96p. Text in Russian.

2262
QUIMBY, Paul Elmore. A Study of the Foreign Policies of Li Hung-chang. Southern California, 1940. 310p. AB: University of Southern California. Abstracts of Dissertations for...1940. p.78-81.
Includes a discussion of Sino-Japanese activities in Korea during the 1880's and the 1890's.

2263
STAROSELTSEV, N. D. Kolonial'naia politika Iaponii v Koree ot "otkrytiia" ee do iapono-kitaiskoi voiny (1876-1894 gg.) [Japan's Colonial Policy in Korea from the "Opening" of the Country to the Sino-Japanese War, 1876-1894]. Moscow, Moskovskii gosudarstvennyi universitet imeni M. V. Lomonosova, 1941. (Candidate of Historical Sciences) xiii, 235p. Text in Russian.

2264
CHEN, Tieh-ming. The Sino-Japanese War, 1894-1895: Its Origin, Development, and Diplomatic Background. California, Berkeley, 1944. 291p.
Includes a discussion of the ways in which the Japanese worked to undermine and to destroy Chinese suzerainty in Korea, 1868-1895. These included Japanese support of an independent Korean government and Japanese encouragement of internal reforms within Korea. See especially Ch.3, "Japan in Korean Politics" (p.57-88), Ch.4, "Chinese Ascendency in Korea, 1885-1894" (p.89-116), and Ch.5, "Revival of Japan's Intense Intervention in Korea" (p.117-48).

2265
SUNOO, Hag-won. A Study of the Korean Treaties: 1876 and 1882. The Opening of Korea. Universita Karlova, 1949/50. 181, xxii p. Diss. ms. available at the University archives, no. AUK 2583.
An account of Korea's isolationist policy under the Taewŏngun (1864-1874), of the conclusion of treaties with Japan and with the United States, and of subsequent Korean reactions (1883-1885) to these developments.
Rel.Publ.: "A Study of the United States-Korean Treaty of 1882," Korean Review, 2 (Sept. 1949), 25-44.

2266
DOTSON, Lillian Ota. The Sino-Japanese War of 1894-1895: A Study in Asian Power Politics. Yale, 1951. 260p. DA 27 (June 1967), 4190-A; UM 67-6898.
Korea's continual role as a pawn in East Asian power politics is illustrated in this study. There is very little information, however, on Korean domestic politics.

2267
TIAGAI, Galina Davidovna. Koreia v 1893-1896 gg.: Krest'ianskoe vosstanie i bor'ba koreiskogo naroda protiv iaponskikh militaristov i ikh amerikanskikh posobnikov [Korea in 1893-1896: Peasant Uprisings and the Struggle of the Korean People against the Japanese Militarists and Their American Accomplices]. Moscow, Institut vostokovedeniia Akademii nauk SSSR, 1951. (Candidate of Historical Sciences degree) viii, 334p. Text in Russian.
Rel.Publ.: Krest'iankie vosstaniia v Koree 1893-1895 gg. Moscow: Izd. Akademii nauk SSSR, 1953. 208p.; Krest'ianskoe vosstanie 1893-1894 godov v Koree," in Akademiia nauk SSSR. Instituta Vostokovedeniia, Uchenye zapiski, 3 (1951), 139-90.

2268
BARTZ, Carl Frederick, Jr. The Korean Seclusion Policy, 1860-1876. California, Berkeley, 1953. 246p.
A descriptive history of the government's seclusion policy directed against the United States, Japan, and certain Western European powers.

2269
REORDAN, Robert Edwin. The Role of George Clayton Foulk in United States-Korean Relations, 1884-1887. Fordham, 1955. 306p. AB: 8p. summary appended to diss. ms.
Contents: The Opening of the Hermit Kingdom; Korea Enters World Affairs; The Progressives Seize Power; Korea Becomes an International Problem; China Tightens Her Control; American Influence in Korea Declines; The Dismissal of Foulk; Retreat from Korea; The Expediency of Secretary Bayard.

2270
SUVOROV, A. S. Ekspansiia SShA v Koree vo vtoroi polovine XIX v. (1866-1882 gg.) [American Expansion in Korea during the Second Half of the Nineteenth Century (1866-1882)]. Moscow, Moskovskii gosudarstvennyi institut mezhdunarodnykh otnoshenii MID SSSR, 1955. (Candidate of Historical Sciences degree) xix, 327p. Text in Russian.

2271
CHOE, Ching-young. A Decade of the Taewŏngun: Reform, Seclusion, and Disaster. Harvard, 1960. vii, 592p. (2v.).
Contents: The Social and Economic Background; The Trend of Reformist Thoughts in Yi Korea; Social Trends on the Eve of the Taewŏngun's Reforms; The Taewŏngun and His Internal Policy; The Taewŏngun's Foreign Policy: (a) The French Invasion of 1866, (b) The American Expedition of 1871, (c) Korean-Japanese Relations, 1864-1873; The Fall of the Taewŏngun's Regime.

2272
NAHM, Andrew Changwoo. Kim Ok-Kyun and the Korean Progressive Movement, 1882-1884. Stanford, 1961. 406p. DA 22 (Nov. 1961), 1603-04; UM 61-4149.
"Focuses upon the goals of the Progressive Party, the forces which nurtured the growth of progressive ideas and the nationalist movement in Korea, and China's policy for reasserting its overlordship in Korea." Also studies the support extended by the United States and Japan to the progressives.
Rel.Publ.: "Korea's Response to International Rivalries: Korean Domestic Policies, 1876-1884," in Michigan Academy of Science, Arts, and Letters, Papers, 50 (1964), 445-65; "Reaction and Response to the Opening of Korea, 1876-1884," in Studies on Asia 1965, ed. by Robert K. Sakai (Lincoln: University of Nebraska Press, 1965), 61-80.

2273
CHIEN, Frederick Foo. The Opening of Korea: A Study of Chinese Diplomacy, 1876-1885. Yale, 1962. 415p.
Contents: The Treaty of Kanghwa; The Initial Modifications of China's Korea Policy; The Opening of Korea: The United States-Korean Treaty of May 1882; The Opening of Korea: Treaties with Other Powers; The Active Policy of China in Korea; The Emeute of 1884; The Inception of International Competition in Korea: To the End of 1884.
Rel.Publ.: The Opening...1885. Hamden, Conn.: Shoe String Press, 1967. xiii, 364p.

2274
CHOI, Soo Book. Political Dynamics in Hermit Korea: The Rise of Royal Power in the Decade of Taewŏnkun, 1864-1873. Maryland, 1963. 239p. DA 24 (June 1964), 5511-12; UM 64-6337.
Contents: The Origins of Confucian Foundation of Power in Yi Choson: 1392-1910 (Fundamentals of the Confucian Symbols for Power, Yi Choson as the Instrument for Confucianism, Structure and Method of the Confucian Power); Eclipse of the Old Order and the Prologue to the Rise of the Royal Power (Unsettling Factors for the Old Equilibrium, Prologue to the Rise of a Strong Man); The Rising Royal Power in Action (Formation of the Inner Circle, Abolition of the Confucian Shrines, Restoration of the Kyong-pok Palace); The Royal Power in Action: The Hermit Kingdom Vindicated (The Roman Catholic Mission: Toleration and Persecution, The French Expedition, 1866, The American Expedition, 1871).

2275
CHUNG, Chai Sik. Protestantism and the Formation of Modern Korea 1884-1894. Boston, 1964. 322p. DA 26 (July 1965), 328; UM 64-11,603.
Analyzes the impact and role of Protestantism.

2276
KIM, Yung Chung. Great Britain and Korea, 1883-1887. Indiana, 1965. 247p. DA 26 (Nov. 1965), 2712; UM 65-10,856.
"Examines British policy toward Korea from the beginning of treaty relations to the withdrawal of the British squadron from Port Hamilton." Contents: Great Britain and the Opening of Korea: The Background; Treaty Relations; Sino-Japanese Intervention; Anglo-Russian Crisis, 1885; Port Hamilton; Great Britain and Chinese Supremacy.

2277
LEE, Yur Bok. Diplomatic Relations between Korea and the United States, 1882-1887: A Study of Foreign Services of Minister Foote and Chargé Foulk in Korea. Georgia, 1965. 303p. DA 27 (Mar. 1967), 2991-A; UM 66-2484.
Indicates that whereas "Foote's major concern for the development and modernization of Korea was his strong desire to bring American business interests into the country, Foulk's main interest...was his concern for the welfare and interest of Korea."
Rel.Publ.: Diplomatic Relations between the United States and Korea, 1866-1887. New York: Humanities, 1969.

2278
MacDONALD, Donald Ross Hazelton. Russian Interest in Korea, to 1895: The Pattern of Russia's Emerging Interest in the Peninsula from the Late Seventeenth Century to the Sino-Japanese War. Harvard, 1966. [Dissertation itself completed in 1957.] xi, 535p.
Contents: Russia and Korea in the Mongol Period; Early Russian Interest in Korea; The Expansion of Russia to the Korean Border, 1850-1860; Russia and Korea: A Korean View, 1860-1884; The Development of Russian Scholarship on Korea (Early Notices on Korea by Members of the Russian Ecclesiastical and Diplomatic Missions in Peking, The Development of Russian Scholarship on the Korean Language, Russian Accounts of Korea in the Nineteenth Century, The Acquisition of Korean Collections and the Development of Korean Studies in Imperial Russia); Russian Travelers in Korea.

2279
DEUCHLER, Martina. The Opening of Korea, 1875-1884. Harvard, 1967. v, 322p.
Contents: Korea on the Eve of the Opening; The Break with the Past: The Conclusion of the Korean-Japanese Treaty (Kuroda Kiyotaka's Mission to Korea, Kim Ki-su's Mission to Japan); Diplomacy and Trade: The Opening of the Korean Ports; Korea on the Threshold of a New Age: Reform and Reaction (Japan's Argumentation for Korea's Opening to the West, China and Korea in a New Context, The Launching of Korea's Self-Strengthening Program); Korea between East and West; Korea after the Opening: Consolidation of Positions (China's Changed Position in Korea, Japan and Korea after 1882, Strengthening of the West's Footholds in Korea, Korea's Readjustment after 1882, The Ports and the Establishment of Foreign Settlements).

2280
PALAIS, James Bernard. Korea on the Eve of the Kanghwa Treaty, 1873-1876. Harvard, 1968. v, 955p. (2v.).
A study of the period immediately preceding the conclusion of the Kanghwa Treaty between Japan and Korea which "attempts to reveal some of the attitudes with which those Koreans who played the leading roles in their own society greeted the new forces of history." Contents: The Taewŏngun's Regime; Overthrow of the Taewŏngun; Abolition of Ch'ing Cash and Fiscal Difficulties; The Mandongmyo and the "Household Cloth" Tax; Grain-Loan Policy; Political Developments; The Response to the West and the Catholic Question; The Taewŏngun's Foreign Policy; Change in Japan Policy; Formal Clothes and the Main Gate, May-September 1875; From the Unyō Incident to Receipt of Chinese Communication; Kanghwa Treaty.

2281
COOK, Harold Francis. Kim Ok-Kyun and the Background of the 1884 Émeute. Harvard, 1969. vi, 708p. (2v.).
Kim Ok-Kyun (1851-1894), the reform-minded Korean leader in the attempted coup d'état of 1884. Contents: The Man and His Antecedents; The Emergence of the Min; Important Contemporary Developments; Genesis of a Reformer; Japan: The First Visit; Japan: The Second Visit; China Reasserts Control; Japan: The Third Visit; The Crescendo of Min Hegemony; The Decision; The Plot; Epilogue.

1895-1910

See also History and International Relations-- 1860-1910 (page 265).

2282
DENNETT, Tyler. Roosevelt and the Russo-Japanese War: A Critical Study of American Policy in Eastern Asia in 1902-1905, Based Primarily upon the Private Papers of Theodore Roosevelt. Johns Hopkins, 1924. 445p.
An investigation of American policies towards Japan, Korea, and China. See especially Ch.5 of the book (p.96-117) entitled "Korea, Japan, and the United States."
Rel.Publ.: Roosevelt...Roosevelt. Garden City, N.Y.: Doubleday, Page, 1925. xi, 357p.; "President Roosevelt's Secret Pact with Japan," Current History, 21 (Oct. 1924), 15-21.

2283
STEINMANN, Friedrich von. Russlands Politik im Fernen Osten und der Staatssekretär Bezobrazov: Ein Beitrag zur Vorgeschichte des russisch-japanischen Krieges [Russia's Policy in East Asia and Secretary of State Bezobrazov: A Contribution to the Antecedents of the Russo-Japanese War]. Berlin, 1931. Text in German. The dissertation in its published form is available at Marburg/Lahn, Universitätsbibliothek, Nr. VII C.
Chapter 2 includes a study of the concessions obtained in Korea.
Rel.Publ.: Russlands...Krieges. Leipzig: Werkgemeinschaft, 1931. 61, iii p.

2284
TAKEUCHI, Sterling Tatsuji. The Control of Foreign Relations in Japan. Chicago, 1931.
One chapter focuses on the Japanese annexation of Korea.
Rel.Publ.: War and Diplomacy in the Japanese Empire. Chicago: University of Chicago Press, 1935. xix, 505p.

2285
CRIST, David Scott. Russia's Manchurian Policy, 1895-1905. Michigan, 1941. vii, 261p.
A narrative account of Russian expansion in Manchuria with considerable information on Russia's Korean policy and its relationship to her Manchurian expansion, and on Russian activity in Korea.

2286
FORD, Harold Perry. Russian Far Eastern Diplomacy, Count Witte, and the Penetration of China, 1895-1904. Chicago, 1950. 428p. AB: United States Department of State, External Research Staff. Abstracts of Completed Doctoral Dissertations for the Academic Year 1950/1951. p.275-80.
Includes a study of the events leading up to the Russo-Japanese War.

2287
MALOZEMOFF, Andrew Alexander. Russian Far Eastern Policy, 1881-1904: With Special Emphasis on the Causes of the Russo-Japanese War. California, Berkeley, 1952. 659p. (2v.).
Includes a discussion of the growth of Russian influence in Korea, 1895-1897.
Rel.Publ.: Russian...War. Berkeley: University of California Press, 1958. 358p.

2288
KIM, Den Do. O zarozhdenii kapitalisticheskikh otnoshenii v Koree (konets XIX-nachalo XX vv.) [The Origins of Capitalist Relations in Korea: The End of the Nineteenth Century and the Beginning of the Twentieth Century]. Moscow, Moskovskii ordena Lenina gosudarstvennyi universitet imeni M. V. Lomonosova, Istoricheskii fakultet, Kafedra Dal'nego Vostoka, 1953 (Candidate of Historical Sciences degree) xxxiv, 317p. Text in Russian. AB: 14p. summary published in 1953.

2289
ARNOLD, Dean Alexander. American Economic Enterprises in Korea, 1895-1939. Chicago, 1954. 515p.
Contents: Korea in 1895; American Concession Hunting, 1895-1897; International Rivalries and American Financial Promotion, 1897-1898; The Greater Concession, 1899-1900; From McKinley's Re-Election to the Russo-Japanese War, November 1900-February 1904; The Russo-Japanese War and American Enterprises in Korea, 1904-1905; The Kapsan Concession, 1905-1915; The Suan Concession, 1905-1924; The Oriental Consolidated Mining Company, 1905-1939.

2290
GRENVILLE, John Ashley Soames. British Foreign Policy, 1899-1902. London, 1954. x, 474p.
Includes a discussion of Anglo-Korean and of Anglo-Japanese relations in 1899.
Rel.Publ.: Lord Salisbury and Foreign Policy: The Close of the Nineteenth Century. London: Athlone Press, 1964. 451p. (University of London Historical Studies, 14)

2291
VERCHAU, Ekkhard. Europa und der Ferne Orient 1894 bis 1898: Studien über Erscheinung und Wesen des Imperialismus in dieser Zeit [Europe and East Asia, 1894-1898: Studies of the Appearance and the Reality of Imperialism during This Period]. Tübingen, 1957. v, 268p. Text in German. Diss. ms. available at Tübingen, Universitätsbibliothek, Nr. UM 7729.
Russian, French, and German penetration into China and Korea; Britain's loss of her dominant position in China; and the struggle between Russia and Japan over conflicting interests in Korea.

2292
LUNG, Chang. La Chine à l'aube du 20e siècle: Les relations diplomatiques de la Chine avec les puissances depuis la guerre sino-japonaise jusqu'à la guerre russo-japonaise [China at the Dawn of the Twentieth Century: China's Diplomatic Relations with the Powers between the Sino-Japanese and Russo-Japanese Wars]. Fribourg, 1962. Text in French.
Includes a very lengthy discussion of the Korean question and of the Sino-Japanese war.
Rel.Publ.: La China...japonaise. Paris: Nouvelles éditions latines, 1962. 503p.

2293
CHAY, Jongsuk. The United States and the Closing Door in Korea: American-Korean Relations, 1894-1905. Michigan, 1965. 192p. DA 27 (Aug. 1966), 435-A; UM 66-6581.
"The objective of this study is to examine America's policy toward Korea during the period 1894-1905 and to evaluate it on the bases of her interests in Korea and the situation in the Far East." Contents: The Bases of American Policy towards Korea; Offer of Good Offices for Korea; Policy of Strict Neutrality; Theodore Roosevelt and Korea: (1) The Policy of Indifference, (2) The Policy of Reality.
Rel.Publ.: "The Taft-Katsura Memorandum Reconsidered," PHR, 37 (Aug. 1968), 321-26.

2294
SYNN, Seung Kwon. The Russo-Japanese Struggle for Control of Korea, 1894-1904. Harvard, 1967. iv, 479p.
"The purpose...is to present a comprehensive analysis of the policies of Russia and Japan toward Korea from 1894 to 1904." Contents: Sino-Japanese Rivalry over Korea, 1873-1893; The Outbreak of the Sino-Japanese War; Japan's Attempt to Seize Korea, 1894-1895; Russian Policy toward Korea, 1894-1895; The Murder of Queen Min; Russo-Japanese Rivalry over Korea, 1896-1898; The Rise of Japanese Influence, 1898-1900; On the Eve of the Russo-Japanese War.

The Japanese Protectorate, 1905-1910

See also History and International Relations--1860-1910 (page 265) and 1895-1910 (pages 268-69).

2295
PRICE, Ernest Batson. The Russo-Japanese Treaties of 1907-1916 Concerning Manchuria and Mongolia. Johns Hopkins, 1933. xii, 158p.
Includes information on the events that led to the Japanese annexation of Korea.
Rel.Publ.: The Russo-Japanese...Mongolia. Baltimore: Johns Hopkins Press, 1933. xiv, 158p.

2296
SEVOSTIANOV, Pavel Petrovich. Imperialisticheskaia ekspansiia Soedinennykh Shtatov Ameriki v Kitae i Koree (1905-1910 gg.) [American Imperialist Expansion in China and in Korea, 1905-1910]. Moscow, Institut mezhdunarodnykh otnoshenii MID SSSR, 1950. (Candidate of Historical Sciences degree) i, 380p. Text in Russian.
Rel.Publ.: Ekspansionistskaia politika SShA na Dalnem Vostoke: V Kitae i Koree v 1905-1911 gg. Moscow, Gospolitizdat, 1958. 311p.

2297
VASILEVSKAIIA , I. I. Politika iaponskogo imperializma v Koree nakanune anneksii (1905-1910 gg.) [The Policy of Japanese Imperialism in Korea on the Eve of the Annexation, 1905-1910]. Moscow, Moskovskii ordena Lenina gosudarstvennyi universitet imeni M. V. Lomonosova, 1953. (Candidate of Historical Sciences degree) xviii, 247p. Text in Russian. AB: 16p. summary published in 1953.
Rel.Publ.: "K voprosu ob ekonomicheskom zakabalenii i ograblenii Korei Iaponskim imperial'izmom v gody protektorata (1905-1910 gg.)," in Akademiia nauk SSSR. Institut Vostokovedeniia, Kratkie soobshcheniia, 34 (1958), 28-34; "Nekotorye voprosy iaponskogo okkupatsionnogo rezhima v Koree v 1904-1905 gg.," in Akademiia nauk SSSR, Institut Vostokovedeniia, Kratkie soobshcheniia, 16 (1955), 57-67.

2298
MERRILL, John Espy. American Official Reactions to the Domestic Policies of Japan in Korea, 1905-1910. Stanford, 1954. 388p. DA 14 (Oct. 1954), 1698; UM 9510.
Pt.1 examines "the foreign attitudes toward the various steps preparatory to the establishment of the protectorate." Pt.2 "deals with the first two years of the protectorate and details the American and European reactions to that government's establishment, to Prince Itō's efforts to reform the Korean government by advisory means, and to the failure of such efforts. ...The third part delineates a period in which the old Emperor of Korea was forced to abdicate and Korean riots and attempted Japanese reforms played an alternating tatoo on the senses of the foreigners in Korea. ...It concludes with foreign reactions, generally acquisescence, to the outstanding events of the last year of the protectorate." Pt.4 focuses on the annexation and on related developments.

2299
KIM, Chong-Ik Eugene. Japan in Korea (1905-1910): The Techniques of Political Power. Stanford, 1959. 333p. DA 20 (Aug. 1959), 722-23; UM 59-2831.
"Evaluates how successfully Japan solved various problems involved in annexing Korea, 1905-1910."
Rel.Publ.: Korea and the Politics of Imperialism, 1876-1910 [by] C. I. Eugene Kim and Han-kyo Kim, Berkeley: University of California Press, 1967. x, 260p. (Publications of the Center for Japanese and Korean Studies); "A Problem in Japan's Control of the Press

in Korea, 1906-1909," PHR, 31 (Nov. 1962), 393-402.

2300
KHAN, Marks. Osvoboditel'naia bor'ba koreiskogo naroda v gody iaponskogo protektorata (1905-1910 gg.) [The Struggle of the Korean People to Liberate Themselves during the Period of the Japanese Protectorate, 1905-1910]. Moscow, Institut narodov Azii Akademii nauk SSSR, 1963. (Candidate of Historical Sciences degree) 177p. Text in Russian.
Rel.Publ.: Osvoboditel'naia...1910 gg. Moscow: Izd. vostochnoi literatury, 1961. 71p.

2301
CHOI, Dong Hoon. The United States Policy toward the Japanese Protectorate and Annexation in Korea, 1904-1910. Fletcher, 1965. iv, 228p. AB: 3p. summary appended to diss. ms.
Contents: Korea and the Outside World: From the Treaty of Kanghwa (1876) to the Japanese Annexation of Korea (1910); Korean-American Relations: From the Treaty of Shimonoseki to the Russo-Japanese War; United States Policy toward the Japanese Protectorate of Korea; United States Policy toward the Japanese Absorption from the Protectorate Agreement to the Hague Affair; United States Policy toward the Japanese Annexation of Korea.

THE PERIOD OF JAPANESE RULE, 1910-1945

General

2302
CHUNG, Henry. Case of Korea: [A] Collection of Evidence on the Japanese Domination of Korea [and] on the Development of [the] Korean Independence Movement. American, 1921. 289p.
Contents: Diplomatic Relations between Korea and Japan; Political and Judicial Oppression; The Official "Paddle"; Prison and Prison Tortures; Economic Exploitation; Intellectual Strangulation; Imposition of Social Evils; Persecution of the Church; Indignities to Missionaries; The Movement to Restore Independence; Japan Amuck; Massacres; "Speaking Officially"; Japan's Alleged Reforms; Korean and Japanese Characters Contrasted.
Rel.Publ.: Case...Movement. New York: F. H. Revell, 1921.

2303
GRAJDANZEV, Andrew Jonah. Modern Korea: Her Economic and Social Development under the Japanese. Columbia, 1945. x, 330p.
The topics covered: population, agriculture, forestry and fishery, power and mineral resources, industrial development, transport and communications, money and banking, public finance, external trade, the government; courts, prisons, police; health, education and religion; problems of Korean independence.
Rel.Publ.: Modern...Japanese. New York: Institute of Pacific Relations, 1944. x, 330p.

2304
SHVER, M. K. Iaponskoe kolonial'noe gospodstvo v Koree i ego krakh [Japanese Colonial Rule in Korea and Its Collapse]. Leningrad, Leningradskii gosudarstvennyi ordena Lenina universitet imeni A. A. Zhdanova, 1947. (Candidate of Economic Sciences degree) iv, 574p. Text in Russian. AB: 3p. summary published in 1948.

2305
SEMENOVA, N. P. Kolonial'naia politika iaponskogo imperializma v Koree i natsional'no-osvoboditel'naia bor'ba koreiskogo naroda (1910-1918 gg.) [Japanese Colonial Policy in Korea and the Korean Struggle for National Liberation, 1910-1918]. Moscow, Ministerstvo kul'tury SSSR, Moskovskii institut vostokovedeniia, 1953. (Candidate of Historical Sciences degree) viii, 454p. Text in Russian. AB: 16p. summary published in 1953.

ARNOLD, Dean A. American Economic Enterprises in Korea, 1895-1939. 1954. See no.2289.

2306
SHIPAEV, Viktor Ivanovich. Natsional'no-osvoboditel'naia bor'ba koreiskogo naroda protiv iaponskogo imperializma (1918-1931) [The National-Liberation Struggle of the Korean People against Japanese Imperialism, 1918-1931]. Moscow, Akademiia nauk SSSR, Institut vostokovedeniia, 1954. (Candidate of Historical Sciences degree) xviii, 282p. Text in Russian. AB: 15p. summary published in 1954.
Rel.Publ.: Koreiskaiia burzhuaziia v natsional'no-osvoboditel'nom dvizhenii. Moscow: "Nauka," 1966. 299p.

2307
KARPOVICH, N. I. Kolonial'naia politika iaponskogo imperializma v Koree (1931-1941 gg.) [The Colonial Policy of Japanese Imperialism in Korea, 1931-1941]. Moscow, Institut vostokovedeniia Akademii nauk SSSR, 1955. (Candidate of Historical Sciences degree) 204p. Text in Russian. AB: 16p. summary published in 1955.

2308
CHEN, Ilen. Kharakternye osobennosti razvitiia promyshlennosti i polozhenie rabochego klassa v Koree nakanune i vo vremia vtoroi mirovoi voiny [The Characteristic Peculiarities of the Development of Industry and the Position of the Working Class in Korea on the Eve of and during the Second World War]. Moscow, Moskovskii ordena Lenina i ordena Trudovogo Krasnogo Znameni gosudarstvennyi universitet imeni M. V. Lomonosova, Ekonomicheskii fakultet, 1956. (Candidate of Economic Sciences degree) 300p. Text in Russian. AB: 16p. summary published in 1956.

2309
MAZUROV, Viktor Mikhailovich. Antiiaponskaia vooruzhennaia bor'ba koreiskogo naroda (1931-1940 gg.) [The Anti-Japanese Armed Struggle of the Korean People, 1931-1940]. Moscow, Institut vostokovedeniia Akademii nauk SSSR, 1958. (Candidate of Historical Sciences degree) 104p. Text in Russian.
Rel.Publ.: Antiiaponskaia...1940 gg. Moscow: Izd. vostochnoi literatury, 1958. 104p. (Akademiia nauk SSSR. Institut Vostokovedeniia)

LIU, John J.-c. An Econometric Model of the Rice Market in the Japanese Empire, 1910-1937. 1960. See no.2115.

2310
USTINOV, V. M. Bor'ba inostrannykh grupp RKP(b) za osushchestvlenie printsipov proletarskogo internatsionalizma: na primere kitaiskikh i koreiskikh kommunisticheskikh organizatsii v Sovetskoi Rossii v 1918-1920 gg. [The Struggle of Foreign Groups within the Russian Communist Party (Bolsheviks) for the Implementation of the Principles of Proletarian Internationalism: The Example of Chinese and Korean Communist Organizations in Soviet Russia, 1918-1920]. Moscow, Institut marksizma-

leninizma pri TsK KPSS, 1960. (Candidate of Historical Sciences degree) 232p. Text in Russian.

2311
LEE, Chong-sik. The Korean Nationalist Movement, 1905-1945. California, Berkeley, 1961. 836p.

A detailed study of Korean efforts to regain national independence. Asserts that the Japanese annexation of Korea awakened and sustained Korean nationalism.

Rel.Publ.: The Politics of Korean Nationalism. Berkeley: University of California Press, 1963. xiv, 342p. (Publications of the Center for Japanese and Korean Studies); "The Origins of the Korean Communist Movement" [by] Robert A. Scalapino and Chong-sik Lee, JAS, 20 (Nov. 1960), 9-31, and 20 (Feb. 1961), 149-67; "Korean Communists and Yenan," China Quarterly, 9 (Jan./Mar. 1962), 182-92; "Witch Hunt among the Guerrillas: The Min-Sheng-T'uan Incident," China Quarterly, 26 (Apr./June 1966), 107-17.

2312
VORONTSOV, Vladilen Borisovich. Koreia v planakh SShA v gody vtoroi mirovoi voiny [Korea in American Planning during the Second World War]. Moscow, Institut narodov Azii Akademii nauk SSSR, 1961. (Candidate of Historical Sciences degree) 222p. Text in Russian.

Rel.Publ.: Koreia...voiny. Moscow: Izd-vo vostochnoi literatury, 1962. 138p. (Institut narodov Azii, Akademiia nauk SSSR); "SShA i problema nezavisimosti Korei v period vtoroi mirovoi voiny," in Institut narodov Azii, Akademiia nauk SSSR, Protiv fal'sifikatsii istorii Vostoka (Moscow, 1961), 113-23.

2313
REW, Joung Yole. A Study of the Government-General of Korea: With an Emphasis on the Period between 1919 and 1931. American, 1962. 312p. DA 23 (Mar. 1963), 3460-61; UM 62-4526.

An analysis of "the administration and the political structure of the Government-General...during the period when administrative reforms were introduced and industry began to rise....Careful consideration was given to the problems regarding (1) the impact of the Government-General of Korea upon Japanese expansion in Asia..., (2) the reactions of the Koreans toward the Government-General..., and (3) the impact of internal Japanese politics and of international affairs upon the development of the Government-General."

WOO, Philip M. The Historical Development of Korean Tariff and Customs Administration, 1875-1958. 1963. See no.2499.

2314
GÖTHEL, Ingeborg. Ker Kampf des koreanischen Volkes für die Schaffung einer nationalen Einheitsfront gegen den japanischen Imperialismus in den Jahren 1930-1940 [The Struggle of the Korean People for the Creation of a National Front against Japanese Imperialism, 1930-1940]. Leipzig, 1964. iv, 139p. Text in German. Diss. ms. available at Leipzig, Universitätsbibliothek; refer to author, title, year, and Nr. U 64.7556.

Studies Korean resistance to Japanese colonial rule during the 1910's and 1920's, the characteristics of Japanese imperialism, the impact of the world economic crisis of the 1930's upon Korea and upon the Korean socio-economic structure, Korea's participation in the international united front against fascism, and the Soviet liberation of Korea in 1945.

2315
SUH, Dae-Sook. Korean Communism and the Rise of Kim. Columbia, 1964. 544p. DA 28 (Dec. 1967), 2317-18-A; UM 67-16,049.

"Attempts to analyze the old Communist movement, to discover and to evaluate its origins and development, and to describe its early relationships with the Russians and the Comintern, its subsequent penetration into Korea, its struggles and spread within Korea, and its activities abroad, both independently and under foreign parties."

Rel.Publ.: The Korean Communist Movement, 1918-1948. Princeton: Princeton University Press, 1967. xix, 406p. (Studies of the East Asian Institute, Columbia University)

2316
DONG, Wonmo. Japanese Colonial Policy and Practice in Korea, 1905-1945: A Study in Assimilation. Georgetown, 1965. 542p. DA 26 (Dec. 1965), 3466-67; UM 65-12,510.

"The study aims at analyzing the Japanese colonial policies and practices in Korea, 1905-1945, with a view toward determining the characteristics, scope, instruments, and some results of assimilation which served as the governing principle of Japanese colonial rule in Korea." In his conclusion the author maintains that "the overemphasis of one common language, in absence of other factors of political socialization, in the pluralistic, colonial society of Korea proved to be most costly in terms of the administration of the colony, and that it inhibited the process of assimilation in a larger sense."

JUHN, Daniel S. Entrepreneurship in an Underdeveloped Economy: The Case of Korea, 1890-1940. 1965. See no.2133.

2317
PAK, Boris Dmitrievich. Osvoboditel'naia bor'ba koreiskogo naroda nakanune pervoi mirovoi voiny [The Struggle of the Korean People to Liberate Themselves on the Eve of the First World War]. Moscow, Moskovskii gosudarstvennyi pedagogicheskii institut imeni V. I. Lenina, 1965. (Candidate of Historical Sciences degree) 297p. Text in Russian. AB: 16p. summary published in 1965.

Rel.Publ.: Osvoboditel'naia...voiny. Moscow: "Nauka", 1967. 167p.; "Iz istorii koreiskoi emigrantskoi pechati (1910-1914)," Narody Azii i Afriki, 3 (1965), 172-78.

SUH, Sang Chul. Growth and Structural Changes in the Korean Economy since 1910. 1967. See no.2104.

2318
CHEN, I-te. Japanese Colonialism in Korea and Formosa: A Comparison of Its Effects upon the Development of Nationalism. Pennsylvania, 1968. 376p. DA 29 (Jan. 1969), 2317-A; UM 69-76.

"In Pt.1 a brief survey of the history of Japanese-Korean and Japanese-Formosan relations is presented in order to ascertain whether nationalism had already developed among Koreans and Formosans before annexation. Pt.2 deals with the impact of Japanese rule on various facets of native life [local government, educational systems and policies, economic effects]....In Pt.3 are presented the different ways in which Koreans and Formosans responded to Japanese rule: the nature of their resistance movements, the techniques they employed, and the repression they invited."

2319
BALDWIN, Frank. The March First Movement: Korean Challenge and Japanese Response. Columbia, 1969. 343p.

Contents: Agent Provocateur: Woodrow Wilson; Doubts and Decisions: November 1918 to January 1919; Planning the Movement: January 28 to February 28, 1919; Korean Demands for Independence, March 1 to December 1919; Self Determination and the Paris Peace Conference; The Japanese Response; The Saitō Administration.

Education

2320
AUH, Paul (Chunsuk). Education as an Instrument of National Assimilation: A Study of the Educational Policy of Japan in Korea. Columbia, 1931. 246p.

The dissertation examines Japan's policy of denationalizing the Korean people by means of an assimilationist educational policy. Among the subjects treated are (1) Korean nationality, (2) political relations between Japan and Korea, (3) education under the Yi Dynasty, (4) Japan's educational policy in Korea, (5) Japan's colonial policy in Korea and education as an instrument of that policy, (6) resistance to the assimilation policy, and (7) the Independence Movement and the student uprising.

2321
KIM, Che-won. Die Volksschule in Korea: Die japanische Assimilationserziehung [Primary Schools in Korea: The Assimilation to Japanese Educational Ideas]. München, 1934. Text in German. The dissertation in its published form is available at Marburg/Lahn, Universitätsbibliothek, Nr. XV C; also at the University of Michigan General Library, no. LA1331.K5.

Studies the accommodation of the Korean primary schools to the Japanese educational system, the goals of elementary education in Korea, and the attitude of the pupils to the authority of their teachers. Also includes Japanese ideas on assimilation.

Rel.Publ.: Die Volksschule...Assimilationserziehung. Antwerpen [Belgium]: "De Sikkel," 1934. 69p.

2322
RIM, Han Young. The Development of Higher Education in Korea during the Japanese Occupation (1910-1945). Columbia (Teachers College), 1952. 246p.

The study includes chapters on the Japanese annexation of Korea, the establishment of Japanese control over education, and Japanese special schools. There is much information on the impact of the Japanese annexation on Korean society, Korean educational reforms, the role of students in the Independence Movement, and institutions of higher education in Korea.

Rel.Publ.: "Japanese Totalitarian Education in Korea, 1910-1945," Koreana Quarterly, 2 (Spring 1960), 85-92.

2323
KIM, In Dia. Shkola i prosveshchenie v Koree (1910-1945 gg.) [Schools and Enlightenment in Korea, 1910-1945]. Moscow, Moskovskii ordena Lenina gosudarstvennyi universitet imeni M. V. Lomonosova, Filosofskii fakultet, 1955. (Candidate of Pedagogical Sciences degree) ii, 243p. Text in Russian. AB: 15p. summary published in 1955.

LEE, Sung-hwa. The Social and Political Factors Affecting Korean Education, 1885-1950. 1958. See no. 2171.

PAK, Hyung Koo. Social Changes in the Educational and Religious Institutions of Korean Society under Japanese and American Occupations. 1965. See no. 2065.

Religion

YUN, Sung Bum. Der Protestantismus in Korea, 1930-1955. 1956. See no. 2531.

2324
LEE, Kun Sam. The Christian Confrontation with Shinto Nationalism: A Historical and Critical Study of the Conflict of Christianity and Shinto in Japan in the Period between the Meiji Restoration and the End of World War II (1868-1945). Amsterdam Vrije Universiteit, 1962.

The introductory chapters examine the development of Shinto nationalism and of Emperor Worship as well as the early confrontations of Christianity with Japan. The main chapters study the conflict between Christianity and Shinto nationalism under the two headings "compromise" and "resistance" and deal with both Japan and Korea.

Rel.Publ.: The Christian...1945. Amsterdam: Van Soest, 1962. 210p.

PAK, Hyung Koo. Social Changes in the Educational and Religious Institutions of Korean Society under Japanese and American Occupations. 1965. See no. 2065.

2325
KIM, Eui Whan. The Korean Church under Japanese Occupation with Special Reference to the Resistance Movement within Presbyterianism. Temple, 1966. 253p. DA 27 (Oct. 1966), 1103-04-A; UM 66-9214.

Contents: The Background in Korea; The Establishment of Missions and the Rise of the National Church; The Growth and Trial of the Church (Its Phenomenal Growth, Its Characteristics, The Christian Encounter with the Early Japanese Persecution); The Challenge of Shintoism to the Korean Church (Introduction of Shintoism by the Japanese Militarists, Early Shinto, Modern Shinto and the Rise of Nationalism); The Korean Church in Conflict with Shinto Nationalism (Christian Education in Conflict with Shintoism, Compromise of the Church with Shinto Government, Christian Resistance within Presbyterian Circles to the Persecution of Shinto Militarists, The Ruling Motive for Resistance); The Struggle of the Korean Church in Larger Perspective: Summary and Conclusion.

2326
KANG, Wi Jo. The Japanese Government and Religions in Korea, 1910-1945. Chicago, 1967. 258p.

Half of the work consists of an historical description of the religious background of the Korean people.

Rel.Publ.: "Belief and Political Behavior in Ch'ondogyo," Review of Religious Research, 10 (Fall 1968), 38-43.

KOREA SINCE 1945

General

2327
IUN, Bon Khym. Kharakter i osobennosti narodno-demokraticheskoi revoliutsii v Koree [The Character and Peculiarities of the People's Democratic Revolution in Korea]. Moscow, Moskovskii gosudarstvennyi universitet imeni V. I. Lomonosova, Kafedra dialekticheskogo i istoricheskogo materializma, Filosofskii fakultet,

1956. (Candidate of Philosophical Sciences degree) 238p. Text in Russian. AB: 17p. summary published in 1956.

2328
HAN, Pyo Wook. The Problem of Korean Unification: A Study of the Unification Policy of the Republic of Korea, 1948-1960. Michigan, 1963. 241p. DA 26 (Feb. 1966), 4776-77; UM 64-12,607.

Contents: Introduction: Background of the Problem; Character of Leadership and Unification Policy in the Formative Stage; Communist Invasion; ROK and Armistice Negotiations; ROK-U.S. Diplomacy on Korean Unification (Rhee-Robertson Talk, Rhee-Dulles Conference); Geneva Conference on Korean Unification; ROK Policy in [the] Post-Geneva Period (ROK Advocates Renewal of War, Renewed Concern over Security, ROK Abandons Militant Posture).

2329
HAH, Chong-Do. The Dynamics of Japanese-Korean Relations, 1945-1963: An Interpretation of International Conflict. Indiana, 1967. 372p. DA 28 (May 1968), 4677-A; UM 68-7234.

Analyzes the various sources of discord, with particular emphasis on the period from 1951 to 1960. Also includes a study on the life of the Korean minority in Japan.

Rel.Publ.: "Bitter Diplomacy: Postwar Japan-Korea Relations," Studies on Asia, 1964, ed. by Robert K. Sakai (Lincoln: University of Nebraska Press, 1964), 63-93; "National Image and the Japanese-Korean Conflict, 1951-1965," Studies on Asia, 1967, ed. by Sidney D. Brown (Lincoln: University of Nebraska Press, 1967), 33-69.

2330
LEE, Soon-won Stewart. Korean-Japanese Discord, 1945-1965: A Case Study of International Conflict. Rutgers, 1967. 304p. DA 28 (Aug. 1967), 752-53-A; UM 67-9253.

Contents: Pt.1: Introduction. Pt.2: Historical Background: Japanese-Korean Relations to 1945. Pt.3: Issues in Conflict: The Issue of Property Claims; The Fishery Line; The Territorial Dispute; Koreans in Japan; Japanese Repatriation of Koreans to North Korea; Political Questions. Pt.4: Negotiations for Normalization: Postwar Developments and Japan-ROK Relations under SCAP; Negotiation Efforts under Syngman Rhee's Regime; Negotiations under Post-Rhee Governments; The Terms of Settlement. Pt.5: Analysis: U.S. Involvement in the Japan-ROK Controversy; Japanese Policy toward the Republic of Korea; ROK's Policy toward Japan.

1945-1950

See also History and International Relations--Korea since 1945: General (page 272).

2331
MEADE, Edward Grant. A Military Government Experiment in Korea. Pennsylvania, 1949. xi, 410p.

"Analyzes the American military government operation in Korea during 1945-1946, the crucial first year of occupation."

Rel.Publ.: American Military Government in Korea. New York: King's Crown Press, 1951. xii, 281p.

2332
FERARU, Arthur N. Le Problème de l'independance de la Corée [The Problem of Korean Independence]. Lyon, 1951. Text in French.

2333
FILIPOVITCH, C. N. La Corée: Problème international [Korea: An International Problem]. Paris, 1951. Text in French.

2334
GANE, William Joseph. Foreign Affairs of South Korea, August 1945 to August 1950. Northwestern, 1951. 444p. AB: Northwestern University. Summaries of Doctoral Dissertations. v.19 (1951), p.352-57.

Focuses particularly on (1) activities of the foreign office of the United States Army Military Government in Korea (e.g. relations with North Korea, SCAP, and Japan), (2) UN efforts to secure unity and independence for all of Korea, and (3) SCAP supervision over Korean affairs, 1945-1948.

2335
HU, Hung-lick. Le Problème coréen [The Korean Problem]. Paris, 1951. Text in French.

Contents: Pt.1: Relations between China and Korea before the Sino-Japanese War: Relations before the Nineteenth Century; The Interruption of These Relations; The Consolidation and Dissolution of Traditional Chinese-Korean Relations. Pt.2: The Loss and Recovery of Independence, 1895-1945. Pt.3: The Question of the Independence and Unification of Korea, 1945-1950: The Efforts of the Joint Commission; The Korean Problem before the UN; The Interim Commission of the General Assembly and the Work of the UN Committee for Korea; The Elections of May 10, 1948, and Their Repercussions. Pt.4: The Korean Problem after the Outbreak of War in 1950; UN Intervention; The Korean Conflict and International Law.

Rel.Publ.: Le Problème coréen. Paris: A. Pedone, 1953. 191p.

2336
KIM, Din Tai. Koreiskaia Narodno-Demokraticheskaia Respublika kak sub"ekt mezhdunarodnogo prava [The Korean People's Democratic Republic as a Subject of International Law]. Leningrad, Leningradskii gosudarstvennyi universitet imeni A. A. Zhdanova, 1951. (Candidate of Legal Sciences degree) 381p. Text in Russian.

2337
SON, E-chen. Obshchestvenno-ekonomicheskie preobrazovaniia v Severnoi Koree posle ee osvobozhdeniia Sovetskoi Armiei ot iaponskogo iga [The Socio-Economic Transformation of North Korea after Its Liberation by the Soviet Army from the Japanese Yoke]. Leningrad, Leningradskii gosudarstvennyi universitet imeni A. A. Zhdanova, 1951. (Candidate of Economic Sciences degree) xxxiii, 386p. Text in Russian.

CHUNG, Han Pom. The Republic of Korea in Power Politics. 1952. See no.2241.

2338
KIM, Georgii Federovich. Pomoshch' Sovetskogo Soiuza v ekonomicheskom i kulturnom stroitel'stve Koreiskoi Narodno-Demokraticheskoi Respubliki (1945-1950 gg.) [Soviet Aid in the Economic and Cultural Construction of the Korean People's Democratic Republic]. Moscow, Institut vostokovedeniia Akademii nauk SSSR, 1952. (Candidate of Historical Sciences) x, 322p. Text in Russian. AB: 21p. summary published in 1952.

Rel.Publ.: "Ekonomicheskoe razvitie Koreiskoi Narodno-Demokraticheskoi Respubliki," Voprosy ekonomiki, 7 (1955), 108-20; "Ekonomicheskoe i kul'turnoe stroitel'stvo v Koreiskoi Narodno-Demokraticheskoi Respublike (1945-1950 gg), Vosprosy istorii, 6, no.6 (1954), 27-42.

2339
TSOI, F. N. Bor'ba Trudovoi partii za sozdanie edinoi nezavisimoi demokraticheskoi Korei (1945-1950 gg.) [The Struggle of the Workers' Party for the Creation of a Unified, Independent, Democratic Korea, 1945-1950]. Moscow, Akademiia Obshchestvennykh nauk pri TsK VKP(b), Kafedra istorii VKP(b), 1952. (Candidate of Historical Sciences degree) i, 352p. Text in Russian. AB: 16p. summary published in 1952.

2340
CHANG, Paul Timothy. Political Effect of World War II On Korea: With Special Reference to the Policies of the United States. Notre Dame, 1953. 270p. DA 15 (Feb. 1955), 285; UM 10,722.
Focuses on the United States occupation of Korea during its early months.

2341
KAIRGELDIN, R. Agressivnaia politika SShA v Koree posle vtoroi mirovoi voiny (1945-1950) [America's Aggressive Policy in Korea after the Second World War, 1945-1950]. Moscow, Moskovskii ordena Lenina gosudarstvennyi universitet imeni M. V. Lomonosova, Istoricheskii fakultet, 1953. (Candidate of Historical Sciences degree) i, 314p. Text in Russian. AB: 16p. summary published in 1953.

2342
KIM, Khen Su. Podgotovka amerikanskoi agressii v Koree (1945-1950 gg.) [The Preparation for American Aggression in Korea, 1945-1950]. Leningrad, Leningradskii gosudarstvennyi ordena Lenina universitet imeni A. A. Zhdanova, 1953. (Candidate of Historical Sciences degree) xxix, 366p. Text in Russian. AB: 21p. summary published in 1953.

2343
LI, A. Natsional'no-osvoboditel'naia bor'ba narodov Iuzhnoi Korei (1945-1952 gg.) [The National-Liberation Struggle of the South Korean People, 1945-1952]. Moscow, Moskovskii gosudarstvennyi universitet imeni M. V. Lomonosova, 1954. (Candidate of Historical Sciences degree) viii, 253p. Text in Russian. AB: 16p. summary published in 1954.

2344
SOROKA-TSIUPA, O. S. Bor'ba Trudovoi Partii Korei za edinyi demokraticheskii otechestvennyi front (1945-1950 gg.) [The Struggle of the Korean Workers' Party for a Unified Democratic Patriotic Front, 1945-1950]. Moscow, Moskovskii institut mezhdunarodnykh otnoshenii MID SSSR, 1954. (Candidate of Historical Sciences degree) xx, 360p. Text in Russian.

2345
TUNKIN, Grigorii Ivanovich. Koreiskii vopros posle 2-oi mirovoi voiny v svete mezhdunarodnogo prava [The Korean Question after the Second World War in the Light of International Law]. Moscow, Moskovskii institut mezhdunarodnykh otnoshenii, 1954. (Doctor of Legal Sciences degree) xviii, 990p. (2v.) Text in Russian.
The dissertation was written in two parts: Pt.1: The Korean Question, 1945-1950. Pt.2: The Korean Civil War and American Aggression.

2346
EVERETT, John Thomas, Jr. The United Nations and the Korean Situation, 1947-1950: A Study of International Techniques of Pacific Settlement. Cincinnati, 1955. 312p. DA 15 (Aug. 1955), 1433-34; UM 12,937.
Focuses on the problem of Korean reunification. Contents: Introduction and Background (Factors in the Development of the Korean Situation as a Problem in Post-World War II International Relations. The Problem of Korea); Techniques and Agencies for the Pacific Settlement of International Disputes; The United States Appeals to the United Nations; The UN Responds; Techniques Used by the General Assembly (The UN Temporary Commission on Korea, The UN Commission on Korea, Continuation of the UN Commission on Korea).

2347
POPOV, V. N. Bor'ba Trudovoi Partii Korei za kulturnoe stroitel'stvo v Severnoi Koree (1945-1950 gg.) [The Struggle of the Korean Workers' Party for Cultural Development in North Korea, 1945-1950]. Moscow, Moskovskii ordena Lenina i ordena Trudovogo Krasnogo Znameni gosudarstvennyi universitet imeni M. V. Lomonosova, 1955. (Candidate of Historical Sciences degree) Text in Russian. AB: 16p. summary published in 1955.

2348
BAGMET, Nikolai Stepanovich. Bor'ba koreiskogo naroda za svobodu i nezavisimost' svoei rodiny i pozitsiia Sovetskogo Soiuza (1945-1954 gg.) [The Struggle of the Korean Nation for the Freedom and Independence of the Motherland and the Position of the Soviet Union, 1945-1954]. Kiev, Kievskii gosudarstvennyi universitet imeni T. G. Shevchenko, Kafedra novoi istorii i istorii mezhdunarodnykh otnoshenii, 1956. (Candidate of Historical Sciences degree) 405p. Text in Russian. AB: 17p. summary published in 1956.
Rel.Publ.: Bor'ba koreiskogo naroda za postroenie sotsializma (1945-1960 gg.). Kiev: Izd. Kievskogo universiteta, 1960. 225p.

2349
GORDENKER, Leon. The United Nations Commissions in Korea, 1947-1950. Columbia, 1958. 435p. DA 19 (July 1958), 161; UM 58-2235.
A study of the activities, successes, and failures of the various UN commissions sent to Korea.
Rel.Publ.: The United Nations and the Peaceful Unification of Korea: The Politics of Field Operations, 1947-1950. The Hague: M. Nijhoff, 1959. xiii, 306p.; "United Nations, the United States Occupation, and the 1948 Election in Korea," Political Science Quarterly, 73 (Sept. 1958), 426-50.

2350
LEE, Tong Won. The United Nations and Korea, 1945-1953. Oxford, 1958.

2351
PAK, L. D. Bor'ba trudovoi partii za ustanovlenie i uprochenie narodno-demokraticheskogo stroia v Severnoi Koree (1945-1950 gg.) [The Struggle of the Workers' Party for the Establishment and Consolidation of a People's Democratic Regime in North Korea, 1945-1950]. Kiev, Kievskii gosudarstvennyi universitet imeni T. G. Shevchenko, 1958. (Candidate of Historical Sciences degree) 248p. Text in Russian.

2352
YOON, Young Kyo. United Nations Participation in Korean Affairs: 1945-1954. American, 1959. 271p. DA 20 (Jan. 1960), 2880; UM 59-3642.

"Reviews the achievement of the UN in the establishment and recognition of the Republic of Korea, and studies the UN collective activities against Communist aggression in the Korean War." Contents: General Background; UN Efforts to Establish and Recognize the Government of the Republic of Korea; USSR Activities Opposing Establishment of the Republic of Korea Government; Korean War and UN Collective Activities; Armistice Negotiations; Post-Armistice Developments.

Rel.Publ.: "United Nations Participation in Korean Affairs: 1947-1951," Koreana Quarterly, 2 (Spring 1960) 22-54; "North Korean Regime's Rejection of the Competence and Authority of the United Nations, Korean Affairs, 2 (1963), 247-63.

2353
CHO, Soon-Sung. United States Policy toward the Unification of Korea: 1943-1950. Michigan, 1960. 384p. DA 20 (June 1960), 4702-03; UM 60-1748.

Argues that "in addition to the uncooperative Soviet attitude and the chaotic developments in internal politics in Korea immediately following the liberation of the country, American foreign policy toward Korea during the postwar period must be considered an important factor contributing to the continued division of Korea." Contents: Pt.1: Legacy of War-Time Diplomacy: Korea in War-Time Conferences (Cairo, Teheran, and Yalta); The Shadow of Roosevelt and the 38th Parallel. Pt.2: Period of Attempted Cooperation: Liberation and Military Occupation of Korea; Initial Negotiations for the Unification and Trusteeship Agreement at Moscow; The Search for Korean Unification and the Failure of the Joint Commission. Pt.3: Era of Containment Policy; United States Policy in the United Nations; The New Republics and Permanent Division of Korea; United States Policy on the Eve of the Korean War.

Rel.Publ.: Korea in World Politics, 1940-1950: An Evaluation of American Responsibility. Berkeley, University of California Press, 1967. 338p. (Publications of the Center for Japanese and Korean Studies); "The Failure of American Military Government in Korea," Korean Affairs, 2 (1963), 331-47; "Hodge's Dilemma: Failure of Korean Trusteeship," Korean Affairs, 4 (1965), 58-74.

2354
LEE, Won Sul. The Impact of the United States Occupation Policy on the Socio-Political Structure of South Korea, 1945-1948. Western Reserve, 1962. 277p.

Contents: Background and Early American Impact on Korean Society; American Preparation and Korean Society at the Time of the Occupation; Social and Political Impact of (1) the Establishment of the American Military Government, September-December 1945, (2) the Trusteeship Controversy, January-May 1946, (3) the Establishment of the Korean Interim Government, June 1945-June 1947, and (4) the Establishment of the Republic of Korea, June 1947-August 1948; Some of the Basic Social Reforms under the American Military Government.

Rel.Publ.: "The Embryo of Korean Bureaucracy in 1945," in [1] Kyung Hee University, Seoul, Theses Collection, 3 (1964), 271-85, and [2] Koreana Quarterly, 7 (Autumn 1965), 32-49; "American Preparedness on the Korean Question in 1945: A Study on the Question of Power and Morality in American Foreign Policy," in Hanguk Yŏngu Tosŏgwan, Seoul, Bulletin of the Korean Research Center: Journal of Social Science and Humanities, 22 (June 1965), 53-68.

NAM, Byung Hun. Educational Reorganization in South Korea under the United States Army Military Government, 1945-1948. 1962. See no.2184.

2355
SOH, Jin Chull. Some Causes of the Korean War of 1950: A Case Study of Soviet Foreign Policy in Korea (1945-1950), with Emphasis on Sino-Soviet Collaboration. Oklahoma, 1963. 266p. DA 24 (Dec. 1963), 2551-52; UM 64-126.

"This study analyzes the role of Soviet foreign policy in the period 1945-1950 as a causative factor in the Korean conflict. Particular emphasis is placed on Sino-Soviet collaboration and the failures of America's Korean policy in the same period. Considerable attention is given to diplomatic and military relations between the USSR, Communist China, and North Korea as reflected in the military and political preparation which took place in North Korea. The role of Soviet Russia and Communist China during the early phases of the war, up to the Communist Chinese intervention in late 1950, after which the war could no longer be portrayed as a simple conflict between two Korean factions, is also considered."

KWAK, Tae-Hwan. United States-Korean Relations: A Core Interest Analysis prior to U.S. Intervention in the Korean War. 1969. See no.2244.

The Korean War, 1950-1953

General

2356
OSTAPENKO, D. D. Interventsiia SShA v Koree: Tiagchaishee mezhdunarodnoe prestuplenie [The Intervention of the United States in Korea: The Gravest International Crime]. Moscow, Akademiia Obshchestvennykh nauk pri TsK VKP(b), Kafedra mezhdunarodnogo prava, 1952. (Candidate of Legal Sciences degree) xx, 449p. Text in Russian. AB: 16p. summary published in 1952.

2357
CHANG, Yu Nan. American Security Problems in the Far East, 1950-1952. Washington, Seattle, 1954. 356p. DA 14 (Nov. 1954), 2114-15; UM 10,002.

Several chapters are devoted to a discussion of the Korean War.

2358
FEER, Mark Cecil Iselin. India's China Policy 1949-1954. Fletcher, 1954. v, 283p. AB: Fletcher School of Law and Diplomacy. Thesis Abstract, 1954. no.4.

Five of the chapters depict India's China policy as it was principally evolved at the United Nations. Considerable information on India's approach to the Korean problem and on Sino-Indian disagreement over Korea may be found in Ch.3, "Birth of a China Policy" (p.61-77), Ch.4, "Policy on Trial" (p.78-94), Ch.5, "Quiescent Interlude" (p.95-103), Ch.6, "Drive for Peace" (p.104-20), and Ch.7, "Watchful Waiting" (p.121-46).

2359
GUPTA, Karunakar. The Korean Crisis and the Indian Union. London, 1954. 448p.

Rel.Publ.: Indian Foreign Policy in Defense of National Interest. Calcutta: Word Press, 1956. 109p.

2360
GRAHAM, Charles John. Republican Foreign Policy, 1939-1952. Illinois, 1955. 334p. DA 16 (Feb. 1956), 368; UM 15,210.
Includes a discussion of the views and criticisms of the Republican Party with regard to the manner in which President Truman and his administration handled the Korean War.

2361
FRASER, Haynes Reynolds. The Korean Conflict with Special Reference to the Theory and Dynamics of Collective Security. Southern California, 1956. 586p. AB: University of Southern California. Abstracts of Dissertations for...1956. p.175-76.
Using the Korean War as a case study, the author analyzes the utility of collective security arrangements as a means of deterring aggression.

2362
AUSTIN, Henry. India in Asia, 1947-1954. American, 1957. 254p.
Ch.4, "India and the Korean Crisis" (p.135-64), includes a discussion of past Indo-Korean contacts, India's role in the Korean War and in UN efforts to achieve a settlement, and Nehru's personal efforts for peace in Korea.

2363
HEIMSATH, Charles Herman, IV. India's Role in the Korean War. Yale, 1957. 342p. DA 26 (Jan. 1966), 4055; UM 66-36.
Discusses "Indian participation in the diplomacy of the Korean War and in the prisoner of war exchange following the armistice."

2364
MAHONEY, James Waite. India in the Commonwealth. Fletcher, 1957. iv, 488p.
A study of India's pre-independent association with the Commonwealth and of her experience in the Commonwealth between the years 1949-1954. Ch.5, "The Korean Triangle" (p.127-77), deals with India's approach to the Korean problem (hostilities in Korea, Chinese intervention, repatriation of prisoners of war, the Neutral Nations Reparatriation Commission, Geneva).

2365
SPANIER, John Winston. The Truman-MacArthur Conflict, June 1950-April 1951. Yale, 1957. 378p.
Contains some information on the role of South Korea in American security. See Ch.1 (p.1-38) in particular.
Rel.Publ.: The Truman-MacArthur Controversy and the Korean War. Cambridge, Mass.: Belknap Press, 1959. xii, 311p.

2366
LYONS, Eugene Martin. The Decline of a Multilateral Policy for Korean Reconstruction: A Case Study of the Relationship of the United Nations to the Conduct of United States Foreign Policy. Columbia, 1958. 392p. DA 20 (Aug. 1959), 726-27; UM 58-2469.
Analyzes certain foreign policy problems that "arose in the history of the relationship between the United States government and the UN Korean Reconstruction Agency (UNKRA), an agency established on December 1, 1950, to undertake a program of relief and rehabilitation in Korea."
Rel.Publ.: Military Policy and Economic Aid: The Korean Case, 1950-1953. Columbus: Ohio State University Press, 1961. xiii, 208p.; "American Policy and the United Nations Program for Korean Reconstruction," International Organization, 12 (Spring 1958), 180-92.

2367
SMITH, Hoke LaFollette. The Reconciliation of Energy and Objectives: A Study of Three Cases in American Foreign Policy. Emory, 1958. 280p. DA 19 (Apr. 1959), 2643; UM 58-5182.
Includes a case study of "the Korean crisis of 1950."

2368
PAIGE, Glenn Durland. The Korean Decision: June 24-30, 1950. Northwestern, 1959. 319p. DA 26 (Nov. 1965), 2852-53; UM 64-12,529.
"The body of the study is composed of a narrative reconstruction of the decision-making activities at the highest level of the United States Government following receipt of the first report that the North Koreans had attacked the Republic of Korea."
Rel.Publ.: The Korean...1950. New York: Free Press, 1968. xxv, 394p.; "The United States Decision to Resist Aggression in Korea: The Application of an Analytical Scheme," Administrative Science Quarterly, 3 (Dec. 1958), 341-78.

2369
CHANG, David Wen-wei. A Comparative Study of Neutralism of India, Burma, and Indonesia. Illinois, 1960. 323p. DA 21 (May 1961), 3509-10; UM 61-99.
"The purpose of this dissertation is to discover what neutralism in the three countries actually means, and how effective neutralism has been in the cold war." The "application of neutralism in three international crises" including the Korean War (Ch.5--p.184-224) is considered.

2370
SMITH, Paul Alan Lawrence. The Impact of International Events upon Domestic Political Behavior. Princeton, 1960. 220p. DA 21 (Apr. 1961), 3149-50; UM 60-5057.
Examines four postwar events--including the North Korean invasion of South Korea in 1950, and the Chinese intervention in the Korean War near the end of 1950--and studies their relationship to American public opinions and voting behavior.

2371
DOODY, Agnes Grace. Words and Deeds: An Analysis of Jawaharlal Nehru's Non-Alignment Policy in the Cold War, 1947-1953. Pennsylvania State, 1961. 311p. DA 22 (May 1962), 4117-18; UM 62-1704.
Includes a study of India's position on the Korean War question. See p.202-30 of Ch.5, "Nehru and Non-Alignment: 1950-1953."

2372
WEHNER, Helfried. Der weltweite Kampf der Volksmassen zur Beendigung der imperialistischen Aggression in Korea 1950-1953 und der Anteil des deutschen Volkes an diesem Kampf [The World-Wide Struggle of the Masses for Ending Imperialistic Aggression in Korea 1950-1953 and the Participation of the German People in This Struggle]. Berlin (Institut für Gesellschaftswissenschaften beim Zentralkomitee der SED), 1961. viii, 387p. Text in German. Diss. ms. available at Berlin, Humboldt Univer-

sitat, Universitätsbibliothek; Refer to author, title, year, and to Nr. U61.1188.

I. The struggle of the masses immediately following the beginning of imperialistic aggression in Korea. II. The struggle against the barbaric manner in which the aggressors fought and the efforts made to prevent them from introducing atomic weapons into Korea. III. The formation of a solidarity movement in the DDR as an expression of proletarian Internationalism. IV. The world-wide struggle of the masses for the suspension of hostilities in Korea.

Rel.Publ.: "Der Kampf der Völker zur Beendigung den imperialistischen Aggression in Korea," Deutsche Aussenpolitik, 5 (1960), 671-80.

2373
PORTER, Brian Ernest. British Opinion and the Far Eastern Crisis, 1945-1954. London, 1962. 310p.

Chapters 5-7 (of the publication) focus on the Korean War.

Rel.Publ.: Britain and the Rise of Communist China: A Study of British Attitudes, 1945-1954. London: Oxford University Press, 1967. ix, 195p.

2374
GOSWAMI, Birendra Nath. The Policies of Some Commonwealth Countries towards the Korean Crisis 1950-1953. Indian School of International Studies, 1963. viii, 319p. Order microfilm copy directly from the Nehru Memorial Museum and Library, New Delhi, India.

"Studies the official policies of certain Commonwealth countries towards the Korean conflict and shows their differences as well as their identity of outlook. Also stresses the efforts of these countries to limit the area of conflict in order to eliminate the possibility of a third world war."

2375
LOFGREN, Charles Augustin. Congress and the Korean Conflict. Stanford, 1966. 250p. DA 27 (Oct. 1966), 1017-A; UM 66-8629.

An analysis of the views that various congressmen held about the Korean War.

2376
CARIDI, Ronald James. The Republican Party and the Korean War. New York, 1967. 481p. DA 30 (Apr. 1970); UM 70-7347.

Studies the manner in which the G.O.P. turned popular discontent with the Korean War into electoral victory in the autumn of 1952. Contents: The Republican Party before Korea; The Commitment: June 25, 1950-July 10, 1950; The Beginning of the Republican Recoil: July 10, 1950-September 15, 1950; The Offensive: September 15, 1950-November 27, 1950; The Great Debate: November 28, 1950-April 11, 1951; MacArthur, Truman, and the Republicans: April 11, 1951-July 8, 1951; Negotiated Peace and Deterrent Power: July 8, 1951-July 7, 1952; The Election of 1952: July 7, 1952-November 4, 1952; The Eisenhower Peace: November 4, 1952-July 26, 1953.

Rel.Publ.: The Korean War and American Politics: The Republican Party as a Case Study. Philadelphia: University of Pennsylvania Press, 1969. 320p.; "The G.O.P. and the Korean War," PHR, 37 (Nov. 1968), 423-44.

2377
DOWELL, Arthur E. Appeasement or Conciliation in Global Crises, 1938 to 1951. Chicago, 1967. 382p.

Pt.1 treats the Korean War in three chapters: (1) McCarthyism paralyzes the governmental process; (2) Attempts to negotiate a settlement are forestalled by MacArthur; (3) Attempts to define appeasement.

2378
EPSTEIN, Laurence Bernard. The American Philosophy of War, 1945-1967. Southern California, 1967. 259p. DA 28 (Feb. 1968), 3092-93-A; UM 68-1188.

Examines "six issues that were prominent in raising debates which brought out the contemporary American attitudes on war...[in order] to ascertain whether or not the American philosophy of war is undergoing change." The Korean War is one of the six cases analyzed.

2379
VOLFSON, S. V. Politicheskaia bor'ba v praviashchikh krugakh SShA po voprosam vneshnei i voennoi politiki v 1950-1951 gg. [The Political Struggle within American Ruling Circles in 1950 and 1951 on Questions of Foreign and Military Policy Regarding the Korean War]. Tomsk, Tomskii gosudarstvennyi universitet imeni V. V. Kuibysheva, 1967. (Candidate of Historical Sciences) 504p. Text in Russian.

2380
CASPARY, William Richard. Public Reactions to International Events. Northwestern, 1968. 209p. DA 29 (Mar. 1969), 3190-A; UM 69-1812.

"This paper reports evidence on the modes in which people react to events and how their attitudes change over time as a sequence of events occur." The author analyzes numerous selections from existing poll data on the United States Public for the period 1946-1962, and in Ch.4 he discusses American reactions to the Korean War, pointing out that public "support for offensive action against China was constant over time."

2381
COLLIER, Joseph Maurice. Editorial Reaction of Certain Catholic Periodicals to United States Department of State Policy in the Far East: 1950. Kansas, 1969. 272p. DA 30 (Jan. 1970); UM 69-21,506. [See also addenda]

2382
STAIRS, Denis Winfield. The Role of Canada in the Korean War. Toronto, 1969. 561p.

"Although the thesis is devoted for the most part to an analysis of Canadian policy from the outbreak of the Korean hostilities in June 1950 to the conclusion of the armistice in July 1953, it includes also an initial chapter which comments briefly on Canada's general strategy in world affairs after 1945, and which considers in detail the Canadian role vis-à-vis the UN Temporary Commission on Korea in 1947-1948. An additional chapter discusses the relations between Canadian and other UN military commanders in the field, and another describes Canada's participation in the Korean phase of the 1954 Geneva Conference."

2383
TWEDT, Michael Stanley. The War Rhetoric of Harry S. Truman during the Korean Conflict. Kansas, 1969. 312p. DA 30 (June 1970); UM 70-11,081.

The United Nations and the War

2384
FRANKENSTEIN, Marc. L'Organisation des Nations Unies devant le conflit coréen [The Organization of the United

Nations and the Korean War]. Paris, 1951. Text in French.

Analyses the competence of the United Nations in settling the Korean conflict. Deals respectively with the Allied intervention and with the Chinese intervention in Korea.

Rel.Publ.: L'Organisation...coréen. Paris: A. Pedone, 1952. 368p.; "Les Initiatives de l'Inde pour le règlement du conflit coréen," Revue politique et parlementaire, 205 (July 1951), 53-62.

2385
BLOKH, Alexandre. L'Indépéndance de la Corée et l'oeuvre des Nations-Unies [Korean Independence and the Actions of the United Nations]. Paris, 1952. Text in French.

2386
VARMA, Shanti Narayan. India's Policy in the United Nations with Special Respect to the Maintenance of International Peace and Security: Being a Study of Selected Questions, Disputes, and Situations. Columbia, 1952. 417p. DA 12 (1952), 552-53; UM 3923.

Ch.9 (p.267-325) includes a study of the Indian position on the Korean question both before and after the Chinese intervention in the war.

2387
FERWERDA, Vernon LeRoy. The United Nations Role in the Maintenance of Peace. Harvard, 1954. 404p. AB: 5p. summary appended to diss. ms.

See Ch.8, "Conflict in Korea: Military Solution?" (p.220-324).

2388
HUANG, William Yung-nien. China's Role with Respect to Major Political and Security Questions under Consideration by the United Nations. Michigan, 1954. 842p. DA 14 (Apr. 1954), 704-05; UM 7669.

Pt.3, Ch.4, "Efforts of China towards Maintaining Peace: Collective Security: The Korean Question" (p.473-563), discusses the war and Nationalist China's efforts to develop "a positive program of United Nations collective action to condemn the aggressors, bar the Peking Government from United Nations membership, and unify the whole country of Korea under a democratic government."

2389
PLOTKIN, Arieh Leopold. Israel's Role in the United Nations: An Analytical Study. Princeton, 1955. 317p. DA 15 (Nov. 1955), 2280-81; UM 13,722.

"This study is an analysis of Israel's role as a member of the United Nations over a period of five years. Its changing relationship to some of the other members is traced, its response to a number of significant problems is examined, and its attempts to contribute to the solution of these problems is reviewed." Ch.6 presents a detailed consideration of Israel's stand and vote on the Korean conflict when it was brought before the UN General Assembly.

2390
RIGGS, Robert Edwon. The Policy of the United States with Respect to Political Questions in the General Assembly of the United Nations. Illinois, 1955. 296p. DA 16 (Feb. 1956), 370; UM 15,257.

A study of the political activities within the General Assembly that led to the UN condemnation of Chinese Communist intervention in Korea is included.

Rel.Publ.: Politics in the United Nations: A Study of United States Influence in the General Assembly. Urbana: University of Illinois Press, 1958. vi, 208p. (Illinois Studies in the Social Sciences, 41)

2391
GONLUBOL, Mehmet. A Critical Analysis of Turkish Participation in the United Nations. New York, 1956. 363p. DA 16 (July 1956), 1274-75; UM 16,767.

A study which points out the active Turkish interest in UN collective security activities and which discusses, among other things, Turkish participation in the UN intervention in Korea.

LEE, Tong Won. The United Nations and Korea, 1945-1953. 1958. See no.2350.

2392
WEISSBERG, Guenter. The International Legal Personality of the United Nations. Columbia, 1959. 539p. DA 20 (Mar. 1960), 3814-15; UM 60-54.

Includes an extensive investigation of "the Korean conflict, in so far as it has had an impact on the personality of the organization."

Rel.Publ.: The International Status of the United Nations. New York: Oceana Publications, 1961. xii, 228p. (The Library of World Affairs)

YOON, Young Kyo. United Nations Participation in Korean Affairs: 1945-1954. 1959. See no.2352.

2393
GOTTLIEB, Paul Herbert. The Commonwealth of Nations at the United Nations. Boston, 1962. 326p. DA 23 (Sept. 1962), 1003; UM 62-3790.

Includes a discussion of the positions taken by the various Commonwealth member-states on the Korean War question.

2394
KAHNG, Tae Jin. The Handling by the Security Council of Legal Questions Involved in International Disputes and Situations. Columbia, 1962. 360p.

Includes a discussion of the competence of the Security Council in the Korean Conflict.

Rel.Publ.: Law, Politics, and the Security Council: An Inquiry into the Handling of Legal Questions Involved in International Disputes and Situations. The Hague: M. Nijhoff, 1964. xiv, 252p.

2395
ATTIA, Gamal el-Din. Les Forces armées des Nations Unies en Corée et au Moyen-Orient [The Armed Forces of the United Nations in Korea and in the Middle East]. Genève, 1963. Text in French.

A legal study exclusively. See Ch.3 (p.113-284), which deals with the situation in Korea.

Rel.Publ.: Les Forces...Moyen-Orient. Genève: Droz, 1963. 467p. (Travaux de droit, d'économie, et de sociologie, 2)

2396
BROWN, Janet Welsh. Burmese Policy in the United Nations: An Analysis of Five Selected Political Questions, 1948-1960. American, 1964. 515p. DA 26 (Apr. 1966), 6146; UM 65-4545.

"The purpose of this dissertation is (1) to analyze and evaluate Burmese foreign policy on political matters from 1948 to 1960, especially with regard to Burma's role in the United Nations, and (2) to contribute to the understanding of 'bloc politics' in the UN by providing examples of the kinds of motivation, deliberation, and decisions which lie behind the voting patterns of one member state." The Korean case is among the questions analyzed. See Ch.4, "Burma and the Korean War: The Cold War" (p.115-207).

2397
YOO, Tae-ho. The Korean War and the United Nations: A Legal and Diplomatic Historical Study. Louvain, 1964.
Contents: The Armed Attack from North Korea and the UN Collective Measures; The Intervention of Communist China in the Korean War and the UN Collective Measures; The Pacific Measures of the United Nations: Armistice; The Korean War and the International Law. [Annotation based on the book.]
Rel.Publ.: The Korean...Study. Louvain, 1964. 215p. (Université catholique de Louvain. Collection de l'Institut des sciences politiques et sociales, 179)

2398
ABU-DIAB, Fawzi. Lebanon and the United Nations, 1945-1958. Pennsylvania, 1965. 229p. DA 26 (Dec. 1965), 3464-65; UM 65-13,305.
A description and analysis of Lebanese participation in the United Nations. Includes much information on the Lebanese stand on the Korean War (see Ch.5, section D).

2399
BOEN, Sharon Elaine. The Leadership Role of the Secretary-General in Times of International Crisis. Virginia, 1965. 424p. DA 26 (Apr. 1966), 6145-46; UM 66-3166.
See Ch.4, "The Secretary-General [of the United Nations] and Collective Security: Korea" (p.181-96).

2400
KIM, Taekhoan. Die Vereinten Nationen und ihre kollektiven Sicherheitsmassnahmen: Studie über die UN-Aktion gegen die Intervention der Volksrepublik China im Korea-Krieg [The United Nations and Its Collective Security Measures: A Study of UN Intervention in the Korean War]. München, 1967. vi, 247p. Text in German. The dissertation in its published form is available at the University of Michigan, General Library, no.37,297.
Rel.Publ.: Die Vereinten...Krieg. München: UNI-Druck, 1967. vi, 247p.

2401
MICHALAK, Stanley Jacob, Jr. The Senate and the United Nations: A Study of Changing Perceptions about the Utilities and Limitations of the United Nations as an Instrument of Peace and Security and Its Role in American National Security Policy. Princeton, 1967. 266p. DA 28 (Feb. 1968), 3246-A; UM 68-2504.
Includes an attempted reconstruction of the Senate's image of international politics during the Korean War period.

2402
RAITT, Walton Archie. American Ideology and the United Nations: A Study in Ambivalence. Claremont, 1968. 301p. DA 29 (Aug. 1968), 660-61-A; UM 68-10,536.
Analyzes the nature of the relationship between the outlook of American ideology and the Charter and early activities of the United Nations. Ch.12 is a case study of the United States, the United Nations, and the Korean War.

The War in Korea

Focuses on military developments in the Korean peninsula, 1950-1953. See also The Korean War, 1950-1953: general (pages 275-77) and the United Nations and the war (pages 277-79).

TUNKIN, Grigorii I. Koreiskii vopros posle 2-oi mirovoi voiny v svete mezhdunarodnogo prava. 1954. See no.2345.

BAGMET, Nikolai S. Bor'ba koreiskogo naroda za svobodu i nezavisimost' svoei rodiny i pozitsiia Sovetskogo Soiuza (1945-1954 gg.). 1956. See no.2348.

2403
BRAZDA, Jaroslav Jan. The Korean Armistice Agreement: A Comparative Study. Florida, 1956. 332p. DA 16 (Dec. 1956), 2506; UM 19,164.
Analyzes "the terms of the armistice and compares them with a number of precedents in order to discover some reasons why the Korean armistice negotiations were so long, drawn-out, and difficult." Concludes that they were prolonged "because (1) modern armistices, involving political considerations, are more difficult to reach than ever before; (2) this armistice reflected the tensions of the cold war; (3) it involved an unprecedented police action on the part of the United Nations; and (4) it reflected significant departures from previous armistice practice."

2404
COOPER, Bernarr. Radio Broadcasting to Chinese and Korean Pow's: A Rhetorical Analysis. Stanford, 1956. 544p. DA 17 (Feb. 1957), 427-28; UM 19,919.
"Through a rhetorical analysis, this study seeks to examine appeals which were contained in radio broadcast communications to Chinese and Korean prisoners of war, held by the United Nations Command. The examination is confined to appeals contained in radio broadcasts designed especially for the Chinese and Korean prisoners of war, and heard by them" in 1952 and 1953.

2405
KHAN, S. A. Druzhba i revoliutsionnoe sotrudnichestvo narodov Korei i Kitaia v bor'be protiv amerikanskogo imperializma 1945-1953 [Friendship and Revolutionary Cooperation between the Koreans and the Chinese People in the Struggle against American Imperialism, 1945-1953]. Moscow, Institut vostokovedeniia Akademii nauk SSSR, 1956. (Candidate of Historical Sciences degree) 242p. Text in Russian. AB: 14p. summary published in 1956.

2406
ALAPATT, George Kappan. The Legal Implications of the Repatriation of War Prisoners in Relation to the Korean Armistice and in View of the Division of Korea. St. Louis, 1958. 235p. DA 19 (May 1959), 3003; UM 59-885.
"Primarily concerned with the work of the Neutral Nations' Repatriation Commission in relation to its legal impact on the problem of the repatriation of prisoners of war."

2407
PAK, Don Din. Zakliuchenie peremiriia v Koree i ego istoricheskoe znachenie [The Conclusion of the Armistice in Korea and Its Historical Significance]. Kiev, Mini-

sterstvo vysshego i srednego spetsial'nogo obrazovaniia SSSR, Kievskii ordena Lenina gosudarstvennyi universitet imeni T. G. Shevchenko, 1959. (Candidate of Historical Sciences degree) Text in Russian. AB: 18p. summary published in 1959.

2408
KIM, Myong Whai. Prisoners of War as a Major Problem of the Korean Armistice, 1953. New York, 1960. 323p. DA 23 (July 1962), 291-92; UM 61-702.

The dissertation is "primarily concerned with the question of repatriation of POW's in the Korean armistice negotiations," and it "attempts to prove that prisoners of war should not be repatriated by force if their refusal to return home is based on good faith."

Rel.Publ.: "A Study on the Korean Armistice, 1953," Korea Observer, 1 (Oct. 1968).

2409
BIDERMAN, Albert David. American Prisoners of War in Korea: Reinterpretation of the Data. Chicago, 1964. 313p.

Contents: Historical Perspectives; Criteria of "Collaboration"; Collaboration and Resistance (Universal Collaboration, POW Cooperation and Resistance in Relation to the Exploitation Objectives and Effectiveness); Mortality (Death Rates and Prisoner Conduct, Inter-Service Comparisons, Death as a Criterion in Captivity Situations, Prisoner Organization and Evaluation of Death Rates); Mistreatment, Coercion, and Atrocities; Military Organization and POW Problems.

Rel.Publ.: March to Calumny: The Story of American POW's in the Korean War. New York: Macmillan, 1963. 326p.; "Effects of Communist Indoctrination Attempts: Some Comments Based on Air Force Prisoner-of-War Study," Social Problems, 6 (Spring 1959), 304-13.

2410
HERMES, Walter G. The United States Army in the Korean War: The Last Two Years, July 1951-July 1953. Georgetown, 1966. 1417p. DA 27 (Aug. 1966), 438-A; UM 66-7282.

"Describes the military and diplomatic events that took place in Korea, in the United States, and elsewhere around the world that had an influence upon the war during its last two years."

Rel.Publ.: Truce Tent and Fighting Front. Washington: Office of the Chief of Military History, U.S. Army, 1966. 571p. (United States in the Korean War, 4)

2411
DAOUST, George Arlington, Jr. The Role of Air Power in U.S. Foreign Policy in the Far East, 1945-1958. Georgetown, 1967. 235p. DA 28 (Feb. 1968), 3243-44-A; UM 68-1901.

A discussion of air power as an element of national power. The use of the United States air force during the Korean War is included within the discussion.

2412
EMERY, Michael Charles. The American Mass Media and the Coverage of Five Major Foreign Events, 1900-1950: The Russo-Japanese War, Outbreak of World War I, Rise of Stalin, Munich Crisis, Invasion of South Korea. Minnesota, 1968. 447p. DA 30 (Aug. 1969), 675-A; UM 69-11,386.

See Ch.5, "Retreat from Seoul" (p.316-78): "From Nightclubs to Foxholes; The Defense of Taejon; The Beachhead."

2413
WITHERSPOON, John Alfred. International Law and Practice Concerning Prisoners of War during the Korean Conflict (1950-1954). Duke, 1968. 396p. DA 29 (Feb. 1969), 2778-79-A; UM 69-3155.

"Concludes that the authorities controlling prisoners in North Korea apparently ignored the moral obligations to abide by the Third Geneva Convention."

2414
MARSHALL, Thomas Lee. The Strategy of Conflict in the Korean War. Virginia, 1969. 366p.

Korea since 1953

For commercial relations with other countries, see Economics--foreign trade (pages 253-54).
See also History and International Relations--Korea since 1945 (pages 272-81).

ALEXANDRIDES, Costas G. The United Nations Economic Assistance to the Republic of Korea: A Case Study of Economic Reconstruction and Development. 1960. See no.2094.

2415
TOLSTIKOV, Vladimir Grigor'evich. Ekspansiia amerikanskogo imperializma v Iuzhnoi Koree i politika Trudovoi Partii po voprosu o mirnom ob"edinenii strany (1953-1960 gg.) [American Imperialist Expansion in Korea and the Policy of the Workers' Party with Regard to the Question of Uniting the Country Peacefully, 1953-1960]. Moscow, Akademiia Obshchestvennykh nauk pri TsK KPSS, 1961. (Candidate of Historical Sciences degree) xii, 295p. Text in Russian.

AVEN, James S. The Organization of American Community Schools in the Far East. 1963. See no.2175.

2416
LEE, Jin Won. Political Issues between Japan and Korea, Post-War Period, 1952-1962. Oxford, 1963/64.

Rel.Publ.: "Brief Survey of Korean-Japanese Relations: Post-War Period," Koreana Quarterly, 1 (Winter 1959), 64-85.

2417
BORNEMANN, Paul. Die Teilnahme politisch geteilter Staaten und der Arbeit internationaler Organisationen [The Participation of Politically Divided States and the Work of International Organizations]. Köln, 1964. xix, 153p. Text in German. The dissertation in its published form is available at the University of Michigan, General Library, no. 29,139.

See especially Pt.D, "The Participation of Germany, Korea, and Vietnam in International Organizations within the U.N." (p.39-119), for detailed information on Korean participation in such organizations as the UN itself, ECAFE, the Universal Postal Union, the Food and Agriculture Organization, and the World Health Organization.

Rel.Publ.: Die Teilnahme...Organisationen. n.p., n.d., 1964. xix, 153p.

2418
CHEE, Choung Il. National Regulation of Fisheries in International Law. New York, 1964. 329p. DA 27 (Sept. 1966), 812-A; UM 65-6624.

"Attempts to study the contemporary development of

international law concerning the control and regulation of sea resources." In Ch.4, the author "investigates several international efforts made for the regulation of fisheries in the high seas, and four postwar fishing disputes--among them the Korea-Japan fishing dispute--are singled out" for detailed analysis.

2419
CHENG, Peter Ping-chii. A Study of John Foster Dulles' Diplomatic Strategy in the Far East. Southern Illinois, 1964. 674p. DA 25 (Apr. 1965), 6043; UM 65-1320.

A study of Dulles' policies in East Asia while serving under President Truman (1950-1952) and as Secretary of State (1953-1959). Dulles' policy with regard to Korea is examined, and the author concludes that in the case of Korea, "Dulles drew a de facto ceasefire line and stood firmly to minimize military hostilities across the line from either side. When the Communists intensified their efforts to cross the line by an open attack by armed forces, Dulles was determined to deter aggression by all means, even at the risk of war."

2420
SALMON, Jack Dean. Limited War and Tactical Nuclear Weapons in East Asia. Kansas, 1965. 246p. DA 27 (July 1966), 236-A; UM 66-6050.

"Reviews the past and present arguments for or against the use of tactical nuclear weapons" in Korea (as well as in the Taiwan Straits area and in Vietnam) and "evaluates the probable advantages or disadvantages of United States' initiation of tactical nuclear warfare in these areas now or in the future."

SEO, Joseph W. Der gegenwärtige Stand der Agrarwirtschaft in Ostasien (Japan, Korea, Taiwan): Unter besonderer Berücksichtigung der handelspolitischen Verflechtung mit der EWG. 1965. See no.2121.

2421
CHAI, Nam Yearl. Asian Attitudes toward International Law: A Case Study of Korea. Pennsylvania, 1967. 303p. DA 28 (June 1968), 5125-26-A; UM 68-9189.

Analyzes the "state practice of the First Republic of Korea (1948-1960) as revealed in three legal disputes: (1) the dispute over Korea's sovereignty over the adjacent seas, (2) the dispute over Japanese claim to property in Korea, and (3) the jurisdictional dispute over Dokto Dok island." Contents: Research Design: Analytical Framework of Inquiry; Korea and International Law during Her Struggle for Independence; Korea and the Law of the Sea; Korea and the Law of War; Korea and the Law of Territorial Jurisdiction.

2422
KIM, Ok Yul. The American Role in Korean-Japanese Relations. Bryn Mawr, 1967. 235p. DA 28 (Apr. 1968), 4239-A; UM 68-4695.

Studies the role of the United States in the achievement of the Normalization Treaty between Japan and Korea.

Rel.Publ.: "American Views of Korean-Japanese Rapprochement," in Hanguk Yŏngu Tosŏgwan, Seoul, Bulletin of the Korean Research Center: Journal of Social Science and Humanities, 28 (June 1968), 18-30.

2423
KIM, Uoong Tack. Sino-Soviet Dispute and North Korea. Pennsylvania, 1967. 385p. DA 28 (Nov. 1967), 1879-A; UM 67-12,766.

"Analyzes North Korea's political development within the overall context of Sino-Soviet relations." Contents: Pt.1: Korea: Historical Background; Korean Communists and the DPRK. Pt.2: Korean War; Modified Soviet Strategy; The Chinese Communes and Volunteers Withdrawal; Taiwan Crisis and Detente with the West. Pt.3: National Economy; The Worsening of the Dispute; Moscow and Peking to the Brink; Khrushchev's Ouster and the 23rd CPSU Congress.

Rel.Publ.: "Sino-North Korean Relations," Asian Survey, 8 (Aug. 1968), 708-22.

2424
MIN, Benjamin Byung-Hui. North Korea's Foreign Policy in the Post-War Decade, 1953-1963: Its Strategy of Korean Unification and Relations with Moscow and Peking. Massachusetts, 1967. 235p. DA 28 (Apr. 1968), 4240-41-A; UM 68-4455.

"Studies North Korea's tactics and strategy in its quest for reunification of Korea under Communist leadership, North Korea's relations with the Soviet Union in the context of Moscow's ideological polemics with China, and Pyongyang's political, cultural, and military relations with Peking in the realm of Sino-Soviet conflict."

2425
CHUNG, Chin Owyee. North Korea's Attitude in the Sino-Soviet Dispute, 1958-1967. Nebraska, 1969. 303p. DA 30 (Jan. 1970); UM 69-22,259.

Contents: Historical Background up to 1957; North Korea in the Growing Sino-Soviet Dispute, 1958-1959; Pyongyang's Neutralism in the Sino-Soviet Rift, 1960-1961; Pyongyang Leans toward Peking, 1962; Pyongyang Sides with Peking in the Sino-Soviet Rift, 1963-October 1964; Pyongyang's New Policy after Khrushchev's Fall.

2426
YIU, Myung Kun. Sino-Soviet Rivalry in North Korea since 1954. Maryland, 1969. 375p.

Contents: Unification of the Workers' Party of Korea by Kim Il-sung as an Internal Factor of Nationalism in North Korea; The Chinese-Soviet Rivalry in North Korea as an External Condition of North Korean Autonomy (1954-1961); North Korean Entente with Communist China Viewed as a Political Maneuver to Limit Soviet Influence in North Korea (1962-1964); Causes of the Turning of North Korea to Peking; The Recent North Korean Rapprochement with the Soviet Union Viewed as a Move to Limit the Influence of Communist China; Nationalism and the Workers' Party of Korea; Current Trends in the Evolution of Kim Il-sung's Policy of Juche and the Sino-Soviet Responses.

Language and Linguistics

APPLIED LINGUISTICS

2427
PULTR, Alois. Učebnice korejštiny [A Textbook of Korean]. Universita Karlova, 1951/52. 170p. Text in Czech. Diss. ms. available at the University archives, no. AUK 2981.
A textbook of modern colloquial Korean intended for practical use.
Rel.Publ.: Učebnice korejštiny. Praha: Státní tiskárna, 1949 [Originally published as a specially inserted supplement to the magazine Nový Orient, v.5 and v.6.]; Učebnice korejštiny. Praha: Nakladatelství Československé akademie, 1954. 279p.; Lehrbuch der koreanischen Sprache. Berlin: Deutsche Verlag der Wissenschaften, 1958. 345p.

2428
KHEGAI, M. A. Leksicheskie zaimstvovaniia iz russkogo iazyka v koreiskikh perevodakh [Lexical Borrowings from the Russian Language in Korean Translations]. Moscow, Akademiia nauk SSSR, Institut iazykoznaniia, 1953. (Candidate of Philological Sciences degree) 204p. Text in Russian. AB: 16p. summary published in 1953.

2429
KHAN, Dyk Pon. Kitaiskie leksicheskie elementy v slovarnom sostave koreiskogo iazyka: Voprosy slovoobrazovaniia [Chinese Lexical Elements in the Vocabulary of the Korean Language: Questions of Word Formation]. Moscow, Ministerstvo Vysshego Obrazovaniia SSSR, Moskovskii institut vostokovedeniia, 1954. (Candidate of Philological Sciences degree) 216p. Text in Russian. AB: 30p. summary published in 1954.

2430
TSOI, Den-Khun. Foneticheskaia struktura zaimstvovannykh kitaiskikh leksicheskikh elementov v koreiskom i iaponskom iazykakh [Phonetic Structure of Borrowed Chinese Lexical Elements in the Korean and Japanese Languages]. Moscow, Moskovskii ordena Lenina gosudarstvennyi universitet imeni M. V. Lomonosova, 1954. (Candidate of Philological Sciences degree) iii, 214p. Text in Russian. AB: 15p. summary published in 1954.

2431
SKALOZUB, L. G. Sopostavitel'noe opisanie soglasnykh sovremennogo russkogo i koreiskogo iazykov [A Comparative Description of Consonants in the Modern Russian and Korean Languages]. Kiev, Kievskii gosudarstvennyi universitet imeni T. G. Shevchenko, 1957(?). (Candidate of Philological Sciences) xv, 481p. Text in Russian.
Rel.Publ.: Sopostavitel'noe opisanie soglasnykh sovremennykh koreiskogo i russkogo iazykov: Itogi eksperimental'no-foneticheskogo issledovaniia i metodika postanovki russkikh soglasnykh u koreitsev. Kiev: Izd. Kievskogo universiteta, 1957. 103p.

Kumata, Hideya. A Factor Analytic Study of Semantic Structures across Three Selected Cultures. 1958. See no.2060.

2432
KNOWLTON, Edgar Colby, Jr. Words of Chinese, Japanese, and Korean Origin in the Romance Languages. Stanford, 1959. 904p. DA 20 (Aug. 1959), 665; UM 59-2822.
"This dissertation contains a set of indexed lists of 298 Chinese, 325 Japanese, and 138 Korean words in the Romance languages. The arrangement is alphabetical by etymon. Indices record all spellings given in quotations or citations from other sources, so that the reader may find (by reference to the etymon) a treatment of any specific Far Eastern word included, together with its Romance language reflexes, or discover to what Far Eastern source a given exoticism may be referred."

2433
KIM, O. M. Osobennosti russkoi rechi koreitsev Uzbekskoi SSR: Fonetiko-morfologicheskii ocherk [Peculiarities in the Russian Spoken by Koreans in the Uzbek Soviet Socialist Republic: A Phonetic-Morphological Essay]. Tashkent, Tashkentskii gosudarstvennyi universitet imeni V. I. Lenina, 1964. (Candidate of Philological Sciences degree) 280p. Text in Russian.

HOWELL, Richard W. Linguistic Choice as an Index to Social Change. 1967. See no.2066.

2434
PAE, Yang Seo. English Loanwords in Korean. Texas, 1967. 199p. DA 28 (June 1968), 5038-39-A; UM 68-4326.
Contents: Historical Survey; Theory of Borrowing (Previous Studies, Identification of Loanwords, Definition of Loanwords); Phonology (Orthography, Symbols, Abbreviations, English Loans versus Other Loans, Three Language Descriptions); Vocabulary (Shortened Forms, Japanized and Koreanized English, Loan Translations, Hybrids, Acronyms and Initials); Internal History of Assimilated Loans; The Cultural Implications of the Loans.

2435
BRODKEY, Dean Guy. A Self-Instructional Program in English Article Usage for Chinese, Japanese, Korean,

and Thai College Students. California, Los Angeles, 1969. 103p. DA 30 (May 1970); UM 70-8119.

Contents: Article and Oriental; Principles of Second-Language Instruction; Patterns of Article Usage; Program Development; Experimental Procedures; Analysis of Data; Conclusions.

GRAMMAR

2436
MAZUR, Iurii Nikolaevich. Padezhi i poslelogi v koreiskom iazyke [Cases and Postpositions in the Korean Language]. Moscow, Moskovskii institut vostokovedeniia, 1953. (Candidate of Philological Sciences degree) 310p. Text in Russian. AB: 17p. summary published in 1953.

Rel.Publ.: Skloneniia v koreiskom iazyke. Moscow: Izd-vo Moskovskogo universiteta, 1962. 116p. (Moskovskii gosudarstvennyi universitet imeni M. V. Lomonosova, Institut vostochnykh iazykov, Kafedra iazykov Dal'nego Vostoka)

2437
KIM, Ben Su. Skazuemoe v sovremennom koreiskom iazyke [The Predicate in the Modern Korean Language]. Moscow: Ministerstvo vysshego obrazovaniia SSSR, Moskovskii institut vostokovedeniia, 1954. (Candidate of Philological Sciences degree) Text in Russian. AB: 15p. summary published in 1954.

2438
LUKOFF, Fred. A Grammar of Korean. Pennsylvania, 1954. 265p. DA 14 (Sept. 1954), 1404-05; UM 8564.

A study of Korean phonology and morphology with a brief sketch of the syntax of the clause. The Korean spoken by educated classes in Seoul is the basis for the analysis, but references also are made to forms found in a number of dialects.

2439
SON, Se Ren. Slovoobrazovanie v koreiskom iazyke [Word Formation in the Korean Language]. Moscow, Moskovskii ordena Lenina gosudarstvennyi universitet imeni M. V. Lomonosova, 1955. (Candidate of Philological Sciences degree) 285p. Text in Russian. AB: 20p. summary published in 1955.

2440
MALKOV, F. V. Morfologiia predikativnykh prilagatel'nykh v koreiskom iazyke [The Morphology of Predicate Adjectives in the Korean Language]. Moscow, Institut vostokovedeniia Akademii nauk SSSR, 1958. (Candidate of Philological Sciences degree) ii, 228p. Text in Russian.

2441
GUSEVA, Evgeniia Konstantinovna. Sistema vidov v sovremennom koreiskom iazyke [The System of Aspects in the Modern Korean Language]. Moscow, Institut vostokovedeniia Akademii nauk SSSR, 1959. (Candidate of Philological Sciences) 211p. Text in Russian.

Rel.Publ.: Sistema...iazyke. Moscow: Izd. vostochnoi literatury, 1961. 119p.

2442
RACHKOV, G. E. Kategoriia vremeni glagola v sovremennom koreiskom iazyke [The Category of Verb Tense in Modern Korean]. Leningrad, Leningradskii gosudarstvennyi universitet imeni A. A. Zhdanova, 1963. (Candidate of Philological Sciences degree) 556p. Text in Russian.

Rel.Publ.: "Dva tipa razdelitel'nykh deeprichastii v koreiskom iazyke," in Leningrad universitet, Vestnik, 20 (1963), 128-31.

2443
DMITRIEVA, V. N. Zalogi v sovremennom literaturnom koreiskom iazyke [Voice in (the Grammar of) the Modern Korean Literary Language]. Moscow, Moskovskii gosudarstvennyi institut mezhdunarodnykh otnoshenii MID SSSR, 1964. (Candidate of Philological Sciences) xviii, 241p. Text in Russian.

2444
KIM, Soon-Ham Park. A Transformational Analysis of Negation in Korean. Michigan, 1967. 167p. DA 28 (Jan. 1968), 2666-A; UM 67-17,795.

"This study presents a syntactic analysis of negation...in the plain style of present-day standard colloquial Korean...Part 1 of the study presents some of the basic rules required for generating Korean sentences, and part 2 analyzes negatives and negative constructions."

2445
LEE, Maeng Sung. Nominalizations in Korean. Pennsylvania, 1967. 180p. DA 29 (July 1968), 249-A; UM 68-9214.

"Ch.2 analyzes sentences containing the nominalizing sentences as the products of the sentence-operator transformation,...Ch.3 analyzes various nominal phrases with a noun in head position,...and Ch.4 discusses somewhat special transformations which yield nominal or nominal-like forms."

2446
SONG, Seok Choong. Some Transformational Rules in Korean. Indiana, 1967. 254p. DA 28 (Mar. 1968), 3660-A; UM 68-2364.

Focuses on the structures of the Korean noun, phrase and verb phrase, various aspects of negation, the problem of converting statement sentences into question sentences, and on numerals and quantity phrases.

2447
REE, Joe Jungno. Some Aspects of Korean Syntax. Indiana, 1969. 301p. DA 30 (Sept. 1969), 1160-A; UM 69-14,715.

"This study is an attempt to characterize in a formal way the syntactic/semantic natures of Subject- and Topic-makers and to examine in detail various aspects of relativization, i.e., postposition deletion, relative clause reduction, the formal distinction between restrictive and non-restrictive relative clauses, etc."

2448
LEE, Hyun Bok. A Study of Korean Syntax. London, 1969. 344p.

A formal consideration of the syntactical structure of standard Korean, with chapters devoted to phonology, word classes, verb structure, phrasing, clause structure, and sentence formation.

HISTORICAL AND COMPARATIVE STUDIES

2449
CHUNG, Kei Won. The Origins of the Korean Alphabet. Princeton, 1938. 130p. DA 12 (1952), 56 [Abstract not available]; UM 2928.

Contents: The Composition of the Yi-do; The Development of the Korean Alphabet; The Source of the Korean Alphabet; Sanskrit through Buddhism; The Seal Character Theory; The Aramaic-Mongolian Theory; The Theory of Sanskrit Origin; Expansion of the Sanskrit Alphabet; Consultation with Whang Ch'an.

2450
PAK, N. F. Glagoly mnogokratnogo znacheniia v russkom iazyke: Privlechennye ekvivalenty koreiskogo i kazakhskogo iazykov dlia sopostavlenii [Verbs with Multiple Meanings in the Russian Language: With Comparative Equivalents in the Korean and the Kazakh Languages]. Alma-Ata, Ministertsvo vysshego obrazovaniia SSSR, Kazakhskii gosudarstvennyi universitet imeni S. M. Kirova, 1956. (Candidate of Philological Sciences degree) Text in Russian. AB: 16p. summary published in 1956.

2451
KIM, F. Z. Zvukovoi sostav koreiskogo iazyka v XV v. i sozdanie pisma khunmin chonym [The Sound Component of the Korean Language of the Fifteenth Century and the Creation of the Hunmin Chŏng'ŭm Writing]. Moscow, Institut vostokovedeniia Akademii nauk SSSR, 1957. (Candidate of Philological Sciences degree) 223p. Text in Russian.

2452
KIM, Boo-Kyom. Gehört die koreanische Sprache zu den altaischen Sprachen? [Does Korean Belong to the Altaic Language Family?]. München, 1959. Text in German. The dissertation in its published form is available at München, Universitätsbibliothek, Nr. U 1959.6480. Phil. D 2933.

Examines previous theories concerning the relationship of Korean to other languages, studies the characteristics of Korean phonetics, and compares Korean substantives, numerals, pronouns, verbs, and adjectives with their equivalents in other languages.

Rel.Publ.: Gehört...Sprachen? Starnberg/See: W. Schraml, 1959. 109p.; "Das koreanische Zahlensystem," in Koreanica: Festschrift: Professor Dr. Andre Eckardt zum 75. Geburtstag, ed. by August Rickel (Baden-Baden: August Lutzeyer, 1960), 85-94; "Gehört die koreanische Sprache zur altaischen Sprachfamilie?" Koreana Quarterly, 5 (Winter 1963), 97-126, and 6 (Spring 1964), 97-128.

2453
KWON, Hyogmyon. Das koreanische Verbum verglichen mit dem altaischen und japanischen Verbum: Zur Typologie des Koreanischen [The Korean Verb Compared with the Altaic Verb and with the Japanese Verb: A Study of the Typology of the Korean Language]. München, 1963. Text in German. The dissertation in its published form is available at Marburg/Lahn, Staatsbibliothek Preussischer Kulturbesitz, Nr. Hsn 45,233; also at the University of Michigan, General Library, no. 30,702.

Surveys various theories centering on the interrelationship of the Korean, Altaic, and Japanese languages; compares polite forms, the imperative and the optative moods, and the structure of the verb in the three languages; and studies various indicative verb forms and various nouns that are derived from verbs. One portion of the dissertation also seeks to determine the origin of the Korean language.

Rel.Publ.: Das koreanische...Koreanischen. München, 1963. xii, 144p.

2454
LEDYARD, Gari Keith. The Korean Language Reform of 1446: The Origin, Background, and Early History of the Korean Alphabet. California, Berkeley, 1966. 472p. DA 27 (Oct. 1966), 1031-32-A; UM 66-8333.

Contents: Writing in Korea prior to the Invention of the Alphabet; The Cultural Background for the Invention of the Alphabet; The Announcement and Early Progress of the Korean alphabet; The Correct Sounds for the Instruction of the People; Translation of Hunmin Chŏng'ŭm and Hunmin Chŏng'ŭm haerye; Early History of the Korean Alphabet; A New Explanation of the Origin of the Korean Alphabet.

2455
KIM, Cher Len. Analiticheskie formy glagola v nanaiskom i drugikh altaiskikh iazykov v sopostavlenii s koreiskim [Analytical Verb Forms in Nanai and in Other Altaic Languages Compared with Those in Korean]. Novosibirsk, Institut istorii, filologii, filosofii Akademii nauk SSSR (Sibirskoe otdelenie), 1968. (Candidate of Philological Sciences degree) 177p. Text in Russian.

LEXICON

2456
PAK, G. A. Izobrazitel'nye slova v koreiskom iazyke [Figurative Words in the Korean Language]. Leningrad, Leningradskii ordena Lenina gosudarstvennyi universitet imeni A. A. Zhdanova, 1959. (Candidate of Philological Sciences degree) i, 149p. Text in Russian. AB: 15p. summary published in 1958.

PHONOLOGY

2457
KHVAN-IUNDIUN, V. A. Foneticheskii stroi koreiskogo iazyka [The Phonetic Structure of the Korean Language]. Moscow, Ministerstvo vysshego obrazovaniia SSSR, Moskovskii institut vostokovedeniia, 1952. (Candidate of Philological Sciences degree) ii, 164p. Text in Russian. AB: 20p. summary published in 1952.

TSOI, Den-Khun. Foneticheskaia struktura zaimstvovannykh kitaiskikh leksicheskikh elementov v koreiskom i iaponskom iazykakh. 1954. See no.2430.

KIM, F. Z. Zvukovoi sostav koreiskogo iazyka v XV v. i sozdanie pisma khunmin chonym. 1957. See no.2451.

SKALOZUB, L. G. Sopostavitel'noe opisanie soglasnykh sovremennogo russkogo i koreiskogo iazykov. 1957. See no. 2431.

2458
SKALIČKOVÁ, Alena. The Korean Consonants. [Exact title not known.] Universita Karlova, 1958(?) Text in English, with summaries in Czech and Russian.

Rel.Publ.: The Korean Consonants. Praha: Nakladatelstvi Československé akademie věd, 1960. 93p. (Rozpravy Československé akademie věd. Rada společenských věd, roč. 70, Seš. 3)

Law and the Judicial System

2459
KOH, Kwang-lim. The Continental Shelf: An Analytical Study of the Draft Articles on the Continental Shelf Adopted by the International Law Commission. Harvard, 1954. [S.J.D. degree] 508, xiv p.
Includes a discussion of the Syngman Rhee line.
Rel.Publ.: "The Continental Shelf and the International Law Commission," Boston University Law Review, 35 (Nov. 1955), 522-40.

2460
KIM, Chin. Renvoi and Characterization in Korean Conflict of Law. Yale, 1958. 252p.
Contents: Renvoi (Logical Bases of Renvoi, Utilitarian Bases of Renvoi); Characterization (Continental Writers, Anglo-American Writers); Renvoi and Characterization in Korean Perspective (Substance and Procedure, Capacity, Marriage, Succession, Real Rights, Obligations); Conclusions.

2461
RYU, Paul Kichyun. The Korean Culture and Criminal Responsibility: An Application of a Scientific Approach to Law. Yale, 1958. 395p.
Contents: Pt.1: Cultural Pattern and Its Significance: Cultural Pattern (A Brief History, Culture Proper, Influence of Other Cultures, Significance of Korean Culture); Legal Significance of Korean Culture (The Ways and Means of Social Control, Cultural Meaning of Criminal Responsibility, Positive Law of Criminal Responsibility). Pt.2: Criminal Responsibility in a "Free Society": Definition of "Free Society"; Criminal Responsibility in a "Free Society" (Introduction, Brief Historical Survey of the Concepts of Guilt and Punishment, Writer's Suggestions). The 89p. appendix contains a translation of the Korean Criminal Code of 1953.

2462
TSCHE, Chong Kil. Die Scheidung im koreanischen materiellen und internationalen Privatrecht [Divorce According to Korean Substantial and International Private Law]. Köln, 1961. Text in German. The dissertation in its published form is available at Marburg/Lahn, Staatsbibliothek Preussischer Kulturbesitz, Nr. Hsn 28,419; also at the University of Michigan, General Library, no. 24,596.
A brief survey of the historical sources of Korean family and inheritance laws and the codification of the new Korean civil code is followed by a study of the historical development of divorce in Korea from early times to 1910, from 1910 to 1923 (when Japanese law was first applied to the matter of divorce), and since 1923. The author also examines the matter of divorce according to Korean international private law, and he translates into German the most important legal norms of Korean law.
Rel.Publ.: Die Scheidung...Privatrecht. Köln: Robert Pulm, 1961. v, 137p.

2463
CHO, Keu-cab. Problems Arising from the Legal Doctrines and Practices of the Korean Marital Law. Yale, 1963. 255p.
Contents: Goal of the Marital Law; Historical Sketch of the Korean Marital Law; Promise of Marriage: The Legal Doctrines and Practices; Formation of Marriage: The Legal Doctrines and Practices; The Effect of Marriage: The Legal Doctrines and Practices; Divorces: The Legal Doctrines and Practices; Evaluation and Recommendations.

LEE, Samuel S.-o. The Effects of Inflation and Legal Remedies on Accounting in Korea Since 1945. 1964. See no.2100.

2464
TSCHE, Kiuon. Die Verfassung der Aktiengesellschaft nach koreanischem Recht im Vergleich mit dem deutschen Aktiengesetz [The Charter of Joint-Stock Companies According to Korean Law and Compared with German Corporation Law]. Bonn, 1965. Text in German. The dissertation in its published form is available at Marburg/Lahn, Staatsbibliothek Preussischer Kulturbesitz, Nr. Hsn 61,361; also at the University of Michigan, General Library, no. 31,990.
After presenting an historical overview of German legislation concerning joint stock companies, 1897-1937, and a brief survey of Korean commercial law, the author examines the charters of joint stock companies first according to German law and then according to Korean law. In his analysis he focuses upon and compares the functions of the head of the company, the supervisory board, and the general membership.
Rel.Publ.: Die Verfassung...Aktiengesetz. Bonn, 1965. vi, 89p.

CHAI, Nam-Yearl. Asian Attitudes toward International Law: A Case Study of Korea. 1967. See no.2421.

Literature

See also History--early to 935 A.D. (pages 262-63) and History--918-1392 (pages 263-64).

2465
PAK, Ten Sik. Sovremennaia koreiskaia literatura posle osvobozhdeniia: Formirovanie i stanovlenie sotsialisticheskogo realizma v koreiskoi literature po tvorchestvu Li Gi Ena [Contemporary Korean Literature after the Liberation: The Inception and the Crystallization of Socialist Realism in Korean Literature as Seen in the Work of Yi Ki-yŏng]. Moscow, Moskovskii ordena Lenina gosudarstvennyi universitet imeni M. V. Lomonosova, 1953. (Candidate of Philological Sciences degree) i, 265p. Text in Russian. AB: 16p. summary published in 1953.

2466
TEN, A. N. Ocherki sovremennoi koreiskoi literatury: Demokraticheskie natsionalnye traditsii i sotsialisticheskii realizm v koreiskoi literature [Essays on Modern Korean Literature: Democratic National Traditions and Socialist Realism in Korean Literature]. Leningrad, Leningradskii gosudarstvennyi pedagogicheskii institut imeni A. I. Gertsena, 1954. (Candidate of Philological Sciences) vii, 512p. Text in Russian. AB: 23p. summary published in 1954.

2467
TSOI, E. M. Otrazhenie velikikh peremen v koreiskoi derevne v romanakh Li Gi Ena [Great Changes in Korean Villages as Reflected in the Novels of Yi Ki-yŏng]. Moscow, Moskovskii ordena Lenina i ordena Trudovogo Krasnogo Znameni gosudarstvennyi universitet imeni M. V. Lomonosova, Filologicheski fakultet, 1955. (Candidate of Philological Sciences degree) i, 241p. Text in Russian. AB: 16p. summary published in 1955.

2468
EREMENKO, Loengrin Efimovich. Zhizn' i tvorchestvo vydaiushchegosia koreiskogo pisatelia Pak Chi Vona (1737-1805) [The Life and Works of the Outstanding Korean Author Pak Chi-wŏn (1737-1805)]. Moscow, Institut vostokovedeniia Akademii nauk SSSR, 1959. (Candidate of Philological Sciences degree) ix, 254p. Text in Russian.

2469
LEE, Peter H. Studien zum Saenaennorae: Altkoreanische Dichtung: Ein Beitrag zur Wertung der japanischen Studium über altkoreanische Dictung [Studies of the Saenaennorae: Early Korean Poetry: A Contribution to the Evaluation of Japanese Studies of Early Korean Poetry]. München, 1958. Text in German. The dissertation in its published form is available at Marburg/Lahn, Universitätsbibliothek, Nr. Z 59.1154.

Studies the development of early Korean poetry (the earliest Korean poems, the Tonnorae and the poetry of the Three Kingdoms, and the Saenaennorae) from an historical, linguistic, and literary viewpoint. Compares various Japanese and Korean interpretations of early Korean poetry through an examination of the ideas of Ogura Shinpei and Yang Chu-dong. Also provides a critically annotated translation of the Saenaennorae.

Rel.Publ.: Studien...Dichtung. München, 1958, 163p.; Studies in the Saenaennorae: Old Korean Poetry. Roma: Istituto italiano per il Medio ed Estremo Oriente, 1959. 212p. (Serie orientale Roma, 22); Introduction to the Saenaennorae: Old Korean Poetry," East and West, 8 (Apr. 1957), 29-42.

2470
IVANOVA, Viktorina Ivanovna. Tvorcheskii put' Li Gi Ena [The Creative Career of Yi Ki-yŏng]. Moscow, Institut vostokovedeniia Akademii nauk SSSR, 1960. (Candidate of Philological Sciences degree) 365p. Text in Russian.

Rel.Publ.: Li Gi En: Zhizn' i tvorchestvo. Moscow: Izd. vostochnoi literatury, 1962. 103p. (Institut narodov Azii, Akademiia nauk SSSR); "Li Gi En: Odin iz osnovopolozhnikov sovremennoi koreiskoi literatury," in International Congress of Orientalists, 25th, Moscow, 1960, Trudy XXV Mezhdunarodnogo Kongressa Vostokovedov (Moscow: Izd-vo vostochnoi literatury, 1963), v.5, 280-85.

2471
HOYT, James. Korean Literature: The Rise of the Vernacular, 1443-1592. California, Berkeley, 1962. 263p.

Discusses the historical development of veracular literature following the invention of the Korean script in 1443 and analyses the thematic nature of this literature.

2472
NIKITINA, M. I. Koreiskaia srednevekovaia poeziia v zhanrakh Sichto i Chan-Sichto [Medieval Korean Poetry: The Genre of Sijo and Ch'angsijo]. Leningrad, Leningradskii gosudarstvennyi universitet imeni A. A. Zhdanova, 1962. (Candidate of Philological Sciences degree) vi, 258p. Text in Russian.

2473
TROTSEVICH, A. F. Istoriia o vernosti Chkhun Khian i

zhanr povesti v koreiskoi srednevekovoi literature [The History of the Loyalty of Ch'unhyang and the Genre of the Novel in Medieval Korean Literature]. Leningrad, Leningradskii gosudarstvennyi universitet imeni A. A. Zhdanova, 1962. (Candidate of Philological Sciences degree) vii, 252p. Text in Russian.

Rel.Publ.: "Ideal cheloveka v koreiskoi srednevekovoi povesti," in Akademiia nauk SSSR, Institut narodov Azii, Kratkie soobshcheniia, 63 (1963), 93-100.

2474
HAN, Ponghum. Schillers Räuber und Hŏ Gyuns Hong Kil-Tong: Vergleichende Untersuchung zur Literatur zweier Kulturkreise [Schiller's Räuber and Ho Kyun's Hong Kil-Tong: A Comparative Study of the Literature of Two Cultural Spheres]. Berlin, Freie Universität, 1963. Text in German. The dissertation in its published form is available at Marburg/Lahn, Staatsbibliothek Preussischer Kulturbesitz, Nr. Hsn 43,887; also at the University of Michigan, General Library, no.29,349.

Compares two dramatic works by J. C. F. von Schiller (1759-1805) and Ho Kyun (1569-1618) respectively. The dissertation studies the historical background and the origins of these two works; their motifs, figures of speech and ideas; the realism in the works; the principles underlying the structure of the compositions; and the grammatical expressions employed within them.

Rel.Publ.: Schillers...Kulturkreise. Berlin: Ernst Reuter, 1963. 161p.

2475
RENTNER, Reta. Studien zur mittelalterlichen Koreanischen Verskunst: "ko. rjo. ka. jo." [Studies of the Medieval Korean Versification "ko. rjo. ka. jo."]. Berlin, Humboldt Universität, 1966. 247p. Text in German.

A genre of ballads of the Koryŏ dynasty.

2476
ELISEEV, D. D. Koreiskaia srednevekovaia literatura pkhesol: Nekotorye problemy proiskhozhdeniia i zhanra [The Korean Literature "Pkhesol" of the Middle Ages: Some Problems of Origins and of Genre]. Leningrad, Institut narodov Azii Akademii nauk SSSR (Leningradskoe otdelenie), 1967. (Candidate of Philological Sciences degree) 258p. Text in Russian. AB: 18p. summary published in 1966.

Rel.Publ.: Koreiskaia...zhanra. Moscow: "Nauka," 1968. 136p.; "O kharaktere literary pkhesol'," Narody Azii i Afriki, 1 (1966), 116-20.

2477
PUCEK, Vladimír. Čchŏ So-hä: představitel literárního hnutí Nový směr. Život a dílo. [Ch'oe So-hae: The Representative Figure of the "New Trends" Literary Movement: His Life and His Work]. Universita Karlova, 1967/68. 151p. Text in Czech.

Presents a general literary-historical account of the subject. Discusses Ch'oe So-hae's participation in Korean literary activities after 1920 and presents a translation of his short story "T' alch' ulgi" ["A Record of the Escape"].

Rel.Publ.: "Hnutie Novýsmer v kórejskej literatúre," in Čchŏ So-hä, tr. by Vladimír Pucek (Bratislava, 1962), 219-31.

2478
LI, V. Koreiskaia proletarskaia literatura: Proza 20-kh - 30-kh gg. [Korean Proletarian Literature: Prose of the 1920's and 1930's]. Moscow, Institut mirovoi literatury imeni A. M. Gorkogo Akademii nauk SSSR, 1968. (Candidate of Philological Sciences degree) 250p. Text in Russian. AB: 16p. summary published in 1967.

Mass Media: Radio, Television, and the Press

2479
KIM, Heun-chun. Die Aufmachung der modernen Zeitung in Ostasien: Japan, China, und Korea [The Make-up of the Modern Newspaper in East Asia: Japan, China and Korea]. Leipzig, 1928. Text in German. The dissertation in its published form is available at Marburg/Lahn, Universitätsbibliothek, Nr. VII C.

Focuses on the historical development of the daily press in East Asia and on the make-up and various parts of the daily newspapers (especially the parts featuring politics, trade, advertisements, local news, and feuilletons). The author also critically compares the press in East Asia with that in Europe, and his appendix contains statistical information on the development and the present-day position of the press in Japan, Korea, and China.

Rel.Publ.: Die Aufmachung...Korea. Leipzig: Twietmeyer, 1928. 61p.

2480
BAK, Yoo Bong. Die Struktur des modernen Pressewesens in Süd-Korea [The Structure of the Modern Press in South Korea]. München, 1960. Text in German. The dissertation in its published form is available at Marburg/Lahn, Universitätsbibliothek, Nr. Z61/3184; also at the University of Michigan, General Library, no.25,563.

A short survey of the press during the Yi dynasty and since 1945 is followed by an examination of the influence of political, economic, and cultural factors upon the Korean press. National and local newspapers are then studied with regard to their lead articles and to the political, economic, and cultural information that they contain, and the development and variety of Korean magazines also are discussed.

Rel.Publ.: Die Struktur...Süd-Korea. München, 1960. 128p.

2481
MOHR, Philip Joe. The Radio and Television Listening Habits and Program Preferences of Eighth U.S. Army Personnel in Korea, Autumn, 1959. Ohio State, 1960. 415p. DA 21 (Apr. 1961), 3193-94; UM 61-932.

A survey and analysis.

CHANG, Yong. Development of Korean Journalism Education Based on American Practices. 1967. See no.2200.

2482
HAN, Kiuk. An Analysis of Government Administration of Communication Media in the Republic of Korea. New York, 1967. 211p. DA 28 (May 1968), 4691-92-A; UM 68-6070.

"An empirical, behavioral study of government control of the mass communication media in the Republic of Korea from 1945 to 1966."

Rel.Publ.: "Influence of Traditional Factors on Effectiveness of Mass Communications in Korea," Korea Journal, 8 (Feb. 1968), 18-25.

Music and the Theatrical Arts

2483
CHUNG, Yung-Ok (Won-ji). Wesen und Werdegang des Koreanischen Maskenspieles: Sandai-keuk, Bongsan-T'al-Ch'um, und O-Kwandai [The Nature and the Development of Korean Folk Mask Plays]. Wien, 1964. 225p. Text in German. Diss. ms. available at the Universitätsbibliothek der Universität Wien, Nr. D 15,707.

A survey of Korean popular drama focusing on the folk mask plays and a detailed exposition of individual aspects of theatrical representation in these plays.

2484
KIM, Jin-Gyun. Musikethnologische Studien über das koreanische Volkslied [An Ethnological Study of the Korean Folksong]. Wien, 1964. 228p. + 29 musical examples. Text in German. Diss ms. available at the Universitätsbibliothek der Universität Wien, Nr. D 12,911.

General remarks on the study of folksongs and an examination of the characteristics of Korean folksongs (e.g. Arirang).

Overseas Korean Communities

2485
MITCHELL, Richard Hanks. The Korean Minority in Japan, 1910-1963. Wisconsin, 1963. 265p. DA 24 (Oct. 1963), 1597-98; UM 63-7655.

"Traces the historical development of this minority and analyzes the various problems that arose between the Korean immigrants and the Japanese." Contents: Relations between Korea and Japan until 1910; The Growth of Korean Nationalism, 1910-1919; The Origins of the Korean Minority Problem, 1920-1930; Communism and Nationalism among Koreans in Japan; The Effect of Japan's War Efforts on the Korean Migrants; The Nonassimilable Koreans; The Korean Minority in Occupied Japan, 1945-1952; The Korean Minority in "New Japan," 1952-1960; Recent Developments, 1960-1963.

Rel.Publ.: The Korean...1963. Berkeley: University of California Press, 1967. 186p.

BURROUGHS, Franklin T. Foreign Students at U.C.L.A.: A Case-Study in Cross-Cultural Education. 1964. See no.2199.

2486
CHUNG, In Teak. The Korean Minority in Manchuria (1900-1937). American, 1966. 213p. DA 28 (Aug. 1967), 584-A; UM 66-13,586.

Studies "the general problems of the Korean minority in Manchuria with particular emphasis on the Korean Communist movements up to 1937."

KIM, Hyung Tae. Relationships between Personal Characteristics of Korean Students in Pennsylvania and Their Attitudes toward the Christian Churches in America. 1966. See no.2537.

SUGIMOTO, Roy Atsuro. The Relationship of Selected Predictive Variables to Foreign Student Achievement at the University of California, Los Angeles. 1967. See no.2201.

Political Science

(Limited primarily to domestic politics during the postwar era)

GENERAL

2487
DEN, Din Tkhai. Sushchnost gosudarstvennoi vlasti Koreiskoi Narodno-Demokraticheskoi Respubliki [The Essence of State Power in the Korean People's Democratic Republic]. Leningrad, Leningradskii gosudarstvennyi universitet imeni A. A. Zhdanova, 1951. (Candidate of Legal Sciences) 352p. Text in Russian.

2488
KIM, Vladimir Aleksandrovich. Gosudarstvennyi stroi Koreiskoi Narodno-Demokraticheskoi Respubliki [The State Structure of the Korean People's Democratic Republic]. Moscow, Institut prava Akademii nauk SSSR, 1952. (Candidate of Legal Sciences) 489p. Text in Russian.

Rel.Publ.: Gosudarstvennyi...Respubliki. Moscow: Gosiurizdat, 1955. 203p.

2489
LI, Tai Din. Narodnye komitety Koreiskoi Narodno-Demokraticheskoi Respubliki [The People's Committees of the Korean People's Democratic Republic]. Moscow, Moskovskii ordena Lenina gosudarstvennyi universitet imeni M. V. Lomonosova, 1952. (Candidate of Legal Sciences degree) Text in Russian. AB: 15p. summary published in 1952.

2490
BAIANOV, Boris Pavlovich. Obshchestvennoe ustroistvo Koreiskoi Narodno-Demokraticheskoi Respubliki [The Social Organization of the Korean People's Democratic Republic]. Moscow, Institut prava Akademii nauk SSSR, 1957. (Candidate of Legal Sciences degree) vii, 360p. Text in Russian.

Rel.Publ.: Narodnaia Koreia na puti k sotsializmu. Moscow: Gospolitizdat, 1959. 144p.

2491
OH, John Kie-chiang. Western Democracy in a Newly Emerging Eastern State: A Case Study of Korea. Georgetown, 1963. 455p.

Contents: Pt.1: Democracy and Traditional, Colonial Korea: The Nature of Democracy; Legacies of the Korean Dynasties; The Impact of Early Foreign Relations; Imprints of the Colonial Rule. Pt.2: Democracy in Republican Korea: National Liberation and Democracy; Birth of the Republic of Korea; Democracy in the First Republic; Caesaristic Rule and the Student Uprising; Democracy in the Second Republic.

Rel.Publ.: Korea: Democracy on Trial. Ithaca: Cornell University Press, 1968. xiv, 240p.; "Role of the United States in South Korea's Democratization," Pacific Affairs, 42 (Summer 1969), 164-77.

2492
PARK, Sung-Jo. Eine Untersuchung der Übertragbarkeit des parlamentarischen oder des präsidentellen Regierungssystem auf ein Entwicklungsland: Unter besonderer Berücksichtigung der koreanischen Staatsentwicklung seit 1945 [A Study of the Transferability of the Parliamentary or Presidential System of Government to a Developing Country: With Special Consideration of the Development of the Korean Government since 1945]. Berlin, Freie Universität, 1963. Text in German. The dissertation in its published form is available at Marburg/Lahn, Staatsbibliothek Preussischer Kulturbesitz, Nr. Hsn 41,308; also at the University of Michigan, General Library, no.28,774.

Studies the problems of transplanting a Western-style constitution into a non-Western environment as illustrated in the case of Korea. Pt.1 defines the concepts "Western democracy," "parliamentary system," and "presidential system" and points out the basic characteristics of developing lands and of Korea in particular. Pt.2 studies Korea's adoption of a Western-style constitution (1948) and Korean constitutional history 1948-1962. Pt.3 analyzes the consequences of adopting either a parliamentary or presidential system of government.

Rel.Publ.: Eine Untersuchung...1945. Berlin: Ernst Reuter, 1963. 113p.

2493
YUN, Kun-shik. Die politische Entwicklung Südkoreas und ihr Hintergrund [The Political Development of South Korea and Its Background]. Göttingen, 1965. Text in German. The dissertation in its published form is available at Marburg/Lahn, Staatsbibliothek Preussischer Kulturbesitz, Nr. Hsn 62,047.

Studies the social background and origins of the Korean constitution and the political development of South Korea prior to 1962. Also surveys the changes in the structure of Korean agriculture and examines the Korean family system and the development of a democratic life style within the country.

Rel.Publ.: Die politische...Hintergrund. Göttingen, 1965. 181p.; "Die Verfassungsentwicklung der Republik Korea seit 1948," Jahrbuch des öffentlichen Rechts, NF Bd. 12 (1963), 461-91.

ELLO, Paul S. The Commissar and the Peasant: A Comparative Analysis of Land Reform and Collectivization in North Korea and North Vietnam. 1967. See no.2123.

2494
LEE, Young Ho. The Political Culture of Modernizing Society: Political Attitudes and Democracy in Korea. Yale, 1969. 291p. DA 30 (Feb. 1970); UM 70-2760.

A study of the political culture of Korea based on personal interviews with respondents selected through a random sample. Three techniques are used: cross-national analysis; cross-sectional analysis--to illustrate the differences among Korean social groups; and multivariate cross-sectional analysis--to illustrate the separate importance of selected social variables in relation to political orientations.

CIVIL BUREAUCRACY AND PUBLIC ADMINISTRATION

2495
NAM, In Kho. Voprosy planirovaniia narodnogo khoziaistva v Koreiskoi Narodno-Demokraticheskoi Respublike (do Otechestvennoi osvoboditel'noi voiny) [Planning the National Economy in the Korean People's Democratic Republic (prior to the Patriotic Liberation War)]. Moscow, Moskovskii gosudarstvennyi ekonomicheskii institut, 1951. (Candidate of Economic Sciences degree) xvii, 427p. Text in Russian.

2496
IM, Khe. Planirovanie narodnogo khoziaistva v Koreiskoi Narodno-Demokraticheskoi Respublike [Planning the National Economy in the Korean People's Democratic Republic]. Moscow, Institut Ekonomiki Akademii nauk SSSR, 1955. (Candidate of Economic Sciences degree) ii, 298p. Text in Russian. AB: 15p. summary published in 1955.

2497
OH, Chung Hwan. The Civil Service of the Republic of Korea. New York, 1961. 352p. DA 27 (Dec. 1966), 1901-02-A; UM 66-9730.

"A study of the efforts of the Korean Government to establish a civil service system--a merit system based on competitive examinations--in the public service." Contents: Korea: The Ecology of Public Administration; Political Authority: Decision-Making Institutions; Public Administration: Organization of the Administrative Agencies; The Nature of the Civil Service; The Selection Process: Appointment and Examination; Classification and Compensation; Changes of Status; Conditions of Work and Employee Relations; Training; Organization for Personnel Management; Conclusions: Problems and Proposed Remedies.

2498
BARK, Dong Suh. Public Personnel Administration in Korea: A Mixed Heritage in Contemporary Practice. Minnesota, 1962. 469p. DA 23 (Apr. 1963), 3959-60; UM 63-2306.

Analyzes and criticizes the system of public personnel administration operating in Korea prior to the military revolution of May 1961 and proposes two steps to bring about a reform of the Korean civil service: (1) "the modification of the old, pre-modern social values," and (2) "the planning of basic changes in the formal personnel system." Contents: Pt.1: Introduction. Pt.2: Historical Background of Korean Public Personnel Administration. Pt.3: The Present System of Korean Public Personnel Administration: Legal Basis for Public Personnel Administration; Classification of the Civil Service; The Problem of Compensation and Ethics; Recruitment, Examination, and Placement; Staff Development; Employee Unions.

Rel.Publ.: Han'guk kwallyo chedo ŭi yŏksajŏk chŏn'gae. Seoul: Han'guk Yŏn'gu Tosŏgwan, 1961. v, 243p.; "Han'guk haengjŏng hyŏnsang ŭi t'uksusŏng," Haengjŏng kwalli, 1 (Dec. 1962), 8-11; "Han'guk kogŭp kongmuwŏn ŭi munjejŏm," Haengjŏng kwalli, 2 (July 1963), 136-45 [Translated and Published as "Korean Higher Civil Servants: Their Social Background and Morale," in (1) Some Problems in Public Administration in Developing Countries (Honolulu: East-West Center, 1966), 1-21. (Institute of Advanced Projects, East-West Center: Occasional Papers of Research Translations, Translation Series, 13), and in (2) Aspects of Administrative Development in South Korea, ed. by Byung Chul Koh (Kalamazoo, Michigan: The Korea Research and Publication, Inc. 1967), 9-29. (Monograph Series on Korea, 4)]; "Chŏngmugwan kwa haengjŏnggwan ŭi kwan'gye," Haengjŏng nonch'ong, 2 (1964), 55-67; "Insa paech'i ŭi chae kŏmt'o," Haenjŏng nonch'ong, 3 (1965), 82-98; "Imyong chedo ŭi chae kŏmto," Kamsa wŏlbo, 3 (Dec. 1965), 9-15; "Kŭndaehwa wa kwallyo ŭi yŏkhwal," Chŏnggyŏng yŏn'gu, 7 (Aug. 1965), 27-36; Bibliography of Korean Public Administration, September 1945-April 1966 [by] Dong Suh Bark and Jai Poong Yoon. Seoul: United States Operations Missions to Korea, 1966. 174p.; "Ch'oegŭn ŭi insa haengjŏng kaejŏng panghyang," Kosigye, 107 (Jan. 1966), 118-22; "Han'guk haengjŏnghak ŭi hyonhang kwa yokhwal," Sabop haengjŏng, 7 (Aug. 1966), 18-23 [Translated and published as "The Status and Role of Korean Public Administration," in Aspects of Administrative Development in South Korea (as above), 1-8]; "An Ecological Analysis of Korean Administration," Koreana Quarterly, 9 (Winter 1967), 55-73.

RO, Chung-Hyun. A Comparative Study of Manpower Administration in Developing Countries: With Special Reference to South and North Korea. 1962. See no.2097.

2499
WOO, Philip Myungsup. The Historical Development of Korean Tariff and Customs Administration, 1875-1958. New York, 1963. 292p. DA 27 (June 1967), 4321-A; UM 64-1792.

The author concludes that "the tariff process pursued by the Korean government is a linear one," i.e., that its formulation, enactment, and execution "are administered by the customs service without implicit consent of the interested public." Contents: The Royal Korean Maritime Customs: Initial Period (1876-1883); The Royal Korean Maritime Customs: European Era (1883-1905); The Japanese Era, I: The Korean Customs in the Period of a Vanished Kingdom (1905-1909); The Japanese Era, II: The Korean Customs (1910-1945); The Japanese Tariff System; Customs: Administration, Postwar Period; Tariff Making Power: Legal Framework of the Customs Institution; Summary Conclusion.

2500
CHO, Suk Choon. Administrative Decentralization in the Government of the Republic of Korea. Minnesota, 1965. 479p. DA 26 (Mar. 1966), 5537; UM 65-15,247.

Contents: Hierarchical Control of Local Governments and Intra-Organizational Distribution of Formal Decision-Making Authorities; The Korean Forces behind Centralization; The Needs in Korea for Administrative Decentralization; Case Studies of Administrative Decentralization in the Korean Government.

Rel.Publ.: "Han'guk haengjŏng kwalli ŭi panghyang," Haengjŏng kwalli, 1 (Nov. 1962), 10-14; "Simnijŏk kaltŭng kwa haengjŏng chidoja," Haengjŏng nonch'ong, 1 (1962), 53-68; "Haengjŏng kaehyŏk kwa chŏhang ŭi munje," Haengjŏng kwalli, 2 (June 1963), 2-7; "Han'guk haengjŏng kwa chojik kwalli ŭi munjejŏm," Haengjŏng kwalli, 2 (Aug. 1963), 21-26; "Che-Sam Konghwaguk kwa haengjŏng kaehyŏk ŭi panghyang," Sin segye, 3 (Feb. 1964), 178-86; "Han'guk esŏui haengjŏngjŏk punkwŏnhwa ŭi p'iryosŏng e kwanhan yŏn'gu," Haengjŏng nonch'ong, 2 (1964), 68-103; "Administrative Decentralization: A Case Study in the South Korean Military Government," Haengjŏng nonch'ong, 4 (1966), 21-39 [Also published in Aspects of Administrative Development in South Korea, ed. by Byung Chul Koh (Kalamazoo, Michigan: The Korea Research and Publication, Inc., 1967), 65-83 (Monograph Series on Korea, 4)].

HAN, Kiuk. An Analysis of Government Administration of Communication Media in the Republic of Korea. 1967 See no.2482.

CHO, Chang-hyun. The System of Local Government in South Korea as Affected by Patterns of Centralized Control. 1968. See no.2514.

2501
WHANG, In-Joung. Elites and Economic Programs: A Study of Changing Leadership for Economic Development in Korea, 1955-1967. Pittsburgh, 1968. 216p. DA 30 (Feb. 1970); UM 69-17,710.

Seeks to determine the manner and the extent to which political change, bureaucratic transformation, and economic development were interrelated in the case of Korea's modernization process during the late 1950's and particularly during the 1960's.

Rel.Publ.: "Elite Change and Program Change in the Korean Government, 1955-1967," Korean Journal of Public Administration, 7 (Apr. 1969), 235-66.

2502
YOO, Jong Hae. National Planning for Development: The Case of Korea. Michigan, 1968. 240p. DA 30 (July 1969), 379-A; UM 69-12,279.

An account of national economic planning in South Korea, 1953-1966. Ch.1 "provides a survey of development planning and of the general situation of the Korean economy and political system up to the present time...Ch.2 treats in chronological order the series of national development plans elaborated in Korea since the early 1950's. It deals specifically with the early efforts at planning by foreign agents, the Three Year Plan of the First Republic, the Draft Five Year Economic Plan of the Second Republic, and the First Five Year Economic Plan of the military government and the Third Republic." Ch.3-5 focus on the substance and process, the administration, and the political aspects of planning. "The final chapter...evaluates the political significance of development planning in Korea."

2503
OH, Suck Hong. A Separate Monitoring Agency in the Administrative Control System: A Study of the Board of Audit and Inspection of the Government of the Republic of Korea. Pittsburgh, 1969. 350p. DA 30 (May 1970); UM 70-5286. [See also addenda entry no.50A.]

CIVILIAN/MILITARY LEADERSHIP, POLITICAL PARTIES, AND ELECTIONS

2504
VINOCOUR, Seymour Murray. Syngman Rhee: Spokesman for Korea (June 23, 1951-October 8, 1952): A Case Study in International Speaking. Pennsylvania State, 1953. xii, 462p. AB: Pennsylvania State University. Abstracts of Doctoral Dissertations. v.16, p.620.

Contents: Background; Rhee's International Speech Methodology: (1) Personal, (2) Delegated; Case Studies of Several Major International Speeches; Rhee's Positions on Major Issues (Re-unification and the Cease-Fire Negotiations, Expansion of ROK Armed Forces, The Pacific Pact); Diplomatic Speaking during the Korean-Japanese Negotiations; The Domestic Political Controversy.

2505
KOH, Kwang Il. In Quest of National Unity and Power: Political Ideas and Practices of Syngman Rhee. Rutgers, 1963. 283p. DA 24 (Sept. 1963), 1231; UM 63-5888.

The author seeks to determine (1) how and why Rhee was inconsistent in his efforts to achieve Korean national unity and unification, (2) the reasons for the conflicting attitudes of various writers towards Rhee, (3) the manner in which Rhee embodied American political theories, and (4) the probable causes for the failure of the Korean presidential system under Syngman Rhee's Presidency.

2506
CHOI, Ki-whan. Das Wahlrecht der Republik Korea in seinen politischen Auswirkungen [The Right to Vote in the Republic of Korea and Its Political Consequences]. Bonn, 1965. Text in German. The dissertation in its published form is available at Bochum, Universitätsbibliothek, Nr. UA 7131; also at the University of Michigan, General Library, no.36,172.

Following a survey of Confucian political thought and of prewar traditional society in Korea, the author studies Korea's postwar modernization, the efforts that were made to prepare a democratic constitution, and the recent changes in the political character of the Korean people. He then explains the influence that the postwar division of the country had upon Korea's political development, presents an historical explanation of political organization in Korea (from the period of Japanese rule to the establishment of the Third Republic), and analyzes both voting rights and voting experiences in South Korea after 1948.

Rel.Publ.: Das Wahlrecht...Auswirkungen, Bonn, 1965. xvi, 153p.

2507
JO, Young Soo. Le Parti libéral coréen [The Korean Liberal Party]. Grenoble, 1965. 280p. Text in French.

2508
CHUNG, Ha Ryong. Les Partis politiques sud-coréens sous le régime de Syngman Rhee [South Korean Political Parties during the Regime of Syngman Rhee]. Paris, 1966. 415p.

2509
HAN, Yung Chul. Traditionalism and the Struggle for Political Modernization in Contemporary Korea: With Special Reference to the Development of Political Parties. New York, 1966. 277p. DA 27 (June 1967), 4311-12-A; UM 67-6026.

"An attempt to explain the causes for the failure of political modernization in South Korea primarily in terms of her traditionalism and traditional leadership by analyzing contemporary party politics."

2510
KIM, Se Jin. Military Revolution in Korea, 1961-1963. Massachusetts, 1966. 345p. DA 28 (Aug. 1967), 741-A; UM 66-10,507.

"Analyzes the socio-economic and political causes of the military revolution in 1961; discusses the civil-military relationship with reference to the conflict of interests between the civilian and military elites; delves into the intra-military structure and the background of the leading military figures...; and examines the impact of the military upon the politics of democratic nation-building in Korea."

2511
KIM, Joungwon Alexander. A Comparative Study of the Role of a Leader in Political Development: Syngman Rhee in South Korea and Kim Il-Song in North Korea. Johns Hopkins, 1968.

2512
LIM, Sang Un. An Analysis of Electoral Behavior in South Korea. Syracuse, 1968. 328p. DA 29 (Dec. 1968), 1934-A; UM 68-13,844.

A study of electoral dynamics and the development of party politics, 1948-1960. Contents: Conceptual Orientation and Analytical Scheme; General Background Materials; Development of Contemporary Parties and Their Politics; Constitutional Structure; Electoral System; Party Development; Candidate Personal Attributes; Political System; Ecological Factors.

LOCAL GOVERNMENT

2513
KANG, Pyung Kun. The Role of Local Government in Community Development in Korea. Minnesota, 1966. 428p. DA 28 (Feb. 1968), 3236-37-A; UM 68-1177.

Includes "an analysis of the structure and power allocation of local governments;" "a survey of the image of local self-government, local service, and community solidarity, as perceived by the citizens and public servants;" and "a comparative study of the urban and rural community."

Rel.Publ.: "Administrative Structure and Management in Regional Development: Case of Korea," _Koreana Quarterly_, 10 (Summer 1968), 121-32.

2514
CHO, Chang-hyun. The System of Local Government in South Korea as Affected by Patterns of Centralized Control. George Washington, 1968. 369p. DA 29 (Nov. 1968), 1588-A; UM 68-14,590.

Contents: Pt.1: Introduction and Description of Local Government: Historical Retrospects; Local Government and the Constitution; Hierarchy of Local Government; Nature of Local Government Functions. Pt.2: Analysis of Central Control Patterns: Institutions of Control: Administrative Law Ordinance; Local Personnel; Local Finance; The Police. Pt.3: Patterns of Local Government Control and Their Determinants: A Summary: Patterns of Centralized Control--Urban versus Rural; Factors Affecting Centralization Patterns.

Religion and Philosophy

BUDDHISM, CONFUCIANISM, AND OTHER NON-CHRISTIAN MOVEMENTS

YUN, Sŏng-sun. The Influences of Confucianism and Christianity upon Korean Education. 1932. See no. 2167.

2515
YOUN, Eul-sou (Abbé Laurent). Le Confucianisme en Corée [Confucianism in Korea]. Paris, 1939. Text in French.

Studies from an historical and politico-social viewpoint the manner in which Confucianism was received by the Koreans and the manner in which it became the basis of their ideology and of their political and social actions. Contents: Philosophical Systems in Korea before the Advent of Confucianism; Introduction of Confucianism into Korea; Development of Neo-Confucianism in Korea; Opposition of Confucianism and of Buddhism; Triumph of Confucianism and Its Influence.

Rel.Publ.: Le Confucianisme...Corée. Paris: P. Téqui, 1939. x, 198, xx p.

2516
KHVAN, Ben In. Tvorcheskoe primenenie marksizma-leninizma tovarishchem Kim Ir Senom v bor'be koreiskogo naroda za edinoe demokraticheskoe nezavisimoe gosudarstvo [Comrade Kim Il-sung's Creative Utilization of Marxism-Leninism in the Struggle of the Korean People for a Unified, Democratic, Independent State]. Moscow, Moskovskii ordena Lenina gosudarstvennyi universitet imeni M. V. Lomonosova, Filosofskii fakultet, 1953. (Candidate of Philosophical Sciences degree) Text in Russian. AB: 12p. summary published in 1953.

2517
PAI, Paul. Les Croyances populaires en Corée [Popular Beliefs in Korea]. Lyon, 1956. 139p. Text in French.

2518
CHUNG, David Tae-wi. Religious Syncretism in Korean Society. Yale, 1959. 306p. DA 30 (Feb. 1970); UM 70-1756.

An historical case study of the religious aspects of those cultural contacts that Korean society had with the outside world (including the West). The author focuses on the process by which Korean society was able to accommodate and to assimilate Confucianism, Taoism, Buddhism, and Christianity; and he concludes that the popular beliefs of Korean society contained elements very congenial to Christian doctrines.

Rel.Publ.: "The Problem of Analogy between Christianity and Confucianism, Koreana Quarterly, 1 (Winter 1959), 115-30.

KOH, Hesung C. Religion, Social Structure, and Economic Development in Yi Dynasty Korea. 1959. See no.2079.

2519
CHOI, Min-hong. Der Einfluss der konfuzianischen Ethik in Korea [The Influence of the Confucian Ethic in Korea]. München, 1961. Text in German. The dissertation in its published form is available at Marburg/Lahn, Staatsbibliothek Preussischer Kulturbesitz, Nr. Hsn 27,635; also at the University of Michigan, General Library, no.25,516.

The study begins with the period of Shamanistic worship in Korea and with the introduction of Confucianism and Buddhism during the period of the Three Kingdoms. It then surveys the Silla and Koryŏ periods, when Buddhist thought predominated, and the Yi dynasty period, when Confucian ideas won a firm hold among the educated classes in Korea. The dissertation concludes with an analysis of the positive and negative influences of Confucianism in Korean history, particularly upon the Korean language, education, and legal thought.

Rel.Publ.: Der Einfluss...Korea. Starnberg/See: W. Schraml, 1960. 83p.

2520
KIM, Yong Choon. The Concept of Man in Ch'ŏndogyo. Temple, 1969. vii, 280p.

A study of Ch'ŏndogyo, a modern, mass religion in Korea whose adherents number over half a million. The major portion of the work deals with the origin and the nature of man, ethics, and eschatology. The Ch'ŏndogyo affirmation of man's essential divinity, of the necessity for treating one's fellowman as God, and of the establishment of the Kingdom of Heaven upon earth are analyzed. The monistic, humanistic, and syncretistic aspects of Ch'ŏndogyo also are evaluated.

2521
SEO, Kyung Bo. A Study of Korean Zen Buddhism Approached through the Chodangjip. Temple, 1969. 429p. DA 30 (Dec. 1969), 2611-A; UM 69-16,815.

Contents: Pt.1: The History or Legend of Zen in India and China, according to the Chodangjip: Zen in India; Zen in China from Bodhidharma to Hui-neng; Zen in China after Hui-neng; The Korean Zen Masters Recorded in the Chodangjip. Pt.2: The Nine Zen Schools of Silla: Hŭiyangsan School; Kajisan School; Tongnisan School; Silsangsan School; Pongnimsan School; Sagulsan School; Sŏngjusan School; Sajasan School; Sumisan School. Pt.3: The Teachings of Master Sunji (Silla

Dynasty). Pt.4: Developments in Korean Zen Subsequent to Silla: Koryŏ Dynasty; Yi Dynasty.

SESSIONS, Eldred S. An Analysis of the Contribution of the Educational Establishment to the Emergence of Korean National Identity: A Case Study of the Role of Education in Formulating a National Ethic in a Developing Country. 1969. See no.2179.

CHRISTIANITY IN KOREA

See also Religion and Philosophy--Buddhism, Confucianism, and other non-Christian Movements (pages 295-96).

2522
PAIK, Lark-June George. The History of Protestant Missions in Korea, 1832-1910. Yale, 1927. 491p. DA 30 (Aug. 1969), 640-41-A; UM 69-12,579.

"An examination has been made of the nature of the Christianity that was propagated; the religious background of the countries from which the faith was introduced; the political, commercial, and other movements connected with the missionary enterprise; the effect of Protestant Christianity upon the people; and the extent of the alteration of Christianity by its environment." Contents: Early Contact with Korea; The Opening of Korea, 1876-1884; The Establishment of Missions, 1885-1890; Occupation of the Field, 1891-1897; The Rise of the Church, 1897-1906; The Revival and the Growth of the Church.

Rel.Publ.: The History...1910. Pyongyang, Korea: Union Christian College Press, 1929. ix, 438, xiii p.

2523
CLARK, Charles Allen. The National Presbyterian Church of Korea as a Test of the Validity of the Nevius Principles of Missionary Method. Chicago, 1929. 366, ix p. AB: University of Chicago. Abstracts of Theses, Humanistic Series, v.7 (1928/29), p.647-52.

A study of the missionary methods suggested by Dr. John L. Nevius in 1886 and implemented by Presbyterian missionaries to Korea in 1890 and thereafter.

Rel.Publ.: Korea and the Nevius Methods. New York: Fleming H. Revell, 1930. 278p.

2524
WASSON, Alfred Washington. Factors in the Growth of the Church in Korea. Chicago, 1931. 229p.

"The History of the Southern Methodist Church Mission in Korea." Contents: Planting the Mission: 1896-1905 (Missionary Factors, Environmental Factors); Five Years of Rapid Growth: 1906-1910 (Activities within the Missionary Enterprise, Contemporaneous Events and Conditions, Current Moving toward the Church); Nine Lean Years: 1911-1919 (Actions of the Government Affecting Missions, The Reactions of the People); Second Period of Rapid Growth: 1920-1924 (The Independence Movement, Government Reforms, The Centenary Advance); Second Period of Arrested Growth: 1925-1928 (Economic Conditions, The World of the Young People, The Church and Society); An Upward Trend: 1929- (The Church Adopts a New Technique, Rural Work, The New Korean Methodist Church).

Rel.Publ.: Church Growth in Korea. Concord, N.H.: Rumford Press, 1934. xii, 175p. (Studies in the World Mission of Christianity, 1)

2525
CHYUNG, Yil Hyung. A Study of Successful Rural Churches and Organizations in America and an Adaption to Korea. Drew, 1935. 267p.

Contents: Pt.1: A Study of Successful American Rural Churches. Pt.2: Research in Literature. Pt.3: The Conditions and Needs in the Korean Rural Church (Korea and Christianity, The Korean Church as It Is). Pt.4: Adaptation of the Factors of Success in American Rural Churches to the Korean Churches.

BASS, Harold J. The Policy of the American State Department toward Missionaries in the Far East. 1937. See no.2240.

2526
STOKES, Charles Davis. History of Methodist Missions in Korea, 1885-1930. Yale, 1947. 421p. DA 25 (Dec. 1964), 3721; UM 64-11,888.

Contents: First Things (1884-1888); Reaching Outward (1889-1895); Open Doors (1896-1905); Revival Years (1906-1910); Advance through Difficulties (1911-1919); Autonomy Achieved (1920-1930).

2527
KAY, Il Seung. Christianity in Korea. Union Theological Seminary in Virginia, 1950. 379p.

Contents: Initial Contacts with the Outside World and with Christianity; Planting the Mission (Founding of the Presbyterian Mission, Founding of the Methodist Episcopal Mission, Medical Work, Education, Orphanage, Initial Missionary Methods, Evangelistic Work, Literary Work, Translation of the Bible); Settlement of the Field (New Societies, The First Council, Comity and Co-operation, City Evangelistic Work, Methods of Work); Korea's Response to Christianity; The Korean Presbyterian Church; The Growth of the Church; Korean Christians; Days of Darkness; After the Storm.

2528
CHUN, Sung-chun. Schism and Unity in the Protestant Churches of Korea. Yale, 1955. 214p.

An historical study of the unifying factors and of the various schisms. Contents: Land and the People: Background for Schism and Unity; Beginning of the Protestant Missions: Harmony and Unity; The Growth of the Missions and Churches; Broadening Churchmanship; The Church Grows among Thorns; Dogmatism and Depression: Two Major Causes of Schism; War and Persecution; Freedom and Unity.

2529
LIEROP, Peter van. The Development of Schools under the Korea Mission of the Presbyterian Church in the U.S.A., 1919-1950. Pittsburgh, 1955. 276p. DA 16 (Jan. 1956), 170; UM 15,109.

Contents: Period of Renewal under the New Reform Movement of Education, 1919-1924; Period of Mission Schools in the Maelstrom of the New Educational Reforms; Period of Determination to Secure Designation from the Government, 1925-1933; Period of High Standing in Higher Education, 1923-1933; Period of Decline under the Imperial Decrees to Pay Homage to the Shinto Shrines, 1933-1945; Period of Reconstruction under the United Nations and the Republic of Korea, 1945-1950.

Rel.Publ.: "The Place of Christian Schools in Korea: Past and Present," in Korean Research Center, Seoul, Seminar Series 1 (1962), 48-63.

2530
PARK, Tae Sun. Prolegomena to a Korean Translation of the Book of Isaiah. Boston, 1956. 253p. DA 16 (Jan.

1956), 169-70; UM 15,339.
Discusses the present Korean-language edition of the Old Testament, illustrating its inadequacies through a critical examination of the Book of Isaiah and pointing out the need for a new translation of the entire text.

2531
Yun, Sung Bum. Der Protestantismus in Korea, 1930-1955 [Protestantism in Korea, 1930-1955]. Basel, 1956. Text in German.
Concerned with the difficulties of the Korean Christian church in regard to the Shinto religion during the 1930's, with the Japanese attempt to compel Korean Christians to revere Shinto in 1938, and with the Church's amazing prosperity during and after the Korean War.

2532
PARK, Pong Nang. Karl Barth's Doctrine of Inspiration of the Holy Scriptures with Special Reference to the Evangelical Churches in Korea. Harvard, 1959. v, 319p.
Contents: Inspiration as a Problem in the Evangelical Church in Korea; The Criterion for Barth's Doctrine of Inspiration; Barth's Criticism of the Three Major Doctrines of Inspiration in the History of the Church; Barth's Positive View of Inspiration; Inspiration and Word; Inspiration and the Work of the Holy Spirit; The Evaluation of the Theological Positions of the Evangelical Churches of Korea with Regard to the Doctrine of Inspiration; Barth's Doctrine of Inspiration with Reference to the Evangelical Churches of Korea.

CHOI, Andreas. L'Érection du premier vicariat apostolique et les origines du catholicisme en Corée 1592-1837. 1961 See no.2237.

2533
LEE, Reverend Gabriel Gab-Soo. Sociology of Conversion: Sociological Implications of Religious Conversion to Christianity in Korea. Fordham, 1961. 308p. DA 22 (Oct. 1961), 1290-91; UM 61-1572.
The dissertation is based on a study of three conversion movements to Christianity in Korean history: (1) an early Catholic conversion movement, 1784-1884, (2) the conversion movement to Protestanism, 1884-1935, (3) the Catholic and Protestant movements, 1945-1960.

2534
BROWN, George Thompson. A History of the Korea Mission, Presbyterian Church, U.S., from 1892 to 1962. Union Theological Seminary in Virginia, 1963. 767p.
Contents: The Hermit Nation prior to 1892; The Founding of the Mission (1891-1895); The First Three Stations; The Great Advance (1905-1910); Against the Tide (1910-1919); The Tide Turns (1920-1931); Advance through Storm (1931-1941); Liberation (1945-1950); The Communist War (1950-1953); New Frontiers (1954-1962).

2535
KIM, Changyup Daniel. Seventy-Eight Years of the Protestant Chruch in Korea. Dallas Theological Seminary, 1963. xvii, 330p.
Contents: The Background in Korea; Planting the Missions (1884-1900); Period of Rapid Growth (1901-1912); Period of Development (1913-1934); Period of Persecution (1935-1945); Rehabilitation and Controversies (1945-1962).

CHUNG, Chai S. Protestantism and the Formation of Modern Korea 1884-1894. 1964. See no.2275.

PALMER, Spencer J. Protestant Christianity in China and Korea: The Problem of Identification with Tradition. 1964. See no.2242.

2536
KO, Hyun Bong. A Historical Study of the Characteristics of the Christian Church in Korea. Dallas Theological Seminary, 1965. xx, 523p.
The table of contents of the dissertation describes the church as being characterized by "the nature of the country, specific persecutions and sufferings, evangelical and fundamental faith, her own mission works, amazing national reforms, intense conflicts and schisms, and by God's providence revealed in the division of Korea."

2537
KIM, Hyung Tae. Relationships between Personal Characteristics of Korean Students in Pennsylvania and Their Attitudes toward the Christian Churches in America. Pittsburgh, 1966. 172p. DA 27 (Feb. 1967), 2415-16-A; UM 66-13,486.
"The problem of this study consisted of four elements: (1) to identify the attitudes of Korean students in Pennsylvania toward the Christian churches as reflected in responses to questions concerning the roles and functions of these churches with respect to American culture; (2) to identify their attitudes toward selected moral and spiritual values; (3) to determine the relationships of selected personal and background factors to their attitudes in both of these areas; and (4) to determine whether there is a relationship between their attitudes toward the churches and their attitudes toward the selected moral and spiritual values."

2538
WEBER, Hans-Ruedi. Asia and the Ecumenical Movement: 1895-1961. Genève, 1966.
A descriptive study of the manner in which Asian Christians and churches have been drawn into the ecumenical movement. Concentrates on Japan, China, and Korea.
Rel.Publ.: Asia...1961. London: S.C.M. Press, 1966. 319p.

2539
WEI, Si Wang Luke. The Juridical Norms Regarding the Conversion of Non-Christians, especially of the Chinese in Korea. Pontifical Urban University, Rome, 1966/67.

2540
CUMMINGS, Malcolm Stanley. A Manual of Personal Evangelism for Korean Christians. Bob Jones, 1967. 241p.
Contents: Personal Evangelism: Its Scriptural Basis; Requirements for Success; Its Basic Method; The Approach; Opportunities; Suggestions for Tract Distribution; Dealing with the Unconcerned and Procrastinators; Dealing with Those Who Offer Sincere Excuses; Dealing with Those Who Believe in Heathen Religions; Dealing with Those Who Believe in False Cults; Summary, Conclusions, and Recommendations.

2541
RO, Bong Rin. Division and Reunion in the Presbyterian Church in Korea, 1959-1968. Concordia Seminary, 1968.

Science, Medicine, and Technology

MEDICINE AND PUBLIC HEALTH

2542
LI, Den Iur. Sostoianie zdoroviia naseleniia i deiatelnost' organov zdravo-okhraneniia KNDR do i posle osvobozhdeniia [The State of Public Health and the Activity of Public Health Organs in the Korean People's Democratic Republic before and after the Liberation]. Moscow, 1-i Moskovskii ordena Lenina meditsinskii institut imeni I. M. Sechenova, 1960. (Candidate of Medical Sciences) Text in Russian. AB: 24p. summary published in 1960.

2543
BRAUN, Wilfried. Über Inhaltsstoffe der weissen koreanischen Ginsengdroge [The Ingredients of the White Korean Genseng Drug]. Bonn, 1963. v, 66p. Diss. ms. available at Bonn, Universitätsbibliothek, Nr. U 4° 63/234.

The author discusses the preparation of ginseng drug extracts, conducts a chromatographic investigation of these extracts and of the chemical substances that are isolated, and describes the procedures that he follows. His chief objective is to isolate crystalline substances from Radix Ginseng.

2544
KIM, Joung Soon. The Epidemiology and Mass Chamotherapy of Paragonimiasis on Che Ju Island. Johns Hopkins, 1967. 122p.

NATURAL SCIENCES

See also Geography (page 261).

2545
SCHRÖTER, Walter. Korea und die Riasverwandten Küsten dieser Halbinsel [The Coasts of the Korean Peninsula and Their Relation to the Lias Period (a subdivision of the Jurassic period)]. Leipzig, 1903. The dissertation in its published form is available at Marburg/Lahn, Universitätsbibliothek, Nr. VI C.

The coastal formation of Korea is presented by means of a tabular survey of measurements pertaining to the peninsula's eastern, southern, and western coasts. Conclusions on the overall development of these coasts are drawn from a study of the geological formations along the eastern coast. A comparison is made between Korea's coasts and similarly formed coasts elsewhere.

Rel.Publ.: Korea...Halbinsel. Leipzig: Metzger & Wittig, 1904. 66, i p.

2546
STEWARD, Albert Newton. The Polygoneae of Eastern Asia. Harvard, 1930. Diss. ms. not available. AB: Harvard University. Summaries of Theses...1930. p.24-25.

An identification as well as a descriptive and contrastive study of the genera Tovara, Koenigia, and Polygonum found in parts of eastern Asia including Korea.

Rel.Publ.: The Polygoneae...Asia. Cambridge: Gray Herbarium of Harvard University, 1930. lxxxviii, 129p. (Contributions from the Gray Herbarium of Harvard University)

2547
WALKER, Egbert Hamilton. A Revision of the Eastern Asiatic Myrsinaceae. Johns Hopkins, 1940.

Korea is included within the scope of coverage.

2548
PAN, Chung-hsiang. The Geology and Metallogenetic Provinces of Eastern Asia. Minnesota, 1947. 298p. + 10 plates.

A study of orogenic movements and igneous activities of Eastern Asia, including Korea, and metallic deposits and metallogenetic provinces.

2549
CHUNG, In-Cho. Manual of the Grasses of Korea. Michigan, 1955. 384p. DA 15 (Sept. 1955), 1483-84; UM 12,554.

Presents "full descriptions, with clear-cut keys to all categories, of all known grasses of Korea, both South and North." Contents: Gramineae; Artificial Key to Genera; Subfamily 1--Panicoideae (Maydeae Andropogoneae, Paniceae, Arundinelleae); Subfamily 2--Pooideae (Zizanieae, Oryzeae, Zoysieae, Stipeae, Agrostideae, Phalarideae, Aveneae, Festuceae, Chlorideae, Hordeae, Bambuseae); Distribution of the Grasses in Korea; The Nearest Systematic and Geographic Relationships of Endemic Species; Classification of the Grasses by Habitats; List of New Names and Combinations.

Rel.Publ.: Korean Grasses. Chicago, 1965.

2550
TSOI, Ik Son. Rezhim pogody nad Koree pri osnovnykh formakh atmosfernoi tsirkuliatsii [The Weather System over Korea and Basic forms of Atmospheric Circulation]. Leningrad, Leningradskii gidrometeoreologicheskii institut, 1957. (Candidate of Geographical Sciences degree) 264p. Text in Russian. AB: 13p. summary published in 1957.

2551
ARNAUD, Paul Henri, Jr. The Heleid Genus Culicoides

in Japan, Korea, and Ryukyu Islands (Insecta: Diptera). Stanford, 1961. 126p. DA 23 (July 1962), 358; UM 62-286.

A "study of the speciation and distribution of the biting midge genus Culicoides" in the area."

2552
MURDOCH, Wallace Pierce. The Female Tabanidae of Japan, Korea, and Manchuria. Utah, 1962. 437p. DA 24 (July 1963), 448; UM 63-1385.

Includes a discussion of their "life history, economic and medical importance, control, morphology, classification, evolution and geologic history, and distribution."

2553
PAEK, Kab-Yong. The Comparative Studies of the Myriapods Fauna of Main Land and Oulpart Island Korea. [sic] Kyungpook Dae Hak Kyo, 1964.

2554
HONG, Wonshic. The Phytogeographical Relationships of the Leafy Hepaticae of South Korea with a Special Consideration of Their Occurrence in North America. Cincinnati, 1965. 202p.

Contents: History of Hepaticae Studies in South Korea; Comparative Geography of South Korea and of North America; Climate and Vegation of South Korean and of North America; The List of South Korean Hepatics with Notes on Their Occurrence (Herbertaceae, Ptilidiaceae, Blepharostomaceae, Trichocoleaceae, Lepidoziaceae, Calypogeiaceae, Cephaloziaceae, Cephaloziellaceae, Lophocoleaceae, Lophoziaceae, Jungermanniaceae, Marsupellaceae, Plagiochilaceae, Scapaniaceae, Porellaceae, Radulaceae, Frullaniaceae, Lejeuneaceae); Discussion of the Geographical Elements of the Leary Hepatics of South Korea; Relationships of the Flora.

2555
PAEK, Un-ha. Aphids of Korea. Seoul Dae Hak Kyo, 1966.

2556
KANG, Che-won. On the Geographical Distribution of Marine [Life?] in Korea. Seoul Dae Hak Kyo, 1967.

TECHNOLOGY

2557
SON, De Gym. Osnovnye printsipy organizatsii zheleznodorozhnogo stroitel'stva v gornykh usloviiakh Korei s uchetom vozomozhnosti elektrifikatsii zheleznykh dorog [Basic Principles for Organizing Railway Construction in the Mountainous Terrain of Korea Taking into Account the Possibilities of Railway Electrification]. Leningrad, Leningradskii ordena Lenina institut inzhenerov zheleznodorozhnogo transporta imeni akad. V. N. Obraztosova, 1953. (Candidate of Technological Sciences degree) Text in Russian. AB: 18p. summary published in 1953.

2558
KHAN, Son Khyb. Izuchenie i analiz opyta dorog SSSR po povysheniiu iznosostoikosti bandazhei kolesynkh par paravozov s tseliiu primeneniia ego na zheleznykh dorogakh Korei [A Study and an Analysis of the Experience of Soviet Railways in Increasing the Wear Resistance of Bands on Locomotive Wheel Couplings and Its Practical Application in the Korean Railway System]. Moscow, Ministerstvo putei soobshchenii SSSR, Moskovskii ordena Lenina i ordena Trudovogo Krasnogo Znameni institut inzhenerov zheleznodorozhnogo transporta imeni I. V. Stalina, 1955. (Candidate of Technological Sciences) Text in Russian. AB: 12p. summary published in 1955.

2559
LI, Ben Don. Nekotorye voprosy elektricheskikh sistem Koreiskoi Narodno-Demokraticheskoi Respubliki: Balans reaktivnoi moshchnosti v sisteme, rabota transformatorov i asinkhronnykh dvigatelei pri izmeneniiakh napriazheniia i chastoty [Some Questions Concerning the Electrical Systems in the Korean People's Democratic Republic: Balance of the Reactive Power in the System; The Work of Transformers and Asynchronous Motors in Connection with Changes in Tension and Frequency]. Moscow, Ministerstvo vysshego obrazovaniia SSSR, Moskovskii ordena Lenina energeticheskii institut imeni V. M. Molotova, 1955. (Candidate of Technological Sciences degree) Text in Russian. AB: 16p. summary published in 1955.

2560
LI, Dia U. Issledovanie elektroprivoda pod"emnykh mashin s asinkhronnym dvigatelem, primenitel'no k skipovomu pod"emu po naklonnym shakhtam v Koree [Research on the Electric Transmission of Lifting Machines with Asynchronous Motors with Respect to Skip-Winding in Inclined Shafts in Korea]. Moscow, Ministerstvo vysshego obrazovaniia, Moskovskii gornyi institut imeni I. V. Stalina, 1955. (Candidate of Technological Sciences) Text in Russian. 15p. summary published in 1955.

2561
TEN, Diai Ren. Osnovnye printsipy blagoustroistva ulits pri vosstanovlenii i rekonstruktsii gorodov KNDR: Po opytu gradostroitelstva v SSSR [Fundamental Principles for Improving City Streets in the KPDR when Restoring and Rebuilding the Cities of that Country: Principles Based on Soviet Experience]. Moscow, Ministerstvo vysshego obrazovaniia SSSR, Moskovskii ordena Trudovogo Krasnogo Znameni inzhenernogo stroitel'stva institut imeni V. V. Kuibysheva, 1955. (Candidate of Technological Sciences degree) Text in Russian. AB: 14p. summary published in 1955.

2562
LI, En Gon. Issledovanie putei razvitiia gorodskogo massovogo passazhirskogo transporta v SSSR dlia primeneniia v praktike gradostroitel'stva v KNDR [Research on the Means of Developing Mass Urban Passenger Transportation in the USSR for Practical Application in City Construction in the KPDR]. Moscow, Moskovskii inzhenerno-stroitel'nyi institut imeni V. V. Kuibysheva, 1956. (Candidate of Technological Sciences degree) 292p. Text in Russian.

Addenda

Information on the following dissertations was received too late to be included in the main body of the bibliography.

JAPAN

1A
ABE, Masatoshi Aloysius. Dynamic Microeconomic Models of Production, Investment, and Technological Change of the U.S. and Japanese Iron and Steel Industries. Wisconsin, 1970. 297p. DA 31 (July 1970); UM 70-8254.
Contents: Introduction; Process Analysis of the U.S. and Japanese Iron and Steel Industries (General Description of Iron and Steelmaking Technology, The Technology Matrix, The Comparison of U.S. and Japanese Technology); Short Run Model of Production Activities and Resource Allocation; Sales Forecast and Production Planning; Investment Activities and Constraints; Simulation Model; Recursive Programming; Conclusions.

2A
ABE, Motoo. A Monetary Model of the Japanese Economy. Pennsylvania, 1969. 443p. DA 30 (June 1970); UM 70-7769.

3A
AKAMATSU, Alfred Saburo. The Function and Type of Program of a Japanese Minority Church in New York City: A Program for the Establishment of the Japanese-American Church of Christ in New York. Columbia (Teachers College), 1948. 268p. AB: Religious Education, 45 (Mar./Apr. 1950), 101-02.
The dissertation seeks to determine the basic policies of the Japanese minority church in New York City and to formulate a program for the church. The American patterns of meeting minority problems, therefore, are reviewed in the light of the treatment of Japanese immigrants to this country.

4A
AZUMI, Koya [addendum to entry no.225].
Rel.Publ.: The Recruitment...Japan. New York: Columbia University, Teachers College Press, 1969.

5A
BANDURA, Iu. N. [addendum to entry no.277].
Rel.Publ.: "Monopol'nye ob"edineniia vo vneshnei torgovle Iaponii, Vneshniaia torgovlia, 7 (1967), 40-41.

6A
BUCKLEY, Edmund. Phallicism in Japan. Chicago, 1895.
Contents: Phallicism in Japan (Temples, Symbols, Festivals, Rituals, Phallicism in the Kojiki); Creed of Phallicism; Place of Phallicism in the Evolution of Religion; Does Phallicism Belong to Shinto?
Rel.Publ.: Phallicism...Japan. Chicago: University of Chicago Press, 1895. 34p.

7A
BUCKLEY, Thomas Hugh. The United States and the Washington Conference, 1921-1922. Indiana, 1961. 321p. DA 22 (Nov. 1961), 1595-96; UM 61-4425.
"Concentrates on the American delegation at the conference and attempts to present a documented description of the negotiations it participated in." Contents: Toward the Washington Conference; Origins: 1921; Preliminaries; Opening the Conference; The Five Power Treaty; The Four Power Treaty; China; The Senate and the Treaties.

8A
CHANG, Richard T. [addendum to entry no.531].
Rel.Publ.: From Prejudice to Tolerance: A Study of the Japanese Image of the West, 1826-1864. Tokyo: Sophia University Press, 1970. xvi, 208p. (Monumenta Nipponica Monograph Series)

9A
CHIANG, Wen-hsien [addendum to entry no.1064].
DA 30 (Dec. 1969), 2591-A; UM 69-21,334.
The dissertation studies General Dohihara's activities in China from 1931 to 1936--particularly his role in the Nakamura Incident, the Mukden Incident, the abduction of Henry P'u-yi, and the North China Autonomy Scheme--and analyzes his attitudes, motives, and ideas during this period. It also considers the judgment of the International Military Tribunal for the Far East regarding Dohihara's responsibility for those events.

10A
DINKEVICH, A. I. [addendum to entry no.340].
Rel.Publ.: "Gosudarstvennye zaimy v poslevoennoi Iaponii," in Institut narodov Azii, Akademiia nauk SSSR, Kratkie soobshcheniia, 79 (1964), 161-75.

11A
DINKEVICH, Anatolii I. [addendum to entry no. 677].
Rel.Publ.: Voennye finansy Iaponii, 1937-1945. Moscow: Izd-vo Vostochnoi literatury, 1958. 114p. (Akademiia nauk SSSR, Institut Vostokovedeniia)

12A
FEENSTRA KUIPER, Jan. Japan en de buitenwereld in de achttiende eeuw [Japan and the Outside World during the Eighteenth Century]. Leiden, 1921. Text in Dutch.
A detailed description of the trade relations between the Netherlands and Japan in the eighteenth century. Also contains considerable information about the development of Dutch learning (rangaku).
Rel.Publ.: Japan...eeuw. 's-Gravenhage: Martinus Nijhoff, 1921. xxiv, 330p.

13A
FRITZE, Adolf. Die Fauna der Liu-Kiu-Insel Okinawa [The Fauna of Okinawa]. Freiburg i.B., 1894. (Habilitationsschrift) Text in German. The dissertation in its published form is available at Freiburg, Bibliothek der Universität, Nr. V 5654.
The author studies the animals of Okinawa, paying particular attention to their habitat, features, and frequency of appearance, and comparing them with the fauna of Japan and of Taiwan. He determines on the one hand that there are close resemblances between the birds and insects found on Okinawa with those in Japan, and he points out on the other that the presence of reptiles on Okinawa indicates that there were early links between the island and Taiwan.
Rel.Publ.: Die Fauna...Okinawa. Jena: G. Fischer, 1894. 77p.; "Die Fauna von Yezo im Vergleich zur Fauna des übrigen Japans," MOAG, Bd 5, 46. Heft (1891), 235-48.

14A
GAMAZKOV, K. A. [addendum to entry no.670].
Rel.Publ.: "'Iuibutsuron kenkiu': Tribuna marksizma-leninizma v Iaponii," Narody Azii i Afriki, 5 (1965), 165-70.

15A
HORIBA, Yutaka. An Input-Output Study of International and Interregional Trade. Purdue, 1969. 205p. DA 30 (May 1970); UM 70-8905.
This study in economic theory proposes a general model of international trade which incorporates two economies characterized by open input-output systems. The Heckscher-Ohlin theorem of trade is used as a model and four regions in Japan--Kinki, Hokkaido, Shikoku, and Tohoku--are selected for observations. For each of the six possible combinations of these regions, the pattern of trade is observed on a bilateral basis, incorporating regionally different production structures so as to study the relationship between the observed trade pattern and the technology.

16A
IATSENKO, B. P. [addendum to entry no.467].
Rel.Publ.: "Sotsial'no-ekonomicheskie usloviia razvitiia promyshlennosti severnykh rainov Iaponii," in Leningrad universitet, Vestnik, 24 (1966), 83-89.

17A
INOUE, Shunichi. Urbanization and Work Force Concentration in Japan. Pennsylvania, 1969. 219p. DA 30 (Dec. 1969), 2637-A; UM 69-21,373.
"The thesis investigates the pattern and intensity of concentration of population and work force in cities in relation to socio-economic development in Japan.... Major attention is focused on development during the intercensal period from 1960 to 1965."

18A
IOFAN, N. A. [addendum to entry no.594].
Rel.Publ.: "Krest'ianskoe dvizhenie posle revoliutsii 1868 g.: Polozhenie Krest'ianstva v period, predshestvovavshii revoliutsii," in Akademiia nauk SSSR, Institut Vostokovedeniia, Uchenye zapiski, 15 (1956), 115-56.

19A
JAQUET, Louis G. M. [addendum to entry no.1188].
Describes the factors (government support, social factors, commercial "dumping") that promoted Japanese industrialization during the 1920's and early 1930's, deals with Japan's trade relations with the Dutch East Indies (1913-1933), and warns against the danger of the Indies becoming too economically dependent upon Japan.
Rel.Publ.: De industrialisatie...Nederlandsch-Indië. Rotterdam: "De Schrijfkamer," 1935. 104p.

20A
KERST, Georg [addendum to entry no.836].
Rel.Publ.: Die Anfänge...Zeitung. Hamburg: Übersee-Verlag, 1953. 174p. (Übersee-Schriftenreihe, H.2)

21A
KIM, Chang Soon. Shinkyoism. Baptist Theological Seminary, 1939.

22A
KIM, Myung Whan [addendum to entry no.1589].
Contents: Introduction; A Vision and Rikurin Ichiro: Two Myths of the Great Wheels; The Vision of the Spiritual World in Yeat's Plays and the Noh; The Place of Symbolism in Yeat's and the Noh; Stasis in Yeats and Yugen in the Noh: The End of Dance and Rhythm.

23A
KUO, Chung-ying. British Trade in China, 1894-1914. Wisconsin, 1947. iii, 289p. AB: University of Wisconsin. Summaries of Doctoral Dissertations. v. 10, p. 310-12.
A discussion of contemporary Anglo-Japanese relations with particular reference to China is included.

24A
LEBRA, Takie Sugiyama. An Interpretation of Religious Conversion: A Millennial Movement among Japanese-Americans in Hawaii. Pittsburgh, 1967. 461p. DA 28 (Sept. 1967), 1134-35-A; UM 67-11,391.
"Research was conducted on a millennial, charismatic sect, the Dancing Religion, in Hawaii predominantly composed of Americans of Japanese ancestry. While the general problem of transculturation among Japanese-Americans underlies the thesis, the central focus of analysis is the individual actor as organizer of his action components....Analysis of the pre-conversion state, the process of conversion, and the post-conversion state constitutes the major part of the thesis."

25A
LEVIN, Maksim G. [addendum to entry no.25A].
Rel.Publ.: Ethnic Origins of the Peoples of Northeastern Asia. Ed. by Henry N. Michael. Toronto: University of Toronto Press, 1963. xii, 355p. (Anthropology of the North: Translations from Russian Sources, 3)

26A
LIDIN, Olof G. [addendum to entry no.1963].
Rel.Publ.: Distinguishing the Way: Ogyū Sorai's Bendō. Tokyo: Sophia University Press, 1970. xiv, 138p. (Monumenta Nipponica Monograph Series)

27A
LINK, Howard Anthony. A Theory on the Identity of Torii Kiyomasu I. Pittsburgh, 1969. 336p. DA 30 (Mar. 1970); UM 70-4534.

Studies the origin and emergence during the late Genroku period of a Torii style of art which "established a standard in the representation of Kabuki subject matter and which was to prove so persuasive that dozens of later artists borrowed the formula." Also investigates the styles and works of Torii Kiyomasu I and of Torii Kiyonobu in order to determine their relationship to one another. Contents: The Torii Enigma; The Art of the Early Torii Masters; The Documentary Evidence. Appendix A catalogues the signed and unsigned books and single-sheets attributed to these men.

28A
MACNAB, John W. [addendum to entry no.193].
The entire second section of the thesis (p. 104-217) is devoted to a consideration of the historical and modern methods of cultivation, describing Kitaki Island in relation to significant historical and social changes in Japan proper, with special consideration being given to this sort of comparative analysis in a 20 page index.

29A
MADDOX, Robert J. [addendum to entry no.1392].
Rel.Publ.: William E. Borah and American Foreign Policy. Baton Rouge: Louisiana State University Press, 1969.

30A
MARKAR'IAN, S. B. [addendum to entry no.185].
REl.Publ.: "Kreditnaia deiatel'nost' sel'skokhoziaistvennykh kooperativov v poslevoennoi Iaponskoi derevne," in Institut narodov Azii, Akademiia nauk SSSR, Kratkie soobshcheniia, 50 (1962), 77-95; "Nekotorye dannye o sel'skokhoziaistvennykh kooperativakh v poslevoennoi iaponskoi derevne," Narody Azii i Afriki, 1 (1962), 59-67.

31A
MODELL, John [addendum to entry no.1774].
Contents: Foundations of the Japanese-American Community; The Maturation of the Japanese Economy; Japanese Community Organization; The White Opposition; Defending the Caste Line: Residential Segregation; The Nisei Dilemma: Schools and Jobs; The Nisei Dilemma: Defining a Generation; The Nisei Dilemma: Ethnic or Class Solidarity (A Case Study); Buildup to War; Relocation and Its Aftermath; Epilogue.

32A
NIEUWENHUIS, Jan E. [addendum to entry no.252].
The dissertation presents a statistical survey of Japanese trade expansion and shipping, 1900-1932, and discusses the impact that Japan's industrialization had upon her overseas trade.

33A
OCHI, Dojun. The Study of the Japanese Religions in America from the Ethical and Socio-Cultural Standpoint. Tōyō, 1963. Diss. ms. available at the National Diet Library, Tokyo.

34A
OUWEHAND, Cornelius. Namazu-e and Their Themes: An Interpretative Approach to Some Aspects of Japanese Folk Religion. leiden, 1964.

A study of the religious meaning of namazu-e ("catfish pictures") based primarily upon an examination of 88 different namazu woodblock colorprints found in the collection of the National Museum of Ethnology in Leiden. Pt.1 of the dissertation surveys the namazu-e repertoire and examines the social context of the prints and the elements of the earthquake legend. Pt.2 analyzes several basic themes in Japanese folk religion. Pt.3 deals with the concepts of theme, symbol, and structure and with the earthquake as a crisis event.

Rel.Publ.: Namazu-e...Religion. Leiden: E. J. Brill, 1964. xvi, 273p.

35A
PIGULEVSKAIA, Evgeniia A. [addendum to entry no.345].
Rel.Publ.: Obnovlenie osnovnogo kapitala iaponskoi promyshlennosti i razvitie poslevoennogo tsikla. Moscow: Izd-vo Akademii nauk SSSR, 1960. 255p. (Akademiia nauk SSSR, Institut Mirovoi Ekonomiki i Mezhdunarodnykh Otnoshenii)

36A
PODPALOVA, Galina I. [addendum to entry no.510].
Rel.Publ.: "Characteristic Features of the Peasant Movement in the XVIIth Century Japan," in International Congress of Orientalists, 25th, Moscow, 1960, Trudy XXV Mezhdunarodnogo Kongressa Vostokovedov (Moscow: Izd-vo vostochnoi literatury, 1963), v.5, 377-82.

37A
POZDNIAKOV, I. G. [addendum to entry no.501].
Rel.Publ.: "O nekotorykh osobennostiakh kewar'ianskikh vosstanii v Iaponii v XV-XVI vv.," in Institut narodov Azii, Akademiia nauk SSSR, Kratkie soobshcheniia, 50 (1962), 35-49; "Progressivnia iaponskaia istoriografiia o kharaktere feodalizma v Iaponii," Narody Azii i Afriki, 3 (1962), 167-77.

38A
RUST, William Charles. The Shin Sect of Buddhism in America: Its Antecedents, Beliefs, and Present Condition. Southern California, 1951. 405p. AB: University of Southern California. Abstracts of Dissertations for...1951. p.217.

A study of the sect's organizational existence in the United States, ca. 1900-1950.

39A
SAMSI SASTRAWIDAGDA [addendum to entry no.248].
After surveying the commercial treaties concluded during the years 1858-1869, 1894-1900, and 1911-1912, and the treaty revisions negotiated during the Meiji period, the author describes the development of Japanese trade policy between 1858 and 1924.

40A
SCHEINER, Irwin [addendum to entry no.608].
Rel.Publ.: Christian Converts and Social Power in Meiji Japan. Berkeley: University of California Press, 1970. (Publications of the Center for Japanese and Korean Studies)

41A
SPENCER, Robert Francis. Japanese Buddhism in the United States, 1940-1946: A Study in Acculturation. California, Berkeley, 1946. 251p.

Discusses the ties of Japanese immigrants to Buddhism during the prewar period and the impact of World War II on these ties and on the process of acculturation in Japanese Buddhism within the United States.

42A
THUNG, Soey-hay [addendum to entry no.937].
The author describes Sino-Japanese relations from the mid-1800's through 1928 and distinguishes between four period: (1) the period without any treates, (2) the period of equality, 1871-1896, (3) the period of good relations and cooperation, 1896-1904, and (4) the period of Japanese imperialism, 1906- .

43A
VOS, Frits [addendum to entry no.1619].
Volume 1 deals with various problems concerning the Ise monogatari such as its formation and date, style, authorship, and its influence on later Japanese literature. The literal translation within it is based upon the Den Teika hippon belonging to the Tempuku version of this uta monogatari. Volume 2 contains notes and indexes.

44A
WASWO, Barbara A. L. [addendum to entry no.648].
"Throughout the Meiji period the rural landlords of Japan formed a wealthy, influential, and respected elite. In the 1920's, however, they became a threatened minority, confronted by widespread tenant unrest and a steady increase in tenancy disputes....This study describes the most important characteristics of these landlords in the late nineteenth and twentieth centuries, examines the reasons for the deterioration of their status and influence in rural society, and analyzes their reactions to tenancy disputes and to the erosion of their economic and social position. The discussion focuses on landlords in two contrasting regions of the country, the economically advanced Kinki and the predominantly agricultural Tōhoku."

45A
WHITMAN, Randal Loring. Interference in Language Learning: A Theory of Contrastive Analysis with Examples from Japanese and English. Pennsylvania, 1969. 126p. DA 30 (Jan. 1970); UM 69-21,457.

46A
YOSHITOMI, Masaomi. Étude sur l'histoire économique de l'ancien Japon: Des origines à la fin du XIIe siècle [A Study of the Economic History of Early Japan: From Its Origins to the End of the 12th Century]. Paris, 1927. 263p. Text in French.

Contents: Pt.1: The People and Society of Ancient Japan: The People; Social Organization; Social Questions. Pt.2: Economic Institutions: Finance; Taxes; Money; Financial Organization. Pt.3: Economic Life: Beginnings of Agriculture and Its Development; Government Agricultural Policy; Industry; Commerce.

Rel.Publ.: Étude...siècle. Paris: Pedone, 1927. 263p.

47A
YU, Yeun-chung. The Development of the Economically Active Population in East Asia, 1947-1966. Pennsylvania, 1969. 303p. DA 30 (May 1970); UM 70-7869.

KOREA

48A
COLLIER, Joseph M. [addendum to entry no.2381].
Shows how editors of seven well known and widely read American Catholic periodicals "reacted editorially to foreign policy problems faced by the U.S. in the Far East in 1950 and to attacks during that year against the State Department for its alleged harboring of Communists."

49A
LEE, Dae Sung [addendum to entry no.2142].
Discusses Korea's international trade and estimates the amount of foreign exchange required if the country's economy is to continue to grow rapidly. Contents: Historical Review of the Korean Economy; Analysis of the Korean Economy and the Source of Growth; International Trade in Underdeveloped Countries; International Trade in the Korean Economy; Economic Growth and Import Requirements in Korea.

50A
OH, Suck Hong [addendum to entry no.2503].
Contents: Basic Concepts; A Control System for the Enforcement of Administrative Responsibility; The Board of Audit and Inspection: Environmental Parameters (Society-at-Large, The Political Regime Type and the Bureaucracy, Political Parties and Pressure Groups, The Legislature, The Judiciary); The Board of Audit and Inspection: Structure and Maintenance (Goals, The Structure in Extrinsic Relations, Service Organizations, Resource Management: Personnel and Budget; Planning, Adaptive Coping, and Support Aspects); The Board of Audit and Inspection: Production Performance.

51A
SHIN, Bong Ju [addendum to entry no.2153].
Contents: Introduction; Economic Characteristics, Growth, and the Pattern of Korean Inflation; Inflation and Economic Growth in Korea, 1948-1967.

52A
SHIN, Roy W. The Politics of Foreign Aid: A Study of the Impact of United States Aid in Korea from 1945 to 1966. Minnesota, 1969. 313p. DA 30 (Dec. 1969), 2588-A; UM 69-20,094.

"This study examines relationships of foreign aid to economic and political developments. The main hypothesis is that U.S. aid influences economic development and contributes to democratic political development. The thesis carries this hypothesis further and argues that democratization is a function of interplay between political leadership and economic progress."

53A
WHEATLEY, Charles William. Military Coups and Political Development: A Comparative Exploratory Study. Columbia, 1969. 495p. DA 30 (Dec. 1969), 2645-46-A; UM 69-15,714.

"This study explores the relationship between military coup sequences and processes of political development in eight contemporary nations [including South Korea, 1961-1963]....It attempts to assess the net developmental effects of the coup sequences examined, and to formulate a system of propositions which in part explain the differing forms and effects of coups observed. Net impact on national political development is weighed in terms of two criteria: evidence of eventual reductions in the scale of coercive political competition and concomitant extensions of institutionalized popular participation in national political life. Causal analysis is concentrated on aspects of coup processes which are linked with the nature and behavior of the 'coup group' undertaking the actions."

54A
YI, He-suk. Generative Phonology of Korean: Lexical Feature Redundancy Rules. Yi Hwa Yeo Ja Dae Hak Kyo, 1968.

JAPAN: PROVENANCE OF DISSERTATIONS BY YEAR AND COUNTRY[a]

JAPAN: 1877-1943

COUNTRY AND PERIOD COVERED	1877/ 1889	1890/ 1899	1900/ 1909	1910/ 1919	'20	'21	'22	'23	'24	'25	'26	'27	'28	'29	'30	'31	'32	'33	'34	'35	'36	'37	'38	'39	'40	'41	'42	'43
Austria (1872-1968)				1														2			1							
Belgium (ca.1895-1965)[b]		1		1							1								1		1							
Canada (ca.1913-1968)				1							1																	
Czechoslovakia (1882-1968)				2																					1			
France (1850-1967)[c]		3	5	1	1				1		2	3	2	1	1	2		5		7	5	4	2	1	2	3	1	
Germany (1880-1969)[d]	2	23	11	16		3	4	2	5	4	4	3	4	4	6	8	7	3	5	6	6	7	6	7	5	6	6	3
Great Britain (1877-1969)			1	1				1	1		1			1			1				1	1	1	1	2	1		
Japan (1882-ca.1966)[b,e]						1																						1
Netherlands (ca.1918-1968)[f]				1		1				1			1	2						3	2	1	1		1	1		
Philippines (1913-ca.1966)																						1			1			
Sweden (1855-ca.1964)	1			1																								
Switzerland (1903-1967)		1					1												1	1				1				
United States (1877-1969)	3	6	16	18	3	4	5	5	4	4	4	12	7	5	3	12	6	8	9	11	6	14	14	14	18	11	10	8
USSR (ca.1930-1969)																						1	1		2	3	1	2
TOTAL FOR EACH YEAR	6	34	33	43	4	9	10	8	11	9	13	18	14	13	10	22	14	18	16	28	22	29	25	24	32	25	18	14

JAPAN: 1944-1969

COUNTRY AND PERIOD COVERED	'44	'45	'46	'47	'48	'49	'50	'51	'52	'53	'54	'55	'56	'57	'58	'59	'60	'61	'62	'63	'64	'65	'66	'67	'68[b]	'69[b]	TOTAL FOR COUNTRY
Australia (1890-1969)											1								2			1	1	3		1	9
Austria (1872-1968)	1		2											1		1	1	2		1	1	2		2	2		20
Belgium (ca.1895-1965)[b]																											5
Brazil[b]																								1			1
Canada (ca.1913-1968)															2			1	1						1		7
Czechoslovakia (1882-1968)							3		2											1				1	1		11
Denmark (1836-1965)															1	1											2
France (1850-1967)[c]	1			2		3	1	3		2		1			3	1	2	1	1			4	5	5			87
Germany (1880-1969)[d]	7	2		4		3	3	5	1	3	5	3	5	7	3	5	8	7	9	9	12	7	3	7	5		289
Great Britain (1877-1969)			1		1	2	2	4	1		3		1	2			3	1	4	2	2		3	6	2	3	57
Hungary (postwar only)																						1					1
India (postwar only)																1				2		1			1	1	6
Italy[b]																		1			1		1	1		1	5
Japan (1882-ca.1966)[b,e]								1					1		1			2		1			1				9
Mexico[b]																				1							1
Netherlands (ca.1918-1968)[f]				1	1		1		1		1	1		1					3	1	2		1				29
New Zealand (1910-1968)																								1			1
Philippines (1913-ca.1966)							1		1								2						1				7
Poland (postwar only)								1																		1	2
Sweden (1855-ca.1964)																						1					3
Switzerland (1903-1967)							1			1			1		1				3			1	3	1			17
United States (1877-1969)	4	6	12	15	25	41	35	27	28	32	40	35	46	45	38	37	38	45	47	49	62	70	83	90	88	69[g]	1347[g]
USSR (ca.1930-1969)	1	1	7	6	3	3	5	8	11	11	14	8	5	1	4	5	2	3	5	8	6	9	6	9	7	2	160
Yugoslavia (1954-1968)																		1									1
TOTAL FOR EACH YEAR	14	9	22	28	30	52	52	49	45	49	64	48	59	57	53	51	56	64	75	75	86	97	108	127	107	78	2077

[a]As defined within the scope of the bibliography, i.e., dissertations dealing in whole or in part with Japan. [b]Records are incomplete. [c]Includes French Algeria, where one dissertation was completed in 1935. [d]Both East and West Germany. Includes 3 dissertations completed at the University of Strassburg before 1914. [e]Western-language dissertations only. [f]Includes the Dutch East Indies, where one dissertation was completed in 1936. [g]Includes 4 dissertations completed in 1969 but not officially accepted until 1970. NOTE: Dissertations recorded as being accepted during an academic year (e.g., 1951/52) are entered under the latter of the two years.

KOREA: PROVENANCE OF DISSERTATIONS BY YEAR AND COUNTRY[a]

KOREA: 1900-1945

COUNTRY AND PERIOD COVERED	1900/ 1919	'20	'21	'22	'23	'24	'25	'26	'27	'28	'29	'30	'31	'32	'33	'34	'35	'36	'37	'38	'39	'40	'41	'42	'43	'44	'45
Austria (1872-1968)																	2										
Belgium (ca.1895-1965)[b]																											
Canada (ca.1913-1969)																											
Czechoslovakia (1882-1968)																											
France (1850-1967)																					1						
Germany (1880-1969)[c]	1		1							1			1	1		1					1						
Great Britain (1877-1969)																											
India (postwar only)																											
Italy[b]																											
Korea (1945-1968)[d]																											
Netherlands (ca.1918-1968)																											
Switzerland (1903-1967)									1																		
United States (1877-1967)			1		2	2	1	1	4	1	1	3	6	2	1	1	4	1	2	1	1	3	4			1	1
USSR (ca.1930-1969)																					1		1				
TOTAL FOR EACH YEAR	1		2		2	2	1	1	5	2	1	3	7	3	1	2	6	1	2	1	4	3	5			1	1

KOREA: 1946-1969

COUNTRY AND PERIOD COVERED	'46	'47	'48	'49	'50	'51	'52	'53	'54	'55	'56	'57	'58	'59	'60	'61	'62	'63	'64	'65	'66	'67	'68[b]	'69[b]	TOTAL FOR COUNTRY
Austria (1872-1968)																			2	1		2			7
Belgium (ca.1895-1965)[b]																			1						1
Canada (ca.1913-1969)																								1	1
Czechoslovakia (1882-1968)					1		1						1										1		4
France (1850-1967)						4	1				1			1						1	1	1			11
Germany (1880-1969)[c]												2	1	1	2	6		6	2	5	1	1	1		35
Great Britain (1877-1969)									2				1				1	2						1	7
India (postwar only)																		1							1
Italy[b]																						1			1
Korea (1945-1968)[d]																			1		1	1		1	4
Netherlands (ca.1918-1968)																	1	1							2
Switzerland (1903-1967)											1						1	1			1				5
United States (1877-1967)		2		4	2	2	5	5	12	11	10	6	12	14	12	16	15	17	18	18	19	38	22	27[e]	331[e]
USSR (ca.1930-1969)	1	1	1		1	6	7	12	11	11	9	4	4	5	4	2	2	5	4	1	1	2	2	1	99
TOTAL FOR EACH NUMBER	1	3	1	4	4	12	14	17	25	22	21	12	19	21	18	24	20	33	28	26	24	46	27	30	509

[a]As defined within the scope of the bibliography, i.e., dissertations dealing in whole or in part with Korea. [b]Records are incomplete. [c]Both East and West Germany. [d]Western-language dissertations only. [e]Includes dissertations completed in 1969 but not officially accepted until 1970. NOTE: Dissertations recorded as being accepted during an academic year (e.g. 1951/52) are entered under the latter of the two years.

Bibliography of Published References

Important bibliographies, checklists, records of theses, and abstracts of dissertations used by the compiler are listed below; publications consulted by various contributors generally have been excluded.

INTERNATIONAL
(Bibliographies covering two or more countries)

Bibliography of Asian Studies. v.7-28, 1947-1968. [Title varies: v.1-15, 1941-1956, issued as the Far Eastern Bibliography.]

Cornwall, Peter G. Unpublished Doctoral Dissertations Relating to Japan Accepted in the Universities of Australia, Canada, Great Britain, and the United States, 1946-1963. Ann Arbor: Center for Japanese Studies, The University of Michigan, 1965. (Reprinted from the Association for Asian Studies Newsletter, v.10, no.2, Dec. 1964.)

Gillis, Frank, and Merriam, Alan P. Ethnomusicology and Folk Music: An International Bibliography of Dissertations and Theses. Middletown, Conn.: Wesleyan University Press, 1966. (Special Series in Ethnomusicology, 1)

McNamee, Lawrence F. Dissertations in English and American Literature: Theses Accepted by American, British, and German Universities, 1865-1964. New York: R. R. Bowker, 1968.

Missionary Research Library. Occasional Bulletin. New York. v.11-19, 1961-1968. [Includes annual list of dissertations on missions and related subjects.]

Nagara, Susumu, and Iseri, Naomi. "A List of Publications in English and Other Western Languages Specially Designed for Use by Students in Japanese Linguistics and by Teachers of Japanese as a Second Language." Mimeographed. Ann Arbor, 1968.

Person, Laura. Cumulative List of Doctoral Dissertations and Masters' Theses on Foreign Missions and Related Subjects as Reported by the Missionary Research Library in the Occasional Bulletin 1950-1960. New York, 1961.

United Nations Educational, Scientific, and Cultural Organization. Thèses de sciences sociales: Catalogue analytique international de thèses inédites de doctorat, 1940-1950. Theses in the Social Sciences: An International Analytical Catalogue of Unpublished Doctoral Theses, 1940-1950. Paris: UNESCO, 1952.

Yuan, Tung-li. "A Guide to Doctoral Dissertations by Chinese Students in Continental Europe, 1907-1962," in Chinese Culture, v.5, no. 3 (Mar. 1964), 98-156 [for France, Belgium, Switzerland]; v.5, no. 4 (June 1964), 81-149 [for Germany]; and v.6, no. 1 (Oct. 1964), 79-98 [for Austria, Netherlands, and Italy].

AUSTRALIA

Tasmania. University. Library. Union List of Higher Degree Theses in Australian University Libraries. Cumulative edition to 1965. Hobart: University of Tasmania Library, 1967.

AUSTRIA

Akler, Lisl. Verzeichnis der an der Universität Wien approbierten Dissertationen. Wien: O. Kerry, 1952-1965. 4v: 1937-1944, 1945-1949, 1950-1957, 1958-1963.

Kroller, Franz. Dissertationen-Verzeichnis der Universität Graz, 1872-1963. Graz: Universitätsbibliothek, 1964. (Biblos-Schriften, 37)

Notring der wissenschaftlichen Verbände Österreichs. Gesamtverzeichnis österreichischer Dissertationen. Wien, 1967. v.1, 1966.

Wien. Universität. Philosophische Fakultät. Verzeichnis über die seit dem Jahre 1872 an der Philosophischen Fakultät der Universität in Wien eingerichten und approbierten Dissertationen. Wien, 1935-1936. 3v.

——— Verzeichnis der 1934 bis 1937 an der Philosophischen Fakultät der Universität in Wien und der 1872 bis 1937 an der Philosophischen Fakultät der Universität in Innsbruck eingerichten und approbierten Dissertationen. Wien, 1937.

BELGIUM

Dargent, J. L. Bibliographie des thèses et mémoires géographiques belges, 1904-1953. Bruxelles: Commission belge de bibliographie, 1953. (Bibliographia belgica, 3)

Louvain. Université. Faculté de philosophie et lettres. Résumé des dissertations présentées pour l'obtention du grade de docteur en philosophie et lettres. Louvain, 1934-1935. Issues for 1930-1931.

CANADA

Gagne, Armand. Catalogue des thèses de l'école des gradués de l'université Laval, 1940-1960. (Etudes et recherches bibliographiques, 1)
Mills, Judy, and Dombra, Irene. University of Toronto Doctoral Theses, 1897-1967. Toronto: University of Toronto Press, 1968.
Ottawa. Canadian Bibliographic Centre. Canadian Graduate Theses in the Humanities and Social Sciences, 1921-1946. Ottawa: E. Cloutier, 1951.
Ottawa. National Library of Canada. Canadian Theses. Thèses canadiennes. Ottawa, 1952-1969. 7v., 1960/61-1967/68.

CZECHOSLOVAKIA

Praha. Universita Karlova. Disertace Pražské University 1882-1953. Praha, 1965. (Sbírka pramenů a příruček k dějinám University Karlovy, 3)

DENMARK

København. Universitet. Bibliotek. Danish Theses for the Doctorate and Commemorative Publications of the University of Copenhagen, 1836-1926: A Bibliography. Copenhagen: Levin & Munksgaard, 1929.
——— Danish Theses for the Doctorate, 1927-1958: A Bibliography. Copenhagen: Copenhagen University Library, 1962. (Library Research Monographs, 6)
København. Universitet. Liste de thèses et d'écrits académiques. Années 1959-1965. n.p., n.d.

FINLAND

Carpelan, Tor, & Tudeer, L. O. Th. Lärare och tjänstemän från ar 1828. Helsingfors, 1925.
Sola, Solmu, & Tudeer, L. O. Th. Opettajat ja virkamiehet vuodesta 1828: Täydennys vuoden 1938 loppuun. Helskinki, 1940.

FRANCE

Bibliographie de la France. Supplément D: Thèses. Paris. 38v., 1930-1967.
Demiéville, Paul. "Organization of East Asian Studies in France," Journal of Asian Studies, 18 (Nov. 1958), 163-81. ["List of Theses Concerning East Asia Completed in France 1946-1958," p.177-81.]
France. Ministère de l'Education Nationale. Catalogue des thèses et écrits académiques. Paris, 1884-1940.
Guigue, Albert. La Faculté des lettres de l'Université de Paris depuis sa fondation (17 mars 1808) jusqu'au 1er janvier 1935. Paris: Libr. Félix Alcan, 1935. ["Listes des thèses de doctorat ès lettres et de doctorat d'université," p.57-184, 207-32.]
Maire, Albert. Répertoire alphabetique des thèses de doctorat ès lettres des universités françaises, 1810-1900. Paris: A. Picard, 1903.
Mourier, Athénaïs, et Deltour, M. F. Catalogue et analyse des thèses latines et françaises admises par les facultés des lettres. Année scolaire 1895-1896. Paris: Delalain frères, 1896.
Paris. Université. Annales de l'Université de Paris. Paris: L'Université de Paris, 1947-1969. v. 17-38, 1947-1968.
Paris. Université. Faculté de droit. Bibliothèque. Catalogue des thèses de droit soutenues devant les Facultés de France. Paris: Recueil Sirey. v.1-5, 1933-1937.
Paris. Université. Faculté des lettres et sciences humaines. Positions des thèses de troisième cycle soutenues devant la Faculté. Paris: Presses Universitaires de France, 1962-1968. v. for 1960/61-1967.

GERMANY

Berlin. Universität. Bibliothek. Verzeichnis der Berliner Universitätsschriften 1810-1885. Berlin: W. Weber, 1899.
Bonn. Universität. Philosophische Fakultät. Jahrbuch der Dissertationen der Philosophischen Fakultät der Rheinischen Friedrich-Wilhelms-Universität zu Bonn. Bonn. 3v, 1951/52-1953/54.
Jahresverzeichnis der deutschen Hochschulschriften. Leipzig: VEB Verlag für Buch- und Bibliothekswesen, 1887-1969. 81v., 1885/86-1965. [Title varies: 1885/86-1935, Jahresverzeichnis der an den deutschen Universitäten erschienenen Schriften. Publisher also varies.]

GREAT BRITAIN

Association of Special Libraries and Information Bureaux. Index to Theses Accepted for Higher Degrees in the Universities of Great Britain and Ireland. London: ASLIB, 1953-1969. 17v., 1950/51-1966/67.
Bloomfield, Barry Cambray. Theses on Asia Accepted by Universities in the United Kingdom and Ireland, 1877-1964. London: Cass, 1967.
——— "Theses on Asia: 1964-1965," Bulletin of the Association of British Orientalists. New Ser., v.4, no.1 (Mar. 1968), 56-65.
Cambridge. University. Abstracts of Dissertations...in the University of Cambridge. Cambridge: Cambridge University Press, 1927-1959. v. for 1925/26-1956/57.
Leeds. University. Publications and Titles of Theses. Leeds. v. for 1938-1950, 1958/59, 1961/62-1964/65.
London. University. Theses and Dissertations Accepted for Higher Degrees. London: University of London, 1946-1968. v. for 1937-1967/68. [Title varies slightly.]
London. University. Institute of Historical Research. Bulletin of the Institute of Historical Research. Theses Supplement. London. v.1-41, 1933-1968.
Oxford. University. Committee for Advanced Studies. Abstracts of Dissertations for the Degree of Doctor of Philosophy. Oxford: Oxford University Press, 1928-1947. 13v., 1925/28-1940.
Yuan, Tung-li. "Doctoral Dissertations by Chinese Students in Great Britain and Northern Ireland, 1916-1961," Chinese Culture, v.4, no.4 (Mar. 1963), 107-37.

INDIA AND PAKISTAN

India. National Archives. Bulletin of Research Theses and Dissertations (in the Union of India). New Delhi: Albion Press. no.1-2, 1955-1956.

JAPAN

Bungaku, Tetsugaku, Shigaku Gakkai Rengō. Kenkyū rombun-shū. Japan Science Review. Literature, Philosophy, and History. Abstracts of Doctoral Dissertations. Tokyo, 1950-1957. no.1-8, 1950-1957.

Japan. Mombushō. Daigaku Gakujutsukyoku. Nippon hakushi roku 1882-1962. Tokyo: Kyōiku Gyōsei Kenkyūsho, 1956-1964. 8v.

——— Nippon hakushi roku 1957-1965. Tokyo: Teikoku Chihō Gyōsei Kakkai, 1967. 4v.

NETHERLANDS

Koninklijke Nederlandse Akademie van Wetenschappen. Sociaal-Wetenschappelijke Raad. Dissertaties 1967-1968 in voorbereiding en in het afgelopen jaar verdedigd aan Nederlandse Universiteiten en Hogescholen. Amsterdam: N. V. Noord-Hollandsche Uitgevers Maatschappij, 1968.

Netherlands Universities Foundation for International Cooperation. Higher Education and Research in the Netherlands. v.1, no.1-v.12, no.4, 1958-1968.

Utrecht. Rijksuniversiteit. Bibliothek. Catalogus van academische geschriften in Nederland. Utrecht. v.1-32, 1925-1955; new ser., v.1-2, 1962-1963. [Title varies: 1924-1941/45, Catalogus van academische geschriften in Nederland en Nederlandsch Indië verschenen.]

NEW ZEALAND

Jenkins, D. L. Union List of Theses of the University of New Zealand, 1910-1954. Wellington: New Zealand Library Association, 1956.

NORWAY

Andresen, Gunnar W. Doctores kreert ved universitetet i Oslo 1817-1961.... Oslo: Universitetsforlaget, 1962.

PHILIPPINES

Philippines. National Science Development Board. Compilation of Graduate Theses Prepared in the Philippines, 1913-1960. Manila, 1964.

Philippines. University. Institute of Public Administration. "A Selected List of Master's Theses and Doctoral Dissertations in Political Science and Related Fields," in Philippine Journal of Public Administration, v.1, p.74-80, 190-99, 421-41; v.2, p.408-14; v.3, p.478-82; v.4, p.363-66; v.5, p.365-68; v.6, p.334-37.

SOUTH AFRICA

Blignaut, F. W. Summaries of Theses Accepted by the University of South Africa in 1966. Pretoria, 1966.

Malan, Stephanus I. Union Catalogue of Theses and Dissertations of the South African Universities. Gesamentlike katalogus van proefskrifte en verhandelinge van die Suid-Afrikaanse Universiteite, 1942-1958. Potchefstroom: Potchefstroomse Universiteit vir Christelike Hoër Onderwys, 1959. [Also supplements 1-4, 1959-1962.]

Robinson, Anthony M. L. Catalogue of Theses and Dissertations Accepted for Degrees by the South African Universities. Katalogus van proefskrifte en verhandelinge vir grade deur die Suid-Afrikaanse universiteite goedgekeur, 1918-1941. Cape Town, 1943.

SWEDEN

Bibliografiska institutet vid Kungl. Biblioteket i Stockholm. Svensk bokkatalog för åren 1951-1955. Stockholm, 1961-1963.

Josephson, Aksel G. S. Avhandlingar och program utgivna vid svenska och finska academier och skolor under åren 1855-1890. Uppsala, 1891-1897. 2v.

Nelson, Axel H. Akademiska afhandlingar vid sveriges universitet och högskolor läsåren 1890/91-1909/10 jämte förtechkning öfver svenskars akademiska afhandlingar vid utländska universitet under samma tid. Uppsala, 1911.

Tuneld, John. Akademiska avhandlingar vid sveriges universitet och högskolor läsåren 1910/11-1939/40: Bibliografi. Lund, 1945.

SWITZERLAND

Blanc, Hermann. Catalogue de l'Université de Genève... des thèses présentées aux diverses facultés pour l'obtention de grades universitaires de 1953 à 1957. Genève: Librairie de l'Université, 1959.

Jahresverzeichnis der schweizerischen Hochschulschriften. Catalogue des écrits académiques suisses. Basel, 1905-1968. v.7-70, 1903/04-1967.

UNITED STATES

Arizona, University. Checklist of Theses Accepted for Higher Degrees, University of Arizona. Tucson. 7v., 1947/51-1965.

California. University. Graduate Division. Record of Theses Submitted in Partial Fulfillment of the Requirements for the Degree of Doctor of Philosophy at the University of California, 1885-1926. Berkeley: University of California, 1926. [Supplements issued for 1926-1931 and 1932-1941.]

Chicago. University. Abstracts of Theses, Humanistic Series.... Chicago. v.1-9, 1922/23-1930/32.

——— Abstracts of Theses, Science Series.... Chicago. v.1-9, 1922/23-1930/32.

——— Annotated List of Graduate Theses and Dissertations. The Department of Education. The University of Chicago. 1900-1931. Chicago, 1932.

——— Doctors of Philosophy, June 1893-April 1931. Chicago: University of Chicago Press, 1931. (The University of Chicago...Announcements. v.31, no. 19; May 15, 1931)

Chicago. University. Library. Far Eastern Library. The University of Chicago Doctoral Dissertations and Masters' Theses on Asia, 1894-1962. Chicago: University of Chicago, 1962.

Clark University. Abstracts of Dissertations and Theses. Worcester. v.1-24, 1929-1952. [Title varies slightly.]

——— Dissertations and Theses. Worcester. (Clark University Bulletin) no.1-16.

Columbia University. List of Theses Submitted by Candidates for the Degree of Doctor of Philosophy in

Columbia University 1872-1910. New York: Columbia University, 1910.

——— Masters' Essays and Doctoral Dissertations. New York. 16v., 1952/53-1967/68.

Columbia University. Libraries. East Asiatic Library. Columbia University Master's Essays and Doctoral Dissertations on Asia, 1875-1956. New York, 1957.

Columbia University. Teachers College. Register of Doctor of Education Reports. New York. v.1-4, 1935/45-1957/63.

Cornell University. Abstracts of Theses. 13v., 1934-1946.

Craven, Akiko A. Theses and Dissertations...at the University of Washington 1946/47-1955/56. Seattle: University of Washington Library, 1959.

Dissertation Abstracts: Abstracts of Dissertations and Monographs in Microform. Ann Arbor, Mich.: University Microfilms, 1938-1970. v.1-30, no.6, 1938-Dec. 1969. [Title varies:1938-1951, Microfilm Abstracts; July 1969- , Dissertation Abstracts International.]

"Dissertations in Geography Accepted by Universities in the United States for the Degree of Doctor of Philosophy, as of May 1935," Association of Geographers Annals, 25 (1935), 211-31.

Doctoral Dissertations Accepted by American Universities, 1933/34-1954/55. Compiled for the Association of Research Libraries. New York: Wilson, 1934-1956. 22v.

Edwards, Sarah Scott. Theses and Dissertations Presented in the Graduate College of the State University of Iowa, 1900-1950. Iowa City: Libraries, State University of Iowa, 1953.

Eells, Walter Crosby. American Dissertations on Foreign Education: Doctor's Dissertations and Master's Theses Written at American Universities and Colleges Concerning Education or Educators in Foreign Countries and Education of Groups of Foreign Birth or Ancestry in the United States, 1884-1959. Washington, D. C.: Committee on International Relations, National Education Association of the United States, 1959.

——— The Literature of Japanese Education, 1945-1954. Hamden, Ct.: Shoe String Press, 1955.

Fletcher School of Law and Diplomacy. Thesis Abstracts. Medford, Mass. v. for 1947-1957.

Fordham University. Dissertations Accepted for Higher Degrees in the Graduate School. New York. no.1-18, 1935-1951.

George Washington University. Bibliography: Titles of Books, Monographs...by...Doctors of Philosophy and Doctors of Civil Law. Washington, D. C., 1904.

——— Summaries of Doctoral Theses. Washington, D. C. (The George Washington University Bulletin) no. for 1925/28-1967.

Hart, Donn V. An Annotated Bibliography of Theses and Dissertations on Asia Accepted at Syracuse University, 1907-1963. Syracuse, New York: Syracuse University Library, 1964.

Harvard University. Doctors of Philosophy and Doctors of Science Who Have Received Their Degree in Course from Harvard University, 1873-1926, with the Titles of Their Theses. Cambridge: Harvard University, 1926.

Harvard University. Graduate School of Arts and Sciences. Summaries of Theses Accepted in Partial Fulfilment of the Requirements for the Degree of Doctor of Philosophy. Cambridge: Harvard University Press. 19v., 1925-1943/45.

"Harvard Ph.D. Theses on East Asian Subjects since 1930," in Harvard University. East Asian Studies at Harvard University (Cambridge, 1964), 50-57. (Official Register of Harvard University, v.61, no.16; Aug. 24, 1964)

Hull, Callie, and West, Clarence J. Doctorates Conferred in the Arts and the Sciences by American Universities, 1921/22. Washington, D. C., 1923. (National Research Council. Reprint and Circular Series, 42)

——— Doctorates Conferred in the Sciences by American Universities, 1925/26-1932/33. Washington, D. C., 1927-1934. (National Research Council. Reprint and Circular Series, no. 75, 80, 86, 91, 95, 101, 104, 105)

Index to American Doctoral Dissertations, 1955/56-1967/68. Compiled for the Association of Research Libraries. Ann Arbor, Mich.: University Microfilms, 1957-1970. 13v.

Iowa. University. Doctoral Dissertations, Abstracts, and References.... Iowa City. v.1-9, 1900/37-1952.

Japan Institute. Doctoral Dissertations on Japan Accepted by American Universities 1912-1939. New York: Japan Institute, Inc., 1940.

Johns Hopkins University. Library. List of Dissertations Submitted in Conformity with the Requirements for the Degrees of Doctor of Philosophy, Doctor of Engineering, and Doctor of Science in Hygiene... 1876-1926. Baltimore: Johns Hopkins Press, 1926. (Johns Hopkins University Circular, 373)

Kozicki, Richard J., and Ananda, Peter. South and Southeast Asia: Doctoral Dissertations and Masters' Theses Completed at the University of California at Berkeley 1906-1968. Berkeley: Center for South and Southeast Asia Studies, University of California, 1969. (Occasional Paper, 1)

Kuehl, Warren. Dissertations in History: An Index to Dissertations Completed in History Departments of U.S. and Canadian Universities, 1873-1960. Lexington: University of Kentucky Press, 1965.

Maryland. University. Graduate School. Abstracts of Dissertations.... College Park, Md. v. for 1938/39-1953/54.

Massachusetts Institute of Technology. Abstracts of Theses. Cambridge. v. for 1951-1954, 1958-1964.

Matsuda, Mitsugu. The Japanese in Hawaii, 1868-1967: A Bibliography of the First Hundred Years. Honolulu: Social Science Research Institute, University of Hawaii, 1968. (Hawaii Series, 1)

Michigan. University. Bureau of Educational Reference and Research. Abstracts of Dissertations and Theses in Education, 1917/1931. Ann Arbor, 1932.

Microfilm Abstracts. See Dissertation Abstracts.

Minnesota. University. A Register of the Ph.D. Degrees Conferred by the University of Minnesota, 1888-1932. Minneapolis: University of Minnesota Press, 1932.

——— Register of the Ph.D. Degrees Conferred by the University of Minnesota, 1938 through June 1956. Minneapolis, 1957.

——— Summaries of Ph.D. Theses.... Minneapolis. v.1-5, 1939-1951.

New York. University. University Bibliography.... New York. 9v., 1942-1953.

New York. University. Washington Square Library. List of Doctors' and Masters' Theses in Education, 1890-June 1936.... New York, 1937. [Supplement for October 1936-June 1940 published in 1941.]

North Carolina. University. The Graduate School Dissertations and Theses. Chapel Hill: University of North Carolina Press, 1947. (University of North Carolina Sesquicentennial Publications) [Supplement for 1946-1959 published in 1960.]

Northwestern University. Summaries of Doctoral Dissertations. Chicago. v.1-20, June/Aug. 1933-June/Sept. 1952.

Ohio State University. Abstracts of Doctoral Dissertations.... Columbus. no.6-67, 1931-1951.

Pennington, Juliana, and Marsh, Paul. The University of Southern California Doctoral Dissertations and Master's Theses on East and Southeast Asia, 1911-1964. Los Angeles, 1965.

Pennsylvania. State University. Abstracts of Doctoral Dissertations.... University Park. v.1-18, 1938-1955.

Radcliffe College. Graduate School of Arts and Sciences. Summaries of Theses...for the Degree of Doctor of Philosophy. Cambridge. 2v., 1931/34-1935/38.

Schlundt, Esther M. Guide to Doctoral Dissertations at Purdue University, 1893-1949. Lafayette, Ind.: Purdue University Libraries, 1956.

Shaughnessy, Amy E. Dissertations in Linguistics: 1957-1964. Washington, D. C.: Center for Applied Linguistics, 1965.

Smith, Esther A. University of Michigan Publications Containing Material of a Scientific or Learned Character. Ann Arbor: University of Michigan, 1922. (University of Michigan General Library Publications, 2)

Southern California. University. Abstracts of Dissertations.... Los Angeles. (The University of Southern California. University Chronicle Series) 22v., 1936-1958.

——— Trends in Scholarship: Annotations of Theses and Dissertations Accepted by the University of Southern California 1910-1935. Los Angeles, 1936.

Stanford University. Abstracts of Dissertations for the Degree of Doctor of Philosophy and Doctor of Education.... Stanford. (Stanford University Bulletin) v.1-27, 1924/26-1950/52.

Stanford University. Library. Degrees Conferred by Stanford University, June 1892-June 1924.... Stanford: Stanford University Press, 1928.

Stucki, Curtis W. American Doctoral Dissertations on Asia, 1933-June 1966.... Ithaca, New York: Cornell University, Southeast Asian Program, 1968. (Cornell University, Southeast Asian Program, Data Paper, 71)

The, Lian, and Van der Veur, Paul W. Treasures and Trivia: Doctoral Dissertations on Southeast Asia Accepted by Universities in the United States. Athens, Ohio, 1968. (Ohio University Center for International Studies. Papers in International Studies. Southeast Asia Series, 1)

United States. Department of State. External Research Staff. Office of Intelligence Research. Abstracts of Completed Doctoral Dissertations for the Academic Year 1950-1951. Washington, D. C., 1952. (External Research Staff Paper, Abstract Series, 1; March 1952)

United States. Library of Congress. Catalog Division. List of American Doctoral Dissertations Printed in 1912-1938. Washington, D. C.: U. S. Government Printing Office, 1913-1939. 26v.

Vanderbilt University. Abstracts of Theses. Nashville. (Bulletin of Vanderbilt University) 19v., 1931-1951/52.

Virginia. University. Absracts of Dissertations.... Charlottesville. 5v., 1931/32-1952.

Washington (State). University. Abstracts of Theses and Faculty Bibliography. Seattle. v.1-9, 1914/31-1944. [Title varies slightly.]

Wilder, Bessie E. University of Kansas, Graduate School, Theses 1888-1947. Lawrence, 1949. (University of Kansas Publications, Library Series, 2) [Supplement for 1948-1958 published in 1961.]

Wisconsin. University. Summaries of Doctoral Dissertations. Madison. v.1-16, 1935/36-1954/55.

Yale University. Graduate School. Doctors of Philosophy of Yale University with the Titles of Their Dissertations, 1861-1927. New Haven: Yale University, 1927. [Supplement for 1928-1930 published in 1931.]

Yang, Key P. "A Guide to Doctoral Dissertations Written by Korean Students in the United States, 1910-1965, and Those Written by Americans on Korean Affairs." Washington, D. C., 1965. Unpublished ms.

Yuan, Tung-li. A Guide to Doctoral Dissertations by Chinese Students in America, 1905-1960. Washington, D. C.: Sino-American Cultural Society, 1961.

YUGOSLAVIA

Beogradski. Univerzitet. Bibliografija doktorskih disertacija 1951-1963. Beograd: Publikacija Rektorata Univerziteta, 1964.

Referativni bilten doktorskih disertacija. Beograd: Savezna Privredna Komora i Institut za Naucno-Tehničku Dokumentaciju i Informacije, 1968. [Postwar coverage only]

Author Index

The name and number following the word "see" in all cross references below refer to the form of the author's name appearing within the bibliography and to the main entry number of the dissertation. Underlined numbers (e.g., 2398) refer to entries in the Korea section; numbers followed by the letter "A" refer to the Addenda. All other numbers refer to entry numbers in the Japan section.

Institutional Index

Underlined numbers (e.g., 2483) refer to entries in the Korea section; numbers followed by the letter "A" refer to the Addenda. All other numbers refer to entry numbers in the Japan section.

Biographical Index

Entries are limited to dissertations focusing on the lives, works, or ideas of individual Japanese and Koreans and to dissertations focusing on the activities of westerners who have lived in Japan or in Korea. Underlined numbers (e.g., <u>2227</u>) refer to entries in the Korea section; numbers followed by the letter "A" refer to the Addenda. All other numbers refer to entry numbers in the Japan section.

Akutagawa Ryūnosuke (1892-1927), 640, 1666
Arai Hakuseki (1657-1725), 515, 537
Arishima Takeo (1878-1923), 640, 1643

Baba Tatsui (1850-1888), 601
Bashō, see Matsuo Bashō

Chikamatsu Monzaemon (1653-1724), 1581, 1584, 1585
Ch'oe Pu (1454-1504), 913, <u>2227</u>
Ch'oe So-hae, <u>2477</u>

Daisetz Suzuki, see Suzuki Daisetzu
Dazai Osamu (1909-1948), 1672
Dōgen (1200-1253), 1914
Dohihara Kenji (1883-1948), 1064, 9A

Ejima Kiseki (1667-1736), 1633
Ennin (794-864), 1610

Foote, Lucius Harwood (1826-1913), <u>2277</u>
Foulk, George Clayton (1856-1893), <u>2269</u>, <u>2277</u>
Fujita Tōko (1806-1855), 531, 533, 8A
Fukuzawa Yukichi (1835-1901), 595, 596
Futabatei Shimei (1864-1909), 1645, 1649, 1662

Hagiwara Sakutarō (1886-1942), 1665, 1670
Hamaguchi Osachi (1870-1931), 665
Hara Kei [Hara Satoshi] (1856-1921), 617, 632
Hatano Seiichi (1877-1950), 1952
Hearn, Lafcadio (1850-1904), 804, 805, 807, 810, 812, 825
Higuchi Ichiyō (1872-1896), 1644
Hiraga Gennai (1728-1780), 538, 1641
Hirata Atsutane (1776-1843), 1962, 1965
Hirota Kōki (1878-1948), 1063
Ho Kyun (1569-1618), <u>2474</u>
Hokusai, see Katsushika Hokusai
Hōnen (1133-1212), 1917
Hozumi Yatsuka (1860-1912), 583

Ichijō Kanera (1402-1481), 495
Ihara Saikaku (1642-1693), 1634, 1635, 1639
Ii Naosuke (1815-1860), 527
Imagawa Ryōshun (1325-1420), 1607
Inukai Tsuyoshi (1855-1932), 551
Ishida Baigan (1685-1744), 6, 1958
Itagaki Taisuke (1837-1919), 564
Itō Jinsai (1627-1705), 1959
Izumi Shikibu (d. <u>ca</u>.1030), 1621

Kaga no Chiyo-jo (fl. 8th c.), 1597
Kagawa Toyohiko (1888-1960), 1928, 1947, 1951
Kaibara Ekiken (1630-1714), 1955
Kamada Ryūkō (1754-1821?), 1966
Kamijima Onitsura (1661-1738), 1604
Kamo no Chōmei (1153-1216), 1623
Kamo Mabuchi (1697-1769), 1956
Katō Hiroyuki (1836-1916), 604
Katsushika Hokusai (1760-1849), 110, 111
Kawakami Hajime (1879-1946), 620, 636
Kawatake Mokuami (1816-1893), 1590
Ki no Tsurayuki (d. 946), 1612
Kido Takayoshi (1833-1877), 593
Kim Il-sung (1912-), <u>2511</u>, <u>2516</u>
Kim Ok-kyun (1851-1894), <u>1151</u>, 1163, <u>2272</u>, <u>2281</u>
Kita Ikki (1883-1937), 615, 645
Kitamura Tōkoku (1868-1894), 1659
Kobayashi Issa (1763-1827), 1601
Kobayashi Takiji (1903-1933), 1656
Kōbō-Daishi (d. 835), 1903
Konoye Fumimaro (1891-1945), 683
Kōtoku Shūsui (1871-1911), 614, 621, 623
Kozaki Hiromichi (1856-1938), 607
Kuki Shūzō (1888-1941), 441
Kumazawa Banzan (1619-1691), 1967
Kunikida Doppo (1871-1908), 1655
Kuroda Kiyotaka (1840-1900), 591
Kurozumi Munetada (1780-1850), 1969

Legendre, Charles William (1830-1899), 920, 922

Maejima Hisoka (1835-1919), 1508
Masaoka Shiki (1867-1902), 1650, 1669
Matsudaira Sadanobu (1758-1829), 1636
Matsuo Bashō (1644-1694), 1600, 1603
Minobe Tatsukichi (1873-1948), 668
Miyamoto Yuriko (1899-1951), 1658
Miyoshi Kiyoyuki (847-918), 489
Montoku Tennō (827-858), 1615
Mori Arinori (1847-1889), 611
Motoori Norinaga (1730-1801), 1964
Mujū Ichien (1226-1312), 1632
Murasaki Shikibu (978-1015?), 1614
Mutsu Munemitsu (1844-1897), 573

Nagai Kafu (1879-1959), 1671
Nakatsukasa no Naishi (fl. <u>ca</u>.950), 1625, 1628
Natsume Sōseki (1867-1916), 1651, 1653
Niijima Noboru [Jō] (1845-1890), 608
Nishi Amane (1829-1897), 577
Nishida Kitarō (1870-1945), 1890, 1891, 1892
Nitobe Inazō (1862-1933), 556, [165]

Ogyū Sorai (1666-1728), 1960, 1963, 26A
Ōkawa Shumei (1886-1957), 661
Ōkubo Toshimichi (1831-1878), 526